In addition to the regions noted, many oils are also sourced from various regions of the world.

THE ESSENTIAL *life*

A Simple Guide to Living the Wellness Lifestyle

Thank you to the many contributors for their collective genius in bringing this work together and sharing a vision of how plants and natural remedies bring new levels of wellness to powerfully impact lives across the globe.

7th EDITION

The information contained in this book has not been evaluated or approved by the U.S. Food and Drug Administration or any other regulatory agency. The information is not intended to diagnose, treat, cure, prevent, or otherwise reduce the effects of any disease or ailment. The information is not, and nothing contained herein is claimed to be, written, edited, endorsed, or researched by a licensed healthcare provider or medical professional or borne out by any specific medical science. In fact, it is not. The information referenced herein is intended for educational purposes only. It is not meant to and should not otherwise be implied to substitute for seeking qualified medical care from a licensed medical doctor. Any information herein should not be used in lieu of a treatment prescribed by any licensed medical professional for a specific health condition. Consult a licensed and qualified healthcare provider for diagnosis, medical care, and treatment. Consult your physician before using any product in a manner not expressly recommended, if you are pregnant, nursing, or otherwise under medical care or treatment.

The information contained in this book does not in any way seek to promote or endorse any specific brand of essential oils, nutritional products, or other products offered or provided by any specific company. Any mention in this book of a specific brand name is not an endorsement or recommendation of any specific product or company.

Any suggested product reference and recommendations are intend only for use with approved oils in accordance with specific methods which are compliant with governmental regulatory standards (see GRAS provisions). Be advised that the use of various oils including, but not limited to, citrus oils, may cause skin sensitivity. Users are advised to avoid sunlight and UV rays for no less than twelve hours after the use of such oils.

The authors of this book have expressed their good faith opinions, which are not established by conventional medical professionals. Total Wellness Publishing, LLC and any contributor to this book expressly disclaim any liability arising from the use of the information contained in this book or for any adverse outcome resulting from the use of the information contained herein for any reason, including but not limited to any misdiagnosis of any condition or any misunderstanding, misapplication, or misinterpretation of the information set forth herein. In no event shall the authors of this book or Total Wellness Publishing, LLC be liable for any direct, indirect, consequential, special, exemplary, or other damages related to the use of the information contained in this book.

DISCLAIMER: Total Wellness Publishing, LLC is a third-party company that does not benefit financially from the sales of essential oils. Total Wellness Publishing, LLC is not affiliated with, sponsored by, or endorsed by any essential oil company. The trademarked and copyrighted names in this publication are owned by dōTERRA Holdings, LLC. Total Wellness Publishing is not affiliated with, sponsored by, or endorsed by dōTERRA Holdings, LLC. The material in this publication is a third-party presentation of and commentary on the essential oils, blends, supplements, and other products produced by dōTERRA, Inc.

TOTAL WELLNESS
PUBLISHING

ISBN 9 781737 692409

TABLE OF CONTENTS

SECTION 1 how-to

SECTION 2 quick reference

SECTION 3 natural solutions

SECTION 4

focus areas

SECTION 5

living

SECTION 6

resources

SECTION 1

HOW-TO

For both the new and the experienced essential oil user, THE ESSENTIAL LIFE is a colllection of everything you need to create positive and profound results. Providing simple quick-reference information to expert-level knowledge, this book brings together the best research and proven solutions to provide you a trusted, credible, and comprehensive guide.

Reach for your oils, refer to this book to guide you, and enjoy THE ESSENTIAL LIFE!

How to Use THIS GUIDE

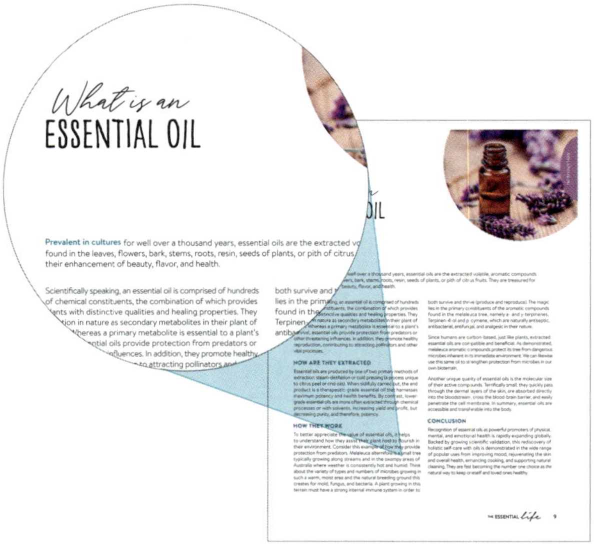

how-to

Establish a foundation of basic knowledge for using essential oils. Learn what oils are, where they come from, and how to use them safely and effectively.

quick reference

Quickly look up any ailment and link it to the top recommended and most-used essential oils with this A-Z index of ailments. Learn basic application methods and find cross-references for more in-depth understanding and to learn about other recommended remedies.

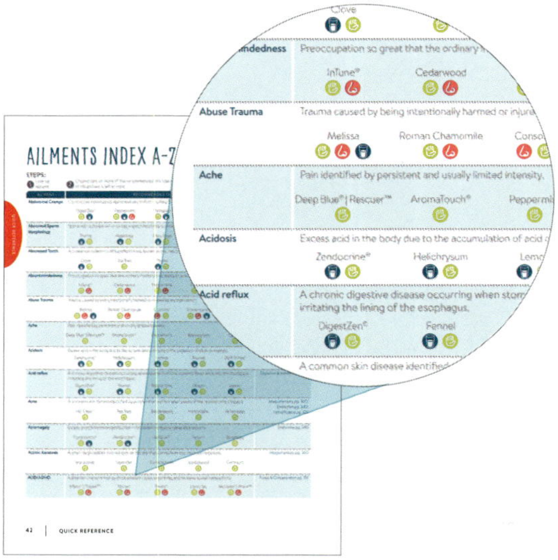

natural solutions

Become familiar with individual essential oils, essential oil blends, and supplementary products. Discover how each oil is derived, common uses, basic emotional benefits, and insights.

focus areas

Reference *Focus Areas* to expand your level of knowledge and learn to address wellness in a more holistic way. Explore both conditions and symptoms to better identify root causes and corresponding protocols.

living

Explore and enjoy the benefits of using essential oils for cleaning, cooking, gardening, fitness, children's activities, pets, on-the-go needs, and more. Integrate the power of essential oils into every part of your life!

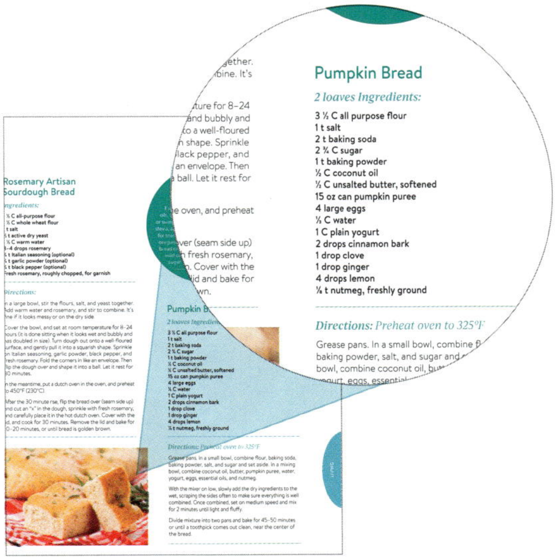

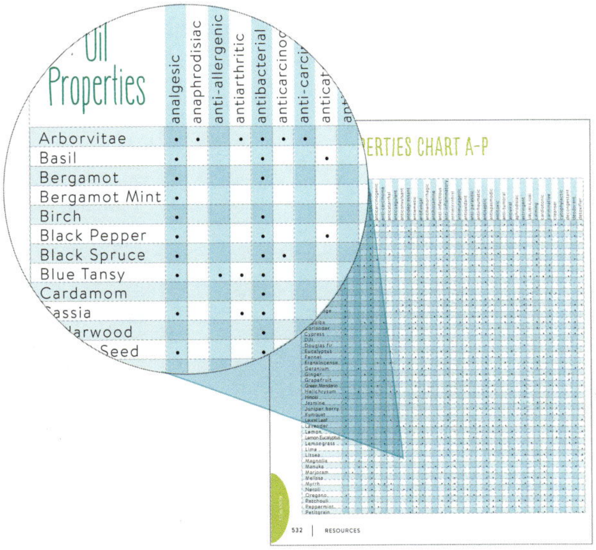

resources

Explore in-depth essential oil chemistry, substitutions, properties, uses through informative charts, research, indexes, and more.

What is an ESSENTIAL OIL

Prevalent in cultures for well over a thousand years, essential oils are the extracted volatile, aromatic compounds found in the leaves, flowers, bark, stems, roots, resin, seeds of plants, or pith of citrus fruits. They are treasured for their enhancement of beauty, flavor, and health.

Scientifically speaking, an essential oil is comprised of hundreds of chemical constituents, the combination of which provides plants with distinctive qualities and healing properties. They function in nature as secondary metabolites in their plant of origin. Whereas a primary metabolite is essential to a plant's survival, essential oils provide protection from predators or other threatening influences. In addition, they promote healthy reproduction, contributing to attracting pollinators and other vital processes.

HOW ARE THEY EXTRACTED

Essential oils are produced by one of two primary methods of extraction: steam-distillation or cold pressing (a process unique to citrus peel or rind oils). When skillfully carried out, the end product is a therapeutic-grade essential oil that harnesses maximum potency and health benefits. By contrast, lower-grade essential oils are more often extracted through chemical processes or with solvents, increasing yield and profit but decreasing purity and, therefore, potency.

HOW THEY WORK

To better appreciate the value of essential oils, it helps to understand how they assist their plant host to flourish in their environment. Consider this example of how they provide protection from predators. Melaleuca alternifolia (commonly known as tea tree) is a small tree typically growing along streams and in the swampy areas of Australia where weather is consistently hot and humid. Think about the variety of types and numbers of microbes growing in such a warm, moist area and the natural breeding ground this creates for mold, fungus, and bacteria. A plant growing in this terrain must have a strong internal immune system in order to both survive and thrive (produce and reproduce). The magic lies in the primary constituents of the aromatic compounds found in tea tree, namely a- and y-terpinenes, Terpinen-4-ol and p-cymene, which are naturally antiseptic, antibacterial, antifungal, and analgesic in their nature.

Since humans are carbon-based, just like plants, extracted essential oils are compatible and beneficial. As demonstrated, tea tree's aromatic compounds protect it from dangerous microbes inherent in its immediate environment. Likewise, we can likewise use this same oil to strengthen protection from microbes in our own bioterrain.

Another unique quality of essential oils is the molecular size of their active compounds. Terrifically small, they quickly pass through the dermal layers of the skin, are absorbed directly into the bloodstream, (in some cases) cross the blood-brain barrier, and easily penetrate the cell membrane. In summary, essential oils are accessible and transferable into the body.

CONCLUSION

Recognition of essential oils as powerful promoters of physical, mental, and emotional health is rapidly expanding globally. Backed by growing scientific validation, this rediscovery of holistic self-care with oils is demonstrated in the wide range of popular uses from improving mood, rejuvenating the skin and overall health, enhancing cooking, and supporting natural cleaning. They are fast becoming the number one choice as *the* natural way to keep oneself and loved ones healthy.

ESSENTIAL OIL *Classifications*

Understanding plant classifications helps one get to know essential oils categorically. This creates a broader knowledge of their general attributes and characteristics, improving one's ability to identify oils that best serve in specific circumstances. Keep in mind that while oils within a classification have common characteristics, each individual oil has far more specific and even unique properties. See ***Oil Properties*** (pg. 532) to learn more.

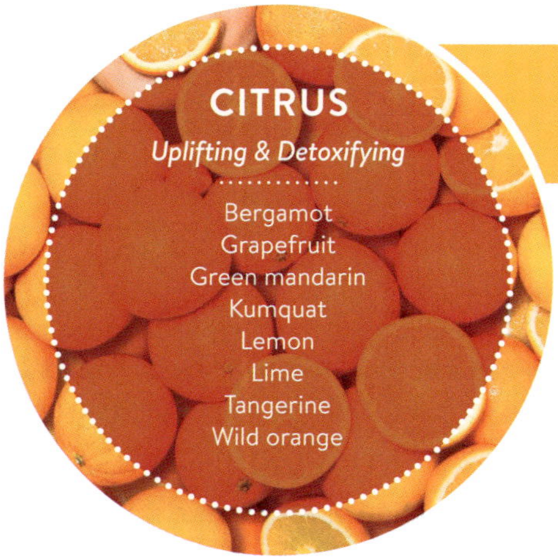

Citrus trees grow juicy, pulpy fruit with and grow in warm climates. These oils are cold-pressed or steam-distilled from the rind.

Top Properties:

- Stimulating
- Uplifting
- Antiseptic
- Calming
- Antimicrobial
- Energizing
- Antioxidant

Positive energy and emotions heightened by citrus oils:

- Invigorated, joyful, energized, validated, feeling worthy, enlivened, restored, productive, mindful

Negative energy and emotions addressed by citrus oils:

- Discouraged, gloomy, distressed, depleted, drained, oppressed, faint, mindless

Florals are flowers. These oils are distilled from the petals or aerial parts of plants.

Top Properties:

- Anti-inflammatory
- Antispasmodic
- Relaxant
- Antihistamine
- Analgesic
- Regenerative
- Antiviral

Positive energy and emotions heightened by floral oils:

- Better able to express oneself, reassured, mended, purposeful, light-filled, loved, exuberant, expressive, sedated, calmed

Negative energy and emotions addressed by floral oils:

- Fearful, worried, hurt, unheard, wounded, neglected, frustrated, depressed, isolated, burdened, tense

Spices are aromatic, flavorful plants. These oils are distilled from the bark, roots, seeds, and buds of the plant.

Top Properties:
- Warming
- Digestive stimulant
- Immunostimulant
- Aphrodisiac
- Antiemetic
- Anti-infectious
- Anti-parasitic

Positive energy and emotions heightened by spice oils:
- Honest, charitable, bold, receptive, supported, participating, activated, empowered, activated

Negative energy and emotions addressed by spice oils:
- Repressed, self-centered, uncertain, denied, dominated, apprehensive, apathetic, somber, disinterested, bored, dispassionate

Herbs are seed-bearing without woody tissue in the stem. These oils are distilled from the green leafy part of these low-growing plants.

Top Properties:
- Immunostimulant
- Detoxifier
- Antiviral
- Antifungal
- Carminative
- Antibacterial
- Anti-parasitic

Positive energy and emotions heightened by herb oils:
- Accepting, yielding, open-minded, invigorated, enhanced, unattached, trusting, progressing, enlightened, relieved

Negative energy and emotions addressed by herb oils:
- Stubborn, angry, unyielding, confused, hindered, degraded, obstinate, doubtful, stalled, limited, inundated, unforgiving

Roots are a plant's fibers that attach it to the ground and receive its water and nourishment. These oils are distilled from roots.

Top Properties:
- Calming
- Nervine
- Grounding
- Neurotonic
- Sedative
- Restorative
- Neuroprotective

Positive energy and emotions heightened by root oils:
- Rooted, flowing, centered, elevated, aware, peaceful, meditative, prioritized

Negative energy and emotions addressed by root oils:
- Ungrounded, obstructed, discontented, erratic, inattentive, agitative, scattered

Leaves are an outgrowth of plant stems that manufacture its nutrients by photosynthesis. These oils are steam distilled from the leaves.

Top Properties:

- Antiseptic
- Invigorating
- Anti-inflammatory
- Insecticide
- Analgesic
- Antibacterial
- Antimicrobial

Positive energy and emotions heightened by leaf oils:

- Accepting, yielding, receiving, invigorated, enhanced, unattached, trusting, progressing, enlightened, relieved

Negative energy and emotions addressed by leaf oils:

- Stubborn, refusing, unyielding, confused, hindered, degraded, obstinate, doubtful, stalled, limited, inundated

Woods typically grow high off the ground and are characterized by a single trunk. These oils are distilled from the leaves, twigs, branches, needles, berries, bark, and wood.

Properties:

- Anticatarrhal
- Regenerative
- Relaxant
- Grounding
- Steroidal
- Analgesic
- Astringent

Positive energy and emotions heightened by wood oils:

- Receiving, devoted, collected, stimulated, progressing, alone, courageous, composed

Negative energy and emotions addressed by wood oils:

- Blocked, uninspired, unsure, congested, stalled, connected, cowardly, overzealous, grieving, sad, ashamed

Resins are the natural sticky substance of certain trees and are insoluble in water. These oils are distilled from hardened resins.

Properties

- Anti-inflammatory
- Cytophylactic
- Analgesic
- Restorative
- Antidepressant
- Immunostimulant
- Antimutagenic

Positive energy and emotions heightened by resin oils:

- Unified, connected, grounded, nurtured, enlightened, inoculated, bonded, awakened

Negative energy and emotions addressed by resin oils:

- Separated, disconnected, stressed, malnourished, unprotected, abandoned, darkened, weak

Why QUALITY MATTERS

As one truly studies the art of growing, harvesting, and distilling essential oils, one discovers the grower's craft and the beauty of this expert human art. Today, we experience the best of tradition in growers' expertise and wisdom handed down through the generations, combined with advancements in science, farming, and distillation practices.

Sourcing

When it comes to sourcing essential oils, the terrain and soil of origin matter. Without exception, sourcing is at its best when plants are grown and harvested in their natural growing conditions and environments where development of their powerful chemistry is encouraged and supported. Additionally, it is vital for the fields, orchards, and so on to not be sprayed with toxic chemicals or have them added to the soil. These compromising practices greatly impact the natural chemistry of the essential oils.

Variations in the natural chemistry of oils are common and are a legitimate expressions of their nature.

Supplier

When it comes to healing, choosing a supplier of essential oils who is well known for product quality and process efficacy is "essential." Every oil has specific constituents, which provide varying levels of therapeutic effects. Therefore, it is necessary to sort through dozens of species of a single plant source from a myriad of geographical locations to find the right combination of therapeutic compounds.

A supplier's greatest task is to search the world for the highest quality plant sources that produce the best possible essential oils nature can provide. This is best accomplished by creating direct and trusted alliances with honest growers and distillers, eliminating middlemen and brokers altogether.

Authenticity

Regulation of therapeutic grade essential oils is limited, and standards are minimal. This leaves suppliers with the responsibility to self-regulate. The term "therapeutic grade" is simply insufficient to identify a level of quality. Yet there exists two distinctly different views. In one, compromised sourcing is permissible and expected; further, synthetic additives are acceptable components. The other maintains true holistic healing requires unadulterated oils that are sourced directly from nature with nothing added. These strict standards allow the oils to remain rich and complex, exactly as nature creates them. One should expect to pay a higher price for genuine, authentic, pure, potent, superior-grade essential oils.

Quality

To be truly therapeutic and superior grade, essential oils must be third-party tested and certified as pure, potent, genuine, and authentic. Each of these terms is important and meaningful in relation to measurements of quality. Although chemists have successfully recreated multiple constituents of plants, they cannot replicate a *complete* essential oil due to extraordinary complexity. Regardless of advancing capacity, replication is common and always results in a synthetic outcome.

Process

To protect and maintain the highest quality essential oils, plants must be patiently harvested by those who are knowledgeable, honest, and committed to gathering only the *one* specie, allowing the plant proper maturation time.

After harvesting, the plant material is ready for distillation. In order to carefully extract the precious constituents, this process must be conducted gently, slowly, and skillfully. Quality distillation requires reduced pressure and temperature, protecting these essences from being oxidized or destroyed by excessive heat. The use of improper temperature, toxic solvents, or chemicals always compromises purity and potency.

Once distillation is complete, most essential oils are moved to distribution companies or middlemen, known as brokers. Most companies that sell essential oils have no ability (or in many cases, no desire) to verify the quality of the oils they buy from their supplier before passing onto their customers. Look for companies who work directly with growers and source from all over the world.

There is a growing number of companies falsely claiming to produce pure essential oils. Yet, 99% of the time, these products use fragrant synthetic chemical substitutes to dilute or replace more expensive essential oil extracts. These claims deceive many consumers who believe they are using natural products.

Essential oils are comprised of only three elements: carbon, hydrogen, and oxygen. The molecules in essential oils are primarily monoterpenes, sesquiterpenes, and their oxygenated derivatives. Essential oils are volatile, organic liquids.

There are no vitamins, minerals, essential fatty acids, or hormones in essential oils. Any claim of such ingredients simply reveals the impurity of a product.

AROMA

One of the most telling ways to detect pure, authentic high-quality oils is by the aroma. Superb aroma is hard-earned and the result of quality plant sourcing, quality distillation processes, and the absence of chemical solvents. The purer an oil, the more it smells like its original plant source. Simply said, genuine and exquisite aroma is the hallmark of quality sourcing and distillation.

SUPPLIER RESPONSIBILITY

It is a distributing company's responsibility to provide consumers with carefully extracted, pure essential oils. Pure oils have no fillers or artificial ingredients. Rigorous quality testing, above and beyond the minimum required, ensures oils are free of contaminants. Look for companies that verify and certify their quality and purity prior to making the product available to consumers. Additionally, the distributor is responsible for labeling products according to FDA GRAS (Generally Regarded As Safe) standards.

MEASURING QUALITY

The highest quality essential oils are authentic, genuine, pure, and potent.

Authentic

In the world of essential oils, the term "authentic" means the following:

- The composition of an oil is equal to the plant specified on the label.
- The oil is not a mixture of plant species, rather only the plant specified.
- The oil is not the product of a mixture of plants or weeds growing alongside the species.
- The oil is comprised of and distilled from only the plant parts clearly identified.
- In total, the oil is precisely characterized so as to clearly identify its healing qualities through consistently occurring compounds.

Genuine

The term "genuine" is equivalent to the term "unadulterated," meaning the following:

- **The essential oil is 100% natural** and contains no addition of any other substances—even other natural substances. It contains NO synthetics, agents, dilutants, or additives.
- **The essential oil is 100% pure** and contains NO similar essential oil or hybrid added to extend supply.
- **The essential oil is 100% complete** and is fully distilled. Almost all essential oils are distilled in a single process. Ylang ylang is an exception, as it passes through more than one distillation to be complete. Distillation processes that are disrupted can produce I, II, III, and "extra" essential oil classes.

Pure

Purity alone does not necessarily mean an oil is good quality. A pure oil can be distilled incorrectly or may be obtained from a particular variety of inferior plant species. Additionally, oils may wrongfully contain contaminants, pesticides, herbicides, solvents, inferior and/or unlabeled plant sources, other unlabeled species, and synthetic compounds. The distillation process may magnify the concentration of these undesirable elements.

Potent

Essential oils are the most potent form of a plant's material. The chemical constituents found in these materials will either increase or decrease the potency of an essential oil. Climate and soil composition directly affect the potency of plant matter. Therefore, sourcing an oil from its native habitat is essential and expected.

PERSONAL RESPONSIBILITY

When it comes to obtaining quality essential oils, the consumer must do their own research and take great care to value quality, above all else. For a plant's purity is its potency. Education is key to becoming a skilled user of these potent plant extracts.

How to Know WHICH OILS TO USE

The greater the number of oils you have at your disposal, the more choices you can make and results create. Yet, deciding which oil to use in certain circumstances can be overwhelming, especially with so many options with overlapping qualities and properties.

The skill to develop is learning to make better choices to create even better results. Remember this: oils move you to a more balanced state of homeostasis to the best of their ability. Necessarily then, ask yourself, "What might I experience on my way to greater balance and wholeness (e.g., temporary discomfort or symptoms due to detoxification from an unhealthy terrain)? Am I providing proper support for my body's needs (e.g., adequate nutrition and rest, proper diet) to help get me where I want to be in the most successful way?"

Following are a number of highly beneficial ways to make oil selections. Enjoy the process of getting to know each oil as if it were a friend you've learned to count on in times of need or want. The most important factors in your decision-making are your preferences based on your own knowledge and experiences. Interactions with the oils vary from person to person. Even with the same condition, people are drawn to and benefited by different solutions. Keep a journal, or simple notations right here in the pages of this book, about what you've learned. Become your own best advocate, knowing greater health and wellness, modeling it for generations to come, and inviting those around you to do the same.

SELECTION TOOLS

On-Hand— In a moment of need, your go-to choices are what you have on hand. Put each of your oils to work for you by looking them up in this book and learning what they do best. As your interest grows in making essential oils your first line of response, identify health issues, desired changes, and results. Research them here in the book, and then increase your personal collection accordingly. It's what you do every day that matters most.

Intuition— Nothing could be more powerful in essential oil use than simply paying attention to what you are attracted to. Trust that feedback and act on it. Intuition is reliable. Again, make notations so you can repeat what you've done before and, with experience, better your results.

Look Things Up in the Book and Do Your Own Research

- **A-Z Quick Reference** (pg. 42)— Search health conditions you want to resolve and choose from the top oils listed.
- **Natural Solutions** (pg. 92)— Look up any oil or blend to discover its origin, chemistry, properties, top uses, application methods, and safety. This section offers education on each oil, blend, and supplement, as well as a way to cross-reference ideas or suggestions from other sections.
- **Oil Properties** (pg. 536)— The last section of this book is a great way to develop your inner oil expert. The oil properties chart is a superb way to learn about how oils work. Notice as well that in every *Focus Area*, you find oils listed by "Related Properties." Certain essential oil properties excel in addressing unique aspects of each body system and area of focus.
- **Focus Areas** (pg. 276)— Look up your health concerns or interests in *Focus Areas*. First, go to the area that relates to your concern (e.g., respiratory for a cough; cardiovascular for a heart or circulation issue). Then, look for specific conditions or symptoms you want to relieve or address. Note both product suggestions and protocols provided.

Online— If you want more detailed knowledge about what to address, first look up your condition online so you better understand it. For example, learn about the different facets of whatever ails you and discover what body parts are involved. With these specific areas of focus identified, utilize the book as described above to pursue your essential oil solutions.

Smell— Like intuition, the value of smelling an oil to discover what you love or are drawn to cannot be overemphasized. This is one of the most wonderful aspects of essential oil use. After all, it is called aromatherapy! Don't limit your thinking to only what is taught. Deliberately choose to make selections by aroma. It is both scientific (every oil has very precise chemistry hence a unique aroma) and traditional to do so. There is a reason why smelling oils prior to selection is so commonplace and one's natural inclination. Even animals and small children quickly identify their favorites and what their body most needs.

Emotions— Perhaps the idea of matching an oil to an emotional state is new to you. However, it is the number one way to narrow selections. Here's why. Consider two people who have arthritis. One is impatient, and the other is resigned. Each has a different emotional profile as well as different needs to be met. Learn more about the connection between essential oils and emotions by first reading *Emotional Well-Being* (pg. 28). The science and chemistry behind this correlation make it well worth your understanding and application. Use the charts in the *Emotions Index* to introduce the connection of what oil for what emotion. Also, see *Mood & Behavior* (pg. 377).

Oil Personalities— Learn your oils by their "personalities" to get a better sense of which oils and blends work best for you. Where and how a plant grows, the parts used, and the chemistry contained are all significant aspects of an oil's "energy" profile. Here is an example: cinnamon, considered a spice oil (see *Emotions Index* pg. 34 to learn more) has warming properties (see pg. 535-538 for more information). This heat both wards off unwanted predators and warms up a cold heart or body, serving as both an immunostimulant and aphrodisiac. Upon use, the user has a sense of feeling more protected, safe, warm, and is thus more willing to be intimate and sexually/emotionally vulnerable.

Individual Test— Utilize a personal digital scan or applied kinesiology, also known as muscle response testing, to quickly identify what resonates as beneficial to your body at the time of evaluation.

Essential Oil ACTIONS

ADAPT	Black Spruce	Cedarwood	Copaiba	Neroli	Lavender
BREATHE	Eucalyptus	Rosemary	Peppermint	Siberian Fir	Cardamom
CALM	Lavender	Bergamot	Petitgrain	Roman Chamomile	Clary Sage
CLARIFY	Tea Tree	Green Mandarin	Rosemary	Lemon Eucalyptus	Geranium
DEODORIZE	Bergamot	Black Spruce	Douglas Fir	Patchouli	Tea Tree
DETOX	Grapefruit	Juniper Berry	Celery Seed	Cilantro	Lemon
DISINFECT	Cilantro	Cassia	Tea Tree	Lemon	Lemon Eucalyptus
ENERGIZE	Peppermint	Spearmint	Basil	Siberian Fir	Tangerine
FOCUS	Vetiver	Cedarwood	Rosemary	Peppermint	Lime
FRESHEN	Lemon	Lime	Spearmint	Green Mandarin	Juniper Berry
GROUND	Siberian Fir	Black Spruce	Frankincense	Douglas Fir	Sandalwood
HARMONIZE	Bergamot	Sandalwood	Ylang Ylang	Jasmine	Roman Chamomile
REGENERATE	Yarrow	Rose	Sandalwood	Helichrysum	Frankincense

RELAX	Marjoram	Roman Chamomile	Coriander	Neroli	Magnolia
RENEW	Helichrysum	Yarrow	Geranium	Blue Tansy	Juniper Berry
REPEL	Lemon eucalyptus	Citronella	Arborvitae	Peppermint	Eucalyptus
RESTORE	Turmeric	Copaiba	Frankincense	Blue Tansy	Black Spruce
SEDATE	Jasmine	Roman Chamomile	Magnolia	Petitgrain	Vetiver
SLIM	Cinnamon Bark	Grapefruit	Lemon	Pink Pepper	Ginger
SOOTHE	Lavender	Roman Chamomile	Frankincense	Celery Seed	Yarrow
STABILIZE	Frankincense	Copaiba	Cedarwood	Spikenard	Rose
STIMULATE	Peppermint	Basil	Rosemary	Eucalyptus	Ginger
THRIVE	Basil	Coriander	Myrrh	Wild Orange	Pink Pepper
TONE	Geranium	Clary Sage	Rose	Marjoram	Siberian Fir
UPLIFT	Wild Orange	Green Mandarin	Bergamot	Melissa	Ylang Ylang
WARM	Wintergreen	Black Pepper	Lemongrass	Clove	Ginger

How to Use ESSENTIAL OILS

Application Methods

AROMATIC

The very term "aromatherapy" was derived from the fact that essential oils are, by nature, aromatic. Their aromas can elicit powerful physiologic, mental, and emotional responses. Essential oils are also volatile, meaning they evaporate quickly, and are rapidly absorbed into the body. The process of conveying aromas to the brain is called olfaction, or is better known simply as smelling. It happens courtesy of the olfactory system.

As a person inhales an essential oil, the molecules of oil go up into the back of each nostril to the postage-sized epithelium patch. There, the molecules attach to receptors on the cilia hairs, which convert to nerves on the other side of the mucous patch. These nerves send the odor information to the olfactory bulb in the brain. This means the essential oil itself is not sent to the brain, but instead, a neural translation or "message" of the complex chemistry it contains is delivered. Then the millions of nerves in the olfactory bulb communicate directly with the amygdala, hippocampus, and other brain structures.

The amygdala, a center for emotions in the limbic system, links our sense of smell to our ability to learn emotionally. Here, aromatic information is connected to present emotions. This capacity to pair the two, information and emotions, is inextricably connected to our ability to survive making essential oils powerful partners in creating and maintaining emotional health. Inhalation of essential oils is also received through the alveoli of the lungs and, from there, into the bloodstream.

The easiest way to aromatically use essential oils is to open a bottle and simply breathe in the aroma through the nose. This technique is known as **direct inhalation**. To enhance this method, place a drop of an oil or blend in the hands, rub them together, and then cup around the nose and mouth (not necessary to make contact with the face), and inhale. Additionally, oil drops can be placed on a piece of cloth or tissue, held close to the face, and the aroma inhaled.

Diffusing essential oils aromatically is one of the most desired and powerful methods for affecting mood, killing airborne pathogens, and changing the aroma of a space such as a room, office, or car. Other uses include a targeted approach for relaxing or stimulating the mind. Diffusing is also one of the most effective ways to impact a respiratory condition. A diffuser can be used as an inhalation device, whether in a room where diffusing is occurring or purposely breathing in the vapor.

Diffusers are devices that evaporate an essential oil into a surrounding environment. There are four main types of diffusers: atomizing, vaporizing or humidification, fan, and heat. Atomizing and employs a cold air pump to force the essential oil through an atomizer, separating the oil into tiny particles to create a micro-fine vapor. The essential oil bottle is, in some manner, directly connected to the diffuser, and no water is involved. Atomizing diffusers are more expensive, create noise due to the mechanisms, and use a lot more of an oil. Vaporizing or humidification diffusers employ water with the essential oil and use ultrasonic waves to emit the oil and water particles into the air. Fan and heat diffusers are usually low-cost and are mainly used for small areas such as cars. The amount of oil used varies with each diffuser type. Most models use anywhere from a few to 10 drops at a time.

Diffusers vary in capacity for covering the square footage of a room or space. Other features may include timers, some allowing both constant and intermittent distribution options.

Another popular method is to add essential oils to water in a glass spray bottle. The mixture can then be sprayed in the air (e.g., air freshener), on surfaces (e.g., countertop) for cleaning, or on the body (e.g., for cooling and soothing benefits).

TOPICAL

Essential oils are fat-soluble. Because of their chemical compounds, they are readily absorbed and enter the bloodstream when they are **applied directly**. This is another reason why the quality of oils is important. Many oils are safe to use neat (e.g., applied topically to the skin with no dilution from a carrier oil). One location, most universally accepted as best for neat application, is the bottoms of the feet.

A primary method of distributing essential oils topically is to combine them with a **carrier oil** (e.g., a different kind of oil used for dilution such as fractionated coconut oil) for both dilution and prevention of evaporation. Using a carrier oil *prior* to applying an oil slows down but does not prohibit the absorption process and therapeutic onset. Applying a carrier oil *after* essential oil application enhances therapeutic onset and sustains absorption. Either way, the carrier oil prevents potential rapid evaporation.

By taking the time to **massage** an essential oil thoroughly into the skin enhances absorption. Massaging increases the blood flow to an area, thus allowing the skin to more efficiently absorb valued compounds. Applying warm heat after oil application, such as a rice bag or moist cloth compress, helps drive oils deeper into tissues. This is especially helpful for muscle pain, body aches, and injured tissue. Use caution when adding heat to hot oils. Carrier oils help protect the skin from irritation. Children, the elderly, and those with sensitive skin or compromised systems, are advised to always use a carrier oil.

Some of the more popular carrier oils are fractionated coconut oil, virgin coconut oil, jojoba oil, grapeseed oil, almond oil, avocado oil, and extra virgin olive oil. Competing aroma is one consideration when selecting the carrier oil of choice. Fractionated coconut oil is a favorite and is created by removing the fatty acids from regular coconut oil, which is solid at 76°F. Fractionating, or removing the fatty acids, keeps the oil in a liquid state, making it easier for use in application (e.g., while giving a massage) and also makes it easier to combine with essential oils in containers such as spray and roll-on bottles. The fractionating process also increases shelf life, removes the potential for rancidity, and makes it odorless and colorless. It's also great on the skin and doesn't clog the pores.

Topical application methods can vary considerably. Most frequently, oils are simply placed either on the skin of any **area of concern** or on the **bottoms of the feet**. Additional methods of distribution can include: combining oils in an unscented lotion or with a carrier oil, or water in a **spray**, **balm**, or **roller bottle**. Limiting the number of drops used and diluting is the best way to safely and effectively use essential oils topically. It's generally unnecessary to use exaggerated amounts to achieve a therapeutic effect. Essential oils contain a robust bouquet of potent chemical constituents capable of delivering powerful effects in sometimes as little as one or a few drops.

The appropriate dosage for topical use of essential oils is different for each individual and should be tailored to their personal circumstances. Consider age and size, as well as overall health status. It is best to use smaller amounts more often rather than greater amounts less often. Start with the lowest amount that makes sense, and then increase as needed to achieve the desired outcome. A topical dose of essential oils is typically repeated every twenty minutes in an acute situation or every two to six hours as needed otherwise. A recommended ratio for essential oil to carrier oil dilution is:

Babies	0.3 % dilution	(1 drop to 1 tablespoon)
Children	1.0 % dilution	(1 drop to 1 teaspoon)
Adults	2.0-4.0% dilution	(3-6 drops to 1 teaspoon)

When applying essential oils topically, avoid sensitive skin areas such as eyes, inner ears, genitals, and, (with some oils), broken, damaged, or injured skin. After applying essential oils, enjoy massaging the residue into the palms for additional therapeutic benefit. Thoroughly wash hands before immediate contact with sensitive areas, such as the eyes or genitals.

Another favorite use for essential oils is in a **bath**, which serves both a topical and aromatic function. Use an emulsifier, such as shampoo, bath gel, milk, or honey, with the essential oils before placing in bath water to disperse the oil throughout the water. Or, add 3 to 10 drops of essential oils to bath salts (use amount per product instructions), or 1 C Epsom salt, and then dissolve in bath.

Essential oils can also be applied to **reflex points** or nerve endings in the feet, hands, or on various points on the rim of the ears (auricular therapy). Refer to *Reflexology* later in this section.

Layering is the process of applying more than one oil to a desired location to intensify the effect or to address multiple concerns at once. For example, frankincense is often used as the first oil applied to an area on the skin to magnify the effects of subsequent oils layered on top. Or, if an individual is sensitive to or dislikes the smell of an oil, they may resist its use. Layering a second and even third oil on top to "deodorize" and create a different aroma can be effective. An example of layering is as follows: apply vetiver, then layer lavender on top. If satisfactory, then the process is complete. If not, add a third oil, such as wild orange or Citrus Bliss®. The last oil applied will be the strongest aroma initially. After time, the more base note oil lingers longer than a top note oil. Putting on socks after application can also "contain" an aroma to a degree.

INTERNAL

Just as plants are eaten fresh, dried for herbs, used in hot water infusions (tea), taken internally for therapeutic benefits, and used to flavor foods, individuals can take essential oils for these same uses. We often consume essential oils when we eat food. Fresh aromatic plants normally contain 1 to 2 percent, by weight, of volatile compounds. When plants are distilled for the extraction of these essential oils, the properties become concentrated. Essential oils are far more potent than their whole plant material. Hence, only small amounts need be used when taking oils internally.

Essential oils are fat-soluble and, therefore, readily delivered to all body organs, including the brain, and easily metabolized. Internal use of essential oils is the most potent method of use. Proper dosing should be followed according to labeling recommendations and other professional guidelines to avoid unnecessary overuse. Just as ingested foods can become overwhelming with excessive consumption, so too can oils.

Some traditional essential oil experts profess internal use of essential oils is not safe. For those using impure oils (99.9%), nothing can be more true. However, FDA approved internal use, by hundreds of thousands of users of certified pure oils, indicates that following appropriate and safe dosing guidelines is appropriately safe. Dosage guidelines for internal use vary depending on the age and size of a person as well as an individual's health status.

Essentials oils can also be ingested **under the tongue**, **in a vegetable capsule** (often referred to as a "veggie cap"), **tea**, **food**, or **water**. As heat affects the compounds of an oil, it is best to add oils to hot liquids after the heating process has occurred.

Another method of internal essential oil use is **vaginal insertion**. Oils can be diluted in a carrier oil and then absorbed into a tampon. The tampon is then inserted and kept in overnight. Essential oils can also be diluted in water and used to irrigate the vaginal area with a vaginal syringe.

Rectal insertion is best accomplished by adding a drop or few of essential oil to an enema, a homemade suppository, or oils can be placed in a capsule, and then inserted in the rectum overnight. Consult trusted sources for guidelines.

As previously stated, a single drop of essential oil is obtained from a large amount of plant material, contains hundreds of constituents, and is very potent. Keep this in mind when determining the amount of an oil to ingest. A common internal dose for an adult is 1 to 3 drops of essential oil every two to six hours (depending on the oils selected), but preferably no more than 25 drops, divided into doses, in a 24-hour period. This methodology allows the body, especially the liver, time to process each dosage. Dosages should be adjusted for a person's age, size, and health status. For extended internal use, a lower daily dose is advised.

Some oils are not considered safe or recommended to ingest. Those include some oils from the needles of trees such as pine and cypress, as well as some varieties of eucalyptus. Oils, such as wintergreen and birch, are required by law to have childproof lids because the blood-thinning properties that could be hazardous to a young child or baby if ingested. Yet, other oils such as cinnamon and oregano, are better when used internally. Verifying a safe for supplemental use or "Supplement Facts" label on an essential oil bottle serves as essential guide for oils that are to be taken internally.

Massage WITH OILS

The application of essential oils topically, combined with massage, is simple to do but very powerful in the healing process. It increases the benefits of massage and the efficacy of essential oils on and within the body. Massage increases circulation and absorption, helps improve lymphatic flow, and aids in the release of toxins. It can also soothe nerve endings, relax muscles, and relieve stress and tension in the body.

HEAD

Apply essential oils to the fingertips and gently massage entire scalp. For headache, massage around the base of the neck and work upward to the base of the scalp.

NECK

Use circular movements, working from the base of the neck, up both sides of the vertebrae, to the base of the scalp. Work to the sides of the neck and repeat the movements, working down again.

ARMS

Massage up toward the armpit on the fatty or muscular areas only.

BACK

Start from the lumbar region of the back, and with two hands stroke all the way up to the shoulders alongside the spine. Slide the hands over the shoulders and return down the sides of the back.

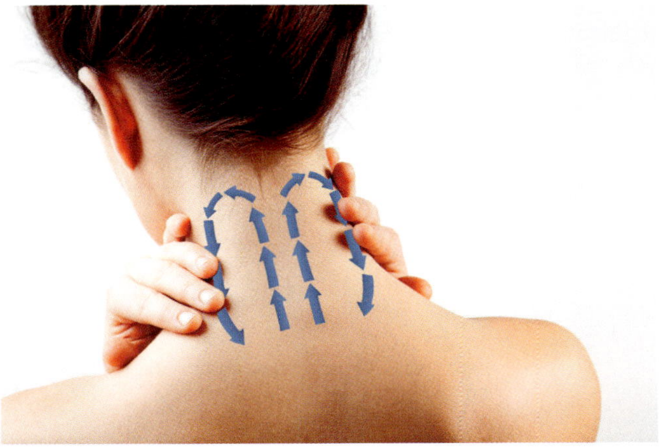

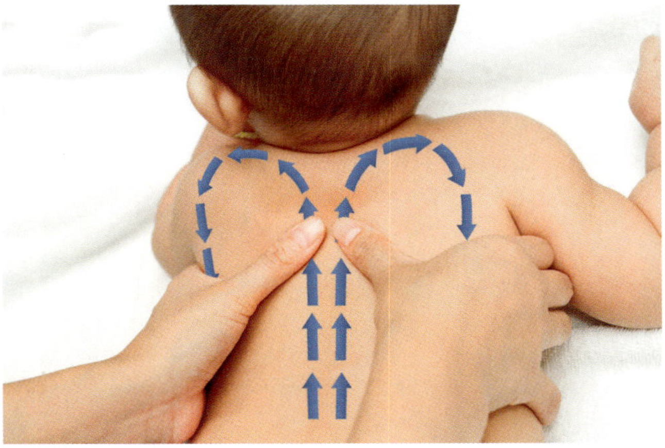

SHOULDERS

Using your thumbs and palms, make firm strokes from the shoulder to the neck and back again.

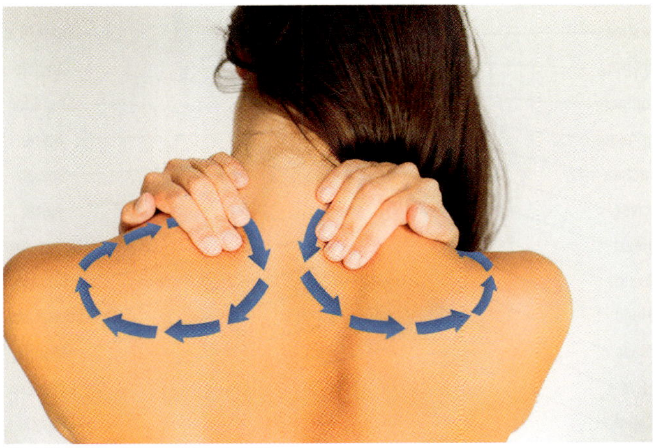

ABDOMEN

Use circular movements only in a clockwise direction.

LEGS

Always massage legs upward on the fatty or muscular areas only and avoid varicose veins.

FEET

Massage from the toes to the heel with thumbs under the foot and fingers on top.

tips

- Massage is most effective when done with the flow of the body—toward the heart, from hand to shoulder, foot to thigh, and so on.
- When massaging children and those who are unwell, use gentle movements.

REFLEXOLOGY

Reflexology is the application of pressure to the feet and hands with specific thumb, finger, and hand techniques without the use of oil or lotion. It is based on a system of zones and reflex areas that reflect an image of the body on the feet and hands with the premise that such work creates a physical change to the body.

Ear Reflexology is a simple and efficient way to relieve stress and pain by applying minimal pressure to the reflex points on the ear. Each ear contains a complete map of the body, rich with nerve endings and multiple connectors to the central nervous system. For example, if the reflex point for the bladder is tender, the body may be in the beginning stages of a bladder infection. One can take preventative measures to head off the bladder infection by applying an essential oil to the reflex point on the ear followed by minimal pressure.

To begin treatment, start at the top of the right ear and slowly work your thumb and forefinger along the outer edges. Hold each point for five seconds before continuing to the end of the earlobe. For best results, repeat this procedure at least five times. Next, work the inner crevices of the ear using the pointer finger and applying minimal pressure. Repeat the procedure on left ear. If any areas in and around the crevices of the ear are sensitive, consult the ear reflexology chart to pinpoint the area of the body that may be out of balance.

This is a great technique to use personally, on family or friends, as well as with those whose hands and feet are not accessible for hand and foot reflexology. Young children are especially receptive to having their outer ears worked on, finding it calming and soothing.

Foot Reflexology is an effective method to bring the body systems into balance by applying pressure to specific places on the feet. Hand reflexology can be utilized in a similar manner. The nerves in the feet correspond with various parts of the body; thus, the entire body is mapped on the feet, telling a story of emotional and physical well-being.

One way to find imbalances in the body is to massage all the areas noted on the foot reflexology chart and feel for triggers or small knots underneath the skin. When a trigger is found, apply an essential oil to the respective location on the foot and continue to massage the trigger until it releases. Another way to use reflexology is to address a specific ailment. For instance, if a person has a headache, locate the brain on the foot chart and the corresponding point on the foot. Apply an essential oil of choice and massage the pad of the big toe to reduce tension. If a person has a tight chest induced by stress, locate the lungs/chest on the foot chart and the corresponding point on the foot. Apply an essential oil of choice followed by a medium to light circular massage on the ball of the foot.

The autonomic nervous system is then engaged, helping to alleviate symptoms and heal the body naturally.

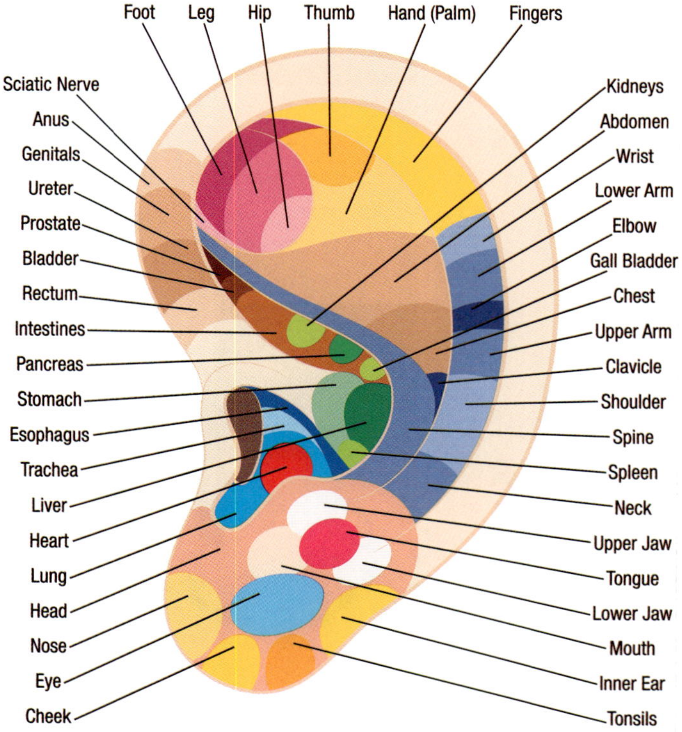

Reflexology Reference

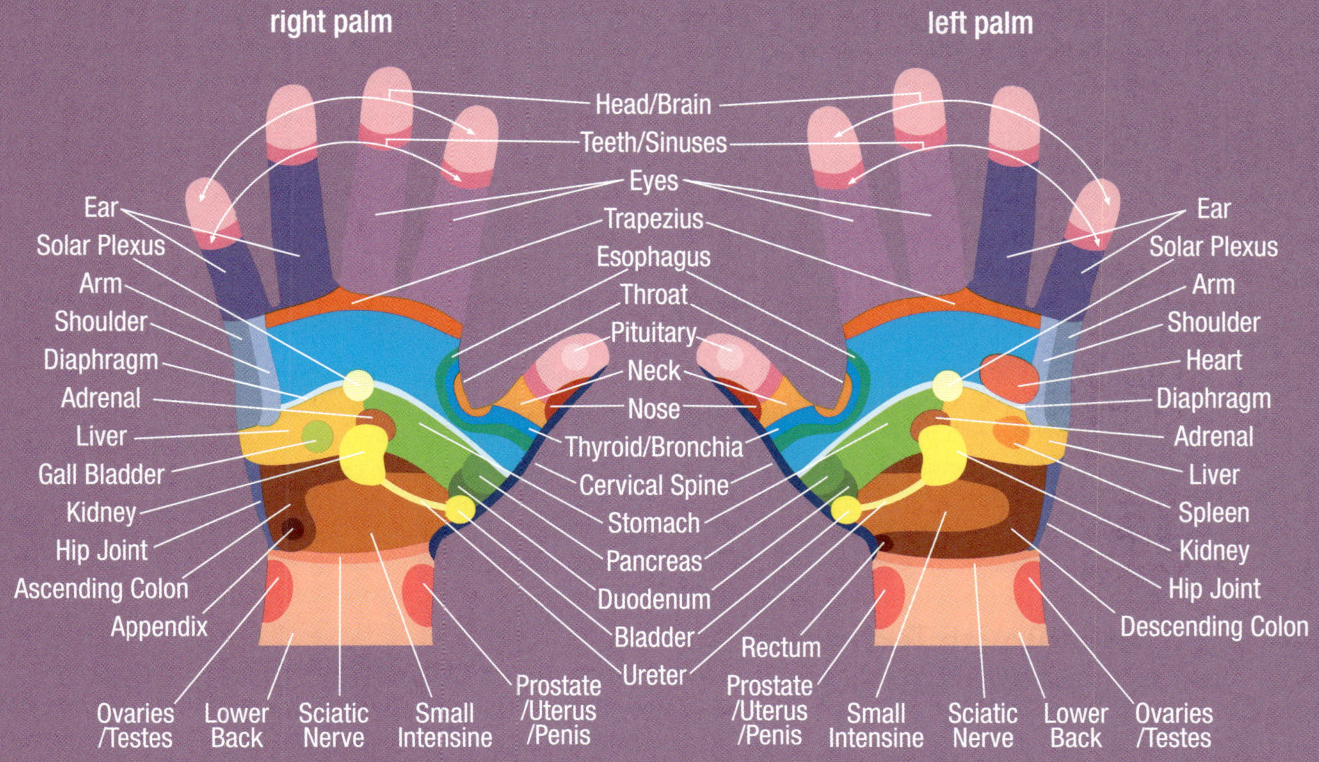

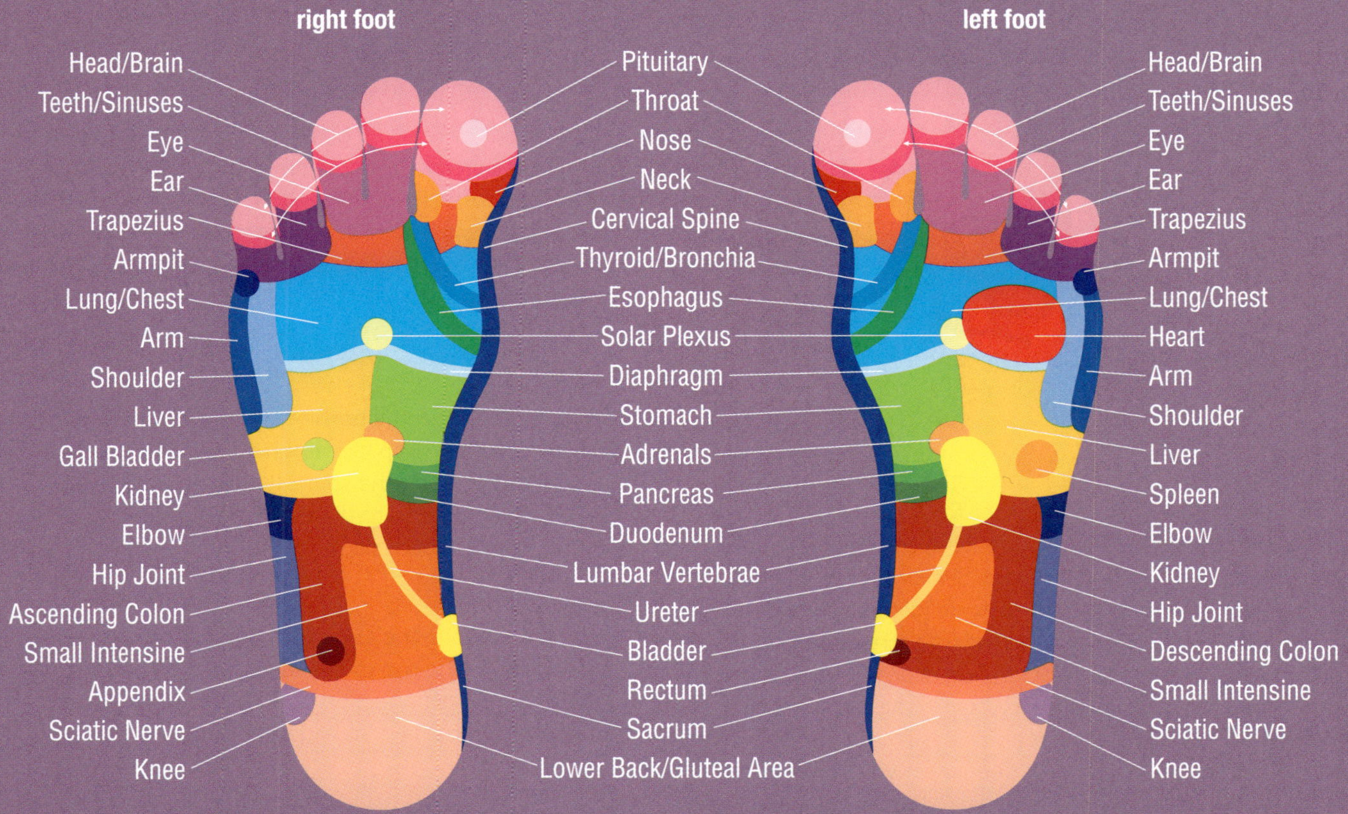

AROMATOUCH *Technique*®

Essential oils have a powerful effect on well-being. These effects are specific and unique to each oil that nature has provided. When we understand these healing properties and how our bodies naturally respond to them, we can use essential oils to promote a superior state of being. The AromaTouch Technique® provides a way to use these gifts to maximizes emotional and physical healing.

The AromaTouch Technique® contains four stages. Each stage utilizes two oils or oil blends. Do not substitute other essential oils. Because these essential oils are applied full strength (neat) to the skin, it is very important that you use only the highest quality essential oil. Oils need to be both pure and potent. The method of distillation, growing and harvesting standards, plant species, even the region of the world from which it comes greatly affect the content of the essential oil. Just as the raw materials entering a factory determine the end product, an Oil Touch is effective if the essential oil used has consistent and whole chemistry.

What is the AromaTouch Technique®?

Oil Touch is an interaction between nature's chemistry and neurology (brain and healing communication system). It supports the body in moving toward a healing state. Health is created as the body achieves and maintains balance. This balance can be interrupted by heightened stress, environmental toxins, or traumas. Oil Touch promotes balance so healing can continue and is recommended as an integral part of preventive care, even for healthy people.

Oil Touch is not a treatment for any specific disease or condition. The body's natural healing abilities are miraculous. Awakening these abilities in others is a simple and precious gift.

How Does it Work?

Balance in your body looks something like a series of connected teeter-totters. To illustrate, consider the process of standing up. In order for you to stand and walk, your body is maintaining a delicate balance between falling forward and falling backward. Similarly, your internal body systems are striving to maintain delicate balances. For example, your nervous system is either in a stressed state or a rested state. Like a teeter-totter, both sides can't be high at the same time. Your immune system is the same and will mirror the nervous system's actions. It is moving infection out of your body or pushing it in deeper for you to deal with later. Your body works this way with regard to your senses too.

When injured, your body sends pain; we call this nociception. When it is not in pain, it sends good sensations that we call proprioception. When all of these are in balance with each other, you become more healthy and heal much better. Oil Touch can help restore this balance. It can be compared to re-booting a computer for optimal functioning. This condition is called homeostasis.

The AromaTouch Technique®

AromaTouch Technique® is divided into four steps. Each step supports a shift in how your body heals and adapts to stress and injury.

Step 1 shifts the nervous system from stress to rest. **Step 2** encourages the body to move from the secondary immune system to the primary immune system. **Step 3** reduces pain and inflammation. During the entire process, good feeling (proprioception) is stimulated. As the technique progresses, the effects compound and a dramatic shift occurs in all three factors.

Once your recipient is in this state, proceed to **Step 4**. In this step, you nudge them back in the other direction. The body takes over and finds its balance. This is why it is like re-booting a computer. You turn it off and then back on. The body knows where to stay to get the healing job done right.

In order to do this, you will need to learn a few easy skills and perform them in the right order.

Setting up for an Oil Touch:

First, find a quiet, comfortable place. Using a massage table is best. A headpiece that angles up and down can be helpful for comfort. You may wish to support the recipient's ankles with a rolled towel or blanket. Your goal is to make your recipient as comfortable as possible. Your recipient will need a blanket for warmth and modesty. They will need to remove their clothing from the waist up and lie face down on the table. They will have their arms at their sides with their shoes and socks off. They will remain in this position for the duration of the technique. Encourage the recipient to completely relax and receive.

Applying Oil

When applying oil, hold the bottle at a 45-degree angle over the recipient and let a drop fall onto the back. You will typically apply 3 to 4 drops along the spine. It is preferable to start at the low back and move up to the neck. In **Step 4**, you will apply a couple of drops to each foot.

Distributing the Oil

Distribute the oil along the spine by spreading it from the base of the low back to the top of the head. This is done by gently using the pads of the fingertips. This is a very light touch and is complete when you have spread the oil along the spine with three passes.

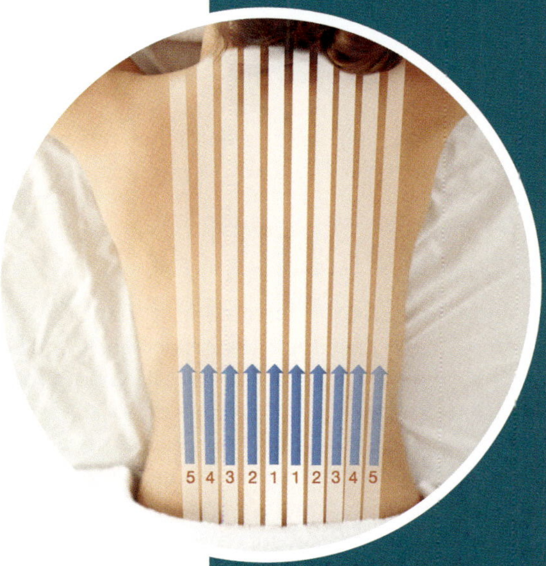

Palm Circles through the Heart Area:

Make a triangle with the thumbs and first fingers, place your hands on the center of the back and at the heart level. Slide the hands in a clockwise fashion over the skin, creating a circle about eight inches wide. Complete three circles and hold for a moment. After pausing, separate the hands, sliding them along the spine. One hand stops on the back of the head while the other hand stops and rests just below the waistline. Pause, leaving your hands in this position. Connect with your recipient, and feel their breathing. Focus on being present with them to find a rhythm that is theirs and not yours.

The Alternating Palm Slide:

This movement is a rhythm created by sliding the hands along the surface of the skin. Stand to the side of the recipient, and place your hand on the low back with your fingers pointing away from you at the level just below their waistline. Place your palm against the far side of the spine. Slide your hand away from you with very mild pressure. That is the basic movement. Begin this motion with your fingertips at the spine and lower your palm to their skin as you slide your hand away from you. The slide ends when your hand starts to turn down the recipient's side. Follow your first slide with a second, using your other hand and, while alternating hands, move up the body toward the head with each horizontal slide. Keep your touch very light and keep it rhythmic. It is kind of like mowing a lawn, one stroke overlapping the other as it moves up the back toward the head. This movement continues up the back, the shoulders, the neck, and finally up on the head until you reach the level just above the ears.

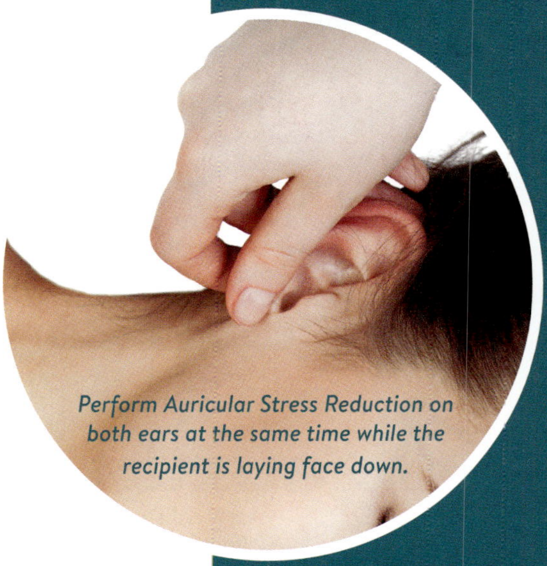

Perform Auricular Stress Reduction on both ears at the same time while the recipient is laying face down.

Repeat this three times, beginning each time at the waistline. Move to the recipient's other side and complete three passes on the opposite side.

Five-Zone Activation:

Imagine broad vertical pinstripes running from the waistline to the shoulders—five to the left of the spine and five to the right running parallel with the spine. The two-inch area directly on either side of the spine is Zone 1. The spaces on both sides directly adjacent to Zone 1 create Zone 2, and so forth. Zone 5 is the farthest out, located on both sides at the angle of the ribs, where they start to turn down to the recipient's sides. Standing at the head of the table, place both hands on either side of the spine at the waistline as close together as you can. Drag your palms with light pressure up the spine, allowing your fingers to trail behind like the train of a wedding dress. Continue this motion through the neck and head, allowing your hands to gently continue the motion lightly to the crown of the head. That completes Zone 1. Now move to Zone 2. Place your hands at the waistline again, but separate them about two inches (this is Zone 2). Pull your palms up toward the shoulders in a straight line as you did for Zone 1. However, once your hands reach the shoulders, turn the fingertips in, drag your palms out along the shoulder blade, rotate the fingers out, and slide them under the front of the shoulders as you drag your palms lightly back to toward the spine, continue up the neck and head as you did for Zone 1. Repeat for Zones 3, 4, and 5 as you did for Zone 2, starting with your hands on the zone just outside the previous one. Complete just one pass per zone.

Auricular Stress Reduction:

Stand at the head of the table. Using your thumbs and forefingers, take hold of both earlobes. Massage them in a circular motion, much like you might rub a penny. Massage along the edge of the ears from the lobe to the top. Drag your fingers back down to the earlobe and repeat three times.

Thumb Walk Tissue Pull:

Stand at your recipient's side near the hips. Place your hands on the back at the waistline with your thumbs on the muscles running directly on either side of the spine. In a circular motion with your thumbs, massage the muscle on either side as you walk up the spine in an alternating fashion until you reach the back of the head. Repeat three times.

Autonomic Balance on the Feet:

There are three steps for the feet. Apply the oils (wild orange and peppermint) together, and spread on the bottom of the foot. You may wish to apply some fractionated coconut oil here, as well.

Grip the foot with your hands and (using a circular motion with your thumbs similar to the thumb tissue pull) wipe the oil into the skin. Start at the side of the heel and move across it horizontally, then move down one-half-inch and work your way across the other direction, almost like you are tilling a garden. Repeat this pattern until you reach the end of the forefoot. You will have just pushed the oil quickly into the skin.

Divide the foot into five zones, just like on the back. The strip running from the heel to the big toe is Zone 1, the strip including the second toe is Zone 2, and so forth. To trigger the reflexes in the foot, place one thumb near the other thumb, starting at the heel on the inside (Zone 1), walk down the foot, pushing into the bottom of the foot with the thumbs using medium pressure. Let one thumb trail the other thumb, so each spot is triggered twice. Complete one pass for each of the five zones, continuing to the tips of the toes.

Gripping the foot, swipe down each zone with your thumb as you slightly compress the foot with your hand. Similar to lightly milking a cow, alternating your hands, swipe Zone 1 three times and then continue through all five zones. Make one pass.

Complete these steps again on the second foot.

The Lymphatic Pump:

If your recipient falls asleep, let them sleep, or perform the Lymphatic Pump. This will help them get moving again and be less disoriented when they arise. Do this by taking both feet in the hands, saddling your thumbs just in front of the heel at the arch. Push toward the head crisply one time, giving them a forward shake. Their body will rebound back toward you. Repeat the motion, matching the rebound. Create a pulse going back and forth. Do this for about ten seconds and repeat a couple of times.

tips

- If for some reason a particular essential oil cannot be used, do not substitute it with another oil. Just remove it from the technique and use fractionated coconut oil on that stage.
- The AromaTouch Technique® is designed to be performed on a massage table. If you do not have access to one, adapt and do the best you can.
- Once you establish contact with your recipient, stay in contact with at least one hand on the body at all times.
- You can use fractionated coconut oil at any time during this process, but if you are using it to lubricate the skin, you are pressing too hard. You should be able to perform this on dry skin. Complete the following steps in order, referencing the descriptions above.

STEP 1 Balance®
- Apply & distribute oil
- Heart Area Circles

Lavender
- Apply & distribute oil
- Alternating Palm Slide
- 5-Zone Activation
- Auricular Stress Reduction

STEP 2 Melaleuca
- Apply & distribute oil
- Alternating Palm Slides
- 5-Zone Activation

On Guard®
- Apply & distribute oil
- Alternating Palm Slides
- 5-Zone Activation
- Thumb Walk Tissue Pull

STEP 3 AromaTouch®
- Apply & distribute oil
- Alternating Palm Slides
- 5-Zone Activation

Deep Blue®
- Apply & distribute oil
- Alternating Palm Slides
- 5-Zone Activation
- Thumb Walk Tissue Pull

STEP 4 Wild orange & Peppermint
- Apply oil to feet
- Autonomic Balance on feet
- Apply & distribute oil to spine
- Heart Area Circles
- Lymphatic Pump

When an Oil DOESN'T SEEM TO BE WORKING

Oils have undeniably potent chemistry and are capable of impacting the body in significant and meaningful ways, yet an oil chosen may still not work due to a number of factors. If confused, consider the following ideas to assist you in identifying ways to enhance results from your essential oil use.

Application Method— There are three basic ways to use essential oils: aromatically, topically, and internally. Each method impacts the body and its numerous layers and parts in different ways. For example, to eliminate a respiratory infection, you may need to combine topical and internal use. As the condition progresses, a change in application methods may be called for. Pay attention to body cues and adjust as needed. Take a moment to consider the variety of aspects of any situation and how you can address them by using more than one oil in more than one way. For further details on how to use essential oils, refer to *Application Methods* (pg. 18). Also, consider learning a special method, *The AromaTouch Technique®*, taught on pg. 24.

Frequency of Use— A best practice of essential oil use is *use less, more often*. With powerful chemistry packed in every drop, a little goes a long way. For example, 1-2 drops of an oil every 20-30 minutes (e.g., in the case of stomach flu or food poisoning, or for a sprained ankle) or every 1-2 hours (e.g., for cold and flu, or exhaustion) until desired relief is achieved, is likely to be far more effective and fast-acting, then 10 drops used one time per day. The body can only chemically process so much at any given time. Therefore, repeated usage, such as every 15-30 minutes for an acute condition and 2-4 times daily for a more chronic or long-lasting condition, is far more likely to drive the results you are looking for. Wondering where to start with your oil use for a particular health goal? Consider using a couple of drops, a couple of times per day, in, on, or around you.

Oil Selection— Most essential oils perform more than 80% of the time consistently. Often, if an oil application is not deemed effective, it is because the issue itself was misidentified. Perhaps a stomach issue was suspected, so a favorite digestion blend was used, yet no effect. In reality ,the gallbladder was the issue, and grapefruit and geranium oils would have been the better selection. Additionally, as individuals' body chemistry, composition, and level of health differ, the effects of oils differ. See the section in this book titled *How to Know Which Oils to Use* on pg. 15 to familiarize yourself with methods of selection. You will discover there are many ways to approach oil choices throughout the book. Dive in and become your own expert user!

Quality— The quality of essential oils offered in the marketplace radically differ. Many are adulterated and deceptively labeled. For example, it's common practice for a broker to dilute pure oils with synthetic counterparts or add a less expensive oil (e.g., add cypress to frankincense or lemongrass to melissa) to extend oil yield. Though the dealer may have found momentary profit, their choice drastically reduces the effects for the end-user. Because chemical profiles have some similarities, common methods of testing for quality are inferior and won't identify the adulterations, allowing for the deception to prevail. Choosing a reliable source is imperative to safely and successfully use. Be sure to read *Why Quality Matters* on pg. 13.

Body Health— What many people don't realize is that essential oils work chemically with and within the body. Acting as messenger molecules, or what is known as exogenous ligands, enters the body like a hired outside management consulting firm, rapidly identifying what's needed and immediately sending instructions to whatever department needs to be involved. Imagine if no one were in the office, nothing would get done. If the body is void of necessary nutrition, then the oils have no way for their powerful instructions to be carried out. One of the most crucial keys for successful results from essential use is a healthy diet, high-quality dietary supplements and vital, daily wellness habits.

Lifestyle— Assessing lifestyle and self-care patterns may be necessary to find the culprits of compromise. Lack of sleep or proper consumption of water, poor quality drinking water, lack of regular exercise or movement, consumption of acid-producing beverages (e.g., carbonated or caffeinated drinks), high levels of stress, etc. may be overriding the benefits of essential oils as the demands on the body are simply too high. It is possible the ratio of offense (e.g., a bad habit) is higher than the ratio of solutions (e.g., good habits like essential oil use), and frequency of oil use may need to be adjusted along with overall changes in personal choices. Oils can make up for a "myriad of sins," but lifestyle has a significant impact on the results you experience.

EMOTIONAL WELL-BEING *with Essential Oils*

There is a significant connection between emotional and physical health. The body releases various chemicals in response to emotions. For example, the body's release of serotonin, dopamine, or oxytocin results in an uplifting emotion and positive sensation in the body. An experience of stress causes the brain to instruct the release of cortisol, and the body's response will be one of urgency and perhaps even fear.

Emotional stress, whether acute or chronic, can have profound effects on the body. A range of illnesses, from headaches to digestive issues, lack of sleep, and heart disease can be the result of emotions such as grief, anxiety, and depression taking a toll on the immune system and other cells, tissues, and organs of the entire body.

Examining activity at a cellular level can assist in the understanding of how emotions can affect body functions. Embedded in the surface of the cell membrane are protein molecules known as receptors. These receptors face outward and continuously scan for, communicate with, and solicit needed chemicals that exist outside the cell.

These solicited chemicals attach to receptors, distribute information, and produce biochemical responses within the cell to adapt to the environment and stimuli. In this way, the receptors play a unique and important role in cellular communication. The binding chemical, called a ligand, is classified as a "messenger molecule" because it sends information to cells that will influence the cell's development and function. A ligand can be a neurotransmitter, hormone, pharmaceutical drug, toxin, part of a virus, or a neuropeptide used by neurons to communicate with each other.

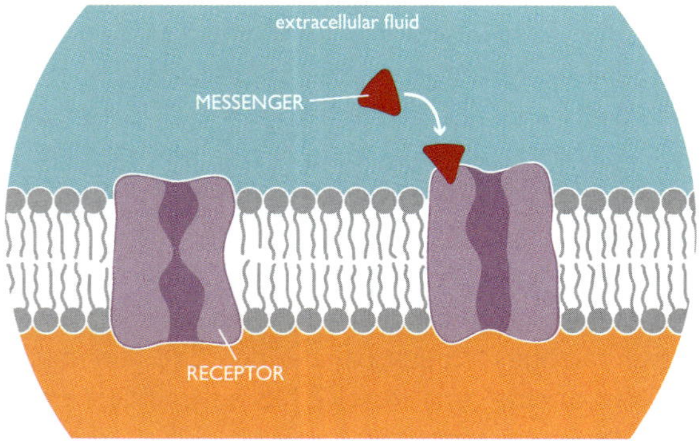

While numerous receptors are found in most cells, each receptor will only bind with ligands of a particular structure, much like how a lock will only accept a specifically shaped key. When a ligand binds to its corresponding receptor, it activates or inhibits the receptor's associated biochemical pathway. There are two types of ligands: endogenous and exogenous. Endogenous ligands, such as serotonin, are produced in the body and can impact emotions. Exogenous ligands are substances that are introduced into the body and have a similar effect. They, too, are messenger molecules and can come from various sources such as medications or essential oils.

The Messages of Emotions

The hypothalamus—the "control and command center" of the brain—converts mental thoughts and emotions into hundreds of different types of ligands, specifically neuropeptides. The emotions triggered by a perceived threat, for example, are powerful and initiate the release of specific messenger molecule chemicals, which, as indicated above, attach to certain receptor sites of cells and affect cell function. What the hypothalamus "believes to be true" determines what the "factory" produces, and chemical production ensues. Neuropeptides affect our chemistry, and our chemistry affects our biology. Bottom line: emotions trigger cell activity!

The Scent Alarm

The sense of smell is our most primal, and it exerts a powerful influence over our thoughts, emotions, moods, memories, and behaviors. A healthy human nose can distinguish over one trillion different aromas through hundreds of distinct classes of smell receptors. By way of comparison, we only have three types of photoreceptors used to recognize visual stimuli. Olfaction is far more complex than sight, and we are ten thousand times more capable of smelling than tasting.

It's accurate to say we "smell" danger. Our sense of smell is inextricably connected to our survival, and it plays a major role in remembering what is and isn't safe and what is pleasurable. Why remember danger, stress, trauma, and pleasure? To learn from experience so we can protect ourselves, survive, and procreate. If it wasn't safe this time, we can avoid it the next time; if it was pleasurable (e.g., food, physical intimacy), we want to participate again. People, environments, food: smelling them is part of everyday life.

Olfactory System

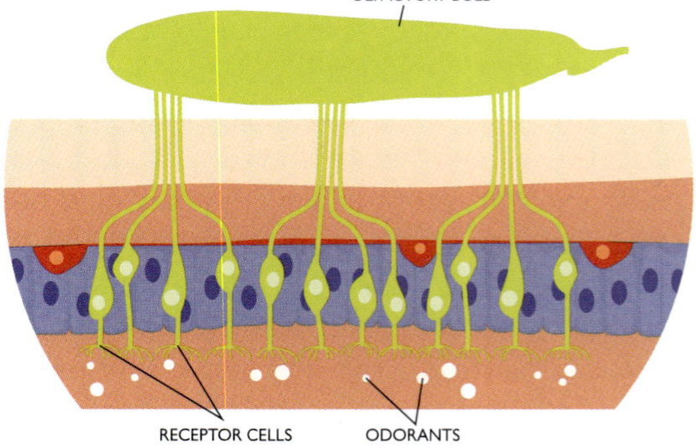

Aromas serve as exogenous ligands. They are received via olfactory receptors, which are highly concentrated in the limbic system, the primitive part of the brain and seat of emotion. In the center lies the amygdala, which instantly receives the incoming scent information before other higher brain centers. By the time the information reaches our "thinking" and decision-making cortex, and we actually figure out what we smelled, the scent has already triggered emotional and body chemistry responses.

The amygdala is the storehouse of traumas and contains the densest concentration of neuropeptides, affecting cellular memory. Smell is the primary sense that unconsciously activates and affects traumatic memories stored there. Acting as the watchdog, the amygdala is constantly on the lookout for danger or threats. As it belongs to the more primitive part of our brain, it doesn't have the intelligence to discern between real threats versus perceived threats (e.g., a saber-toothed tiger versus a missed bus stop or being late to work and an angry boss). It passes on its concerns and notifies the hypothalamus when safety and security are at risk, which then in turn notifies the pituitary, which alerts the adrenal glands, which sets off the alarm for fight-or-flight stress response and releases cortisol and adrenaline. Bottom line: emotional stress triggers the release of stress hormones.

Many researchers agree that physical illnesses are often the result of an emotional inflammatory response to trauma or negative experiences. What can begin as "emotional inflammation" can later become physical issues and disease. Although medical technology is not advanced enough to see them, memories, trauma, and painful emotions are stored in the body and eventually manifest as physical inflammation when the body's tissues follow suit.

Food & Mood

What you put in your mouth has a direct impact on emotions. Nutritional deficiencies, food sensitivities, blood sugar imbalances, substance abuse, and stimulants (like caffeine) affect biochemistry and contribute to mood fluctuations and compromised emotional states.

Additives in processed foods generate adverse chemical reactions within the body and drastically affect mood and behavior in many children and adults. Some of these synthetic substances are labeled "excitotoxins" by nutritionists and wellness experts. These include additives such as high fructose corn syrup, trans-fats, artificial flavors, artificial colors, artificial sweeteners, MSG, and other preservatives. These chemicals deliver messages to the brain and cells of the body just like any exogenous ligand. More than one specific ligand can "fit" into a receptor. As heroin fits in the same opiate site as endorphins, so can these toxic food chemicals unlock receptor sites in our brain and transmit influences that, if we knew, we would never let in.

So once again, we have a choice as to what chemical soup we want to ingest. The old adage, "we are what we eat," could not ring more true. Or perhaps, it gets rewritten here: we emote or express emotionally what we eat.

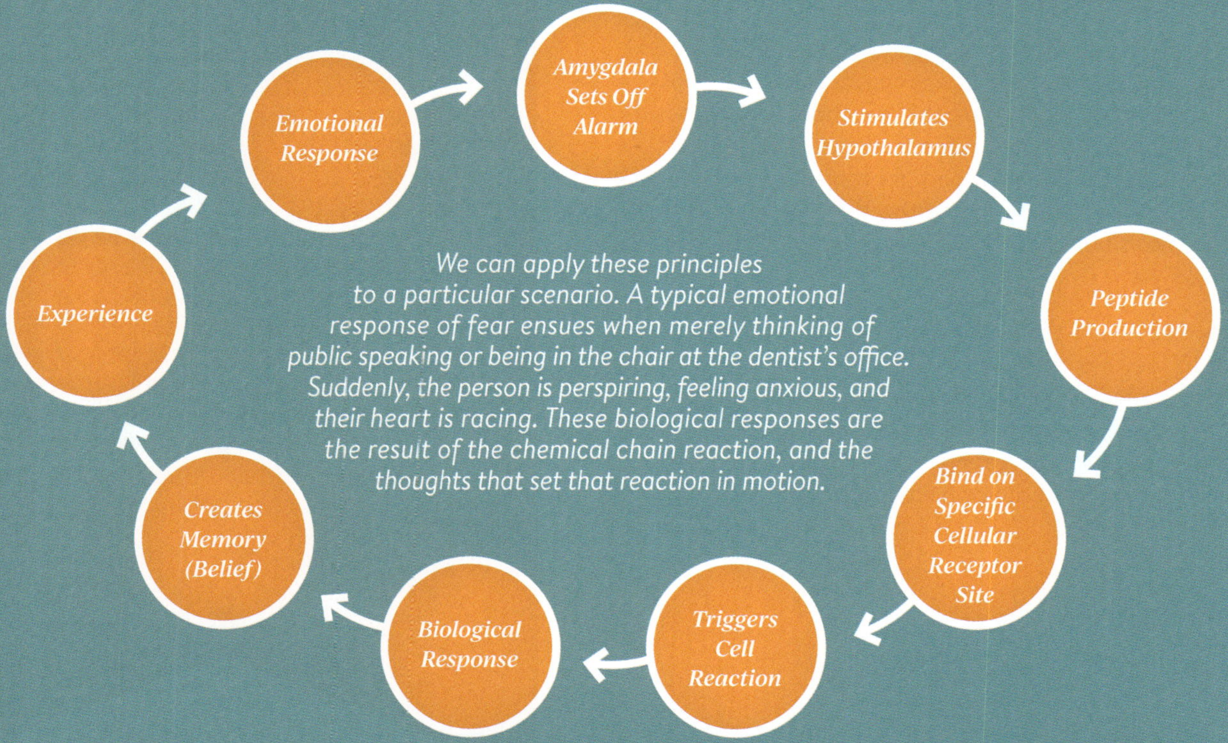

We can apply these principles to a particular scenario. A typical emotional response of fear ensues when merely thinking of public speaking or being in the chair at the dentist's office. Suddenly, the person is perspiring, feeling anxious, and their heart is racing. These biological responses are the result of the chemical chain reaction, and the thoughts that set that reaction in motion.

The Importance of the Sense of Smell

Smell can be used beneficially in healing efforts as well. Scents are experienced long before words. Whether for relieving stress, stabilizing mood, improving sleep, eliminating pain, relieving nausea, or improving memory and energy levels, scents can actually change nervous system biochemistry.

Essential oils can facilitate a rapid emotional response in the brain and the body to facilitate such a release. Essential oils are powerful biochemical agents for emotional balance, wellness, and toxic release, which can be paired or partnered with any holistic or medically-derived program to create a successful approach to mental and emotional wellness.

The Power of Essential Oils Choose Your Mood

Moods are often perceived as having chosen us as if they are happening *to* us. Rather, the chemical impact of our emotions and other exogenous ligands are the real chooser of moods. That's why we reach for certain foods, sugar, caffeine, or a drug of choice (see "Food & Mood" for more information), interact with certain people, do certain things, and act out certain behaviors because of how it makes us feel and to get a "chemical" hit.

What if we could use this knowledge to choose the mood we want to feel and then actually feel it—without harmful substances or recreational drugs? What if we could think of a desired mood and then choose to use a healthful exogenous ligand that is capable of creating it? With essential oils, we have the ability to direct our own emotional traffic!

Our Second Brain

Digestive issues and disorders are growing rampant, in part because of the refined and processed foods that are prevalent in today's diets. The gut is considered the body's "second brain" because of its impact on mood states. In recent years, scientists have discovered that there are more neurotransmitters (a type of ligand) in the gut than there are in the brain, and, among other things, healthy mood management depends on how well these neurotransmitters relay messages to each other.

Serotonin is a chemical responsible for maintaining mood balance, social behavior, appetite, and digestion, sleep, memory, and sexual desire and function. The majority of the body's serotonin, between 80-90 percent can be found in the gastrointestinal tract. Gut health, then, promotes emotional health and mood stabilization. How can an individual hope to experience healthy moods if their cells are depleted of nutrition and if their neurotransmitters reside in an area with blockages and inflammation? How can the over one hundred million neurons embedded in the gut influence healthy emotions when inflammation, blockages, candida, and other harmful bacteria are overpopulated, and system imbalances are standard?

Detoxifying the body can improve emotional health. Toxicity symptoms in the body can directly mirror many depressive symptoms and may include insomnia, foggy thinking, low energy, digestive issues, dampened immune function, and allergies. New studies even suggest that depression may be a type of "allergic reaction" to inflammation.

Chemical compounds found in essential oils stimulate a range of gentle to more intense detoxification effects (depending on use) and promote a natural cleanse for the digestive, endocrine, immune, and lymphatic and other detoxification systems and channels of the body. This, in turn, boosts mood and restores mental and physical energy.

Blood sugar imbalances can also trigger depressive symptoms. Certain essential oils, like cinnamon bark, coriander, and fennel, support metabolic function and assist in moderating blood sugar levels. Omega 3-fatty acids, TerraZyme®, chelated minerals, and B and D vitamins found in a MicroPlex VMz®, antioxidants, and polyphenol supplements also help to regulate blood sugar levels, as well as reduce inflammation, boost energy, and support the gut with the right combination of good fats and other nourishing components.

Rather than feeling victimized by our emotional states, what if we had our own apothecary of essential oils in the home? Such a collection offers a cornucopia of emotional states for ready access. Like an eager child opening a box of candy, relishing the array of colors and designs and imagining the flavors, waiting to tantalize her tongue and brighten her spirit. We, too, can delight in selecting and influencing moods with the use of essential oils.

As natural exogenous ligands, essential oils can powerfully influence our emotions, much like mood-altering drugs like morphine but with healthful results. Unlike synthetic medications or drugs that are designed to alter behavior, their complex molecular structure allows them to intelligently bind to the receptor sites of cells in our body and support a desired effect to restore balance and healthy function.

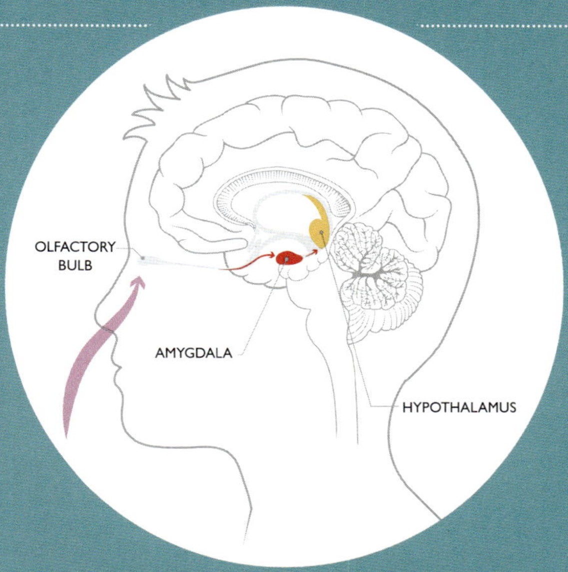

Taking It to the Next Level

Emotional healing and rebalancing of moods is accomplished when a new stimulus is introduced to the same chain of command in the brain. As we've already discussed, an aroma (stimulus) enters the olfactory system, and in turn, the limbic system and amygdala, hypothalamus, and other parts of the brain and body. Depending on the aroma introduced and the information it conveys determines the brain's response. Traumatic memories stored in the amygdala can be released by utilizing the sense of smell and essential oils. If the significance an individual attaches to a past experience can be shifted, the amygdala can release the trauma of the memory. This is what makes aromatherapy a wonderful means for emotional healing and rebalancing moods. Here is an example:

If an individual is deficient in serotonin for an extended period of time, their habitual response to life's situations might be more anxious or angry, more hopeless, more sad, more phobic, more thoughts of "what-if?". If he begins using wild orange, for example, a known antidepressant oil due to its capacity to uplift, detoxify, and calm, he would find himself irresistibly more happy and with a plausible capacity to be more hopeful, trusting, less reactive, and more calm. He also, therefore, has the potential to react to experiences and respond to memories differently.

Here's another example: a young child experiences a high level of trauma, such as a parent suffering from cancer who subsequently passes away. The child's body experiences tremendous chemical expenditures to support the experiences of stress, trauma, and grief. And then, if more trauma occurs, say the deceased parent is replaced and the surviving parent remarries, additional chemicals are released to cope with a new stepparent and step-siblings.

Her coping capacity is chemically diminished if her chemical reserves are not replenished during or after the traumatic seasons of this child's life. She might find herself crying more, experiencing meltdowns more easily, perhaps being teased for being a crybaby, or simply coping less effectively with everyday life. A missed homework deadline, low grade, or athletic performance failure may seem a crushing blow. The same exact events could happen to another person with full reserves who moves through it gracefully. What's the difference?

One of the most important chemicals we have to work in these kinds of situations is endorphins. The name itself reveals it to be an endogenous ligand: "endo-morphine," self-made morphine or *endorphin*. When endorphins are lacking, coping challenges arise. Endorphins serve us not only in our ability to experience pleasure but also to appropriately buffer us from pain, both physical and emotional. The craving for its benefits will drive any number of behaviors when levels are low.

Typically, two types of addictions may arise. One is generally met by abnormally intense levels of thrill or pleasure, as intensity is required in order to get the chemical "hit." The endogenous ligand, endorphins, is the body's "drug" of choice, received on an opiate receptor site. Activities of greater and greater intensity may be pursued to increase the production of endorphins. Bungee jumping, pornography use, playing intense video games, exaggerated sexual activity, gambling, overconsumption of comfort foods, or other behaviors are known to generate endorphins become appealing in an attempt to fill a need.

The second addiction is usually focused on exogenous ligands in the form of pain-numbing opiate drugs, including opium, heroin, Vicodin, oxycodone, and other prescription pain medications. Opiate drugs are received on the same opiate receptor sites. Either type of addiction is powerful as chemical needs remain unmet.

Returning to the story of the child who lost her parent, one of the main chemicals likely low, based on circumstances described, is endorphins. If those diminished reserves of endorphins were never replenished, she would potentially grow into an adult continually experiencing the inability to cope with life or fully experience pleasure, never fully recovering from the trauma, ever searching for ways to numb the pain and meet her emotional needs. Her body is simply lacking the chemical capacity to fully heal. The body needs to increase its reserves and the ability to manufacture the chemicals needed.

Now to explore a potential solution, the essential oil of helichrysum. Helichrysum has powerful analgesic and pain-relieving therapeutic benefits. It is high in many chemical constituents, including one known as ketones, a compound with powerful, regenerative benefits. As the child-turned-adult uses this oil, and her body experiences this chemistry, she is exposed to generous amounts of healthy pain-killing/numbing chemicals. What science has yet to identify is what happens in the body from here.

Whether a chemical need is met or a pathway of reception is opened up is not known. What is happening potentially for the woman, however, is she finally feels relief from "pain." Her coping capacity is increased. She handles life better. With natural, healing chemicals onboard in rich supply, she may finally experiences healing.

The diverse and concentrated chemical constituents in essential oils work to cleanse, ground, lift, balance, and calm the central nervous system and the emotional body. Some essential oils—like frankincense, patchouli, and sandalwood—have high concentrations of sesquiterpene molecules that have been clinically demonstrated to cross the blood-brain barrier. These molecules have significant oxygen supporting effects on the brain and, when combined with aromatic stimulation, can assist the amygdala in releasing the effects of stored memories.

Here are some additional demonstrated mental and emotional benefits:

- Cleanse negative memories
- Reduce stress, anxiety, and tension
- Offset mental fatigue
- Uplift mood
- Calm the central nervous system
- Relax muscular tension
- Induce restful sleep
- Invigorate the senses
- Increase feelings of courage and determination
- Promote a cathartic effect (facilitating the release of stuck emotions)
- Support DNA correction and expression

In conclusion, aromatherapy offers many practical healing advantages, but perhaps one of the most fascinating is the relationship it has with emotional well-being. Inhalation of essential oils with the resulting aromatic exposure is the most effective method of impacting the brain for emotional wellness. Some studies demonstrate that essential oils have the highest bio-frequency of any consumable natural substance.

Essential oils offer a fresh, effective support tool to aid in the emotional healing process and to shift out of old habits and ineffective coping patterns. Aromatherapy allows the individual to harness the olfactory power of plants for healing or simply enhance a state of well-being using scents to create a powerful influence over how one thinks, feels, and behaves.

Move it, Move it

Studies indicate that moderate exercise of thirty minutes a day for three days a week has an antidepressant effect on a large percentage of depressed subjects. However, many who are anxious or depressed lack the energy or sensory motivation to begin an exercise regime. Essential oils like peppermint, cypress, and wintergreen support the flow of blood and oxygen and the sensory "oomph" to engage in physical activity-other oils aid in relieving muscle tension and assisting with muscle recovery. Helichrysum, for example, contains natural chemical components that have a regenerative effect both physically and emotionally.

Practical Application

As essential oils are used topically, aromatically, and internally, the body's vibration is raised, and its emotional frequencies are impacted, as is the capacity for emotional well- being. Each individual oil, with its diverse chemistry, has the ability to be a tremendous multi-tasker and work in multiple areas of interest simultaneously. Additional benefits to essential oil use come from combining oils to create synergistic blends. See Application Methods earlier to learn more.

Application methods also impact the body's response to aromatherapy in emotional health and healing:

- Aromatic use is the fastest way to access the mood center of the brain and invite the release of negative emotions. It is also helpful to use the oils aromatically when resetting new, healthy belief patterns.
- Topical use assists the body in moving from a stress response to a repair or restore response necessary to create an environment where emotional healing can take place.
- Internal use of essential oils supports healthy chemical reactions in the body, nourishment of cells, and release of toxins. This internal support fosters a healthy and balanced emotional environment. Internal use of essential oils supports healthy chemical reactions in the body, nourishes cells, and releases toxins

Sweet Dreams

Adequate sleep is crucial to mental health and brain function. Insomnia and restless sleep are a problem for many who experience depressed or anxious mood states. Pairing a resin or tree essential oil like vetiver, cedarwood, sandalwood, or frankincense with a citrus oil like wild orange, lime, lemon, or bergamot has been found to stabilize mood fluctuations, ground the body, and promote a relaxation response in preparation for sleep. Flower oils like lavender, Roman chamomile, clary sage, geranium, and ylang ylang aid in quieting mental chatter and calming the nervous system.

Similarly, many studies have been conducted on the powerful mental, physical, and emotional benefits of meditation. Meditation is a practice that seeks to achieve a focused state of relaxation. The essential oils listed above can help to still the mind, open air pathways, and calm the mind and heart.

EMOTIONS *Index*

Essential oils are some of nature's most powerful remedies for emotional health. Below are lists designed to help you associate a particular oil an emotion or vice versa. This may serve you as an ongoing wellness resource. Select specific targeted emotional states to address and then identify corresponding oils. **If you want to research specific mood conditions, refer to *Focus & Attention* (pg. 351) and *Mood & Behavior* (pg. 377) sections of this book.**

ESSENTIAL OIL	UN-BALANCED EMOTION	BALANCED EMOTION
Arborvitae	Overzealous	Composed
Basil	Inundated	Relieved
Bergamot	Inadequate	Worthy
Bergamot Mint	Listless	Perky
Birch	Cowardly	Courageous
Black pepper	Repressed	Honest
Black spruce	Halted	Acclaimed
Blue tansy	Overwhelmed	Encouraged
Cardamom	Self-centered	Charitable
Cassia	Uncertain	Bold
Cedarwood	Alone	Connected
Celery seed	Aggravated	Reconciled
Cilantro	Obsessed	Easygoing
Cinnamon bark	Denied	Receptive
Citronella	Punished	Averting
Clary sage	Limited	Enlightened
Clove	Dominated	Supported
Copaiba	Plagued	Directed
Coriander	Apprehensive	Participating
Cypress	Stalled	Progressing
Dill	Avoiding	Intentional
Douglas fir	Upset	Renewed
Eucalyptus	Congested	Stimulated
Fennel	Unproductive	Flourishing
Frankincense	Separated	Unified
Geranium	Neglected	Mended
Ginger	Apathetic	Activated
Grapefruit	Rejected	Validated
Green Mandarin	Distressed	Carefree
Helichrysum	Wounded	Reassured
Hinoki	Muddled	Poised
Jasmine	Hampered	Liberated
Juniper berry	Denying	Insightful
Kumquat	Divided	Integrous
Laurel leaf	Self-sabotaging	Victorious
Lavender	Unheard	Expressed
Lemon	Mindless	Energized
Lemon eucalyptus	Concealed	Revealing
Lemongrass	Obstructed	Flowing
Lime	Faint	Enlivened
Litsea	Encumbered	Purified
Magnolia	Disturbed	Confident
Manuka	Bothered	Revived
Marjoram	Doubtful	Trusting
Melissa	Depressed	Light-filled
Myrrh	Disconnected	Nurtured
Neroli	Afflicted	Released
Oregano	Obstinate	Unattached
Patchouli	Degraded	Enhanced
Peppermint	Hindered	Invigorated
Petitgrain	Conflicted	Harmonized
Pink Pepper	Impeded	Aroused
Ravintsara	Inflicted	Untroubled
Red Mandarin	Troubled	Resilient
Roman chamomile	Frustrated	Purposeful
Rose	Isolated	Loved
Rosemary	Confused	Open-minded
Sandalwood	Uninspired	Devoted
Siberian fir	Excluded	Empowered
Spearmint	Weary	Refreshed
Spikenard	Agitated	Tranquil
Tangerine	Oppressed	Restored
Tea Tree	Unsure	Collected
Thyme	Unyielding	Yielding
Tulsi	Run-down	Enduring
Turmeric	Compromised	Assured
Vanilla	Aloof	Delighted
Vetiver	Ungrounded	Rooted
White fir	Blocked	Receiving
Wild orange	Drained	Productive
Wintergreen	Stubborn	Accepting
Yarrow	Invaded	Shielded
Ylang ylang	Burdened	Exuberant

If you want to feel the positive emotion listed, use the associated oil.

Accepting	wintergreen
Acclaimed	black spruce
Activated	ginger
Aroused	pink pepper
Assured	turmeric
Averting	citronella
Bold	cassia
Carefree	green mandarin
Charitable	cardamom
Collected	tea tree
Composed	arborvitae
Confident	magnolia
Connected	cedarwood
Courageous	birch
Delighted	vanilla
Devoted	sandalwood
Directed	copaiba
Easygoing	cilantro
Empowered	Siberian fir
Encouraged	blue tansy
Enduring	tulsi
Energized	lemon
Enhanced	patchouli
Enlightened	clary sage
Enlivened	lime
Expressed	lavender
Exuberant	ylang ylang
Flourishing	fennel
Flowing	lemongrass
Guided	red mandarin
Harmonized	petitgrain
Honest	black pepper
Insightful	juniper berry
Integrous	kumquat, laurel leaf
Intentional	dill
Invigorated	peppermint
Liberated	jasmine
Light-filled	melissa
Loved	rose
Mended	geranium
Nurtured	myrrh
Open-minded	rosemary
Participating	coriander
Perky	bergamot mint
Poised	hinoki
Productive	wild orange
Progressing	cypress
Purified	litsea
Purposeful	Roman chamomile
Reassured	helichrysum
Receiving	white fir
Receptive	cinnamon bark
Reconciled	celery seed
Refreshed	spearmint
Released	neroli
Relieved	basil
Renewed	Douglas fir
Restored	tangerine
Revealing	lemon eucalyptus
Revived	manuka
Rooted	vetiver
Shielded	Yarrow
Stimulated	eucalyptus
Supported	clove
Tranquil	spikenard
Trusting	marjoram
Unattached	oregano
Unified	frankincense
Untroubled	ravintsara
Validated	grapefruit
Victorious	laurel leaf
Worthy	bergamot
Yielding	thyme

If you are feeling the negative emotion listed, use the associated oil.

Afflicted	neroli
Agitated	spikenard
Aggravated	celery seed
Alone	cedarwood
Aloof	vanilla
Apathetic	ginger
Apprehensive	coriander
Avoiding	dill
Blocked	white fir
Bothered	manuka
Burdened	ylang ylang
Compromised	turmeric
Concealed	lemon eucalyptus
Conflicted	petitgrain
Confused	rosemary
Congested	eucalyptus
Cowardly	birch
Degraded	patchouli
Denied	cinnamon bark
Denying	juniper berry
Depressed	melissa
Disconnected	myrrh
Distressed	green mandarin
Disturbed	magnolia
Divided	kumquat
Dominated	clove
Doubtful	marjoram
Drained	wild orange
Encumbered	litsea
Excluded	Siberian fir
Faint	lime
Frustrated	Roman chamomile
Halted	black spruce
Hampered	jasmine
Hindered	peppermint
Impeded	pink pepper
Inadequate	bergamot
Inflicted	ravintsara
Inundated	basil
Invaded	Yarrow
Isolated	rose
Limited	clary sage
Listless	bergamot mint
Mindless	lemon
Muddled	hinoki
Neglected	geranium
Obsessed	cilantro
Obstinate	oregano
Obstructed	lemongrass
Oppressed	tangerine
Overwhelmed	blue tansy
Overzealous	arborvitae
Plagued	copaiba
Punished	citronella
Rejected	cilantro
Repressed	black pepper
Run-down	tulsi
Self-centered	cardamom
Self-sabotaging	laurel leaf
Separated	frankincense
Stalled	cypress
Stubborn	wintergreen
Troubled	red mandarin
Uncertain	cassia
Ungrounded	vetiver
Unheard	lavender
Uninspired	sandalwood
Unproductive	fennel
Unsure	tea tree
Unyielding	thyme
Upset	Douglas fir
Weary	spearmint
Wounded	helichrysum

Be a POWER USER

The Essential Life supports focusing on core elements of wellness where YOU hold the power to create personal health success. This section teaches one how to become a confident essential oil *Power User* with the healing tools needed to elevate your essential life.

Live an Essential Lifestyle

The first step to balanced living is considering and implementing components that contribute to wellness, or lack of wellness when neglected. Focus your efforts and actions on each of these key areas.

What you put into your body becomes your body. If you want a high-energy, vibrant, high-functioning body, then put high-energy, vibrant, high-functioning food, & fuel into your body! **Add vitality supplements and energizing oils to a great diet.**

Your body was built to move. As you enjoy some kind of active moment every day, your body systems have good reason to stay active and healthy. **Enhance activity with oils for muscle, joint, and respiratory support.**

Meaningful rest is necessary for every body system to reset and regenerate. Commit daily to giving yourself adequate time to recover through quality sleep and personal care. **Use oils that your body responds to for optimal relaxation and sleep.**

Emotional and physical stressors are at the root of all illness and disease. Intentionally discover the best tools to reduce stress in your life. **Pause briefly throughout each day to support emotional balance with your oils.**

Toxicity is found in our water, air, household cleaners and chemicals, and many more things we put into our bodies. **Minimize toxicity and create a clean environment inside your body. Use oils to safely clean your home and detox your body.**

Knowing how to use safe, effective natural remedies is empowering. It allows you to restore health, prevent unwanted issues, and be prepared for the unexpected. **Discover your solutions and how to put them to work for you.**

Good Health Loves Preparation

Be prepared for anything by always keeping your essential oils easily accessible. A few suggestions:

- **Around the House.** Keep frequently used oils by your bedside, in the bathroom, kitchen, and main family living areas. You'll use them more often, see better results, and engage more users if they're easily accessible.
- **Purse or Keychain.** Have an oil-specific small bag with those you need for mood, digestive, and immune support for when out and about or traveling. If not carrying a purse or bag, use a special keychain that holds small vials (5/8 dram) of your favorite oils.
- **Car.** Bring oils for focus and stress management in your car to turn driving time into useful rejuvenation time. Don't leave your oils in a hot car. Heat destroys the compounds.
- **Diaper Bag or Stroller.** Kids love to do the unexpected. Choose to be ready for those bumps and bruises, skin irritations, and temper tantrums.

tip Consistency brings the magic. While oils are fast-acting, consistency breeds the best long-term results.

tip Frequency trumps quantity. Use smaller amounts of oils more frequently to maximize results.

Find Brilliant Answers

Learn how to take greater ownership of your personal and family's health and wellness. Seem overwhelming? Don't know where to turn for resources that are trustworthy and up-to-date?

The Essential Life team is dedicated to helping you eliminate the stress of learning to take charge of your health and wellness by providing additional resources at **www.EssentialLife.com**

Go to EssentialLife.com to:

- **Buy** *The Essential Life*, *The Essential Basics*, *The Essential Quick Reference* books or booklets.
- **Download** *The Essential Life* app to look up remedies on the go and stay in sync with the EL community as they share their remedies and insights.

Explore Different Usage Methods

- **Aromatic.** Keep a diffuser in high-traffic areas in the home and in sleeping areas. Diffusers are a great way to let everyone around enjoy the benefits of the oils.
- **Topical.** Have a carrier oil, like fractionated coconut oil, on hand for use with sensitive skin and as a remedy if someone experiences sensitivity after an oil has been applied. Try recipes for skin creams and lotions with your oils.
- **Internal.** Keep veggie capsules near your oils for easy internal use. Put some in a small plastic baggie so they are ready to grab on the go. Remember to only use oils internally if they are tested and certified pure.

tip Blending oils is a lot of fun! Also, try layering oils. Apply one oil topically at a time, wait several seconds, and then apply another, and so on.

tip Focus your efforts. You'll achieve greater results as you concentrate your efforts on just a few key wellness goals.

Supercharge Your Oils

While oils can be used in an infinite number of ways, find methods that work best for you and your family. Try some of these tips to enhance the effectiveness of your oils:

- **Add heat.** Use a hot compress to drive the oils in deeper when using topically. Avoid use of heat with "hot" oils.
- **Add frankincense.** Frankincense enhances the therapeutic effects of many protocols and offers exceptional healing properties.
- **Massage.** Massaging oils into an area of need stimulates circulation and increases absorption. It provides benefits for the person giving and the person receiving the massage.
- **Combine oils that complement each other.** Don't be afraid to try different oil combinations. You can find an ocean of essential oil recipes and protocols in this book and online. Try different combinations, and enjoy the process of discovering what resonates with your body.

SAFETY *and* STORAGE

Every individual can safely use essential oils but needs to be educated with proper information first.

Essential oils are concentrated, potent plant extracts and should be used with reasonable care. Essential oils are very effective and safe when used appropriately. It takes a small amount to induce a powerful therapeutic benefit.

Never apply essential oils directly to eyes or ear canals. After applying, take care to avoid eye contact or the touching of sensitive areas. If oils enter eyes, place a drop of carrier oil, such as fractionated coconut or olive oil, in the eye and blink until it's clear. Never use water, as oils and water don't mix, and water does not help with dilution.

SENSATION

Some oils are considered "warm" or even "hot," creating a heat-like sensation on the skin. These are best diluted with a carrier oil when used topically. These oils include birch, cassia, cinnamon, clove, eucalyptus, ginger, lemongrass, oregano, peppermint, thyme, tulsi, and wintergreen. With babies, children, and those with sensitive skin or compromised health, it is particularly important to exercise caution or avoidance with these oils, as they can be a temporary or even severe irritant to delicate skin. When using these oils internally, it is best to consume in a vegetable capsule.

PHOTOSENSITIVITY

Some oils contain furocoumarins, a constituent that can cause the skin to be photosensitive. Photosensitive oils react to sources of UV rays (e.g., sunshine, tanning bed, etc.). The higher the concentration of furanoids, the greater the sensitivity. Oils with concentrated amounts of furanoids include any cold-pressed citrus oil such as bergamot, grapefruit, lemon, and lime, with lesser amounts in wild orange. Internal use of these oils is typically not a problem. It is best to wait a minimum of twelve hours after topical application of these photosensitive oils before being exposed to UV rays. Be sure to consult a healthcare provider before incorporating products into your routine.

PREGNANCY & NURSING

Most essential oils applied topically and used reasonably are safe to be used during pregnancy and nursing. Some individuals prefer to avoid internal use during pregnancy, and some use essential oils only aromatically during the first trimester. Several oils may be helpful during and after delivery. Internal use of peppermint essential oil should be avoided while nursing as it may reduce milk supply. Be sure to consult your healthcare provider before incorporating products into your routine. To learn more about oil usage during pregnancy and nursing, see *Pregnancy, Labor & Nursing* (pg. 403).

CRITICAL HEALTH

Persons with critical health conditions should consult a healthcare professional before using essential oils and may want to research individual oils prior to using them. In general, those with low seizure thresholds should be cautious in using, or avoid altogether, fennel, basil, rosemary, birch, and any digestive blend that contains fennel. Those with high blood pressure should be cautious with or avoid thyme and rosemary essential oils.

CLEANSING REACTION

Occasionally, a person may experience a cleansing reaction, which takes place when the body is trying to rid itself of toxins faster than it is able. When this happens, increase water intake and decrease application of essential oils, or change the area of application.

STORAGE

The compounds in essential oils are best preserved when stored and kept from light, heat, air, and moisture. Extended exposure to oxygen can break down and change the chemical makeup of an essential oil. This process is called oxidation, and an oil is said to have "oxidative breakdown." This process is slow but can, over time, promote skin sensitivity with some oils. Citrus oils and blue-tinted oils and those high in aldehydes are especially prone to this breakdown.

For optimum storage of these types of oils, and for longer than a year, refrigeration is best. A carrier oil can also be added to slow the oxidation process. Keep air space in essential oil bottles to a minimum for those that are opened and kept for a longer period of time. Consider combining partially used bottles. Some oils with compounds such as sesquiterpenes (e.g., myrrh and sandalwood) can actually get better with age. Essential oils can be flammable and should be kept clear of open flame, spark, or fire hazards.

CHILDREN & BABIES

The general rule is dilute oils for babies and children. Before applying an oil, it is best to check the oil's profile in *Natural Solutions* for any safety warnings or precautions. Use extra care when an oil is "hot" (as previously mentioned on this page). Be sure to keep oils out of reach of children. To understand more about applying oils to babies and children, refer to *Children* (pg. 325) for further information and dosage recommendations.

safety tips

- Refer to the internal use guidelines on pg. 20 prior to ingesting oils.
- Avoid oils in eyes, ears, and nose.
- Avoid exposing areas of application to sunlight for 12 hours after using citrus oils topically.
- Dilute oils for sensitive skin
- Refer to *Natural Solutions* for specific oil safety and usage recommendations for each oil and blend.

SECTION 2

QUICK REFERENCE

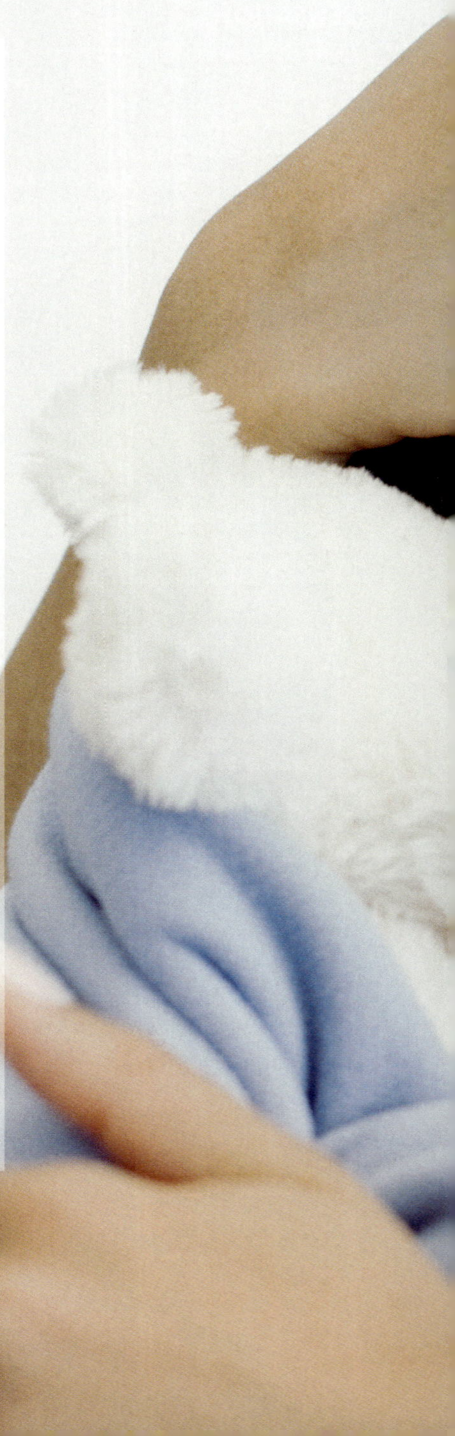

How to Use This Section

Ailments are listed alphabetically. Start by searching for the ailment in question, then note the recommended essential oils for each ailment. Oils are listed in order of most common use. Application methods are also recommended for each oil. Here are key applications for you to choose from:

= Aromatic:

Diffuse with a diffuser.
Inhale from cupped hands (your personal diffuser).
Inhale directly from oil bottle.
Wear an oil pendant.

= Topical:

Apply to area of pain or concern (dilute as needed).
Apply under nose, to back of neck, forehead, or wrists.
To affect entire body, apply to bottoms of feet, spine, or navel.
To affect specific organs or body systems, apply to reflex points on the ears, hands, or feet (See *Reflexology* pg. 22).
*Add warm compress or massage to drive oils deeper into body tissues.

= Internal:

Put a drop or two of oil under tongue, hold a few seconds, and then swallow.
Drink a few drops in a glass of water.
Put a few drops of oil in an empty capsule and swallow.
Put a drop of oil on the back of your hand and lick.

For more specific instruction, see *Application Methods* on page 18. For more in-depth information, see *Be a Power User* on page 36.

Frequency:
For acute conditions, use every fifteen to twenty minutes until symptoms subside, then apply every two to six hours as needed. For chronic or ongoing conditions, repeat one to 2x's per day, typically morning, and evening.

For more information on a particular ailment, see the corresponding *Focus Areas* page.

AILMENTS INDEX A-Z

STEPS:

1. Look up ailment.
2. Choose one or more of the recommended oils. Use oil(s) as indicated. Order of recommendation of oils and use is left to right.
3. Learn more in corresponding focus area.

AILMENT	RECOMMENDED OILS & USE	FOCUS AREA
Abdominal Cramps	Constrictive intermittent abdominal discomfort resulting from the spasm of an internal organ. DigestZen® · Peppermint · Petitgrain · Ginger · ClaryCalm®	Digestive & Intestinal pg. 331; Women's Health pg. 436; Pain & Inflammation pg. 392
Abnormal Sperm Morphology	Sperm with a double tail or no tail; a sperm head that is crooked, has double heads, or is too large. Thyme · Rosemary · Clary Sage · DDR Prime® · Zendocrine®	Men's Health pg. 374
Abscessed Tooth	A contained collection of liquefied tissue, known as pus, reacting as a defense to foreign material. Clove · Tea Tree · Thyme · Frankincense · Purify | Abōde™	Oral Health pg. 389
Absentmindedness	Preoccupation so great that the ordinary insistence on attention is avoided. InTune® · Cedarwood · Peppermint · Patchouli · Vetiver	Brain pg. 300; Focus & Concentration pg. 351
Abuse Trauma	Trauma caused by being intentionally harmed or injured by another person. Melissa · Roman Chamomile · Console® · Frankincense · Elevation	Mood & Behavior pg. 377; Limbic pg. 371
Ache	Pain identified by persistent and usually limited intensity. Deep Blue® | Rescuer™ · AromaTouch® · Peppermint · Wintergreen · Cypress	Muscular pg. 381; Skeletal pg. 415; Pain & Inflammation pg. 392; Immune & Lymphatic pg. 355
Acidosis	Excess acid in the body due to the accumulation of acid or the depletion of alkaline reserves. Zendocrine® · Helichrysum · Lemon · Fennel · DDR Prime®	Detoxification pg. 326
Acid reflux	A chronic digestive disease occurring when stomach acid or content flows back into the food pipe irritating the lining of the esophagus. DigestZen® · Fennel · Peppermint · Ginger · Lemon	Digestive & Intestinal pg. 331
Acne	A common skin disease identified by pimples that surface when pores of the skin become clogged. HD Clear® · Tea Tree · Sandalwood · Immortelle · Arborvitae	Integumentary pg. 360; Endocrine pg. 340; Detoxification pg. 326
Acromegaly	Excess growth hormone production in the anterior pituitary gland after puberty. Frankincense · Zendocrine® · Balance® · Peace® · Rosemary	Endocrine pg. 340
Actinic Keratosis	A small rough reddish colored spot on the skin that comes from too much sun exposure. Immortelle · Lavender · Frankincense · Sandalwood · Geranium	Integumentary pg. 360
ADD/ADHD	A disorder characterized by short attention span, impulsivity, and (in some cases) hyperactivity. InTune® | Thinker™ · Vetiver · Peace® · Lavender · Motivate® | Brave™	Focus & Concentration pg. 351

Aromatic: Inhale from cupped hands or diffuse into the air.
Topical: Apply directly to affected area(s) or bottom of feet.
Internal: Take in a capsule, glass of water, or on/under tongue.
TIP Adults: Use 2-3 drops; Children: Use 1-2 drops.

AILMENT	RECOMMENDED OILS & USE	FOCUS AREA
Addictions	The repeated involvement with a substance or activity, despite the potential substantial harm it may cause, because that involvement was (and may continue to be) pleasurable and/or valuable. Copabia (Internal); Helichrysum (Internal); Black Pepper (Internal); Bergamot (Internal, Topical); Cinnamon Bark (Internal)	Endocrine pg. 340; Autoimmune pg. 292
Addison's Disease	A long-term endocrine disorder in which the adrenal glands do not produce enough steroid hormones. Clove (Internal, Topical); Basil (Internal, Topical); Cinnamon Bark (Internal, Topical); Zendocrine® (Internal, Topical); Rosemary (Internal, Topical)	Endocrine pg. 340; Autoimmune pg. 292
Adrenal Fatigue	A decrease in the adrenal glands' ability produce a diversity of hormones essential to life, commonly caused by chronic stress. Rosemary (Topical, Internal, Aromatic); Basil (Topical, Internal, Aromatic); Geranium (Topical, Internal, Aromatic); Zendocrine® (Topical, Internal); Ylang Ylang (Topical, Internal, Aromatic)	Endocrine pg. 340; Energy & Vitality pg. 344
Age Spots	Flat tan, brown, or black spots that vary in size that usually appear on the face, hands, shoulders, and arms. Immortelle (Topical); Frankincense (Topical); Sandalwood (Topical); Spikenard (Topical); Petitgrain (Topical)	Integumentary pg. 360; Other pg. 323
Agitation	A feeling of restlessness associated with increased motor activity. Serenity® | Calmer™ (Topical, Aromatic); Deep Blue® (Topical, Aromatic); Peace® (Topical, Aromatic); Balance® | Steady™ (Topical, Aromatic); Lavender (Topical, Aromatic)	Mood & Behavior pg. 377; Focus & Concentration pg. 351
AIDS or HIV	A disease in which there is a severe loss of the body's cellular immunity, greatly lowering the resistance to infection and malignancy. Cinnamon Bark (Topical, Internal); On Guard® | Stronger™ (Topical, Internal, Aromatic); Melissa (Topical, Internal, Aromatic); Tea Tree (Topical); DDR Prime® (Topical, Internal)	Immune & Lymphatic pg. 355
Alcohol Addiction	The frequent intake of large amounts of alcohol, commonly noted by the impairment of regular functioning. Helichrysum (Internal, Aromatic, Topical); Forgive® (Aromatic, Topical); Cinnamon Bark (Internal); Zendocrine® (Internal); Slim & Sassy® (Internal)	Addictions pg. 280; Limbic pg. 371
Alertness	A measure of being mentally keen, active, and rapidly aware of one's environment. Peppermint (Topical, Aromatic); Rosemary (Topical, Aromatic); Motivate® (Topical, Aromatic); Breathe® (Topical, Aromatic); InTune® | Thinker™ (Topical, Aromatic)	Brain pg. 300; Focus & Concentration pg. 351; Energy & Vitality pg. 344
Alkalosis	Uncommonly high alkalinity of blood and body fluids. Geranium (Internal, Topical); Balance® (Topical, Aromatic); On Guard® (Internal, Topical, Aromatic); Citrus Bliss® (Topical, Aromatic); Rosemary (Internal, Topical)	Detoxification pg. 326
Allergies (Insect)	A hypersensitive reaction to an insect allergen. Lavender (Topical, Internal); Abōde™ | Purify (Topical); Roman Chamomile (Topical); Arborvitae (Topical); Blue Tansy (Topical)	First Aid pg. 347; Integumentary pg. 360; Allergies pg. 284
Allergies (Pet Dander)	An overreaction of the immune system to ordinarily harmless pet dander resulting in skin rash, sneezing, or wheezing. Lavender (Aromatic, Topical, Internal); Roman Chamomile (Aromatic, Topical, Internal); Zendocrine® (Aromatic, Topical, Internal); Breathe® (Aromatic, Topical); Abōde™ | Purify (Aromatic, Topical)	Allergies pg. 284
Allergies (Respiratory)	Uncommon reactions of the respiratory system that arise in response to otherwise inoffensive substances. Lavender (Internal, Aromatic, Topical); Lemon | Melissa (Internal, Aromatic, Topical); Peppermint (Internal, Aromatic, Topical); Roman Chamomile (Internal, Aromatic, Topical); Breathe® (Aromatic, Topical)	Respiratory pg. 409; Allergies pg. 284; First Aid pg. 347; Digestive & Intestinal pg. 331
Alzheimer's Disease	A progressive neurological disease that destroys memory and other important mental functions. DDR Prime® (Internal, Topical); Frankincense | Black Spruce (Internal, Topical | Topical); Thyme (Internal, Topical); Clove | Turmeric (Internal, Aromatic); Cilantro (Internal, Topical)	Brain pg. 300

QUICK REFERENCE

*Avoid eyes, ear canals, and nasal passages.

STEPS:

1. Look up ailment.
2. Choose one or more of the recommended oils. Use oil(s) as indicated. Order of recommendation of oils and use is left to right.
3. Learn more in corresponding focus area.

AILMENT	RECOMMENDED OILS & USE	FOCUS AREA
Amenorrhea	Three or more missed menstrual periods in a row or the lack of menstruation by age 15. ClaryCalm® · Basil · Rosemary · DDR Prime® · Clary Sage	Women's Health pg. 436
Amnesia	A partial or total loss of memory. Peppermint · InTune® · Forgive® · Peace® · Frankincense	Brain pg. 300
Amyotrophic Lateral Sclerosis (ALS) / Lou Gehrig's Disease	Also known as Lou Gehrig's disease, ALS is a neurological disease that attacks the nerve cells that control voluntary muscles. Cypress · DDR Prime® · Melissa · Patchouli · Frankincense	Autoimmune pg. 292; Nervous System pg. 385; Muscular pg. 381
Anemia	A condition in which there is an unusually low number of red blood cells in the bloodstream. Zendocrine® · Cinnamon Bark · Helichrysum · Geranium · DDR Prime®	Cardiovascular pg. 308
Aneurysm	Excessive localized enlargement or ballooning of an artery caused by a weakening of the artery wall. Helichrysum · Cypress · DDR Prime® · Frankincense · Marjoram	Cardiovascular pg. 308
Anger	A strong feeling of annoyance, displeasure, or hostility. Forgive® · Balance® | Steady™ · Helichrysum · Peace® · Serenity® | Calmer™	Mood & Behavior pg. 377; Children pg. 317; Focus & Concentration pg. 351;
Angina	A condition marked by severe pain in the chest caused by an inadequate blood supply to the heart. Douglas Fir · Thyme · Basil · Cinnamon Bark · Rosemary	Cardiovascular pg. 308
Ankylosing Spondylitis	An inflammatory arthritis affecting the spine and large joints. Wintergreen · AromaTouch® · Birch · Balance® · Deep Blue®	Skeletal pg. 415; Pain & Inflammation pg. 392
Anorexia	An emotional disorder characterized by an obsessive desire to lose weight by refusing to eat. Grapefruit · Patchouli · Slim & Sassy® · Bergamot · Peace®	Eating Disorders pg. 336; Addictions pg. 280; Weight pg. 431
Anosmia	Loss of the sense of smell, usually caused by a nasal condition or brain injury. Peppermint · Basil · Lemongrass · Helichrysum · Arborvitae	Respiratory pg. 409
Anthrax	A rare but serious bacterial illness typically affecting livestock but can be spread to humans affecting the intestines, skin, or lungs. Oregano · Melissa · Thyme · Clove · Frankincense	Immune & Lymphatic pg. 355
Anxiety	A mental health disorder characterized by feelings of worry, nervousness, or fear that are strong enough to interfere with one's daily activities. Serenity® | Calmer™ · Adaptiv™ · Lavender + Wild Orange · Peace® | Roman Chamomile · Balance®	Mood & Behavior pg. 377; Stress pg. 423; Focus & Concentration pg. 351
Apathy	A lack of, absence, indifference, or suppression of emotion. Ginger · Motivate® · Passion® · Ylang Ylang · Citrus Bliss®	Mood & Behavior pg. 377

Discover other ways essential oil enthusiasts are getting results in the app.

Aromatic: Inhale from cupped hands or diffuse into the air.
Topical: Apply directly to affected area(s) or bottom of feet.
Internal: Take in a capsule, glass of water, or on/under tongue.
TIP Adults: Use 2-3 drops; Children: Use 1-2 drops.

(A = Aromatic, T = Topical, I = Internal)

AILMENT	RECOMMENDED OILS & USE	FOCUS AREA
Appetite (Loss of)	Absence of the desire to eat. Peace® (T, A); Slim & Sassy® (I, T); Console® (A, T); Wild Orange (I, A, T); Cardamom (I, T)	Digestive & Intestinal pg. 331; Stress pg. 423; Eating Disorders pg. 336; Weight pg. 431
Appetite (Overactive)	Excessive feelings of hunger. Slim & Sassy® (I, T, A); Grapefruit (I, A); Ginger (I, T, A); Cinnamon Bark (I, T); Peppermint (I, T, A)	Weight pg. 431; Eating Disorders pg. 336; Addictions pg. 280
ARDS	Acute Respiratory Distress Syndrome is a condition in which fluid collects in the lungs' air sacs, depriving organs of oxygen. Rosemary (T, A); Melissa (T, A); Eucalyptus (T, A); Breathe® (T, A); Cardamom (T, A)	Respiratory pg. 409
Arrhythmia	An irregularity in the strength or rhythm of the heartbeat. Lavender (T, A); Ylang Ylang (I, T, A); Basil (I, T, A); Rosemary (I, T, A); Melissa (I, T)	Cardiovascular pg. 308
Arteriosclerosis	A chronic disease involving the thickening and hardening of the walls of the arteries, occurring typically in old age. Black Pepper (T, I); Lemongrass (I, T); Cinnamon Bark (I); Juniper Berry (I, T); On Guard® (I, T)	Cardiovascular pg. 308
Arthritic Pain	Inflammation and stiffness of the joints followed by pain, and swelling that can worsen with age. Deep Blue® | Rescuer™ (T); Copaiba (I); Turmeric (T, I); Frankincense (T, I); Black Pepper (T, I)	Skeletal pg. 415; Pain & Inflammation pg. 392
Arthritis (Reactive)	A chronic form of arthritic joint pain and swelling triggered by an infection. Deep Blue® | Rescuer™ (T); Lemongrass (T, I); On Guard® (T, I); AromaTouch® (T); Wintergreen (T)	Immune & Lymphatic pg. 355; Pain & Inflammation pg. 392; Autoimmune pg. 292; Skeletal pg. 415
Asthma	A respiratory condition characterized by spasms in the bronchi of the lungs, causing difficulty in breathing. Typically results from an allergic reaction or other forms of hypersensitivity. Breathe® (T, A); Eucalyptus (T, A); Rosemary (T, A, I); Peppermint (I, T, A); Cardamom (I, T, A)	Respiratory pg. 409; Allergies pg. 284; Digestive & Intestinal pg. 331
Ataxia	Loss of the full control to coordinate bodily muscular movement. Frankincense (T, I); Sandalwood (T, I); Helichrysum (T, I); Marjoram (T, I); DDR Prime® (I, T)	Brain pg. 300; Muscular pg. 381
Atherosclerosis	The increase of a waxy plaque on the inside of blood vessels. Marjoram (I, T); Lemongrass (I, T); Slim & Sassy® (I, T); Cinnamon Bark (I, T); On Guard® (I, T)	Cardiovascular pg. 308
Athlete's Foot	A fungus infection that typically begins between the toes in which the skin starts cracking and peeling away, becoming itchy and sore. Tea Tree (T); Cinnamon Bark (T, I); Oregano (T, I); HD Clear® (T); Arborvitae | Citronella (T)	Athletes pg. 288; Candida pg. 304; Integumentary pg. 360
Auditory Processing Disorder	A disorder affecting the ability to understand speech in noisy environments, follow directions, and distinguish between similar sounds. Helichrysum (T); Basil (T, A, I); Peace® (T, A); Douglas Fir (T, A); DDR Prime® (T, I)	Brain pg. 300; Nervous System pg. 385
Autism / Asperger's	A serious developmental disorder, present from early childhood, that impairs the ability to communicate, interact, and regulate behavior. Clary Sage (T, A); Serenity® | Calmer™ (T, A); Balance® | Steady™ (T, A); Zendocrine® (T, I, A); Frankincense | DDR Prime® (T, A, I)	Brain pg. 300; Mood & Behavior pg. 377; Nervous System pg. 385

*Avoid eyes, ear canals, and nasal passages.

STEPS:

1. Look up ailment.
2. Choose one or more of the recommended oils. Use oil(s) as indicated. Order of recommendation of oils and use is left to right.
3. Learn more in corresponding focus area.

AILMENT — **RECOMMENDED OILS & USE** — **FOCUS AREA**

Autoimmune Disorder
A disease in which the body's immune system attacks healthy cells.
DDR Prime® · Turmeric · Lemongrass · Zendocrine® · Thyme
Focus area: Autoimmune pg. 292

Autointoxication
Poisoning by toxins or metabolic waste formed within the body itself.
Zendocrine® · Cilantro · Clove · Geranium · Thyme
Focus area: Detoxification pg. 326; Weight pg. 431

Avoidant Restrictive Food Intake Disorder
A type of eating disorder where the consumption of certain foods is limited based on the food's appearance, smell, taste, texture, or a past negative experience with the food. Previously known as selective eating disorder (SED).
Slim & Sassy® · Patchouli · Passion® · Forgive® · Bergamot
Focus area: Eating Disorders pg. 336

Back Muscle Fatigue
A state of fatigue or loss of strength and/or muscle endurance following arduous activity associated with the accumulation of lactic acid in muscles.
AromaTouch® · Deep Blue® · Ginger · Wintergreen · Marjoram
Focus area: Muscular pg. 381

Back Pain
A pain in the lumbar regions of the back varying in sharpness and intensity.
Deep Blue® | Rescuer™ · Copaiba · Wintergreen · Siberian Fir · Frankincense
Focus area: Pain & Inflammation pg. 392; Skeletal pg. 415; Muscular pg. 381

Back Stiffness
Persistent throbbing or stiffness anywhere along the spine from the base of the neck to the tailbone.
AromaTouch® · Peppermint · Deep Blue® | Rescuer™ · Siberian Fir · PastTense®
Focus area: Pain & Inflammation pg. 392; Muscular pg. 381; Skeletal pg. 415

Bacteria
Single-celled microorganisms that can exist either as independent (free-living) organisms or as parasites (dependent on another organism for life) that thrive in diverse environments.
Tea Tree · Oregano · Cinnamon Bark · Abōde™ | Purify · Cilantro
Focus area: Immune & Lymphatic pg. 355

Bags Under the Eyes
The appearance of mild swelling or puffiness in the tissues under the eyes caused by fluid buildup.
Lime · Immortelle · Juniper Berry · Cedarwood · Roman Chamomile
Focus area: Integumentary pg. 360; Sleep pg. 419

Balance Problems
Symptoms include light-headedness to dizziness and may be caused by viral or bacterial infections in the ear, a head injury, or blood circulation disorders that affect the inner ear or brain.
Rosemary · Cedarwood · Frankincense · Ylang Ylang · Douglas Fir
Focus area: Brain pg. 300; Cardiovascular pg. 308; Immune & Lymphatic pg. 355

Baldness
Having little or no hair on the scalp.
DDR Prime® · Ylang Ylang · Rosemary · Thyme · Clary Sage
Focus area: Integumentary pg. 360; Men's Health pg. 374

Basal Cell Carcinoma
A slow-growing form of skin cancer with a low metastatic risk. It is the most common skin cancer.
DDR Prime® · Frankincense · Sandalwood · Zendocrine® · Melissa
Focus area: Cellular Health pg. 313; Integumentary pg. 360

Bed Bugs
Small, oval, brownish parasitic insects that live on the blood of animals or humans.
TerraShield® · Arborvitae · Eucalyptus · Siberian Fir · Peppermint
Focus area: On the Go pg. 504

Bed Sores
A painful reddened area of ulcerated skin caused by pressure and lack of movement.
Lavender · Myrrh · Geranium · Frankincense · Cypress
Focus area: Integumentary pg. 360

Bed-wetting
Involuntary urination while asleep after the age at which bladder control typically happens.
Cypress · Juniper Berry · Cinnamon Bark · Copaiba · Peace®
Focus area: Children pg. 317; Urinary pg. 428; Mood & Behavior pg. 377

Aromatic: Inhale from cupped hands or diffuse into the air.
Topical: Apply directly to affected area(s) or bottom of feet.
Internal: Take in a capsule, glass of water, or on/under tongue.
TIP Adults: Use 2-3 drops; Children: Use 1-2 drops.

AILMENT	RECOMMENDED OILS & USE	FOCUS AREA
Bee Sting	An injury caused by the venom of bees, usually followed by swelling and pain. Purify | Abōde™; Lavender; Roman Chamomile; Clove; Basil	First Aid pg. 347
Bell's Palsy	A weakness or paralysis of the muscles on one side of the face causing that side of the face to droop. Usually the result of a virus, respiratory, cranial, nerve or blood sugar issue. Frankincense; Basil; Thyme; On Guard®; Helichrysum	Nervous System pg. 385; Immune & Lymphatic pg. 355; Muscular pg. 381
Benign Prostatic Hyperplasia	A noncancerous case of the prostate that causes overgrowth of the prostate tissue, obstructing urination. Clary Sage; Thyme; DDR Prime®; Juniper Berry; Sandalwood	Cellular Health pg. 313; Men's Health pg. 374
Binge Eating Disorder (BED)	A serious eating disorder characterized by recurrent episodes of compulsively consuming unusually large amounts of food quickly and feeling unable to stop. A person with BED will not use compensatory behaviors, such as self-induced vomiting or over-exercising after binge eating. Slim & Sassy®; Cinnamon Bark; Elevation; Console®; Adaptiv™ | Cedarwood	Eating Disorders pg. 336; Digestive & Intestinal pg. 331; Weight pg. 431
Bipolar Disorder	A mood disorder characterized by extreme episodes of mania and depression. Individuals with severe episodes may experience psychotic symptoms. Also known as manic-depressive illness. Melissa; Elevation; Peace®; Serenity® | Calmer™; Bergamot	Limbic pg. 371
Bladder Control	Urinary incontinence is unexpected loss of urine that is sufficient enough in regularity and amount to cause physical and/or emotional concern in the person experiencing it. Forgive®; Thyme; Rosemary; Coriander; Spearmint	Urinary pg. 428; Mood & Behavior pg. 377
Bladder Infection (Cystitis)	Inflammation of the urinary bladder, typically due to a bacterial infection of the bladder. Lemongrass; Wintergreen; Oregano; Thyme; Lemon	Urinary pg. 428; Candida pg. 304
Bleeding	The discharge of blood from the vascular system as a result of harm to a blood vessel. Helichrysum; Yarrow | Pom; Geranium; Lavender; Frankincense	Cardiovascular pg. 308; First Aid pg. 347
Blisters from Sun	A local swelling of the skin that contains watery fluid, caused by overexposure to the sun. Lavender; Myrrh; Immortelle; Helichrysum; Sandalwood	Integumentary pg. 360
Blisters on Feet	A local swelling of the skin that contains watery fluid, caused by moisture or friction. Myrrh; Frankincense; Patchouli; Lavender; Eucalyptus	Integumentary pg. 360
Bloating	Any abnormal general swelling of the abdominal area with symptoms including feeling full, tight, or in pain. Peppermint; Ginger; DigestZen® | Tamer™; Fennel; Slim & Sassy®	Digestive & Intestinal pg. 331; Holiday pg. 476
Blood Clot	A thickened lump in the blood formed to stop bleeding, such as at the site of a cut. Coriander; DDR Prime®; Fennel; Helichrysum; AromaTouch®	Cardiovascular pg. 308
Blood Pressure (High)/ Hypertension	A condition in which the force of the blood against the artery walls is too strong. Commonly known as hypertension. Marjoram; Ylang Ylang; Celery Seed; Lavender | Petitgrain; Clove	Cardiovascular pg. 308 Urinary pg. 428

*Avoid eyes, ear canals, and nasal passages.

STEPS:

1. Look up ailment.
2. Choose one or more of the recommended oils. Use oil(s) as indicated. Order of recommendation of oils and use is left to right.
3. Learn more in corresponding focus area.

AILMENT	RECOMMENDED OILS & USE	FOCUS AREA
Blood Pressure (Low)/Hypotension	A condition in which a person's blood pressure is not satisfactory for tissue oxygenation. Commonly known as hypotension. Thyme · DDR Prime® · Basil · Rosemary · Lime	Cardiovascular pg. 308; Endocrine pg. 340
Blood Sugar (Low) Hypoglycemia	An uncommonly low concentration of glucose in the circulating blood. Cassia · Lavender · Zendocrine® · Cypress · Juniper Berry	Blood Sugar pg. 297; Endocrine pg. 340
Blood Sugar (High) Hyperglycemia	A condition in which the body does not handle glucose effectively. Blood glucose levels may fluctuate outside of the body's optimal blood glucose range. Coriander · Cinnamon Bark · Cassia · Slim & Sassy® · Fennel	Blood Sugar pg. 297; Endocrine pg. 340;
Blood Toxicity or Poisoning	Occurs when bacteria-causing infection in another part of the body enters the bloodstream. Geranium · Zendocrine® · Celery Seed | Turmeric · DDR Prime® · Frankincense	Blood Sugar pg. 297; Endocrine pg. 340;
Body Dysmorphic Disorder	A type of chronic mental illness in which one cannot stop thinking about a minor or imagined flaw in appearance. Appearance seems so shameful that the individual does not want to be seen by anyone. Clove · Frankincense · Arborvitae · DDR Prime® · Rosemary	Brain pg. 300; Limbic pg. 371; Mood & Behavior pg. 377
Body Myositis	Inflammation of a muscle, especially a voluntary muscle, characterized by pain, tenderness, and sometimes spasm in the affected area. Marjoram · Lemongrass · AromaTouch® · Cypress · Wintergreen	Muscular pg. 381; Pain & Inflammation pg. 392
Body Odor	An unpleasant smell produced by bacteria on the skin that breaks down the acids in perspiration. Petitgrain · Cilantro · Purify | Abōde™ · Zendocrine® · Arborvitae	Detoxification pg. 326; Personal Care pg. 508
Boils	Painful, pus-filled bumps under the skin caused by infected, inflamed hair follicles. Myrrh · Immortelle · Tea Tree · Purify · Lavender	Integumentary pg. 360
Bone Pain	Any pain that is associated with an unusual condition within a bone, such as osteomyelitis. Deep Blue® · Helichrysum · Wintergreen · Siberian Fir · Birch	Skeletal pg. 415; Pain & Inflammation pg. 392
Bone Spurs	Bony projections that develop along the edges of bones. Also referred to as osteophytes. Cypress · Eucalyptus · Basil · Lemongrass · Wintergreen	Skeletal pg. 415
Brain Fog	A condition defined by decreased clarity of thought, confusion, and forgetfulness which may lead to minor depression. Peppermint · Motivate® · Rosemary · Lemon · Douglas Fir	Brain pg. 300; Focus & Concentration pg. 351;
Brain Injury	A comprehensive term for any injury occurring in the brain that is typically traumatic. Frankincense · Balance® · DDR Prime® · Forgive® · Bergamot	Brain pg. 300
Breastfeeding (Milk Supply)	Giving a baby milk from the breast, suckling or nursing. Clary Sage · ClaryCalm® · Basil · Fennel · Geranium	Pregnancy, Labor & Nursing pg. 401

Aromatic: Inhale from cupped hands or diffuse into the air.
Topical: Apply directly to affected area(s) or bottom of feet.
Internal: Take in a capsule, glass of water, or on/under tongue.
TIP Adults: Use 2-3 drops; Children: Use 1-2 drops.

AILMENT	RECOMMENDED OILS & USE	FOCUS AREA
Breathing Problems	A condition in which respiratory function is insufficient to meet the needs of the body when physical activity increases. Breathe® | Eucalyptus (Aromatic, Topical); Air-X™ (Internal, Aromatic); Siberian or Douglas Fir (Topical, Aromatic); Cardamom | Rosemary (Topical, Internal, Aromatic); Peppermint (Topical, Aromatic, Internal)	Respiratory pg. 409
Brittle Nails	Brittleness with breakage of finger or toenails. Myrrh (Topical); Lemon (Topical); Frankincense (Topical); Grapefruit (Topical); Eucalyptus (Topical)	Integumentary pg. 360
Broken Bone	A break in continuity of bone. Siberian Fir (Topical); Birch (Topical); Helichrysum (Topical, Internal); Deep Blue® (Topical); Wintergreen (Topical)	Skeletal pg. 415
Broken Capillaries	Break in the tiniest blood vessels with the smallest diameter. Cypress (Topical); Geranium (Internal, Topical); Helichrysum (Internal, Topical); Yarrow | Pom (Internal, Topical); Lavender (Internal, Topical)	Cardiovascular pg. 308
Broken Heart Syndrome	A severe but short-term condition in which extreme stress can lead to heart muscle failure, feeling similar to the sensation of a heart attack. Console® (Aromatic, Topical); Ylang Ylang (Aromatic, Topical, Internal); Geranium (Aromatic, Topical, Internal); Lime (Aromatic, Topical, Internal); Clary Sage (Aromatic, Topical, Internal)	Cardiovascular pg. 308; Mood & Behavior pg. 377; Emotions pg. 28
Bronchitis	Inflammation of the lining of bronchial tubes, which carry air to and from the lungs, resulting in hoarseness and a vigorous cough. Breathe® | Eucalyptus (Topical); Air-X™ (Topical, Aromatic, Internal); Cardamom (Internal, Topical); Thyme (Internal, Topical); On Guard® (Internal, Topical)	Respiratory pg. 409; Immune & Lymphatic pg. 355
Bruise	An injury appearing as an area of discolored skin on the body, caused by a blow or impact rupturing underlying blood vessels. Siberian Fir (Topical); Roman Chamomile (Topical); Geranium (Topical); Helichrysum (Topical); Deep Blue® (Topical)	Cardiovascular pg. 308; Integumentary pg. 360; First Aid pg. 347
Bruised Muscles	A deep bruise on a muscle can occur when the underlying fibers and connective tissue of the muscle are crushed without breaking through the skin. Also known as a contusion. Deep Blue® | Rescuer™ (Topical); Helichrysum (Topical); Birch (Topical); AromaTouch® (Topical); Siberian Fir (Topical)	Muscular pg. 381
Buerger's Disease	A blood vessel disease with swelling and blockage from blood clots. Typically caused by smoking. Clary Sage (Aromatic, Topical, Internal); Arborvitae (Aromatic, Topical); Cypress (Aromatic, Topical); Lemongrass (Aromatic, Topical, Internal); Cinnamon Bark (Aromatic, Topical, Internal)	Cardiovascular pg. 308
Bulimia	A chronic eating disorder involving repeated episodes of uncontrolled eating followed by self-induced purging. Melissa (Internal, Topical); Cinnamon Bark (Internal, Topical, Aromatic); Grapefruit (Topical, Internal, Aromatic); Forgive® (Topical, Aromatic); Patchouli (Topical, Internal, Aromatic)	Eating Disorders pg. 336; Addictions pg. 280
Bunions	A bony bump that forms on the joint at the base of the big toe. Eucalyptus (Topical); Cypress (Topical); Ginger (Topical); Wintergreen (Topical); Basil (Topical)	Skeletal pg. 415
Burns	Injuries to tissues caused by electricity, radiation, heat, friction, or chemicals. Lavender (Topical); Peppermint (Topical); Immortelle (Topical); Myrrh (Topical); Helichrysum (Topical)	Integumentary pg. 360; First Aid pg. 347
Bursitis	Inflammation of the fluid-filled pads that act as cushions to the joints. Deep Blue® (Topical); Birch (Topical); Wintergreen (Topical); Siberian Fir (Topical); Cypress (Topical)	Skeletal pg. 415

*Avoid eyes, ear canals, and nasal passages.

STEPS:

1. Look up ailment.
2. Choose one or more of the recommended oils. Use oil(s) as indicated. Order of recommendation of oils and use is left to right.
3. Learn more in corresponding focus area.

AILMENT	RECOMMENDED OILS & USE	FOCUS AREA
Calcified Spine	A spine that is hardened by calcium deposits. Birch · DDR Prime® · Lemongrass · Deep Blue® · Wintergreen	Skeletal pg. 415
Calluses	A thickened and hardened part of the skin or soft tissue, especially in an area that has been subjected to friction. Roman Chamomile · Cypress · HD Clear® · Siberian Fir · Oregano	Integumentary pg. 360
Cancer (Bladder)	A growth of abnormal cells forming masses called tumors in the bladder. Frankincense · DDR Prime® · Lemongrass · Rosemary · Cinnamon Bark	Cellular Health pg. 313
Cancer (Blood)	A cancer of blood-forming tissues, hindering the body's ability to fight infection. Also known as Leukemia. Frankincense · DDR Prime® · Turmeric · Helichrysum · Siberian Fir	Cellular Health pg. 313
Cancer (Bone)	A skeletal malignancy typified by a mass of unusual cells growing in a bone. Frankincense · DDR Prime® · Helichrysum · Lemongrass + Turmeric · Siberian Fir	Cellular Health pg. 313
Cancer (Brain)	A mass or growth of abnormal cells in the brain or central spinal canal. Arborvitae · DDR Prime® · Clove · Frankincense · Thyme	Cellular Health pg. 313
Cancer (Breast)	The development of uncontrolled breast cells causing a malignant tumor. Usually only occurs in women but sometimes is present in men. DDR Prime® | Frankincense · Pink Pepper · Thyme · Grapefruit · Eucalyptus	Cellular Health pg. 313
Cancer (Cervical)	A malignant tumor of the cervix, the lowermost part of the uterus. Frankincense · DDR Prime® · Siberian Fir · Tangerine · Sandalwood	Cellular Health pg. 313
Cancer (Colon)	A cancer of the colon or rectum, located at the digestive tract's lower end. Geranium · Zendocrine® · Rosemary · Turmeric · DDR Prime®	Cellular Health pg. 313
Cancer (Follicular thyroid)	Occurs when cells in the thyroid undergo genetic changes (mutations). The mutations allow the cells to multiply and grow rapidly. Characterized by capsular invasion and vascular invasion by tumor cells. Rosemary · Clary Sage · Frankincense · Tangerine · Sandalwood	Cellular Health pg. 313
Cancer (Hurthle Cell Thyroid)	An unusual form of cancer that affects the thyroid gland. Melissa · Frankincense · DDR Prime® · Clary Sage · Thyme	Cellular Health pg. 313
Cancer (Liver)	A rare form of cancer that is either initiated in the liver or spread from another part of the body. Zendocrine® · Turmeric · Tangerine · DDR Prime® · Clove	Cellular Health pg. 313
Cancer (Lung)	Malignant growths of the lung believed to be caused by inhaled carcinogens. Air-X™ · DDR Prime® · Breathe® | Ravintsara · Abōce™ · Frankincense	Cellular Health pg. 313

Discover other ways essential oil enthusiasts are getting results in the app.

Aromatic: Inhale from cupped hands or diffuse into the air.
Topical: Apply directly to affected area(s) or bottom of feet.
Internal: Take in a capsule, glass of water, or on/under tongue.
TIP Adults: Use 2-3 drops; Children: Use 1-2 drops.

AILMENT	RECOMMENDED OILS & USE	FOCUS AREA
Cancer (Lymph)	A cancer characterized by the formation of solid tumors in the immune system which impact white blood cells. Also known as lymphoma. Lemongrass · Frankincense · DDR Prime® · Tangerine · Turmeric	Cellular Health pg. 313
Cancer (Mouth)	Cancer that develops in any part of the mouth typically induced by tobacco use, heavy alcohol use, and HPV. Also known as oral cavity cancer. Myrrh · Turmeric · DDR Prime® · Frankincense · Black Pepper	Cellular Health pg. 313
Cancer (Ovarian)	A cancer that begins in the female organs that produce eggs (ovaries). Frankincense · Tangerine · Zendocrine® · Grapefruit · DDR Prime®	Cellular Health pg. 313
Cancer (Pancreatic)	An uncontrolled multiplication of cells in the pancreas (the organ lying behind the lower part of the stomach) that impacts endocrine and exocrine functions. Turmeric · DDR Prime® · Cinnamon Bark · Zendocrine® · Frankincense	Cellular Health pg. 313
Cancer (Prostate)	A disease in which cells in the prostate gland become atypical and start to grow uncontrollably, forming tumors. Thyme · Zendocrine® · Oregano · Turmeric · DDR Prime®	Cellular Health pg. 313
Cancer (Skin)	The abnormal growth of skin cells caused by genetics, chemical carcinogens, fumes, or overexposure to the sun or other sources of ultraviolet light. Immortelle · Arborvitae | Sandalwood · Turmeric · Tangerine · Frankincense	Cellular Health pg. 313
Cancer (Throat)	A group of cancers of the mouth, sinuses, nose, tonsils, or throat. Frankincense · DDR Prime® · Thyme · Lavender · Cinnamon Bark	Cellular Health pg. 313
Cancer (Thyroid)	A disease in which malignant cells are found in the tissues of the thyroid gland. DDR Prime® · Turmeric · Thyme · Lemongrass · Frankincense	Cellular Health pg. 313
Cancer (Tongue)	A form of cancer that begins in the cells of the tongue. Geranium · DDR Prime® · Turmeric · Frankincense · Zendocrine®	Cellular Health pg. 313
Cancer (Uterine)	Cancer of the womb (uterus) is a common cancer that affects the female reproductive system. It's also called uterine cancer and endometrial cancer. Clary Sage · DDR Prime® · Turmeric · Frankincense · Geranium	Cellular Health pg. 313
Candida	A variety of yeast like fungi that are generally part of the normal flora of the mouth, skin, intestinal tract, and vagina, but can cause an array of infections. Thyme · Oregano · DDR Prime® · Pink Pepper + Tea Tree · Arborvitae	Candida pg. 304
Canker Sores	Small white or yellow colored sores or ulcers that grow inside the mouth. They are painful to the touch, self-healing, and can reappear. On Guard® · Myrrh · Black Pepper · Tea Tree · Birch	Oral Health pg. 389

*Avoid eyes, ear canals, and nasal passages.

STEPS:

1. Look up ailment.
2. Choose one or more of the recommended oils. Use oil(s) as indicated. Order of recommendation of oils and use is left to right.
3. Learn more in corresponding focus area.

AILMENT	RECOMMENDED OILS & USE					FOCUS AREA
Cardiovascular Disease	Heart conditions that include diseased vessels, structural problems, and blood clots.					Cardiovascular pg. 308
	AromaTouch®	Black Pepper	Basil	Cypress	PastTense®	
Carpal Tunnel Syndrome	A numbness, tingling, and weakness in the hand and arm caused by a pinched nerve in the wrist.					Nervous System pg. 385
	Deep Blue®	Lemongrass	Cypress	Ginger	Copaiba	
Cartilage Injury	An injury to the fibrous, flexible, and connective tissue found in adults resulting in joint pain and stiffness.					Skeletal pg. 415; Athletes pg. 288
	Deep Blue®	Lemongrass	Helichrysum	Birch	Wintergreen	
Cataracts	A medical condition in which the lens of the eye becomes progressively opaque, resulting in blurred vision and may lead to blindness.					Nervous System pg. 385
	Lemongrass	Clary Sage	Cardamom	Immortelle	Black Pepper	
Cavities	The decayed part of a tooth that has developed into a hole.					Oral Health pg. 389
	Clove	On Guard®	Birch	Wintergreen	Helichrysum	
Celiac Disease	A genetic disease defined by malabsorption of nutrients from food and an immune response to eating gluten (a protein found in wheat, barley, and rye).					Autoimmune pg. 292; Digestive & Intestinal pg. 331
	Celery Seed | Lemongrass	DigestZen®	Cardamom	Slim & Sassy®	Zendocrine®	
Cellulite	A fatty deposit causing an uneven or dimpled appearance, commonly found around the thighs.					Detoxification pg. 326; Weight pg. 431
	Eucalyptus	Grapefruit	Slim & Sassy®	Spikenard	Lemongrass	
Chapped Skin	Skin that is rough, cracked, or reddened by exposure to cold or excessive moisture.					Integumentary pg. 360; Children pg. 317
	Roman Chamomile	Petitgrain	Sandalwood	Immortelle	Myrrh	
Chemical Imbalance	A disequilibrium of one or more neurotransmitters. Chemical imbalances show a strong association with mental illnesses.					Brain pg. 300; Mood & Behavior pg. 377
	Zendocrine®	Elevation	Cilantro	DDR Prime®	Melissa	
Chemical Sensitivity Reaction	An allergic condition attributed to extreme sensitivity to various environmental chemicals, such as water, food, air, building materials, or fabrics.					Allergies pg. 284
	Zendocrine®	Cilantro	Purify | Abōde™	Coriander	Arborvitae	
Chest Infection	An infection in the airways or lungs, commonly resulting in coughing up yellow or green phlegm (thick mucus).					Immune & Lymphatic pg. 355
	Zendocrine®	On Guard®	Breathe® | Eucalyptus	Air-X™	Tea Tree | Stronger™	
Chest Pain	A sharp, burning, or crushing sensation in the chest.					Cardiovascular pg. 308; Stress pg. 423; Respiratory pg. 409; Pain & Inflammation pg. 392
	Marjoram	Douglas Fir	AromaTouch®	Basil | Ylang Ylang	On Guard®	
Chicken Pox	A highly contagious viral infection causing an itchy, blister-like rash on the skin and fever. Most cases occur in children under the age of 16.					Immune & Lymphatic pg. 355
	Tea Tree	Patchouli	Blue Tansy	On Guard®	Thyme	

Discover other ways essential oil enthusiasts are getting results in the app.

[Aromatic] Aromatic: Inhale from cupped hands or diffuse into the air.
[Topical] Topical: Apply directly to affected area(s) or bottom of feet.
[Internal] Internal: Take in a capsule, glass of water, or on/under tongue.
TIP Adults: Use 2-3 drops; Children: Use 1-2 drops.

AILMENT	RECOMMENDED OILS & USE	FOCUS AREA
Chiggers	Red bugs similar to a tick from the Trombiculidae family; however, chiggers do not burrow into the skin but have feeding structures that insert into the skin. Lemongrass [Topical]; Purify | Abōde™ [Aromatic, Topical]; TerraShield® [Topical]; Lavender [Topical]; Clove [Topical, Internal]	Parasites pg. 398; First Aid pg. 347
Cholera	A bacterial disease causing severe diarrhea and dehydration, usually spread in water. Cinnamon Bark [Internal, Topical, Aromatic]; Rosemary [Internal, Topical, Aromatic]; Zendocrine® [Internal, Topical, Aromatic]; Breathe® [Topical, Aromatic]; Melissa [Topical, Internal, Aromatic]	Immune & Lymphatic pg. 355
Cholesterol (High)	Abnormally high levels of cholesterol (a waxy substance found in the fats in the blood) that can lead to an increased risk of heart disease. Slim & Sassy® [Internal, Topical]; Lemongrass [Internal, Topical]; Coriander [Internal, Topical]; Cinnamon Bark [Internal, Topical]; Lemon [Internal, Topical]	Cardiovascular pg. 308
Chondromalacia Patella	Damage to the cartilage under the kneecap, also known as "runner's knee." AromaTouch® [Topical]; Helichrysum [Topical, Internal]; Birch [Topical]; Siberian Fir [Topical]; Sandalwood [Topical]	Skeletal pg. 415
Chronic Fatigue	A disease characterized by profound fatigue, sleep abnormalities, pain, and other symptoms that are made worse by exertion. Rosemary [Internal, Topical, Aromatic]; Passion® | Tulsi [Topical, Aromatic]; Geranium [Internal, Topical]; Black Pepper [Internal, Topical]; Basil [Internal, Topical, Aromatic]	Energy & Vitality pg. 344; Limbic pg. 371; Endocrine pg. 340
Chronic Pain	Persistent pain that lasts weeks to years from a disease or unknown cause. Deep Blue® [Topical]; Helichrysum [Topical, Internal]; Copaiba [Topical, Internal]; Wintergreen [Topical]; Peppermint [Topical, Internal]	Pain & Inflammation pg. 392; Muscular pg. 381; Skeletal pg. 415; Sleep pg. 419
Circulation (Poor)	A poor circulation of blood and lymph through the body, consisting of the heart, blood vessels, blood, lymph, and the lymphatic vessels and glands. Cypress [Topical]; AromaTouch® [Topical]; Geranium [Topical, Internal]; Cassia [Internal, Topical]; Peppermint [Topical, Internal]	Cardiovascular pg. 308; Other pg. 323
Cirrhosis	A continual degenerative disease in which normal liver cells are impaired and then replaced by scar tissue. Zendocrine® [Internal, Topical]; Geranium [Internal, Topical, Aromatic]; Myrrh [Internal, Topical]; Helichrysum [Internal, Topical]; Marjoram [Internal, Topical]	Digestive & Intestinal pg. 331; Other pg. 323
Clogged Pores	A plug of sebum and keratin within a hair follicle. HD Clear® [Topical]; Cedarwood [Topical]; Juniper Berry [Topical, Internal]; DDR Prime® [Topical, Internal]; Petitgrain [Topical, Internal]	Integumentary pg. 360; Other pg. 323
Club Foot	A condition in which one or both feet are twisted into an unusual position before birth. Basil [Topical]; AromaTouch® [Topical]; Wintergreen [Topical]; Marjoram [Topical, Internal]; Helichrysum [Topical, Internal]	Skeletal pg. 415; Muscular pg. 381; Other pg. 323
Cold Body Temperature	A body temperature below 97.6 degrees Fahrenheit (36.4 degrees Celsius). "Normal" body temperature is 98.6 degrees Fahrenheit (37 degrees Celsius). Passion® [Topical]; Cypress [Topical]; AromaTouch® [Topical]; Wintergreen [Topical]; Eucalyptus [Topical]	Cardiovascular pg. 308; Other pg. 323
Cold (Common)	A viral infection of the upper respiratory system including the throat, nose, and sinuses. Sneezing, coughing, and temperature are common symptoms. On Guard® [Topical, Internal, Aromatic]; Black Pepper [Topical, Internal]; Breathe® [Topical, Aromatic]; Thyme [Topical, Internal, Aromatic]; Yarrow | Pom [Topical, Internal, Aromatic]	Immune & Lymphatic pg. 355; Other pg. 323
Cold Hands/Feet/ Nose	Relative to problems with poor blood circulation, small blood vessels, and the body attempting to maintain its natural core temperature. AromaTouch® [Topical]; Motivate® [Topical, Aromatic]; Cassia [Topical, Internal]; DDR Prime® [Topical, Internal]; Passion® [Topical, Aromatic]	Cardiovascular pg. 308; Other pg. 323

*Avoid eyes, ear canals, and nasal passages.

STEPS:

1. Look up ailment.
2. Choose one or more of the recommended oils. Use oil(s) as indicated. Order of recommendation of oils and use is left to right.
3. Learn more in corresponding focus area.

AILMENT	RECOMMENDED OILS & USE	FOCUS AREA
Cold Sores/Fever Blisters	Infection with the herpes simplex virus around the border of the lips. Tea Tree; Melissa; Arborvitae; On Guard®; Bergamot	Oral Health pg. 389; Immune & Lymphatic pg. 355
Colic	Persistent, unexplained crying in a healthy baby between two weeks and five months of age. DigestZen® | Tamer™; Fennel; Roman Chamomile; Serenity® | Adaptiv™; Ylang Ylang	Children pg. 317; Digestive & Intestinal pg. 331;
Colitis	An inflammatory reaction in the colon or large bowel, often resulting in ulcers. Cardamom; DigestZen®; Peppermint; Copaiba; Ginger	Digestive & Intestinal pg. 331
Coma	A state of severe unresponsiveness, in which an individual shows no voluntary movement or behavior. Frankincense; Spikenard; Vetiver; Ginger; Cedarwood	Brain pg. 300; Blood Sugar pg. 297
Concentration (Poor)	The inability to focus the mind or concentrate. InTune® | Thinker™; Vetiver & Lavender; Peace®; Cedarwood; Motivate® | Brave™	Focus & Concentration pg. 351; Brain pg. 300
Concussion	A trauma-induced change in mental status with or without a brief loss of consciousness. Frankincense; Sandalwood; Cedarwood; Clove; Petitgrain	Athletes pg. 288; Brain pg. 300
Confidence (Lack of)	The low belief that you have in yourself and your abilities. Self-esteem affects how you think and act, how you feel about others, and how successful you are in life. Bergamot; Motivate®; Patchouli; Jasmine; Passion®	Mood & Behavior pg. 377
Confusion	Impaired orientation in terms of time, place, or person; a disturbed mental state or lack of clarity or discernment. Peppermint; Frankincense; Rosemary; Douglas Fir; Motivate®	Mood & Behavior pg. 377; Focus & Concentration pg. 351;
Congenital Heart Disease	An abnormality in the heart's structure that develops before birth. Geranium; Ylang Ylang; Helichrysum; Basil; Passion®	Cardiovascular pg. 308
Congestion	The existence of an unusual amount of fluid in a vessel or organ causing obstruction. Lemon; Peppermint; DigestZen®; Breathe® | Eucalyptus; Air-X™	Respiratory pg. 409; Allergies pg. 284; Digestive & Intestinal pg. 331
Conjunctivitis (Pink Eye)	Inflammation or infection of the outer membrane of the eyeball and the inner eyelid. Lavender; Tea Tree; Douglas Fir; Rosemary; Melissa	Immune & Lymphatic pg. 355; Children pg. 317
Connective Tissue Injury	Injury to tissue that binds and supports other connecting ligaments and tendons. Lemongrass; Helichrysum; Wintergreen | Deep Blue®; Siberian Fir; Copaiba	Skeletal pg. 415; Muscular pg. 381
Constipation	A condition in which bowel movements occur less often than normal or consist of hard, dry stools that are painful and difficult to pass. DigestZen® | Tamer™; Marjoram; Zendocrine®; Ginger; Peppermint	Digestive & Intestinal pg. 331; Children pg. 317
Convalescence	Recuperation time spent recovering from an illness or medical treatment. Petitgrain; Frankincense; Spikenard; Console®; Myrrh	Brain pg. 300

Aromatic: Inhale from cupped hands or diffuse into the air.
Topical: Apply directly to affected area(s) or bottom of feet.
Internal: Take in a capsule, glass of water, or on/under tongue.
TIP Adults: Use 2-3 drops; Children: Use 1-2 drops.

AILMENT	RECOMMENDED OILS & USE	FOCUS AREA
Convulsions	A sudden violent contraction of a group of muscles. Also referred to a seizures. Petitgrain, Sandalwood, Spikenard, Frankincense, Clary Sage	Brain pg. 300
Corns	Thick and hardened layers of skin caused by friction and pressure, usually found on a toe. Arborvitae, Lemon, DDR Prime®, Clove, Ylang Ylang	Integumentary pg. 360
Cortisol Imbalance	An imbalance in the naturally produced cortisol hormone generated from the adrenal glands that helps the body use sugar and fat for energy, and to manage stress. Geranium, Adaptiv™, Ylang Ylang, Black Spuce | Tulsi, Petitgrain	Endocrine pg. 340
Cough	A strong release of air from the lungs that can be heard. Coughing protects the respiratory system by clearing it of secretion and irritants. Breathe®, Rosemary, DigestZen® | Air-X™, Cardamom, Lemon	Respiratory pg. 409;
Cough (Whooping)	A highly contagious respiratory tract infection causing spasms of uncontrollable coughing. Clary Sage, Roman Chamomile, Breathe®, Blue Tansy, Cardamom	Respiratory pg. 409
Cradle Cap	White or yellow scaly patches on an infant's scalp. Lavender, Tea Tree, Sandalwood, Frankincense, Immortelle	Children pg. 317
Cramps (Intestinal)	An uncontrolled, spasmodic muscular contraction in the lower abdomen causing severe pain. DigestZen® | Tamer™, Marjoram, Ginger, Turmeric, Cardamom	Digestive & Intestinal pg. 331
Creutzfeldt-Jakob Disease	A degenerative neurological disorder that leads to dementia and is incurable. Also called a human form of mad cow disease. Spikenard, Frankincense, DDR Prime®, Clove, Zendocrine®	Brain pg. 300; Immune & Lymphatic pg. 355
Crohn's Disease	A type of inflammatory bowel disease (IBD), followed by swelling and dysfunction of the intestinal tract. DigestZen® | Tamer™, Copaiba, Celery Seed | Frankincense, Peppermint, Pink Pepper	Autoimmune pg. 292 Digestive & Intestinal pg. 331
Croup	An upper airway infection that blocks breathing and has a distinctive barking cough, typical to children. Thyme, Lemon, Eucalyptus, Marjoram, Breathe®	Children pg. 317 Respiratory pg. 409
Crying Baby	A sudden, loud automatic or voluntary vocalization in response to fear, pain, or a startle reflex. Serenity®, Roman Chamomile, Peace® | Tamer™, Lavender, Console®	Children pg. 317
Cushing's Syndrome	A condition that occurs from exposure to inappropriately high cortisol levels over a long period of time. Clove, Black Pepper, DDR Prime®, Geranium, Citrus Bliss®	Endocrine pg. 340
Cuts	The separation of skin or other tissue created by a sharp edge. Tea Tree, Frankincense, Geranium, Lavender, Helichrysum	First Aid pg. 347 Integumentary pg. 360

*Avoid eyes, ear canals, and nasal passages.

STEPS:

1. Look up ailment.
2. Choose one or more of the recommended oils. Use oil(s) as indicated. Order of recommendation of oils and use is left to right.
3. Learn more in corresponding focus area.

AILMENT	RECOMMENDED OILS & USE						FOCUS AREA
Cyst	An abnormal membranous sac or cavity in the body containing semisolid material or liquid.	Douglas Fir	On Guard®	Lemon	Thyme	Cardamom	Integumentary pg. 360
Cystic Fibrosis	An inherited life-threatening disorder that damages the lungs and digestive system.	Eucalyptus	Lemon	Douglas Fir	Breathe®	Frankincense	Respiratory pg. 409
Dandruff	A common scalp condition in which small pieces of dry skin flake off of the scalp.	Tea Tree	Wintergreen	Patchouli	Rosemary	Petitgrain	Integumentary pg. 360
Deep Vein Thrombosis	A blood clot in a deep vein, usually in the legs.	Frankincense	Cypress	Wintergreen	DDR Prime®	Zendocrine®	Cardiovascular pg. 308
Dehydration	A condition that occurs when the loss of body fluids, mostly water, exceeds the amount that is taken in.	Wild Orange	Lemon	Slim & Sassy®	Zendocrine®	Juniper Berry	First Aid pg. 347 Athletes pg. 288 Urinary pg. 428
Dementia	A chronic disorder of the mental processes caused by brain disease or injury and marked by memory disorders, personality changes, and impaired reasoning.	DDR Prime®	Frankincense	Thyme	Sandalwood	Clove	Brain pg. 300
Dengue Fever	A mosquito-borne viral disease occurring in tropical and subtropical areas. Symptoms include fever, headache, muscle and joint pain, and a measle-like rash.	Eucalyptus	Melissa	On Guard®	Thyme	Tea Tree	Immune & Lymphatic pg. 355
Dental Infection	An infection of the jaw, face mouth, or throat that begins as a tooth cavity or infection.	Clove	On Guard®	Myrrh	Tea Tree | Stronger™	Cinnamon Bark	Oral Health pg. 389
Depression	A mental state of altered mood associated by feelings of despair, sadness, and discouragement.	Melissa	Elevation	Cheer®	Frankincense	Neroli	Mood & Behavior pg. 377 Limbic pg. 371 Pregnancy, Labor & Nursing pg. 401
Deteriorating Spine	A deterioration of the series of vertebrae that provide support and form a flexible bony case for the spinal cord.	Wintergreen	Birch	DDR Prime®	Helichrysum	Siberian Fir	Skeletal pg. 415
Detoxification	The process of removing toxic substances or qualities from the body which is mainly carried out by the liver.	Zendocrine®	Grapefruit | Siberian Fir	Slim & Sassy® | Air-X™	Clove | DDR Prime®	Green Mandarin	Detoxification pg. 326
Diabetes	A disease identified by an inability to process sugars in the diet, due to a decrease in or total absence of insulin production.	Cinnamon Bark	Coriander	Slim & Sassy®	Juniper Berry	Cassia	Blood Sugar pg. 297
Diabetes (Gestational)	A condition in which women without previously diagnosed diabetes show high blood glucose levels during pregnancy, especially after the third trimester.	Cinnamon Bark	Zendocrine®	Coriander	Cassia	Juniper Berry	Pregnancy, Labor & Nursing pg. 401 Blood Sugar pg. 297

Discover other ways essential oil enthusiasts are getting results in the app.

Aromatic: Inhale from cupped hands or diffuse into the air.
Topical: Apply directly to affected area(s) or bottom of feet.
Internal: Take in a capsule, glass of water, or on/under tongue.
TIP Adults: Use 2-3 drops; Children: Use 1-2 drops.

AILMENT	RECOMMENDED OILS & USE	FOCUS AREA
Diabetic Sores	Open wounds or sores that normally occur on the bottom of the feet over weight-bearing areas. Myrrh (Topical); Lavender (Topical); Patchouli (Topical); Sandalwood | Tulsi (Topical); Geranium (Topical)	Integumentary pg. 360; Blood Sugar pg. 297
Diaper Rash	Irritation of the genitals, buttocks, lower abdomen, or thigh folds of an infant or toddler. Balance® | Steady™ (Topical); Roman Chamomile (Topical); Lavender (Topical); Myrrh (Topical); Patchouli (Topical)	Children pg. 317
Diarrhea	The fast movement of fecal matter through the intestines resulting in poor absorption of nutritive elements and persistent watery stools. DigestZen® | Tamer™ (Topical, Internal | Topical); Cardamom (Internal, Topical); Black Pepper (Internal, Topical); Tea Tree (Topical); Ginger (Internal, Topical)	Digestive & Intestinal pg. 331
Digestive Discomfort	Symptoms may include bloating, diarrhea, gas, stomach pain, and stomach cramps. DigestZen® | Tamer™ (Topical, Internal | Topical); Cardamom (Internal, Topical); Peppermint (Internal, Topical); Ginger (Internal, Topical); Fennel (Internal)	Digestive & Intestinal pg. 331
Diphtheria	A contagious disease that commonly involves the throat, nose, and air passages. Eucalyptus (Topical, Aromatic); Breathe® (Topical, Aromatic); On Guard® (Internal, Topical, Aromatic); DigestZen® (Internal, Topical, Aromatic); Thyme (Internal, Topical, Aromatic)	Respiratory pg. 409 Immune & Lymphatic pg. 355
Diverticulitis	An inflammation or infection in one or more small pouches in the digestive tract. DigestZen® (Internal, Topical); Slim & Sassy® (Internal, Topical); Basil (Internal, Topical); DDR Prime® (Internal, Topical); AromaTouch® (Topical)	Digestive & Intestinal pg. 331
Dizziness	A disturbed sense of relationship to space involving light-headedness and a sensation of unsteadiness. Rosemary (Topical, Aromatic, Internal); Peppermint (Topical, Aromatic, Internal); Cedarwood (Topical, Aromatic); Arborvitae (Aromatic, Topical); Zendocrine® (Topical, Internal)	Cardiovascular pg. 308
Do Quervain's Tenosynovitis	Inflammation of the tendons on the side of the wrist at the base of the thumb. Commonly causes pain when grasping anything, turning the wrist, or making a fist. Lemongrass (Topical); Cypress (Topical); AromaTouch® (Topical); Deep Blue® (Topical); Birch (Topical)	Muscular pg. 381; Skeletal pg. 415
Down Syndrome	A genetic chromosome 21 disorder causing developmental and intellectual delays. Balance® | Steady™ (Aromatic, Topical); Frankincense (Topical, Internal); Melissa (Internal, Topical); DDR Prime® (Topical, Internal); Cedarwood (Topical, Aromatic)	Brain pg. 300
Drug Addiction	An overwhelming desire to continue taking a drug because of a particular effect, typically an alteration of mental status. Zendocrine® (Internal, Topical); Serenity® | Calmer™ (Aromatic, Topical); Peppermint (Internal, Topical, Aromatic); Motivate® (Aromatic, Topical); Purify (Topical)	Addictions pg. 280
Dry Skin	Epidermis that lacks sebum or moisture, often identified by a pattern of fine lines, scaling, and itching. Myrrh (Topical); Petitgrain (Topical); Patchouli (Topical); Sandalwood (Topical); Immortelle (Topical)	Integumentary pg. 360
Dumping Syndrome	A condition which occurs when food, especially sugar, moves from the stomach into the small bowel too quickly. Can develop after bypass stomach surgery. Fennel (Internal, Topical); Ginger (Internal, Topical); Frankincense (Internal, Topical); Helichrysum (Internal, Topical); DigestZen® (Internal, Topical)	Digestive & Intestinal pg. 331
Dysentery	An infection of the intestines resulting in severe diarrhea with potential mucus and flood in feces. Peppermint (Internal, Topical); Ginger (Internal, Topical); On Guard® (Internal, Topical); Myrrh (Topical, Internal); Spearmint (Topical, Internal)	Digestive & Intestinal pg. 331
Dysmenorrhea	The existence of painful cramps during menstruation. ClaryCalm® (Topical); Clary Sage (Topical, Internal); AromaTouch® (Topical); Marjoram (Topical, Internal); Thyme (Topical, Internal)	Women's Health pg. 436

*Avoid eyes, ear canals, and nasal passages.

STEPS:

1. Look up ailment.
2. Choose one or more of the recommended oils. Use oil(s) as indicated. Order of recommendation of oils and use is left to right.
3. Learn more in corresponding focus area.

AILMENT	RECOMMENDED OILS & USE	FOCUS AREA
Dysphagia	Difficulty swallowing foods or liquids arising from the throat or esophagus. Peppermint · Arborvitae · Black Pepper · Serenity® · Lavender	Digestive & Intestinal pg. 331; Oral Health pg. 389
Earache	A pain in the ear, sensed as dull, sharp, intermittent, burning or constant.* Tea Tree · Helichrysum · Basil · Lavender · Rosemary	Respiratory pg. 409
Ear Infection	The existence and growth of bacteria or viruses in the ear.* On Guard® · Thyme · Basil · Tea Tree | Stronger™ · Helichrysum	Respiratory pg. 409
Ear Mites	The existence of tiny parasites that feed on the wax and oils in the ear canal.* Purify | Abōde™ · Cedarwood · Thyme · Clove · Tea Tree	Parasites pg. 398; Respiratory pg. 409
E. Coli	Bacteria found in the environment, foods, and intestines of warm-blooded organisms. Most E. Coli are harmless but some can cause serious infection. Cinnamon Bark · On Guard® · Cassia · Oregano · Clove	Immune & Lymphatic pg. 355
Eczema	Chronic or acute noncontagious inflammation of patches of the skin. Defined mainly by itchy red lesions that may become scaly and encrusted. Cedarwood · Neroli · HD Clear® · Yarrow | Pom · Black Spruce	Integumentary pg. 360; Candida pg. 304
Edema	A condition of unusually large fluid volume in the circulatory system or in the tissue between the body's cells. Cypress · Lemon · Lemongrass · Celery Seed | Juniper Berry · Grapefruit	Cardiovascular pg. 308; Pregnancy, Labor & Nursing pg. 401
Ehrlichiosis	A bacterial illness transmitted by ticks that causes flu-like symptoms ranging from mild body aches to severe fever. Oregano · On Guard® · Thyme · Zendocrine® · Rosemary	Immune & Lymphatic pg. 355
Electrical Hypersensitivity Syndrome	A group of symptoms caused by exposure to electromagnetic fields resulting in effects similar to allergic reactions. Vetiver · Frankincense · Zendocrine® · Balance® · Abōde™ | Purify	Limbic pg. 371
Emotional Trauma	An extremely disturbing, overwhelming, and stressful event that exceeds one's ability to cope that can lead to emotional impairment. Frankincense · Melissa · Helichrysum · Forgive® · Peace®	Mood & Behavior pg. 377; Limbic pg. 371
Emphysema	A progressive disease of the lungs that primarily causes shortness of breath due to over-inflation of the air sacs in the lung. Douglas Fir · Breathe® | Eucalyptus · Air-X™ · Black Pepper · Frankincense	Respiratory pg. 409
Endometriosis	A condition in which part of the tissue similar to the lining of the uterus grows in other parts of the body. Clary Sage · Thyme · Geranium · DDR Prime® · Rosemary	Women's Health pg. 436
Endurance (Poor)	A weak ability to continue an activity over an extended period of time. Peppermint · Basil · Slim & Sassy® · Breathe® · Motivate®	Energy & Vitality pg. 344;

Discover other ways essential oil enthusiasts are getting results in the app.

Aromatic: Inhale from cupped hands or diffuse into the air.
Topical: Apply directly to affected area(s) or bottom of feet.
Internal: Take in a capsule, glass of water, or on/under tongue.
TIP Adults: Use 2-3 drops; Children: Use 1-2 drops.

AILMENT	RECOMMENDED OILS & USE	FOCUS AREA
Energy (Lack of)	The strength and vitality required for sustained physical or mental activity. Peppermint (Topical, Internal, Aromatic) · Pink Pepper (Topical, Aromatic, Internal) · Citrus Bliss® (Topical, Aromatic) · Motivate® (Aromatic, Topical) · Passion® (Aromatic, Topical)	Energy & Vitality pg. 344
Engorgement	A condition where the breasts become painfully firm and swollen from being overfull with milk. Peppermint (Topical) · AromaTouch® (Topical) · Deep Blue® (Topical) · PastTense® (Topical) · Ginger (Topical)	Pregnancy, Labor & Nursing pg. 401;
Epilepsy	A neurological disorder defined by recurrent seizures with or without a loss of consciousness. Spikenard (Topical, Aromatic) · Frankincense (Topical, Internal, Aromatic) · Clary Sage (Topical) · Cedarwood (Topical, Aromatic) · DDR Prime® (Topical, Internal)	Brain pg. 300
Epstein-Barr (EBV)	The most common viral infection in humans and the best known cause of mononucleosis. Zendocrine® (Internal, Topical) · Rosemary (Topical, Internal) · Basil (Topical, Internal) · Ylang Ylang (Topical, Internal) · Passion® (Topical)	Immune & Lymphatic pg. 355; Energy & Vitality pg. 344
Erectile Dysfunction	The inability to achieve or sustain an erection for satisfactory sexual activity; also known as impotence. Cypress (Topical) · Zendocrine® (Internal, Topical) · Sandalwood (Topical) · Ylang Ylang (Topical) · Passion® (Topical)	Men's Health pg. 374; Intimacy pg. 366
Esophagitis	Inflammation that damages the tube running from the throat to the stomach (esophagus). Peppermint (Internal, Topical) · DigestZen® (Internal, Topical) · Frankincense (Internal, Topical) · Fennel (Internal, Topical) · Coriander (Internal, Topical)	Digestive & Intestinal pg. 331
Estrogen Imbalance	A condition where a woman can have deficient or excessive levels of estrogen but has little or no progesterone to balance its effects in the body. Grapefruit (Topical, Internal) · Thyme (Internal, Topical) · ClaryCalm® | Clary Sage (Topical) · Zendocrine® (Internal) · Basil (Internal, Topical)	Women's Health pg. 436; Detoxification pg. 326
Exhaustion	A state of extreme loss of mental or physical abilities caused by illness or fatigue. Motivate® | Thinker™ (Topical, Aromatic) · Passion® (Topical, Aromatic) · Basil (Topical, Internal, Aromatic) · Citrus Bliss® (Topical, Aromatic) · Wild Orange (Topical, Internal, Aromatic)	Energy & Vitality pg. 344; Endocrine pg. 340; Athletes pg. 288
Eyes (Dry)	Dryness of the cornea caused by a deficiency of tear secretion resulting in a gritty sensation and irritation.* Sandalwood (Topical) · Frankincense (Topical, Internal) · Lavender (Topical) · Wild Orange (Internal, Topical) · Zendocrine® (Internal)	Respiratory pg. 409
Eyes (Swollen)	Uncommon enlargement around the eyes not due to an underlying disease.* Immortelle (Topical) · Cypress (Topical) · Lemon (Internal) · Frankincense (Topical, Internal) · Zendocrine® (Internal)	Nervous System pg. 385
Fainting	Loss of consciousness caused by a brief lack of oxygen to the brain. Peppermint (Topical, Aromatic) · Rosemary (Topical) · Citrus Bliss® (Topical, Aromatic) · Sandalwood (Internal, Topical, Aromatic) · Frankincense (Internal, Topical)	Cardiovascular pg. 308; First Aid pg. 347
Fatigue	Physical and/or mental exhaustion that can be triggered by stress, overwork, medication, or physical and mental illness or disease. Motivate® | Thinker™ (Topical, Aromatic) · Passion® (Topical, Aromatic) · Basil (Topical, Internal) · Citrus Bliss® (Topical, Aromatic) · Wild Orange (Topical, Internal, Aromatic)	Energy & Vitality pg. 344
Fear	A feeling of dread and agitation caused by the presence or imminence of danger or perceived threat. Peace® or Adaptiv™ (Aromatic, Topical) · Motivate® (Aromatic, Topical) · Console® (Aromatic, Topical) · Bergamot (Aromatic, Topical) · Passion® (Aromatic, Topical)	Mood & Behavior pg. 377
Fear of Flying	A fear of being on an airplane or other flying vehicle, such as a helicopter, while in flight. It is also referred to as flying phobia. Causes anxiety or panic attacks. Peace® | Brave™ (Aromatic, Topical) · Balance® | Steady™ (Aromatic, Topical) · Serenity® | Calmer™ (Aromatic, Topical) · Cassia (Topical, Aromatic, Internal) · On Guard® | Stronger™ (Topical, Aromatic, Internal)	Mood & Behavior pg. 377

*Avoid eyes, ear canals, and nasal passages.

STEPS:

1. Look up ailment.
2. Choose one or more of the recommended oils. Use oil(s) as indicated. Order of recommendation of oils and use is left to right.
3. Learn more in corresponding focus area.

AILMENT	RECOMMENDED OILS & USE	FOCUS AREA
Fever	Any body temperature elevation above 100° F (37.8° C). Peppermint; Spearmint; Eucalyptus; Pink Pepper; Yarrow | Pom	Immune & Lymphatic pg. 355
Fibrillation	Fast, uncoordinated contractions of the lower or upper chambers of the heart. Ylang Ylang; Black Pepper; Lime; Marjoram; AromaTouch®	Cardiovascular pg. 308
Fibrocystic Breasts	Noncancerous changes that give a breast a lumpy or rope-like texture. Grapefruit | Pink Pepper; Thyme | DDR Prime®; Frankincense; Sandalwood; Geranium | Clary Sage	Endocrine pg. 340; Women's Health pg. 436
Fibroids (Uterine)	Growths in the uterus which are non-cancerous (benign). Oregano; DDR Prime®; Thyme; Magnolia | Clary Sage; Frankincense	Immune & Lymphatic pg. 355; Women's Health pg. 436;
Fibromyalgia	A chronic neuRosensory disorder defined by widespread joint stiffness, muscle pain, and fatigue with pain moving throughout the body. DDR Prime®; AromaTouch®; Ginger; Deep Blue® | Rescuer™; Oregano	Muscular pg. 381
Fifth's Disease (Human Parvovirus B19)	A common and highly contagious childhood ailment causing a distinctive face rash. Sometimes referred to as "slapped-cheek disease." On Guard®; DDR Prime®; Black Pepper; Oregano; Purify | Stronger™	Children pg. 317 Immune & Lymphatic pg. 355
Fleas	Small flightless external parasites of warm-blooded animals, living by hematophagy off the blood of mammals. Lemon Eucalyptus | Eucalyptus; Arborvitae; Abōde™ | Cedarwood; TerraShield®; Lavender	Parasites pg. 398 First Aid pg. 347 Pets pg. 512
Floaters	Spots in vision that look like black or gray specks or strings that drift across the eye.* Immortelle; Sandalwood; Frankincense; Lavender; DDR Prime®	Nervous System pg. 385
Flu (Influenza)	A common viral infection of the nose and throat with common symptoms including chills, fever, runny nose, sore throat, muscle pain, and fatigue. On Guard®; Thyme; Melissa; Yarrow | Pom; Oregano	Immune & Lymphatic pg. 355 Children pg. 317
Focal Brain Dysfunction (Brain Injury)	Injuries confined to one specific area of the brain, often the result of a severe head trauma. Helichrysum; Frankincense; DDR Prime®; Sandalwood; Balance® | Steady™	Brain pg. 300 Limbic pg. 371
Focus	The ability to concentrate or direct one's attention or efforts. InTune® | Thinker™; Frankincense + Wild Orange; Vetiver + Lavender; Cedarwood; Peppermint	Focus & Concentration pg. 351;
Food Addiction	A compulsive behavior of uncontrolled eating, often consuming food past the point of being comfortably full, followed by feelings of guilt and depression. Grapefruit; Slim & Sassy®; Peppermint; Ginger; Basil	Addictions pg. 280; Weight pg. 431
Food Poisoning	Illness caused by food contaminated with bacteria marked by diarrhea, cramps, nausea, vomiting, and fever. DigestZen®; Zendocrine®; Tea Tree; Clove; Lemon	Digestive & Intestinal pg. 331; Parasites pg. 398; Immune & Lymphatic pg. 355

Aromatic: Inhale from cupped hands or diffuse into the air.
Topical: Apply directly to affected area(s) or bottom of feet.
Internal: Take in a capsule, glass of water, or on/under tongue.
TIP Adults: Use 2-3 drops; Children: use 1-2 drops.

AILMENT	RECOMMENDED OILS & USE	FOCUS AREA
Fragile Hair	Damaged or dry hair that is prone to breaking because of weakness. Rosemary (Topical); DDR Prime® (Topical, Internal); Thyme (Topical); Cedarwood (Topical); Geranium (Topical)	Integumentary pg. 360
Frozen Shoulder	A condition characterized by stiffness and pain in the shoulder joint. Also known as adhesive capsulitis. Deep Blue® (Topical); Wintergreen (Topical); Siberian Fir (Topical); Lemongrass (Topical); Birch (Topical)	Skeletal pg. 415; Muscular pg. 381
Fungal Skin Infection	Any inflammatory skin condition caused by a fungus, including athlete's foot, ringworm, jock itch, and yeast infections. Tea Tree (Topical); HD Clear® (Topical); DDR Prime® (Topical, Internal); Turmeric (Topical); Myrrh (Topical, Internal)	Integumentary pg. 360; Candida pg. 304
Fungus	A condition in which primitive organisms duplicates by spores. Oregano (Topical, Internal, Aromatic); DDR Prime® (Topical, Internal, Aromatic); Cinnamon Bark (Topical, Internal, Aromatic); Tea Tree (Topical, Aromatic); Abōde™ | Arborvitae (Topical, Aromatic)	Immune & Lymphatic pg. 355; Candida pg. 304; Integumentary pg. 360
Gallbladder Issues	Disruptions that affect normal function of the gallbladder. Geranium (Topical, Internal); Grapefruit (Internal, Topical); Zendocrine® (Topical, Internal); Slim & Sassy® (Internal, Topical); Turmeric (Internal, Topical)	Digestive & Intestinal pg. 331; Detoxification pg. 326
Gallbladder Infection	Generally categorized as inflammation of the gallbladder which can be caused by gallstones, excessive alcohol consumption, infections, or tumors causing bile buildup. Zendocrine® (Topical, Internal); Slim & Sassy® (Topical, Internal); On Guard® (Topical, Internal); Cinnamon Bark (Topical, Internal); Rosemary (Topical, Internal)	Digestive & Intestinal pg. 331
Gallstones	Small stone-like masses in the gallbladder that are formed by excessive bile or calcium salt buildup. Geranium (Internal, Topical); Celery Seed + Juniper Berry (Internal, Topical); Lemon + Grapefruit (Internal, Topical); Zendocrine® (Internal, Topical); Wintergreen (Topical)	Digestive & Intestinal pg. 331
Ganglion Cyst	Round or oval lumps that most frequently develop in the wrist and are filled with a jelly-like fluid. DDR Prime® (Topical, Internal); Frankincense (Topical, Internal); Lemongrass (Topical, Internal); Lemon (Topical, Internal); Basil (Topical, Internal)	Skeletal pg. 415; Cellular Health pg. 313
Gangrene	The death or decay of a tissue or an organ caused by a lack of blood supply. Cypress (Topical); AromaTouch® (Topical, Aromatic); Slim & Sassy® (Topical, Internal); Cinnamon Bark (Topical, Internal); Myrrh (Topical)	Cardiovascular pg. 308; Immune & Lymphatic pg. 355; Blood Sugar pg. 297
Gas (Flatulence)	An overabundance of gas in the digestive tract. Ginger (Internal, Topical); DigestZen® (Topical, Internal) | Tamer™ (Topical); Black Pepper (Internal, Topical); Coriander (Internal, Topical); Peppermint (Internal, Topical)	Digestive & Intestinal pg. 331
Gastritis	Inflammation of the lining of the stomach. Symptoms include abdominal discomfort or burning. Peppermint (Internal, Topical); DigestZen® (Internal, Topical); Coriander (Internal, Topical); Petitgrain (Internal, Topical); Fennel (Internal, Topical)	Digestive & Intestinal pg. 331
Gastroenteritis/ stomach flu	An intestinal infection marked by diarrhea, cramps, nausea, vomiting, and fever. Cardamom (Internal, Topical); Peppermint (Internal, Topical); Ginger (Internal, Topical); DigestZen® (Internal, Topical); Thyme (Internal, Topical)	Digestive & Intestinal pg. 331; Children pg. 317
Gastroesophageal Reflux Disease (GERD)	A digestive disease in which stomach acid or bile irritates the food pipe lining. Zendocrine® (Internal, Topical); Lemon (Internal, Topical); DigestZen® (Internal, Topical); Ginger (Internal, Topical); Coriander (Internal, Topical)	Digestive & Intestinal pg. 331
Genital Warts	Growths in the genital area generated by a sexually transmitted papillomavirus. Frankincense (Topical, Internal); Arborvitae (Topical); Thyme (Topical, Internal); Melissa (Topical, Internal); Geranium (Topical, Internal)	Immune & Lymphatic pg. 355; Women's Health pg. 436; Men's Health pg. 374; Integumentary pg. 360

*Avoid eyes, ear canals, and nasal passages.

STEPS:

1. Look up ailment.
2. Choose one or more of the recommended oils. Use oil(s) as indicated. Order of recommendation of oils and use is left to right.
3. Learn more in corresponding focus area.

Ailment	Description and Recommended Oils	Focus Area
Giardia	An intestinal infection caused by a microscopic parasite that causes watery diarrhea alternating with greasy stools. Thyme, Oregano, Rosemary, Cardamom, On Guard®	Parasites pg. 398 Digestive & Intestinal pg. 331
Gingivitis	Inflammation of the gums, identified by redness and swelling. Myrrh, Clove, On Guard®, Frankincense, Black Pepper	Oral Health pg. 389
Glaucoma	A condition that is linked to a buildup of pressure inside the eye that can lead to loss of vision and even blindness.* Lemongrass, DDR Prime®, Frankincense, Black Pepper, Immortelle	Nervous System pg. 385
Goiter	A swelling of the thyroid gland, sometimes leading to a swelling of the larynx (voice box) or neck. Myrrh, Lemongrass, DDR Prime®, Frankincense, Patchouli	Autoimmune pg. 292; Endocrine pg. 340
Gout	A form of intense arthritis that causes severe swelling, tenderness, and pain in the joints. Copaiba, Lemongrass, Turmeric, Wintergreen, Deep Blue®	Skeletal pg. 415; Pain & Inflammation pg. 392
Grave's Disease	A thyroid dysfunction characterized by generalized overactivity of the entire gland. Myrrh, Frankincense, Lemongrass, Rosemary, Zendocrine®	Endocrine pg. 340
Grief	The commonly emotional response to an external and consciously recognized loss. Console®, Elevation, Peace® | Brave™, Serenity® | Calmer™, Magnolia	Mood & Behavior pg. 377
Growing Pains	Pains in the joints and limbs of children or adolescents frequently appearing at night and often attributed to rapid growth. Cypress, AromaTouch®, Siberian Fir, Marjoram, Deep Blue® | Rescuer™	Children pg. 317; Muscular pg. 381
Gulf War Syndrome	A prominent condition affecting Gulf War Veterans with symptoms including fatigue, headaches, joint pain, indigestion, insomnia, dizziness, respiratory problems, and memory issues. Frankincense, Clove, Thyme, Patchouli, Passion®	Limbic pg. 371; Nervous System pg. 385; Pain & Inflammation pg. 392; Digestive & Intestinal pg. 331
Gum Disease	Often appears in the form of gingivitis and bone loss due to toxins produced by bacteria in plaque collecting along the gum line. On Guard® | Stronger™, Myrrh, Clove, Tea Tree, Cinnamon Bark	Oral Health pg. 389
Gums (Bleeding)	Gums that bleed during and after tooth brushing. Myrrh, Helichrysum, Frankincense, Clove, Tea Tree	Oral Health pg. 389
H. Pylori	Spiral-shaped bacteria that grow in the digestive tract and have a tendency to attack the stomach lining. Responsible for the majority of stomach and intestine ulcers. Cassia | Cinnamon Bark, Black Pepper, Oregano, Ginger, Thyme	Immune & Lymphatic pg. 355; Digestive & Intestinal pg. 331
Hair (Dry)	Occurs when the scalp does not produce enough oil to moisturize the hair or the hair does not absorb moisture. Sandalwood, Patchouli, Geranium, Copaiba, Rosemary	Integumentary pg. 360

Aromatic: Inhale from cupped hands or diffuse into the air.
Topical: Apply directly to affected area(s) or bottom of feet.
Internal: Take in a capsule, glass of water, or on/under tongue.
TIP Adults: Use 2-3 drops; Children: use 1-2 drops.

AILMENT	RECOMMENDED OILS & USE	FOCUS AREA
Hair Loss	The lack of all or a significant part of the hair on the head or other parts of the body. Clary Sage (Topical, Internal); DDR Prime® (Topical, Internal); Thyme (Topical, Internal); Rosemary (Topical, Internal); Arborvitae (Topical)	Integumentary pg. 360
Hair (Oily)	Excessive sebum production caused by heredity, unhealthy eating habits, medications, or improper hygiene. Petitgrain (Topical, Internal); Lemon (Topical, Internal); Arborvitae (Topical); Rosemary (Topical, Internal); Citronella (Topical)	Integumentary pg. 360
Halitosis	The condition of having revolting-smelling breath. Peppermint (Internal); Spearmint (Internal); Slim & Sassy® (Internal); On Guard® (Internal); Cardamom (Internal)	Oral Health pg. 389
Hallucinations	Seeing, hearing, or experiencing sensations that appear to be real but are actually created within the mind. Balance® | Steady™ (Aromatic, Topical); Frankincense (Topical, Aromatic, Internal); Cedarwood (Topical, Aromatic); Peace® (Aromatic, Topical); Serenity® | Calmer™ (Topical, Aromatic)	Limbic pg. 371
Hand, Foot & Mouth Disease	A mild, contagious viral infection common in young children that is defined by sores in the mouth and a rash on the feet and hands. Thyme (Internal, Topical); Cinnamon Bark (Internal, Topical); Tea Tree (Topical); Melissa (Internal, Topical); Wintergreen (Topical)	Immune & Lymphatic pg. 355
Hangover	A group of disagreeable physical effects, including thirst, nausea, headache, fatigue, and irritability, resulting from the heavy consumption of alcohol and/or certain drugs. Zendocrine® (Internal, Topical); Slim & Sassy® (Internal); Lemon (Internal); Geranium (Internal); PastTense® (Topical)	Addictions pg. 280; Detoxification pg. 326
Hardening of Arteries	A chronic condition defined by hardening and thickening of the arteries and the build-up of plaque on the arterial walls. Black Pepper (Internal, Topical); Lemongrass (Internal, Topical); Cinnamon Bark (Internal, Topical); Grapefruit (Internal, Topical); Lemon (Internal, Topical)	Cardiovascular pg. 308
Hashimoto's Disease	An autoimmune disease of the thyroid gland in which immune cells mistakenly attack healthy thyroid tissue, causing inflammation. DDR Prime® (Internal, Topical); Myrrh (Topical, Internal); Zendocrine® (Topical, Internal); Lemongrass (Topical, Internal); Peppermint (Topical, Internal, Aromatic)	Endocrine pg. 340; Autoimmune pg. 292
Hay Fever	An allergic reaction caused by an abnormal sensitivity to airborne pollen, typically defined by nasal discharge and itchy/watery eyes.* Lavender (Internal, Topical, Aromatic); Lemon (Internal, Topical, Aromatic); Breathe® (Aromatic, Topical); Abōde™ | Purify (Topical, Aromatic); Cilantro (Internal, Topical, Aromatic)	Allergies pg. 284; Respiratory pg. 409
Headache	A painful sensation in any part of the head, ranging from sharp to dull. PastTense® (Topical); Peppermint (Topical, Aromatic); Siberian Fir (Internal, Topical); Copaiba (Topical, Internal); Frankincense (Topical, Aromatic)	Pain & Inflammation pg. 392; Nervous System pg. 385; Muscular pg. 381; Women's Health pg. 436
Headaches (Blood Sugar)	Pain in the head caused by blood sugar levels being either too high or too low. Cassia (Internal); Zendocrine® (Topical, Internal); Slim & Sassy® (Internal); On Guard® (Internal); Coriander (Topical, Aromatic, Internal)	Blood Sugar pg. 297
Headache (Sinus)	The buildup of pressure in the sinuses resulting in sensitive pressure which may worsen when bending over. Basil (Topical, Aromatic, Internal); Cedarwood | Tulsi (Topical, Aromatic); Rosemary (Topical, Internal, Aromatic); Peppermint (Topical, Aromatic, Internal); Eucalyptus (Topical, Aromatic)	Pain & Inflammation pg. 392; Respiratory pg. 409
Headache (Tension)	A common form of headache that is defined by severe muscle contractions triggered by overexertion or stress. PastTense® (Topical); Peppermint (Topical); Deep Blue® | Rescuer™ (Topical); AromaTouch® (Topical); Frankincense | Tulsi (Topical)	Muscular pg. 381; Pain & Inflammation pg. 392

*Avoid eyes, ear canals, and nasal passages.

QUICK REFERENCE

STEPS:

1. Look up ailment.
2. Choose one or more of the recommended oils. Use oil(s) as indicated. Order of recommendation of oils and use is left to right.
3. Learn more in corresponding focus area.

AILMENT	RECOMMENDED OILS & USE	FOCUS AREA
Hearing in a Tunnel	The ability to hear only one thing at a time with the accompanying sensation of hearing noise as if standing in a tunnel.* Helichrysum · Lemon · Clary Sage · Cardamom · Purify	Respiratory pg. 409
Hearing Problems	An impairment of any degree of the ability to apprehend sound.* Helichrysum · Basil · Lemon · Frankincense · Patchouli	Respiratory pg. 409
Heartburn	A burning pain or discomfort in the upper chest. DigestZen® · Peppermint · Cardamom · Black Pepper · Zendocrine®	Digestive & Intestinal pg. 331; Pregnancy, Labor & Nursing pg. 401
Heart Failure	A chronic, progressive condition in which the heart muscle is unable to pump enough blood to meet the body's needs for blood and oxygen. Lemongrass · Marjoram · Ylang Ylang · Thyme · Rosemary	Cardiovascular pg. 308
Heart Issues	Generally refers to conditions that involve narrowed or blocked blood vessels that can lead to a heart attack, chest pain or stroke. Ylang Ylang · Cypress · Marjoram | Tulsi · Geranium · AromaTouch®	Cardiovascular pg. 308
Heat Exhaustion	A condition deriving from exposure to intense heat. Defined by dizziness, abdominal cramp, and prostration. Also called heat prostration. Peppermint · Lime · Lemon · Petitgrain · Eucalyptus	First Aid pg. 347; Athletes pg. 288; Outdoors pg. 506
Heatstroke	A serious condition caused by the body overheating, usually as a result of prolonged exposure to or physical exertion in high temperatures. Defined by a core temperature of 104° F (40° C) or higher, altered mental state, nausea, and rapid heart rate & breathing. Peppermint · Petitgrain + Lemon · Black Pepper · Zendocrine® · Spearmint	First Aid pg. 347; Athletes pg. 288; Outdoors pg. 506
Heavy Metal Toxicity	The toxic buildup of heavy metals in the soft tissues of the body, most commonly associated with lead, mercury, arsenic and cadmium. Cilantro · Zendocrine® · Arborvitae | Tulsi · Thyme · Black Pepper	Detoxification pg. 326
Hematoma	A localized swelling filled with blood emerging from a break in a blood vessel. Cypress · Helichrysum · Geranium · AromaTouch® · Lemongrass	Cardiovascular pg. 308
Hemochromatosis	An inherited blood disorder that causes the body to retain more than normal amounts of iron, leading often to cirrhosis of the liver. Zendocrine® · DDR Prime® · Arborvitae · Geranium · Helichrysum	Digestive & Intestinal pg. 331
Hemophilia	One of a group of inherited bleeding disorders that cause abnormal or exaggerated bleeding and poor blood clotting. Geranium · Helichrysum · Lavender · Roman Chamomile · Vetiver	Cardiovascular pg. 308
Hemorrhage	An emergency condition in which a ruptured blood vessel causes bleeding that is difficult to control. Helichrysum · Yarrow | Pom · Geranium · Lemon · Lavender	Cardiovascular pg. 308

Aromatic: Inhale from cupped hands or diffuse into the air.
Topical: Apply directly to affected area(s) or bottom of feet.
Internal: Take in a capsule, glass of water, or on/under tongue.
TIP Adults: Use 2-3 drops; Children: use 1-2 drops.

AILMENT	RECOMMENDED OILS & USE	FOCUS AREA
Hemorrhoids	Swollen and inflamed veins in the rectum and anus that cause discomfort and bleeding. Cypress (Topical); Helichrysum (Topical, Internal); Yarrow | Pom (Internal); Myrrh (Topical); Balance® | Steady™ (Topical)	Cardiovascular pg. 308; Digestive & Intestinal pg. 331; Integumentary pg. 360; Pregnancy, Labor & Nursing pg. 401
Hepatitis	An inflammation of the liver, with accompanying liver cell damage or cell death. Created frequently by viral infection but also by certain poisons, drugs, or chemicals. Zendocrine® (Internal, Topical); Tea Tree (Topical); Myrrh (Internal, Topical); Helichrysum (Internal, Topical); Geranium (Topical, Internal)	Digestive & Intestinal pg. 331; Immune & Lymphatic pg. 355
Hernia, Hiatal	Occurs when part of the stomach pushes upward through the diaphragm. Basil (Topical, Internal); Arborvitae (Topical); Helichrysum (Topical, Internal); Ginger (Topical, Internal); Juniper Berry (Topical)	Digestive & Intestinal pg. 331
Hernia, Incisional	A type of hernia caused by an incompletely-healed surgical wound. Helichrysum (Topical); Geranium (Topical); Basil (Topical); Arborvitae (Topical); Cypress (Topical)	Integumentary pg. 360
Herniated Disc	A condition which refers to a swelling or fragmented disc between the spinal bones. Birch (Topical); Wintergreen (Topical); Siberian Fir (Topical); Eucalyptus (Topical); AromaTouch® (Topical)	Skeletal pg. 415; Pain & Inflammation pg. 392
Herpes Simplex	A virus causing contagious sores, most often around the mouth or on the genitals. Melissa (Topical, Internal); Tea Tree (Topical); Peppermint (Topical, Internal); On Guard® (Internal, Topical); Basil (Topical, Internal)	Immune & Lymphatic pg. 355; Autoimmune pg. 292
Hiccups	The outcome of an involuntary, spasmodic contraction of the diaphragm followed by the closing of the throat. Zendocrine® (Internal, Topical); Peppermint (Internal, Topical); Serenity® | Calmer™ (Topical); Arborvitae (Topical); Basil (Internal, Topical)	Respiratory pg. 409; Children pg. 317
Hives	An allergic skin reaction resulting in localized redness, swelling, and itching. Roman Chamomile (Topical); Rosemary (Topical, Internal); Frankincense (Topical, Internal); Peppermint (Topical, Internal); Lavender (Internal, Topical)	Allergies pg. 284; Children pg. 317
Hoarse Voice	An inflammation of the voice box from overuse, irritation, or infection. Lemon or Lime (Internal); Ginger (Internal); Myrrh (Internal); Peppermint (Internal); Cinnamon Bark (Internal)	Oral Health pg. 389
Hodgkin's Disease	A malignant form of lymphoma defined by painless enlargement of the lymph nodes, liver, and spleen. Cardamom (Internal, Topical); DDR Prime® (Internal, Topical); Frankincense | Lemongrass (Internal, Topical); Myrrh (Internal, Topical); Frankincense (Internal, Topical)	Cellular Health pg. 313
Hormonal Imbalance (Female)	Subtle changes in the endocrine system with an estrogen decline causing a change in the ratio of estrogen to testosterone in the body. ClaryCalm® (Topical); Geranium (Internal, Topical); Clary Sage (Topical, Internal); Whisper® (Topical, Aromatic); Ylang Ylang (Topical, Aromatic)	Women's Health pg. 436; Detoxification pg. 326
Hormone Imbalance (Male)	A testosterone decline with advancing age which causes a change in the ratio of estrogen to testosterone in the body. Sandalwood (Topical, Aromatic); Juniper Berry (Internal, Topical); Rosemary (Topical, Internal, Aromatic); Balance® | Steady™ (Topical, Aromatic); Ylang Ylang (Aromatic, Topical, Internal)	Men's Health pg. 374; Detoxification pg. 326

QUICK REFERENCE

*Avoid eyes, ear canals, and nasal passages.

STEPS:

1. Look up ailment.
2. Choose one or more of the recommended oils. Use oil(s) as indicated. Order of recommendation of oils and use is left to right.
3. Learn more in corresponding focus area.

AILMENT	RECOMMENDED OILS & USE	FOCUS AREA
Hot Flashes	Troublesome warmth beginning in the upper chest, neck, and face followed by chills and sweating. ClaryCalm® · Peppermint · Eucalyptus · Clary Sage · PastTense®	Women's Health pg. 436
Huntington's Disease	A rare hereditary condition that causes mental deterioration and progressive jerky muscle movements that ends in dementia. DDR Prime® · Frankincense · Clove · Thyme · Rosemary	Brain pg. 300; Nervous System pg. 385; Autoimmune pg. 292
Hydrocephalus	An unusual expansion of cavities (ventricles) within the brain that is caused by the accumulation of cerebrospinal fluid. Spikenard · Frankincense · Basil · Juniper Berry · Sandalwood	Brain pg. 300
Hyperactivity	Excessive or abnormally increased muscular activity or function. Vetiver · Lavender · InTune® | Thinker™ · Petitgrain · Peace®	Focus & Concentration pg. 351; Children pg. 317; Energy & Vitality pg. 344
Hyperpnea	Fast and deep respiration that appears normally after exercise or abnormally when associated with fevers or other disorders. Peppermint · Cardamom · Patchouli · Breathe® · Ylang Ylang	Respiratory pg. 409
Hypersomnia	Excessive daytime sleepiness. People who have hypersomnia can fall asleep at any time, even while driving. Zendocrine® · Peppermint · Lemon · Douglas Fir · Eucalyptus	Sleep pg. 419; Focus & Concentration pg. 351; Energy & Vitality pg. 344
Hyperthyroidism	A medical condition that results from an excess of thyroid hormone in the blood. DDR Prime® · Rosemary · Myrrh · Ginger · Juniper Berry	Endocrine pg. 340
Hypoglycemia	Occurs when blood glucose or blood sugar concentrations fall below a level necessary to support the body's need for energy stability at the cellular level. Cassia · Lavender · Zendocrine® · Cypress · Juniper Berry	Blood Sugar pg. 297
Hypothermia	A condition in which core temperature drops below the needed temperature for normal metabolism and body functions which is defined as 95.0° F (35.0° C). Cinnamon Bark · Clove | Black Pepper · Ginger · Wintergreen · AromaTouch®	First Aid pg. 347
Hypothyroidism	A condition in which the thyroid gland doesn't produce enough thyroid hormone. Clove · Peppermint · Blue Tansy · Lemongrass · Myrrh	Endocrine pg. 340
Hysteria	A psychiatric disorder characterized by violent emotional outbreaks, disturbances of sensory and motor functions. Roman Chamomile · Melissa · Neroli · Balance® | Steady™ · Petitgrain	Mood & Behavior pg. 377; Women's Health pg. 436
Ichthyosis Vulgaris	An inherited skin condition that occurs when the skin does not shed its dead cells. Also known as "fish scale disease" because of the similar appearance. Frankincense · Geranium · Sandalwood · Patchouli · Cedarwood	Integumentary pg. 360

Aromatic: Inhale from cupped hands or diffuse into the air.
Topical: Apply directly to affected area(s) or bottom of feet.
Internal: Take in a capsule, glass of water, or on/under tongue.
TIP Adults: Use 2-3 drops; Children: use 1-2 drops.

AILMENT	RECOMMENDED OILS & USE	FOCUS AREA
Impetigo	A highly contagious skin infection that causes red sores on the face. Geranium (Topical); Oregano (Topical); Vetiver (Topical); Purify | Abōde™ (Topical); Lavender (Topical)	Integumentary pg. 360
Impotence	The inability to maintain or achieve an erection long enough to engage in sexual intercourse. Cypress (Topical, Aromatic); Passion® (Topical, Aromatic); Ylang Ylang (Topical, Aromatic); Ginger (Topical); AromaTouch® (Topical)	Men's Health pg. 374; Intimacy pg. 366
Incontinence	Loss of bladder control, varying from a slight loss of urine after sneezing, coughing, or laughing to complete inability to control urination. Cypress (Topical); Basil (Topical, Internal); Thyme (Topical, Internal); AromaTouch® (Topical); Lemongrass (Topical, Internal)	Urinary pg. 428; Men's Health pg. 374; Women's Health pg. 436
Indigestion	A broad term covering a group of universal symptoms in the digestive tract including bloating, heartburn, nausea, or gas discomfort. DigestZen® (Topical, Internal) | Tamer™ (Topical); Peppermint (Internal, Topical); Black Pepper (Internal, Topical); Slim & Sassy® (Internal, Topical); Cardamom (Internal, Topical)	Digestive & Intestinal pg. 331; Weight pg. 431; Detoxification pg. 326
Infant Reflux	A condition where the contents of the stomach are spit out shortly after feeding. Also known as infant acid reflux. Fennel (Topical, Internal); DigestZen® or Tamer™ (Topical); Peppermint (Internal, Topical); Lavender (Topical); Roman Chamomile (Topical, Internal)	Children pg. 317
Infected Wounds	Infiltration of microorganisms in body tissues. Tea Tree (Topical); Purify (Topical); Frankincense (Topical); Copaiba (Topical); On Guard® | Stronger™ (Topical)	Integumentary pg. 360; First Aid pg. 347
Infection	Multiplication of microorganisms in body tissues, mainly causing cellular injury due to competitive toxins. Oregano (Topical, Internal); On Guard® (Topical, Internal, Aromatic); Cinnamon Bark (Topical, Internal); Thyme (Topical, Internal); Melissa (Internal, Topical, Aromatic)	Immune & Lymphatic pg. 355
Infertility	The inability to conceive a pregnancy after trying for at least one full year. Thyme (Internal, Topical); Clary Sage (Topical, Internal); Spikenard (Internal, Topical); Jasmine | Ylang Ylang (Topical, Internal); Grapefruit + Zendocrine® (Internal, Topical)	Men's Health pg. 374; Women's Health pg. 436
Inflammation	A protective tissue response process by which the body's white blood cells and substances they produce protect from infection. Frankincense (Topical, Internal); Peppermint (Topical, Internal); AromaTouch® + Deep Blue® (Topical); DDR Prime® (Topical, Internal); Turmeric (Topical, Internal)	Pain & Inflammation pg. 392
Inflammatory Bowel Disease	A chronic disorder of the gastrointestinal tract defined by inflammation of the intestine and resulting in persistent diarrhea and abdominal cramping. DigestZen® (Internal, Topical); Ginger (Internal, Topical); Marjoram (Topical, Internal); Copaiba (Internal, Topical); Basil (Topical, Internal)	Digestive & Intestinal pg. 331; Autoimmune pg. 292
Inflammatory Myopathies	A disease featuring weakness and inflammation of muscles. Another term for chronic muscle tissue inflammation is myositis. Lemongrass (Topical, Internal); AromaTouch® (Topical); Deep Blue® (Topical); Siberian Fir (Topical); Wintergreen (Topical)	Muscular pg. 381; Autoimmune pg. 292
Ingrown Toenail	Abnormal growth of a toenail with one edge growing deeply into the nail groove and surrounding tissues. Arborvitae (Topical); DDR Prime® | Lemongrass (Topical); Eucalyptus (Topical); Myrrh (Topical); Tea Tree (Topical)	Integumentary pg. 360

QUICK REFERENCE

*Avoid eyes, ear canals, and nasal passages.

STEPS:

1. Look up ailment.
2. Choose one or more of the recommended oils. Use oil(s) as indicated. Order of recommendation of oils and use is left to right.
3. Learn more in corresponding focus area.

AILMENT	RECOMMENDED OILS & USE	FOCUS AREA
Injury	Harm or damage caused to the body, specifically to the muscles, bones, or other connective tissue. Helichrysum; Deep Blue® | Rescuer™; Lemongrass; Wintergreen; Copaiba	First Aid pg. 347; Muscular pg. 381; Skeletal pg. 415
Insect Bites	An adverse response to a bite or sting of an insect such as bees, wasps, hornets, ticks, mosquitoes, or ants. Lavender; Purify | Abōde™; Roman Chamomile; Blue Tansy; Basil	First Aid pg. 347; Allergies pg. 284
Insect Repellent	A substance applied to clothing or skin which discourages insects from landing or climbing on that surface. TerraShield®; Abōde™ | Citronella; Cedarwood; Lemon Eucalyptus | Eucalyptus; Arborvitae	First Aid pg. 347; Outdoors pg. 506
Insomnia	The inability to access a satisfactory amount or quality of sleep. Serenity® | Calmer™; Lavender; Petitgrain; Roman Chamomile; Vetiver	Sleep pg. 419
Insulin Imbalances	Irregular levels of insulin produced by the pancreas to help the body use glucose for storing energy. Coriander; Cinnamon Bark; Slim & Sassy®; Cassia; Geranium	Blood Sugar pg. 297
Insulin Resistance	A physiological condition in which cells fail to respond to the normal actions of the hormone insulin. Lavender; Slim & Sassy®; Turmeric or Ginger; Zendocrine®; Oregano	Blood Sugar pg. 297
Iris Inflammation	Inflammation of the iris caused by eye trauma.* Juniper Berry; Helichrysum; Patchouli; Frankincense; Arborvitae	Nervous System pg. 385
Irritable Bowel Syndrome	An intestinal disorder causing pain in the belly, gas, diarrhea, and constipation. DigestZen® | Tamer™; Ginger | Celery Seed; Peppermint; Cardamom; Zendocrine®	Digestive & Intestinal pg. 331
Itching	An acute disturbing irritation or tickling sensation that may be felt all over the skin's surface or confined to just one area. Roman Chamomile; Zendocrine®; Blue Tansy; Lavender; Myrrh	Integumentary pg. 360; Allergies pg. 284
Jaundice	A yellowish tinge to the skin, whites of the eyes, and mucous membranes caused by elevated levels of the bile pigment bilirubin. (See dilution recommendation for infants) Frankincense; Lemon; Geranium; Zendocrine®; Juniper Berry	Digestive & Intestinal pg. 331
Jet Lag	A condition marked by insomnia, fatigue, and irritability that is caused by air travel through changing time zones, probably as the result of disrupting circadian rhythms in the body. Peppermint; Serenity® | Calmer™; Rosemary; Citrus Bliss®; Slim & Sassy®	Sleep pg. 419; Energy & Vitality pg. 344; On the Go pg. 504
Jock Itch	A fungal infection that causes an itchy, red rash to the skin of the groin area, inner thighs, and buttocks. Tea Tree; Myrrh; Cedarwood; Thyme; Patchouli	Men's Health pg. 374; Candida pg. 304
Joint Pain	Discomfort, pain, and/or inflammation originating from any part of the joint. Turmeric & Copaiba; Deep Blue® | Rescuer™; Siberian Fir; Pink & Black Pepper; Wintergreen	Skeletal pg. 415; Pain & Inflammation pg. 392

Aromatic: Inhale from cupped hands or diffuse into the air.
Topical: Apply directly to affected area(s) or bottom of feet.
Internal: Take in a capsule, glass of water, or on/under tongue.
TIP Adults: Use 2-3 drops; Children: use 1-2 drops.

AILMENT	RECOMMENDED OILS & USE	FOCUS AREA
Kidney Infection	The condition that occurs when microbes from the bladder or blood (bacteria, fungi, or viruses) invade the tissues of the kidney(s) and reproduce. Lemongrass (Internal, Topical); Juniper Berry (Internal, Topical); Thyme (Internal, Topical); Cinnamon Bark (Internal, Topical); Cardamom (Internal, Topical)	Urinary pg. 428
Kidney Stones	Small, hard mineral deposits that form inside the kidneys. Lemon (Internal, Topical); Eucalyptus (Topical); Wintergreen (Topical); Lemongrass (Topical, Internal); Celery Seed (Internal, Topical)	Urinary pg. 428
Kidneys	A bean-shaped organ that regulates fluid and excretes waste products through urine. Juniper Berry (Internal, Topical); Lemon (Internal, Topical); DDR Prime® (Internal, Topical); Rosemary (Topical, Internal); Eucalyptus (Topical)	Urinary pg. 428
Knee Cartilage Injury	When damage occurs to the cartilage (tough, flexible connective tissue) in the knee, resulting in pain, stiffness, and inflammation. Lemongrass (Topical); Wintergreen or Birch (Topical); Helichrysum (Topical); Copaiba (Topical); Siberian Fir (Topical)	Skeletal pg. 415
Labor	The process during which the uterus contracts and the cervix opens to allow the transition of a baby into the vagina. Ylang Ylang (Topical, Aromatic); ClaryCalm® (Topical, Aromatic); Serenity® (Topical, Aromatic); Clary Sage (Topical, Aromatic); Frankincense (Topical, Aromatic)	Pregnancy, Labor & Nursing pg. 401;
Lactation Problems	Conditions which prevent or discourage breastfeeding, including engorged breasts, sore nipples, mastitis (infection), thrush, and low milk supply that new nursing mothers may experience. Fennel (Topical, Internal); Basil (Topical, Internal); Clary Sage (Topical, Internal); Ylang Ylang (Internal, Topical); Deep Blue® (Topical)	Pregnancy, Labor & Nursing pg. 401;
Lactose Intolerance	Failure of the body to digest lactose, a compound found in dairy products, due to lack of the enzyme lactase in the small intestine. Cardamom (Internal, Topical); DigestZen® (Internal, Topical); Ginger (Internal, Topical); Slim & Sassy® (Internal, Topical); Coriander (Internal, Topical)	Digestive & Intestinal pg. 331; Allergies pg. 284
Laryngitis	Inflammation of the larynx followed by hoarseness of the voice and a painful cough. Lemon (Internal, Topical); On Guard® (Internal, Topical); Myrrh (Internal, Topical); Sandalwood | Stronger™ (Topical); Frankincense (Topical, Internal)	Respiratory pg. 409; Oral Health pg. 389
Lead Poisoning	A potentially fatal buildup of lead in the body, usually over months or years. Cilantro (Internal, Topical); Zendocrine® (Internal, Topical); Helichrysum (Internal, Topical); Rosemary (Internal, Topical); Frankincense (Internal, Topical)	Detoxification pg. 326
Leaky Gut Syndrome	A type of gastrointestinal tract dysfunction that allows bacteria, fungi, toxins, and parasites to permeate the intestinal wall and leak into the bloodstream. Celery Seed (Internal, Topical); Myrrh (Internal, Topical); Lemongrass (Internal, Topical); Cardamom (Internal, Topical); DigestZen® (Internal, Topical)	Digestive & Intestinal pg. 331
Learning Difficulties	An impairment or significantly reduced ability to learn, understand, organize, retain and/or use new information. Vetiver & Lavender (Topical, Aromatic); Balance® (Topical, Aromatic); InTune® | Thinker™ (Topical, Aromatic); Motivate® | Peppermint (Topical, Aromatic); Cedarwood (Topical, Aromatic)	Focus & Concentration pg. 351; Brain pg. 300
Leg Cramps	An abrupt, involuntary, spasmodic muscular contraction causing severe pain, often existing in the leg or shoulder as the result of chill or strain. AromaTouch® (Topical); Marjoram (Topical); Basil (Topical); Deep Blue® | Rescuer™ (Topical); Douglas Fir (Topical)	Muscular pg. 381; Pregnancy, Labor & Nursing pg. 401

*Avoid eyes, ear canals, and nasal passages.

STEPS:

1. Look up ailment.
2. Choose one or more of the recommended oils. Use oil(s) as indicated. Order of recommendation of oils and use is left to right.
3. Learn more in corresponding focus area.

AILMENT	RECOMMENDED OILS & USE	FOCUS AREA
Legg-Calve-Perthes Disease	Occurs when too little blood is supplied to the ball part of the hip joint. Without ample blood flow, the bone stops growing, begins to die and breaks more easily. AromaTouch® [topical]; Lemongrass [topical] [internal]; Peppermint [topical]; Cypress [topical]; Cassia [topical]	Children pg. 317; Skeletal pg. 415
Legionnaires' Disease	A severe form of pneumonia (lung inflammation caused by infection) which is typically caused by inhaling a bacteria called legionella. Tea Tree [topical] [aromatic]; Black Pepper [topical] [aromatic] [internal]; Thyme [topical] [aromatic] [internal]; Eucalyptus [topical] [aromatic]; Birch [topical] [aromatic]	Respiratory pg. 409; Immune & Lymphatic pg. 355
Leukemia	A progressive, malignant cancer of blood-forming tissues, hindering the body's ability to fight infection. Frankincense [internal] [topical]; DDR Prime® [internal] [topical]; Lemongrass [internal] [topical]; Zendocrine® [internal] [topical]; Geranium [internal] [topical]	Cellular Health pg. 313
Libido (Low) for Men	The inhibition of a man's sex drive or natural desire for sexual activity. Ylang Ylang [topical] [aromatic]; Patchouli [topical] [aromatic]; Passion® [topical] [aromatic]; Cinnamon Bark [topical] [aromatic]; Neroli [topical] [aromatic]	Intimacy pg. 366; Men's Health pg. 374
Libido (Low) for Women	The inhibition of a woman's sex drive or natural desire for sexual activity. Ylang Ylang [topical] [aromatic]; Whisper® [topical] [aromatic]; Jasmine [topical] [aromatic]; Passion® [topical] [aromatic]; Neroli [topical] [aromatic]	Intimacy pg. 366; Women's Health pg. 436
Lice/Crabs	A wingless parasite that spends their entire lives on the human hair and feeding exclusively on human blood. Transmitted in crowded conditions (e.g., crabs). Cinnamon Bark [topical] [internal]; Arborvitae [topical]; Eucalyptus [topical]; Rosemary [topical] [internal]; Thyme [topical] [internal]	Parasites pg. 398; Integumentary pg. 360; First Aid pg. 347
Lichen Nitidus	A chronic inflammatory skin condition defined by small, glistening, skin-colored bumps on the surface of the skin. Purify [topical]; Patchouli [topical]; DDR Prime® [topical]; Zendocrine® [topical]; Geranium [topical]	Integumentary pg. 360
Lipoma	A benign, rubbery, encapsulated tumor of fatty tissue that is not tender and feels doughy to the touch. DDR Prime® [topical]; Clove [topical]; Arborvitae [topical]; Frankincense [topical]; Eucalyptus [topical]	Cellular Health pg. 313
Lips (Dry)	Skin on the lips that has lost moisture, often due to dehydration, too much sun or wind, or constant licking or picking. Myrrh [topical]; Geranium [topical]; Sandalwood [topical]; Lavender [topical]; Frankincense [topical]	Integumentary pg. 360
Listeria Infection	A foodborne bacterial illness that is often contracted by eating improperly processed deli meats and unpasteurized dairy products. Cinnamon Bark [internal] [topical]; Oregano [internal] [topical]; On Guard® [internal] [topical]; Tea Tree | Stronger™ [topical]; Purify [topical] [aromatic]	Immune & Lymphatic pg. 355
Liver Disease	Any condition or damage that lowers or stops the functioning of the liver. Zendocrine® [internal] [topical]; Geranium [internal] [topical]; Copaiba [internal] [topical]; Turmeric [internal] [topical]; Lemon + Grapefruit [internal] [topical]	Digestive & Intestinal pg. 331
Lockjaw (Tetanus)	An early symptom of tetanus that affects the central nervous system by causing painful muscular contractions that result in difficulty opening the jaw. Deep Blue® [topical]; Cypress [topical]; Rosemary [topical]; Clove [topical]; Eucalyptus [topical]	Immune & Lymphatic pg. 355; Nervous System pg. 385; Muscular pg. 381
Long QT Syndrome	A heart rhythm disorder that can cause fast, chaotic heartbeats, which may trigger a seizure, sudden fainting spell, or death. Ylang Ylang [topical] [aromatic] [internal]; Melissa [internal] [topical]; Rosemary [internal] [topical]; On Guard® [internal] [topical]; Zendocrine® [internal] [topical]	Cardiovascular pg. 308

Aromatic: Inhale from cupped hands or diffuse into the air.
Topical: Apply directly to affected area(s) or bottom of feet.
Internal: Take in a capsule, glass of water, or on/under tongue.
TIP Adults: Use 2-3 drops; Children: use 1-2 drops.

AILMENT	RECOMMENDED OILS & USE	FOCUS AREA
Lou Gehrig's Disease (ALS)	A rapidly progressive neurodegenerative disease that attacks and kills the nerve cells responsible for controlling voluntary muscles. Melissa (Internal, Topical); DDR Prime® (Topical, Internal); Frankincense (Topical, Internal); Copaiba (Internal, Topical); Cypress (Topical)	Nervous System pg. 385; Autoimmune pg. 292; Muscular pg. 381
Lumbago	An old term used to describe pain in the muscles and joints of the lower back. Deep Blue® (Topical); AromaTouch® (Topical); Frankincense (Topical); Siberian Fir (Topical); Cardamom (Topical)	Muscular pg. 381; Skeletal pg. 415
Lupus	A chronic inflammatory disease caused when the immune system attacks its own tissues. DDR Prime® (Internal, Topical); Zendocrine® (Internal, Topical); Clove (Internal, Topical); Copaiba (Internal, Topical); AromaTouch® (Topical)	Autoimmune pg. 292
Lyme Disease	An inflammatory disease caused by bacteria carried by ticks. Oregano (Internal); Thyme (Topical, Internal); Clove (Topical, Internal); Cassia (Internal, Topical); Frankincense (Internal, Topical, Aromatic)	Immune & Lymphatic pg. 355
Lymphoma	A type of blood cancer that starts in the lymphatic tissues of the body, causing white blood cells to behave abnormally. DDR Prime® (Internal, Topical); Frankincense (Internal, Topical); Thyme (Internal, Topical); Clove (Internal, Topical); Wild Orange (Internal, Topical, Aromatic)	Cellular Health pg. 313
Macular Degeneration	A progressive deterioration of a critical region of the retina called the macula which can cause severe vision impairment.* Immortelle (Topical); Helichrysum (Topical, Internal); Coriander (Topical, Internal); Juniper Berry (Internal, Topical); Frankincense (Topical, Internal)	Nervous System pg. 385
Malabsorption Syndrome	A condition that prevents absorption of nutrients through the small intestine. Sandalwood (Topical, Internal); Fennel (Topical, Internal); Citrus Bliss® (Topical); DigestZen® (Topical, Internal); Ginger (Topical, Internal)	Digestive & Intestinal pg. 331
Malaria	A life-threatening blood disease transmitted by the bite of infected mosquitoes. Thyme (Internal, Topical); Cinnamon Bark (Internal, Topical); Zendocrine® (Topical, Internal); Lemon Eucalyptus | Eucalyptus (Topical, Aromatic); TerraShield® (to avoid) (Topical, Aromatic)	Immune & Lymphatic pg. 355; Parasites pg. 398
Marfan Syndrome (Connective Tissue Disorder)	A genetic disorder that affects connective tissue and causes excessive bone elongation, joint flexibility, and abnormalities of the cardiovascular system. Lemongrass (Topical, Internal); Helichrysum (Topical, Internal); AromaTouch® (Topical); Siberian Fir (Topical); Basil (Topical, Internal)	Cardiovascular pg. 308; Skeletal pg. 415; Muscular pg. 381
Mastitis	A bacterial infection in the mammary glands of the breast which typically only occurs in women who are breastfeeding. Lavender (Topical); DDR Prime® (Internal, Topical); Thyme (Internal); Peppermint (Topical, Internal); Oregano (Internal)	Pregnancy, Labor & Nursing pg. 401
Measles	A highly contagious viral infection which causes full-body rash and other symptoms, mostly in children. On Guard® (Internal, Topical, Aromatic); Yarrow | Pom (Topical, Internal); Tea Tree | Stronger™ (Topical, Aromatic); Coriander (Topical, Internal); Blue Tansy (Topical)	Immune & Lymphatic pg. 355
Melanoma	The least common but most deadly form of skin cancer which typically develops in pigment-containing cells. Frankincense (Topical, Internal); Sandalwood (Topical, Internal); DDR Prime® (Internal, Topical); Immortelle (Topical); Lemongrass (Topical, Internal)	Cellular Health pg. 313
Melatonin Imbalances/ Insufficiencies	Melatonin is a hormone produced at the onset of darkness to aid in sleep. Imbalances or insufficiencies may lead to sleep deprivation or sleeping disorders. Vetiver (Internal, Topical, Aromatic); Lavender (Internal, Topical, Aromatic); Serenity® | Calmer™ (Topical, Aromatic); Petitgrain (Internal, Topical, Aromatic); Roman Chamomile (Internal, Topical, Aromatic)	Endocrine pg. 340; Sleep pg. 419

*Avoid eyes, ear canals, and nasal passages.

STEPS:

1. Look up ailment.
2. Choose one or more of the recommended oils. Use oil(s) as indicated. Order of recommendation of oils and use is left to right.
3. Learn more in corresponding focus area.

AILMENT	RECOMMENDED OILS & USE	FOCUS AREA
Memory (Poor)	The weak mental capacity of retaining facts or recalling previous experiences. Peppermint · Rosemary · Frankincense · Thyme · Sandalwood	Focus & Concentration pg. 351; Brain pg. 300
Meningitis	Inflammation of brain and spinal cord membranes, typically caused by a viral or bacterial infection, characterized by serious symptoms. Tea Tree | Stronger™ · On Guard® · Clove · DDR Prime® · Basil	Immune & Lymphatic pg. 355
Meniere's Disease	Inner disorder with symptoms including vertigo, tinnitus, hearing loss, and a sensation of pressure. Helichrysum · Frankincense · Juniper Berry · Ginger · Basil	Women's Health pg. 436
Menopause	The period of permanent cessation of menstruation, typically occurring between the ages of 45 and 55. ClaryCalm® · Zendocrine® · Passion® · Thyme · Clary Sage	Women's Health pg. 436
Menorrhagia (Excessive Menstrual Bleeding)	Extremely heavy menstrual flow with cycles of normal length or prolonged uterine bleeding lasting longer than seven days. ClaryCalm® · Helichrysum · Zendocrine® · Geranium · DDR Prime®	Women's Health pg. 436
Menstrual Cycle (Irregular or Scanty)	Uncommonly slight or infrequent menstrual flow. ClaryCalm® · Geranium · Rosemary · Yarrow | Pom · Zendocrine®	Women's Health pg. 436
Menstrual Pain/ Cramps	Also referred to as dysmenorrhea, a female condition of painful, debilitating menstrual cycles that ranges from dull to severe. ClaryCalm® · Clary Sage · Marjoram · PastTense® · Copaiba	Women's Health pg. 436
Mental Fatigue	A cognitive or emotional state associated with decreased ability to function, typically caused by prolonged mental exertion or emotional duress. Rosemary · Basil · Peppermint · Citrus Bliss® | Motivate® · Tulsi	Brain pg. 300
Mesenteric Lymphadentis	Painful inflammation of the lymph nodes that attach the intestine to the abdominal wall, typically a temporary condition in children. Purify | Abōde™ · DDR Prime® · Basil · Cardamom · Zendocrine®	Immune & Lymphatic pg. 355
Mesothelioma	A cancerous tumor of the epithelium lining the lungs, heart, or abdomen often associated with exposure to asbestos dust. Air-X™ · Ravintsara · Laurel Leaf | Breathe® · DDR Prime® · Abōde™	Cellular Health pg. 313
Metabolic Muscle Disorders	A condition that interferes with the body's ability to draw and utilize energy from food, resulting in muscle weakness or pain. Basil · Cypress · Ginger · Peppermint · Cassia	Muscular pg. 381
Metabolism (Low)	A low basal metabolic rate normally leads to low energy expenditure. As a result, the number of calories a person normally expends is likely less than the number of calories consumed. Grapefruit · Slim & Sassy® · Cinnamon Bark · DDR Prime® · Clove	Weight pg. 431
Migraine	A severe recurring headache over the course of 3 hours to 4 days associated with sharp pain nausea, and/or sensitivity to light. Peppermint · Copaiba · Frankincense · Lavender · PastTense®	Pain & Inflammation pg. 392; Muscular pg. 381

(A) Aromatic: Inhale from cupped hands or diffuse into the air.
(T) Topical: Apply directly to affected area(s) or bottom of feet.
(I) Internal: Take in a capsule, glass of water, or on/under tongue.
TIP Adults: Use 2-3 drops; Children: use 1-2 drops.

AILMENT	RECOMMENDED OILS & USE	FOCUS AREA
Milk Supply (Low)	Milk supply is considered low when there is not enough breast milk being produced to meet the need of the baby. Fennel (T)(I) · Basil (T)(I) · Cardamom (I)(T)(A) · Clary Sage (I)(T) · Lavender (T)(I)(A)	Pregnancy, Labor & Nursing pg. 401
Miscarriage (Prevention)	The spontaneous and unexpected loss of a pregnancy resulting in a complex and often difficult emotional healing process afterward. Console® (T)(A) · Patchouli (T)(A) · Immortelle (T) · Thyme (I)(T) · DDR Prime® (I)(T)	Pregnancy, Labor & Nursing pg. 401
Miscarriage (Recovery)	The spontaneous and unexpected loss of a pregnancy resulting in a complex and often difficult emotional healing process afterward. Zendocrine® (T) · DDR Prime® (I)(T) · Clary Sage (I)(T) · Console® (T) · ClaryCalm® (T)	Pregnancy, Labor & Nursing pg. 401
Mitral Valve Prolapse	Improper closure of the valve between the heart's upper and lower left chambers, typically not serious. Helichrysum (T)(I) · Marjoram (T)(I) · PastTense® (T) · AromaTouch® (T) · DDR Prime® (I)(T)	Cardiovascular pg. 308
Mold/Mildew	Fungi; mold typically grows on food whereas mildew typically grows on damp surfaces such as walls, cardboard, etc. Tea Tree (A)(T) · Oregano (A)(T) · Thyme (A)(T) · Abōde™ | Purify (A)(T) · Arborvitae (A)(T)	Allergies pg. 284; Detoxification pg. 326
Moles	A common skin condition, moles are pigmented and slightly raised blotches on the outer layer of the skin. Frankincense (T) · HD Clear® (T) · DDR Prime® (T) · Zendocrine® (T) · Juniper Berry (T)	Integumentary pg. 360
Molluscum	A viral skin disorder characterized by groups of small, smooth, painless, pinkish nodules with a central depression that yields a milky fluid when squeezed. Melissa (T) · HD Clear® (T) · Roman Chamomile (T) · Tea Tree (T) · Sandalwood (T)	Children pg. 317; Integumentary pg. 360
Mononucleosis	An infectious disease typically spread through saliva resulting in severe fever, sore throat, enlarged lymph nodes, and extreme fatigue. Melissa (I)(T) · Thyme (I)(T) · Cinnamon Bark (I)(T) · Eucalyptus | Stronger™ (T)(A) · On Guard® (I)(T)(A)	Immune & Lymphatic pg. 355
Mood Swings	An unpredictable alteration of a person's emotional state between periods of depression and euphoria. Balance® | Steady™ (T)(A) · Cheer® | Brave™ (T)(A) · Forgive® (T)(A) · Adaptiv™ | Neroli (T)(A) · Elevation (T)(A)	Mood & Behavior pg. 377; Candida pg. 304; Women's Health pg. 436
Morning Sickness	Vomiting and nausea beginning in the morning upon arising, common during early pregnancy. DigestZen® | Tamer™ (T)(I) | (T) · Peppermint (A)(T)(I) · Ginger (I)(T)(A) · Coriander (I)(T)(A) · Fennel (I)(T)(A)	Pregnancy, Labor & Nursing pg. 401;
Mosquito Bites	Itchy bumps that appear after a mosquito has pierced the skin to consume blood. Purify | Abōde™ (T) · Lavender (T) · Roman Chamomile (T) · Blue Tansy (T) · Tea Tree (T)	First Aid pg. 347
Motion Sickness	The uncomfortable nausea which people experience when their sense of balance and equilibrium is disturbed by constant motion. Ginger (I)(A)(T) · Basil (I)(T)(A) · Peppermint (A)(I)(T) · Cassia (I)(A) · DigestZen® | Tamer™ (I) | (T)	Digestive & Intestinal pg. 331; First Aid pg. 347
Mouth Ulcers	Ulcers of the oral mucosa commonly caused by a secondary bacterial infection of less severe mucosal lesions. Clove (T)(I) · On Guard® (T)(I) · Cinnamon Bark (T)(I) · Tea Tree (T) · Myrrh (T)(I)	Oral Health pg. 389; Autoimmune pg. 292

*Avoid eyes, ear canals, and nasal passages.

QUICK REFERENCE

STEPS:

1. Look up ailment.
2. Choose one or more of the recommended oils. Use oil(s) as indicated. Order of recommendation of oils and use is left to right.
3. Learn more in corresponding focus area.

AILMENT	RECOMMENDED OILS & USE	FOCUS AREA
MRSA	An infection caused by a type of staph bacteria that has become resistant to many of the antibiotics used to treat ordinary staph infections. Cinnamon Bark, Oregano, Thyme, On Guard®, Clove	Immune & Lymphatic pg. 355
Mucus	A thick, gel-like, viscous material that functions to protect and moisten inner body surfaces. Lemon, DigestZen®, Fennel, Eucalyptus, Cardamom	Respiratory pg. 409; Digestive & Intestinal pg. 331; Allergies pg. 284
Multiple Chemical Sensitivity Reaction	A medical condition identified by symptoms to low-level chemical exposure. Substances include pesticides, smoke, plastics, petroleum products, scents, and paints. Cilantro, Zendocrine®, Douglas Fir, Geranium, Coriander	Allergies pg. 284
Multiple Sclerosis	A potentially disabling disease of the brain and spinal cord in which the immune system eats away at the protective covering of nerves. Zendocrine®, Frankincense, Sandalwood, DDR Prime®, Cypress	Nervous System pg. 385; Autoimmune pg. 292
Mumps	A mild short-term viral infection of the salivary glands that commonly occurs during childhood. On Guard®, DDR Prime®, Zendocrine®, Yarrow | Pom, Lavender	Immune & Lymphatic pg. 355
Muscular Cramps / Charley Horse	An immediate, uncontrolled, spasmodic muscular contraction causing severe pain, often occurring in the leg or shoulder as the result of a strain or chill. Marjoram, AromaTouch®, Deep Blue®, PastTense®, Siberian Fir	Athletes pg. 288; Muscular pg. 381
Muscle Pulls, Strains	Partial or total breach of muscle fibers due to sudden applied force or overuse. Copaiba, Lemongrass, Deep Blue® | Rescuer™, Marjoram, AromaTouch®	Muscular pg. 381; Athletes pg. 288; Pain & Inflammation pg. 392
Muscle Pain	Pain in a muscle or group of muscles that is typically shared by a feeling of unease. AromaTouch®, Deep Blue® | Rescuer™, Siberian Fir, Marjoram, Peppermint	Muscular pg. 381; Athletes pg. 288; Pain & Inflammation pg. 392
Muscle Spasms	A quick, involuntary contraction of a muscle or group of muscles. AromaTouch®, Marjoram, Copaiba, Roman Chamomile, Basil	Muscular pg. 381; Athletes pg. 288; Sleep pg. 419
Muscle Stiffness	The rigidity of muscles due to inadequate use and movement. PastTense®, AromaTouch® | Rescuer™, Siberian Fir, Ginger, Marjoram	Muscular pg. 381; Athletes pg. 288
Muscle Weakness / Lack of Growth	Muscle development from exercise and exertion. When a muscle is pushed to its limits, it will repair and rebuild itself for future exertion. Wintergreen or Birch, Helichrysum, Ginger, Lemongrass, Siberian Fir	Muscular pg. 381; Athletes pg. 288
Muscular Dystrophy	A group of inherited disorders in which muscle bulk and strength gradually drop. Lemongrass, Frankincense, PastTense®, DDR Prime®, Marjoram	Muscular pg. 381
Myasthenia Gravis	A weakness and rapid fatigue of muscles under voluntary control. Helichrysum, Ginger, Lemongrass, Cypress, DDR Prime®	Muscular pg. 381; Autoimmune pg. 292
Myelofibrosis	A severe bone marrow disorder that disrupts the body's normal production of blood cells. Helichrysum, Zendocrine®, Ginger, Frankincense, Siberian Fir	Skeletal pg. 415

Discover other ways essential oil enthusiasts are getting results in the app.

Aromatic: Inhale from cupped hands or diffuse into the air.
Topical: Apply directly to affected area(s) or bottom of feet.
Internal: Take in a capsule, glass of water, or on/under tongue.
TIP Adults: Use 2-3 drops; Children: use 1-2 drops.

AILMENT	RECOMMENDED OILS & USE	FOCUS AREA
Myotonic Dystrophy	A genetic disorder that causes progressive muscle weakness. Douglas Fir (Topical); DDR Prime® (Internal, Topical); Helichrysum (Internal, Topical); Siberian Fir (Topical); Lemongrass (Internal, Topical)	Muscular pg. 381
Nails	The hard, cutaneous plate on the dorsal surface of the end of a finger or toe. Sandalwood (Topical); Lemon (Topical); Wild Orange (Topical); Arborvitae (Topical); ClaryCalm® (Topical)	Integumentary pg. 360
Narcolepsy	A disorder distincted by extreme daytime sleepiness, cataplexy and uncontrollable sleep attacks. Sandalwood (Internal, Topical, Aromatic); Console® (Topical, Aromatic); Motivate® | Brave™ (Topical, Aromatic); Wild Orange (Aromatic, Internal, Topical); InTune® | Thinker™ (Topical, Aromatic)	Sleep pg. 419; Brain pg. 300
Nasal Polyp	A rounded, stretched piece of pulpy, dependent mucosa that projects into the nasal cavity. Rosemary (Topical, Aromatic); Melissa (Topical); Breathe® (Topical, Aromatic); On Guard® (Topical, Aromatic); Sandalwood (Topical, Aromatic)	Respiratory pg. 409; Cellular Health pg. 313
Nausea	An undesirable queasy sensation including an urge to vomit. DigestZen® | Tamer™ (Topical, Internal, Aromatic | Topical, Aromatic); Ginger (Internal, Topical, Aromatic); Peppermint (Internal, Topical, Aromatic); Pink Pepper (Internal, Topical, Aromatic); Zendocrine® (Internal, Topical, Aromatic)	Digestive & Intestinal pg. 331
Neck Pain	Pain in response to injury or another stimulus that resolves when the injury stimulus is removed or healed. Deep Blue® (Topical); PastTense® (Topical); Copaiba (Topical); AromaTouch® (Topical); Wintergreen (Topical)	Muscular pg. 381
Nerves, Weakened / Damaged	A dysfunction or breakdown of the nervous system. Vetiver (Topical); Helichrysum (Topical, Internal); Petitgrain (Topical, Internal); Copaiba (Topical, Internal); Patchouli (Topical)	Nervous System pg. 385
Nervous Fatigue	A form of fatigue associated with changes in the synaptic concentration of neurotransmitters within the central nervous system. Peppermint (Topical, Aromatic, Internal); Citrus Bliss® (Topical, Aromatic); Basil (Topical, Aromatic, Internal); Yarrow | Pom (Topical, Internal); Zendocrine® (Topical, Aromatic)	Energy & Vitality pg. 344; Stress pg. 423
Nervousness	A state of concern, accompanied by great physical and mental unrest. Peace® (Topical, Aromatic); Balance® | Steady™ (Topical, Aromatic); Serenity® | Calmer™ (Topical, Aromatic); Motivate® | Brave™ (Topical, Aromatic); Petitgrain (Internal, Topical, Aromatic)	Mood & Behavior pg. 377; Stress pg. 423
Neuralgia	Characterized as an extreme stabbing or burning pain caused by irritation of or damage to a nerve. Helichrysum (Topical, Internal, Aromatic); PastTense® (Topical); Wintergreen (Topical); Clove | Neroli (Topical, Internal | Topical); Douglas Fir (Topical)	Nervous System pg. 385; Muscular pg. 381; Pain & Inflammation pg. 392
Neuritis	The inflammation of a nerve or group of nerves that is defined by loss of reflexes, pain, and atrophy of the affected muscles. Cardamom (Topical, Internal); Patchouli (Topical, Internal); Helichrysum (Topical, Internal); Ginger (Topical, Internal); Deep Blue® | Rescuer™ (Topical)	Nervous System pg. 385
Neuromuscular Disorders	A broad term that encompasses many different diseases that affect the function of the skeletal muscles that move the limbs and trunk. Marjoram (Topical); Arborvitae (Topical); Ginger (Topical); Basil (Topical); AromaTouch® (Topical)	Muscular pg. 381
Neuropathy	A condition affecting the nerves supplying the legs and arms. Cypress (Topical); AromaTouch® (Topical); Deep Blue® (Topical); Basil (Topical); Wintergreen (Topical)	Nervous System pg. 385
Night Eating Syndrome (NES)	An eating disorder characterized by abnormal food intake patterns during the night, not to be confused with binge eating disorder. Cinnamon Bark (Internal, Aromatic); Slim & Sassy® (Internal, Aromatic); Grapefruit (Internal, Aromatic, Topical); Ginger (Internal, Aromatic, Topical); Peppermint (Internal, Aromatic, Topical)	Eating Disorders pg. 336; Weight pg. 431

*Avoid eyes, ear canals, and nasal passages.

STEPS:

1. Look up ailment.
2. Choose one or more of the recommended oils. Use oil(s) as indicated. Order of recommendation of oils and use is left to right.
3. Learn more in corresponding focus area.

QUICK REFERENCE

AILMENT	RECOMMENDED OILS & USE	FOCUS AREA
Night Sweats	Profuse episodes of sweating at night that soak nightclothes or bedding. Peppermint · DDR Prime® · ClaryCalm® · Whisper® · Spearmint	Women's Health pg. 436
Nighttime Urination	Nocturia, or nocturnal polyuria, is the medical term for excessive urination during the night. Rosemary · Cypress · Juniper Berry · Slim & Sassy® · Thyme	Children pg. 317
Nipples, Sore	Increased sensitivity due to breastfeeding, friction, running, or hormonal imbalances. Myrrh · Tea Tree · Sandalwood · Frankincense · Geranium	Pregnancy, Labor & Nursing pg. 401
Nose (Dry)	Irritation caused from insufficient mucus in the nasal cavity.* Myrrh · Wild Orange · Geranium · Sandalwood · Lavender	Respiratory pg. 409
Nosebleed	Bleeding from the nose, either spontaneous or induced by nose picking or trauma.* Helichrysum · Geranium · Myrrh · On Guard® | Stronger™ · Lavender	Respiratory pg. 409
Numbness	Loss of sensation or feeling. Peppermint · Cypress · PastTense® · Ginger · Basil	Nervous System pg. 385; Cardiovascular pg. 308
Obesity	Obesity is an uncommon quantity of body fat, usually 20% or more over an individual's ideal body weight. Slim & Sassy® · Cinnamon Bark · Grapefruit · Ginger · Bergamot	Weight pg. 431; Endocrine pg. 340; Stress pg. 423; Blood Sugar pg. 297
Obsessive-Compulsive Disorder (OCD)	A type of anxiety disorder marked by distressing excessive thoughts (obsessions) that lead to repetitive ritualized behaviors (compulsions) that interfere with daily life. Adaptiv™ | Cedarwood · Serenity® | Calmer™ · Forgive® · InTune® | Thinker™ · Ylang Ylang	Mood & Behavior pg. 377; Limbic pg. 371
Ocular Rosacea	A common inflammatory condition affecting the eyes. Often develops in individuals who have rosacea, a chronic condition that affects the face and chest.* Myrrh · Frankincense · Zendocrine® · Immortelle · Sandalwood	Nervous System pg. 385; Integumentary pg. 360; Respiratory pg. 409
Olfactory Loss	The inability to perceive odor or loss of the sense of smell. Also known as anosmia. Lavender | Helichrysum · Peppermint · Adaptiv™ | Basil · DDR Prime® · Arborvitae	Respiratory pg. 409; Allergies pg. 284
Oppositional Defiant Disorder	A disorder in a child marked by defiant and disobedient behavior to authority figures. Peace® | Calmer™ · PastTense® · Forgive® · Cardamom · Cheer®	Mood & Behavior pg. 377
Oral Health	The state of health of the mouth, throat, tooth and other capacities to allow for biting, chewing, smiling, and speaking. Topical use can indicate brushing with or rubbing oil(s) on affected area. Myrrh · Clove · Peppermint · On Guard® · Turmeric	Oral Health pg. 389; Personal Care pg. 508
Osgood-Schlatter Disease	A childhood repetitive-use injury that causes a painful lump below the kneecap. Cypress · Ginger · Lemongrass · AromaTouch® · Birch	Skeletal pg. 415

Aromatic: Inhale from cupped hands or diffuse into the air.
Topical: Apply directly to affected area(s) or bottom of feet.
Internal: Take in a capsule, glass of water, or on/under tongue.
TIP Adults: Use 2-3 drops; Children: Use 1-2 drops.

AILMENT	RECOMMENDED OILS & USE	FOCUS AREA
Osteoarthritis	A form of arthritis, occurring commonly in older persons, that is defined by chronic degeneration of the cartilage of the joints. Black Pepper (Topical, Internal); Frankincense (Topical, Internal); Siberian Fir (Topical); Deep Blue® (Topical); Wintergreen (Topical)	Skeletal pg. 415; Pain & Inflammation pg. 392
Osteomyelitis	Inflammation of bone caused by infection, generally in the legs, arm, or spine. Thyme (Topical); Melissa (Topical); Lemongrass (Topical); Wintergreen (Topical); Clove (Topical)	Immune & Lymphatic pg. 355; Skeletal pg. 415
Osteoporosis	A disease defined by loss in bone mass and density, occurring commonly in postmenopausal women, resulting in a predisposition to fractures and bone deformities such as vertebral collapse. Siberian Fir (Topical); Clove (Internal, Topical); Wintergreen (Topical); Geranium (Topical, Internal); Lemongrass (Topical, Internal)	Skeletal pg. 415
Ovarian Cyst	A solid or fluid-filled sac or pocket within or on the surface of an ovary. Commonly benign. Zendocrine® (Internal, Topical); DDR Prime® (Internal, Topical); Clary Sage (Internal, Topical); Basil (Internal, Topical, Aromatic); Rosemary (Topical, Internal)	Women's Health pg. 436; Cellular Health pg. 313
Overactive Bladder (OAB)	The leakage of urine in large amounts at unexpected times, including during sleep. Cypress (Topical); Thyme (Internal, Topical); Juniper Berry (Topical, Internal); Ginger (Topical, Internal); Zendocrine® (Topical, Internal)	Urinary pg. 428
Overeating	Uncontrolled ingestion of sizable quantities of food in a discrete interval, usually with a lack of control over the activity. Slim & Sassy® (Topical, Internal); Coriander (Topical, Internal, Aromatic); Grapefruit (Topical, Internal, Aromatic); Cinnamon Bark (Topical, Internal, Aromatic); Ginger (Topical, Internal)	Weight pg. 431; Stress pg. 423; Eating Disorders pg. 336
Over-Exercised	Overuse of muscle and connective tissue that may cause injury or exhaustion. Peppermint (Topical); Deep Blue® | Rescuer™ (Topical); AromaTouch® (Topical); Marjoram (Topical); Eucalyptus (Topical)	Muscular pg. 381; Athletes pg. 288
Overheated	An elevated body temperature due to failed thermoregulation. Peppermint (Topical, Internal); Eucalyptus (Topical); PastTense® (Topical); Petitgrain (Topical, Internal); Spearmint (Topical)	First Aid pg. 347; Athletes pg. 288
Overwhelmed	To feel overcome completely in mind or body, usually by large amounts of stress. Peace® (Aromatic, Topical); InTune® | Thinker™ (Aromatic, Topical); Rosemary (Aromatic, Topical); Adaptiv™ | Serenity® (Aromatic, Topical); Lemon (Aromatic, Topical)	Mood & Behavior pg. 377
Ovulation (Lack of)	The failure of an egg to rupture from the ovary at mid-cycle. The cause is a lack of progesterone. Basil (Topical, Internal); ClaryCalm® (Topical, Aromatic); Thyme (Topical, Internal); Ylang Ylang (Topical, Aromatic); Clary Sage (Topical)	Women's Health pg. 436; Blood Sugar pg. 297
Paget's Disease	A disease that disrupts the replacement of old bone tissue with new bone tissue. DDR Prime® (Internal, Topical); Myrrh (Topical); Wintergreen (Topical); Clove (Topical, Internal); ClaryCalm® (Topical)	Skeletal pg. 415; Cellular Health pg. 313
Pain	An undesirable sensation occurring in varying degrees of severity as a consequence of disease, injury, or emotional disorder. Turmeric or Copaiba (Topical, Internal); Peppermint (Topical, Internal); Deep Blue® | Rescuer™ (Topical); Helichrysum (Topical, Internal); Wintergreen | Birch (Topical)	Pain & Inflammation pg. 392
Palpitations	A sensitivity in which a person is aware of an intermittent, hard, or rapid heartbeat. Ylang Ylang (Topical, Internal, Aromatic); Petitgrain (Internal, Topical); Lavender (Aromatic, Topical, Internal); Neroli (Topical); Rosemary (Aromatic, Topical, Internal)	Cardiovascular pg. 308
Pancreatitis	An inflammation of the pancreas, an organ that is essential in digestion. Coriander (Internal, Topical); Rosemary (Internal, Topical); Geranium (Internal, Topical); Cinnamon Bark (Internal, Topical); Zendocrine® (Internal, Topical)	Endocrine pg. 340

*Avoid eyes, ear canals, and nasal passages.

STEPS:

1. Look up ailment.
2. Choose one or more of the recommended oils. Use oil(s) as indicated. Order of recommendation of oils and use is left to right.
3. Learn more in corresponding focus area.

QUICK REFERENCE

AILMENT	RECOMMENDED OILS & USE	FOCUS AREA
Panic Attacks	Periods of intense apprehension or fear typically characterized by hyperventilation that occur suddenly and of variable duration from minutes to hours. Petitgrain · Adaptiv™ | Serenity® · Neroli | Calmer™ · Magnolia · Balance® | Steady™	Mood & Behavior pg. 377
Paralysis	Complete or partial loss of strength or muscle function. Frankincense · Cypress · Melissa · Ginger · DDR Prime®	Nervous System pg. 385; Muscular pg. 381; Cardiovascular pg. 308; Immune & Lymphatic pg. 355; Autoimmune pg. 292
Parasites	An organism that feeds, grows, and is sheltered on or in a different organism while contributing nothing to the survival of its host. Clove · Oregano · Thyme · Turmeric · Lemongrass	Parasites pg. 398; Detoxification pg. 326; Digestive & Intestinal pg. 331; Integumentary pg. 360
Parathyroid Disorder	Overactivity of one or more of the parathyroid lobes, which make too much parathyroid hormone, causing a potentially serious calcium imbalance. ClaryCalm® · Zendocrine® · Melissa · Ginger · Citrus Bliss®	Endocrine pg. 340
Parkinson's Disease	A gradual nervous disease appearing most often after the age of 50, associated with the ruin of brain cells that produce dopamine. Copaiba + Frankincense · Zendocrine® · Marjoram · Bergamot | Melissa · DDR Prime®	Brain pg. 300; Nervous System pg. 385; Muscular pg. 381; Addictions pg. 280
Pelvic Pain Syndrome	Pain in the pelvis that arises in endometritis, appendicitis, and oophoritis. Ginger · Geranium · Thyme · Copaiba · Rosemary	Women's Health pg. 436; Digestive & Intestinal pg. 331
Perforated Ear Drum	Occurs when there is a rupture or hole in the eardrum (the thin membrane that separates the outer ear canal from the middle ear).* Basil · Ylang Ylang · On Guard® · Arborvitae · Patchouli	Respiratory pg. 409
Pericardial Disease	Occurs when there is too much fluid buildup around the heart. Rosemary · Juniper Berry · Marjoram · Lemongrass · Zendocrine®	Cardiovascular pg. 308
Perimenopause	The three to five year period before menopause during which progesterone and estrogen levels decline and symptoms of hormone deprivation begin. Zendocrine® · Whisper® · DDR Prime® · Clary Sage · Rosemary	Women's Health pg. 436
Perineal Tearing, Lack of Elasticity	An unintended laceration of women's skin and other soft tissue structures which separate the vagina from the anus. Geranium · Frankincense · Sandalwood · Roman Chamomile · Lavender	Pregnancy, Labor & Nursing pg. 401;
Periodic Limb Movement Disorder	Repetitive cramping or jerking of the legs during sleep. AromaTouch® · PastTense® · Marjoram · Basil · Lavender	Sleep pg. 419
Pernicious Anemia	A severe anemia associated with poor intake or absorption of vitamin B12, defined by defective production of red blood cells. Helichrysum · Geranium · Zendocrine® · Cinnamon Bark · Lemon	Autoimmune pg. 292; Cardiovascular pg. 308

Aromatic: Inhale from cupped hands or diffuse into the air.
Topical: Apply directly to affected area(s) or bottom of feet.
Internal: Take in a capsule, glass of water, or on/under tongue.
TIP Adults: Use 2-3 drops; Children: Use 1-2 drops.

AILMENT	RECOMMENDED OILS & USE	FOCUS AREA
Perspiration (Excessive)	An inherited disorder of the eccrine sweat glands in which emotional stimuli cause abnormal amounts of sweating. Coriander · Geranium · Petitgrain · Zendocrine® · Douglas Fir	Endocrine pg. 340; Athletes pg. 288; Urinary pg. 428; Detoxification pg. 326
Phantom Pains	Pain, itching, tingling, or numbness in the place where amputated parts used to be. Helichrysum · Basil · Frankincense · Deep Blue® | Rescuer™ · AromaTouch®	Pain & Inflammation pg. 392; Nervous System pg. 385
Phlebitis	Inflammation of the walls of a vein. Cypress · Helichrysum · Zendocrine® · Basil · Lemongrass	Cardiovascular pg. 308
Pica	Craving and chewing substances that have no nutritional value, such as ice, clay, soil, or paper. Microplex VMz® | A2Z · Patchouli · Cilantro · Cinnamon Bark · Peppermint	Eating Disorders pg. 336; Children pg. 317
Pinkeye	Inflammation or infection of the outer membrane of the eyeball and the inner eyelid, causing the eye to become pink in color.* Frankincense · Tea Tree · Spikenard · Lavender · Clary Sage	Immune & Lymphatic pg. 355; Children pg. 317
Pinworms	A parasitic nematode worm infecting the rectum, colon, and anus of humans. Clove · Oregano · Thyme · Lemongrass · On Guard®	Parasites pg. 398
Plantar Fasciitis	An inflammation of a thick band of tissue that connects the heel bone to the toes. Copaiba · Lemongrass · AromaTouch® · Wintergreen · Siberian Fir	Skeletal pg. 415; Muscular pg. 381
Plantar Warts	An unpleasant verrucous lesion on the sole of the foot. Cinnamon Bark · Melissa · Purify · Oregano · Frankincense	Integumentary pg. 360
Plaque	An semi-hardened accumulation of substances from fluids that surround an area. Examples include dental plaque and cholesterol plaque. On Guard® · Clove · Thyme · Myrrh · Lemon	Oral Health pg. 389; Cardiovascular pg. 308
Pleurisy	An infection of the membrane that surrounds and protects the lungs. Cinnamon Bark · Breathe® · Rosemary · Eucalyptus · Melissa	Respiratory pg. 409
Pneumonia	Infection that inflames air sacs in one or both lungs which many fill with fluid. Air-X™ · Breathe® | Ravintsara · Copaiba · Roman Chamomile · Abōde™ | Arborvitae	Respiratory pg. 409
Poison Ivy	A poisonous North American vine or shrub that is well known for causing itching, irritation, and rash on skin that has come in contact with its leaves. Geranium · Purify | Abōde™ · Roman Chamomile · Lavender · Frankincense	First Aid pg. 347; Integumentary pg. 360; Outdoors pg. 506
Polio	A highly infectious viral disease that may attack the central nervous system and can cause paralysis. Melissa · Lemongrass · Patchouli · Spikenard · Frankincense	Immune & Lymphatic pg. 355; Nervous System pg. 385
Polycystic Ovary Syndrome (PCOS)	A hormonal disorder causing enlarged ovaries with small cysts on the outer edges. Hormonal symptoms include acne and facial hair. Thyme · Basil · Geranium · Zendocrine® · DDR Prime®	Women's Health pg. 436; Blood Sugar pg. 297; Cellular Health pg. 313

*Avoid eyes, ear canals, and nasal passages.

STEPS:

1. Look up ailment.
2. Choose one or more of the recommended oils. Use oil(s) as indicated. Order of recommendation of oils and use is left to right.
3. Learn more in corresponding focus area.

AILMENT	RECOMMENDED OILS & USE	FOCUS AREA
Polymyositis	A disease featuring inflammation of the muscle fibers. Ginger; Black Pepper; Balance® | Steady™; Deep Blue®; DDR Prime®	Muscular pg. 381; Pain & Inflammation pg. 392
Polyps	A tumor with a small flap that attaches itself to the wall of different vascular organs such as the rectum, uterus, and nose. Rosemary; Ginger; Peppermint; Clove; Lemongrass	Digestive & Intestinal pg. 331; Cellular Health pg. 313; Women's Health pg. 436; Respiratory pg. 409
Porphyria	Disorders resulting from buildup of certain chemicals related to red blood cell proteins. Zendocrine®; Frankincense; Lemongrass; Geranium; DDR Prime®	Nervous System pg. 385; Integumentary pg. 360; Detoxification pg. 326
Postpartum Depression	An emotional disorder that starts after childbirth and typically lasts beyond six weeks. Cheer®; Frankincense; Clary Sage; Zendocrine®; Elevation	Pregnancy, Labor & Nursing pg. 401
Post-Traumatic Stress Disorder (PTSD)	A disorder characterized by failure to recover after experiencing or witnessing a terrifying event. Individuals who are triggered can relive the event as if it was happening again in the present. Melissa; Roman Chamomile; Helichrysum + Vetiver; Adaptiv™ | Balance®; Neroli	Limbic pg. 371; Mood & Behavior pg. 377
Precocious Puberty	A condition in which a child's body begins changing into that of an adult too soon. Zendocrine®; Frankincense; Whisper®; ClaryCalm®; DDR Prime®	Endocrine pg. 340; Women's Health pg. 436; Men's Health pg. 374
Preeclampsia	A condition during pregnancy that results in high blood pressure, large amounts of protein in the urine, and swelling that doesn't go away. Also called toxemia. Marjoram; Frankincense; Zendocrine®; AromaTouch®; Cypress	Pregnancy, Labor & Nursing pg. 401
Pregnancy	The time from conception until birth, typically lasting 9 months or 40 weeks, with three stages or trimesters. DigestZen®; Lavender; Geranium; Ylang Ylang; Slim & Sassy®	Pregnancy, Labor & Nursing pg. 401; Women's Health pg. 436
Pregnancy (Post-term)	Delivery on or after 41 weeks plus three days of gestation, or 10 days over the estimated date of delivery. Myrrh; Clary Sage; Zendocrine®; Basil; Whisper®	Pregnancy, Labor & Nursing pg. 401
Premenstrual Syndrome	A group of symptoms including irritability, bloating, and fatigue that occur in women, typically between ovulation and a period. ClaryCalm®; Geranium; DDR Prime®; Clary Sage; Whisper®	Women's Health pg. 436; Mood & Behavior pg. 377
Preterm Labor	Labor before the thirty-seventh week of pregnancy. Marjoram; Ylang Ylang + Wild Orange; Lavender | Neroli; Balance® | Steady™; Serenity® | Calmer™	Pregnancy, Labor & Nursing pg. 401
Pre-Workout Muscle Prep	To help insure a good workout and decrease chance of injury, preparation or stretching should be implemented before a workout. Deep Blue® | Rescuer™; Peppermint; Marjoram; Wild Orange; Slim & Sassy®	Athletes pg. 288
Prostatitis	Enlargement or inflammation of the prostate gland which is relatively typical in adult males. Rosemary; Balance®; Juniper Berry; DDR Prime®; Cypress	Men's Health pg. 374; Cardiovascular pg. 308

Discover other ways essential oil enthusiasts are getting results in the app.

Aromatic: Inhale from cupped hands or diffuse into the air.

Topical: Apply directly to affected area(s) or bottom of feet.

Internal: Take in a capsule, glass of water, or on/under tongue.

TIP Adults: Use 2-3 drops; Children: Use 1-2 drops.

AILMENT	RECOMMENDED OILS & USE	FOCUS AREA
Psoriasis	A continual, non-contagious skin disease defined by inflamed lesions covered with silvery-white scabs of dead skin. Zendocrine® [Internal]; Roman Chamomile [Topical, Internal]; Turmeric [Topical, Internal]; Copaiba [Internal, Topical]; Geranium [Topical, Internal]	Integumentary pg. 360; Digestive & Intestinal pg. 331; Candida pg. 304; Parasites pg. 398
Purging Disorder	An eating disorder characterized by recurrent self-induced vomiting, misuse of laxatives, diuretics, or enemas to control weight or shape in the absence of binge eating episodes. Melissa [Internal, Topical]; Cinnamon Bark [Internal, Topical, Aromatic]; Balance® [Aromatic, Topical]; Patchouli [Aromatic, Internal, Topical]; Slim & Sassy® [Internal, Topical]	Eating Disorders pg. 336
Pyorrhea	A serious gum infection that damages gums and can destroy the jawbone. Clove [Topical]; Myrrh [Topical, Internal]; Cedarwood [Topical]; Frankincense [Topical, Internal]; On Guard® [Topical, Aromatic]	Oral Health pg. 389
Q Fever	A sickness caused by a type of Coxiella burnetii bacteria and resulting in a rash and fever. Oregano [Internal, Topical]; On Guard® [Topical, Internal]; Thyme [Internal, Topical]; Eucalyptus [Topical]; Arborvitae [Topical]	Immune & Lymphatic pg. 355
Radiation Damage	Radiation can damage the DNA inside a cell's nucleus, and if the DNA becomes sufficiently damaged, the cell can become cancerous. Peppermint [Internal, Topical]; Zendocrine® [Internal, Topical]; Patchouli | Tulsi [Topical]; Cilantro [Internal, Topical]; Geranium [Internal, Topical]	Cellular Health pg. 313; Detoxification pg. 326
Rashes	A spotted, pink, or red skin outbreak that may be followed by itching. Cedarwood [Topical]; Zendocrine® [Internal]; Neroli [Topical]; Lavender [Topical]; Immortelle [Topical]	Integumentary pg. 360; Allergies pg. 284; Autoimmune pg. 292; Parasites pg. 398
Raynaud's Disease	A disorder in which the toes or fingers suddenly experience reduced blood circulation. Black Pepper [Internal, Topical]; Cypress [Topical]; AromaTouch® [Topical]; Lemongrass [Internal, Topical]; Console® [Topical]	Cardiovascular pg. 308; Endocrine pg. 340
Reactive Attachment Disorder (RAD)	A rare but severe condition in which an infant or young child does not establish healthy attachments with parents or caregivers, resulting in markedly disturbed and developmentally inappropriate ways of relating socially. Frankincense [Topical, Aromatic]; Balance® | Steady™ [Topical, Aromatic]; Forgive® [Topical, Aromatic]; Console® [Topical, Aromatic]; Peace® | Calmer™ [Topical, Aromatic]	Limbic pg. 371; Mood & Behavior pg. 377; Stress pg. 423
Reiter's Arthritis	Joint pain and swelling triggered by an infection in another part of the body. Basil [Topical, Internal]; Thyme [Topical, Internal]; Deep Blue® [Topical]; AromaTouch® [Topical]; Forgive® [Topical]	Immune & Lymphatic pg. 355; Digestive & Intestinal pg. 331; Skeletal pg. 415
Renal Artery Stenosis	The narrowing of one of the renal arteries that can impede blood flow to the target kidney, resulting in a secondary type of high blood pressure. Zendocrine® [Internal, Topical]; Ylang Ylang [Internal, Topical]; Lemon [Internal, Topical]; Citrus Bliss® [Topical]; Lemongrass [Internal, Topical]	Cardiovascular pg. 308; Urinary pg. 428
Respiratory Issues	Respiratory problems can be as minor as the common cold or as serious as pneumonia. They may affect the upper respiratory system (nose, mouth, sinuses, and throat) or the lower bronchial tubes and lungs. Breathe® [Aromatic, Topical]; Air-X™ | Cardamom [Topical, Internal, Aromatic]; Ravintsara | Rosemary [Aromatic, Topical, Internal]; Arborvitae [Aromatic, Topical]; Eucalyptus | Laurel Leaf [Topical, Aromatic]	Respiratory pg. 409
Restless Leg Syndrome	A condition characterized by a nearly irresistible urge to move the legs, typically in the evenings. AromaTouch® [Topical]; Deep Blue® [Topical]; PastTense® [Topical]; Cypress [Topical]; Serenity® [Topical]	Cardiovascular pg. 308; Sleep pg. 419
Restlessness	A failure to achieve relaxation; perpetually agitated or in motion; unquiet or uneasy. Balance® | Steady™ [Topical, Aromatic]; Lavender [Topical, Aromatic]; Peace® [Topical, Aromatic]; Patchouli [Topical, Aromatic]; Adaptiv™ | Serenity® [Topical, Aromatic]	Sleep pg. 419; Energy & Vitality pg. 344; Mood & Behavior pg. 377

*Avoid eyes, ear canals, and nasal passages.

STEPS:

1. Look up ailment.
2. Choose one or more of the recommended oils. Use oil(s) as indicated. Order of recommendation of oils and use is left to right.
3. Learn more in corresponding focus area.

AILMENT	RECOMMENDED OILS & USE	FOCUS AREA
Retinitis Pigmentosa	An eye disease in which the back wall of the eye (retina) is damaged.* Patchouli · Helichrysum · Juniper Berry · DDR Prime® · Cardamom	Nervous System pg. 385
Rheumatic Fever	A sickness which emerges as a complication of untreated or inadequately treated strep throat. Oregano · Ginger · Wintergreen · Eucalyptus · Thyme	Immune & Lymphatic pg. 355; Pain & Inflammation pg. 392
Rheumatism	Any disease marked by inflammation and pain in the joints, muscles, or fibrous tissue (especially rheumatoid arthritis). Turmeric · Deep Blue® · Celery Seed · Lemongrass · Siberian Fir	Muscular pg. 381; Skeletal pg. 415
Rheumatoid Arthritis	A chronic disease of the musculoskeletal system defined by swelling and inflammation of the joints (hands, wrists, knees, and feet). Deep Blue® · Frankincense · AromaTouch® · Siberian Fir · Marjoram	Skeletal pg. 415; Pain & Inflammation pg. 392; Autoimmune pg. 292
Rhinitis	An infection of the mucous lining of the nose.* Breathe® · On Guard® · Peppermint · Eucalyptus · Oregano	Respiratory pg. 409
Ringworm	A highly contagious fungal infection of the skin or scalp. Petitgrain · Thyme · Tea Tree · Citronella · Coriander	Integumentary pg. 360; Immune & Lymphatic pg. 355
Rosacea	A condition that causes redness and often small, red, pus-filled bumps on the face. Roman Chamomile · Sandalwood · Helichrysum · Myrrh · DDR Prime®	Integumentary pg. 360; Nervous System pg. 385; Parasites pg. 398
Roseola	A common viral infection in young children that may cause high fever and a rash. Melissa · Tea Tree | Stronger™ · On Guard® · Copaiba · Myrrh	Children pg. 317; Immune & Lymphatic pg. 355
RSV (Respiratory Syncytial Virus)	A virus that causes infections of the lungs and respiratory tract. The virus is so common that most children have been infected by age two. Breathe® · Eucalyptus · Laurel Leaf | Rosemary · Air-X™ | Melissa · Siberian Fir	Children pg. 317; Respiratory pg. 409
Rubella	An extremely contagious viral disease, spread through contact with discharges from the throat and nose of an infected person. On Guard® · Tea Tree · Lime · Thyme · Clove	Immune & Lymphatic pg. 355
Rumination Disorder	An eating disorder in which a person (usually an infant or young child) brings back up and re-chews partially digested food that has already been swallowed. DigestZen® · Zendocrine® · Grapefruit · Balance® | Steady™ · Peppermint	Eating Disorders pg. 336
Scabies	A somewhat contagious infection caused by a tiny burrowing mite. Abōde™ | Purify · Peppermint · Thyme · Arborvitae | Stronger™ · On Guard®	Parasites pg. 398; Integumentary pg. 360
Scarlet Fever	An acute contagious bacterial illness that develops in some individuals who have strep throat. Produces a bright red rash that covers most of the body. Oregano · On Guard® · Tea Tree | Stronger™ · Sandalwood · Thyme	Children pg. 317; Immune & Lymphatic pg. 355

(Aromatic icon) Aromatic: Inhale from cupped hands or diffuse into the air.
(Topical icon) Topical: Apply directly to affected area(s) or bottom of feet.
(Internal icon) Internal: Take in a capsule, glass of water, or on/under tongue.
TIP Adults: Use 2-3 drops; Children: Use 1-2 drops.

AILMENT	RECOMMENDED OILS & USE	FOCUS AREA
Scarring	The fibrous tissue that replaces normal tissue ruined by disease or injury. Frankincense (Topical); Helichrysum (Topical); Lavender (Topical); Sandalwood + Neroli (Topical); Immortelle (Topical)	Integumentary pg. 360
Schizophrenia	A long-term mental disorder characterized by extremely impaired emotions, thinking, hallucinations, and behaviors. Frankincense (Topical, Internal, Aromatic); Roman Chamomile (Topical, Internal, Aromatic); Juniper Berry (Topical, Internal, Aromatic); Spikenard (Topical, Internal, Aromatic); Patchouli (Topical, Aromatic)	Brain pg. 300; Limbic pg. 371; Mood & Behavior pg. 377
Schmidt's Syndrome	A combination of Addison's disease with autoimmune hypothyroidism and/or type 1 diabetes. Zendocrine® (Internal, Topical); Spikenard (Topical); Motivate® (Aromatic, Topical); Cardamom (Internal); On Guard® (Internal, Topical, Aromatic)	Autoimmune pg. 292; Endocrine pg. 340; Nervous System pg. 385
Sciatica	An inflammation of the sciatic nerve, commonly defined by pain and tenderness along the course of the nerve through the leg and thigh. Deep Blue® (Topical); Douglas Fir (Topical); Frankincense (Topical); Siberian Fir (Topical); Basil (Topical)	Nervous System pg. 385; Pain & Inflammation pg. 392; Athletes pg. 288
Scleroderma	A gradual hardening and contraction of the skin and connective tissue, either locally or throughout the body. Sandalwood (Topical, Internal); Helichrysum (Topical, Internal); Douglas Fir (Topical, Aromatic); Ginger (Topical, Internal); Coriander (Topical, Internal)	Autoimmune pg. 292; Integumentary pg. 360; Skeletal pg. 415; Muscular pg. 381
Scoliosis	An abnormal side-to-side curve of the spine. Deep Blue® (Topical); Lemongrass (Topical); Helichrysum (Topical); AromaTouch® (Topical); Wintergreen (Topical)	Skeletal pg. 415
Scurvy	Disease caused by a deficiency of vitamin C. Cypress (Topical); Zendocrine® (Internal, Topical); Lemon (Internal, Topical); Helichrysum (Internal, Topical); Ginger (Internal, Topical)	Immune & Lymphatic pg. 355; Energy & Vitality pg. 344
Seasonal Affective Disorder (SAD)	A type of depression that tends to occur as the days grow shorter in the fall and winter. Bergamot | Melissa (Topical, Aromatic, Internal); Elevation | Neroli (Topical, Aromatic); Cheer® (Topical, Aromatic); Passion® (Topical, Aromatic); Motivate® | Brave™ (Topical, Aromatic)	Mood & Behavior pg. 377; Limbic pg. 371
Sebaceous Cyst	Noncancerous small bumps beneath the skin that can appear anywhere on the skin, but are most common on the face, neck and trunk. Fennel (Internal); Cedarwood (Topical, Internal); Basil (Topical, Internal); Black Pepper (Topical, Internal); Coriander (Topical, Internal)	Integumentary pg. 360
Seizures	A convulsion or attack, commonly from a stroke or epileptic fit. Spikenard (Topical, Internal, Aromatic); Frankincense (Topical, Internal, Aromatic); Petitgrain (Internal, Topical, Aromatic); Cedarwood (Aromatic, Topical); Sandalwood (Aromatic, Topical, Internal)	Brain pg. 300; Children pg. 317
Sepsis	A bacterial infection in the body tissues or bloodstream. This is a very broad term covering the presence of many types of microscopic disease-causing organisms. Oregano (Topical, Internal); Marjoram (Topical, Internal); Thyme (Topical, Internal); Copaiba (Topical, Internal); On Guard® (Topical, Internal, Aromatic)	Immune & Lymphatic pg. 355
Sex Drive (Excessive)/ Hypersexuality	An obsession with sexual thoughts, urges, or behaviors that may cause distress and negatively affect one's health, job, relationships, or other parts of life. Marjoram (Topical, Internal, Aromatic); Arborvitae (Aromatic, Topical); Zendocrine® (Internal); Neroli (Aromatic, Topical); Console® (Aromatic, Topical)	Intimacy pg. 366
Sex Drive (Low)	The inhibition of the sex drive or natural desire for sexual activity. Passion® (Topical); Jasmine (Topical); Cinnamon Bark (Topical); Ylang Ylang (Topical); Whisper® (Topical)	Intimacy pg. 366; Men's Health pg. 374; Women's Health pg. 436

QUICK REFERENCE

*Avoid eyes, ear canals, and nasal passages.

STEPS:

1. Look up ailment.
2. Choose one or more of the recommended oils. Use oil(s) as indicated. Order of recommendation of oils and use is left to right.
3. Learn more in corresponding focus area.

AILMENT	RECOMMENDED OILS & USE	FOCUS AREA
Shigella Infection	An intestinal disease caused by a family of bacteria known as shigella. The main sign of shigella infection is bloody diarrhea. Eucalyptus · Clove · Black Pepper · Thyme · On Guard®	Immune & Lymphatic pg. 355; Digestive & Intestinal pg. 331
Shingles	A viral infection that causes a painful rash, most often as a stripe of blisters that wraps around the torso. Patchouli · Melissa · Yarrow | Pom · Tea Tree · Black Pepper	Immune & Lymphatic pg. 355; Nervous System pg. 385
Shin Splints	Acute pain in the shin and lower leg caused by moderate to heavy physical activity. Commonly occurs in athletes who have recently intensified or changed their training routines. AromaTouch® · Deep Blue® · Lemongrass · Wintergreen · Basil	Skeletal pg. 415; Athletes pg. 288
Shock	Critical condition brought on by a sudden drop in blood flow through the body often accompanying severe injury or illness. Peppermint · Peace® | Adaptiv™ · Lavender · Roman Chamomile · Balance® | Steady™	First Aid pg. 347; Nervous System pg. 385; Stress pg. 423
Sickle Cell Anemia	Disorder of the blood characterized by distorted red blood cells which are fragile and prone to rupture. The decrease in number of red blood cells results in anemia. Zendocrine® · Frankincense · Lemongrass · Geranium · Cassia	Cardiovascular pg. 308; Detoxification pg. 326
Silent Thyroiditis	Inflammation of the thyroid gland, commonly occurring in the middle-aged women. Zendocrine® · Basil · DDR Prime® · AromaTouch® · Console®	Autoimmune pg. 292; Endocrine pg. 340
Sinus Congestion	Blockage of the nasal passage, also known as a stuffy nose.* Breathe® · Eucalyptus | Stronger™ · Rosemary · On Guard® · Helichrysum	Respiratory pg. 409; Digestive & Intestinal pg. 331
Sinusitis	Inflammation of the nasal sinus.* Peppermint · Breathe® · Cedarwood · Passion® · Thyme	Respiratory pg. 409
Sjogren's Syndrome	A chronic, autoimmune disease characterized by dryness of the mouth and eyes.* Cinnamon Bark · Black Pepper · Zendocrine® · Roman Chamomile · DDR Prime®	Autoimmune pg. 292
Skin (Dry)	Chapped or flaky skin caused from dehydration, lack of omega 3s, or sun or wind damage. Sandalwood · Cedarwood · Copaiba · Immortelle · Myrrh	Integumentary pg. 360
Skin (Oily)	Excessively oily skin caused by excessive discharge of sebum from the sebaceous glands. HD Clear® · Petitgrain · Lemon · Wild Orange · Ylang Ylang	Integumentary pg. 360
Skin Issues	A variety of issues that occur on the skin, causing irritation, outbreaks, or a breach in the surface. Lavender · Immortelle · Geranium | Tulsi · Sandalwood · Frankincense	Integumentary pg. 360
Skin Ulcers	A lesion of a mucous membrane or the skin. Frankincense · Helichrysum · Lavender · Geranium · Myrrh	Integumentary pg. 360
Sleep Apnea	Disorder characterized by one or more pauses in breathing or shallow breaths while asleep. Breathe® · Thyme · Rosemary | Tulsi · Peppermint · Lemongrass	Sleep pg. 419; Respiratory pg. 409

Discover other ways essential oil enthusiasts are getting results in the app.

Aromatic: Inhale from cupped hands or diffuse into the air.
Topical: Apply directly to affected area(s) or bottom of feet.
Internal: Take in a capsule, glass of water, or on/under tongue.
TIP Adults: Use 2-3 drops; Children: Use 1-2 drops.

AILMENT	RECOMMENDED OILS & USE	FOCUS AREA
Sleepwalking	Purposeful moving or walking while in a deep stage of sleep. Vetiver (Topical, Aromatic); Serenity® | Calmer™ (Topical, Aromatic); Lavender (Topical, Aromatic); Peace® | Brave™ (Topical, Aromatic); Balance® | Steady™ (Topical, Aromatic)	Sleep pg. 419
Smell (Loss of)	Inability to perceive odor.* Basil (Topical, Aromatic); Sandalwood (Topical); Peppermint (Aromatic, Topical); Lavender | Adaptiv™ (Topical, Aromatic); Arborvitae | Helichrysum (Topical, Aromatic)	Immune & Lymphatic pg. 355; Respiratory pg. 409
Smoking Addiction	A physical addiction or strong craving for nicotine, a chemical found in tobacco products. Black Pepper (Internal, Topical); Clove (Topical, Internal, Aromatic); On Guard® (Topical, Aromatic, Internal); Cilantro (Internal); Zendocrine® (Topical, Internal)	Addictions pg. 280; Mood & Behavior pg. 377
Snake Bites	A bite from a snake which may be nonpoisonous or poisonous. Basil (Topical); Purify | Abōde™ (Topical); On Guard® | Stronger™ (Topical); Myrrh (Topical); Zendocrine® (Topical)	First Aid pg. 347
Snoring	A sound achieved during sleep by vibration of loose tissue in the upper airway. To breathe during sleep with harsh, snorting noises caused by pulsing of the soft palate. Breathe® (Topical, Aromatic); Peppermint (Topical, Aromatic); Rosemary (Topical, Aromatic); Eucalyptus (Topical, Aromatic); Douglas Fir (Topical, Aromatic)	Respiratory pg. 409; Sleep pg. 419
Social Anxiety Disorder	Excessive and unreasonable fear of social situations, arising from a fear of being closely watched, judged, and criticized by others. Peace® | Adaptiv™ (Topical, Aromatic); Serenity® | Calmer™ (Topical, Aromatic); Bergamot | Patchouli (Topical, Aromatic); Douglas Fir | Cedarwood (Topical, Aromatic); Console® (Topical, Aromatic)	Brain pg. 300; Mood & Behavior pg. 377
Sore Feet	Pain or discomfort in the foot. AromaTouch® (Topical); Deep Blue® | Rescuer™ (Topical); Ginger (Topical); Copaiba (Topical); Wintergreen (Topical)	Athletes pg. 288; Muscular pg. 381; Skeletal pg. 415
Sore Muscles	Pain and stiffness felt in muscles several hours to days after unaccustomed or strenuous exercise. AromaTouch® (Topical); Deep Blue® | Rescuer™ (Topical); Peppermint (Topical); PastTense® (Topical); Marjoram (Topical)	Muscular pg. 381; Pain & Inflammation pg. 392; Athletes pg. 288
Sore Throat	Any of various inflammations of the pharynx, tonsils, or larynx defined by pain in swallowing. On Guard® (Internal, Topical); Tea Tree | Stronger™ (Topical); Myrrh (Internal); Lime (Internal, Topical); Thyme (Internal)	Oral Health pg. 389; Immune & Lymphatic pg. 355; Respiratory pg. 409
Spina Bifida	Birth defect of the spine in which part of the spinal cord is exposed through a gap in the backbone. Siberian Fir (Topical); Clove (Topical); DDR Prime® (Topical, Internal); Wintergreen (Topical); Deep Blue® (Topical)	Skeletal pg. 415; Nervous System pg. 385
Sprains	An injury to a ligament when the joint is carried through a range of motion larger than its normal range without dislocation or fracture. Deep Blue® (Topical); Lemongrass (Topical); Marjoram (Topical); Copaiba | Rescuer™ (Topical); Wintergreen (Topical)	Muscular pg. 381; Pain & Inflammation pg. 392; First Aid pg. 347
Staph Infection	Infections caused by staphylococcus bacteria. On Guard® (Topical, Internal); Purify | Abōde™ (Topical); Geranium (Topical, Internal); Oregano (Topical, Internal); Myrrh (Topical, Internal)	Immune & Lymphatic pg. 355
Stevens-Johnson Syndrome	Disorder of the skin and mucous membranes in which cell death causes the epidermis to separate from the dermis. Zendocrine® (Topical, Internal); Tea Tree (Topical); Frankincense (Topical, Internal); Myrrh (Topical); Arborvitae (Topical)	Integumentary pg. 360

*Avoid eyes, ear canals, and nasal passages.

STEPS:

1. Look up ailment.
2. Choose one or more of the recommended oils. Use oil(s) as indicated. Order of recommendation of oils and use is left to right.
3. Learn more in corresponding focus area.

AILMENT	RECOMMENDED OILS & USE	FOCUS AREA
Stomach Ache	Pain in the abdomen or stomach area. DigestZen® | Tamer™, Peppermint, Ginger, Wild Orange, Black Pepper	Digestive & Intestinal pg. 331
Strep Throat	A sore throat with fever caused by streptococcal infection. Oregano, On Guard®, Tea Tree | Stronger™, Lemon, Cinnamon Bark	Immune & Lymphatic pg. 355
Stress	An organism's total response to environmental pressures or demands. Adaptiv™ or Peace®, Balance® | Steady™, Lavender, Serenity® | Calmer™, Neroli	Stress pg. 423
Stress Fractures	A fracture of bone caused by replicated application of a heavy load, such as the constant pounding on a surface by runners, dancers, and gymnasts. Birch, Helichrysum, Siberian Fir, Wintergreen, Deep Blue®	Skeletal pg. 415
Stretch Marks	Streaks or stripes on the skin, especially the abdomen, caused by prolonged stretching of the skin. Immortelle, Geranium, Sandalwood, Lavender, Frankincense	Integumentary pg. 360; Pregnancy, Labor & Nursing pg. 401; Weight pg. 431
Stroke	The sudden death of brain cells in a localized area due to insufficient blood flow. Cassia, Helichrysum, Cypress, Basil, Fennel	Brain pg. 300
Stye	Infection of the sebaceous gland of an eyelash.* Tea Tree, DDR Prime®, Patchouli, Frankincense, Myrrh	Respiratory pg. 409
Sunburn	Overexposure to the sun that causes redness and inflammation. Lavender, Peppermint, Immortelle, Frankincense, Helichrysum	Integumentary pg. 360; First Aid pg. 347; Outdoors pg. 506
Swimmer's Ear	Infection of the outer ear canal that runs from the eardrum to the outside of the head. Often caused by water remaining in the ear after swimming.* Rosemary, Clove, On Guard®, Lavender, Oregano	Respiratory pg. 409;
Swimmer's Itch	Rash usually caused by an allergic reaction to parasites that burrow into the skin while swimming or wading in warm water. Purify | Abōde™, Lemongrass, Zendocrine®, Frankincense, Roman Chamomile	Parasites pg. 398; Integumentary pg. 360
Tachycardia	A fast heart rate which is above 100 beats per minute in an adult. Balance® | Steady™, Ylang Ylang, Lavender | Calmer™, Rosemary, Melissa	Cardiovascular pg. 308
Taste, Loss	Loss of taste functions of the tongue. Also refers to alterations in taste (such as metallic taste, etc.). Peppermint, Lime, Zendocrine®, Melissa, Helichrysum	Respiratory pg. 409; Nervous System pg. 385
Tear Duct (Blocked)	A blocked nasolacrimal duct which typically moves tears from the eyes to the nose.* Myrrh, Lavender, Clary Sage, Eucalyptus, Tea Tree	Respiratory pg. 409

Discover other ways essential oil enthusiasts are getting results in the app.

Aromatic: Inhale from cupped hands or diffuse into the air.
Topical: Apply directly to affected area(s) or bottom of feet.
Internal: Take in a capsule, glass of water, or on/under tongue.
TIP Adults: Use 2-3 drops; Children: Use 1-2 drops.

AILMENT	RECOMMENDED OILS & USE	FOCUS AREA
Teeth, Discolored	Occurs when the outer layer of the tooth is stained by smoking, coffee, wine, cola or other drinks or foods. Wintergreen · Lemon · Peppermint · Lime · Zendocrine®	Oral Health pg. 389; Personal Care pg. 508
Teeth Grinding	The habit of grinding and clenching one's teeth at night during sleep. Roman Chamomile · Lavender · Marjoram · Serenity® · Geranium	Oral Health pg. 389
Teething Pain	Pain experienced when an infant's first teeth emerge through the gums. Clove · Roman Chamomile | Calmer™ · Myrrh · On Guard® | Stronger™ · Helichrysum	Oral Health pg. 389; Children pg. 317
Tendonitis	The inflammation of a tendon, a hard rope-like tissue that connects muscle to bone. Deep Blue® · AromaTouch® · Copaiba + Marjoram · Lemongrass · Siberian Fir	Muscular pg. 381; Athletes pg. 288
Tennis Elbow	Inflammation of the tendons of the elbow caused by overuse of the muscles of the forearm. AromaTouch® · Deep Blue® · Basil · Ginger · Lemongrass	Skeletal pg. 415; Muscular pg. 381
Tension (Muscle)	Condition in which muscles of the body remain semi-contracted for an extended period. PastTense® · AromaTouch® | Rescuer™ · Peppermint · Marjoram · Ginger	Muscular pg. 381;
Testosterone (Low)	Abnormally low levels of testosterone, a hormone required for male development and sexual function. Sandalwood · Rosemary · Passion® · Rose | Ylang Ylang · Black Spruce	Men's Health pg. 374
Thrush	A contagious disease caused by a Candida albicans, fungus that appears most often in children and infants, defined by small whitish outbreaks on the mouth, throat, and tongue. Spikenard · Arborvitae · Clary Sage · Tea Tree · Myrrh	Candida pg. 304; Children pg. 317; Pregnancy, Labor & Nursing pg. 401; Women's Health pg. 436
Tick Bites	Bites from any of numerous small bloodsucking parasitic arachnids of the group Ixodidae and Argasidae, many of which spread febrile diseases. Purify · HD Clear® · Abōde™ | Tea Tree · Lemon Eucalyptus | Eucalyptus · Peppermint	Parasites pg. 398; First Aid pg. 347
Tinnitis	Hearing buzzing, ringing, or other sounds without an external cause.* Helichrysum · Basil · Cypress · Zendocrine® · Juniper Berry	Respiratory pg. 409
TMJ (TempoRo-mandibular Joint Dysfunction)	Pain in the jaw joint and in the muscles that control jaw movement. AromaTouch® · Marjoram · PastTense® · Siberian Fir · Deep Blue®	Muscular pg. 381; Oral Health pg. 389
Toe Fungus	A nail fungus causing thickened, brittle, crumbly, or ragged nails. Tea Tree · Cinnamon Bark · Copaiba · HD Clear® | Abōde™ Arborvitae | Citronella	Athletes pg. 288; Candida pg. 304; Integumentary pg. 360
Tonsillitis	A swelling and infection of the tonsils, which are oval-shaped masses of lymph gland tissue located on both sides of the back of the throat. On Guard® · Myrrh · Lemon · Tea Tree | Stronger™ · Eucalyptus	Immune & Lymphatic pg. 355; Oral Health pg. 389
Toothache	A soreness or pain around or within a tooth, indicating inflammation and possible infection. Clove · Birch · Helichrysum · On Guard® | Stronger™ · Tea Tree	Oral Health pg. 389

*Avoid eyes, ear canals, and nasal passages.

QUICK REFERENCE

STEPS:

1. Look up ailment.
2. Choose one or more of the recommended oils. Use oil(s) as indicated. Order of recommendation of oils and use is left to right.
3. Learn more in corresponding focus area.

AILMENT	RECOMMENDED OILS & USE	FOCUS AREA
Tourette Syndrome	Disorder of the nervous system characterized by involuntary tics and/or vocalizations. Spikenard, DDR Prime®, Patchouli, Frankincense, Vetiver	Nervous System pg. 385; Brain pg. 300; Mood & Behavior pg. 377
Toxemia	Blood poisoning by toxins from a local bacterial infection. Frequently used to refer to preeclampsia, a condition in pregnancy characterized by high blood pressure. Zendocrine®, Slim & Sassy®, Patchouli, Cypress, Frankincense	Pregnancy, Labor & Nursing pg. 401
Toxicity	The degree to which a substance can damage an organism. Zendocrine®, Air-X™, Green Mandarin, DDR Prime®, Celery Seed	Detoxification pg. 326; On the Go pg. 504; Personal Care pg. 508
Transverse Myelitis	Inflammation across both sides of one level, or segment, of the spinal cord. Patchouli, Clove, Spikenard, Wintergreen, Roman Chamomile	Nervous System pg. 385
Trigeminal Neuralgia	A disorder of the trigeminal nerve that causes episodes of stabbing, sharp pain in the lips, cheek, gums, or chin on one side of the face. Wintergreen, Juniper Berry, Helichrysum, Spikenard, Roman Chamomile	Nervous System pg. 385
Tuberculosis	Infectious bacterial disease characterized by the growth of nodules in the tissues, especially the lungs. Thyme, Black Pepper, Rosemary, Eucalyptus, Breathe®	Respiratory pg. 409; Immune & Lymphatic pg. 355
Tularemia	Rare infectious disease that typically attacks the skin, eyes, lymph nodes and lungs, characterized by ulcers, fever, and loss of weight. Oregano, Tea Tree, Zendocrine®, Rosemary, Thyme	Immune & Lymphatic pg. 355
Tumor	An uncommon growth of tissue resulting from uncontrolled, continuous multiplication of cells. DDR Prime®, Frankincense, Thyme, Copaiba, Sandalwood	Cellular Health pg. 313
Turner Syndrome	Chromosomal disorder affecting only females characterized by the absence of part or all of a second sex chromosome in some or all cells. Thyme, Clary Sage, Myrrh, Ylang Ylang, Frankincense	Endocrine pg. 340
Typhoid	An infectious bacterial fever with an eruption of red spots on the chest and abdomen and severe intestinal irritation. Clove, Oregano, Eucalyptus, Cinnamon Bark, Peppermint	Immune & Lymphatic pg. 355
Ulcers (Duodenal)	An ulcer that occurs in the duodenum, the beginning of the small intestine. Frankincense, Myrrh, Wintergreen, DigestZen®, Fennel	Digestive & Intestinal pg. 331
Ulcers (Gastric)	An ulcer of the inner wall of the stomach. DigestZen®, Peppermint, Bergamot, Yarrow | Pom, Geranium	Digestive & Intestinal pg. 331
Ulcers (Leg)	An ulcer in the leg. Geranium, Frankincense, AromaTouch®, Yarrow | Pom, Helichrysum	Integumentary pg. 360; Cardiovascular pg. 308

Aromatic: Inhale from cupped hands or diffuse into the air.
Topical: Apply directly to affected area(s) or bottom of feet.
Internal: Take in a capsule, glass of water, or on/under tongue.
TIP Adults: Use 2-3 drops; Children: Use 1-2 drops.

AILMENT	RECOMMENDED OILS & USE	FOCUS AREA
Ulcers (Peptic)	Ulcers in the upper duodenum and stomach (first portion of the small intestine) caused by a bacterium and stomach acid called Helicobacter pylori. Cinnamon Bark (Internal); Fennel (Internal, Topical); Peppermint (Internal, Topical); DigestZen® (Internal, Topical); Juniper Berry (Internal, Topical)	Digestive & Intestinal pg. 331
Ulcers (Varicose)	Loss of skin surface in the drainage area of a varicose vein, typically in the leg, emerging from stasis and infection. PastTense® (Topical); Helichrysum (Topical, Internal); Cypress (Topical); Geranium (Topical); Coriander (Topical, Internal)	Cardiovascular pg. 308; Integumentary pg. 360
Ureter Infection	Infection in the tube that transfers urine from the kidney to the bladder. Coriander (Internal, Topical); On Guard® (Internal, Topical); Lemongrass (Internal, Topical); DDR Prime® (Internal, Topical); Cinnamon Bark (Internal, Topical)	Urinary pg. 428; Immune & Lymphatic pg. 355
Urinary Tract Infection (UTI)	An infection in any part of the urinary system; ureters, kidneys, bladder, and urethra. Lemon (Topical, Internal); Geranium (Topical, Internal); Lemongrass (Internal, Topical); Juniper Berry (Topical, Internal); Cypress (Topical)	Urinary pg. 428; Immune & Lymphatic pg. 355
Urination (Painful/Frequent)	Discomfort or burning with urination, usually felt in the urethra or perineum. Cinnamon Bark (Internal, Topical); Tea Tree (Topical); Lemongrass (Internal, Topical); Zendocrine® (Internal, Topical); On Guard® (Topical, Internal)	Urinary pg. 428
Urine Flow (Poor)	Abnormally slight or infrequent urination. Zendocrine® (Internal, Topical); Slim & Sassy® (Internal); Juniper Berry (Topical, Internal); Cypress (Topical); AromaTouch® (Topical)	Urinary pg. 428
Uterine Bleeding	Any loss of blood from the uterus. ClaryCalm® (Topical); Helichrysum (Internal, Topical); Geranium (Internal, Topical); Frankincense (Internal, Topical); Lavender (Internal, Topical)	Pregnancy, Labor & Nursing pg. 401; Women's Health pg. 436
Uvetitis	An infection of the uveal tract, which lines the inside of the eye behind the cornea.* Myrrh (Topical, Internal); Juniper Berry (Topical, Internal); Frankincense (Topical, Internal); Immortelle (Topical); Sandalwood (Topical, Internal)	Nervous System pg. 385
Vaginal Yeast Infection	Fungal infection that causes irritation, discharge and intense itchiness of the vagina and the vulva. Tea Tree (Topical); Spikenard (Topical, Internal); Thyme (Internal, Topical); Frankincense | Myrrh (Internal, Topical); DDR Prime® (Internal, Topical)	Candida pg. 304; Women's Health pg. 436
Vaginitis	Vaginal inflammation. Tea Tree (Topical); Patchouli (Internal, Topical); Spikenard (Topical, Internal); Yarrow | Pom (Internal, Topical); Rosemary (Topical, Internal)	Candida pg. 304; Women's Health pg. 436
Varicose Veins	Tortuous, dilated, elongated superficial veins that are commonly seen in the legs. Cypress (Topical); Helichrysum (Topical); Coriander (Internal, Topical); Yarrow | Pom (Internal, Topical); Bergamot (Internal, Topical)	Cardiovascular pg. 308; Integumentary pg. 360
Vertigo	A feeling of whirling or irregular motion, either of oneself or of external objects, generally caused by inner ear disease. Frankincense (Topical, Aromatic); Rosemary (Topical, Aromatic); Ylang Ylang (Topical, Aromatic); Ginger (Topical, Aromatic); Balance® | Steady™ (Topical, Aromatic)	Brain pg. 300; Cardiovascular pg. 308
Virus	A microorganism that cannot grow or reproduce apart from a living cell. A virus invades living cells and uses their chemical machinery to keep itself alive and to replicate itself. Melissa (Internal, Topical); Thyme (Internal, Topical); Black Pepper (Internal, Topical); Yarrow | Pom (Internal, Topical); Oregano (Internal, Topical)	Immune & Lymphatic pg. 355

*Avoid eyes, ear canals, and nasal passages.

STEPS:

1. Look up ailment.
2. Choose one or more of the recommended oils. Use oil(s) as indicated. Order of recommendation of oils and use is left to right.
3. Learn more in corresponding focus area.

AILMENT	RECOMMENDED OILS & USE	FOCUS AREA
Vision (Blurred)	The loss of sharpness of eyesight, making objects appear out of focus and hazy.* DDR Prime® · Lemongrass · Helichrysum · Frankincense · Immortelle	Nervous System pg. 385
Vision (Poor)	Decreased ability to see to a degree that causes problems not fixable by usual means, such as glasses. DDR Prime® · Immortelle · Cypress · Lemongrass · Juniper Berry	Nervous System pg. 385
Vitiligo	A condition in which the pigment is lost from areas of the skin, causing whitish patches. Zendocrine® · Whisper® · Vetiver · DDR Prime® · Sandalwood	Autoimmune pg. 292; Integumentary pg. 360
Vomiting	Forcible elimination of contents of stomach through the mouth. DigestZen® | Tamer™ · Peppermint · Fennel · Ginger · Pink Pepper	Digestive & Intestinal pg. 331; Immune & Lymphatic pg. 355; Eating Disorders pg. 336
Warts	Small, benign growths generated by a viral infection of the mucous or skin membrane. Melissa · Arborvitae · Oregano · Frankincense · Lemongrass	Integumentary pg. 360
Wasp Sting	Painful stings or bites from bees, yellow jackets, hornets, wasps, and ants. These stings are generally harmless; however, more serious allergic reactions may occur which can be deadly. Purify | Abōde™ · Roman Chamomile · Lavender · Basil | Peppermint · Cedarwood	First Aid pg. 347
Water Retention	Excessive buildup of fluid in the circulatory system, body tissues, or cavities in the body. Lemon · Cypress · Slim & Sassy® · Juniper Berry · Celery Seed	Urinary pg. 428; Cardiovascular pg. 308; Pregnancy, Labor & Nursing pg. 401
Weight Issues	Having more or less body fat than is optimally healthy. Slim & Sassy® · Grapefruit · Zendocrine® · Bergamot · DDR Prime®	Weight pg. 431
Whiplash	Neck injury due to forceful, rapid back-and-forth movement of the neck. PastTense® · Siberian Fir · Lemongrass · Deep Blue® | Rescuer™ · AromaTouch®	Muscular pg. 381
Withdrawal Symptoms	Unpleasant physical or mental symptoms that accompany the process of ceasing to take an addictive drug. Motivate® | Calmer™ · Frankincense · Spikenard · Zendocrine® · Cheer® | Brave™	Addictions pg. 280; Mood & Behavior pg. 377; Focus & Concentration pg. 351
Workout Recovery	The period of time following sustained exercise needed for the body to recuperate and for muscles to repair. AromaTouch® · Lemon · Deep Blue® | Rescuer™ · Peppermint · PastTense®	Athletes pg. 288; Muscular pg. 381
Worms	A family of parasites that mainly reside in the intestinal tract, but can also live in the brain or muscles. Clove · Oregano · Thyme · Lemongrass · Blue Tansy	Parasites pg. 398; Digestive & Intestinal pg. 331
Wounds	An injury to living tissue caused by a cut, blow, or other impact, typically one in which the skin is cut or broken. Tea Tree · Lavender · Yarrow | Pom · Helichrysum · Frankincense	Integumentary pg. 360; First Aid pg. 347

Aromatic: Inhale from cupped hands or diffuse into the air.
Topical: Apply directly to affected area(s) or bottom of feet.
Internal: Take in a capsule, glass of water, or on/under tongue.
TIP Adults: Use 2-3 drops; Children: Use 1-2 drops.

AILMENT	RECOMMENDED OILS & USE	FOCUS AREA
Wrinkles	A fold, ridge, or crease in the skin typically appearing as a result of aging processes. Immortelle [Topical]; Petitgrain [Topical]; Spikenard [Topical]; Geranium & Neroli [Topical]; Sandalwood [Topical]	Integumentary pg. 360
Xenoestrogens	A type of xenohormone that imitates estrogen and creates byproduct estrogen metabolites as it is utilized by the body. Lemon [Internal, Topical]; ClaryCalm® [Topical]; Zendocrine® [Internal, Topical]; Thyme [Internal, Topical]; Ginger [Internal, Topical]	Women's Health pg. 436; Detoxification pg. 326
Xerophthalmia	Abnormal dryness of the eyes.* Lavender [Internal, Topical]; Sandalwood [Topical, Internal]; Lemon [Internal]; Immortelle [Topical]; Zendocrine® [Internal, Topical]	Respiratory pg. 409
Yeast	Overgrowth of the Candida fungi, which live on the surfaces of the body, causing systemic infection. Tea Tree [Topical]; Thyme [Internal, Topical]; Oregano [Internal, Topical]; DDR Prime® [Internal, Topical]; Lemongrass [Internal, Topical]	Candida pg. 304; Women's Health pg. 436; Children pg. 317

*Avoid eyes, ear canals, and nasal passages.

SECTION 3

NATURAL SOLUTIONS

Becoming familiar with the qualities and benefits of essential oils is key to living THE ESSENTIAL LIFE. As you become versed in the powerful characteristics of each oil, blend, and supplement, you will develop confidence in turning to nature as your first resource for wellness. Nature's vast diversity provides answers for any health interest—physical, mental, emotional, and beyond.

SINGLES/BLENDS

SUPPLEMENTS

ESSENTIAL OILS

This section provides a detailed reference for the origins, qualities, purposes, and safety of essential oils. The top uses of each oil are presented in this succinct guide, and more detailed uses are highlighted in *Focus Areas*.

Please note the symbols (aromatic icon) =aromatic (topical icon) =topical (internal icon) =internal that specify recommended usage. While all oils are meant to be used aromatically and most topically, only verified pure therapeutic essential oils are intended for internal use (see *Why Quality Matters* and *How to Use Essential Oils* for further detail).

ABŌDE™

REFRESHING BLEND

refreshing
cleansing
purifying

MAIN INGREDIENTS
Distilled lime
Litsea
Cassia
Lemon eucalyptus
Tea tree
Arborvitae
Eucalyptus
Cilantro
Lavandin
Lemon myrtle

SUBSTITUTE WITH
Air-X™
Arborvitae
Cassia
Cilantro
Eucalyptus
Lemon eucalyptus
Lemon myrtle
Lime
Niaouli
Purify
Tea tree

SAFETY
Not safe for internal use. Dilution recommended. Possible skin irritation. Avoid exposure to sunlight or UV rays for up to 12 hours after application.

With the threat of toxic exposure at every turn, green cleaning for air and home has never been more important and sought after. Time and time again, essential oils have outperformed toxic synthetic counterparts in purifying any surface or space.

TOP USES

REFRESHING ENVIRONMENT
Diffuse (A) to energize, uplift, and refresh home, office, and/or personal space.

BODY, AIR & ODOR CLEANSING, AIRBORNE PATHOGENS
Diffuse (A). Apply (T) to underarm area or add to body wash.

URINARY ISSUES & PARASITES
Apply (T) to bottoms of feet, and/or over kidney area or lower abdomen.

VIRUSES & BACTERIA, RESPIRATORY CONGESTION & LYMPHATIC TOXICITY
Diffuse (A). Apply (T) to bottoms of feet, chest and back, and/or underarms.

SURFACE & BATHROOM CLEANING
Add (T) 6-8 drops and 1 T vinegar to glass spray bottle filled with water.

LAUNDRY BOOST & DRYER BALL
Add (T) with laundry soap to each wash load and/or drop onto laundry balls placed in with dryer load.

DISHWASHER BOOST
Add (T) a few drops onto dishwasher soap before starting cycle.

INSECT REPELLENT
Diffuse (A) and/or spray on surfaces and apply (T) to exposed skin and clothing.

EMOTIONAL BALANCE
Use (A) aromatically and (T) topically to go from Toxic → Cleansed.

(A) = Aromatically (T) = Topically (I) = Internally

ADAPTIV™

CALMING BLEND

uplifting • invigorating • refreshing

MAIN INGREDIENTS
Wild orange
Lavender
Copaiba
Spearmint
Magnolia
Rosemary
Neroli
Sweetgum

SUBSTITUTE WITH
Cedarwood
Copaiba
Magnolia
Neroli
Rosemary
Wild orange

SAFETY
Not safe for internal use.

TOP USES

CHAOTIC ENVIRONMENTS & SITUATIONS, LACK OF TRANQUILITY
Diffuse and apply to bottoms of feet.

LOSS OF COMPOSURE, POOR COPING CAPACITY & ANXIETY
Diffuse and apply up spine, on back of neck, and bottoms of feet.

MENSTRUATION & MENOPAUSE-RELATED MOODINESS & DEPRESSION
Apply to abdomen, reflex points for ovaries, and to bottoms of feet.

ADDICTIVE, OBSESSIVE/COMPULSIVE BEHAVIORS/OVERTHINKING
Diffuse and apply over liver area and to bottoms of feet.

LACK OF MOTIVATION & MENTAL FATIGUE
Diffuse and apply on back of neck.

LACK OF FOCUS & CONCENTRATION, INABILITY TO STAY ON TASK, RESTLESSNESS
Apply to back of neck, across forehead, and on bottoms of feet as needed.

UPSET BABY, COLIC
Diffuse and apply diluted in circular motion on abdomen and/or to bottoms of feet.

TIRED, ACHY, WEAK OR RUN DOWN
Apply to back of neck and bottoms of feet, forehead, or over adrenal area.

LOSS OF SENSE OF SMELL
Apply across forehead and under nostrils.

BRAIN ISSUES, ALZHEIMER'S, ELEVATED CORTISOL LEVELS
Apply to back of neck, bottoms of feet, across forehead, and/or over adrenal area.

PERSONAL SCENT
Wear to enhance mood and promote relaxation and euphoria.

Sweet gum, a lesser known essential oil with its sweet forest-like aroma, has a chemical composition reminiscent of a mixture of copaiba, frankincense, and Douglas fir.

= Aromatically = Topically = Internally

clearing
purifying
eliminating

AIR-X™

AIR BLEND

MAIN INGREDIENTS
Litsea
Tangerine
Grapefruit
Frankincense
Cardamom

SUBSTITUTE WITH
Abōde™
Breathe®
DDR Prime®
HD Clear®
Lemongrass
Litsea
Melissa

SAFETY
Avoid exposure to sunlight or UV rays for up to 12 hours after application.

TOP USES

ASTHMA, COUGH, BRONCHITIS, PNEUMONIA, SINUSITUS
Diffuse and apply diluted to forehead, chest, and back.

CONGESTION & DIGESTIVE DISCOMFORT
Take in a capsule or under tongue. Apply diluted to chest or abdomen.

INJURED RESPIRATORY TISSUE DUE TO OXIDATIVE STRESS
Diffuse or inhale and apply to bottoms of feet, chest, and back. Dilute if needed.

ODORS & AIRBORNE PATHOGENS
Diffuse in home or workspace during day or overnight as needed.

KIDNEY, GALLBLADDER & LIVER CLEANSING
Take in a capsule. Apply diluted to abdomen and/or back.

MENTAL CLARITY, FOCUS & CONCENTRATION
Apply diluted with peppermint under nose and on back of neck. Diffuse .

SOOTHING & CLEARING MASSAGE
Apply with a carrier oil with emphasis on back and chest to clear airways.

TOXIC OR FEARFUL THINKING
Diffuse or inhale . Apply diluted to forehead, back of neck, and behind ears.

This blend was originally formulated to support those residing in areas of the world where extreme air pollution is the norm.

ALIGN

YOGA CENTERING BLEND

encouraging
centering
flowing

MAIN INGREDIENTS
Bergamot
Coriander
Marjoram
Peppermint
Jasmine
Rose

SUBSTITUTE WITH
Arborvitae
Black spruce
Copaiba
Northern Escape

SAFETY
Not safe for internal use. Avoid exposure to sunlight or UV rays for up to 12 hours after application.

TOP USES

SCATTERED & OVERWHELMED
Apply under nose and across forehead. Inhale deeply from cupped hands.

ALIGNED, SINGLEMINDED, TRANQUIL & FOCUSED
Diffuse. Apply to crown, neck area, and/or forehead.

ACCEPTED & WORTHY
Diffuse. Apply under nose, over heart, spleen, and/or solar plexus.

MEDITATION & PRAYER
Diffuse or inhale deeply. Apply over heart and forehead.

APATHETIC & LOW ENERGY
Diffuse. Apply to pulse points, over heart, and on bottoms of feet.

ANGER, RAGE & IMBALANCED MOOD
Diffuse or inhale from cupped hands. Apply to back of neck and over heart.

PERFUME
Apply to pulse points, chest, behind ears, and/or on ankles.

AFFIRMATION:
I know, accept, and am true to myself.

COMPLEMENTARY YOGA POSES:
Seated Meditation, Warrior II, Triangle, and Gate Pose.

stabilizing • centering • sweet

AMAVI®

MEN'S FORTIFYING BLEND

MAIN INGREDIENTS
Buddha wood
Balsam fir
Black pepper
Hinoki
Patchouli
Cocoa extract

SUBSTITUTE WITH
Balance®
Black spruce
Hinoki

SAFETY
Not safe for internal use.

TOP USES

COLOGNE OR AFTERSHAVE
Apply to pulse points, neck, and behind ears, or apply to face.

FOCUSED HEART, MIND & BODY
Diffuse. Apply over heart, to forehead, and/or bottoms of feet.

MENTAL CLARITY, MEDITATION & TRANQUILITY
Diffuse. Apply to forehead, over heart, and bottoms of feet.

DISCOURAGED, ENRAGED, AGITATED & IRRITATED
Diffuse. Apply over heart, to back of neck, spine, and/or bottoms of feet.

SCATTERED, RUSHED, STRESSED
Diffuse. Apply to pulse points and/or bottoms of feet.

WOMEN'S PERFUME
Blend with jasmine or Beautiful. Apply to pulse points, back of neck, or behind ears.

Intentionally replacing colognes made with synthetic ingredients with essential oil blends is a great way to choose to reduce tonic exposure.

ANCHOR

YOGA STEADYING BLEND

stabilizing
harmonizing
centering

MAIN INGREDIENTS
Lavender
Cedarwood
Frankincense
Cinnamon bark
Sandalwood
Black pepper
Patchouli

SUBSTITUTE WITH
Arborvitae
Balance®
Black spruce
Cedarwood
Frankincense
Patchouli
Sandalwood

SAFETY
Not safe for internal use.

TOP USES

MEDITATION, PRAYER & FOCUS
Diffuse. Apply to forehead, behind ears, along spine, and/or bottoms of feet.

ANCHORED, COURAGEOUS & AUTHENTIC, STABLE
Diffuse. Apply to ankles, along spine, and/or bottoms of feet.

COMPOSED, CALM & RESTED
Diffuse. Apply to back of neck, along spine, and/or bottoms of feet.

ROOTED TO THE EARTH, GROUNDED, SPEAKING TRUTH
Diffuse. Apply to throat area, along spine, and/or bottoms of feet.

FEARFUL & DISCONNECTED, RESISTANT, WITHHOLDING
Diffuse or inhale deeply from cupped hands. Apply over heart.

PERFUME
Apply to pulse points, chest, and behind ears.

AFFIRMATION:
I am living who I really am.

COMPLEMENTARY YOGA POSES:
Seated Meditation, Seated Twist, and Bhu Mudra.

= Aromatically = Topically = Internally

ARBORVITAE

THUJA PLICATA

woody
majestic
strengthening

WOOD PULP

STEAM DISTILLED

SOURCED
Canada

MAIN CONSTITUENTS
Methyl thujate
Methyl-myrtenate
Terpinen-4-ol

TOP PROPERTIES
Antiviral
Antifungal
Antibacterial
Stimulant

FOUND IN
Abōde™
Forgive®

SUBSTITUTE WITH
Abōde™
Align
Anchor
Cedarwood
Clary sage
Jasmine
Petitgrain
Roman chamomile

SAFETY & RESEARCH
Not safe for internal use. Dilution recommended. Possible skin sensitivity. For research, see page 540.

TOP USES

CANDIDA & FUNGAL ISSUES
Apply to bottoms of feet or area of concern.

VIRUSES & FEVER
Apply to bottoms of feet. Diffuse.

COLD SORES & WARTS
Apply to area of concern frequently.

RESPIRATORY ISSUES & COUGH
Apply to chest and back.

INSECT REPELLENT
Diffuse, spray on surfaces, and/or apply to exposed areas or clothing.

SKIN CANCER
Apply to affected area.

LYMPHATIC CONGESTION
Apply under nose, on back of neck, and/or bottoms of feet.

CHLAMYDIA & STAPH
Apply to area of concern. Dilute when applied to sensitive areas.

PSORIASIS & HAIR LOSS
Apply to troubled skin or scalp, or add with shampoo.

MEDITATION & MINDFULNESS
Diffuse to enhance practice and invite a calm state of mind.

EMOTIONAL BALANCE
Use aromatically and topically to go from Overzealous → Composed.

Arborvitae means "Tree of Life," and these trees often live for over 800 years.

ARISE

YOGA ENLIGHTENING BLEND

rising
connecting
aligning

MAIN INGREDIENTS
Grapefruit
Lemon
Osmanthus
Melissa
Siberian fir

SUBSTITUTE WITH
Beautiful
Citrus Bloom™
Elevation
Hinoki
Melissa

SAFETY
Not safe for internal use. Avoid exposure to sunlight or UV rays for up to 12 hours after application.

TOP USES

CONNECTEDNESS WITH SELF AND HIGHER POWER
Diffuse. Apply to crown, over heart, and along spine.

INTENTIONAL, ACTION-ORIENTED & MANIFESTING
Diffuse. Apply to ankles, along spine, and bottoms of feet.

UPLIFTED, COURAGEOUS & EMPOWERED
Diffuse. Apply to forehead, over heart, and bottoms of feet.

OVERWHELMED, MENTAL CHATTER, LACK OF CLARITY & FOCUS
Diffuse. Apply to forehead, toes, and behind ears.

FEELING CHALLENGED, DEPRESSION & MOOD SWINGS
Diffuse. Apply to crown, over heart, behind ears, bottoms of feet, and pulse points.

PERFUME
Apply to pulse points, chest, behind ears, and/or on ankles.

AFFIRMATION:
I am one with the Divine.

COMPLEMENTARY YOGA POSES:
Volcano, Standing Side Stretch, and Half Moon.

relieving • renewing • circulating

AROMATOUCH®

MASSAGE BLEND

MAIN INGREDIENTS
Cypress
Peppermint
Marjoram
Basil
Grapefruit
Lavender

SUBSTITUTE WITH
Basil
Coriander
Cypress
Marjoram

SAFETY
Not safe for internal use. Avoid exposure to sunlight or UV rays for up to 12 hours after application.

ESSENTIAL OILS

TOP USES

MUSCLE TENSION, ACHES & CRAMPS
Apply to areas of concern.

HEADACHE, NECK & BACK PAIN, ARTHRITIS
Apply to neck, shoulders, and/or along spine and/or areas of concern.

NEUROPATHY & RESTLESS LEG
Apply to areas of concern to stimulate nerves and circulation.

CONNECTIVE TISSUE, LIGAMENT & TENDON ISSUES
Apply to areas of concern.

LYMPHATIC CONGESTION
Apply to bottoms of feet and/or under arms, back of knees, and neck.

HIGH BLOOD PRESSURE
Apply to bottoms of feet.

POOR CIRCULATION & COLD EXTREMITIES
Apply to arms, hands, legs, and/or feet.

This blend relaxes and soothes muscles, enhances blood flow, and encourages muscle tissue healing.

= Aromatically = Topically = Internally

BALANCE®

GROUNDING BLEND

stabilizing
centering
sweet

MAIN INGREDIENTS
Spruce
Ho wood
Frankincense
Blue tansy
Blue chamomile
Osmanthus

Life's stressful surprises can leave one feeling unstable and more physically or mentally rigid in an effort to self protect. Balance® encourages feelings of restoration, stability, and groundedness.

TOP USES

STRESS & ANXIETY
Apply to bottoms of feet. Diffuse or inhale from cupped hands.

JET LAG & TRAVEL ANXIETY
Inhale from cupped hands and/or apply under nose.

MOOD SWINGS
Diffuse, apply under nose, and/or on back of neck.

NEUROLOGICAL CONDITIONS, CONVULSIONS, EPILEPSY, PARKINSON'S, BRAIN INJURY
Apply to back of neck, along spine, and/or bottoms of feet, especially on toes.

FEELING UNSTABLE OR INFLEXIBLE
Apply to bottoms of feet and/or diffuse.

TRANQUILITY & MEDITATION
Apply under nose, across forehead, and or inhale from cupped hands.

ANGER & RAGE, FEAR, GRIEF & TRAUMA
Diffuse, apply under nose, and on back of neck.

SUBSTITUTE WITH
Amavi®
Anchor
Black spruce
Frankincense
Steady™

SAFETY
Not safe for internal use.

regenerating • uplifting • stimulating

BASIL

OCIMUM BASILICUM

TOP USES

ADRENAL & CHRONIC FATIGUE
Apply under nose, to bottoms of feet, back of neck, forehead, and/or over adrenal area.

EARACHE & CONGESTION, ALLERGIES, CHRONIC COLDS, CHILLS, MALARIA
Apply behind and around ear, swab ear canal. Apply to spine, bottoms of feet, and chest. Take in a capsule.

LOSS OF SENSE OF SMELL
Apply under nose and to toes to regain or increase sense of smell.

LOW BLOOD PRESSURE, DIZZINESS, FAINTING, MIGRAINES
Apply to temples and back of neck, and/or bottoms of feet.

MENTAL FATIGUE & LACK OF FOCUS, AUTISM, SEIZURES
Breathe in, diffuse, and/or apply across forehead and/or on back of neck.

LACK OF OVULATION, OVARIAN CYSTS, SCANT & PAINFUL MENSTRUATION, INFERTILITY, LABOR & TRANSITION, ENGORGEMENT
Apply to ovary and/or uterine areas. Take in a capsule.

DIABETES, LACK OF PERSPIRATION, LOW DOPAMINE, PARKINSON'S
Take in a capsule.

TIRED & WEAK MUSCLES, CRAMPS & SPASMS
Apply to affected areas.

NAUSEA & ABDOMINAL CRAMPING
Take in a capsule. Apply to abdomen.

BUG, SNAKE, & SPIDER BITES
Diffuse or wear to repel insects. Apply to affected areas.

EMOTIONAL BALANCE
Use aromatically and topically to go from Inundated → Relieved.

One of the most universally applicable oils, basil is from the Greek word meaning "king." Ancient Greeks believed it opened the gateways to heaven.

LEAVES

STEAM DISTILLED

SOURCED
Egypt

MAIN CONSTITUENT
Linalool
1,8-cineole (eucalyptol)
Bergamotene

TOP PROPERTIES
Stimulant
Neurotonic
Steroidal
Regenerative
Antispasmodic
Anti-inflammatory
Antibacterial
Digestive

FOUND IN
Align
AromaTouch®
Motivate®
PastTense®

SUBSTITUTE WITH
AromaTouch®
Coriander
Fennel
Marjoram
Rosemary
Tulsi

SAFETY & RESEARCH
Dilution recommended. Possible skin sensitivity. Caution with pregnancy and epilepsy. For research, see page 540.

BEAUTIFUL

CAPTIVATING BLEND

alluring
equisite
lovely

MAIN INGREDIENTS
Lime
Osmanthus
Bergamot
Frankincense

SUBSTITUTE WITH
Arise
Beautiful Body Mist
Citrus Bloom™
Elevation
Magnolia

SAFETY
Not safe for internal use
Avoid exposure to sunlight or UV rays for up to 12 hours after application.

TOP USES

PERFUME
Apply to pulse points, chest, back of neck, and behind ears.

ENERGIZE & UPLIFT MOOD & ENVIRONMENT
Apply to pulse points, back of neck, and/or bottoms of feet. Diffuse.*

STRESSED & ANXIOUS
Apply to forehead, back of neck, and over heart. Diffuse.*

FOCUSED HEART, MIND & BODY
Apply to forehead, back of neck, and/or bottoms of feet. Diffuse.*

MEDITATION & TRANQUILITY, EMPOWERMENT & SELF WORTH
Apply to pulse points, back of neck, and bottoms of feet. Diffuse.*

ENCOURAGE BEING TRUE TO SELF
Apply to pulse points, back of neck, along spine, and/or bottoms of feet. Diffuse.*

MAGNIFY RADIANCE & FEMININE ENERGY
Apply to pulse points, back of neck, along spine, and/or bottoms of feet. Diffuse.*

**Apply roller blend to diffuser jewelry.*

Replace toxic and endocrine-disrupting synthetic perfumes with pure essential oil blends that support healthy hormones and a happier mood.

uplifting • assuring • restoring

BERGAMOT

CITRUS BERGAMIA

TOP USES

ADDICTIONS & DOPAMINE
Apply to back of neck and bottoms of feet or diffuse. Take in a capsule.

SELF-WORTH ISSUES & DEPRESSION
Apply over heart or gut and diffuse.

APPETITE EXCESS OR LOSS & ANOREXIA
Breathe in and take in a capsule.

ACNE, OILY SKIN, PSORIASIS & ECZEMA, WOUNDS, BOILS
Apply to affected area.

FUNGAL ISSUES, VAGINAL ITCHING, & CANDIDA
Apply to affected areas and/or take in a capsule.

BLADDER & URINARY TRACT INFECTIONS
Take in a capsule.

COUGHS & BRONCHITIS, TONSILITIS, SORE THROAT
Apply to chest and/or throat area. Gargle and take in a capsule.

INSOMNIA
Inhale or diffuse before sleep.

STRESS & AGITATION
Apply to back of neck and bottoms of feet and/or diffuse.

JOINT ISSUES & MUSCLE CRAMPS
Apply to affected areas.

EMOTIONAL BALANCE
Use aromatically and topically to go from Inadequate ⟶ Worthy.

Used in the first eau de cologne, Bergamot is now used to flavor Earl Grey tea.

RIND

COLD PRESSED

SOURCED
Italy

MAIN CONSTITUENTS
Limonene
Linalyl acetate
Linalool
Terpinene
β-pinene

TOP PROPERTIES
Neurotonic
Anti-inflammatory
Antidepressant
Antibacterial
Antifungal
Digestive stimulant

FOUND IN
Align
Citrus Bliss®
ClaryCalm®
Forgive®
Hope®
Whisper®

SUBSTITUTE WITH
Citrus Bliss®
Hope®
Magnolia
Neroli
Petitgrain
Pink pepper
Whisper®

SAFETY & RESEARCH
Possible skin sensitivity. Avoid sunlight or UV rays to applied area for up to 12 hours. For research, see page 540.

ESSENTIAL OILS

= Aromatically = Topically = Internally

BERGAMOT MINT

MENTHA CITRATA

LEAVES & STEMS

STEAM DISTILLED

SOURCED
India

MAIN CONSTITUENTS
Linalool
Linalyl acetate

TOP PROPERTIES
Antioxidant
Calming
Invigorating
Analgesic
Antidepressant

SUBSTITUTE WITH
Clary sage
Island Mint®
Lavender
Petitgrain
Spearmint

SAFETY & RESEARCH
Not safe for internal use.
For research, see page 540.

refreshing
revitalizing
invigorating

TOP USES

CLEAR & REVITALIZE MIND, MEDITATION & MINDFULNESS
Diffuse Ⓐ or apply Ⓣ under nose, on forehead, back of neck, and/or toes.

CALM, CENTER, & RELAX
Diffuse Ⓐ or apply Ⓣ to pulse points, back of neck, along spine, and/or bottoms of feet.

LOW ENERGY, LACK OF MOTIVATION, PESSIMISM
Diffuse Ⓐ or apply Ⓣ under nose, over heart, and across forehead.

MUSCLE ACHES & PAINS, TENSION
Apply Ⓣ to areas of concern.

UNSETTLED OR RESTLESS, SLEEP ISSUES
Diffuse Ⓐ. Apply Ⓣ under nose and on bottoms of feet, especially at bedtime.

BLOATING, GAS, NAUSEA & UPSET STOMACH
Apply Ⓣ to abdomen, bottoms of feet, and under nose. Repeat as often as needed.

CONSTRICTED BREATHING & CONGESTION
Diffuse Ⓐ with citrus oil and/or inhale from cupped hands. Apply Ⓣ to chest, forehead, bottoms of feet, and/or along spine.

MENSTRUAL DISCOMFORT & MOODS
Diffuse Ⓐ. Apply Ⓣ under nose and on lower abdomen.

FUNGUS & PARASITES, IMMUNE BOOST
Apply Ⓣ to areas of concern, abdomen, spine, and/or bottoms of feet.

HOUSEHOLD ODORS
Diffuse Ⓐ to clear odors such as cooking smells or a musty closet.

EMOTIONAL BALANCE
Use Ⓐ aromatically and Ⓣ topically to go from Listless → Perky.

Despite the name, bergamot mint is not related to the bergamot fruit in any way. Rather, it comes from a flowering, perennial herb that is part of the mint family.

Ⓐ = Aromatically Ⓣ = Topically Ⓘ = Internally

BIRCH

BETULA LENTA

invigorating
activating
soothing

WOOD
STEAM DISTILLED

SOURCED
Canada

MAIN CONSTITUENT
Methyl salicylate

TOP PROPERTIES
Analgesic
Neurotonic
Anti-rheumatic
Stimulant
Steroidal
Warming

SUBSTITUTE WITH
Deep Blue®
PastTense®
Wintergreen

SAFETY & RESEARCH
Not safe for internal use.
Avoid during pregnancy.
Not for use by epileptics.
For research, see page 540.

Birch is used to make root beer.

TOP USES

CONNECTIVE TISSUE, MUSCLE, OR TENDON INJURIES, WHIPLASH
Apply to affected area.

BROKEN BONES & TOOTH PAIN
Apply to area of concern.

ARTHRITIS & RHEUMATISM, & GOUT
Apply to affected area.

MUSCLE PAIN, SPASMS, LACK OF TONE
Apply to area(s) of concern for steroidal support.

FEVER
Apply on spine.

WEAK-WILLED, UNSUPPORTED
Diffuse or inhale from cupped hands. Apply to bottoms of feet.

BONE SPURS, GALLSTONES, KIDNEY STONES, CATARACTS
Apply to bottoms of feet or over areas of concern.

SKIN INFLAMMATION, ECZEMA, PSORIASIS, BOILS
Apply to areas of concern.

EDEMA, BLOOD, TOXICITY, CONGESTED LYMPH
Apply to bottoms of feet or ankles.

ULCERS & CRAMPS
Apply to abdomen.

EMOTIONAL BALANCE
Use aromatically and topically to go from Cowardly → Courageous.

spicy • warming • circulating

BLACK PEPPER

PIPER NIGRUM

TOP USES

CONSTIPATION, DIARRHEA, GAS
Take in capsule or apply to abdomen.

RESPIRATORY & LYMPHATIC DRAINAGE, LACK OF PERSPIRATION
Use a drop under tongue. Inhale or diffuse. Apply to affected area.

POOR CIRCULATION & COLD EXTREMITIES, DIZZINESS, APHRODISIAC
Apply to increase circulation and blood flow to areas of concern or interest.

CATARACTS
Take in a capsule. Apply under second and third toes.

COLD & FLU, ACHES & CHILLS
Take in a capsule. Apply to bottoms of feet and along spine.

CONGESTED AIRWAYS
Diffuse and apply to chest. Dilute if needed.

LOSS OF APPETITE & ANOREXIA, ANEMIA
Take under tongue or in a capsule.

LACK OF COURAGE & POOR STAMINA
Diffuse or inhale from cupped hands. Apply under nose and over heart.

JOINT PAIN & STIFFNESS, SPRAINS, MUSCLE & UTERINE CRAMPS
Apply to affected areas.

SMOKING & ADDICTIONS
Take under tongue. Inhale or diffuse.

TOOTHACHE
Apply to affected area.

FOOD FLAVOR
Enhance foods by adding a drop for flavor.

EMOTIONAL BALANCE
Use aromatically and topically to go from Repressed → Honest.

Archaeological evidence shows this spice going back to at least 2000 B.C. In fact, in the oldest known cookbook in existence, 80 percent of the recipes use black pepper.

PEPPERCORN

STEAM DISTILLED

SOURCED
Madagascar

MAIN CONSTITUENT
β-caryophyllene
Limonene
Sabinene
α-pinene
ß-Pinene
δ-3-carene

TOP PROPERTIES
Antioxidant
Antispasmodic
Digestive stimulant
Expectorant
Neutronic
Rubefacient
Stimulant

FOUND IN
Amavi®
Tamer™

SUBSTITUTE WITH
Balsam fir
Copaiba
Hinoki
Juniper berry
Yarrow|Pom
Ylang ylang

SAFETY
Dilution recommended. Possible skin sensitivity if old or oxidized. For research, see page 540.

= Aromatically = Topically = Internally

ESSENTIAL OILS

TOP USES

OVERSTRIVING, ADRENAL/NERVOUS EXHAUSTION & FATIGUE, MELANCHOLIC
Diffuse and apply to forehead, over heart, and/or above kidney area.

CHRONIC JOINT/BACK PAIN
Apply to areas of concern.

FEELING DISCONNECTED FROM POTENTIAL, THWARTED, STUCK, UNFORGIVING
Diffuse and apply to pulse points and over heart.

ASTHMA, BRONCHITIS, SINUSITIS, SPASTIC & MOIST COUGHS
Apply to warm/wet washcloth and place on chest or add to hot water, cover head with towel, and inhale vapors.

HORMONE & STRESS-RELATED SKIN OUTBREAKS, HIGH BLOOD PRESSURE
Apply to areas of concern and/or bottoms of feet.

INSECURITY & INDECISIVENESS
Diffuse and apply over heart and on pulse points.

PITUITARY & THYMUS ISSUES, HYPERTHYROIDISM, HYPOTHALAMUS
Apply to spine, base of skull, neck, across forehead, and on bottoms of feet.

LOW CORTICOSTEROIDS
Apply to bottoms of feet.

WOUND HEALING, POST SURGERY, CANCER, AGE SPOTS
Apply to areas of concern. Dilute for sensitive skin.

LOW TESTOSTERONE
Apply to wrists, feet, and gonad reflex points.

INSATIABLE EATING DUE TO ANXIETY
Diffuse and/or apply under nose and to pulse points.

TRAUMATIC MEMORIES
Diffuse and apply to forehead and back of neck.

STRESS-INDUCED SHORT-TERM MEMORY LOSS, ALZHEIMER'S
Apply to back of neck, across forehead, and to underside of toes.

EMOTIONAL BALANCE
Use aromatically and topically to go from Halted → Acclaimed.

The Lakota Native American tribe used black spruce in ointments and salves to treat skin issues and during spiritual rituals.

= Aromatically = Topically = Internally

BLACK SPRUCE

PICEA MARIANA

NEEDLES/ BRANCHES

STEAM DISTILLED

SOURCED
Canada

MAIN CONSTITUENTS
Bornyl acetate
α-pinene
Camphene
δ-3-carene

TOP PROPERTIES
Anti-inflammatory
Steroidal
Expectorant
Calming
Grounding
Restorative

FOUND IN
Balance®
Forgive®
Island Mint®
Midnight Forest
Northern Escape

SUBSTITUTE WITH
Align
Amavi®
Anchor
Balance®
Forgive®
Hinoki
Jasmine
Lavender
Northern Escape
Petitgrain
Siberian fir

SAFETY & RESEARCH
Not safe for internal use.
For research, see page 540.

UE TANSY

ANACETUM ANNUUM

eliminating • relieving • depending

FLOWER/LEAF & STEM

STEAM DISTILLED

SOURCED
Northern Morocco

MAIN CONSTITUENTS
Sabinene
Chamazulene
p-Cymene
α-Phellandrene
ß-Pinene
Camphor

TOP PROPERTIES
Sedative
Relaxant
Antidepressant
Aphrodisiac
Decongestant
Stomachic

FOUND IN
Balance®
Deep Blue®

SUBSTITUTE WITH
Deep Blue®
Juniper berry
Roman chamomile
Rosemary
Tulsi
Yarrow|Pom

SAFETY & RESEARCH
Not safe for internal use. Can be harmful to small animals. Possible skin sensitivity. May stain surfaces, fabrics, and skin. For research, see page 540.

TOP USES

ALLERGIES, ITCHING, RASHES, WATERY EYES, SNEEZING
Apply to bottoms of feet and/or affected areas. Diffuse.

ACNE, ECZEMA, PSORIASIS, SUNBURN
Apply to affected areas.

FIBROMYALGIA, SCIATICA, ARTHRITIS, & RHEUMATISM
Apply to affected areas.

FUNGAL & SKIN INFECTIONS
Apply to affected areas.

ASTHMA & RESPIRATORY ISSUES, HICCUPS
Diffuse and apply to chest.

TENSION & SINUS HEADACHES, MIGRAINES, TOOTHACHE
Massage into temples, forehead, sides of nose or jaw.

INDIGESTION, STOMACH ULCERS, INTESTINAL WORMS
Apply to abdomen.

COLD & FLU, MUMPS, CHICKEN POX, MUSCLE ACHES
Apply to affected areas or bottoms of feet.

ADDICTIONS & LOW SELF-CONFIDENCE
Diffuse or inhale from cupped hands.

BUG BITES, SCABIES, INSECT REPELLENT
Apply to affected areas, Diffuse or add to a spray and apply to defer.

THYROID & THYMUS ISSUES
Apply over thyroid area, to chest, and back of neck.

EMOTIONAL BALANCE
Use aromatically and topically to go from Overwhelmed → Encouraged.

Tansy comes from the Greek word "Athanaton," meaning immortal.

empowering
assuring
invigorating

BRAVE™

CHILDREN'S COURAGE BLEND

TOP USES

DISCOURAGED & LOW ENERGY
Apply under nose, to back of neck, over heart, and/or bottoms of feet.

TIRED & WEARY
Apply under nose, to back of neck, forehead, and/or bottoms of feet.

LACK OF DETERMINATION & CONVICTION
Apply under nose, along spine, over heart, and/or bottoms of feet.

AFRAID & SCARED
Apply under nose, to back of neck, along spine, and/or bottoms of feet.

LACK OF CONFIDENCE & MOTIVATION
Apply under nose, to chest, back, and/or bottoms of feet.

CONFUSED & OVERWHELMED
Apply under nose, to back of neck, and forehead.

DIGESTIVE UPSET, NERVOUS & AGITATED
Apply to abdomen, forehead, and/or bottoms of feet.

ACHES & PAINS
Apply to areas of concern.

MAIN INGREDIENTS
Wild orange
Amyris
Osmanthus
Cinnamon bark

SUBSTITUTE WITH
Harvest Spice
Holiday Joy
Passion®
Wild orange

SAFETY
Not safe for internal use. Avoid exposure to sunlight or UV rays for up to 12 hours after application.

Brave™ promotes feelings of confidence, courage, and belief in oneself while helping to manage stress and anxiety and counteract negative emotions of doubt, pessimism, and cynicism.

Children's blends are intentionally pre-diluted and uniquely formulated with milder aromas to work best with smaller or more sensitive bodies. Designed to indicate when a blend is best suited for mind, heart, or body, icon-coded bottles help children and adults alike learn how to use safe and fun roll-on applications to attend to feelings, listen to the body's needs, and solve everyday issues for a healthier, happier life.

ESSENTIAL OILS

= Aromatically = Topically = Internally

BREATHE®

RESPIRATION BLEND

airy
expanding
supportive

ESSENTIAL OILS

MAIN INGREDIENTS
Laurel leaf
Peppermint
Eucalyptus
Tea tree
Lemon
Cardamom
Ravintsara

SUBSTITUTE WITH
Air-X™
Eucalyptus
Laural leaf
Peppermint
Ravintsara

SAFETY
Not safe for internal use. Dilution recommended. Possible skin sensitivity. Avoid exposure to sunlight or UV rays for up to 12 hours after application.

TOP USES

COUGH & CONGESTION, RUNNY NOSE
Diffuse and/or apply under or over bridge of nose, to chest, and bottoms of feet.

PNEUMONIA & ASTHMA
Diffuse and/or apply under nose, and on chest and back.

ALLERGIES & POLLEN SENSITIVITY
Inhale from cupped hands and/or apply under nose and on forehead. Diffuse.

BRONCHITIS & INFLUENZA
Diffuse and/or apply to chest, back, and on bottoms of feet.

SINUSITIS & NASAL POLYPS
Apply across forehead and under nose.

SLEEP ISSUES
Diffuse and/or apply to bottoms of feet before bed.

CONSTRICTED BREATHING
Diffuse and apply to chest and back.

EXERCISE-INDUCED ASTHMA
Diffuse and apply to chest and/or bottoms of feet before and during activity.

Healthy airflow and oxygen supply bring life and energy with each breath. Enjoy a more energized day and restful sleep with this blend.

pacifying • relaxing • unwinding

CALMER™

CHILDREN'S RESTFUL BLEND

MAIN INGREDIENTS
Lavender
Cananga
Buddha wood
Roman chamomile

SUBSTITUTE WITH
Console®
Lavender
Roman chamomile
Serenity®
Ylang ylang

TOP USES

UNSETTLED & RESTLESS, SLEEP ISSUES
Apply under nose and to bottoms of feet.

STRESSED & ANXIOUS
Apply under nose, to back of neck, and forehead.

FUSSY, EASILY UPSET & STARTLED
Apply to chest and/or bottoms of feet.

UPTIGHT & WOUND UP, MOODY
Apply under nose and across forehead or inhale deeply from cupped hands.

MUSCLE ACHES & GROWING PAINS
Apply to areas of concern.

ANGRY, AGITATED & IRRITABLE
Apply to bottoms of feet, spine, and under nose.

BATH & BEDTIME ROUTINE
Apply before or after bath, under nose, to forehead, along spine, and/or bottoms of feet.

Calmer™ can help quiet the mind before bedtime, support restful sleep, and encourage relaxation.

Children's blends are intentionally pre-diluted and uniquely formulated with milder aromas to work best with smaller or more sensitive bodies. Designed to indicate when a blend is best suited for mind, heart, or body, icon-coded bottles help children and adults alike learn how to use safe and fun roll-on applications to attend to feelings, listen to the body's needs, and solve everyday issues for a healthier, happier life.

SAFETY
Not safe for internal use.

= Aromatically = Topically = Internally

invigorating • relaxing • cleansing

CARDAMOM

ELETTARIA CARDAMOMUM

SEEDS

STEAM DISTILLED

SOURCED
Guatelama

MAIN CONSTITUENT
α-Terpinyl acetate,
Linalyl acetate
1,8-cineole (eucalyptol)

TOP PROPERTIES
Digestive stimulant
Antispasmodic
Anti-inflammatory
Decongestant
Expectorant
Tonic
Stomachic
Carminative

FOUND IN
Air-X™
Breathe®
DigestZen®
Passion®

SUBSTITUTE WITH
Celery seed
Coriander
DigestZen®
Dill
Eucalyptus
Passion®

SAFETY & RESEARCH
Not safe for internal use. For research, see page 540.

TOP USES

RESPIRATORY CONGESTION & BREATHING DIFFICULTIES
Apply to chest, bridge of nose, forehead, and diffuse.

STOMACH ACHE & CONSTIPATION
Take in a capsule and/or apply to abdomen.

COLITIS & DIARRHEA, LOSS OF APPETITE
Apply to abdomen and/or take in a capsule.

GASTRITIS & STOMACH ULCERS
Take in a capsule. Apply to abdomen.

MENSTRUAL & MUSCULAR PAIN
Apply to area of concern.

SORE THROAT & FEVER
Gargle and apply to throat area, back of neck, forehead, and/or bottoms of feet.

CATARACTS
Take in a capsule. Apply under second and third toes.

MENTAL FATIGUE & CONFUSION
Apply under nose and to back of neck.

PANCREATITIS & SLOW METABOLISM
Apply over pancreas area and on bottoms of feet. Take in a capsule.

BAD BREATH & HOUSEHOLD ODORS
Take in a capsule or lick off back of hand. Diffuse to clear odors.

SKIN IRRITATIONS & FUNGUS
Apply to areas of concern.

COOKING
Use to season foods and enhance flavors.

EMOTIONAL BALANCE
Use aromatically and topically to go from Self-centered ⟶ Charitable.

Known as one of the most expensive cooking spices, cardamom is a close relative of ginger.

spicy
strong
warming

CASSIA

CINNAMOMUM CASSIA

BARK

STEAM DISTILLED

SOURCED
China

MAIN CONSTITUENTS
Transcinnamaldehyde
Cinnamyl acetate

TOP PROPERTIES
Decongestant
Carminative
Detoxifier
Cardiotonic
Antimicrobial
Antiviral
Antifungal
Antispasmodic

FOUND IN
Abōde™
Harvest Spice
Holiday Joy

SUBSTITUTE WITH
Abōde™
Cinnamon

SAFETY & RESEARCH
Dilution recommended. Possible skin sensitivity. Can reduce milk supply in lactating women. For research, see page 540.

Sweeter than cinnamon, cassia's medicinal properties were highly valued by ancient Chinese healers who then spread them widely to other parts of the world.

TOP USES

COLD EXTREMITIES & POOR CIRCULATION
Apply diluted to bottoms of feet.

UPSET STOMACH & VOMITING
Take in a capsule.

DETOX FOR EAR, NOSE, THROAT, LUNGS & LYMPH
Take in a capsule.

WATER RETENTION & KIDNEY INFECTION
Take in a capsule or apply on bottoms of feet to kidney reflex points.

VIRUSES & BACTERIA, FUNGUS & CANDIDA
Take in a capsule and diffuse.

IMBALANCED BLOOD SUGAR & INSULIN RESISTANCE
Take in a capsule before meals.

SLOW METABOLISM
Take in a capsule before meals.

LOW SEX DRIVE
Diffuse or inhale aroma from bottle or apply diluted to bottoms of feet.

FLAVORING
Add a drop to a favorite recipe for a sweet cinnamon flavor.

EMOTIONAL BALANCE
Use aromatically and topically to go from Uncertain → Bold.

= Aromatically = Topically = Internally

CEDARWOOD

JUNIPERUS VIRGINIANA

WOODS

STEAM DISTILLED

SOURCED
South-Eastern USA

MAIN CONSTITUENTS
α-cedrene
Cedrol
Thujopsene

TOP PROPERTIES
Anti-inflammatory
Diuretic
Astringent
Antiseptic
Insecticidal
Sedative

FOUND IN
Anchor
ClaryCalm®
Harvest Spice
Hygge™
Northern Escape
Serenity®
Stronger™
TerraShield®

SUBSTITUTE WITH
Adaptiv™
Anchor
Arborvitae
Copaiba
Frankincense
Holiday Peace
Hygge™
Sandalwood
Serenity®
Spikenard
Stronger™
TerraShield®

SAFETY & RESEARCH
Not safe for internal use. Dilution recommended. Possible skin sensitivity. For research, see page 540.

Used by Native Americans for over 400 years to treat colds and fevers.

ESSENTIAL OILS

TOP USES

ADD, ADHD, LOW GABA OR DOPAMINE LEVELS
Apply to back of neck, across forehead, and diffuse or inhale.

PSORIASIS & ECZEMA, SKIN INFECTIONS
Apply to affected area.

ULCERS
Inhale or apply to back of neck, bottoms of feet and/or abdomen.

COUGH, SINUS & LUNG ISSUES
Apply to chest and forehead. Diffuse and/or inhale from cupped hands.

STROKE & SEIZURE, ANXIETY
Apply on back of neck and bottoms of feet.

JOINT INFLAMMATION, STIFF NECK, MUSCLE TENSION
Apply to area of concern.

URINARY TRACT, BLADDER & VAGINAL INFECTION, EDEMA
Apply to lower abdomen or ankles.

GUM ISSUES
Apply along jawline.

INSECT REPELLENT
Apply to exposed skin and clothing. Diffuse.

ACNE & OILY SKIN, GRAY HAIR, AFTERSHAVE
Apply with a drop of tea tree to blemishes, add to shampoo, or use after shaving.

EMOTIONAL BALANCE
Use aromatically and topically to go from Alone → Connected.

= Aromatically = Topically = Internally

CELERY SEED

APIUM GRAVEOLENS

SEEDS

STEAM DISTILLED

SOURCED
India

MAIN CONSTITUENTS
Limonene
ß-Selinene

TOP PROPERTIES
Diuretic
Detoxifier
Digestive stimulant
Hypertensive
Purifier

SUBSTITUTE WITH
Cardamom
Dill
Green mandarin

SAFETY & RESEARCH
Not safe for internal use. For research, see page 540.

detoxing

dispersing

reinstating

TOP USES

CELERY SEED TONIC
Take (Internally) 4 drops per 8 ounces of purified water.

ULCERS, GERDS, STOMACH OR INTESTINAL LINING ISSUES
Take (Internally) in capsule and apply (Topically) to abdomen.

WATER RETENTION & EDEMA, URINARY ISSUES
Take (Internally) in water or juice . Apply (Topically) on lower abdomen and bottoms of feet.

BLOOD & LIVER TOXICITY
Take (Internally) in capsule and apply (Topically) to bottoms of feet and over liver.

WEAK & STIFF JOINTS, GOUT, ARTHRITIS & RHEUMATISM, OSTEOPOROSIS
Apply (Topically) to bottoms of feet and areas of concern.

HIGH BLOOD PRESSURE & RESTRICTED BLOOD FLOW
Apply (Topically) over heart, liver, and bottoms of feet.

INDIGESTION, FLATULENCE, DIARRHEA, POOR APPETITE
Take (Internally) in capsule or apply (Topically) to abdomen.

PERIPHERAL NERVE DAMAGE & NEUROPATHY, WEAKENED SPINAL DISCS
Apply (Topically) to back of neck, up spine, bottoms of feet, and/or areas of concern.

BLADDER, KIDNEY OR GALLSTONES
Take (Internally) in capsule.

MUSCLE ACHE, CRAMPS & SPASMS
Apply (Topically) to areas of concern.

HEADACHE & DIZZINESS, EPILEPSY & STROKE
Apply (Topically) to areas of concern, spine, across forehead, and back of neck.

IRREGULAR MENSTRUAL FLOW & CRAMPS, UTERINE ISSUES
Apply (Topically) in clockwise motion on lower abdomen.

INSECT REPELLENT
Apply (Topically) to clothing and exposed areas of skin.

SEASONING
Use 1-2 drops (Internally) as an alternative celery seasoning. Add 10-12 drops to ½ cup sea salt and salt foods to flavor.

EMOTIONAL BALANCE
Use (Aromatically) aromatically and (Topically) topically to go from Aggravated ⟶ Reconciled.

Conventionally grown celery is one of the most heavily sprayed vegetables and has been found to contain as many as 19 different pesticides, routinely exceeding government-established human tolerance standards. CPTG® essential oils are thoroughly screened for the presence of pesticides, both pre- and post-distillation.

CHEER®

UPLIFTING BLEND

gladdening
illuminating
resilient

MAIN INGREDIENTS
Wild orange
Clove
Star anise
Lemon myrtle
Nutmeg
Vanilla bean extract
Ginger
Cinnamon bark
Zdravetz

Go from discouraged, distressed, or disinterested to an uplifted and resilient state of mind with this blend.

TOP USES

DEPRESSION & DISCOURAGEMENT
Diffuse Ⓐ or inhale from cupped hands. Apply Ⓣ to pulse points, under nose and/or across forehead.

HYSTERIA OR ANXIETY
Diffuse Ⓐ or inhale from cupped hands. Apply Ⓣ to pulse points, under nose, and/or across forehead.

DISCONNECTION
Diffuse Ⓐ or inhale from cupped hands. Apply Ⓣ to pulse points, under nose, and/or across forehead.

PMS
Diffuse Ⓐ or inhale from cupped hands. Apply Ⓣ to pulse points, under nose, and/or across forehead.

CELLULAR HEALTH
Apply Ⓣ to bottoms of feet.

INFLAMMATION & STIFFNESS
Apply Ⓣ diluted to affected area.

INDIGESTION & IRRITABLE BOWELS
Apply Ⓣ diluted to abdomen and bottoms of feet.

IMBALANCED BLOOD SUGAR & HIGH CHOLESTEROL
Apply Ⓣ diluted to bottoms of feet, back of neck, or chest.

SUBSTITUTE WITH
Elevation
Harvest Spice
Holiday Joy
Motivate®
Vanilla
Wild orange

SAFETY
Not safe for internal use. Avoid exposure to sunlight or UV rays for up to 12 hours after application.

fresh awakening cleansing

CILANTRO

CORIANDRUM SATIVUM

TOP USES

HEAVY METAL TOXICITY & FREE RADICAL DAMAGE
Take Ⓘ in a capsule.

AUTISM, PARKINSON'S, ALZHEIMER'S, MULTIPLE SCLEROSIS
Take Ⓘ in a capsule and apply Ⓣ to toes.

GAS, BLOATING & CONSTIPATION
Apply Ⓣ over abdomen.

ALLERGIES
Apply Ⓣ over liver and to bottoms of feet to ease allergies by reducing liver toxicity.

LIVER & KIDNEY TOXICITY
Take Ⓘ in a capsule or apply Ⓣ over liver or kidney area.

FUNGAL & BACTERIAL INFECTIONS, CANDIDA
Take Ⓘ in a capsule and apply Ⓣ to infected area.

BODY ODOR
Take Ⓘ in a capsule.

ANXIETY, OBSESSIVE-COMPULSIVE BEHAVIOR
Inhale Ⓐ or diffuse Ⓐ and take Ⓘ in a capsule.

FLAVORING
Dip toothpick and add Ⓘ to favorite salad, dip, or guacamole.

EMOTIONAL BALANCE
Use Ⓐ aromatically and Ⓣ topically to get from Obsessed → Expansive.

Cilantro and coriander essential oils come from the same plant. Cilantro is extracted from the leaves and coriander from the seeds.

LEAVES

STEAM DISTILLED

SOURCED
USA

MAIN CONSTITUENT
Linalool
Trans-2- Decenal

TOP PROPERTIES
Antioxidant
Antifungal
Detoxifying
Antibacterial

FOUND IN
Abōde™
PastTense®
Purify
Zendocrine®

SUBSTITUTE WITH
Abōde™
Citronella
Coriander
Lemon eucalyptus
Marjoram
Melissa

SAFETY & RESEARCH
Not safe for internal use.
For research, see page 540.

Ⓐ = Aromatically Ⓣ = Topically Ⓘ = Internally

CINNAMON BARK

CINNAMOMUM ZEYLANICUM

SEEDS

STEAM DISTILLED

SOURCED
Madagascar

MAIN CONSTITUENTS
Transcinnamaldehyde
Cinnamyl acetate
Eugenol

TOP PROPERTIES
Antiseptic
Antimicrobial
Antioxidant
Antifungal
Antiviral
Aphrodisiac

FOUND IN
Anchor
Brave™
Cheer®
Harvest Spice
On Guard®
Passion®
Slim & Sassy®
Whisper®

SUBSTITUTE WITH
Cassia
Clove
On Guard®
Passion®
Slim & Sassy®
Tulsi

SAFETY & RESEARCH
Dilution recommended.
Possible skin sensitivity.
For research, see page 540.

Used in biblical times and by the ancient Egyptians, cinnamon bark was often traded. Its origin was a closely guarded secret.

TOP USES

DIABETES & HIGH BLOOD SUGAR
Take in a capsule.

COLD & FLU, VIRUSES, RESPIRATORY INFECTION
Take in a capsule or apply to bottoms of feet. Diffuse.

POOR CIRCULATION, COLD EXTREMITIES, HIGH CHOLESTEROL & HEART ISSUES
Apply diluted to bottoms of feet. Take in a capsule.

ORAL INFECTIONS
Gargle a drop in water.

FUNGAL & BACTERIAL INFECTION, PARASITES, SCABIES
Take in a capsule. Apply highly diluted to area of concern.

KIDNEY INFECTION OR BLADDER
Take in a capsule.

CANDIDA & VAGINITIS
Take in a capsule.

LOW LIBIDO & SEXUAL FRIGIDITY
Take in a capsule. Apply highly diluted on location to warm and stimulate.

MUSCLE STRAIN & PAIN
Apply highly diluted to warm and relieve.

DIVERTICULITIS & DIARRHEA, INTESTINAL INFECTION
Take in a capsule.

FLAVORING
Add to drinks, dishes, or baking recipes.

EMOTIONAL BALANCE
Use aromatically and topically to go from Denied → Receptive.

= Aromatically = Topically = Internally

ESSENTIAL OILS

repelling
reckoning
freshening

TOP USES

FLEA & TICK REPELLENT
Diffuse Ⓐ and apply Ⓣ to exposed skin. Add to glass spray bottle to treat surfaces or apply to clothing.

GREASY HAIR & LICE, DETANGLER
Add Ⓣ to shampoo or conditioner.

DIGESTIVE & INTESTINAL INFLAMMATION, REACTION TO SPICY FOODS & CARRAGEENAN
Apply Ⓣ to bottoms of feet and over upper abdomen and liver area.

SIDE EFFECTS FROM DRUGS, ALCOHOL, NARCOTICS & TOXINS
Diffuse Ⓐ and apply Ⓣ to bottoms of feet and affected areas.

FUNGAL & BACTERIAL INFECTIONS OF INTESTINAL & URINARY TRACTS, PARASITES
Apply Ⓣ to lower abdomen, bottoms of feet, and/or reflex points.

POOR HORMONE OR ENZYME SECRETION, PROSTATE ISSUES
Apply Ⓣ to lower abdomen, on bottoms of feet, and/or corresponding gland or organ area.

ACNE, ATHLETE'S FOOT & NAIL FUNGUS
Apply Ⓣ to areas of concern.

POOR PERSPIRATION OR TOXIN ELIMINATION, FEVERS
Apply Ⓣ to bottoms of feet and over liver area.

OXIDATIVE STRESS & CELL MUTATION, TUMORS
Diffuse Ⓐ and apply Ⓣ to bottoms of feet and over liver area.

POST-SURGERY PAIN, SWOLLEN JOINTS & ARTHRITIS
Apply Ⓣ to areas of concern.

POOR CIRCULATION & HEART PALPATIONS, SEIZURES, HIGH BLOOD PRESSURE
Apply Ⓣ over heart, to bottoms of feet and extremities.

ANXIETY & DEPRESSION, INSOMNIA, LOW ENERGY
Diffuse Ⓐ and apply Ⓣ to neck and forehead, up spine, and on bottoms of feet.

SURFACE CLEANSING & AIR FRESHENING
Add 6-8 drops + 1 T vinegar to glass spray bottle filled with water. Diffuse Ⓐ.

EMOTIONAL BALANCE
Use Ⓐ aromatically and Ⓣ topically to go from Punished to Averting.

Single synthetic chemical compounds used in common bug repellents are relatively easy for insects to develop resistance to. However, it is virtually impossible to do so with an essential oil like citronella due to the chemical complexity.

Ⓐ = Aromatically Ⓣ = Topically Ⓘ = Internally

CITRONELLA

CYMBOPOGON WINTERIANUS

GRASS

STEAM DISTILLED

SOURCED
Indonesia

MAIN CONSTITUENTS
Citronellal
Geraniol

TOP PROPERTIES
Insect Repellent
Insecticidal
Detoxifier
Cleanser
Bactericidal
Antifungal
Astringal
Astringent
Fungicidal
Deodorant

FOUND IN
Forgive®
Purify
TerraShield®

SUBSTITUTE WITH
Cilantro
Laural leaf
Lemon eucalyptus
Rose
TerraShield®

SAFETY & RESEARCH
Not safe for internal use. Dilution recommended for possible skin sensitivity. For research, see page 540.

CITRUS BLISS®

INVIGORATING BLEND

alleviating
pacifying
easing

MAIN INGREDIENTS
Wild orange
Lemon
Grapefruit
Mandarin
Bergamot
Tangerine
Clementine
Vanilla bean absolute

SUBSTITUTE WITH
Citrus Bloom™
Grapefruit
Lemon
Red mandarin
Tangerine
Vanilla
Wild orange

SAFETY
Not safe for internal use. Avoid exposure to sunlight or UV rays for up to 12 hours after application.

TOP USES

LOW ENERGY & EXHAUSTION
Diffuse, apply under nose, and/or back of neck to energize and uplift.

STRESS, ANXIETY & DEPRESSION
Diffuse. Apply under nose, and/or back of neck.

EATING DISORDERS
Diffuse or inhale from cupped hands. Apply to abdomen.

LYMPHATIC & IMMUNE BOOST
Diffuse. Apply under nose, on back of neck, and/or bottoms of feet.

AIR FRESHENER
Diffuse to clear air of odors and uplift.

ANTISEPTIC CLEANER
Mix with water in a glass bottle and apply to surfaces.

PERFUME
Apply to pulse points.

LAUNDRY
Add to eliminate odors, freshen aroma, and kill germs.

Diffuse to uplift and invigorate the senses with this blend of citrus essential oils, and find increased energy and zest for life.

exhilarating
delighting
uplifting

CITRUS BLOOM™

SPRINGTIME BLEND

MAIN INGREDIENTS
Wild orange
Grapefruit
Lavender
Roman chamomile
Magnolia

SAFETY
Not safe for internal use. Avoid exposure to sunlight or UV rays for up to 12 hours after application.

SUBSTITUTE WITH
Arise
Beautiful
Citrus Bliss®
Elevation
Magnolia

TOP USES

CLOSED MINDEDNESS, HOPELESSNESS OR RESIGNATION
Diffuse (A) or inhale deeply from cupped hands. Apply (T) to belly button, over heart, and on forehead to open up to new possibilities.

CHAOTIC ENVIRONMENTS & SITUATIONS
Diffuse (A) and/or apply (T) to forehead, bottoms of feet, and over heart.

SELF-WORTH ISSUES
Diffuse and/or inhale (A). Apply (T) over solar plexus and heart areas, and back of neck to create connections with heart, mind, and body.

AFTERNOON SLUMP & PESSIMISTIC OUTLOOK
Diffuse and inhale (A). Apply (T) under nose, on forehead, and over heart.

BODY ODOR
Apply (T) as a deodorizing body spray or swipe over armpit area prior to applying deodorant.

PERFUME SCENT
Apply (T) to pulse points, behind ears, and on ankles.

Bring the uplifting and powerful benefits of spring indoors with this exotic combination of citrus and fragrant florals.

(A) = Aromatically (T) = Topically (I) = Internally

ESSENTIAL OILS

CLARYCALM®

WOMEN'S MONTHLY BLEND

MAIN INGREDIENTS
Clary sage
Lavender
Bergamot
Roman chamomile
Ylang ylang
Cedarwood
Geranium
Fennel
Carrot seed
Palmarosa
Vitex

SUBSTITUTE WITH
Clary sage
Geranium
Jasmine
Roman chamomile
Serenity®
Ylang ylang

SAFETY
Not safe for internal use. Avoid exposure to sunlight or UV rays for up to 12 hours after application.

TOP USES

IMBALANCED HORMONES
Apply to back of neck, reflex points, lower abdomen, and/or bottoms of feet.

HEAVY PERIODS, PMS & CRAMPS, BREAST TENDERNESS
Apply to lower abdomen, back of neck, and/or bottoms of feet. For added soothing, combine with marjoram and cover with a moist, warm washcloth.

PRE & PERIMENOPAUSE
Apply to abdomen, back of neck, and/or bottoms of feet.

HOT FLASHES
Apply to lower abdomen, back and sides of neck, and/or bottoms of feet.

MOOD SWINGS
Apply over heart, across forehead, on back of neck, and/or bottoms of feet.

LOW SEX DRIVE
Apply to lower abdomen.

SKIN ISSUES & WOUNDS
Apply to areas of concern.

This gentle and safe blend brings harmony by helping to balance and stabilize hormones.

balancing • musky • feminine

CLARY SAGE

SALVIA SCLAREA

TOP USES

ENDOMETRIOSIS & BREAST CANCER
Apply diluted to breasts or take in capsule to help regulate estrogen.

BREAST ISSUES OR ENLARGEMENT
Apply to breast areas.

PARKINSON'S, SEIZURES & CONVULSIONS, THICK BLOOD
Apply to back of neck to support healthy brain function.

CHILD BIRTH & LOW MILK SUPPLY
Apply diluted down spine or over abdomen to help bring on labor. Apply to each breast for increased lactation.

INFERTILITY & IMPOTENCE, PROSTATE/UTERINE ISSUES
Use in a capsule or apply to abdomen and uterine reflex points.

PMS & CRAMPS, PERIMENOPAUSE, MENOPAUSE
Take in a capsule or apply to abdomen or bottoms of feet.

POSTPARTUM DEPRESSION & ANXIETY, FRIGIDITY
Inhale/diffuse or apply over heart and on bottoms of feet.

HOT FLASHES
Combine with peppermint and spritz on back of neck for cooling relief. Take in a capsule.

PINK EYE & CATARACTS
Apply around eye area. Take in a capsule, and apply under second and third toes.

INSOMNIA & RESTLESSNESS
Take under the tongue or apply to bottoms of the feet. Diffuse at bedtime.

WHOOPING COUGH
Apply to chest and take under tongue.

EMOTIONAL BALANCE
Use aromatically and topically to go from Limited → Enlightened.

= Aromatically = Topically = Internally

FLOWER

STEAM DISTILLED

SOURCED
France

MAIN CONSTITUENT
Linalyl acetate
linalool

TOP PROPERTIES
Emmenagogue
Galactagogue
Neurotonic
Mucolytic
Anticoagulant
Sedative
Antispasmodic

FOUND IN
ClaryCalm®
Elevation

SUBSTITUTE WITH
Bergamot mint
ClaryCalm®
Davana
Jasmine
Lavender
Magnolia
Petitgrain
Roman chamomile

SAFETY & RESEARCH
Exercise caution during earlier stages of pregnancy. For research, see page 540.

Clary sage is derived from Latin meaning, "clear eyes." Medieval monks favored it for eye troubles.

ESSENTIAL OILS

CLOVE

EUGENIA CARYOPHYLLATA

warm • spicy • protecting

BUDS

STEAM DISTILLED

SOURCED
Madagascar

MAIN CONSTITUENTS
Eugenol
Eugenyl acetate
β-caryophyllene

TOP PROPERTIES
Antioxidant
Antiviral
Antifungal
Expectorant
Nervine
Anti-parasitic
Vermicide

FOUND IN
Cheer®
Harvest Spice
On Guard®
Passion®
Slim & Sassy®
Whisper®

SUBSTITUTE WITH
Cinnamon
DDR Prime®
On Guard®
Oregano
Thyme
Tulsi

SAFETY & RESEARCH
Dilution recommended. Possible skin sensitivity. To reduce potential liver stress when taken internally, take with Zendocrine®, helichrysum, cumin, green mandarin, geranium, or Roman chamomile. For research, see page 540.

TOP USES

ALZHEIMER'S & MEMORY LOSS
Dilute and apply diluted to bottoms of feet. Take in a capsule.

COLD & FLU, VIRAL OR RESPIRATORY INFECTION, LUPUS
Apply diluted to bottoms of feet and take in a capsule. Diffuse .

POOR CIRCULATION, LEG ULCERS, BLOOD CLOTS, HYPERTENSION
Apply highly diluted to spine, bottoms of feet, and/or area of concern.

TOOTH PAIN & CAVITIES
Dilute and apply to affected area to numb and ease pain.

THYROID ISSUES & SLOW METABOLISM
Apply diluted to base of big toe and/or take in a capsule.

CANDIDA & PARASITES, INTESTINAL INFECTION, HEPATITIS
Take in a capsule.

SMOKING ADDICTION
Take with black pepper under tongue.

NERVE INFLAMMATION, MUSCLE DEGENERATION, OSTEOPOROSIS, VISION PROBLEMS
Take in a capsule. Apply diluted to bottoms of feet.

WARTS, SKIN INFECTIONS, ULCERS, ATHLETE'S FOOT
Apply highly diluted to area of concern.

LYMPHOMA & LEUKEMIA
Take in a capsule.

EMOTIONAL BALANCE
Use aromatically and topically to go from Dominated → Supported.

Clove is one of the most powerful antioxidants on the planet. As a dried spice, it measures 300,000 on the ORAC scale and as an essential oil, measures over 1 million.

a sustaining
reconciling
alleviating

CONSOLE®

COMFORTING BLEND

MAIN INGREDIENTS
Frankincense
Patchouli
Ylang ylang
Laudanum
Amyris
Sandalwood
Rose
Osmanthus

SUBSTITUTE WITH
Calmer™
Deep Blue®
Frankincense
Geranium
Helichrysum
Myrrh
Patchouli
Rose
Ylang ylang

SAFETY
Not safe for internal use. Avoid exposure to sunlight or UV rays for up to 12 hours after application.

TOP USES

GRIEF & SADNESS, HEARTACHE
Diffuse or apply under nose and over heart.

EMOTIONAL RELEASE & REASSURANCE
Diffuse and apply under nose, over heart, and across forehead.

FEAR & EMOTIONAL PAIN RELIEF
Diffuse or apply under nose and to chest.

BRAIN IMPAIRMENT
Apply to forehead, back of neck, and toes.

SPIRITUAL CONNECTIVITY & MEDITATION
Apply to forehead and chest. Diffuse and/or inhale from cupped hands.

LOW LIBIDO
Diffuse or apply to abdomen.

SKIN REPAIR & ANTI-AGING
Apply to affected area and/or add to moisturizer for ease of application.

LUNG & BRONCHIAL INFECTION
Apply to chest, bottoms of feet, and/or diffuse.

URINARY INFECTION, EDEMA & CONSTIPATION
Apply over abdomen or to bottoms of feet.

IRREGULAR & RACING HEARTBEAT
Apply under nose and to chest.

= Aromatically = Topically = Internally

When the loss of something loved or treasured occurs, use this blend to provide comfort through times of sadness or grief and encourage to move forward in life.

COPAIBA

COPAIFERA OFFINCINALIS

RESIN

STEAM DISTILLED

SOURCED
Brazil

MAIN CONSTITUENTS
β-caryophyllene

TOP PROPERTIES
Anti-inflammatory
Antiarthritic
Analgesic
Antifungal
Antibacterial
Antioxidant
Anti-carcinoma
Carminative
Anti-microbial

FOUND IN
Adaptiv™
Rescuer™

SUBSTITUTE WITH
Adaptiv™
Align
Black pepper
Cedarwood
Deep Blue®
Deep Blue® Stick
Rescuer™
Tulsi
Ylang ylang

SAFETY & RESEARCH
Possible skin sensitivity. To reduce potential liver stress when taken internally, take with Zendocrine®, helichrysum, cumin, green mandarin, geranium, or Roman chamomile. For research, see page 540.

commanding
comforting
magnifying

TOP USES

PAIN & INFLAMMATION, ARTHRITIS, GOUT & MUSCLE CRAMPS
Diffuse, inhale from cupped hands, and/or apply to area of concern.

LIVER TOXICITY & ISSUES, CANCER
Take in a capsule or in water.

TENDONITIS, PLANTAR FASCIITIS & HEEL SPURS
Apply to area of concern.

RESPIRATORY & TONSIL ISSUES, SORE THROAT
Diffuse or inhale from cupped hands. Apply to throat area, under nose, and/or to chest.

DOPAMINE DEFICIENCY & ADDICTIONS
Take in a capsule.

BEDWETTING & INCONTINENCE
Apply to abdomen and/or take in a capsule.

COLITIS & INTESTINAL INFECTIONS
Apply to abdomen and/or take in a capsule.

CANCER & AUTOIMMUNE DISORDERS
Take in a capsule. Apply to bottoms of feet, and/or along spine. Combine with frankincense and Siberian fir.

FUNGAL, BACTERIAL & VIRAL INFECTIONS
Take in a capsule, apply to areas of concern, bottoms of feet, and/or along spine.

NAUSEA, VOMITING, ABDOMINAL PAIN & BLOATING
Take in a capsule and/or apply to abdomen.

DRY SKIN & HAIR, ACNE, ECZEMA, PSORIASIS
Apply to areas of concern or with skin and hair care products.

AGING SKIN & COLLAGEN PRODUCTION, WOUND HEALING
Apply to areas of concern.

HEADACHES & MIGRAINES
Apply to temples and forehead. Take in a capsule.

ENDOMETRIOSIS & PMS
Take in a capsule. Apply to lower abdomen.

HIGH BLOOD PRESSURE & ATHEROSCLEROSIS
Take in a capsule and apply over heart and on bottoms of feet.

ANXIETY & SLEEP ISSUES
Diffuse or inhale form cupped hands. Apply to bottoms of feet and/or under nose.

BLISTERS, BITES, BURNS, BRUISING & SPRAINS
Apply to areas of concern.

EMOTIONAL BALANCE
Use aromatically and topically to go from Plagued → Directed.

Copiaba is extracted from mature trees between 30-50 years in age found in the Amazon rain forest and considered one of the most anti-inflammatory substances on earth.

= Aromatically = Topically = Internally

ESSENTIAL OILS

CORIANDER

CORIANDRUM SATIVUM

calming

restoring

stimulating

SEEDS

STEAM DISTILLED

SOURCED
Russia

MAIN CONSTITUENTS
Linalool
α-pinene
γ-terpinene
Camphor

TOP PROPERTIES
Analgesic
Antioxidant
Anti-inflammatory
Digestive stimulant
Antibacterial
Antispasmodic

FOUND IN
Align
DigestZen®
Motivate®
Steady™

SUBSTITUTE WITH
AromaTouch®
Basil
Cardamom
Cilantro
DigestZen®
Magnolia

SAFETY & RESEARCH
For research, see page 540.

TOP USES

GAS & NAUSEA, COLIC, DIARRHEA, FOOD POSIONING
Apply to abdomen. Take in a capsule.

HIGH BLOOD SUGAR & DIABETES
Take in a capsule before meals.

ITCHY SKIN & RASHES, ACNE, CANDIDA, FUNGAL ISSUES
Apply to area of concern.

CARTILAGE & JOINT PAIN OR INJURY
Apply directly to area of concern.

NEUROPATHY
Apply to bottoms of feet. Take in a capsule.

LOSS OF APPETITE, ANOREXIA
Take in a capsule and/or inhale from cupped hands.

BODY ODOR
Take in a capsule. Apply diuted under arms.

LOW ENERGY & NERVOUS EXHAUSTION
Inhale from cupped hands. Apply to back of neck and/or bottoms of feet .

UPTIGHT & IRRITABLE, FEARFUL
Apply to bottoms of feet and/or inhale from cupped hands.

MEASLES, COLD & FLU
Take in a capsule. Diffuse . Apply to bottoms of feet.

EMOTIONAL BALANCE
Use aromatically and topically to go from Apprehensive → Participating.

Coriander comes from the seeds of the same plant as the cilantro herb. Cilantro essential oil comes from the leaves.

clearing • tonifying • energizing

CYPRESS

CUPRESSUS SEMPEVIRENS

TOP USES

RESTLESS LEG, POOR CIRCULATION & COLD EXTREMITIES
Apply Ⓣ to areas of concern.

POOR URINE FLOW, EDEMA & TOXEMIA
Apply Ⓣ to lower abdomen, legs, and/or bottoms of feet.

BED WETTING & INCONTINENCE
Apply Ⓣ over bladder area and/or bladder reflex point on foot.

VARICOSE VEINS & HEMORRHOIDS, BROKEN CAPILLARIES, NOSE BLEED
Apply Ⓣ to areas of concern.

STROKE & CONCUSSION
Apply Ⓣ to back of neck, forehead, and on bottoms of feet.

CELLULITE, LACK OF PERSPIRATION
Apply Ⓣ over areas of concern.

WHOOPING & SPASTIC COUGH, RESPIRATORY INFECTION, PLEURISY
Apply Ⓣ over lung area followed by a warm compress and/or to bottoms of feet. Diffuse Ⓐ.

PROSTATE & PANCREAS INSUFFICIENCIES, OVARIAN CYSTS
Apply Ⓣ over area of concern and/or on corresponding reflex point.

LIVER & GALLBLADDER CONGESTION
Apply Ⓣ to liver reflex point and over liver area.

IRREGULAR OR HEAVY PERIODS, ENDOMETRIOSIS & FIBROIDS, EPISIOTOMY
Apply Ⓣ to lower abdomen or over affected area.

BONE SPUR, BUNION, WEAK CONNECTIVE TISSUE, JOINT STIFFNESS
Apply Ⓣ to area of concern.

LOW ENERGY
Inhale Ⓐ from cupped hands and/or diffuse.

EMOTIONAL BALANCE
Use Ⓐ aromatically and Ⓣ topically to go from Stalled ⟶ Progressing.

Ⓐ = Aromatically Ⓣ = Topically Ⓘ = Internally

LEAVES

STEAM DISTILLED

SOURCED
Kenya

MAIN CONSTITUENTS
α-pinene
δ-3-carene

TOP PROPERTIES
Antibacterial
Antiseptic
Anti-rheumatic
Stimulant
Vasoconstrictor
Tonifying

FOUND IN
AromaTouch®
Midnight Forest
Northern Escape

SUBSTITUTE WITH
AromaTouch®
Douglas fir
Hinoki
Juniper berry
Neroli
Northern Escape
Siberian fir

SAFETY & RESEARCH
Not safe for internal use.
For research, see page 540.

The ancient Greeks loved cypress so much they dedicated it to one of their gods, Pluto.

ESSENTIAL OILS

DDR PRIME®

CELLULAR COMPLEX BLEND

regenerating • correcting • repairing

MAIN INGREDIENTS
Frankincense
Wild orange
Litsea
Thyme
Clove
Summer savory
Niaouli
Lemongrass

SUBSTITUTE WITH
Air-X™
Clove
Frankincense
Lemongrass
Pink pepper
Thyme
Tulsi
Wild orange

SAFETY
Dilution recommended. Possible skin sensitivity. Avoid exposure to sunlight or UV rays for up to 12 hours after application.

TOP USES

CANCER & TUMORS
Take in a capsule. Apply diluted to back of neck, along spine, and/or on bottoms of feet.

LOW PROGESTERONE, ESTROGEN & THYROID ISSUES
Take in a capsule and/or apply to bottoms of feet.

CANDIDA & FUNGAL ISSUES
Apply to bottoms of feet and/or take in a capsule.

PAIN & INFLAMMATION
Apply diluted to area of concern.

NERVE DAMAGE
Apply diluted to affected area. Take in a capsule.

AUTOIMMUNE DISORDERS
Take in a capsule. Apply diluted to back of neck, along spine, and/or on bottoms of feet.

SEIZURES & BRAIN ISSUES, ALZHEIMER'S, FREE RADICALS
Apply diluted to back of neck, along spine, and/or on bottoms of feet. Take in a capsule.

BREAST ISSUES
Apply diluted to breasts and/or bottoms of feet. Take in a capsule.

HOT FLASHES & NIGHT SWEATS
Apply to bottoms of feet and/or take in a capsule.

CELLULAR TOXICITY & VIRUSES
Apply to bottoms of feet. Take in a capsule.

Cellular damage from free radicals is an underlying contributor to many of today's diseases. This powerful antioxidant blend helps promote cellular health and protect long-term wellness.

cooling
warming
soothing

DEEP BLUE®

SOOTHING BLEND

MAIN INGREDIENTS
Wintergreen
Camphor
Peppermint
Ylang ylang
Helichrysum
Blue tansy
Blue chamomile
Osmanthus

SUBSTITUTE WITH
Blue Tansy
Copaiba
Helichrysum
PastTense®
Peppermint
Rescuer™
Wintergreen

SAFETY
Not safe for internal use.
Possible skin sensitivity.

TOP USES

MUSCLE, BACK & JOINT PAIN
Apply (topically) to areas of discomfort.

ARTHRITIS & RHEUMATISM, GOUT
Apply (topically) to areas of discomfort.

PRE- & POST-WORKOUT
Apply (topically) to muscles, joints, and, already stressed areas before and/or after activity.

NEUROPATHY & CARPAL TUNNEL
Apply (topically) to areas of discomfort.

BRUISING & BROKEN BONES
Apply (topically) to affected area to reduce inflammation and scar tissue.

FIBROMYALGIA & LUPUS
Apply (topically) to areas of concern.

WHIPLASH & TENSE, STRAINED, OR SPRAINED MUSCLES
Apply (topically) to areas of discomfort.

HEADACHE & NECK PAIN
Apply (topically) to back of neck, shoulders, and temples.

GROWING PAINS
Apply (topically) to affected area.

This blend naturally helps reduce pain and inflammation and makes a great toxin-free substitute for synthetically derived ointments and creams.

= Aromatically = Topically = Internally

ESSENTIAL OILS

DIGESTZEN®

DIGESTION BLEND

stimulating
moving
settling

MAIN INGREDIENTS
Peppermint
Coriander
Ginger
Caraway
Cardamom
Fennel
Anise

Travelers of all kinds reach for DigestZen® to deal with motion sickness, food poisoning, queasiness, stomach upset, and the heat. Recently, emerging research led to a reformulation of this blend to provide better efficacy, aroma, and flavor. New research inspired cardamom to be added and ginger, coriander, and peppermint to play a more prominent role in this blend.

TOP USES

BLOATING, GAS, HEARTBURN, NAUSEA & INDIGESTION
Apply over abdomen and take in a capsule.

REFLUX & COLIC
Take in water or in a capsule. Apply diluted to an infant's abdomen or bottoms of feet.

DRY OR SORE THROAT
Drop directly onto back of throat.

MORNING SICKNESS & HEARTBURN
Apply to chest, pulse points, abdomen, and/or take in a glass of water.

MOTION & TRAVEL SICKNESS
Inhale or apply under nose, and/or drink in water or drop under tongue.

COLITIS & IRRITABLE BOWEL
Take in a capsule, water, and/or massage onto abdomen.

DIARRHEA & CONSTIPATION
Take in a capsule or water until symptoms subside.

CROHN'S DISEASE & CHRONIC FATIGUE
Take in a capsule and/or rub on abdomen.

FOOD POISONING
Take in a capsule or water frequently until symptoms subside. Add tea tree.

COUGH & SINUS CONGESTION
Apply diluted to navel and over bridge of nose and/or drink in water.

SUBSTITUTE WITH
Cardamom
Coriander
Fennel
Ginger
Peppermint
Tamer™

SAFETY
Possible skin sensitivity. Dilute for sensitive skin.

detoxing
disinfecting
cleansing

DILL

ANETHUM GRAVEOLENS

WHOLE PLANT

STEAM DISTILLED

SOURCED
India

MAIN CONSTITUENT
Limonene
Carvone
α-phellandrene

TOP PROPERTIES
Antispasmodic
Expectorant
Stimulant
Galactagogue
Carminative
Emmenagogue
Hypertensive
Antibacterial

SUBSTITUTE WITH
Cardamom
Celery seed
DigestZen®
Fennel
Peppermint
Spearmint

SAFETY & RESEARCH
Not safe for internal use.
For research, see page 540.

Used extensively in soft drinks and alcoholic beverages.

TOP USES

MUSCLE SPASMS
Apply Ⓣ to calm muscles.

NERVOUSNESS
Inhale Ⓐ from cupped hands or apply Ⓣ under nose or back of neck with Roman chamomile to calm.

SUGAR ADDICTION & PANCREAS ISSUES
Take Ⓘ in a capsule.

LOW BREAST MILK SUPPLY
Apply Ⓣ to chest and/or take Ⓘ in a capsule.

DETOX & ELECTROLYTE BALANCE
Take Ⓘ in a capsule as part of a detox program.

CHOLESTEROL & HIGH BLOOD PRESSURE
Take Ⓘ in a capsule.

RESPIRATORY ISSUES
Apply Ⓣ diluted to chest and/or take Ⓘ in a capsule. Diffuse Ⓐ.

GAS, BLOATING & INDIGESTION
Take Ⓘ in a capsule or in water.

LACK OF MENSTRUATION
Apply Ⓣ diluted over abdomen.

COLIC
Apply Ⓣ diluted to bottoms of feet or abdomen.
Apply Ⓣ highly diluted for an infant.

EMOTIONAL BALANCE
Use Ⓐ aromatically and Ⓣ topically to go from Avoiding → Intentional.

Ⓐ = Aromatically Ⓣ = Topically Ⓘ = Internally

DOUGLAS FIR

PSEUDOTSUGA MENZIESII

cleansing
promoting
grounding

NEEDLES & BRANCHES

STEAM DISTILLED

SOURCED
New Zealand

MAIN CONSTITUENTS
β-pinene
α-pinene
δ-3-carene
Sabinene

TOP PROPERTIES
Antioxidant
Analgesic
Antimicrobial
Antiseptic
Anticatarrhal
Astringent
Diuretic
Expectorant
Laxative
Sedative
Stimulant
Tonic

FOUND IN
Holiday Peace

SUBSTITUTE WITH
Cypress
Frankincense
Northern Escape
Pink pepper
Siberian fir
Yarrow|Pom

SAFETY
Not safe for internal use.
For research, see page 540.

TOP USES

MENTAL FOG & LOW ENERGY
Apply to temples and forehead or diffuse to clear mind and revive enthusiasm.

DEPRESSION & TENSION
Apply to temples, forehead, and back of neck or diffuse to relax and ground.

CONGESTION & SINUS ISSUES
Apply to chest or bridge of nose.

RESPIRATORY INFECTION & COUGH
Apply to throat, chest and/or diffuse.

MUSCLE & JOINT SORENESS
Apply with wintergreen to affected area.

RHEUMATIC & ARTHRITIC CONDITIONS
Apply to affected areas.

CONSTIPATION
Apply diluted to abdomen.

SKIN IRRITATIONS & CUTS
Apply diluted to affected areas.

CELLULITE & SKIN CLEANSING
Apply diluted with grapefruit onto areas of concern.

EMOTIONAL BALANCE
Use aromatically and topically to go from Upset → Renewed.

In 1859, Douglas fir trees were introduced to New Zealand to produce needed timber. The trees thrived, so much that they invaded huge areas of land and prevented indigenous plant growth. In order to reclaim farmland and return balance to the native ecosystem, harvesting Douglas Fir is imperative to preventing the further spread of this invasive species.

happy • citrus • sweet

ELEVATION

JOYFUL BLEND

TOP USES

ELEVATE MOOD & MIND
Diffuse (A) or inhale. Apply (T) under nose, on pulse points, back of neck, and/or forehead.

DEPRESSION & MOOD DISORDERS
Diffuse (A) or inhale. Apply (T) to back of neck, on forehead, and over heart.

ENERGIZE & REFRESH
Diffuse (A) and inhale from cupped hands. Apply (T) under nose, across forhead, and/or on neck and chest.

STRESS & ANXIETY
Apply (T) under nose on ears, back of neck and inhale (A) from cupped hands or diffuse.

GRIEF & SORROW
Diffuse (A) and inhale. Apply (T) over heart and on back of neck.

STIMULATE & UPLIFT
Apply (T) under nose, on back of neck, forehead, and/or inhale (A) from cupped hands or diffuse.

BODY ODOR
Apply (T) as a deodorizing body spray or swipe over armpit area prior to applying deodorant.

MAIN INGREDIENTS
Lavandin
Tangerine
Lavender
Amyris
Clary sage
Hawaiian sandalwood
Ylang ylang
Ho wood
Osmanthus
Lemon myrtle
Melissa

SUBSTITUTE WITH
Arise
Beautiful
Cheer®
Citrus Bloom™
Melissa

SAFETY
Not safe for internal use. Avoid exposure to sunlight or UV rays for up to 12 hours after application.

Use this blend to uplift both mood and mind and invite more joyful states of being.

(A) = Aromatically (T) = Topically (I) = Internally

EUCALYPTUS

EUCALYPTUS RADIATA

LEAVES

STEAM DISTILLED

SOURCED
Australia

MAIN CONSTITUENTS
1,8-cineole (Eucalyptol)
α-terpineol

TOP PROPERTIES
Antiviral
Antibacterial
Expectorant
Analgesic
Insecticidal
Hypotensive
Disinfectant
Catalyst

FOUND IN
Abōde™
Breathe®
Harvest Spice
HD Clear®
On Guard®

SUBSTITUTE WITH
Abōde™
Breathe®
Cardamom
Laurel leaf
Ravintsara
Rosemary

SAFETY
Not safe for internal use.
Dilution recommended.
Possible skin sensitivity.
For research, see page 540.

enlivening

fresh

clearing

TOP USES

CONGESTION, COUGH, BRONCHITIS, PNEUMONIA, ASTHMA, SINUSITIS
Apply Ⓣ to chest, bridge of nose, forehead, and bottoms of feet. Diffuse Ⓐ or inhale from cupped hands.

SHINGLES, MALARIA, COLD & FLU, HERPES
Apply Ⓣ to bottoms of feet or spine. Diffuse Ⓐ.

LICE & PARASITES
Apply Ⓣ to affected areas, scalp, or bottoms of feet.

FEVER & HEAT SENSITIVITY
Apply Ⓣ down the spine for cooling effect.

BITES, WOUNDS & CUTS, BLISTERS
Apply Ⓣ to area of concern.

HYPOGLYCEMIA, HIGH BLOOD PRESSURE & POOR CIRCULATION
Apply Ⓣ to bottoms of feet.

EARACHES & SORE THROAT
Dilute and apply Ⓣ around and below ear or on neck.

MENTAL SLUGGISHNESS & HEADACHES
Inhale Ⓐ with rosemary from cupped hands.

KIDNEY STONES & BLADDER ISSUES
Gently massage Ⓣ over kidney area or lower abdomen.

BREAST ISSUES & CANCER, FIBROIDS, ENDOMETRIOSIS
Dilute and massage Ⓣ into breast tissues, and/or on bottoms of feet.

MUSCLE FATIGUE & NERVE INFLAMMATION
Dilute and massage Ⓣ into affected areas.

CELLULITE & EDEMA, BODY ODOR
Apply Ⓣ diluted to area of concern or under arms.

CLEANING DISINFECTANT & DUST MITES
Add 10-15 drops Ⓣ to a glass spray bottle of water and use to clean or defer.

EMOTIONAL BALANCE
Use Ⓐ aromatically and Ⓣ topically to go from Congested ⟶ Stimulated.

Eucalyptus was widely used in World War I to control infections and influenza.

FENNEL

FOENICULUM VULGARE

strong • purifying • supporting

SEEDS

STEAM DISTILLED

SOURCED
Egypt

MAIN CONSTITUENTS
Trans-Anethole
α-pinene
Limonene

TOP PROPERTIES
Antispasmodic
Emmenagogue
Galactagogue
Diuretic
Mucolytic
Digestive
Anti-inflammatory

FOUND IN
ClaryCalm®
DigestZen®

SUBSTITUTE WITH
Basil
Cardamom
DigestZen®

SAFETY & RESEARCH
Dilution recommended. Possible skin sensitivity. Caution during pregnancy and with children under 5 years old. Not for use with epileptics. For research, see page 540.

TOP USES

NAUSEA, COLIC & FLATULENCE, VOMITING
Take in a capsule or water. Apply. Apply to abdomen. Dilute for infant.

MENSTRUAL ISSUES & PMS
Take in a capsule and/or apply to lower abdomen.

MENOPAUSE & PREMENOPAUSE
Take in a capsule. Apply to lower abdomen.

CRAMPS & SPASMS, LACK OF UTERUS TONE
Dilute and rub onto area of need.

LOW BREAST MILK SUPPLY
Take in a capsule or water.

OVERLY ACIDIC, TOXICITY, KIDNEY STONES, GOUT
Take in a capsule or glass of water.

EDEMA & FLUID RETENTION, CYSTITIS
Combine with grapefruit and massage over affected areas. Take in a capsule.

COUGH & CONGESTION, EARACHES
Apply diluted to chest, throat, or around ears.

INTESTINAL PARASITES & SLUGGISH BOWELS
Take with lemon in a capsule.

BLOOD SUGAR IMBALANCE & SLOW METABOLISM
Take in a capsule or add to glass of water.

HUNGER PAINS & SUGAR CRAVINGS
Take under or drop on tongue or sip in water.

STROKE & BLOOD CLOTS
Take in a capsule. Massage on back of neck.

EMOTIONAL BALANCE
Use aromatically and topically to go from Unproductive → Flourishing.

Ancient Roman warriors used fennel because it was believed it gave them strength during battle.

relieve

release

liberate

FORGIVE®

RENEWING BLEND

TOP USES

LACK OF FORGIVENESS, REPRESSED EMOTIONS, HOLDING A GRUDGE
Apply to temples, back of neck, over heart, and/or diffuse.

ANGER, FRUSTRATION, IRRITABILITY, EXCESSIVE JUDGMENT, PUNISHING
Diffuse or inhale. Apply under nose, across forehead, on back of neck, and/or over heart.

SPIRITUAL & EMOTIONAL TOXICITY HELD IN BODY TISSUES
Diffuse and apply under nose and/or to chest. Apply to affected area.

ADDICTIONS & UNHEALTHY ATTACHMENTS
Diffuse and apply to pulse points and/or over heart.

ULCER & LIVER ISSUES
Apply over upper abdomen and/or liver area.

SKIN INFECTION & DAMAGE
Apply to affected areas. Dilute if needed.

CIRCULATION ISSUES
Apply to chest and/or bottoms of feet.

FUNGUS & PARASITES
Apply to bottoms of feet or affected areas.

HAIR LOSS, PROSTATE ISSUES & LOW SEX DRIVE
Apply to affected areas, lower abdomen, and/or bottoms of feet.

INCONTINENCE
Apply over lower abdomen or bottoms of feet and over bladder reflex points.

MAIN INGREDIENTS
Spruce
Bergamot
Juniper berry
Myrrh
Arborvitae
Nootka
Thyme
Citronella

SUBSTITUTE WITH
Arborvitae
Black spruce
Holiday Peace
Northern Escape
Thyme

SAFETY
Not safe for internal use. Dilution recommended. Possible skin sensitivity. Avoid exposure to sunlight or UV rays for up to 12 hours after application.

Whether feeling stubborn, attached, guilty, bitter, angry, or judgmental, this blend invites one to let go, trust the process of life, and become renewed.

= Aromatically = Topically = Internally

restoring

repairing

regenerating

TOP USES

CANCER & TUMORS, CELLULAR & IMMUNE HEALTH
Take in capsule or under tongue with oil(s) that target area of need. Massage over affected area.

SEIZURES & TRAUMA, CONCUSSION
Drop under the tongue and apply along hairline.

ALZHEIMER'S, DEMENTIA, PARKINSON'S & BRAIN INJURY, LACK OF MOTOR CONTROL
Use or apply under nose and on back of neck. Diffuse or inhale from cupped hands.

WOUNDS, WRINKLES, SKIN ULCERS, BOILS, MOLES
Apply to affected areas.

SCARS & STRETCH MARKS
Combine with myrrh or sandalwood and apply .

SCIATICA, BACK PAIN & HEADACHES, MIGRAINES
Apply over affected area and/or take in a capsule.

DEPRESSION & ANXIETY, POSPARTUM
Diffuse . Drop under tongue or press onto roof of mouth. Apply over heart and on back of neck.

LIVER TOXICITY, JAUNDICE, HEPATITIS, CIRRHOSIS
Take in a capsule. Apply to abdomen and/or on bottoms of feet over organ reflex points.

AUTOIMMUNE DISORDERS
Take in a capsule. Apply to bottoms of feet and over spleen.

CONSTRICTED BREATHING, ALLERGIES, LARYNGITIS
Diffuse and/or inhale . Apply to chest and throat. Take in a capsule.

BREAST CANCER PREVENTION & FIBROCYSTIC BREASTS
Apply diluted to breast tissue twice per day for 30 days, 2-4 times per year. Take in a capsule.

VANGINITIS & GENITAL WARTS, HEAVY MENSTRUATION
Apply to tip of tampon and insert or to area of concern. Take in a capsule.

PROLAPSED UTERUS, FIBROIDS, MISCARRIAGE RECOVERY
Apply to lower abdomen.

WARTS & BITES
Apply to affected area.

MEDITATION, PRAYER & FOCUS
Apply under nose, or back of neck, and diffuse .

EMOTIONAL BALANCE
Use aromatically and topically to go from Separated → Unified.

Nearly all religions have used frankincense in their spiritual practices including ancient Egyptians, Greeks, Romans, Christians, Jews, Muslims, Hindus, and Buddhists.

= Aromatically = Topically = Internally

FRANKINCENSE

BOSWELLIA FREREANA

RESIN

STEAM DISTILLED

SOURCED
Oman/Somalia

MAIN CONSTITUENTS
α-pinene
Limonene
α-thujene

TOP PROPERTIES
Immunostimulant
Anticancer
Anti-inflammatory
Antidepressant
Restorative

FOUND IN
Air-X™
Anchor
Balance®
Console®
DDR Prime®
Holiday Joy
Holiday Peace
Hope®
Hygge™
Immortelle
InTune®
Midnigh Forest
Northern Escape
PastTense®
Stronger™

SUBSTITUTE WITH
Anchor
Balance®
DDR Prime®
Douglas fir
Ginger
Immortelle
InTune®
Myrrh
Pink Pepper
Siberian fir
Spikenard
Stronger™
Turmeric

SAFETY & RESEARCH
Not safe for internal use. For research, see page 540.

GERANIUM

PELARGONIUM GRAVEOLENS

strengthening
releasing
stabilizing

A powerful floral oil often referred to as the "poor man's rose." No rose? Reach for geranium!

WHOLE PLANT

STEAM DISTILLED

SOURCED
Madagascar

MAIN CONSTITUENTS
Citronellol
Citronellyl formate
Geraniol
Guaiadene
Menthone

TOP PROPERTIES
Hemostatic
Detoxifier
Regenerative
Anti-allergenic
Antihemorrhagic
Antitoxic

FOUND IN
Align
ClaryCalm®
HD Clear®
TerraShield®
Zendocrine®

SUBSTITUTE WITH
ClaryCalm®
Console®
Davana
HD Clear®
Helichrysum
Lavender
Neroli
Rose
Zendocrine®

SAFETY & RESEARCH
Dilution recommended.
Possible skin sensitivity.
For research, see page 540.

ESSENTIAL OILS

TOP USES

BLOOD TOXICITY, BLEEDING, VARICOSE VEINS & BROKEN CAPILLARIES
Take in a capsule. Apply to troubled areas.

LIVER & GALLBLADDER ISSUES, GALLSTONES, BILE DUCT OBSTRUCTION
Take in a capsule.

HORMONE IMBALANCE, ADRENAL FATIGUE, EXCESSIVE EMOTIONALITY
Diffuse or inhale and take in a capsule

ENDOMETRIOSIS, IRREGULAR OR PROLONGED MENSTRUATION, PMS, PELVIC PAIN, STERILITY
Take in a capsule. Apply to lower abdomen and reflex points.

BLOOD SUGAR IMBALANCE, PANCREAS ISSUES
Take in a capsule. Apply to bottoms of feet.

CUTS & WOUNDS, BURNS, SCARS
Apply to area of concern.

WEAK, BROKEN OR WOUNDED HEART
Diffuse or inhale. Apply over heart.

NERVE PAIN & DEGENERATION, SPINAL CALCIFICATION, OSTEOPOROSIS
Apply to affected area and/or bottoms of feet. Take in a capsule.

ECZEMA, CELLULITIS, DERMATITIS, IMPETIGO, RINGWORM
Apply to affected area. Take in a capsule.

DRY OR OILY HAIR & SKIN
Apply to scalp or troubled skin.

BREAST TENDERNESS, ENGORGEMENT, MISCARRIAGE RECOVERY
Apply diluted to breast area, lower abdomen, and/or take in a capsule.

EMOTIONAL BALANCE
Use aromatically and topically to go from Neglected → Mended.

warming

accelerating

stimulating

GINGER

ZINGIBER OFFICINALE

ROOT

STEAM DISTILLED

SOURCED
Kenya

MAIN CONSTITUENT
α-zingiberene
β-sesquiphellandrene

TOP PROPERTIES
Anti-inflammatory
Antispasmodic
Digestive stimulant
Laxative
Analgesic
Stimulant
Decongestant
Neurotonic

FOUND IN
Cheer®
DigestZen®
Passion®
Slim & Sassy®
Tamer™

SUBSTITUTE WITH
Cedarwood
DigestZen®
Frankincense
Slim & Sassy®
Tamer™
Turmeric

SAFETY & RESEARCH
Dilution recommended.
Possible skin sensitivity.
For research, see page 540.

Ginger has been used as a medicinal herb for centuries.

TOP USES

NAUSEA, INDIGESTION, VOMITING, MORNING SICKNESS, LOSS OF APPETITE, ANOREXIA
Diffuse Ⓐ. Take Ⓘ in a glass of water or capsule. Apply Ⓣ diluted to abdomen and/or bottoms of feet.

MOTION SICKNESS & VERTIGO
Inhale Ⓐ from cupped hands and/or take Ⓘ in a capsule.

SPASMS, CRAMPS & SORE MUSCLES, SPRAIN
Dilute and apply Ⓣ to area of discomfort.

CONSTIPATION, DIARRHEA & INTESTINAL CRAMPS
Apply Ⓣ diluted over abdomen or take Ⓘ in a glass of warm water or capsule.

HEAD CONGESTION, SORE THROAT & LARYNGITIS, TONSILITIS
Dilute and apply Ⓣ on chest, forehead, and/or throat area. Diffuse Ⓐ. Take Ⓘ with lemon or gargle.

POOR CIRCULATION & COLD EXTREMITIES, WEAK HEART
Apply Ⓣ diluted to areas of concern and/or bottoms of feet.

MEMORY & BRAIN ISSUES, NEUROTRANSMITTER DEFICIENCIES
Inhale Ⓐ from cupped hands and/or take Ⓘ in a capsule.

HEARTBURN & REFLUX
Take Ⓘ in a capsule or under tongue as often as needed.

HORMONE & BLOOD SUGAR IMBALANCES
Take Ⓘ in a capsule. Apply Ⓣ to bottoms of feet.

COLD & FLU, CHILLS & FEVER, SCURVY
Take Ⓘ in a capsule. Apply Ⓣ to bottoms of feet.

BROKEN BONES, JOINT OR MUSCLE PAIN
Dilute Ⓣ and apply to affected areas.

DEBILITY & NERVOUS EXHAUSTION
Take Ⓘ in a capsule and/or apply Ⓣ diluted to bottoms of feet.

LOW SEX DRIVE & IMPOTENCE
Apply Ⓣ highly diluted to warm and stimulate areas of concern.

ALCOHOL ADDICTION, POWERLESSNESS
Take Ⓘ in a capsule. Diffuse Ⓐ with other related oils.

EMOTIONAL BALANCE
Use Ⓐ aromatically and Ⓣ topically to go from Apathetic → Activated.

Ⓐ = Aromatically Ⓣ = Topically Ⓘ = Internally

GRAPEFRUIT

CITRUS X PARADISI

RIND

COLD PRESSED

SOURCED
USA

MAIN CONSTITUENTS
d-limonene

TOP PROPERTIES
- Diuretic
- Antioxidant
- Antiseptic
- Astringent
- Antitoxic
- Purifier
- Expectorant

FOUND IN
- Air-X™
- Arise
- AromaTouch®
- Citrus Bliss®
- Citrus Bloom™
- Holiday Peace
- Slim & Sassy®

SUBSTITUTE WITH
- Citrus Bliss®
- Green mandarin
- Tangerine
- Wild orange

SAFETY & RESEARCH
Avoid exposure to sunlight or UV rays for up to 12 hours after application. For research, see page 540.

TOP USES

WEIGHT LOSS & OBESITY
Take in water or a capsule.

FOOD ADDICTIONS & SUGAR CRAVINGS, ANOREXIA & BULIMIA
Diffuse . Take in a capsule or sip in water.

UTERINE ISSUES, LACK OF PROGESTERONE, MISCARRIAGE PREVENTION
Take in a capsule. Apply diluted to area of concern or reflex points.

BREAST ISSUES
Apply to breast area and take in a capsule. Use with pink pepper.

CANCER & CELLULAR HEALTH
Take in a capsule.

DETOXIFICATION & CELLULITE, SAGGING SKIN
Drink in water or take in a capsule. Apply diluted to problem areas and/or bottoms of feet.

GALLSTONES & GALLBLADDER SUPPORT
Take with geranium in a capsule.

LYMPHATIC & KIDNEY TOXICITY, EDEMA
Take in water. Apply diluted over lymph nodes, kidney area, or bottoms of feet.

HEADACHES & MIGRAINES, LIVER & BLOOD TOXICITY
Apply over liver and take in a capsule.

HANGOVER & JET LAG
Take in a capsule.

ADRENAL FATIGUE & NERVOUS EXHAUSTION
Apply diluted with basil over adrenal area, to bottoms of feet or back of neck. Take in a capsule.

OILY SKIN & ACNE, HAIRLOSS
Apply to areas of concern or add to shampoo.

EMOTIONAL BALANCE
Use aromatically and topically to go from Divided ⟶ Validate.

Grapefruit juice chemically differs from its essential oil counterpart when cold-pressed from the rind. Therefore, experts suggest reasonable use of the oil is not likely to cause major interaction with blood pressure medications.

= Aromatically = Topically = Internally

TOP USES

DEPRESSED, AGITATED, AFRAID NERVOUS, INNER CHILD WORK
Take under tongue. Apply to pulse points and/or inhale from cupped hands or diffuse.

SITUATIONAL ANXIETY
Apply under nose, diffuse or inhale from cupped hands.

GAS, POOR DIGESTION, CONSTIPATION, HEARTBURN & ULCERS
Apply over area of concern and/or take in water or under tongue.

POOR CIRCULATION, CONGESTED LYMPH, WATER RETENTION & EDEMA
Take with black pepper under tongue or in a capsule.

LIVER & KIDNEY TOXICITY, SLUGGISH OR OBSTRUCTED BILE FLOW
Take with juniper berry or lemon in a capsule.

ACNE, OILY SKIN, WOUNDS, SCARS
Combine with skin care products and apply to areas of concern.

IMBALANCED BLOOD SUGAR, FAT METABOLISM & CHOLESTEROL
Take daily in a capsule.

COUGH & RESPIRATORY ISSUES, DAIRY INTOLERANCE
Diffuse with spearmint. Apply to chest and back. Take under tongue with pink pepper.

SKIN & BREAST CANCER
Take in a capsule or under tongue. Apply to areas of concern.

LACK OF MENTAL ENERGY OR ALERTNESS, DEMENTIA
Apply to palms of hands, rub together, inhale deeply, then rub on base of neck. Diffuse .

WRINKLES, FINE LINES & AGE SPOTS, STRETCH MARKS
Add to skin care products and apply to areas of concern.

FLAVORING & NATURAL FOOD PRESERVATIVE
Add to dishes, frostings, smoothies, or cut fruit.

PERFUME
Apply with neroli to pulse points.

ODOR & SURFACE CLEANING
Diffuse or spritz, diluted in water.

EMOTIONAL BALANCE
Use aromatically and topically to go from Distressed → Carefree.

The only citrus oil without photosensitivity warning, this oil is safe to apply before going in the sun. This fruit was offered as a gift to rulers in China as a sign of respect and represented abundance and happiness during Chinese New Year celebrations.

= Aromatically = Topically = Internally

GREEN MANDARIN

CITRUS NOBILIS

RIND OF UNRIPE FRUIT

COLD PRESSED

SOURCED
Brazil

MAIN CONSTITUENTS
Limonene
γ-Terpinene

TOP PROPERTIES
Uplifting
Refreshing
Digestive stimulant
Cleanser
Expectorant
Calming

FOUND IN
Citrus Bliss®

SUBSTITUTE WITH
Celery seed
Grapefruit
Tangerine
Wild orange

SAFETY & RESEARCH
For research, see page 540.

HARVEST SPICE

GATHERING BLEND

heartwarming
protecting
nestling

MAIN INGREDIENTS
Cinnamon bark
Clove
Eucalyptus
Cedarwood
Cassia
Nutmeg

This special blend of spices, combined with leaves and wood, has mastered the capacity to warm the soul and protect the body, while suggesting to the mind to be gathered in as the season begins to change.

TOP USES

WARM & INVITE, SAFEGUARD
Diffuse Ⓐ and/or apply Ⓣ to pulse points, back of neck, along spine, and/or bottoms of feet.

DELIGHT & SNUGGLE
Diffuse Ⓐ and/or drop onto seasonal décor or potpourri as a passive diffuser. Apply Ⓣ diluted on bottoms of feet prior to covering with warm socks or wrapping up in a blanket.

UPLIFT & STIMULATE MIND, MOOD & BODY
Apply Ⓣ under nose, back of neck, and/or inhale Ⓐ from cupped hands.

IMMUNE BOOST, COLD & FLU PREVENTION
Diffuse Ⓐ and/or apply Ⓣ to bottoms of feet, back of neck, and/or along the spine.

COLD EXTREMITIES & POOR CIRCULATION, CHILLS
Apply Ⓣ diluted to extremities, bottoms of feet, and/or along spine.

SEASONAL AFFECTIVE DISORDER & BLUES, DEPRESSION
Diffuse Ⓐ and/or inhale from cupped hands. Apply Ⓣ to bottoms of feet and base of skull.

EMOTIONAL BALANCE
Use Ⓐ aromatically and Ⓣ topically to go from Frigid → Warmed.

SUBSTITUTE WITH
Brave™
Cheer®
Holiday Joy
On Guard®
Passion®
Tulsi

SAFETY
Not safe for internal use.
Dilution recommended.
Possible skin sensitivity.

cleansing

clearing

calming

HD CLEAR®

SKIN CLEARING BLEND

MAIN INGREDIENTS

Black cumin
Ho wood
Tea tree
Litsea
Eucalyptus
Geranium

SUBSTITUTE WITH

Abōde™
Air-X™
DDR Prime®
Forgive®
Geranium
Litsea
Tea tree

SAFETY

Not safe for internal use.
Possible skin sensitivity.

TOP USES

ACNE & PIMPLES
Apply to areas of concern.

OILY SKIN & OVERACTIVE SEBACEOUS GLANDS
Apply to areas of concern.

SKIN BLEMISHES & IRRITATIONS
Apply to areas of concern.

DERMATITIS & ECZEMA
Apply to areas of concern.

FUNGAL & BACTERIAL ISSUES
Apply to areas of concern.

This blend is cleansing and calming to the skin. It helps reduce two components that encourage acne: bacteria and inflammation.

ESSENTIAL OILS

HELICHRYSUM

HELICHRYSUM ITALICUM

FLOWERS

STEAM DISTILLED

SOURCED
Corsica,
Albania

MAIN CONSTITUENT
Neryl acetate
α-pinene
γ-curcumene

TOP PROPERTIES
Antispasmodic
Anticatarrhal
Neuroprotective
Neurotonic
Vasoconstrictor
Hemostatic
Nervine
Analgesic

FOUND IN
Deep Blue®
Immortelle

SUBSTITUTE WITH
Deep Blue®
Geranium
Immortelle
Ravintsara
Yarrow|Pom

SAFETY & RESEARCH
For research, see page 540.

TOP USES

NOSEBLEEDS, BLEEDING & HEMORRHAGING, BROKEN CAPILLARIES, PHLEBITIS, HEMATOMA, STROKE
Apply to area of concern. Take in a capsule.

LIVER OR PANCREAS CONGESTION & OBSTRUCTED BILE DUCT, GALL BLADDER INFECTION, HEAVY METAL & BLOOD TOXICITY, HIGH OR LOW CHOLESTEROL
Take in a capsule or under tongue.

SCARS, WOUNDS & BRUISING, BURNS
Apply to area of concern.

ALCOHOL ADDICTION & CIRRHOSIS
Apply to abdomen and over liver area.

VARICOSE VEINS & HEMORRHOIDS
Massage with cypress into affected areas.

WRINKLES & STRETCH MARKS, AGE SPOTS
Apply to areas of concern.

BONE BRUISING, SCIATICA, TENNIS ELBOW, NERVE DAMAGE
Apply to area of concern.

SHOCK, ANGER & DEEP EMOTIONAL WOUNDS
Diffuse and apply under nose and over heart. Dilute or blend as desired.

SINUS INFECTION & HEADACHE, LOSS OF TASTE, CONSTRICTED BREATHING, SWOLLEN EYES
Apply to forehead, swab nostrils. Diffuse.

PSORIASIS & ECZEMA, BOILS, FIBROIDS, SKIN ISSUES, REDNESS & DISCOLORATION
Apply to area of concern. Take in a capsule.

JOINT & BACK PAIN, INFLAMMATION
Apply to area of discomfort.

TINNITIS & EARACHE, VERTIGO
Apply behind the ears or back of neck.

VIRUSES, HERPES, STAPH, HIV/AIDS, SPLEEN ISSUES
Take in a capsule or under tongue.

EMOTIONAL BALANCE
Use aromatically and topically to go from Wounded → Released.

This precious oil is often hand-picked on the island of Corsica and commonly referred to as "liquid stitches."

= Aromatically = Topically = Internally

dissipating • harmonizing • restoring

HINOKI

CHAMAECYPARIS OBTUSA

WOOD/BARK

STEAM DISTILLED

SOURCED
Japan

MAIN CONSTITUENTS
α-pinene
Δ-cadinene
Δ-amorphene
α-muurolene

TOP PROPERTIES
Anti-inflammatory
Antifungal
Grounding
Deodorant
Antibacterial
Uplifting
Stimulant

FOUND IN
Northern Escape

SUBSTITUTE WITH
Amavi®
Black pepper
Black spruce
Cypress
Douglas fir
Frankincense
Juniper berry
Northern Escape
Siberian fir

SAFETY & RESEARCH
Not safe for internal use.
For research, see page 540.

TOP USES

OVERACTIVE MIND, OVERSTIMULATED OR FRAZZLED NERVES
Diffuse or inhale deeply from palms. Apply to bottoms of feet and base of skull.

BRONCHITIS, SINUSITIS, COUGH & COLDS
Diffuse. Apply to chest and back, and bottoms of feet.

OVERLY TIRED, MOODY, UNSETTLED AT BEDTIME
Diffuse. Apply to bottoms of feet, and/or combine with Epsom salts in a warm bath.

HIGH BLOOD PRESSURE & POOR CIRCULATION, EDEMA & WATER RETENTION
Apply over heart, on lower legs, and bottoms of feet.

TENSE, OVERWORKED & TIRED MUSCLES, HEADACHES & EYESTRAIN
Apply to areas of concern and/or across forehead and back of neck.

EXCESSIVE EXPOSURE TO CELL PHONE, COMPUTER & EMFs
Diffuse and inhale deeply from palms at the end of the day. Apply to bottoms of feet and base of skull.

BODY ODOR & LYMPHATIC DETOX
Apply under arms and slightly down ribcage, and to bottoms of feet.

RASHES, SWELLING, WOUNDS, SCARS, WRINKLES
Apply to areas of concern or on face and neck with moisturizer.

INSECT REPELLENT, AIRBORNE & LOCALIZED FUNGUS
Diffuse or apply to exposed areas.

CUTTING BOARDS, WOOD PRESERVATION, TERMITES, ROT PREVENTION
Add to glass spray bottle with water or an oil base to treat surfaces or apply to wooden items.

EMOTIONAL BALANCE
Use aromatically and topically to go from Muddled → Poised.

In Japan, parks populated with these most enduring trees are designated for forest bathing therapy to clear oneself from the energetic congestion and toxicity of city living. This essential oil is distilled from wood considered unusable for building materials.

festive

warming

spicy

HOLIDAY JOY

HOLIDAY BLEND

TOP USES

INVITE JOYFUL GATHERINGS
Diffuse or inhale from cupped hands.

PROTECTING
Apply to back of neck, pulse points, and/or bottoms of feet.

IMMUNE BOOST
Diffuse or inhale from cupped hands.

COLD & FLU PREVENTION
Diffuse or inhale from cupped hands.

HEADACHE & MIGRAINE
Apply diluted to temples and back of neck.

TENSION & STRESS
Apply to pulse points and diffuse.

NECK & SHOULDER PAIN, ARTHRITIS
Apply diluted to areas of discomfort.

MAIN INGREDIENTS
Wild orange
Clove
Cassia
Siberian fir
Frankincense
Styrax
Ginger Co2
Balsam fir
Cistus

SUBSTITUTE WITH
Brave™
Cheer®
Harvest Spice
On Guard®
Passion®
Tulsi

SAFETY
Not safe for internal use. Dilution recommended. Possible skin sensitivity. Avoid exposure to sunlight or UV rays for up to 12 hours after application.

This blend inspires the joy of the holidays while also stimulating immunity and offering seasonal protection.

= Aromatically = Topically = Internally

HOLIDAY PEACE

HOLIDAY BLEND

reassuring
grounding
collecting

MAIN INGREDIENTS
Siberian fir
Grapefruit
Douglas fir
Himalayan fir
Frankincense
Vetiver

SUBSTITUTE WITH
Cedarwood
Northern Escape
Siberian fir

SAFETY
Not safe for internal use. Dilution recommended. Possible skin irritation. Avoid exposure to sunlight or UV rays for up to 12 hours after application.

TOP USES

TRANQUIL, HARMONIOUS, GROUNDED & CALM
Diffuse and/or apply to pulse points, back of neck, along spine, and/or bottoms of feet.

PEACEFUL & FESTIVE
Diffuse and/or apply to diffusing ornaments, garlands, and/or holiday décor. Apply to wrist pulse points to exude a holiday aroma.

UPLIFT & STIMULATE MIND, MOOD & BODY
Apply under nose, on back of neck, and/or inhale from cupped hands.

CONGESTED AIRWAYS & RESPIRATORY ISSUES
Diffuse and inhale from cupped hands. Apply to bridge of nose or forehead, and chest.

SKIN ISSUES
Apply to area of concern.

POOR CIRCULATION
Apply to extremities.

SEASONAL DEPRESSION
Diffuse and inhale from cupped hands.

AIR FRESHENER & DEODORIZER
Diffuse. Drop on laundry balls or add 10-20 drops with vinegar to glass spray bottle filled with water and apply to freshen linens or carpet.

EMOTIONAL BALANCE
Use aromatically and topically to go from Rushed → Peaceful.

Bring the forest home with this blend of trees and roots that delight the senses and invite one to leave their cares at the door in exchange for a comforting occasion.

comforting • relaxing • quieting

HYGGE™

COZY BLEND

TOP USES

RELAXATION & TOGETHERNESS, CLOSENESS
Diffuse while applying to base of neck, shoulders, and bottoms of feet on self and/or others while gathered. Follow up with fuzzy socks, blankets, and cuddle time.

SEASONAL DEPRESSION & WINTER BLAHS
Diffuse and/or inhale from cupped hands. Apply over heart and forehead, on base of neck, and/or bottoms of feet.

PONDERING, CREATIVE, WARM & COLLECTED
Diffuse and apply to base of neck, and/or pulse points.

MINDFUL & MINIMALISTIC, MEDITATION
Diffuse and/or inhale from cupped hands. Apply to base of neck, bottoms of feet, and/or pulse points.

VULNERABLE & COMPROMISED, LONELY
Apply over heart, on back of neck, along spine, and/or bottoms of feet.

OBSESSED WITH PAST EVENTS & HOLDING ON TO NEGATIVE THINKING
Add to bath salts and soak in warm tub to relax and unwind. Diffuse while sleeping.

EMOTIONAL BALANCE
Use aromatically and topically to go from Distanced ⟶ Close.

MAIN INGREDIENTS
Wild orange
Cedarwood
Amyris
Frankincense
Myrrh
Cistus
Vetiver
Tonka bean

SAFETY
Not safe for internal use.

SUBSTITUTE WITH
Anchor
Cedarwood
Frankincense
Harvest Spice
Holiday Joy
InTune®
Peace®
Steady™

What is hygge (hoo-guh)? It's a Danish word with no English translation, and it's meaning resembles a description of a warm, cuddly winter evening. It represents a way of creating an atmosphere that invites rest and reflection, while enjoying the good things in life with good people.

= Aromatically = Topically = Internally

IMMORTELLE

ANTI-AGING BLEND

regenerating
youthful
replenishing

MAIN INGREDIENTS
Frankincense
Hawaiian sandalwood
Lavender
Myrrh
Helichrysum
Rose

SUBSTITUTE WITH
Frankincense
Helichrysum
Lavender
Myrrh
Rose
Sandalwood
Yarrow|Pom

SAFETY
Not safe for internal use.

TOP USES

WRINKLES & FINE LINES, AGE SPOTS
Apply to face, neck, and hands as part of skin care routine.

SUNBURN & DAMAGE & SKIN CANCER
Apply to affected areas.

WOUNDS & CUTS, SCARS & STRETCH MARKS
Apply to affected areas.

FACIAL REDNESS & CAPILLARIES, BLEMISHES & ACNE, BLOTCHY SKIN
Apply to affected areas.

POSTPARTUM PERINEUM RECOVERY
Apply to affected area.

CATARACTS
Apply under eyes, and under second & third toes.

TENSION & MOOD BALANCE
Apply to heart, back of neck, forehead, pulse points, and/or under nose.

MEDITATION
Apply under nose or to pulse points.

A beautiful blend with time-honored essential oils for radiant skin and beyond.

grounding
earthy
clarifying

INTUNE®

FOCUS BLEND

TOP USES

LACK OF MENTAL CLARITY, FOCUS OR CONCENTRATION, OVERWHELMED
Apply under nose and back of neck.

ADD/ADHD, HYPERACTIVITY
Apply to back of neck, spine, and/or bottoms of feet. Inhale from cupped hands.

OVER & UNDER ACTIVE BRAIN ACTIVITY
Apply to back of neck and spine.

ANXIOUS & UNGROUNDED, NERVOUSNESS
Apply under nose, back of neck, and/or on bottoms of feet.

DEPRESSION
Apply under nose, on bottoms of feet, and back of neck. Inhale from cupped hands.

STRESSFUL CLASROOM ENVIRONMENT
Apply to back of neck and under nose.

MID-AFTERNOON SLUMP
Apply under nose and/or back of neck. Inhale from palms.

SEIZURES & HEADACHES
Apply to back of neck, up spine, and/or to bottoms of feet.

MAIN INGREDIENTS
Amyris
Patchouli
Frankincense
Lime
Ylang ylang
Hawaiian sandalwood
Roman chamomile

SUBSTITUTE WITH
Frankincense
Hawaiian sandalwood
Patchouli
Peace®
Serenity®
Thinker™
Vetiver

SAFETY
Not safe for internal use. Avoid exposure to sunlight or UV rays for 12 hours after application.

Focused attention has become a difficult task for a growing population. InTune® helps balance activity in unique ways for each part of the brain.

= Aromatically = Topically = Internally

ISLAND MINT®

SUMMERTIME BLEND

delighting
refreshing
reviving

ESSENTIAL OILS

MAIN INGREDIENTS
Lime
Distilled lemon
Peppermint
Spruce

Powerful aromas invite the senses to transport the self to a new state of mind and presence. Simply diffuse this summer blend to be instantly carried away to a vacation-like state, any moment, anywhere.

TOP USES

CALM, RELAXING & RENEWING ATMOSPHERE
Diffuse during a party, gathering, or staycation to solicit feelings of a relaxed and refreshing getaway.

ENERGIZE & UPLIFT MOOD AND ENVIRONMENT
Diffuse or apply to pulse points, along spine, on back of neck, and/or bottoms of feet.

RENEWED FOCUS
Diffuse. Apply to back of neck, across forehead, and to bottoms of feet as needed.

TIRED & LOW ENERGY, MIDDAY SLUMP
Diffuse or inhale from cupped hands. Apply under the nose or on back of neck.

MELANCHOLY & WEARY
Diffuse or inhale from cupped hands and/or apply over heart and across forehead.

CONGESTED AIRWAYS & RESPIRATORY ISSUES
Diffuse or inhale from cupped hands. Apply to forehead, bridge of nose, and chest.

EMOTIONAL BALANCE
Use aromatically and topically to go from Overworked → Revitalized.

SUBSTITUTE WITH
Bergamot mint
Peppermint
Spearmint
Tamer™

SAFETY
Not safe for internal use. Avoid exposure to sunlight or UV rays for up to 12 hours after application.

euphoric • splendorous • joyful

JASMINE

JASMINUM GRANDIFLORUM

TOP USES

UTERINE HEALTH, LABOR & DELIVERY, BREAST MILK SUPPLY
Apply (T) diluted over abdomen and to reflex points or diffuse (A).

LACK OF SELF ASSURANCE, POOR SELF EXPRESSION, LARYNGITIS
Wear (T) as a personal perfume and apply (T) to neck/throat area. Blend as desired.

HORMONE IMBALANCE, PMS, MENSTRUAL CRAMPS
Apply (T) to lower abdomen. Inhale (A).

LACK OF SEXUAL INTEREST OR DRIVE, FRIGIDITY
Apply (T) diluted to back of neck and on pulse points.

LACK OF OVULATION & INFERTILITY
Apply (T) diluted over lower abdomen and/or on ovary and uterine reflex points.

FINE LINES & WRINKLES, OILY SKIN
Add to moisturizer and apply (T).

LOW DOPAMINE LEVELS
Inhale (A) from cupped hands. Apply (T) to back of neck and forehead.

DEPRESSION & ANXIETY, UPSET OR EMOTIONALLY TENSE OR EXHAUSTED
Inhale (A) from cupped hands or apply (T) diluted under nose and back of neck.

IRRITATED & DRY SKIN
Apply (T) diluted to affected area.

WEAK PROSTATE, GONADS, OR SEXUAL PERFORMANCE
Apply (T) to ankle reflex points or before intimacy.

PERFUME
Apply (T) to neck and wrist pulse points and behind ears. Blend as desired.

EMOTIONAL BALANCE
Use (A) aromatically and (T) topically to go from Hampered ⟶ Liberated.

(A) = Aromatically (T) = Topically (I) = Internally

FLOWERS

ABSOLUTE

SOURCED
Egypt

MAIN CONSTITUENT
Benzyl acetate
Benzyl benzoate

TOP PROPERTIES
Antidepressant
Aphrodisiac
Antispasmodic
Calming
Regenerative
Carminative

FOUND IN
Align
Passion®
Whisper®

SUBSTITUTE WITH
Arborvitae
Clary sage
Davana
Magnolia
Neroli
Passion®
Petitgrain
Roman chamomile
Rose
Whisper®
Ylang ylang

SAFETY & RESEARCH
Not safe for internal use. Best diluted due to aromatic potency. For research, see page 540.

In India, jasmine is known as "Queen of the Night" because it typically blossoms in the night.

ESSENTIAL OILS

JUNIPER BERRY

JUNIPERUS COMMUNIS

FLOWER/LEAF & STEM

STEAM DISTILLED

SOURCED
Albania

MAIN CONSTITUENTS
α-pinene
Sabinene

TOP PROPERTIES
Detoxifier
Diuretic
Antiseptic
Antispasmodic
Astringent
Anti-rheumatic
Carminative
Anti-parasitic

FOUND IN
Forgive®
Midnight Forest
Zendocrine®

SUBSTITUTE WITH
Black pepper
Blue tansy
Celery seed
Coriander
Cypress
Rosemary
Yarrow|Pom
Zendocrine®

SAFETY & RESEARCH
For research, see page 540.

detoxing

revitalizing

toning

TOP USES

JAUNDICE, LIVER & KIDNEY TOXICITY
Take in a capsule or under tongue.

EXCESS URIC ACID, WATER RETENTION, LACK OF PERSPIRATION
Combine with lemon and apply and take in a capsule.

URINARY, BLADDER, KIDNEY INFECTIONS & STONES
Take in a capsule and/or apply over area of concern.

ENLARGED PROSTATE, POOR URINE FLOW, HAIRLOSS
Take in a capsule or under tongue.

SORE JOINTS & MUSCLES, GOUT
Apply to area of concern. Take in a capsule.

RESPIRATORY INFECTIONS & CONTAGIONS, TINNITUS
Apply to chest, forehead, and/or take in a capsule.

ALCOHOL OR FOOD ADDICTIONS
Take in a capsule or under tongue.

HIGH CHOLESTEROL & BLOOD SUGAR LEVELS
Take in a capsule or under tongue.

ACNE, PSORIASIS & ECZEMA, CELLULITIS
Apply to area of concern, diluting as needed.

SCANT OR IRREGULAR MENSTRUATION, CRAMPS, UTERUS ISSUES
Apply to lower abdomen, ankle reflex points, and/or take in a capsule.

TENSION, STRESS & DEPRESSION
Diffuse or inhale deeply from cupped hands, and/or apply under nose.

EMOTIONAL BALANCE
Use aromatically and topically to go from Denying → Insightful.

A favorite oil for its fragrance, juniper berries are also used for making gin.

KUMQUAT

FORTUNELLA JAPONICA

self-affirming
sweet
fulfilling

ESSENTIAL OILS

PEEL

STEAM DISTILLED

SOURCED
India

MAIN CONSTITUENTS
Limonene

TOP PROPERTIES
Antiseptic
Antimicrobial
Immunostimulant
Digestive stimulant
Refreshing

SUBSTITUTE WITH
Grapefruit
Green mandarin
Tangerine
Wild orange

SAFETY & RESEARCH
Avoid exposure to sunlight or UV rays for up to 12 hours after application. For research, see page 540.

TOP USES

WINTER BLAHS, INAUTHENTICITY & PRETENSE, LACK OF PERSPECTIVE
Diffuse or inhale from cupped hands. Apply over heart and on forehead.

BRAIN FOG & POOR FOCUS
Combine with green mandarin and vetiver. Diffuse or inhale. Apply under nose.

DIABETES, IMBALANCED INSULIN & GLUCOSE LEVELS, HIGH CHOLESTEROL
Take in a capsule with fennel.

ULCERS
Take in a capsule.

BACTERIAL, FUNGAL & VIRAL INFECTIONS, PARASITES
Apply to areas of concern. Take in a capsule.

SORE THROAT & SWOLLEN GLANDS
Diffuse. Gargle and/or take in a capsule.

OVERWEIGHT, EXCESSIVE APPETITE
Take in a capsule.

MACULAR DEGENERATION & CATARACTS
Take in a capsule.

FLAVORING
Add to salad dressings, baked goods, frostings, beverages, or cut fruit.

EMOTIONAL BALANCE
Use aromatically and topically to go from Divided → Integrous.

Kumquat essential oil is typically anywhere from 70%-95% limonene, but of its other 105 known constituents, 46 have not been found in any other essential oil. The kumquat peel is sweet and its flesh bitter, the reverse of most citrus fruits.

purging • clearing • thwarting

LAUREL LEAF

LAURUS NOBILIS

TOP USES

CONGESTION, COUGH, BRONCHITIS & PNEUMONIA
Apply to chest and down bridge of nose. Diffuse or inhale from cupped hands.

VIRUSES, COLD & FLU, EARACHES
Combine with Siberian fir and diffuse or inhale from cupped hands. Apply under nose, to chest, or around ear.

ACNE, RASH, POISON OAK OR IVY, BRUISING
Apply to affected areas as often as needed. Consider combining with a soothing oil.

CONFIDENT & COURAGOUS, UPLIFTING ENVIRONMENT
Diffuse and apply under nose and over heart.

MENTAL FOCUS, CONCENTRATION & CLARITY
Apply under nose, to forehead, and back of neck.

MUSCLE SPASMS, RHEUMATISM, SCIATICA, HEADACHES
Apply to areas of concern prior to or after exertion, for a soothing massage, or before soaking in a warm bath.

HIGH BLOOD PRESSURE
Apply with marjoram under nose, back of neck, and/or bottoms of feet.

HEAVY METAL DETOX, BIO ABSORBENT, WATER TREATMENT
Apply on bottoms of feet twice daily during a detox program. Add to water supply to purify.

CLEANING DISINFECTANT
Combine with lemon in a glass spray bottle with water as a surface cleaner.

INSECT OR PATHOGEN REPELLENT
Diffuse. Apply to exposed areas of skin and clothing before going outdoors.

EMOTIONAL BALANCE
Use aromatically and topically to go from Divided → Integrous.

= Aromatically = Topically = Internally

LEAF

STEAM DISTILLED

SOURCED
Albania

MAIN CONSTITUENT
1,8-cineole (eucalyptol)
α-Terpinyl acetate

TOP PROPERTIES
Anticatarrhal
Antiviral
Expectorant
Antibacterial
Analgesic
Antioxidant
Detoxifier
Antimicrobial

FOUND IN
Breathe®

SUBSTITUTE WITH
Breathe®
Cardamom
Eucalyptus
Ravintsara
Rosemary

SAFETY
Not safe for internal use. For research, see page 540.

Laurel leaves were a symbol of victory and highest status in both the Greek and Roman cultures, worn in head wreaths by both emperors and athletes. It is also the common cooking herb known as bay leaves.

TOP USES

SLEEP ISSUES, INSOMNIA, RESTLESSNESS, JET LAG
Apply under nose, on bottoms of feet, and/or diffuse to promote better sleep.

UPSET, UPTIGHT, STRESSED & ANXIOUS, TEETH GRINDING
Apply over heart, on back of neck. Inhale from cupped hands and diffuse.

SUNBURNS & SUNSTROKE, BURNS & SCARS, STRETCH MARKS
Apply to areas of concern.

ALLERGIES & HAY FEVER, EARACHE
Take in a capsule or under tongue. Inhale from cupped hands.

BUG BITES & STINGS, HIVES, RASHES, ITCHING, POISON IVY, IMPETIGO, DANDRUFF
Apply on site to soothe or area of concern.

COLIC & UPSET BABY, DIAPER RASH, THRUSH
Massage diluted on abdomen, bottoms of feet, and/or area of concern.

CUTS, WOUNDS & BLISTERS, DIABETIC SORES, BRUISES
Apply to area of concern.

SHOCK, HYSTERIA, GRIEF, SORROW
Diffuse or inhale. Apply over heart.

HIGH BLOOD PRESSURE
Apply on pulse points, over heart, and to bottoms of feet. Take in a capsule.

LABOR PAINS, WEAK CONTRACTIONS, PLACENTA DELIVERY, POSTPARTUM RECOVERY & DEPRESSION, MASTITIS, BREAST TENDERNESS
Apply to lower abdomen, breasts, and/or bottoms of feet. Diffuse or inhale from cupped hands.

NOSEBLEEDS & PINK EYE, COLD SORES
Apply across bridge of nose, diluted around eye, or on lips.

PARKINSON'S, SEIZURES & CONVULSIONS, DIZZINESS
Apply to back of neck and forehead, and/or on bottoms of feet. Take under tongue.

INJURIES, SPRAINS, MUSCLE TENSION, NERVE PAIN
Apply to area of concern.

MIGRAINES & HEADACHES
Inhale and apply to temples and back of neck.

EMOTIONAL BALANCE
Use aromatically and topically to go from Unheard → Expressed.

Lavender means "to wash" in Latin. It is likely the most used essential oil globally, and for good reason, as it serves in all things calming! When in doubt, use lavender!

= Aromatically = Topically = Internally

LAVENDER

LAVANDULA ANGUSTIFOLIA

FLOWERS

STEAM DISTILLED

SOURCED
Bulgaria

MAIN CONSTITUENTS
Linalool
Linalyl acetate
Ocimene

TOP PROPERTIES
Sedative
Antihistamine
Cytophylactic
Hypotensive
Nervine
Relaxing
Soothing
Antibacterial
Regenerative

FOUND IN
Adaptiv™
Anchor
AromaTouch®
Calmer™
Citrus Bloom™
ClaryCalm®
Elevation
Immortelle
PastTense®
Rescuer™
Serenity®

SUBSTITUTE WITH
Adaptiv™
Anchor
Bergamot mint
Black pepper
Black spruce
Calmer™
Clary sage
Geranium
Immortelle
Petitgrain
Serenity®

SAFETY & RESEARCH
For research, see page 540.

LEMON

CITRUS LIMON

RIND

COLD PRESSED

SOURCED
Italy

MAIN CONSTITUENTS
Limonene
β-pinene
γ-terpinene

TOP PROPERTIES
Antiseptic
Diuretic
Antioxidant
Antibacterial
Detoxifier
Disinfectant
Mucolytic
Astringent
Degreaser

FOUND IN
Arise
Breathe®
Citrus Bliss®
Island Mint®
Purify
Slim & Sassy®

SUBSTITUTE WITH
Citrus Bliss®
Green mandarin
Lime
Purify

SAFETY & RESEARCH
Avoid exposure to sunlight or UV rays for up to 12 hours after application. For research, see page 540.

uplifting
invigorating
refreshing

TOP USES

LIVER & KIDNEY TOXICITY, CELLULITE
Take (I) in a capsule. Apply (T) to bottoms of feet or areas of concern.

TOXICITY & LOW GLUTATHIONE LEVELS
Take (I) in a capsule or under tongue.

KIDNEY & GALLSTONES
Apply (T) diluted over kidney area with eucalyptus or take (I) in a capsule with geranium for gallstones.

EDEMA & WATER RETENTION, HIGH BLOOD PRESSURE
Take (I) in a capsule or glass of water. Apply (T) to lower legs and bottoms of feet.

WATER & AIR POLLUTION, HANGOVER, FOOD POISONING
Diffuse (A). Take (I) under tongue or in a glass of water.

RUNNY NOSE & ALLERGIES
Diffuse (A). Take (I) with lavender and peppermint under tongue, in a glass of water, or capsule.

EXCESS ACIDITY & LYMPHATIC CONGESTION
Take (I) in a capsule. Apply (T) to bottoms of feet.

CONGESTION & MUCUS
Apply (T) to chest and forehead. Diffuse (A). Take (I) in a capsule.

DEPRESSION & LOW ENERGY
Diffuse (A). Take (I) under tongue. Apply (T) with rosemary.

GOUT, RHEUMATISM & ARTHRITIS
Take (I) in a glass of water or capsule.

BRAIN FOG, LACK OF LOGICAL THINKING DIMINISHED LEFT BRAIN ACTIVITY
Diffuse (A) or inhale, and/or take (I) in a capsule with rosemary.

HIGH CHOLESTEROL & CLOGGED ARTERIES, EXCESS APPETITE
Take (I) in a capsule and/or sip in water. Apply (T) to bottoms of feet.

HEARTBURN & REFLUX, LARYNGITIS & TONSILITIS
Take (I) with ginger in a capsule, glass of water, or under tongue.

VARICOSE VEINS & BROKEN CAPILLARIES
Apply (T) diluted with cypress to areas of concern.

OILY SKIN & HAIR
Apply (T). Add to toner or shampoo.

DEGREASER, FURNITURE POLISH, STICKY RESIDUE REMOVAL
Apply (T) to surface. Caution with plastic or varnished surfaces.

FLAVORING
Add (I) to favorite recipe or beverage.

EMOTIONAL BALANCE
Use (A) aromatically and (T) topically to go from Mindless → Energized.

It takes approximately 45 lemons to produce a 15mL bottle of lemon essential oil.

ESSENTIAL OILS

LEMON EUCALYPTUS

EUCALYPTUS CITRIODORA

LEAVES

STEAM DISTILLED

SOURCED
Kenya

MAIN CONSTITUENTS
Citronellal
Citronellol

TOP PROPERTIES
Expectorant
Analgesic
Insect Repellent
Rubefacient
Cleanser

FOUND IN
Abōde™

SUBSTITUTE WITH
Abōde™
Cilantro
Citronella
TerraShield®

SAFETY & RESEARCH
Not safe for internal use.
For research, see page 540.

resolving
stimulating
refreshing

TOP USES

INSECT, TICKS & MOSQUITOES REPELLENT
Diffuse Ⓐ. Apply Ⓣ to exposed areas of skin and on clothing. Spray on outdoor surfaces.

AIRBORNE PATHOGENS & VIRUSES, MALARIA
Diffuse Ⓐ. Apply Ⓣ on bottoms of feet, especially when vulnerable to exposure.

BRONCHITIS, ASTHMA, COUGHS, SINUSITIS, FLU
Diffuse Ⓐ and/or apply Ⓣ on chest and back.

FEAR & FEELING UNSAFE OR OVERLY VULNERABLE TO OUTSIDE INFLUENCES, UNPROTECTED SPACES
Diffuse Ⓐ or inhale from cupped hands and/or apply Ⓣ.

DANDRUFF, ATHLETE'S FOOT & JOCK ITCH, SKIN FUNGUS
Add to shampoo or apply Ⓣ to areas of concern.

OSTEOARTHRITIS, RHEUMATIC & JOINT PAIN, HEADACHES
Apply Ⓣ to areas of concern and/or bottoms of feet.

BURNS, FEVERS, HEAT EXHAUSTION & OVEREXERTION
Apply Ⓣ to areas of concern, spine, across forehead, and/or bottoms of feet.

POOR CIRCULATION & BLOOD OXYGENATION
Apply Ⓣ to bottoms of feet and over liver.

CHRONIC CONSTIPATION, POOR DIGESTION & BLOATING, INTESTINAL CRAMPS, PARASITES
Apply Ⓣ in clockwise motion all over abdomen.

CUTS & WOUNDS, COLD SORES
Apply Ⓣ to area of concern.

HOUSEHOLD SMELLS & BODY ODOR
Diffuse Ⓐ or add Ⓣ to body wash.

SURFACE DISINFECTING
Add with vinegar to glass spray bottle filled with water.

EMOTIONAL BALANCE
Use Ⓐ aromatically and Ⓣ topically to go from Concealed → Revealing.

By its chemistry, lemon eucalyptus is as if lemon, citronella, and eucalyptus had a baby.

Ⓐ = Aromatically Ⓣ = Topically Ⓘ = Internally

LEMONGRASS

CYMBOPOGON FLEXUOSUS

electrifying · regenerating · purifying

Lemongrass essential oil is used in the pharmaceutical industry for the synthesis of Vitamin A.

LEAVES

STEAM DISTILLED

SOURCED
India

MAIN CONSTITUENTS
Geranial
Neral
Geraniol

TOP PROPERTIES
Anti-inflammatory
Antimicrobial
Analgesic
Anti-carcinoma
Antimutagenic
Decongestant
Regenerative
Anti-rheumatic

FOUND IN
DDR Prime®
TerraShield®

SUBSTITUTE WITH
Abōde™
Air-X™
DDR Prime®
Litsea
Melissa
TerraShield®

SAFETY & RESEARCH
Dilution recommended.
Possible skin sensitivity.
For research, see page 540.

TOP USES

CONNECTIVE TISSUE INJURY & WHIPLASH
Apply diluted to affected area.

JOINT, TENDON & LIGAMENT PAIN, CARPAL TUNNEL, FROZEN SHOULDER
Apply diluted to affected area.

CANCER & TUMORS, FREE RADICALS
Take in a capsule.

LYMPHATIC & RESPIRATORY CONGESTION, TOXIC ACCUMULATIONS
Take in a capsule and/or apply to bottoms of feet.

HYPO OR HYPERTHYROID, HASHIMOTO'S, GRAVE'S DISEASE
Take in a capsule. Apply under big toe.

BLADDER & KIDNEY INFECTION OR STONES, CANDIDA
Use in a capsule or apply diluted over lower abdomen or back.

BLOOD PRESSURE & CHOLESTEROL, POOR CIRCULATION
Take in a capsule. Apply to bottoms of feet.

COLITIS & LACTOSE INTOLERANCE
Take in a capsule.

CONSTIPATION & WATER RETENTION
Take in a capsule. Apply to bottoms of feet.

CATARACTS & POOR EYESIGHT
Take in a capsule. Apply under second and third toes.

CRAMPS & LACTIC ACID ACCUMULATION
Apply to area of concern.

COOKING
Add to flavor dishes.

EMOTIONAL BALANCE
Use aromatically and topically to get from Obstructed → Flowing.

renewing • energizing • purifying

LIME

CITRUS AURANTIFOLIA

TOP USES

SORE THROAT, COLD & FLU, FEVER
Gargle, take in a capsule, or lick off back of hand.

RESPIRATORY/LYMPH CONGESTION, CROUP
Take in a capsule or apply over areas of concern with Breathe®.

LIVER & BLOOD TOXICITY, CELLULITE, LOW GLUTATHIONE LEVELS
Take in a capsule or under tongue. Apply to affected areas.

URINARY & DIGESTIVE ISSUES
Take in a glass of water or capsule.

EXHAUSTION & DEPRESSION
Apply to back of neck with spearmint and/or diffuse.

WEAK PANCREAS & GALLBLADDER, GALLSTONES
Take in a capsule, water, or under tongue.

MEMORY LOSS & LACK OF MENTAL CLARITY
Inhale or diffuse. Apply to forehead with rosemary.

HERPES & COLD SORES, CHICKEN POX
Take in a capsule and/or apply to outbreaks.

BACTERIA, LOW BLOOD CELL COUNT
Take in a capsule or under tongue.

INSECT BITES & STINGS, CELLULITIS
Apply to area of concern.

HEAD LICE
Add 20 drops and 20 drops tea tree to bottle of shampoo and apply.

EMOTIONAL BALANCE
Use aromatically and topically to go from Faint → Enlivened.

A popular oil in perfumery for men. In times past, British sailors drank lime juice to prevent scurvy.

RIND

COLD PRESSED

SOURCED
Brazil

MAIN CONSTITUENT
Limonene
β-pinene
γ-terpinene

TOP PROPERTIES
Anti-inflammatory
Antiseptic
Antioxidant
Antibacterial
Tonic
Uplifting
Detoxifier
Disinfectant
Diuretic

FOUND IN
Abōde™
InTune®
Island Mint®
Purify

SUBSTITUTE WITH
Abōde™
Black pepper
Lemon
Purify

SAFETY & RESEARCH
Avoid exposure to sunlight or UV rays for up to 12 hours after application. For research, see page 540.

= Aromatically = Topically = Internally

cleansing
refreshing
uplifting

Sweeter than lemongrass, without the musty note, and more citrusy in scent than melissa.

TOP USES

ASTHMA ATTACK, SPASTIC COUGHS, BRONCHITIS, ALLERGIES
Apply diluted to chest with Breathe® or inhale from cupped hands.

ACUTE & CHRONIC BACK OR MUSCLE PAIN
Apply diluted to affected area.

HIGH BLOOD PRESSURE, IRREGULAR HEARTBEAT, ANXIETY
Apply to chest, back of neck, under nose, and/or bottoms of feet.

COLD, CHILLS & INFECTIONS
Apply to chest, back of neck, or along spine.

ECZEMA, ACNE & OILY SKIN
Apply diluted to affected areas.

SEASONAL BLUES, NEGATIVE THINKING & SPEAKING
Diffuse or inhale from cupped hands.

NAUSEA, MOTION SICKNESS, INDIGESTION, POOR APPETITE
Apply diluted in circular motion on upper abdomen.

CELLULITE, EXCESSIVE PERSPIRATION, ATHLETE'S FOOT
Apply to areas of concern.

BRAIN FOG, LACK OF MOTIVATION, FATIGUE, SLEEP ISSUES
Apply diluted across forehead, on temples. Diffuse and/or inhale from cupped hands.

NERVOUS TENSION & HEADACHES
Apply diluted across forehead and on temples. Diffuse and/or inhale from cupped hands.

MENSTRUAL DISCOMFORT
Apply to abdomen or area of concern.

LUNG CANCER
Apply diluted to chest and back.

PET SHAMPOO, INSECT REPELLENT
Apply diluted to exposed areas or add to shampoo.

SURFACE & AIR CLEANSER
Spray on with tea tree and water in place of toxic chemical cleaners or diffuse.

FLAVORING
Add a dipped toothpick to a favorite dish.

EMOTIONAL BALANCE
Use aromatically and topically to go from Encumbered ⟶ Purified.

= Aromatically = Topically = Internally

LITSEA

LITSEA CUBEBA

FRUIT

STEAM DISTILLED

SOURCED
China

MAIN CONSTITUENTS
Geranial
Neral
Limonene

TOP PROPERTIES
Refreshing
Detoxifier
Uplifting
Antibacterial
Antifungal
Antispasmodic
Disinfectant
Digestive stimulant

FOUND IN
Abōde™
Air-X™
DDR Prime®
HD Clear®
Stronger™

SUBSTITUTE WITH
Abōde™
Air-X™
Lemon
Lemongrass
Melissa
Stronger™

SAFETY & RESEARCH
Not safe for internal use. Dilution recommended. May stain surfaces, fabrics, and skin. For research, see page 540.

MAGNOLIA

MICHELIA X ALBA

FLOWER PETALS

STEAM DISTILLED

SOURCED
China

MAIN CONSTITUENTS
Linalool

TOP PROPERTIES
Sedative
Relaxant
Antidepressant
Aphrodisiac
Decongestant
Stomachic

FOUND IN
Adaptiv™
Citrus Bloom™
Steady™

SUBSTITUTE WITH
Beautiful
Bergamot
Citrus Bloom™
Clary sage
Coriander
Jasmine
Neroli
Petitgrain
Rose
Steady™
Ylang ylang

SAFETY & RESEARCH
Not safe for internal use. Avoid keeping in hot places (e.g. glove box of car) to prevent oxidation. For research, see page 540.

TOP USES

ANXIETY, DEPRESSION & LACK OF ENERGY
Apply to back of neck, forehead, under nose, and/or over heart. Inhale from cupped hands.

PMS & MENSTRUAL CRAMPS, HORMONE IMBALANCES
Apply in clockwise motion over lower abdomen, wrists, and/or ankles.

IRRITABILITY, ANGER & RAGE, HYSTERIA, PANIC, GRIEF & SHOCK
Apply to back of neck, forehead, under nose, over heart, and/or bottoms of feet. Inhale from cupped hands.

RESPIRATORY, SINUS & LYMPHATIC CONGESTION
Apply to chest, back, and/or to bottoms of feet. Combine with cardamom or eucalyptus.

LOW SEX DRIVE, BREAST & PROSTATE ISSUES
Apply to wrists, chest, back of neck, and/or reproductive organ reflex points.

STRESSED, WORRIED, UPTIGHT & TENSE
Apply to back of neck, forehead, under nose, and/or bottoms of feet. Inhale from cupped hands.

LACK OF ABILITY TO RECEIVE LOVE, BROKEN-HEARTED
Apply over heart and across forehead. Inhale from cupped hands.

ABRASIONS & WOUNDS, SKIN IRRITATIONS, SCARS
Apply to areas of concern and combine with tea tree, frankincense, or geranium.

ACNE & DRY SKIN, WRINKLES
Add to skin care routine and apply.

INSOMNIA & RESTLESSNESS
Apply to back of neck, forehead, and/or under nose. Inhale from cupped hands.

PERFUME
Apply to pulse points. Layer with jasmine or neroli if desired.

EMOTIONAL BALANCE
Use aromatically and topically to go from Disturbed → Confident.

Fossilized Magnolia genus is over 20 million years old, a time prior to the presence of bees, and was pollinated by beetles. For the purpose of producing the essential oil, it's harvested at night when blooms are most fragrant. Magnolia was traditionally used in ceremonies to enhance confidence and well-being.

supporting · transforming · harmonizing

MANUKA

LEPTOSPERMUM SCOPARIUM

ESSENTIAL OILS

BRANCHES & LEAVES

SOURCED
New Zealand

MAIN CONSTITUENT
Leptospermone
E-calamenene
α-pinene
Cadina-3
5-diene

TOP PROPERTIES
Anti-allergenic
Antihistamine
Antibacterial
Anti-inflammatory
Anti-fungal
Antiviral
Relaxant

SUBSTITUTE WITH
Patchouli
Spikenard
Ylang ylang

SAFETY & RESEARCH
Not safe for internal use.
For research, see page 540.

The Maori people use all parts of this plant in their natural medicine. The concentration of its constituents varies with the height of the tree and where the leaves were extracted.

TOP USES

ACHY JOINTS & MUSCLE PAIN
Massage diluted into affected areas.

DANDRUFF, SCALP ISSUES
Apply to scalp or add to shampoo or conditioner.

ATHLETE'S FOOT, NAIL FUNGUS
Apply to bottoms of feet and/or drop into foot soak.

IRRITATED & CHAFFED SKIN, ACNE, RASHES
Apply to affected areas. Dilute as needed.

INTESTINAL, RESPIRATORY, URINARY TRACT BACTERIAL INFECTION
Apply to bottoms of feet, abdomen, and/or chest.

COLD, FEVER, COUGH, SINUS CONGESTION, ASTHMA
Diffuse, inhale from cupped hands, apply to chest.

MUSCLES SPASMS & CONTRACTIONS
Apply diluted with eucalyptus over affected area.

INDIGESTION & SPICY FOOD ISSUES, TOXICITY
Apply to abdomen.

ALLERGIES & SENSITIVITIES TO DUST, PETS & DANDER
Diffuse or inhale from cupped hands. Apply to bottoms of feet.

BITES, STINGS & BURNS
Apply to affected area.

EAR & FUNGAL INFECTIONS, HERPES
Apply around ears and/or on affected areas.

DAMAGED SKIN & SCARS, WOUNDS, RADIATION TREATMENT SIDE EFFECTS
Apply to affected areas.

MENTAL STRESS, ANXIETY & HIGH BLOOD PRESSURE
Diffuse or inhale from cupped hands. Apply to back of neck, forehead, and/or chest.

EMOTIONAL BALANCE
Use aromatically and topically to go from Bothered → Revived.

---

relaxing
connecting
pleasing

MARJORAM

ORIGANUM MAJORANA

TOP USES

CARPAL TUNNEL, BONE SPURS, TENDINITIS & ARTHRITIS
Apply to areas of discomfort.

MUSCLE CRAMPS & SPRAINS
Apply to areas of concern.

HIGH BLOOD PRESSURE & EDEMA, HEART ISSUES, PROLAPSED MITRAL VALUE
Apply over heart, to pulse points, and/or bottoms of feet. Take in a capsule.

CROUP & BRONCHITIS, ASTHMA
Apply to neck, chest, and upper back.

PANCREATITIS & LIVER/SPLEEN OBSTRUCTIONS
Apply over affected area.

OVERACTIVE SEX DRIVE
Apply to lower abdomen and/or bottoms of feet. Inhale.

VIRAL & BACTERIAL INFECTIONS, SHINGLES, BOILS, COLD SORES & RINGWORM
Take in a capsule and/or apply to affected area.

MIGRAINES & HEADACHES
Apply on back of neck and temples.

COLIC & CONSTIPATION
Take in a capsule and/or massage diluted onto lower abdomen.

STRESS & ANXIETY, TENSION, SHOCK
Rub on back of neck and bottoms of feet. Diffuse.

EMOTIONAL BALANCE
Use aromatically and topically to go from Doubtful ⟶ Trusting.

= Aromatically = Topically = Internally

LEAVES

STEAM DISTILLED

SOURCED
Egypt

MAIN CONSTITUENTS
Terpinen-4-ol
Trans-sabinene hydrate
γ-terpinene

TOP PROPERTIES
Vasodilator
Antispasmodic
Digestive stimulant
Antibacterial
Antifungal
Hypotensive
Sedative

FOUND IN
Align
AromaTouch®
PastTense®
Serenity®

SUBSTITUTE WITH
AromaTouch®
Basil
Cilantro
PastTense®
Tea tree

SAFETY & RESEARCH
Caution during earlier stages of pregnancy.
For research, see page 540.

Also known as "Joy of the Mountains," marjoram symbolized happiness to the ancient Greeks and Romans.

MELISSA

MELISSA OFFICINALIS

LEAVES & TOPS

STEAM DISTILLED

SOURCED
Bulgaria

MAIN CONSTITUENTS
Geranial
Germacrene D
Neral
β-caryophyllene

TOP PROPERTIES
Antioxidant
Antibacterial
Antidepressant
Antispasmodic
Antihistamine
Antiviral
Hypotensive
Nervine
Sedative

FOUND IN
Arise
Elevation
Motivate®

SUBSTITUTE WITH
Air-X™
Arise
Black pepper
Cilantro
Elevation
Lemongrass
Litsea
On Guard+™

SAFETY & RESEARCH
Dilute as needed to prevent skin sensitivity. For research, see page 540.

awakening
authentic
restorative

TOP USES

FEVERS, COLDS & VIRAL INFECTIONS
Apply diluted along spine, bottoms of feet, or take in a capsule.

COLD SORES & FEVER BLISTERS, HERPES, CHICKEN POX
Apply directly to sores or take in a capsule.

DEPRESSION, ANXIETY, SHOCK & PTSD, OVERCOME BY DARKNESS, DESPAIR
Apply to back of neck and ears. Diffuse. Apply to thumb pad and press to roof of mouth and hold for 5-10 seconds.

BITES, STINGS & WARTS
Apply directly to area of concern.

ALLERGIES & ASTHMA
Inhale from cupped hands, and/or apply to chest. Take in a capsule, or under tongue.

HYPERTENSION, PALPITATIONS & HIGH BLOOD PRESSURE
Diffuse. Take in a capsule, or apply diluted to back of neck and over heart.

VERTIGO
Take in a capsule and/or apply behind ears and on back of neck.

ECZEMA & ACNE
Apply diluted to affected areas.

INFERTILITY, STERILITY, IRREGULAR OVULATION & MENSTRUAL ISSUES
Apply diluted to lower abdomen. Take in a capsule.

DYSENTERY & INDIGESTION
Take in a capsule or apply over abdomen.

HIGH BLOOD SUGAR & ELEVATED TRIGLYCERIDE LEVELS
Take in a capsule and apply to bottoms of feet.

ALZHEIMER'S & DEMENTIA
Take in a capsule. Apply diluted to back of neck and/or on big toe.

EMOTIONAL BALANCE
Use aromatically and topically to go from Depressed → Light-filled.

Melissa is Greek for "honey bee," and its sweet fragrance was known to attract bees. It requires 66 lbs/30 kgs of plant matter to create one precious 5mL bottle of melissa.

MOTIVATE®

ENCOURAGING BLEND

motivating
energizing
believing

MAIN INGREDIENTS
Peppermint
Clementine
Coriander
Basil
Yuzu
Melissa
Rosemary
Vanilla bean absolute

SUBSTITUTE WITH
AromaTouch®
Cheer®
Clementine
Hope®
Peppermint

SAFETY
Not safe for internal use. Avoid sunlight or UV rays to applied area for up to 12 hours.

TOP USES

LACK OF CONFIDENCE, COURAGE OR MOTIVATION
Diffuse. Apply under nose, on forehead, back of neck, and/or over heart.

CONFUSION & OVERWHELM
Inhale. Apply under nose, on forehead, back of neck, and/or chest.

MENTAL FATIGUE & EXHAUSTION
Diffuse and inhale from cupped hands. Apply to temples and back of neck.

DEPLETION & STAGNATION
Inhale from cupped hands and apply to bottoms of feet.

DEPRESSION & RESIGNATION
Diffuse and/or apply over heart area, on forehead, and back of neck.

ADRENAL EXHAUSTION
Inhale from cupped hand. Apply under nose, over adrenal area, and/or on bottoms of feet.

DIGESTIVE ISSUES
Apply to upper abdomen and/or on bottoms of feet.

BRONCHITIS & ASTHMA
Diffuse. Apply to neck and chest.

ACHES & PAINS
Apply to affected areas.

Squelch the frustration and doubt that can halt progress with this blend's ability to encourage productivity, creativity, and confidence.

drying • healing • nurturing

MYRRH

COMMIPHORA MYRRHA

TOP USES

GUM DISEASE & BLEEDING, GINGIVITIS, MOUTH ULCERS
Apply directly to gums.

FINE LINES & DRY SKIN, STRETCH MARKS, CRACKED HEELS
Apply to areas of concern.

THYROID ISSUES, HASHIMOTO'S
Apply to base of neck and bottoms of feet.

DIGESTIVE UPSET & CRAMPING, ULCERS, DIARRHEA
Apply to abdomen and/or take in capsule.

ECZEMA, SKIN ULCERS, SYPHILLIS, LEPROSY
Apply to affected area, especially weeping skin.

FUNGAL INFECTIONS, ATHLETE'S FOOT, CANDIDA, RINGWORM, VAGINAL THRUSH
Take in a capsule and/or apply to area of concern.

VIRAL INFECTION, HERPES
Take in a capsule and/or apply to bottoms of feet.

RESPIRATORY INFECTION, SORE THROAT, CONGESTION & MUCUS
Apply to chest and forehead, diffuse, and/or take in a capsule.

CIRRHOSIS, VIRAL HEPATITIS
Take in a capsule or under tongue.

DEPRESSION & ANXIETY
Diffuse or inhale from cupped hands with melissa or a citrus oil.

MEDITATION
Diffuse and inhale from cupped hands.

EMOTIONAL BALANCE
Use aromatically and topically to go from Disconnected → Nurtured.

Myrrh means "bitter" and was referred to in the Bible as the balm of Gilead. It was given as a gift to the Christ child and also presented at His death to be used prior to burial.

RESIN

STEAM DISTILLED

SOURCED
Somaliland

MAIN CONSTITUENTS
Furanoeudesma1 3-diene
Curzerene
Lindestrene

TOP PROPERTIES
Anti-inflammatory
Antiviral
Antimicrobial
Expectorant
Anti-infectious
Carminative
Antifungal

FOUND IN
Forgive®
Hygge™
Immortelle

SUBSTITUTE WITH
Frankincense
Immortelle
InTune®
Patchouli
Sandalwood
Spikenard
Turmeric
Vetiver

SAFETY & RESEARCH
For research, see page 540.

= Aromatically = Topically = Internally

TOP USES

LOSS OF SEXUAL INTEREST OR AROUSAL, ERECTILE DYSFUNCTION
Apply under nose, to reproductive areas, and/or wear as a personal scent on pulse points. Inhale from cupped hands.

UNSETTLED, STRESSED OUT, DEPRESSED, ELEVATED CORTISOL LEVELS
Diffuse and/or inhale from cupped hands. Apply diluted to chest, solar plexus, back of neck, temples, and/or under nose.

DAMAGED, DRY, WRINKLED, SAGGING & SCARRED SKIN
Apply diluted to area of concern.

PREGNANCY & CHILDBIRTH
Apply under nose and/or to lower abdomen. Apply diluted to lower back to ease anxiety during labor.

HEART PALPITATIONS, HIGH BLOOD PRESSURE & SEIZURES
Apply over heart, on back of neck, forehead, and/or bottoms of feet.

MENOPAUSE & CHRONIC INSOMNIA, PMS, ESTROGEN IMBALANCE, MENSTRUAL CRAMPS
Inhale from cupped hands. Apply to lower abdomen, forehead, and/or ankle reflex points.

HYSTERIA, PANIC, GRIEF, SHOCK, IRRITATION & ANGER
Diffuse and/or inhale from cupped hands. Apply across forehead and over heart.

OVERTHINKING, OVERWHELM, CONFUSION, TENSION HEADACHES
Apply under nose, across forehead. Diffuse or inhale from cupped hands.

MUSCLE CRAMPS, SPASTIC COUGHS
Apply to area of concern or chest.

INTESTINAL CRAMPS, COLITIS, DIARRHEA & FOOD POISONING
Massage diluted onto abdomen.

ACNE & RELATED DARK SPOTS, ECZEMA, RASHES
Apply diluted to affected areas.

WOUND DISINFECTANT, ATHLETE'S FOOT, RINGWORM, PAINFUL INJECTION SITE
Apply diluted to area of concern.

DEODORANT, PERFUME
Apply diluted to underarms and/or wrist and neck pulse points.

EMOTIONAL BALANCE
Use aromatically and topically to go from Afflicted → Released.

One ton of blossoms are needed to produce 1 kg of neroli oil. This historically desired fragrance can be heavily diluted and still remain highly effective.

= Aromatically = Topically = Internally

NEROLI

CITRUS AURANTIUM

FLOWERS

STEAM DISTILLED

SOURCED
Egypt

MAIN CONSTITUENTS
Linalool
Linalyl acetate
Limonene
Nerolidol
Terpineol
Terpinyl acetate

TOP PROPERTIES
Antidepressant
Anti-inflammatory
Antimutagenic
Aphrodisiac
Cytophylactic
Neurotonic
Regenerative
Sedative
Warming

FOUND IN
Adaptiv™

SUBSTITUTE WITH
Adaptiv™
Bergamot
Cypress
Geranium
Jasmine
Magnolia
Petitgrain

SAFETY & RESEARCH
Not safe for internal use.
Dilution recommended.
Possible skin sensitivity.
For research, see page 540.

NORTHERN ESCAPE

WOODLAND BLEND

clearing
renewing
grounding

MAIN INGREDIENTS
Black spruce
Siberian fir
Balsam fir
Lavandin
Cedarwood
Cypress
Hinoki
Frankincense
Nootka
Cananga
Clove

Like Japanese forest bathing, the tree aromas in this blend have the capacity to help the body release acquired negative energies and invite harmony and peace.

TOP USES

FOREST THERAPY
Diffuse. Apply under nose, over heart, on back of neck, and/or bottoms of feet.

MENTAL STRESS & CLUTTERED THINKING
Diffuse or inhale from cupped hands. Apply under nose, across forehead, and/or on back of neck.

OVERSTIMULATION FROM SCREENTIME
Apply under nose, across forehead, and on back of neck.

UNINSPIRED OR UNMOTIVATED
Diffuse. Apply under nose, on forehead and back of neck, and/or over heart.

RESPIRATORY ISSUES
Diffuse or inhale from cupped hands. Apply under nose, across forehead, and/or around ears.

CHAOTIC ENERGY FIELDS, AGITATION
Diffuse. Apply to pulse points and/or bottoms of feet.

POLLUTED AIR & ODORS
Diffuse in areas or spaces in need of air purification.

BATH & BEDTIME ROUTINE
Apply under the nose, on forehead, and bottoms of feet. Add to Epsom salts for a relaxing bath.

JOINTS, MUSCLE ACHES & PAINS
Apply to area of concern.

COLOGNE/PERFUME
Apply to pulse points, neck, and behind the ears for a grounding natural fragrance.

SUBSTITUTE WITH
Align
Black spruce
Cypress
Douglas fir
Forgive®
Hinoki
Holiday Peace
Siberian fir
Tulsi

SAFETY
Not safe for internal use.

defensive • shielding • warming

ON GUARD®

PROTECTIVE BLEND

MAIN INGREDIENTS
Wild orange
Clove
Cinnamon leaf
Cinnamon bark
Eucalyptus
Rosemary

SUBSTITUTE WITH
Cheer®
Cinnamon
Clove
Harvest Spice
Holiday Joy
Passion®
Stronger™
Tulsi

SAFETY
Dilution recommended. Possible skin sensitivity. Avoid exposure to sunlight or UV rays for up to 12 hours after application.

TOP USES

AIRBORNE PATHOGENS
Diffuse and apply to chest and under nose.

SEASONAL IMMUNE BOOST
Diffuse and take in water or a capsule.

COLDS & FLU
Take in a capsule and/or apply to bottoms of feet.

STAPH, STREP THROAT & COUGH
Gargle in water. Apply to chest, throat, and/or take in a capsule or with water.

COLD SORES, WARTS & INFECTED WOUNDS
Apply diluted to affected areas.

ORAL HEALTH & TOOTHBRUSH CLEANING
Gargle and/or use as a mouthwash. Apply to bristles.

FUNGUS & PARASITE ISSUES
Apply to affected area and take in a capsule.

URINARY TRACT INFECTIONS
Take in a capsule. Apply to bottoms of feet.

CHRONIC FATIGUE & AUTOIMMUNE DISEASE
Take in a capsule and/or apply to bottoms of feet.

SURFACE CLEANER & LAUNDRY BOOST
Add with water and vinegar and apply to surfaces. Add to laundry detergent.

SMOKING ADDICTION
Take in a capsule. Inhale from cupped hands.

Use this blend to stay healthy when seasonal threats are high.

= Aromatically = Topically = Internally

OREGANO

ORIGANUM VULGARE

LEAVES

STEAM DISTILLED

SOURCED
Turkey

MAIN CONSTITUENTS
Carvacrol
Thymol

TOP PROPERTIES
Antibacterial
Antifungal
Anti-parasitic
Antiviral
Immunostimulant

FOUND IN
On Guard® softgels

SUBSTITUTE WITH
Clove
On Guard+™
Thyme

SAFETY & RESEARCH
Dilution recommended. Possible skin sensitivity. To reduce liver stress, use with Zendocrine®, helichrysum, cumin, green mandarin, geranium or Roman chamomile. For research, see page 540.

strengthening
resolving
powerful

ESSENTIAL OILS

This powerful and potent essential oil packs a punch. It works well against antibiotic-resistant bacteria.

TOP USES

VIRAL & BACTERIAL INFECTION, COLD/FLU
Take in a capsule and/or sip in warm water from a mug that contains one drop each oregano, peppermint, On Guard®, and/or lemon.

STREP THROAT & TONSILLITIS
Gargle and/or take in a capsule.

STAPH INFECTION & MRSA
Apply diluted to affected area and/or take in a capsule.

INTESTINAL WORMS & PARASITES
Take in a capsule.

WARTS, CALLUSES & CANKER SORES
Apply diluted to affected areas. Inhale steam from a bowl that contains hot water and one drop oregano, Breathe®, and/or On Guard®.

PNEUMONIA & TUBERCULOSIS, WHOOPING COUGH
Apply diluted to bottoms of feet.

LOW PROGESTERONE, URINARY INFECTION
Take in a capsule.

OBESITY & SLOW METABOLISM
Take in a capsule.

ATHLETE'S FOOT, RINGWORM & CANDIDA
Apply diluted to area of concern and/or take in a capsule.

MUSCLE PAIN & INFLAMMATION, CARPAL TUNNEL & RHEUMATISM
Take in a capsule. Apply diluted to area of concern.

EMOTIONAL BALANCE
Use aromatically and topically to go from Obstinate → Unattached.

PASSION®

INSPIRING BLEND

spontaneous · enlivening · daring

MAIN CONSTITUENTS
Cardamom
Cinnamon bark
Ginger
Clove
Sandalwood
Jasmine
Vanilla bean absolute
Damiana

SUBSTITUTE WITH
Cardamom
Cinnamon
Ginger
Harvest Spice
Holiday Joy
Jasmine
On Guard®

TOP USES

APATHY, DEPRESSION & ENERGY ISSUES
Diffuse or inhale from cupped hands to energize and uplift.

LOW LIBIDO & SEXUAL PERFORMANCE, FRIGIDITY
Diffuse and/or inhale from cupped hands. Apply to bottoms of feet, and/or lower abdomen.

MENTAL FOG & MEMORY ISSUES
Apply to big toe and under nose. Diffuse and/or inhale from cupped hands.

SLUGGISH DIGESTION & ELIMINATION
Apply diluted to lower abdomen.

LUNG & SINUS CONGESTION
Diffuse or inhale from hands.

POOR CIRCULATION & COLD EXTREMITIES
Apply to bottoms of feet to warm and stimulate blood flow.

MENSTRUATION & MENOPAUSE ISSUES
Apply diluted to lower abdomen or pressure points below inside and/or outside of ankle bones.

INFECTIONS
Diffuse and apply on area of concern. Dilute if needed.

PERFUME
Apply diluted to wrists and neck.

SAFETY
Not safe for internal use.
Dilution recommended.
Possible skin sensitivity.

This blend invites the natural desire to embrace new and exciting experiences with passion and courage.

relieving
renewing
awakening

PASTTENSE®

TENSION BLEND

MAIN INGREDIENTS
Wintergreen
Lavender
Peppermint
Frankincense
Cilantro
Marjoram
Roman chamomile
Basil
Rosemary

SUBSTITUTE WITH
AromaTouch®
Basil
Deep Blue®
Marjoram
Motivate®
Peppermint
Wintergreen

SAFETY
Not safe for internal use.
Possible skin sensitivity.

TOP USES

HEADACHES & MIGRAINES
Apply to temples, forehead, back of neck, and/or reflex points.

MUSCLE ACHES, SWELLING & CRAMPING
Apply to areas of concern.

HANGOVER
Apply under nose and to back of neck.

HOT FLASHES & COOLING
Apply to abdomen and/or back of neck to cool and calm.

BRUISES & BURNS
Apply to area of concern.

TENSION & STRESS
Apply to pulse points and/or inhale from cupped hands.

JOINT, NECK & SHOULDER PAIN, ARTHRITIS
Apply to areas of discomfort.

RESTFUL SLEEP
Apply to back of neck.

Tension causes many neurological complaints including headaches. This blend helps relieve tension and increase blood flow.

= Aromatically = Topically = Internally

PATCHOULI

POGOSTEMON CABLIN

calming · recovering · stabilizing

LEAVES

STEAM DISTILLED

SOURCED
Indonesia

MAIN CONSTITUENT
Patchouli alcohol
α-Bulnesene
α-Guaiene

TOP PROPERTIES
Aphrodisiac
Sedative
Diuretic
Antifungal
Antispasmodic
Insecticide
Antidepressant

FOUND IN
Amavi®
Anchor
Whisper®
InTune®

SUBSTITUTE WITH
Anchor
Console®
InTune®
Myrrh
Sandalwood
Spikenard
Vetiver
Whisper®

SAFETY & RESEARCH
For research, see page 540.

Patchouli has a long history in the perfume trade, but became famous from the 1960's hippie movement.

TOP USES

ANXIETY & DOPAMINE DEFICIENCY, NERVOUS EXHAUSTION, DEPRESSION
Diffuse. Apply under nose, on back of neck, and/or bottoms of feet.

SHINGLES & HERPES
Apply to area of concern, bottoms of feet, and/or take in a capsule.

DRY SKIN & IMPETEGO, ACNE, ECZEMA
Apply to areas of concern or add to body or face wash.

OILY HAIR & DANDRUFF
Add to shampoo or conditioner.

NERVE & CNS ISSUES
Apply to bottoms of feet. Take in a capsule.

LOW LIBIDO, ERECTILE DYSFUNCTION, LOW TESTOSTERONE, DIFFICULTIES DURING PUBERTY
Take in a capsule and apply to pulse points and/or bottoms of feet. Diffuse with another aphrodisiac oil.

INTERNAL TOXICITY, FLUID RETENTION, BODY ODOR
Take in a capsule. Apply to underarm area.

APPETITE & WEIGHT ISSUES
Take in a capsule or under tongue.

STRETCH MARKS & WRINKLES, UV EXPOSURE
Apply to affected areas.

INSECT & MOSQUITO REPELLENT
Diffuse and apply to exposed areas of skin and clothing when outdoors.

INSECT BITES & STINGS, SNAKE BITES, HIVES, RASHES
Apply to affected areas.

EMOTIONAL BALANCE
Use aromatically and topically to go from Degraded → Enhanced.

brave · composed · flowing

PEACE®

REASSURING BLEND

TOP USES

INSECURITY & WORRY
Apply under nose, on back of neck, and/or forehead. Diffuse or inhale from cupped hands.

NERVOUSNESS & IRRITABILITY
Apply under nose, on back of neck, and/or forehead. Diffuse or inhale from cupped hands.

RESTLESSNESS & CONFUSION
Inhale and apply to forehead and back of neck.

ADD, ADHD & FOCUS ISSUES
Diffuse or inhale and apply to forehead and/or back of neck.

STRESS, MENTAL STRAIN & HYPERACTIVITY
Apply under nose, on back of neck, and/or forehead. Diffuse or inhale from cupped hands.

ADDICTIONS & ANOREXIA
Apply under nose and/or inhale from cupped hands.

CHILDBIRTH & RECOVERY
Apply to lower abdomen, massage into feet, and/or diffuse.

ALLERGIES & OVERREACTION TO LIFE'S CIRCUMSTANCES
Apply to affected area, bottoms of feet, and/or diffuse.

COLIC & UPSET BABY
Apply diluted to bottoms of feet and abdomen.

INFERTILITY & FRIGIDITY
Apply under nose, over abdomen, and/or to pulse points. Diffuse.

MEDITATION
Diffuse and apply under nose.

MAIN INGREDIENTS
Vetiver
Lavender
Ylang ylang
Frankincense
Clary sage
Marjoram
Labdanum
Spearmint

SUBSTITUTE WITH
Anchor
Hygge™
InTune®
Lavender
Serenity®
Thinker™
Vetiver
Ylang ylang

SAFETY
Not safe for internal use. Caution during earlier stages of pregnancy.

No matter what may be happening, this blend helps to release fear and worry and assure a sense of safety and security.

PEPPERMINT

MENTA PIPERITA

LEAVES

STEAM DISTILLED

SOURCED
USA

MAIN CONSTITUENTS
Menthol
Menthone
1,8-cineole (eucalyptol)

TOP PROPERTIES
Anti-inflammatory
Analgesic
Antispasmodic
Warming
Invigorating
Cooling
Expectorant
Vasoconstrictor
Stimulating

FOUND IN
Align
AromaTouch®
Breathe®
Deep Blue®
DigestZen®
Island Mint®
Motivate®
PastTense®
Slim & Sassy®
TerraShield®
Thinker™

SUBSTITUTE WITH
Breathe®
Deep Blue®
DigestZen®
Island Mint®
Motivate®
PastTense®
Spearmint
Tamer™
Thinker™

SAFETY & RESEARCH
Because of its stimulating properties, avoid use at bedtime. Dilution recommended. Possible skin sensitivity. For research, see page 540.

driving
invigorating
cooling

TOP USES

NAUSEA, INDIGESTION, VOMITING, HEARTBURN, GASTRITIS, IBS
Take (I) in a capsule or water, and/or apply (T) over upper abdomen. Dilute as needed.

MENTAL OR CHRONIC FATIGUE, JETLAG, FAINTING, SHOCK
Inhale (A) or apply (T) diluted under nose or on back of neck.

FEVERS & HOT FLASHES
Apply (T) on back of neck, spine, and/or bottoms of feet. Dilute if needed.

HEADACHES & MIGRAINES
Apply (T) to temples, above ears, and/or on back of neck.

BURNS & SUNBURN, HEATSTROKE
Apply (T) neat or diluted to affected area and/or back of neck to cool.

RESPIRATORY CONGESTION, ASTHMA & SINUSITIS, TUBERCULOSIS
Apply (T) diluted to chest, back, and/or bottoms of feet. Take (I) in a capsule.

BRAIN FOG & MEMORY ISSUES, AUTISM, SEIZURE, CONCUSSION
Apply (T) on back of neck, spine, and/or bottoms of feet. Use while studying and then again during times of recall.

ALLERGIES & HIVES, SCABIES
Take (I) in a capsule or water. Apply (T) under nose, and/or to bottoms of feet.

MUSCLE STIFFNESS & TENSION, CHARLEY HORSE, TENNIS ELBOW
Apply (T) directly to area of need, and/or apply pre-workout.

POOR CIRCULATION & VARICOSE VEINS
Apply (T) diluted to affected areas and extremities.

NERVE DAMAGE, MYELIN SHEATH, SCIATICA, PARALYSIS
Apply (T) to area of concern and bottoms of feet.

MENSTRUAL CRAMPS & IRREGULARITIES, PREGNANCY & LABOR DISCOMFORT
Apply (T) diluted over lower back and/or abdomen.

CRAVINGS & APPETITE ISSUES
Inhale (A) or apply (T) under nose. Take a drop (I) on tongue before meals.

INSECT & RODENT REPELLENT
Diffuse (A) and spray of infested surfaces.

BAD BREATH & HANGOVER
Gargle (I) with water, drop on tongue, or take a beadlet.

DECREASE BREAST MILK SUPPLY
Apply (T) diluted to breasts. Take (I) in a capsule or water.

LOSS OF SENSE OF SMELL
Inhale (A) or apply (T) diluted over bridge of nose.

GAMMA RADIATION EXPOSURE
Take (I) in a capsule. Apply to bottoms of feet and/or base of skull.

EMOTIONAL BALANCE
Use (A) aromatically and (T) topically to go from Hindered → Invigorated.

Peppermint's chemistry makes it a powerhouse essential oil. When ingested, menthol, peppermint's main constituent, works with the ion channels of the body to influence nerve impulses and muscle contraction. This relaxes smooth colon muscles that keep bowels moving. Menthol also gives peppermint its cooling properties so it can deliver instant relief from pervasive heat.

ESSENTIAL OILS

(A) = Aromatically (T) = Topically (I) = Internally

relaxing
calming
resolving

Farmers in Paraguay grow, harvest, and distill the plants on their own land to produce Petitgrain essential oil. Once the plant matter has been distilled, it is used again to fuel boilers for future distilling and also as mulch.

TOP USES

BACTERIAL INFECTIONS & WOUNDS
Apply to affected area or take in a capsule.

SPASTIC COUGH & CONGESTION
Apply to chest, diffuse, or take in a capsule.

ABDOMINAL & MUSCLE CRAMPS OR SPASMS
Apply diluted to affected area.

CONVULSIONS & SEIZURES
Apply to back of neck, and/or bottoms of feet.

FEARFUL & ANXIOUS THINKING
Diffuse or inhale from cupped hands.

SUDDEN ANGER, SHOCK, HYSTERIA
Diffuse or inhale from cupped hands.

WEAKENED NERVES & INSOMNIA
Diffuse before going to bed or apply with lavender or bergamot to bedding.

PALPITATIONS & HYPERTENSION
Apply over heart, back of neck, and on bottoms of feet.

NERVOUSNESS & ANXIETY
Diffuse. Take in a capsule. Apply to bottom of feet.

BODY ODOR & EXCESSIVE SWEATING
Apply on underarms or blend with other oils and apply as perfume.

CONVALESCENCE & LONELINESS
Diffuse and apply to back of neck and over heart.

DRY, CRACKED SKIN, ACNE
Apply to areas of concern and/or add to face care regimen.

DANDRUFF & OILY HAIR
Add to shampoo and/or conditioner.

EMOTIONAL BALANCE
Use aromatically and topically to go from Conflicted → Harmonized.

= Aromatically = Topically = Internally

PETITGRAIN

CITRUS AURANTIUM

LEAVES & TWIGS

STEAM DISTILLED

SOURCED
Paraguay

MAIN CONSTITUENTS
Linalyl acetate
Linalool
α-terpineol

TOP PROPERTIES
Antidepressant
Antiseptic
Antispasmodic
Cardiotonic
Detoxifier
Immunostimulant
Nervine
Sedative
Tonic
Uplifting

SUBSTITUTE WITH
Arborvitae
Bergamot mint
Black spruce
Clary sage
Jasmine
Lavender
Magnolia
Neroli
Roman chamomile

SAFETY & RESEARCH
Dilution recommended.
Possible skin sensitivity.
For research, see page 540.

PINK PEPPER

SCHINUS MOLLE

PEPPERCORN

STEAM DISTILLED

SOURCED
Kenya

MAIN CONSTITUENTS
Limonene
α-Phellandrene
Myrcene

TOP PROPERTIES
Invigorating
Purifier
Anti-inflammatory
Antioxidant
Refreshing
Antimicrobial
Digestive stimulant

SUBSTITUTE WITH
DDR Prime®
Douglas fir
Frankincense

SAFETY & RESEARCH
Because of stimulating properties, avoid use at bedtime. Dilution recommended. For research, see page 540.

eliminating
clarifying
enlivening

TOP USES

LYMPHATIC CONGESTION, CANCER, CANDIDA
Combine with frankincense and take in water or a capsule.

CROHN'S DISEASE, NAUSEA & VOMITING, GAS & BLOATING, POOR APPETITE
Apply to areas of concern. Take under tongue or in a capsule.

PAIN MED ADDICTION
Combine with copaiba and black pepper and take in a capsule.

GOUT, RHEUMATISM & ARTHRITIS
Apply to areas of concern and/or take in a capsule.

PMS, MENSTRUAL CRAMPS, BREAST ISSUES & CANCER
Apply to areas of concern. Take in a capsule.

RESPIRATORY ISSUES & BRONCHITIS, DAIRY INTOLERANCE
Apply to chest and back, over lung area, and take under tongue. Diffuse.

DEPRESSION & ANXIETY
Diffuse with green mandarin, lavender, or Roman chamomile. Apply over heart.

INFECTION & FEVER, PROMOTE PERSPIRATION
Take or apply. Dilute as needed.

MUSCLE TENSION, CRAMPS & PAIN
Apply with marjoram to areas of concern. Dilute as needed.

FATIGUE & LACK OF ALERTNESS
Diffuse or inhale from cupped hands. Apply to chest and bottoms of feet.

APHRODISIAC, EUPHORIC, WARMING & INVIGORATING
Apply on abdomen with ylang ylang or jasmine.

METABOLIC SYNDROME & OBESITY, HIGH BLOOD SUGAR, CHOLESTEROL
Take in a capsule with grapefruit and black pepper.

POOR CIRCULATION
Take or apply diluted to areas of concern.

FLAVORING
Add to favorite recipe as a subtle pepper flavor.

EMOTIONAL BALANCE
Use aromatically and topically to go from Impeded → Aroused.

This powerhouse faux pepper (or fake, because it's not hot) potentizes a number of other essential oils in highly complimentary ways.

PURIFY

CLEANSING BLEND

regenerating · corrective · repairing

MAIN INGREDIENTS
Lemon
Siberian fir
Citronella
Lime
Tea tree
Cilantro

SUBSTITUTE WITH
Abōde™
Cilantro
Citronella
Lemon
Lime
Siberian fir
Tea tree

SAFETY
Not safe for internal use. Avoid exposure to sunlight or UV rays for up to 12 hours after application.

TOP USES

GERMS & MICROBES
Diffuse spray on surfaces from glass spray bottle filled with water.

AIR POLLUTION & ODORS
Diffuse to clear the air.

ACNE
Add to skin care routine and apply to areas of concern.

SURFACE CLEANING
Add 6-8 drops and 1 T vinegar to glass spray bottle filled with water.

BUG BITES & STINGS
Apply with lavender to affected areas.

INSECT REPELLENT
Diffuse. Apply to clothing and/or exposed areas of skin.

LAUNDRY
Add 2-4 drops to each load of laundry to dispel odors and kill germs.

DEODORANT
Apply diluted on underarms. Blend to soften aroma.

LYMPHATIC DETOX
Apply diluted to skin or neat to bottoms of feet.

ALLERGIES
Apply to chest, bottoms of feet, and/or diffuse.

ADDICTIONS & DISCOURAGEMENT
Diffuse or apply under nose, across forehead, and/or on bottoms of feet.

Using synthetic chemicals to clean the home can be counterproductive to wellness goals and potentially hazardous. Add Purify to water for a powerful natural surface cleaner or to bring new life to smelly laundry.

expanding
expelling
invigorating

RAVINTSARA

CINAMOMUM CAMPHORA

LEAF

STEAM DISTILLED

SOURCED
Madagascar

MAIN CONSTITUENTS
1,8-cineole (eucalyptol)
Sabinene
α-terpineol

TOP PROPERTIES
Antibacterial
Energizing
Mucolytic
Relaxant
Cleanser
Analgesic
Antifungal
Anti-parasitical
Antimicrobial

FOUND IN
Breathe®

SUBSTITUTE WITH
Breathe®
Eucalyptus
Helichrysum
Laurel leaf

SAFETY & RESEARCH
Not safe for internal use.
Dilution recommended.
Possible skin sensitivity.
For research, see page 540.

Ravintsara tree leaves, also known as Ho leaf, cultivated in Madagascar, contain high levels of eucalyptol and do not contain any camphor.

TOP USES

COLD & FLU, RESPIRATORY OR EAR ISSUES
Diffuse or inhale (A) from cupped hands. Apply (T) under nose, to chest and back, and/or around ears.

SITUATIONAL ANXIETY & WORRY
Diffuse or inhale (A) from cupped hands. Apply (T) under nose and on back of neck.

RESTFUL SLEEP, SLEEP APNEA
Diffuse (A) with Serenity® and/or apply (T) on bottoms of feet.

SORE JOINTS & MUSCLES, LYMPHATIC CONGESTION
Apply (T) to areas of concern. Dilute as needed.

FUNGUS & PARASITES, STAPH, EZCEMA
Apply (T) to areas of concern. Dilute as needed.

LACK OF FOCUS, NERVOUS FATIGUE
Diffuse or inhale (A) from cupped hands. Apply (T) under nose, on forehead, back of neck, and/or over adrenal gland area.

BATH & BEDTIME ROUTINE
Use in bath with Epsom salts or apply (T) to bottoms of feet.

AIR FRESHENER & INSECT REPELLENT
Diffuse (A) in a desired area or space as often as needed.

EMOTIONAL BALANCE
Use (A) aromatically and (T) topically to go from Inflicted → Untroubled.

(A) = Aromatically (T) = Topically (I) = Internally

relieving

cleansing

renewing

ESSENTIAL OILS

TOP USES

ACNE & OILY SKIN, WOUNDS
Apply to areas of concern.

BLOATING, GAS, HICCUPS & INDIGESTION, IBS, COLIC, LEAKY GUT
Apply to chest, back, and/or forehead. Take under tongue or in a capsule.

CONGESTION, SEVERE & SPASTIC COUGHS
Apply to chest, back, or forehead. Take under tongue.

WRINKLES, AGE SPOTS, SCARS, STRETCH MARKS
Add to daily skin care products and apply to areas of concern.

BACTERIAL, FUNGAL & VIRAL INFECTIONS
Apply to areas of concern. Take in a capsule.

NERVOUS AFFLICTIONS, TENSION, HYPERACTIVITY IN CHILDREN
Apply under nose and to bottoms of feet. Diffuse. Take under tongue.

INCREASE APPETITE, ULCERS, UPSET STOMACH, ESOPHAGEAL SPASMS
Take under tongue or in a capsule. Apply for relief.

LIVER, URINARY & LYMPHATIC TOXICITY, EDEMA & POOR BILE FLOW
Take in a capsule daily. Apply to reflex points.

DEPRESSION & MENTAL FATIGUE, CONVULSIONS
Diffuse or inhale. Apply under nose and to bottoms of feet. Take in a capsule or under tongue.

FEAR, FATIGUE, IRRITABILITY, TANTRUMS & HYSTERIA
Diffuse. Apply under nose and on back of neck. Take under tongue as needed.

LACK OF SLEEP & RESTLESSNESS
Diffuse. Apply to back of neck and under nose. Spritz on pillowcase.

GOUT, ARTHRITIS & RHEUMATISM
Take and apply to area of concern.

VARICOSE VEINS & POOR CIRCULATION
Apply to areas of concern. Take in a capsule.

ODOR & SURFACE CLEANING
Diffuse. Add 20 drops to 16 oz glass spray bottle with water and vinegar.

FLAVORING & PROTECT FOOD FROM BACTERIA
Add to dishes, frostings, smoothies, or cut fruit.

EMOTIONAL BALANCE
Use aromatically and topically to go from Troubled → Resilient.

Mandarins are often confused with tangerines and although their taste and tree appearance are similiar, Mandarins are lighter, smoother, and easier to peel.

= Aromatically = Topically = Internally

RED MANDARIN

CITRUS RETICULATA

PEEL

COLD PRESSED

SOURCED
Brazil

MAIN CONSTITUENTS
Limonene

TOP PROPERTIES
Antimicrobial
Antiseptic
Detoxifying
Digestive stimulant
Cytophylactic
Immunostimulant
Antispasmodic
Uplifting

SUBSTITUTE WITH
Grapefruit
Green mandarin
Lemon
Tangerine
Wild orange

SAFETY & RESEARCH
Avoid exposure to sunlight or UV rays or up to 12 hours after application. For research, see page 540.

RESCUER™

CHILDREN'S SOOTHING BLEND

alleviating
calming
comforting

MAIN INGREDIENTS
Copaiba
Lavender
Spearmint
Zanthoxylum

TOP USES

MUSCLE ACHES & TENSION
Apply to areas of concern.

GROWING PAINS
Apply to areas of concern.

HEADACHE & NECK PAIN
Apply to back of neck, forehead, temples, and shoulders.

BRUISES & INJURIES
Apply to areas of concern.

SHOCK, DISTRESS & FEAR
Apply under nose, back of neck, forehead, and/or bottoms of feet.

BATH & BEDTIME ROUTINE
Apply bottoms of feet before or after a warm bath or at bedtime.

Rescuer™ helps unwind and relax after a busy day, reduce feelings of tension in the neck and shoulders, as well as pacify daily bumps and bruises.

Children's blends are intentionally pre-diluted and uniquely formulated with milder aromas to work best with smaller or more sensitive bodies. Designed to indicate when a blend is best suited for mind, heart, or body, icon-coded bottles help children and adults alike learn how to use safe and fun roll-on applications to attend to feelings, listen to the body's needs, and solve everyday issues for a healthier, happier life.

SUBSTITUTE WITH
Copaiba
Deep Blue®
Deep Blue® Stick
Lavender
Spearmint

SAFETY
Not safe for internal use.

calming · relaxing · soothing

ROMAN CHAMOMILE

ANTHEMIS NOBILIS

TOP USES

STRESS & SHOCK, HYSTERIA
Diffuse or inhale Ⓐ from cupped hands. Apply Ⓣ to back of neck.

ALLERGIES & ITCHY EYES, HIVES OR RASHES
Take Ⓘ in a capsule. Apply Ⓣ diluted around eyes, to bottoms of feet, or areas of concern.

DRY, IRRITATED & AGING SKIN, ECZEMA, PSORIASIS, SORE NIPPLES
Apply Ⓣ to areas of concern.

HIGH BLOOD PRESSURE
Apply Ⓣ over heart, on back of neck, and/or bottoms of feet. Take Ⓘ in a capsule.

INSOMNIA & OVEREXCITEMENT
Diffuse Ⓐ and apply Ⓣ to back of neck and forehead.

INSECT BITES, BEE & HORNET STINGS
Apply Ⓣ to area of concern.

ANXIETY, ANGER, IRRITABILITY & AGITATION
Diffuse Ⓐ and/or apply Ⓣ under nose or back of neck.

PARASITES & WORMS, DYSENTERY
Apply Ⓣ to abdomen and take Ⓘ in a capsule.

ANOREXIA, ADDICTIONS, LOW DOPAMINE LEVELS, DEPRESSION, LOW SEROTONIN
Apply Ⓣ under nose, on forehead, and/or back of neck. Take Ⓘ in a capsule.

INFANT/CHILD TEETHING PAIN, CRYING, IRRITABILITY
Apply Ⓣ neat or diluted to bottoms of feet or over area of concern. Diffuse Ⓐ.

FEVERS & EARACHES
Apply Ⓣ to bottoms of feet and/or around ears.

BILE DUCT OBSTRUCTION, HEADACHES & MIGRAINES
Apply Ⓣ over liver area, back of neck, and/or forehead. Take Ⓘ in a capsule.

PMS & CRAMPS, SPRAINS
Apply Ⓣ to lower abdomen or areas of discomfort.

SCIATICA & LOWER BACK PAIN
Apply Ⓣ to areas of concern.

EMOTIONAL BALANCE
Use Ⓐ aromatically and Ⓣ topically to go from Frustrated → Purposeful.

Ⓐ = Aromatically Ⓣ = Topically Ⓘ = Internally

FLOWERS

STEAM DISTILLED

SOURCED
USA

MAIN CONSTITUENT
4-methyl amyl angelate
Isobutyl angelate
Isoamyl tiglate

TOP PROPERTIES
Antihistamine
Antibacterial
Antifungal
Sedative
Immunostimulant

FOUND IN
Calmer™
Citrus Bloom™
ClaryCalm®
InTune®
PastTense®
Serenity®

SUBSTITUTE WITH
Arborvitae, Blue tansy, Calmer™, ClaryCalm®, Clary sage, Jasmine, Lavender, Palmarosa, Petitgrain, Serenity®

SAFETY & RESEARCH
For research, see page 540.

Ancient Romans used Roman chamomile before battle to empower them with courage and clear minds.

encompassing
connecting
clarifying

ESSENTIAL OILS

Known as the "Queen of Flowers," it requires about 12,000 rose blossoms to make one 5mL bottle.

TOP USES

LOW LIBIDO, SEXUAL DEBILITIES, FRIGIDITY, LACK OF SEXUAL CONFIDENCE
Diffuse or inhale Ⓐ from cupped hands. Apply Ⓣ to lower abdomen, bottoms of feet, or areas of interest.

BACTERIAL INFECTIONS, MRSA/STAPH, POISON OAK
Apply Ⓣ a drop to areas of concern.

GRIEF & DEPRESSION, BROKEN-HEARTED, LONELY, HEART ISSUES & PALPITATIONS
Diffuse Ⓐ and apply Ⓣ to back of neck, forehead, and/or over heart.

CHILDBIRTH & BABY BLUES
Diffuse Ⓐ and apply Ⓣ to back of neck and over heart.

IRREGULAR OVULATION & MENSTUATION, MISCARRIAGE, PROLAPSED, SCARRED, OR CONGESTED UTERUS, EXCESSIVE BLEEDING
Apply Ⓣ over lower abdomen and to ankle reflex points.

SEIZURES, BRAIN & NERVE ISSUES
Apply Ⓣ to back of neck and bottoms of feet.

FINE LINES, SCARS, WRINKLES, FACIAL CAPILLARIES & REDNESS
Apply Ⓣ to areas of concern. Add to skincare routine.

LOW SEMEN PRODUCTION, IMPOTENCY, & PROSTATE ISSUES
Apply Ⓣ to navel, bottoms of feet, and ankle reflex points.

PERFUME
Combine with jasmine or neroli and apply Ⓣ as desired.

EMOTIONAL BALANCE
Use Ⓐ aromatically and Ⓣ topically to go from Isolated ⟶ Loved.

Ⓐ = Aromatically Ⓣ = Topically Ⓘ = Internally

ROSE

ROSA DAMASCENA

FLOWERS

STEAM DISTILLED

SOURCED
Bulgaria

MAIN CONSTITUENTS
Citronellol
Geraniol
Nonadecane
Nerol

TOP PROPERTIES
Antidepressant
Aphrodisiac
Antispasmodic
Emmenagogue
Sedative
Tonic

FOUND IN
Align
Immortelle
Stronger™
Whisper®

SUBSTITUTE WITH
Citronella
Console®
Davana
Geranium
Immortelle
Jasmine
Magnolia
Stronger™
Whisper®
Ylang ylang

SAFETY & RESEARCH
Not safe for internal use. Dilution recommended due to highly concentrated and powerful aroma. For research, see page 540.

ROSEMARY

ROSMARINUS OFFICINALIS

LEAVES

STEAM DISTILLED

SOURCED
Bulgaria

MAIN CONSTITUENTS
1,8-cineole (eucalyptol)
α-pinene
Camphor

TOP PROPERTIES
Analgesic
Anticatarrhal
Stimulant
Neurotonic

FOUND IN
Adaptiv™
Motivate®
On Guard®
PastTense®
Thinker™
Zendocrine®

SUBSTITUTE WITH
Basil
Blue tansy
Eucalyptus
Juniper berry
Laurel leaf
Thinker™

SAFETY & RESEARCH
Caution with use with epileptics, during pregnancy, and high blood pressure. For research, see page 540.

In ancient times, rosemary was commonly used to drive away evil spirits.

TOP USES

MENTAL, ADRENAL & CHRONIC FATIGUE, HEADACHE
Diffuse. Apply under nose and/or on neck and shoulders. Take in a capsule.

RESPIRATORY INFECTIONS & CONDITIONS, LOSS OF SMELL
Apply to chest, bottoms of feet, and/or diffuse.

POOR MEMORY & LACK OF FOCUS
Apply under nose and across forehead, and/or diffuse.

PROSTATE ISSUES & NIGHTTIME URINATION
Apply to bottoms of feet. Take in a capsule.

FAINTING, DIZZINESS, LOW BLOOD PRESSURE, RAPID HEARTBEAT
Inhale from cupped hands. Apply under nose, on back of neck, and bottoms of feet.

HAIR THINNING & LOSS, DANDRUFF, OILY HAIR
Apply to scalp, and/or add to shampoo.

TIRED OR WEAK MUSCLES & BONE PAIN, GOUT, NATURAL STEROID
Apply to area of concern.

MALARIA & PARASITES, JAUNDICE, LIVER & KIDNEY ISSUES
Apply to bottoms of feet and take in a capsule.

NERVOUSNESS, DEPRESSION, ADDICTIONS & LOW DOPAMINE
Apply under nose or diffuse. Take in a capsule.

JET LAG
Apply under nose, on back of neck, and/or diffuse.

CELLULITE & LYMPHATIC DRAINAGE, CONGESTION, CHEMICAL TOXICITY OR EXPOSURE
Take in a capsule. Apply to areas of concern.

BELL'S PALSY & MULTIPLE SCLEROSIS, PARALYSIS
Apply to bottoms of feet and/or take in a capsule.

CANCER, HEPATITIS, DIABETES
Take in a capsule. Apply to bottoms of feet.

EMOTIONAL BALANCE
Use aromatically and topically to go from Confused → Open-minded.

---

stabilizing · regenerating · solving

SANDALWOOD

SANTALUM ALBUM

WOOD

STEAM DISTILLED

SOURCED
India
Hawaii

MAIN CONSTITUENT
α- & ß-santalols
α- & ß-santalenes

TOP PROPERTIES
Anti-inflammatory
Anti-carcinoma
Astringent
Antidepressant
Calming
Sedative

FOUND IN
Anchor
Console®
Passion®
Whisper®

SUBSTITUTE WITH
Anchor
Cedarwood
Immortelle
InTune®
Myrrh
Patchouli
Spikenard
Vetiver

SAFETY
Not safe for internal use.
For research, see page 540.

Sandalwood has been used for various spiritual and religious uses. Today, Hindus still use it to anoint the temple floor and walls to enhance spiritual ambiance.

TOP USES

DRY SKIN & SCALP, RASHES
Use topically or add to shampoo.

SCARS & BLEMISHES, VITILIGO, MOLES, UV SKIN DAMAGE
Apply directly to affected area.

WOUND CARE & SKIN INFECTIONS
Apply to affected area.

LOW SEX DRIVE, LOW TESTOSTERONE & IMPOTENCE
Take in a capsule. Apply to lower abdomen or pulse points. Wear combined with black spruce to boost testosterone.

CANCER & TUMORS
Take in a capsule and/or apply to bottoms of feet and back of neck.

ALZHEIMER'S, CONFUSION, PITUITARY & PINEAL GLAND ISSUES
Take in a capsule. Apply to bottoms of feet, back of neck, and forehead.

INSOMNIA & RESTLESSNESS
Apply under nose, to bottoms of feet, and/or diffuse.

MEDITATION & YOGA
Inhale from cupped hands or diffuse.

DEPRESSION, LOW SEROTONIN OR DOPAMINE
Diffuse or inhale from cupped hands. Take in a capsule.

MYELIN SHEATH DISEASE, SCIATICA, LOU GEHRIG'S
Apply to affected areas and/or take in a capsule.

SINUS INFECTION, SORE THROAT, LARYNGITIS
Apply over bridge of nose or throat area. Inhale from cupped hands. Take in a capsule or gargle.

SPASMS & CRAMPS
Apply over area of concern.

EMOTIONAL BALANCE
Use aromatically and topically to go from Uninspired → Devoted.

recuperating

relaxing

calming

SERENITY®

RESTFUL BLEND

TOP USES

INSOMNIA & SLEEP ISSUES
Diffuse (A), apply (T) under nose, down spine, and/or bottoms of feet.

STRESS & ANXIETY, RESTLESSNESS
Apply (T) under nose, on back of neck, and/or diffuse (A).

FUSSY BABY & RESTLESS CHILD
Diffuse (A). Apply (T) to bottoms of feet or down spine to calm. Dilute as desired.

TENSION & MOOD SWINGS
Diffuse (A) or inhale from cupped hands. Apply (T) to back of neck and/or over heart.

FEARS & NERVOUSNESS
Apply (T) to back of neck, diffuse (A), and/or inhale from cupped hands.

BATH & BEDTIME ROUTINE
Use in bath or apply (T) to back of neck, along spine, and bottoms of feet to relax and unwind at night.

ANGER, AGITATION & IRRITABILITY
Diffuse (A), apply (T) under nose, and/or to bottoms of feet.

SKINCARE
Apply (T) to areas of concern.

MUSCLE TENSION
Apply (T) to areas of concern.

PERFUME
Apply (T) to pulse points and wear as a personal scent. Blend as desired.

MAIN INGREDIENTS
Lavender
Cedarwood
Ho wood
Ylang ylang
Marjoram
Roman chamomile
Vetiver
Vanilla bean absolute
Hawaiian sandalwood

SUBSTITUTE WITH
Calmer™
Cedarwood
ClaryCalm®
Frankincense
InTune®
Lavender
Peace®
Ylang ylang

SAFETY
Not safe for internal use.
Possible skin sensitivity.

Create a tranquil feeling and transport oneself to a state of blissful rest by calming the mind and emotions, soothing the senses, and supporting a deeper sleep with this grounding aroma.

ESSENTIAL OILS

TOP USES

PAIN & INFLAMMATION, RHEUMATISM, ARTHRITIS & GOUT, TIRED & ACHY MUSCLES
Take in a capsule or massage into area of concern.

CONSTRICTED BREATHING, CONGESTION, COLD, FLU, FEVER & SORE THROAT, COUGH
Apply to chest, bottoms of feet, along spine. Diffuse and/or inhale from cupped hands.

BROKEN BONES & OSTEOPOROSIS
Apply diluted with helichrysum, cypress, and wintergreen. Take in a capsule.

CANDIDA & URINARY INFECTIONS
Take in a capsule. Apply to lower abdomen.

POOR CIRCULATION, HEMORRHOIDS, LOW BLOOD PRESSURE
Apply to area of concern, and/or to bottoms of feet.

SLUGGISH DIGESTION & METABOLISM LIVER FUNCTION, CELLULITE
Massage onto abdomen and/or take in a capsule.

BODY ODOR
Apply diluted under arms. Take in a capsule to detox.

CANCER & AUTOIMMUNE DISORDERS
Take in a capsule. Apply to area of concern, and/or bottoms of feet.

BURNS, WOUNDS, ECZEMA, DERMATITIS
Apply to area of concern. Dilute as needed.

HORMONE IMBALANCES & PROSTATITIS
Take in a capsule. Apply on lower abdomen, and/or reflex points.

ANXIETY, BRAIN FOG & EXHAUSTION
Apply under nose, across forehead, and/or on bottoms of feet. Diffuse and/or inhale from cupped hands.

AIRBORNE PATHOGENS
Diffuse in affected spaces.

SURFACE DISINFECTANT
Spray on surfaces and wipe.

EMOTIONAL BALANCE
Use aromatically and topically to go from Excluded → Empowered.

Siberian fir is believed to have the finest scent of all the firs.

= Aromatically = Topically = Internally

SIBERIAN FIR

ABIES SIBIRICA

NEEDLES, TWIGS

STEAM DISTILLED

SOURCED
Russia

MAIN CONSTITUENTS
Bornyl acetate
Camphene
δ-3-Carene
α-Pinene

TOP PROPERTIES
Analgesic
Anti-fungal
Anti-inflammatory
Detoxifier
Energizing
Expectorant
Refreshing
Antiseptic

FOUND IN
Arise
Holiday Joy
Holiday Peace
Midnight Forest
Northern Escape
Purify

SUBSTITUTE WITH
Black spruce
Cypress
Douglas fir
Frankincense
Hinoki
Holiday Peace
Northern Escape
Purify

SAFETY & RESEARCH
Dilution recommended.
For research, see page 540.

SLIM & SASSY®

METABOLIC BLEND

cleansing
spicy
refreshing

MAIN INGREDIENTS
Grapefruit
Lemon
Peppermint
Ginger
Cinnamon bark

Balancing appetite, reducing cravings, and balancing blood sugar levels are all important precursors to weight loss success.

TOP USES

WEIGHT LOSS, OBESITY & SLOW METABOLISM
Take 5 drops up to 5 times daily in capsule or water.

CELLULITE
Apply diluted to areas of concern.

EATING DISORDERS
Take in a capsule or with water. Apply to bottoms of feet or diffuse.

EXCESS OR DIMINISHED APPETITE & CRAVINGS
Drop under tongue or add to drinking water. Inhale from bottle or apply under nose.

CONGESTION & COLDS
Take in a capsule or in water.

URINARY TRACT INFECTION
Take in a capsule or in water.

BLOOD SUGAR IMBALANCE
Take in a capsule or in water.

LIVER, LYMPH, URINARY TOXICITY
Take in a capsule or in water.

UPSET OR SLUGGISH DIGESTION OR ELIMINIATION
Take in a capsule or in water.

HIGH CHOLESTEROL
Take in a capsule or in water.

GALLBLADDER ISSUES & STONES
Take in a capsule or in water.

SUBSTITUTE WITH
Cinnamon
Ginger
Grapefruit
Lemon
Peppermint

SAFETY
Dilution recommended for topical use. Avoid exposure to sunlight or UV rays for up to 12 hours after application.

relieving · uplifting · promoting

SPEARMINT

MENTHA SPICATA

TOP USES

INDIGESTION, NAUSEA & COLIC, CONSTIPATION OR DIARRHEA
Apply over abdomen. Dilute as needed. Take in a capsule.

BRONCHITIS & RESPIRATORY ISSUES
Apply to chest and back or diffuse.

OVERHEATED, HEATSTROKE, FEVER
Apply to back of neck, on spine, and/or bottoms of feet.

CYSTITIS, INCONTINENCE, KIDNEY STONES
Take in a capsule or glass of water. Apply on back over kidney areas.

BAD BREATH & SORE GUMS
Swish and swallow in water.

SLOW METABOLISM/FAT BURNING, APPETITE IMBALANCES
Take in a capsule or glass of water.

DEPRESSION & FATIGUE, MENTAL STRAIN OR LACK OF FOCUS
Diffuse and apply to back of neck.

HEADACHES & MIGRAINES
Diffuse and apply to temples and/or back of neck.

ACNE, SORES & SCARS, ECZEMA
Apply to area of concern.

HIGH BLOOD PRESSURE, DIZZINESS, LOSS OF EQUILIBRIUM
Apply to bottoms of feet and back of neck.

SLOW OR HEAVY MENSTRUATION, VAGINITIS, DIFFICULT LABOR
Diffuse and apply over abdomen or back of neck.

EMOTIONAL BALANCE
Use aromatically and topically to go from Weary ⟶ Refreshed.

= Aromatically = Topically = Internally

WHOLE PLANT

STEAM DISTILLED

SOURCED
India

MAIN CONSTITUENT
Carvone
Limonene

TOP PROPERTIES
Anti-inflammatory
Digestive stimulant
Carminative
Antiseptic

FOUND IN
Adaptiv™
Rescuer™
Tamer™

SUBSTITUTE WITH
Bergamot mint
Island Mint®
Peppermint
Rescuer™
Tamer™
Turmeric

SAFETY & RESEARCH
For research, see page 540.

A common flavor for toothpaste & candy, the ancient Greeks enjoyed bathing with spearmint.

SPIKENARD

NARDOSTACHYS JATAMANSI

healing • rejuvenating • uplifting

ROOTS

STEAM DISTILLED

SOURCED
Nepal

MAIN CONSTITUENT
Jatamansone
Gurjunene

TOP PROPERTIES
Anti-inflammatory
Antispasmodic
Sedative
Antibacterial
Antifungal
Deodorant
Laxative
Tonic

SUBSTITUTE WITH
Cedarwood
Myrrh
Patchouli
Ylang ylang

SAFETY & RESEARCH
Not safe for internal use. For research, see page 540.

TOP USES

AGING & IRRITATED SKIN
Add to facial cleanser or moisturizer.

INSOMNIA, STRESS, MUSCLE TENSION & SPASMS
Diffuse and apply to bottoms of feet and/or area of concern.

PMS & MENSTRUAL ISSUES, INFERTILITY
Apply to lower abdomen, back of neck, and pulse points.

CANDIDA & VAGINAL THRUSH
Apply to affected area diluted.

BRAIN ISSUES, CONVULSIONS & SEIZURES
Apply to back of neck or affected area.

DETOXING, DIURETIC & CELLULITE
Apply to affected area or bottoms of feet.

TERMINALLY ILL & HOSPICE
Apply to bottoms of feet and/or diffuse.

ULCERS, GAS & INDIGESTION
Apply to abdomen.

PINK EYE & RASHES
Apply diluted to affected area or around eye.

GROUNDING MEDITATION
Diffuse during meditation session and/or apply to bottoms of feet.

ANXIETY, DEPRESSION & PERSISTENT EMOTIONAL BLOCKS
Apply to back of neck, forehead. Diffuse.

EMOTIONAL BALANCE
Use aromatically and topically to go from Agitated → Tranquil.

Spikenard, one of the Romans' favorite perfumes, is featured in the Bible several times and was traditionally used to annoint those of high honor.

balancing
steadying
quieting

STEADY™

CHILDREN'S GROUNDING BLEND

TOP USES

UNCOOPERATIVE & OBSTINATE, OUT OF CONTROL
Apply (Topically) to chest, forehead, and/or bottoms of feet.

OVERSTIMULATED & OVERWHELMED
Apply (Topically) under nose, to back of neck, and forehead.

DISCONNECTED FROM REALITY, UNGROUNDED OR UNSTABLE
Apply (Topically) under nose, and/or to bottoms of feet.

FOCUS ISSUES & MOOD SWINGS
Apply (Topically) under nose, over heart, and/or to forehead.

RESTLESS & WOUND UP
Apply (Topically) under nose, to back of neck, along spine, and/or bottoms of feet.

ANGER & FRUSTRATION, TANTRUMS
Apply (Topically) under nose, to back of neck, along spine, over heart, and/or bottoms of feet.

GRIEF & SADNESS, DISAPPOINTMENT
Apply (Topically) under nose, to chest, forehead, and/or bottoms of feet.

BATH & BEDTIME ROUTINE
Apply (Topically) to bottoms of feet before or after a warm bath or at bedtime.

MAIN INGREDIENTS
Amyris
Balsam fir
Coriander
Magnolia

SUBSTITUTE WITH
Balance®
Hygge™
InTune®
Magnolia

SAFETY
Not safe for internal use.

Steady™ helps to balance mood and soothe upset feelings when emotions seem close to the surface. Use when a child seems to be extra sensitive. Goes great alongside naps, extra snuggles, and one-on-one time.

Children's blends are intentionally pre-diluted and uniquely formulated with milder aromas to work best with smaller or more sensitive bodies. Designed to indicate when a blend is best suited for mind, heart, or body, icon-coded bottles help children and adults alike learn how to use safe and fun roll-on applications to attend to feelings, listen to the body's needs, and solve everyday issues for a healthier, happier life.

= Aromatically = Topically = Internally

STRONGER™

CHILDREN'S PROTECTIVE BLEND

fortifying • shielding • boosting

MAIN INGREDIENTS
Cedarwood
Litsea
Frankincense
Rose

SUBSTITUTE WITH
Cedarwood
Frankincense
Holiday Joy
Litsea
On Guard®
Rose

SAFETY
Not safe for internal use.

TOP USES

BACTERIA & VIRUSES, AIRBORNE PATHOGENS
Apply to areas of concern, bottoms of feet, under nose, and/or across forehead.

FLU, WEAK IMMUNITY, POOR RECOVERY
Apply under nose, over heart, along spine, and/or bottoms of feet.

EMOTIONAL DISTRESS & POOR BOUNDARIES
Inhale deeply from cupped hands. Apply to bottoms of feet and over heart.

STAPH, STREP THROAT & COUGH
Apply to throat/neck, chest, along spine, and/or bottoms of feet.

COLD SORES, WARTS & INFECTED WOUNDS
Apply to areas of concern.

CUTS & SCRAPES
Apply to areas of concern.

FUNGUS & PARASITES
Apply to areas of concern, over abdomen, along spine, and on bottoms of feet.

CHRONIC FATIGUE & AUTOIMMUNE CONDITIONS
Apply to chest, back, and/or bottoms of feet.

Stronger™ helps to strengthen the mind and body, promote natural immune defense, and soothe emotions and skin during times of distress.

Children's blends are intentionally pre-diluted and uniquely formulated with milder aromas to work best with smaller or more sensitive bodies. Designed to indicate when a blend is best suited for mind, heart, or body, icon-coded bottles help children and adults alike learn how to use safe and fun roll-on applications to attend to feelings, listen to the body's needs, and solve everyday issues for a healthier, happier life.

alleviating • pacifying • easing

TAMER™

CHILDREN'S DIGESTIVE BLEND

TOP USES

MOTION, TRAVEL & MORNING SICKNESS
Apply to upper or lower abdomen and/or to bottoms of feet.

BLOATING, GAS, NAUSEA & UPSET STOMACH
Apply to upper or lower abdomen and/or to bottoms of feet.

CONSTIPATION, DIARRHEA, IRRITABLE BOWEL SYNDROME, CROHN'S DISEASE
Apply to upper and lower abdomen and/or to bottoms of feet.

BRONCHITIS, ASTHMA, COUGH, CHEST COLD
Apply to chest and back.

FEVER & CHILLS, COLD/FLU, BODY ACHES
Apply to chest, back, forehead, areas of discomfort, and/or bottoms of feet.

HOT FLASHES, OVERHEATED, HEATSTROKE OR EXHAUSTION
Apply to back of neck, forehead, and/or bottoms of feet.

EDEMA
Massage onto lower legs and feet.

ACNE & SKIN BLEMISHES
Apply to areas of concern after cleansing skin's surface and prior to moisturizing.

Tamer™ is perfect for little ones who are experiencing unpleasant tummy troubles, helping to soothe and cool.

Children's blends are intentionally pre-diluted and uniquely formulated with milder aromas to work best with smaller or more sensitive bodies. Designed to indicate when a blend is best suited for mind, heart, or body, icon-coded bottles help children and adults alike learn how to use safe and fun roll-on applications to attend to feelings, listen to the body's needs, and solve everyday issues for a healthier, happier life.

MAIN INGREDIENTS
Spearmint
Japanese peppermint
Ginger
Black pepper
Parsley

SUBSTITUTE WITH
DigestZen®
Ginger
Island Mint®
Peppermint
Spearmint

SAFETY
Not safe for internal use.

TANGERINE

CITRUS RETICULATA

RIND

COLD PRESSED

SOURCED
Brazil

MAIN CONSTITUENTS
Limonene

TOP PROPERTIES
Energizing
Sedative
Uplifting
Antioxidant
Cytophylactic
Detoxifier
Mucolytic
Stomachic

FOUND IN
Air-X™
Citrus Bliss®
Elevation
Zendrocrine®

SUBSTITUTION WITH
Citrus Bliss®
Grapefruit
Green mandarin
Wild orange

SAFETY & RESEARCH
Avoid exposure to sunlight or UV rays for up to 12 hours after application. For research, see page 540.

TOP USES

ANTIOXIDANT, IMMUNE BOOST & CELL PROTECTION
Take in water or in a capsule.

SADNESS & IRRITABILITY, IMPULSIVENESS
Diffuse or inhale from cupped hands. Appy under nose and over heart.

SLEEP ISSUES & ANXIETY, NERVOUSNESS
Diffuse or inhale from cupped hands. Appy under nose, and/or take in water.

DIGESTIVE & INTESTINAL DISORDERS, PARASITES, LIVER & GALLBLADDER ISSUES
Take in water or a capsule and apply to upper or lower abdomen.

OVERTHINKING & FEELING STUCK
Diffuse or inhale from cupped hands and apply under nose and across forehead.

EDEMA, CELLULITE
Massage onto area of concern and take in water or a capsule.

DRY, CRACKED & IRRITATED SKIN, RASHES & BURNS, DANDRUFF
Apply diluted to area of concern or add to shampoo.

CONGESTION, COUGHS, ASTHMA
Apply to chest and back (over lung area). Take in water or a capsule.

SLOW METABOLISM & WEIGHT ISSUES
Take in water or a capsule.

POOR CIRCULATION, CONVULSIONS
Apply to area of concern, back of neck, or bottoms of feet. Take in a capsule.

ACHY TENSE OR FATIGUED MUSCLES & ARTHRITIS
Massage onto area of concern.

ARTHRITIS & MUSCLE PAIN, TENSION
Massage onto area of concern.

EMOTIONAL BALANCE
Use aromatically and topically to go from Oppressed → Restored.

Tangerine has been used for over 3000 years and remains valuable in integrative medicine.

= Aromatically = Topically = Internally

TEA TREE

MELALEUCA ALTERNIFOLIA

LEAVES

STEAM DISTILLED

SOURCED
Australia

MAIN CONSTITUENTS
Terpinen-4-ol
γ-terpinene
α-terpinene

TOP PROPERTIES
Antiseptic
Antibacterial
Antifungal
Anti-parasitic
Antiviral
Analgesic
Decongestant

FOUND IN
Abōde™
Breathe®
HD Clear®
Purify

SUBSTITUTE WITH
Abōde™
HD Clear®
Marjoram

SAFETY & RESEARCH
Tea tree remains on the FDA's GRAS list. For research, see page 540.

powerful

cleansing

resolving

TOP USES

CUTS, WOUNDS & ASSOCIATED PAIN
Apply to affected area.

BACTERIA, VIRUSES, DIARRHEA, FOOD POSIONING, ULCERS
Take in a capsule and/or apply to abdomen.

CANKERS & COLD SORES, HERPES, WARTS
Apply on affected area to treat or prevent from emerging.

ATHLETE'S FOOT & CANDIDA ISSUES, RINGWORM, VAGINAL THRUSH
Take in a capsule. Apply diluted to affected area.

SORE THROAT & TONSILLITIS, MUMPS
Take in a capsule or gargle with warm water.

DANDRUFF, SCABIES, LICE
Apply to affected area and/or add to shampoo.

EAR INFECTIONS
Apply behind and around ear.

SHOCK
Apply under nose or along spine.

ACNE, PINK EYE, STAPH INFECTION & MRSA, BOILS
Take in a capsule or apply on or around affected area.

BRONCHITIS, COLD & FLU
Use in a capsule, rub on throat, and diffuse.

HIVES, RASHES & ITCHY EYES, SHINGLES, MEASLES
Take in a capsule and/or apply to affected area or bottoms of feet.

CAVITIES & GUM DISEASE
Use in a capsule and apply on affected area.

EMOTIONAL BALANCE
Use aromatically and topically to go from Unsure → Collected.

With 12 times the antiseptic power of a phenol, Australian Aborigines have used tea tree for centuries, often crushing leaves in their hands and inhaling the aroma for colds and illnesses.

= Aromatically = Topically = Internally

TERRASHIELD®

REPELLENT BLEND

guarding
repelling
protecting

MAIN CONSTITUENTS
Citronella
Lemongrass
Thyme
Cedarwood
Geranium
Peppermint

SUBSTITUTE WITH
Abōde™
Arborvitae
Citronella
Lemon eucalyptus
Lemongrass
Thyme

SAFETY
Not safe for internal use.

TOP USES

INSECT REPELLENT
Apply to exposed areas of skin and clothing before going outdoors. Diffuse and spray on outdoor surfaces.

CELLULAR HEALTH & ANTIOXIDANT
Apply to pulse points and bottoms of feet to promote healthy cell function.

SKIN COMPLAINTS
Apply diluted with lavender to troubled skin.

POOR EMOTIONAL BOUNDARIES, EASILY BUGGED OR BOTHERED
Diffuse or apply to strengthen one's resolve and maintain healthy emotional boundaries.

WOOD POLISH
Mix 4 drops with fractionated coconut oil to polish and preserve wood.

A toxic-free alternative to guard against bugs and pests. Sesame seed oil helps the blend stay on the skin longer, prolonging its effect.

anchoring • enlivening • signaling

THINKER™

CHILDREN'S FOCUS BLEND

TOP USES

LACK OF MENTAL CLARITY, FOCUS & CONCENTRATION
Apply under nose, to forehead, along spine, back of neck, and/or bottoms of feet.

ADD/ADHD, HYPERACTIVITY
Apply under nose, to forehead, along spine, back of neck, and/or bottoms of feet.

OVER & UNDERACTIVE BRAIN ACTIVITY
Apply under nose, to forehead, along spine, back of neck, and/or bottoms of feet.

OVERWHELMED & APATHETIC, CHECKED OUT, AFTERNOON SLUMP
Apply under nose, to forehead, along spine, back of neck, and/or bottoms of feet.

STRESSED OUT & UNGROUNDED
Apply under nose, to forehead, along spine, back of neck, and/or bottoms of feet.

NERVOUS, ANXIOUS & MOODY
Apply under nose, to forehead, along spine, back of neck, and/or bottoms of feet.

SEIZURES
Apply under nose, to forehead, along spine, back of neck, and/or bottoms of feet.

MAIN INGREDIENTS
Vetiver
Peppermint
Clementine
Rosemary

SUBSTITUTE WITH
InTune®
Peace®
Peppermint
Rosemary
Vetiver

SAFETY
Not safe for internal use. Avoid sunlight or UV rays to applied area for up to 12 hours.

Thinker™ can help instill a sense of alertness and focus while doing homework, during tests, or anytime concentration is needed while reducing mental stress and fatigue.

Children's blends are intentionally pre-diluted and uniquely formulated with milder aromas to work best with smaller or more sensitive bodies. Designed to indicate when a blend is best suited for mind, heart, or body, icon-coded bottles help children and adults alike learn how to use safe and fun roll-on applications to attend to feelings, listen to the body's needs, and solve everyday issues for a healthier, happier life.

= Aromatically = Topically = Internally

THYME

THYMUS VULGARIS

LEAVES

STEAM DISTILLED

SOURCED
Kenya

MAIN CONSTITUENTS
Thymol
Paracymene

TOP PROPERTIES
Analgesic
Mucolytic
Stimulant
Antioxidant
Anti-rheumatic
Antiviral
Expectorant

FOUND IN
DDR Prime®
Forgive®
TerraShield®

SUBSTITUTE WITH
Clove
DDR Prime®
Forgive®
Oregano
TerraShield®
Tulsi

SAFETY & RESEARCH
Caution with use with epileptics, during pregnancy, and high blood pressure. For research see page 540.

resolving
powerful
expelling

TOP USES

COLD, FLU & VIRUSES, SORE THROAT, BACTERIAL INFECTIONS
Take in a capsule. Apply to bottoms of feet.

ASTHMA, CROUP & PNEUMONIA, WHOOPING COUGH, LARYNGITIS, TONSILITIS, PLEURISY
Dilute and massage onto chest, inhale from cupped hands. Take in a capsule.

CANDIDA & PARASITES, FUNGAL INFECTIONS, ECZEMA, PSORIASIS
Take in a capsule or inhale . Apply highly diluted to affected areas.

INFERTILITY, LOW PROGESTERONE, BREAST, OVARY & PROSTATE ISSUES, IRREGULAR MENSTRUATION
Apply to reflex points on feet and take in a capsule.

POOR MEMORY OR CONCENTRATION, ALZHEIMER'S, DEMENTIA, AGING
Inhale and apply highly diluted on back of neck and/or under toes on brain reflex points.

LOW BLOOD PRESSURE
Apply to bottoms of feet and pulse points.

INCONTINENCE & BLADDER INFECTION, CYSTITIS, EDEMA
Take in a capsule.

UTERINE FIBROIDS, FIBROCYSTIC BREAST, CANCER
Take in a capsule.

RHEUMATIC PAIN & SORE MUSCLES
Take in a capsule. Apply highly diluted to areas of concern.

FATIGUE, STRESS & DEPRESSION
Take in a capsule.

HAIR LOSS OR BALDNESS, OILY OR FRAGILE HAIR
Add a few drops to shampoo and apply .

RADIATION WOUNDS
Apply highly diluted to affected area.

EMOTIONAL BALANCE
Use aromatically and topically to go from Unyielding → Yielding.

Thyme means "to fumigate" in Greek and is one of the most potent antioxidant essential oils.

= Aromatically = Topically = Internally

TULSI

OCIMUM SANCTUM

FLOWERING TOPS / LEAVES

STEAM DISTILLED

SOURCED
India

MAIN CONSTITUENTS
Eugenol
1,8-cineole (eucalyptol)
Methyl chavicol

TOP PROPERTIES
Relaxant
Antibacterial
Antiviral
Antifungal
Anti-inflammatory
Analgesic
Disinfectant

SUBSTITUTE WITH
Basil
Blue tansy
Clove
Copaiba
Coriander
Fennel

SAFETY & RESEARCH
Not safe for internal use. For research, see page 540.

correcting
balancing
harmonizing

TOP USES

MENTAL & ADRENAL FATIGUE, POOR MEMORY & COGNITION, REPEATED TENDENCY TOWARD ERRORS & SLOW REACTION TIME
Diffuse or inhale from cupped hands. Apply diluted under nose and/or to pulse points.

IMBALANCED BLOOD SUGAR & DIABETES-RELATED ISSUES, POOR CIRCULATION, HIGH CHOLESTEROL
Apply to bottoms of feet and over pancreas and/or liver areas.

PHYSICAL, HEART, CHEMICAL, METABOLIC & PSYCHOLOGICAL STRESS, ELEVATED CORTISOL LEVELS & ANXIETY
Diffuse or inhale from cupped hands. Apply diluted under nose, over heart, on back of neck, and/or bottoms of feet.

HEADACHES, STRESS-INDUCED MUSCLE TENSION & INFLAMMATION
Diffuse. Apply to forehead and/or areas of concern. Dilute as needed.

EYE ISSUES & INFECTION, CATARACTS, COMPROMISED EYESIGHT
Apply highly diluted around eye area and under 2nd and 3rd toes.

LACK OF VITALITY, SELF-ASSURANCE, RESILIENCY OR ADAPTABILITY
Diffuse or inhale from cupped hands. Apply diluted under nose and/or to pulse points.

FEVER, SINUS PRESSURE & PAIN, CONSTRICTED BREATHING & RESPIRATORY ISSUES, ASTHMA, SLEEP APNEA
Diffuse. Apply on forehead, back of neck, chest, along spine, and/or bottoms of feet. Dilute as needed.

CANCER & PREVENTION, CHEMICAL-INDUCED SKIN, LIVER, ORAL, & LUNG CANCER, FREE RADICALS
Apply to bottoms of feet, chest, and/or other areas of concern. Dilute as needed.

CHEMICAL & HEAVY METAL TOXICITY, RADIATION, PH IMBALANCE, EXAGGERATED IMMUNE RESPONSE
Diffuse or inhale from cupped hands. Apply under nose, on forehead, back of neck, and/or bottoms of feet.

ACNE, COLD SORES, WARTS & INFECTED WOUNDS, SKIN IRRITATIONS
Apply to areas of concern. Dilute as needed.

DANDRUFF & SCALP ISSUES, HAIR LOSS
Apply to scalp or add to shampoo or conditioner.

GRIEF, DISAPPOINTMENT, SADNESS, & FEAR
Diffuse or inhale from cupped hands. Apply diluted under nose and over heart.

INTESTINAL PARASITES, & COMPROMISED MUCOSAL LINING
Apply to bottoms of feet and/or diluted on lower abdomen.

DISPEL ODORS & AIRBORNE PATHOGENS, DISINFECT SURFACES & SANITIZE HAND
Diffuse to eliminate odors and clean the air. Spray on surfaces from glass bottle mixed with water, or apply to hands.

EMOTIONAL BALANCE
Use aromatically and topically to go from Run-down → Enduring.

Known as the "elixir of life" and native to India, Holy Basil is considered a sacred plant called the "incomparable one" and kept in a special place in Hindu courtyards to invite divine presence.

ESSENTIAL OILS

Turmeric, or "sacred earth" in Latin, is renowned for a myriad of profound properties, including its powerful action against cancer and inflammation. On an energetic level, it also cleanses chakras and energy fields and promotes feelings of prosperity.

TOP USES

JOINT PAIN & SWELLING, ARTHRITIS, GOUT, RHEUMATISM
Apply Ⓣ to areas of concern. Take Ⓘ in a capsule.

CANCER & TUMORS, AUTOIMMUNE DISORDERS
Take Ⓘ in a capsule. Apply Ⓣ to affected areas.

FUNGAL, BACTERIAL OR VIRAL INFECTIONS
Take Ⓘ and apply Ⓣ to affected areas.

ALZHEIMERS, STROKE, POOR BLOOD SUPPLY
Take Ⓘ in a capsule. Inhale Ⓐ from cupped hands. Apply Ⓣ to forehead, bottoms of feet, and/or along spine.

BLOOD & LYMPH, LIVER & GALLBLADDER DETOX
Take Ⓘ in a capsule as part of a detox program. Apply Ⓣ to reflex points and/or bottoms of feet.

INTESTINAL WORMS & PARASITES
Take Ⓘ in a capsule.

ACNE, ECZEMA & PSORIASIS
Add to skin care routine and apply Ⓣ to affected areas. Take Ⓘ in a capsule.

DEPRESSION & DISCOURAGEMENT, TENSION & ANXIETY
Diffuse Ⓐ. Apply Ⓣ to back of neck and/or along spine.

ULCERS, GAS & BLOATING, INDIGESTION, COMPROMISED INTESTINAL FLORA
Take Ⓘ in a capsule. Apply Ⓣ to area of concern.

POOR CIRCULATION, DIABETES & METABOLISM, HIGH CHOLESTEROL
Take Ⓘ in a capsule. Apply Ⓣ to bottoms of feet.

COUGH, RESPIRATORY ISSUES & BRONCHITIS
Apply Ⓣ to chest and back. Take Ⓘ in a capsule.

SORE MUSCLES & MENSTRUAL CRAMPS
Combine with AromaTouch® or marjoram and apply Ⓣ to areas of concern.

CAVITIES & ORAL HEALTH
Add Ⓘ to toothpaste or mouthwash. Gargle, swish, and spit or use as part of an oil pulling routine.

COOKING
Add Ⓘ to dishes for a savory flavor.

EMOTIONAL BALANCE
Use Ⓐ aromatically and Ⓣ topically to go from Compromised → Assured.

Ⓐ = Aromatically Ⓣ = Topically Ⓘ = Internally

TURMERIC

CURCUMA LONGA

ROOT

STEAM DISTILLED

SOURCED
Nepal

MAIN CONSTITUENTS
ar-turmerone
Turmerone

TOP PROPERTIES
Anti-inflammatory
Anticarcinogenic
Detoxifier
Antibacterial
Antioxidant
Antimutagenic
Anticancer
Anti-tumoral
Decongestant
Antiviral

SUBSTITUTE WITH
Ginger
Myrrh
Spearmint

SAFETY & RESEARCH
The essential oil does not have the same skin-coloring and fabric staining properties or warning as powdered form. Can be toxic to plants. For research, see page 540.

ESSENTIAL OILS

blissful · elating · enriching

VANILLA

VANILLA PLANIFOLIA

BEANS (PODS)

SOLVENT (OR CO^2) EXTRACTION

SOURCED
Madagascar

MAIN CONSTITUENTS
Vanillin

TOP PROPERTIES
Calming
Relaxant

FOUND IN
Cheer®
Citrus Bliss®
Hope®
Hygge™
Motivate®
Passion®
Serenity®
Whisper®

SUBSTITUTE WITH
Cheer®
Citrus Bliss®
Hope®
Whisper®

SAFETY & RESEARCH
Not safe for internal use.
Dilution recommended.
Possible skin sensitivity.
For research, see page 540.

In 1841, 12-year-old slave, Edmond Albius, discovered a way to hand-pollinate the flowers while working on a vanilla plantation on the island of Réunion. That same process is used today for nearly all vanilla grown across the world.

TOP USES

EUPHORIC, WARMING & INVIGORATING
Combine with favorite citrus, flower, spice, and/or tree oils. Diffuse or inhale from cupped hands. Add to fractionated coconut oil and apply under nose, to back of neck, along spine, and/or on bottoms of feet as a personal scent.

RELAXATION & TRANQUILITY, COMFORT
Combine with favorite calming oil. Diffuse. Apply diluted to pulse points, back of neck, along the spine, and/or bottoms of feet.

RESTLESS & SLEEP ISSUES
Diffuse and apply under nose and to bottoms of feet.

APHRODISIAC, LOSS OF LIBIDO & FRIGIDITY, IMPOTENCE, ERECTILE DYSFUNCTION
Combine with other aphrodisiac oils such as ylang ylang, jasmine, and/or cinnamon. Diffuse and/or inhale from cupped hands. Add to a base of fractionated coconut oil and apply to lower abdomen and/or reproductive organ reflex points and/or wear as a personal scent.

NERVOUSNESS, STRESS, ANXIETY & DEPRESSION
Diffuse and apply diluted under nose and to bottoms of feet. Dilute.

NEUROLOGICAL ISSUES
Diffuse and apply diluted under nose and to bottoms of feet or area of need.

CANCER & TUMORS, PREVENTION
Diffuse and apply diluted under nose, to bottoms of feet and/or area of need.

ALBUMIN (PROTEIN) GLYCATION
Apply to bottoms of feet and toes and/or affected skin.

LOW BLOOD PRESSURE RELATED TO INFECTION
Diffuse and apply diluted under nose and to bottoms of feet.

BATH & BEDTIME ROUTINE
Mix with Epsom salts and add to bath water or apply to bottoms of feet and/or spine prior to a warm, relaxing soak.

PERFUME
Combine with other favorite oils in a roller bottle topped off with fractionated coconut oil and wear to enhance mood and delight the senses.

EMOTIONAL BALANCE
Use aromatically and topically to go from Aloof → Delighted.

---

regenerating

reassuring

enduring

VETIVER

VETIVERIA ZIZANIOIDES

TOP USES

ADD, ADHD, LACK OF FOCUS & CONCENTRATION
Apply to back of neck, along spine, and/or under nose. Combine with lavender.

LEARNING DIFFICULTIES & POOR RETENTION
Apply to back of neck, and/or under nose. Diffuse during learning times with lavender.

INSOMNIA & IRRITABILITY
Apply to bottoms of feet or back of neck.

NERVE ISSUES & DEBILITY, NUMBNESS
Apply to affected area.

PTSD, DEPRESSION & ANXIETY, SHOCK, FEAR, TRAUMA
Apply to back of neck, forehead, and pulse points. Diffuse with lavender.

STRETCH MARKS, AGING SKIN, DISCOLORATION & SCARS, VITILIGO, ACNE, WOUNDS & CUTS
Apply to affected areas.

POSTPARTUM DEPRESSION & FATIGUE
Apply to back of neck, under nose, and on pulse points. Diffuse with Citrus Bliss®.

BREAST ENLARGEMENT
Apply diluted to breasts.

LACK OF ENDURANCE & SUSCEPTIBILITY TO GETTING ILL
Take in capsule. Apply under nose.

ANOREXIA
Apply to back of neck or across forehead.

PARATHYROID
Apply to back of neck. Take in capsule.

TUBERCULOSIS
Apply to feet, spine, and chest.

EMOTIONAL BALANCE
Use aromatically and topically to go from Ungrounded → Rooted.

= Aromatically = Topically = Internally

ROOTS

STEAM DISTILLED

SOURCED
Haiti

MAIN CONSTITUENT
Isovalencenol
Khusimol

TOP PROPERTIES
Stimulant
Tonic
Sedative
Antiseptic
Immunostimulant
Vermifuge
Antispasmodic
Rubaficient

FOUND IN
Holiday Peace
Hygge™
Serenity®
Thinker™
Whisper®

SUBSTITUTE WITH
InTune®
Myrrh
Patchouli
Peace®
Sandalwood
Thinker™
Whisper®

SAFETY & RESEARCH
For research, see page 540.

Vetiver is a natural tranquilizer, and in Ayurvedic medicine is known as the oil of "tranquility."

WHISPER®

WOMEN'S PERFUME BLEND

seducing
balancing
euphoric

MAIN INGREDIENTS
Patchouli
Bergamot
Hawaiian sandalwood
Rose
Vanilla bean absolute
Jasmine
Cinnamon bark
Vetiver
Labdanum
Cocoa bean
Ylang ylang

SUBSTITUTE WITH
Bergamot
Jasmine
Neroli
Patchouli
Rose
Sandalwood
Vanilla
Vetiver
Ylang ylang

SAFETY
Not safe for internal use. Avoid exposure to sunlight or UV rays for up to 12 hours after application.

Each woman's unique body chemistry makes the scent of this blend her own.

TOP USES

PERFUME
Apply to wrists and base of neck.

LACK OF SEX DRIVE OR SEXUAL INTEREST
Apply to wrists, neck, and/or chest.

IMBALANCED HORMONES
Apply to pulse points, back of neck, and bottoms of feet.

HOT FLASHES
Apply to base of neck and/or lower abdomen.

LACK OF SELF-EXPRESSION OR PRESENCE
Inhale from cupped hands, apply under nose, and on wrist and neck to pulse points.

LACK OF SELF-CONFIDENCE & CREATIVITY
Inhale from cupped hands, and/or apply to forehead and over heart.

ANGER & IRRITABILITY
Inhale from cupped hands, and/or apply to pulse points.

stimulating

clearing

calming

WHITE FIR

ABIES ALBA

NEEDLES

STEAM DISTILLED

SOURCED
Austria

MAIN CONSTITUENTS
Limonene
β-pinene
Bornyl acetate

TOP PROPERTIES
Analgesic
Antiarthritic
Antiseptic
Stimulant
Antioxidant

SUBSTITUTE WITH
Arborvitae
Douglas fir
Grapefruit
Neroli
Northern Escape
Pink pepper
Siberian fir

SAFETY & RESEARCH
Not safe for internal use.
For research, see page 540.

Used to decorate homes as Christmas trees. Native Americans used this tree to clear respiratory problems.

TOP USES

SINUSITIS & ASTHMA
Apply to bridge of nose and chest or diffuse to ease breathing.

MUSCLE & JOINT PAIN
Massage diluted on affected areas.

MUSCLE FATIGUE & REGENERATION
Apply diluted to areas of concern.

BURSITIS & RHEUMATISM
Apply to affected areas.

AIRBORNE PATHOGENS
Diffuse to fight germs.

CIRCULATION ISSUES & BRUISING
Massage into affected areas.

STRESS & FOGGY MIND
Diffuse with frankincense for increased focus and clarity.

BRONCHITIS & CONGESTION
Apply to chest or bridge of nose.

COLDS & FLU
Apply to chest and diffuse.

URINARY INFECTION & EDEMA
Apply over lower abdomen.

FURNITURE POLISH
Apply to surfaces using a cloth.

EMOTIONAL BALANCE
Use aromatically and topically to go from Blocked → Receiving.

= Aromatically = Topically = Internally

WILD ORANGE

CITRUS SINENSIS

RIND

COLD PRESSED

SOURCED
Brazil

MAIN CONSTITUENTS
Limonene

FOUND IN
Energizing
Sedative
Anti-carcinoma
Carminative
Antiseptic
Antidepressant
Immunostimulant

FOUND IN
Adaptiv™
Brave™
Cheer®
Citrus Bliss®
Citrus Bloom™
DDR Prime®
Holiday Joy
Hygge™
Midnight Forest
On Guard®

SUBSTITUTE WITH
Adaptiv™
Cheer®
Citrus Bliss®
DDR Prime®
Grapefruit
Green mandarin
Tangerine

SAFETY & RESEARCH
Avoid exposure to sunlight or UV rays for up to 12 hours after application. For research, see page 540.

The Chinese first recognized the value of the peel of an orange for treating coughs and colds.

ESSENTIAL OILS

TOP USES

DEPRESSION, FEAR, ISOLATION, IRRITABILITY
Apply under nose, across forehead, or pulse points. Diffuse or inhale from cupped hands.

LACK OF ENERGY, CREATIVITY & PRODUCTIVITY OR CONCENTRATION
Take in a capsule, apply under nose, or diffuse.

CANCER & TISSUE OR CELLULAR REGENERATION
Take in a capsule and/or apply to affected areas.

HEARTBURN & SLUGGISH BOWELS, DIARRHEA, COLIC, JAUNDICE
Take in a capsule with ginger or apply diluted to abdomen.

TOXICITY, EDEMA, OBESITY & HIGH CHOLESTEROL
Take in a glass of water or capsule.

DIGESTIVE UPSET DUE TO ANXIETY
Take in a capsule and inhale from cupped hands.

INSOMNIA, STRESS & ANXIETY, ADDICTION WITHDRAWALS, EXCESSIVE APPETITE
Diffuse or inhale from cupped hands or take a few drops under tongue at bedtime.

MENOPAUSE & WEAKENED BONES, PROLAPSED UTERUS
Apply to abdomen, pulse points, and diffuse. Take in a capsule.

DULL, OILY DAMAGED SKIN & WRINKLES
Apply to areas of concern.

SCURVY & COLDS, MOUTH ULCERS
Diffuse or apply to bottoms of feet.

COOKING
Add a drop to dishes, frostings, and smoothies for a sweet, rich citrus flavor.

EMOTIONAL BALANCE
Use aromatically and topically to go from Drained → Productive.

= Aromatically = Topically = Internally

TOP USES

ARTHRITIS, GOUT & RHEUMATISM
Dilute and apply Ⓣ to affected areas.

POOR CIRCULATION & COLD EXTREMITIES, HIGH BLOOD PRESSURE
Dilute and apply Ⓣ to affected areas.

MUSCLE PAIN, CRAMPS & LACK OF TONE
Dilute and apply Ⓣ to area of concern.

BONE OR NERVE PAIN, SCIATICA
Apply Ⓣ diluted to affected area.

BROKEN BONES, SPURS, CARTILAGE INJURY & BRUISING OSTEOPOROSIS
Dilute and apply Ⓣ to affected area.

ROTATOR CUFF ISSUES & FROZEN SHOULDER, TENDINITIS
Dilute and apply Ⓣ to affected areas.

DANDRUFF
Add to shampoo and apply Ⓣ to scalp.

DERMATITIS, ECZEMA, ACNE
Dilute and apply Ⓣ to affected areas.

LYMPHATIC CONGESTION, CHRONIC MUCUS DISCHARGE, EDEMA, OBESITY, GALLSTONES
Apply Ⓣ diluted to bottoms of feet, chest, or abdomen.

BLADDER INFECTION & KIDNEY STONES, FEVER
Dilute and apply Ⓣ over lower abdomen, midback, or back of neck.

EMOTIONAL BALANCE
Use Ⓐ aromatically and Ⓣ topically to go from Stubborn → Accepting.

A naturally occurring compound found in wintergreen, "methyl salicylate" is related to the chemical found in aspirin.

Ⓐ = Aromatically Ⓣ = Topically Ⓘ = Internally

WINTERGREEN

GAULTHERIA FRAGRANTISSIMA

LEAVES

STEAM DISTILLED

SOURCED
Nepal

MAIN CONSTITUENTS
Methyl salicylate

TOP PROPERTIES
Anti-inflammatory
Analgesic
Anti-rheumatic

FOUND IN
Deep Blue®
PastTense®

SUBSTITUTE WITH
AromaTouch®
Birch
Deep Blue®
PastTense®

SAFETY & RESEARCH
Not safe for internal use.
Dilution recommended.
Possible skin sensitivity.
For research, see page 540.

YARROW | POM

ACHILLEA MILLEFOLIUM

AERIAL PARTS

STEAM DISTILLED

SOURCED
Bulgaria

MAIN CONSTITUENTS
Punicic acid
β-caryophyllene
Chamazulene

TOP PROPERTIES
Antihemorrhagic
Anti-rheumatic
Antiviral
Emmenagogue
Regenerative

SUBSTITUTE WITH
Black pepper
Blue tansy
Douglas fir
Helichrysum
Immortelle
Juniper berry
Ylang ylang

SAFETY & RESEARCH
Dilution recommended. Possible skin sensitivity. May stain surfaces, fabric, and skin. For research, see page 540.

purging

relieving

mending

TOP USES

BLEEDING, HEMORRHAGING, INTERNAL WOUNDS & SCARRING
Take [internally] in a capsule or in water.

VARICOSE VEINS & HEMORRHOIDS, SAGGING, DRY OR AGING SKIN, POOR COLLAGEN PRODUCTION
Apply [topically] to affected area. Add a hot compress to take deeper.

IRREGULAR OR ABSENT MENSTRUATION & EARLY MENOPAUSE
Apply [topically] to abdomen, drop in a sitz bath, and/or take [internally] in a capsule.

DEPRESSION, ANXIETY & FATIGUE
Inhale [aromatically] from cupped hands, apply [topically] under nose, and/or bottoms of feet.

PAIN & INFLAMMATION, ARTHRITIS, RHEUMATISM
Apply [topically] to area of concern, and/or take [internally] in a capsule.

FEVER, VIRUSES & ALLERGIES
Take [internally] in a capsule, apply [topically] to bottoms of feet, and/or along spine.

BRAIN OR NERVE DYSFUNCTION, POOR COGNITION OR MEMORY RECALL
Take [internally] in a capsule. Apply [topically] to back of neck, forehead, and/or bottoms of feet.

CANCER, FREE RADICAL DAMAGE, OVARY & BREAST ISSUES
Take [internally] in a capsule. Apply [topically] to affected areas.

ACNE, ECZEMA, HAIR LOSS & SCALP ISSUES
Apply [topically] to areas of concern or add to skin or hair care products.

BLOOD TOXICITY & SLUGGISH LIVER
Take [internally] in a capsule or massage [topically] onto upper abdomen.

TOOTHACHE OR LOOSE TEETH
Apply [topically] to gums and teeth.

INDIGESTION, BELCHING, BLOATING & ULCERS
Take [internally] in a capsule and/or massage [topically] into abdomen.

LOW PERSPIRATION & POOR CIRCULATION
Apply [topically] to bottoms of feet and/or area of concern. Use in a steam bath to promote sweating and release toxins.

METABOLIC DISORDERS & BLOOD SUGAR IMBALANCE
Take [internally] in a capsule.

EMOTIONAL BALANCE
Use [aromatically] aromatically and [topically] topically to go from Invaded → Shielded.

In ancient Greece, Achilles was said to use yarrow to ease a painful Achilles tendon.

[aromatically] = Aromatically [topically] = Topically [internally] = Internally

YLANG YLANG

CANANGA ODORATA

exotic · sedating · seducing

FLOWERS

STEAM DISTILLED

SOURCED
Madagascar

MAIN CONSTITUENT
Germacrene D
β-Caryophyllene
Farnesene

TOP PROPERTIES
Hypotensive
Aphrodisiac
Antispasmodic
Sedative

FOUND IN
ClaryCalm®
Console®
Deep Blue®
Elevation
InTune®
Peace®
Serenity®
TerraShield®
Whisper®

SUBSTITUTE WITH
Black pepper
Calmer™
ClaryCalm®
Console®
Copaiba
Hope®
Jasmine
Magnolia
Peace®
Rose
Tulsi
Whisper®
Yarrow|Pom

SAFETY & RESEARCH
For research, see page 540.

TOP USES

LOW LIBIDO, IMPOTENCE, INFERTILITY, HORMONE IMBALANCE, LOW TESTOSTERONE
Apply to lower abdomen, pulse points, and/or take in a capsule.

ADRENAL OR MENTAL FATIGUE, APATHY OR LOSS OF WILL
Diffuse or inhale from cupped hands. Apply over heart. Take in a capsule.

IRREGULAR HEARTBEAT & PALPITATIONS
Apply to bottoms of feet and over the heart. Inhale from cupped hands. Take in a capsule

DISTRESS, GRIEF, HEARTBREAK, CRYING, FEAR, SHOCK, TRAUMA
Diffuse or inhale from cupped hands. Apply over heart, and/or back of neck. Take in a capsule.

ANXIETY, FRUSTRATION, INSOMNIA, STRESS
Diffuse or inhale from cupped hands. Apply under nose, and on bottoms of feet.

LACK OF EQUILIBRIUM & HIGH BLOOD PRESSURE
Apply to back of neck, across forehead, and behind ears. Inhale from cupped hands. Take under tongue, or in a capsule.

OILY SKIN & INSECT BITES
Apply to area of concern.

HAIR LOSS & SPLIT ENDS
Massage into scalp to stimulate hair growth and/or on ends with conditioner.

COLIC & STOMACH ACHE, CONSTIPATION
Apply diluted to abdomen and/or take in a capsule.

EMOTIONAL BALANCE
Use aromatically and topically to go from Burdened → Exuberant.

In Java, ylang ylang flowers adorn the newlyweds' bed and are often used as an aphrodisiac.

refreshing
detoxing
clearing

ZENDOCRINE®

DETOXIFICATION BLEND

MAIN INGREDIENTS
Tangerine
Rosemary
Geranium
Juniper berry
Cilantro

SUBSTITUTE WITH
Cilantro
Forgive®
Geranium
Juniper berry
Rosemary
Tangerine

SAFETY
Avoid exposure to sunlight or UV rays for up to 12 hours after application.

TOP USES

KIDNEY, GALLBLADDER & LIVER TOXICITY & ISSUES
Take in a capsule and/or apply diluted over organ area and/or reflex points on feet.

HEAVY METAL DETOXIFICATION
Take in a capsule. Apply on bottoms of feet.

CONSTIPATION & URINARY TRACT INFECTION
Take and/or apply diluted over abdomen.

WEIGHT LOSS & DETOXIFICATION
Take in a capsule.

COLITIS & JAUNDICE
Take in a capsule and/or apply diluted to abdomen or bottoms of feet.

ENDOCRINE & HORMONE IMBALANCE
Take in a capsule and/or apply diluted to abdomen or bottoms of feet.

ADRENAL FATIGUE & EXHAUSTION, HANGOVER
Take in a capsule and/or apply diluted to back of neck, or bottoms of feet.

A regular detoxification regime helps ensure healthy kidney and liver function. Take 1-3 drops in a capsule, fresh juice, or tea 2x's/day during a cleansing program.

= Aromatically = Topically = Internally

ESSENTIAL OILS

SUPPLEMENTARY PRODUCTS

Is your energy low? Do you experience chronic pain or discomfort? Dealing with challenges in sustaining energy and concentration throughout the day, along with maintaining adequate immune and physical health, are the norm for many. However, virtually any health compromise or issue can be traced to some kind of underlying deficiency or toxicity. Numerous studies have been conducted over decades to determine the optimal nutritional state for the human body. The scientific community agrees that virtually everyone falls short in obtaining the bare minimum of recommended daily nutritional requirements in at least some areas.

These nutritional deficiencies can be attributed to two main factors. The first is a rise in compromised farming practices and interest by growers to genetically modify foods. Even those eating a wholesome, balanced diet find it challenging to consume adequate levels of certain nutrients. The second factor is the over consumption of refined, processed, nutrient-void foods that are loaded with empty calories. Such declines have been advancing for decades. Similarly, adults and children alike are also consuming excessive amounts of animal protein, while eating far too few fresh fruits and vegetables.

With these drastic changes in both food supply and consumption, examining one's own nutritional status is a worthy course of action. Ask asking yourself if you have any diet, health, or lifestyle compromises that contribute to an overall lack in wellness and vitality. Then make adjustments accordingly. Whether actually healthy or not, everyone certainly benefits from supplemental nutrition to intentionally bridge these widening gaps.

A2Z CHEWABLE™

Multivitamin, mineral and botanical chewable for children and adults that have difficulty swallowing. Blended with antioxidants and herbal compounds that increase overall health and wellness.

TOP USES

Low energy and fatigue, compromised digestion and immunity, brain fog, oxidative cell damage, malnutrition, and poor health.

INGREDIENTS

- Vitamins A, C, D3, E, K, and full B-complex: antioxidants and cellular energy, bringing synergy and vital nutrients to the cells of the body and brain. Also supports a healthy immune function.
- Calcium, copper, iron, iodine, magnesium, manganese, potassium and zinc: bioavailable minerals which lay the foundation for bone health and nerve cell functions. Also supports fluid transportation and utilization by the cells.
- Superfood blend of pineapple, pomegranate extract, lemon bioflavonoids, spirulina, sunflower oil, rice bran, beet greens, broccoli, brown rice, carrot, mango, cranberry, rose hips, acerola cherry extract, spinach: blend of antioxidants and whole food nutrients to support healthy cell function and increase utilization of other nutrients throughout the body.
- Cellular vitality complex of tomato extract, turmeric extract, boswellia serrata extract, grape seed extract, marigold flower extract: synergistic blend of natural anti-inflammatories, antioxidants and cellular repair compounds.

SAFETY

No GMOs, gluten, wheat, dairy, soy, or nut products. Pregnant or lactating women should consult a physician or healthcare provider before use.

Selected vitamins and trace elements support immune function by strengthening epithelial barriers and cellular and humoral immune responses, Maggini S, Wintergerst ES, Beveridge S, Hornig DH, British Journal of Nutrition, 2007

Contribution of selected vitamins and trace elements to immune function, Wintergerst ES, Maggini S, Hornig DH, Ann Nutr Met, 2007

Minerals and vitamins in bone health: The potential value of dietary enhancement, Bonjour JP, Gueguen L, Palacios C, et al, Bri J Nutr, 2009

The immunological functions of the vitamin D endocrine system, Hayes CE, Nashold FE, Spach KM & Pedersen LB, Cell Molec Biol, 2003

Possible role for dietary lutein and zeaxanthin in visual development, Hammond BR, Nutr Rev, 2008

ADAPTIV™ CAPSULES

Liquicap combining a supportive blend of essential oils with clinically proven botanicals. Supports relaxation, and encouragement when adapting to stressful situations or acclimating to new surroundings. Intended as a tool to help manage effects of stress, tension, uneasiness, and worry that come during everyday life.

TOP USES

Manage stress, boost mood, balance mind and body, promote positive attitude, improve state of mind, invite resiliency, agility, and mental well-being.

INGREDIENTS

- Lavender oil: highly versatile, best known for calming and relaxing properties; major uses include promoting peaceful sleep, easing emotional and physical tension.
- Coriander oil: eases stomach upset and balances blood sugar (both of which are aggravated by states of stress), while promoting feelings of relaxation.
- Wild orange oil: stress-protective antioxidants and anti-inflammatory properties, calms emotionally-based digestive upset, energizes and uplifts mind and body.
- Fennel oil: curbs cravings for sweets, soothes digestive upset, addresses blood sugar imbalances—all due to prolonged stress, helps move a person out of emotionally-paralyzed inactivity with relaxing properties.
- Sceletium root extract: unique phytochemical, stirs "alert serenity," supports healthy emotional responses to everyday stressors, stimulates production of mood stabilizing hormones, improves cognitive function while combating occasional nervousness, promotes sense of well-being and euphoria.
- GABA: quieting neurotransmitter, promotes relaxation through natural comforting effects, helps reduce feelings of apprehension and fear by decreasing neuronal excitability, moving the brain and body into a lower gear by lowering activity of neural cells and central nervous system.
- Ahiflower seeds: superior omega-rich oil, contains higher quality and quantity of omegas than any other seed oils, known for capacity to help maintain self-confidence, emotional stability, positive attitude while reducing restlessness.

SAFETY

Keep out of reach of children. If pregnant, nursing, or under a doctor's care, consult physician. Vegan friendly. Store in cool, dry place.

ALPHA CRS®+

A capsule that delivers potent antioxidants, natural anti-inflammatories, and energy cofactors. This blend of synergistic herbs will give life and energy to the cells and a sense of well being to the body.

TOP USES

Pain and inflammation, arthritis, osteoarthritis, fibromyalgia, foggy brain, cirrhosis, jaundice, cellular repair, fatigue, mood, and cancer prevention.

INGREDIENTS

- Boswellia serrata gum resin: inflammatory modulator (helps regulate and decrease inflammation and pain).
- Scutellaria root (baicalin): inflammatory modulator and cellular damage repair, supports liver and kidney health.
- Milk thistle (silymarin): powerful liver protectant and free radical scavenger.
- Polygonum cuspidatum (resveratrol): increases healthy cell proliferation and decreases free radical damage from cells.
- Green tea leaf (EGCG): powerful antioxidant, free radical scavenger, and anticancer properties.
- Pomegranate fruit extract: antioxidant shown to lower LDL cholesterol, blood pressure, and increase heart health.
- Pineapple (bromelain): an enzyme shown to decrease pain and inflammation.
- Turmeric extract (curcumin): powerful anti-inflammatory and anticancer compound.
- Grape seed extract: proanthocyanidins shown to decrease free radical damage and increase cellular repair.
- Sesame seed extract: antioxidant shown to protect liver from oxidative damage.
- Pine bark extract (pycnogenol): antioxidant shown to increase vasodilation of the arteries and decrease free radical damage.
- Gingko Biloba leaf: increases circulation to the brain and brings mental clarity.
- Acetyl-L-Carnitine: increases energy production by the mitochondria and increases glutathione (internal antioxidant) levels in the body.
- Alpha-Lipoic acid: antioxidant vital for cellular energy and neutralizing free radicals.
- Coenzyme Q10: plays a significant role in energy production for the heart and muscle cells.
- Quercetin: potent antioxidant flavonoid known to decrease cell damage and increase recovery.
- Stomach comfort blend of peppermint, ginger and caraway: calms and soothes the digestive processs.

SAFETY

For men, women, and teens. Pregnant or lactating women should consult a physician or healthcare provider before use.

Gene Expression Profiling of Aging in Multiple Mouse Strains: Identification of Aging Biomarkers and Impact of Dietary Antioxidants, Park SK, Kim K, Page GP, Allison DB, Weindruch R, Prolla TA, Aging Cell, 2009

Antioxidative and anti-inflammatory activities of polyhydroxyflavonoids of Scutellaria baicalensis GEORGI, Huang WH, Lee AR, Yang CH, Biosci Biotechnol Biochem, 2006 Oct

New therapeutic aspects of flavones: the anticancer properties of Scutellaria and its main active constituents Wogonin, Baicalein and Baicalin, Li-Weber M, Cancer Treat Rev, 2009 Feb

The SIRT1 activator resveratrol protects SK-N-BE cells from oxidative stress and against toxicity caused by alpha-synuclein or amyloid-beta (1-42) peptide, Albani D, Polito L, Batelli S, De Mauro S, Fracasso C, Martelli G, Colombo L, Manzoni C, Salmona M, Caccia S, Negro A, Forloni G, J Neurochem, 2009

Resveratrol induces mitochondrial biogenesis in endothelial cells, Csiszar A, Labinskyy N, Pinto JT, Ballabh P, Zhang H, Losonczy G, Pearson K, de Cabo R, Pacher P, Zhang C, Ungvari Z, Am J Physiol Heart Circ Physiol, 2009 Jul

In vitro effects of tea polyphenols on redox metabolism, oxidative stress, and apoptosis in PC12 cells, Raza H, John A, Ann N Y Acad Sci, 2008 Sep

Orally administered green tea polyphenols prevent ultraviolet radiation-induced skin cancer in mice through activation of cytotoxic T cells and inhibition of angiogenesis in tumors, Mantena SK, Meeran SM, Elmets CA, Katiyar SK, J Nutr, 2005 Dec

Grape seed and red wine polyphenol extracts inhibit cellular cholesterol uptake, cell proliferation, and 5-lipoxygenase activity, Leifert WR, Abeywardena MY, Nutr Res, 2008 Dec

Quercetin increases brain and muscle mitochondrial biogenesis and exercise tolerance, Davis JM, Murphy EA, Carmichael MD, Davis B, Am J Physiol Regul Integr Comp Physiol, 2009 Apr

Mineral and vitamin deficiencies can accelerate the mitochondrial decay of aging, Ames BN, Atamna H, Killilea DW, Mol Aspects Med, 2005 Aug-Oct

Boswellic acid inhibits growth and metastasis of human colorectal cancer in orthotopic mouse model by downregulating inflammatory, proliferative, invasive and angiogenic biomarkers, Yadav, VR, Prasad S, Sung, B, Gelovani, JG, Guha, S, Krishnan, S, Aggarwal, BB Int. J. Cancer, 2012

Plant food supplements with anti-inflammatory properties: A systematic review, Di Lorenzo C, Dell'agli M, Badea M, et al, Critical Reviews in Food Science and Nutrition, 2013

Polyphenols, inflammation, and cardiovascular disease, Tangney CC, Rasmussen HE, Curr Atheroscler Rep, 2013

Bioavailability and activity of phytosome complexes from botanical polyphenols: The silymarin, curcumin, green tea, and grape seed extracts, Kidd PM, Alternative Medicine Review, 2009

Open, randomized controlled clinical trial of Boswellia serrata extract as compared to valdecoxib in osteoarthritis of knee, Sontakke S, Thawani V, Pimpalkhute S, Kapra P, Babhulkar S, Hingorani L, Indian Journal of Pharmacology. 2007

Baicalin, an emerging multi-therapeutic agent: pharmacodynamics, pharmacokinetics, and considerations from drug development perspectives, Srinivas NR, Xenobiotica, 2010

BONE

NUTRIENT COMPLEX

A capsule of whole food created vitamins, minerals and other cofactors necessary for bone integrity, strength and overall health. Not just for women, this complex is bioavailable to the body so the cells not only will recognize but also utilize the compounds for bone reformation.

TOP USES

Weak or fragile bones, osteopenia and osteoporosis-prone individuals, bone fractures, growing individuals, and anyone needing more bone density.

INGREDIENTS

- Vitamin C: protective role in building strong bones and preventing fractures.
- Vitamin D2 and D3: increases the absorption of calcium and other minerals by the intestines, increasing utilization of minerals for bone density.
- Biotin: increase efficiency of bone marrow cell function as well as plays a role in the growth of hair, skin, and nails.
- Calcium, magnesium, zinc, copper, manganese, and boron: work synergistically to build the foundation of bone tissue and integrity.

SAFETY

Safe for use by women, teens, and men. Pregnant or lactating women should consult a physician or healthcare provider before use. GMO and gluten-free.

Association between serum 25-hydroxyvitamin d levels, bone geometry, and bone mineral density in healthy older adults, Mosele M, Coin A, Manzato E, et al, The Journals of Gerontology Series A: Biological Sciences and Medical Sciences. 2013

Nutritional aspects of the prevention and treatment of osteoporosis, Peters BS, Martini LA, Arquivos Brasileiros de Endocrinologia & Metabologia, 2010

Minerals and vitamins in bone health: the potential value of dietary enhancement, Bonjour JP, Gueguen L, Palacios C, et al, 2009

Magnesium and osteoporosis: current state of knowledge and future research directions, Castiglioni S, Cazzaniga A, Albisetti W, Maier JA, Nutrients, 2013

The physiological effects of dietary boron, Devirian TA, Volpe SL, Critical Reviews in Food Science and Nutrition, 2003

BREATHE®

RESPIRATORY DROPS

A blend of essential oils in a convenient, organically sweetened throat lozenge for the use of opening the airways and supporting the respiratory system.

TOP USES

Congestion, head cold, sore throat, bronchitis, asthma, allergies, cough, sinusitis, bad breath, and motion sickness.

INGREDIENTS

- Cardamom oil: clears and opens respiratory system, promotes digestion, decreases nausea and motion sickness.
- Peppermint oil: bronchodilator, soothes digestion, anti-inflammatory, and stimulates brain.
- Eucalyptus oil: decreases fevers, congestion and body pains; has antiviral effects on respiratory system.
- Lemon oil: antioxidant, antiseptic, promotes physical energy, health and cleansing.
- Thyme oil: strong antioxidant and antiseptic, supports healthy immune system; antiviral effects
- Melissa oil: antiviral properties and supports against respiratory ailments.

SAFETY

Be aware with small children that are prone to choking.

COPAIBA
SOFTGELS

A convenient, easy-to-swallow softgel that delivers the internal benefits of Copaiba essential oil, including supporting the healthy functioning of the circulatory system and soothing anxious feelings.

TOP USES

Cardiovascular, immune, and digestive system support, powerful antioxidant; addresses lungs, respiratory, and mood concerns.

INGREDIENTS

- Copaiba essential oil: promotes healthy immune function and response, while supporting cellular health and function.

SAFETY

Keep out of reach of small children. If pregnant or lactating, women should consult a physician or healthcare provider before use.

Effect of Moringa oleifera Leaf Capsules on Glycemic Control in Therapy-Naïve Type 2 Diabetes Patients: A Randomized Placebo Controlled Study, R. Taweerutchana, N. Lumlerdkij, S. Vannasaeng, P. Akarasereenont, and A. Sriwijitkamol, Evid.-Based Complement. Altern. Med. ECAM, 2017

Phytochemicals, antioxidant activity and hepatoprotective effect of ginger, A. Fahmi, N. Hassanen, M. Abdur-Rahman, and E.

Shams-Eldin, Biomarkers, 2019

Gastroprotective mechanisms of Citrus lemon (Rutaceae) essential oil and its majority compounds limonene and β-pinene: involvement of heat-shock protein-70, vasoactive intestinal peptide, glutathione, sulfhydryl compounds, nitric oxide and prostaglandin E2, A.L. Rozza et al., Chem. Biol. Interact., 2011

Gastroprotective activity of essential oils from turmeric and ginger, V.B. Liju, K. Jeena, and R. Kuttan, J. Basic Clin. Physiol. Pharmacol., 2015

DDR PRIME®
SOFTGELS

A softgel filled with a blend of essential oils that have been shown in clinical studies to help protect cells against free radical damage while supporting cellular function through apoptosis of damaged and mutated cells, and proliferation of healthy cells.

TOP USES

Damaged or mutated cellular diseases, oxidative stress, autoimmune diseases and anything that requires cellular regeneration and healthy cellular function.

INGREDIENTS

- Frankincense oil: anti-inflammatory and immune-stimulant properties. Is often used to help support the body's response to cancer and other cellular diseases.
- Wild orange oil: high levels of d-Limonene, which helps inhibit cancer tumor growth and reduction of cholesterol.
- Lemongrass oil: anti-inflammatory and antiseptic and has the ability to inhibit cancer cell growth and to induce apoptosis (cellular death).
- Thyme oil: strong antioxidant and antiseptic. Supports the brain as it ages.
- Summer savory oil: antifungal and anti-inflammatory properties. Shows ability to reduce DNA damage from oxidative stress.
- Clove oil: powerful antioxidant and anti-infectious and helps support healthy liver and thyroid function.
- Niaouli oil: powerful antifungal and anti-inflammatory, helps protect against radiation, and helps to regenerate damaged tissues.
- Litsea oil: high in geranial, neral and limonene; helps with multi-tasking.

SAFETY

Not for small children. If pregnant or lactating, women should consult a physician or health care provider before use.

DEEP BLUE

POLYPHENOL COMPLEX®

A capsule containing a blend of powerful polyphenols clinically tested to help soreness and discomfort from physical activities and daily life.

TOP USES

Joint pain, inflammation, arthritis, rheumatoid arthritis and anything "-itis", fibromyalgia, sore muscles, Alzheimer's disease, and cancer prevention.

INGREDIENTS

- Frankincense (boswellia serrata) gum resin extract: inflammatory modulator which helps regulate and decrease inflammation and pain.
- Curcumin: extract from turmeric, has been shown to inhibit amyloid beta plaque formation and decrease risk of Alzheimer's Disease. Also shows powerful anti-inflammatory properties.
- Ginger root extract: reduces pain and inflammation, warming effect and increases circulation.
- Green tea leaf extract (caffeine-free): powerful anti-oxidant, free radical scavenger, and anticancer properties.
- Pomegranate fruit extract: antioxidant shown to lower LDL cholesterol, blood pressure, and increase heart health.
- Grape seed extract: 95% polyphenols shown to decrease free radical damage and increase cellular repair.
- Resveratrol: increases healthy cell proliferation and inhibits proliferation of damaged and mutated cells.
- Stomach comfort blend of peppermint, ginger, caraway: helps soothe the digestive process and tames the stomach.

SAFETY

Not for use for children. If pregnant or lactating, women should consult a physician or healthcare provider before use. Gluten-free.

J Biol Chem. 2005 Feb 18;280(7):5892-901. Epub 2004 Dec 7.Curcumin inhibits formation of amyloid beta oligomers and fibrils, binds plaques, and reduces amyloid in vivo.Yang F1, Lim GP, Begum AN, Ubeda OJ, Simmons MR, Ambegaokar SS, Chen PP, Kayed R, Glabe CG, Frautschy SA, Cole GM.
BMC Cancer. 2015;15(1):1119. doi: 10.1186/s12885-015-1119-y. Epub 2015 Mar 5 Resveratrol suppresses epithelial-to-mesenchymal transition in colorectal cancer through TGF-1/Smads signaling pathway mediated Snail/E-cadherin expression. Ji Q1, Liu X, Han Z, Zhou L, Sui H, Yan L, Jiang H, Ren J, Cai J, Li Q.
Yadav, V.R., Prasad S., Sung, B., Gelovani, J. G., Guha, S., Krishnan, S. and Aggarwal, B.B. Boswellic acid inhibits growth and metastasis of human colorectal cancer in orthotopic mouse model by downregulating inflammatory, proliferative, invasive and angiogenic biomarkers. Int. J. Cancer: 2012 130: 2176–2184.
Di Lorenzo C, Dell'agli M, Badea M, et al. Plant food supplements with anti-inflammatory properties: A systematic review. Critical Reviews in Food Science and Nutrition. 2013;53(5):507-516.
Int J Rheum Dis. 2013 Apr;16(2):219-29. doi: 10.1111/1756-185X.12054. Epub 2013 Apr 4. Protective effects of ginger-turmeric rhizomes mixture on joint inflammation, atherogenesis, kidney dysfunction and other complications in a rat model of human rheumatoid arthritis.
Ramadan G1, El-Menshawy O.
Tangney CC, Rasmussen HE. Polyphenols, inflammation, and cardiovascular disease. Curr Atheroscler Rep. 2013;15:324-334.
Kidd PM. Bioavailability and activity of phytosome complexes from botanical polyphenols: The silymarin, curcumin, green tea, and grape seed extracts. Alternative Medicine Review. 2009;14(3):226-246
Sontakke S, Thawani V, Pimpalkhute S, Kapra P, Babhulkar S, Hingorani L. Open, randomized controlled clinical trial of Boswellia serrata extract as compared to valdecoxib in osteoarthritis of knee. Indian Journal of Pharmacology. 2007;39:27-29.

DIGESTTAB®

TABLETS

A convenient chewable tablet that combines the acid-neutralizing benefits of calcium carbonate with the digestive health-supporting benefits of essential oils that help maintain overall digestive health.

TOP USES

Upset stomach, poor digestive health, belching and bloating, heartburn, and acid indigestion/reflux.

INGREDIENTS

- Anise oil: promotes healthy digestion.
- Peppermint oil: supports healthy gastrointestinal function and aids in digestion.
- Ginger oil: renowned for its ability to soothe stomach upset and ease indigestion.
- Caraway oil: acts as a natural carminative while supporting a healthy gastrointestinal tract.
- Coriander oil: eases occasional stomach upset.
- Tarragon oil: promotes healthy digestion.
- Fennel oil: helps relieve indigestion and a myriad of stomach issues.

SAFETY

Keep out of reach of children. Not intended to be used with other acid reducers. If taking a prescription drug, consult a physician or healthcare provider before use. Vegan friendly. GMO and gluten-free.

P. N. Maton and M. E. Burton, "Antacids revisited: a review of their clinical pharmacology and recommended therapeutic use," Drugs, vol. 57, no. 6, pp. 855–870, Jun. 1999
S. K. Lam, "Antacids: the past, the present, and the future," Baillieres Clin. Gastroenterol., vol. 2, no. 3, pp. 641–654, Jul. 1988
M. Robinson, S. Rodriguez-Stanley, P. B. Miner, A. J. McGuire, K. Fung, and A. A. Ciociola, "Effects of antacid formulation on postprandial oesophageal acidity in patients with a history of episodic heartburn," Aliment. Pharmacol. Ther., vol. 16, no. 3, pp. 435–443, Mar. 2002
M. Valussi, "Functional foods with digestionenhancing properties," Int J Food Sci Nutr, vol. 63 Suppl 1, pp. 82–89, Mar. 2012
"Herbal remedies for dyspepsia: peppermint seems effective," Prescrire Int, vol. 17, no. 95, pp. 121–123, Jun. 2008
Freise and S. Köhler, "[Peppermint oil-caraway oil fixed combination in non-ulcer dyspepsia--comparison of the effects of enteric preparations]," Pharmazie, vol. 54, no. 3, pp. 210–215, Mar. 1999

DIGESTZEN®

SOFTGELS

A softgel to internally deliver the synergistic blend of essential oils that help ease digestion and increase digestive health.

TOP USES

Upset stomach, constipation, diarrhea, IBS, vomiting, heartburn, and acid indigestion/reflux.

INGREDIENTS

- Ginger oil: renowned for its ability to soothe stomach upset and ease indigestion.
- Peppermint oil: supports healthy gastrointestinal function and aids in digestion.
- Tarragon oil: promotes healthy digestion.
- Fennel oil: helps relieve indigestion and a myriad of stomach issues.
- Caraway oil: acts as a natural carminative while supporting a healthy gastrointestinal tract.
- Coriander oil: eases occasional stomach upset.
- Anise oil: promotes healthy digestion.

SAFETY

Can be taken with food. Useful for all ages that can swallow capsules. Keep out of reach of small children.

FIBER

DIETARY SUPPLEMENT

A convenient whole food fiber supplement powder that supports a healthy and regular digestive system and many different health functions within the body, including the cardiovascular and the immune systems.

TOP USES

Weight management, metabolic issues, cardiovascular concerns, unhealthy lifestyle, Vitamin C source.

INGREDIENTS

- Prebiotic blend (Fructooligosaccharide-from chicory root & Jerusalem Artichoke, Isomaltooligosaccharide Xylooligosaccharide): provides food for probiotics in the gut to support a healthy microbiome and immune system.
- Fiber Blend (apple fiber, tapioca fiber): supports a healthy and regular digestive system.
- Flaxseed powder: provides high dietary fiber content.
- Lemon oil: provides natural vitamin C and a unique prebiotic blend.

SAFETY

Keep out of reach of small children. If pregnant or lactating, consult a physician or healthcare provider before use. Keep in a cool, dryplace. GMO and gluten-free.

Effect of Prebiotic on Microbiota, Intestinal Permeability, and Glycemic Control in Children With Type 1 Diabetes, J. Ho et al., J. Clin. Endocrinol. Metab., 2019

Prebiotics Reduce Body Fat and Alter Intestinal Microbiota in Children Who Are Overweight or With Obesity, A. C. Nicolucci, M. P. Hume, I. Martínez, S. Mayengbam, J. Walter, and R. A. Reimer, Gastroenterology, 2017

Effect of Chicory-derived Inulin on Abdominal Sensations and Bowel Motor Function, F. Azpiroz et al., J.Clin. Gastroenterol., 2017

Effect of consumption of chicory inulin on bowel function in healthy subjects with constipation: a randomized, double-blind, placebo-controlled trial, A. Micka, A. Siepelmeyer, A. Holz, S. Theis, and C. Schön, Int. J. Food Sci. Nutr., 2017

Effect of Dietary Fiber on Morphineinduced Constipation in Rats, T. Niwa et al., Biosci. Biotechnol. Biochem., 2002

GINGER

DIGESTIVE DROPS

A blend of ginger and lemon essential oils that reduces occasional feelings of nausea associated with motion and supports healthy digestion.

TOP USES

Upset stomach, indigestion, nausea, morning and motion sickness.

INGREDIENTS

- Ginger oil: renowned for its ability to soothe stomach upset and ease indigestion.
- Lemon oil: help support natural cleansing and healthy digestion.
- Organic cane sugar: natural sweetener.
- Organic brown rice syrup: natural sweetener.

SAFETY

Be aware with small children that are prone to choking. For children under 5 years, consult a physician before use.

Gastroprotective mechanisms of Citrus lemon (Rutaceae) essential oil and its majority compounds limonene and β-pinene: involvement of heat-shock protein-70, vasoactive intestinal peptide, glutathione, sulfhydryl compounds, nitric oxide and prostaglandin E2, A.L. Rozza et al., Chem. Biol. Interact., 2011

Gastroprotective activity of essential oils from turmeric and ginger, V.B. Liju, K. Jeena, and R. Kuttan, J. Basic Clin. Physiol. Pharmacol., 2015

GREENS

DIETARY SUPPLEMENT

A convenient and tasty whole-food fruit and vegetable supplement powder that includes a special superfood blend and essential oils to enhance overall wellness.

TOP USES

Weight management, metabolic issues, poor nutrition; gluten-free and vegan alternatives, source of dietary fiber.

INGREDIENTS

- Green blend (kale, spinach, broccoli, dandelion leaf, parsley, alfalfa, barley grass): supports healthy immune function, digestion, weight management, and energy.
- Superfood blend (moringa leaf, noni fruit, acai berry): provides a nutritious boost.
- Fruit blend (pineapple, mango, guava, acerola cherry): provides body with essential nutrients and acts as a natural sweetener.
- Essential oil blend (lemon and ginger essential oils, ginger root extract): help support natural cleansing and healthy digestion.
- Monkfruit: low-glycemic natural sweetener

SAFETY

Keep out of reach of small children. If pregnant or lactating, women should consult a physician or healthcare provider before use. Vegan friendly. Keep in a cool, dry place. GMO and gluten-free.

Effect of Moringa oleifera Leaf Capsules on Glycemic Control in Therapy-Naïve Type 2 Diabetes Patients: A Randomized Placebo Controlled Study, R. Taweerutchana, N. Lumlerdkij, S. Vannasaeng, P. Akarasereenont, and A. Sriwijitkamol, Evid.-Based Complement. Altern. Med. ECAM, 2017

Phytochemicals, antioxidant activity and hepatoprotective effect of ginger, A. Fahmi, N. Hassanen, M. Abdur-Rahman, and E. Shams-Eldin, Biomarkers, 2019

Gastroprotective mechanisms of Citrus lemon (Rutaceae) essential oil and its majority compounds limonene and β-pinene: involvement of heat-shock protein-70, vasoactive intestinal peptide, glutathione, sulfhydryl compounds, nitric oxide and prostaglandin E2, A.L. Rozza et al., Chem. Biol. Interact., 2011

Gastroprotective activity of essential oils from turmeric and ginger, V.B. Liju, K. Jeena, and R. Kuttan, J. Basic Clin. Physiol. Pharmacol., 2015

GX ASSIST®

SOFTGELS

Enteric coated softgel containing a blend of essential oils and caprylic acid that support a healthy gastrointestinal (GI) tract by decreasing the overgrowth of pathogens in the gut; thereby increasing gut integrity and creating a healthy environment for new, good bacteria to thrive.

TOP USES

For overgrowth of candida albicans and other negative pathogens, autoimmune diseases, compromised digestive system, brain fog, illness, and infections.

INGREDIENTS

- Oregano oil: anti-fungal, anti-bacterial, anti-parasitic, decreases allergies, heartburn and bloating.
- Tea tree oil: fights bad bacteria, fungus, and yeast infections and supports the immune system.
- Lemon oil: antioxidant, anti-microbial, increases liver health and glutathione (internal antioxidant) production.
- Lemongrass oil: anti-inflammatory, anti-microbial, supports immunity and digestive health.
- Peppermint oil: soothes digestion, decreases heartburn and upset stomach.
- Thyme oil: decreases inflammation, nausea and fatigue, anti-parasitic, and fights bad bacteria.
- Caprylic acid: medium-chain fatty acid potent antibacterial, antifugal, and anti-inflammatory properties.

SAFETY

Keep out of reach of small children. If pregnant or lactating, women should consult a physician or healthcare provider before use.

Effect of thyme oil on small intestine integrity and antioxidant status, phagocytic activity and gastrointestinal microbiota in rabbits, Placha I, Chrastinova L, Laukova A, et al, Acta Veterinaria Hungarica. 2013

Antimicrobial activity of essential oils against Helicobacter pylori, Ohno T, Kita M, Yamaoka Y, et al, Helicobacter, 2003

Inhibition of enteric parasites by emulsified oil of oregano in vivo, Force M, Sparks WS, Ronzio RA, Phytotherapy Research, 2000

Antimicrobial activity of five essential oils against origin strains of the Enterobacteriaceae family, Penalver P, Huerta B, Borge C, et al, APMIS, 2005

In vitro antibacterial activity of some plant essential oils, Prabuseenivasan S, Jayakumar M, Ignacimuthu S, BMC Complementary and Alternative Medicine, 2006

Antimicrobial and antioxidant activities of three Mentha species essential oils, Mimica-Dukic N, Bozin B, Sokovic M, et al, Planta Med, 2003

IQ MEGA

SUPPLEMENT

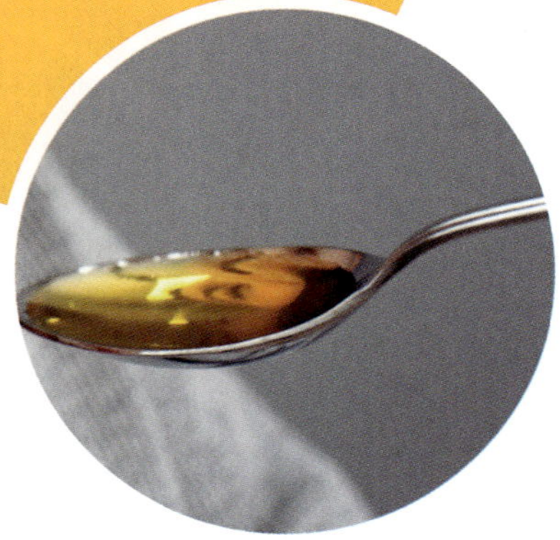

Easy to swallow, potent omega-3 supplement with both eicosapentaenoic acid (EPA) and docosahexaenoic acid (DHA) which combine to make up a balance of omega-3 essential fatty acids in fish oil form. Blended with wild orange essential oil to bring a less fishy and more pleasant flavor.

TOP USES

Brain fog, ADD/ADHD, cardiovascular disease, dry skin, joint pain and arthritis, anything "-itis", weak muscles, and compromised immune system.

INGREDIENTS

- Fish oil (from cod, saithe, haddock) concentrate: high content omega-3 fatty acids extensively tested to ensure the oils are free of toxins and heavy metals. Supports brain function, increase mood, heart and cardiovascular function, increase attention, memory, concentration, and skin health.
- DHA: essential fatty acid shown to increase brain function, concentration, attention, memory, joint health, cell membrane integrity, nerve cell function, immunity, and decrease inflammation.
- EPA: essential fatty acid shown to increase mood, well being, cognitive function, nerve cell function, and overall health of joints and inflammation in the body.
- Wild orange: for flavor and energy.

SAFETY

Keep out of reach of small children, keep refrigerated after opening.

Omega-3 fatty acid intakes are inversely related to elevated depressive symptoms among United States women, Beydoun MA, Kuczmarski MTF, Beydoun HA, et a, J Nutr 2013

Low blood long chain omega-3 fatty acids in UK children are associated with poor cognitive performance and behavior: A cross-sectional analysis from the DOLAB study, Montgomery P, Burton JR, Sewell RP, et al, PLoS ONE. 2013

Omega-3 fatty acids; Their beneficial role in cardiovascular health, Schwalfenberg G, Can Fam Physician. 2006

Omega-3 polyunsaturated fatty acids and the treatment of rheumatoid arthritis; a meta-analysis, Lee YH, Bae SC, Song GG, Arch Med Res, 2012

Effect of omega-3 fatty acids supplementation on endothelial function: A meta-analysis of randomized controlled trials, Wang Q, Liang X, Wang L, et al, Atherosclerosis. 2012

The importance of the ratio of omega-6/omega-3 essential fatty acids, Simopoulos AP, Biomed Pharmacother, 2002

MICROPLEX

VMz®

A micronutrient supplement providing naturally balanced amounts of all vitamins, minerals, trace elements, phytonutrients and antioxidants that give the body the most beneficial amounts needed for long term health and vitality.

TOP USES

Overall health, low energy and fatigue, compromised digestion and immunity, oxidative cell damage, malnutrition, poor health, and imbalanced nutrition.

INGREDIENTS

- Water soluble vitamins, B-complex, and C: support energy and enhances macronutrient metabolism, transportation and elimination; enhances immunity and cognitive function, and strengthens the viscosity of the mucosa membranes lining the smooth muscle of the GI tract.
- Fat soluble vitamins A, E and K: increases free radical scavenging, enhances utilization of macro-minerals and increases immune function.
- Vitamin D3: Immune system regulator. enhances macro-mineral absorption, hormone balance, muscle health. Increases cognitive function.
- Macro-minerals (calcium, iron, iodine, magnesium, zinc, selenium, copper, manganese and chromium): supports and enhances bone strength and density, proper bowel health, muscle contraction and release, fluid balance, nervous system health, cell function, immunity, anti-oxidation and hormone health.
- Polyphenol blend (grape seed extract, quercetin, rutin, pomegranate fruit extract, citrus fruit polyphenol extract, resveratrol, Indian Kino tree wood extract): enhances free radical scavenging, decreases inflammation, increases proper cellular function and proliferation.
- Whole foods blend (kale leaf extract, dandelion leaf powder, parsley leaf powder, spinach leaf powder, broccoli aerial parts powder, cabbage leaf extract, Brussels sprout immature inflorescences powder): a blend of whole foods and phytonutrients which enhance digestion and absorption of micronutrients and give balanced nutrition.
- Stomach comfort blend of ginger, peppermint extract, and caraway: calms and soothes the digestive process.

SAFETY

Can be taken by all ages that can swallow capsules. Wheat used in the fermentation process. However, no gluten detected in the final product.

Selected vitamins and trace elements support immune function by strengthening epithelial barriers and cellular and humoral immune responses, Maggini S, Wintergerst ES, Beveridge S, Hornig DH, British Journal of Nutrition. 2007

Contribution of selected vitamins and trace elements to immune function, Wintergerst ES, Maggini S, Hornig DH, Ann Nutr Met, 2007

Efficacy and tolerability of a fixed combination of peppermint oil and caraway oil in patients suffering from functional dyspepsia, May B, Kohler S, Schneider B, Aliment Pharmacol Therapy. 2000

The immunological functions of the vitamin D endocrine system, Hayes CE, Nashold FE, Spach KM & Pedersen LB, Cell Molec Biol, 2003

Use of calcium or calcium in combination with vitamin D supplementation to prevent fractures and bone loss in people aged 50 years and older: a meta-analysis, Tang BMP, Eslick GD, Nowson C, et al, The Lancet, 2007

MICROPLEX

VMz® VEGAN

A comprehensive vegan dietary supplement for a lifetime of vitality and wellness. Provides the same benefits as Microplex VMz®, but comprised of vegan-friendly sources.

TOP USES

Overall health, low energy and fatigue, compromised digestion and immunity, oxidative cell damage, malnutrition, poor health, imbalanced nutrition, GMO-free and vegan alternatives.

INGREDIENTS

- Water soluble vitamins, B-complex, and C: support energy and enhances macronutrient metabolism, transportation and elimination; enhances immunity and cognitive function, and strengthens the viscosity of the mucosa membranes lining the smooth muscle of the GI tract.
- Fat soluble vitamins A, E and K: increases free radical scavenging, enhances utilization of macro-minerals and increases immune function.
- Vitamin D3: Immune system regulator. enhances macro-mineral absorption, hormone balance, muscle health. Increases cognitive function.
- Macro-minerals (calcium, iron, iodine, magnesium, zinc, selenium, copper, manganese and chromium): supports and enhances bone strength and density, proper bowel health, muscle contraction and release, fluid balance, nervous system health, cell function, immunity, anti-oxidation and hormone health.
- Polyphenol blend (grape seed extract, quercetin, rutin, pomegranate fruit extract, citrus fruit polyphenol extract, resveratrol, Indian Kino tree wood extract): enhances free radical scavenging, decreases inflammation, increases proper cellular function and proliferation.
- Whole foods blend (kale leaf extract, dandelion leaf powder, parsley leaf powder, spinach leaf powder, broccoli aerial parts powder, cabbage leaf extract, Brussels sprout immature inflorescences powder, Kelp stern and leaf powder): a blend of whole foods and phytonutrients which enhance digestion and absorption of micronutrients and give balanced nutrition.
- Stomach comfort blend of ginger, peppermint extract, and caraway: calms and soothes the digestive process.

SAFETY

Not for children. Keep out of reach of small children. If pregnant or lactating, women should consult a physician or healthcare provider before use. Vegan friendly. GMO and gluten-free.

Maggini S, Wintergerst ES, Beveridge S, Hornig DH. Selected vitamins and trace elements support immune function by strengthening epithelial barriers and cellular and humoral immune respons- es. British Journal of Nutrition. 2007; 98:S29-S35

Wintergerst ES, Maggini S, Hornig DH. Contribution of selected vitamins and trace elements to immune function. Ann Nutr Met. 2007; 51:301-323

Hayes CE, Nashold FE, Spach KM & Pedersen LB. The immunological functions of the vitamin D endocrine system. Cell Molec Biol. 2003; 49:277 -300

Tang BMP, Eslick GD, Nowson C, et al. Use of calcium or calcium in combination with vitamin D supplementation to prevent fractures and bone loss in people aged 50 years and older: a metaanalysis. The Lancet. 2007;370:657-666

MITO2MAX®

COMPLEX

A capsule containing a blend of adaptogenic herbs and extracts with energy co-factors made to increase mitochondrial biogenesis and overall energy while decreasing the stress response due to physical activity and daily life.

TOP USES

Body fatigue and tiredness, adrenal fatigue, hormonal imbalance, libido, physical stress, anxiety, and poor circulation.

INGREDIENTS

- Acetyl-l-carnitine HCL: increases energy production by the mitochondria and increases glutathione (internal antioxidant) levels in the body.
- Alpha-lipoic acid: antioxidant vital for cellular energy and neutralizing free radicals.
- Coenzyme Q10: plays a significant role in energy production for the heart and muscle cells.
- Lychee fruit extract and green tea leaf polyphenol extract: increases circulation, decreases inflammation, and decreases oxidative stress.
- Quercetin dihydrate: potent antioxidant flavonoid known to decrease cell damage and increase recovery.
- Cordyceps mycelium: an adaptogen which enhances respiratory health and physical endurance, hormonal health, increased libido and liver function.
- Ginseng (panax quinquefolius) root extract: increases energy and adaption to stress as well as stimulates the immune system by increasing the amount of white blood cells in the blood.
- Ashwagandha (withania somnifera) root extract: powerful adaptogen that lowers cortisol by decreasing the mental and physical stress response. Also gives energy and vitality to the body.

SAFETY

Not for children. Keep out of reach of small children. If pregnant or lactating, women should consult a physician or healthcare provider before use. GMO and gluten-free.

Ginkgo biloba special extract EGb 761 in generalized anxiety disorder and adjustment disorder with anxious mood: A randomized, double-blind, placebo-controlled trial, Woelk H, Arnoldt KH, Kieser M, Hoerr R, Journal of Psychiatric Research 2007

Effects of ginkgo biloba on mental functioning in healthy volunteers, Cieza A, Maier P, Poppel E, Archives of Medical Research, 2002

Translating the basic knowledge of mitochondrial functions to metabolic therapy: role of L-carnitine, Marcovina SM, Sirtori C, Peracino A, et al, Translational Research 2013

Effects of lipoic acid on mtDNA damage following isolated muscle contractions, Fogarty MC, Deviot G, Hughes CM, et al, Med Sci Sports Exerc, 2013

The effects and mechanisms of mitochondrial nutrient a-lipoic acid on improved age-associated mitochondrial and cognitive dysfunction: An overview, Liu J, Neurochem Res, 2008

Effect of Cs-4 (Cordyceps sinensis) on exercise performance in healthy older subjects: A double-blind, placebo controlled trial, Chen S, Li Z, Krochmal R, et al, The Journal of Alternative and Complementary Medicine. 2010

ON GUARD+™

SOFTGELS

A blend of several essential oils in a convenient softgel that protect the immune system from pathogens.

TOP USES

Sore or dry throat, cough, cold and flu, illness, laryngitis, preventative care, and compromised immunity.

INGREDIENTS

- Wild orange oil: antioxidant and anti-inflammatory properties, antimicrobial, and promotes healthy digestion.
- Clove oil: powerful antioxidant, anti-parasitic and anti-fungal properties, improves blood circulation, decreases pain (numbing agent) and inflammation, and inhibits pathogenic activity.
- Black pepper oil: antiseptic, anti-catarrhal, and expectorant properties. Helps respiratory system by promoting blood flow and circulation.
- Cinnamon bark oil: highly antibacterial, antifungal, and antimicrobial, promotes healthy blood sugar and insulin balance.
- Eucalyptus oil: decreases fevers, congestion and body pains, and has antiviral effects on the respiratory system.
- Oregano oil: powerful antibacterial, antiviral, and antifungal properties. Helps support the immune system against ailments.
- Rosemary oil: great expectorant/decongestant, increases memory and concentration, inflammation and has a balancing effect on the endocrine system.
- Melissa oil: antiviral properties and supports against respiratory ailments.

SAFETY

Not for children. Keep out of reach of small children. If pregnant or lactating, women should consult a physician or healthcare provider before use.

ON GUARD®

TABLETS

A blend of essential oils combined with specific immune-boosting nutrients and contained in a chewable tablet designed to support the immune system when it needs strengthening.

TOP USES

Compromised immune function, and high seasonal and environmental threats.

INGREDIENTS

- Wild orange peel: protects the body against seasonal threats.
- Clove bud: supports a healthy immune system.
- Cinnamon leaf/bark: promotes healthy immune function.
- Eucalyptus leaf: purifying and cleansing properties.
- Rosemary flower/leaf: may help support the digestive system.
- Vitamin C: prevents UV skin damage; even skin tone, reverse damage caused by sun exposure; boost cellular energy and nutrient absorption.
- Vitamin D: immune system and calcium regulator.
- Zinc: reduces inflammation and boosts immune health.
- Beta glucan: stimulates the immune system by increasing body chemicals which prevent infections, and a soluble source of fiber.

SAFETY

Keep out of reach of small children. If pregnant or lactating, women should consult a physician or healthcare provider before use. Keep in a cool, dry place. Vegan friendly, sugar-free, non-GMO, and gluten-free.

ON GUARD®

THROAT DROPS

A blend of essential oils in a convenient, organically-sweetened lozenge that soothes the throat and protects the immune system from pathogens.

TOP USES

Sore or dry throat, cough, cold and flu, illness, laryngitis, preventative care, and compromised immunity.

INGREDIENTS

- Wild orange oil: antioxidant, and anti-inflammatory, and antimicrobial properties; promotes healthy digestion.
- Clove: powerful antioxidant, anti-parasitic and anti-fungal properties, improves blood circulation, decreases pain (numbing agent) and inflammation, and inhibits pathogenic activity.
- Cinnamon bark: highly antibacterial, antifungal, and antimicrobial, promotes healthy blood sugar and insulin balance.
- Eucalyptus: decreases fevers, congestion and body pains, and has antiviral effects on respiratory system.
- Rosemary: great expectorant/decongestant, increases memory and concentration, inflammation and has a balancing effect on endocrine system.
- Myrrh: supports blood flow to gums and teeth, antioxidant properties.
- Organic cane juice: natural sweetener
- Organic brown rice syrup: natural sweetener

SAFETY

Be aware with small children that are prone to choking. Gluten-free.

PB ASSIST®+

PROBIOTIC

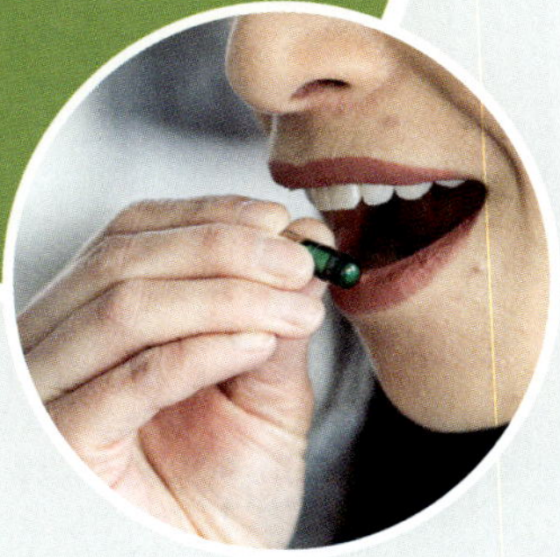

A proprietary formula in a unique doublelayer vegetable capsule with six different strains of good bacteria and prebiotic fiber for maximum delivery and cultivation of healthy gut flora.

TOP USES

Flatulence, constipation or diarrhea, malabsorption, irritable bowel, compromised immune system, leaky gut, allergies, autoimmune diseases, anxiety and depression, mental disorders, and infections.

INGREDIENTS

- L. acidophilus, L. salivarius, L. casei: Lactobacillus strains of bacteria which increase the integrity of the villi of the upper intestinal tract to improve the absorption of other nutrients. Also enhancing immunity and the gut-brain connection increasing proper neurotransmitter and brain function.
- B. lactis, B. bifidum, B. longum: Bifidobacterium strains that help digestion and immunity of the large intestines and enhance overall colon health. Also increasing the functions of the brain and improving mood.
- FOS (fructo-oligosaccharides) prebiotic: Indigestible fibers that enhance the growth and cultivation of good bacteria while decreasing growth of bad bacteria.

SAFETY

If pregnant or lactating, women should consult a physician or healthcare provider before use. Keep in a cool, dry place. GMO and gluten-free.

Rupa P, Mine Y. Recent advances in the role of probiotics in human inflammation and gut health. Journal of Agricultural and Food Chemistry. 2012;60:8249-8256

Ng SC, Lam EFC, Lam TTY, et al. Effect of probiotic bacteria on the intestinal microbiota in irritable bowel syndrome. Journal of Gastroenterology and Hepatology. 2013;28:1624-1631

Hempel S, Newberry SJ, Maher AR, et al. Probiotics for the prevention and treatment of antibiotic-associated diarrhea. Journal of the American Medical Association. 2012;307(18):1959-1969

Messaoudi S, Manai M, Kergourlay G, et al. Lactobacillus salivarius: Bacteriocin and probiotic activity. Food Microbiology. 2013;36:296-304

Elazab N, Mendy A, Gasana J, et al. Probiotic administration in early life, atopy, and asthma: a meta-analysis of clinical trials. Pediatrics. 2013;123:e666-e676

PB ASSIST JR®+

PROBIOTIC

A powdered encapsulated probiotic supplement for children or adults who have trouble swallowing pills with six different strains of good bacteria and prebiotic fiber for maximum delivery and cultivation of healthy gut flora.

TOP USES

Flatulence, constipation or diarrhea, malabsorption, irritable bowel, compromised immune system, leaky gut, allergies, autoimmune diseases, kidney health, and urinary tract infection.

INGREDIENTS

- L. rhamnosus. L. salivarius, L. plantarum (LP01, LP02), B. breve, B. lactic strains selected for unique stability at room temperature, ability to survive harsh extremes of digestive system, reach the intestines safely, and benefits among children. Also to maintain healthy intestinal microflora balance and support healthy function of digestive, immune, female reproductive systems, and GI tract (particularly the intestines and colon), kidneys, bladder, and urinary tract. Promotes optimal metabolism and absorption of nutrients and healthy lung and respiratory tract function. Also enhancing healthy brain and nervous system function and establishing health benefits for long-term well-being.
- FOS prebiotic to help sustain a healthy balance of beneficial friendly flora.

SAFETY

For all ages. Can be consumed with or without food. NOTE: Do not mix with hot water. Non-GMO and gluten-free.

M. E. Segers and S. Lebeer, "Towards a better understanding of Lactobacillus rhamnosus GG--host interactions," Microb. Cell Factories, vol. 13 Suppl 1, p. S7, Aug. 2014

S. Liu, P. Hu, X. Du, T. Zhou, and X. Pei, "Lactobacillus rhamnosus GG supplementation for preventing respiratory infections in children: a meta-analysis of randomized, placebo-controlled trials," Indian Pediatr., vol. 50, no. 4, pp. 377–381, Apr. 2013

H. Szajewska, M. Wanke, and B. Patro, "Metaanalysis: the effects of Lactobacillus rhamnosus GG supplementation for the prevention of healthcare-associated diarrhoea in children," Aliment. Pharmacol. Ther., vol. 34, no. 9, pp. 1079–1087, Nov. 2011

Q. Hao, B. R. Dong, and T. Wu, "Probiotics for preventing acute upper respiratory tract infections," Cochrane Database Syst. Rev., vol. 2, p. CD006895, 2015

M. Ozen, G. Kocabas Sandal, and E. C. Dinleyici, "Probiotics for the prevention of pediatric upper respiratory tract infections: a systematic review," Expert Opin. Biol. Ther., vol. 15, no. 1, pp. 9–20, Jan. 2015

Y. E. Borre, G. W. O'Keeffe, G. Clarke, C. Stanton, T. G. Dinan, and J. F. Cryan, "Microbiota and neurodevelopmental windows: implications for brain disorders," Trends Mol. Med., vol. 20, no. 9, pp. 509–518, Sep. 2014

A. Evrensel and M. E. Ceylan, "The Gut-Brain Axis: The Missing Link in Depression," Clin. Psychopharmacol. Neurosci. Off. Sci. J. Korean Coll. Neuropsychopharmacol., vol. 13, no. 3, pp. 239–244, Dec. 2015

P. M. Grin, P. M. Kowalewska, W. Alhazzan, and A. E. Fox-Robichaud, "Lactobacillus for preventing recurrent urinary tract infections in women: meta-analysis," Can. J. Urol., vol. 20, no. 1, pp. 6607–6614, Feb. 2013.

PEPPERMINT

SOFTGELS

An enteric coated capsule ensures peppermint essential oil passes through the stomach undissolved for small intestine delivery where it's most effective for specific and intended purposes.

TOP USES

Help ease and relax gastrointestinal muscles, while calming stomach and intestinal tract; helpful to an irritable bowel or spastic colon with conditions such as IBS, Crohn's disease, and colitis.

INGREDIENTS

- Peppermint: with high menthol content, gastrointestinal applications include appetite reduction, relief of gas, bloating, and stomach upset, soothing digestion and heartburn. Other internal use benefits can include helping ease respiratory congestion, improve alertness, stimulate brain, decrease breast milk supply, overcome loss of sense of smell.

SAFETY

Keep out of reach of children. If pregnant, nursing, or under a doctor's care, consult physician. Store in cool, dry place.

Kline RM, Kline JJ, Di Palma J, Et Al. Enteric-coated, pH-dependent peppermint oil capsules for the treatment of irritable bowel syndrome in children. J Pediatr. 2001;138(1):125-128.

Liu JH, Chen GH, Yeh HZ, Et Al. Enteric-coated peppermint-oil capsules in the treatment of irritable bowel syndrome: a prospective, randomized trial. J Gastroenterol. 1997;32(6):765-768.

Wu H, Fu CC, Yu DD et al. Repellent activity screening of 11 kinds of essential oils against Aedes albopictus Skuse: microcapsule preparation of Herba Schizonepetae oil and repellent bioassay on hand skin. Trans R Soc Trop Med Hyg. 2013;107(8):471-479.

PHYTOESTROGEN

COMPLEX

A blend of standardized extracts of plant (phyto) estrogens and lignans delivered in a capsule to help create a balance of hormones throughout the body and eliminate unwanted metabolites. Designed for pre-pubescent, perimenopausal, and menopausal women.

TOP USES

Menopause, perimenopause, andropause, estrogen dominance and deficiency, hormonal imbalances, endometriosis, uterine fibroids, fibrocystic breasts, prostate inflammation, gynecomastia, painful menstruation, night sweats, hot flashes, PMS, and mood swings (PMS).

INGREDIENTS

- Genistein (soy extract): an isoflavone antioxidant that promotes healthy breast and uterine tissue and brings balance to hormones in both men and women. Also shown to help prevent prostate cancer in men and ovarian and breast cancer in women.
- Flax seed extract (lignans): decreases estrogen metabolites for further hormone balance and protection of the sex organ tissues and cells.
- Pomegranate extract: powerful antioxidant shown to help the reduction of free radical damage to the cells.

SAFETY

Not for children. Keep out of reach of small children. Okay for men and women. If pregnant or lactating, women should consult a physician or healthcare provider before use.

PROTEIN

WHEY DIETARY SUPPLEMENT

A convenient and nutritionally complete protein supplement crucial for building muscle, managing appetite, providing the body with energy, and keeping the body functioning at optimal capacity.

TOP USES

Weight management, poor nutrition, GMO, soy, and gluten free alternatives, weak immune system, amino acid imbalance, high protein/low carb diets, unhealthy lifestyle.

INGREDIENTS

- Whey protein: helps body's anabolic processes step in to build muscle and create new, different amino acids.
- Monk fruit extract: acts as a natural sweetener.
- Flaxseed powder: provides high dietary fiber content.
- Comes in both chocolate and vanilla.

SAFETY

Keep out of reach of small children. If pregnant or lactating, women should consult a physician or health care provider before use. Keep in a cool, dry place. Soy, GMO and gluten-free.

Effects of whey protein supplement in the elderly submitted to resistance training: systematic review and meta-analysis, T. Colonetti et al., Int. J. Food Sci. Nutr., 2017

Effectiveness of whey protein supplements on the serum levels of amino acid, creatinine kinase and myoglobin of athletes: a systematic review and meta-analysis, F.-C. Lam, T. M. Khan, H. Faidah, A. Haseeb, and A. H. Khan, Syst. Rev., 2019

Effect of whey protein supplementation on long and short term appetite: A meta-analysis of randomized controlled trials, M. Mollahosseini, S. Shab-Bidar, M. H. Rahimi, and K. Djafarian, Clin. Nutr. ESPEN, 2017

Effect of whey protein supplementation on body composition changes in women: a systematic review and metaanalysis, R. E. Bergia, J. L. Hudson, and W. W. Campbell, Nutr. Rev., 2018"

PROTEIN

PLANT DIETARY SUPPLEMENT

A convenient and nutritionally complete plant-based protein supplement crucial for building muscle, managing appetite, providing the body with energy, and keeping the body functioning at optimal capacity.

TOP USES

Weight management, poor nutrition, GMO, soy, and gluten free alternatives, weak immune system, amino acid imbalance, high protein/low carb diets, unhealthy lifestyle.

INGREDIENTS

- Pea protein: provides strong protein levels, along with an amazing amino acid profile with a broad balance of all 20 amino acids.
- Protein blend (brown rice protein, seed protein, pumpkin seed protein): complementary sources of protein which helps round out the flavor and texture.
- Monk fruit extract: acts as a natural sweetener.
- Quinoa grain powder: provides high fiber content.

SAFETY

Keep out of reach of small children. If pregnant or lactating, women should consult a physician or healthcare provider before use. Keep in a cool, dry place. Vegan friendly. Dairy, soy, GMO, and gluten-free.

Flaxseed dietary fibers lower cholesterol and increase fecal fat excretion, but magnitude of effect depend on food type, M. Kristensen et al., Nutr. Metab., 2012

Pea proteins oral supplementation promotes muscle thickness gains during resistance training: a double-blind, randomized, Placebocontrolled clinical trial vs. Whey protein, N. Babault et al., J. Int. Soc. Sports Nutr., 2015

Effects of Whey and Pea Protein Supplementation on Post-Eccentric Exercise Muscle Damage: A Randomized Trial, D. C. Nieman et al., Nutrients, 2020

Effect of different protein sources on satiation and short-term satiety when consumed as a starter, R. Abou-Samra, L. Keersmaekers, D. Brienza, R.

Mukherjee, and K. Macé, Nutr. J., 2011 Flaxseed dietary fiber supplements for suppression of appetite and food intake, S. Ibrügger, M. Kristensen, M. S. Mikkelsen, and A. Astrup, Appetite, 2012'

SUPPLEMENTARY PRODUCTS

SERENITY®

SOFTGELS

A softgel containing a blend of lavender essential oil and natural plant extracts to enhance a restful night's sleep by promoting relaxation without feeling groggy or sleepy the next day.

TOP USES

Insomnia, inability to fall asleep or wake up easily, groggy feelings upon rising in morning, lack of adequate sleep, negative impact due to lack of sleep: decreased ability to lose weight, learn, or control emotions; poor reaction time, increased presence of stress hormones, decreased sense of well-being.

INGREDIENTS

- Lavender oil: long history of traditional internal use to encourage restful sleep, calm the nervous system, reduce stress.
- L-Theanine (non-protein amino acid found in green tea [camellia sinensis]): promotes pre-sleep relaxation and quality sleep without feeling groggy or drowsy the next day. Improves mood, calmness, and general relaxation.
- Lemon balm oil: calming effects for anxiety, sleep problems, restlessness. Used for attention deficit, hyperactivity, hysteria, tension headaches, and rapid heartbeat due to nervousness. Boosts alertness upon waking, improves memory, problem-solving, brain protection, and mood.
- Passionflower oil: used for insomnia, nervous stomach/ulcers, anxiety, nervousness, drug withdrawal, hysteria, attention deficit, hyperactivity, excitability, heart palpitations, an overactive mind, stress.
- German chamomile oil: acts as a mild sedative, promotes healthy serotonin levels. Used traditionally to treat nervous stomach or bowels, anxiety, tension headaches, and at bedtime for insomnia. Promotes body's healing and restorative capacity and ability to get rid of dark circles under eyes.

SAFETY

Keep out of reach of children. If pregnant, nursing, or under a doctor's care, consult a physician.

Rodriguez, Damian. doTERRA Serenity Restful Complex Research Clinical Trial. doTERRA.

SLIM & SASSY®

SOFTGELS

A blend of essential oils in convenient softgels to help manage hunger throughout the day while boosting metabolism and promoting a positive mood, cleansing the body, aiding digestion, curbing appetite, providing a stimulating and positive effect on the endocrine system, and assisting weight loss.

TOP USES

Slow metabolism, overweight or obese individuals, lack of energy (fatigue), diabetes, toxic liver, and compromised endocrine system.

INGREDIENTS

- Grapefruit oil: promotes cleansing and detoxifying, decreases appetite, and induces lipolysis (mobilization of fat cells from stored fat).
- Lemon oil: cleanses, aids digestion, powerful antioxidant, increases lipolysis, and elevates the mood.
- Peppermint oil: helps manage hunger cravings, soothes digestion, and invigorates the mind.
- Ginger oil: promotes healthy digestion and enhances metabolism and thermogenesis (increased heat through metabolic stimulation).
- Cinnamon bark oil: positively impacts on the endocrine system to assist with weight loss, lowers blood sugar, and balances insulin response. Also inhibits adipogenesis (fat storage).

SAFETY

Not for children. Keep out of reach of small children. If pregnant or lactating, women should consult a physician or healthcare provider before use.

*Also available in Slim & Sassy® Gum

TERRAZYME®

A capsule of several, active, whole-food enzymes as well as mineral cofactors that help the breakdown of proteins, fats, complex carbohydrates, sugars, and fiber, giving the body better digestion nutrients readily available for absorption and utilization.

TOP USES

Poor nutrition, heartburn or indigestion, slow metabolism, upset stomach, bloating, and flatulence.

INGREDIENTS

- Protease: breaks down protein to peptides and amino acids.
- Papain: breaks down protein.
- Amylase: breaks down carbohydrates, starches, and sugars.
- Lipase: breaks down fats and oils to be absorbed in the intestine.
- Lactase: breaks down lactose in milk sugars.
- Alpha galactosidase: breaks down complex polysaccharide sugars in legumes and cruciferous vegetables that can cause bloating and gas.
- Cellulase: breaks down fiber to help digest fruits and vegetables.
- Sucrase: breaks down sucrose to fructose and glucose for energy.
- Anti-gluten enzyme blend: assists in breaking down gluten.
- Glucoamylase: breaks down starch.
- Betaine HCL: aids in protein digestion.
- Stomach comfort peppermint, ginger, caraway: helps soothe the digestive process and tames the stomach.

SAFETY

Can be taken by all ages that can swallow capsules. If pregnant or lactating, women should consult a physician or healthcare provider before use.

A broader view: Microbial enzymes and their relevance in industries, medicine, and beyond, Gurung N, Ray S, Bose S, Rai V, Biomed Res Int 2013

Enzyme replacement therapy for pancreatic insufficiency: Present and future, Fieker A, philpott J, Armand M, Clinical and Experimental Gastroenterology, 2011

Randomised clinical trial: A 1-week, double-blind, placebo-controlled study of pancreatin 25000 Ph. Eur. Minimicrospheres for pancreatic exocrine insufficiency after pancreatic surgery, with a 1-year open-label extension, Seiler Cm, Izbicki J, Varga-Szabo L, et al, Aliment Pharmacol Ther, 2013

Fate of pancreatic enzymes during small intestinal aboral transit in humans, Layer P, Go VLW, DiMagno EP, Intraluminal Fate of Pancreatic Enzymes, 1986

Effects of different levels of supplementary alpha-amylase on digestive enzyme activities and pancreatic amylase mRNA expression of young broilers, Jiang Z, Zhou Y, Lu F, et al, Asian-Aust J Anim Sci. 2008

TRIEASE®

SOFTGELS

A blend of essential oils to use when attending outdoor events, when seasonal or environmental elements are particularly high, or on a daily basis during allergy season to promote clear breathing and overall respiratory health.

TOP USES

Seasonal allergies, hay fever, congestion, head colds and headaches, bronchitis, asthma, and sinusitis.

INGREDIENTS

- Lemon oil: antioxidant, antiseptic, promotes respiratory health and cleansing.
- Lavender oil: renowned for its calming and balancing effects, both internally and externally.
- Peppermint oil: bronchodilator, soothes digestion, stimulates brain and helps decrease allergy symptoms.

SAFETY

Be aware with small children that are prone to choking.

TURMERIC

DUAL CAPSULES

Unique dual chamber capsule provides a proprietary bundling of an inner layer of the botanical extract curaiminoids and outer layer of essential oil tumerones, a synergy that maximizes effectiveness and benefits in a convenient delivery system. Turmeric is chemically diverse in composition, with more than 235 chemical constituents identified.

TOP USES

Cancer, tumors, leukemia, cellular and immune health, autoimmune conditions, joint pain and swelling, arthritis, gout, rheumatism; neurological diseases, fungal, bacterial, viral infections; cognitive dysfunction, stroke, poor circulation and blood supply to brain, epilepsy; high blood sugar and cholesterol, poor metabolism; blood, liver and lymph toxicity; intestinal worms and parasites, acne, eczema, psoriasis, ulcers, gas, bloating, cough, bronchitis, menstrual cramps, cavities, oral health, bites, stings, skin health.

INGREDIENTS

- Turmeric oil: increases bioavailability of curcuminoids for better potency and absorption, supports healthy nervous, glucose, immune response, helps prevent cancer cells from forming, multiplying.
  - ar-Turmerone and Turmerone: Antioxidant, anti-inflammatory, inhibits reception of pain, promotes stem cell proliferation and differentiation in brain for self-repair and recovery of brain function, stomach, liver ailments; reproductive problems, infectious diseases, blood disorders.
- Turmeric extract: anti-inflammatory, anticancer compounds, help fight foreign invaders, heart disease, cancer, metabolic syndrome, Alzheimer's, degenerative conditions.
  - Curlone: antioxidant, antifungal, antibacterial; clogged arteries, stroke or heart attack, blood sugar control.
  - Curcumin extract: antioxidant, stimulates body's own antioxidant enzymes, decreases risk of Alzheimer's disease, helping to improve learning and memory; boosts growth and development of new neurons, improving symptoms related to neurodegenerative and psychiatric disorders.

SAFETY

Keep out of reach of children. If pregnant, nursing, or under a doctor's care, consult physician. Store in cool, dry place.

SUPPLEMENTARY PRODUCTS

Efficacy of Turmeric Extracts and Curcumin for Alleviating the Symptoms of Joint Arthritis: A Systematic Review and Meta-Analysis of Randomized Clinical Trials, James W. Daily, Mini Yang, and Sunmin Park, Journal of Medicinal Food, Aug 2016.717-729

Effects of Turmeric (Curcuma longa) on Skin Health: A Systematic Review of the Clinical Evidence, Vaughn, A. R., Branum, A., & Sivamani, R. K., Phytotherapy Research, 1243-1264, , Aug 2016

vEO MEGA®

COMPLEX

A unique blend of plant- and algae-sourced omega fatty acids to help support joint, cardiovascular, and brain health, as well as healthy immune function.

TOP USES

Compromised immune system, brain fog, arthritis, joint pain, poor mobility, cardiovascular disease, dry skin and skin issues.

INGREDIENTS

- Flax seed oil: ALA essential fatty acid that support the production of EPA and DHA in the body increasing all the benefits of omega-3 fatty acids.
- Algae oil (DHA): essential fatty acid that support brain function and increase mood, heart, and cardiovascular function, decreases LDL and triglyceride levels, increased attention, memory, concentration, joint health, skin health, immunity and decreases inflammation.
- Inca Inchi seed oil: essential fatty acid that promotes inflammatory modulation and decreases oxidative stress.
- Borage oil: GLA essential fatty acid that supports inflammatory markers in the body, clears skin, and balances out the mood and hormones.
- Cranberry oil: shown to decrease LDL and triglyceride levels, enhances mood and concentration as well as provides beneficial fats for skin health.
- Pomegranate oil: antioxidant oil that increases skin health and decreases inflammation in the skin.
- Pumpkin oil: helps to increase HDL (good) cholesterol and can promotes energy in the brain.
- Grape oil: promotes a reduction in LDL (bad) cholesterol and triglyceride levels.
- Natural vitamin E: protects cell membranes against oxidative damage and promotes eye health.
- Astaxanthin: powerful carotenoid that promotes cellular regeneration, heart and cardiovascular strength, decreases macular degeneration and strengthens the eyes.
- Lutein: shown to increase strength of the eyes, heart and cells.
- Zeaxanthin: potent antioxidant good for the eyes and cardiovascular system.
- Lycopene: fights free radicals and strengthens the integrity of the cell membranes.
- Alpha and beta carotene: antioxidants that promote eye health and fight free radicals.
- Essential oil blend of clove, frankincense, thyme, cumin, wild orange, peppermint, ginger, caraway, and German chamomile: powerful antioxidant properties, immune system properties, promotes healthy digestion, cellular function, and anti-inflammation.

SAFETY

Keep out of reach of children. If pregnant, nursing, or under a doctor's care, consult physician. Vegan friendly. GMO, and gluten-free.

Bernstein AM, Ding EL, Willett WC, Rimm EB. A meta-analysis shows that docosahexaenoic acid from algal oil reduces serum triglycerides and increases HDL-cholesterol and LDL-cholesterol in person without coronary heart disease. The Journal of Nutrition. 2012;142:99-104

Kidd P. Astaxanthin, cell membrane nutrient with diverse clinical benefits and anti-aging potential. Alternative Medicine Review. 2011;16(4):355-364

Pan A, Chen M, Chowdhury R, et al. ■-Linolenic acid and risk of cardiovascular disease: a systematic review and meta-analysis. The American Journal of Clinical Nutrition. 2012;96:1262-1273

Rodriguez-Leyva D, Bassett CMC, McCullough R, Pierce GN. The cardiovascular effects of flaxseed and its omega-3 fatty acid, alpha-linolenic acid. Can J Cardiol. 2010;26(9):489-496. Alexander DE. Macular pigment optical density and eye health. Kemin Technical Literature. 2010.

xEO MEGA®

COMPLEX

A blend of marine base and land base omega essential fatty acids in a unique assimilation capsule with essential oils and fat-soluble vitamins.

TOP USES

Inflammation and pain, arthritis, anything "-itis," compromised immune system, brain fog, concentration, ADD/ADHD, aging skin, PMS, post-partum depression, anxiety and depression, cardiovascular disease, dry skin and skin issues.

INGREDIENTS

- Fish oil (from anchovy, sardine, mackerel, and calamari) concentrate: EPA and DHA essential fatty acids that support brain function and increase mood, heart and cardiovascular function, decrease LDL and triglyceride levels, increase attention, memory, concentration, joint health, skin health, immunity, and decrease inflammation.
- Echium plantagineum seed oil: a blend of ALA, SDA, and GLA essential fatty acids that support the cardiovascular system, decrease LDL and increase HDL triglyceride levels, balances inflammatory markers, enhances mood, brain, and skin health.
- Pomegranate oil: antioxidant oil that increases skin health and decreases inflammation in the skin.
- Vitamin A (as alpha and beta carotene): antioxidants that promote eye health and fight free radicals.
- Vitamin D3 (as natural cholecalciferol): supports immune system function, enhances macro-mineral absorption, hormone balance, muscle health, and increases cognitive function.
- Vitamin E: protects cell membranes against oxidative damage and promotes eye health.
- Astaxanthin: powerful carotenoid that promotes cellular regeneration, heart and cardiovascular strength, decreases macular degeneration and strengthens the eyes.
- Lutein: shown to increase strength of the eyes, heart, and cells.
- Zeaxanthin: potent antioxidant good for the eyes and cardiovascular system.
- Essential oil blend of caraway, clove, cumin, frankincense, German chamomile, ginger, peppermint, thyme, and wild orange: powerful antioxidant properties, immune system properties, promotes healthy digestion, cellular function, and anti-inflammation.

SAFETY

Can be taken by all ages that can swallow capsules. If pregnant or lactating, consult a physician or healthcare provider before use.

SUPPLEMENTARY PRODUCTS

Serum and macular responses to multiple xanthophyll supplements in patients with early age-related macular degeneration, Huang YM, Yan SF, Ma L, et al, Nutrition, 2013

a-Linolenic acid and risk of cardiovascular disease: a systematic review and meta-analysis, Pan A, Chen M, Chowdhury R, et al, The American Journal of Clinical Nutrition, 2012

Protective effect of borage seed oil and gamma linolenic acid on DNA: In Vivo and In Vitro Studies, Tasset-Cuevas I, Fernandez-Bedmar Z, Lozano-Baena MD, et al, PLoS ONE, 2013

Fish oil omega-3 fatty acids and cardio-metabolic health, alone or with statins, Minihane AM, European Journal of Clinical Nutrition, 2013

Essential fatty acids as potential anti-inflammatory agents in the treatment of affective disorders, Song C, Mod Trends Pharmacopsychiatry, 2013

YARROW | POM

CAPSULES

A blend of essential oils and extracts designed to combat oxidative stress and help maintain skin's youthful appearance from the inside out. Outstanding for anti-aging, vitality, overall wellness, and skin health with powerful antioxidants and anti-inflammatory compounds.

TOP USES

Cellular, skin, immune and nervous system support; metabolic health, improve skin firmness, reduce skin imperfections, illuminate and brighten complexion, and calm mind and body.

INGREDIENTS

- Yarrowlpom: skin healing accelerator; sagging, aging skin and surface veins; scars, acne, eczema.
- Pomegranate: superior moisturizing ability, nourishing and softening skin.
- Celery seed: promote detoxification, blood purification; facilitate elimination of toxins, excess fluid.
- Frankincense: lift, tighten skin, slow signs of aging; help reduce acne blemishes, appearance of large pores; prevent wrinkles, repair cellular damage.
- Palmarosa: cell renewal benefits; nourish, restore skin health, harmony; regulate skin moisture and oil production.
- Turmeric: skin lightening, reduce facial hyper-pigmentation, fine lines, wrinkles, acne.
- Melissa: tighten and hydrate skin, improve elasticity, smooth wrinkles, overcome sensitive skin.
- Grape seed extract: increase cellular repair, help reverse or reduce aging and wrinkling effects.
- Zinc citrate: vital to collagen formation and healthy tissue development.
- Vitamin C: prevent UV skin damage; even skin tone, reverse damage caused by sun exposure; boost cellular energy and nutrient absorption.
- Melon extract: extremely hydrating, helps reduce signs and progression of aging, wrinkles; improve skin radiance.

SAFETY

Keep out of reach of children. If pregnant, nursing, or under a doctor's care, consult physician. Store in cool, dry place.

ZENDOCRINE®

COMPLEX

This capsule is a proprietary blend of 14 active whole-food extracts in a patented enzyme delivery system that supports healthy cleansing and filtering functions of the liver, kidneys, colon, lungs, and skin.

TOP USES

Toxic liver, jaundice, cirrhosis, bloating, toxic gallbladder, pancreatitis, kidney damage, respiratory issues, colon issues, and constipation.

INGREDIENTS

- Barberry leaf, milk thistle seed, burdock root, clove bud, dandelion root, garlic fruit, red clover leaf: targets the cleansing and support of the liver and helps filter the blood of toxins.
- Turkish rhubarb stem, burdock root, clove bud, dandelion root: targets the cleansing of the kidneys while bringing strength and integrity to it.
- Psyllium seed husk, turkish rhubarb stem, acacia gum bark, marshmallow root: helps to strengthen the elimination process of the colon and colon health.
- Osha root, safflower petals: helps to strengthen and cleanse the lungs from environmental and other toxins.
- Kelp, milk thistle seed, burdock root, clove bud, garlic fruit: helps support the cleansing of toxins from the skin.
- Enzyme assimilation system of amylase and cellulase their natural mineral cofactors magnesium and manganese: increases digestion and utilization of the rest of the ingredients.

SAFETY

Not for children. Keep out of reach of small children. If pregnant or lactating, women should consult a physician or healthcare provider before use.

ZENDOCRINE®

SOFTGELS

A softgel blend of synergistic essential oils that support natural detoxification of the body to help cleanse it of toxins and free radicals that can slow body systems down, leaving a heavy, weighted feeling.

TOP USES

Toxic liver, jaundice, cirrhosis, bloating, toxic gallbladder, pancreatitis, kidney damage, and hormonal imbalances.

INGREDIENTS

- Tangerine: antioxidant and cleansing properties of the liver and kidneys.
- Rosemary: supports a healthy liver and gallbladder as well as reduces xenoestrogens (foreign estrogens form plastics, growth hormones and environmental toxins).
- Geranium: cleanses liver, gallbladder and balances hormones and rids the body of unwanted estrogens.
- Juniper berry: powerful detoxifier of the kidneys and decreases water retention.
- Cilantro: powerful cleansing agent that eliminates toxins from the body, including heavy metals.

SAFETY

Not for children. Keep out of reach of small children. If pregnant or lactating, women should consult a physician or healthcare provider before use.

Tips for TAKING SUPPLEMENTS

- **Partner with quality.** Use supplements with optimal, not exaggerated or deficient, levels of nutrients by buying from a reputable source.
- **Dose diligence.** All products provide dose recommendations. Maximum benefit comes from the consistent use of a variety of specific and complementary supplements. When first starting a program, some individuals may choose to start with a lower dose and work up. The basic recommendations may be adequate or even excessive for a healthy person who has implemented a healthy diet, lifestyle, and regular supplementation program. However, someone with longstanding health issues may require an extensive regimen that may include consumption beyond label recommendations when safe.
- **Start slowly.** Over the course of the first week, start with a few supplements at lower doses and then add from there. This will support awareness of how individual supplements make you feel. Gradually add others and increase doses of each supplement. Synergy between supplements coupled with using the proper therapeutic dose is generally required to achieve optimal benefit. Most supplements can be taken at the same time.

- **Time it right.** Most people do better taking supplements with food while digestive processes are in action. Consumption on an empty stomach (except at bedtime) can trigger nausea. Just a few bites of food can be enough (e.g., half a banana). Avoid taking with tea, coffee, soda, or even some dairy products as these can interfere with absorption. Dinner and bedtime are also excellent times of day as the body's repair mode and hormone secretions are at their highest capacity while sleeping. Most products recommend dividing doses, say two or three times during the day. Spreading consumption over the course of the day maximizes absorption.
- **Make it a habit.** Consider targeting two set times per day to establish routine or ritual for basic daily nutrition habits. This is what most people can handle and remember. Add additional times for other supplemental needs. In the beginning, or as needed, place reminders in line of sight or set alarms.
- **Be practical.** Keep your supplements in locations that provide easy access. Most do not require refrigeration, so keeping them out on kitchen and bathroom counters creates visibility and supports routine use. Many people find it useful to purchase some kind of pill box or container that allows a week's worth of supplements to be pre-counted and organized for each day. This way, consumption can be accomplished quickly or supplements easily placed in a pocket or small container to consume later. Marking on bottle lids with markers or posting a sheet on the inside of a cupboard door for dose instruction can also be helpful. Use a small cup or glass to put the capsules for convenience and ease of swallowing. Keep it close by for reuse.
- **Stay the course.** Most people experience an increased sense of well-being when beginning a supplementation program. Some individuals are an exception and feel worse before starting to feel better. A few common causes of discomfort are the elimination of microbes or dealing with chronic illness or disease. In Lyme disease treatment, this phenomenon is referred to as a Herxheimer reaction, but it can occur with any microbial infection. If a new symptom occurs that can be specifically defined as a side effect to a particular supplement (such as nausea after taking a certain supplement), consider first if it was taken with food. If an exacerbation of symptoms occurs, reduce the dose of supplements until symptoms ease and then gradually increase the dose again over time. If adverse reactions occur that seem beyond these parameters, consider discontinuing use until issues can be addressed or a more suitable choice can be made.
- **Make supplements part of your lifestyle.** Supplements to support general health can be continued indefinitely and are an excellent component of a healthy lifestyle. Supplements that support immune function, reduce inflammation, and provide antimicrobial properties should be continued at the higher doses recommended until symptoms subside, when doses may be reduced or supplements discontinued completely. Rotate different supplements over time as needed. Consider intermittent programs to maintain health results. For example, engage in a quarterly detox program for the duration of fourteen to thirty days as a complementary commitment to a basic daily routine.
- **Take them along.** When you travel, take your supplements with you. Get a pill box that contains specific, marked sections for different times of the day. Most allow for a week's worth of doses. Plastic baggies can hold capsules for single use or to contain individual products. Use a permanent marker to label the baggies "AM" or "PM" or identify the product contained.
- **Store them right.** Keep supplements out of windowsills or away from other sources of bright light. Store in dark or opaque bottles away from microwaves and otherelectromagnetic sources.

Tip

At the beginning of each *Focus Areas* is a list of supplements that have specific merit for each area. Those of particular significance are bolded.

Additional Information

- **Herxheimer reactions.** Die-off of bacteria can intensify symptoms of fatigue, muscle pain, and feeling flu-like. Generally, herxheimer reactions are more common and more intense with conventional antibiotic therapy, but they can still occur with natural supplements. If you feel that you are having herxheimer reactions, back off on dose and then increase gradually and slowly.

- **Excessive stimulation.** One of the greatest benefits of natural supplementation is an increased energy and reserves. Generally, this is welcomed during the day but can be a problem at night while trying to sleep. If you notice an effect, take primary supplements in the morning and afternoon.

- **Dealing with adverse effects:** Adverse effects associated with taking natural supplements are uncommon, but possible. Fortunately, most are mild and transient and should be easy to work through by reducing dosages.

- **Upset stomach.** The most common adverse effects are an upset stomach, indigestion, mild nausea, and discomfort mid-chest or on the left side under the lower rib cage (where the stomach is located). First consider if consumption occurred on an empty or overly full stomach and adjust accordingly. Otherwise, if necessary, take a break from the supplements for a few days to a week. Consider adding an essential oil such as ginger, peppermint, or digestive blend to soothe upset. If chronic digestive issues already existed, additional considerations may need to be made.

SECTION 4

FOCUS AREAS

Take a holistic approach to wellness by learning to address your health in terms of body systems and focus areas. Think beyond the disease-symptom model, and instead focus on supporting systems that determine the well-being of your entire body.

***A holistic approach to wellness** promotes living with an intentional mindset, while addressing root causes when symptoms and needs arise.*

A HEALTHY BODY is like a finely tuned symphony orchestra. An orchestra is divided into sections, and sections are comprised of individual instruments. Similarly, the body is divided into sections called body systems that are comprised of individual organs.

During a musical performance, when out-of-tune sounds come from a single instrument, it affects that section and the quality of music coming from the entire orchestra. The conductor's role is to identify the underlying cause behind the affected sound, tuning and refining where necessary. So, too, is every individual the conductor of their own internal orchestrations and harmony in partnership with the body itself and its messaging.

Take a Holistic Approach

Thinking beyond a disease-symptom model and focusing on the systems that govern the function of the entire body and its parts allows one to shift from an ambulance mentality of "if it ain't broke don't fix it" to true whole-body thinking and a prevention mindset. By addressing wellness in terms of body systems, a ho istic approach to wellness ensues.

AMBULANCE MENTALITY APPROACH

HOLISTICALLY-MINDED APPROACH

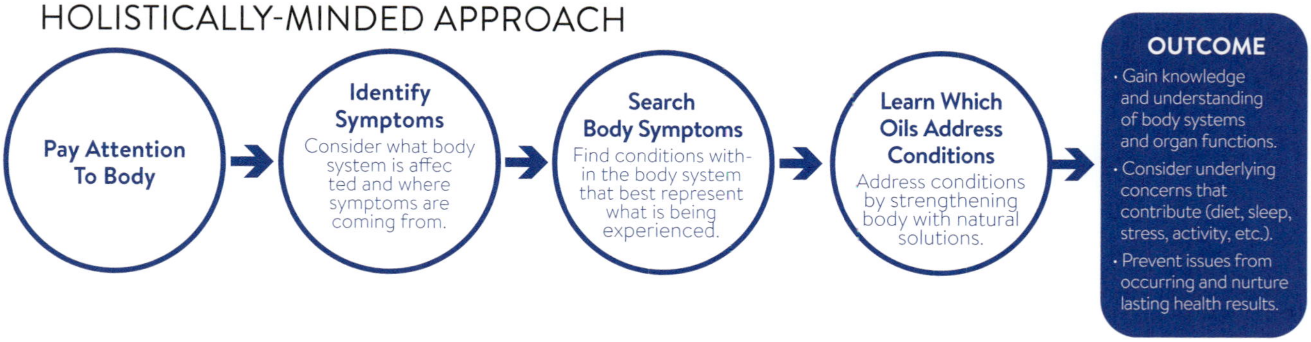

The Body—A System of Interconnectivity

Because body systems are interconnected, when one system is hindered or malfunctions, other are impacted. Likewise, when one is repaired and strengthened the whole body benefits and functions are restored.

When it comes to creating true and long-lasting wellness, learn to use natural healing solutions in terms of the body systems—exactly as this section is designed.

Biological Terrain

- Nutrients
- Water
- Oxygen
- Waste removal
- Chemical and temperature regulation

↓

Cellular Health

- Healthy cells are the result of a healthy bioterrain.
- Unhealthy cells, caused by deficiencies and toxicities, are at the core of ailments and diseased body tissues.

↓

Specialized Tissue

- Body tissues are comprised of cells, both of which specialize in certain functions depending on the organs and systems they belong to.

↓

Body Systems

- Body systems, like a section of an orchestra, are comprised of specialized tissues designed to perform certain body functions, the failure of which is the manifestation of ailment and disease.

tips

The Body Talks

Use the *Focus Areas* to search by conditions for specific solutions. The body uses symptoms as messages, or what's being called "conditions," to communicate it has unmet needs.

The Long and the Short of It

Essential oils provide support to cells, tissues, organs, and systems so the body can better resolve current conditions as well as root causes for improved long-term results.

The Multi-Taskers

Although an essential oil or blend is chosen to support one need, their complex chemistry can't help but support other systems and organs simultaneously.

Using the Focus Areas Effectively

The *Focus Areas* section of this book is designed to create an opportunity to learn, first, about a body system itself, gaining a basic understanding of its purpose or role, working parts, and what can potentially go wrong. Second, each section focuses on key oils and supplements as first responses to solutions, usage tips, solutions to numerous conditions, and user-recommended protocols.

An additional component of each *Focus Area* is "Related Properties" and is to be used to search for solutions by related properties to certain oils. For example, if one wanted to sleep better, one would search for a properties category such as "Calming" and find an oil such as lavender or Roman chamomile. To take this process to a *Power User* (pg. 36) level, use the properties chart in the back of the book and learn of the numerous properties for each oil and the multiplicity of actions they are capable of.

In conclusion, the desired outcome from the use of *Focus Areas* is to become a more experienced oil user, knowing how to "think for yourself," shifting from a symptoms focus instead to addressing root causes, finding solutions, and taking intentional actions.

Addictions

See also Limbic

THE WORD "ADDICT" has a negative connotation, leading people to think of base individuals living among the dregs of society, but anyone can develop an addiction. To the brain, all addictions, regardless of the type, have similar damaging effects. The only difference is to the degree to which they occur. Although the substance or the body releases chemicals which enhance a "high," or feeling of euphoria, the pleasure response or relief from pain is only temporary.

Drug addiction is a powerful force that can take control of user's lives. In the past, addiction was thought to be a weakness of character, but now research is proving that addiction is also a matter of brain chemistry.

Dr. Nora Volkow, the director of the National Institute on Drug Abuse, says, "The way a brain becomes addicted to a drug is related to how a drug increases levels of the naturally occurring neurotransmitter dopamine, which modulates the brain's ability to perceive reward reinforcement. The pleasure sensation that the brain gets when dopamine levels are elevated creates the motivation for us to proactively perform actions that are indispensable to our survival (like eating or procreation). Dopamine is what conditions us to do the things we need to do."

Volkow continues, "Using addictive drugs floods the limbic brain with dopamine—taking it up to as much as five or ten times the normal level. With these levels elevated, the user's brain begins to associate the drug with an outsize neurochemical reward. Over time, by artificially raising the amount of dopamine, our brains think is 'normal,' the drugs create a need that only they can meet."

When the body starts to expect and incorporate this extra chemical release as part of normal body function, the addict experiences chemical addiction and will suffer from withdrawal symptoms if they try to stop. To make matters worse, most addicts suffer from worsening problems in interpersonal relationships as their psychological and physical need for relief takes over and replaces all other responsibilities that would enable them to lead a healthy, normal life such as working, fully participating in family and social relationships. The results of addiction are typically nothing short of debilitating and eventually devastating.

There are many types of addiction, including but not limited to: alcohol, drugs, food, sugar, exercise, computer (including computer games and social media), pornography (online or other), sex, shopping, gambling, emotional intimacy (including unreasonable expectations and compulsive patterns of romance, sexuality, and relationships), texting, risky behaviors, or thrill-seeking ("adrenaline junkies"), and more.

Addictions that center on ingested substances (known as exogenous addictions) change body chemistry; addictions to activities or behaviors (known as endogenous addictions) cause the body to produce extra endorphins and other chemicals that make a person feel good temporarily. Either way, changes in body chemistry creates a dependency on the activity or substance. The greater the exposure, the more the body becomes desensitized to the excess chemicals.

Individuals who are addicted to substances or activities often feel helpless, frustrated, and ashamed of their situation. Often, most don't realize or admit they are addicted until they try to stop, only to find that they keep regressing to participation in the addictive behavior. Until an addict is ready to be honest and take responsibility for their choices, ask for help, and fully participate in successful rehabilitation programs (such as treatment programs, counseling, and twelve-step programs), they faces a downward spiral that can include marital/family ruin or dissolution, financial devastation, criminal activity, and/or sickness or death.

Because they are chemical in nature, essential oils can assist recovering addicts with emotional and chemical support for the brain as they are seeking to get their lives under control again. To gain additional insight on how they powerfully affect the brain, read the introduction to *Limbic*.

There are essential oils that can help reprogram the body's cravings for specific substances and that can strengthen the resolution to abstain. Essential oils are also able to support and strengthen the very emotional areas of pain that caused the individual to participate in the addictive behavior in the first place, leading the individual to adopt a healthier lifestyle. Loved ones often suffer alongside the addict, as they feel helpless to prevent the collateral damage they see happening right in front of their eyes; essential oils can be a tremendous emotional support for these individuals as well.

top solutions

Single Oils

Copaiba— boosts dopamine levels (pg. 136)

Grapefruit, Black pepper, Clove, and Cinnamon bark— dissipate cravings, support detoxification and renewed energy (pgs. 154, 111, 134, 126)

Melissa— clears negative thought patterns that block change; alleviates depression (pg. 188)

Bergamot— promotes sense of self-worth (pg. 107)

Peppermint— supports sense of buoyancy, recovery, and reprieve from painful emotions (pg. 202)

Blends

Serenity®— promotes calm, peaceful, tranquil state of being; quiets mind (pg. 219)

Zendocrine®— promotes elimination, detoxification of toxins (pg. 251)

Motivate®— promotes self-confidence, trust (pg. 190)

Balance®— restores sense of solidity/feeling grounded in life (pg. 104)

Slim & Sassy®, On Guard®, Purify— subdue cravings, detoxify (pgs. 222, 195, & 208)

Elevation, Citrus Bloom™— uplift, boost mood, promote positive outlook (pgs. 131, 145)

Supplements

Adaptiv™ Capsules (pg. 253), Alpha CRS®+, DDR Prime® Softgels, Fiber, Greens, **IQ Mega** (pg. 260), Microplex VMz®, **Mito2Max®** (pg. 262), On Guard® Throat Drops or Beadlets, Protein, **Slim & Sassy® Softgels** (pg. 267), TerraZyme®, **xEO Mega®** (pg. 271), Zendrocrine® Complex

usage tips

For best support for addiction recovery:

- **Aromatic:** Diffuse or inhale oils from a bottle or hands. Wear as a perfume/cologne.
- **Topical:** Apply under nose, behind ears, to base of skull (especially in suboccipital triangles), forehead, and on roof of mouth (closest location to the amygdala; place on pad of thumb, hold on roof of mouth, then suck on thumb). Place oils in locations that best match emotional states, such as over the heart. Use a carrier oil as needed for sensitive skin or "hot" oils.
- **Internal:** For immediate impact, in addition to inhalation, place a drop or two of a chosen oil under tongue, hold for 30 seconds then swallow. Take oils in capsule or glass of water. Consider detoxification products/oils or a program— see *Detoxification.*

Related Ailments

Adrenaline, Alcohol Addition, Drug Addiction, Food Addiction, Smoking Addiction, Video Game Addiction, Withdrawal Symptoms, Work Addiction

By Related Properties

For more, see *Oil Properties* on pages 535-538

Anaphrodisiac— arborvitae, marjoram

Analgesic— bergamot, birch, black pepper, blue tansy, clary sage, clove, copaiba, eucalyptus, fennel, frankincense, helichrysum, juniper berry, lavender, litsea, marjoram, oregano, peppermint, pink pepper, Siberian fir, tea tree, turmeric, wild orange, wintergreen, yarrow|pom

Antidepressant— bergamot, cinnamon bark, clary sage, frankincense, geranium, lavender, lemongrass, magnolia, melissa, neroli, oregano, patchouli, pink pepper, ravintsara, sandalwood, tangerine, wild orange

Anti-parasitic— bergamot, blue tansy, cinnamon bark, clove, frankincense, lavender, oregano, rosemary, tangerine, thyme, tea tree, tulsi, turmeric

Antitoxic— bergamot, black pepper, cinnamon bark, citronella, coriander, fennel, geranium, grapefruit, juniper berry, lavender, lemon, lemongrass, patchouli, thyme

Calming— bergamot, black pepper, black spruce, blue tansy, cassia, clary sage, copaiba, coriander, frankincense, geranium, juniper berry, lavender, litsea, magnolia, oregano, patchouli, Roman chamomile, sandalwood, tangerine, vetiver, yarrow|pom

Regenerative— cedarwood, clove, coriander, geranium, jasmine, lemongrass, manuka, myrrh, neroli, patchouli, sandalwood, wild orange, yarrow|pom

Relaxing— basil, blue tansy, cassia, cedarwood, clary sage, cypress, fennel, geranium, green mandarin, jasmine, lime, manuka, neroli, patchouli, rosemary, sandalwood, spearmint

Restorative— basil, black spruce, frankincense, lime, patchouli, rosemary, sandalwood, spearmint

Sedative— bergamot, blue tansy, cedarwood, clary sage, frankincense, geranium, juniper berry, lavender, magnolia, marjoram, melissa, neroli, patchouli, Roman chamomile, rose, spikenard, tangerine, yarrow|pom, ylang ylang

Stimulant— basil, bergamot, black pepper, blue tansy, cardamom, clove, coriander, fennel, grapefruit, juniper berry, lime, patchouli, pink pepper, rosemary, Siberian fir, tangerine, tea tree, thyme, tulsi

Stomachic— blue tansy, cardamom, cinnamon bark, clary sage, coriander, fennel, ginger, juniper berry, marjoram, melissa, peppermint, rosemary, tangerine, wild orange, yarrow|pom

Uplifting— cardamom, cedarwood, clary sage, cypress, grapefruit, green mandarin, lemon, lime, litsea, melissa, pink pepper, tangerine, wild orange

conditions

Accountability, lack of– fennel, ginger, Balance®

Anesthetize pain, attempting to– birch, clove, helichrysum, wintergreen, Deep Blue®

Anguish– helichrysum, melissa, Citrus Bloom™, Elevation

Antisocial– cardamom, cedarwood, marjoram, Balance®

Anxiety– basil, bergamot, bergamot mint, black spruce, cedarwood, frankincense, juniper berry, lavender, magnolia, vanilla, vetiver, ylang ylang, Adaptiv™, Balance®, Elevation, Motivate®, Peace®, Serenity®

Appetite stimulant– blue tansy, ginger, wild orange, Slim & Sassy®; see *Digestive & Intestinal*

Appetite, excessive– cassia, cinnamon bark, ginger, grapefruit, peppermint, tulsi, Slim & Sassy®; see *Digestive & Intestinal, Eating Disorders, Weight*

Checked out– basil, cedarwood, clary sage, frankincense, patchouli, ravintsara, sandalwood, Balance®, InTune® or Passion®

Control, loss of– blue tansy, clove, Balance®

Cravings– cilantro, cinnamon bark, clove, grapefruit, peppermint, Balance®, Serenity®, Slim & Sassy®

Deceptive/lying/secretive– clary sage

Despairing/hopeless– bergamot, clary sage, lemongrass, melissa, Citrus Bloom™, Elevation, Forgive®, Motivate®, Peace®

Dishonest– black pepper, clary sage, frankincense, lavender, melissa, Abōde™, ClaryCalm®, Purify, Serenity®

Dopamine levels, low– basil, bergamot, cedarwood, copaiba, frankincense, jasmine, lemon, patchouli, Roman chamomile, rosemary, sandalwood, wild orange, Cheer®, Whisper®

Financial issues– wild orange, Motivate®

Guilt– bergamot, lemon, peppermint, Forgive®, HD Clear®

Hangover– cassia, cinnamon bark, geranium, grapefruit, lemon, PastTense®, Slim & Sassy®, Zendocrine®

Irrational– cedarwood, lemon, Adaptiv™, InTune®

Irresponsible– fennel, ginger, Balance®

Irritable– cardamom, Forgive®, Serenity®

Obsession/fixation with drug of choice– cilantro, cypress, patchouli, ylang ylang, Adaptiv™, Balance®; see *Limbic "Obsessive/compulsive thoughts/behaviors"*

Relapsing– clove, ginger, lavender, melissa, ravintsara, InTune®, Motivate®, Passion®, Zendocrine®,

Stealing– black pepper, cassia, clary sage, frankincense, geranium, lavender, vetiver, ylang ylang, Abōde™, ClaryCalm®, Purify, Serenity®, Zendocrine®

Stress management, poor– lavender, Serenity®; see *Stress*

Thrill seeking, excessive– birch, clove, frankincense, helichrysum, oregano, peppermint, Siberian fir, tulsi, wintergreen, Deep Blue®

Urges, intense– black spruce, cedarwood, patchouli

Withdrawal– cilantro, cinnamon bark, copaiba, frankincense, grapefruit, juniper berry, lavender, marjoram, sandalwood, spikenard, wild orange, Adaptiv™, Citrus Bloom™, DDR Prime®, Elevation, Motivate®, Passion®, Peace®, citrus essential oils

protocols

DOPAMINE BOOST: Take 1 drop patchouli, 1 drop bergamot, 1 drop copaiba in a capsule or under tongue.

ALCOHOL CRAVINGS & LIVER SUPPORT

- Take 1 -2 drops copaiba on tongue when cravings hit.
- Consume 2 drops of helichrysum 2x's a day in a capsule or under tongue. Apply diluted over liver and/or bottoms of feet.

CHEWING TOBACCO CRAVINGS: Apply black pepper to lips and/or on thumb then press to roof of mouth.

TOBACCO/NICOTINE CRAVINGS (top oils: black pepper, clove, On Guard®)

- Inhale black pepper from cupped hands or diffuse.
- Apply clary sage, patchouli, spikenard.
- Put a drop of On Guard® or clove oil on toothbrush prior to brushing.
- Combine 2 drops each of clove, frankincense and peppermint. Inhale from palms, apply to bottoms of feet, and/or add to drinking water.
- Take On Guard® on tongue or in water when an urge strikes. Additional considerations: clove or cinnamon bark.

PORNOGRAPHY ADDICTION RECOVERY SUPPORT: Use 1-2 drops frankincense under tongue 1-2x's per day. Apply helichrysum or vetiver over lower abdomen as least once per day. Combine with basil, cardamom, frankincense, grapefruit, helichrysum, Purify, Balance®, and/or On Guard® to create a desirable blend that can be worn daily and/or inhaled when needed.

WORK ADDICTION: Diffuse oils in workspace for a minimum of 2-3 hours per day. Combine as desired: basil, geranium, wild orange, ylang ylang, and/or Serenity® to equal 5-10 drops and diffuse.

Suggested combinations:

- 3 drops wild orange and 2 drops ylang ylang.
- 2 drops each geranium and ylang ylang and 3 drops Whisper®.
- 2 drops basil, 3 drops wild orange, and 2 drops ylang ylang.
- 6 drops Serenity® and 1-2 drops ylang ylang.

ENERGY DRINK & CAFFEINE ADDICTION: Place 3 drops basil oil on bottom of each foot and inhale regularly throughout the day. Take 5 drops Zendocrine® in a capsule 3-5x's daily. Place one drop grapefruit under tongue, hold for 30 seconds, and swallow anytime experiencing cravings.

DRUG & ALCOHOL ADDICTION: Place 2-3 drops of any one or more oil listed on bottoms of feet, abdomen (specifically over liver area), and forehead. Choose from basil, copaiba, bergamot and/or Zendocrine®. Dilute with fractionated coconut oil as needed or desired.

ADDICTION EMOTIONAL RECOVERY: Combine 10 drops each Adaptiv™, copaiba, melissa, and Roman chamomile in 10mL roller bottle, topped of with carrier oil. Apply over heart, on forehead, pulse points, and/or bottoms of feet.

Oils to Address Emotional States for Addiction Recovery:

For emotional states associated with addictions— see *Mood & Behavior*

Singles

Basil— overcomes chronic fatigue (creates desire for stimulants); release toxins
Bergamot— encourages self-love, restores sense of self worth
Cardamom— helps overcoming objectifying (common problem with addictions)
Cedarwood— supports healthy GABA (anti-excitatory), serotonin levels
Clary sage— dispels darkness and illusion
Clove— restores healthy boundaries
Copaiba— boosts dopamine levels
Coriander— effective with any addiction
Frankincense— connects to divine love/ acceptance, purpose, higher brain function
Geranium— assists with love and acceptance
Ginger— supports being fully present, taking full responsibility
Grapefruit— reduces cravings; restores relationship with body's natural energy
Helichrysum— supports healing from deep, intense pain, trauma
Juniper berry— supports accessing, releasing unaccessed/unresolved fears
Lemon— supports restoration of logical thinking; clears generational patterns
Melissa— restores connection to reality, truth, light; instills courage
Patchouli— grounds and stabilizes; get the "guts" to take a leap of faith
Peppermint— promotes sense of recovery
Roman chamomile— helps one live true to one's self
Siberian fir— clears inherited/passed on addictions; tendencies in families
Thyme— releases and resolves toxic emotions
Vetiver— gets to "root" cause and face it head on; supports amygdala
Wild orange— supports creative thoughts, expression; restores playfulness
Ylang ylang— releases trauma; recovers connection to the heart, to feel/trust again

Blends

Adaptiv™— brings transquility and motivation and stirs a coping capacity
Balance®— restores sense of solidity/feeling grounded in life; brings electrical balance to body and focus to mind
DDR Prime®— supports knowing what's worth keeping vs. releasing
Deep Blue®— supports deep emotional healing; restores normal endorphin levels
Elevation— soothes heart, balances emotions; stabilizes mood, supports serotonin
InTune®— normalizes, stabilizes brain activity; invites acceptance of reality
PastTense®— invites releasing fears, relaxing and enjoying life again
Purify, **Abōde™**— supports detoxification; provides freedom from past habits/patterns
Serenity®— quiets mind; encourages facing issues; helps balance expectations
Slim & Sassy®— supports restoration of a positive relationship to one's body and natural sources of energy
Zendocrine®— supports detox processes; detoxing old habits, beliefs

Solutions for Specific Addictions:

Adrenaline— basil, bergamot, black spruce, clary sage, geranium, patchouli, rosemary, Adaptiv™, Balance®, Console®, InTune®, Motivate®, Serenity®, Zendocrine®
Alcohol*— basil, cassia, citronella, copaiba, eucalyptus, frankincense, ginger, grapefruit, helichrysum, juniper berry, lavender, lemon, marjoram, melissa, Roman chamomile, rosemary, Balance®, Cheer®, Forgive®, Peace®, Serenity®
Anger— black spruce, geranium, helichrysum, magnolia, marjoram, rosemary, thyme, wintergreen, Abōde™, Cheer®, Elevation, Forgive®, Motivate®, Peace®, Purify, Serenity®, Whisper®; see *Mood & Behavior*
Caffeine*— basil, grapefruit, patchouli, Passion®, Peace®, Slim & Sassy®, Zendocrine®
Controlling, overly/"control freak"— cilantro, cinnamon bark, cypress, patchouli, sanda wood, wintergreen, Passion®, Citrus Bliss®, Slim & Sassy®
Cutting/self harm/self inflicted pain— bergamot, geranium, myrrh, rose, wintergreen, ClaryCalm®, Console®, Elevation, Forgive®, HD Clear®, Immortelle, On Guard®, Peace®, Whisper®
Drugs*— basil, citronella, clary sage, copaiba, grapefruit, patchouli, Roman chamomile, Cheer®, Console®, Motivate®, Passion®, Peace®, Zendocrine®
Eating Disorders (anorexia, bulimia)— bergamot, cardamom, cinnamon bark, grapefruit, melissa, patchouli, Air-X™, Breathe® Respiratory Drops, Citrus Bliss®, Console®, Elevation, Forgive®, Passion®, Peace®, Slim & Sassy®; see *Eating Disorders*
Entertainment— peppermint, vetiver, Balance®, Console®, Elevation, Passion®, Serenity®
Fear— black spruce, cassia, cinnamon bark, ginger, juniper berry, myrrh, patchouli, Peace®; see *Mood & Behavior*
Food— basil, cardamom, ginger, grapefruit, peppermint, myrrh, Console®, Motivate®, Passion®, Peace®, Slim & Sassy®; see *Eating Disorders*
Gaming— Cheer®, Console®, Deep Blue®, Elevation, HD Clear®, TerraShield®, Whisper®
Irritable— rose, ClaryCalm®, Serenity®, Whisper®
Marijuana— basil, black pepper, copaiba, patchouli, ylang ylang, Passion®, Peace®
Nicotine— bergamot, black pepper, cassia, cinnamon bark (on tongue), clove, eucalyptus, ginger, Adaptiv™, Passion®, Peace®, On Guard®, On Guard® Throat Drops; see "Tobacco" below
Pain meds— birch, clove, copaiba, eucalyptus, patchouli, pink pepper, wintergreen, Deep Blue®, Console®, Passion®, Peace®
Pornography*— basil, cardamom, frankincense, grapefruit, helichrysum, Abōde™, Balance®, Console®, On Guard®, Purify
Sex— arborvitae, basil, cardamom, geranium, marjoram, sandalwood, Passion®, Peace®, Motivate®, Whisper®
Sugar— cardamom, cassia, cinnamon bark, clove, grapefruit, helichrysum, Cheer®, Motivate®, Passion®, Peace®, Slim & Sassy®
Technology— patchouli, peppermint, Cheer®, InTune®, Forgive®, Motivate®, Passion®; see "Entertainment"
Tobacco/chewing*— bergamot, black pepper, cassia, cinnamon bark, clove, coriander, frankincense, Cheer®, Forgive®, On Guard®, On Guard® Throat Drops, Passion®, Peace®
Tobacco/smoking*— basil, bergamot, black pepper, cassia, cinnamon bark, clove, eucalyptus, frankincense, patchouli, peppermint, spikenard, Air-X™, Breathe®, Cheer®, Forgive®, On Guard® Throat Drops or Beadlets, Passion®, Peace®
Work*— arborvitae, basil, cedarwood, geranium, lavender, marjoram, wild orange, ylang ylang, Adaptiv™, Cheer®, Forgive®, Peace®

*See Protocols on pg. 282

Allergies

See also Immune & Lymphatic

ALLERGIC REACTIONS occur when the immune system reacts to foreign substances in the environment that are normally harmless to most people, such as pollen, bee venom, or pet dander. A substance that causes a reaction is called an allergen. These reactions are generally considered to be acquired. A true allergic reaction is an immediate form of hypersensitivity and is distinctive because the immune response over-activates specific white blood cells that are triggered by antibodies.

When allergies occur, the immune system identifies a particular allergen as harmful—even if it isn't—and creates antibodies to fight it. When contact is made with the allergen, the immune system's reaction will typically inflame skin, sinuses, airways, or digestive system. This reaction is known as an inflammatory response.

The severity of allergies varies from person to person and can range from minor irritation to anaphylaxis, which is a severe reaction to an allergen that can be a life-threatening emergency. Common triggers for severe reactions include insect bites or stings (wasps, bees) and certain food allergies (e.g., peanuts, shellfish). It is important to note that not all reactions or intolerances are forms of allergic responses.

Allergy symptoms depend on the allergens/substances involved and can impact the airways, sinuses and nasal passages, skin, digestive system, and other body parts. Allergies are typically categorized as either respiratory or systemic (involving multiple organs—especially digestive, respiratory, and circulatory).

Common allergens include airborne particles (e.g., animal hair, car exhaust, cigarette smoke, dust, dust mites, fragrances, fungi, herbicides, mold, paint fumes, perfume, pesticides, pet dander, pollens, weeds); chemicals, latex, petroleum, and automotive products; foods (e.g. peanuts, genetically modified soy products); insect stings and bites; insect or reptile venom; medications (e.g., aspirin, antibiotics such as penicillin or sulfa drugs).

Traditional treatments for allergies include avoiding known allergens or administering steroids that modify the immune system in general and medications such as antihistamines and decongestants to reduce symptoms. Essential oils have the ability to chemically support the body in its capacity to reduce and overcome acute or chronic hypersensitivity. For allergy support specifically, it is especially important to be familiar with three properties of oils and the particular oils associated with the related actions: anti-allergenic (e.g., geranium, helichrysum), antihistamine (e.g., lavender, melissa, Roman chamomile), and steroidal (e.g., basil, rosemary). See "By Related Properties" for more information. Additionally, for numerous related respiratory needs refer to *Respiratory*.

top solutions

Single Oils

Basil, Rosemary– reduce inflammatory response and support adrenal glands (pgs. 105, 216)

Blue tansy, Lavender, Melissa– act as an antihistamine and calm irritation (pgs. 114, 175, 188)

Lemon– decongests and reduces mucus (pg. 176)

Peppermint– discharges phlegm and reduces inflammation (pg. 202)

Blends

Breathe®, Air-X™– support reduction of and recovery from allergic responses, open airways (pg. 116, 97)

Zendocrine®– supports permanent reduction of reactivity (pg. 251)

Purify, Abōde™– alleviate allergic responses to bites and stings, cleanse air (pg. 208, 95)

DigestZen®– supports digestion to calm food allergy responses (pg. 142)

On Guard®– supports immune system (pg. 195)

Serenity®– acts as an antihistamine (pg. 219)

Supplements

Alpha CRS®+, **Breathe® Respiratory Drops** (pg. 255), Microplex VMz®, Mito2Max®, **TerraZyme®** (pg. 268), **TriEase® Softgels** (pg. 268), Zendrocrine® Complex, **Zendocrine® Softgels** (pg. 273)

usage tips

For best support for overcoming allergies:

- **Internal:** Take oils in water and drink, in a capsule, or place a drop on or under tongue.
- **Aromatic:** Diffuse chosen oils, apply to palms and inhale, and/or under nostrils, on chest, clothing, or bedding.
- **Topical:** Apply oils to forehead, cheeks (avoid eyes), chest, and bottoms of feet.

Related Ailments

Chemical Sensitivity Reaction [Detoxification, Immune & Lymphatic], Hay Fever [Immune & Lymphatic, Respiratory], Hives [Integumentary], Lactose Intolerance, Loss of Smell, Multiple Chemical Sensitivity Reaction, Olfactory Loss, Pet Dander

By Related Properties

For more, see *Oil Properties* on pages 535-538

Anti-allergenic– blue tansy, geranium, helichrysum, turmeric

Antihistamine– blue tansy, lavender, manuka, melissa, Roman chamomile, yarrow|pom

Anti-inflammatory– arborvitae, basil, bergamot, birch, black pepper, blue tansy, cardamom, cassia, cedarwood, cinnamon bark, copaiba, coriander, cypress, eucalyptus, fennel, frankincense, geranium, ginger, helichrysum, lavender, lemongrass, lime, manuka, myrrh, neroli, oregano, patchouli, peppermint, Roman chamomile, rosemary, sandalwood, Siberian fir, tangerine, tea tree, turmeric, yarrow|pom

Antitoxic– bergamot, black pepper, coriander, grapefruit, juniper berry, lavender, lemon, lemongrass, thyme

Calming– basil, bergamot, black pepper, blue tansy, cassia, clary sage, copaiba, coriander, fennel, frankincense, geranium, jasmine, juniper berry, lavender, litsea, magnolia, patchouli, Roman chamomile, sandalwood, tangerine, vetiver, yarrow|pom

Cleanser– arborvitae, cilantro, eucalyptus, grapefruit, green mandarin, juniper berry, lemon, thyme, wild orange

Detoxifier– cilantro, green mandarin, juniper berry, lime, litsea, patchouli, tangerine, turmeric, wild orange, yarrow|pom

Steroidal– basil, bergamot, birch, cedarwood, clove, fennel, patchouli, rosemary, thyme

protocols

ALLERGY POWER TRIO: Take 2 drops each lavender, lemon, and peppermint one of the following ways:

1. Under the tongue, hold there for thirty seconds, swallow; repeat as necessary.
2. Mix in a cup of water, drink; repeat as necessary until symptoms subside.
3. Consume in a capsule; repeat as necessary. OR take TriEase® Softgels.

EYE ALLERGIES: Layer 2 drops lavender and blue tansy under the pads of the index toe and middle toe and then rub in. Use a few drops lavender at the temples and gently rubbed in. Take care to stay close to the hairline to avoid eye contact.

SKIN RASH/HIVES: Dilute lavender and/or Roman chamomile with carrier oil and apply to area of concern.

THE ALLERGY BOMB: Take 2-3 drops each melissa and lavender in a capsule.

ALLERGY RELIEF COMBINATION: Combine 1-2 drops each lemon, lavender, and Roman chamomile in a capsule to help relieve hay fever or other airborne, allergy-type symptoms that result in sneezing, runny nose, watery eyes, and so on.

ALLERGIES

Ingredients:

2 drops lavender
1 drop Roman chamomile
2 drops blue tansy
1 drop peppermint
1 drop melissa

Directions:

Combine in palms with carrier oil, rub together, and then apply behind ears, on temples, and over thymus area. Repeat as needed. Also consume the same blend (except blue tansy) in a capsule.

LIVER FLUSH: Take 2-3 drops each Zendocrine® and Roman chamomile in a capsule 2x's per day to help relieve liver stagnation or congestion that can contribute to chronic, reoccuring allergies.

For more ideas, download the app on Android or iOS.

conditions

Abdominal cramping/spasms– See *Digestive & Intestinal*

Adrenal fatigue– See *Endocrine*

Airways, narrowing/constriction– birch, blue tansy, cinnamon bark, Douglas fir, eucalyptus, frankincense, helichrysum, laurel leaf, lavender, lemon, marjoram, myrrh, peppermint, ravintsara, rosemary, Siberian fir, thyme. wintergreen, Air-X™, Breathe®, Breathe® Respiratory Drops, DDR Prime®, Motivate®, Serenity®

Allergies, chronic– basil, ginger, lemon, lemongrass. thyme

Allergies, general*– cilantro, frankincense, lavender, peppermint, tea tree, yarrow|pom, Console®, Peace®, Zendocrine®

Anxiety– See *Mood & Behavior*

Blood pressure, high or low– see *Cardiovascular*

Chemical sensitivity– arborvitae, cilantro, coriander, Douglas fir, eucalyptus, lemon, peppermint, sandalwood, wild orange, Abōde™, DDR Prime®, Purify, Zendocrine®

Congestion– See *Respiratory*

Cough– See *Respiratory*

Energy, loss of/fatigue, chronic– See *Energy & Vitality*

Facial pressure and pain– helichrysum, myrrh, DDR Prime®, DigestZen®

Glands, enlarged/swollen– arborvitae, cilantro, lemon, lime, oregano, Roman chamomile, wintergreen, On Guard®

Hay fever*– cilantro, lavender, lemon, tea tree, yarrow|pom, Abōde™, Air-X™, Breathe®, Motivate®, Purify

Headache– See *Pain & Inflammation*

Hives*– basil, cilantro, frankincense, lavender, lemongrass, peppermint, Roman chamomile, rosemary, tea tree, DDR Prime®

Inflammation, joints– See *Skeletal*

Inflammation, skin– See *Integumentary*

Immune system, overactive– peppermint, rosemary, Elevation

Insect bite– lavender, Purify; see *First Aid*

Itching/urge to scratch, burning– See *Integumentary*

Itchy eyes/mouth/throat*– blue tansy, cilantro, lavender, lemon, peppermint, tea tree, Motivate®, Purify, Slim & Sassy®, Zendocrine®, TriEase® Softgels

Joint pain– See *Skeletal*

Liver– See *Digestive & Intestinal*

Liver, toxic load– See *Digestive & Intestinal*; see "Anti-allergenic" property

Mold sensitivity– arborvitae, oregano, tea tree, thyme, Abōde™, Air-X™, Purify, Zendocrine®

Nasal congestion/drip– See *Respiratory*

Nausea– See *Digestive & Intestinal*

Poison oak– See *First Aid*

Pollen sensitivity– blue tansy, cilantro, juniper berry, lavender, Abōde™, Air-X™, Breathe®, Purify, Zendocrine®

Rapid pulse– cardamom, cedarwood, frankincense, rosemary, ylang ylang, Elevation, Motivate®, Purify, Serenity®; see *Cardiovascular*

Rash*– arborvitae, blue tansy, cedarwood, frankincense, lavender, lemon, neroli, Roman chamomile, sandalwood, tangerine, tea tree, ClaryCalm®, Immortelle, Purify, Serenity®, Slim & Sassy®, Zendocrine®

Reaction– blue tansy, lavender, Roman chamomile

Runny nose– grapefruit, lavender, lemon, myrrh, peppermint, DigestZen®, Motivate®, Zendocrine®

Shock– See *First Aid*

Skin bumps– See *Integumentary*

Skin cracking/peeling/scaling– See *Integumentary*

Skin flushed– See *Integumentary*

Skin irritation– blue tansy, neroli, peppermint, tea tree, yarrow|pom, DigestZen®, Purify, Serenity®, Slim & Sassy®, Correct-X

Skin reddening– See *Integumentary*

Smoke sensitivity– black pepper, lavender, peppermint, Serenity®, Zendocrine®

Sneezing– blue tansy, Douglas fir, lavender, lemon, peppermint, Abōde™, Air-X™, Breathe®, Motivate®, Purify

Swallowing, difficulty– lavender, Motivate®, Zendocrine®

Swelling of lips, face, tongue, throat, etc.– lavender, wintergreen, Purify, Zendocrine®

Throat, dry or sore– See *Respiratory*

Voice, loss of/raspy/hoarseness– See *Respiratory*

Vomiting– See *Digestive & Intestinal*

Watery/itchy/red eyes*– blue tansy, eucalyptus, laurel leaf, lavender, lemon, ravintsara, Roman chamomile, tea tree, Purify, Zendocrine®

Welts– arborvitae, myrrh, vetiver, Roman chamomile, Purify

Wheezing– birch, lavender, wintergreen, Air-X™, Breathe®

*See Protocols on pg. 286

Athletes

AS THEY PREPARE for their sport of preference, many athletes participate in one or more training programs that can include but are not limited to: circuit training (develops a broad range of skills by providing stations with various exercises); interval training (short periods of vigorous activity interspersed with shorter resting periods; helps build speed endurance); Plyometrics (bounding exercises to help improve strength and speed); tempo training (exercisce that is faster-paced than is comfortable to increase endurance ability); strength training (the use of various pieces of equipment increases muscle resistance and inspires faster conditioning); resisted and/or assisted training (helps develop faster speed as the athlete uses resistance equipment, such as bands, or participates in assistance-based exercise, such as running downhill).

As athletes push their bodies for greater conditioning and/or endurance in fitness training or sports, the potential for injury is present. Often these injuries are a result of inadequate recovery (rest) time for muscles/body tissues to adequately rebuild or repair.

Some of these injuries include the following:

- Muscle pain and soreness
- Overusing tendons
- "Runner's Knee"—a generic term to describe anterior knee pain
- IT Band (iliotibial band) stress/injury—affects approximately 12 percent of runners
- Shin splints
- Pain in Achilles tendon
- Stress fracture

Other common conditions athletes may experience during training/sports:

- Exercise-induced asthma
- Exercise-associated collapse
- Effects resulting from over training—lack of concentration, depression, heart rate (resting) changes, increased injuries, insomnia/restless sleep, insatiable thirst, motivation and/or diminshed self esteem, muscle soreness lasting more than 72 hours, personality changes, progress hindered, sick more often

Athletes can combine sound principles of sports medicine (icing, heating, resting, etc., as appropriate) with natural remedies to increase the body's recovery time. There are oils known specifically for their ability to support connective tissue (involved in all sports injuries), to reduce inflammation, to support cellular regeneration for faster recovery time, and/or to help warm up/cool down muscle groups for better overall performance.

Adding whole-food, bio-available supplements gives cells the support they need to enhance restorative and repairing activities. Supplementation can also increase energy levels during a workout to reduce fatigue. An easily digestible protein drink consumed just after a cardio workout gives the body readily accessible protein so it doesn't have to break down proteins in the body. All these good practices help to minimize breakdown and overuse injuries in the first place, help provide energy, and increase the body's capacity to restore tissues to good health quickly.

top solutions

Single Oils

Wintergreen– supports joints, circulation, pain relief, and warming (pg. 247)

Frankincense, Copaiba– relieves pain and inflammation (pgs. 151, 136)

Peppermint– pre-exercise support, cooling, pain relief (pg. 202)

Lemongrass– connective tissue repair (pg. 180)

Marjoram– muscle repair and tension relief (pg. 187)

Blends

AromaTouch®, **Deep Blue®**, **Deep Blue® Rub** or **Stick**– pre- or post-exercise recovery and pain relief (pgs. 103, 141)

Breathe®, **Air-X™**– open airways and ease breathing (pgs. 116, 97)

Rescuer™– gentle relief and recovery support (pg. 212)

Supplements

Adaptiv™ Capsules, Alpha CRS®+, **Bone Nutrient Complex** (pg. 255), **Copaiba Softgels** (pg. 256), DDR Prime® Softgels, **Deep Blue Polyphenol Complex®** (pg. 257), Microplex VMz®, **Mito2Max®** (pg. 262), **Protein** (pg. 266), **Slim & Sassy® Softgels** (pg. 267), **Turmeric Dual Capsules** (pg. 269), xEO Mega®

usage tips

For best methods of use for athletes:

- **Topical:** Apply to areas of concern and/or performance.
- **Aromatic:** Inhale oils before and during workouts to invigorate, energize, and improve respiration, as well as before amd during performance or competition for energy or an emotional boost.

ATHLETES

By Related Properties

For more, see *Oil Properties* on pages 535-538

Analgesic– basil, birch, black pepper, blue tansy, clove, copaiba, eucalyptus, ginger, helichrysum, lavender, lemongrass, litsea, peppermint, pink pepper, rosemary, Siberian fir, tea tree, wintergreen, yarrow|pom

Anti-inflammatory– arborvitae, basil, birch, black pepper, blue tansy, cedarwood, copaiba, cypress, frankincense, geranium, ginger, helichrysum, lavender, lemongrass, lime, manuka, oregano, patchouli, peppermint, rosemary, Siberian fir, spearmint, spikenard, tea tree, turmeric, wintergreen, yarrow|pom

Energizing– basil, cypress, ginger, grapefruit, lemongrass, lime, Siberian fir, tangerine, wild orange, yarrow|pom

Regenerative– basil, frankincense, geranium, helichrysum, lavender, lemongrass, myrrh, neroli, patchouli, tea tree, wild orange, yarrow|pom, ylang ylang

Relaxing– basil, blue tansy, cedarwood, cypress, helichrysum, lavender, litsea, manuka, marjoram, neroli, Roman chamomile, wild orange, ylang ylang

Steroidal– basil, bergamot, birch, cedarwood, clove, fennel, patchouli, rosemary, thyme

Vasodilator– lemongrass, marjoram, peppermint, rosemary, Siberian fir, thyme

Warming– birch, black pepper, cassia, cinnamon bark, ginger, marjoram, peppermint, pink pepper, wintergreen

protocols

PRE/POST-WORKOUT TIPS

- Sniff peppermint and/or Citrus Bliss® before workout to give a boost of energy, uplift mood, and reduce fatigue.
- Add 2 drops lemon or Slim & Sassy® to water to keep hydrated.
- Apply peppermint alone or with cypress, lemongrass, marjoram, peppermint, and/or pink pepper before a workout routine to increase circulation, warm and oxygenate muscles, and reduce possibility of injury.
- After workout, apply a Deep Blue® product with copaiba.
- For a more intense post-workout treatment, layer fractionated coconut oil, lemongrass, and/or marjoram, and then add a layer of Deep Blue® Rub to relieve aching muscles, reduce inflammation, improve recovery, and/or support injury repair.

FOR OVERHEATED/HEAT STROKE/HEAT EXHAUSTION: Apply 1 drop peppermint on back of neck. Make a peppermint spritzer bottle with water for future use.

FOR OXYGEN UPTAKE: Place a few drops of peppermint or Slim & Sassy® in water and sip. Swipe a drop of frankincense under nose.

FOR NAUSEA: Place a few drops of peppermint in water or use Beadlets.

FOR INFLAMMATION/PAIN/STIFFNESS: Mix together 30 drops Deep Blue® and 25 drops frankincense in a 10mL roller bottle and fill with fractionated coconut oil. Shake to blend. Apply onto affected areas as needed.

AFTER-SPORTS MASSAGE OR BATH: Use 2 drops each AromaTouch®, marjoram, and turmeric, and 1 drop each lavender, Roman chamomile, helichrysum, peppermint, and black pepper. Combine with carrier oil and massage on areas of concern OR add to 1 C Epsom salt, stir, and add to warm bath and soak. Consider multiplying recipe in a 10mL roll-on.

SHIN SPLINTS AND RUNNER'S KNEE REMEDIES

- Step 1: In a 10mL roller bottle, create one of the following blends. Add fractionated coconut oil to fill remainder of bottle. Shake to blend. Apply frequently. Massage into areas of concern.
  - Recipe #1: 10-12 drops each lemongrass and rosemary
  - Recipe #2: 10 drops lemongrass, 8 drops marjoram, 8 drops wintergreen
- Step 2 (optional): Apply a layer of Deep Blue® blend or Rub and massage in.

MUSCLE RELAXANT BATH SALTS: Combine 1 drop copaiba, 3 drops frankincense, 1 drop peppermint with 1 C Epsom salt. Add to bath water for relaxation and relief.

LINIMENT: Combine the following in a 2 oz. bottle: 10 drops copaiba with 5 drops each lemongrass and AromaTouch®. Fill remainder of bottle with fractionated coconut oil. Add 4 drops peppermint to intensify blend. Apply to sore muscles and joints.

FIRST AID: In a 2 oz glass bottle, combine 11 drops copaiba, 5 drops frankincense, 4 drops helichrysum, 3 drops lavender with 1 oz. aloe vera gel. Shake to blend. Apply 2-3x's a day or as needed to assist body's natural healing processes.

"TONE" UP YOUR MUSCLES: Combine 4 drops basil, 3 drops cypress, 3 drops rosemary, and 3 drops lavender with 1 t carrier oil. Rub into muscles before workout to enhance muscle tone and prevent soreness.

conditions

Appetite, excessive– bergamot, cassia, cinnamon bark, ginger, grapefruit, lemon, tulsi, Slim & Sassy®; see *Weight*

Appetite, imbalanced– wild orange, Slim & Sassy®; see *Weight*

Appetite, loss of– bergamot, black pepper, ginger, lemon, Slim & Sassy®; see *Weight*

Athlete's foot– arborvitae, cardamom, cinnamon bark, clove, copaiba, lavender, lemon eucalyptus, lemongrass, myrrh, oregano, tea tree, DDR Prime®, HD Clear®; see *Candida*

Blood pressure, low– rosemary, thyme; see *Cardiovascular*

Body temperature, too cool– black pepper, cinnamon bark, ginger, oregano, wintergreen; see "Warming" property

Body temperature, too high– bergamot, eucalyptus, peppermint, spearmint, Deep Blue®, PastTense®

Bone, pain– birch, cedarwood, cypress, eucalyptus, helichrysum, Siberian fir, wintergreen, Deep Blue®; see *Skeletal*

Breathing, constricted– Douglas fir, ravintsara, Air-X™, AromaTouch®, Breathe®, Deep Blue®; see *Respiratory*

Breathing, labored– ravintsara, Air-X™, Breathe®; see *Respiratory*

Cartilage injury– basil, birch, helichrysum, marjoram, lemongrass, peppermint, Siberian fir, wintergreen, Deep Blue®; see *Skeletal*

Circulation, poor– basil, cypress, Douglas fir, ginger, marjoram, pink pepper, turmeric, yarrow|pom, AromaTouch®; see *Cardiovascular*

Concussion– bergamot, cedarwood, clove, cypress, frankincense, sandalwood, Balance®. InTune®; see *Brain*

Consciousness, loss of– basil, frankincense, peppermint, rosemary; see *Brain*

Dehydration– lemon, peppermint, Slim & Sassy®

Dizziness– See *Brain*

Fatigue/Exhaustion– basil, bergamot, bergamot mint, cinnamon bark, cypress, Douglas fir, eucalyptus, frankincense, green mandarin, laurel leaf, lavender, lemon, peppermint, pink pepper, ravintsara, rosemary, sandalwood, wild orange, yarrow|pom, ylang ylang, Adaptiv™, Citrus Bliss®, DDR Prime®, Elevation, Slim & Sassy®, Zendocrine®; see *Energy & Vitality*

Feet, sore– lemongrass, marjoram, AromaTouch®

Headache– See *Pain & Inflammation*

Heat exhaustion/stroke*– bergamot, bergamot mint, eucalyptus, lemon, peppermint, petitgrain, spearmint, PastTense®, Zendocrine®

Inflammation*– birch, copaiba, cypress, frankincense, lavender, peppermint, rosemary, turmeric, wintergreen, Alpha CRS®+, DDR Prime®, Deep Blue®; see "Anti-inflammatory" property

Injury– birch, helichrysum, lemongrass, Siberian fir, wintergreen, AromaTouch®; see *Skeletal, Muscular*– see the area of injury: muscles, bones, connective tissue, bruising/skin, etc.

Involuntary muscle contractions– clary sage, geranium, lavender, marjoram; see *Nervous*

Jock itch– See *Men's Health*

Joint, inflammation/stiffness*– arborvitae, basil, birch, cinnamon bark, clove, cypress, Douglas fir, eucalyptus, frankincense, ginger, lavender, marjoram, peppermint, ravintsara, rosemary, Siberian fir, thyme, wintergreen, DDR Prime®, Deep Blue®, Zendocrine®; see *Skeletal*

Lactic acid buildup– juniper berry, lemon, lemongrass

Ligaments/tendons/connective tissue– basil, clove (dilute for topical use), eucalyptus, helichrysum, lemongrass, Siberian fir; see "Tendonitis", *Skeletal*

Lower back pain– birch, eucalyptus, frankincense, lavender, lemongrass, ginger, marjoram, peppermint, Siberian fir, wintergreen, AromaTouch®, DDR Prime®, Deep Blue®, PastTense®; see *Skeletal*

Lymphatic, congestion– ginger, grapefruit, lavender, lemon, lemongrass, ravintsara, sandalwood, Air-X™, AromaTouch®, Purify; see *Immune & Lymphatic*

Mental strength/clarity– basil, patchouli, peppermint, vetiver, Adaptiv™, Balance®, InTune®; see *Focus & Concentration*

Muscle, cramps/charley horse– basil, cypress, lemongrass, marjoram, peppermint, ravintsara, Siberian fir, spikenard, wintergreen, AromaTouch®, Deep Blue®, PastTense®; see *Muscular*

Muscle, fatigue/overworked– basil, black pepper, bergamot mint, cypress, Douglas fir, eucalyptus, laurel leaf, marjoram, ravintsara, rosemary, Siberian fir, AromaTouch®; see *Muscular*

Muscle, pain/sprain/strain/injury*– clove (dilute for topical use), copaiba, Douglas fir, eucalyptus, ginger, lavender, lemongrass, marjoram, peppermint, ravintsara, rosemary, Siberian fir, thyme, vetiver, wintergreen, AromaTouch®, Deep Blue®; see *Muscular*

Muscle spasms– arborvitae, basil, birch, black pepper, cardamom, coriander, cypress, eucalyptus, frankincense, ginger, laurel leaf, lavender, lemongrass, marjoram, myrrh, oregano, patchouli, peppermint, Roman chamomile, rosemary, spearmint, wild orange, wintergreen, yarrow|pom; see *Muscular*

Muscle, stiffness/tension*– basil, bergamot mint, Douglas fir, ginger, grapefruit, rosemary, Siberian fir, AromaTouch®, Deep Blue®, PastTense®; see *Muscular*

Muscle, weak– basil, bergamot, birch, black pepper, clary sage, clove, coriander, cypress, frankincense, ginger, helichrysum, lavender, lemongrass, jasmine, marjoram, patchouli, rosemary, wintergreen; see *Muscular*

Nausea/Vomiting*– See *Digestive & Intestinal*

Nerve damage– bergamot, frankincense, helichrysum, peppermint, Serenity®; see *Nervous*

Nerve pain– basil, birch, ginger, helichrysum, wintergreen, Deep Blue®; see *Nervous*

Pain*– birch, cypress, eucalyptus, helichrysum, lemongrass, peppermint, wintergreen, Deep Blue®; see *Pain & Inflammation*

Perspiration, excess– cypress, lemongrass, peppermint, petitgrain; see *Detoxification, Integumentary*

Perspiration, lack of– black pepper, cilantro, coriander, cypress, ginger, yarrow|pom; see *Detoxification*

Pulse, rapid– cedarwood, lavender, rosemary, ylang ylang, Serenity®; see *Cardiovascular*

Pulse, weak– cinnamon bark, coriander, ginger; see *Cardiovascular*

Sciatica, issues with– basil, birch, cardamom, cypress, Douglas fir, frankincense, helichrysum, laurel leaf, lavender, peppermint, sandalwood, Siberian fir, thyme, wintergreen, Deep Blue®; see *Skeletal*

Stamina, lack of– peppermint, rosemary; see *Energy & Vitality*

Stress, performance– bergamot, clary sage, sandalwood, tulsi, Balance®, Peace®, Serenity®; see *Stress*

Tendonitis– basil, birch, cardamom, cypress, eucalyptus, helichrysum, lavender, lemon, lemongrass, marjoram, oregano, peppermint, rosemary, wintergreen, AromaTouch®, Deep Blue®; see *Skeletal*

*See Protocols on pg. 290

ATHLETES

Autoimmune

See also Immune & Lymphatic

AUTOIMMUNE DISEASES occur when the body has either an abnormally low immune response to pathogens or when the body's immune system fails to distinguish the difference between pathogens and healthy body tissues. When normal body tissue is identified as a pathogen or invader, the adaptive immune system creates antibodies that target the destruction of these tissues.

Because they attack the body's organs in a similar manner, many autoimmune disorders tend to have similar symptoms, making it difficult to diagnose them. It is possible for individuals to have multiple conditions simultaneously. There are no known medical cures for autoimmune conditions, so treatment focuses on using medications to suppress the immune response, leaving the individual vulnerable to sickness and disease, and to manage symptoms.

Approximately 75 percent of those suffering from autoimmune disorders are women. Autoimmune disorders are among the top ten causes of death in women. A number of factors contribute to conditions leading to an autoimmune disorder. These factors include genetics, toxins from heavy metals, candida, Epstein-Barr, herpes simplex virus, nerve damage due to excessive exposure to neurotoxins, and chronic inflammation related to food sensitivities, particularly gluten intolerance.

Some of the symptoms characteristic of autoimmune conditions include joint and/or muscle pain, weakness, tremors, weight loss, insomnia, heat intolerance, rapid heartbeat, recurrent rashes or hives, sun sensitivity, difficulty concentrating or focusing, glandular imbalances such as hypothyroidism or hyperthyroidism, fatigue, weight gain, cold intolerance, hair loss, white patches on skin or inside mouth, abdominal pain, blood or mucus in stool, diarrhea, mouth ulcers, dry eyes/mouth/skin, numbness or tingling in the extremities, blood clots, and multiple miscarriages.

Eighty percent of the immune system is directly connected to gut health, making it a vital area of focus to restore health. Using natural remedies together with a healthy diet can be an effective, non-invasive way to improve gut health. By using a consistent program such as a Microplex VMz®, xEO Mega®, and Alpha CRS®+ in a consistent program, along with TerraZyme®, Zendrocrine® Complex, lemon oil, GX Assist®, and a defensive probiotic, an individual can nourish and support the body in an effort to reclaim health.

Repeating a healthy cleanse the first three to four months in a row can also help the body improve its capacity to take care of itself. Targeted support using natural remedies for certain conditions individualizes a program and targets symptoms of discomfort and disease. It is empowering to exercise options for natural solutions to target root causes, since most modern medical approaches to autoimmune conditions seek to only manage symptoms.

Additionally, a great way to help the immune system function optimally and reduce environmental stress on the body is to perform the AromaTouch Technique®. It is explained in the introduction to this book. The technique is a systematic application of eight different essential oils that strengthen the immune system, eliminate pathogens, reduce stress, and bring the body into homeostasis, enabling the body to function more optimally. A weekly application for three to four months is ideal. See AromaTouch Technique®, page 24.

top solutions

Single Oils

Lemongrass– stimulates nerves and supports digestion (pg. 180)

Juniper berry– antioxidant and supports digestion (pg. 170)

Copaiba, Frankincense– anti-inflammatory, anti-infectious, pain reliever (pgs. 136, 151)

Ginger– invigorates nerves and cleanses (pg. 153)

Clary sage– invigorates nerves and supports endocrine system (pg. 133)

Turmeric– antioxidant and anti-inflammatory (pg. 239)

Blends

DDR Prime®– supports nerves and glands (pg. 140)

Zendocrine®– detoxifies and supports proper digestive function (pg. 251)

Slim & Sassy®– antioxidant and improves digestion (pg. 222)

DigestZen®– supports digestion and elimination (pg. 142)

Supplements

Alpha CRS®+ (pg. 254), Bone Nutrient Complex, **DDR Prime® Softgels** (pg. 256), **Deep Blue Polyphenol Complex®** (pg. 257), DigestZen® Softgels, IQ Mega, Microplex VMz®, Mito2Max®, **On Guard+™ Softgels** (pg. 262), On Guard® Throat Drops, **PB Assist®+** (pg. 264), Peppermint Softgels, **TerraZyme®** (pg. 268), **xEO Mega®** (pg. 271)

usage tips

For best support in resolving autoimmune conditions:

- **Internal:** Take oils in a capsule, water, or drop under tongue (hold 30 seconds, swallow).
- **Topical:** Use AromaTouch Technique® at least one to 1-2x's weekly if possible. Apply oils on bottoms of feet, down spine, and on any specific area of concern.
- **Aromatic:** Diffuse chosen oils, most especially to open airways and promote positive moods.

Related Ailments

Addison's Disease (adrenals) [Endocrine], Autoimmune Hepatitis (liver) [Digestive & Intestinal], Celiac Sprue Disease (GI tract) [Digestive & Intestinal], Crohn's Disease [Digestive & Intestinal], Diabetes Type 1 [Blood Sugar], Glomerulonephritis (kidneys) [Urinary], Grave Disease (thyroid) [Endocrine], Gout (joints, big toe) [Skeletal], Hashimoto's (thyroid) [Endocrine], Huntington's Disease (nerve cells in brain) [Brain, Nervous], Inflammatory Bowel Disease, Inflammatory Myopathies [Muscles], Lou Gehrig's/ALS (nerve cells in brain, spinal cord) [Brain, Nervous], Lupus (any part of the body such as skin, joints, and/or organs), Multiple Sclerosis (myelin sheath) [Nervous], Myasthenia Gravis, Pernicious Anemia (failure to produce red blood cells [Cardiovascular] and failure to absorb vitamin B12– liver) [Digestive & Intestinal], Rheumatoid Arthritis (joints in hands, feet) [Skeletal], Sarcoidosis/Sarcoid (primarily lungs, lymph nodes) [Respiratory, Immune & Lymphatic; Digestive & Intestinal (leaky gut)], Schmidt's Syndrome, Scleroderma (connective tissue) [Muscles, Skeletal], Sjogrens (salivary, tear duct glands) [Oral Health, Respiratory], Vitiligo (skin pigment cells) [Integumentary, Endocrine (thyroid), Women's Health, Stress]

By Related Properties

For more, see *Oil Properties* on pages 535-538

Analgesic– basil, birch, blue tansy, cassia, cinnamon bark, clary sage, clove, copaiba, coriander, eucalyptus, fennel, frankincense, helichrysum, lavender, litsea, peppermint, Siberian fir, tea tree, tumeric, wintergreen, yarrow|pom

Antiarthritic– arborvitae, basil, birch, blue tansy, cassia, copaiba, cypress, ginger, manuka, turmeric, wintergreen

Antidepressant– bergamot, clary sage, frankincense, geranium, jasmine, lavender, lemon, magnolia, melissa, neroli, pink pepper, rose, tangerine, ylang ylang

Anti-infectious– basil, bergamot, cedarwood, cinnamon bark, clove, copaiba, cypress, frankincense, geranium, lavender, litsea, marjoram, patchouli, rosemary, tea tree, turmeric

Anti-inflammatory– basil, birch, blue tansy, cardamom, cassia, cedarwood, cinnamon bark, copaiba, coriander, cypress, eucalyptus, frankincense, geranium, helichrysum, lemongrass, lime, litsea, manuka, melissa, myrrh, neroli, peppermint, rosemary, sandalwood, Siberian fir, spikenard, tangerine, turmeric, wintergreen, yarrow|pom

Antioxidant– basil, black pepper, cassia, cilantro, cinnamon bark, clove, copaiba, frankincense, ginger, grapefruit, helichrysum, juniper berry, lemongrass, lime, neroli, oregano, tangerine, tea tree, thyme, turmeric, vetiver, wild orange, yarrow|pom

Anti-parasitic– blue tansy, cinnamon bark, clove, frankincense, juniper berry, lavender, oregano, rosemary, tangerine, tea tree, thyme

Regenerative– cedarwood, clove, coriander, frankincense, geranium, helichrysum, jasmine, manuka, myrrh, neroli, patchouli, sandalwood, turmeric, wild orange, yarrow|pom

Stomachic– blue tansy, cardamom, cinnamon bark, clary sage, coriander, fennel, ginger, juniper berry, marjoram, melissa, peppermint, pink pepper, rose, rosemary, tangerine, turmeric, wild orange, yarrow|pom

Tonic– arborvitae, basil, birch, cardamom, cedarwood, clary sage, coriander, cypress, fennel, frankincense, geranium, ginger, grapefruit, green mandarin, lavender, lemon, marjoram, melissa, myrrh, neroli, patchouli, Roman chamomile, rose, rosemary, sandalwood, Siberian fir, tangerine, thyme, vetiver, wild orange, ylang ylang, yarrow|pom

Uplifting– bergamot, cardamom, cedarwood, clary sage, cypress, grapefruit, green mandarin, lime, litsea, melissa, sandalwood, tangerine, wild orange, ylang ylang

protocols

Critical Autoimmune Supplementation Program:

- **Microplex VMz®** as a high potency multivitamin/mineral
- **xEO Mega®** with land and sea omega sources, astaxanthin (use a IQ Mega for children and elderly who can't swallow pills)
- **Alpha CRS®+** to supply powerful antioxidants, flavonoids, and provide cellular support
- **TerraZyme®** for proper digestion; add DigestZen® Softgels as needed for additional digestive comfort

Add as needed for desired target support:

- **Bone Nutrient Complex** necessary for numerous cellular, structural functions
- **DDR Prime® Softgels** to establish and maintain healthy cell vitality and apoptosis
- **Deep Blue Polyphenol Complex®** to reduce or eliminate pain/inflammation and improve inflammatory responses
- **PB Assist®+** to establish and maintain healthy gut flora, eliminate harmful microorganisms
- **Mito2Max®** with CoQ10 for energy, improve circulation
- **Turmeric Dual Capsules** to supply additional antioxidants, cellular support
- **Zendrocrine® Complex** and **Zendocrine®** to promote detoxification and proper elimination

For ALL autoimmune diseases consider the following:

- See *Digestive & Intestinal* for digestive/intestinal issues, leaky gut
- See *Immune & Lymphatic* to eliminate harmful microorganisms
- See *Candida* to manage/eliminate/prevent candida
- AromaTouch Technique® or massage— see page 24

AUTOIMMUNE

For the following specific autoimmune conditions, all suggestions are recommended *in addition* to using the suggested Critical Autoimmune Supplementation Program.

CELIAC DISEASE PROTOCOL

Take in a capsule or water 2-4x's daily:

2 drops lemon (tonic for liver)
2 drops grapefruit (dissolves toxins stored in fat cells)
2 drops ginger (digestive support)
1 drop cinnamon bark (regulates blood sugar levels)
OR
6-7 drops of Slim & Sassy®

Additional suggestions:

- Rub DigestZen® on stomach. Take 2-4 drops in capsule OR use 1-2 DigestZen® Softgels during digestive discomfort or upset stomach.
- Diffuse frankincense, Elevation, and/or Citrus Bliss® to combat depression or irritability.

CROHN'S DISEASE

In addition to, or as part of, taking the Critical Autoimmune Supplemental Program, add any or all of the following:

- Take PB Assist®+ 3x's daily for six months.
- Take 1-2 TerraZyme® per meal.
- Rub DigestZen® on abdomen 2x's daily for 2 months.
- Rub DigestZen® and ginger on bottoms of feet twice daily for 6 months.
- Combine 2 drops each DigestZen® and frankincense in a capsule. Take twice a day for 2 weeks. Then change blend to 5 drops ginger, 5 drops peppermint or marjoram, and 4 drops frankincense for 2 weeks. Keep alternating if needed.
- Apply pink pepper, DigestZen®, and/or copaiba for abdominal pain or discomfort.
- Apply or diffuse lavender or Serenity® to help manage stress.

Consider a candida cleanse. See Candida for details (pg. 304).

SJOGREN'S

In addition to taking the Critical Autoimmune Supplementation Program twice per day, take 2-3 drops of frankincense 2-4x's daily under tongue or in a capsule. Use additional oils as symptoms occur; Deep Blue® for painful joints, DigestZen® for digestive problems, lavender or geranium for skin problems, and so on.

Additional suggestions:

Candida cleanse and other detoxing programs— see *Candida* (pg. 304) and *Detoxification* (pg. 326).

CHRONIC DRY EYE

Gently dab diluted lavender, frankincense, myrrh, and/or sandalwood on facial bones surrounding eye, being careful to avoid the eye itself. Within minutes dry, irritated eyes should feel better. Should you accidentally get oil in eye, dilute with carrier oil, not water!

CHRONIC DRY MOUTH

Oil pull on pg. 330 for one week to stimulate salivary glands. Continue as needed for sustainable results.

Oil Pulling recipe:

1 T coconut oil
2 drops Zendocrine®
2 drops peppermint

Place mixture in mouth, swish for 20 minutes, then spit into the trash. Repeat daily.

See *Detoxification— Oil Pulling* (pg. 330) for additional instructions.

HASHIMOTO'S

Choose from the following protocols. Consider progressive use of each.

Protocol 1

Combine 20 drops each Balance® and geranium in 10mL roller bottle topped of with carrier oil.

Combine 15 drops lemongrass with 20 drops myrrh in a different 10mL roller bottle topped of with carrier oil.

Shake blends initially and before each application. Alternate use weekly. Apply directly to thyroid area and reflex points at base of big toe 3x's daily. Use for 4 weeks.

Protocol 2

15 drops lemongrass
15 drops clove
8 drops frankincense
4 drops peppermint

Combine oils in 10mL roller bottle topped of with fractionated coconut oil. Apply topically to thyroid area and on big toe reflexology points 3x's daily.

Protocol 3

Apply 2-3 drops of frankincense and 1 drop peppermint topically to thyroid area and big toe 3x's daily. Dilute if needed.

LUPUS

Cleanse (in addition to basic critical supplementation):

Do a candida cleanse. See *Candida* for details (pg. 304).

Address Inflammation

- Ingest citrus oils as a daily priority. Use your favorite 3-5 drops 3x's per day in water or veggie capsule.
- For liver and anti-inflammatory support:
  - › Place 4 drops each geranium, helichrysum or lemongrass, rosemary oils in a capsule and take daily.
  - › Apply 2 drops Zendocrine® over liver area or take 1-2 Softgels.

For localized pain, apply Deep Blue®, wintergreen, or copaiba.

For systemic pain, take in a capsule, every four hours or as often as needed:

2-4 drops clove
2-4 drops helichrysum
2-4 drops copaiba
2-4 drops turmeric

Additionally, for a soothing bath:

Add 2 drops each of any 4 suggested oils below to 1 C Epsom salt. Add to warm bath water and soak for 20 minutes. Consider: coriander, frankincense, ginger, helichrysum, lavender, copaiba, Roman chamomile, wintergreen, Deep Blue®, and/or AromaTouch®. Change oil choices/combinations as needed and desired.

SCLERODERMA

Initial Cleanse– two to four weeks as needed.

- Take Critical Autoimmune Supplementation Program (pg. 294).
- Do a candida cleanse. See *Candida* for details. Repeat the cleanse twice. Take a 10 day break in between the first and second rounds. Then repeat every other month as needed. Follow up each round with 5 days of increased amounts of PB Assist®+.
- Take 2-3 drops of frankincense under tongue 4x's a day.
- Apply the following blends to bottoms of feet, along spine, and outside of ears. Use both alternating, two or more times daily:
  - › Blend #1: 3 drops each lavender, Deep Blue®, and lemongrass.
  - › Blend #2: 4 drops each copaiba and turmeric.

Ongoing Support

- Continue critical supplementation program.
- Daily:
  - › Apply Deep Blue® to areas of concern as often as needed.
- Morning:
  - › Apply peppermint to bottoms of feet.
  - › Take 3-4 drops peppermint, DigestZen®, frankincense, and basil in capsule.
- Throughout:
  - › Consume 3 drops tangerine in 16 oz. drinking water at least 3x's per day.
- Evening:
  - › Take 3-4 drops each peppermint, lemongrass, and marjoram in capsule.
  - › Apply 2-3 drops frankincense to bottoms of feet. Layer with 1-2 drops geranium, AromaTouch®, and wintergreen.

Specific Issues:

- Breathing– Apply 2-4 drops cardamom and/or Breathe® on chest back, and under nose.
- Digestive– Rub 3-4 drops DigestZen® over abdomen in clockwise motion.

AUTOIMMUNE

conditions

Abdominal pain– marjoram, turmeric, AromaTouch®; see *Digestive & Intestinal, Muscles*

Blood clots– Deep Blue®, Motivate®, On Guard®, PastTense®; see *Cardiovascular*

Blood in stool– birch (ulcer), geranium (bleeding), helichrysum, (bleeding), yarrow|pom, wintergreen (ulcer); see *Digestive & Intestinal (Ulcers)*

Blood pressure changes– celery seed, clary sage, ylang ylang (if too high); rosemary, Siberian fir, thyme (if too low); see *Cardiovascular*

Cold intolerance– black pepper, cinnamon bark, eucalyptus, DDR Prime®; see *Endocrine (Thyroid), Cardiovascular (Poor circulation; Warming property)*

Diarrhea or constipation– black pepper, cardamom, Douglas fir, ginger, DigestZen®, Motivate®; see *Digestive & Intestinal*

Dry eyes, mouth, or skin*– See *Respiratory, Oral Health, Integumentary*

Hair loss– clary sage, eucalyptus, rosemary, tulsi, yarrow|pom, Motivate®; see *Integumentary*

Heat intolerance– eucalyptus, peppermint; see *Endocrine (Thyroid)*

Inflammation– birch, copaiba, cypress, peppermint, turmeric, wintergreen, Motivate®; see *Pain & Inflammation*

Insomnia– lavender, frankincense, neroli, vetiver, wild orange, InTune®, Peace®, Serenity®; see *Sleep*

Joint pain– celery seed, copaiba, lemongrass, turmeric, AromaTouch®, Deep Blue®; see *Skeletal, Pain & Inflammation*

Lack of concentration or focus– basil, rosemary, InTune®, Motivate®; see *Focus & Concentration*

Mucus in stool– cardamom, ginger, DigestZen®, Motivate®; see *Digestive & Intestinal*

Muscle pain, weakness, tremor, or cramps– copaiba, marjoram, AromaTouch®, Deep Blue®, Passion®; see *Muscular, Pain & Inflammation*

Mouth ulcers– clove, myrrh, tulsi, wild orange; see *Oral Health*

Multiple miscarriages– blue tansy, clary sage, grapefruit, thyme, Motivate®; see *Women's Health*

Numbness or tingling in the hands or feet– cypress, peppermint, AromaTouch®, Deep Blue®; see *Nervous*

Overactive immune system– basil, frankincense, helichrysum, lavender, neroli, Balance®

*See Protocols on pg. 294-295.

For more ideas, download the app on Android or iOS.

Paralysis, facial– helichrysum, patchouli, peppermint, Motivate®; see *Nervous*

Rapid heartbeat– frankincense, sandalwood, ylang ylang; see *Cardiovascular*

Rashes or hives– blue tansy, lavender, Roman chamomile; see *Allergies*

Salt cravings– celery seed; see "Critical Autoimmune Supplementation Program"

Skin pigmentation– cedarwood, sandalwood, Immortelle; see *Integumentary*

Sore throat, chronic– basil, cassia, cinnamon bark, eucalyptus, fennel, ginger, lemon, oregano, thyme, Breathe®, On Guard®

Sun sensitivity– arborvitae, helichrysum, lavender, myrrh, xEO Mega® with astaxanthin; see *Integumentary*

Tiredness or fatigue– cinnamon bark, cypress, Douglas fir, peppermint, Cheer®, Motivate®; see *Energy & Vitality*

Weight gain or loss– cinnamon bark, ginger, Slim & Sassy®; see *Weight*

White patches on skin, inside mouth– myrrh, sandalwood; see *Integumentary*

Blood Sugar

See also Endocrine

INSULIN is a hormone that regulates blood sugar levels, shuttling the right amount of glucose into the cells where it is used for energy. When the body doesn't have enough insulin, blood-sugar levels become too high, and cells don't have enough energy to function properly.

Diabetes is the most common endocrine disorder; it occurs when the pancreas doesn't produce enough insulin (type 1—typical onset is before age 20), or if the body is unable to use insulin (type 2—typically over age 40). The onset age for type 2 is decreasing with an increasingly younger population suffering from what is a preventable disease. A third type, gestational diabetes, can occur during pregnancy and create potential long-term issues for both mother and child.

Hypoglycemia is a condition characterized by too little glucose in the blood. When severe, it is also called "insulin reaction" or "insulin shock" and can lead to accidents, injuries, even coma and death.

When we consume healthy sources of carbohydrates with plenty of good fats and protein, the glucose from the meal enters the blood slowly, and the pancreas responds by secreting a measured amount of insulin. Keeping blood sugar balanced throughout the day is the best way to avoid "sugar highs" and "sugar lows." A healthy individual can easily go three hours or more between meals without experiencing sugar cravings or feeling shaky, irritable, or tired.

Eating habits can influence the likelihood of developing blood sugar issues. When individuals consume foods too high in sugar or refined carbohydrates, these simple carbs enter the bloodstream almost immediately through the intestines, resulting in higher-than-normal blood sugar levels. The body then needs to produce more insulin to process the excess glucose. As the presence of elevated insulin levels becomes chronic, the body's sensitivity to insulin decreases (known as insulin resistance), forcing blood glucose levels to rise. Insulin is also an inflammatory agent.

Additionally, blood sugar imbalances and elevated insulin levels affect a number of functions, from hormones to heart to mood to cellular health to fertility, and perpetuate inflammation, which is considered a prime contributor to disease. One lesser-known fact is that high blood pressure is another common symptom caused by increased circulating levels of insulin in the blood. Common conditions resulting from blood sugar issues can be found in *Endocrine* and *Cardiovascular*.

Insulin and glucose levels are easily improved by positive changes in lifestyle, exercise, and diet. One of the benefits of stable blood sugar is the natural reduction of inflammation and the resulting balance of hormones. Healthy dietary changes (elimination of harmful sugars and refined carbohydrates), commitments, and consistencies are therefore significant. A study reported in the Journal of the American Medical Association (JAMA) stated, "Duration and degree of sugar exposure correlated significantly with diabetes prevalence while declines in sugar exposure correlated with significant subsequent declines in diabetes rates."*

Natural solutions can be incredibly effective in supporting the body to generate a healthy insulin response and blood sugar regulation. Because stable blood sugar levels diminish or eliminate sugar and carb cravings, even stubborn weight can melt away, and longevity may be extended.

In addition to necessary dietary and lifestyle commitments, essential oils are powerful allies in achieving and maintaining healthy blood sugar and insulin levels, improving insulin receptivity, and resolving a surprising number of related health concerns. Additionally, essential oils support bringing other body systems into balance, which is particularly helpful given the number of diabetes-related disorders. Essential oils positively impact blood sugar management. For example, coriander oil lowers glucose levels by normalizing insulin levels and supporting pancreatic function. Cinnamon bark oil aids in managing blood glucose levels and strengthens the circulatory and immune systems.

NOTE: Every blood sugar-related condition listed in this section is considered potentially related to or associated with imbalanced blood sugar and/or insulin levels. Addressing both blood sugar and insulin levels through diet, supplementation, and the use of essential oils is critical to success. The use of suggestions below to manage symptoms is intended to be paired with these critical diet and lifestyle changes.

**JAMA, 2004; Diabetes Care, 2010; PLOS ONE, 2013. Reported by Business Insider: www.businessinsider.com/effects-of-eating-too-much-sugar-2014-3#ixzz3UKTXOpuy*

top solutions

Single Oils

Cinnamon bark, Cassia– help balance blood sugar levels and promote a healthy insulin response (pgs. 126, 119)

Coriander, Tulsi– promote a healthy insulin response (pgs. 138, 236)

Basil– stress reducer, key for helping diabetics stabilize sugar (pg. 105)

Ginger– prevents blood sugar from spiking (pg. 153)

Pink pepper– supports blood sugar and metabolism (pg. 206)

Turmeric– supports blood sugar and cleanses liver (pg. 239)

Blends

DDR Prime®– supports nerves and glands (pg. 140)

Zendocrine®– detoxifies and supports proper digestive function (pg. 251)

Slim & Sassy®– reduce sugar cravings and keep blood sugar from spiking (pg. 222)

DigestZen®– supports digestion and elimination (pg. 142)

Supplements

Alpha CRS®+ (pg. 254), DigestZen® Softgels, Microplex VMz®, **Slim & Sassy® Softgels** (pg. 267), xEO Mega®

Related Ailments

Blood Sugar Headache, Blood Sugar Imbalance, Diabetes, Diabetic Sores, Hypoglycemia, Insulin, Insulin Imbalance, Insulin Resistance, Low Blood Sugar

BLOOD SUGAR

By Related Properties

For more, see *Oil Properties* on pages 535-538

Antifungal– bergamot, blue tansy, cinnamon bark, clove, copaiba, coriander, fennel, helichrysum, lemongrass, litsea, oregano, Siberian fir, tea tree, thyme, turmeric

Anti-inflammatory– birch, blue tansy, cardamom, cassia, cinnamon bark, clove, copaiba, coriander, frankincense, ginger, lavender, lemongrass, litsea, manuka, myrrh, neroli, oregano, patchouli, pink pepper, rosemary, Siberian fir, spikenard, tangerine, turmeric, yarrow|pom

Antioxidant– black pepper, cinnamon bark, copaiba, coriander, frankincense, ginger, helichrysum, juniper berry, lemon, lemongrass, neroli, oregano, tangerine, turmeric vetiver, wild orange, yarrow|pom

Detoxifier– arborvitae, cassia, cilantro, geranium, juniper berry, lemon, lime, litsea, patchouli, tangerine, yarrow|pom

Invigorating– grapefruit, lemon, litsea, peppermint, pink pepper, Siberian fir, wild orange

Stimulant– basil, blue tansy, cedarwood, cinnamon bark, coriander, Siberian fir, tangerine, thyme, wintergreen

Stomachic– blue tansy, cardamom, cinnamon bark, clary sage, coriander, eucalyptus, juniper berry, marjoram, melissa, peppermint, rosemary, tangerine, wild orange, yarrow|pom

Vasodilator– blue tansy, copaiba, lemongrass, litsea, manuka, marjoram, neroli, rosemary, thyme

protocols

HIGH BLOOD SUGAR REDUCER

Ingredients:

3 drops coriander or basil
3 drops Slim & Sassy®
1 drop oregano

Directions:

Take 2-3x's per day in a capsule around meal times.

BLOOD SUGAR & PANCREAS SUPPORT

Ingredients:

2 drops grapefruit
2 drops cassia
3 drops coriander

Directions:

Add to empty capsule and take AM and PM.

LOW BLOOD SUGAR (use to improve)

Ingredients:

2 drops rosemary
1 drop geranium
1 drop juniper berry

Directions:

Apply to bottoms of feet. Take in a capsule.

BLOOD SUGAR BALANCE BLEND

- Recipe #1: 2 drops cinnamon bark + 2 drops cassia + 4 drops and coriander + 4 drops turmeric. Combine in 10mL roller bottle and fill remainder with carrier oil. Apply to bottoms of feet, focus on arch of foot to target pancreas reflex point.
- Recipe #2: 1 drop cinnamon bark + 3 drops tulsi + 2 drops Zendocrine® + 2 drops cypress. Combine in palm of one hand, dilute, and then apply on bottoms of feet and on abdomen, just below the ribs over pancreas area.

DAILY HEALTHY BLOOD SUGAR ROUTINE

- Dilute and apply 1-2 drops Slim & Sassy® on bottoms of feet and abdomen around both AM and PM meals.
- Take "High Blood Sugar Reducer" remedy 3x's daily.
- Apply 1-2 drops turmeric on feet at bedtime.

Clear And Balance

Combine 2 drops each On Guard® and pink pepper in a capsule. Consider adding fennel, coriander, tulsi, and/or turmeric.

Neuropathy Neutralizer

Apply 3-4 drops each cypress, coriander, pink pepper, and Deep Blue® to lower legs all the way to bottoms of feet. Use at least AM and PM.

Blood Sugar Balancing Tea

Place 1-2 drops cinnamon bark or Slim & Sassy® in 2 cups warm water. Add 1-2 drops wild orange or lemon for added flavor as desired.

Grapefruit Detox Delight

Add 1 drop cassia or cinnamon bark + 3 drops grapefruit to 24 ozs. of water. Shake up and drink out of glass container. Repeat 3 x's per day.

Emotional Relief and Pancreas Support

Apply 1-2 drops each geranium and tulsi to bottoms of feet and over pancreas area. Diluted if desired.

usage tips

For best success at targeting blood sugar and insulin levels:

- **Internal:** Place 1-5 drops in water to drink, take in a capsule, place under tongue, or lick off back of hand.
- **Topical:** Apply on bottoms of feet, targeting reflex points for pancreas and other endocrine partners such as adrenal and thyroid locations; see *Reflexology*.

conditions

Anxiety– cilantro, coriander, peppermint, tea tree, Balance®, PastTense®, Serenity®, Zendocrine®; see *Mood & Behavior*

Apple-shaped body/abdominal excess weight– See "Insulin resistance," "Insulin, excessive," "Blood Sugar, high," *Weight*

Blood sugar, high (hyperglycemia)*– basil, cinnamon bark, coriander, eucalyptus, fennel, geranium, ginger, juniper berry, lemon, oregano, pink pepper, rosemary, tulsi, turmeric, ylang ylang, Slim & Sassy®, Zendocrine®

Blood sugar, low (hypoglycemia)*– cassia, cypress, eucalyptus, geranium, juniper berry, lavender, lemongrass, rosemary, Zendocrine®

Blurred/compromised vision– cilantro, coriander, helichrysum, juniper berry, lemongrass, melissa, rose, thyme, tulsi, DDR Prime®, Elevation, Immortelle, Zendocrine®

Circulation issues/foot issues/gangrene– See *Cardiovascular*

Cravings for sweets– cassia, cinnamon bark, grapefruit, Slim & Sassy®; see *Eating Disorders, Weight*

Concentration, poor/brain fog– See *Focus & Concentration*

Depression– bergamot, geranium, wild orange, ylang ylang, Elevation; see *Mood & Behavior*

Digestive issues/chronic constipation or diarrhea– See *Digestion & Intestinal*

Dizziness– helichrysum, DDR Prime®, Zendocrine®; see "Glucose levels, low (hypoglycemia)"

Energy dips/fatigue/drowsiness– basil, cinnamon bark, ginger, lemon, lime, peppermint, rosemary, tulsi, wild orange, wintergreen, Cheer®, Slim & Sassy®; see *Energy & Vitality*

Feeling frequent urination– Zendocrine®; see *Urinary*

Glycation– juniper berry, vanilla

Headache– frankincense, lavender, peppermint, wintergreen, PastTense®, Slim & Sassy®, Zendrocrine®; see *Pain & Inflammation*

Heart palpitations/irregular/rapid heartbeat– See *Cardiovascular*

High blood pressure (due to the circulation of excessive insulin)– See "Glucose levels, high (hyperglycemia)"

Hunger/excessive hunger– See *Weight*

Infections, skin/vaginal– tea tree, On Guard®

Insulin, excessive– coriander, fennel, lemongrass, tulsi, turmeric

Insulin, insufficient– tulsi, wild orange; see "Blood sugar, high"

Insulin resistance or **poor response to**– cassia, coriander, cypress, juniper berry, lavender, lemongrass, oregano, rosemary, tulsi, turmeric, ylang ylang, DDR Prime®, On Guard®, Purify, Slim & Sassy®, Zendocrine®

Irritability– See *Mood & Behavior*

Kidney/urinary issues– lemon, lemongrass, oregano; see *Urinary*

Mood swings– geranium, patchouli, Balance®, Citrus Bloom™, Elevation, InTune®, Serenity®; see *Mood & Behavior*

Nausea– basil, bergamot, ginger, juniper berry, DigestZen®; see *Digestion & Intestinal*

Nerve damage* (e.g. neuropathy, painful cold or insensitive feet, loss of hair on the lower extremities, or erectile dysfunction, tingling skin)– basil; see *Nervous*

Nervousness, sudden– cedarwood, frankincense, petitgrain, Balance®, Serenity®; see *Mood & Behavior*

Shaky/weak– black pepper, frankincense, vetiver, Elevation, PastTense®, Serenity®

Skin, pale– cypress, wild orange, AromaTouch®

Sleep, difficulty– geranium, lavender, marjoram, patchouli, Roman chamomile, ylang ylang; see *Sleep*

Sleep, want excessive amount– geranium, wild orange

Sweating/hot flashes (blood sugar imbalance)– eucalyptus, peppermint

Thirst, excessive/increased– grapefruit, lemon, Slim & Sassy®

Urination, frequent– basil, cinnamon bark, cypress, AromaTouch®, On Guard®, Zendocrine®; see *Urinary*

Weight loss, sudden/excessive– cinnamon bark, Slim & Sassy®; see *Weight*

Wound healing, poor/slow– cypress, frankincense, helichrysum, lavender, myrrh, Siberian fir, tulsi, Immortelle; see *First Aid*

See *Endocrine* for additional suggestions for pancreas support.

BLOOD SUGAR

Brain

THE BRAIN, an organ the size of a small head of cauliflower, resides in the skull and is the body's control center. The brain is the most vital organ to everyday life. The brain, spinal cord, and peripheral nerves make up the central nervous system, which directs, coordinates, and regulates voluntary (conscious) and involuntary (unconscious) processes. Sensory nerves throughout the body constantly gather information from the environment and send it to the brain via the spinal cord. The brain rapidly interprets the data and responds by sending messages with motor neurons to the rest of the body.

Scientists have found that certain parts of the brain perform certain functions. The frontal lobe, where the limbic system is located, helps regulate emotions and trauma, assists with reasoning, planning, and problem-solving, and is involved with some language skills. The parietal lobe aids with recognition and interpreting data, orientation, and movement. The occipital lobe is connected to visual processing, and the temporal lobe supports perception, auditory processing, memory, and speech.

Due to its important role in managing and directing all organs, systems, and body processes, the brain has several layers of protection, including the skull, the meninges (thin membranes), and cerebrospinal fluid. The brain also has what has come to be called the "blood-brain barrier," which keeps cells of the nervous system separate from cells throughout the vascular system (the rest of the body).

Essential oils powerfully benefit brain function and processes. When used aromatically, such as diffusing oils into the air or inhaling oils directly from bottle or palms of the hands, essential oils directly access the brain through the olfactory bulb and are able to initiate almost immediate physical and emotional responses in the brain.

Due to their unique chemical constituents and the fact that they are carbon-based, essential oils are able to permeate the protective blood-brain barrier and provide support for such things as headaches, migraines, vertigo (or other balance issues), emotions, and mood. Certain essential oils comprised of specific chemical constituents like sesquiterpenes, such as frankincense and sandalwood, have a particular affinity for supporting the brain. Essential oils with antioxidant and anti-inflammatory properties are also particularly important for maintaining a healthy brain.

top solutions

Single Oils

Frankincense, Sandalwood– promote optimal brain function and repair; cross blood-brain barrier, anti-aging (pgs. 151, 218)

Cedarwood, Arborvitae– calm, stimulate, and protect brain; supports GABA levels (cedarwood) (pgs. 120, 101)

Rosemary, Patchouli– enhance brain, cognitive performance; relieve mental fatigue and boost dopamine levels (pgs. 216, 200)

Clove, Thyme– provide brain protective antioxidants (pgs. 134, 234)

Petitgrain– calms and soothes the brain (pg. 205)

Turmeric– brain protection and antioxidant (pg. 239)

Blends

Adaptiv™– supports brain function and helps mitigate repetitive thoughts (pg. 96)

DDR Prime®– provides strong antioxidants and brain protection (pg. 140)

InTune®– supports oxygen and blood flow to brain, crosses blood brain barrier (pg. 167)

Thinker™– supports brain function, especially in children (pg. 233)

Zendocrine®– supports relief from mental fatigue and toxins (pg. 251)

Supplements

Adaptiv™ Capsules (pg. 253), **Alpha CRS®+** (pg. 254), **DDR Prime® Softgels** (pg. 256), **IQ Mega** (pg. 260), Microplex VMz®, **xEO Mega®** (pg. 271), Zendrocrine® Complex

usage tips

Best ways to apply oils and make them more accessible for brain health:

- **Topically:** Apply to forehead, back of skull (especially on occipital triangles), under nose, and/or on roof of mouth (place oil on pad of thumb, place on roof of mouth).

  Use reflex points on foot, namely big toe, underside pad.
- **Aromatically:** Diffuse oils of choice to stimulate brain, allowing entry through nose to olfactory system.

Related Ailments

Absentmindedness, Alertness, Alzheimer's Disease, Amnesia, Ataxia, Autism [Focus & Concentration], Balance Problems, Bipolar Disorder [Mood & Behavior], Body Dysmorphic Disorder, Brain Fog, Brain Injury/Focal Brain Dysfunction, Chemical Imbalance [Endocrine], Coma, Concussion, Creutzfeldt-Jakob Disease [Immune & Lymphatic], Dementia, Down Syndrome, Epilepsy, Huntington's Disease [Nervous], Hydrocephalus, Learning Difficulties, Lou Gehrig's Disease, Meniere's Disease, Memory (poor), Mental Fatigue, Narcolepsy, Obsessive-Compulsive Disorder, Parkinson's Disease, Schizophrenia, Seizures, Social Anxiety Disorder [Mood & Behavior], Stroke, Vertigo

By Related Properties

For more, see *Oil Properties* on pages 535-538

Anticonvulsant– clary sage, fennel, geranium, lavender, neroli, tangerine

Anti-inflammatory– basil, bergamot, birch, black pepper, blue tansy, cardamom, cedarwood, celery seed, cinnamon bark, clove, copaiba, coriander, eucalyptus, fennel, frankincense, geranium, helichrysum, lavender, lemongrass, lime, litsea, manuka, melissa, myrrh, oregano, neroli, patchouli, peppermint, pink pepper, Roman chamomile, rosemary, sandalwood, Siberian fir, spearmint, tangerine, tea tree, turmeric, wild orange, wintergreen, yarrow|pom

Antioxidant– arborvitae, basil, black pepper, black spruce, cassia, celery seed, cilantro, cinnamon bark, clove, copaiba, coriander, eucalyptus, frankincense, ginger, grapefruit, helichrysum, juniper berry, lemon, lemongrass, lime, oregano, neroli, rosemary, tangerine, tea tree, thyme, turmeric, vetiver, wild orange, yarrow|pom

Anti-parasitic– bergamot, blue tansy, cinnamon bark, clove, fennel, frankincense, juniper berry, oregano, Roman chamomile, rosemary, tangerine, tea tree, thyme, turmeric

Nervine– basil, clary sage, clove, helichrysum, green mandarin, juniper berry, lavender, lemongrass, melissa, patchouli, peppermint, rosemary, thyme

Neuroprotective– frankincense, lavender, magnolia, Roman chamomile, thyme, turmeric, vetiver

Neurotonic– arborvitae, basil, bergamot, black pepper, clary sage, cypress, ginger, neroli, tea tree

Regenerative– frankincense, geranium, helichrysum, manuka, neroli, patchouli, rose, sandalwood, tea tree, wild orange, yarrow|pom

Stimulant– arborvitae, basil, bergamot, birch, black pepper, blue tansy, cardamom, cedarwood, cinnamon bark, clove, coriander, cypress, eucalyptus, fennel, ginger, grapefruit, juniper berry, lime, tea tree, patchouli, pink pepper, rosemary, Siberian fir, spearmint, tangerine, thyme, vetiver, wintergreen, ylang ylang

protocols

BRAIN

ALZHEIMER'S PROTOCOL

Internal:

- Take Mito2Max® and Lifelong Vitality (LLV) trio twice daily.
- Take 2 drops each frankincense, copaiba, thyme, patchouli, and turmeric in a capsule AM and PM.
- Consume 4-5 drops each clove, melissa, vetiver in a capsule 3x's per week.
- Consume 1 t of virgin coconut oil daily. Work up to 3 T as part of a healthy diet. Great on toast and excellent to cook with.
- Take 1-2 drops Slim & Sassy® under tongue 3-5x's per day and/or chew Slim & Sassy® gum to maintain healthy blood sugar.

Topical:

- Apply frankincense and Imortelle on base of skull and back of neck twice daily. Rotate with InTune® and patchouli.

Aromatic:

- Diffuse: Adaptiv™, copaiba, frankincense, patchouli, turmeric, vanilla, and/or vetiver.

Brain-Fog Buster (for overall brain support)**:**
Layer 1 drop each cedarwood, frankincense, patchouli, sandalwood, and vetiver on back of neck with carrier oil to enhance brain circulation. Carrier oil can be applied before, mixed with, or after essential oils.

Cognitive Improvement:
Apply diluted 1-2 drops each melissa, frankincense, and patchouli on suboccipital triangles at base of skull, on bottoms of feet, and take under tongue twice daily to help improve cognition and dispel agitation and depression.

AUTISM SUPPORT PROTOCOL

- **Overall Brain Support & Detox**– bedtime routine immediately follows detox.
  - Step 1: Apply Thinker™, InTune® and/or 1 drop each rosemary and wild orange on bottoms of feet.
  - Step 2: Apply 2 drops Zendocrine® on bottoms of feet.
- **Gut Cleanse**– dosages depend on age, weight, and capacity to swallow pills.
  - Take 2 A2Z Chewable™ or LLV 1 each twice daily.
  - Take 1 GX Assist® daily or use a good quality powder or liquid GI cleansing supplement.
  - Take 1 PB Assist® Jr Sachet.
- **Brain Recharge & Repair**
  - Take IQ Mega® twice daily.
  - Apply 1 drop DDR Prime® diluted on base of skull AM and PM, or more often if needed.
- **Emotional Support**– Choose from the following as needed or desired. Diffuse and/or apply, diluting for smaller bodies.
  - **Adaptiv™** for inflexibility.
  - **Brave™** to lift mood and instill courage.
  - **Peace®** when feeling overstimulated or overwhelmed.
  - **Patchouli** when feeling agitated.
  - **Roman chamomile** or **Adaptiv™** to soothe nerves and calm excessive responses or over reactivity.
  - **Stronger™** on bottom of feet to increase sense of security and protection.

conditions

Alzheimer's*— black spruce, cilantro, clove, frankincense, lemon, melissa, oregano, sandalwood, thyme, turmeric, vanilla, vetiver, Adaptiv™, Balance®, Console®, DDR Prime®, Forgive®, InTune®; see *Focus & Concentration*

Autism*— basil, bergamot, clary sage, frankincense, geranium, peppermint, rosemary, vetiver, Balance®, DDR Prime®, InTune®, Serenity®, Zendrocrine®

Balance/equilibrium— See "Dizziness" and "Vertigo" below

Blood-brain barrier— cedarwood, frankincense, ginger, myrrh, patchouli, sandalwood, Siberian fir, vetiver, ylang ylang, Balance®, Whisper®

Brain— arborvitae, cedarwood, clove, eucalyptus, frankincense, ginger, patchouli, rosemary, sandalwood, thyme, turmeric vetiver, yarrow|pom, Balance®, DDR Prime®, Motivate®, InTune®, On Guard®, Zendocrine®

Brain, aging— clove, copaiba, Douglas fir, frankincense, neroli, oregano, thyme, vanilla, Adaptiv™, Alpha CRS®+, Balance®, Console®, InTune®, On Guard®, Peace®; see "Brain" above

Brain, aneurysm— bergamot, frankincense, helichrysum, myrrh, yarrow|pom, DDR Prime®

Brain, blood flow— basil, black spruce, cedarwood, cypress, eucalyptus, ginger, laurel leaf, lemongrass, oregano, patchouli, peppermint, ravintsara, rosemary, sandalwood, tangerine, thyme, AromaTouch®, DDR Prime®, Whisper®, Mito2Max®

Brain, injury— arborvitae, bergamot, frankincense, helichrysum, lemon, myrrh, peppermint, spikenard, Balance®, Console®, DDR Prime®, Forgive®

Brain, lesions— frankincense, peppermint, rosemary, sandalwood, Balance®, DDR Prime®

Central nervous system— bergamot, black pepper, myrrh, patchouli, rosemary, sandalwood, vanilla

Chemical imbalance— cilantro, cinnamon bark, frankincense, geranium, melissa, patchouli, rosemary, wild orange, Adaptiv™, Cheer®, DDR Prime®, Elevation, InTune®, Zendocrine®

Coma— cedarwood, clove, frankincense, ginger, helichrysum, myrrh, sandalwood, spikenard, vetiver, Balance®, DDR Prime®, Motivate®

Concussion— bergamot, cedarwood, clove, cypress, frankincense, petitgrain, sandalwood, Balance®, InTune®

Dizziness— arborvitae, cedarwood, Douglas fir, frankincense, ginger, lavender, rosemary, spearmint, tulsi, Air-X™, Balance®, Citrus Bliss®, Console®, DDR Prime®, InTune®, Zendocrine®

Free radicals, neutralization of— black spruce, cilantro, cinnamon bark, clove, coriander, ginger, lemongrass, rosemary, tulsi, vanilla, any citrus oil; see oils with "Antioxidant" properties

GABA, lack of— basil, black spruce, cedarwood, rosemary, thyme, ylang ylang, Adaptiv™, Balance®, Citrus Bliss®, InTune®, Motivate®, Serenity®; see *Endocrine (adrenals)*

Heat stroke— bergamot, black pepper, lemon, peppermint, Air-X™, Deep Blue®, PastTense®, Zendocrine®

Heavy metal toxicity— cilantro, Zendocrine®; see *Detoxification*

Mental fatigue*— basil, bergamot, cardamom, frankincense, lavender, lemon, lemongrass, peppermint, pink pepper, ravintsara, rose, rosemary, sandalwood, Siberian fir, spearmint, tulsi, ylang ylang, Adaptiv™, Air-X™, Breathe®, Citrus Bliss®, Citrus Bloom™, Console®, Forgive®, Motivate®, Peace®, Thinker™

Memory loss— arborvitae, black spruce, myrrh, Siberian fir, thyme

Memory, poor— black spruce, clove, Douglas fir, frankincense, ginger, rosemary, peppermint, sandalwood, Siberian fir, InTune®

Oxygen, lack of— cedarwood, cypress, eucalyptus, frankincense, ginger, patchouli, sandalwood, Siberian fir, vetiver; see oils with "Antioxidant" properties

Parasites— See oils with "Anti-parasitic" properties, *Parasites*

Parkinson's— basil, bergamot, cedarwood, clary sage, clove, cypress, frankincense, geranium, helichrysum, jasmine, juniper berry, lemon, marjoram, melissa, patchouli, peppermint, Roman chamomile, rosemary, sandalwood, Siberian fir, thyme, vetiver, wild orange, Balance®, Cheer®, Console®, DDR Prime®, Serenity®, Zendocrine®; see *Addictions (oils to support dopamine levels)*

Seizures/convulsions, involuntary— basil, cardamom, cedarwood, celery seed, clary sage, Douglas fir, fennel, frankincense, geranium, lavender, myrrh, neroli, peppermint, petitgrain, rose (delay onset), sandalwood, spikenard, tangerine, Cheer®; see oils with "Anticonvulsant" properties

Senility/Dementia— frankincense, sandalwood; see oils with "Stimulant" properties

Sensory systems, closed/blocked— birch, wintergreen

Speech, slurred words/trouble speaking/difficulty understanding speech— arborvitae, patchouli, Whisper®, Zendocrine®

Stroke— basil, bergamot, cassia, cedarwood, celery seed, cypress, fennel, frankincense, helichrysum, turmeric, wintergreen, Abōde™, DDR Prime®, Purify, On Guard®; see oils with "Anti-inflammatory" and "Antioxidant" properties

Vertigo— cedarwood, frankincense, ginger, helichrysum, lavender, melissa, rosemary, Air-X™, Balance®, Citrus Bliss®, DDR Prime®, InTune®, Peace®

*See Protocols on pg. 302

Candida

See also Immune & Lymphatic

CANDIDA ALBICANS is a type of yeast that grows on the warm interior membranes of the body, such as the digestive, respiratory, gastrointestinal, female reproductive organs, and urogenital tracts. Candidiasis, the overgrowth of candida, can have detrimental effects on the body's systems. It occurs when the balance between candida organisms and helpful bacteria in the gastrointestinal tract is disrupted. Candida mutates and grows rapidly in such situations, and that overgrowth can cause frustrating and/or dangerous conditions in the body.

Conditions that can result from candidiasis include headaches, autoimmune diseases, allergies, fatigue, digestive disorders (including IBS), yeast infections, infertility, skin and nail conditions/infections (such as toenail fungus or psoriasis), and strong sugar cravings or addiction.

Certain factors increase the risk of candidiasis. Becoming aware of these risk factors is important for prevention.

- Candida and other microorganisms thrive when there is a lack of competing healthy organisms. A lack of friendly bacteria predisposes one to candidiasis.
- Diets high in sugar, high-fructose corn syrup, processed foods, yeast, or alcohol can depress the immune system and/or offset the delicate bacterial balance in the gut, allowing opportunity for candida to multiply.
- A single round of antibiotics is enough to kill both good and bad bacteria, leaving opportunity for harmful candida organisms to encroach. Prolonged or repeated use of antibiotics or other medications (e.g., contraceptive pills, steroidal drugs) increases risk dramatically.
- Poorly digested food particles, especially proteins, are known irritants that often stimulate mucus production as a part of the body's defense or coping mechanism. These affected areas can become feasting ground for microorganisms like candida albicans.

Use of probiotic supplements is one of the most effective ways to restore gut flora when compromised.

A diet rich in raw, live food as well as supplementing with digestive enzymes assists in restoring proper digestion. Utilizing these enzymes as well as essential oils like DigestZen® helps to clear both unwanted food particles and mucus accumulation.

Stress can lead to candida in one of two ways:

- First, the body can respond to stressful situations by releasing cortisol, a hormone that elicits the same responses as excess sugar.
- Second, stress can weaken the immune system and adrenal glands, leading to exhaustion or lack of energy. Individuals in this weakened state typically don't eat well, further decreasing the body's ability to respond to pathogens such as candida.

Use of immune-boosting essential oil blends, such as On Guard®, as well as caring for adrenal gland health with proper rest, nutrition, and essential oils such as rosemary or basil helps preserve the body's defense system.

One of candida albicans' toxic byproducts is estrogenic, and its presence "tricks" the body, influencing delicate hormonal states in both men and women. This toxic state undermines important functions such as fertility, stable weight, and impacts prostate inflammation. This kind of activity can go undetected for years and is a culprit of many other health issues.

Use of essential oils such as clary sage and thyme combined supports the body's ability to correct exaggerated estrogen and deficient progesterone levels. Grapefruit, oregano, and thyme essential oils demonstrate positive effects on healthy progesterone levels.

While it is important to work with expert medical professionals, especially when candidiasis has caused extensive system upset in the body, restoring the body's bioterrain to a balanced state can be done very effectively with natural remedies. Essential oils help clear toxins and harmful microorganisms gently and effectively from the gastrointestinal tract, address improved insulin response, and support digestion. Probiotics help restore balance and immune support.

top solutions

Single Oils

Tea tree– helps eliminate yeast overgrowth and prevents mutation (pg. 230)

Oregano, Thyme– help eliminate and prevent yeast and fungus overgrowth (pgs. 196, 234)

Turmeric, Pink Pepper– create an environment unfriendly yeast overgrowth, cleanse blood and lymph (pgs. 239, 206)

Blends

DDR Prime®– restores health of cells (pg. 140)

Zendocrine®– detoxifies and eliminates free radicals (pg. 251)

On Guard®– helps eliminate candida/fungus (pg. 195)

HD Clear®– cleanses skin (pg. 159)

Supplements

Fiber (pg. 258), Greens, **GX Assist®** (pg. 260), Microplex VMz®, **PB Assist®+** (pg. 264), Protein, **TerraZyme®** (pg. 268), xEO Mega®, Zendrocrine® Complex

Related Ailments

Athlete's foot, Candidiasis, Fungal Skin Infection, Fungus, Yeast

By Related Properties

For more, see *Oil Properties* on pages 535-538

Anti-carcinogenic– arborvitae, clove, frankincense, lemongrass, myrrh, tangerine, turmeric, wild orange, yarrow|pom

Antifungal– arborvitae, blue tansy, cardamom, cassia, cedarwood, cilantro, cinnamon bark, clary sage, clove, copaiba, coriander, ginger, helichrysum, lemongrass, marjoram, melissa, myrrh, oregano, patchouli, pink pepper, ravintsara, rosemary, Siberian fir, spearmint, tangerine, tea tree, thyme, turmeric, yarrow|pom

Antimicrobial– arborvitae, blue tansy, cassia, cilantro, cinnamon bark, copaiba, fennel, lemongrass, litsea, manuka, myrrh, neroli, oregano, Siberian fir, spearmint

Antimutagenic– ginger, lavender, lemongrass, turmeric

Antioxidant– basil, cassia, cinnamon bark, clove, copaiba, coriander, juniper berry, lemongrass, neroli, tangerine, tea tree, thyme, turmeric

Vermifuge– arborvitae, black pepper, fennel, frankincense, geranium, lavender, lemon, Roman chamomile, turmeric

**See Protocols on pg. 306*

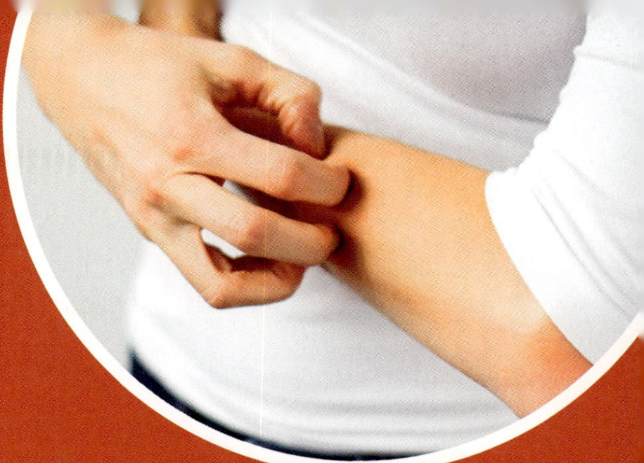

conditions

Athlete's foot– arborvitae, cardamom, clove, copaiba, lavender, lemon eucalyptus, lemongrass, myrrh, neroli, oregano, tea tree, AromaTouch®; see "Antifungal" property

Autoimmune disease– See *Autoimmune*

Brain fog– See *Focus & Concentration*

Candidiasis– See "Antifungal" property in column one

Concentration, poor– See *Focus & Concentration*

Cravings, sugar/refined carbohydrate– See *Weight*

Fatigue– See *Energy & Vitality*

Focus, lack of– See *Focus & Concentration*

Intestinal Flora, restore– Turmeric

Memory, poor– See *Focus & Concentration*

Moodiness– depression/irritability– See *Mood & Behavior*

Severe seasonal allergies– See *Allergies*

Sinus infection, chronic– arborvitae, cardamom, melissa, myrrh, oregano, rosemary, Siberian fir (diluted) ; consider a chronic fungal condition; see "Antifungal" property in column one

Skin or nail infection– see *Integumentary*

Skin, eczema/psoriasis*– arborvitae, bergamot, birch, blue tansy, cedarwood, copaiba, geranium, helichrysum, juniper berry, melissa, myrrh, neroli, patchouli, peppermint, Roman chamomile, rosemary, Siberian fir, spearmint, thyme, wintergreen, yarrow|pom

Thrush– arborvitae, bergamot, clary sage, clove (diluted), fennel, lavender, lemon, oregano (diluted), tea tree, turmeric, wild orange, On Guard® (diluted), Slim & Sassy®

Urinary infection/fungal– basil, blue tansy, cypress, eucalyptus, juniper berry, lemon, lemongrass, pink pepper, Siberian fir, tea tree, thyme, Forgive®, On Guard®, Purify, Zendocrine®; consider a chronic fungal condition; see "Antifungal" property

Vagina, mild discharge– bergamot, spikenard

Vaginal inflammation/infection*– cinnamon bark (internal or diluted on bottoms of feet only), spearmint, spikenard, (internal or diluted on bottoms of feet only), Whisper®; see *Women's Health*

Vaginal itching*– bergamot, frankincense, neroli, spikenard, tea tree, Whisper®; see *Women's Health*

Vaginal thrush*– blue tansy, frankincense (topical, internal), oregano (internal or diluted on bottoms of feet only), spikenard, tea tree (topical– diluted, internal); see *Women's Health*

Weak immune system– cinnamon bark, Siberian fir, Abōde™, On Guard®; see *Immune & Lymphatic*

Weakness, chronic– copaiba, frankincense, rosemary, Motivate®, On Guard®; see *Energy & Vitality*

protocols

CANDIDA SIMPLE TREATMENT

Dilute thyme and tea tree and massage onto bottoms of feet.

CANDIDA MONTHLY PROTOCOL

- **Step 1:** 1 GX Assist® 3x's per day with meals for 10 days.
- **Step 2:** 1 capsule PB Assist®+ each meal daily for at least next 10 days.
- **Step 3:** Continue PB Assist®+ if desired; rest for 10 days.
- **Step 4:** Repeat steps 1 and 2 monthly as needed.
- For the entire 30 days consume:
  - 1-3 capsules TerraZyme® with meals and/or on an empty stomach
  - 1-2 Zendrocrine® Complex with AM and PM meals
  - 2 drops Zendocrine® in capsule 2x's per day with meals
  - 2 drops lemon 3x's per day in a capsule or in drinking water

CANDIDA QUARTERLY MAINTENANCE CLEANSE

- **Step 1:** Place 2-3 drops each tea tree, lemon, and choose from lemongrass, thyme, and/or oregano in a capsule. Take AM and PM for 2 weeks. If oregano was utilized, after 10 days, take a break and replace with thyme or lemongrass.
- **Step 2:** After 2 weeks of usage, reduce consumption to one capsule of above combination per day for 2 weeks.
- **Step 3:** Take 2-4 PB Assist®+ per day for at least 10 days.
- **Step 4:** Repeat cleanse every 3 months or more frequently as needed.

CANDIDA SUPPOSITORY

Ingredients:

1 drop tea tree
1 drop oregano
1 drop thyme

Directions:

Combine essential oils with 1 T virgin coconut oil and roll into 3-4 bullet-shaped suppositories. Refrigerate or freeze until solid and leave until ready to use. Insert into vagina prior going to bed for at least 30 minutes. Overnight is best.

CANDIDA FACIAL & SKIN OIL

Ingredients:

3 drops clary sage
2 drops frankincense
2 drops geranium
2 drops myrrh
1 drop patchouli

Directions:

Combine oils in 30mL glass bottle and fill remainder of bottle with fractionated coconut oil. Apply to affected areas to soothe and relieve irritated skin until symptoms subside.

**Optional - add oils to nearly full Rose Touch*

CANDIDA SKIN RELIEF

Create a paste with ½ C aluminum-free baking soda and a few tabelespoons fractionated coconut oil. Then add

Ingredients:

4 drops lavender
3 drops tea tree
3 drops rosemary

Directions:

Use paste in shower as cleanser and exfoliator. Apply all over body; gently scrub for a few minutes. Repeat at least twice a week to kill the candida living on the skin.

CANDIDA RELIEF TOPICAL BLEND

Ingredients:

9 drops cassia
6 drops cinnamon bark
8 drops clove
4 drops oregano

Directions:

Blend oils into a 10mL roller bottle and fill remainder with carrier oil. Apply to affected areas.

CANDIDA BOMB

Ingredients:

3 drops cassia
2 drops oregano

Directions:

Place oils in a capsule. Take with meals twice a day for up to 10 days. Add 1 drop melissa or 4 drops On Guard® as needed for more chronic cases where conditions have lasted for long periods of time or are stubborn to resolve.

ECZEMA AND PSORIASIS

Ingredients:

4 drops DDR Prime®
3 drops Roman chamomile
3 drops geranium
2 drops turmeric
2 drops rosemary
Carrier oil in a 10mL roller bottle

Directions:

Apply to skin twice per day. Massage in as tolerated. Take TerraZyme® twice daily on empty stomach

CANDIDA RASH

Ingredients:

12 drops Siberian fir
6 drops patchouli
5 drops frankincense
6 drops geranium
6 drops thyme
Carrier oil

Directions:

Dilute in 5mL glass bottle. Apply to areas of concern. Consider a candida detox.

CANDIDA TAMPON VAGINAL SUPPOSITORY

Ingredients:

2 T fractionated coconut oil
5 drops frankincense or tea tree

Directions:

Dip a tampon into mixture about half-way up. Squeeze out excess. Insert. Wear a panty liner. Use only when menstruating. Alternate oils as desired. May sting initially and then subside. Reduce quantity of oil used if needed. Use a probiotic simultaneously.

Store in a glass bottle for future use. Repeat nightly.

CANDIDA DOUCHE

Ingredients:

1 drop lavender
1 drop tea tree
1 t vinegar
1 C purified water

Directions:

Combine into squeeze bottle. Douche three days a week.

CANDIDA RELIEF INTERNAL BLEND

Ingredients:

2 drops cinnamon bark + 2 drops clove

Directions:

Take combined in a capsule 3x's per day.

candida program

A 30-day program designed to help achieve a balanced body system, while avoiding unneccessary discomfort throughout a cleanse.

CORE PROGRAM

Take 2 each twice daily:

- **Microplex VMz®**— basic core nutrition for body's daily needs
- **xEO Mega®**— vital essential fatty acids
- **Alpha CRS®+**— provides powerful antioxidant and cellular vitality support
- **Lemon**— balance and maintain healthy pH; antioxidant and detox support
- **TerraZyme®**— help with digestion of food and waste elimination
- **Optional**— add DigestZen® for unresolved digestive upset

STEP 1

Days 1-13:

- **PB Assist®+**— populates gut with friendly bacteria

STEP 2

Add detox supplement- take 1-2 twice daily

Day 14:

- **Zendrocrine® Complex**— for detoxification and elimination (add to program sooner if bowels tend to be sluggish) with TerraZyme®.
- **Zendocrine® Softgels**— for detoxification

Consider increasing the length of time for consumption, such as extending for 1-3 months, if needed.

CHOOSE OILS BY EMOTIONAL STATE

Another method of selecting target oils is to search for those that most closely relate to both the physical *and* emotional states one is experiencing.

Below are a few suggestions that relate to candida specifically. *See Emotional Well-Being on page 28 to learn more.*

The following oils address candida-related emotions:

Bitterness, resentment	thyme, geranium
Blame/victim mentality/defensive	tea tree
Deprived	myrrh
Used, betrayed	coriander, rose
Feeling out of control/invaded	oregano
Parasitical/co-dependent relationships	clove
Powerless/unprotected	cassia/cinnamon bark, frankincense, turmeric

Oils that support empowerment (such as ginger) are excellent for correcting candida overgrowth. The body is being invaded and overpowered by microorganisms and fungi, often promoting an emotional sense of powerlessness, anger, blame, defensiveness, feeling out of control, and/or vulnerability.

STEP 3

Take for 10 days - 1-2 softgels once or twice daily

Day 14

- **GX Assist®**— for gut detoxification (start with only 1 per day, work up to 2-3; take less if discomfort arises)
- **DDR Prime® Softgels**— for cellular detoxification

Consider taking these products one at a time versus stacking if a slower detoxification pace is needed.

STEP 4

Choose additional antifungal target support:

Day 21 and beyond: Consider additional antifungal oils to target specific areas of concern. Can be added at a later time if a need arises. Although specific oils are suited for specific areas or organs of the body, all oils listed in this section are antifungal and assist the body in restoring and balancing the bioterrain.

- **Adrenals**— rosemary, ginger, geranium, Zendocrine®
- **Brain**— cedarwood, clary sage, frankincense, rosemary, sandalwood
- **Heavy Metals**— cilantro, frankincense, laurel leaf, tulsi, Abōde™, Purify, Zendocrine®
- **Intestinal**— marjoram, oregano, tea tree, thyme, Zendocrine®, On Guard®
- **Liver**— helichrysum, lemon, lemongrass, geranium, Zendocrine®
- **Mouth**— bergamot, lavender, oregano, tea tree, Slim & Sassy®, On Guard®
- **Mucous membrane** (e.g. stomach, intestines, uro-genital)— lemon, fennel, tea tree
- **Pancreas**— cassia, cinnamon bark, coriander, tulsi, Slim & Sassy®
- **Reproductive**— female/infertility— clary sage, fennel, geranium, oregano, rose, thyme, frankincense, rosemary
- **Reproductive**— male/infertility/prostate— clary sage, cypress, frankincense, geranium, thyme, ginger
- **Respiratory**— arborvitae, cardamom, myrrh, oregano, rosemary, melissa, eucalyptus, Air-X™, Breathe®
- **Skin** (e.g. eczema, psoriasis)— arborvitae, bergamot, cedarwood, geranium, helichrysum, juniper berry, lavender, melissa, myrrh, oregano, patchouli, peppermint, Roman chamomile, rosemary, spearmint, thyme, wintergreen
- **Thyroid**— clove, lemongrass, myrrh, rosemary, frankincense, DDR Prime®, On Guard®
- **Urinary**— basil, cinnamon bark, cypress, eucalyptus, juniper berry, lemon, lemongrass, tulsi, Purify, Zendocrine®
- **Vaginal**— cinnamon bark, thyme, basil, marjoram, spearmint, tea tree
- **Weight, excessive**— oregano, ginger, grapefruit, Slim & Sassy®

STEP 5

Repopulate gut

After completing detoxification program, take PB Assist®+, 2 capsules at bedtime, for 10 days to repopulate gut.

CARDIOVASCULAR

THE HEART and circulatory system make up the cardiovascular system. The heart works as a pump that pushes blood to the body's organs, tissues, and cells. Blood delivers oxygen and nutrients to every cell and removes carbon dioxide and waste products made by those cells. Blood is carried from the heart to the rest of the body through a complex network of arteries, arterioles, and capillaries. Blood is returned to the heart through venules and veins. Many blood vessels are smaller than a hair and only allow one blood cell at a time to circulate. If all the vessels of this network were laid end to end, they would extend for about 60,000 miles (more than 96,500 kilometers), which is far enough to circle the planet more than twice.

In pulmonary circulation, the roles are reversed. The pulmonary artery brings oxygen-poor blood into the lungs, and the pulmonary vein sends oxygen-rich blood back to the heart.

The oxygen and nutrient-rich blood that bring life and health to all the cells and tissues of the body also transport essential oils. When applied topically, essential oils are absorbed through the skin. They move through the circulatory system within thirty seconds and can then permeate cells and tissues throughout the body for targeted support within fourteen to twenty minutes.

Cardiovascular diseases comprise the leading cause of death globally and can refer to any disease involving the heart or blood vessels. The most common cardiovascular disease is related to arteriosclerosis/atherosclerosis, a process by which plaque causes the blood vessels to harden, stiffen, suffer a loss of elasticity, and narrow. The narrower vessels make blood flow more difficult, and blood clots can more easily block blood flow and cause serious conditions, including death. The good news is that 90% of cardiovascular disease is preventable with good lifestyle choices, including adequate rest, exercise, and nutrition. Risk factors are vast and include stress, excessive use of alcohol or caffeine, high blood pressure, smoking, diabetes, poor diet, obesity, and certain medications.

Any serious issue involving the cardiovascular system should immediately be seen by a qualified medical professional. It should be noted that natural solutions can support heart health, both preventatively and restoratively. Using certain essential oils has been shown to reduce blood pressure and heart rate. As heart disease, one of the leading causes of death, is almost entirely preventable, solutions offered with essential oils and the shifting from an ambulance mentality to a prevention mindset is most prudent.

top solutions

Single Oil

Cypress, cinnamon bark— promote proper circulation and blood flow throughout body (pgs. 139, 126)

Ylang ylang— balances heart rate and reduces high blood pressure (pg. 250)

Marjoram— supports the heart muscle (pg. 187)

Helichrysum, Yarrow|pom— repair damaged blood vessels; stop bleeding; (pgs. 160, 248)

Black and Pink pepper— warm and tone blood vessels; decongest circulatory/lymphatic (pgs. 111, 206)

Geranium— supports heart, healthy blood, and blood vessel integrity (pg. 152)

Blends

Purify— decongests circulatory/lymphatic congestion (pg. 208)

Passion®— promotes healthy blood flow (pg. 198)

AromaTouch®— stimulates circulation and blood flow, especially to extremities (pg. 103)

Supplements

Adaptiv™ Capsules, **Alpha CRS®+** (pg. 254), DDR Prime® Softgels, Deep Blue Polyphenol Complex®, **Fiber** (pg. 258), **Greens** (pg. 259), Microplex VMz®, **Mito2Max®** (pg. 262), PB Assist®+, Phytoestrogen Complex, **xEO Mega®** (pg. 271)

usage tips

Best methods of use for cardiovascular and circulatory support consider:

- **Topical:** Apply oils directly to chest, bottoms of feet, down spine, and/or on specific areas of concern.
- **Aromatic:** Diffuse 5-10 drops of oils of choice (especially stress-reducing options), inhale from cupped hands, or apply a few drops to clothing and inhale.
- **Internal:** Place 1-5 drops in water to drink, take in a capsule, or place under tongue to affect internal activities that impact circulation and healthy heart activity.

Related Ailments

Anemia (iron deficiency), Aneurysm, Angina, Arrhythmia, Arteriosclerosis, Atherosclerosis, Balance Problems, Bleeding, Blood Clot, Body Temperature issues, Broken Capillaries, Broken Heart Syndrome [Mood & Behavior], Bruise [Integumentary], Cardiomyopathy, Cardiovascular Disease, Cholesterol, Circulation (poor), Cold [Endocrine (Thyroid)], Cold Hands/Feet/Nose, Congenital Heart Disease, Deep Vein Thrombosis (blood clot in vein), Dizziness, Edema (water retention), Fainting [First Aid], Fibrillation (atrial), Fibrillation (ventricular), Gangrene [Immune & Lymphatic], Hardening of Arteries, Hematoma, Hemophilia, Hemorrhage, Hemorrhoids, Hypertension (high blood pressure), Hypotension (low blood pressure), Long QT Syndrome, Marfan Syndrome (connective tissue disorder), Mitral Valve Prolapse, Palpitations, Pericardial Disease, Phlebitis (inflammation of the vein), Pulmonary Embolism, Raynaud's Disease, Renal Artery Stenosis, Restless Leg, Syndrome, Sickle Cell, Tachycardia, Thrombosis, Varicose Veins [Integumentary], Vertigo

By Related Properties

For more, see *Oil Properties* on pages 535-538

Anticoagulant— clary sage, helichrysum, lavender
Antihemorrhagic— geranium, helichrysum, lavender, lemon, lemongrass, myrrh, oregano, patchouli, rosemary, sandalwood, spearmint, tea tree, thyme, yarrow|pom
Anti-inflammatory— arborvitae, basil, bergamot, black pepper, blue tansy, cinnamon bark, clary sage, copaiba, coriander, cypress, eucalyptus, frankincense, geranium, helichrysum, lavender, lemongrass, lime, litsea, manuka, melissa, neroli, patchouli, peppermint, Siberian fir, spikenard, tangerine, turmeric, wintergreen, yarrow|pom
Antitoxic— bergamot, black pepper, cinnamon bark, coriander, fennel, geranium, grapefruit, juniper berry, lavender, lemon, lemongrass, patchouli, thyme
Calming— basil, blue tansy, clary sage, copaiba, coriander, frankincense, jasmine, lavender, magnolia, patchouli, Roman chamomile, sandalwood, tangerine, vetiver, yarrow|pom
Cardiotonic— cassia, copiaba, cypress, ginger, lavender, litsea, marjoram, pink pepper, tangerine, turmeric, yarrow|pom
Decongestant— basil, black pepper, cardamom, copaiba, cypress, eucalyptus, ginger, grapefruit, lemon, lemongrass, litsea, patchouli, pink pepper, tangerine, tea tree, turmeric, yarrow|pom
Detoxifier— arborvitae, celery seed, cilantro, cypress, geranium, juniper berry, lemon, lime, patchouli, tangerine, yarrow|pom
Hypertensive— celery seed, melissa, rosemary, Siberian fir, thyme
Hypotensive— blue tansy, clary sage, copaiba, eucalyptus, lavender, lemon, marjoram, neroli, Siberian fir, yarrow|pom, ylang ylang
Regenerative— basil, cedarwood, clove, frankincense, geranium, helichrysum, jasmine, lavender, lemongrass, manuka, myrrh, neroli, patchouli, tea tree, wild orange, yarrow|pom
Relaxing— basil, blue tansy, cypress, geranium, lavender, litsea, manuka, marjoram, neroli, Roman chamomile, ylang ylang
Rubefacient— bergamot, birch, black pepper, black spruce, eucalyptus, ginger, green mandarin, helichrysum, juniper berry, lavender, lemon, lemon eucalyptus, magnolia, pink pepper, red mandarin, rosemary, Siberian fir, thyme, vetiver
Tonic— basil, bergamot, cypress, fennel, frankincense, geranium, lavender, lemon, lemongrass, neroli, patchouli, sandalwood, Siberian fir, tangerine, thyme, vetiver, wild orange, yarrow|pom
Vasoconstrictor— cypress, helichrysum, peppermint, Siberian fir, ylang ylang
Vasodilator— blue tansy, copaiba, lemongrass, litsea, manuka, marjoram, neroli, rosemary, thyme
Warming— birch, black pepper, cassia, cinnamon bark, clary sage, clove, eucalyptus, ginger, lemongrass, marjoram, neroli, oregano, peppermint, pink pepper, thyme, turmeric, wintergreen

conditions

Anemia (iron deficiency)*– basil, cinnamon bark, geranium, helichrysum, lemon, rosemary, DDR Prime®, OnGuard®, Zendocrine®, Microplex VMz®

Aneurysm*– cypress, frankincense, helichrysum, marjoram, DDR Prime®

Bleeding/hemorrhaging– arborvitae, cypress, frankincense, geranium, helichrysum, lavender, myrrh, yarrow|pom, ylang ylang, DDR Prime®, Purify, Zendocrine®

Blood clot*– clary sage, clove, coriander, fennel, frankincense, helichrysum, marjoram, myrrh, patchouli, peppermint, tea tree, thyme, wintergreen, AromaTouch®, DDR Prime®, Deep Blue®, Motivate®, Purify

- **Pain**– ylang ylang, AromaTouch®, Deep Blue®
- **Significant swelling**– clary sage, DDR Prime®, OnGuard®, Purify
- **Redness**– melissa, tea tree, ylang ylang, OnGuard®, Zendocrine®
- **Warmth**– fennel, melissa, ylang ylang, AromaTouch®, PastTense®, Whisper®, Zendocrine®

Blood, dirty/toxic– basil, cassia, clove, frankincense, geranium, grapefruit, helichrysum, lime, Roman chamomile, Siberian fir, turmeric, DDR Prime®, Zendocrine®

Blood flow, blocked*– celery seed, cypress, fennel, lavender (arteries), lemon (arteries), ylang ylang, AromaTouch®, DDR Prime®, Motivate®, Purify, Zendocrine®, Mito2Max®

Blood pressure, high (hypertension)*– birch, blue tansy, celery seed, copaiba, clove, cypress, eucalyptus, laurel leaf, lavender, lemon, lime, marjoram, melissa, neroli, patchouli, Roman chamomile, spearmint, thyme, wintergreen, ylang ylang, Breathe®, Cheer®, Citrus Bliss®

Blood pressure, low (hypotension)– basil, cardamom, helichrysum, lime, rosemary, Siberian fir, thyme, DDR Prime®, Purify, Zendocrine®

Blood vessels, blocked/obstructed– arborvitae, cinnamon bark, cypress, lemongrass, marjoram, Motivate®, OnGuard®

Blood vessels /capillaries, broken– cypress, frankincense, geranium, helichrysum, lavender, lemon, lime, Zendocrine®

Blood vessel integrity, lack of– black pepper, helichrysum, lemongrass, marjoram, Zendocrine®

Breathing problems– Air-X™, Breathe®; see *Respiratory*

Bruising– arborvitae, blue tansy, copaiba, cypress, fennel, geranium, helichrysum, lavender, neroli, oregano, Roman chamomile, Siberian fir, ylang ylang, DDR Prime®, Purify, Zendocrine®

Chest pain/pressure (angina)– basil, cinnamon bark, ginger, marjoram, rosemary, thyme, wild orange (for false angina), DDR Prime®, OnGuard®, Purify; see *Stress*

Cholesterol/triglycerides, elevated or imbalanced*– cinnamon bark, coriander, cypress, green mandarin, helichrysum, juniper berry, lemon, lemongrass, marjoram, pink pepper, rosemary, tulsi, turmeric, thyme, Cheer®, Slim & Sassy®

Circulation, poor/cold extremities*– arborvitae, basil, black pepper, black spruce, cassia, cedarwood, cinnamon bark, citronella, clove, cypress, eucalyptus, geranium, ginger, lemon eucalyptus, neroli, peppermint, pink pepper, rose, rosemary, Siberian fir, turmeric, wintergreen, yarrow|pom, AromaTouch®, Cheer®, Console®, DDR Prime®, Motivate®, OnGuard®, Passion®, Peace®, Whisper®, Mito2Max®

Circulatory system tonic*– basil, cypress, fennel, lemon, rosemary, tea tree, tulsi, turmeric, wild orange, AromaTouch®, Deep Blue®, Forgive®, Immortelle, PastTense®

Cold, need localized warming– birch, black pepper, cinnamon bark, eucalyptus, pink pepper, turmeric, AromaTouch®

Cold, need overall or systemic warming– black pepper, birch, cassia, cinnamon bark, cypress, eucalyptus, ginger, lemongrass, pink pepper, turmeric, wintergreen, AromaTouch®, Forgive®, Passion®

Confusion or trouble walking– arborvitae, Douglas fir, eucalyptus, frankincense, myrrh, peppermint, rosemary, wild orange, Motivate®, InTune®, Purify; see *Brain*

Dizziness/loss of balance/unsteady/lightheaded– black pepper, celery seed, Douglas fir, grapefruit, marjoram, oregano, patchouli, rosemary, tea tree, tangerine, ylang ylang, Breathe®, DDR Prime®, On Guard®, PastTense®, Whisper®, Zendocrine®

Edema (water retention, swelling in hands/ankles/feet)– basil, blue tansy, celery seed, cypress, ginger, green mandarin, juniper berry, lemon, lemongrass, rosemary, spikenard, Siberian fir, tangerine, PastTense®; see *Urinary, Detoxification*

Fainting/near fainting– basil, bergamot, cinnamon bark, cypress, frankincense, lavender, patchouli, peppermint, rosemary, sandalwood, wintergreen, Citrus Bliss®, Motivate®

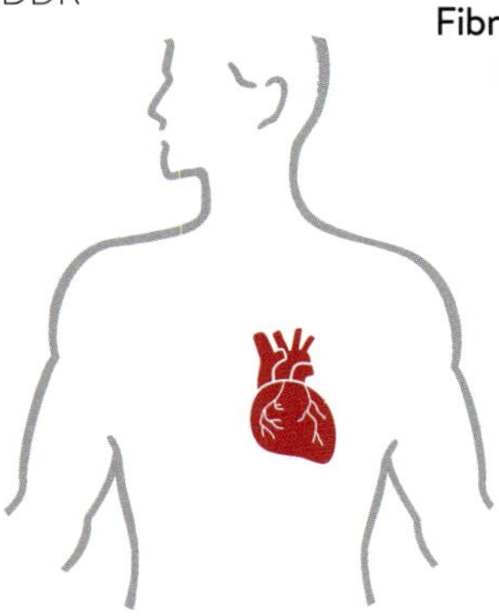

Fibrillation/atrial fibrillation– arborvitae, black pepper, Douglas fir, ginger, lime, marjoram, ylang ylang, AromaTouch®, Breathe®, DDR Prime®, Purify

Gangrene– arborvitae, cinnamon bark, cypress, geranium, melissa, myrrh, patchouli, tea tree, AromaTouch®, DDR Prime®, OnGuard®, Slim & Sassy®, Zendocrine®

Hardening of the arteries (arteriosclerosis)– arborvitae, basil, black pepper, cardamom, cinnamon bark, cypress, juniper berry, lavender, lemongrass, marjoram, rosemary, sandalwood, wild orange, InTune®, OnGuard®, Forgive®, Slim & Sassy®

Heart– blue tansy, copaiba, cinnamon bark, frankincense, geranium, lime, patchouli, sandalwood, tulsi, ylang ylang, AromaTouch®, Purify, Zendocrine®

Heart attack, prevention– cassia, cinnamon

Heartbroken– geranium, lime, rose, tulsi, ylang ylang, Console®

Heart infection– oregano; see *Immune & Lymphatic*

Heart murmur– Douglas fir, patchouli, peppermint, Siberian fir, thyme, AromaTouch®, Purify, Whisper®

Heart muscle, thickening (cardiomyopathy)– basil, marjoram, rose, rosemary, ylang ylang, Purify

Heart muscle, lack of tone– cassia, helichrysum, rose, Forgive®

Heart, weak– cinnamon bark, coriander, ginger, rosemary, tulsi, AromaTouch®

Heartbeat, irregular (arrhythmia)– basil, cedarwood, cinnamon bark, citronella, lavender, lemon, melissa, rosemary, ylang ylang, Console®, DDR Prime®, Peace®, OnGuard®

Heartbeat, rapid/racing (tachycardia)– arborvitae, blue tansy, cardamom, cedarwood, lavender, melissa, neroli, oregano, rosemary, tulsi, wild orange, ylang ylang, Serenity®, Zendocrine®

Heartbeat, slow (bradycardia)– Douglas fir, patchouli, AromaTouch®, Motivate®, Zendocrine®

Hematoma– basil, cypress, frankincense, geranium, helichrysum, marjoram, myrrh, lemongrass, AromaTouch®, Forgive®, Immortelle

*See Protocols on pg. 312

Hemorrhoids*— cypress, frankincense, geranium, helichrysum, juniper berry, myrrh, patchouli, Roman chamomile, rosemary, Siberian fir, yarrow|pom, DigestZen®, Forgive®, Zendocrine®

Numbness/tingling/paralysis in arm, face, leg— arborvitae, basil, cardamom, cypress, frankincense, geranium, ginger, patchouli, peppermint, AromaTouch®, DDR Prime®, PastTense®, Purify, Zendocrine®

Palpitations— blue tansy, cardamom, cedarwood, cinnamon bark, frankincense, lavender, neroli, oregano, petitgrain, rose, rosemary, thyme, ylang ylang, AromaTouch®, On Guard®, Peace®, Serenity®, Zendocrine®

Phlebitis— basil, cypress, helichrysum, lavender, lemon, lemongrass, marjoram, Zendocrine®

Plaque, clogged arteries (atherosclerosis)— basil, clove, copaiba, ginger, lemon, lemongrass, marjoram, patchouli, rosemary, thyme, wintergreen, AromaTouch®, DDR Prime®, Motivate®, On Guard®, Purify, Zendocrine®

Prolapsed mitral valve— marjoram, myrrh, patchouli, AromaTouch®, PastTense®

Red blood cells, poor production— geranium, lemon

Redness on tip of nose— patchouli, ylang ylang, TerraShield®

Redness on tip of tongue— arborvitae, ylang ylang, Purify, Whisper®

Restless leg syndrome— arborvitae, basil, cardamom, cypress, wintergreen, AromaTouch®, Deep Blue®, PastTense®; see *Sleep*

Ringing in ears (see tinnitus)— arborvitae, cypress, TerraShield®, Zendocrine®,

Stenosis (vessel narrowing)— arborvitae, lemon, oregano, patchouli, rosemary, DDR Prime®, Purify, Zendocrine®

Stroke— See *Brain*

Skin, cold/clammy/cold sweats— patchouli, ylang ylang, AromaTouch®

Skin, color changes to skin on face, feet, hands (bluish cyanosis, grayish, pale/white)— cypress, Douglas fir, lemon, patchouli, ylang ylang, Purify

Thrombosis, deep vein/blood clot— see "Blood clot" on previous page

Tongue, inflamed/red/sore— See *Heart*

Ulcers, leg/varicose— clove, cypress, frankincense, geranium, helichrysum, lavender, marjoram, AromaTouch®, DDR Prime®, PastTense®, Slim & Sassy®, Zendocrine®

Varicose veins*— bergamot, cardamom, coriander, cypress, geranium, helichrysum, lemon, lemongrass, marjoram, tea tree, patchouli, peppermint, rosemary, yarrow|pom, PastTense®, Peace®, Zendocrine®

Vein inflammation (phlebitis)— cypress, frankincense, marjoram, myrrh, DDR Prime®, PastTense®, Zendocrine®

Vertigo/sense room is spinning/sense of falling/loss of equilibrium (disequilibrium)— melissa, peppermint, rosemary, Balance®, Citrus Bliss®, DDR Prime®, Peace®; see *Brain*

Vessels:

- **Narrowing (stenosis)**— patchouli, Zendocrine®
- **Leaking (regurgitation/insufficiency)**— grapefruit, ylang ylang, On Guard®
- **Improper closing (prolapse)**— melissa, Zendocrine®

Vision, abnormal or jerking eye movements (nystagmus)— DDR Prime®

Vision, blurred— arborvitae, Douglas fir, juniper berry, lemongrass, peppermint, tulsi, DDR Prime®, Purify, Zendocrine®

Vision, trouble with seeing in one or both eyes— arborvitae, cypress, Douglas fir, lemongrass, DDR Prime®

Vision, see spots (consider low blood pressure)— arborvitae, rosemary, thyme; see *Nervous*

Weakness in arms/muscles; reduced ability to exercise— coriander, ginger, helichrysum, lemongrass, rosemary, tangerine

**See Protocols on pg. 312*

protocols

CHOLESTEROL FIGHTER: Take 2 drops each frankincense, turmeric, and lemongrass in a capsule 2x's per day.

CHOLESTEROL BUILD UP BUSTER

Ingredients:

2 drops lemongrass
2 drops Slim & Sassy®
2 drops marjoram
2 drops turmeric

Directions:

Place in capsule. Take 2x's per day.

CIRCULATION MOVER: Apply cypress. Cover with a warm, moist towel to help drive oil deeper into tissue and increase circulation.

PROMOTE CIRCULATION & OXYGENATION: Use AromaTouch® twice per day on legs and feet.

VARICOSE VEIN SOOTHER: Apply cypress and/or Aromatouch® on affected areas at least once per day or as needed.

VARICOSE VEIN REPAIR: Apply cypress and helichrysum with fractionated coconut oil to affected veins twice daily.

ANEMIA RESOLVE

Ingredients:

3 drops geranium
2 drops helichrysum

Directions:

Apply diluted to bottoms of feet and over liver area.

ANEURYSM SUPPORT & PREVENTION

Ingredients:

5 drops frankincense
1 drop peppermint
1 drop helichrysum

Directions:

Combine and apply diluted to base of skull, along spine, and/or bottoms of feet.

BLOOD CLOT SUPPORT

Ingredients:

4 drops grapefruit
3 drops lemon
3 drops clove
2 drops helichrysum

Directions:

Combine and take in capsule. Apply diluted to bottoms of feet and/or aea of concern to support blood flow.

HEMORRHOID SUPPORT

Ingredients:

10 drops cypress
10 drops helichrysum
10 drops lavender
5 drops basil
5 drops geranium
5 drops yarrow|pom or Balance®

Directions:

Place oils in 2 oz bottle with orifice-reducer seal, mix and fill remainder with fractionated coconut oil. Apply 10 drops of mixture to affected areas at least twice per day and/or following bowel movement. Additionally, keep a witch hazel bottle with 5 drops lavender in it beside toilet area. Spray on affected area and use with last wipe when using bathroom. Alternatively, a spritzer may be made with above listed oils.

HIGH BLOOD PRESSURE RELIEVER

Ingredients:

12 drops helichrysum
12 drops ylang ylang
8 drops cinnamon bark
8 drops frankincense
8 drops marjoram

Directions:

Combine in 10mL roller bottle and fill remainder with fractionated coconut oil. Apply blend to bottoms of feet, wrists, along breastbone, massage over heart, carotid arteries, and/or on back of neck at least 2x's per day.

RAYNAUD'S REMEDY

Ingredients:

12 drops cypress
8 drops geranium
10 drops black pepper
12 drops AromaTouch®
1 T carrier oil

Directions:

Combine in a 15mL glass bottle with a dropper top. Place 5 drops of mixture in palms and massage into hands and feet as often as needed, especially when vulnerable to getting chilled. To make a larger quantity of blend, and fill up the bottle, multiply the recipe.

CARDIOVASCULAR

For more ideas, download the app on Android or iOS.

Cellular Health

See also Immune & Lymphatic

CELLS are the smallest units of life for all living organisms. Cells replicate themselves through a process called mitosis. They perform specialized functions depending on their type; there are epithelial, sensory, blood, and hormone-secreting cells. At the end of their life cycle, cells experience apoptosis, a pre-programmed, healthy, cellular death. To achieve optimal health, it is important to nourish and support the cells throughout each stage of their life cycle.

In his book, *Never Be Sick Again*, Dr. Raymond Francis teaches that there's only one disease—a malfunctioning cell; there are two causes of disease—deficiency and toxicity; and there are six pathways to health and disease—nutrition, toxins, psychological/emotional state, physical, genetic, and medical. These ideas certainly simplify and highlight the most important areas on which to focus to achieve a healthy body. When cells do not operate efficiently, tissue and organ function is compromised, which in turn can diminish physical well-being and invite a host of health conditions and diseases. By nourishing the cells, the entire body system is supported.

Safeguarding the DNA (located in the cell's nucleus) and providing energy for all body processes are two of the most critical cellular activities. Research has shown that a diet low in antioxidants and other important phytonutrients, and environmental exposure to toxins such as pesticides, can damage DNA. This damage, called "mutation," can affect the cells' ability to produce energy. It can cause cells to die early, resulting in weakened tissue or inflammation, or even worse. And it can also cause cells to replicate themselves in their mutated form.

When using essential oils to support cellular function, it is important to remember that essential oils operate chemically within the body; they do not provide nutrition. When essential oils enter the body, they bring powerful instructions to help "remind" and support cells of their healthy function— but unless the cells are properly nourished, they won't have the energy necessary to perform their desired functions. Eating nutrient-dense raw foods is always a top priority, but many individuals have difficulty eating the quantities and types of quality food that assist cellular health. If this is the case, it's a good idea to find high-quality, bioavailable supplements, such as a whole-food nutrient supplement and xEO Mega®, to assist with keeping cells well-nourished and safeguarded.

Essential oils are a powerful addition to any regimen targeting cellular health. They can actually permeate the cell membrane and provide powerful support to the structures found within the cell, including safeguarding against inside threats such as viruses. Synthetic or adulterated essential oils cannot bypass the cell membrane and, therefore, cannot assist on a cellular level in the body.

top solutions

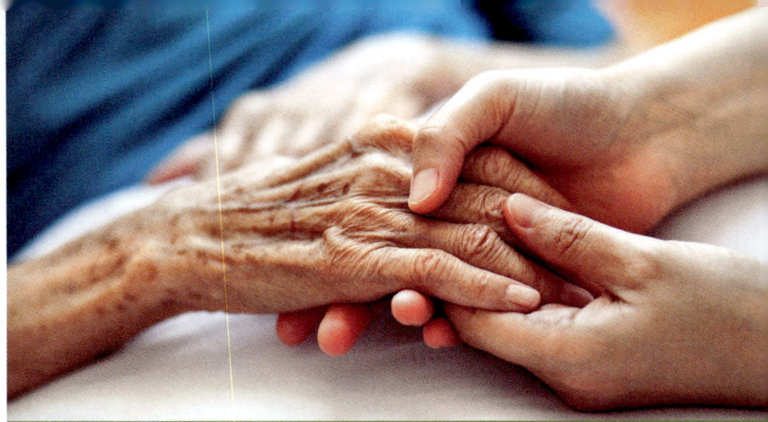

Single Oils

Turmeric– cellular health and antioxidant (pg. 239)

Frankincense, Sandalwood– promote healthy apoptosis and cellular health (pgs. 151, 218)

Lemongrass– cellular detoxifier and repairer (pg. 180)

Tangerine, Wild orange– encourage healthy DNA and optimal glutathione levels (pgs. 228, 244)

Cinnamon bark, Tulsi– promote healthy cellular response to glucose and inflammation (pgs. 126, 236)

Patchouli, Yarrow|pom– support cell in eliminating harmful toxins (pgs. 200, 248)

Clove, Thyme, Pink pepper– powerful antioxidants, support cellular and DNA repair (pgs. 134, 234, 206)

Arborvitae– stimulates immune support and cellular repair (pg. 101)

Blends

DDR Prime®– promotes cellular health and DNA repair (pg. 140)

Zendocrine®– helps eliminate toxins, free radicals and heavy metals (pg. 251)

Air-X™– antioxidant; neutralizes free radicals, supports cellular health (pg. 97)

Purify, Abōde™– detoxify cells and lymphatic system (pgs. 208, 95)

Supplements

Alpha CRS®+ (pg. 254), Copaiba Softgels, **DDR® Prime Softgels** (pg. 256), Deep Blue Polyphenol Complex®, DigestZen® Softgels, **Fiber** (pg. 258), Greens, GX Assist®, Microplex VMz®, Mito2Max®, PB Assist®+, **Turmeric Dual Capsules** (pg. 269), xEO Mega®

usage tips

For best success at supporting cellular health:

- **Topical:** Apply oils on bottoms of feet, spine, and/ or on any specific area of concern. Use AromaTouch Technique® regularly as desired or able.
- **Internal:** Consume oils in capsules, drop under tongue, or sip in water.

Related Ailments

Basal Cell Carcinoma, Benign Prostatic Hyperplasia, Bone Cancer, Brain Cancer, Breast Cancer, Cells [Integumentary], Cervical Cancer, Colon Cancer, Endometrial Cancer, Hodgkin's Disease, Leukemia, Lipoma, Liver Cancer, Lung Cancer, Lymphoma (Non-Hodgkin's), Melanoma, Mesothelioma, Mouth Cancer, Ovarian Cancer, Paget's Disease, Pancreatic Cancer, Polyps, Prostate Cancer, Radiation Damage [Immune & Lymphatic], Skin Cancer, Throat Cancer, Tongue Cancer, Tumor, Uterine Cancer

By Related Properties

For more, see *Oil Properties* on pages 535-538

Anticarcinogenic– arborvitae, black spruce, frankincense, myrrh, peppermint, tangerine, turmeric, yarrow|pom

Anti-carcinoma– arborvitae, copaiba, frankincense, grapefruit, lemon, lemongrass, litsea, myrrh, rosemary, sandalwood, tangerine, turmeric, wild orange

Anti-inflammatory– basil, bergamot, black pepper, blue tansy, cassia, cinnamon bark, clove, copaiba, coriander, cypress, eucalyptus, frankincense, geranium, ginger, lavender, lemongrass, litsea, manuka, melissa, neroli, oregano, patchouli, peppermint, pink pepper, Roman chamomile, Siberian fir, spearmint, tangerine, turmeric, yarrow|pom

Antimutagenic– cinnamon bark, copaiba, ginger, lavender, lemongrass, neroli, tangerine, turmeric

Antioxidant– arborvitae, basil, black pepper, cassia, cilantro, cinnamon bark, clove, copaiba, coriander, eucalyptus, frankincense, ginger, grapefruit, green mandarin, helichrysum, juniper berry, lemon, lemongrass, lime, neroli, oregano, patchouli, peppermint, pink pepper, rosemary, tangerine, thyme, turmeric, vetiver, wild orange, yarrow|pom

Antitoxic– black pepper, cinnamon bark, coriander, fennel, geranium, grapefruit, lemongrass, patchouli, thyme

Anti-tumoral– arborvitae, clove, copaiba, frankincense, lavender, myrrh, sandalwood, turmeric, vanilla

Cleanser– cilantro, grapefruit, lemon, thyme, wild orange

Cytophylactic– arborvitae, frankincense, geranium, lavender, manuka, neroli, red mandarin, rosemary, tangerine

Detoxifier– cassia, cilantro, geranium, green mandarin, litsea, juniper berry, patchouli, tangerine, turmeric, yarrow|pom

Purifier– cinnamon bark, eucalyptus, grapefruit, lime, marjoram, manuka, Siberian fir, tangerine, tea tree, wild orange, yarrow|pom

Regenerative– basil, cedarwood, citronella, clove, coriander, frankincense, geranium, helichrysum, jasmine, lavender, lemongrass, manuka, myrrh, neroli, patchouli, sandalwood, tea tree, wild orange, yarrow|pom

Tonic– arborvitae, basil, birch, cardamom, coriander, frankincense, geranium, lemon, lemongrass, melissa, Roman chamomile, sandalwood, Siberian fir, ylang ylang, yarrow|pom

CELLULAR HEALTH

conditions

Cellular Health:

Acidic, overly– arborvitae, fennel, frankincense, lemon, lime, rosemary, wild orange, Balance®, DDR Prime®, Slim & Sassy®, Zendocrine®

Activity, poor– cinnamon bark, clove, frankincense, geranium, ginger, rosemary, DDR Prime®, DigestZen®, Immortelle, On Guard®, Zendocrine®

Cellular health, poor/premature aging– neroli, tangerine, Console®, DDR Prime®, Immortelle, Peace®; see "Antioxidant" property

Cellular malfunction*– arborvitae, black pepper, cedarwood, citronella, clove, frankincense, geranium, lavender, lemongrass, rosemary, Siberian fir, tangerine, thyme, turmeric, wild orange, DDR Prime®, Forgive®, Immortelle, On Guard®

Free radicals, excess damage– arborvitae, basil, cassia, cardamom, cilantro, cinnamon bark, clove, frankincense, ginger, grapefruit, lemon, lemongrass, lime, rosemary, tangerine, tea tree, thyme, turmeric, yarrow|pom, Citrus Bliss®, DDR Prime®, Forgive®, Immortelle, On Guard®; see "Antioxidant" property

Hardening of cell membrane– arborvitae, cinnamon bark, clove, frankincense, rosemary, sandalwood, tangerine, thyme, vetiver, Breathe®, DDR Prime®, Immortelle; see "Antioxidant" property

Inflammation– basil, bergamot, birch, black pepper, black spruce, cinnamon bark, clove, copaiba, coriander, cypress, Douglas fir, eucalyptus, frankincense, geranium, lavender, melissa, patchouli, peppermint, Roman chamomile, rosemary, thyme, turmeric, wintergreen, Console®, DDR Prime®, Deep Blue®; see "Anti-inflammatory" property, *Pain & Inflammation*

Nutrient absorption, poor/cellular starvation– cinnamon bark, ginger, Slim & Sassy®

Oxygen flow to cell, poor– black pepper, cilantro, cypress, frankincense, peppermint, sandalwood, Siberian fir, Breathe®, Slim & Sassy®

Radiation damage– arborvitae, cilantro, clove, copaiba, frankincense, geranium, patchouli, peppermint, sandalwood, tulsi, DDR Prime®, Zendocrine®

Toxic/autointoxication– arborvitae, bergamot, copaiba, Douglas fir, frankincense, grapefruit, lemon, lime, sandalwood, Siberian fir, turmeric, wild orange, DDR Prime®, Immortelle, InTune®, Purify, Slim & Sassy®, Zendocrine®

Vitality, lack of– bergamot, cedarwood Douglas fir, wild orange, yarrow|pom, ylang ylang, Citrus Bliss®, DDR Prime®, Purify, Zendocrine

**See Protocols on pg. 316*

Support By Body Parts Or Areas:

Bladder– basil, cinnamon bark, cypress, frankincense, juniper berry, lemongrass, rosemary, turmeric, AromaTouch®, DDR Prime®, Slim & Sassy®

Blood– basil, clary sage, clove, frankincense, geranium, lavender, lemongrass, myrrh, rosemary, thyme, turmeric, DDR Prime®, On Guard®, Purify, Zendocrine®

Bone– clary sage, clove, frankincense, helichrysum, lemon, lemongrass, sandalwood, thyme, turmeric, Siberian fir, DDR Prime®

Brain– arborvitae, cedarwood, clove, frankincense, grapefruit, green mandarin, helichrysum, melissa, myrrh, patchouli, pink pepper, rosemary, sandalwood, thyme, wild orange, DDR Prime®, Immortelle

Breast*– arborvitae, cinnamon bark, clary sage, frankincense, grapefruit, lavender, lemongrass, marjoram, oregano, pink pepper, rosemary, sandalwood, thyme, vanilla, DDR Prime®, Immortelle, Whisper®

Cervix– clary sage, frankincense, geranium, lemon, patchouli, rosemary, sandalwood, Siberian fir, thyme, vetiver, DDR Prime®, Immortelle, On Guard®, Whisper®, Zendocrine®

Fatty tissue– frankincense, grapefruit, helichrysum, lemon, lemongrass, Slim & Sassy®

General– arborvitae, basil, clary sage, clove, eucalyptus, frankincense, geranium, grapefruit, lavender, lemongrass, myrrh, rose, rosemary, sandalwood, tangerine, wild orange, DDR Prime®, Immortelle, On Guard®, Purify, Whisper®, Zendocrine®

Large intestines/colon/rectum– arborvitae, basil, cardamom, clove, Fiber, frankincense, geranium, ginger, lavender, lemongrass, oregano, rosemary, sandalwood, thyme, turmeric, wild orange, DDR Prime®, Immortelle, Purify, Whisper®, Zendocrine®

Liver– clove, copaiba, frankincense, geranium, grapefruit, helichrysum, lavender, lemon, lemongrass, rosemary, tangerine, thyme, tulsi, turmeric, wild orange, DDR Prime®, Zendocrine®

Lung– blue tansy, cinnamon bark, eucalyptus, frankincense, lauel leaf, lavender, lemon, litsea, melissa, ravintsara, rosemary, sandalwood, thyme, tulsi, wild orange, Air-X™, Breathe®, DDR Prime®, On Guard®, Purify, Whisper®, Zendocrine®

Lymphatic system/lymph/nodes– basil, bergamot, cardamom, cilantro, cinnamon bark, clary sage, clove, frankincense, lavender, lemon, lemongrass, myrrh, rosemary, sandalwood, tea tree, thyme, turmeric, Air-X™, DDR Prime®, Elevation, On Guard®, Purify, Zendocrine®

Mouth/oral– bergamot, black pepper, frankincense, geranium, myrrh, peppermint, tea tree, thyme, tulsi, turmeric, DDR Prime®

Mucus membrane– arborvitae, frankincense, geranium, lavender, lemongrass, peppermint

Ovaries– clary sage, frankincense, geranium, lemon, myrrh, rosemary, sandalwood, turmeric, vetiver, wild orange, Balance®, DDR Prime®, Immortelle, Slim & Sassy®, Whisper®, Zendocrine®

Pancreas– cinnamon bark, coriander, frankincense, rosemary, tulsi, turmeric, DDR Prime®, On Guard®, Purify, Slim & Sassy®, Zendocrine®

Prostate– arborvitae, basil, cardamom, cassia, cedarwood, cinnamon bark, clary sage, cypress, frankincense, juniper berry, oregano, neroli, rose, rosemary, sandalwood, thyme, turmeric, DDR Prime®, Immortelle, InTune®, On Guard®, Slim & Sassy®, Zendocrine®

Skin– arborvitae, Douglas fir, frankincense, geranium, grapefruit, green mandarin, lavender, lemon, melissa, myrrh, rosemary, sandalwood, tangerine, tea tree, thyme, tulsi, turmeric, wild orange, DDR Prime®, Immortelle, On Guard®, Whisper®, Zendocrine®

Throat– cinnamon bark, frankincense, lavender, lemon, lime, myrrh, rosemary, thyme, turmeric, DDR Prime®, On Guard®, Whisper®, Zendocrine®

Thyroid– blue tansy, clary sage, frankincense, lemon, melissa, rosemary, sandalwood, thyme, DDR Prime®, Forgive®, Passion®

Tongue– bergamot, cassia, cinnamon bark, clove, frankincense, geranium, ginger, lavender, myrrh, peppermint, tea tree, thyme, turmeric, DDR Prime®, DigestZen®, Zendocrine®

Tissue– clove, frankincense, geranium, grapefruit, lemongrass, melissa, myrrh, patchouli, sandalwood, wild orange, DDR Prime®, On Guard®, Purify, Whisper®, Zendocrine®

Uterus– clary sage, cypress, frankincense, geranium, ginger, grapefruit, lemon, lemongrass, rosemary, sandalwood, turmeric, DDR Prime®, Immortelle, Purify, On Guard®, Whisper®, Zendocrine®

protocols

Notes:

Diet, exercise, and stress, as well as emotional and spiritual issues, all add to the development of any degenerative diseases including cancer. These contributing factors need to be addressed in order to truly heal any condition.

Engage the support and care of trusted professional healthcare providers.

CELLULAR HEALTH PROGRAM

Engage in the following:

- **Adjust and fortify diet.**
  - › Add Greens, Fiber, and/or Protein to smoothies or water.
- **Supply vital nutrients.**
  - › Microplex VMz®— 2 capsules AM and PM
  - › Alpha CRS®+— 2 capsules AM and PM; increase as needed
  - › xEO Mega®— 2 capsules AM and PM
  - › A2Z Chewable™, IQ Mega®— for kids
- **Support healthy digestion & elimination.**
  - › TerraZyme®— 1-2 capsules each meal
  - › PB Assist®+— 2 capsules at bedtime; add more as needed
  - › DigestZen®— for digestive/intestinal upset or sluggishness
  - › Tamer™ & PB Assist® Jr— for kids
- **Use citrus oils daily** to raise glutathione levels in body.
  - › 2-5 drops grapefruit, tangerine, and/or wild orange 2-3 x's per day in drinking water or take in capsule.
- **Remove toxins** from diet and lifestyle as well as exposure to harmful chemicals.
- **Open channels of elimination:**
  - › Zendrocrine® Complex— 1-2 capsules AM and PM with food
  - › See *Detoxification* for further ideas (pg. 326)

SUPPORT LIVER AND HELP RID BODY OF HEAVY METAL TOXICITY.

Choose one of following based on condition(s):

- **Recipe #1:** Take 4 drops Zendocrine® 2x's per day.
- **Recipe #2:** Take 2-3 drops each cilantro, geranium, grapefruit, and rosemary in a capsule 2x's per day.
- **Recipe #3:** Take 2 drops each helichrysum and Zendocrine® in a capsule 2x's per day.

PROMOTE CELLULAR HEALTH, DNA REPAIR, AND HEALTHY APOPTOSIS

Take daily:

- › Take DDR Prime® Softgels— 2 per meal AM and PM.
- › Take 2 Turmeric Dual Capsules AM and PM.
- › Apply DDR Prime® on bottoms of feet— 2-4 drops per foot 2x's per day.
- › Take 2 drops frankincense under tongue 2x's daily. Hold for 30 seconds and then swallow.

Add one or more of following:

- › Take 4 drops each Siberian fir, lemongrass, sandalwood, and frankincense in a capsule 3x's per day.
- › Take 2-3 drops each clove, grapefruit, Siberian fir, and DDR Prime® in capsule 2-3x's per day.
- › Research and create own blend using oils that are specific to condition(s).

CREATE AND MAINTAIN A HEALTHY EMOTIONAL STATE

- › See *Mood & Behavior* (pg. 377)
- **Support a healthy immune system**—
  - › Take On Guard® or see *Immune & Lymphatic* (pg. 355).
  - › Consider candida detox program— see *Candida* (pg. 304).

MANAGE PAIN

- › Take Deep Blue Polyphenol Complex®.
- › Take Copaiba Softgels.
- › See *Pain & Inflammation* (pg. 392), *Muscular* (pg. 381) , *Nervous* (pg. 385), *and/or Skeletal* (pg. 415).

MAINTAIN ENERGY LEVELS

- › Take Mito2Max® twice daily.
- › See *Energy & Vitality* (pg. 344)
- **Use a specified topical application** once or more per day.

Choose from the following:

- › Apply the Basic Application Technique once daily.
- › Choose a Topical Application Recipe or create one. See next column for instructions.

BASIC APPLICATION TECHNIQUE

1. Apply a base coat of fractionated coconut oil.
2. Layer the following oils on back, about 5-6 drops each up the spine and across back. Massage lightly. Repeat until all oils are applied:

   Clove or thyme, frankincense, lemongrass, rosemary, sandalwood, and DDR Prime®. Apply more carrier oil as needed.

Alter recipe according to needs and conditions. Choose oils from lists on previous page.

TOPICAL APPLICATION RECIPES

Apply selected blend below, diluted with carrier oil, to affected areas 2x's daily.

Recipes may be multiplied and stored in a glass bottle for use in future applications. Mix in the following ratios:

Breast

1 drop each frankincense, Siberian fir, pink pepper, and grapefruit. IF lymph glands are also affected, add 1 drop lemongrass. Add aloe vera gel for additional soothing effect.

Lung

3 drops Breathe® + 2 drops clove or tulsi + 2 drops myrrh + 3 drops frankincense + 1 drop rosemary or ravintsara

Lymph

5 drops lemongrass + 3 drops clove + 3 drops frankincense

Ovaries

3 drops pink pepper + 1 drop basil + 1 drop geranium

Skin

3 drops lavender + 4 drops frankincense + 3 drops sandalwood + 2 drops tulsi

BREAST DETOX SALVE

16 drops pink pepper
16 drops grapefruit
24 drops frankincense
8 drops ylang ylang
2 drops tulsi

Melt 2 T shea butter over low heat until liquified. Cool to room temperature. Add essential oils. When salve begins to solidify, stir well.

Cover and use within about two weeks.

For more ideas, download the app on Android or iOS.

CELLULAR HEALTH

CHILDREN'S HEALTH involves both physical and mental well-being. Physical health concerns range from irritating (e.g., diaper rash, crying, colic) to concerns that can quickly become serious if not addressed (e.g., scarlet fever, strep throat). Once a child begins socializing outside the home, exposure to bacterial and viral infections becomes commonplace. Since their immune systems are immature, children can more easily succumb to infectious diseases. They are also exposed to a number of compromising situations that increase risk for injury. See *First Aid* for tips on addressing issues resulting while engaged in typical childhood play.

Just like adults, children have mental health needs and are affected by perceived stress and trauma, responding with typical emotions such as fear, sadness, and anger. Parents and caregivers often feel poorly equipped with the knowledge and tools they need to properly care for their children. It is difficult and frustrating to have limited resources when trying to help a child resolve emotional upset, stress, hyperactivity, sadness, illness, injury, and any other potential concern.

Children are particularly responsive to aromas and healthy touch. Simply smelling or experiencing the application of an essential oil followed by a simple massage technique is very comforting to a child and can support rapid changes in behavior and responsiveness to trauma or difficult situations. Many real life situations have demonstrated that a room full of children under a variety of circumstances have a nearly universal positive response in mood, outlook, and behavior through the diffusing or dispersing of essential oils into the air.

Most children naturally love essential oils, and many seem to know what they need and when to use them. They respond particularly well to opportunities to discover their favorite oils and make their own personalized roller-bottle blend (see *Blending and Layering* for further information). For further ideas for mood support, see *Mood & Behavior*.

While proper medical care is always advised when needed, there are many situations in the home and family when natural solutions can be used as a first line of defense. Parents and caregivers are more intimately acquainted with their children than anyone else and typically have excellent insight into the nature or causes of many issues their children encounter. It is empowering to know a few natural remedy basics that support health and wellness and may help prevent potential issues.

Teaching children self-care at an early age creates an empowering environment in which they may grow and advance as confident and balanced individuals. Essential oils offer an excellent opportunity to participate in this self-care process. When partnered with children's nutritional supplements and a healthy diet, a foundation of health is laid that positively affects a young person's health status for decades to come.

top solutions

Single Oils

Lavender— the most used essential oil for children and for all things calming (pg. 175)

Wild orange— gentle, powerful, calming, uplifting, offers digestive and immune/anti-infectious support, promotes sense of abundance: "there is enough for me!" (pg. 244)

Frankincense— supports brain, mood, wound healing, feeling grounded; promotes a sense of safety and security (pg. 151)

Roman chamomile— supports sense of calm and relaxation, has a sedative effect, diffuses agitated negative thoughts or moods; detoxifies (pg. 213)

Blends

Brave™— encourages a sense of self-confidence (pg. 115)

Calmer™— supports sense of peace and calm (pg. 117)

Rescuer™— supports injury recovery and pain relief (pg. 212)

Steady™— supports feeling grounded and stable (pg. 225)

Stronger™— supports and boosts immune system (pg. 226)

Tamer™— supports digestion and elimination (pg. 227)

Thinker™— supports focus and concentration (pg. 233)

Also consider any single oil or blend offered as a Touch® roll-on.

Supplements

a2z Chewable™ (pg. 253), Fiber, Greens, **IQ Mega** (pg. 260), **PB Assist® Jr** (pg. 264), Protein (pg. 266)

CHILDREN

usage tips

Children are wonderfully responsive to the use of essential oils.

They love to learn and be involved in the process of selecting what oils they use. They also love to nurture others with the oils and participate in making their own personalized roller bottle blends. Allowing a child to smell an oil prior to use creates a sense of connection and trust.

- **Aromatic:** Diffuse, inhale from cupped hands, wear on pulse points for peace and calm as well as mental focus and concentration before school or at bedtime.
- **Topical:** Apply with a carrier oil and massage on back, abdomen, or feet. With smaller body weight, and depending on age, just a drop or two diluted, or even less for infants, can be highly effective and appropriate for safety.

Related Ailments

Colic, Crying Baby, Diaper Rash, Fifth's Disease (human parvovirus B19), Gastroenteritis (stomach flu) [Digestive & Intestinal; Immune & Lymphatic], Growing Pains, Hand, Foot and Mouth Disease [Immune & Lymphatic— Viral], Infant Reflux, Legg-Calve-Perthes Disease [Skeletal], Molluscum, Roseola, RSV, Scarlet Fever, Thrush [Candida]

By Related Properties

For more, see *Oil Properties* on pages 535-538

Antibacterial— arborvitae, bergamot, black pepper, blue tansy, cardamom, cedarwood, cinnamon bark, copaiba, eucalyptus, ginger, lemongrass, litsea, manuka, marjoram, myrrh, oregano, patchouli, rosemary, Siberian fir, tangerine, tea tree, thyme, turmeric

Anticatarrhal— black pepper, frankincense, helichrysum, myrrh, neroli, rosemary, Siberian fir, spearmint

Antidepressant— basil, bergamot, clary sage, coriander, frankincense, geranium, lemon, lemongrass, neroli, rose, sandalwood, tangerine, wild orange

Anti-inflammatory— arborvitae, basil, bergamot, blue tansy, cedarwood, copaiba, coriander, cypress, eucalyptus, frankincense, geranium, ginger, helichrysum, lavender, lemongrass, lime, litsea, manuka, marjoram, myrrh, neroli, peppermint, Roman chamomile, rosemary, sandalwood, Siberian fir, tangerine, tea tree, turmeric, wintergreen, yarrow|pom

Antiseptic— basil, bergamot, black pepper, cardamom, cedarwood, clary sage, copaiba, cypress, geranium, helichrysum, jasmine, lavender, lemon, lime, manuka, marjoram, melissa, neroli, oregano, patchouli, ravintsara, rosemary, sandalwood, Siberian fir, tangerine, tea tree, thyme, wild orange, yarrow|pom, ylang ylang

Antiviral— arborvitae, blue tansy, cassia, cinnamon bark, clove, copaiba, eucalyptus, lime, litsea, manuka, melissa, oregano, Siberian fir, tea tree, thyme, turmeric, yarrow|pom

Calming— basil, black spruce, blue tansy, copaiba, lavender, litsea, magnolia, patchouli, Roman chamomile, tangerine, vetiver, yarrow|pom

Decongestant— copaiba, cypress, eucalyptus, lemon, melissa, rosemary, Siberian fir, yarrow|pom

Expectorant— cardamom, eucalyptus, fennel, helichrysum, jasmine, lemongrass, marjoram, oregano, rosemary, sandalwood, Siberian fir, tea tree, thyme

Immunostimulant— arborvitae, cassia, cinnamon bark, clove, copaiba, eucalyptus, frankincense, lime, melissa, rosemary, Siberian fir, wild orange, yarrow|pom

Invigorating— grapefruit, lemon, litsea, peppermint, pink pepper, Siberian fir, spearmint, wild orange, wintergreen

Mucolytic— basil, cedarwood, clary sage, copaiba, cypress, fennel, helichrysum, lemon, myrrh, tangerine, yarrow|pom

Regenerative— basil, cedarwood, clove, cypress, frankincense, geranium, helichrysum, lavender, lemongrass, manuka, neroli, patchouli, sandalwood, tea tree, yarrow|pom

Relaxing— basil, blue tansy, cassia, cedarwood, geranium, jasmine, lavender, litsea, manuka, marjoram, myrrh, neroli, ravintsara, Roman chamomile, ylang ylang

Sedative— basil, bergamot, blue tansy, cedarwood, coriander, frankincense, juniper berry, lavender, magnolia, neroli, patchouli, Roman chamomile, sandalwood, tangerine, vetiver, ylang ylang, yarrow|pom

Stomachic— basil, cardamom, fennel, ginger, juniper berry, peppermint, pink pepper, rosemary, turmeric, yarrow|pom

Uplifting— bergamot, cardamom, cedarwood, clary sage, cypress, grapefruit, litsea, sandalwood, tangerine, wild orange

conditions

Emotional/Mental States*

Children naturally experience any number of emotional states, as do adults. Common expressions can be anxious or stressed, defiant, excessive crying, willful, grumpy, overly reactive or over-sensitive, shy, sad, whiny, and excessively wound-up or hyperactive. See *Mood & Behavior* for suggested solutions. For attention deficits or issues with focus and concentration, see *Focus & Concentration*

Physical States

Acne, baby– tea tree, HD Clear® (dilute); see *Integumentary*

Allergies– blue tansy, cilantro, lavender, lemon, peppermint, tea tree, Zendocrine®; see *Allergies*

Antibiotic recovery– cilantro, Zendocrine®, PB Assist® Jr; see *Candida*

Bed-wetting*– black pepper, cilantro, cinnamon bark, copaiba, cypress, juniper berry, rosemary, spearmint, Peace®, Rescuer™, Zendocrine®

Birth– arborvitae, clary sage, frankincense, melissa, myrrh, neroli, patchouli, sandalwood, tea tree, wild orange, Calmer™, Motivate®, Steady™, Thinker™; see *Pregnancy, Labor & Nursing*

Bronchitis– cardamom, clary sage, copaiba, eucalyptus, pink pepper, Siberian fir, Breathe®, Motivate®, On Guard®; see *Respiratory*

Bug bites/stings– blue tansy, copaiba, lavender, Purify; see *First Aid*

Bumps/bruises– fennel, geranium, helichrysum, lavender, Deep Blue®; see *First Aid*

Colic*– bergamot, black pepper, cardamom, cilantro, clove, coriander, cypress, fennel, ginger, lavender, marjoram, Roman chamomile, rosemary, spearmint, wild orange, ylang ylang, Adaptiv™, Calmer™, DigestZen®, Tamer™; see *Digestive & Intestinal*

Common cold/flu*– cardamom, cedarwood, lemon, melissa, ravintsara, rose, rosemary, sandalwood, tangerine, tea tree, thyme, Breathe®, Stronger™; see *Immune & Lymphatic*

Constipation– cardamom, cilantro, Douglas fir, ginger, lemongrass, marjoram, rosemary, wild orange, DigestZen®, Tamer™, Zendocrine®; see *Digestive & Intestinal*

Cradle cap*– clary sage, frankincense, geranium, lavender, lemon, sandalwood, tea tree, Immortelle, Correct X; see *Integumentary*

Croup– arborvitae, Douglas fir, eucalyptus, lemon, marjoram, patchouli, sandalwood, thyme, wild orange, Breathe®, Stronger™; see *Respiratory*

Cuts– copaiba, frankincense, lavender, magnolia, myrrh, sandalwood, tea tree, yarrow|pom, Correct X; see *First Aid*

Diaper rash*– dilute: frankincense, lavender, patchouli, Roman chamomile, tea tree, ylang ylang; see *Integumentary*

Dry lips/above lips– cedarwood, jasmine, myrrh, sandalwood, Correct-X, fractionated coconut oil; see *Integumentary*

Dry skin– arborvitae, black spruce, copaiba, lavender, lemon (skin cleansing), myrrh, neroli, sandalwood, tea tree, Immortelle, diluted; see *Integumentary*

Earache*– basil, clary sage, cypress, fennel, ginger, helichrysum, lavender, neroli, Roman chamomile, tea tree, thyme, wild orange, Rescuer™; see *Respiratory*

Eczema/Psoriasis– arborvitae, black spruce, cedarwood, Douglas fir, geranium, helichrysum, myrrh, neroli, patchouli, ravintsara, Roman chamomile, sandalwood, Siberian fir, turmeric, yarrow|pom, ylang ylang, Correct-X, fractionated coconut oil; see *Integumentary*

Fever*– birch, eucalyptus, juniper berry, lavender, lemon eucalyptus, lime, peppermint, pink pepper, Roman chamomile, Siberian fir, spearmint, wintergreen, yarrow|pom, Citrus Bliss®, PastTense®; see *Immune & Lymphatic*

Growing Pains– see *Leg Aches* below

Foot fungus (Athlete's foot)– basil, copaiba, neroli, tea tree, On Guard®; see *Candida*

Hand, foot and mouth– arborvitae, cassia, cinnamon bark, clove, helichrysum, lemongrass, melissa, oregano, rosemary, tea tree, thyme, turmeric, wild orange, wintergreen, On Guard®, Stronger™; see *Immune & Lymphatic*

Headache– lavender, peppermint, frankincense, wintergreen, Rescuer™, Zendocrine®; see *Pain & Inflammation*

Hiccups– arborvitae, basil, blue tansy, clary sage, fennel, helichrysum, lemon, peppermint, sandalwood, wild orange, Serenity®, Zendocrine®

Hives– basil, cilantro, frankincense, lavender, peppermint, Roman chamomile, rosemary, tea tree; see *Allergies*

Immune system boost– Stronger™; see *Immune & Lymphatic*

Infant reflux– lavender, peppermint, Roman chamomile, DigestZen®; Tamer™; see *Digestive & Intestinal*

Jaundice*– frankincense, geranium, helichrysum, juniper berry, lemon, lemongrass, lime, rosemary, wild orange, Zendocrine®; see *Digestive & Intestinal*

Leg aches/growing pains– arborvitae, bergamot mint, birch, cypress, ginger, lavender, lemongrass, marjoram, melissa, rosemary, Siberian fir, wintergreen, Adaptiv™, AromaTouch®, Rescuer™; see *Pain & Inflammation*

Pinkeye (conjunctivitis)– clary sage, Douglas fir, frankincense, lavender, spikenard, tea tree, Correct X; see *Immune & Lymphatic*

Rash– arborvitae, cedarwood, lavender, lemon, Roman chamomile, rose, sandalwood, tea tree, Rescuer™, Zendocrine®; see *Integumentary*

Respiratory support– eucalyptus, laurel leaf, ravintsara, rosemary, Air-X™, Breathe®; see *Respiratory*

Runny nose– basil, cedarwood, lemon/lavender/peppermint (use together), Breathe®, Stronger™; see *Allergies, Immune & Lymphatic, Respiratory*

Seizures– cedarwood, celery seed, Douglas fir, frankincense, petitgrain, rose (will delay onset), sandalwood, spikenard; see *Brain*

Sleep, disturbed/irregular/nighttime waking*– lavender, tangerine, vetiver, Balance®, Calmer™; see *Sleep*

Sleep, trouble getting to*– lavender, neroli, Roman chamomile, Calmer™, Steady™; see *Sleep*

Stomach flu* (Gastroenteritis)– basil, bergamot, cardamom, clove, ginger, thyme, DigestZen®, Stronger™, Tamer™; see *Digestive & Intestinal*

Stuffy nose– Douglas fir, lemon, sandalwood, Breathe®, DigestZen®; see *Allergies, Immune & Lymphatic, Respiratory*

Sunburn– blue tansy, frankincense, helichrysum, lavender, peppermint, sandalwood, Immortelle; see *Integumentary*

Teeth grinding– black spruce, frankincense, geranium, marjoram, lavender, Roman chamomile, wild orange, Calmer™, Serenity®; see *Parasites*

Teething pain– blue tansy, clove, frankincense, helichrysum, lavender, Roman chamomile, sandalwood, yarrow|pom; dilute and apply directly to gums, Rescuer™

Thumb sucking– clove or any other internally safe, unpleasant-tasting oil (diluted)

Thrush*– bergamot, clary sage, clove, copaiba, geranium, fennel, lavender, lemon, oregano, tea tree, thyme, wild orange, On Guard®, Slim & Sassy®; see *Candida*

Tired, overly– lavender, neroli, Roman chamomile, yarrow|pom, Calmer™, Forgive®, Motivate®, Serenity®, Steady™; see *Sleep*

Tooth decay– clove, copaiba, helichrysum, tea tree; see *Oral Health*

Tooth infection– clove, helichrysum, tea tree, Stronger™; see *Oral Health*

Tummy ache– bergamot mint, blue tansy, cardamom, fennel, ginger, peppermint, yarrow|pom, DigestZen®, Tamer™; see *Digestive & Intestinal*

Vomiting– bergamot, cardamom, clove, ginger, pink pepper, On Guard® (dilute), DigestZen®, Purify, Tamer™, Zendocrine®; see *Digestive & Intestinal*

Warts– arborvitae, cinnamon bark, clove, copaiba, frankincense, lemon, lemongrass, lime, melissa, oregano, thyme, On Guard®; see *Integumentary*

Whooping Cough, spastic/persistent cough– cardamom, clary sage, cypress, Douglas fir, eucalyptus, frankincense, lavender, neroli, petitgrain, Roman chamomile, rosemary, yarrow|pom, Breathe®, Purify, Serenity®, Stronger™; see *Respiratory*

*See Protocols on pg. 320-321

protocols

CHILDREN

ANGER MANAGEMENT FOR LITTLE ONES

Apply Calmer™, Steady™, and/or Forgive® Touch to palms, rub together, cup over face (without touching), and inhale deeply. Then rub excess oils on back of neck and over heart.

Other options: Serenity®, Roman chamomile, and/or magnolia.

NO WET BED

Younger children: Apply 1 drop diluted cypress and/or juniper berry on bottoms of feet.

Older children who can swallow capsules: In addition to above, take 1 drop coriander in a capsule 1x per day. Increase number of times per day as needed.

CHILL OUT

Ingredients:

4 drops cypress
5 drops frankincense
10 drops lavender
3 drops vetiver
6 drops Roman chamomile
2 drops ylang ylang
1 drop cedarwood

Directions:

Add oils to 10mL roller bottle and top off with carier oil. Double number of drops for older children. Triple for adults. Apply to back of neck, pulse points, base of neck, and/or along spine.

Other options: Steady®, Serenity®, and/or Peace® Touch

COLIC CALMING

Apply Tamer™ or DigestZen® Touch on abdomen, lower back, and/or on bottoms of feet. Repeat until relief is achieved. Layer with Calmer™ or Lavender Touch® if needed. Burp baby and use warm compress if needed.

COMMON COLD BLEND

Add 4 drops tea tree, 2 drops lemon, and 4 drops On Guard® to a 5mL roller bottle and top off with carrier oil. Massage on chest, back, and bottoms of feet. **Other options:** Stronger™ and Breathe® Touch.

tips

- To calm an upset baby, apply Lavender Touch® or Calmer™ on chest and bottoms of feet.
- Scent children's clothes with their favorite essential oils by applying to cotton balls and then placing in corners of drawers and/or hang with clothes.
- To signal safety, comfort, or time for sleep, diffuse lavender, Balance®, and/or Serenity®.
- Create a nighttime routine by putting on pajamas, applying oils, reading a story, and being tucked into bed.
- For a calming and relaxing bedtime bath: add 2-4 drops each Roman chamomile and lavender or Serenity® with ½ C Epsom salt to warm bath water.
- To soothe baby's sore gums, swab 1 drop or less Roman chamomile, Siberian fir, or clove without touching lips or cheeks.

CRADLE CAP

In a 5mL roller bottle, blend 1-3 drops each lemon, tea tree, geranium, and cedarwood or sandalwood, topped off with fractionated coconut oil. Apply a small amount one or more times daily.

DIAPER RASH RELIEF

Use diaper cream, Correct-X®, or a combination of 1 drop each Roman chamomile, frankincense, and lavender diluted with fractionated coconut oil.

EARACHE BLEND

Add 1 drop each basil, tea tree, and helichrysum to a cotton ball and place on the surface of outer ear canal. Avoid putting inside ear itself. Rub oils diluted behind/around ear, down neck, and along jaw.

FEVER

Apply Tamer™ or 1 drop diluted spearmint on back of neck, bottoms of feet, across forehead, back of neck, and/or along spine.

FLU

Diffuse 5 drops On Guard®. Add 1-2 drops each cypress, lemon, and tea tree to ½ C Epsom salt for a relieving bath.

JAUNDICE

Apply, highly diluted, geranium, frankincense and juniper berry over liver area and liver reflex points on feet.

PINK EYE

Mix 1 drop each lavender and tea tree with a few drops of carrier oil. Apply a small amount around eye area. Avoid the eye itself. Additionally, apply oil mixture to crooks of 2nd and 3rd toes.

LIGHTS OUT!

Ingredients:

2 drops vetiver
2 drops cedarwood
2 drops patchouli
2 drops Serenity®
3 drops ylang ylang, OR Calmer™, Serenity®, OR Peace® Touch

Directions:

Combine oils in 10mL roller bottle, topped off with carrier oil. Roll on bottoms of feet and/or along spine at bedtime.

THRUSH BLEND

Ingredients:

5 drops lemon
1 drop clary sage
1 drop lavender
3 yarrowlpom dropperfuls

Directions:

Combine in empty 5mL bottle. Apply a small amount to nipples before each nursing, and/or with a clean finger rub in baby's mouth to coat tongue, gums, and inside of cheeks.

TRANSITION BLEND

Use when children are facing stressful social environments and changes, such as going to daycare or a new school, public speaking, moving, or for any activity outside of their normal routine. Choose from: Balance® or Peace® Touch, Brave™, Steady™, or Calmer™.

Apply to back of neck, forehead, over heart, and/or on bottoms of feet the night before, the morning of, and if possible, just before any significant event.

WINTER CHEEKS BALM

Ingredients:

20 drops neroli Touch
5 drops blue tansy
5 drops yarrowlpom
2 T shea butter

Directions:

Place shea butter in a small glass jar. Lower into a saucepan partially filled with warm water. On low heat, stir until melted. Remove from heat and let cool a few minutes. Add oils. Mix to combine. Then let cool until hardened. Rub balm over reddened cheeks to soothe and protect. Store in small tin.

did you know?

- Talc is found in most commercial baby powders and is a known lung irritant and harmful toxin.
- Many baby products are made with synthetic fragrances that can cause respiratory, neurological, skin, and eye damage.
- You can make natural, safe, gentle, and uniquely scented DIY products for babies, children, and the entire family for a fraction of the cost of chemically-laden, over-the-counter remedies.

CHILDREN

kid's lifestyle

Begin and end a child's day with loving connections through positive physical touch and pure plant power. Offer proven support to meet children's daily needs by integrating these simple solutions into regular activities and routines. Make selections based on each child's needs and preferences.

Morning

- **Morning Wake-Up**– apply diluted peppermint, wild orange, or Motivate® under nose, on wrists, and/or up spine.
- **Morning Empowerment**– apply Brave™ or Motivate® under nose, and then as they move their body as they speak positive empowering affirmations.
- **Morning Nourishment**– add Protein, Greens, IQ Mega®, and/or citrus oil to a shake/smoothie.
- **School Prep**– apply Thinker™ on temples and forehead.
- **Finicky/picky eating**–
  - > Apply Peace® Touch to pulse points and under nose.
  - > Take fennel, wild orange, or cardamom in a capsule or in small glass of water. Apply on abdomen and under nose.
- **Stay Healthy**– apply Stronger™ to neck, feet, and/or spine. Take TerraZyme® and PB Assist® Jr.
- **Soothe & Calm Fears**– apply Brave™, Calmer™, Steady™, lavender, or Roman chamomile diluted over heart.
- **Avoid Meltdowns**– apply Calmer™ or Steady™ under nose and on back of neck.
- **Clinging to Parents/Others**– apply Brave™ under nose and over heart, and give a 10-second reassuring embrace.
- **Ease with the Flow of Life & Release Control**– apply cypress across forehead.

Afternoon

- **Homework**– apply Thinker™, rosemary, or peppermint onto wrists and inhale deeply from cupped hands.
- **Invite focus**– apply InTune® or Thinker™, along spine, forehead, and bottoms of feet. Inhale.
- **Encourage/cheer up**– diffuse Cheer®. Apply Brave™ on wrists, behind knees, and bottoms of feet. Inhale.
- **Increase movement or exercise**– apply Brave™ under nose, on wrists, and bottoms of feet. Apply Rescuer™ after a long day of activity, or to soothe growing pains, or on area of discomfort.

Night

- **Unplug from screen time**– apply diluted spearmint or Northern Escape under nose and on outer rim of ears.
- **Reset**– apply frankincense and Balance® and practice box breathing. Breathe in for a count of 4, hold for 4, and breathe out for 4, hold for 4. Repeat several times.
- **Bath time**– apply Steady™, sandalwood, Siberian fir, or Calmer™ prior to taking a warm bath. Add Epsom salt if desired.
- **Soothe & calm**– apply vetiver, Calmer™, or Serenity® on back of neck and bottoms of feet.
- **Deep, peaceful rest**– apply Roman chamomile, lavender, or Calmer™ along spine and back of neck. Take 1 Serenity® Softgel with older children if able to swallow capsule.
- **Nighttime ritual**– apply Serenity®, vetiver + lavender or Calmer™ on bottoms of feet, and/or diffuse by bed.
- **Nightmares & night terrors**– apply Brave™, Calmer™, or diluted juniper berry on back of neck, bottoms of feet, and chest to help promote restful and calming sleep.
- **Boost immunity**– apply Stronger™ on spine and bottoms of feet.

Other

- **Sugar craving**– add tangerine to drinking water.
- **Food addictions/overeating**– add grapefruit to drinking water.
- **Successful play**– diffuse wild orange to uplift mood and energy levels.
- **Promote sharing**– use rose, bergamot, cardamom, Roman chamomile, frankincense, lavender, myrrh, and/or patchouli. Choose one or more and diffuse or apply to children playing together.
- **Stay steady**– apply Steady™ to back of neck and bottoms of feet.
- **Anger**– apply Forgive® Touch or Calmer™ over heart and pulse points with a quiet moment to regain composure.
- **Forgiveness**– apply Forgive® Touch over heart and forehead.
- **Receive discipline & direction**– apply Calmer™ and Thinker™.
- **Increase love after discipline**– apply Forgive® Touch with a 10-second hug and statements of love and assurance.
- **Move past and/or break an old habit**– write on a helium balloon and release along with applying Brave™.
- **Overheated**– apply diluted spearmint or Tamer™ on shoulders, back of neck, and feet for a cooling sensation.
- **Itchy eyes**– apply diluted lavender on bridge of nose and across forehead.
- **Irritated skin**– apply diluted lavender or eucalyptus to desired areas.
- **Stubbed toe**– apply Rescuer™ to area of concern.
- **Skinned knee**– combine and apply lavender and tea tree on site. Apply Correct-X thereafter.
- **Stinky shoes or gym bag**– place a few drops Purify or Abōde™ on a cotton ball and place inside shoes or bag.
- **Car rides**– apply Tamer™ or DigestZen® Touch to palms, rub together, and inhale deeply. Diffuse in car with a car diffuser or add oils to cotton ball and placed in air vents of vehicle.
- **Successful travel**– apply Tamer™ to abdomen and bottoms of feet.
- **Plane trips**– apply Tamer™ under nose and on abdomen before take-off and landing.
- **Church, performance, or quiet/calm activity**– apply Calmer™, Roman chamomile, lavender, or Serenity® on pulse points, under nose, along spine, and/or back of neck.
- **Quiet time**– to transition or unwind before quiet time, apply Calmer™, Roman chamomile, or Serenity® Touch to bottoms of feet or back of neck.

tips

Children are naturally drawn to essential oils and can access all the power natural solutions have to offer as caregivers introduce, educate, and support usage. Integrate oils alongside daily routines to address needs and observe how incorporating them increases healthy behaviors.

- Use high-quality essential oils to ensured purity and potency.
- Use smaller doses of essential oils relative to a child's smaller body mass, development, and skin maturity.
- Dilute essential oils with a carrier oil to avoid skin sensitivities (e.g., 1 drop of an essential oil to 5 drops of carrier oil)
- Topical use of citrus oils is only recommended outside of 12 hours to UV rays exposure.
- Store essential oils in a safe place and out of reach of children.
- Guide children to understand and use essential oils appropriately for their age.
- Consumption of adult supplements by children is based on half or quarter doses based on age, weight, and capacity to swallow pills. Consult healthcare provider.
- Be Informed. Always read and follow labels and manufacturer's recommendations.

Recommended Dosage*

Application	Ideal	24 hour max.
Topical	1-2 drops	3-12 drops

Avoid applying oils to inner ear (use cotton ball instead), inside nostrils, or directly in eyes.

KID'S COLLECTION USE RECOMMENDATIONS

Stronger™	Brave™	Thinker™	Steady™	Calmer™	Rescuer™	Tamer™
Boundaries	Discouraged	ADD/ADHD	Uncooperative	Sleep issues	Muscle aches & tension	Bloating, gas, nausea
Susceptibility	Unexcited	Lack of focus & concentration	Obstinate or out of control	Stressed & anxious	Growing pains	Constipation, diarrhea, Crohn's, IBS
Vulnerable	Tired & weary	Lack of logical or creative thinking	Restless & wound up	Skin irritations	Bruises & injury	Motion, travel/ morning sickness
Lack of protection	Afraid & scared	Distracted	Overstimulated	Need relaxation	Loneliness	Bronchitis, asthma, cough, chest cold
Poor immunity	Lack of confidence	Daydreaming	Angry	Worried & restlessness	Headache & migraine	Acne & skin blemishes
Clear skin	Overwhelmed	Nervous	Frustrated	Easily upset	Distress, fear	Edema
Bacteria & viruses	Bullied	Anxious	Tantrums	Uptight	Shock	Trouble "digesting" experiences
Cold sores, warts, infected wounds	Unsure	Afternoon slump	Grief	Moody	Pain from grief	Feeling overheated
Cuts & scrapes	Apathetic	Disconnected	Disappointed	Angry, irritated	Chaos	Unclear
Fungus & parasites	Unenthusiastic	Inattentive	Disconnected from earth + reality	Bed & bath routine	Overwhelmed	Incongruent
Chronic fatigue, autoimmune disease	Aches & pain	Seizures	Bath & bedtime	Over scheduled	Avoiding	Codependent

usage tips

FOR THE PARENTS

Parents and caretakers have a profound responsibility to manage the care of their children. This involves educating oneself about nutrition, supplementation, preventative care options, and treatment of illnesses and injuries.

Doctors bring a wealth of medical skills and deep knowledge of disease to their work. Few have more than a cursory understanding of health maintenance essentials like supplements and nutrition. Most have little to no knowledge about effective natural health care solutions like essential oils.

A parent who educates him or herself appropriately can choose a healthcare provider for their family who is open to natural solutions. Together, they can partner intelligently to provide the child an effective health lifestyle with powerful natural remedies when needed. Essential oils can play a key role in both.

Use wisdom when researching solutions online. Most information available about aromatherapy reflects the assumption that the product used will contain synthetic compounds. In the case of adulterated products, warnings should be heeded as legitimate.

But when pure, unadulterated, genuine essential oils are selected, a parent can care for the family with confidence. In fact, when quality oils are used, parents and children alike can enjoy experimenting, much like experimenting with healthy options in the kitchen. One child might thrive on a particular grain; another might find it upsets the tummy and prefers a different selection. But no harm is done. Oil selection is the same. Individualized, experimental, and fun!

Know it isn't about being perfect. It is about being effective. Be flexible and teachable. If something isn't generating desired results, change it up, try something different, diversify efforts. Obtain fearless confidence by freely playing with the oils until you (and your children) figure them out and discover what is right for you.

keep it safe

FOR THE CHILDREN

Essential oils are very effective with children of all ages. However, because their skin tends to be more sensitive than that of adults, it is important to take certain precautionary measures, especially when using what are considered to be "hot" oils, such as birch, cassia, cinnamon, clove, eucalyptus, ginger, lemongrass, oregano, peppermint, thyme, tulsi, and wintergreen. When using these oils topically with children and infants, either highly dilute with a carrier oil, or make another choice. When using an oil neat (undiluted), it is often best applied on the bottoms of a child's feet.

To determine quantities, consider a child's body weight and apply a fraction of an adult recommended dosage. For example, if an adult were to apply 1-2 drops of an oil directly to the skin, those same number of drops could be placed in a roller bottle, highly diluted with a carrier oil, and applied on an infant.

Avoid putting undiluted peppermint or eucalyptus the chest, face, or throat area of a young child (under 3 years), as the sensation and effect can startle an infant and cause them to hold their breath momentarily. Use these oils diluted on the bottoms of the feet or in a blend such as Breathe®.

Consider consistently using pre-made Kid's Collection or Touch® products such as a pre-diluted Breathe® or Peppermint.

Keep oils away from eyes and out of reach of children.

PREMATURE BABIES: Since premature babies have very thin and sensitive skin, a very conservative and highly diluted use of essential oils is recommended.

Detoxification

DETOXIFICATION (detoxing or cleansing) is the term used to describe the deliberate use of programs, products, dietary, and lifestyle changes to support the body in eliminating unwanted substances and circumstances. Releasing toxins allows the body, heart, and mind to dedicate greater amounts of energy to thriving rather than just coping and surviving.

We live, eat, and breathe toxic substances every day. Consider the paint on the walls, the carpet, laundry and cleaning products, pesticides, extermination products, preservatives and chemicals in foods, the "stuff" that goes in and out of cars; personal care products and makeup also contribute to higher toxicity levels in the body. Even when trying to limit exposure to toxins, it is difficult to live toxin-free. Contact occurs daily with chemicals and other toxic agents as we eat, breathe, live, and sleep.

When overwhelmed by toxins, the body cannot properly perform its functions with full efficiency. Metabolism, immunity, elimination of waste, absorption of nutrients, production of important brain chemicals, reproduction, circulation, respiration, etc., are all affected. Toxins can compromise even hydration. Toxic overload may reveal itself as fevers, headaches, acne, fatigue or lack of energy, sneezing, coughing, vomiting, diarrhea, rashes, allergies, excess weight, cellulite, brain fog or lack of mental clarity, decreased immunity, chronic pain, poor moods, and much more. Sometimes these symptoms are interpreted as sickness, when in reality, the body may be trying to eliminate toxins through different systems—and the symptoms are mere side effects. Avoiding toxins and detoxifying are necessary to be healthy, happy, and free of disease.

Essential oils have unique properties that support health on a cellular level, including detoxing. When the body is overwhelmed by excess toxins, the liver will safeguard vital organs by insulating toxins in fat cells. There are oils that help release toxins from fat cells, break them down, and flush them out of the body with good hydration. Other oils stimulate cell receptor sites to greater, more efficient activity. And there are oils that are helpful in clearing the gut of harmful bacteria and restoring balance for healthy digestion and immunity. Consider what actions can reduce the intake of toxins and how to consistently detox to maintain optimal health.

top solutions

Single Oil

Grapefruit, Lemon– antioxidants, superb detoxifiers (pgs. 154, 176)

Lemongrass– powerhouse decongestant for any system and cells of the body (pg. 180)

Celery seed– blood and liver detoxifier, digestive stimulator (pg. 122)

Cilantro– heavy metal detoxifier, liver and kidney support (pg. 125)

Clove– powerful antioxidant, blood and cellular cleanser (pg. 134)

Blends

Abōde™, Purify– detox lymph, blood, kidneys, skin (pgs. 95, 208)

Air-X™– detox lymph, respiratory, blood, gut (pg. 97)

DDR Prime®– detox lymph, cells, gut, brain (pg. 140)

Slim & Sassy®– detox fat, liver, gallbladder (pg. 222)

Zendrocrine®– detox liver, gallbladder, gut, kidneys, lungs, skin (pg. 251)

Supplements

Alpha CRS®+, **DDR Prime® Softgels** (pg. 256), **Fiber** (pg. 258), **Greens** (pg. 259), **GX Assist®** (pg. 260), Microplex VMz®, Mito2Max®, TerraZyme®, xEO Mega®, **Zendocrine® Complex** (pg. 272), **Zendocrine® Softgels** (pg. 273)

Related Ailments

Acidosis, Alkalosis, Autointoxication, Blood Detoxification, Body Odor, Hangover, Lead Poisoning, Metal Toxicity, Xenoestrogens

By Related Properties

For more, see *Oil Properties* on pages 535-538

Antitoxic– bergamot, black pepper, cinnamon bark, coriander, fennel, geranium, grapefruit, juniper berry, lavender, lemon, lemongrass, patchouli, thyme

Detoxifier– arborvitae, cassia, celery seed, cilantro, citronella, cypress, geranium, green mandarin, juniper berry, lemon, lime, litsea, patchouli, rosemary, tangerine, turmeric, wild orange, yarrowlpom

usage tips

To improve or enhance any detox program results:

- **Internal:** Internal consumption of essential oils and supplements is one of the most effective ways to deliver detox "instructions" to specific organs and tissues of the body. Consume oils in a capsule, under tongue, or in water.
- **Topical:** Invite tissue and organs to release fat and toxins by directly applying oils to targeted areas. Massage after application to ensure absorption. Apply oils to bottoms of feet to impact the blood and lymphatic fluids of the body vital to detoxification processes. Additionally, use the AromaTouch Technique® to enhance the success of any detox program.
- **Aromatic:** Consider addressing toxic emotional states during a program, as mood directly impacts health. Negative emotions and toxins are inextricably and chemically connected. Aromatic application immediately and directly impacts the amygdala, the center of emotions in the brain. See *Mood & Behavior* or the charts on pgs. 34, 35 of *Emotional Well-being* to select oils related to specific emotional states.

Why Detox

The body strategically stores toxins in fatty tissue to keep harmful substances away from critical organs and functions. A detox program, *especially when nutrients are provided and proper dietary parameters are observed,* encourages the body to release toxins and excess fat. Long-lasting results can be achieved when diet and lifestyle habits continue to be supportive.

Detox Response Too Intense?

Diarrhea can be a common detox discomfort and indicative of a lack of probiotics and fiber in the diet. It can also indicate a detox program is simply pushing the body faster than it can handle. Solutions can include increased consumption of dietary or supplemental fiber, probiotics, and, if necessary, cutting back on detox products. For example, to ease diarrhea, cut back on Zendrocrine® or DDR Prime® Softgels.

If constipation is an issue, increase the very same products along with TerraZyme® and drink more water. If other adverse symptoms occur, such as congestion, skin eruptions, etc., see the correlating section of this book for suggested solutions—*Respiratory, Integumentary*, etc.

Basic Detox Program

DETOXIFICATION

Two-Week Program

CLEAN UP DIET	
Make the necessary dietary adjustments to achieve desired results. If results are not being achieved, make additional adjustments. Eliminate refined sugars, junk foods, dairy. Add Greens and Fiber to program.	
PROVIDE PROPER NUTRIENTS & GUT SUPPORT	
MicroPlex VMz®	1-2 capsules AM and PM
xEO Mega®	1-2 capsules AM and PM
Alpha CRS®+	1-2 capsules AM and PM
TerraZyme®	1-2 capsules with meals Bonus: 1-2 capsules on empty stomach in AM and/or bedtime
PB Assist®+	2 capsules at bedtime
USE DETOX TOOLS	
Tangerine	3 drops in 24 oz. of water 3 times a day
Zendocrine® Complex	1-2 capsules AM and PM
Zendocrine®	5 drops in capsule or 1-2 softgels AM and PM

Bonus

SUPERCHARGE CLEANSE	
DDR Prime® Softgels	5 drops in capsule or 1-2 softgels twice daily
DAILY ENERGY SUPPORT	
Mito2Max®	1-2 capsules AM and afternoon as needed
TISSUE & CELLULAR RELEASE	
AromaTouch Technique®	Weekly
TARGET EMOTIONS	
When negative emotions are retained, so are associated toxins. They are inextricably and chemically connected. Consider targeting toxic emotional states during a program. Use Balance® or choose your own. See *Mood & Behavior* to select emotions and oils for a program.	

Dosage levels are best tied to body weight, tolerance, and intended results. Adjust accordingly.

**To take a cleansing commitment to the next level, see* Weight *or* Candida *for additional detox programs.*

conditions

Blood toxicity– basil, cassia, cinnamon bark, clove, frankincense, geranium, grapefruit, helichrysum, lemongrass, Roman chamomile, thyme, turmeric, Siberian fir, DDR Prime®, Zendrocrine®; see *Cardiovascular*

Brain– arborvitae, basil, bergamot, cedarwood, clove, fennel, frankincense, melissa, rosemary, sandalwood, thyme, turmeric, vanilla, DDR Prime®, InTune®, Thinker™

Candida toxicity– arborvitae, basil, lemongrass, tea tree, oregano, Siberian fir, thyme, yarrowlpom, InTune®, Thinker™; see *Candida*

Cellular toxicity– arborvitae, clove, frankincense, helichrysum, lemongrass, pink pepper, Siberian fir, tangerine, thyme, turmeric, vanilla, wild orange, yarrowlpom, DDR Prime®; see *Cellular Health*

Cellulite– birch, cypress, Douglas fir, eucalyptus, ginger, grapefruit, lemon, lemongrass, Siberian fir, spikenard, thyme, wild orange, Slim & Sassy®; see *Weight*

Chemical toxicity– celery seed, cilantro, lemon, vanilla, Abōde™, Purify

EMF toxicity– hinoki, Northern Escape

Gallbladder toxicity– geranium, grapefruit, lemongrass, lime, tangerine, turmeric, DDR Prime®, Slim & Sassy®, Zendrocrine®; see *Digestive & Intestinal*

Gut toxicity– bergamot, black pepper, cardamom, celery seed, cinnamon bark, fennel, ginger, Roman chamomile, tangerine, wild orange, DigestZen®, Zendrocrine®; see *Digestive & Intestinal*

Heavy metal toxicity*– arborvitae, black pepper, cilantro, clove, coriander, frankincense, geranium, grapefruit, helichrysum, juniper berry, rosemary, thyme, tulsi, Purify, Zendrocrine®

Kidney/urinary toxicity– bergamot, blue tansy, cardamom, cassia, celery seed, cilantro, coriander, eucalyptus, fennel, geranium, green mandarin, juniper berry, lemon, lemongrass, rosemary, Siberian fir, thyme, Citrus Bliss®, Motivate®; see *Urinary*

Liver toxicity– basil, bergamot, citronella, clove, copaiba, cypress, geranium, grapefruit, green mandarin, helichrysum, juniper berry, lemon, lemongrass, marjoram, peppermint, Roman chamomile, rose, rosemary, turmeric, yarrowlpom, Slim & Sassy®, Zendrocrine®; see *Digestive & Intestinal*

Lymphatic toxicity– arborvitae, cypress, lemon, lemongrass, myrrh, pink pepper, rosemary, tangerine, tea tree, Abōde™, Air-X™, AromaTouch®, Motivate®, Purify; see *Immune & Lymphatic*

Lung/respiratory toxicity– arborvitae, blue tansy, cardamom, cedarwood, cinnamon bark, Douglas fir, eucalyptus, laurel leaf, lemon, lemongrass, lime, ravintsara, Air-X™, Breathe®, Motivate®, Northern Escape, On Guard®, Purify, Zendrocrine®; see *Respiratory*

Nerve toxicity– arborvitae, basil, bergamot, black pepper, clary sage, cypress, frankincense, ginger, helichrysum, lemongrass, myrrh, patchouli, peppermint, petitgrain, Roman chamomile, Balance®; see *Nervous*

Pancreas toxicity– cilantro, cinnamon bark, citronella, coriander, fennel, lemongrass, rosemary, tulsi, vanilla

Parasite, intestinal toxicity– blue tansy, clove, fennel, oregano, Roman chamomile, thyme, turmeric, On Guard®; see *Parasites*

Skin toxicity*– cedarwood, frankincense, geranium, lavender, lemon, myrrh, sandalwood, vetiver, turmeric, yarrowlpom, ylang ylang, HD Clear®, Immortelle; see *Integumentary*

Xenoestrogen toxicity– clary sage, ginger, grapefruit, lemon, neroli, oregano, thyme, ClaryCalm®, DDR Prime®, Zendrocrine®; see *Men's or Women's Health*

*See Protocols →

protocols

HEAVY METAL DETOX

Ingredients:

2 drops geranium
4 drops helichrysum
2 drops Zendrocrine®
4 drops cilantro
2 drops cypress
2 drops frankincense

Directions:

Combine oils in a 5mL roller bottle. Fill with fractionated coconut oil. Apply to bottoms of feet and over liver area AM and PM.

DETOX FOOT SOAK

Ingredients:

1 C Epsom salt
1 C baking soda
⅓ C sea salt
⅓ C Redmond Clay powder
Selected essential oil(s)

Directions:

- Mix dry ingredients in a jar and store with a lid. When a foot soak is desired, put ¼ C of the dry mix in a foot bath tub, then mix in oils.
- Add enough warm-to-hot (100-115° F) water to cover feet completely.
- Add 3-4 drops of selected oils chosen to detox a specific area of focus. See "Conditions" in this chapter for suggestions.

DETOX BODY SCRUB

Ingredients:

2 C salt or sugar (e.g. sea salt, mineral salts, organic sugar)
1 C almond oil
4 drop wild orange
4 drops basil
4 drops lemongrass
4 drops lime
4 drops thyme
4 drops rosemary
4 drops grapefruit
4 drops lavender
4 drops Zendocrine®

Directions:

Combine ingredients and store in a glass jar. Apply desired amount and gently massage onto skin for exfoliation. Rinse.

EVERYDAY MORNING DETOX

Ingredients:

1 T organic apple cider vinegar with Mother
1 t honey (optional)
2 drops grapefruit
2 drops ginger
2 drops celery seed
1 drop pink pepper
10 oz. warm water

Directions:

Mix in a glass and drink first thing in morning.

SKIN DETOX

Ingredients:

½ C aluminum-free baking soda
A few Ts of fractionated coconut oil
4 drops lavender
4 drops rosemary
4 drops tea tree
4 drops geranium

Directions:

Create a paste, adding more or less coconut oil to achieve desired consistency. Use in shower as a cleanser and exfoliator. Apply over entire body and gently scrub for a few minutes, then rinse. Repeat at least twice a week. The skin naturally serves as a pathway for detoxification. Keeping it "open" will aid the body in other detoxification processes.

Oil Pulling

Oil pulling is an ancient practice and cleansing technique that involves the simple swishing of a specific pure food grade oil in the mouth for about 20 minutes daly. One of the main purposes for the habit is "pulling" a variety of toxins from the bloodstream.

Benefits include positive changes in cellular health, immunity, the ridding of unwanted toxins such as heavy metals and microorganisms, increased energy, improved gum health, whiter teeth, clearer skin, elimination of bad breath, and a more vibrant complexion.

To enhance oil pulling benefits, add an essential oil of choice that targets an area of interest. For example, add frankincense for cellular health or clove for oral health.

Instructions

- Oil pull first thing in the morning on an empty stomach prior to consumption of any liquids (including water) or foods. It is not recommended to be done at any other time of day.
- Choose a "swishing" oil. Top choices include sesame, olive (cold-pressed, extra virgin), coconut, cod liver, cedar nut, avocado, walnut, castor, or black cumin. Each oil has particular properties that bring specific results. More information is available online and in written resources regarding oil choices.
- Choose an essential oil that supports your particular health or detox goals. See "Conditions" in this on any other chapter of this book for recommendations by organ or body system.

Step One

Put 1 T of selected "swishing" oil in mouth via a spoon. Add 1-2 drops of selected essential oil.

Step Two

Swish oil all around in mouth, including pulling it through the teeth. DO NOT swallow it. Use the tongue to help create the movement. Do not tilt head back. The oil will begin to get watery as it mixes with saliva. Keep swishing. If jaw muscles get sore while swishing, relax jaw and use tongue more to help move liquid.

This gentle and relaxed process lasts for about 20 minutes. When done correctly, it feels comfortable, especially with repeated practice. As the oil/saliva mixture is saturated with toxins, it becomes more whitish or milk-like in consistency, depending on oil used. Each session varies in results and timing for such an effect. Again, twenty minutes is the general rule.

Step Three

At the end of the oil pulling session, spit the oil combination out in a trash can— not down the drain nor in the toilet (can clog the drain).

Rinse mouth with warm water. Add ½ t salt to 2 oz. water (a good quality sea salt or such) to provide antimicrobial action and cleansing to help rinse any residual mouth toxins.

tips

If experiencing an urge to swallow during an oil pulling session prior to the 20 minute mark, spit the oil out and begin again. Resume the session until the above described change in the liquid has occurred to indicate completion. With practice, these urges diminish over time.

Digestive & Intestinal

THE DIGESTIVE SYSTEM is comprised of the gastrointestinal (GI) tract and is a series of connected organs along a thirty-foot pathway responsible for chewing food, digesting and absorbing nutrients, and expelling waste. The organs involved in the digestive process are the mouth (chewing), the esophagus (swallowing), the stomach (mixing food with digestive juices), small intestine (mixing food with digestive juices of the pancreas, liver/gallbladder, and intestine, and pushing food forward for further digestion), large intestine (absorbing water and nutrients, changing remaining waste into stool), and the rectum (storing and expelling stool from the body).

The digestive tract works closely with the immune system to protect the body from pathogens and invaders. The GI tract is exposed to high quantities of outside substances, including bacteria and viruses, and can almost be considered to be an exterior body surface. Without the immune system (lymphoid tissue in the GI produces about 60 percent of the total immunoglobulin produced daily), the long, dark, moist GI tract would be ideal for pathogenic colonization. In return, the digestive system assists the immune system in protecting the rest of the body by breaking down bacteria and pathogens at various stages, starting with lysozyme in the saliva.

There are over one hundred million neurons embed in the gut, which is more than exist in the spinal column or peripheral nervous system. This mesh-like network of neurons, known as the enteric nervous system (sometimes called the second brain) works together with the central nervous system to oversee every aspect of digestion. It follows then, that brain-gut interactions are highly connected to emotional health; there is a proven correlation between stress, anxiety, and gut disorders such as Crohn's disease and irritable bowel syndrome.

Digestive and eliminative problems are becoming increasingly more prevalent. They create pain, gas, bloating, excessive diarrhea, inability to absorb nutrients, and more. Mood management and emotional health issues are also on the rise. How can the neurons embed in the gut influence healthy emotions when inflammation, blockages, candida, and other harmful bacteria are overpopulated, and system imbalances are standard? They can't.

When digestive system problems are present, natural remedies offer ample opportunity for balance and restoration (see *Candida* for additional understanding of GI tract imbalances). Start with good nutrition, clear the primary pathways of elimination so waste and toxins can be eliminated, use essential oils specifically targeted to help remove harmful bacteria, take a good prebiotic to encourage the growth of good bacteria, and ingest a probiotic to repopulate the gut with live strains of helpful bacteria.Re-establishing health and balance in the gut can literally be a life-changing experience.

top solutions

Single Oils

(Sorted by ailment)

Stomach– black pepper, cardamom, fennel, ginger, peppermint, wild orange

Stomach/intestinal lining– celery seed, grapefruit

Intestines– basil, cardamom, ginger, green mandarin, marjoram, peppermint

Liver– basil, cilantro, geranium, grapefruit, green mandarin, helichrysum, lemon, rosemary

Gallbladder– geranium, grapefruit, turmeric

Pancreas– fennel, geranium, ginger, thyme

Blends

DigestZen®, Tamer™– support digestion and elimination (pgs. 142, 227)

Slim & Sassy®– supports stomach, intestines, pancreas, liver, gallbladder, fat digestion, and satiation (pg. 222)

AromaTouch®– supports peristalsis and bowel tone (pg. 103)

Zendocrine®– supports gallbladder, liver, and pancreas (pg. 251)

Supplements

Adaptiv™ Capsules, Bone Nutrient Complex, DDR Prime® Softgels, **DigestTabs®**, **DigestZen® Softgels** (pg. 258), **GX Assist®** (pg. 260), IQ Mega, Microplex VMz®, **Peppermint Softgels, PB Assist®+** (pg. 264), **TerraZyme®** (pg. 268), xEO Mega®, **Zendocrine® Softgels** (pg. 273), **Zendocrine® Complex** (pg. 272)

usage tips

For best effect on digestive and intestinal activity:

- **Internal:** Place 1-5 drops in water and drink, take in capsule, lick off back of hand, or place drop(s) on or under tongue to allow impact directly in stomach and intestines.
- **Topical:** Apply oils topically on abdomen and/or bottoms of feet for relief.

Related Ailments

- **Digestive:** Abdominal Cramps, Acid Reflux, Bloating, Esophagitis, Flatulence, Food Poisoning [Immune & Lymphatic], Gastritis, GERD, Heartburn, Hemochromatosis, Hernia (Hiatal), Indigestion, Inflammatory Bowel Disease, Metabolism, Motion Sickness, Nausea, Ulcers [Duodenal, Gastric, and Peptic],Stomach ache, Vomiting [Detoxification]
- **Intestinal:** Appendicitis, Celiac, Colitis, Constipation, Crohn's Disease, Diarrhea, Dumping Syndrome, Diverticulitis, Dysentery, Giardia [Immune & Lymphatic], Irritable Bowel Syndrome, Leaky Gut Syndrome, Malabsorption Syndrome
- **Liver and Gallbladder:** Cirrhosis, Liver Disease, Gallbladder Infection, Gallbladder Stones, Jaundice [Children]

By Related Properties

For more, see *Oil Properties* on pages 535-538

Calming– basil, blue tansy, celery seed, copaiba, coriander, jasmine, litsea, oregano, Roman chamomile, sandalwood, tangerine, vetiver, yarrowlpom
Carminative– basil, bergamot, blue tansy, cardamom, cassia, cilantro, cinnamon bark, clary sage, clove, copaiba, coriander, cypress, fennel, ginger, jasmine, juniper berry, lavender, lemon, lemongrass, litsea, melissa, myrrh, neroli, oregano, patchouli, peppermint, Roman chammile, rose, rosemary, sandalwood, spearmint, tangerine, thyme, vetiver, wild orange, wintergreen, yarrowlpom
Detoxifier– arborvitae, cassia, cilantro, citronella, cypress, geranium, green mandarin, lavender, lime, litsea, patchouli, tangerine, turmeric, yarrowlpom
Digestive Stimulant– basil, bergamot, black pepper, cardamom, celery seed, cinnamon bark, clary sage, coriander, fennel, frankincense, grapefruit, helichrysum, juniper berry, lemon eucalyptus, lemongrass, litsea, marjoram, myrrh, oregano, patchouli, spearmint, tangerine, tea tree, wild orange, yarrowlpom
Laxative– bergamot, black pepper, blue tansy, cilantro, copaiba, fennel, ginger, lemongrass, tangerine, yarrowlpom
Regenerative– frankincense, geranium, helichrysum, lavender, manuka, myrrh, neroli, wild orange, yarrowlpom
Stimulant– arborvitae, basil, birch, black pepper, blue tansy, cardamom, cedarwood, cinnamon bark, fennel, ginger, grapefruit, juniper berry, Siberian fir, spearmint, tangerine, thyme, vetiver, wintergreen
Stomachic– basil, cardamom, celery seed, cinnamon bark, clary sage, coriander, fennel, ginger, green mandarin, juniper berry, marjoram, melissa, peppermint, pink pepper, rosemary, tangerine, turmeric, wild orange, yarrowlpom

protocols

DIGEST-EASE: Take 1-2 drops each DigestZen® and Zendrocrine® in a capsule. Apply one or both diluted to ease digestive discomfort, stomach pain, and/or bloating.

SOOTHING BATH: Add 10-15 drops of a favorite digestive/intestinal soothing oil(s) to Epsom salt. Stir oils into salt and place in hot (as is tolerable) bathwater and soak for 20 minutes.

HOT COMPRESS: Apply digestive/intestinal soothing oil(s) with carrier oil to abdomen. Place warm, moist cloth over top to create soothing compress. Repeat as needed.

INTERNALIZE: Take favorite digestive/intestinal soothing oil(s) internally. Methods include: 1-2 drops under tongue and hold for 30 seconds before swallowing, sip a few drops of in a glass of water, and/or take in a capsule. Consume every 20-60 mins. in acute situations until symptoms subside. Then reduce intake to every few hours or twice per day as needed.

MASSAGE MAGIC FOR RELIEF

- Apply oil(s) diluted to upper or lower abdomen, in clockwise motion, depending on location of discomfort.
- Apply oil(s) to bottoms of feet using digestive organ reflexology points provided on charts in *Reflexology* (pg. 23)

NO MORE NAUSEA: Aromatic use of an essential oil can reduce the influence of nausea-triggering smells. Try:

- Diffusing essential oil of choice to dispel offensive smells or toxic fumes.
- Swiping an oil under nose so unpleasant odors are overridden by an essential oil aroma.
- Applying a few drops to palms, cupped over nose, and inhaled as often as needed.

TUMMY SOOTHER: Place 1 drop cardamom in belly button to help eliminate gas and pain or other digestive discomfort.

NAVEL APPLICATION: Place a single drop of selected oil (e.g. DigestZen®) onto navel for digestive and/or intestinal relief.

CIRRHOSIS

Ingredients:

8 drops Zendocrine®
3 drops frankincense
3 drops geranium
4 drops helichrysum
2 drops myrrh
2 drops rosemary
3 drops marjoram

Directions:

Place oils in 10mL roller bottle and fill remainder with fractionated coconut oil. Apply over liver area twice per day.

BEFORE THE BLOAT (IBS RELIEF)

Ingredients:

4 drops frankincense
2 drops peppermint
2 drops fennel
2 drops ginger
2 drops celery seed

Directions:

Combine oils in a capsule. Consume 3x's a day before meals. Add GX Assist®, PB Assist®+, and Microplex VMz® to support, rebuild the gut, and restore natural function.

TRAVELER'S DIARRHEA:

Take 1-2 DigestZen® Softgels or 3-4 drops DigestZen® in a capsule or water 3x's per day.

OR

Take 1 drop each tea tree and DigestZen® under tongue every 30 minutes until symptoms subside.

CONSTIPATION ROLLER BLEND

Ingredients:

7 drops wild orange
5 drops cardamom
4 drops green mandarin
4 drops DigestZen®
2 drops ginger

Directions:

Combine in 10mL roller bottle, topped of with carrier oil. Rub on belly in clockwise motion as often as needed. Take 1 drop of each oil in a capsule to complement.

GUT SUPPORT

Ingredients:

Fractionated coconut oil
2 drops grapefruit or tangerine
2 drops ginger
2 drops blue tansy
1 drop helichrysum

Directions:

Combine oils in 10mL roller bottle and top off with carrier oil. Shake gently to blend. Apply to abdomen and inhale.

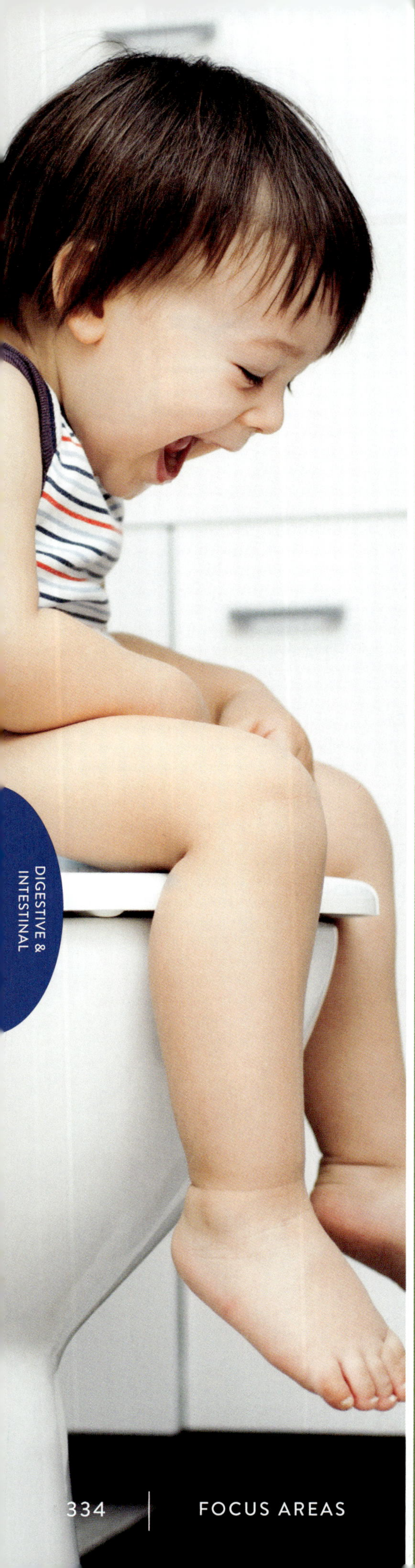

conditions

Abdominal cramps/pain*– basil, birch, cardamom, cinnamon bark, clove, copaiba, fennel, ginger, lavender, lemon eucalyptus, lemongrass, marjoram, melissa, patchouli, peppermint, petitgrain, AromaTouch®, DigestZen®, Forgive®, Passion®, Tamer™, Zendrocrine®

Acid reflux/regurgitation– cardamom, fennel, ginger, lemon, peppermint, thyme, DigestZen®

Alcohol-related conditions– See *Addictions*

Anus, itching– cypress, geranium, helichrysum, lavender, oregano (internal), DDR Prime®, Immortelle

Anus, prolapsed– thyme, wild orange

Appendix– basil, ginger, DigestZen®, Zendrocrine®

Appetite, exaggerated– cassia, cinnamon bark, fennel, ginger, grapefruit, peppermint, Slim & Sassy®

Appetite, reduced/loss of– cardamom, celery seed, ginger, grapefruit, lavender, lemon, wild orange, Motivate®, PastTense®, Peace®, Slim & Sassy®

Belching/burping– cardamom, fennel, ginger, lavender, thyme, vetiver, yarrowlpom, DigestZen®, Zendrocrine®

Bloating/swollen belly– cedarwood, cilantro, ginger, melissa, myrrh, peppermint, pink pepper, tangerine, turmeric, DigestZen®; see *Gaseousness* next page

Bowel constrictions/obstructions– basil, marjoram, rosemary, thyme, Motivate®, Passion®, Zendrocrine®

Bowel inflammation– basil, ginger, peppermint, thyme, DDR Prime®, Zendrocrine®

Bowel, lack of tone– cardamom, ginger, lemongrass, marjoram

Bowel, lining (hyperpermeability/ ulcerations)– basil, celery seed, frankincense, geranium, helichrysum, lavender, lemongrass, myrrh, tulsi, wild orange, DDR Prime®

Bowel, pockets (diverticula)– arborvitae (topical), black pepper, cedarwood(topical), geranium, tangerine, wild orange, Zendrocrine®

Breath, bad (halitosis)– bergamot, cardamom, cilantro, juniper berry, lavender, patchouli, peppermint, spearmint, Cheer®, DDR Prime®, DigestZen®, Slim & Sassy®, Zendrocrine®

Burp, need to– ginger, peppermint

Cirrhosis– frankincense, geranium, helichrysum, lemon, marjoram, myrrh, Roman chamomile, Passion®, Zendrocrine®

Colic– bergamot, black pepper, cardamom, cilantro, clove (dilute), coriander, cypress (topical only), fennel, ginger, lavender, marjoram, Roman chamomile, rosemary, spearmint, wild orange, ylang ylang, Adaptiv™, Cheer®, Console®, DigestZen®, Serenity®, Tamer™

Colon polyps– arborvitae, basil, cardamom, coriander, eucalyptus, frankincense, ginger, lemongrass, peppermint, rosemary, DigestZen®

Constipation/sluggish bowels/inability to defecate despite urgency*– arborvitae, black pepper, cardamom, cilantro, copaiba, Douglas fir, fennel, ginger, green mandarin, lemon, lemon eucalyptus, lemongrass, marjoram, patchouli, peppermint, rosemary, spearmint, tangerine, vetiver, ylang ylang, Console®, DigestZen®, Forgive®, Motivate®, Tamer™, Zendrocrine®

Dehydration– green mandarin, lemon, wild orange, Slim & Sassy®

Diarrhea/urgency to pass stool*– arborvitae, black pepper, cardamom, celery seed, cinnamon bark, clove, coriander, cypress, frankincense, geranium, ginger, jasmine, lemon, lemongrass, melissa, myrrh, patchouli, peppermint, Roman chamomile, spearmint, tangerine, vetiver, wild orange, Cheer®, Console®, DigestZen®, Forgive®, Tamer™, Zendrocrine®

Digestive disorders*– coriander, fennel, ginger, green mandarin, peppermint, tangerine, DigestZen®, Tamer™, Zendrocrine®

Digestion, poor/sluggish*– cassia, cinnamon bark, coriander, geranium, green mandarin, lemon, lemon eucalyptus, spearmint, Motivate®, Tamer™

Distended abdomen (many possible contributors)– cardamom, fennel, ginger, DigestZen®, Zendrocrine®

Diverticulitis– arborvitae, basil, cedarwood, cilantro, cinnamon bark, ginger, lavender, DDR Prime®, DigestZen®, Slim & Sassy®, Zendrocrine®

Failure to thrive– patchouli, DDR Prime®

Fat digestion– grapefruit, lemon, tangerine, Slim & Sassy®

Flatulence– black pepper, celery seed, cilantro, coriander, fennel, ginger, lavender, melissa, myrrh, Roman chamomile, rosemary, sandalwood, spearmint, tangerine, DigestZen®, Slim & Sassy®, Zendrocrine®

Food poisoning– black pepper, cinnamon bark, clove, coriander, juniper berry, lemon, peppermint, oregano, rosemary, tea tree, thyme, DDR Prime®, DigestZen®, Tamer™, Zendrocrine®

Fullness, uncomfortable (lasts longer than it should)– arborvitae, DigestZen®

*See Protocols on pg. 333

Gallbladder, disease– juniper berry, grapefruit, helichrysum, lemongrass

Gallbladder– basil, cypress, geranium, grapefruit, helichrysum, lime, rosemary, tangerine, turmeric, DDR Prime®, Slim & Sassy®, Zendrocrine®

Gallstones– bergamot, birch, celery seed, cilantro, clove, geranium, grapefruit, juniper berry, lavender, lemon, lime, patchouli, rosemary, wild orange, wintergreen, DDR Prime®, Forgive®, Peace®, Zendrocrine®

Gaseousness/bloating– bergamot mint, black pepper, blue tansy, cardamom, cilantro, cinnamon bark, clove, fennel, frankincense, geranium, ginger, green mandarin, lavender, lemongrass, lime, melissa, neroli, peppermint, pink pepper, turmeric, DigestZen®, Peace®, Tamer™

Gastric juices, poor production of– cinnamon bark

Heartburn– black pepper, cardamom, cedarwood (topical), fennel, ginger, green mandarin, lemon, peppermint, wild orange, DDR Prime®, DigestZen®, Slim & Sassy®, Zendrocrine®

Hemorrhoids– cypress, geranium, helichrysum, myrrh, patchouli, Roman chamomile, yarrowlpom, DDR Prime®, DigestZen®, Zendrocrine®

Hiatal hernia– arborvitae, basil, cypress, ginger, helichrysum, melissa, patchouli, peppermint, Zendrocrine®

Hunger pains– fennel, lavender, Slim & Sassy®

Indigestion*– arborvitae, black pepper, blue tansy, ginger, lavender, lemon, lemongrass, melissa, neroli, peppermint, spearmint, thyme, turmeric, ylang ylang, DigestZen®, Passion®, Slim & Sassy®, Tamer™

Indigestion, nervous– cardamom, Tamer™

Inflammation, gut/intestinal– copaiba, fennel, ginger, lemongrass, peppermint, Roman chamomile, spearmint, thyme, tulsi, turmeric, DigestZen®, Passion®

Intestinal parasites– blue tansy, citronella, clove, fennel, lemon eucalyptus, oregano, ravintsara, thyme, tulsi

Intestinal peristalsis, lack of/spastic– marjoram, neroli, AromaTouch®, DigestZen®

Jaundice/excess bilirubin– basil, frankincense, geranium, helichrysum, juniper berry, lemon, lemongrass, lime, rosemary, wild orange, Purify, Slim & Sassy®, Zendrocrine®

Lactose issues– cardamom, coriander, lemongrass, DDR Prime®, DigestZen®, TerraZyme®, Zendrocrine®

Leaky gut/gut permeability/weak intestinal lining/malabsorption– arborvitae, cardamom, ginger, grapefruit, lemongrass, myrrh, patchouli, tulsi, DDR Prime®, DigestZen®

Liver– basil, cilantro, clove, copaiba, cypress, frankincense, geranium, ginger, grapefruit, helichrysum, jasmine, juniper berry, lemon, rosemary, Cheer®, Console®, DDR Prime®, Forgive®, Zendrocrine®

Liver, blocked bile duct/obstruction– cumin, cypress, geranium, marjoram, patchouli, Zendrocrine®

Liver congestion– geranium, helichrysum, peppermint, rose, rosemary, Motivate®

Liver, fatty– grapefruit, lemon, rosemary, turmeric, Slim & Sassy®

Liver headaches/migraines– grapefruit, helichrysum, Zendrocrine®

Liver, hepatitis– copaiba, frankincense, geranium, helichrysum, jasmine, lemon, myrrh, tea tree, Zendrocrine®

Liver, low bile production– geranium, green mandarin, helichrysum, lavender, peppermint, Roman chamomile, rosemary, Zendrocrine®

Liver, overloaded/sluggish/toxic- celery seed, cilantro, clove, helichrysum, lemon, Motivate®, Zendrocrine®

Liver, scarring– helichrysum, myrrh

Liver, weak– celery seed, geranium, lemon, lime, Roman chamomile, rose

Nausea/motion sickness*– basil, black pepper, cardamom, cassia, clove, coriander, fennel, ginger, lavender, melissa, patchouli, peppermint, petitgrain, pink pepper, Roman chamomile, rosemary, sandalwood, spearmint, DigestZen®, Forgive®, Peace®, Slim & Sassy®, Zendrocrine®

Pancreas*– basil, cinnamon bark, coriander, fennel, frankincense, geranium, ginger, DDR Prime®, On Guard®, Slim & Sassy®

Pancreatic, duct blocked– cardamom, helichrysum, Zendrocrine®

Rectal bleeding– geranium, helichrysum, DDR Prime®

Rectal, fissures– geranium, helichrysum, Zendrocrine®

Rectal pain– frankincense, geranium, helichrysum, Zendrocrine®

Saliva, lack of– cardamom

Spasms, digestive– cardamom, cassia, cinnamon bark, clove, coriander, fennel, spearmint, tangerine, wild orange, Forgive®, Passion®, Tamer™

Spasms, esophageal– wild orange

Stomach, ache/cramp/pain/inflammation*– basil, cardamom, cinnamon bark, coriander, ginger, helichrysum, peppermint, Roman chamomile, sandalwood, ylang ylang, Citrus Bliss®, Console®, DDR Prime®, DigestZen®, Tamer™, Zendrocrine®

Stomach flu (viral gastroenteritis)– arborvitae, oregano, tea tree, thyme, Citrus Bliss® (topical), On Guard®, Zendrocrine®

Stomach, lack of tone– black pepper, rose, tangerine

Stomach lining– celery seed

Stomach, nervous (due to worry/anxiety/stress)– black spruce, cardamom, wild orange, Balance®, Serenity®

Stomach, upset (indigestion)*– cardamom, cinnamon bark, clove, fennel, frankincense, ginger, grapefruit, jasmine, lavender, thyme, wild orange, Citrus Bliss® (topical), Forgive®, Tamer™

Stools, bloody– frankincense, geranium, helichrysum (bleeding); birch, wild orange, wintergreen (ulcer)

Stools, mucus– black pepper, On Guard®, Zendrocrine®

Stools, pale in color/clay-like– Zendrocrine®, DigestZen® Softgels

Swallowing, difficulty (dysphagia)– arborvitae, black pepper, frankincense, lavender, peppermint, wild orange, DDR Prime®, Serenity®

Swallowing, painful/tight throat– cardamom, wild orange, On Guard®, Zendrocrine®

Ulcer, duodenal (located in duodenum/upper intestines)– birch, bergamot, ginger, fennel, frankincense, geranium, myrrh, wintergreen, Adaptiv™, Deep Blue®, DDR Prime®, DigestZen®, Purify, Zendrocrine®

Ulcer, gastric (located in stomach)– bergamot, birch, blue tansy, celery seed, frankincense, geranium, green mandarin, myrrh, peppermint, rose, turmeric, wintergreen, yarrowlpom, Adaptiv™, Console®, DDR Prime®, DigestZen®, Zendrocrine®

Vomiting– basil, black pepper, cardamom, cassia, clove, fennel, geranium, ginger, melissa, patchouli, peppermint, pink pepper, sandalwood, tea tree, Console®, DigestZen®, Purify, Tamer™, Zendrocrine®

Yeast– See *Candida*

Eating Disorders

See also Limbic

EATING DISORDERS comprise a group of serious disruptions in eating behavior and weight regulation that adversely impact physical, psychological, and social well-being. The most common are anorexia nervosa, bulimia nervosa, and binge-eating disorder. While an individual may start by simply eating more or less food than normal, the tendency increases until he or she is eating portions outside of a healthy range and the urge to manage weight or food intake spirals out of control. While the majority of those with eating disorders are women, men have them also. An exception is binge-eating disorder, which appears to affect almost as many men as women.

Eating disorders are often accompanied by depression, substance abuse, or anxiety disorders. While they can become life-threatening if proper care is not received, it is important to remember that they are treatable medical illnesses. Such treatments usually involve psychotherapy, nutrition education, family counseling, medications, and may include hospitalization.

Anorexia nervosa is characterized by an obsession with food and being thin, even to the point of near starvation. Symptoms of this disorder may include refusal to eat and denial of hunger, intense fear of weight gain, excessive exercising, lack of emotion, irritability, fear of eating in public, social withdrawal, trouble sleeping, menstrual irregularities or loss of menstruation (amenorrhea), constipation, abdominal pain, dry skin, irregular heart rhythms.

Alternating episodes of binging and purging are the primary symptoms of bulimia nervosa. During these episodes, an individual typically eats a large amount of food in a short duration and then tries to expel the extra calories through vomiting or excessive exercise. Additional symptoms may include eating to the point of discomfort or pain, laxative use, an unhealthy focus on body shape and weight, going to the bathroom after eating or during meals, abnormal bowel function, damaged teeth and gums, and swollen salivary glands in the cheeks.

Even though eating disorders manifest as a physical condition with physical consequences, many experts in the field believe that they actually originate from an individual's mental or emotional state. Many individuals with eating disorders may suffer from low self-esteem or self-worth or even feel helpless and thus choose to control something that is in their immediate control (the food that does or does not go into their body). Due to the unique direct relationship between emotional and physical well being with eating disorders, natural remedies can be a very effective part of treatment since they can support individuals emotionally as they work with professionals to learn new habits and ways of coping.

Essential oils have a powerful effect on the brain. Aromas have direct access through the olfactory senses, which connect directly to glands and areas such as the hypothalamus and amygdala, allowing oils to initiate rapid responses both physically and emotionally in the brain and the rest of the body. Inhalation and aromatic exposure are powerful methods of impacting the brain with essential oils. Oils offer an extremely effective way of supporting the body with eating disorders.

top solutions

Single Oils

Grapefruit— helps heal relationship with body, curb cravings, and balance appetite (pg. 154)

Patchouli— supports restoring connection to and acceptance of body (pg. 200)

Bergamot— helps with addictions and dopamine levels, balances hormones, promotes sense of self-worth (pg. 107)

Cinnamon bark, Tulsi— balance glucose levels and metabolism; promote sense of safety (pgs. 126, 236)

Copaiba— supports healthy dopamine levels (pg. 136)

Blends

Slim & Sassy®— balances metabolism/insulin levels (pg. 222)

Balance®— balances emotions and promotes a feeling of tranquility (pg. 104)

Purify— encourages release of toxic emotions (pg. 208)

Adaptiv™— promotes emotional agility and resiliency (pg. 96)

Supplements

Adaptiv™ Capsules (pg. 253), Alpha CRS®+, **DigestZen® Softgels** (pg. 258), **Microplex VMz®** (pg. 261), PB Assist®+, Phytoestrogen Complex, TerraGreens®, **TerraZyme®** (pg. 268), xEO Mega®

usage tips

Best methods of use for eating disorders:

- **Aromatic:** Have oils of choice on hand to diffuse, inhale directly from bottle or cupped hands, swipe under nose, wear as a perfume/cologne, and place on clothing, bedding, and jewelry.
- **Internal:**
  - Drink oils to satisfy cravings or compulsions by placing a few drops in water.
  - Plan ahead for typical cravings by taking supportive oils in a capsule prior to when urges hit.
  - For more instant effects, lick a drop off back of hand to help pacify a craving.
  - Apply oils to roof of mouth. Place oil on pad of thumb and then place pad on roof of mouth.
- **Topical:** Apply under nose, behind ears, to base of skull (especially in suboccipital triangles), and forehead. For daily grounding, apply to bottoms of feet.

Related Ailments

Anorexia Nervosa (AN) [Weight], Avoidant/Restrictive Food Intake Disorder (ARFID), Binge Eating Disorder (BED), Bulimia Nervosa (BN) [Weight], Night Eating Syndrome (NES) [Sleep, Weight], Pica, Purging Disorder, Rumination Disorder

By Related Properties

For more, see *Oil Properties* on pages 535-538

Analgesic— basil, birch, blue tansy, cinnamon bark, clary sage, copaiba, cypress, eucalyptus, frankincense, ginger, helichrysum, jasmine, lavender, lemongrass, litsea, tea tree, oregano, ravintsara, Siberian fir, turmeric, wintergreen, yarrowlpom

Antidepressant— bergamot, cinnamon bark, clary sage, frankincense, geranium, lavender, lemon, lemongrass, neroli, patchouli, pink pepper, rose, sandalwood, tangerine, wild orange, ylang ylang

Antispasmodic— black pepper, blue tansy, cardamom, cassia, clary sage, clove, cypress, fennel, ginger, helichrysum, jasmine, lavender, lemon, litsea, marjoram, melissa, neroli, peppermint, ravintsara, rosemary, sandalwood, Siberian fir, spearmint, tangerine, vetiver, wintergreen, yarrowlpom

Calming— bergamot, black pepper, blue tansy, clary sage, copaiba, coriander, geranium, juniper berry, lavender, litsea, oregano, Roman chamomile, tangerine, vetiver, yarrowlpom

Carminative— bergamot, blue tansy, cassia, clary sage, clove, copaiba, fennel, green mandarin, jasmine, juniper berry, lemongrass, litsea, neroli, patchouli, peppermint, sandalwood, spearmint, tangerine, turmeric, wintergreen, yarrowlpom

Energizing— basil, clove, grapefruit, lemongrass, peppermint, rosemary, Siberian fir, tangerine, wild orange, yarrowlpom

Grounding— black spruce, blue tansy, clary sage, cypress, magnolia, tea tree, Siberian fir, vetiver

Relaxing— blue tansy, cassia, cedarwood, clary sage, cypress, lavender, litsea, manuka, magnolia, marjoram, neroli, ravintsara, Roman chamomile, ylang ylang

Stomachic— blue tansy, cardamom, cinnamon bark, clary sage, fennel, ginger, melissa, pink pepper, rosemary, tangerine, turmeric, wild orange, yarrowlpom

conditions

Abdominal pain— ginger, lavender; see *Digestive & Intestinal*

Abuse, history of, healing from— frankincense, melissa, Roman chamomile; see *Mood & Behavior*

Anger— basil, bergamot, black spruce, cedarwood, frankincense, helichrysum, magnolia, Roman chamomile, rose, Balance®, InTune®, Serenity®; see *Mood & Behavior*

Anorexia*— bergamot, black pepper, cardamom, cinnamon bark, coriander, frankincense, ginger, grapefruit, melissa, patchouli, Roman chamomile, rose, vetiver, Citrus Bliss®, Elevation, Peace®, Serenity®, Slim & Sassy®

Anxiety— bergamot, black spruce, cedarwood, clary sage, frankincense, green mandarin, lavender, magnolia, pink pepper, tangerine, tulsi, turmeric, vanilla, vetiver, wild orange, yarrow|pom, Adaptiv™, Balance®, InTune®, Peace®, Serenity®; see *Mood & Behavior*

Apathetic/emotionally flat/lack of emotion— lime, ylang ylang; see *Mood & Behavior*

Appetite, lack of/refusal to eat— blue tansy, cardamom, fennel, grapefruit, Slim & Sassy®, red mandarin; see *Digestive & Intestinal*

Appetite, loss of control— ginger, peppermint, Slim & Sassy®; see *Digestive & Intestinal, Weight*

Binging/overeating until "stuffed"*— basil, cedarwood, cinnamon bark, ginger, grapefruit, peppermint, thyme, Elevation, Slim & Sassy®

Bulimia*— arborvitae, bergamot, cinnamon bark, ginger, grapefruit, melissa, patchouli, Balance®, DigestZen®, Forgive®, Passion®, Slim & Sassy®

Cold, frequently being— black pepper, cassia, cinnamon bark, ginger, oregano, patchouli; see *Cardiovascular*

Constipation— cardamom, cilantro, fennel, ginger, green mandarin, lavender, lemongrass, marjoram, DigestZen®, Tamer™, Zendrocrine®; see *Digestive & Intestinal*

Control, feeling out of, of behavior— black spruce, Adaptiv™; see *Mood & Behavior*

Dehydration— cypress, juniper berry; see *Urinary*

Denial of hunger— cardamom, fennel, Slim & Sassy®

Depression— bergamot, grapefruit, magnolia, wild orange, ylang ylang, Adaptiv™, Cheer®, Citrus Bliss®, Elevation; see *Mood & Behavior*

Digestive issues— cardamom, fennel, ginger, green mandarin, peppermint, lavender, DigestZen®, Tamer™; see *Digestive & Intestinal*

Dry skin— cedarwood, geranium, myrrh, patchouli, sandalwood, Immortelle; see *Integumentary*

Emotionality/overly emotional— cypress, geranium, vanilla, Adaptiv™

Excessive exercising— cypress, patchouli, vetiver, Balance®, Purify

Expressing/managing emotions/feelings, difficulty— Balance®, InTune®; see *Mood & Behavior*

Family patterns/runs in family— cedarwood, lemon, Siberian fir

Fear of eating in public— cardamom, wild orange, Serenity®, Slim & Sassy®

Guilt— bergamot, coriander, geranium, lemon, Siberian fir, Breathe®, HD Clear®, Purify, TerraShield®

Gum damage— clove, myrrh, Immortelle; see *Oral Health*

Helpless— cedarwood, clove, ginger, Siberian fir, tangerine, Citrus Bliss®, DigestZen®, On Guard®, PastTense®

Hormone imbalance— See *Men's* or *Women's Health*

Impatient— basil, vanilla, Breathe®, ClaryCalm®, Elevation, PastTense®

Intense fear of gaining weight— cypress, juniper berry, melissa

Irregular heartbeat (arrhythmia)— basil, lavender, ylang ylang; see *Cardiovascular*

Irritability— coriander, jasmine, Roman chamomile, rose, tangerine; see *Mood & Behavior*

Loneliness— black spruce, cedarwood, frankincense, marjoram, myrrh, Roman chamomile, Citrus Bliss®, Immortelle, Purify,

Low blood pressure— basil, cardamom, helichrysum, lavender, lime, rosemary, thyme, DDR Prime®, Purify; see *Cardiovascular*

Low self-esteem/self-worth— bergamot, cassia, grapefruit, jasmine, lemon, patchouli, rose, spearmint, tangerine, Slim & Sassy®; see *Mood & Behavior*

Menstrual irregularities or loss of menstruation (amenorrhea)— basil, clary sage, fennel, geranium, juniper berry, rosemary, ylang ylang, ClaryCalm®; see *Women's Health*

Obsessive/compulsive— oregano, Adaptiv™, Balance®, Serenity®; see *Mood & Behavior*

Out of sync with natural urges of body— ravintsara, thyme, Forgive®

People-pleasing— black pepper, cinnamon bark, lavender, lime, peppermint, Purify

Perfectionistic— cypress, melissa, tangerine, Balance®, TerraShield®

Preoccupation with food— cypress, grapefruit, lavender, vetiver, Elevation

Purging urge— Douglas fir, lime, patchouli, rose, tangerine, wintergreen, Slim & Sassy®, Zendrocrine®

Self image, distorted/negative— bergamot, grapefruit, spearmint, Slim & Sassy®

Shame— bergamot, cypress, Douglas fir, frankincense, thyme, On Guard®

Shame, body— grapefruit, patchouli, Slim & Sassy®

Social withdrawal— cassia, cinnamon bark, cedarwood, frankincense, ginger, myrrh, spearmint

Sores, throat and mouth— frankincense, lemon, melissa, myrrh, tea tree, thyme, Breathe®, DDR Prime®; see *Oral Health*

Sores, scars, calluses on knuckles or hands— see *Integumentary*

Stress— black spruce, frankincense, lavender, lime, ylang ylang, wild orange, Adaptiv™, Citrus Bliss®, Elevation, Serenity®; see *Stress*

Swollen salivary glands in cheeks— marjoram, vetiver, Citrus Bliss®, Elevation, PastTense®, Purify

Teeth damage— birch, clove, helichrysum, wintergreen, On Guard®; see *Oral Health*

Trouble sleeping— basil, lavender, Roman chamomile, vetiver, Serenity®; see *Sleep*

Vomiting, addiction to forcing— Douglas fir, fennel, ginger, grapefruit, lavender, DigestZen®, Slim & Sassy®

*See Protocols →

protocols

ANOREXIC ASSIST

Ingredients:

2 drops vetiver
4 drops bergamot

Directions:

Combine and diffuse around meal times or during times of vulnerability. Apply Peace® or Adaptiv™ to calm unhealthy behaviors.

BULIMIA OR ANOREXIA

- Place 1 drop bergamot, grapefruit, and/or DigestZen® under tongue each morning.
- Inhale and/or diffuse emotional oils(s) of choice throughout day.
- Take in water or a capsule. Choose from bergamot, cinnamon bark, grapefruit, melissa, patchouli, thyme, DigestZen®, and/or Slim & Sassy®. Use individually or combine as desired.

Example regime:

- Drink 5 drops Slim & Sassy® in glass of water 3x's per day.
- Wear 3 drops patchouli + 2 drops bergamot as a perfume on wrists and neck.
- Take 1 drop cinnamon bark, 2 drops melissa, and 1 drop thyme in a capsule.

OVEREATING CONTROL

Ingredients:

2 drops black pepper
1 drops ginger
2 drops grapefruit
2 drops peppermint

Directions:

Apply to bottoms of feet and take in a capsule before eating. Additionally, diffuse any or all of the listed oils.

KILL SUGAR CRAVINGS

Choose one or more as needed:

- Basil or tulsi (smell)
- Cinnamon bark (lick, capsule)
- Grapefruit (drink, smell, capsule)
- Thyme (capsule)
- Slim & Sassy® (drink, capsule)

For more ideas, download the app on Android or iOS.

Endocrine

ENDOCRINE

THE ENDOCRINE SYSTEM consists of glands in the body that produce and secrete hormones directly into the circulatory system. The hormones travel to targeted organs and tissues, which bind only to cells with necessary specific receptor sites. The endocrine system is responsible for bodily functions and processes such as cell growth, tissue function, sleep, sexual and reproductive functions, metabolism, blood sugar management, injury and stress management, energy, water and electrolyte balance, and more. It basically tells the cells in the body exactly what to do.

The glands of the endocrine system include the pituitary gland (the master gland which helps regulate the others within the endocrine system), pineal gland, thyroid and parathyroid glands, adrenal glands, hypothalamus, thalamus, pancreas, gastrointestinal tract and reproductive glands (ovaries/testicles). Many organs that are part of other body systems (such as the liver, kidneys, and heart) also secrete hormones, and this is recognized as a secondary endocrine function. The exocrine system also secretes hormones but uses glands with ducts, such as sweat glands or salivary glands to deliver these secretions.

Endocrine disorders are common and include such conditions as obesity, thyroid malfunction, and diabetes. Endocrine disorders typically occur when hormone levels are too high or too low, a condition that can be caused by unregulated hormone release, cellular messaging problems (lack of response to signaling), when endocrine glands are not operating at full capacity, or when important organs/tissues become enlarged or malfunctioned.

Stress, electrolyte or fluid imbalances in the blood, infection, tumors, and medication can also affect endocrine function. Hypofunction of endocrine glands means there isn't enough endocrine activity, whereas hyperfunction refers to too much activity; both types of imbalance can cause serious problems.

Because of the unique delivery system of the endocrine system, the hormones travel to targeted organs and tissues, which bind only to cells with necessary specific receptor sites. Essential oils are able to profoundly benefit cells they encounter throughout the body as they circulate. There are also specific oils that have been shown to be incredibly supportive of certain gland/organ functions. Individuals can work together with their medical providers, when necessary, to consider the benefits of natural solutions as well as modern medical treatment options.

top solutions

Single Oils

Frankincense, Sandalwood— for pineal, pituitary, and hypothalamus support (pgs. 151, 218)

Geranium, Tulsi, Ylang ylang— for hormone/glandular and adrenal support (pgs. 152, 236, 250)

Blue tansy, Clove, Lemongrass— for thyroid support (pgs. 114, 134, 180)

Basil, Rosemary— stimulate glands and brain function; and provide adrenal support (pgs. 105, 216)

Blends

DDR Prime®— nerve repair; glandular support (pg. 140)

Zendrocrine®— adrenal and glandular support (pg. 251)

Supplements

a2Z Chewable™, **Adaptiv™ Capsules** (pg. 253), Alpha CRS®+, Bone Nutrient Complex, **DDR Prime® Softgels** (pg. 256), IQ Mega®, Microplex VMz®, **Mito2Max®** (pg. 262), **xEO Mega®** (pg. 271), YarrowlPom Capsules

General Gland Support

Adrenal— basil, geranium, rosemary, tulsi, ylang ylang, Citrus Bliss®, Citrus Bloom™, Zendrocrine®

Glandular sluggishness— black spruce, citronella, clove, DDR Prime®

Hypothalamus— cardamom, cedarwood, clove, frankincense, jasmine, sandalwood, Siberian fir, Balance®, DDR Prime®, InTune®

Pancreas— basil, cassia, cinnamon bark, coriander, eucalyptus, fennel, geranium, ginger, grapefruit, helichrysum, jasmine, lavender, lemon, lemongrass, oregano, rosemary, wild orange, ylang ylang, Cheer®, On Guard®, Serenity®, Slim & Sassy®

Parathyroid— basil, clary sage, clove, geranium, ginger, melissa, Roman chamomile, Balance®, ClaryCalm®

Pineal— arborvitae, basil, cedarwood, frankincense, helichrysum, lavender, sandalwood, Balance®, Immortelle

Pituitary— basil, black spruce, cedarwood, frankincense, geranium, ginger, patchouli, sandalwood, ylang ylang, Abōde™, Citrus Bliss®, DDR Prime®, On Guard®, Purify

Thalamus— clary sage, frankincense, jasmine, melissa, Siberian fir, vetiver, Abōde™, Purify

Thymus— blue tansy, clary sage, lemongrass, Breathe®, On Guard®; see *Immune & Lymphatic*

Thyroid— blue tansy, clove, geranium, lemongrass, myrrh, DDR Prime®, On Guard®, Purify

usage tips

For endocrine support, a variety of methods can be successful. Suggestions:

- **Internal:** Consume selected oils in capsule, under tongue, or place in water to drink.
- **Topical:** Apply selected oils directly over location of gland and on bottoms of feet on reflex points (see *Reflexology*) twice daily. Use a carrier oil to prevent sensitivity.
- **Aromatic:** Diffuse 5-10 drops of oils of choice and/or inhale from bottle or self-made blend. Apply a few drops to clothing or use other inhalation methods.

Related Ailments

- **Adrenal:** Addison's Disease [located in Autoimmune], Adrenal Fatigue/Exhaustion, Cortisol Imbalance, Cushing's Syndrome
- **Pancreas:** Pancreatitis; for pancreas ailments related to blood sugar management see *Blood Sugar*
- **Thyroid:** Goiter, Night sweats [Immune & Lymphatic, Women's Health], Grave's Disease [located in Autoimmune], Hashimoto's Disease [located in Autoimmune], Hyperthyroidism, Hypothyroidism, Silent Thyroiditis, Thyroid
- **Additional Endocrine Ailments:** Acromegaly, Endocrine System, Glands, Growth Problems, Melatonin Imbalances/Insufficiencies, Parathyroid, Pineal, Pituitary, Precocious Puberty, Schmidt's Syndrome (adrenals, thyroid) [located in Autoimmune], Thymus, Turner Syndrome

By Related Properties

For more, see *Oil Properties* on pages 535-538

Anti-inflammatory— arborvitae, basil, blue tansy, cassia, cinnamon bark, clary sage, clove, copaiba, eucalyptus, fennel, helichrysum, jasmine, lemongrass, litsea, manuka, myrrh, neroli, patchouli, peppermint, pink pepper, rosemary, Siberian fir, spikenard, tangerine, turmeric, yarrowlpom

Calming— basil, black pepper, blue tansy, cassia, copaiba, frankincense, green mandarin, juniper berry, litsea, magnolia, melissa, oregano, Roman chamomile, tangerine, yarrowlpom

Detoxifier— arborvitae, cilantro, citronella, geranium, green mandarin, lime, litsea, tangerine, turmeric, yarrowlpom

Regenerative— clove, coriander, helichrysum, manuka, neroli, sandalwood, wild orange, yarrowlpom

Relaxing— blue tansy, cedarwood, clary sage, geranium, litsea, manuka, marjoram, myrrh, neroli

Sedative— basil, bergamot, blue tansy, coriander, geranium, lavender, magnolia, melissa, neroli, patchouli, rose, spikenard, tangerine, ylang ylang, yarrowlpom

Stimulant— basil, blue tansy, cardamom, cinnamon bark, coriander, ginger, grapefruit, myrrh, Siberian fir, spearmint, tangerine

Uplifting— bergamot, clary sage, lemon, litsea, tangerine

Vasodilator— lemongrass, marjoram, rosemary, Siberian fir, thyme

conditions

Adrenal

Adrenal cortex, sluggish– basil, cinnamon bark, frankincense, geranium, rosemary, DDR Prime®, On Guard®, Zendocrine®

Adrenal fatigue/exhaustion– basil, black pepper, black spruce, geranium, ginger, rosemary, tulsi, wild orange, ylang ylang, Citrus Bliss®, Console®, Motivate®, Passion®, Zendrocrine®; see *Energy & Vitality*

Constantly feeling sick– bergamot, lemon, DDR Prime®, On Guard®, Zendrocrine®; see *Immune & Lymphatic*

Cortisol, balance– basil, bergamot, black spruce, clove, lavender, magnolia, rosemary, tulsi, wild orange, ylang ylang, Adaptiv™

Cortisol, high– black spruce, cedarwood, clary sage, geranium, lavender, magnolia, marjoram, neroli, ylang ylang, Adaptiv™

Cortisol, low– basil, birch, thyme, wintergreen

DHEA levels– clary sage, frankincense, geranium, lavender, Roman chamomile, ylang ylang, Whisper®

Difficulty concentrating– cedarwood, vetiver, InTune®; see *Focus & Concentration*

Mild depression– basil, bergamot, geranium, jasmine, magnolia, lavender, wild orange, Cheer®, Citrus Bliss®, Citrus Bloom™, Elevation; see *Mood & Behavior*

Trouble sleeping– lavender; see *Sleep*

Weight gain– ginger, grapefruit, lemon, Slim & Sassy®; see "Thyroid" below, *Weight*

Pancreas

Blood sugar issues (too high/too low)– See *Blood Sugar*

Eyesight, poor/vision– coriander, frankincense, geranium, helichrysum, lemongrass, sandalwood, tulsi, DDR Prime®, Immortelle

Hunger pains– fennel, peppermint; see *Digestive & Intestinal*

Low sex drive– cinnamon, clary sage, jasmine, ylang ylang, Whisper®; see *Intimacy*

Obesity– cinnamon bark, fennel, ginger, grapefruit, lemon, peppermint, Slim & Sassy®; see *Weight*

Pancreatic duct, congested/blocked– cardamom, clary sage, geranium, green mandarin, helichrysum, rosemary

Pancreas, congested– grapefruit, tulsi, Zendrocrine®; see *Detoxification*

Pancreas sluggish/under-active*– black pepper, helichrysum, lime, Passion®

Pancreas support*– cinnamon bark, fennel, frankincense, geranium, ginger, tulsi, Cheer®, Passion®, Slim & Sassy®

Pancreatitis– basil, cinnamon bark, coriander, geranium, lemon, marjoram, rosemary, thyme, DDR Prime®, On Guard®, Slim & Sassy®, Zendrocrine®; see *Immune & Lymphatic*

Urinary issues associated with pancreatic/blood sugar imbalances– juniper berry, tulsi; see *Blood Sugar, Urinary*

Thyroid

Body temp, cold– black pepper, cinnamon bark, clove, eucalyptus, ginger, rosemary, On Guard®, Slim & Sassy®; see *Cardiovascular* "Warming" property

Cold intolerance– black pepper, cinnamon bark, eucalyptus; see *Cardiovascular* "Warming" property

Compromise– basil

Constipation– cardamom, ginger, DigestZen®; see *Digestive & Intestinal*

Grave's disease– clove, frankincense, ginger, lemongrass, rosemary, On Guard®, Slim & Sassy®; see *Autoimmune*

Hashimoto's– blue tansy, frankincense, ginger, lemongrass, myrrh, patchouli, rosemary, DDR Prime®, On Guard®, Zendrocrine®; see *Autoimmune*

Hair falling out– arborvitae, cedarwood, clary sage, Douglas fir, eucalyptus, frankincense, geranium, juniper berry, Roman chamomile, rosemary, sandalwood, tulsi, wintergreen, yarrowlpom, ylang ylang, DDR Prime®, Whisper®; see *Integumentary*

Heat intolerance– eucalyptus, peppermint, spearmint, PastTense®, Tamer™

Hyperthyroid*– black spruce, cedarwood, clary sage, clove, frankincense, geranium, ginger, jasmine, juniper berry, lavender, lemon, lemongrass, myrrh, neroli, peppermint, rosemary, sandalwood, ylang ylang, DDR Prime®

Hypothyroid*– bergamot, black pepper, blue tansy, cedarwood, clove, frankincense, geranium, ginger, lemongrass, myrrh, peppermint, spearmint, DDR Prime®, Zendrocrine®

Overheated/night sweats/hot flashes– cedarwood, clary sage, eucalyptus, ginger, lemon, lime, peppermint, AromaTouch®, ClaryCalm®, PastTense®, spearmint, Whisper®; see "Hypothyroid" above, *Blood Sugar*, *Women's Health*

Thyroid hormones, false– lemongrass, myrrh, neroli; see *Candida*

*See Protocols →

For more ideas, download the app on Android or iOS.

protocols

GLANDULAR HEALTH BASIC PROGRAM

Supplement daily with:

Microplex VMz®
xEO Mega®
Mito2Max®
Alpha CRS®+

Choose to add one or both for additional support:

DDR Prime® and/or Slim & Sassy®.
Consider candida program— See *Candida*

ADRENAL ENERGY PUMP UP— Take Mito2Max® 2 capsules twice per day.

ADRENAL AID

Ingredients:

3 drops tulsi
5 drops lemon
8 drops basil
8 drops rosemary

Directions:

Combine in a 10mL bottle/roller bottle and fill remainder with carrier oil. Apply above kidneys (on both sides of back just below rib cage). Follow with a warm, damp washcloth as a compress.

SIMPLE ADRENAL SUPPORT

Take 2 drops basil and/or rosemary in water or under tongue 1-2x's per day. Massage diluted over adrenal area.

PANCREATIC PROMOTER

Ingredients:

30 drops basil
25 drops Zendocrine®
25 drops DDR Prime®

Directions:

Combine in 10mL roller bottle. Fill remainder with carrier oil. Apply over pancreas (on abdomen just below sternum) morning and evening for pancreatic support.

THYROID BOOST

Ingredients:

20 drops clove
20 drops myrrh
25 drops frankincense
15 drops lemongrass
10 drops peppermint

Directions:

Combine in a 10mL roller bottle. Fill remainder with carrier oil. Apply at least once daily over thyroid area (on both sides of neck).

INTERNAL THYROID ASSIST

Ingredients:

- Take DDR Prime® Softgels AM and PM.
- Take 2 drops each frankincense, clove, peppermint and 1 drop each myrrh and lemongrass in a capsule 3x's per day.

THYROID CALMER

Ingredients:

1 drop myrrh
1 drop DDR Prime®

Directions:

Apply with carrier oil to thyroid area on both sides of neck and on bottoms of feet, focusing on base of big toe.

THYROID REMEDIES

- Use one of following recipes in 10mL roller bottle. Initially, apply to thyroid area and/or bottoms of feet 2-4x's per day to boost activity. As progress is made, apply 1-2x's per day.
  - **Recipe #1:** 10 drops myrrh, 10 drops lemongrass, 2-3 drops clove, 2-3 drops peppermint. Add carrier oil to fill.
  - **Recipe #2:** 25 drops each lemongrass, clove, peppermint. Fill remainder with carrier oil.

Other variations:

- Apply 1 drop of any single thyroid oil alone or combine with one or two others to thyroid area twice per day. Use with carrier oil.

Choose from:

- Clove, frankincense, lemongrass, myrrh, Immortelle
- OR trade off weekly— first week, lemongrass and myrrh; second week, geranium and Balance®; repeat.

Energy & Vitality

LACK OF ENERGY or diminished vitality can be described as tiredness, weariness, lethargy or fatigue and can contribute to symptoms like depression, decreased motivation, or apathy. Lack of energy can be a normal response to inadequate sleep, overexertion, overworking, stress, lack of exercise, or even boredom. When lack of energy is part of a normal response, it's often resolved with adequate rest and sleep, stress management, and good nutrition.

Persistent lack of energy that does not resolve with routine self-care may be an indication of an underlying physical or psychological disorder. Common causes may include allergies and asthma, anemia, cancer and its treatments, chronic pain, heart disease, infection, depression, eating disorders, grief, sleeping disorders, thyroid problems, medication side effects, alcohol use, or drug use.

Observing patterns and symptoms of lack of energy may be helpful in discovering its cause. Persistent fatigue with no clear diagnosis may result from chronic fatigue syndrome, which can start with a flu-like illness and may not be relieved with rest. Other symptoms, such as cognitive difficulties, long-term exhaustion and illness after activity, muscle or joint pain, sore throat, headache, and tender lymph nodes, are common.

Lack of energy by itself is rarely an emergency and can be addressed successfully with effective supplementation and natural solutions. However, if it develops suddenly or is accompanied by other serious symptoms, it may require immediate evaluation to avoid serious complications.

Resolving issues of lack of energy and fatigue can be simple. First considerations include a focus on rest, proper diet, nutrition and supplementation, and balanced blood sugar. Certain essential oils are very effective partners in creating and supporting energy. Basil oil, for example, is superb for overall energy and vitality (if used in higher amounts has the opposite effect—calming). Lemongrass has an overall whole-body stimulating effect. Lavender helps balance body systems where energy might be squandered unnecessarily in one area. Any citrus oil and blend is considered refreshing, uplifting, and rejuvenating. One of the most popular choices for an immediate, invigorating effect is peppermint oil.

top solutions

Single Oils

Basil— stimulates and revives (pg. 105)

Peppermint— invigorates and energizes (pg. 202)

Wild orange— uplifts and rejuvenates (pg. 244)

Lemon— cleanses and refreshes (pg. 176)

Lime— energizes and enlivens (pg. 181)

Blends

Citrus Bliss®, Citrus Bloom™— rejuvenate and energize (pgs. 130, 131)

Breathe®— invigorates and revives (pg. 116)

Motivate®, Brave™— stimulate, renew, and strengthen (pgs. 190, 115)

Passion®— promotes excitement, passion and joy (pg. 198)

Elevation— uplifts and energizes (pg. 145)

Purify— refreshes and cleanses (pg. 208)

Supplements

a2z Chewable™, **Alpha CRS®+** (pg. 254), DDR Prime® Softgels, **Microplex VMz®** (pg. 261), **Mito2Max®** (pg. 262), xEO Mega®

usage tips

For best success in supporting optimal energy and vitality:

- **Internal:** Consume energy-producing oils and supplements. For oils, place a few drops in a capsule, add to drinking water, or drop under tongue.
- **Topical & Aromatic:** Rub selected energy-producing oils on tired/sore shoulders, neck, back, legs and feet to invigorate, improve circulation, and increase blood flow and oxygen levels in the body.

Related Ailments

Chronic Fatigue, Exhaustion, Fatigue, Nervous Fatigue, Poor Endurance, Scurvy

By Related Properties

For more, see *Oil Properties* on pages 535-538

Antidepressant— basil, bergamot, clary sage, coriander, frankincense, geranium, jasmine, lemongrass, magnolia, neroli, oregano, pink pepper, sandalwood, tangerine, wild orange, ylang ylang

Energizing— basil, clove, cypress, grapefruit, lemongrass, rosemary, Siberian fir, wild orange, yarrowlpom

Immunostimulant— cassia, cinnamon bark, clove, copaiba, eucalyptus, frankincense, ginger, lemon, lime, melissa, rosemary, Siberian fir, spearmint, tea tree, vetiver, wild orange, yarrowlpom

Invigorating— grapefruit, lemon, litsea, peppermint, Siberian fir, spearmint, wild orange, wintergreen

Refreshing— cypress, geranium, grapefruit, green mandarin, lemon, lime, peppermint, pink pepper, Siberian fir, tea tree, wild orange, wintergreen

Restorative— basil, black spruce, frankincense, lime, neroli, patchouli, rosemary, sandalwood, spearmint, tangerine

Stimulant— arborvitae, basil, black spruce, bergamot, birch, black pepper, blue tansy, cardamom, cedarwood, cinnamon bark, clove, coriander, cypress, eucalyptus, fennel, ginger, grapefruit, juniper berry, lime, myrrh, patchouli, rosemary, Siberian fir, spearmint, tangerine, tea tree, thyme, vetiver, wintergreen, ylang ylang

conditions

Adrenal exhaustion/fatigue— basil, black spruce, geranium, rosemary, tulsi, ylang ylang; see *Endocrine (Adrenals)*

Alertness, decreased/drowsiness—basil, frankincense, ginger, lemon, lemongrass, lime, peppermint, rosemary, ylang ylang, Siberian fir, Adaptiv™, Breathe®, Citrus Bliss®, InTune®, Motivate®; see *Focus & Concentration*

Debility— cinnamon bark, Douglas fir, ginger, helichrysum, lavender, lemon, lime, neroli, On Guard®, Purify, Zendrocrine®

Energy, lack of*— basil, black pepper, cardamom, cinnamon bark, coriander, cypress, eucalyptus, ginger, grapefruit, jasmine, juniper berry, lemon, lime, melissa, patchouli, peppermint, rosemary, sandalwood, Siberian fir, tangerine, thyme, tulsi, wild orange, Air-X™, Breathe®, Citrus Bliss®, Forgive®, Motivate®, On Guard®, Purify

Exhaustion/fatigue*— arborvitae, basil, bergamot mint, black spruce, cinnamon bark, Douglas fir, eucalyptus, geranium, green mandarin, jasmine, lemon, lime, patchouli, peppermint, pink pepper, rosemary, sandalwood, tulsi, wild orange, wintergreen, ylang ylang, AromaTouch®, Brave™, Breathe®, Citrus Bliss®, DDR Prime®, Motivate®, Passion®, Purify, Slim & Sassy®, Zendrocrine®

Hyperactivity/restlessness/wound up— cedarwood, coriander, frankincense, lavender, patchouli, Roman chamomile, vetiver, wild orange, Adaptiv™, Balance®, Calmer™, InTune®, Serenity®; see *Focus & Concentration*

Jet lag— geranium, grapefruit, patchouli, peppermint, DDR Prime®, Motivate®; see *Sleep*

Lethargy/lack of motivation— Douglas fir, grapefruit, helichrysum, jasmine, lemon, lime, lemongrass, spearmint, yarrowlpom, Adaptiv™, Brave™, Breathe®, Citrus Bliss®, Purify, Motivate®

Nervous exhaustion— arborvitae, basil, black spruce, cedarwood, cinnamon bark, coriander, ginger, grapefruit, helichrysum, lemongrass, patchouli, rosemary, tulsi, Breathe®, Motivate®, PastTense®

Oxygen, lack of— frankincense, geranium, laurel leaf, peppermint, Siberian fir, Air-X™, Breathe®; see *Respiratory*

Weakness, physical after illness— basil, Douglas fir, frankincense, thyme, On Guard®, Purify, Zendrocrine®

*See Protocols →

ENERGY & VITALITY

protocols

ENERGY BOOST DAILY ROUTINE

- Take daily: Mito2Max®, Alpha CRS®+, xEO Mega®, Microplex VMz®, TerraZyme®.
- Rub 1-2 drops Motivate® on bottoms of feet AM and PM.
- Take 2-3 drops frankincense under tongue AM and PM.
- Apply and inhale wild orange and peppermint for an immediate awakening and refreshing.
- Add lime and grapefruit to drinking water and consume throughout the day.
- Use any of the blends listed below, as needed, to create additional energy and vitality.
- Rub 2-3 drops of DDR Prime®, followed by lavender or Serenity®, on bottoms of feet at night prior to sleep.

BRING THE ZING

Use grapefruit alone or in combination with frankincense, geranium, and/or bergamot. Diffuse, inhale, and apply to bottoms of feet and back of neck. Dilute as desired.

ENERGY KICK

Ingredients:

6 drops Slim & Sassy®
3 drops peppermint
3 drops wild orange

Directions:

Take oils in capsule 2x's per day.

INVIGORATING BLAST

Ingredients:

1 drop frankincense
1 drop peppermint
2 drops wild orange

Directions:

Inhale from cupped hands and massage onto back of neck.

MID AFTERNOON SLUMP BUSTER

Ingredients:

15 drops peppermint
20 drops wild orange

Directions:

Combine in 10mL roller bottle and fill remainder with carrier oil. Apply to back of neck, base of skull, across forehead, and inhale from cupped hands.

ENERGY BOOSTING DIFFUSER BLEND

Diffuse 3-4 drops each tangerine, spearmint, and rosemary.

For more ideas, download the app on Android or iOS.

FIRST AID RESPONSE is required whenever an injury, illness, or emergency must be immediately addressed. Situations requiring first aid can include insect bites and stings, snake bites, scratches and cuts, bleeding and hemorrhaging, burns, bruises, shock, sudden vertigo, heart issues, breathing issues, fever, food poisoning, sprained muscles, broken and dislocated bones, heat exhaustion and sunstroke, hypothermia, and more.

In these situations, it is important to have basic equipment readily available, such as antibiotic ointments, adhesive bandages, splints, etc., and to know how to respond in the event emergency personnel are required.

Essential oils and natural remedies make a great addition to complete any first aid kit. Particular oils have powerful antibiotic properties, help lower or raise body temperature, assist the respiratory system, help to settle nausea and other digestive problems, address burns, help to slow or stop bleeding, and more. Best of all, if the lids are secure and the first aid kit is kept in temperatures under 120° F, the oils typically last much longer than over-the-counter medications.

When assembling a first aid kit, it is important to consider lifestyle and risk factors for specific activities (e.g., hiking, camping, boating, traveling, etc.) and use common sense to anticipate future needs.

top solutions

Single Oils

Clove— powerful analgesic for numbing wounds (pg. 134)

Frankincense— universal healing properties, wound antiseptic/analgesic/healing, anti-scarring (pg. 151)

Helichrysum, Yarrowlpom— stop bleeding, wound repair/healing, powerful pain reliever (pgs. 160, 248)

Roman chamomile, Lavender, Blue tansy— antihistamine activity, wound/burn care, shock treatment, bite/sting recovery (pgs. 213, 175, 114)

Lemon— sanitizes, neutralizes acid, universal for immune, skin, respiratory needs (pg. 176)

Lemongrass— connective tissue, ligament repair (pg. 180)

Marjoram— muscle repair, digestive/eliminative support, sore muscle/cramp relief (pg. 187)

Tea tree— gentle/powerful wound antiseptic, antimicrobial activity (pg. 230)

Copaiba, Oregano— anti-inflammatory, powerful antibacterial, antiviral, antifungal (pgs. 136, 196)

Peppermint— cooling, burn care, pain relief, relieves nausea and vomiting (pg. 202)

Blends

DDR Prime®— cellular, cognitive, and trauma recovery support (pg. 140)

Purify, Abōde™— antiseptic properties; sanitize, bug bite/sting recovery (pgs. 208, 95)

Zendrocrine®— anti-allergenic, blood cleansing, anti-infectious support (pg. 251)

DigestZen®, Tamer™— excellent to resolve nausea, vomiting, and stomach upset (pgs. 142, 227)

AromaTouch®— for injured tissue recovery; sore muscle/cramp relief (pg. 103)

On Guard®, Stronger™— immune protection, analgesic (pgs. 195, 226)

TerraShield®— bug repellent (pg. 232)

Serenity®, Calmer™— shock, trauma recovery (pgs. 219, 117)

HD Clear®— antiseptic, wound care (pg. 159)

Deep Blue®, Rescuer™— bone, pain, sore muscle, and cramp relief (pgs. 141, 212)

Supplements

Bone Nutrient Complex, **Copaiba Softgels** (pg. 256), Correct-X®, **Deep Blue Polyphenol Complex®** (pg. 257), **DigestZen® Softgels** (pg. 258), **TriEase® Softgels** (pg. 268), Mito2Max®

Related Ailments

Bee Sting, Chiggers, Fainting, Heat Exhaustion, Heat Illness/Dehydration, Heat Stroke, Hypothermia, Injury, Insect Bite, Insect Repellent, Mosquito Bites, Shock, Snake Bites, Tick Bites, Wasp Sting, Wounds

By Related Properties

For more, see *Oil Properties* on pages 535-538

Analgesic— arborvitae, basil, bergamot, birch, black pepper, blue tansy, cassia, cinnamon bark, clary sage, clove, copaiba, cypress, eucalyptus, fennel, frankincense, ginger, helichrysum, juniper berry, lavender, lemongrass, litsea, marjoram, oregano, peppermint, ravintsara, rosemary, Siberian fir, tea tree, turmeric, wild orange, wintergreen, yarrowlpom

Anti-allergenic— blue tansy, geranium, helichrysum, manuka

Anticonvulsant— clary sage, fennel, geranium, lavender, neroli, tangerine

Antihemorrhagic— geranium, helichrysum, myrrh, yarrowlpom

Anti-infectious— arborvitae, basil, cardamom, cedarwood, cinnamon bark, clove, copaiba, cypress, eucalyptus, frankincense, geranium, lavender, litsea, marjoram, myrrh, patchouli, Roman chamomile, rosemary, tea tree, turmeric

Anti-inflammatory— bergamot, black pepper, blue tansy, cassia, cinnamon bark, clove, copaiba, cypress, eucalyptus, fennel, frankincense, ginger, jasmine, lemongrass, litsea, manuka, myrrh, neroli, oregano, patchouli, peppermint, pink pepper, rosemary, sandalwood, Siberian fir, spikenard, tangerine, tea tree, turmeric, wintergreen, yarrowlpom

Antiseptic— arborvitae, bergamot, black pepper, cedarwood, cinnamon bark, clove, copaiba, frankincense, ginger, grapefruit, helichrysum, juniper berry, lemon, marjoram, neroli, oregano, rosemary, Siberian fir, tangerine, tea tree, thyme, vetiver, wild orange, ylang ylang

Antispasmodic— basil, blue tansy, cardamom, cassia, cinnamon bark, clove, eucalyptus, fennel, helichrysum, lavender, lemon, litsea, marjoram, neroli, peppermint, rosemary, sandalwood, Siberian fir, spearmint, tangerine, thyme, vetiver, wintergreen, yarrowlpom, ylang ylang

Calming— bergamot, black pepper, blue tansy, clary sage, copaiba, coriander, frankincense, geranium, green mandarin, juniper berry, lavender, litsea, patchouli, Roman chamomile, tangerine, vetiver, yarrowlpom

Hypotensive— blue tansy, clary sage, copaiba, lavender, lemon, litsea, manuka, neroli, yarrowlpom, ylang ylang

Insect repellent— arborvitae, birch, blue tansy, cedarwood, celery seed, cinnamon bark, citronella, eucalyptus, geranium, laurel leaf, lemon eucalyptus, lemongrass, litsea, patchouli, pink pepper, ravintsara, thyme, turmeric, vetiver, ylang ylang

Vasoconstrictor— helichrysum, peppermint, Siberian fir

Warming— birch, black pepper, cassia, cinnamon bark, clary sage, clove, eucalyptus, ginger, lemongrass, marjoram, neroli, oregano, peppermint, pink pepper, tulsi, thyme, wintergreen

FIRST AID

conditions

Allergies to insect bite or sting— basil, blue tansy, lavender, lemon, melissa, peppermint, Roman chamomile, rosemary, tea tree, thyme, Abōde™, Air-X™, Breathe®, Purify, TerraShield®, Zendrocrine®; see *Allergies*

Bed Bugs— arborvitae, blue tansy, cedarwood, citronella, eucalyptus, lavender, lemon eucalyptus, peppermint, tea tree, Abōde™

Bites, insect— arborvitae, basil, blue tansy, cinnamon bark, copaiba, coriander, eucalyptus, frankincense, lavender, lemon, lemongrass, melissa, patchouli, Roman chamomile, tea tree, thyme, ylang ylang, Abōde™, Passion®, Peace®, Purify

Bleeding/hemorrhaging— frankincense, geranium, helichrysum, lavender, myrrh, wild orange, yarrowlpom, Console®; see *Cardiovascular*

Blood vessels, broken— cypress, frankincense, geranium, helichrysum, lemon, lime, yarrowlpom, Purify, Zendrocrine®; see *Cardiovascular*

Breathing, shortness of breath— eucalyptus, peppermint, Air-X™, Breathe®; see "Allergies to insect bite or sting", *Respiratory*

Bruising— arborvitae, blue tansy, clove, copaiba, cypress, fennel, geranium, grapefruit, helichrysum, lavender, neroli, oregano, Roman chamomile, Siberian fir, ylang ylang, AromaTouch®, Citrus Bliss®, DDR Prime®, Deep Blue®, Passion®, Purify, Peace®, Rescuer™, Zendrocrine®

Burns— copaiba, eucalyptus, frankincense, geranium, helichrysum, lavender, lemon eucalyptus, myrrh, peppermint, sandalwood, Siberian fir, spearmint, tangerine, Immortelle, InTune®, Tamer™, Stronger™

Cellulitis— lime, oregano (internally), On Guard®; see *Immune & Lymphatic*, *Integumentary*

Chills (shock)— basil, grapefruit, lemon, melissa, peppermint, Roman chamomile, rosemary, tea tree, wild orange, ylang ylang, Balance®, Citrus Bliss®, Motivate®, On Guard®, Slim & Sassy®, Stronger™

Cuts/wounds, cleaning*— black spruce, blue tansy, cassia, cedarwood, copaiba, cypress, frankincense, juniper berry, lavender, lemon, lemongrass, (superb disinfectant), magnolia, myrrh, tea tree, Abōde™, HD Clear®, On Guard®, Peace®, Stronger™

Cuts/wounds, healing*— basil, black spruce, copaiba, cypress, eucalyptus, frankincense, geranium, helichrysum (apply to cleaned wound), lavender, lemon eucalyptus, lime, magnolia, myrrh, peppermint, petitgrain, sandalwood, Siberian fir, tea tree, vetiver, yarrowlpom, HD Clear®, Immortelle, Purify

Cuts/wounds, pain (numbing)*— cassia, clove, copaiba, eucalyptus, frankincense, helichrysum, neroli, Siberian fir, tea tree, tulsi, yarrowlpom, On Guard®

Dehydration— cypress, juniper berry, lemon, petitgrain, wild orange, Slim & Sassy®, Zendrocrine®

Dizziness/lightheaded— geranium, ginger, peppermint, rosemary, Balance®, DDR Prime®, Deep Blue®, PastTense®, Zendrocrine®

Drop in blood pressure (allergic reaction)— cypress, helichrysum, lavender, peppermint, rosemary, Siberian fir, thyme, ylang ylang; see *Allergies*, "Allergies to insect bite or sting" in previous column

Fainting— basil, peppermint, rosemary, Balance®, Citrus Bliss®, Motivate®

Fleas— arborvitae, cedarwood, citronella, eucalyptus, lavender, lemon, lemon eucalyptus, lemongrass, peppermint, Abōde™, Purify, TerraShield®

Food poisoning— black pepper, cinnamon bark, clove, ginger, juniper berry, lemon, oregano, tea tree, thyme, DigestZen®, On Guard®, Purify, Tamer™, Zendrocrine®

Heat exhaustion*— basil, bergamot, eucalyptus, lemon, lemon eucalyptus, lime, peppermint, spearmint, tulsi, Deep Blue®, PastTense®, Tamer™

Hypothermia— birch, cassia, cinnamon bark, clove, cypress, eucalyptus, ginger, lemongrass, marjoram, oregano, patchouli, peppermint, thyme, tulsi, wild orange, wintergreen, AromaTouch®, DDR Prime®, On Guard®, Stronger™

Infections— juniper berry, oregano, tea tree, On Guard®, Purify, Stronger™; see *Immune & Lymphatic*

Insect repellent— arborvitae, basil, bergamot, birch, blue tansy, cedarwood, celery seed, cinnamon bark, citronella, cypress, Douglas fir, eucalyptus, geranium (mosquito), laurel leaf, lavender (flies, gnat, midge, mosquito), lemon eucalyptus, lemongrass, lime, patchouli, pink pepper, rosemary, thyme, turmeric, vetiver, ylang ylang, Abōde™, Forgive®, Passion®, Purify, TerraShield®

Itching, excessive— blue tansy, cilantro, lavender, lemon, melissa, patchouli, peppermint, Roman chamomile, tea tree, vetiver, wild orange, Immortelle, Slim & Sassy®, Zendrocrine®; see *Integumentary*

Lice— citronella, geranium, rosemary, tea tree, thyme, Abōde™, TerraShield®; see *Parasites*

Mites (e.g. chiggers, scabies)— See *Parasites*

Mosquito bites— arborvitae, juniper berry, lavender, Roman chamomile, tea tree, Abōde™, Purify; see "Bites, insect"

Motion sickness— bergamot, ginger, peppermint, Cheer®, DigestZen®, Tamer™; see *Digestive & Intestinal*

Nausea/vomiting— basil, bergamot, cardamom, cassia, clove, coriander, fennel, ginger, lavender, melissa, pink pepper, DigestZen®, Tamer™; see *Digestive & Intestinal*

Nosebleeds— cypress, helichrysum, geranium, lavender, lemon, lime, yarrowlpom; see *Cardiovascular*

Poison— black pepper, juniper berry, lemongrass, Abōde™, Passion®

Poison ivy— frankincense, geranium, lavender, lemon, Roman chamomile, tea tree, Abōde™, Immortelle, Purify

Poison oak— clove, laurel leaf, lavender, rose, vetiver, Immortelle

Shivering/low body temp— See "Hypothermia"

Shock— bergamot, coriander, Douglas fir, frankincense, geranium, helichrysum, lavender, magnolia, marjoram, melissa, neroli, peppermint, Roman chamomile, tangerine, tea tree, vetiver, wild orange, ylang ylang, Console®, DDR Prime®, InTune®, Motivate®, PastTense®, Peace®, Serenity®

Snake bite— basil, clove, coriander, helichrysum, frankincense, geranium, patchouli, sandalwood, tea tree, Purify

Spider bite*— basil, juniper berry, lavender, melissa, Roman chamomile, tea tree, thyme, Abōde™, On Guard®, Purify

Stinging nettle— clove, lemon (neutralizes acid), Abōde™, Citrus Bliss®, Purify

Stings— basil, cinnamon bark, clove, lavender, lemon, lime, Roman chamomile, tea tree, thyme, Abōde™, Purify

Sunburn— arborvitae, bergamot mint, blue tansy, eucalyptus, frankincense, geranium, helichrysum, lavender, peppermint, sandalwood, spearmint, Immortelle

Sunstroke/heatstroke— Douglas fir, eucalyptus, lavender, lemon, peppermint, rosemary, spearmint, PastTense®, Tamer™, Zendrocrine®

Tick bites— lavender, tea tree; see *Parasites*

Tick prevention— lemon eucalyptus, TerraShield®

Trauma— cypress, frankincense, geranium, juniper berry, myrrh, Balance®, Calmer™, DDR Prime®, Immortelle, Motivate®, Purify, Serenity®, Steady™, TerraShield®; see "Shock"

*See Protocols on pg. 350

protocols

SPIDER BITE RECOVERY: Combine basil, Purify, rosemary, and lemon to take the "sting" away and reduce inflammation. Add helichrysum at end of treatment to bite location to encourage faster healing and prevent scarring.

WOUND CLEANSING SPRAY

Ingredients:

5 drops lemon
10 drops tea tree
5 drops frankincense
5 drops eucalyptus

Directions:

Place oils in a glass spray bottle with ½ t salt and 4 oz of distilled water. Spray area each time before applying fresh bandage. Repeat twice first day. Then use healing spray.

WOUND HEALING SPRAY

Ingredients:

5 drops frankincense
10 drops tea tree
10 drops lavender
5 drops helichrysum

Directions:

Add with water to 2 oz glass spray Apply repeatedly.

HEAT EXHAUSTION RECOVERY

Place 1 drop peppermint in drinking water and sip to cool down. Place 2-4 drops lemon in drinking water and sip to rehydrate. Combine the two as desired.

QUELL THE SWELL

5 drops each: peppermint, wintergreen, frankincense, eucalyptus, cypress, and rosemary

Directions:

Combine in 10mL roller, topped off with carrier oil. Massage into swollen and/or painful areas twice per day, or as often as needed.

AFTER SUN SPRAY RELIEF

1 C aloe vera juice
1/4 C fractionated coconut oil
1-2 dropperfuls yarrowlpom
8 drops each lavender, Roman chamomile, and peppermint

Directions:

Combine in 16 oz glass spray bottle. Shake and spray on skin.

BYE-BYE BRUISES

10 drops helichrysum
10 drops copaiba
10 drops cypress

Directions:

Add to 10mL roller bottle, topped off with carrier oil. Massage lightly onto bruised area at least twice per day.

DITCH THE ITCH

1 drop lavender
1 drop Roman chamomile
1 drop eucalyptus
1 drop peppermint

Directions:

Apply to areas affected by poison ivy. Add a cold compress if needed. Repeat until relief and healing are achieved.

FIRST AID

usage tips

- **Topical:**
  - Apply oils directly to an area of concern such as on cuts, bruises, bites, stings, injury sites, and burns whenever possible. Otherwise, get as close to site as possible or use bottoms of feet as alternative location.
  - **For acute situations,** apply oils frequently, even every few minutes as needed for pain relief, to stop bleeding, etc. Always clean the site of a cut/wound (e.g., with tea tree) prior to applying an oil like helichrysum that can help stop bleeding and seal up the site.
  - **To cool or raise body temperature,** apply diluted cooling or warming oils on back of neck, down spine, bottoms of feet, or spray on an oil/water (cooling only) mixture (shake first). For sunburn, apply to site.
  - **To clean a wound,** apply a disinfecting type oil (e.g., tea tree) followed by Correct-X to promote healing.
  - **To stop bleeding,** quickly apply lavender or geranium; apply helichrysum and/or yarrowlpom after wound is cleaned.
  - **For splinters** deep under the skin, apply clove to bring splinter to surface. Then apply 1 drop Deep Blue® to affected area.
  - **For stings,** apply Purify to neutralize venom and then lavender to soothe and help stop swelling.
  - **For blister relief,** apply 2 drops each lavender and tea tree. Repeat often for the first day and continue use until resolved.
- **Aromatic:** Offer immediate support in times of shock or trauma with inhalation from a bottle, or cupped hands, or a swipe under nose. Diffuse or apply topically for ongoing aroma exposure.
- **Internal:** For any allergic response, place a drop of an anti-histamine like oil (e.g., lavender, Roman chamomile) under tongue (for older children/adults) and/or on bottoms of feet for any age (dilute for infants/toddlers). Inhale. For nausea/vomiting, place oils on abdomen, lick off back of hand, drop on tongue, and/or place on bottoms of feet, depending on age.

For more ideas, download the app on Android or iOS.

Focus & Concentration

See also Brain

THE ABILITY TO FOCUS requires adequate neural connections in the brain to process incoming sensory data (sights, sounds, smells, etc.). When the brain is unable to assimilate this data, the stimuli become overwhelming or "noisy," and symptoms such as frustration, irritation, and even fatigue can occur. An increasing number of individuals of any age are experiencing a decreasing ability to focus and concentrate. It is important to consider factors that contribute to the decline of optimal focus and concentration in order to reverse or prevent this trend.

Given the innate complexity of the human brain, it is not surprising that issues of focus and concentration and contributing factors are vast. Tiredness or lack of sleep, stress, hormonal changes (such as during pregnancy or puberty), medication side effects, alcohol, drugs, chronic illness, infection, brain injury, anxiety, depression, bipolar disorder, and emotional trauma are just a few that impact neural connections necessary to make sense of the vast sensory stimuli the brain receives moment to moment. For example, individuals with ADHD consistently struggle to "think over the noise" in their brains as stimuli come in without the necessary processing ability to make sense of it all.

The very nature of the brain's structure allows for improvements in function and ability. To summarize this complex process in a simple way: the more neurons available to make connections with other neurons, the easier and more efficient focus and learning will be. While traditional medicine and neurological specialists contribute great expertise to the science of improving brain activity, there are a myriad of natural remedies that can greatly impact and benefit brain activity, specifically in the area of focus and concentration.

When an individual inhales an essential oil (or other aroma) the olfactory bulb is activated and directly links to brain processes that stimulate and encourage neural connections. The simple act of diffusing an essential oil like lavender in the classroom, or inhaling peppermint from a bottle, can have immediate and effective impact on the learner. Simple yet powerful suggestions through both single oils or blends and remedies have demonstrated that essential oils and nutritional support are powerful tools for improving focus, concentration, and much more!

top solutions

Single Oils

Roman chamomile— reduces anxiety, promotes confidence (pg. 213)

Vetiver— hones focus, concentration, improves dendrite function (pg. 241)

Lavender— calms the mind, supports mental adaptability (pg. 175)

Clary sage— supports a calm, clear, focused mind (pg. 133)

Cedarwood— quiets mind, supports improved mental performance (pg. 120)

Peppermint— stimulates and invigorates the mind (pg. 202)

Blends

InTune®, Thinker™— calm and stimulates the mind (pgs. 167, 233)

Motivate®, Brave®— promote motivation, mental stimulation and movement (pgs. 190, 115)

Balance®, Steady™— promote a grounded state of mind (pgs. 104, 225)

Adaptiv™— supports mental agility and resilience, enhances focus, promotes a positive outlook (pg. 96)

Serenity®, Calmer™— relax mind (pgs. 219, 117)

Supplements

Adaptiv™ Softgels (pg. 253), Alpha CRS®+, Bone Nutrient Complex, **DDR Prime® Softgels** (pg. 256), **IQ Mega** (pg. 260), Microplex VMz®, **Mito2Max®** (pg. 262), PB Assist®+, TerraZyme®, **xEO Mega®** (pg. 271), Zendocrine® Complex, Zendocrine® Softgels

FOCUS & CONCENTRATION

usage tips

For best methods of use for focus and concentration consider:

- **Aromatic:** Diffuse 5-10 drops of oils of choice, inhale from product bottle or a self-made blend, apply a few drops to clothing, bedding, or any other method that supports inhalation for oils to enter brain via nose and olfactory system.
- **Topical:** Apply on forehead, under nose, back of neck (especially in suboccipital triangles), roof of mouth (place oil on pad of thumb, place on roof, "suck"), and forehead.

Related Ailments

Absentmindedness, ADD or ADHD [Brain], Concentration, Confusion, Focus, Hyperactivity [Mood & Behavior], Mental strength/clarity, Poor Concentration, Poor Memory [Brain]

By Related Properties

For more, see *Oil Properties* on pages 535-538

Antidepressant— bergamot, frankincense, green mandarin, lemon, melissa, neroli, ravintsara, Roman chamomile, tangerine, wild orange

Antifungal— arborvitae, bergamot, blue tansy, cedarwood, cinnamon bark, clary sage, copaiba, coriander, litsea, manuka, myrrh, oregano, sandalwood, Siberian fir, tangerine, tea tree, thyme, turmeric

Antioxidant— bergamot, clove, copaiba, helichrysum, grapefruit, juniper berry, lemongrass, litsea, neroli, rosemary, patchouli, tangerine, tea tree, thyme, turmeric, yarrowlpom

Calming— black spruce, blue tansy, cedarwood, clary sage, copaiba, coriander, fennel, jasmine, lavender, litsea, magnolia, patchouli, Roman chamomile, sandalwood, tangerine, vetiver, yarrowlpom

Energizing— basil, bergamot, cinnamon bark, cypress, ginger, peppermint, rosemary, Siberian fir, tangerine, wild orange, yarrowlpom

Grounding— black spruce, blue tansy, cedarwood, frankincense, magnolia, Siberian fir, vetiver, ylang ylang

Invigorating— lemon, lime, lemongrass, litsea, peppermint, pink pepper, Siberian fir, wild orange

Neuroprotective— frankincense, magnolia, myrrh, Roman chamomile, sandalwood, turmeric

Refreshing— any citrus oil, Siberian fir, tea tree

Relaxing— blue tansy, cypress, geranium, green mandarin, litsea, magnolia, neroli, Roman chamomile

Sedative— bergamot, blue tansy, cedarwood, clary sage, frankincense, lavender, magnolia, melissa, neroli, patchouli, Roman chamomile, tangerine, vetiver, yarrowlpom, ylang ylang

Stimulant— arborvitae, basil, bergamot, black pepper, black spruce, blue tansy, cardamom, cedarwood, cinnamon bark, coriander, cypress, eucalyptus, ginger, grapefruit, juniper berry, lime, pink pepper, rosemary, Siberian fir, spearmint, tangerine, tea tree, vetiver, wintergreen

Uplifting— bergamot, grapefruit, green mandarin, lime, litsea, melissa, tangerine, wild orange

conditions

Emotional States

(See *Mood & Behavior* for additional emotional support)

Afraid/unadventurous— black pepper, patchouli, ravintsara, Brave™

Agitated*— arborvitae, bergamot, black spruce, patchouli, Balance®, Deep Blue®, InTune®, Serenity®, Thinker™

Angry*— bergamot, cardamom, cedarwood, frankincense, geranium, helichrysum, Roman chamomile, Balance®, InTune®, Serenity®

Antisocial— bergamot, black pepper, cedarwood, oregano, patchouli

Anxious— basil, cedarwood, frankincense, juniper berry, patchouli, vetiver, Adaptiv™, Balance®, InTune®, Serenity®

Apathetic/lacking of motivation*— bergamot mint, birch, black pepper, cardamom, frankincense, jasmine, juniper berry, melissa, patchouli, ravintsara, rose, vetiver, wild orange, ylang ylang, Adaptiv™, Balance®, Breathe®, Elevation, InTune®, Motivate®, Passion®

Defensive— ginger, lemon, patchouli, tea tree, wintergreen, ClaryCalm®, Deep Blue®, On Guard®, PastTense®, TerraShield®

Depressed— bergamot, green mandarin, jasmine, patchouli, Roman chamomile, vetiver, wild orange, ylang ylang, Cheer™, Citrus Bliss®, Citrus Bloom™, Elevation, Passion®

Easily bugged/bothered— black spruce, lemongrass, rose, Siberian fir, TerraShield®

Fearful— frankincense, juniper berry, wild orange, ylang ylang, Balance®, Air-X™, Brave™, Breathe®, On Guard®, Serenity®, Zendrocrine®

Frustrated*— black spruce, cardamom, ylang ylang, Calmer™, InTune®, Serenity®

Hypersensitive— lavender, melissa, Roman chamomile, rosemary, vanilla, vetiver

Obsessed/preoccupied— cedarwood, cilantro, frankincense, jasmine, oregano, sandalwood, vetiver, Adaptiv™, InTune®, Serenity®

Performance stress/stage fright— bergamot, patchouli, ravintsara, rose, wild orange, ylang ylang, Adaptiv™, Breathe®

Shy/timid/unsure— bergamot, cassia, clove, ginger, jasmine, juniper berry, laurel leaf, melissa, patchouli, ravintsara, spearmint, yarrowlpom, ylang ylang, Brave™, Breathe®, InTune®, Motivate®, Passion®

Stubborn/willful— birch, ginger, lemongrass, oregano, tea tree, wintergreen, Calmer™

Unsafe/vulnerable, feeling*— bergamot, cardamom, cilantro, cinnamon bark, ginger, jasmine, oregano, ravintsara, Roman chamomile, vanilla, ylang ylang, Air-X™, AromaTouch®, Breathe®, On Guard®, Serenity®, TerraShield®, Whisper®

Mental States

Attention deficit— lavender, vetiver, Adaptiv™, Calmer™, InTune®, Motivate®, Peace®, Serenity®, Thinker™

Autistic— basil, bergamot, clary sage, frankincense, geranium, lemon, peppermint, rosemary, vanilla, vetiver, Balance®, DDR Prime®, Deep Blue®, Immortelle, InTune®, Northern Escape, Serenity®

Brain fogged*— arborvitae, bergamot, Douglas fir, eucalyptus, frankincense, juniper berry, lemon, lime, peppermint, Siberian fir, Air-X™, Breathe®, InTune®, Motivate®, Northern Escape, Thinker™

Brain oxygen, lack of— cedarwood, cypress, eucalyptus, frankincense, ginger, lemon, patchouli, peppermint, sandalwood, vetiver, Passion®; see "Antioxidant" property

Chemically imbalanced— See *Brain*

Concentration/focus, lack of*— arborvitae, cedarwood, Douglas fir, eucalyptus, frankincense, laurel leaf, lavender, lemon, lime, patchouli, peppermint, ravintsara, rosemary, vetiver, Adaptiv™, Calmer™, InTune®, Motivate®, Thinker™

Confusion/disorganized— arborvitae, frankincense, peppermint, rosemary, Siberian fir, vetiver, Balance®, Citrus Bloom™, Elevation, InTune®, Motivate®, Thinker™

Coping skills, lack of— bergamot, black spruce, clove, eucalyptus, ginger, juniper berry, lavender, oregano, rosemary, wintergreen, Adaptiv™, Balance®, Calmer™, Citrus Bliss®, Citrus Bloom™, Deep Blue®, Elevation, InTune®, PastTense®, Serenity®

Daydreamer— cedarwood, frankincense, peppermint, ravintsara, rosemary, vetiver, ylang ylang, AromaTouch®, Breathe®, InTune®, Motivate®, Thinker™

Dendrite and neuron support— vetiver

Distracted/bored easily— frankincense, peppermint, Roman chamomile, vetiver, wild orange, Citrus Bliss®, Citrus Bloom™, Motivate®

Environmental tension— lemon, wintergreen, yarrowlpom, Steady™

Equilibrium/balance, lack of— arborvitae, frankincense, lavender, rosemary, spearmint, ylang ylang, Balance®, Citrus Bliss®, InTune®, Steady™, Zendrocrine®

Fatigued— basil, bergamot mint, black spruce, cassia, cinnamon bark, coriander, ginger, lemon, pink pepper, thyme, tulsi DDR Prime®, Motivate®, Slim & Sassy®, Zendrocrine®; see *Energy & Vitality*

Fixated— black pepper, lemongrass, tangerine, ylang ylang, Northern Escape

Hyperactive/restlessness/wound up*— coriander, frankincense, lavender, lemon, ravintsara, Roman chamomile, vetiver, Adaptiv™, Balance®, Breathe®, Calmer™, Peace®, Serenity®, Thinker™

Impulsive/acting without thinking— cedarwood, Siberian fir, Balance®

Learning difficulties— cedarwood, patchouli, peppermint, vetiver, Balance®, InTune®, Motivate®, Passion®, Thinker™

Left brain, lack of activity— lemon

Mentally fatigued— basil, bergamot, black spruce, cardamom, Douglas fir, frankincense, laurel leaf, lavender, lemon, lemongrass, peppermint, rose, rosemary, sandalwood, spearmint, Siberian fir, ylang ylang, Breathe®, Citrus Bliss®, Console®, Motivate®, Passion®

Mentally sluggish— basil, eucalyptus, laurel leaf, peppermint, pink pepper, rosemary, Siberian fir, Motivate®

Mentally strained/stressed— bergamot, cedarwood, grapefruit, lavender, Roman chamomile, spearmint, tulsi, Adaptiv™, Calmer™, Immortelle, Thinker™

Memory, lack of/unreliable/poor sense of time— bergamot, Douglas fir, lemon, lemongrass, lime, juniper berry, melissa, peppermint, thyme, tulsi, Elevation, InTune®, Passion®

Memory, poor*— black spruce, frankincense, ginger, peppermint, rosemary, sandalwood, thyme, tulsi, Adaptiv™, InTune®, Motivate®, Passion®

Memory, loss of short term— basil, black spruce, cedarwood, peppermint, rosemary, tulsi, ylang ylang, Adaptiv™, Balance®, Forgive®, InTune®, Peace®

Neurotransmitter production capacity, compromised— fennel, ginger

Oxygen deprived (brain)— cedarwood, cypress, eucalyptus, frankincense, ginger, lemon, patchouli, peppermint, sandalwood, tea tree, vetiver, On Guard®; see "Antioxidant" above

Restless/fidgety/squirming*— bergamot mint, lavender, ravintsara, vanilla, vetiver, wild orange, Adaptiv™, Balance®, Breathe®, Citrus Bliss®, Serenity®, Steady™

Right brain, lack of activity— Douglas fir, Roman chamomile, wild orange

Sensory systems, closed/blocked— birch, wintergreen, Motivate®

FOCUS & CONCENTRATION

*See Protocols on pg. 354

protocols

CONCENTRATION: Apply a drop or two each of vetiver and lavender on bottoms of feet and base of neck before heading off to school or work. Blend can also be worn on a diffuser pendant throughout the day. If aroma is offensive, add an oil such as wild orange to "deodorize" as desired.

FOCUS SUPPORT: Blend and dilute 2-4 drops each spearmint and rosemary. Massage on back of neck and inhale.

FOCUS, MEMORY, RECALL

- **Option #1:** Combine frankincense with wild orange or peppermint. Inhale or sniff and/or take under tongue.
- **Options #2:** In a 10mL roller bottle, combine 20 drops each wild orange and peppermint. Fill rest of bottle with fractionated coconut oil, shake, and apply.
- **Option #3:** Combine 10-15 drops each cedarwood, cinnamon, and grapefruit in a 10mL roller bottle with a carrier oil

FRUSTRATION/ANGER: Choose from calming oils: frankincense, helichrysum, lavender, magnolia, ylang ylang, Balance®, and/or Serenity®. Combine as desired and apply to feet, back of neck, behind ears, knees, and/or over heart. Diffuse.

BEDTIME ROUTINE: Allow individual to choose up to 3 favorite oils by smelling for preference. Make a personal blend and massage on bottoms of feet prior to bedtime. Then cover with weighted blankets.

HYPERACTIVITY: Healthy touch is often a welcomed experience, and the action of applying oils can create a calming effect. Combine Balance® and Serenity®. Apply and massage onto back of neck, spine, and bottoms of feet.

PEACE AND CALM: Combine 10 drops lavender, 20 drops vetiver, and 10 drops Serenity® in a 10mL roller bottle. Top off with fractionated coconut oil. Shake and apply to feet and back of neck. Diffuse or inhale. Use at least 2x's per day.

CHILL PILL

Ingredients:

10 drops clary sage
15 drops bergamot
20 drops grapefruit
25 drops wild orange
15 drops frankincense
10 drops cedarwood

Directions:

Combine oils in an empty 15mL bottle. Diffuse 3-5 drops of blend, and/or apply diluted to base of skull, back of neck, along spine, behind ears, over heart, and on wrists.

MOTIVATION POWER

Ingredients:

3 drops basil
3 drops grapefruit
2 drops bergamot
2 drops sandalwood
1 drop rosemary
1 drop ylang ylang

Directions:

Combine oils and diffuse.

CALM AND COMPOSED

Ingredients:

5-10 drops vetiver or black spruce
2-4 drops lavender
2-4 drops ylang ylang
1-2 drop frankincense
1-2 drop clary sage
1-2 drop marjoram

Directions:

Combine oils in a 10mL roller bottle. Fill remainder of bottle with fractionated coconut oil. Apply behind ears, on occipital triangle area, bottoms of feet, and/or along the spine before bedtime and as needed. Choose fewer drops for a child and more for an adult from recipe.

MELLOW OUT

Ingredients:

10 drops Balance®
10 drops vetiver
10 drops frankincense
10 drops Serenity® or Calmer™

Directions:

Combine oils in a 10mL roller bottle. Fill remainder of bottle with fractionated coconut oil. Rub behind ears, on suboccipital triangle area, bottoms of feet, and/or down the spine before bedtime and as needed.

FIDGET FIXER

Ingredients:

3-6 drops cedarwood
6-12 drops Balance®
2-4 drops frankincense
2-4 drops lavender
3-6 drops Adaptiv™

Directions:

Combine oils in a 10mL roller bottle. Fill remainder of bottle with fractionated coconut oil. Apply to ears, forehead, back of neck, up spine, and on bottoms of feet. Massage into tissue to enhance absorption. Consider age, size, need, and tolerance of intended recipient to determine strength of blend.

FOCUS DIFFUSER BLEND OPTIONS:

- 5 drops lime, 3 drops eucalyptus, 2 drops spearmint
- 2 drops grapefruit, 2 drops wild orange, 1 drop lime, 1 drop spearmint
- 4 drops black spruce, 3 drops bergamot, 2 drops peppermint

For more ideas, download the app on Android or iOS.

Immune & Lymphatic

THE IMMUNE SYSTEM and lymphatic system work closely together to protect the body from harmful pathogens and disease. These systems include white blood cells, bone marrow, the spleen, tonsils, adenoids, appendix, thymus, lymph, and lymph nodes. A healthy immune response consists of the body's ability to properly identify a pathogen and engage in a series of responses designed to prevent pathogens from entering targeted cells/tissues.

The immune system consists of two smaller systems:

- The innate immune system—prevents pathogens from entering the body; it also provides a generalized response that destroys any pathogens that bypass the barriers.
- The adaptive immune system—analyzes the pathogen so the body can respond with an army of protective cells created specifically to destroy that particular pathogen. This system also supports the immune system by delivering nutrients to the cells and removing toxins and waste products.

The lymphatic system includes two biological substances:

- Bone marrow—creates T-cells and creates and grows B-cells to maturation. B-cells travel via the blood system to destroy any lurking pathogens. T-cells, which attack pathogens and any toxic molecules, travel to the thymus, where they mature and later join the B-cells. These T-cells and B-cells are lymphocytes that travel in the lymph.
- Lymph—a yellowish, watery fluid that carries white blood cells. It circulates through tissues, picks up unwanted fats, bacteria, and other substances, and filters it through the lymphatic system.

The first line of defense is the innate immune system, which includes physical barriers, such as skin, fingernails, mucous membranes, tears, and earwax that help prevent invaders from entering the body, and chemical barriers, such as fatty acids, stomach acid, proteins, and secretions that naturally help destroy pathogens.

When pathogens are undeterred by the innate immune response, the adaptive immune system, which is more complex than the innate, processes the pathogen in a way that allows it to design specific immune cells to combat it effectively. Then it produces huge numbers of those cells to attack the pathogen and any toxic molecules it creates. The cells that carry out this specific immune response are called lymphocytes and are created and delivered by the lymph system.

As part of the adaptive immune system response, humans have sophisticated defense mechanisms that include the ability to adapt over time to recognize specific pathogens more efficiently. This is accomplished by creating immunological memory after the initial response is rendered, leading to an enhanced response to subsequent encounters with that same pathogen.

Certain lifestyle choices can either provide great strength or can seriously weaken immune response. Nutrition is a key factor in a healthy immune system; if cells don't have the energy they need to provide critical safeguards for the body, pathogens can more easily penetrate and multiply. Detoxification is another critical activity that helps promote the body's natural defenses; often when an individual gets sick, it is simply the body's way to eliminate toxins naturally.

Natural essential oils, which have a chemical footprint compatible with the human body, have the unique ability to help the immune system balance because they are lipophilic (soluble in fat) and thus can penetrate the cell membrane. Viruses are also lipophilic. Most pure essential oils are naturally drawn to the inside of the cell to help the body eradicate threats within the cell.

Interestingly, when essential oils are adulterated because the oil is synthetic (created in a laboratory), the signal molecule approaching the cell is the mirror-image of what it should be and thus is limited in the support it can give the body.

Note that for threats that exist outside the cell, namely, bacterial infections, essential oils can assist in warding off such risks. Oregano essential oil, for example, also has hydrophilic properties that allow it to effectively target threats that exist in the extracellular fluid (outside the cell). Knowledge of these powerful properties can help individuals provide effective reinforcements for the immune system.

Additional consideration for immune support:
When threats to the body from various pathogens are combined with a weakened immune system, illness can occur. Ideally, one would target pathogens within the body while simultaneously strengthening the immune system. The AromaTouch Technique® discussed in the *Introduction* accomplishes both objectives. The AromaTouch Technique® is a systematic application of eight different essential oils that serve to strengthen the immune system, eliminate pathogens, reduce stress, and bring the body into homeostasis, enabling the body to function more optimally. See *AromaTouch Technique®*, page 24.

top solutions

Single Oils

Tea tree— fights bacteria and viruses (pg. 230)

Cassia, Cinnamon bark— fight bacteria and viruses (pgs. 119, 126)

Copaiba— fights bacteria and viruses (pg. 136)

Black or Pink pepper— support digestion and boosts immunity (pgs. 111, 206)

Oregano, Thyme— fight bacteria and viruses (pgs. 196, 234)

Cilantro, Rose— fight and kill bacteria (pgs. 125, 215)

Blends

On Guard®, Stronger™— stimulates immune system and fights bacteria/viruses (pgs. 195, 226)

Zendrocrine®— supports proper detoxification (pg. 251)

DDR Prime®— manages abnormal cell activity and stimulates immune system (pg. 140)

Abōde™, **Purify**— disinfects and sanitizes (pgs. 95, 208)

Supplements

a2z Chewable™, Alpha CRS®+, Bone Nutrient Complex, Copaiba Softgels, Correct-X®, **DDR Prime® Softgels** (pg. 256), **GX Assist®** (pg. 260), Microplex VMz®, **On Guard® Softgels** (pg. 262), **On Guard® Throat Drops** and **Tablets** (pg. 263), **PB Assist®+** (pg. 264), TerraZyme®, TriEase® Softgels, xEO Mega®, YarrowlPom Capsules, **Turmeric Dual Capsules** (pg. 269), Zendocrine® Complex

IMMUNE & LYMPHATIC

usage tips

For most effective use of essential oils for immune and lymphatic benefits:

- **Topical:** Apply oils on bottoms of feet, especially on back side of toes, down spine, and/or on any specific area of concern. Use the AromaTouch Technique®.
- **Internal:** Take oils in capsule, place under or on tongue near back of throat, or sip from a glass of water.
- **Aromatic:** Diffuse to clear pathogens from air, open airways, and add airborne benefits.
- **Surfaces:** Sanitize surfaces with essential oils mixed with water, an emulsifier, and/or vinegar.

Related Ailments

Adenitis, AIDS or HIV, Anthrax, Antiseptic, Bacteria, Body Temperature Issues, Chemical Sensitivity Reaction [Allergies], Chest Infections, Chicken Pox, Cholera, Common Cold, Conjunctivitis (Pink Eye), Cystitis, Cytomegalovirus Infection, Dengue Fever, E. Coli, Ebola, Epstein-Barr, Ehrlichiosis, Fever, Flu, H.Pylori, Hand Foot & Mouth Disease, Hepatitis, Herpes Simplex, Infection, Legionnaires' Disease, Listeria Infection, Lockjaw (Tetanus), Lyme Disease, Measles, Meningitis, Mesenteric Lymphadenitis, Mold, Mononucleosis, MRSA, Mumps, Plague, Polio [Nervous], Q Fever, Radiation Damage [Cellular Health], Rubella [Integumentary], Reiter's Arthritis, Scurvy, Sepsis, Shigella Infection, Shingles, Staph Infection, Strep Throat [Oral Health], Tularemia, Typhoid, Virus

By Related Properties

For more, see *Oil Properties* on pages 535-538

Antibacterial— arborvitae, basil, black pepper, blue tansy, cassia, cedarwood, cilantro, cinnamon bark, clove, copaiba, coriander, eucalyptus, frankincense, geranium, ginger, lemongrass, lime, litsea, manuka, marjoram, melissa, myrrh, oregano, peppermint, ravintsara, rosemary, Siberian fir, tangerine, tea tree, thyme, turmeric, ylang ylang

Antifungal— arborvitae, blue tansy, cassia, cedarwood, cinnamon bark, copaiba, coriander, cypress, eucalyptus, fennel, ginger, lemon, lemon eucalyptus, lemongrass, litsea, manuka, myrrh, oregano, rosemary, Siberian fir, tangerine, tea tree, turmeric, wild orange

Anti-infectious— bergamot, cardamom, cinnamon bark, copaiba, cypress, eucalyptus, frankincense, geranium, laurel leaf, litsea, myrrh, Roman chamomile, rose, rosemary, tea tree

Anti-inflammatory— arborvitae, bergamot, black pepper, cardamom, blue tansy, cinnamon bark, clary sage, clove, copaiba, coriander, fennel, frankincense, helichrysum, lavender, litsea, manuka, melissa, neroli, oregano, peppermint, pink pepper, Roman chamomile, Siberian fir, spikenard, tangerine, turmeric, wintergreen, yarrowlpom

Antimicrobial— arborvitae, basil, blue tansy, cassia, cilantro, copaiba, cypress, fennel, frankincense, helichrysum, laurel leaf, lavender, lemongrass, litsea, manuka, melissa, neroli, patchouli, ravintsara, Siberian fir, thyme

Antioxidant— black pepper, cassia, cinnamon bark, clove, copaiba, frankincense, grapefruit, helichrysum, lemon, lime, neroli, oregano, tangerine, tea tree, turmeric, vetiver, wild orange, yarrowlpom

Antiseptic— basil, bergamot, cardamom, cedarwood, clary sage, copaiba, cypress, geranium, ginger, helichrysum, jasmine, lavender, lemon, lime, marjoram, melissa, myrrh, neroli, manuka, peppermint, ravintsara, rosemary, Siberian fir, spearmint, tangerine, thyme, vetiver, wild orange, wintergreen

Antiviral— basil, black pepper, blue tansy, cassia, cinnamon bark, clove, copaiba, eucalyptus, ginger, helichrysum, laurel leaf, lemon eucalyptus, litsea, manuka, melissa, myrrh, peppermint, ravintsara, rose, Siberian fir, thyme, tea tree, turmeric, yarrowlpom

Immunostimulant— arborvitae, cassia, cinnamon bark, clove, copaiba, eucalyptus, fennel, frankincense, ginger, lemon, lime, melissa, oregano, ravintsara, rosemary, Siberian fir, spearmint, tea tree, thyme, vetiver, wild orange, yarrowlpom

Stimulant— arborvitae, basil, blue tansy, cardamom, cedarwood, clove, cypress, eucalyptus, fennel, grapefruit, myrrh, pink pepper, Siberian fir, spearmint, tangerine, tea tree, vetiver, wintergreen, ylang ylang

Warming— birch, black pepper, cassia, cinnamon bark, clary sage, clove, eucalyptus, ginger, lemongrass, marjoram, neroli, oregano, peppermint, pink pepper, thyme, tulsi, wintergreen

protocols

LYME DISEASE SUPPORT

Ingredients:

Important *facts* regarding chemistry of essential oils and Lyme:

- **Oregano**— 60-90% carvacrol, kills bacteria, interrupts communication (quorum sensing) between harmful bacteria
- **Thyme**— 55% thymol, 10% carvacrol; protective agent for neurological tissue in brain
- **Clove**— 85% eugenol, controls symptoms, kills bacteria
- **Carvacrol, eugenol, thymol**— are some of the most effective compounds for destroying pathogens and are often even more powerful when combined
- **Cassia**— 80-90% cinnamaldehyde; COX2 inhibitor, antibacterial
- **Cinnamon bark**— 50% cinnamaldehyde; COX2 inhibitor, antibacterial
- **Melissa**— 65% aldehydes, 35% sesquiterpenes; antiviral, antibacterial; disrupts microorganism communication, immunostimulant, anti-inflammatory, antidepressant
- **On Guard®**— contains both cinnamon bark and clove
- **Frankincense**— 87% monoterpenes, 24% sesquiterpenes, analgesic, anti-inflammatory, effective for pain management
- **Patchouli**— 63% sesquiterpenes, antioxidant, offers relief from secondary neurological effects of chronic Lyme

LYME DISEASE INTENSE RESOLVE BLEND

Ingredients:

3 drops oregano
3 drops thyme
3 drops clove
3 drops cassia or cinnamon bark
2 drops On Guard®
2 drops melissa
2 drops frankincense

Directions:

Internal: Place oils in capsule and take 1-2 times daily for 2 weeks depending upon intensity of symptoms. Rest from the blend for one week. Repeat this pattern until symptoms have ceased for at least 2 months.

Topical (use while taking a break from internal use or instead of): Apply diluted 2 drops lemongrass + 1 drop oregano to bottoms of feet before bed. Add oils such as melissa and/or On Guard® as needed or desired.

NOTE: If rash or other discomfort occurs, reduce number of drops used or take a break until resolved. Consider greater dilution with a carrier oil. Improve intestinal elimination, remove certain foods from diet (foods that encourage microorganism over growth), and drink more water.

LYME DISEASE BOMB CAPSULE

Ingredients:

2 drops cinnamon bark or clove
2 drops cassia
2 drops oregano or thyme (alternate; use oregano in 10-day cycles then take a break for 20 days; repeat as long as needed)
2 drops frankincense

Directions

Take oils in a capsule twice daily. Dilute with carrier oil if needed. Add melissa, On Guard®, and/or GX Assist® as needed.

ADDITIONAL LYME SUPPORT

- **Receive an AromaTouch Technique® weekly.** See page 24 in this book.
- **Apply patchouli to bottoms of feet** twice per day to support nervous system. Add other oils as desired. Consider frankincense and wild orange.
- **Supplementation program**— minimum 4 month program:
  - **Foundation:** Microplex VMz®, xEO Mega®, Alpha CRS®+
  - **Digestive/intestinal:** TerraZyme®, PB Assist®+, Zendocrine® Complex
  - **Anti-inflammatory/pain relief:** Deep Blue Polyphenol Complex®, Copaiba Softgels, and/or Turmeric Dual Capsules
  - **Cellular vitality:** DDR Prime® Softgels
  - **Immune Support:** On Guard®
  - **GI cleanse:** GX Assist®

See *Candida* for a detox program also beneficial for Lyme.

PAIN REMEDY

Ingredients:

10 drops copaiba
8 drops AromaTouch®
8 drops Deep Blue®
8 drops rosemary
6 drops lemongrass

Directions

Combine above oils in 10mL roller bottle. Fill remainder with carrier oil and shake well. Apply directly to painful joints and bottoms of feet several times each day as needed.

Additional recipes; use as needed:

- **Mo better:**
  Apply 1-3 drops each On Guard®, melissa, frankincense, and patchouli to bottoms of feet.
- **Sleep** (see *Sleep*):
  Apply 3 drops each vetiver, juniper berry, and lavender to bottoms of feet.
- **Better by morning:**
  Rub 1 drop each basil and lemon at night behind ears to clear symptoms of physical illness by morning.
- **Range of motion:**
  Apply a few drops each bergamot and Siberian fir to muscles affected. Also see *Muscular*, *Skeletal*.

IMMUNE & LYMPHATIC

For more ideas, download the app on Android or iOS.

SKIN WOUND ANTISEPTIC

Ingredients:

6 drops lavender
5 drops tea tree
4 drops frankincense
3 drops geranium
1 oz aloe vera gel

Directions:

Blend in a glass bottle or bowl. Apply using cotton swab to affected areas of skin. Follow with Correct-X®.

COLD & FLU TONIC

Ingredients:

1 drop lavender
2 drops lemon
1 drop peppermint
2 drops tea tree
1 drop Siberian fir

Directions:

Mix oils in 1 C warm water, stir, and drink.

COLD & FLU BOMB

Ingredients:

2 drops On Guard®
3 drops thyme
3 drops lemon
2 drops frankincense
1 drop peppermint

Directions:

Take in a capsule. Repeat every 3-4 hours until symptoms subside.

WINTER-TO-SPRING BLEND

Ingredients:

2 drops thyme
2 drops black pepper
4 drops grapefruit
2 drops lavender

Directions:

Combine and apply diluted on bottoms of feet 5 consecutive nights to help navigate seasonal and environmental changes.

SUMMER-TO-FALL BLEND

Ingredients:

2 drops clove
4 drops Siberian fir
4 drops lemon

Directions:

Apply diluted on bottoms of feet 5 consecutive nights to help transition with seasonal and environmental changes.

NIP-IT-IN-THE-BUD STEAMER

If a cold is coming on, blend Siberian fir, eucalyptus, and tea tree and place a few drops of each in a pan of steaming water. Inhale steam. Place a towel over head to make a tent to trap steam for greater potency. Take caution with hot pan.

HIV/AIDS SUPPORT

As a foundation, use Critical Autoimmune Supplementation Program- See *Autoimmnune.*

Initial Cleanse:

- Take 2-4 drops lemon in water daily (glass container only).
- Take 2-4 drops each On Guard®, melissa, and peppermint in a capsule daily for 10 days followed by 5 days of PB Assist®+. Repeat as long as needed.
- Avoid processed foods and beverages, refined sugars; increase fresh fruits and vegetables.

Ongoing Support- use twice daily

- Take 2-4 drops lemon in water (glass container only).
- Take 3-4 drops each frankincense, On Guard®, and rosemary in capsule.
- Rub 2-3 drops each Balance® and On Guard® on bottoms of feet. Apply 2-4 drops lavender for stress relief or as a sleep aid at bedtime.
- Rub 1-2 drops frankincense on base of neck.
- Diffuse Elevation or Adaptiv™ to uplift and stabilize and Serenity® at night for relaxation.
- Use a hot compress for 15 minutes after lightly applying with soothing or calming oils onto back and along spine for comfort and relief.
- For other specific issues, refer to a respective *Focus Area.*

Perform the AromaTouch Technique®

once a week. See *AromaTouch Technique®*. Benefits include:

- Strengthening immune system.
- Relieving stress inflammation and supressed moods.

ENHANCE IMMUNITY SUGAR SCRUB

Ingredients:

2 C brown or organic sugar
1 C fractionated coconut oil
15 drops black spruce
6 drops tea tree
5 drops eucalyptus
5 drops lemon

Directions:

Mix and store in glass container. Scrub extremities gently and rinse. For added benefits, soak in bath after scrubbing.

conditions

Abnormal cellular activity– frankincense, DDR Prime®; see *Cellular Health*

AIDS/HIV*– arborvitae, cassia, cinnamon bark, clove, helichrysum, melissa, myrrh, ravintsara, rosemary, tea tree, thyme, DDR Prime®, On Guard®

Airborne germs and bacteria– arborvitae, cedarwood, eucalyptus, Siberian fir, tulsi, Abōde™, Air-X™, Breathe®, On Guard®, Purify; see "Antimicrobial" property

Allergies*– See *Allergies*

Bacteria– arborvitae, basil, black pepper, blue tansy, cassia, cedarwood, cilantro, cinnamon bark, citronella, clove, copaiba, coriander, eucalyptus, frankincense, geranium, lemongrass, lime, marjoram, melissa, myrrh, neroli, oregano, petitgrain, ravintsara, rose, rosemary, Siberian fir, tangerine, tea tree, thyme, Abōde™, DDR Prime®, On Guard®, Purify, Zendrocrine®

Bacteria, staph– arborvitae, celery seed, cilantro, cinnamon bark, helichrysum, melissa, rose, rosemary, Cheer®; see "Antibacterial" property

Boils/carbuncles– eucalyptus, frankincense, lavender, marjoram, myrrh, sandalwood, Immortelle

Body temperature issues, too cold– See "Warming" property

Body temperature issues, too hot–bergamot, bergamot mint, black pepper, eucalyptus, lemon, peppermint

Catch colds/get sick easily– see "Weakened/suppressed immune system" on next page

Cellulitis– cardamom, geranium, juniper berry, lemongrass, oregano, sandalwood, tea tree, see "Antibacterial" property

Chicken Pox– black pepper, blue tansy, eucalyptus, frankincense, patchouli, tea tree, thyme, On Guard®, Stronger™

Chills– basil, black pepper, cinnamon bark, ginger, wintergreen, On Guard®, Stronger™; see "Warming" property

Cholera– black pepper, cinnamon bark, eucalyptus, melissa, rosemary, Zendrocrine®; see "Antibacterial" property

Cold, chronic– basil, cardamom, cypress, On Guard®, Stronger™, Zendrocrine®

Cold/flu– black pepper, blue tansy, cassia, celery seed, cinnamon bark, clove, eucalyptus, frankincense, ginger, juniper berry, lemon, lime, oregano, peppermint, rose, rosemary, Siberian fir, tea tree, thyme, wild orange, YarrowlPom, Air-X™, Breathe®, tea tree, On Guard®, Stronger™; see "Antiviral" property

Cold/flu, reduce aches/pains from†– black pepper, cypress, cedarwood, coriander, laurel leaf, magnolia, oregano, peppermint, ravintsara, thyme, Siberian fir, wild orange, Air-X™, AromaTouch®, Breathe®, Deep Blue®, On Guard®, PastTense®

**See Protocols on pg. 357-358*

IMMUNE & LYMPHATIC

Cold sores— arborvitae, bergamot, clove, geranium, helichrysum, lavender, lemon, lemon eucalyptus, melissa, myrrh, tea tree, tulsi, On Guard®, Zendrocrine®; see "Antiviral" property, *Oral Health*
Common Cold— See "Cold/flu"
Conjunctivitis/pinkeye— clary sage, Douglas fir, frankincense, lavender, jasmine, melissa, rosemary, spikenard, tea tree, Correct-X ointment; see "Antibacterial" property
Contagious diseases— clove, cinnamon bark, ginger, juniper berry, DDR Prime®, On Guard®, Purify; see "Antibacterial, Anti-infectious, Antimicrobial, Antiviral" properties
Earache— basil, cypress, ginger, helichrysum, laurel leaf, lavender, ravintsara, Breathe®, Citrus Bliss®, Deep Blue®, Passion®; see *Respiratory*
Epidemics— basil, Douglas fir, ginger, juniper berry, lemon, peppermint, DDR Prime®, On Guard®
Fever— arborvitae, basil, birch, black pepper, cypress, eucalyptus, helichrysum, juniper berry, lavender, lemon, lemon eucalyptus, lemongrass, lime, patchouli, peppermint, pink pepper, Roman chamomile, rose, Siberian fir, spearmint, wild orange, YarrowlPom, Forgive®, Passion®, PastTense®
Fever blisters— see "Cold sores" above
Flu— See "Cold/flu"
Fungus/candida— arborvitae, basil, blue tansy, cassia, cedarwood, cilantro, cinnamon bark, clove, copaiba, coriander, lemongrass, marjoram, myrrh, oregano, patchouli, rosemary, Siberian fir, tea tree, thyme, turmeric, Purify; see *Candida*,
Germs— blue tansy, grapefruit, lemon, lemon eucalytpus, lime, wild orange, Abōde™, Citrus Bliss®, On Guard®, Purify; see "Antimicrobial, Antiseptic" properties
Glands, swollen— cardamom, cypress, Douglas fir, frankincense, ginger, lemon, rosemary, sandalwood, tea tree, Breathe®, On Guard®, Purify, Stronger™
Herpes simplex— basil, bergamot, black pepper, clove, eucalyptus, frankincense, helichrysum, lavender, melissa, myrrh, oregano, patchouli, peppermint, sandalwood, tea tree, thyme, Console®, On Guard®; see "Antiviral" property
Illness prevention— clove, cinnamon bark, oregano, thyme, Adaptiv™, On Guard®
Illness recovery— cinnamon bark, Douglas fir, juniper berry, lemon, lemongrass, thyme, wild orange, Adaptiv™, Slim & Sassy®
Immune, weakness— cinnamon bark, clove, copaiba, Douglas fir, frankincense, green mandarin, petitgrain, sandalwood, tangerine, tea tree, Citrus Bliss®, DDR Prime®, On Guard®, TerraShield®, Zendrocrine®
Infection— black pepper, cardamom, cassia, cinnamon bark, clove, lavender, melissa, oregano, tea tree, thyme, wintergreen, On Guard®; see "Antibacterial", "Anti-infectious", "Antimicrobial", "Antiviral" properties
Infectious diseases— bergamot, cassia, lemongrass, melissa, oregano, rosemary, thyme; see "Antibacterial", "Anti-infectious", "Antimicrobial", "Antiviral" properties
Leprosy— arborvitae, cedarwood, frankincense, melissa, myrrh, peppermint, sandalwood, thyme, DDR Prime®
Lymph, congestion/stagnation— birch, cassia, cypress, Douglas fir, frankincense, geranium, grapefruit, laurel leaf, lavender, lemon, lemongrass, lime, petitgrain, pink pepper, sandalwood, tangerine, wintergreen, tea tree, Air-X™, Citrus Bliss®, Motivate®, Passion®, Purify; see *Respiratory*
Malaria— bergamot, cardamom, cinnamon bark, Douglas fir, eucalyptus, laurel leaf, lemon, lemongrass, ravintsara, tea tree, thyme, Breathe®, Zendrocrine®; see *Parasites*
Measles— blue tansy, clove, coriander, eucalyptus, juniper berry, lavender, tea tree, wild orange, DDR Prime®, On Guard®; see "Antiviral" property
Microorganisms (bacterial/viral)— black pepper, cinnamon bark, clove, copaiba, lemongrass, oregano, Siberian fir, tangerine, tea tree, thyme, YarrowlPom, On Guard®
MRSA— cinnamon bark, cilantro, clove, frankincense, geranium, juniper berry, lemon, melissa, oregano, peppermint, rose, tea tree, thyme, DDR Prime®, On Guard®; see "Antibacterial" property
Mumps— basil, blue tansy, cinnamon bark, lavender, lemon, rosemary, tea tree, DDR Prime®, On Guard®, Zendrocrine®
Night sweats— ginger, lime, peppermint, DDR Prime®, DigestZen®, Zendrocrine®; see *Women's Health, Endocrine (Thyroid)*
Parasites— clove; see *Parasites*
Paralysis, facial— frankincense, helichrysum, marjoram, melissa, rosemary, thyme, DDR Prime®
Rheumatic fever— arborvitae, basil, coriander, eucalyptus, ginger, melissa, oregano, patchouli, thyme, wintergreen
Rubella— basil, black pepper, clove, frankincense, lemon, melissa, oregano, tea tree, thyme, On Guard®, Slim & Sassy®
Ringworm— geranium, neroli, oregano, Roman chamomile, tea tree, thyme, HD Clear®; see *Integumentary*
Scurvy— cypress, geranium, ginger, grapefruit, helichrysum, lemon, lemongrass, Zendrocrine®
Sore throat— cinnamon bark, copaiba, lemon, melissa, oregano, Siberian fir, tea tree, thyme, Breathe®, On Guard®
Spleen— bergamot, cardamom, clary sage, lemon, rose, On Guard®
Spleen, congestion— cinnamon bark, fennel, helichrysum, lemon, sandalwood, InTune®
Spleen obstruction— basil, frankincense, ginger, marjoram, melissa
Staph— cilantro, cinnamon bark, frankincense, geranium, lemon, melissa, oregano, peppermint, ravintsara, rose, tea tree, thyme, Abōde™, HD Clear®, On Guard®, Purify
Strep— cinnamon bark, frankincense, lemon, oregano, On Guard®
Sexually transmitted diseases:
- **Chlamydia**— arborvitae, basil, clove, tea tree, thyme, On Guard®
- **Gonorrhea**— basil, copaiba, frankincense, rosemary, sandalwood, tea tree
- **Syphilis**— black pepper, frankincense, tea tree, melissa, myrrh, rosemary

Stomach flu (viral gastroenteritis)— arborvitae, celery seed, oregano, thyme, DDR Prime®, On Guard®, Zendrocrine®; see "Antiviral" property
Strep throat— cardamom, cinnamon bark, eucalyptus, lemon, oregano, tea tree, thyme, Breathe®, On Guard®; see "Antibacterial" property
Throat, sore— cinnamon bark, geranium, lavender, lemon, lime, oregano, thyme, Breathe®, On Guard®, Passion®; see *Respiratory*
Tonsillitis— cinnamon bark, copaiba, eucalyptus, frankincense, ginger, lavender, lemon, myrrh, Roman chamomile, tea tree, Breathe®, On Guard®; see *Oral Health*
Typhoid fever— basil, blue tansy, cinnamon bark, clove, eucalyptus, lemon, oregano, peppermint, tea tree, On Guard®, Zendrocrine®
Virus— arborvitae, bergamot, black pepper, blue tansy, cassia, cinnamon bark, clove, copaiba, eucalyptus, frankincense, helichrysum, laurel leaf, marjoram, melissa, myrrh, oregano, patchouli, peppermint, ravintsara, rose, rosemary, tea tree, thyme, turmeric, YarrowlPom, Console®, On Guard®; see "Antiviral" property
Viral, hepatitis— basil, cedarwood, clove, geranium, myrrh, rosemary, Motivate®, Zendrocrine®
Virus, spinal— melissa, tea tree, thyme, wintergreen; see "Antiviral" property
Weakened/suppressed immune system— frankincense, myrrh, tea tree, thyme, Forgive®, On Guard®, Stronger™
White blood cells (leukocytes), low count/lack of formation— frankincense, lavender, lemon, lime, myrrh
Zoonosis— cedarwood, clove, eucalyptus, frankincense, melissa, myrrh, tea tree, thyme, On Guard®, Stronger™

Integumentary

Hair, Skin, & Nails

INTEGUMENTARY

THE INTEGUMENTARY SYSTEM consists of the skin, hair, and nails. On the broadest scale, this system supports immune function and regulates homeostasis. It constitutes the body's first line of defense against things that would disrupt its delicate balance and registers external stimuli through sensory receptors that communicate touch, pain, and pressure.

With a surface area averaging eighteen square feet, the skin is the largest organ of the body. It has two layers: the inner layer is called the dermis. The epidermis, or outer layer, consists of several strata that produce keratin, which gives strength and elasticity to the skin; melanin, which gives it its color; Merkel's cells, which facilitate touch reception; and Langerhans' cells, which produce antigens to support the immune system. And as a living organ, deep-level cells continually divide and push older cells to the surface to be worn off—millions every day—leaving behind a new epidermis every five to seven weeks.

The skin protects the internal organs, guards against infection, regulates temperature change and hydration levels through perspiration, and stores water, fat, and glucose. It excretes waste, generates vitamin D when exposed to ultraviolet light, and secretes melanin to protect against sunburn. It also has the capacity to form new cells to repair minor cuts and abrasions.

The array of dermatological conditions that may afflict people ranges from warts, eczema, acne, and moles to psoriasis, vitiligo, and a variety of skin cancers. Hair and nail conditions can be unsightly, uncomfortable, or even painful. Since many skin, hair, and nail conditions are an outward reflection of other imbalances going on inside the body, it is important to focus on detoxing, cleansing, and supplementing vital nutrition to the cells and internal organs in addition to essential oil applications that can easily target the area of concern.

Natural solutions are very effective and can be used as a first line of defense toward various integumentary conditions. If problems or conditions persist or cause concern, proper medical attention should be sought. Keep in mind that natural solutions can be used safely together with medical treatments if the latter becomes necessary. Many essential oils that are beneficial for integumentary support are diverse in the conditions they can impact. Some oils are more obvious choices, such as lavender and geranium, with their marvelous healing properties. Other oils target more of the underlying factors. For example, birch oil is great when used in ointments, creams, and compresses, especially for inflamed skin (eczema, boils, dermatitis, psoriasis, ulcers, etc.). There are a diverse number of oils and solutions that can be realized.

top solutions

Single Oil

Lavender, Magnolia– calm reactions, support healing and maintaining healthy tissue (pgs. 175, 184)

Sandalwood, Myrrh– soothe, promote regeneration and toning (pgs. 218, 191)

Geranium, Neroli– regenerate tissue and tone skin (pgs. 152, 193)

Frankincense, Cedarwood– cleanse, restore, invigorate skin, reduce inflammation (pgs. 151, 120)

Helichrysum, Yarrow|Pom– regenerate tissue and reduce scarring (pgs. 160, 248)

Blends

Immortelle– restores and tones skin, promotes anti-aging (pg. 166)

HD Clear®– cleanses skin and reduces inflammation, helps eliminate blemishes and acne (pg. 159)

Supplements

Alpha CRS®+, **Bone Nutrient Complex** (pg. 255), GX Assist®, **IQ Mega** (pg. 260), Microplex VMz®, PB Assist®+, TerraZyme®, **xEO Mega®** (pg. 271), **Yarrow|Pom Capsules** (pg. 272), Zendocrine® Complex

usage tips

For best support of hair, skin and nails:

- **Topical:** Apply oils directly to hair, scalp, nails, and skin. Use a carrier oil to dilute and reduce sensitivity to skin when necessary, especially with infants, elderly, and compromised skin.
- **Internal:** Consume specified oils either by capsule or under tongue. Gut health is a major component of integumentary health. See *Digestive & Intestinal, Candida.*

Related Ailments

Acne, Actinic Keratosis, Age Spots, Bags Under Eyes, Baldness, Bed Sores, Blisters, Blisters from Sun, Boils, Brittle Nails, Burns, Calluses, Chapped Skin, Clogged Pores, Cold Sores, Corns, Cuts, Cyst [Cellular Health], Dandruff, Dehydrated Skin, Dry Hair, Dry Lips, Dry Skin, Eczema, Excessive Perspiration, Fragile Hair, Genital Warts, Hair Loss, Head Lice, Hernia (incisional), Ichthyosis Vulgaris, Impetigo [Immune], Infected Wounds, Ingrown Toenail, Itching [Allergies], Lichen Nitidus, Moles [Cellular Health], Molluscum Oily Hair, Oily Skin, Plantar Warts, Poison Ivy [Allergies], Porphyria, Psoriasis, Rashes [Allergies], Ringworm, Rosacea, Scabies, Scarring, Sebaceous Cyst, Skin Ulcers, Stevens-Johnson Syndrome, Stretch Marks [Pregnancy], Sunburn, Swimmer's Itch [Candida], Tissue Regeneration [Cellular Health, Muscular], Ulcers—Leg and Varicose [Cardiovascular], Vitiligo, Warts, Wounds, Wrinkles

By Related Properties

For more, see *Oil Properties* on pages 535-538

Analgesic– arborvitae, basil, black pepper, blue tansy, cassia, cinnamon bark, copaiba, coriander, cypress, eucalyptus, fennel, frankincense, ginger, juniper berry, lavender, litsea, peppermint, rosemary, Siberian fir, tea tree, tulsi, turmeric, yarrowlpom
Antifungal– arborvitae, blue tansy, cassia, cinnamon bark, clary sage, copaiba, coriander, ginger, helichrysum, lemon eucalyptus, lemongrass, litsea, manuka, patchouli, ravintsara, Siberian fir, spearmint, tea tree, thyme, turmeric
Anti-infectious– cedarwood, cinnamon bark, clove, copaiba, cypress, frankincense, geranium, lavender, litsea, marjoram, Roman chamomile, rosemary, tea tree
Anti-inflammatory– arborvitae, basil, birch, black pepper, blue tansy, cedarwood, cinnamon bark, clove, copaiba, coriander, fennel, frankincense, ginger, lavender, lime, litsea, manuka, myrrh, neroli, patchouli, Siberian fir, spearmint, spikenard, tangerine, turmeric, wintergreen, yarrowlpom
Antimicrobial– basil, blue tansy, cardamom, cinnamon bark, clary sage, copaiba, cypress, frankincense, helichrysum, green mandarin, laurel leaf, lemon, lemongrass, litsea, manuka, myrrh, neroli, oregano, ravintsara, rosemary, Siberian fir, thyme
Antimutagenic– cinnamon bark, copaiba, ginger, lavender, lemongrass, neroli, tangerine, turmeric, vanilla
Antiseptic– bergamot, birch, clary sage, clove, copaiba, fennel, frankincense, ginger, grapefruit, juniper berry, lavender, lemon eucalyptus, manuka, marjoram, myrrh, neroli, oregano, ravintsara, sandalwood, Siberian fir, spearmint, tangerine, tea tree, vetiver, wintergreen, yarrowlpom, ylang ylang
Antiviral– arborvitae, basil, blue tansy, cassia, clove, copaiba, eucalyptus, ginger, helichrysum, lime, litsea, manuka, melissa, myrrh, rose, turmeric, Siberian fir, yarrowlpom
Astringent– cassia, cedarwood, clary sage, cypress, geranium, grapefruit, green mandarin, helichrysum, lemon, litsea, myrrh, sandalwood, wintergreen, yarrowlpom
Cytophylactic– arborvitae, frankincense, geranium, lavender, manuka, neroli, rosemary, tangerine, tulsi
Deodorant– bergamot, clary sage, citronella, copaiba, cypress, eucalyptus, geranium, lavender, lemon eucalyptus, lemongrass, litsea, manuka, neroli, patchouli, Siberian fir, spikenard
Insect repellent– arborvitae, birch, blue tansy, cedarwood, cinnamon bark, eucalyptus, geranium, laurel leaf, lemongrass, litsea, patchouli, ravintsara, thyme, vetiver, ylang ylang
Regenerative– basil, cedarwood, clove, coriander, geranium, jasmine, lavender, lemongrass, manuka, myrrh, neroli, patchouli, sandalwood, tea tree, wild orange, yarrowlpom
Revitalizer– coriander, juniper berry, lemon, lemongrass, lime, manuka
Tonic– arborvitae, basil, birch, cardamom, clary sage, coriander, cypress, fennel, frankincense, geranium, ginger, grapefruit, green mandarin, lavender, lemon, lime, marjoram, myrrh, neroli, patchouli, pink pepper, Roman chamomile, rose, rosemary, sandalwood, Siberian fir, tangerine, thyme, wild orange, ylang ylang, yarrowlpom

conditions

Hair

Dandruff— cedarwood, cypress, lavender, lemon eucalyptus, patchouli, petitgrain, rosemary, tangerine, tea tree, thyme, wintergreen, Abōde™, Cheer®, Elevation, Purify

Dirty— lemon, lime, Citrus Bliss®, Purify

Dry— copaiba, geranium, lavender, patchouli, rosemary, sandalwood, spikenard, wintergreen, Breathe®, ClaryCalm®, Elevation, Zendrocrine®

Dull— lemongrass, lime (has mild bleaching action), rosemary, tea tree, Breathe®, TerraShield®

Fragile/brittle— clary sage, cedarwood, geranium, lavender, Roman chamomile, rosemary, sandalwood, thyme, wintergreen, Breathe®, DDR Prime®

Greasy/oily*— arborvitae, basil, cedarwood, citronella, cypress, geranium, juniper berry (scalp), lemon, peppermint, petitgrain, rosemary, tea tree, thyme, Breathe®, Elevation

Growth, poor— cedarwood, clary sage, geranium, ginger, grapefruit, lavender, lemon, rosemary, thyme, ylang ylang, Citrus Bliss®, Elevation, Motivate®

Lice*— arborvitae, cedarwood, cinnamon, citronella, clove, eucalyptus, geranium, oregano, rosemary, tea tree, thyme, Abōde™, TerraShield®, Zendrocrine®; see *Parasites*

Loss*— arborvitae, cedarwood, clary sage, cypress, eucalyptus, grapefruit, juniper berry, lavender, lemongrass, myrrh, Roman chamomile, rosemary, thyme, tulsi, wintergreen, yarrowlpom, ylang ylang, DDR Prime®

Scalp, itchy/flaky— cedarwood, lavender, rosemary, wintergreen, Forgive®, Zendrocrine®

Split ends— cedarwood, clary sage, lavender, rosemary, ylang ylang, Zendrocrine®

Nails

Brittle Nails— arborvitae, cypress, eucalyptus, frankincense, grapefruit, lavender, lemon, marjoram, myrrh, Roman chamomile, rosemary, sandalwood, wild orange, ClaryCalm®, Immortelle; see *Cardiovascular*

Fungus†— arborvitae, blue tansy, citronella, copaiba, eucalyptus, geranium, oregano, lemongrass, myrrh, ravintsara, tea tree, thyme, Abōde™, DDR Prime®, HD Clear®, On Guard®, Purify, Zendrocrine®; see *Candida*

Hangnail*— basil, black pepper, cilantro, coriander, lavender, rosemary, sandalwood, ylang ylang, Breathe®

Missing (injury)— eucalyptus, frankincense, myrrh, Elevation, On Guard®, TerraShield®

Ridges— eucalyptus, tea tree, thyme, Zendrocrine®

Ripped/split*— eucalyptus, geranium, lemon, tea tree, Citrus Bliss®, Elevation, HD Clear®

Soft/weak*— eucalyptus, fennel, frankincense, grapefruit, lemon, lime, Siberian fir, Citrus Bliss®, Purify

Swelling/red/tender— arborvitae, eucalyptus, lemongrass, myrrh, tea tree, thyme, DDR Prime®, On Guard®, Zendrocrine®

Yellowed/infected— eucalyptus, frankincense, lemon, myrrh, tea tree, thyme, AromaTouch®, Elevation, On Guard®, Zendrocrine®

Skin

NOTE: See *First Aid* for Bites & Stings; *Allergies* for Hives, Rashes, etc. for additional suggestions.

Acne— arborvitae, bergamot, black spruce, blue tansy, citronella, copaiba, cedarwood (astringent), clary sage, coriander, cypress, frankincense, geranium, grapefruit, green mandarin, helichrysum, juniper berry, lavender, lemon, magnolia, myrrh, neroli, patchouli, petitgrain, rosemary, sandalwood, Siberian fir, spearmint, tea tree, thyme, tulsi, wintergreen, yarrowlpom, ylang ylang, DDR Prime®, Forgive®, HD Clear®, Immortelle, Purify

Aging/age spots— basil, copaiba, coriander, fennel, frankincense, geranium, helichrysum, lavender, lemon, lime, magnolia, myrrh, neroli, petitgrain, Roman chamomile, rose, sandalwood, spikenard, tangerine, vanilla, vetiver, yarrowlpom, DDR Prime®, Immortelle, Whisper®

Athlete's foot— arborvitae, cinnamon bark, citronella, clove, coriander, lemon eucalyptus, lemongrass, myrrh, oregano, patchouli, tea tree, thyme, DDR Prime®, Purify; see *Candida*

Appearance, poor/dull— basil, cedarwood, Douglas fir, fennel, frankincense, geranium, lemon, lemongrass, lime, myrrh, sandalwood, wild orange, HD Clear®, Immortelle

Bags under eyes— cedarwood, frankincense, helichrysum, juniper berry, lavender, lemon, lime, Roman chamomile, sandalwood, Immortelle, Serenity®, Zendrocrine®

Blister, friction/heat/liquid-filled— copaiba, eucalyptus, frankincense, lavender, myrrh, patchouli, sandalwood, Immortelle

Body odor— arborvitae, cilantro, citronella, copaiba, coriander, Douglas fir, eucalyptus, lemon eucalyptus, lemongrass, neroli, patchouli, Siberian fir, tangerine, tea tree, Elevation, Whisper®, Zendrocrine®

Boils/carbuncles— bergamot, frankincense, helichrysum, lavender, marjoram, myrrh, neroli, Roman chamomile, sandalwood, Immortelle

Bruises— arborvitae, blue tansy, copaiba, clove, cypress, fennel, geranium, helichrysum, lavender, Roman chamomile, Siberian fir, ylang ylang, AromaTouch®, DDR Prime®, Deep Blue®, Zendrocrine®

Bumps— clary sage, frankincense, patchouli, wild orange, Slim & Sassy®, Zendrocrine®

Burns— copabia, eucalyptus, frankincense, geranium, helichrysum, lavender, lemon eucalyptus, myrrh, peppermint, Roman chamomile, Siberian fir, spearmint, tangerine, Immortelle; see *First Aid*

Calluses— cypress, Douglas fir, lavender, oregano, Roman chamomile, Siberian fir, HD Clear®

Capillaries, broken— geranium, helichrysum, lemon, yarrowlpom; see *Cardiovascular*

Cell renewal— arborvitae, basil, cedarwood, frankincense, helichrysum, jasmine, lavender, lemongrass, lime, magnolia, myrrh, patchouli, rosemary, sandalwood, spearmint, tea tree, thyme, wild orange, DDR Prime®, Immortelle

Cellulitis— See *Immune & Lymphatic*

Chapped/cracked/dry/peeling— copaiba, frankincense, green mandarin, jasmine, magnolia, myrrh, neroli, patchouli, petitgrain, sandalwood, spearmint, tangerine, turmeric, Immortelle, Purify, Correct-X®

Circulation, poor— geranium, lemongrass, marjoram, rose

Collagen, lack of— helichrysum, lemongrass, sandalwood, yarrowlpom

Corns— arborvitae, clove, grapefruit, lemon, peppermint, ylang ylang, Citrus Bliss®, DDR Prime®, TerraShield®

Cuts/wounds*— basil, cardamom, frankincense, geranium, green mandarin, lavender, magnolia, helichrysum, juniper berry, lavender, lemongrass, marjoram, myrrh, rose, sandalwood, tea tree, tulsi, yarrowlpom, On Guard®

Damaged— arborvitae, basil, cedarwood, cilantro, cypress, frankincense, geranium, helichrysum, lemongrass, lime, neroli, sandalwood, wild orange, DDR Prime®, Immortelle

Dermatitis*— black spruce, blue tansy, geranium, helichrysum, patchouli, Siberian fir, thyme, Elevation, HD Clear®
Diseased— birch, cedarwood, geranium, lavender, oregano, thyme, wintergreen, Zendrocrine®
Eczema/psoriasis*— arborvitae, bergamot, birch, black spruce, blue tansy, cedarwood, copaiba, Douglas fir, geranium, helichrysum, juniper berry, lavender, melissa, myrrh, neroli, oregano, patchouli, peppermint, Roman chamomile, rosemary, Siberian fir, spearmint, thyme, turmeric, wintergreen, yarrowlpom, ylang ylang, Adaptiv™, Forgive®, HD Clear®; see *Candida*
Facial, thread veins— rose, Immortelle
Fine lines or cracks— lavender, sandalwood, vetiver, DDR Prime®, Immortelle; see "Aging/age spots" on previous page
Flushed— wild orange, Breathe®, Purify
Fungus— arborvitae, blue tansy, cedarwood, clove, frankincense, lavender, lemon eucalyptus, myrrh, patchouli, Roman chamomile, tea tree, thyme, turmeric, Zendrocrine®, HD Clear®; see *Candida*
Growth, small/fleshy/rough/grainy— fennel, grapefruit, thyme, HD Clear®, Elevation, Slim & Sassy®, Zendrocrine®
Heels, cracked— copaiba, myrrh, sandalwood, vetiver, Correct-X
Hemorrhoids— cypress, geranium, helichrysum, myrrh, patchouli, Roman chamomile, sandalwood, yarrowlpom, AromaTouch®, DigestZen®, Zendrocrine®
Hernia, incision— arborvitae, basil, geranium, helichrysum, lemongrass, melissa, On Guard®, Zendrocrine®
Impetigo— geranium, lavender, oregano, vetiver, Purify, Whisper®, Zendrocrine®
Infection— arborvitae, cassia, cinnamon bark, clove, copaiba, Douglas fir, eucalyptus, frankincense, juniper berry, lavender, melissa, myrrh, oregano, patchouli, peppermint, rose, sandalwood, tea tree, thyme, tulsi, On Guard®, Purify
Inflammation/redness— cedarwood, geranium, jasmine, juniper berry, lavender, helichrysum, magnolia, peppermint, Roman chamomile, rose, sandalwood, wild orange, ylang ylang, DDR Prime®, Immortelle, On Guard®, Serenity®
Itching— blue tansy, cilantro, lavender, magnolia, patchouli, peppermint, Roman chamomile, sandalwood, tea tree, vetiver, wild orange, Immortelle, Slim & Sassy®, Zendrocrine®
Lips, chapped/cracked/dry/peeling— cedarwood, jasmine, lavender, myrrh, sandalwood, Whisper®, Correct-X®
Moles— frankincense, geranium, juniper berry, lavender, oregano, sandalwood, wild orange, DDR Prime®, Elevation, HD Clear®, TerraShield®, Zendrocrine®
Oily— bergamot, cedarwood, coriander, frankincense, geranium, grapefruit, green mandarin, jasmine, petitgrain, sandalwood, wild orange, ylang ylang, Breathe®, Forgive®, HD Clear®
Pores, clogged— cedarwood, lemon, tea tree, juniper berry, petitgrain, sandalwood, tea tree, DDR Prime®, HD Clear®, Immortelle, Purify
Pores, enlarged— lemongrass, sandalwood, DDR Prime®, HD Clear®, Immortelle; see "Acne" on previous page
Perspiration, excessive— cilantro, coriander, cypress, Douglas fir, geranium, lemon, lemongrass, peppermint, petitgrain, Zendrocrine®
Perspiration, lack of— arborvitae, basil, black pepper, citronella, cypress, ginger, Siberian fir, tea tree, wild orange, yarrowlpom, Zendrocrine®
Pigmentation, excess— basil, cedarwood, frankincense, lavender, lemon, Roman chamomile, sandalwood, spearmint, ylang ylang, Citrus Bliss®, Immortelle, Whisper®
Pigmentation, lack of— bergamot, cedarwood, Douglas fir, sandalwood, vetiver, DDR Prime®, Immortelle
Radiation wounds— arborvitae, basil, cedarwood, clove, frankincense, geranium, helichrysum, jasmine, lavender, myrrh, patchouli, rosemary, sandalwood, tea tree, thyme, tulsi, wild orange, DDR Prime®, Immortelle
Rashes— arborvitae, blue tansy, frankincense, lavender, lemon, Roman chamomile, sandalwood, tea tree, vetiver, ClaryCalm®, Immortelle, Purify, Serenity®, Slim & Sassy®, Zendrocrine®; see *Candida*
Ringworm— cardamom, clove, geranium, lemongrass, tea tree, neroli, oregano, petitgrain, Roman chamomile, tea tree, thyme, HD Clear®
Rough, dry, scaly cracked— black spruce, cedarwood, jasmine, lavender, magnolia, myrrh, Roman chamomile, sandalwood, yarrowlpom, Whisper®, Correct-X
Sagging— basil, coriander, frankincense, geranium, grapefruit, helichrysum, jasmine, juniper berry, lime, myrrh, sandalwood, tea tree, yarrowlpom, Citrus Bliss®, DDR Prime®, Immortelle
Scabs— arborvitae, basil, birch, coriander, eucalyptus, frankincense, geranium, helichrysum, juniper berry, lavender, lemon, lemongrass, lime, spearmint, Citrus Bliss®, Elevation, Immortelle
Scarring— cypress, frankincense, geranium, helichrysum, lavender, magnolia, neroli, rose, sandalwood, yarrowlpom, vetiver, Immortelle
Sensitive/tender— arborvitae, frankincense, ginger, helichrysum, jasmine, lavender, magnolia, marjoram, rosemary, tea tree, wild orange, DDR Prime®, Elevation, TerraShield®, Whisper®
Skin disorders— arborvitae, black pepper, cilantro, coriander, frankincense, geranium, helichrysum, oregano, rosemary, tangerine, wild orange, Immortelle
Skin tags— cedarwood, coriander, frankincense, geranium, lavender, oregano, sandalwood
Sores— lavender, myrrh, patchouli, sandalwood, spearmint, On Guard®, Purify; see "Cuts/wounds" on previous page
Stretch marks— arborvitae, cypress, Douglas fir, frankincense, geranium, lavender, magnolia, myrrh, neroli, sandalwood, tangerine, AromaTouch®, ClaryCalm®, Immortelle; ;see *Pregnancy* for protocols
Sunburns*— arborvitae, blue tansy, eucalyptus, frankincense, geranium, helichrysum, lavender, myrrh, peppermint, sandalwood, spearmint, Immortelle
Sunburns, prevent (sunscreen)— arborvitae, helichrysum, lavender, myrrh
Tightened/hardened— frankincense, patchouli, DDR Prime®, Purify, Zendrocrine®
Tone, lack of/imbalanced*— arborvitae, basil, cypress, Douglas fir, frankincense, lemon, lemongrass, rose, sandalwood, ylang ylang, Citrus Bliss®, Immortelle
Ulcers (open crater, red, tender edges)— cedarwood, coriander, frankincense, geranium, helichrysum, lavender, lemongrass, myrrh, sandalwood, tea tree, wild orange, Immortelle
UV radiation— clove, coriander, helichrysum, lavender, myrrh, sandalwood, DDR Prime®
Varicose ulcer— cedarwood, coriander, frankincense, geranium, yarrowlpom, AromaTouch®, DDR Prime®
Varicose veins— bergamot, cardamom, cypress, geranium, helichrysum, lemon, lemongrass, rosemary, yarrowlpom, AromaTouch®, DDR Prime®, DigestZen®
Vitiligo— bergamot, sandalwood, vetiver, Immortelle, DDR Prime®, Whisper®, Zendrocrine®
Warts*— arborvitae, cedarwood, cinnamon bark, clove, frankincense, lemon, lemongrass, lime, melissa, oregano, tea tree, thyme, tulsi, DDR Prime®, AromaTouch®, Forgive®, On Guard®
White patches on skin, inside mouth— bergamot, black pepper, frankincense, myrrh, sandalwood, tea tree
Wounds, weeping (yellow/green pus)*— bergamot, clary sage, copaiba, frankincense, helichrysum, tea tree, wild orange, yarrowlpom
Wrinkles— arborvitae, Douglas fir, fennel, geranium, grapefruit, green mandarin, frankincense, helichrysum, jasmine, lavender, magnolia, myrrh, neroli, petitgrain, Roman chamomile, rose, sandalwood, Siberian fir, spikenard, wild orange, yarrowlpom, Forgive®, Immortelle

*See Protocols on pg. 364

protocols

Skin

DERMATITIS/ECZEMA BLEND

Ingredients:

10 drops frankincense
10 drops lavender
10 drops cedarwood
10 drops helichrysum
3 drops lemongrass
4 drops juniper berry
5 drops geranium
45 drops fractionated coconut oil

Directions:

Add ingredients to 15mL glass amber bottle. Add a sprayer top. Apply at least twice daily and as needed.

GRAPEFRUIT EXFOLIATING SCRUB– to boost circulation and tone skin. Do not use on sensitive or inflamed skin.

Ingredients:

30 mL fractionated coconut oil
3 oz fine sea salt or sugar
40 drops grapefruit
10 drops Douglas fir

Directions:

- Pour carrier oil into a glass bowl for blending, add essential oils, mix slightly. Add sea salt in stages, stirring until a thick paste is formed. Add more carrier oil or salt to adjust consistency as desired.
- Place mixture in dark glass jar to preserve. Make note of date it was made. Keeps for 6 months.
- **Application:** Massage scrub in circular motion directly onto skin. Rinse with warm water.

NATURAL ACNE BLEND

Ingredients:

4 drops copaiba
4 drops frankincense
1 oz witch hazel
3 drops green mandarin
3 drops lavender or tulsi

Directions:

Combine into 2 oz glass sprayer bottle and spray on affected area.

REFRESHING SUGAR SCRUB:

Scrub: Mix 2 C brown sugar, ½ C coconut oil, and 20 drops each tangerine and spearmint. Store in an airtight glass container.

SKIN REJUVENATION

Layer magnolia and neroli, followed by 1 drop each lavender, Roman chamomile, and yarrowlpom.

SKIN TONE AND TEXTURE HEALTH

Ingredients:

10 drops yarrowlpom
10 drops helichrysum
6 drops lavender
8 drops lemongrass
4 drops patchouli
5 drops myrrh

Directions:

Add to 10mL roller bottle and top off with carrier oil. Gently shake to mix before each use. Apply to desired areas of skin 2-4x's daily.

SUNBURN REMEDY

Ingredients:

25 drops lavender
25 drops helichrysum
10 drops peppermint
10 drops frankincense

Directions:

Add to 10mL roller or glass spray bottle. Fill with carrier oil and apply gently to sunburn.

WART

Use 1 drop Abōde™ with less than a drop of diluted oregano (depending on size of area) twice daily for two weeks.

WOUND CARE– To help heal and prevent infection, apply 1 drop tea tree to affected area to clean. Then apply Correct-X®.

Nails

ANTIFUNGAL NAIL BLEND

Ingredients:

5 drops Abōde™
2 drops myrrh
Carrier oil

Directions:

Mix and apply around and under affected nails 2-3x's per day until gone. Avoid contact with eyes.

HANGNAIL: Apply 1 drop arborvitae to area of concern and massage.

NAIL GROWTH: Combine 30 drops each lemon and rosemary in a 10mL roller bottle. Top off with fractionated coconut oil. Apply to nail bed and massage in and upward.

NAIL SOAK AND CUTICLE CURE— to stimulate circulation and promote healthy shine

Ingredients:

4 drops lavender
2 drops lemon
3 drops sandalwood
Carrier oil

Directions:

Soak for 10 minutes. Buff and moisturize.

NAIL STRENGTHENER

Ingredients:

2 drops lemon
2 drops frankincense
2 drops myrrh
Fractionated coconut oil

Directions:

Combine in glass bowl. Dip fingernails in blend. Massage. Use twice per week.

NOURISH YOUR NAILS

Ingredients:

15 drops lavender
10 drops lemon
4 drops myrrh
2 T carrier oil

Directions:

Mix in 2 oz glass bottle with a dropper lid. Fill remainder with the coconut oil. Apply 1 drop of mixture per nail and massage.

SPLIT OR DAMAGED NAIL REPAIR

Ingredients:

4 drops sandalwood
2 drops ClaryCalm®
1 drop wild orange
1 drop myrrh
½ t carrier oil

Directions:

Soak nail in formula each night. Massage in thoroughly to promote absorption. Wipe off excess with tissue.

Hair

LICE OUT BLEND:

Ingredients:

25 drops arborvitae
25 drops tea tree
25 drops rosemary
25 drops TerraShield®
25 drops lemon eucalyptus
OR 75 drops Abōde™

Directions:

Combine in a 4 oz glass spray bottle topped off with distilled water. Spray head and scalp liberally. Let set 20 minutes. Shampoo and then lice comb. Reapply after shampooing. Repeat daily until resolved. Spray works well for pillows, mattresses and other surfaces as well.

GREASY HAIR RESOLVE:

Ingredients:

1 t natural shampoo
1 drop petitigrain and/or lemon

Directions:

Combine shampoo and essential oil. Massage gently into scalp with fingertips. Rinse.

HAIR GROWTH: Add 2 drops each rosemary and lavender with 2 t of jojoba, and stir. Massage into scalp using a circular motion with fingertips. Leave on for 30 minutes and then wash hair with shampoo.

DANDRUFF RESOLVE: Add 3-4 drops Abōde™, tea tree, lemon eucalyptus, and/or tulsi to shampoo prior to a single application. Apply copaiba and patchouli to scalp after towel drying hair prior to drying.

HAIR LOSS REMEDIES:

- Add 1-2 drops each cedarwood, clary sage, tulsi, and rosemary with each shampooing.
- Blend 2 drops each of oils listed above with 2 t fractionated coconut oil. Massage into scalp, cover with a shower cap, and let sit for a few hours or overnight. Then shampoo and condition.
- Combine 8 drops rosemary + 10 drops tulsi + 10 drops sandalwood + 10 drops cedarwood + 10 drops tea tree per 3 oz of shampoo. Work blend into scalp 3-5x's per week and let sit for 20 minutes before rinsing.

Intimacy

INTIMACY

ALL HUMANS have a basic need to love and feel loved. Emotional, intellectual, social, and sexual intimacy contribute to the connection couples experience. Because of past experiences and current health concerns, physical intimacy can often present inherent challenges, including low sex drive, exhaustion/fatigue, aches and pains, chronic illness, hemorrhoids, yeast infections, endometriosis, vaginal dryness, impotence, lack of nitric oxide, oxytocin production, etc.

At times, individuals may be interested in an aphrodisiac, a substance that enhances or stimulates passion and sexual arousal. An aphrodisiac can also help reduce physical, psychological, or emotional conditions that interfere with passion and sexual arousal. Certain essential oils have long been praised for their aphrodisiac qualities. One of the reasons why they are so effective is that their natural chemical composition works quickly on the circulatory, endocrine, and reproductive systems when applied to the skin (usually diluted).

Additionally, essential oils are an effective aphrodisiac because their aromatic qualities affect mood, thought, and feelings via olfaction. Once inhaled, the odor molecules register a response in the limbic portion of the brain, which is also responsible for sexual behavior and memory and can influence the body's sexual response.

Essential oils can produce desired effects for oneself and/or one's partner. Most aphrodisiac essential oils work by raising the body temperature through their warm and rich aromas. Once the body has reached an ideal temperature, essential oils' sensual and euphoric properties are most effective.

Essential oils can also help balance hormones, reduce fatigue and exhaustion, help support the body's physical health, and promote emotional wellness, which in turn promotes emotional and physical intimacy. Additionally, certain essential oil applications can help individuals relax and "get in the mood."

top solutions

Single Oils

Cinnamon Bark, Jasmine, Neroli, Magnolia– enhance mood, libido, and euphoria (pgs. 126, 168, 193, 184)

Ylang ylang– supports a healthy libido and endocrine function (pg. 250)

Patchouli– improves circulation, raises body temperature, enhances mood (pg. 200)

Black Spruce, Sandalwood– boost testosterone levels (pgs. 113, 218)

Clary sage– supports the endocrine system, enhances libido (pg. 133)

Bergamot, Pink pepper– balance hormones, enhance libido (pgs. 107, 206)

Blends

Whisper®– stimulating aroma, supports healthy libido (pg. 242)

Passion®– promotes passion, excitement and joy (pg. 198)

Elevation– uplifts mood, energizes (pg. 145)

AromaTouch®– supports circulation, relieves tension (pg. 103)

Supplements

Alpha CRS®+, DDR Prime® Softgels, **Deep Blue Polyphenol Complex®** (pg. 257), GX Assist®, Microplex VMz®, **Mito2Max®** (pg. 262), **xEO Mega®** (pg. 271), Zendocrine® Complex, Zendocrine® Softgels

usage tips

For best results, and to support optimal intimacy:

- **Aromatic:** Set the mood by diffusing oils of choice that are calming, warming, and arousing to both parties.
- **Topical:** Enjoy using specified oils to obtain desired results. When applying to sensitive areas, be sure to dilute with a carrier oil.

Related Ailments

Erectile Dysfunction, Impotency, Loss of Libido

By Related Properties

For more, see *Oil Properties* on pages 535-538

Anaphrodisiac– arborvitae, marjoram (avoid if interested in libido enhancement)
Antidepressant– bergamot, cinnamon bark, coriander, frankincense, geranium, grapefruit, jasmine, lavender, lemon, lemongrass, magnolia, neroli, patchouli, ravintsara, sandalwood, tangerine, wild orange, ylang ylang
Aphrodisiac– black pepper, black spruce, cardamom, cinnamon bark, clary sage, clove, coriander, jasmine, juniper berry, magnolia, neroli, patchouli, peppermint, pink pepper, ravintsara, rose, rosemary, sandalwood, spearmint, vanilla, vetiver, wild orange, ylang ylang
Calming– basil, bergamot, black pepper, blue tansy, cassia, clary sage, copaiba, coriander, frankincense, geranium, jasmine, juniper berry, lavender, litsea, oregano, patchouli, sandalwood, tangerine, vetiver, yarrow|pom
Energizing– basil, clove cypress, grapefruit, lemongrass, rosemary, Siberian fir, tangerine, wild orange
Grounding– basil, black spruce, blue tansy, cedarwood, clary sage, cypress, Siberian fir, tea tree, vetiver, ylang ylang
Invigorating– grapefruit, lemon, litsea, peppermint, spearmint, Siberian fir, wild orange, wintergreen
Relaxing– basil, black spruce, blue tansy, cassia, cedarwood, clary sage, cypress, fennel, geranium, lavender, magnolia, myrrh, neroli, ravintsara, Roman chamomile, Siberian fir, turmeric, ylang ylang
Rubefacient– bergamot, birch, juniper berry, lavender, lemon, magnolia, rosemary, Siberian fir, vetiver
Sedative– bergamot, blue tansy, cedarwood, coriander, frankincense, geranium, juniper berry, lavender, magnolia, melissa, neroli, Roman chamomile, rose, sandalwood, spikenard, tangerine, vetiver, ylang ylang, yarrow|pom
Stimulant– basil, bergamot, birch, black pepper, black spruce, blue tansy, cinnamon bark, clove, cypress, eucalyptus, fennel, ginger, grapefruit, juniper berry, lime, myrrh, patchouli, pink pepper, rosemary, Siberian fir, spearmint, tangerine, vetiver, ylang ylang
Uplifting– bergamot, cedarwood, clary sage, cypress, green mandarin, lemon, lime, litsea, melissa, sandalwood, tangerine, wild orange
Vasodilator– blue tansy, copaiba, lemongrass, litsea, manuka, marjoram, neroli, rosemary, thyme
Warming– birch, cassia, cinnamon bark, clary sage, ginger, neroli, patchouli, pink pepper, tulsi, turmeric, wintergreen

protocols

ACTIVATE HER APHRODITE

Ingredients:

4 drops ylang ylang
2 drops clary sage
2 drops geranium
2 drops patchouli
2 drops sandalwood
1 drop bergamot
1 drop vanilla

Directions:

Combine and store in a glass bottle. Apply to pulse points, or diffuse.

APHRODISIAC AROUSER ROLL-ON: Combine 12 drops sandalwood, 5 drops ylang ylang, 3 drops cinnamon bark, 1 drop each jasmine and vanilla with carrier oil in a 10mL roller bottle or in a partially empty magnolia or neroli Touch® bottle. Apply on back of neck, behind ears, or wherever desired.

TURN UP THE HEAT MASSAGE OIL

Ingredients:

2 drops rose or geranium
3 drops sandalwood
2 drops ylang ylang
3 drops vanilla
3 drops clary sage
2 drops cinnamon bark

Directions:

In a 2 oz glass bottle, add oils, swirl, top off with carrier oil. Use as a massage blend to warm the body and create arousal.

ECSTASY EXTENDER: Combine 1-2 drops each geranium, cinnamon bark, ginger, pink pepper, and peppermint in a 2 oz glass bottle with a dropper top. Fill remainder with fractionated coconut oil. Use to support reaching and prolonging climax. Use 10-15 drops at a time and massage lightly on genitals.

KISS AND MAKE UP: Layer Peace®, Console®, and Forgive® to "diffuse" an argument or calm a partner. Apply over heart and forehead.

PRE-INTIMACY RELAXATION BATH: Add 1-2 cups pink Himalayan salt to warm bath and swish until dissolved. Layer rose, jasmine, and neroli with 2 drops green mandarin, on body, and step into a blissful bath. Add ½ cup of milk or cream for a soothing skin treatment.

LET'S GET IT ON – a men's formula

Ingredients:

4 drops sandalwood
4 drops ylang ylang
1 drop clary sage
2 drops wild orange
4 drops black spruce

Directions:

Combine and apply to pulse points and diluted on desired areas of stimulation. Diffuse.

WARM-IT-UP!: In a 15mL glass bottle, combine: 10 drops neroli, 8 drops wild orange, 2 drops pink pepper, 8 drops ginger, 2 drops black pepper. Shake and then fill with fractionated coconut oil. Apply to erogenous zones to support sexual arousal.

EDIBLE MASSAGE AND LUBRICATING BLEND: Melt ½ C organic coconut oil and 2 t raw honey in a jar or bowl placed over hot water. Add 2 drops cinnamon and 4 drops wild orange and stir. Use warm, not hot. Can be stored for up to 6 months in airtight container. Rewarm as desired. Adjust oils as desired.

SHEET SPRITZER

Ingredients:

10 drops sandalwood
6 drops ylang ylang
14 drops bergamot
3 oz distilled water

Directions:

Add essential oils to a 4 oz glass spray bottle and fill with water. Spray lightly on sheets for a romantic evening.

SEXY TOUCH LOTION

Ingredients:

2 drops ylang ylang
1 drop black pepper
1 drop ginger
1 drop wild orange

Directions:

Add to lotion or massage oil and apply to legs, arms, and body.

Diffuser Blends

Drop any of these combinations into a diffuser and enjoy:

APHRODISIAC: 1 drop each Siberian fir, cinnamon bark, patchouli, rosemary, sandalwood, and ylang ylang

LOVE POTION: 4 drops each jasmine and geranium

MOOD MAKER: 1 drop each cinnamon bark, black spruce, patchouli, sandalwood, and ylang ylang

For more ideas, download the app on Android or iOS.

Arousal Bubble Bath

Ingredients:

1 ½ cups liquid castile soap
2 T vegetable glycerin
½ T white sugar
30 drops cedarwood
20 drops clary sage
10 drops ylang ylang
6 drops patchouli

Directions:

Stir together ingredients in a large glass or ceramic bowl until the sugar has dissolved. Pour into bottle, shake, and let sit for 24 hours before using. To use, pour about ¼ cup of bubble bath under hot running water.

Did you know?

Essential oils have been used throughout history to increase sensuality and passion by helping providea lovely ambience, relieve emotional tension, exhaustion, and even increase libido.

Essential oils used for the purpose of sensuality are typically used topically and aromatically. Different oils appeal to different people. Part of the fun and delight is discovering what oils create the best results for each partner and the couple.

Exotic Cinnamon Love Balm

Ingredients:

2 ½ T carrier oil
1 T cocoa butter
1 ½ t vegetable glycerin
1 t beeswax
6 drops cinnamon bark

Directions:

Warm ingredients, except essential oil, over low heat until the cocoa butter and beeswax are melted. Remove from heat and add essential oil. Beat mixture until it begins to thicken and becomes opaque. Add to a storage container. Cool for 15 minutes before capping. Let sit for 4 hours before using it.

Steamy After-Bath Rub

Ingredients:

30 drops bergamot
10 drops sandalwood
5 drops juniper berry
4 drops ginger
4 drops ylang ylang
2 drops jasmine or lavender
3 ½ oz fractionated coconut oil

Directions:

Combine ingredients in a 4 oz glass bottle. Mix and apply. Enjoy the deep, intoxicating effects of essential oils with sensual touch and massage to arouse intense desire.

conditions

Depression– bergamot, rose, wild orange, ylang ylang, Citrus Bliss®, Citrus Bloom™, Elevation, Motivate® ; see *Mood & Behavior*

Emotional issues, female sexuality*– clary sage, jasmine, magnolia, Roman chamomile, rose, ylang ylang, *Motivate*®, Whisper®; see *Mood & Behavior, Women's Health*

Exhaustion/fatigue– arborvitae, bergamot, black spruce, cinnamon bark, cypress, grapefruit, pink pepper, peppermint, wild orange, DDR Prime®, Motivate®, Passion®, Zendocrine®; see *Energy & Vitality*

Frigidity*– cinnamon bark, jasmine, neroli, patchouli, rose, sandalwood, vanilla, ylang ylang, Passion®, Peace®; see *Mood & Behavior*

Headache– cinnamon bark, frankincense, geranium, lavender, peppermint, rose, wintergreen, PastTense®; see *Pain & Inflammation*

Hemorrhoids– cypress, helichrysum, myrrh, Roman chamomile, sandalwood, DigestZen®, Zendocrine®; see *Cardiovascular*

Impotence*– cinnamon bark, clary sage, cypress, geranium, ginger, neroli, rose, sandalwood, thyme, turmeric, vanilla, ylang ylang, Forgive®, Passion®, Purify, Whisper®; see *Men's Health*

Lack of confidence– bergamot, blue tansy, cedarwood, jasmine, lime, melissa, ravintsara, rose, Citrus Bliss®, InTune®, Peace®; see *Mood & Behavior*

Lack of nitric oxide– cinnamon bark, AromaTouch Technique®

Oxytocin production– clary sage, fennel, geranium, myrrh, ylang ylang

Sex drive, excessive– arborvitae, marjoram

Sex drive, low (low libido)*– black pepper, black spruce, cardamom, cassia, cinnamon bark, clary sage, clove, coriander, geranium, ginger, jasmine, juniper berry, magnolia, neroli, patchouli, peppermint, pink pepper, Roman chamomile, rose, rosemary, sandalwood, spearmint, tangerine, vanilla, vetiver, wild orange, ylang ylang, Cheer®, Console®, Forgive®, Passion®, Peace®, Whisper®; see *Men's Health* and *Women's Health*

Sexual Tension– black spruce, geranium, jasmine, lavender, magnolia, neroli, peppermint, rose, vanilla, wild orange, ylang ylang, Adaptiv™, AromaTouch®, Console®, Forgive®, PastTense®, Peace®, Serenity®; see *Muscular*

Vaginal dryness– clary sage, Balance®

Warming, localized– bergamot, birch, cassia, cinnamon bark, clary sage, juniper berry, lavender, lemon, neroli, patchouli, pink pepper, rosemary, Siberian fir, tulsi, vanilla, vetiver, wintergreen; see *Cardiovascular*

Yeast Infection– basil, clary sage, coriander, frankincense, lemon, tea tree; see *Candida*

*See Protocols on pgs. 368-369

Limbic

LOCATED IN THE CENTER of both hemispheres of the brain just under the cerebrum, the limbic system includes the amygdala, hippocampus, hypothalamus, olfactory cortex, and thalamus. The limbic system is a busy part of the brain, responsible for regulating both our emotional lives and higher mental functions such as learning, motivating, formulating, and storing memories. It also controls adrenaline and autonomic response and regulates hormones and sexual response, sensory perception (optical and olfactory), and motor function.

Since the limbic system is involved in so many of the body's activities, and because it works so closely with several other systems, the actual anatomical parts of the limbic system are somewhat controversial. It is the reason there is pleasure in activities such as eating and sexual intimacy, and why stress manifests in the physical body and directly impacts health.

The limbic system is directly responsible for the processes of intercellular communication that affect how an individual responds to situations and all sensory stimuli and forms and stores memories about those situations and the resulting emotions. The limbic system works closely with the endocrine system to help with hormone regulation. It partners with the autonomic nervous system, the part of the body responsible for the "fight-or-flight" response that helps the body recuperate during rest periods, regulates heart rate and body temperature, and controls gastrointestinal functions. It also works with the nucleus accumbens, the brain's pleasure center, which is involved with sexual arousal and euphoric response to recreational drugs.

Deep in the core of the limbic system lies the amygdala, which is involved in many of the limbic activities listed above. It serves as the "watchtower," evaluating situations to help the brain recognize potential threats and prepare for fight-or-flight reactions. One of the ways it performs its duties is through the sense of smell. Through the olfactory system, aromas have a quick, unfiltered route to the amygdala, where emotions and memories are stored. Why? Because the sense of smell is necessary for survival.

The sense of smell is one of the more complex and discerning senses and is ten thousand times more powerful than our sense of taste. Aromas have a direct and profound effect on the deepest levels of the body systems, emotions, and psyche. Interestingly, we have only three types of receptors for sight but an amazing one hundred distinct classes of smell receptors. We can distinguish an infinite number of smells even at very low concentrations. It is the *only* sense linked directly to the limbic brain. The response is instant, and so are the effects on the brain's mental and emotional responses and our body chemistry.

Herein lies the power and beauty of using essential oils for limbic health. Their aromas are one hundred to ten thousand times more concentrated and more potent than the solid form of a plant. Due to their unique ability to bypass the blood-brain barrier and their concentrated aromatic compounds, pure essential oils can significantly benefit individuals who desire to improve limbic system function.

When inhaled, essential oils enter the olfactory system and directly affect the amygdala and therefore impact mood and emotional response. As a result, they can be beneficial in reprogramming the significance that individuals have attached to past experiences and can initiate rapid responses both physically and emotionally in the brain and the rest of the body. Inhaling essential oils with the resulting aromatic exposure is the most effective method of impacting the brain.

It is important to know that many apparently physical and seemingly unrelated symptoms are associated with limbic system imbalance because activities of the limbic system are so deeply integrated with other body systems. For any other related condition not listed in this section, see the corresponding body system in which the symptom tends to occur. For example, chronic fatigue—see *Energy & Vitality*; anxiety, depression, or irritability—see *Mood & Behavior*.

Specific sections in this book are complementary to the topic of limbic health. See *Addictions*, *Eating Disorders*, and *Mood & Behavior* following this section and *Emotional Usage* later in the book.

top solutions

Single Oils

Melissa– helps relieve depression and supports trauma recovery (pg. 188)

Juniper berry– helps release fears, trauma, and nightmares (pg. 170)

Frankincense, Balance®– balance brain activity; supports a sense of protection, safety and helps release traumatic memories (pgs. 151, 104)

Patchouli– sedates, grounds, stabilizes; supports central nervous system (pg. 200)

Copaiba, Turmeric– antioxidant and anti-inflammatory (pgs. 136, 239)

Petitgrain, Lavender– calm fight, flight, or freeze tendencies, worry, agitation (pgs. 205, 175)

Blends

Calmer™, Peace®, Serenity®– calm feelings of fear, anger, jealousy, and rage (pgs. 117, 201, 219)

Cheer®, Passion®– bring feelings of cheerfulness, optimism and positivity (pgs. 124, 198)

Motivate®, Thinker™– stimulate self-belief, courage and confidence (pgs. 190, 233)

Brave™, Elevation– stabilize mood and promote courage and cheerfulness (pgs. 115, 145)

Balance®, Steady™– calm an overactive mind; promote sense of connectivity (pgs. 104, 225)

Adaptiv™, Console®, Forgive®– help to let go, heal, and move on (pgs. 96, 135, 149)

Supplements

Adaptiv™ Capsules (pg. 253), Alpha CRS®+, Copaiba Softgels, Microplex VMz®, **Mito2Max®** (pg. 262), **Serenity® Softgels** (pg. 219), Turmeric Dual Capsules, **xEO Mega®** (pg. 271)

LIMBIC

usage tips

The best way to affect the limbic system with essential oils is to inhale them, giving the oils the most direct access to through the olfactory bulb.

- **Aromatic:** Diffuse oils of choice, inhale from bottle, apply a few drops to clothing, or any other method that supports inhalation for oils to enter brain via nose.
- **Topical:** Apply oils as close to brain as possible such as on forehead, under nose, back of neck (especially in suboccipital triangles), roof of mouth (place oil on pad of thumb, place thumb on roof of mouth and hold). Applying oils on chest allows breathing in the vapors.

Related Ailments

Electrical Hypersensitivity Syndrome, Focal Brain Dysfunction (brain injury), Gulf War Syndrome, Hallucinations, Hypersexuality (excessive sex drive), Obsessive Compulsive Disorder, Post Traumatic Stress Disorder (PTSD)

By Related Properties

For more, see *Oil Properties* on pages 535-538

Antidepressant– frankincense, green mandarin, lavender, magnolia, melissa, neroli, tangerine, vetiver

Calming– black spruce, blue tansy, copaiba, frankincense, litsea, melissa, patchouli, sandalwood, tangerine, vanilla, vetiver, yarrow|pom

Grounding– black spruce, blue tansy, cedarwood, clary sage, cypress, magnolia, Siberian fir, vetiver, ylang ylang

Relaxing– blue tansy, cedarwood, clary sage, cypress, lavender, litsea, manuka, myrrh, neroli, ravintsara, Roman chamomile, Siberian fir, vanilla, ylang ylang

Sedative– bergamot, blue tansy, cedarwood, clary sage, frankincense, magnolia, lavender, melissa, neroli, patchouli, rose, sandalwood, tangerine, vetiver, ylang ylang, yarrow|pom

Examples of other ailments that are associated with limbic imbalance:

Chronic Fatigue Syndrome– See *Energy & Vitality*
Fibromyalgia– See *Muscular*
Food Sensitivity– See *Allergies*
Chronic Pain– See *Pain & Inflammation*

conditions

Bipolar disorder*— bergamot, cedarwood, frankincense, lavender, magnolia, melissa, vetiver, Balance®, Citrus Bliss®, Elevation, Peace®, Serenity®; see *Mood & Behavior*

Delusions (false belief)— black pepper, clary sage, frankincense, green mandarin, helichrysum, juniper berry, neroli, patchouli, pink pepper, vetiver, Adaptiv™, Balance®, Deep Blue®, Elevation, Forgive®, Motivate®, Passion®

Environmental sensitivity— bergamot, lemon eucalyptus, lemongrass, ylang ylang, Abōde™, Balance®, Citrus Bliss®, DDR Prime®, Serenity®, TerraShield®

Excessive sex drive— arborvitae, marjoram

Hallucinations— cedarwood, cilantro (small amounts), clove, coriander (small amounts), frankincense, juniper berry, melissa, myrrh, sandalwood, thyme, vetiver, Balance®, DDR Prime®, InTune®

Nightmares*— bergamot, cinnamon bark, clary sage, cypress, eucalyptus, geranium, grapefruit, juniper berry, lavender, melissa, neroli, Roman chamomile, Siberian fir, wild orange, vetiver, ylang ylang, Balance®, Elevation, Serenity®; see *Sleep*

Obsessive/compulsive thoughts/behaviors*— bergamot, black pepper, cedarwood, cilantro, cypress, frankincense, geranium, lavender, patchouli, sandalwood, vanilla, vetiver, ylang ylang, Adaptiv™, Balance®, Elevation, Forgive®, InTune®, Serenity®; see *Mood & Behavior*

Overreacting— black spruce, cedarwood, clary sage, magnolia, melissa, Roman chamomile, sandalwood, vetiver, wintergreen, Adaptiv™, Balance®, Calmer™, On Guard®, Steady™, TerraShield®

Psychiatric conditions (not a substitute for medical care)— bergamot, jasmine, melissa, neroli, sandalwood, Balance®, Elevation, Forgive®, InTune®, Serenity®

PTSD/Stress, traumatic (past, present)*— blue tansy, cedarwood, frankincense, helichrysum, jasmine, lavender, magnolia, melissa, neroli, patchouli, Roman chamomile, sandalwood, vetiver, wild orange, ylang ylang, Adaptiv™, Balance®, Citrus Bliss®, Console®, Deep Blue®, Elevation, Forgive®, Motivate®, Peace®, Serenity®; see *Stress*

*See Protocols →

protocols

BIPOLAR BLENDS: Diffuse, inhale, and/or apply on backof neck and wrists.

- Recipe #1: 3 drops bergamot and 2 drops clary sage
- Recipe #2: 1 drop each lavender and ylang ylang with 3 drops grapefruit
- Recipe #3: 2 drops frankincense, 1 drop lemon, layered with jasmine

POST TRAUMATIC STRESS BLEND: Combine 2 drops each cedarwood, frankincense, sandalwood, lavender, and vetiver with a small amount of carrier oil and apply to back of neck, forehead, and bottoms of feet. Then inhale deeply from cupped hands.

RELEASING OBSESSIONS & COMPULSIONS: In a 5mL roller bottle, combine 25 drops patchouli, 30 drops Balance® and 25 drops Adaptiv™, and apply behind ears, on wrists, bottoms of feet, and cup over nose and inhale deeply 2-3x's daily.

NIGHTMARES BE GONE

- Dilute 1 drop juniper berry and Roman chamomile with fractionated coconut oil and apply to back of neck, forehead, behind ears, and bottoms of feet at bedtime.
- Diffuse juniper berry and Roman chamomile at bedtime.

CLEAR MINDED

Ingredients:

9 drops frankincense
9 drops ylang ylang
6 drops cedarwood
6 drops melissa
15 drops wild orange

Directions:

Combine oils in a 10mL roller bottle and fill remainder with fractionated coconut oil. Roll onto forehead, back of neck, and inside of wrists. Inhale from cupped hands.

RESET ENTHUSIASM: Combine 1 drop ylang ylang with 3 drops wild orange and diffuse.

OH HAPPY DAY! Diffuse Elevation, Cheer®, Motivate® and/or Adaptiv™ throughout the day to promote a sense of joy and well-being.

OBSESS NO MORE: Apply InTune® or Serenity® + Balance® to back of neck and forehead.

PEACEFUL PERFUME

Ingredients:

3 drops ylang ylang
2 drops geranium
1 drop patchouli
1 drop juniper berry

Directions:

Combine oils in a partially empty magnolia, neroli, or jasmine Touch® 10mL roller bottle. Roll onto forehead, back of neck, and inside of wrists. Inhale from cupped hands.

MEN'S HEALTH refers to the state of overall and complete physical, mental, and social well-being, as experienced by men–not merely the absence of disease. It encompasses issues that are unique to men as well as those that are particularly challenging.

The primary sex organs in the male reproductive system have dual functions. The testes produce sperm and the hormone testosterone. The penis allows sperm access to the female reproductive system during intercourse and also serves an excretory function for urine. Testosterone is primarily secreted by the testicles in men, and small amounts are also secreted by the adrenal glands. It is the principal male sex hormone and an anabolic steroid. It is responsible for the development of the testes and prostate as well as secondary sex characteristics, including increased muscle and bone mass, body hair, and a deeper voice. Testosterone levels gradually decrease over a man's lifetime.

The prostate is located beneath the bladder and connects the bladder and seminal vesicles to the penis. It produces part of the seminal fluid that is alkaline, which helps lengthen the life of sperm as they enter the vagina. It also has involuntary muscles that contract to expel the sperm during ejaculation. Normally it is a little larger than a walnut in size, but the cells that make up the prostate continue to multiply throughout a man's life. The enlarged organ can become a problem (benign prostatic hyperplasia) if it pinches off the urethra that runs through it, causing difficulty in emptying the bladder. Symptoms include urgency to urinate, hesitancy, frequency, incontinence, and an inability to completely empty the bladder. This can also lead to infection, stones, damaged bladder and kidneys, and erectile dysfunction. As men age, they are at greater risk for prostate cancer as well. Next to skin cancer, prostate cancer is the most common cancer in men.

Sexual health is important for a healthy lifestyle. The ability for a man to participate in intercourse depends on hormones, the brain, nerves, and blood vessels that supply the penis. For an erection to occur, all these mechanisms need to be in place. Erectile dysfunction or impotence can be caused by a complication in any of these areas and may be attributed to diabetes, peripheral vascular disease, smoking, medications, prostate cancer, and more.

As far as general health goes, compared to women, men make more risky or unhealthy choices, smoke and drink more, and put off making health decisions. Some of the most common health issues men deal with are heart disease, high blood pressure, liver disease, influenza and pneumococcal infection, skin cancer, and diabetes (which can contribute to impotence and low testosterone levels, which can, in turn, contribute to depression and anxiety). Regardless of the cause, many men suffer from depression that goes untreated. This can be a byproduct of a decline in physical health and can affect their self-confidence. It is common for men to hide negative emotions as they continue to function daily.

Since men are independent by nature, empowering themselves with knowledge and practical application of natural remedies can help them reduce health risks while managing mood and helping the body maintain better overall health.

top solutions

Single Oils

Frankincense, Thyme– promote longevity, support brain and prostate health (pgs. 151, 234)

Juniper berry, Celery seed– support urinary and prostate health, wound healing (pgs. 170, 122)

Black Spruce, Sandalwood– boost testosterone levels (pgs. 113, 218)

Tea tree– fights bacteria and fungus with antiseptic action (pg. 230)

Cardamom– supports digestive, muscular, and respiratory health (pg. 118)

Lemon– detoxifies and has an alkalizing effect (pg. 176)

Blends

Balance®– great cologne, aftershave; brain support (pg. 104)

On Guard®– supports cardiovascular and immune health (pg. 195)

Zendocrine®– supports urinary, prostate; prevents hair loss (pg. 251)

DDR Prime®– assists with cellular repair and longevity (pg. 140)

Supplements

Alpha CRS®+ (pg. 254), **DDR Prime® Softgels** (pg. 256), **Deep Blue Polyphenol Complex®** (pg. 257), **Microplex VMz®** (pg. 261), **Mito2Max®** (pg. 262), **xEO Mega®** (pg. 271)

usage tips

Best results for men's health:

- **Get oils in, on, and around you.** Start with a couple drops per day and go from there.
- **Use common sense.** Take oils in a capsule, glass of water, or under tongue for internal use; use as an aftershave, apply them to bottoms of feet or on an area of concern for topical use; smell or diffuse for aromatic purposes.

Related Ailments

Abnormal Sperm Morphology, Erectile Dysfunction, Men's Hormonal Imbalance, Impotence, Infertility, Libido (low) for Men, Prostate, Prostate Problems, Prostatitis, Testes, Testosterone (low)

By Related Properties

For more, see *Oil Properties* on pages 535-538

Anti-inflammatory– arborvitae, basil, bergamot, birch, black pepper, blue tansy, cardamom, cassia, cedarwood, cinnamon bark, copaiba, coriander, cypress, eucalyptus, frankincense, geranium, ginger, helichrysum, jasmine, lavender, lemongrass, lime, litsea, manuka, melissa, myrrh, neroli, oregano, patchouli, peppermint, roman chamomile, sandalwood, Siberian fir, spearmint, spikenard, tea tree, tangerine, turmeric, wild orange, wintergreen, yarrow|pom

Cardiotonic– cassia, copaiba, cypress, ginger, lavender, litsea, manuka, marjoram, pink pepper

Restorative– basil, frankincense, lime, neroli, patchouli, rosemary, sandalwood, spearmint, tangerine

Steroidal– basil, bergamot, birch, cedarwood, clove, fennel, patchouli, rosemary, tulsi, thyme

conditions

Baldness*— cedarwood, cypress, geranium, lavender, rosemary, thyme, tulsi, ylang ylang, Console®, Zendocrine®

Dihydrotestosterone, levels too high (male pattern baldness, enlarged prostate)— See "Testosterone (DHT), high" below

Estrogen dominance— basil, clary sage, geranium, thyme

Genital warts— arborvitae, frankincense, geranium, melissa, lemongrass, tea tree, thyme

Hormones, imbalanced— black spruce, citronella, clary sage, thyme, ylang ylang, Cheer®, Console®, DDR Prime®, Whisper®, Zendocrine®

Impatient— Balance®; see *Mood & Behavior*

Impotence, erectile dysfunction*— cassia, cinnamon bark, clary sage, clove, cypress, Douglas fir, ginger, jasmine, neroli, pink pepper, sandalwood, tulsi, vanilla, ylang ylang, AromaTouch®, DDR Prime®, Passion®, Whisper®, Zendocrine®

Infertility— basil, celery seed, cinnamon bark, clary sage, geranium, jasmine, melissa, rosemary, sandalwood, spikenard, thyme, ylang ylang, DDR Prime®, Passion®, Zendocrine®

Jock itch— cypress, lavender, lemon eucalyptus, myrrh, patchouli, petitgrain, tea tree; see *Candida*

Prostate issues*— basil, cinnamon bark, clary sage, fennel, frankincense, helichrysum, jasmine, juniper berry, magnolia, myrrh, rose, rosemary, thyme, Cheer®, DDR Prime®, Passion®

Prostate, congested— cinnamon bark, cypress, juniper berry, lemon, lemongrass, peppermint, rosemary, thyme, Air-X™, DDR Prime®, Passion®, Zendocrine®

Prostate infection— citronella, neroli, oregano, thyme; see *Immune & Lymphatic*

Prostate, enlarged— fennel; see *Detoxification*

Prostate, inflamed*— basil, cypress, Douglas fir, eucalyptus, juniper berry, lavender, Roman chamomile, rosemary, sandalwood, Siberian fir, thyme, AromaTouch®, DDR Prime®, Forgive®, On Guard®

Semen production, low— celery seed, frankincense, rose, thyme, DDR Prime®, Purify, Whisper®, Zendocrine®

Sperm count, low— basil, cedarwood, celery seed, clary sage, geranium, ginger, juniper berry

Testosterone, low— black spruce, cassia, celery seed, clary sage, fennel, ginger, myrrh, rose, rosemary, sandalwood, ylang ylang, Passion®, Whisper®

Testosterone (DHT), high— celery seed, juniper berry, rosemary, tulsi, DDR Prime®, Zendocrine®

For more ideas, download the app on Android or iOS.

MEN'S HEALTH

protocols

GIDDY UP (for erectile dysfunction)

- **Restore:** Layer Immortelle + 3 drops black spruce to genital area 2-3x's per day.
- **Encourage and stimulate hormone balance:** 1 drop sandalwood, 2 drops clary sage, 1 drop ylang ylang and 2 drops pink pepper. Apply on lower abdomen, diffuse, and take in a veggie capsule.
- **Circulation support:** Apply 1-2 drops cypress, pink pepper, or AromaTouch® to inner thighs and lower abdomen.
- **Anxiety and stress relief:** Diffuse 1-2 drops basil, lavender, and/or ylang ylang. Inhale from cupped hand. Put a few drops on pillow.
- **Support healthy nutrition:** Take xEO Mega®, Microplex VMz®, Alpha CRS®+.

PROSTATE RELIEF

- Consume 2 DDR Prime® Softgels 2x's daily at mealtimes.
- Apply diluted clary sage, thyme, and juniper berry.
- Consume 3-5 drops rosemary under tongue or in capsule AM and PM.
- Apply 2-3 drops Balance® to bottoms of feet AM and PM before sleep.

HAIR STAY THERE STIMULATOR

Ingredients:

24 drops rosemary		40 drops rosemary
18 drops cedarwood		25 drops basil
14 drops geranium		20 drops lemon
12 drops peppermint	OR	15 drops tulsi
8 drops lavender		10 drops lemongrass
40 drops carrier oil		10 drops peppermint

Directions:

Combine oils in 15mL dropper bottle. Apply daily before bed and/or just after shower. Generously apply blend and massage blend into scalp, paying special attention to thinning or balding spots. For an intensified treatment, wrap head with plastic wrap, warm towel, and/or shower cap, and leave on for 45 mins. twice a week. Shampoo and condition after treatments.

AFTERSHAVE: Combine 1-2 drops frankincense, lavender, black spruce, and yarrow|pom together in palms, then apply gently to the neck and face in an upward motion.

ANTI-FUNGAL ROLL ON

Ingredients:

35 drops tea tree
8 drops lavender

Directions:

Combine essential oils in a 10mL roller bottle topped off with fractionated coconut oil. Apply to affected areas between and behind toes, and behind and around toenails.

SHOE DEODORIZER

Drop 2 drops each peppermint and wild orange or 4 drops Abōde™ on cotton balls/rounds and place in shoes overnight.

Mood & Behavior

See also Limbic

MOOD CHALLENGES and disorders are becoming more prevalent, especially in industrialized nations where computers, technology, and other conveniences have become a way of life. People are increasingly disconnected in their personal relationships, although they may have upward of half a million "friends" on social media sites. It isn't uncommon to see teenagers texting each other rather than conversing while standing right next to each other!

Digestive issues and disorders are rampant, in part because of the refined and processed foods that many individuals eat. In recent years, scientists have discovered that there are more neurotransmitters in the gut than there are in the brain, and, among other things, healthy mood management depends on how well these neurotransmitters relay messages to each other. How can an individual hope to experience healthy moods if their cells are depleted of nutrition, their emotional needs for social connection are unmet, and if their neurotransmitters reside in an area with blockages and inflammation? The list of contributors to mood challenges is extensive.

The limbic system in the brain has glands that help relay and respond to emotions. It includes the amygdala, hippocampus, hypothalamus, and thalamus. The hippocampus, specifically, is involved in storing memories and producing emotions. It works effectively at full capacity when it is producing new neurons and solid nerve connections to assist with these key activities. When an individual experiences stress, the blood flow around the hippocampus changes—and individuals in their later years can often experience up to 20% loss in the nerve connections of the hippocampus, which can drastically affect mood and memory.

One of the challenges with balancing brain functions is that the brain is well-protected by a layer of high-density cells called the blood-brain barrier that restricts the passage of all but a small, select group of substances. This is actually a good thing; this layer of cells helps keep neurotoxins, viruses, and other invaders out of the body's control center. Among the few substances that can bypass this barrier are natural fat-soluble substances such as sesquiterpenes, a compound found in many essential oils.

Since the brain is the origin and relayer of messages that produce emotions, and the brain functions on a chemical level, it stands to reason that natural remedies with strong chemical messages (signal or messenger molecules) can help balance and cleanse the very processes that need assistance. Essential oils can assist with cleansing and balancing the GI tract (see *Digestive & Intestinal*, *Detoxification* sections for further information), benefit brain functions, specifically those involving focus, concentration (see *Focus & Concentration*), mood, and memory through both aromatic and topical application.

When inhaled, natural aromatic compounds enter the olfactory system and pass the olfactory bulb, which leads directly to the limbic center of the brain. Oils can be inhaled by smelling directly from the bottle, rubbing a drop of essential oil in the palms of the hands and cupping over the nose, or by utilizing a diffuser (a device that disperses essential oils into the air.) Inhalation is the fastest way to get an essential oil into the body and has significant benefits on mood as it alters the chemical messages being relayed within the limbic system.

When applying essential oils topically to assist mood, it is important to get the oils as close to the limbic system as possible and apply them where they can best bypass the blood-brain barrier. Directly below the base of the skull, on both sides of the neck, there is an "indentation" that can be felt with the fingers. This area is called the suboccipital triangle. When pure essential oils are applied here, they can enter the brain's circulatory system before entering the body's circulatory system. Oils may also be topically applied on the mastoid bones behind the ears, across the front of the forehead, directly under the nose, and may even be applied to the roof of the mouth (place oil on pad of thumb and then place on roof of mouth) for more direct access to the limbic system.

top solutions

Single Oils

Lavender– calms and relaxes, increases the ability to express feelings (pg. 175)

Wild orange, Tangerine– melt away anxiousness and energize (pgs. 244, 228)

Cedarwood– grounds, promotes a sense of belonging and feeling connected socially (pg. 120)

Bergamot, Copaiba– help increase self-confidence and boost dopamine levels (pgs. 107, 136)

Neroli, Magnolia– calm and sedate (pgs. 193, 184)

Melissa, Spikenard– help alleviate depression and to feel spiritually connected (pgs. 188, 224)

Blends

Adaptiv™– promotes adaptibility, agility, and resiliency; supports GABA levels; promotes a sense of composure (pg. 96)

Citrus Bliss®, Cheer®– stimulates the mind and mood; encourages creativity (pgs. 130, 124)

Elevation, Passion®– energizes, balances hormones; restores a sense of exhilaration (pgs. 145, 198)

Serenity®, Forgive®– support letting go, encourage a tranquil state of mind (pgs. 219, 149)

Motivate®, Brave™ stimulate belief, courage, and confidence (pgs. 190, 115)

Balance®, Steady™– promote a state of balance and calm (pgs. 104, 225)

Peace®, Console®– supports emotional recovery, helps release worry, fear, and irritability (pgs. 201, 135)

Supplements

Adaptiv™ Capsules, **Copaiba Softgels**, DDR Prime® Softgels, **IQ Mega** (pg. 260), Microplex VMz®, **Mito2Max®** (pg. 262), **Phytoestrogen Complex** (pg. 265), **Serenity® Softgels** (pg. 219), TerraZyme®, **xEO Mega®** (pg. 271)

usage tips

For best effect for mood and behavior:

- **Aromatic:** Diffuse oils of choice, inhale from hands, apply a few drops to clothing, or any other method that supports inhalation for oils to enter brain via nose.
- **Topical:** Apply oils as close to brain as possible such as under nose, on forehead, and back of neck (especially in suboccipital triangles). Applying oils on chest allows breathing in vapors.
- **Internal:** Place 1-5 drops of chosen oil in water to drink or take in a capsule, drop under tongue, lick a drop off back of hand, or apply to roof of mouth (place oil on pad of thumb and then place pad on roof of mouth).

Related Ailments

Abuse Trauma, Agitation, Agoraphobia, Anger, Anxiety, Apathy, Attachment Disorder (RAD), Depression, Emotional Trauma, Fear, Fear of Flying, Grief, Hysteria, Lack of Confidence, Mood Swings, Nervousness, Oppositional Defiant Disorder, Overwhelm, Panic Attacks, Seasonal Affective Disorder, Social Anxiety Disorder

By Related Properties

For more, see *Oil Properties* on pages 535-538

Antidepressant– arborvitae, basil, bergamot, cinnamon bark, clary sage, coriander, frankincense, geranium, grapefruit, jasmine, lavender, lemon, lemongrass, melissa, neroli, oregano, patchouli, ravintsara, rose, sandalwood, tangerine, wild orange, ylang ylang

Calming– bergamot, birch, black pepper, black spruce, blue tansy, cassia, clary sage, copaiba, coriander, fennel, frankincense, geranium, jasmine, juniper berry, lavender, litsea, melissa, oregano, patchouli, Roman chamomile, sandalwood, tangerine, vetiver, yarrow|pom

Energizing– basil, clove, cypress, grapefruit, pink pepper, lemongrass, ravintsara, rosemary, Siberian fir, spearmint, tangerine, wild orange, yarrow|pom

Grounding– arborvitae, basil, birch, black spruce, blue tansy, cedarwood, clary sage, cypress, magnolia, patchouli, Siberian fir, tea tree, vetiver, ylang ylang

Invigorating– grapefruit, lemon, litsea, peppermint, spearmint, Siberian fir, wild orange, wintergreen

Relaxing– basil, cassia, blue tansy, cedarwood, clary sage, cypress, fennel, geranium, jasmine, lavender, litsea, manuka, marjoram, myrrh, neroli, ravintsara, Roman chamomile, Siberian fir, vanilla, ylang ylang

Sedative– basil, bergamot, blue tansy, cedarwood, clary sage, coriander, frankincense, geranium, jasmine, juniper berry, lavender, lemongrass, marjoram, melissa, neroli, patchouli, Roman chamomile, rose, sandalwood, spikenard, tangerine, vetiver, ylang ylang, yarrow|pom

Stimulant– arborvitae, basil, bergamot, birch, black pepper, blue tansy, cardamom, cedarwood, cinnamon bark, clove, coriander, cypress, eucalyptus, fennel, ginger, grapefruit, juniper berry, laurel leaf, lime, myrrh, patchouli, rosemary, Siberian fir, spearmint, tangerine, tea tree, thyme, vetiver, wintergreen, ylang ylang

Uplifting– bergamot, cardamom, cedarwood, clary sage, cypress, grapefruit, lemon, lime, litsea, melissa, sandalwood, tangerine, wild orange, ylang ylang

conditions

Abandoned– birch, cilantro, clary sage, frankincense, myrrh, Forgive®, InTune®

Abuse, healing from– frankincense, geranium, juniper berry, melissa, Roman chamomile, Siberian fir, spikenard, ylang ylang, Console®, Forgive®, Motivate®, Serenity®

Angry– bergamot, blue tansy, cardamom, cedarwood, copaiba, frankincense, helichrysum, magnolia, melissa, neroli, Roman chamomile, rose, spearmint, tangerine, thyme, wild orange, ylang ylang, Balance®, Console®, Forgive®, PastTense®, Serenity®

Antisocial– black pepper, clove, lemongrass, marjoram, oregano, patchouli, rosemary, spearmint, yarrow|pom, Purify

Anxious or worried– arborvitae, basil, bergamot, bergamot mint, cedarwood, cilantro, clary sage, copaiba, cypress, Douglas fir, frankincense, geranium, grapefruit, green mandarin, jasmine, juniper berry, lavender, lemon, lime, magnolia, marjoram, melissa, neroli, patchouli, petitgrain, pink pepper, Roman chamomile, rose, sandalwood, Siberian fir, spikenard, tangerine, vanilla, vetiver, wild orange, yarrow|pom, ylang ylang, Adaptiv™, Balance®, InTune®, PastTense®, Peace®, Motivate®, Northern Escape, Serenity®, Whisper®

Apathetic/indifferent– basil, cardamom, cassia, coriander, eucalyptus, fennel, ginger, jasmine, lemon, lime, rosemary, peppermint, wild orange, ylang ylang, Breathe®, Cheer®, Citrus Bliss®, Citrus Bloom™, Elevation, InTune®, Motivate®, Passion®, Zendocrine®

Betrayed/deceived– cardamom, cinnamon bark, green mandarin, juniper berry, lemon, marjoram, melissa, peppermint, rose, Console®, Forgive®, Motivate®, Whisper®

Blaming/bitter*– black spruce, cardamom, cinnamon bark, geranium, helichrysum, lemon, oregano, pink pepper, rosemary, thyme, wintergreen, Calmer™, Forgive®, Passion®, Purify, Zendocrine®

Confidence, lack of/timid/self-rejection– bergamot, black spruce, blue tansy, Douglas fir, grapefruit, jasmine, juniper berry, melissa, patchouli, Roman chamomile, rosemary, Siberian fir, spearmint, vetiver, yarrow|pom, Adaptiv™, Balance®, Brave®, Breathe®, Cheer®, Console®, DigestZen®, HD Clear®, InTune®, Motivate®, Passion®

Conflicted– clary sage, frankincense, geranium, juniper berry, patchouli, pink pepper, Roman chamomile, rosemary, sandalwood, Adaptiv™, Brave™, Console®, Immortelle, Steady™, Whisper®, Zendocrine®

Confused– basil, cedarwood, cinnamon bark, clary sage, cypress, frankincense, ginger, jasmine, juniper berry, lemon, neroli, peppermint, patchouli, wild orange, Adaptiv™, Citrus Bliss®, InTune®, Motivate®, Peace®

Crying– cypress, frankincense, geranium, lavender, neroli, Roman chamomile, rose, Siberian fir, wild orange, ylang ylang, Balance®, Cheer®, Console®, Elevation, Serenity®

Denial/dishonest– birch, black pepper, cinnamon bark, coriander, grapefruit, juniper berry, marjoram, peppermint, thyme, Forgive®, Purify, Zendocrine®

Depressed/sad*– basil, bergamot, black spruce, Douglas fir, frankincense, geranium, grapefruit, green mandarin, helichrysum, jasmine, lavender, lemon, lime, melissa, neroli, patchouli, peppermint, Roman chamomile, rose, sandalwood, spearmint, rose, thyme, tangerine, wild orange, ylang ylang, Adaptiv™, Cheer®, Citrus Bliss®, Citrus Bloom™, ClaryCalm®, Elevation, Motivate®, Passion®

Discernment, lack of/double-minded– arborvitae, basil, cinnamon bark, clary sage, frankincense, juniper berry, lavender, melissa, pink pepper, Roman chamomile, rosemary, sandalwood, Siberian fir, Brave™, Motivate®

Disconnected– cedarwood, cinnamon bark, coriander, frankincense, green mandarin, marjoram, myrrh, neroli, Roman chamomile, rose, Siberian fir, wintergreen, vetiver, Balance®, Elevation, Motivate®, Whisper®

Distrusting/suspicious– black pepper, cedarwood, cilantro, eucalyptus, frankincense, lavender, marjoram, rose, Siberian fir, spearmint, spikenard, tea tree, Adaptiv™, Breathe®, Citrus Bliss®, Motivate®, Peace®

Expression, lack of– birch, fennel, lavender, ravintsara, Roman chamomile, wild orange, Motivate®, Passion®, Whisper®

Fearful/lack of courage/nervousness– basil, bergamot, birch, black pepper, black spruce, copaiba, coriander, Douglas fir, frankincense, green mandarin, jasmine, juniper berry, patchouli, tangerine, turmeric, wild orange, yarrow, ylang ylang, Balance®, Brave™, Console®, Motivate®, Passion®, On Guard®, Peace®, Serenity®, TerraShield®

Frustrated– black spruce, cardamom, lemongrass, rosemary, wintergreen, ylang ylang, Adaptiv™, InTune®, Serenity®, Whisper®

Grieving– bergamot, cedarwood, frankincense, geranium, helichrysum, magnolia, marjoram, melissa, neroli, rose, sandalwood, tangerine, Balance®, Console®, Deep Blue®, Elevation, Forgive®, Peace®, Serenity®, Steady™

Heartbroken– geranium, lime, magnolia, rose, spikenard, wild orange, ylang ylang, Console®, Elevation, Serenity®, Whisper®

Hopeless– jasmine, lime, patchouli, rose, vetiver, wild orange, ylang ylang, Elevation

Humiliated– bergamot, birch, cassia, fennel, grapefruit, myrrh, patchouli, ylang ylang, On Guard®, Stronger™

Impatient– arborvitae, cardamom, cilantro, frankincense, grapefruit, lavender, lemongrass, marjoram, ravintsara, Roman chamomile, Siberian fir, wintergreen, Adaptiv™, Calmer™, PastTense®, Peace®, Serenity®

Indecisive– cassia, cinnamon bark, ginger, lemon, magnolia, marjoram, rosemary, tea tree, Adaptiv™, On Guard®, Zendocrine®

Insecure/feeling unsafe or vulnerable– bergamot, black spruce, clary sage, copaiba, grapefruit, myrrh, ravintsara, Roman chamomile, Siberian fir, tea tree, yarrow|pom, ylang ylang, AromaTouch®, Breathe®, On Guard®, Stronger™

Irritable/agitated– arborvitae, bergamot, black spruce, coriander, geranium, green mandarin, lavender, lemon, magnolia, neroli, Roman chamomile, rose, tangerine, wild orange, Adaptiv™, Calmer™, Console®, Forgive®, Serenity®, TerraShield®

Jealous– cinnamon bark, grapefruit, myrrh, patchouli, Roman chamomile, rose, Siberian fir, ylang ylang, Forgive®, Serenity®

Melancholy– basil, bergamot, ginger, grapefruit, jasmine, lemon, lime, melissa, spearmint, tangerine, wild orange, yarrow|pom, Citrus Bliss®, Elevation

Night terrors/nightmares– clove, juniper berry, melissa, neroli, pink pepper, Roman chamomile, sandalwood, vetiver, Adaptiv™, Brave™, On Guard®, Peace®, TerraShield®

Obsessive/compulsive– arborvitae, bergamot, black pepper, clary sage, cedarwood, cypress, frankincense, grapefruit, lavender, neroli, oregano, patchouli, Roman chamomile, sandalwood, vetiver, ylang ylang, Adaptiv™, Balance®, Elevation, Forgive®, InTune®, Serenity®

Overwhelmed/burdened– basil, black spruce, blue tansy, clary sage, Douglas fir, lemon, lemongrass, neroli, pink pepper, rosemary, tangerine, wild orange, ylang ylang, Balance®, Console®, Citrus Bliss®, Elevation, InTune®, Motivate®, PastTense®, Peace®, Serenity®

Over sensitive or reactive/defensive– black spruce, clove, geranium, ginger, lavender, lemon, tea tree, melissa, patchouli, Roman chamomile, rosemary, Siberian fir, spikenard, tea tree, vetiver, wintergreen, Adaptiv™, Brave™, Deep Blue®, On Guard®, PastTense®, Serenity®, Steady™, TerraShield®

Powerless, feeling– bergamot, black spruce, cedarwood, cinnamon bark, coriander, fennel, frankincense, ginger, grapefruit, jasmine, lime, tea tree, rose, Siberian fir, vetiver, wild orange, Adaptiv™, Brave™, On Guard®, Whisper®

Rejected– bergamot, fennel, frankincense, geranium, grapefruit, lime, patchouli, Citrus Bliss®, Elevation, Forgive®, Whisper®

MOOD & BEHAVIOR

*See Protocols on pg. 380

Resentful— cardamom, frankincense, geranium, lemon, lemongrass, oregano, Roman chamomile, thyme, Purify

Restless— lavender, lemon, neroli, patchouli, Siberian fir, vanilla, vetiver, yarrow|pom, Adaptiv™, Balance®, InTune®, Peace®, Serenity®, Whisper®; See "Anxious" above

Selfish— arborvitae, cardamom, cedarwood, oregano, thyme, wintergreen, Forgive®

Sexual frustration— See *Intimacy*

Shame, feel— bergamot, fennel, grapefruit, helichrysum, jasmine, lavender, oregano, vetiver, ylang ylang, Brave™

Shocked— bergamot, frankincense, geranium, helichrysum, magnolia, neroli, Roman chamomile, InTune®; see *First Aid*

Sluggish/stuck— black spruce, cypress, ginger, juniper berry, lemongrass, peppermint, rosemary, Adaptiv™, AromaTouch®, DigestZen®, DDR Prime®

Spiritual connection, lack of— cinnamon bark, frankincense, juniper berry, melissa, Roman chamomile, sandalwood, Siberian fir, spikenard, yarrow|pom, Elevation, Forgive®

Stiffnecked/arrogant— cedarwood, cypress, Douglas fir, lemongrass, oregano, Siberian fir, thyme, wintergreen, AromaTouch®, Northern Escape, PastTense®, Steady™

Stubborn/willful/defiant/controlling— black spruce, cardamom, coriander, lemongrass, oregano, thyme, wintergreen, Balance®, Calmer™, Forgive®, PastTense®, Peace®

Tense/uptight— basil, juniper berry, lavender, magnolia, marjoram, neroli, patchouli, petitgrain, turmeric, vetiver, ylang ylang, Adaptiv™, Forgive®, Northern Escape, Serenity®

Terror/panicked/hysterical— clary sage, jasmine, lavender, magnolia, melissa, neroli, patchouli, Roman chamomile, spikenard, wild orange, ylang ylang, Balance®, Brave™, Peace®, Serenity®

Traumatized— basil, frankincense, helichrysum, melissa, rose, spikenard, tangerine, Balance®, Brave™, Console®, Deep Blue®, Motivate®, Peace®, Serenity®

Weary/faint— black spruce, cassia, cinnamon bark, lime, peppermint, rosemary, spearmint, wild orange, Citrus Bliss®, Elevation

Wounded, deep emotionally*— birch, copaiba, eucalyptus, frankincense, geranium, helichrysum, lime, myrrh, neroli, Roman chamomile, rose, Siberian fir, spikenard, yarrow|pom, Deep Blue®, Cheer®, Console®, Immortelle, Motivate®, Stronger®

Worthless— bergamot, black pepper, b lack spruce, blue tansy, clove, frankincense, geranium, grapefruit, myrrh, patchouli, rose, wild orange, ylang ylang, Brave™, Elevation, On Guard®, Whisper®, Stronger™

MOOD & BEHAVIOR

protocols

DIFFUSER BLENDS:

Directions:
Combine all ingredients and diffuse. Enjoy the pure, vibrant, energizing aroma to help manage emotions.

NOTE: Recipes can be made into topical blends. Place oils in a 10mL roller bottle, multiplying the number of drops by approximately 4 and filling remainder with carrier oil. Use on "perfume" points.

ORANGE YOU HAPPY

Ingredients:
3 drops basil
3 drops wild orange

HEART'S DESIRES

Ingredients:
3 drops jasmine, rose or magnolia
3 drops sandalwood
1 drop rose or geranium
1 drop wild orange or bergamot
1 drop ylang ylang

BRIGHTEN

Ingredients:
3 drops bergamot
1 drop grapefruit
1 drop ylang ylang

REFRESH

Ingredients:
2 drops bergamot
2 drops clary sage
1 drop frankincense

LIFT

Ingredients:
3 drops bergamot or wild orange
2 drops clary sage
2 drops frankincense
1 drop jasmine or ylang ylang
1 drop lemon

CLEAR-THE-AIR

Ingredients:
4 drops Adaptiv™
4 drops wild orange
2 drops tea tree
2 drops lemon

BETTER THAN BITTER AND BROODING

Ingredients:
1 drop bergamot
1 drop helichrysum
1 drop Roman chamomile

Directions:
Place in palms, rub together, cup hands, and inhale.

AGGRESSION-LESS

(to reduce aggression)

Ingredients:
4 drops bergamot
3 drops sandalwood
3 drops ylang ylang
2 drops lemon
2 drops Siberian fir

Directions:
Combine in 15mL bottle/roller bottle and fill with carrier oil. Put 4-5 drops in palms, rub on bottoms of feet, at base of rib cage over liver area, cup hands and then slowly inhale.

NOT SO SAD

Ingredients:
3 drops grapefruit
2 drops bergamot

Directions:
Combine in palm, rub hands together, and then apply on pulse points, back of neck into hairline, and then slowly inhale. For a 5mL roller bottle blend, multiply by 4 for 12 and 8 drops respectively. Fill with carrier oil; use throughout day.

UNCONDITIONAL LOVE

Ingredients:
9 drop wild orange
4 drops frankincense
6 drops bergamot
2 drop ylang ylang
2 drop geranium

Directions:
Combine in 10mL roller bottle and fill remainder with carrier oil. Apply to pulse points, rub on neck, center of back. Then cup hands together and inhale. For more potency, double the amount of oils. Combine without carrier oil as a diffuser blend.

For more ideas, download the app on Android or iOS.

Muscular

THE MUSCULAR SYSTEM consists of 650 muscles in three main categories: skeletal, smooth, and cardiac muscles. It is controlled by the nervous system via two pathways: somatic and autonomic. Only skeletal muscles fall into the somatic category, meaning that they are under voluntary control; these are the muscles attached to the skeleton. They are striated in appearance and provide strength, balance, posture, movement, and heat for the body.

Tendons are bands of fibrous tissue attached to the skeletal muscles that allow movement in the body. When a skeletal muscle contracts, it pulls on the tendon to which it is attached, causing the tendon to pull on the bone and resulting in movement. Ligaments, on the other hand, are the fibrous material that connects bone to bone and holds the skeletal structure together. Once injured, both require long healing times and are prone to weakness or re-injury. Rest is required, as scar tissue usually takes at least ninety days to form. Once formed, the fibers can take up to another seven to nine months to reach maximum strength again.

Autonomic muscles contract and relax involuntarily and include both smooth and cardiac muscles. Smooth muscles are non-striated and are typically found in layers, one behind the other. They can be found in the walls of internal organs (excluding the heart), such as blood vessels, intestines, bladder, digestive system, and stomach. They are constantly at work, performing their functions throughout the body.

Cardiac muscles are specific to the heart and are also known as myocardium. These involuntary muscles contract to pump blood through the heart, then relax to allow blood to return after it has carried vital oxygen and nutrients to the body.

The muscular system is constantly in motion and supporting vital body functions. Essential oils have a unique ability to affect muscles and connective tissue and to support muscle function on a cellular level. Once oils are applied, users often experience near-instant relief. Minor issues and injuries are easily managed with either topical and internal application. For more serious muscle and tendon issues, professional medical care is appropriate. Traditional treatment methods can be enhanced and supported with essential oil and nutritional supplement solutions.

top solutions

Single Oils

Marjoram, Basil, Frankincense— relax and help heal muscles and decrease spasms (pgs. 187, 105, 151)

Cypress, Siberian Fir— promote blood flow to muscles and connective tissue, reduce pain and spasms (pgs. 139, 221)

Copaiba— reduces muscle aches and pain (pg. 136)

Lemongrass— soothes muscle aches, supports connective tissue repair (pg. 180)

Peppermint, Eucalyptus— cool and stimulate muscles (pgs. 202, 146)

Wintergreen, Ginger— warm and stimulate muscles (pgs. 247, 153)

Blends

AromaTouch®— promotes circulation and relieves pain (pg. 103)

Deep Blue®, Rescuer™— soothe muscles, joint pain, and inflammation (pgs. 141, 212)

PastTense®— soothes sore muscles and tissue; releases tension (pg. 199)

DDR Prime®— helps with connective tissue repair and soothes pain (pg. 140)

Supplements

Alpha CRS®+ (pg. 254), **Bone Nutrient Complex** (pg. 255), **Copaiba Softgels**, **DDR Prime® Softgels** (pg. 256), **Deep Blue Polyphenol Complex®** (pg. 257), Microplex VMz®, **Mito2Max®** (pg. 262), **Turmeric Dual Capsules** (pg. 269), **xEO Mega®** (pg. 271), Zendocrine® Softgels

MUSCULAR

usage tips

For best results with muscles and connective tissue:

- **Topical:** Apply oils directly on area of concern, massage in thoroughly whenever possible. Drive oils in with heat, cold, or moisture. Use carrier oil as needed or desired. Layer multiple oils over affected area, one at a time. Place a carrier oil or lotion atop to enhance absorption.
  - **Acute:** Apply often, every 20-30 minutes, until symptoms subside, then reduce to every 2-6 hours.
  - **Chronic:** Apply 2-3x's times daily.
- **Internal:** Consume oils in a capsule or under the tongue to resolve inflammation.

Related Ailments

Aches, Back Muscle Fatigue, Back Pain, Back Stiffness, Body Myositis, Bruised Muscles, Connective Tissue Injury, Convulsions, Cramps/Charley Horse, Do Quervain's Tenosynovitis, Fibromyalgia, Frozen Shoulder, Growing Pains, Headache, Inflammatory Myopathies, Leg Cramps, Lumbago, Metabolic Muscle Disorders, Migraine, Muscle Pain, Muscle Spasms, Muscle Stiffness, Muscle Strains, Muscle Weakness, Muscular Dystrophy, Myasthenia Gravis, Myotonic Dystrophy, Neck Pain, Neuromuscular Disorders (drooping eyelids, double vision, slurred speech, difficulty swallowing, difficulty breathing), Over-exercised, Polymyositis, Rheumatism, Sore Feet, Sore Muscles, Sprains, Tendonitis, Tension, Tension Headache, Tissue Pain, Tissue Regeneration, TMJ, Whiplash

By Related Properties

For more, see *Oil Properties* on pages 535-538

Analgesic— basil, bergamot, birch, black pepper, blue tansy, cinnamon bark, clove, copaiba, coriander, eucalyptus, fennel, frankincense, helichrysum, juniper berry, laurel leaf, lavender, lemongrass, litsea, marjoram, oregano, peppermint, pink pepper, ravintsara, rosemary, Siberian fir, tea tree, turmeric, wintergreen, yarrow|pom

Anticonvulsant— clary sage, fennel, geranium, lavender, neroli, tangerine

Anti-inflammatory— arborvitae, basil, birch, black pepper, blue tansy, cardamom, cassia, cedarwood, cinnamon bark, copaiba, coriander, cypress, eucalyptus, fennel, frankincense, geranium, ginger, helichrysum, jasmine, lavender, lemongrass, lime, litsea, manuka, tea tree, melissa, myrrh, neroli, oregano, patchouli, peppermint, pink pepper, Roman chamomile, rosemary, Siberian fir, sandalwood, spearmint, spikenard, tangerine, tea tree, turmeric, wild orange, wintergreen, yarrow|pom

Antispasmodic— basil, bergamot, birch, black pepper, blue tansy, cardamom, cassia, cinnamon bark, clary sage, clove, coriander, cypress, eucalyptus, fennel, ginger, helichrysum, jasmine, juniper berry, lavender, lemon, lime, litsea, marjoram, melissa, neroli, patchouli, peppermint, ravintsara, Roman chamomile, rosemary, sandalwood, Siberian fir, spearmint, tangerine, thyme, vetiver, wild orange, wintergreen, yarrow|pom, ylang ylang

Energizing— clove, cypress, grapefruit, lemongrass, pink pepper, rosemary, Siberian fir, tangerine, wild orange, yarrow|pom

Regenerative— basil, cedarwood, clove, coriander, frankincense, geranium, helichrysum, jasmine, lavender, lemongrass, manuka, myrrh, neroli, patchouli, sandalwood, tea tree, wild orange, yarrow|pom

Relaxing— basil, blue tansy, cassia, cedarwood, clary sage, cypress, fennel, geranium, jasmine, lavender, litsea, manuka, marjoram, myrrh, magnolia, neroli, ravintsara, Roman chamomile, Siberian fir, ylang ylang

Steroidal— basil, bergamot, birch, cedarwood, clove, fennel, patchouli, rosemary, thyme, wintergreen

Tonic— arborvitae, basil, bergamot, birch, cardamom, cedarwood, clary sage, coriander, cypress, eucalyptus, fennel, frankincense, geranium, ginger, grapefruit, juniper berry, lavender, lemon, lemongrass, lime, marjoram, melissa, myrrh, neroli, patchouli, Roman chamomile, rose, rosemary, sandalwood, Siberian fir, tangerine, thyme, vetiver, wild orange, yarrow|pom, ylang ylang

Warming— birch, black pepper, cassia, cinnamon bark, clary sage, ginger, marjoram, neroli, peppermint, tulsi, wintergreen

conditions

Bruising— birch, black pepper, blue tansy, copaiba, fennel, geranium, helichrysum, laurel leaf, lavender, neroli, Roman chamomile, Siberian fir, AromaTouch®, Deep Blue®, Rescuer™

Circulation (increase)— basil, black spruce, cedarwood, cypress, eucalyptus, green mandarin, lavender, marjoram, pink pepper, turmeric, AromaTouch®, Deep Blue®, HD Clear®, Motivate®, Northern Escape; see *Cardiovascular*

Collagen, lack of— helichrysum, lemongrass, sandalwood

Connective tissue/fascia (tendons)— basil, birch, clove, cypress, geranium, ginger, helichrysum, lavender, lemongrass, marjoram, oregano, peppermint, Roman chamomile, rosemary, Siberian fir, thyme, vetiver, wintergreen, AromaTouch®, Deep Blue®, PastTense®

Cramping/charley horse*— arborvitae, basil, birch, black pepper, blue tansy, cardamom, cedarwood, celery seed, cilantro, cinnamon bark, clary sage, clove, copaiba, cypress, Douglas fir, grapefruit, jasmine, lavender, lemongrass, marjoram, peppermint, Roman chamomile, rosemary, Siberian fir, vetiver, wintergreen, AromaTouch®, Cheer®, Deep Blue®, PastTense®, Rescuer™, Peace®, Zendocrine®

Fatigued/overused— basil, black pepper, cinnamon bark, cypress, Douglas fir, eucalyptus, grapefruit, marjoram, peppermint, ravintsara, rosemary, Siberian fir, tangerine, thyme, Adaptiv™, AromaTouch®, DDR Prime®, Motivate®, Zendocrine®

Fibromyalgia— basil, birch, blue tansy, clove, copaiba, frankincense, marjoram, oregano, peppermint, ginger, helichrysum, lavender, Roman chamomile, rosemary, Siberian fir, thyme, tulsi, wintergreen, AromaTouch®, DDR Prime®, Deep Blue®, Zendocrine®

Headaches— frankincense, lavender, laurel leaf, peppermint, tulsi, wintergreen, Cheer®, Deep Blue®, PastTense®; see *Pain & Inflammation*

Headaches, migraine— basil, helichrysum, Roman chamomile; see *Pain & Inflammation*

Heart— cassia, cinnamon bark, copaiba, Douglas fir, frankincense, geranium, marjoram, lavender, peppermint, rosemary, sandalwood, ylang ylang, AromaTouch®

Hernia, inguinal— fennel, frankincense, ginger, helichrysum, lavender, vetiver

Inflammation, acute (with swelling, redness or pain)*— basil, blue tansy, clary sage, clove, coriander, eucalyptus, frankincense, ginger, helichrysum, laurel leaf, marjoram, peppermint, rosemary, sandalwood, Siberian fir, tulsi, wintergreen, AromaTouch®, Cheer®, Deep Blue®, PastTense®; see *Pain & Inflammation*

Inflammation, chronic— basil, birch, copaiba, cypress, eucalyptus, frankincense, marjoram, oregano, peppermint, patchouli, rosemary, sandalwood, Siberian fir, vetiver, wintergreen, AromaTouch®, Deep Blue®; see *Pain & Inflammation*

Injuries— birch, black spruce, frankincense, helichrysum, lavender, lemongrass, myrrh, sandalwood, Siberian fir, wintergreen, yarrow|pom, AromaTouch®, Deep Blue®, Rescuer™

Muscle development— basil, birch, Douglas fir, lemongrass, marjoram, rosemary, wintergreen, AromaTouch®, Deep Blue®

Muscle, neuralgia— basil, Douglas fir, eucalyptus, frankincense, lemongrass, marjoram, neroli, peppermint, rosemary, wintergreen, AromaTouch®, Deep Blue®, PastTense®; see *Pain & Inflammation*

Numbness— arborvitae, basil, cypress, frankincense, ginger, lemongrass, patchouli, wintergreen, AromaTouch®, Rescuer™

Pain, burning/intense— black pepper, eucalyptus, frankincense, juniper berry, lavender, petitgrain, peppermint, spearmint, turmeric, DDR Prime®, Deep Blue®, PastTense®; see *Pain & Inflammation*

Pain, dull/chronic/achy*— bergamot mint, black pepper, blue tansy, celery seed, copaiba, eucalyptus, ginger, helichrysum, lemongrass, marjoram, pink pepper, rosemary, Siberian fir, wintergreen, AromaTouch®, Deep Blue®, Immortelle; see *Pain & Inflammation*

Pain, sharp/acute— basil, birch, black pepper, black spruce, blue tansy, copaiba, frankincense, ginger, helichrysum, lemongrass, peppermint, rosemary, Siberian fir, turmeric, wintergreen, yarrow|pom, AromaTouch®, Deep Blue®, PastTense®; see *Pain & Inflammation*

Paralysis— basil, Douglas fir, frankincense, ginger, lavender, lime, melissa, patchouli, peppermint, rosemary, sandalwood, AromaTouch®, Balance®, DDR Prime®, Motivate®, PastTense®

Parkinson's disease— See *Brain, Addictions* "Conditions Associated with Addictions— Dopamine"

Spasms*— basil, bergamot, black pepper, celery seed, cypress, laurel leaf, marjoram, melissa, neroli, peppermint, rosemary, thyme, yarrow|pom, AromaTouch®, Motivate®, Passion®, PastTense®

Sprain/strain— birch, black pepper, black spruce, clove, copaiba, eucalyptus, frankincense, ginger, helichrysum, jasmine, lavender, lemongrass, marjoram, Roman chamomile, rosemary, Siberian fir, thyme, vetiver, wintergreen, AromaTouch®, Deep Blue®, PastTense®, Peace®, Rescuer™

Tender tissues, swollen, red— frankincense, helichrysum, lemongrass, myrrh, wintergreen, Deep Blue®, PastTense®, Zendocrine®

Tendons/tendonitis— copaiba, lemongrass, Siberian fir; see "Connective Tissue"

Tension/stiffness, nervous— basil, bergamot, bergamot mint, black spruce, cedarwood, celery seed, copaiba, coriander, cypress, Douglas fir, frankincense, ginger, grapefruit, helichrysum, lavender, lemongrass, marjoram, melissa, patchouli, peppermint, petitgrain, Roman chamomile, rosemary, sandalwood, Siberian fir, tulsi, turmeric, vetiver, wild orange, wintergreen, ylang ylang, AromaTouch®, Deep Blue®, Motivate®, Northern Escape, Passion®, PastTense®, Peace®, Rescuer™

Tingling— cedarwood, frankincense, ginger, Siberian fir, AromaTouch®, DDR Prime®, Deep Blue®, PastTense®

Walking on toes— basil, rosemary, Siberian fir, Balance®, DDR Prime®, Rescuer™, Zendocrine®

Weakness/loss of mass or tone/degeneration— basil, bergamot, birch, black pepper, clove, coriander, cypress, lavender, marjoram, melissa, rosemary, wintergreen, Adaptiv™, DDR Prime®, Deep Blue®, PastTense®, Whisper®

Whiplash— birch, coriander, frankincense, helichrysum, lemongrass, peppermint, Siberian fir, Deep Blue®, PastTense®

*See Protocols on pg. 384

protocols

FOOT LOVE

Ingredients:

1 drop frankincense
2 drops of spearmint or peppermint
4 drops of rosemary

Directions:

Stir oils into 1 C Epsom salt, mix well, and add to warm water foot bath. Soak for 20 minutes.

ACHE-Y BRAKE-Y BATH (muscle relief)

Ingredients:

4 drops Siberian fir
4 drops bergamot
1 drop clove

Directions:

Stir oils into 1 C Epsom salt, mix well, and add to hot (as is tolerable) bath water. Soak for 20 minutes.

ANTI-SPAZ (for muscle spasms)

Ingredients:

12 drops Siberian fir
9 drops lemongrass
6 drops basil
6 drops copaiba

Directions:

Combine oils in 10mL roller bottle and fill remainder with carrier oil. Apply to affected area.

COLD COMPRESS RELIEF RECIPES

Apply oils on areas of concern. Dip washcloth in cold water. Wring out. Apply moistened cloth directly to muscle.

- **Muscular Pain Relief**
  3 drops Roman chamomile
  3 drops lavender
- **Muscle Inflammation Relief**
  3 drops peppermint
  3 drops yarrow|pom
- **Pulled Muscle Relief:**
  3 drops lemongrass
  2 drops marjoram

READY ROLLERBALL RECIPES

Combine in a 5mL roller bottle and fill remainder with carrier oil. Apply to affected area as needed.

- **Leg Muscle Cramps**
  4 drops ginger
  8 drops black pepper
  8 drops cinnamon bark
- **Loosen Tight Muscles**
  4 drops ginger
  8 drops lavender
  8 drops rosemary
- **Muscle Spasm Relief**
  6 drops cypress
  3 drops lemongrass
  8 drops marjoram
  4 drops ginger
- **Soothe Aching Muscles**
  2 drops cardamom
  4 drops lemongrass
  5 drops ginger
  6 drops lavender

MUSCULAR

MASSAGE IN A BOTTLE

Apply AromaTouch® and/or Deep Blue® to any unhappy muscle. Reapply every 30 minutes for acute pain and twice per day for more chronic or reduced situations.

AROMA TOUCH

Add to a 5mL glass bottle: 7 drops blue tansy, 3 drops lavender, 4 drops frankincense, 6 drops copaiba. Fill remainder of bottle with carrier oil. Shake well and apply as desired to sore muscles.

MUSCLE & PAIN RELIEF

Add 3 drops each celery seed and marjoram with fractionated coconut oil. Gently massage on affected areas. Alternatively, add with ½ C Epsom salt to tub of warm water for a relaxing foot soak.

MUSCLE-RELAXING BLEND

Ingredients:

8 drops black spruce
6 drops Roman chamomile
6 drops cedarwood
4 drops copaiba
4 drops turmeric

Directions:

Combine in 10mL roller bottle with carrier oil. Apply for an overall relaxing massage or to tense, overexerted muscles.

MUSCLE RELIEF BLEND

Ingredients:

6 drops turmeric
6 drops marjoram
3 drops black pepper
3 drops rosemary
3 drops peppermint
3 drops copaiba

Directions:

Combine in 10mL roller bottle and top off with carrier oil. Apply to areas of concern. Repeat as needed.

For more ideas, download the app on Android or iOS.

THE NERVOUS SYSTEM is a complex system of nerves and specialized cells that allows the body to transmit and receive messages. It serves as the body's primary control and communications center, responsible for transmitting and receiving messages between every other system in the body.

The sensory function involves transmitting data from sensory receptors, which register internal and external stimuli to the central nervous system (CNS), where it is processed by the brain. The CNS relies on the conscious and subconscious signals from the body's sensory receptors to make it aware of any threats. It is also charged with the higher functions of language, imagination, emotion, and personality.

When the CNS receives sensory input, a complex network of neurons in the brain and brain stem evaluates, categorizes, and files this information, making it available for decision-making and future retrieval. After the incoming sensory signals are evaluated, a signal is sent through the nerves of the peripheral nervous system (PNS) to effector cells, which release hormones or otherwise cause the body to respond to the stimulus.

The somatic nervous system (SNS), which is part of the PNS, directs the conscious, voluntary movements of the body. The autonomic nervous system (ANS), on the other hand, controls all the involuntary neurons, those that do not require conscious direction to function, such as cardiac, visceral, and glandular tissues.

The ANS is further divided into the sympathetic and parasympathetic systems. The sympathetic system is responsible for the body's fight-or-flight response which, when activated, increases respiration, heart rate, and adrenaline and stress hormone levels in the blood while suppressing digestive functions. The parasympathetic system takes over when the body rests and digests. This system tries to undo what the sympathetic system does when it encounters a threat, e.g., decreasing respiration and heart rate, while increasing digestion and waste elimination.

The enteric nervous system (ENS) is yet another division of the autonomic nervous system and is in charge of regulating the digestive system. As mentioned above, it receives input from both the sympathetic and parasympathetic divisions of the ANS, instructing it what to do. The majority of the ENS's functions, however, are regulated independently, warranting the nickname "the second brain," and rightly so, for it alone boasts as many neurons as exist in the spinal cord.

Essential oils can facilitate the complex messaging that occurs throughout the nervous system. They help with homeostasis, circulation, and brain function (see Limbic System) as the brain interprets and sends out data. They even help the neurons transmitting and receiving messages to be more efficient due to their regenerative and soothing properties. They address root causes of ailments connected to the nervous system, helping improve symptoms because the body has support in helping itself.

top solutions

Single Oils

Helichrysum— invigorates nerves and relieves pain (pg. 160)

Peppermint— stimulates nerves and supports repair (pg. 202)

Lemongrass— stimulates nerves and electrical system of body (pg. 180)

Patchouli— provides nerve protection and supports regeneration; removes toxins (pg. 200)

Basil— stimulates, energizes and restores nerves; relaxes tension (pg. 105)

Frankincense— provides nerve protection and supports regeneration (pg. 151)

Neroli, Magnolia, Rose, Vanilla— relax, sedate, regenerate; nerve tonic (pgs. 193, 184, 215, 240)

Blends

InTune®, Thinker™— support central nervous system, reduce inflammation (pgs. 167, 233)

AromaTouch®— increases circulation (pg. 103)

Deep Blue®— invigorates and stimulates nerves (pg. 141)

DDR Prime®— regenerates and protects nerves (pg. 140)

Immortelle— regenerates nerves and increases clarity (pg. 166)

Supplements

Alpha CRS®+(pg. 254), **Bone Nutrient Complex** (pg. 255), **DDR Prime® Softgels** (pg. 256), Deep Blue Polyphenol Complex®, **IQ Mega** (pg. 260), **Microplex VMz®**, Mito2Max®, **xEO Mega®** (pg. 271), TerraZyme®

usage tips

For best success in support the nerves and nervous system

- **Topical:** Apply selected oil(s) directly to any area of concern, remembering to use a carrier oil if necessary to prevent sensitivity.
- **Internal:** Consume oils in a capsule or under tongue to address nervous system issues and bring a particular chemical message to affected areas.
- **Aromatic:** Inhaling from a preparation or diffusing selected oils can have direct impact on brain and nervous system via olfactory pathways.

Targeted Nervous System Support

Autonomic nervous system— basil, bergamot, fennel, lemon, Balance®, DigestZen®, Serenity®

Central nervous system— basil, black pepper (circulation to nerves), frankincense, grapefruit, lavender, patchouli, peppermint, rosemary (stimulant), DDR Prime®, Immortelle

Parasympathetic nervous system— lavender, lemongrass (regulates), marjoram, patchouli, wild orange, Balance®, Breathe®, PastTense®, Serenity®

Sympathetic nervous system— cedarwood, eucalyptus, fennel (stimulant), ginger, grapefruit (stimulant), peppermint, DDR Prime®

Related Ailments

Bell's Palsy, Blurred Vision, Carpal Tunnel Syndrome, Cataracts, Floaters, Glaucoma, Iris Inflammation, Macular Degeneration, Neuralgia, Neuritis, Neuropathy, Numbness, Multiple Sclerosis, Optic Neuritis, Ocular Rosacea, Phantom Pains, Poor Taste, Poor Vision, Porphyria, Retinitis Pigmentosa, Sciatica, Shock, Spina Bifida, Tourette Syndrome, Transverse Myelitis, Trigeminal Neuralgia, Uveitis

By Related Properties

For more, see *Oil Properties* on pages 535-538

Analgesic— arborvitae, basil, bergamot, birch, blue tansy, cassia, cinnamon bark, clary sage, copaiba, coriander, eucalyptus, fennel, frankincense, ginger, jasmine, juniper berry, lavender, lemongrass, litsea, marjoram, oregano, peppermint, ravintsara, rosemary, Siberian fir, tea tree, wild orange, wintergreen, yarrow|pom

Anti-inflammatory— arborvitae, basil, bergamot, birch, black pepper, blue tansy, cardamom, cassia, cedarwood, cinnamon bark, copaiba, coriander, cypress, eucalyptus, fennel, frankincense, geranium, ginger, helichrysum, jasmine, lavender, lemongrass, lime, litsea, manuka, melissa, myrrh, oregano, neroli, patchouli, peppermint, Roman chamomile, rosemary, sandalwood, Siberian fir, spearmint, spikenard, tangerine, tea tree, turmeric, wild orange, wintergreen, yarrow|pom

Calming— bergamot, birch, black pepper, black spruce, blue tansy, cassia, clary sage, copaiba, coriander, fennel, frankincense, geranium, jasmine, juniper berry, lavender, litsea, melissa, oregano, patchouli, Roman chamomile, sandalwood, tangerine, vanilla, vetiver, yarrow|pom

Grounding— basil, black spruce, blue tansy, cedarwood, clary sage, cypress, vetiver, Siberian fir, tea tree, ylang ylang

Nervine— basil, clary sage, clove, helichrysum, juniper berry, lavender, lemongrass, melissa, patchouli, peppermint, rose, rosemary, thyme

Neuroprotective— frankincense, lavender, magnolia, Roman chamomile, thyme, turmeric, vetiver

Neurotonic— arborvitae, basil, bergamot, black pepper, clary sage, cypre ss, ginger, neroli, tea tree

Regenerative— basil, cedarwood, citronella, clove, coriander, frankincense, geranium, helichrysum, lavender, lemongrass, manuka, myrrh, neroli, patchouli, sandalwood, tea tree, wild orange, yarrow|pom

Relaxing— basil, blue tansy, cassia, cedarwood, cypress, fennel, geranium, jasmine, lavender, litsea, magnolia, manuka, marjoram, myrrh, neroli, ravintsara, Roman chamomile, Siberian fir, ylang ylang

Steroidal— basil, bergamot, birch, cedarwood, clove, fennel, patchouli, rosemary, thyme, tulsi, wintergreen

Stimulant— arborvitae, basil, bergamot, birch, black pepper, black spruce, blue tansy, cardamom, cedarwood, cinnamon bark, clove, coriander, cypress, eucalyptus, fennel, ginger, grapefruit, juniper berry, lime, myrrh, patchouli, pink pepper, rosemary, Siberian fir, spearmint, tangerine, tea tree, thyme, vetiver, wintergreen, ylang ylang

conditions

Carpal tunnel, pain/tingling– basil, cypress, ginger, lemongrass, marjoram, oregano, peppermint, spearmint, AromaTouch®, DDR Prime®, Deep Blue®; see *Skeletal*

Decreased ability to taste– black pepper, ginger, peppermint, spearmint

Dendrites, lack of– vetiver

Dizziness– basil, bergamot, black pepper, clove, frankincense, ginger, juniper berry, peppermint, Roman chamomile, tangerine, Citrus Bliss®, DDR Prime®, Slim & Sassy®, Whisper®, Zendocrine®

Dropsy– basil, black pepper, frankincense, ginger, juniper berry, marjoram, myrrh, patchouli, peppermint, vetiver, wintergreen, AromaTouch®, Breathe®, DDR Prime®, Immortelle, On Guard®, Serenity®

Eyes

Caution– do not put oils in eyes; place oils on skin near eyes; use very small amounts, dilute with carrier oil. Use reflex point on toes for eyes– See *Reflexology* chapter in this book.

- **Cataracts**- birch, black pepper, cardamom, clary sage, frankincense, lemongrass, tulsi
- **Dry, itchy, red/redness, tear duct (blocked), watery**– See *Respiratory*
- **Fatigue**– cypress, lavender
- **Optical nerve**– arborvitae, frankincense, juniper berry (regeneration), patchouli, Immortelle
- **Pain**– frankincense, lavender, tea tree
- **Sensitivity to light/glare**– arborvitae, basil, frankincense, helichrysum, patchouli, Roman chamomile, vetiver, DDR Prime®, Immortelle
- **Stinging/burning/scratching**– frankincense, helichrysum, lavender, patchouli, rosemary, DDR Prime®
- **Swollen**– cypress, frankincense
- **Vision, clouded/blurred/poor**– basil, bergamot, black pepper, cardamom, clary sage, clove, cypress, frankincense, ginger, helichrysum, juniper berry, lemongrass, tea tree, DDR Prime®, Immortelle
- **Vision, double in one eye**– clary sage, helichrysum, lavender, lemongrass
- **Vision, fading or yellowing of colors**– basil, black pepper, clary sage, cypress, frankincense, lavender, vetiver, AromaTouch®, DDR Prime®
- **Vision, weak**– clove, frankincense, helichrysum, lemongrass, Immortelle

Headache– basil, copaiba, frankincense, lavender, neroli, patchouli, peppermint, Siberian fir, thyme, wintergreen, PastTense®

Headache, migraine– blue tansy, copaiba, frankincense, lavender, marjoram, melissa, peppermint, Roman chamomile, spearmint, PastTense®; see *Pain & Inflammation*

Huntington's disease– See *Autoimmune*

Impaired gait, posture, and balance– frankincense, marjoram, patchouli, peppermint, thyme, Balance®, Immortelle

Increased sensitivity to sound– helichrysum, Immortelle, Northern Escape

Multiple Sclerosis– bergamot, clove, copaiba, cypress, frankincense, helichrysum, melissa, oregano, patchouli, peppermint, rosemary, sandalwood, Console®, DDR Prime®, Immortelle, InTune®; *see Autoimmune*

Myelin sheath, compromised– frankincense, patchouli, peppermint, rosemary, sandalwood, vetiver, Immortelle

Nausea– basil, bergamot, fennel, ginger, juniper berry, lavender, DigestZen®, Tamer™, Zendocrine®; see *Digestive & Intestinal*

Nerve damage*– basil, ginger, helichrysum, lemongrass, patchouli, Deep Blue®

Nerve degeneration*– basil, citronella, copaiba, frankincense, geranium, helichrysum, juniper berry, patchouli, peppermint, Deep Blue®, Immortelle, InTune®, Motivate®, Zendocrine®

Nerve inflammation– blue tansy, cedarwood, clove, copaiba, eucalyptus, frankincense, juniper berry, lavender, lemongrass, magnolia, patchouli, peppermint, Roman chamomile, turmeric, vetiver, wintergreen, Deep Blue®, InTune®

Nerve, lack of tone– black pepper, cardamom, fennel, patchouli, peppermint, sandalwood, spearmint, Forgive®

Nerve pain (neuralgia)– basil, bergamot, birch, cedarwood, cinnamon bark, clove, coriander, eucalyptus, frankincense, geranium, ginger, helichrysum, juniper berry, lavender, marjoram, neroli, patchouli, peppermint, Roman chamomile, rosemary, thyme, wintergreen, Deep Blue®, Immortelle, PastTense®

Nerve problems*– black pepper, cinnamon bark, grapefruit, lemon, lime, patchouli, peppermint, Roman chamomile, sandalwood, vetiver, Citrus Bliss®, Forgive®, Peace®; see *Blood Sugar*

Nerve, virus– clove, frankincense, lemongrass, melissa, myrrh, turmeric, DDR Prime®, Motivate®

Nervous debility/exhaustion– coriander, ginger, grapefruit, helichrysum, patchouli, Deep Blue®

Nervous disorders– bergamot, blue tansy, cedarwood, citronella, frankincense, melissa, neroli, patchouli, Roman chamomile, spikenard, vetiver, Deep Blue®, InTune®, Peace®

Nervous tension– basil, bergamot, black spruce, Douglas fir, geranium, grapefruit, jasmine, lavender, melissa, Roman chamomile, rose, sandalwood, turmeric, vetiver, wild orange, ylang ylang, Adaptiv™, Calmer™, PastTense®, Rescuer™

Neurons, impaired activity– Roman chamomile, vetiver, PastTense®

Neuropathy, peripheral– celery seed, tulsi

Numbness/prickling– basil, cypress, helichrysum, marjoram, wintergreen, AromaTouch®, Deep Blue®, PastTense®

Paralysis– cardamom, cypress, Douglas fir, frankincense, geranium, ginger, helichrysum, juniper berry, lemongrass, melissa, peppermint, sandalwood, AromaTouch®, Balance®, DDR Prime®, Purify

Paralysis, side of face– helichrysum, marjoram, patchouli, peppermint, rose, rosemary, thyme; see "Paralysis" above

Paralysis, temporary– frankincense, rosemary, AromaTouch®

Sciatica, issues with– basil, birch, blue tansy, cardamom, copaiba, cypress, Douglas fir, frankincense, helichrysum, laurel leaf, lavender, peppermint, sandalwood, Siberian fir, thyme, wintergreen, Deep Blue®

Sedation, need– cedarwood, coriander, geranium, magnolia, melissa, neroli, patchouli, wild orange, ylang ylang

Shock– bergamot, frankincense, helichrysum, magnolia, neroli, peppermint, Roman chamomile, Adaptiv™, Peace®; see *First Aid*

Speech impediment– frankincense, rosemary, InTune®

Teeth grinding– frankincense, geranium, lavender, marjoram, Roman chamomile, wild orange, Serenity®; see *Parasites*

*See Protocols on pg. 388

protocols

NERVE REPAIR

Ingredients:

2-4 drops frankincense
2-4 drops thyme
2-4 drops clove

Directions:

Combine oils and take in a capsule twice daily.

CENTRAL NERVOUS SYSTEM REVITALIZER

Ingredients:

7 drops helichrysum
7 drops patchouli
6 drops sandalwood
5 drops Roman chamomile
3 drops cypress
2 drops pink pepper

Directions:

Combine in a 5mL roller bottle. Fill remainder with carrier oil. Apply to mastoid bone behind ears, back of neck into hairline, and on forehead, AM and PM.

CALM SYMPATHETIC RESPONSE ROUTINE

- Use as directed Alpha CRS®+, DDR Prime® Softgels, xEO Mega®, Mito2Max®, Microplex VMz®, PB Assist®+.
- Rub 1-2 drops Balance® on bottoms of feet AM and PM.
- Place 1-2 drops frankincense, and/or turmeric under tongue AM and PM.
- Consume water with favorite citrus oil throughout day.
- Layer Immortelle and InTune® up back of neck into hairline.
- Diffuse favorite calming oil/blend at bedtime.

NERVE DAMAGE REPAIR

Ingredients:

28 drops frankincense
20 drops helichrysum
20 drops Roman chamomile
16 drops vetiver
12 drops peppermint

Directions:

Combine in 10mL roller bottle. Fill remainder with carrier oil. Massage onto spine or affected area 3x's daily.

SHINGLES SPRITZER

Ingredients:

10 drops eucalyptus
8 drops marjoram
20 drops melissa
20 drops patchouli

Directions:

Combine in 2 oz spritzer bottle. Fill remainder of bottle with half fractionated coconut oil and half purified water. Spray affected area every 20-30 minutes. Shake bottle before each use.

SIMPLE SHINGLES REMEDY

Combine equal parts tea tree and frankincense in 5-10mL roller bottle. Use NEAT (directly on skin without dilution).

For more ideas, download the app on Android or iOS.

Oral Health

ORAL HEALTH

ALTHOUGH ORAL HEALTH is often treated separately from the body as a whole, the health of the oral cavity (the mouth and its tissues) impacts overall health. Poor oral health may cause a more serious underlying disease process, or it may predispose an individual to other health conditions.

The mouth is colonized by hundreds of different bacterial species that inhabit dental plaque. These species adhere in layers to oral surfaces. They are not easily eliminated by the body's natural immune responses and must be mechanically removed. Bacteria increase tenfold when the mouth is not sufficiently cleaned.

A clean mouth contains several hundred billion bacteria, and this number increases when poor oral care exists. Using saliva and gingival fluid to supply their nutrients, bacteria inhabit all areas of the mouth, threatening oral and systemic health. Bacteria beneath the gums, or gingiva, have been reported to be involved in numerous systemic diseases. Oral health care, primarily proper cleaning and caution in the consumption of and ongoing exposure to intensely acidic and sugary foods (e.g., soda pop), contributes to a healthy lifestyle.

Essential oils are a particularly effective means of supporting oral health, partly because they are antibacterial and antifungal in nature. Clove oil helps relieve oral pain, cinnamon bark and peppermint are effective against plaque and gum disease, tea tree is soothing and helpful in eradicating canker sores, and lavender is soothing to sore muscles that result from teeth grinding. Oil pulling is also particularly beneficial to restoring and maintaining oral health. Specific essential oils can be chosen as part of that routine to target desired results. See *Detoxification* for further instruction.

top solutions

Single Oils

Myrrh– fights gum disease, infections and sores; soothes gums (pg. 191)

Clove– protects nerves, soothes pain; prevents tooth decay (pg. 134)

Peppermint– freshens breath; reduces swelling, inflammation, and tenderness (pg. 202)

Wintergreen– protects nerves, soothes pain; prevents tooth decay (pg. 247)

Turmeric– relieves pain and inflammation (pg. 239)

Blends

On Guard®– helps fight infection and bacteria; prevents tooth decay (pg. 195)

DDR Prime®– protects nerves, soothes pain; prevents tooth decay (pg. 140)

PastTense®– reduces tension, inflammation, swelling, and pain in jaw (pg. 199)

Supplements

Alpha CRS®+, **Bone Nutrient Complex** (pg. 255), TerraZyme®, **Greens** (pg. 259), Microplex VMz®, **On Guard+™ Softgels** and **Tablets** (pgs. 262, 263) xEO Mega®, Zendrocrine® Softgels

ORAL HEALTH

usage tips

For oral health support:

- **Topical:** Apply oils that are safe for internal use directly to area of concern in mouth such as gums, teeth, tongue, sores, etc. To relieve pain, also apply pain-relieving oils to outside cheek/jaw area (use with a carrier oil). Apply frequently as needed for acute situations.
- **Internal:** Place oils on toothbrush and brush teeth with selected internal use oils to affect surface of teeth. Ingest oils (e.g., lemon) to change pH (alkalize) in body/mouth which affects tooth and oral health.

Related Ailments

Abscess (tooth), Bleeding Gums, Canker Sores, Cavities, Dental Infection, Dysphagia [Digestive & Intestinal], Gingivitis, Gum Disease, Hoarse Voice, Halitosis, Laryngitis, Mouth Ulcers, Plaque, Pyorrhea, Sore Throat [Respiratory], Teeth Grinding, Teething Pain, Tonsillitis, Toothache

By Related Properties

For more, see *Oil Properties* on pages 535-538

Analgesic– arborvitae, bergamot, black pepper, blue tansy, cassia, cinnamon bark, clove, copaiba, coriander, cypress, eucalyptus, fennel, frankincense, ginger, jasmine, juniper berry, lavender, lemongrass, litsea, marjoram, oregano, ravintsara, Siberian fir, tea tree, turmeric, wild orange, wintergreen, yarrow|pom

Antibacterial– arborvitae, basil, bergamot, birch, black pepper, cardamom, cassia, cedarwood, cilantro, cinnamon bark, clary sage, clove, copaiba, coriander, cypress, eucalyptus, geranium, ginger, grapefruit, helichrysum, lemongrass, lime, litsea, manuka, marjoram, melissa, myrrh, oregano, patchouli, peppermint, pink pepper, ravintsara, rosemary, Siberian fir, sandalwood, spearmint, spikenard, tangerine, tea tree, thyme, turmeric, wild orange, ylang ylang

Anti-infectious– arborvitae, bergamot, cardamom, cedarwood, cinnamon bark, clove, copaiba, cypress, eucalyptus, frankincense, geranium, lavender, litsea, marjoram, myrrh, Roman chamomile, rosemary, tea tree

Anti-inflammatory– arborvitae, bergamot, birch, black pepper, blue tansy, cardamom, cassia, cedarwood, cinnamon bark, copaiba, coriander, eucalyptus, fennel, frankincense, geranium, ginger, helichrysum, jasmine, lavender, lemongrass, lime, litsea, manuka, myrrh, neroli, oregano, patchouli, peppermint, Roman chamomile, rosemary, sandalwood, Siberian fir, spearmint, spikenard, tangerine, tea tree, turmeric, wild orange, wintergreen, yarrow|pom

Detoxifier– arborvitae, cassia, geranium, juniper berry, lemon, lime, litsea, rosemary, tangerine, yarrow|pom

Immunostimulant– arborvitae, cassia, cinnamon bark, clove, copaiba, eucalyptus, fennel, frankincense, ginger, lemon, lime, melissa, oregano, ravintsara, rosemary, Siberian fir, spearmint, tea tree, thyme, turmeric, vetiver, wild orange, yarrow|pom

protocols

COLD SORE ROLLER BOTTLE

Ingredients:

6 drops peppermint
6 drops tea tree
1 drop helichrysum
2 drops clove
3 drops lavender
2 drops cinnamon bark

Directions:

Add to a 5mL roller bottle. Fill remainder with carrier oil and apply to area until healed and then one day more.

CANKER SORE REMEDY

Ingredients:

1 drop melissa
2 drops geranium
2 drops helichrysum
2 drops black pepper
1 drop clove

Directions:

Combine with carrier oil and apply as needed.

BRACES PAIN: Place helichrysum or PastTense® on outside jaw area. Dilute if needed.

TMJ: Use Serenity® or PastTense® on neck and jaw. Dilute if needed.

MOUTHWASH

Ingredients:

5 drops frankincense
5 drops peppermint
3 drops clove
2 drops cinnamon bark
2 drops myrrh

Directions:

Combine in a 4 oz glass bottle. Fill remainder with purified water. Shake before use.

For more ideas, download the app on Android or iOS.

conditions

Bleeding gums— cardamom, clove, frankincense, helichrysum, lemon, lime, myrrh, oregano, patchouli, peppermint, rosemary, spearmint, tea tree, thyme, wild orange, DDR Prime®, On Guard®, Zendocrine®

Bleeding, tooth extraction— cardamom, frankincense, helichrysum, lavender, lemon, lime, DDR Prime®, Zendocrine®

Breath, bad (halitosis)— bergamot, cardamom, cilantro, juniper berry, lavender, peppermint, spearmint, turmeric, DDR Prime®, DigestZen®, Slim & Sassy®, Zendocrine®

Canker sore*— birch, black pepper, helichrysum, myrrh, oregano, tea tree, tulsi, wild orange, DDR Prime®, On Guard®, Slim & Sassy®

Cavities— see *Tooth decay*

Cold sores*— arborvitae, basil, bergamot, clove, fennel, geranium, lavender, lemon, marjoram, melissa, myrrh, oregano, tea tree, tulsi, wild orange, DDR Prime®, On Guard®, Zendocrine®

Fever blisters— see "Cold sores" above

Gum disease— cinnamon bark, clove, grapefruit, myrrh, tea tree, On Guard®

Gums, infection— basil, geranium, myrrh, DDR Prime®, On Guard®

Gums, inflammation— birch, cinnamon bark, clove, myrrh, peppermint, tea tree, Console®, On Guard®

Gums, receding— clove, geranium, myrrh, DDR Prime®, On Guard®

Gums, tender— birch, cardamom, cinnamon bark, clove, frankincense, helichrysum, lavender, lemon, lime, myrrh, peppermint, rosemary, spearmint, tea tree, thyme, wild orange, DDR Prime®, On Guard®

Headache, jaw-related— basil, frankincense, lavender, marjoram, peppermint, wintergreen, Balance®, DDR Prime®, PastTense®, Serenity®

Mouth, dry— frankincense, grapefruit, lemon, tangerine, wild orange

Mouth, infection— bergamot, cinnamon bark, clove, frankincense, helichrysum, lavender, lemon, lime, oregano, rosemary, tea tree, thyme, turmeric, DDR Prime®, On Guard®

Mouth, injury/trauma— frankincense, helichrysum, myrrh, Siberian fir, On Guard®

Mouth ulcers and sores— basil, bergamot, cinnamon bark, clove, frankincense, geranium, helichrysum, lavender, lemon, marjoram, melissa, myrrh, oregano, tea tree, wild orange, DDR Prime®, On Guard®, Zendocrine®

Oral Health— green mandarin, turmeric

Pain with pressure of chewing/biting— helichrysum, myrrh, thyme, Zendocrine®

Plaque— clove, grapefruit, lemon, lime, myrrh, tangerine, thyme, wild orange, On Guard®, Zendocrine®

Root canal— copaiba, turmeric

Salivary glands, blocked/congested— cypress, grapefruit, lemon, lemongrass, AromaTouch®, Citrus Bliss®, On Guard®, Purify, Zendocrine®

Swallowing, difficulty/inability/gagging— peppermint, rosemary

Swollen cheek— basil, cypress, frankincense, helichrysum, peppermint, wintergreen, AromaTouch®, Deep Blue®

Tartar— black pepper, coriander, lemon, lime, tangerine, On Guard®, Slim & Sassy®, Zendocrine®

Teeth grinding— frankincense, lavender, marjoram, Roman chamomile, Serenity®; see *Parasites*

Teeth, new spaces between— clary sage, frankincense, patchouli, DDR Prime®

Teeth, sensitivity to hot/cold— frankincense, helichrysum, lavender, myrrh, DDR Prime®, On Guard®, Zendocrine®

Tooth abscess— cinnamon bark, clove, frankincense, helichrysum, lavender, myrrh, rosemary, tea tree, thyme, DDR Prime®, On Guard®

Throat, sore— cinnamon bark, helichrysum, lemon, myrrh, tea tree, thyme, wild orange, Breathe®, DDR Prime®, On Guard®; see *Respiratory*

Throat, tickling/raw— frankincense, helichrysum, rosemary, wild orange, On Guard®

Tingling/burning sensation in mouth— grapefruit, lemon, Zendocrine®

Tongue, indentations— On Guard®

Tonsils, red/swollen/white patches— oregano, tea tree

Tooth abscess— cinnamon bark, clove, frankincense, helichrysum, lavender, myrrh, rosemary, tea tree, thyme, DDR Prime®, On Guard®

Toothache— bergamot, birch, black pepper, blue tansy, clove, cinnamon bark, frankincense, helichrysum, lavender, myrrh, peppermint, Roman chamomile, tea tree, wintergreen, yarrow|pom, On Guard®, Zendocrine®

Tooth decay— birch, clove, copaiba, green mandarin, helichrysum, tea tree, wintergreen, On Guard®

Tooth enamel, worn— Siberian fir, wintergreen

Tooth, loose— bergamot, cinnamon bark, clove, frankincense, green mandarin, helichrysum, lavender, myrrh, peppermint, rose, rosemary, yarrow|pom, DDR Prime®, On Guard®

Tooth stains, black/brown/white— frankincense, lemon, lime, myrrh, peppermint, wild orange

Voice, weak, hoarse, or loss/laryngitis— basil, cardamom, cinnamon bark, eucalyptus, fennel, frankincense, ginger, lavender, lemon, lemongrass, lime, myrrh, peppermint, rosemary, sandalwood, thyme, vetiver, wintergreen, ylang ylang, Breathe®, On Guard®, PastTense®, Purify, Zendocrine®

← **See Protocols*

Pain & Inflammation

INFLAMMATION is the body's biological response to anything the body considers harmful, including pathogens, irritants, infection, allergens, injury, and pain. Healthy inflammation is part of the innate immune system (see *Immune*), which responds to pathogens with an "automatic" generalized response aiming to clear tissues and cells of harmful stimuli and initiate cellular repair. It works closely with the local vascular system to deliver the plasma and leukocytes that are the "first responders." Sometimes, trying to reduce swelling too quickly can actually slow down the body's healing processes! Symptoms of inflammation can include swelling, redness, pain, heat, and at times, reduced function. Healthy inflammation is necessary for the body to prevent breakdown of body tissues due to pathogens or injury. Note that inflammation is not infection but is part of the body's response to it.

There are two types of inflammation: acute and chronic. Acute inflammation occurs when there is a one-time trigger or event, and the body responds immediately to that trigger by moving plasma and leukocytes into the compromised tissues. Situations that can cause acute inflammation are intense physical training, cold or flu, an infected ingrown toenail, a scratch or cut, sore throat, appendicitis, etc.

Chronic inflammation is long-term inflammation and can occur because the body was unable to repair the initial cause of acute inflammation or because of an autoimmune response, in which the body mistakes healthy tissue as harmful and thus attacks healthy tissue on an ongoing basis. Conditions contributing to chronic inflammation include asthma, arthritis, any chronic condition, and any autoimmune condition.

While wounds, infections, and diseases would not be able to heal without acute inflammation, chronic inflammation can cause a myriad of undesirable diseases or conditions that can include cancers, other chronic conditions, and hay fever. When chronic inflammation occurs, the type of cells at the site shift, and the result is the concurrent repair and destruction of the tissue. Inflammation must be regulated to serve as nature intended.

Cortisol, which is a hormone produced by the adrenal glands, is the most powerful anti-inflammatory substance in the body. When the adrenal glands become stressed or fatigued, insufficient amounts of cortisol are produced, resulting in increased inflammation. Therefore, proper care of the adrenal glands is a critical component to ensuring an appropriate inflammatory response.

Pain, which is very closely related to inflammation, can be slight, moderate or severe, and can manifest in a myriad of ways including constant stabbing, pinching, or throbbing. Pain is a significant problem in modern medicine: The National Institute of Health National Pain Consortium estimates that one-third of America's population deals with significant pain issues that cost between $560 and 635 billion dollars each year. England's chief medical officer estimated that while more than five million people in the UK develop chronic pain each year, only two-thirds recover. In addition to the extreme discomfort it causes, chronic pain can lead to loss of ability to work or function in relationships, addiction to pain medications, and feelings of frustration and helplessness.

There are several ways to classify pain. These include the following:

- **Acute:** typically intense and short-lived, caused by an injury that heals in time, with pain subsiding
- **Chronic:** Ongoing, can be mild or intense
- **Nociceptive:** includes somatic and visceral pain
  - Somatic: Includes all musculoskeletal pain, includes sore/strained muscles, cuts on skin, etc.
  - Visceral: Refers to internal organs and body cavities such as the thorax, abdomen and pelvis; includes cramping and aching sensations
- **Non-nociceptive:** Includes neuropathic and sympathetic
  - Neuropathic: Refers to nerve pain that can be caused by nerves between tissues and the spinal cord, or between the spinal cord and the brain—sometimes referred to as pinched nerves; this can also be caused by degenerative disease (e.g., stroke or loss of myelin sheath) or infection, as in the case of shingles
  - Sympathetic: Refers to pain of the sympathetic nervous system (controls blood flow, etc.) which typically occurs after a fracture or soft-tissue injury. Though there are no specific pain receptors, the affected area can become extremely sensitive, causing temporary disuse of the injured limb or area.
- **Referred pain:** When pain is felt in an area other than the original site of injury/infection, such as when the arm or back hurts in the case of a heart attack

When considering how best to treat pain, medical professionals take into account the original site of pain, what other areas are affected, the type of pain, what activities lessen or worsen the pain, when pain is more aggravated, and the effect the pain has on an individual's mood and ability to function.

Responding to both inflammation and pain with natural remedies can be highly effective, since both these topics involve systematic bodily responses to injury or disease; natural remedies support the body in doing its job. When dealing with chronic injury and/or inflammation, it is important to participate in a wellness regimen that interrupts the continuation of chronic inflammation, so that the body can be liberated to properly address acute conditions that occur. Supplementation is critical so that cells and tissues have the nourishment they need to subdue more chronic conditions, and when the cells and tissues are well-nourished they respond readily to the powerful chemical influence of pure essential oils.

top solutions

Single Oils

Copaiba, Turmeric, Frankincense— relieve pain and inflammation (pgs. 136, 239, 151)

Helichrysum— reduces pain; accelerates healing; chelates toxins (pg. 160)

Wintergreen— soothes aches and pain, warms, promotes circulation; cortisone-like effect; supports bone healing (pg. 247)

Peppermint— reduces inflammation and pain, cools, invigorates, and stimulates (pg. 202)

Ginger— invigorates nerves, promotes circulation and healing to bones and muscles (pg. 153)

Black pepper— reduces inflammation, relieves pain, increases circulation (pg. 111)

Basil, Rosemary— calm nerves, improves circulation and healing; steroidal action (pgs. 105, 216)

Blends

Deep Blue®— invigorates nerves and reduces pain and inflammation (pg. 141)

DDR Prime®— protects cells against free-radical damage while supporting healthy cellular function and renewal (pg. 140)

PastTense®— relieves headaches and tension, soothes joints and tissues (pg. 199)

AromaTouch®— stimulates circulation and blood flow, soothes sore muscles (pg. 103)

Supplements

Alpha CRS®+ (pg. 254), **Bone Nutrient Complex**, **Copaiba Softgels** (pg. 256), **DDR Prime® Softgels** (pg. 256), **Deep Blue Polyphenol Complex®** (pg. 257), **IQ Mega** (pg. 260), Microplex VMz®, PB Assist®+, **Turmeric Dual Capsules** (pg. 269), **xEO Mega®** (pg. 271)

usage tips

Best practices for essential oil use for relief from pain and inflammation:

- **Topical:** Very effective in relieving pain resulting from a structural issue. Apply oils directly to any area of concern. Use a carrier oil if necessary to prevent sensitivity. Apply often, every 20-30 minutes, until symptoms subside, then reduce to every 2-6 hours for acute pain. For chronic pain, apply 2-3x's daily. Layering is very effective for using multiple oils at the same time.
- **Internal:** Highly effective for more chronic or internal pain. Place oils in a capsule or drop under tongue (hold for 30 seconds, swallow).

Related Ailments

Aches, Back pain, Chronic pain, Inflammation, Pain, Rheumatic fever

For other ailments leading to Pain & Inflammation, see the appropriate section. For example:

Autoimmune, Brain, Cellular Health, Digestive & Intestinal, Endocrine, Immune & Lymphatic, Muscular, Nervous, Skeletal, Urinary. Pain and inflammation can occur in any region or part of the body.

By Related Properties

For more, see *Oil Properties* on pages 535-538

Analgesic— arborvitae, basil, bergamot, birch, black pepper, blue tansy, cassia, cinnamon bark, clary sage, clove, copaiba, coriander, cypress, eucalyptus, frankincense, ginger, helichrysum, jasmine, juniper berry, lavender, lemongrass, litsea, marjoram, oregano, peppermint, rosemary, Siberian fir, tea tree, turmeric, tulsi, wild orange, wintergreen, yarrow|pom

Anti-inflammatory— arborvitae, basil, bergamot, birch, black pepper, blue tansy, cardamom, cassia, cedarwood, cinnamon bark, copaiba, coriander, eucalyptus, fennel, frankincense, geranium, ginger, helichrysum, jasmine, lavender, lemongrass, lime, litsea, manuka, melissa, myrrh, neroli, oregano, patchouli, peppermint, Roman chamomile, sandalwood, Siberian fir, spearmint, spikenard, tangerine, tea tree, turmeric, wild orange, wintergreen, yarrow|pom

Calming— bergamot, birch, black pepper, blue tansy, cassia, clary sage, copaiba, coriander, fennel, frankincense, geranium, jasmine, juniper berry, lavender, litsea, melissa, oregano, patchouli, Roman chamomile, sandalwood, tangerine, vetiver, yarrow|pom

Neurotonic— arborvitae, basil, bergamot, black pepper, clary sage, cypress, ginger, neroli, tea tree

Purifier— arborvitae, cinnamon bark, eucalyptus, grapefruit, lemongrass, lime, manuka, marjoram oregano, Siberian fir, tangerine, tea tree, wild orange, yarrow|pom

Relaxing— basil, blue tansy, cassia, cedarwood, clary sage, cypress, fennel, geranium, jasmine, lavender, litsea, manuka, marjoram, myrrh, neroli, ravintsara, Roman chamomile, Siberian fir, ylang ylang

Sedative— basil, bergamot, blue tansy, cedarwood, clary sage, coriander, frankincense, geranium, jasmine, juniper berry, lavender, lemongrass, magnolia, marjoram, melissa, neroli, patchouli, Roman chamomile, rose, sandalwood, spikenard, tangerine, vetiver, ylang ylang, yarrow|pom

Steroidal— basil, bergamot, birch, black spruce, cedarwood, clove, fennel, magnolia, patchouli, rosemary, thyme, wintergreen conditions

General:

Emotional cause– basil, bergamot, black spruce, cardamom, frankincense, geranium, patchouli, Adaptiv™, Brave™, Deep Blue®, Rescuer™, Serenity®, Whisper®; see *Mood & Behavior*

Inflammation*– birch, bergamot, cardamom, cassia, cinnamon bark, clove, copaiba, coriander, cypress, frankincense, geranium, jasmine, lavender, peppermint, Roman chamomile, rosemary, turmeric, wintergreen, AromaTouch®, DDR Prime®, Deep Blue®, Elevation, Forgive®, PastTense®, Peace®, Rescuer™, Whisper®

Pain, acute/sharp*– black pepper, black spruce, clove, copaiba, ginger, helichrysum, lavender, peppermint, rosemary, turmeric, wintergreen, AromaTouch®, DDR Prime®, Deep Blue®, PastTense®, Serenity®, Rescuer™

Pain, chronic*– birch, black pepper, cardamom, cilantro, cinnamon bark, clary sage, clove, copaiba, coriander, cypress, eucalyptus, frankincense, ginger, helichrysum, juniper berry, lavender, lemon, lemongrass, magnolia, marjoram, oregano, peppermint, Roman chamomile, rosemary, sandalwood, Siberian fir, tea tree, tulsi, turmeric, vetiver, wintergreen, AromaTouch®, Console®, DDR Prime®, Deep Blue®, Motivate®, PastTense®, Peace®, Purify, Rescuer™, Whisper®, Zendocrine®

Unexplained/undefined– arborvitae, frankincense, helichrysum, Adaptiv™, Console®, DDR Prime®, Deep Blue®, Forgive®, PastTense®, Purify, Rescuer™, Zendocrine®; see *Cellular Health*

Viscera (organ pain):

Abdominal, lower or side/back– bergamot, black pepper, cardamom, clary sage, cypress, ginger, lemongrass, Purify, Zendocrine®; see *Urinary*

Abdominal, upper/mid– cardamom, cinnamon bark, fennel, frankincense, ginger, lavender, marjoram, peppermint, petitgrain, DigestZen®, Tamer™; see *Digestive & Intestinal, Parasites*

Breathing issues– blue tansy, cardamom, cypress, Douglas fir, eucalyptus, frankincense, peppermint, Air-X™, Breathe®, Deep Blue®; see *Respiratory, Skeletal*

Chest– marjoram, ylang ylang, AromaTouch®, Immortelle; see *Cardiovascular*

Deep, glandular– basil, myrrh, tulsi, Balance®, DDR Prime®, Immortelle, Zendocrine®; see *Endocrine*

Illness/infection– cinnamon bark, helichrysum, melissa, peppermint, rosemary, yarrow|pom, On Guard®; see *Immune & Lymphatic*

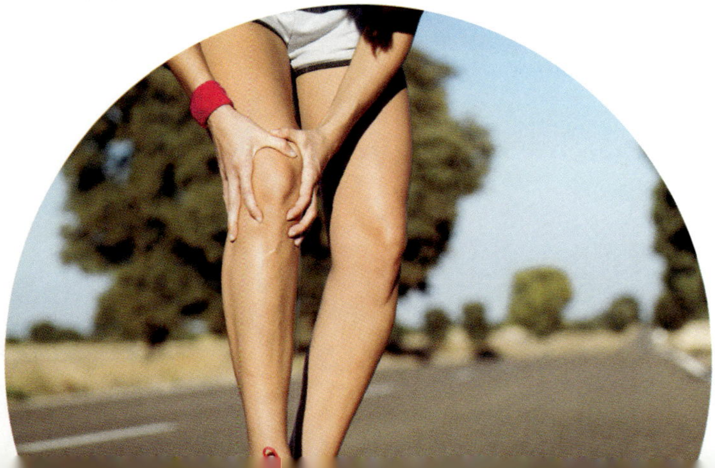

Somatic (Skeletal muscular pain):

Backaches– basil, bergamot, birch, copaiba, coriander, cypress, eucalyptus, frankincense, helichrysum, lavender, lemongrass, marjoram, peppermint, turmeric, wintergreen, ylang ylang, AromaTouch®, DDR Prime®, Deep Blue®, Rescuer™; see *Skeletal*

Cramping/charley horse– arborvitae, basil, cypress, laurel leaf, lemongrass, marjoram, peppermint, pink pepper, AromaTouch®, Deep Blue®; see *Muscular*

Headache*– basil, blue tansy, cardamom, cilantro, copaiba, frankincense, helichrysum, juniper berry, laurel leaf, lavender, lemongrass, marjoram, peppermint, rose, rosemary, Siberian fir, thyme, wintergreen, Balance®, Cheer®, DDR Prime®, Deep Blue®, Forgive®, Passion®, Peace®, PastTense®, Serenity®

Headache, migraine*– basil, bergamot, clove, coriander, frankincense, helichrysum, lavender, melissa, patchouli, peppermint, marjoram, Roman chamomile, rosemary, rose, spearmint, AromaTouch®, Cheer®, Forgive®, Passion®, PastTense®, Peace®, Zendocrine®

Joints*– birch, copaiba, ravintsara, Siberian fir, turmeric, Deep Blue®, Rescuer™; see *Skeletal*

Referred– frankincense, helichrysum, juniper berry, DDR Prime®, Deep Blue®, PastTense®, Rescuer™

Spinal conditions– birch, lemongrass, Siberian fir, DDR Prime®, Deep Blue®; see *Skeletal*

Tissue damage/injury– birch, cedarwood, clary sage, copaiba, frankincense, helichrysum, lemongrass, marjoram, myrrh, sandalwood, vetiver, Deep Blue®, Rescuer™; see *First Aid*

Neuropathic (damaged nerve fiber pain):

Facial nerve– arborvitae, basil, clary sage, clove, frankincense, neroli, patchouli, DDR Prime®, Deep Blue®, Serenity®; see *Nervous*

Nerve damage– arborvitae, black pepper, clary sage, clove, frankincense, ginger, helichrysum, lavender, lemongrass, yarrow|pom, vanilla, Balance®, DDR Prime®, PastTense®; see *Nervous*

Phantom pains– arborvitae, basil, copaiba, cypress, frankincense, helichrysum, lavender, turmeric, DDR Prime®, AromaTouch®, Deep Blue®, Rescuer™, PastTense®; see *Nervous*

Shooting/burning– arborvitae, basil, bergamot, black pepper, clary sage, clove, frankincense, helichrysum, juniper berry, lavender, patchouli, peppermint, Roman chamomile, thyme, vetiver, DDR Prime®, Deep Blue®, Passion®

Spinal cord injury– arborvitae, basil, clary sage, frankincense, helichrysum, lemongrass, thyme, DDR Prime®, Deep Blue®, Immortelle, PastTense®; see *Nervous*

Tingling/numbness– arborvitae, basil, black pepper, clary sage, clove, cypress, DDR Prime®, Immortelle, PastTense®; see *Nervous*

For more ideas, download the app on Android or iOS.

PAIN & INFLAMMATION

See Protocols on pg. 396

protocols

ARTHRITIS RUB

Mix 2 drops each wintergreen, lemongrass, copaiba, frankincense, and eucalyptus with a small amount of fractionated coconut oil and massage into painful areas.

JOINT & ARTHRITIS PAIN RELIEF

Ingredients:

4 drops copaiba
3 drops marjoram
3 drops Roman chamomile
3 drops ginger
3 drops helichrysum

Directions:

Mix essential oils in roller bottle with 1 t carrier oil, shake, and use as needed OR add essential oils to ½ C Epsom salt, stir, and use in a hot bath.

MIGRAINE INTERRUPTER: Place 1-2 drops juniper berry and helichrysum on back of neck. Dilute if desired.

HEADACHE RESOLVE (also works to reduce swelling): Layer or mix 1-2 drops each cedarwood, peppermint, and frankincense to areas of need. Reapply every 30 minutes until headache or swelling is gone. Dilute as desired.

HEADACHE BLEND

Ingredients:

7 drops peppermint
5 drops lavender
5 drops frankincense

Directions:

Combine oils into a 5mL roller bottle. Fill bottle with fractionated coconut oil or carrier oil. Apply as needed. Reapply every 30 minutes until relief is achieved.

PAIN AWAY: Apply helichrysum, Deep Blue®, and frankincense on affected area. Reapply frequently (every 20-60 minutes) until relief is achieved. Continue and apply at least 2-3x's/day to support healing process.

SORE MUSCLE SALVE

Ingredients:

1 T beeswax
4 T carrier oil
10-30 drops each wintergreen, lemongrass, marjoram and copaiba

Directions:

Gently melt beeswax with carrier oil over very low heat, stirring frequently. Remove from heat and allow to cool. While still soft, stir essential oils into mixture. Pour into small glass storage container or tin. Cool completely before putting on lid. Apply to sore muscles or any aches or pains.

SORE MUSCLE SOAK

Mix 4 drops black pepper, 2 drops rosemary, 1 drop ginger with 1 C Epsom salt. Add to warm bath and soak for up to 30 minutes. Drink lots of water while soaking and thereafter.

Parasites

A PARASITE is an organism that lives on or in another organism and gets food at the expense of its host. The majority of human parasites are microscopic (not visible to the naked eye), and contrary to common belief, can actually infest tissues all over the body—not just in the intestines. Not all parasites cause sickness, but those that do can cause incredible damage to the human body. Most parasites reproduce very quickly and infest human tissues and organs. There are over a thousand types of parasites, which can be broken down into six major categories:

1. Protozoa make up about 70 percent of parasites that invade humans. They are one-celled microscopic organisms that can quickly colonize the intestinal tract and from there move on to blood and other tissues and organs. A well-known protozoa parasite is giardia lamblia.

2. Nematoda are worm-like, multicellular organisms that reproduce by laying eggs that typically grow in soil or within an intermediate host before infecting humans. Many people don't show signs of nematode infestation unless it is very heavy. Experts estimate that 75 percent of the world's population has some type of parasite infestation. Commonly known nematodes are roundworm, hookworm, and pinworm. Nematodes typically infect the intestinal tract, blood, and tissues. Ascaris parasites are roundworms typically found in the intestines. Ascaris lumbricoides are probably the best-known parasite in humans. Throughout its life cycle, this parasite infects various organs/tissues of the body that can include the intestines, the lungs, and the brain. When these organisms infiltrate sensitive tissues, they can cause serious health problems.

3. Platyhelminthes such as cestodes, or tapeworms, can be seen with the naked eye. The head attaches to the intestinal wall, and they feed on partially digested particles in the intestinal tract. As long as the head is intact, new tapeworms can grow. Beef, pork, fish, and dog tapeworms are well-recognized in the cestode category. Trematodes, also called flatworms or flukes, are leaf-shaped flatworm parasites that originate from infected snails. They can penetrate human skin or infiltrate a human host after the host has eaten an infected fish, plant, or crustacean. They can infect the intestines, blood, liver, and lungs. Common trematodes include Intestinal flukes, blood flukes, and liver flukes.

4. Acanthocephala, or thorny-headed worms, live in the intestines in their adult form. They are considered by many to be the intermediary between nematodes and cestodes. They have elongated appendages with spines they use to pierce and attach to the organ walls of their hosts. Infections by acanthocephalans in humans are relatively rare.

5. Arthropod are part of a classification called ectoparasites. This includes every kind of arthropod that receives its nourishment from other hosts (such as mosquitoes), but more specifically refers to the arthropods that burrow into and attach to the skin and remain for a time. These include chiggers, ticks, fleas, lice, scabies, and mites. Arthropods cause disease, and are common transmitters of pathogens that cause disease.

Certain dietary and lifestyle habits encourage parasitic invasion. Poorly and improperly digested food particles, mucus-forming foods, and sick/unhealthy tissue and organs encourage the proliferation of internal parasitic populations that rely on such substances or conditions for their food. Unsanitary habits, contact with infected individuals, certain outdoor activities such as walking barefoot in infested sand or soil, swimming in infested water, and even improper hand washing can bring exposure.

Symptoms of parasitic infestation are: diarrhea, constipation, gas, history of food poisoning, difficulty sleeping, difficulty staying asleep, skin irritations, unexplained skin rashes, hives, rosacea, eczema, teeth grinding (during sleep), pain or aching in muscles or joints, fatigue, exhaustion, depression, feelings of apathy, feeling satiated only after meals, iron-deficiency anemia. Since many of these symptoms are commonly associated with other conditions, it is important to work with a medical professional who can properly diagnose the presence of parasites.

The use of essential oils has at times been referred to as "intelligent medicine" because these oils have a unique ability to recognize what is supposed to be present in an organism and what should be eliminated. Parasites can be especially threatening due to their mobile nature. They move from tissue to tissue, wreaking havoc in their wake, and are able to reproduce quickly. Essential oils should be considered as part of a well-planned approach to regain systemic balance after parasitic damage is discovered.

usage tips

For parasite elimination:

The goal is to get essential oils to the location(s) where the parasites lives, such as on the skin or in the gut. Consume internally or apply accordingly. Use a carrier oil to prevent sensitivity wherever needed with topical applications.

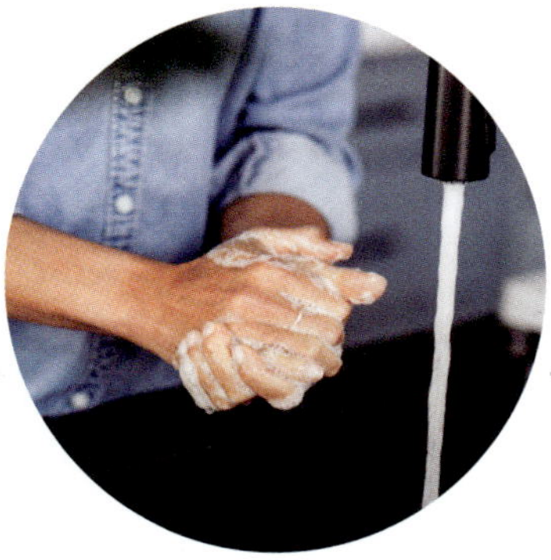

top solutions

Single Oil

Blue tansy (pg. 114), **Cinnamon bark** (pg. 126), **Clove** (pg. 134), **Lemongrass** (pg. 180), **Oregano** (pg. 196), **Roman chamomile** (pg. 213), **Thyme** (pg. 234), **Tulsi** (pg. 236), **Turmeric** (pg. 239)– use to establish an unfriendly environment for parasites and encourage elimination

Blends

Abōde™ (pg. 114), **DDR Prime®** (pg. 140), **Purify** (pg. 208), **Zendocrine®** (pg. 251), **DigestZen®** (pg. 142), **On Guard®** (pg. 195), **HD Clear®** (pg. 159)– to establish an unfriendly environment for parasites and encourage elimination

Supplements

DDR Prime® Softgels (pg. 256), DigestZen® Softgels, **Fiber**, **GX Assist®** (pg. 260), **PB Assist®+** (pg. 264), TerraZyme®, **Turmeric Dual Capsules** (pg. 269), **Zendocrine® Complex** (pg. 272)

When engaging in a parasite cleanse, it is essential to support intestinal tract elimination to prevent autointoxication.

Related Ailments

Ear Mites, Head Lice, Malaria [Immune & Lymphatic], Parasites, Pinworms, Swimmer's Itch, Worms

By Related Properties

For more, see *Oil Properties* on pages 535-538

Anti-parasitic– bergamot, bergamot mint, black pepper, blue tansy, cinnamon bark, citronella, clove, fennel, frankincense, juniper berry, lavender, lemon eucalyptus, oregano, ravintsara, Roman chamomile, rosemary, tangerine, tea tree, thyme, tulsi, turmeric

Vermicide (a substance toxic to worms)– blue tansy, clove, lavender, oregano, wintergreen

Vermifuge (an agent that destroys or expels parasitic worms)– arborvitae, basil, bergamot, cedarwood, cinnamon bark, clove, eucalyptus, fennel, geranium, lavender, lemon, peppermint, Roman chamomile, rosemary, tea tree, thyme, vetiver, wild orange, wintergreen

protocols

PARASITE CLEANSE

Ingredients:

2 drops cinnamon bark
4 drops clove
2 drops thyme
3 drops oregano
3 drops lemon
3 drops lemongrass

Directions:

Take in capsule or dilute with water in a shot glass. Take 2-3x's per day for 10-14 days. Drink 4 drops lemon in water 4x's a day for 2 weeks as well.

- **Tapeworms**— Combine cinnamon bark + clove + cypress; OR lemon + oregano + sandalwood + thyme
- **Thorny-headed worms**— Combine 6-8 drops each arborvitae, peppermint, thyme, and wintergreen in 10mL roller bottle, topped off with carrier oil. Apply on abdomen and bottoms of feet 2-3x's per day for 10-14 days.

MITES BE GONE (topical formula for chiggers and scabies)

- Blend 4 drops each peppermint and lavender with carrier oil (recipe can be multiplied and stored in a glass bottle for future use) and apply generously to all affected areas of skin at least twice per day, preferably after bathing. Do a patch test first to ensure there is no skin irritation.
- For a bath: add 2 drops each lavender and rosemary mixed in a 1 t of milk to encourage elimination of mites.
- To assist skin in recovery from dry, blotchy patches, apply lavender and myrrh, 2 drops each with carrier oil. Apply at least twice per day.

MITE CONTROL (for household invasion)

Use eucalyptus, lemon, lavender, peppermint, and tea tree. Eucalyptus being the most important, so use if nothing else. Blend 35 drops each of above oils in 24 ozs of water in a glass spray bottle. Add 2 ozs witch hazel (optional). Generously spray carpets, beds, curtains, pillows, furniture, etc.

Clean mattress with 1 C of baking soda and 4 to 5 drops of the above recommended oils mixed into a small mason jar (makes enough for a single twin mattress). Use a screen on top of jar or punch holes in lid. Sprinkle on mattress and let sit for 1-2 hours. Vacuum up residue.

COMBAT LICE

- **Prevent**— add 10 drops TerraShield® or Abōde™ to a 30mL glass spray bottle and fill with water. Spray on scalp each day before school.
- **Treat & Repel**— mix 5 drops each tea tree, arborvitae, and TerraShield® with shampoo. Massage thoroughly into hair and scalp. Let sit at least 20 minutes and rinse well. Add 2 drops tea tree to conditioner. Follow with regular comb-through protocol.

BED BUGS

Use arborvitae, eucalyptus, peppermint, and Siberian fir to repel bed bugs. Use arborvitae and Siberian fir to kill them. For a concentrated dose, add 1 drop of each on corners of mattress each week. For a spray solution, add 15 drops of each oil with 16 oz water to a glass spray bottle. Spray across mattress every 2 weeks to prevent or multiple times per day to rid.

PARASITES

conditions

Fleas— arborvitae, cedarwood, eucalyptus, lavender, lemon, lemongrass, peppermint, Abōde™, Purify, TerraShield®

Giardia— bergamot, cardamom, clove, frankincense, ginger, lavender, oregano, patchouli, rosemary, tea tree, thyme, Zendocrine®

Lice, head*— arborvitae, cedarwood, cinnamon bark, clove, eucalyptus, geranium, lavender, lemon eucalyptus, oregano, rosemary, tea tree, thyme, Abōde™, Citrus Bliss®, TerraShield®, Zendocrine®

Lice, pubic or crab— tea tree, rosemary

Mites, ear*— arborvitae, basil, cedarwood, clove, lavender, lemongrass, oregano, rosemary, tea tree, thyme, Abōde™, InTune®, Purify, TerraShield®

Parasites, general*— arborvitae, cinnamon bark, clove, lemongrass, oregano, tulsi, turmeric, On Guard®

Parasites, intestinal worms— bergamot, citronella, clove, geranium, lemon, lemon eucalyptus, peppermint, Roman chamomile, thyme, tulsi, turmeric, HD Clear®, On Guard®, Zendocrine®

Scabies (caused by Sarcoptes scabiei mite) - bergamot, blue tansy, cinnamon bark, clove, frankincense, lavender, oregano, peppermint, Roman chamomile, rosemary, tea tree, thyme, Abōde™, Cheer®, DDR Prime®, Deep Blue®, HD Clear®, On Guard®, Purify

Tick bites— eucalyptus, juniper berry, lavender, lemon, lemongrass, peppermint, tea tree, Abōde™, HD Clear®, Purify; see *First Aid*

Trombiculosis (caused by chiggers mite)— arborvitae, clove, lavender, lemongrass, peppermint, tea tree, thyme, vetiver, Abōde™, On Guard®, TerraShield®

Worms— black pepper, blue tansy, cinnamon bark, clove, fennel, lavender, lemon, lemon eucalyptus, lemongrass, oregano, Roman chamomile, thyme, turmeric, Abōde™, Forgive®

Flukes— clove, oregano, tulsi, turmeric, Purify

Hookworms— clove, thyme, turmeric

Pinworms— bergamot, clove, lemon, lemongrass, oregano, Roman chamomile, thyme, turmeric, Abōde™, On Guard®

Roundworms— blue tansy, cypress, geranium, oregano, sandalwood, turmeric

Tapeworms— cinnamon bark, clove, cypress, lemon, oregano, sandalwood, thyme, turmeric

Thorny-headed worms— arborvitae, peppermint, thyme, wintergreen

For more ideas, download the app on Android or iOS.

← *See Protocols

Pregnancy, Labor & Nursing

PREGNANCY can be a unique, exciting, and joyous time in a woman's life. For a woman to become pregnant, she must release an egg from her ovary—ovulation. Next, the egg and sperm must meet and form a single cell—fertilization. Then pregnancy begins when and if the fertilized egg attaches to a woman's uterus and begins to grow—implantation.

The growing fetus depends entirely on its mother's healthy body for all needs. Pregnant women must take steps to remain as healthy and well-nourished as they possibly can. After an approximate nine-month gestation period, a woman's body begins the work of opening up and pushing the baby out into the world. This work is called labor. Labor is a process by which the baby inside the womb adjusts itself to its surroundings and passes out of the uterus to be born as an infant into the world. Every woman's labor is different. It can be long or short, very difficult or not. Each labor experience, however, follows a basic pattern:

- Contractions (labor pains) open the cervix
- The womb pushes the baby down through the vagina
- The baby is born
- The placenta (afterbirth) is born

Once the baby is born, it no longer receives nutrients from the umbilical cord. Breastfeeding is the body's way of providing young infants the nutrients they need for healthy growth and development. Typically most mothers can breastfeed, provided they have accurate information. Exclusive breastfeeding is recommended up to six months of age, with continued breastfeeding along with appropriate complementary foods as desired.

It is difficult to get all the proper vitamins and minerals needed in a normal diet, so supplementation is usually necessary both during pregnancy and while nursing. Taking in whole food nutrients is key. This makes the vitamins and minerals bioavailable to the body so it is better equipped to provide adequate nutrition for both mother and baby. Many synthetic or non-food-based supplements are not able to be absorbed by the body and can sometimes cause more harm than good.

Essential oils can assist with some of the uncomfortable changes that take place in a woman's body during pregnancy, labor, and postpartum periods as well as during breastfeeding. The oils may be applied topically, diffused, or ingested for issues including breast soreness, constipation, depression, fatigue, high blood pressure, nausea/ vomiting, sleep, stretch marks, swelling, and more.

top solutions

Pregnancy

Single Oils

Wild orange, Rose— energize and lift mood (pgs. 244, 215)

Ginger— relieves nausea and morning sickness (pg. 153)

Peppermint— relieves digestive upsets, morning sickness, headaches; supports memory (pg. 202)

Blends

Deep Blue®— soothes aches and pains (pg. 141)

PastTense®— relieves tension and headaches (pg. 199)

Slim & Sassy®— balances glucose levels and metabolism (pg. 222)

DigestZen®, Tamer™— support digestion and relieve morning sickness (pgs. 142, 227)

Whisper®— balances hormones (pg. 242)

Labor

Single Oils

Clary sage— broad-spectrum support to labor process (pg. 133)

Jasmine— assists with labor and afterbirth (pg. 169)

Geranium— supports perineum, labor performance, mood and healing (pg. 152)

Lavender, Neroli— calm and soothe mood and tissues (pgs. 175, 193)

Frankincense— lessens stress and trauma; promotes healing (pg. 151)

Basil— relieves pain; enhances labor performance (pg. 105)

Helichrysum, YarrowlPom— slow/stop bleeding and promote healing (pgs. 160, 248)

Blends

Balance®— improves coping capacity (pg. 104)

PastTense®— relieves tension (pg. 199)

ClaryCalm®— enhances labor performance (pg. 132)

Deep Blue®— soothes aches and pains (pg. 141)

Nursing

Single Oils

Fennel— promotes milk production; prevents clogged ducts, infection, and thrush (pg. 148)

Ylang ylang— alleviates tender breasts and depression (pg. 250)

Clary sage— promotes milk supply and hormone balancing; boosts mood (pg. 133)

Lavender— promotes milk production; prevents/heals tender, sore breasts, nipples, and clogged milk ducts (pg. 175)

Blends

Whisper®— balances hormones and helps increases libido (pg. 242)

Adaptiv™, Elevation— support mood and alleviate depression (pgs. 96, 145)

Supplements

Alpha CRS®+ (pg. 254), **Bone Nutrient Complex** (pg. 255), DDR Prime® Softgels, **DigestTab®** (pg. 257), **DigestZen® Softgels** (pg. 258), **Fiber** (pg. 258), Ginger Drops, **Greens** (pg. 259), **Microplex VMz®** (pg. 261), Protein, **PB Assist®+** (pg. 264), **TerraZyme®** (pg. 268), **xEO Mega®** (pg. 271)

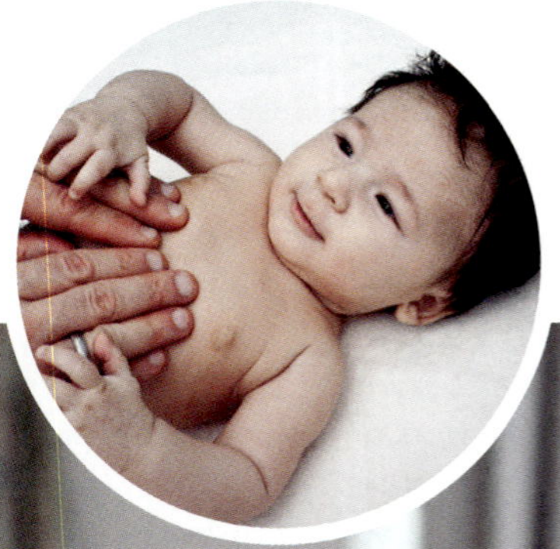

By Related Properties

For more, see *Oil Properties* on pages 535-538

Analgesic— arborvitae, basil, bergamot, blue tansy, cassia, cinnamon bark, clary sage, copaiba, fennel, frankincense, ginger, helichrysum, litsea, peppermint, ravintsara, rosemary, Siberian fir, turmeric, wintergreen, yarrow|pom

Antidepressant— bergamot, clary sage, frankincense, geranium, grapefruit, jasmine, lemon, melissa, neroli, patchouli, rose, sandalwood, tangerine, wild orange, ylang ylang

Anticoagulant— clary sage, helichrysum, lavender, tangerine

Antiemetic— basil, cardamom, cassia, clove, copaiba, coriander, fennel, ginger, lavender, patchouli, peppermint, pink pepper

Antihemorrhagic— geranium, helichrysum, lavender, myrrh, yarrow|pom

Antispasmodic— basil, bergamot, black pepper, blue tansy, cardamom, cassia, cinnamon bark, clary sage, clove, cypress, eucalyptus, fennel, ginger, helichrysum, laurel leaf, lavender, lemon, litsea, marjoram, neroli, patchouli, peppermint, pink pepper, Roman chamomile, rose, rosemary, sandalwood, Siberian fir, spearmint, tangerine, vetiver, wild orange, wintergreen, ylang ylang, yarrow|pom

Calming— bergamot, bergamot mint, clary sage, copaiba, frankincense, geranium, jasmine, lavender, patchouli, Roman chamomile, sandalwood, tangerine, vetiver, yarrow|pom

Carminative— basil, bergamot, blue tansy, cardamom, cinnamon bark, clary sage, copaiba, fennel, ginger, green mandarin, lavender, lemon, litsea, myrrh, neroli, patchouli, peppermint, Roman chamomile, rosemary, sandalwood, spearmint, tangerine, turmeric, vetiver, wild orange, wintergreen, yarrow|pom

Digestive stimulant— basil, bergamot, black pepper, cardamom, cinnamon bark, coriander, fennel, frankincense, grapefruit, litsea, myrrh, patchouli, spearmint, tangerine, wild orange, yarrow|pom

Energizing— basil, cypress, grapefruit, lemongrass, rosemary, Siberian fir, wild orange, tangerine, yarrow|pom

Galactagogue— basil, clary sage, fennel, jasmine, lemongrass, wintergreen

Immunostimulant— arborvitae, cassia, cinnamon bark, clove, copaiba, frankincense, ginger, lemon, lime, melissa, oregano, rosemary, Siberian fir, spearmint, tea tree, thyme, vetiver, wild orange, yarrow|pom

Invigorating— grapefruit, lemon, litsea, peppermint, spearmint, Siberian fir, wild orange, wintergreen

Regenerative— basil, cedarwood, clove, coriander, frankincense, geranium, helichrysum, jasmine, lavender, manuka, myrrh, neroli, patchouli, peppermint beadlets, sandalwood, tea tree, wild orange, yarrow|pom

Relaxing— basil, blue tansy, cassia, cedarwood, clary sage, cypress, fennel, geranium, jasmine, lavender, litsea, manuka, marjoram, myrrh, neroli, ravintsara, Roman chamomile, Siberian fir, tea tree, vanilla, ylang ylang

Sedative— basil, bergamot, blue tansy, cedarwood, clary sage, frankincense, geranium, jasmine, lavender, magnolia, marjoram, melissa, neroli, patchouli, Roman chamomile, rose, sandalwood, tangerine, vetiver, ylang ylang

Stomachic— blue tansy, cardamom, cinnamon bark, clary sage, coriander, fennel, ginger, marjoram, peppermint, rosemary, tangerine, turmeric, wild orange, yarrow|pom

Uplifting— bergamot, clary sage, grapefruit, lemon, lime, litsea, melissa, sandalwood, tangerine, wild orange, ylang ylang

Warming— birch, black pepper, cassia, cinnamon bark, clary sage, clove, eucalyptus, ginger, lemongrass, marjoram, oregano, peppermint, pink pepper, thyme, tulsi, wintergreen

Essential Oil Usage For Pregnant & Nursing Women

Essential oil use during pregnancy can be one of the most poignant decisions a woman makes on behalf of her own care as well as that of her developing baby. The oils offer some of the most powerful support nature has to offer and in the most diverse of ways, with benefits continuing through birth and beyond.

Along with the decision to partner essential oils with pregnancy comes the responsibility to understand that quality matters. Impure oils simply aren't safe, most especially for mother and child. Claims are common but purity is not.

Choose to partner with an essential oil source that provides certification based on rigorous 3rd party testing, guaranteeing purity, potency, and authenticity. Peace of mind is earned and not to be assumed. See *Quality Matters* on page 13 to learn more.

Safety guidelines when selecting oils for use during pregnancy:

- **Read labels to ensure oils are certified safe,** free from adulteration and harmful contaminants. Some companies care more about profit, while others care more to ensure benefits for their customers. Pure oils offer outstanding benefits.
- **Be aware.** Pure oils are powerful and are best used in smaller amounts. Consult the application methods and *Safety* in the *How To* section as well as in this chapter.
- **Err on the side of safety**. Use prudence, intuition, and avoid anything that simply doesn't feel right.
- **Be a wise steward.** During the first trimester, while the baby is developing more rapidly, be thoughtful and use careful considerations.
- **Use oils aromatically** as a safe method during pregnancy. They are excellent for boosting mood, energy, and creating an uplifting environment. They also help reduce feelings of stress and tension and promote a good night's sleep.
- **Pay attention to how the body responds** to dosages**.** As body weight increases and hormones change, there may be a need to change application quantities or frequencies accordingly. Also, notice any heightened sensitivity. Once again, pay attention to the body's responses. Make it a habit to dilute oils for topical applications. The bottoms of feet are an excellent, conservative location, hence commonly used with children.
- **Recommendations.** Avoid the use of clary sage if there is a history of preterm labor or miscarriage. Avoid peppermint while breastfeeding, as regular use can significantly reduce milk supply for some women.

conditions

Pregnancy:

Appetite cravings/blood sugar imbalance– Slim & Sassy®

Backache– peppermint, rosemary, AromaTouch®, Deep Blue®

Bleeding– geranium, helichrysum, lavender, myrrh, yarrow|pom; see *Cardiovascular*

Blood pressure, high– clove, eucalyptus, laurel leaf, lavender, lemon, marjoram, ylang ylang

Breast tenderness– geranium, grapefruit, lavender, ylang ylang, ClaryCalm®

Constipation– cilantro, copaiba, fennel, ginger, green mandarin, lemon, lemongrass, marjoram, peppermint, DigestZen®, Tamer™, Zendocrine®; see *Digestive & Intestinal*

Cramps– arborvitae, basil, cypress, marjoram, AromaTouch®, Deep Blue®

Depression– basil, bergamot, frankincense, geranium, lavender, lemon, melissa, patchouli, ravintsara, rose, sandalwood, vanilla, vetiver, wild orange, ylang ylang, Adaptiv™, Balance®, Citrus Bliss®, ClaryCalm®, Elevation; see *Mood & Behavior*

Energy, low/fatigue– black spruce, cypress, grapefruit, green mandarin, lemon, peppermint, pink pepper, wild orange, Adaptiv™, Citrus Bliss®, Elevation, Motivate®; see *Energy & Vitality*

Headaches– frankincense, green mandarin, lavender, peppermint, tulsi, wintergreen, Deep Blue®, PastTense®

Heartburn/gas/bloating – green mandarin, peppermint, pink pepper, wild orange, DigestZen®, Tamer™; see *Digestive & Intestinal*

Hemorrhoids*– See "Varicose veins" below

Infection– lemon, oregano, tea tree, On Guard®

Labor, preterm/cramping– arborvitae, frankincense, laurel leaf, lavender, marjoram, neroli, patchouli, Roman chamomile, wild orange + ylang ylang, ClaryCalm®, Whisper®, Zendocrine®

Leg cramps– basil, cypress, lavender, lemongrass, marjoram, wintergreen, Adaptiv™, AromaTouch®, Deep Blue®, PastTense®

Miscarriage, prevents– blue tansy, myrrh, patchouli, rose, thyme, Console®, DDR Prime®, Elevation, Immortelle

Miscarriage, recovery– clary sage, frankincense, geranium, grapefruit, lavender, myrrh, patchouli, Roman chamomile, rose, ClaryCalm®, DDR Prime®, Deep Blue®, Elevation, Immortelle, Purify, Zendocrine®

Miscarriage, process, and recovery– clary sage, lavender, Siberian fir, ClaryCalm®, Console®, DDR Prime®, Deep Blue®, Purify

Morning sickness/nausea– arborvitae, bergamot, cardamom, cinnamon bark, coriander, fennel, geranium, ginger, lavender, lemon, peppermint, Deep Blue®, DigestZen®, Tamer™, Zendocrine®

Muscles, sore– arborvitae, basil, bergamot mint, birch, black pepper, clary sage, copaiba, coriander, frankincense, geranium, helichrysum, juniper berry, marjoram, peppermint, Siberian fir, turmeric, wintergreen, Adaptiv™, AromaTouch®, Breathe®, Deep Blue®

Preeclampsia– cinnamon bark, cypress, frankincense, ginger, lavender, marjoram, Roman chamomile, AromaTouch®, Serenity®, Slim & Sassy®

Postbirth healing– cypress, frankincense, geranium, helichrysum, lavender, myrrh, Roman chamomile, yarrow|pom, On Guard®

Progesterone, low– geranium, grapefruit, oregano, thyme

Skin, itching/pregnancy mask– frankincense, geranium, lavender, Roman chamomile, sandalwood, yarrow|pom, Immortelle

Sleep, restless/insomnia– frankincense, lavender, Roman chamomile, wild orange, Adaptiv™, Balance®, Serenity®; see *Sleep*

Stretch marks*– cypress, frankincense, geranium, green mandarin, helichrysum, lavender, myrrh, sandalwood, tangerine, wild orange, yarrow|pom, AromaTouch®, Citrus Bliss®, Forgive®, Immortelle,

Uterus, weak– clary sage, frankincense, ginger, jasmine, lemongrass, marjoram, AromaTouch®, DDR Prime®, Forgive®

Urinary tract infections– basil, cassia, cinnamon bark, cypress, lemon, lemongrass, tea tree, oregano, tea tree, thyme, On Guard®

Varicose veins– bergamot, cardamom, cypress, geranium, helichrysum, lemon, lemongrass, tea tree, patchouli, peppermint, rosemary, yarrow|pom, Zendocrine®; see *Cardiovascular*

Water retention (edema)/blood pressure elevated– cypress, ginger, green mandarin, juniper berry, lavender, lemon, patchouli, spikenard, AromaTouch®, Citrus Bliss®; see *Cardiovascular, Urinary*

Labor:

Afterbirth/placenta delivery– clary sage, geranium, jasmine, lavender, magnolia, petitgrain

Bleeding– geranium, helichrysum, myrrh, ClaryCalm®, Serenity®

Calm nerves, relax mind– basil, bergamot mint, frankincense, jasmine, lavender, magnolia, vanilla, Balance®, Motivate®, Serenity®

Contractions, slow/weak/stalled labor*– cinnamon bark, clary sage, fennel, jasmine, lavender, myrrh, AromaTouch®, Balance®, Elevation, Motivate®, Zendocrine®

Coping, poor/overwhelmed, low confidence/fearful mindset, mood issues– basil, clary sage, geranium, jasmine, lavender, neroli, peppermint, wild orange, Adaptiv™, AromaTouch®, Balance®, Calmer™, Citrus Bliss®, Deep Blue®, Elevation, Motivate®, Serenity®

Difficult– basil, cedarwood, clary sage, fennel, geranium, lavender, myrrh, neroli, rose, spearmint, AromaTouch®, Balance®, Serenity®

Increase awareness, lift mood– basil, bergamot, lavender, magnolia, Citrus Bliss®, Citrus Bloom™, Elevation

Labor pains, management/lower back/support circulation– arborvitae, basil, birch, black pepper, clary sage, coriander, cypress, frankincense, geranium, helichrysum, juniper berry, laurel leaf, lavender, marjoram, neroli, Siberian fir, wintergreen, AromaTouch®, Balance®, Deep Blue®, Peace®, Serenity®

Overall support for optimal labor– basil, clary sage, geranium, ClaryCalm®, Peace®

Overheated– birch, eucalyptus, peppermint, wintergreen

Pain– cypress, lavender, marjoram, Deep Blue®, PastTense®

Perineum, prep/avoid episiotomy– frankincense, geranium, lavender, myrrh, Roman chamomile, sandalwood

Position of baby needs work– peppermint

Prep for labor– basil, clary sage, geranium, jasmine, ClaryCalm®

Tension, excess– clary sage, geranium, lavender, magnolia, neroli, ylang ylang, Adaptiv™, AromaTouch®, Calmer™, PastTense®, Serenity®

Transition– basil, Whisper®

Uterus, performance during labor– clary sage, frankincense, jasmine, myrrh, rose, ClaryCalm®, Elevation

PREGNANCY

Post-Delivery & Nursing:

After pains/uterine cramping that occurs while nursing– basil, bergamot, birch, clary sage, coriander, frankincense, helichrysum, laurel leaf, myrrh, AromaTouch®, Whisper®

Breasts, tender– frankincense, geranium, grapefruit, lavender, ylang ylang, ClaryCalm®; see *Women's Health*

Clogged milk ducts– cypress, fennel, grapefruit, lavender, patchouli, pink pepper, Purify

Constipation– cilantro, Douglas fir, fennel, ginger, lemon, lemongrass, marjoram, peppermint, DigestZen®, Tamer™, Zendocrine®; see *Digestive & Intestinal*

Depression, postpartum*– bergamot, black spruce, clary sage, frankincense, geranium, grapefruit, lemon, Roman chamomile, sandalwood, vanilla, vetiver, wild orange, ylang ylang, Adaptiv™, Cheer®, Citrus Bliss®, Citrus Bloom™, ClaryCalm®, Console®, DDR Prime®, Elevation, Peace®, Whisper®, Zendocrine®; see *Mood & Behavior*

Engorgement– peppermint, AromaTouch®, Deep Blue®

Episiotomy/healing from– black pepper, cypress, frankincense, helichrysum, myrrh, yarrow|pom, Immortelle

Infection (mastitis)– fennel, frankincense, lavender, patchouli, rosemary, tea tree, wild orange, Citrus Bliss®, DDR Prime®, Purify; for internal use only– cinnamon bark, clove, lemongrass, oregano, tea tree, thyme

Milk production (lactation), lack of*– basil, cardamom, clary sage, fennel, geranium, jasmine, lavender, lemongrass (avoid nipple area if applying topically); *avoid peppermint or blends with peppermint as it can decrease milk supply

Milk production, to stop– peppermint

Nipple vasospasms (nipple compressed after nursing)– lime, Whisper®

Nipples dry, cracked/sore– clary sage, copaiba, fennel, frankincense, geranium, helichrysum, lavender, myrrh, neroli, Roman chamomile, sandalwood, wild orange, yarrow|pom, Immortelle, Zendocrine®; see "Thrush" below

Recovery from childbirth– clary sage, coriander, cypress, geranium, frankincense (soothe perineum or circumcision), helichrysum, jasmine (supports expulsion of placenta), lavender (supports expulsion of placenta; soothes perineum or circumcision), neroli, sandalwood, Siberian fir, ylang ylang, Adaptiv™, Balance® (for emotional stability, recovery), Immortelle (cesarean-section recovery), Serenity® (to overcome distress, deal with newness of breastfeeding), Whisper® (supports hormone rebalancing)

Thrush– clary sage, copaiba, fennel, frankincense, lavender, lemon, Siberian fir, tea tree, wild orange, yarrow|pom; see *Candida*

PREGNANCY

**See Protocols on pgs. 407-408*

usage tips

Pregnancy

- **Allergy support**– take 2 drops each of lemon, peppermint, and lavender in a capsule or water.
- **Baby brain development support**– take 2 xEO Mega® 2x's daily during pregnancy and nursing.
- **Calming emotional support**– apply Balance® and Serenity® to bottoms of feet.
- **Headache relief**– apply PastTense® or peppermint on forehead, temples, back of neck, and/or under nose.
- **Fatigue**– add 2-3 drops of lemon, grapefruit, or wild orange to drinking water, 2-3x's per day.
- **Heartburn**– apply DigestZen®, Tamer™, diluted peppermint, and/or ginger directly on breastbone. Dilute as needed.
- **Increase sex drive**– diffuse or apply wild orange or ylang ylang; see *Intimacy*.
- **Morning sickness**– use peppermint, DigestZen®, Tamer™, fennel, or ginger and apply under nose, put in water, or a capsule. Apply Zendocrine® and take Zendocrine® Complex during first trimester.
- **Muscle cramps**– apply basil, marjoram, and/or AromaTouch®
- **Relaxation and deep sleep**– apply lavender or Serenity® under nose, on forehead, over heart, and/or on bottoms of feet.
- **Sciatica and muscle pain**– apply Deep Blue® and/or AromaTouch® to area of concern.
- **Swelling**– apply AromaTouch®, Deep Blue®, and/or cypress to bottoms of feet and/or area of swelling. Add a few drops of lemon to drinking water or take in a capsule.

Labor & Delivery

- **Back pain during labor**– apply peppermint, bergamot mint, and/or AromaTouch® on back to help ease pain.
- **Energy during labor**– apply peppermint and/or add to drinking water on ice.
- **Increase perineum elasticity**– massage myrrh and/or helichrysum on perineum prior to labor.
- **Protect birth canal from group B strep**– add 1 drop each frankincense and basil, highly diluted, to douche prior to birth.
- **Promote or induce labor**– apply ClaryCalm® to abdomen, ankles, and pressure points if labor has stalled.
- **To support labor**– apply jasmine and clary sage to ankles and other pressure points to help contractions increase/improve.
- **Baby's first bath**– apply a small amount of diluted neroli.

Post Partum

- **After-birth pains**– apply Deep Blue® and copaiba to abdomen.
- **Body aches and pains**– apply magnolia, Deep Blue®, AromaTouch®, and/or clary sage to areas of concern.
- **Bowels moving**– take 2-3 drops of DigestZen® in water or capsule.
- **Engorgement**– apply basil around breast.
- **Depression**– apply Adaptiv™, Elevation, frankincense, melissa, Citrus Bloom™ and/or Citrus Bliss® under nose and on ears
- **Fatigue**– take 4 drops Slim & Sassy® with 2 drops each peppermint and wild orange twice daily in a capsule.
- **Hemorrhoids**– apply Balance® and/or cypress directly to affected area.
- **Increase milk production**– apply fennel and/or rosemary to breasts. Take in a capsule.
- **Prevent infection for mom & baby**– apply highly diluted frankincense and Rescuer™ on baby's spine and bottoms of feet.
- **Sleep support**– apply a few drops of lavender or Serenity® on bottoms of feet at nap or bedtime. Place a couple drops in bath water, diffuse 30 minutes before bedtime, and/or add to a DIY linen spray.
- **Sore nipples**– apply helichrysum directly to nipples.
- **Tearing, inflammation, and soreness**– apply frankincense, helichrysum, and/or lavender; drop lavender and frankincense on frozen feminine pads and/or in peri-wash.
- **Uplifting emotional support**– apply Adaptiv™, Elevation, or Citrus Bloom™ under nose, to ears, and/or on bottoms of feet.

Newborn

- **For swelling, baby blemishes, or skin discoloration**– apply frankincense diluted to any area of concern.
- **To assist baby's transition and release any trauma**– diffuse frankincense or Balance® and apply diluted along baby's spine and bottoms of feet.
- **To help avoid infection and release umbilical cord remains**– place a few drops of myrrh on umbilical cord.

PREGNANCY

protocols

Optimal Pregnancy and Post-pregnancy Success Suggestions

BASIC SUPPLEMENT PROGRAM

Benefits: core nutrition; energy and stamina; emotional stability; healthy blood pressure; proper digestion, absorption of nutrients, and gut health; rich breast milk supply; healthy immunity; muscular and structural health and flexibility; healthy cervix

- **Microplex VMz®**— delivers multivitamins and minerals
- **xEO Mega®**— supplies essential fatty acids
- **Alpha CRS®+**— provides powerful antioxidants
- **TerraZyme®**— provides digestive enzyme support
- **PB Assist®+**— provides and promotes prebiotics and probiotics
- **Bone Nutrient Complex**— supplies needed calcium, magnesium, and more

In addition to the above, choose, as needed, from the following:

- **Morning sickness**— take or apply diluted DigestZen®, Tamer™, ginger, and/or peppermint
- **Liver/gallbladder support**— take lemon, grapefruit, pink pepper, turmeric, and/or Zendocrine®
- **Heartburn**— take DigestZen®, DigestTab®
- **Stay calm, grounded**— use 1-2x's daily:
  - Frankincense, wild orange, Balance®, and/or Serenity®
- **Balance metabolism, sugar cravings, appetite**— add 3-5 drops grapefruit or Slim & Sassy® to drinking water:
- **Antioxidant support**— take 1-2x's daily:
  - DDR Prime®, Zendocrine®, lemon, and/or other citrus oils
- **Gut detox**— 2 drops each lemon, celery seed, and thyme 2x's a day for 10 days, follow with extra PB Assist®+ for 10 days
- **Leg/muscle/ligament cramps or spasms**—
  - Apply: basil, cypress, lavender, marjoram, AromaTouch®, and/or Deep Blue®. Dilute as needed

PREGNANCY SWELLING RELIEF

Ingredients:

3 drops ginger
2 drops cypress
2 drops lavender

Directions:

Combine oils with carrier oil and massage onto legs and feet.

NO MORE STRETCH MARKS

Ingredients:

10 drops lavender
10 drops wild orange
5 drops geranium
5 drops myrrh
5 drops helichrysum
4 drops frankincense

Directions:

Combine in a 10mL roller bottle and remainder with carrier oil. Apply twice daily and massage into areas of concern.

STRETCH MARK RELIEF

2 drops each green mandarin, helichrysum, lavender, and myrrh mixed with ½— 1 t carrier oil (depending on area intended to cover) and apply to abdomen.

For more ideas, download the app on Android or iOS.

ITCHY BELLY BUTTER

Ingredients:

½ cup shea butter
¼ cup carrier oil
¼ cup sweet almond oil
5 drops frankincense
5 drops lavender

Directions:

Add to glass bowl. Place in a couple inches of water in a pot. Melt over medium heat until translucent. Remove, cool slightly. Then add carrier and essential oils. Stir. Place in refrigerator until solid. Whip for 2-3 minutes into buttery consistency. Spoon into jar, cover, and refrigerate one more hour. Apply directly to belly or itchy spots to nourish and moisturize skin. Store for up to 6 months at room temperature.

HEALING HEMORRHOIDS

Ingredients:

20 drops helichrysum
20 drops geranium
20 drops arborvitae or cypress
10 drops peppermint

Directions:

Mix oils in 2 oz glass spray bottle and fill remainder with carrier oil. Apply 1-2x's daily and/or after every bowel evacuation.

THE FINAL COUNTDOWN ROLL-ON (to help reduce swelling and bleeding as well as improve experience during labor.)

Ingredients:

10 drops clary sage
10 drops ginger
10 drops lavender
10 drops lemon
10 drops AromaTouch®

Directions:

Combine oils in 10mL roller bottle and fill remainder with carrier oil. Apply blend to low back and ankles at least once daily during the last week of pregnancy. Massage in thoroughly. BONUS: Add a layer of diluted jasmine.

JUMPSTART CONTRACTIONS

If labor has begun but is stalled, apply 1-2 drops each myrrh and clary sage to wrists and abdomen as well as on uterine and cervical reflex points on under inside ankle bones.

INCREASE MILK SUPPLY

Ingredients:

7 drops basil
8 drops fennel
6 drops clary sage
4 drops geranium

Directions:

Combine 4 t carrier oil with 2 t beeswax. Melt over low heat. Cool. While still soft, add oils and stir. Rub on breasts after each nursing.

HELLO WORLD!— Diffuse or apply fennel, frankincense, lavender, lemon, and/or Elevation, highly diluted, at least 2x's daily to support optimal recovery for mom and bonding with baby.

POSTPARTUM DEPRESSION

Apply or diffuse:

- Recipe #1: 1 drop wild orange and 3 drops sandalwood, topped with diluted rose
- Recipe #2: 1 drop each lavender and ylang ylang, 3 drops grapefruit
- Recipe #3: 1 drop each bergamot, grapefruit, clary sage, and wild orange with 3 drops frankincense

To fill a 10mL roller bottle, multiply any of these recipes by 5-10 and top off with fractionated coconut oil.

Pure essential oils are powerful and superb aids during pregnancy. They offer natural, safe, and effective options, without side effects, for everyday needs and common discomforts.

AFTERBIRTH TEAR RELIEF

Ingredients:

1 bottle witch hazel
4 drops lavender
3 drops frankincense
4 drops tea tree
10 drops yarrow|pom
Aloe vera gel

Directions:

Add oils to witch hazel and shake well. Cut large menstrual pads into thirds, spray with solution, squirt aloe gel down center, and freeze. Use immediately after birth or while area is inflamed. Options: add same solution with water to peri bottle or simply add 5 drops each Balance® and yarrow|pom to frozen pad.

PREGNANCY

RESPIRATORY

RESPIRATION is the process of inhaling, warming, filtering, controlling the humidity of, and exhaling air. Lungs exchange oxygen for carbon dioxide, and the heart pumps oxygenated blood to the rest of the body. Additionally, the cilia in the lungs secrete mucus as they move back and forth, carrying out of the lungs dust and germs and expelling those by sneezing, coughing, spitting, and swallowing.

Breathing is controlled by the diaphragm, located at the base of the ribcage. When the diaphragm contracts, it pulls down on the thoracic cavity, causing the lungs to expand and air to be inhaled. When the diaphragm relaxes, the lungs retract and air is exhaled. The breathing process, one of the most basic and important functions performed by the body, is often taken for granted–until something goes wrong. For some individuals, breathing can be challenging, especially if they suffer from some type of respiratory condition or disease.

Respiratory disease is a broad term used to refer to a series of conditions that affect the respiratory system. Therefore, any condition that affects the lungs, bronchial tubes, upper respiratory tract, trachea, pleural cavity, or even nerves and muscles used for breathing can be termed as a respiratory disease.

Infection, histamine reaction, or prolonged irritation can negatively impact the respiratory system. A variety of ailments may result, ranging from mild allergies or stuffy nose to more severe asthma or diphtheria.

In general, a respiratory illness can have a debilitating effect on one's overall health. Many people mistake respiratory illnesses for other health problems, particularly when they experience an overall feeling of fatigue and malaise. Loss of appetite, indigestion, severe weight loss, and headaches are also quite common in respiratory diseases.

Medical attention and diagnosis is absolutely essential for any respiratory ailment that is severe or persistent. However, milder conditions can be easily resolved with the support of natural and simple home remedies. The scope of home remedies is vast. They can be used alone or in combination with conventional treatments.

top solutions

Single Oils

Black or Pink pepper- reduce inflammation and mucus (pgs. 113, 206)

Eucalyptus, Cardamom— open airways, support proper respiratory function (pgs. 146, 118)

Peppermint— opens airways, expels mucus (pg. 202)

Rosemary, Laurel leaf, Ravintsara— help prevent, relieve, and resolve a multitude of respiratory issues (pgs. 216, 173, 209)

Blends

Breathe®, Air-X™— address a broad spectrum of respiratory issues (pgs. 116, 97)

On Guard®— fights respiratory infections, helps resolve respiratory issues (pg. 195)

Purify, Abōde™— decongest (pgs. 208, 95)

Supplements

Breathe Respiratory Drops (pg. 255), DDR Prime® Softgels, DigestZen® Softgels, Microplex VMz®, **On Guard® Throat Drops** (pg. 263), **PB Assist®+** (pg. 264), **Peppermint Softgels** (pg. 265), TerraZyme®, **TriEase® Softgels** (pg. 268), xEO Mega®

usage tips

Whether for preventative measures (to clear airborne pathogens and sterilize air) or to resolve respiratory conditions, essential oils are excellent for "clearing the air" in both the environment and the body's respiratory system, as well as addressing contributing factors such as poor digestion.

- **Aromatic:** Diffuse (using a diffuser) or inhale selected oils. For a quick treatment, drop oil(s) in hands, rub together, cup around nose and mouth area (can avoid touching face) and repeatedly, deeply inhale through mouth and nose. Additionally, oils can be applied under the nose, on clothing or bedding, or on jewelry made for diffusing purposes or to create long-lasting inhalation exposure.
- **Topical:** Rub oils on chest (for aromatic benefits as well), back, forehead (sinuses), and on back side of toes and ball of foot (reflex points for head and chest).
- **Internal:** Place drops of oils in a capsule or in water for systemic support.
- **Surfaces**: Make a spray mixing essential oils in water with witch hazel for surfaces, such as countertops and door knobs, for cleaning purposes and eradicating bacteria, viruses, fungi, or other harmful germs.

Related Ailments

Acute Respiratory Distress Syndrome (ARDS), Anosmia, Asthma, Auditory Processing Disorder, Blocked Tear Duct, Breathing Problems, Bronchitis, Congestion, Cough, Croup, Cystic Fibrosis, Diphtheria, Dry Eyes, Dry Nose, Earache, Ear Infection (Otitis Media), Emphysema, Hearing in a Tunnel, Hearing Problems, Hiccups, Hyperpnea (increased deep and/or rapid breathing to meet demand following exercise, lack of oxygen, high altitude, as the result of anemia), Legionnaire's Disease, Loss of smell, Mucus, Nasal Polyp [Cellular Health], Nosebleed, Perforated Eardrum, Pleurisy, Pneumonia (viral, bacterial), Rhinitis [allergies], Sinus Congestion, Sinus Headache, Sinusitis (sinus infection), Sleep Apnea, Snoring, Stye (Eye), Swollen Eye, Tinnitus, Tuberculosis, Whooping Cough, Xerophthalmia

By Related Properties

For more, see *Oil Properties* on pages 535-538

Antidepressant— arborvitae, basil, bergamot, cinnamon bark

Anticatarrhal— basil, black pepper, cardamom, clary sage, eucalyptus, fennel, frankincense, helichrysum, laurel leaf, neroli, oregano, ravintsara, rosemary, sandalwood, Siberian fir, spearmint, wild orange

Anti-inflammatory— arborvitae, basil, bergamot, birch, black pepper, blue tansy, cardamom, cassia, cedarwood, cinnamon bark, copaiba, coriander, cypress, eucalyptus, fennel, frankincense, geranium, ginger, helichrysum, jasmine, lavender, lemongrass, litsea, manuka, melissa, myrrh, neroli, oregano, patchouli, peppermint, Roman chamomile, rosemary, sandalwood, Siberian fir, spearmint, spikenard, tangerine, tea tree, turmeric, wild orange, wintergreen, yarrow|pom

Antispasmodic— blue tansy, clary sage, litsea, neroli, Roman chamomile, Siberian fir, tangerine, yarrow|pom

Decongestant— basil, black spruce, cardamom, cassia, copaiba, cypress, eucalyptus, ginger, grapefruit, green mandarin, laurel leaf, lemon, lemongrass, ravintsara, tea tree, patchouli, Siberian fir, turmeric, yarrow|pom

Expectorant— arborvitae, basil, black pepper, black spruce, cardamom, cedarwood, clove, eucalyptus, fennel, frankincense, ginger, green mandarin, helichrysum, jasmine, marjoram, myrrh, laurel leaf, lemon eucalyptus, oregano, peppermint, pink pepper, ravintsara, rosemary, sandalwood, Siberian fir, tea tree, thyme, turmeric, white fir

Immunostimulant— arborvitae, basil, black pepper, cassia, cinnamon bark, clove, copaiba, eucalyptus, fennel, frankincense, ginger, lemon, lime, magnolia, melissa, oregano, ravintsara, rosemary, sandalwood, Siberian fir, spearmint, tea tree, thyme, vetiver, wild orange, yarrow|pom

Mucolytic— basil, cardamom, cedarwood, cinnamon bark, clary sage, copaiba, cypress, fennel, helichrysum, lemon, myrrh, sandalwood, tangerine, wild orange, yarrow|pom

Steroidal— basil, birch, cedarwood, clove, fennel, patchouli, rosemary, thyme conditions

Bronchial

Infection (e.g. bronchitis)*– cardamom, cedarwood, clary sage, clove, copaiba, eucalyptus, frankincense, green mandarin, lavender, lime, marjoram, oregano, peppermint, pink pepper, rosemary, spearmint, thyme, turmeric, Air-X™, Breathe®, Breathe® Respiratory Drops, Console®, Forgive®, On Guard®, Peace®

Inflammation– basil, cardamom, cedarwood, clove, cypress, laurel leaf, magnolia, ravintsara, rosemary, Siberian fir, spearmint, wild orange, Breathe®, Breathe® Respiratory Drops

Breathing, *General Need To Improve*

General– cinnamon bark, eucalyptus, laurel leaf, patchouli, peppermint, thyme, Air-X™, Breathe®, Breathe® Respiratory Drops, Cheer®, Motivate®, Northern Escape, Purify

Constricted/tight airways– arborvitae, bergamot mint, birch, black spruce, blue tansy, cardamom, cinnamon bark, clove, Douglas fir, eucalyptus, frankincense, helichrysum, laurel leaf, lavender, lemon, lemongrass, marjoram, peppermint, ravintsara, rosemary, Siberian fir, thyme, tulsi, wild orange, wintergreen, Air-X™, Breathe®, Breathe® Respiratory Drops, Console®, Motivate®, Passion®, Serenity®

Difficulty (hyperpnea)– cardamom, clary sage, patchouli, peppermint, Abōde™, Air-X™, Breathe®, Purify

Labored– cinnamon bark, ylang ylang, Purify, Serenity®

Rapid– melissa, DDR Prime®, Serenity®

Shortness of breath/breathlessness/difficulty breathing (dyspnea)– blue tansy, cinnamon bark, eucalyptus, frankincense, laurel leaf, patchouli, peppermint, ravintsara, Air-X™, Breathe®, DDR Prime®, Northern Escape, Peace®, Purify

Shortness of breath/breathlessness/discomfort while lying down (orthopnea)– Roman chamomile, tea tree, ylang ylang, Abōde™, Purify

Shortness of breath/breathlessness with exertion or during exercise or activity– myrrh, oregano, wintergreen, ylang ylang, Abōde™, Air-X™, Breathe®, Peace®, Purify, Whisper®, Zendocrine®

Sleep apnea– eucalyptus, laurel leaf, lemongrass, peppermint, ravintsara, rosemary, thyme, tulsi, wintergreen, Abōde™, Air-X™, Balance®, Breathe®, On Guard®, Purify, Whisper®

Wheezing– birch, cinnamon bark, clary sage, clove, eucalyptus, fennel, frankincense, helichrysum, lavender, lemon, marjoram, myrrh, peppermint, rosemary, Siberian fir, thyme, wintergreen, Abōde™, Air-X™, Breathe®, On Guard®, Purify, Serenity®, Whisper®

Congestion, General *(Mucus/Sputum/Phlegm, Catarrh)*

General– bergamot mint, blue tansy, cardamom, cassia, cypress, Douglas fir, eucalyptus, fennel, frankincense, ginger, helichrysum, laurel leaf, lemon, lemon eucalyptus, lime, magnolia, marjoram, myrrh, peppermint, petitgrain, ravintsara, rosemary, Siberian fir, tangerine, Abōde™, Air-X™, Breathe®, Breathe® Respiratory Drops, Console®, DigestZen®, Forgive®, Motivate®, Passion®, Slim & Sassy®, Zendocrine®

Clear mucus– black pepper, cardamom, clove, eucalyptus, ginger, laurel leaf, lavender, lemon, melissa, peppermint, ravintsara, sandalwood, tangerine, Abōde™, Air-X™, Purify

Chronic discharge of mucus– basil, eucalyptus, wintergreen

Thick mucus– bergamot, birch, cardamom, cassia, cypress, eucalyptus, lemon, pink pepper, myrrh, ravintsara, thyme, wild orange, Abōde™, Air-X™, Breathe®, Citrus Bliss®, DDR Prime®, Forgive®, On Guard®, Passion®, Peace®, Purify, Slim & Sassy®

Yellow, green mucus– basil, cilantro, eucalyptus, ginger, laurel leaf, lemongrass, ravintsara, On Guard®, Slim & Sassy®

Cough, General*

General– arborvitae, black spruce, blue tansy, cardamom, cedarwood, copaiba, Douglas fir, eucalyptus, frankincense, ginger, green mandarin, helichrysum, juniper berry, laurel leaf, lemon eucalyptus, magnolia, oregano, ravintsara, Siberian fir, tea tree, thyme, turmeric, wild orange, Air-X™, Breathe®, Breathe® Respiratory Drops, Northern Escape, On Guard®

Barking (e.g. croup)– basil, bergamot, cinnamon bark, grapefruit, lemon, lemongrass, marjoram, oregano, patchouli, sandalwood, thyme, wild orange, Air-X™, Breathe®, DDR Prime®, DigestZen®, On Guard®

Chronic– cardamom, cassia, cinnamon bark, eucalyptus, helichrysum, laurel leaf, lemon, melissa, oregano, ravintsara, rosemary, thyme, On Guard®

Coughing up blood– blue tansy, cardamom, eucalyptus, geranium, helichrysum, lavender, myrrh, oregano, rose, wild orange, wintergreen, yarrow|pom, On Guard®, Purify, Whisper®; see "Lung–infections" below (consider radon poisoning)

Dry– eucalyptus, frankincense, lavender, Siberian fir, ylang ylang, Air-X™, Breathe®, Whisper®

GERD– See *Digestive & Intestinal*

Heavy mucus– arborvitae, cinnamon bark, clary sage, eucalyptus, fennel, frankincense, ginger, green mandarin, laurel leaf, lemon, myrrh, oregano, pink pepper, ravintsara, tea tree, wintergreen, Air-X™, Citrus Bliss®, Console®, DigestZen®, Motivate®, Passion®

Moist (sputum-producing)– eucalyptus, ginger, lemon, oregano, On Guard®, Purify, Slim & Sassy®

Spastic/persistent (e.g. whooping cough)– basil, black spruce, cardamom, citronella, clary sage, cypress, frankincense, helichrysum, lavender, melissa, oregano, petitgrain, Roman chamomile, rosemary, sandalwood, thyme, yarrow|pom, Forgive®, Peace®, Purify, Serenity®

Worsens with activity/from exposure to irritant– ginger, ylang ylang, Northern Escape, On Guard®, Purify

Ears

Auditory processing challenges– helichrysum, thyme, Purify, Whisper®; see *Brain*

Earache/pain– basil, clary sage, cypress, fennel, ginger, helichrysum, lavender, peppermint, Roman chamomile, tea tree, Citrus Bliss®, Deep Blue®, On Guard®, Passion®, Zendocrine®

Eardrum, perforated– arborvitae, basil, patchouli, ylang ylang, On Guard®, Purify

Ear, infection– basil, helichrysum, lavender, lemon, rosemary, tea tree, On Guard®

Ear mites– basil, blue tansy, cedarwood, myrrh, wild orange, DigestZen®, InTune®; see *Parasites*

Hearing problems– basil, clary sage, frankincense, helichrysum, lemon, patchouli, tea tree, Deep Blue®, PastTense®, Slim & Sassy®

Ringing/noise in the ear (tinnitus)– arborvitae, basil, cypress, frankincense, helichrysum, juniper berry, lemongrass, peppermint, tea tree, Purify, TerraShield®, Zendocrine®

RESPIRATORY

*See Protocols on pgs. 413-414

Eyes

Caution: Use only highly diluted oils around eye area. Do not put oils in the eyes. Use eye reflex point on toes; see *Reflexology*.

Dry– lavender, myrrh, sandalwood

Itchy– lavender, oregano, patchouli, wild orange, Citrus Bliss®, DDR Prime®, Zendocrine®

Stringy mucus in or around eyes– clary sage, fennel, tea tree, DDR Prime®

Tear duct, blocked– clary sage, eucalyptus, frankincense, lavender, lemongrass, myrrh, tea tree, Purify

Watery/teary– arborvitae, basil, black pepper, blue tansy, frankincense, lime, patchouli, wild orange, DDR Prime®, Immortelle, On Guard®, Purify, Zendocrine®

Infection– frankincense, lavender, tulsi, Correct-X®

General Respiratory

Infection, general respiratory*– black pepper, cardamom, cinnamon bark, eucalyptus, frankincense, green mandarin, lemon, magnolia, melissa, oregano, pink pepper, ravintsara, rose, turmeric, Air-X™, Breathe®, Forgive®, Motivate®, On Guard®

Inflammation*– birch, black pepper, coriander, cypress, eucalyptus, ginger, laurel leaf, marjoram, melissa, myrrh, rose, peppermint, spearmint, tea tree, Air-X™, Breathe®, On Guard®, Slim & Sassy®

Virus– cassia, cinnamon bark, clove, eucalyptus, laurel leaf, melissa, oregano, ravintsara, rosemary, thyme, Air-X™, Breathe®, On Guard®

Lung

Infection (e.g. pneumonia)– black pepper, cedarwood, cinnamon bark, copaiba, Douglas fir, eucalyptus, frankincense, juniper berry, laurel leaf, lavender, melissa, oregano, ravintsara, rose, sandalwood, Siberian fir, thyme, vetiver, Console®, On Guard®

Problems/conditions*– arborvitae, basil, bergamot, birch, cardamom, cinnamon bark, copaiba, Douglas fir, eucalyptus, fennel, frankincense, ginger, laurel leaf, lemon, lemongrass, tea tree, melissa, oregano, peppermint, ravintsara, rosemary, sandalwood, Siberian fir, tea tree, thyme, tulsi, wild orange, wintergreen, AromaTouch®, Breathe®, Cheer®, Motivate®, Purify

Nose

Bleeding– cypress, geranium, helichrysum, lavender, myrrh, yarrow|pom, AromaTouch®, DDR Prime®, Deep Blue®, On Guard®, Purify, Serenity®

Itchy– lavender, lemon, lemongrass, On Guard®, Purify,

Nasal polyps– eucalyptus, frankincense, geranium, lemongrass, ravintsara, rosemary, sandalwood, Citrus Bliss®, melissa, myrrh, Breathe®, Deep Blue®, On Guard®, Purify, TerraShield®

Postnasal drip– cinnamon bark, lavender, lemon, On Guard®, Purify

Runny– lavender, lemon, peppermint, Purify, Whisper®, Zendocrine®

Smell, decreased/loss of (anosmia)– arborvitae, basil, frankincense, helichrysum, lavender, lemongrass, peppermint, Roman chamomile, rose, sandalwood, Adaptiv™, DDR Prime®, On Guard®, PastTense®

Smell, loss of (nerve damage)– helichrysum, patchouli

Sneezing– cilantro, coriander, lavender, lemon, peppermint, Purify, Whisper®, Zendocrine®

Stuffy– cardamom, cassia, eucalyptus, fennel, frankincense, ginger, jasmine, laurel leaf, lemon, lime, marjoram, myrrh, patchouli, peppermint, ravintsara, rosemary, Siberian fir, Air-X™, Breathe®, DigestZen®, On Guard®, Zendocrine®

Sinus

Facial, forehead pain/pressure/tenderness; swelling/pressure around eyes, cheeks, nose, or forehead– blue tansy, cinnamon bark, lemongrass, peppermint, thyme, tulsi, On Guard®, Purify

Infection/inflammation– basil, bergamot, cedarwood, clove, Douglas fir, eucalyptus, helichrysum, lemon, lemongrass, melissa, peppermint, rosemary, sandalwood, Siberian fir, Air-X™, Breathe®, DigestZen®, Forgive®, Northern Escape

Pain in teeth– arborvitae, lavender, lemon, myrrh, DDR Prime®, On Guard®, Purify, Serenity®

Throat

Dry– cypress, grapefruit, lemon, lime, peppermint, wild orange, Breathe®, Breathe® Respiratory Drops, Purify, Zendocrine®

Sore, infection*– basil, cardamom, cinnamon bark, eucalyptus, lemon, lemongrass, lime, myrrh, myrrh + lemon, oregano, patchouli, rosemary, sandalwood, thyme, On Guard®, On Guard® Throat Drops, Purify, Zendocrine®

Swollen, glands– lavender, lemon, peppermint, Slim & Sassy®

Voice

Hoarse, Loss of (laryngitis)– cinnamon bark, eucalyptus, fennel, frankincense, ginger, jasmine, lavender, lemon, lemongrass, lime, peppermint, sandalwood, thyme, ylang ylang, Console®, On Guard®, Purify, Zendocrine®

Other Respiratory Issues

Airborne germs/bacteria– arborvitae, cassia, cedarwood, cinnamon bark, clove, eucalyptus, grapefruit, lavender, lemon, tea tree, Siberian fir, thyme, Abōde™, Air-X™, Breathe®, On Guard®, Purify

Breath, bad– patchouli, peppermint or beadlets, ylang ylang, DDR Prime®, DigestZen®, DigestZen® Softgels

Chest pain– Douglas fir, consider cardiac association; see *Cardiovascular*

Hiccups– arborvitae, basil, blue tansy, lemon, peppermint, sandalwood, Zendocrine®; see *Children*

Mouth, dry– lemon, lemongrass, tangerine, vetiver, wild orange, Citrus Bliss®, On Guard®, Slim & Sassy®, Whisper®

Pleura, inflammation of– birch, cinnamon bark, cypress, eucalyptus, lemon, melissa, rosemary, thyme, Air-X™, Breathe®

Smoking, quit– See *Addictions*

Snoring*– eucalyptus, geranium, laurel leaf, patchouli, peppermint, ravintsara, Air-X™, Breathe®, On Guard®, Purify, Zendocrine®

Taste, loss of– cinnamon bark, helichrysum, lemongrass, lime, melissa, peppermint, tangerine, Zendocrine®

RESPIRATORY

protocols

ULTIMATE RESPIRATORY PROTECTION PROGRAM

ESSENTIAL NUTRITION:

Microplex VMz®, xEO Mega®, Alpha CRS®+ — take as directed

Immune support and sources of Vitamin C, D, and zinc:

YarrowlPom Capsules, On Guard Tablets® — take as directed

Choose one or more, as needed, from each of the following:

RESPIRATORY TARGETED SUPPORT & CLEANSING:

Air-X™, *Breathe®, eucalyptus, laurel leaf, ravintsara, rosemary, *Siberian fir

- Diffuse 5-10 drops of selected oil(s) at least 4 hours per day, especially during nighttime sleep— preferably for 8 hours.
- Apply oils to forehead, chest, over and under nose, and/or along spine.
- Take 2-4 drops of selected oil(s) 2-4x's per day (for those labeled for internal consumption).

IMMUNE TARGETED SUPPORT:

Black pepper, copaiba, grapefruit, green mandarin, melissa, *On Guard®, rosemary, *Siberian fir, tea tree, thyme

- Take take 2-4 drops of selected oil(s) 2-4x's per day as needed.

CLARIFYING AND DETOXIFICATION:

Zendocrine® (blend or softgels)

- Take 2-4 drops or 1-2 softgels 2-4x's per day.

CELLULAR HEALTH, REPAIR, AND ANTIOXIDANT SUPPORT:

***Air- X™, clove, *DDR Prime®, frankincense, lemongrass, thyme, *Turmeric Dual Capsules**

- Take 2-4 drops of selected oil(s) or 1-2 softgels/capsules 2-4x's per day.

GUT CLEARING AND FORTIFYING:

***Terrazyme, *PB Assist+®, DigestZen®, ginger, Slim & Sassy®**

- Take as directed; increase consumption if needed.

PUBLIC PROTECTION:

Spearmint, manuka, hyssop

- Take or apply before, during, or after exposure to the public.

CLEAR THE AIR & REPEL:

Abōde™, lemon, eucalyptus

- Diffuse a few hours each day to keep home/office space air clean.

**Highly recommended as primary choices.*

ALLERGY POWER TRIO

Ingredients:

2 drops lavender
2 drops lemon
2 drops peppermint

Directions:

Place drops in 4 ozs of water. Drink. Repeat every 30 minutes as needed or take 1-2 TriEase® Softgels 2-4x's per day.

GARGLE— Combine salt, warm water, and 1-2 drops of an essential oil of choice and gargle at least twice per day to soothe throat and clear congestion.

CLEAR THE AIR (for snoring, respiratory/lung issues) Add essential oils to a diffuser and run 8-10 hours per day. Suggested combinations:

Recipe #1: 3 drops each Siberian fir and Breathe®
Recipe #2: 5-10 drops Breathe® or Air-X™
Recipe #3: 8 drops On Guard® + 2 drops rosemary
Recipe #4: 3 drops each Douglas fir, wild orange, and eucalyptus
Recipe #5: 2 drops each cardamom, rosemary, and lime

ALL STEAMED UP (moist air supports respiratory resolve) Use a humidifier (suitable for essential oils), steam from a pan, sauna, or shower and add a few drops of Breathe® or eucalyptus. Inhale for 15 minutes 3x's a day. When possible, drape a towel over head and source of steam.

HOT TEA: Add a few drops of essential oils to warm water. Slowly inhale steam, and then sip water when slightly cooled to relieve sore throat or breathing issues. Options: cinnamon bark, clove, cardamom, lemon, oregano, rosemary, thyme, and/or On Guard®.

SORE THROAT/LARYNGITIS REMEDY: Add 1 drop ginger and 3 drops lemon to honey. Oils can also be added to warm water to drink or licked off back of hand.

CLEAR RESPIRATORY INFECTION: Apply diluted tea tree and thyme on chest and back. Consider adding black or pink pepper and eucalyptus for additional support.

FLU-BUSTING, LUNG-STIMULATING SMOOTHIE

Ingredients:

1 C orange fresh juice
½ C lemon juice
½ C chopped pineapple
1-2 t raw honey (to taste)
1 T coconut oil
¼ t cayenne pepper
1-2 drops ginger
1-2 drops peppermint

Directions:

Blend with a little ice and greens and enjoy.

IMMUNE BOOSTING INHALATION

Use 2 drops each pink pepper, peppermint, tea tree, and lavender in a diffuser, or place 1 drop each in palms of hands, rub together, cup over face, inhale, and then rub on chest. Dilute with carrier oil as needed.

COUGH BUSTER RUB

Ingredients:

¾ C virgin coconut oil
¾ C fractionated coconut oil
4 T beeswax

Directions:

Melt in glass container (double boiler or glass jar in a pot of water) Remove from heat and add:

Ingredients:

2 T Vitamin E oil
40 drops basil
40 drops cardamom
40 drops lime
40 drops marjoram
15 drops peppermint
5 drops eucalyptus
5 drops rosemary
5 drops lemon
5 drops frankincense

Directions:

Mix and let cool. Rub on chest as needed.

thin it out

2 drops fennel
2 drops green mandarin
1 drop peppermint
Mix oils in warm water as a tea or take in a capsule every 2-4 hours to relieve congestion and clear mucus.

HOMEMADE COUGH SYRUP

Ingredients:

½ C honey, warmed
8 drops peppermint
8 drops lemon
8 drops lavender
8 drops frankincense
3 drops clove
3 drops wild orange
1 drop cinnamon bark

Directions:

Mix and take 1 t every three hours as needed. Thin with warm water if desired.

SINGER'S OR SPEAKER'S VOICE RECOVERY SPRAY

Ingredients:

8 drops lemon
8 drops On Guard®
4 drops peppermint
2 drops myrrh
1 drop oregano or thyme
1 drop clove
1 drop sandalwood

Directions:

Add all oils to 15mL glass spray bottle. Add distilled water and shake. Spray on back of throat frequently (every 20-60 minutes) to obtain desired results.

CONGESTION RELIEF STEAM BLENDS

To a bowl of steamy water, add:

Ingredients:

Option 1: 2 drops copaiba, 1 drop lemon, 3 drops tea tree, 4 drops eucalyptus.

Option 2: 2 drops each Siberian fir, cardamom, lime, and tea tree.

Directions:

Drape a towel over head to trap steam. With eyes closed, inhale through nose. Breathe deeply for five minutes, or until oils evaporate and relief is achieved.

Skeletal

THE BODY'S SKELETAL STRUCTURE comprises the framework upon which all other organs and tissues depend for proper placement and coordination. But bones are not inert material; they are alive, and need blood and oxygen to metabolize nutrients and produce waste. They respond to external stresses by changing shape to accommodate new mechanical demands. The skeleton is often referred to in terms analogous to a tree: the trunk, or torso, supports the limbs, and so on. This system accounts for about 20 percent of the body's overall weight.

The backbone, also called the spine or vertebral column, is made up of twenty-four movable bone segments called vertebrae and is divided into three sections. The top seven are cervical vertebrae, which support the cranium, or skull. The thoracic vertebrae, twelve in all, comprise the mid-back area and support the ribs. The lower back, or lumbar spine, consists of five vertebrae that connect to the pelvis at the sacrum. Each vertebra is stacked upon another and is separated and cushioned by intervertebral discs held in place by tendons and cartilage. Through a channel formed by a hole in each of the stacked vertebrae runs the spinal cord, off of which branch root nerves. This nerve network enables communication between the brain, the muscles, and the organs of the body system.

In addition to providing a structure to keep other body systems from lying in a heap on the floor, the skeleton protects the softer body parts. The cranium fuses around the brain, forming helmet-like protection. The vertebrae protect the spinal cord from injury, and the rib cage creates a barrier around the heart and lungs. Similarly, the majority of hematopoiesis, or the formation of blood cells, occurs in the soft, red marrow inside bones themselves.

Ligaments connect bones to each other and help to stabilize and move joints. They are composed essentially of long, elastic collagen fibers, which can be torn or injured if overworked. Gentle stretching before any strenuous activity protects the ligaments and prevents injury to joints and muscles. If ligaments are injured, healing can take ninety days and up to nine months for the fibers to regain their maximum strength.

The skeleton's dynamic functions are facilitated by a simple yet sophisticated network of levers, cables, pulleys, and winches actuated by muscles and tendons. When muscles contract, they shorten their length, thus drawing in an adjacent bone that pivots around a connecting joint, much like the boom, stick, and hydraulic lever system of a backhoe.

The skeletal system is in a constant state of use, undergoing perpetual repair and rejuvenation. It is therefore vulnerable, as is any body system, to imbalance and disease. The joints, in particular, are susceptible to damage due to constant friction, impact, and leverage. As we grow older, we may also experience challenges stemming from calcium or other mineral deficiencies—calcium being the primary material of which bones are made.

Proper pH balance in the body supports a strong skeletal structure. When pH balance is off and the body is too acidic, the blood is compelled to take minerals from the bones and organs, which can cause disease and depletion in the skeletal system. Sugar, refined and processed foods, and overconsumption of meat and dairy make the body more acidic-throwing off the pH balance. Certain essential oils like lemon, fennel, or lemongrass can help reduce acidity by creating a more alkaline environment. Maintaining an alkaline environment helps promote healing. Similarly, adequate nourishment with bioavailable vitamins, minerals, and trace minerals helps to maintain a proper pH balance in the blood. Adequate, high-quality supplementation will manage any chronic inflammation, and a topical use of anti-inflammatory essential oils will support joint health.

When there is a skeletal injury, essential oils can accelerate the healing process and recovery time. For example, in the case of a broken bone, wintergreen and birch have been demonstrated to be useful in relieving and resolving inflammatory conditions and supporting injury recovery. Additionally, lemongrass supports the healing of any connective tissue damage.

top solutions

Single Oils

Copaiba, Frankincense, Turmeric– relieve pain and inflammation (pgs. 136, 151, 239)

Lemongrass– enhances connective tissue repair (pg. 180)

Wintergreen– reduces aches, pains, and inflammation; stimulates bone repair (pg. 247)

Helichrysum– relieves pain and inflammation; accelerates bone repair (pg. 160)

Siberian fir– eases bone and joint pain; reduces inflammation (pg. 221)

Cypress, Cedarwood– improve blood circulation through bones (pgs. 139, 120)

Blends

Deep Blue®– soothes, relaxes, and relieves aches and pains; helps with after injuries/surgery healing (pg. 141)

PastTense®– helps relieve and resolve tension, soreness, and stiffness (pg. 199)

DDR Prime®– reduces/resolves inflammation and regenerates tissue (pg. 140)

Supplements

Alpha CRS®+ (pg. 254), **Bone Nutrient Complex** (pg. 255), **Copaiba Softgels** (pg. 256), DDR Prime® Softgels, **Deep Blue Polyphenol Complex®** (pg. 257), **IQ Mega** (pg. 260), Greens, Microplex VMz®, PB Assist®+, TerraZyme®, **Turmeric Dual Capsules** (pg. 269), **xEO Mega®** (pg. 271)

SKELETAL

usage tips

For best results with skeletal and connective tissue issues:

- **Topical:** Apply oils directly on areas of concern. Massage in thoroughly whenever possible. Add heat, cold, or moisture to further drive oils into tissue. Use a carrier oil as needed or desired. Consider layering oils one on another to create a multiplicity of effects. Place a lotion or carrier oil on top of layered oils to optimize absorption.
  - **Acute:** Apply often, every 20-30 minutes, until symptoms subside, then reduce to every 2-6 hours.
  - **Chronic:** Apply 2-3x's times daily.
- **Internal:** Consume oils (to support resolving inflammation and bone repair) in a capsule or under tongue. Place oils in a capsule or drop under tongue (hold for 30 seconds, swallow).

Related Ailments

Amyotrophic Lateral Sclerosis, Ankylosing Spondylitis, Arthritis Pain [Pain & Inflammation], Bone Pain, Bone Spurs, Broken Bone, Bunions, Bursitis, Calcified Spine, Cartilage Injury, Chondromalacia Patella, Club foot, Deteriorating Spine, Frozen Shoulder, Ganglion Cyst, Gout, Herniated Disc, Joint Pain, Knee Cartilage Injury, Marfan Syndrome, Myelofibrosis, Osgood-Schlatter Disease, Osteoarthritis [Pain & Inflammation], Osteomyelitis [Immune], Osteoporosis, Paget's Disease, Plantar Fasciitis [Muscular], Rheumatism, Rheumatoid Arthritis, Scoliosis, Shin Splints, Spina Bifida [Nervous], Tennis Elbow [Muscular]

By Related Properties

For more, see *Oil Properties* on pages 535-538

Analgesic– arborvitae, basil, bergamot, birch, black pepper, blue tansy, cassia, cinnamon bark, clary sage, clove, copaiba, coriander, cypress, eucalyptus, fennel, frankincense, ginger, helichrysum, juniper berry, lavender, lemongrass, litsea, marjoram, oregano, peppermint, ravintsara, rosemary, Siberian fir, tea tree, turmeric, wild orange, wintergreen, yarrow|pom

Antiarthritic– arborvitae, black spruce, blue tansy, cassia, copaiba, ginger, manuka, neroli, Siberian fir, yarrow|pom

Anti-inflammatory– arborvitae, basil, bergamot, birch, black pepper, blue tansy, cardamom, cassia, cedarwood, celery seed, cinnamon bark, copaiba, coriander, cypress, eucalyptus, fennel, frankincense, geranium, ginger, helichrysum, jasmine, lavender, lemongrass, lime, litsea, manuka, melissa, myrrh, neroli, oregano, patchouli, peppermint, Roman chamomile, rosemary, sandalwood, Siberian fir, spearmint, spikenard, tangerine, tea tree, turmeric, wild orange, wintergreen, yarrow|pom

Anti-rheumatic– birch, black spruce, blue tansy, cassia, celery seed, clove, copaiba, coriander, cypress, Douglas fir, eucalyptus, ginger, juniper berry, laurel leaf, lavender, lemon, lemongrass, lime, manuka, oregano, rosemary, Siberian fir, thyme, turmeric, wintergreen, yarrow|pom

Regenerative– basil, cedarwood, clove, coriander, frankincense, geranium, helichrysum, jasmine, lavender, lemongrass, manuka, myrrh, neroli, patchouli, sandalwood, tea tree, wild orange, yarrow|pom

Steroidal– basil, bergamot, birch, black spruce, cedarwood, clove, fennel, patchouli, rosemary, thyme, tulsi, wintergreen

conditions

Aching pain in/around ear– arborvitae, basil, bergamot, black pepper, cedarwood, cilantro, cinnamon bark, clary sage, clove, cypress, eucalyptus, ginger, helichrysum, myrrh, oregano, Siberian fir, wintergreen, AromaTouch®, DDR Prime®, Deep Blue®, Whisper®

Arthritis– basil, black pepper, black spruce, birch, blue tansy, celery seed, copaiba, cypress, Douglas fir, eucalyptus, frankincense, ginger, lavender, lemongrass, marjoram, pink pepper, rosemary, Siberian fir, turmeric, wintergreen, yarrow|pom, AromaTouch®, DDR Prime®, Deep Blue®, Forgive®; see *Pain & Inflammation*

Back/lower back, pain*– birch, black pepper, copaiba, eucalyptus, frankincense, lemongrass, peppermint, Roman chamomile, Siberian fir, wintergreen, AromaTouch®, Deep Blue®, PastTense®; see *Pain & Inflammation*

Bones, tender– birch, geranium, helichrysum, juniper berry, myrrh, Roman chamomile, wintergreen, DDR Prime®, Deep Blue®, On Guard®, Purify

Bones, bruised– basil, birch, clary sage, frankincense, helichrysum, wintergreen, DDR Prime®, Deep Blue®, On Guard®

Bones, breaking easily– basil, birch, clove, helichrysum, myrrh, oregano, Siberian fir, wild orange, wintergreen, DDR Prime®, Deep Blue®

Bones, broken/fractured*– birch, cypress, frankincense, ginger, helichrysum, Siberian fir, wintergreen, Deep Blue®

Bones, bumps under skin on– birch, cypress, marjoram, myrrh, oregano, rosemary, Siberian fir, wintergreen, AromaTouch®, DDR Prime®, Deep Blue®

Bones, porous– birch, clove, cypress, geranium, helichrysum, lemongrass, peppermint, Siberian fir, wintergreen

Bones, spurs– basil, copaiba, cypress, eucalyptus, frankincense, helichrysum, ginger, peppermint, wintergreen, AromaTouch®

Bunions– basil, cypress, eucalyptus, ginger, lemongrass, thyme, wintergreen, AromaTouch®

Breathing difficulty– cardamom, cypress, Douglas fir, eucalyptus, marjoram, myrrh, oregano, peppermint, Siberian fir, wintergreen, Air-X™, AromaTouch®, Breathe®, Deep Blue®, PastTense®; see *Respiratory*

Cartilage, inflamed/injured*– basil, birch, copaiba, coriander, eucalyptus, helichrysum, lemongrass, marjoram, peppermint, sandalwood, Siberian fir, wintergreen, Deep Blue®; see *Pain & Inflammation*

Cartilage, generate– helichrysum, sandalwood, Siberian fir

Chewing difficulty– basil, clary sage, frankincense, oregano, Siberian fir, wintergreen, AromaTouch®, DDR Prime®, Deep Blue®, PastTense®

Club foot– arborvitae, basil, copaiba, ginger, helichrysum, lavender, lemongrass, marjoram, peppermint, Roman chamomile, rosemary, wintergreen, AromaTouch®

Connective tissue/fascia (ligaments)*– basil, birch, clary sage, copaiba, helichrysum, ginger, lemongrass, sandalwood, Siberian fir, Air-X™, Deep Blue®, HD Clear®

Connective tissue (ligaments), injured/weak/aches and pains*– basil, birch, black spruce, copaiba, clove, cypress, geranium, ginger, helichrysum, lemongrass, marjoram, oregano, peppermint, Roman chamomile, rosemary, Siberian fir, thyme, vetiver, wintergreen, Air-X™, AromaTouch®, Deep Blue®, PastTense®

Headaches– basil, clary sage, clove, copaiba, eucalyptus, frankincense, geranium, helichrysum, lavender, myrrh, oregano, peppermint, Roman chamomile, Siberian fir, spearmint, thyme, tulsi, wintergreen, DDR Prime®, Deep Blue®, PastTense®, On Guard®

Hearing loss– basil, birch, clary sage, helichrysum, oregano, Siberian fir, PastTense®

Inflamed/deteriorating/disc– birch, celery seed, cypress, eucalyptus, frankincense, helichrysum, peppermint, thyme, turmeric, wintergreen, AromaTouch®, DDR Prime®, Deep Blue®

Inflammation– basil, birch, clove, copaiba, eucalyptus, frankincense, ginger, peppermint, Roman chamomile, sandalwood, Siberian fir, turmeric, vetiver, wintergreen, Deep Blue®, Forgive®, Northern Escape, PastTense®

Joint, clicking– birch, marjoram, myrrh, wintergreen, DDR Prime®, Deep Blue®, On Guard®

Joint, grinding sensation– bergamot, birch, rosemary, Siberian fir, wintergreen, DDR Prime®, Purify

Joint, inflammation*– arborvitae, basil, bergamot, blue tansy, cardamom, cedarwood, cinnamon bark, clove, copaiba, coriander, cypress, Douglas fir, eucalyptus, frankincense, ginger, helichrysum, lavender, lemon, lemon eucalyptus, marjoram, peppermint, pink pepper, ravintsara, Roman chamomile, rosemary, Siberian fir, thyme, turmeric, vetiver, wild orange, wintergreen, DDR Prime®, Deep Blue®, Northern Escape, Zendocrine®

Joint, locking– basil, birch, clary sage, helichrysum, marjoram, Siberian fir, wintergreen, AromaTouch®, DDR Prime®, Deep Blue®, On Guard®

Joint, pain/stiffness*– arborvitae, basil, birch, black pepper, cardamom, celery seed, cinnamon bark, copaiba, coriander, Douglas fir, eucalyptus, frankincense, geranium, lemongrass, Siberian fir, thyme, turmeric, wintergreen, AromaTouch®, Deep Blue®

Joint, swollen/warm/red/tender– citronella, eucalyptus, frankincense, lavender, Roman chamomile, AromaTouch®, Deep Blue®

Ligament strain*– copaiba, frankincense, lemongrass, marjoram, Siberian fir, Air-X™, DDR Prime®, Deep Blue®

Rheumatism– basil, birch, black spruce, blue tansy, cassia, celery seed, copaiba, cypress, Douglas fir, eucalyptus, ginger, juniper berry, lavender, lemon eucalyptus, lemongrass, pink pepper, spikenard, Siberian fir, thyme, turmeric, AromaTouch®, Cheer®, DDR Prime®, Deep Blue®, Forgive®; see *Pain & Inflammation*

Rheumatoid arthritis*– basil, bergamot, birch, black spruce, cardamom, copaiba, cypress, Douglas fir, frankincense, ginger, lavender, lemon, marjoram, pink pepper, wintergreen, AromaTouch®, Deep Blue®, PastTense®

Sciatic issues– See *Nervous*

Shoulder, frozen– basil, birch, lemongrass, oregano, peppermint, Siberian fir, wintergreen, DDR Prime®, Deep Blue®

Shoulder, rotator cuff– birch, Siberian fir, wintergreen, Deep Blue®, PastTense®

Shin splints– basil, frankincense, helichrysum, lavender, lemongrass, marjoram, myrrh, patchouli, wintergreen, AromaTouch®, Deep Blue®

Stiff/limited range of motion– birch, frankincense, marjoram, Siberian fir, wintergreen, Deep Blue® or rub, PastTense®

Vertebral misalignment– helichrysum, marjoram, rose, Siberian fir, AromaTouch®, Deep Blue®

**See Protocols on pg. 418*

protocols

BROKEN BONE FIX MIX

Ingredients:

7 drops frankincense
6 drops Siberian fir
2 drops wintergreen
11 drops helichrysum
4 drops lemongrass
4 drops cedarwood

Directions:

Combine oils in 10mL roller bottle and fill remainder with carrier oil. Apply on or near affected area every 2 hours for 2 days and every 4 hours for the following 3 days. If applying to area of concern is not possible due to casting, apply to bottoms of feet and on specific related reflex point and/or to an area in same circulation flow.

BONE SPUR RESOLVE

Ingredients:

5 drops frankincense
6 drops cypress
7 drops wintergreen
5 drops marjoram
4 drops helichrysum
3 drops lemongrass

Directions:

Combine in a 10mL roller bottle and fill remainder with carrier oil. Apply to affected area AM and PM. Continue for an additional 2 weeks, even after spur is gone.

EASE-E-FLEX (for joint pain and inflammation)

Ingredients:

20 drops turmeric
20 drops copaiba
20 drops Deep Blue®
20 drops frankincense

Directions:

Combine in a 10mL roller bottle and fill remainder with carrier oil. Apply topically on or near affected area as needed.

CONNECT REPAIR (for carpal tunnel, tendon, ligaments)

Ingredients:

15 drops lemongrass
15 drops helichrysum
10 drops Siberian fir
10 drops ginger
10 drops copaiba
10 drops marjoram
2 drops peppermint
2 drops wintergreen
10 drops turmeric

Directions:

Combine in 10mL roller bottle and fill remainder with carrier oil. Apply to affected area.

OH MY ACHING BACK

Ingredients:

10 drops frankincense
10 drops helichrysum
10 drops cypress
10 drops Siberian fir
10 drops peppermint
10 drops turmeric

Directions:

Add to 10mL roller bottle and fill remainder with carrier oil. Apply along back and spine 2-4x's per day. Massage in thoroughly. Place 2 drops each oil in 1 C Epsom salt in warm bath and soak.

RHEUMATIC PAIN

Ingredients:

3 drops thyme
3 drops Siberian fir
3 drops lemongrass
3 drops turmeric

Directions:

Combine in a 5mL roller bottle and fill remainder with carrier oil. Apply to affected area as needed.

For more ideas, download the app on Android or iOS.

SLEEP DESCRIBES the period when the body ceases to engage in most voluntary bodily functions, providing an opportunity for the body to focus on restoration and repair. During this time, conscious brain activity is fully or partially suspended, a state that contributes to restoring and maintaining emotional, mental, and physical health. In recent years, doctors and organizations such as the National Sleep Foundation have encouraged the wide acceptance of sleep as one of the three pillars of health, together with nutrition and exercise.

All sleep can be divided into two states: REM and Non-REM. REM is an acronym for Rapid Eye Movement sleep, and represents a period when brain waves have fast frequency and low voltage, similar to brain activity during waking hours. However, during REM sleep all voluntary muscles cease activity except those that control eye movements. Dreams take place during REM sleep. It is the period of sleep where the body is in a deeply subconscious state, and much healing, repair, and restoration occurs.

Non-REM sleep can be further subdivided into three stages: Stage N1 sleep is the state between wakefulness and sleep; it is very light, and some people don't even recognize they are asleep during this stage. Stage N2 is a true deep sleep. Stage N3 is deep sleep or delta sleep. Interestingly, sleep typically occurs in 90-120 minute cycles, with transitions from the N-stages of sleep in the first part of the night to REM sleep in the latter.

Age plays a huge factor in normal sleeping patterns. Newborns need between sixteen to eighteen hours of sleep a day, preschoolers need ten to twelve hours, and school-age children and teenagers need nine or more hours. Because deeper N3 and REM sleep states diminish as individuals age, older adults experience more difficulty getting to sleep and staying asleep. At a time when individuals tend to need more reparative and restorative sleep, they actually receive less.

Some of the most common sleep disorders include insomnia (difficulty getting to sleep and staying asleep), sleep apnea (where breathing may stop or be blocked for brief periods during sleep), sleep deprivation (not getting enough sleep), restless leg syndrome (an uncontrollable need to move legs at night, at times accompanied by tingling or other discomfort), narcolepsy (a central nervous system disease that results in daytime sleepiness and other issues, including loss of muscle tone and more), and problem sleepiness (when daytime sleepiness interferes with regular responsibilities, such as working or studying).

In addition to sleeping disorders, lack of necessary sleep can cause a myriad of other physical and emotional problems. It contributes to adrenal fatigue, poor digestion, weight gain and/or obesity, grogginess, decreased focus and concentration, memory problems, increased irritability and frustration levels and other mood challenges, heart disease, a compromised immune system, and a higher likelihood of chronic or autoimmune conditions.

When children don't get the sleep they need, both physical and emotional development can be negatively affected. The necessity for regular, healthy sleeping patterns is apparent when one considers the serious difficulties and disorders caused by lack of sleep.

Countless individuals have turned to natural remedies to promote ease in falling asleep, staying asleep, and reaching the deeper levels of sleep. There are supplements and essential oils that work together to reduce symptoms of the more serious sleeping disorders and should be considered as a viable addition or alternative to sleep treatments as advised by medical professionals. The benefits of using essential oils such as lavender to promote healthy sleep are numerous and astounding, and the results can be life-altering for the chronically sleep-deprived.

top solutions

Single Oils

Lavender, Petitgrain– calm, relax, and sedate; support parasympathetic system (pgs. 175, 205)

Vetiver, Cedarwood– ground and promote tranquility (pgs. 241, 120)

Roman chamomile– balances hormones; sedates, calms, and relaxes (pg. 213)

Magnolia– relaxes and sedates (pg. 184)

Basil– helps overcome adrenal fatigue-driven insomnia (pg. 105)

Blends

Serenity®, Calmer™– calm mind/emotions; promote relaxation and restful sleep (pgs. 219, 117)

Balance®, Steady™– promote sense of well being and support autonomic nervous system (pgs. 104, 225)

InTune®, Peace®– balance brain activity and calm overstimulation (pgs. 167, 201)

Adaptiv™– supports healthy GABA levels and the leveling of mood (pg. 96)

Supplements

Adaptiv™ Capsules (pg. 253), Alpha CRS®+, **Bone Nutrient Complex** (pg. 255), **IQ Mega®** (pg. 260), Microplex VMz®, Mito2Max®, PB Assist®+, Phytoestrogen Complex, **Serenity® Softgels** (pg. 219), **xEO Mega®** (pg. 271), Zendocrine® Complex, Zendocrine® Softgels

usage tips

To support optimal and restful sleep, inhale or use essential oils topically to access to the brain through smell, relax tense muscles, and calm an overactive mind.

- **Aromatic:** Diffuse selected oil(s), apply to clothing, bedding (e.g., pillow), or any other method that supports inhalation. Start exposure 30 minutes before bedtime.
- **Topical:** Combine oils with soothing and relaxing massage techniques. Apply oils on forehead, back, shoulders, under nose, and especially bottoms of feet. Applying oils on chest allows breathing in vapors. For additional relaxation or to overcome sleep issues, use the AromaTouch Technique® regularly.

Related Ailments

Hypersomnia, Insomnia, Jet Lag, Narcolepsy, Periodic Limb Movement Disorder (PLMD), Sleep Apnea, Sleepwalking, Restless Leg Syndrome (RLS)

By Related Properties

For more, see *Oil Properties* on pages 535-538

Analgesic– arborvitae, basil, bergamot, birch, black pepper, blue tansy, cassia, cinnamon bark, clary sage, clove, copaiba, coriander, cypress, eucalyptus, fennel, frankincense, ginger, helichrysum, jasmine, juniper berry, lavender, lemongrass, litsea, marjoram, tea tree, oregano, peppermint, ravintsara, rosemary, Siberian fir, wild orange, wintergreen, yarrow|pom

Antidepressant– clary sage, coriander, frankincense, geranium, jasmine, lavender, lemongrass, magnolia, melissa, neroli, oregano, patchouli, ravintsara, rose, sandalwood, tangerine, wild orange, ylang ylang

Calming– bergamot, birch, black pepper, black spruce, blue tansy, cassia, clary sage, copaiba, coriander, fennel, frankincense, geranium, jasmine, juniper berry, lavender, litsea, melissa, oregano, patchouli, Roman chamomile, sandalwood, tangerine, vetiver, yarrow|pom

Detoxifier– arborvitae, cassia, cilantro, cypress, geranium, juniper berry, lemon, lime, litsea, patchouli, rosemary, tangerine, wild orange, yarrow|pom

Grounding– basil, black spruce, blue tansy, cedarwood, clary sage, cypress, Douglas fir, Siberian fir, vetiver, ylang ylang

Relaxing– basil, blue tansy, cassia, cedarwood, clary sage, cypress, fennel, geranium, jasmine, lavender, magnolia, manuka, marjoram, myrrh, neroli, petitgrain, ravintsara, Roman chamomile, Siberian fir, vanilla, ylang ylang

Restorative– basil, frankincense, lime, neroli, patchouli, rosemary, sandalwood, spearmint, tangerine

Sedative– basil, bergamot, blue tansy, cedarwood, clary sage, coriander, frankincense, geranium, jasmine, juniper berry, lavender, lemongrass, marjoram, melissa, neroli, patchouli, Roman chamomile, rose, sandalwood, spikenard, tangerine, vetiver, yarrow|pom, ylang ylang

conditions

Conditions (Contributors to Sleep Issues):

Alcohol, issues with– See *Addictions*

Anxiety*– See *Mood & Behavior*

Bedtime, chronically late– See "Night owl" below

Brain injury– See *Brain*

Breathing issues– See *Respiratory*

Caffeine (avoid consuming within 4-6 hours of bedtime)– See *Addictions*

Chronic pain– See *Pain & Inflammation*

CPAP machine, difficulties with– See *Respiratory*

Daytime napping– See *Energy & Vitality*

Depression– See *Mood & Behavior*

Dreaming, excessive– clary sage, frankincense, geranium, juniper berry, lavender, patchouli, Roman chamomile, Balance®, PastTense®, Serenity®

Drug abuse– See *Addictions*

Drug withdrawals– See *Addictions*

Emotional discomfort– bergamot, clary sage, geranium, juniper berry, melissa, ravintsara, ylang ylang; see *Mood & Behavior*

Eating, excessive, late at night– See *Eating Disorders, Weight*

Cold extremities, poor circulation– black pepper, cypress, coriander, pink pepper; see *Cardiovascular*

Fear (of sleeping, etc.)– bergamot, cardamom, coriander, patchouli, ravintsara, Roman chamomile, Balance®, Deep Blue®, Serenity®; see *Mood & Behavior*

Grief– Console®; see *Mood & Behavior*

Heart symptoms (e.g. rapid heart rate)– magnolia, ylang ylang; see *Cardiovascular*

Hormone imbalances– clary sage; see *Men's Health* or *Women's Health*

Illness/chronic illness– See *Immune & Lymphatic*

Insomnia– See "Sleeplessness" and "Sleeplessness, chronic" on next page

Insomnia, nervous tension– basil, blue tansy, lavender, magnolia, marjoram, petitgrain, Roman chamomile, rosemary, vetiver, AromaTouch®, PastTense®, Peace®, Serenity®; see *Nervous*

Interferences in normal sleep schedule– See "Jet lag" below

Jet lag, can't go to sleep– lavender, patchouli, peppermint, wild orange, Serenity®; see "Sleeplessness" next page

Jet lag, overly tired– arborvitae, basil, grapefruit, lemon, lemongrass, rosemary, tangerine, wild orange, Citrus Bliss®, InTune®, Motivate®, Slim & Sassy®

Melatonin levels low, irregular sleep cycles (REM)– black pepper, cedarwood, frankincense, ginger, lime, myrrh, rosemary (use during day), sandalwood, tangerine, ylang ylang, vetiver, InTune®, Serenity®

Mental chatter/over-thinking*– basil, bergamot mint, black spruce, cedarwood, lavender, magnolia, neroli, rosemary, vanilla, ylang ylang, Adaptiv™, Balance®, Serenity®

Muscle cramps/charley horses– See *Muscular*

Nervous tension– basil, bergamot, black spruce, Douglas fir, geranium, grapefruit, jasmine, lavender, melissa, Roman chamomile, rose, sandalwood, vanilla, vetiver, wild orange, ylang ylang, AromaTouch®, Balance®, Citrus Bliss®, PastTense®, Serenity®; see *Mood & Behavior, Nervous*

Nicotine– cinnamon bark, clove, On Guard®; See *Addictions*

Night eating syndrome– See *Eating Disorders, Weight*

Night owl– cedarwood, lavender, vetiver, wild orange, wintergreen, Balance®, Serenity®; see "Sleeplessness," "Sleeplessness, chronic" below

Night sweats– clary sage, Douglas fir, eucalyptus, ginger, lime, peppermint, AromaTouch®, ClaryCalm®, DDR Prime®, Whisper®, Zendocrine®; see *Endocrine (Thyroid), Immune & Lymphatic, Women's Health*

Nightmares– cinnamon bark, clary sage, cypress, eucalyptus, geranium, grapefruit, juniper berry, lavender, magnolia, melissa, neroli, Roman chamomile, Siberian fir, wild orange, vetiver, Balance®, Serenity®

Over-excited/over-stimulated– bergamot mint, lavender, magnolia, patchouli, Roman chamomile, sandalwood, vanilla, wild orange; see *Mood & Behavior*

Pain or discomfort at night– copaiba, turmeric, Deep Blue®, Rescuer™; see *Pain & Inflammation*

Periodic limb movement– basil, marjoram, AromaTouch®; see "Twitching" below

Psychiatric disorder– See *Mood & Behavior*

Restless legs– basil, cypress, geranium, ginger, grapefruit, lavender, neroli, patchouli, peppermint, Roman chamomile, spearmint, vanilla, wintergreen, AromaTouch®, Deep Blue®, PastTense®, Serenity®

Restlessness*– bergamot, bergamot mint, black pepper, cedarwood, frankincense, lavender, neroli, patchouli, Roman chamomile, tangerine, vetiver, wild orange, yarrow|pom, Adaptiv™, AromaTouch®, Balance®, Elevation, PastTense®, Serenity®

Routine/schedule, poor– Balance®; see "Melatonin levels low" below

Serotonin levels low (precursor to melatonin)– bergamot, cedarwood, clary sage, grapefruit, melissa, patchouli, Roman chamomile, ylang ylang, Adaptiv™; see *Mood & Behavior*

Sleep apnea– eucalyptus, lemongrass, peppermint, ravintsara, rosemary, thyme, tulsi, wintergreen, Air-X™, Balance®, Breathe®, On Guard®, Purify, Whisper®; see *Respiratory*

Sleep-walking– black pepper, geranium, lavender, vetiver, Balance®, DDR Prime®, Peace®, Serenity®

Snoring*– Douglas fir, eucalyptus, geranium, patchouli, peppermint, rosemary, Breathe®, On Guard®, Purify, Zendocrine®; see *Respiratory*

Stimulants, use of (medications, caffeine, energy drinks, supplements)– See *Addictions*

Stress– clary sage, frankincense, lavender, lime, vanilla, vetiver, wild orange, Citrus Bliss®, Citrus Bloom™, Elevation, Serenity®; see *Stress*

Teeth grinding– frankincense, geranium, lavender, marjoram, Roman chamomile, wild orange, Serenity®; see *Parasites*

Tranquility, lack of– cinnamon bark, clary sage, jasmine, melissa, neroli, Roman chamomile, vanilla, Adaptiv™, PastTense®

Twitching/muscle spasms– basil, clary sage, coriander, cypress, eucalyptus, ginger, jasmine, lemongrass, marjoram, neroli, AromaTouch®, Balance®, Deep Blue®; see *Muscular*

*See Protocols on pg. 422

Conditions (Related to, Result of Sleep Issues):

Adrenal fatigue– tulsi; see *Endocrine (Adrenals)*

Alertness, lack of | poor daytime learning | mental fatigue; See *Energy & Vitality, Focus & Concentration*

Depression– See "Serotonin levels low" above, *Mood & Behavior*

Difficulty controlling emotions– See *Mood & Behavior*

Driving, can't stay awake (pull over!)– basil, peppermint, pink pepper, rosemary, Breathe®

Drowsiness, daytime– basil, grapefruit, lemon, rosemary, wild orange, Citrus Bliss®, InTune®; see *Energy & Vitality*

Focus, concentration compromised– See *Focus & Concentration*

Memory, poor/slow recall or response– bergamot, frankincense, rosemary, tulsi; see *Focus & Concentration*

Narcolepsy– basil, frankincense, lavender + wild orange, patchouli, sandalwood, vetiver, Console®, InTune®, Motivate®, Serenity®; see *Brain*

Night eating syndrome– See *Eating Disorders, Mood & Behavior, Weight*

Physical discomfort/pain– frankincense, Deep Blue®; see *Pain & Inflammation*

Screentime, excess– cedarwood, cilantro, petitgrain, magnolia, Arise, Balance®, InTune®, Northern Escape, Peace, Serenity®

Sleep, lack of/deprivation– geranium, lavender, patchouli, tulsi, DDR Prime®, PastTense®, Zendocrine®; see *Energy & Vitality*

Sleep, poor– lavender, marjoram, Roman chamomile, sandalwood, vetiver, Serenity®

Sleeplessness– basil, bergamot mint, cedarwood, clary sage, frankincense, geranium, lavender, magnolia, patchouli, petitgrain, ravintsara, Roman chamomile, sandalwood, vetiver, wild orange, Balance®, Console®, Forgive®, Peace®, Serenity®

Sleeplessness, chronic– bergamot, bergamot mint, cedarwood, copaiba, cypress, jasmine, lavender, melissa, neroli, peppermint, petitgrain, Roman chamomile, sandalwood, tangerine, thyme, vetiver, wild orange, ylang ylang, Balance®, Cheer®, Console®, Forgive®, Passion®, Serenity®

Weakened immunity– See *Immune & Lymphatic*

Weight gain– See *Weight*

protocols

Avoid using stimulating essential oils before bed, such as rosemary and peppermint. Instead, opt for oils that relax, such as vetiver and Roman chamomile.

SLEEP-PROMOTING BATH RECIPES

- **To help fall asleep:** Add a few drops lavender to 1 C Epsom salt; dissolve in hot bath (Epsom salt is a good source of magnesium, which supports relaxation).
- **Sleep tonight, sleep in tomorrow:** Mix 5 drops patchouli, 2 drops wild orange, and 1 drop frankincense with 1 C Epsom salt; soak 15-20 minutes.

STOP SNORING BLEND

Ingredients:

18 drops Douglas fir
12 drops geranium
12 drops lavender
8 drops eucalyptus
5 drops cedarwood

Directions:

Combine in glass spray bottle. Mist room generously, lightly spray pillow, apply to throat, bridge of nose, and forehead. Inhale.

SLEEP & ANXIETY ROLLER BOTTLE REMEDIES

Use a 10mL roller bottle. Choose your recipe. Combine oils and fill remainder with carrier oil. Apply to bottoms of feet, back of neck, and chest.

- Recipe #1: 20 drops Serenity®, 10 drops vetiver, 10 drops wild orange
- Recipe #2: 5 drops juniper berry, 20 drops Balance®, 10 drops vetiver, 5 drops patchouli, 3 drops ylang ylang

RESTFUL SLEEP

Combine 2 drops each Adaptiv™, Roman chamomile, and clary sage. Diffuse at night to promote quality sleep.

DREAMMAKER BLEND

Combine 25 drops frankincense, 20 drops bergamot, and 15 drops Roman chamomile in a 10mL roller bottle and fill remainder with carrier oil. Apply at bedtime.

SLEEPY-TIME MASSAGE RUB (Yield: ½ C)

Ingredients:

¼ C cocoa butter
¼ C coconut oil
20 drops lavender
6 drops Douglas fir
6 drops cedarwood
10 drops of frankincense

- Substitution oils if an aroma alternative is desired: ylang ylang, Roman chamomile, vetiver, cedarwood, clary sage.
- **Instructions:** Warm coconut oil and cocoa butter in a small pan until melted. Cool for 10 minutes. Once cooled, add essential oils. Place in fridge for 1 hour. Whip on high with electric mixer until softened. Apply and massage into feet and neck before bed. Save remainder for additional treatments. Store remainder in a cool place.

GOING TO STAY ASLEEP

In empty 15mL bottle, combine:

20 drops each cedarwood, patchouli, Balance®, vetiver, Roman chamomile
50 drops Serenity®
30 drops wild orange

Diffuse 5-10 drops at bedtime.

BEDTIME RELAXATION TEA

Steep chamomile tea and add 2 drops lavender. Make sure pajamas are on before finishing tea.

QUIET THE MIND & BODY

- **Stop the mind chatter:** 1-3 drops Balance® and Serenity®, layer on bottoms of feet, back of neck, and inhale deeply.
- **For more restful sleep:** 3 drops Roman chamomle on bottoms feet at night

DREAMY TOUCH

Combine 2 drops Adaptiv™ and 4 drops sandalwood with carrier oil. Add a layer of magnolia or rose. Apply under nose, across forehead, and/or back of neck.

Stress

UNDER NORMAL conditions, individuals are able to maintain homeostasis, a state where one is healthy, alert, and effective, and where body systems are operating as they should. Conversely, stress is the body's physiological response to overwhelming stimuli, a condition that directly challenges the body's ability to maintain homeostasis. When a stressful event or condition is perceived, the sympathetic nervous system is activated, which causes a fight-or-flight response in the body.

The fight-or-flight response initiates a chain reaction of activity in the body, starting with the central nervous system. Various parts of the brain, adrenal glands, peripheral nervous system (PNS), and other body systems work together to secrete hormones, such as adrenaline and cortisol, into the bloodstream. These hormones send messages instructing the immediate suspension of uncritical activities, such as those of the digestive, reproductive, and immune systems. All bodily energy and resources are directed to supporting heart and brain function.

Once the body's response to stress has been activated, a number of physical changes immediately occur. Stress reduces the blood-brain barrier's ability to block hormones and chemicals from entering the brain, thereby allowing corticosteroids to speed up the brain's ability to process information and make a decision. Cortisol deactivates the immune system, which does not cause serious problems as long as it is only a temporary, acute, response to stress.

When stress becomes chronic, however, some extremely serious situations can result. Over time, neuroplasticity of the brain is compromised, which results in the atrophy and destruction of neuron dendrites, and the brain loses the ability to form new connections or even process new sensory information (both being vital brain functions). When the immune system is repressed for an extended period of time, the body pays a significant toll. Risk of heart attack and stroke increases, anxiety and depression are more likely, and infertility can result, as well as a number of other chronic conditions including asthma, back pain, fatigue, headaches, serious digestive issues, and more.

It stands to reason that individual interpretation of relationships and other stimuli directly impact the level of stress experienced. When an individual can honestly assess a situation and choose to interpret it differently, this simple change in thinking can help reprogram an individual's stress response.

Essential oils are excellent support for effectively reprogramming the stress response on a chemical level. For example, when the cell membrane is hardened, cells suspend activity, rich nutrients and oxygen from the blood are not able to enter the cell, and toxic waste inside the cell is unable to escape. The chemical compounds in citrus oils, when inhaled, help cells to return to their normal state, thus allowing the interchange of nutrients and release of toxins to resume. On a physiological cellular level, the body's descent into fight-or-flight is interrupted, and the body is quickly able to shift towards homeostasis. There are numerous viable essential oils solutions that can interrupt unhealthy stress responses and prevent additional negative results.

top solutions

Single Oil

Roman chamomile, Lavender, Petitgrain— calm and relieve stress (pgs. 213, 175, 205)

Tangerine, Wild orange, Green mandarin— energize while reducing anxiety and depression (pgs. 228, 244, 157)

Frankincense— reduces depression, trauma, and tension (pg. 151)

Vetiver— improves focus and sedates (pg. 241)

Blends

Adaptiv™, Citrus Bliss®, Citrus Bloom™, Elevation— energize while reducing anxiety and depression (pgs. 96, 130, 131, 145)

Balance®, Steady™— balance mood while reducing stress and trauma (pgs. 104, 225)

Serenity®, Calmer™— reduce anxiety and stress (pgs. 219, 117)

PastTense®— relieves tension and stress (pg. 199)

Whisper®— balances hormones and calms anxiety (pg. 242)

Supplements

Adaptiv™ Softgels, Alpha CRS®+, **Bone Nutrient Complex** (pg. 273), **Copaiba Softgels** (pg. 256), DigestZen® Softgels, **IQ Mega** (pg. 260), **Microplex VMz®** (pg. 261), **Mito2Max®** (pg. 262), Phytoestrogen Complex, **Serenity® Softgels** (pg. 219), **xEO Mega®** (pg. 271)

STRESS

usage tips

Essential oils are extremely effective for managing and eliminating stress. Any method of application can be successful. Here are some primary methods:

- **Aromatic:** Smell an aroma for an immediate invitation to relax, calm down, and get focused. Diffuse favorite oils, inhale from a bottle or hands, apply to clothing or under nose.
- **Topical:** Apply to tense or tired muscles on back, shoulders, neck, legs, or anywhere stress is affecting the body. Topical use also allows for an aromatic experience. Consider use on chest, gland locations, base of skull (especially in suboccipital triangles), behind ears, across forehead, and perfume points.
- **Internal:** Stress often affects internal activity such as digestion. Choose and use oils according to needs. Take in a capsule or water.

By Related Properties

For more, see *Oil Properties* on pages 535-538

Calming— bergamot, birch, black pepper, black spruce, blue tansy, cassia, clary sage, copaiba, coriander, fennel, frankincense, geranium, jasmine, juniper berry, lavender, melissa, oregano, patchouli, Roman chamomile, sandalwood, tangerine, vetiver, yarrow|pom

Energizing— basil, bergamot, clove, cypress, grapefruit, lemon, lemongrass, lime, pink pepper, rosemary, Siberian fir, tangerine, wild orange, yarrow|pom

Grounding— basil, black spruce, blue tansy, cedarwood, clary sage, cypress, Douglas fir, vetiver, Siberian fir, ylang ylang

Refreshing— bergamot, bergamot mint, cypress, geranium, grapefruit, green mandarin, lemon, lime, peppermint, pink pepper, Siberian fir, spearmint, wild orange

Relaxing— basil, blue tansy, cassia, cedarwood, clary sage, cypress, fennel, geranium, jasmine, lavender, litsea, marjoram, magnolia, manuka, myrrh, neroli, ravintsara, Roman chamomile, Siberian fir, vanilla, ylang ylang

Uplifting— bergamot, bergamot mint, cardamom, cedarwood, clary sage, cypress, grapefruit, lemon, lime, litsea, melissa, ravintsara, sandalwood, tangerine, wild orange, ylang ylang

conditions

For more emotions associated with stress (e.g. anxiety, depression)— see *Mood & Behavior*

Accelerated aging— frankincense, jasmine, sandalwood, ylang ylang, Immortelle, Slim & Sassy®

Anxiety*— bergamot, bergamot mint, black spruce, cedarwood, clary sage, frankincense, lavender, magnolia, neroli, petitgrain, pink pepper, ravintsara, spikenard, tangerine, turmeric, vanilla, vetiver, wild orange, yarrow|pom, Adaptiv™, Anchor, Balance®, Calmer™, Citrus Bliss®, Citrus Bloom™, Forgive®, InTune®, Peace®, Serenity®; see *Mood & Behavior*

Behavioral stress— See *Addictions, Eating Disorders, Weight*

Busy-ness— juniper berry, Anchor, Balance®, Serenity®

Chest pain— basil, cypress, lavender, marjoram, rosemary, sandalwood, thyme, wild orange, ylang ylang, AromaTouch®, DDR Prime®, Deep Blue®, On Guard®; see *Cardiovascular*

Constricted breathing— bergamot, blue tansy, frankincense, lavender, ravintsara, Roman chamomile, Air-X™, Balance®, Breathe®, Citrus Bliss®, Passion®; see *Respiratory*

Cortisol, low or high— tulsi; see *Endocrine*

Depression— bergamot, frankincense, laurel leaf, neroli, wild orange, ylang ylang, Adaptiv™, Citrus Bliss®, Citrus Bloom™, ClaryCalm®, Elevation, Serenity®; see *Mood & Behavior*

Energy, lack of stress— See *Energy & Vitality*

Endure stress and avoid illness— vetiver; see *Immune & Lymphatic*

Environmental stress— cinnamon bark, frankincense, geranium, juniper berry, lemon eucalyptus, sandalwood, wild orange, Air-X™, Balance®, Citrus Bliss®, Forgive®, Northern Escape

Fainting— basil, bergamot, cinnamon bark, cypress, frankincense, lavender, peppermint, rosemary, sandalwood, wild orange; see *Cardiovascular*

Fatigue/exhaustion*— basil, bergamot, bergamot mint, black spruce, cinnamon bark, green mandarin, lemon, lime, pink pepper, Siberian fir, Adaptiv™, Citrus Bliss®, Elevation, Passion®, Motivate®, Slim & Sassy®, Zendocrine®; see *Energy & Vitality*

Headache and migraine— copaiba, frankincense, lavender, peppermint, tulsi, wintergreen, Deep Blue®, PastTense®; see *Pain & Inflammation*

Heart disease— geranium, lime, ylang ylang; see *Cardiovascular*

Illness, stress-related— bergamot, copaiba, lemon, rosemary, On Guard®, Stronger™; see *Immune & Lymphatic*

Insomnia— lavender, magnolia, marjoram, neroli, Roman chamomile, vetiver, Balance®, Calmer™, Serenity®; see *Sleep*

Mind/thought-related/poor memory stress— tulsi, InTune®, Thinker™; see *Brain, Focus & Concentration*

Mood-related, moodiness driven stress— See *Mood & Behavior*

Muscle tension or pain— marjoram, peppermint, wintergreen, AromaTouch®, Deep Blue®, PastTense®, Rescuer™; see *Muscular, Skeletal, Pain & Inflammation*

Nervous tension— black spruce, Douglas fir, Calmer™, InTune®, Northern Escape, Serenity®; see *Mood & Behavior, Nervous*

Obesity/overeating— bergamot, blue tansy, cinnamon bark, clary sage, geranium, ginger, grapefruit, jasmine, patchouli, sandalwood, Siberian fir, tusli, ylang ylang, Adaptiv™, Citrus Bliss®, Slim & Sassy®, Whisper®; see *Weight, Eating Disorders*

Physical stress— geranium, lavender, AromaTouch®, Citrus Bliss®, Deep Blue®, Peace®; see *Athletes*

Sex drive, change in— neroli, ylang ylang, Passion® Whisper®; see *Intimacy*

Shock— bergamot, frankincense, geranium, helichrysum, magnolia, peppermint, Roman chamomile, tea tree, Adaptiv™, Brave™, Calmer™, Motivate®, Peace®, Serenity®; see *First Aid*

Sleep problems— basil, lavender, petitgrain, Roman chamomile, wild orange, Balance®, Serenity®; see *Sleep*

Stomach, upset— DigestZen®, Tamer™; see *Digestive & Intestinal*

Stress, lack of management— blue tansy, coriander, wintergreen

Teeth grinding— black spruce, cilantro, frankincense, geranium, lavender, magnolia, marjoram, petitgrain, Roman chamomile, wild orange, Serenity®; see *Parasites*

Tension— cedarwood, copaiba, ginger, lavender, lemongrass, peppermint, vanilla, Siberian fir, wintergreen, Balance®, Calmer™, PastTense®, Serenity®; see *Muscular*

Trauma stress, intense— cedarwood, frankincense, jasmine, lavender, melissa, Roman chamomile, vetiver, ylang ylang, Adaptiv™, Balance®, Brave™, Calmer™, InTune®, Serenity®, Steady™; see *Limbic, Mood & Behavior*

**See Protocols on pg. 426*

protocols

Roller Bottle Remedies

Directions:
*Combine oils in 5-10mL roller bottle and fill remainder with carrier oil. Apply to pulse points and behind the ears.

LIFT AND CALM BLEND*
Ingredients:
10 drops frankincense
12 drops Citrus Bliss®
8 drops lavender
4 drops peppermint

ANXIETY BLEND*
Ingredients:
10 drops green mandarin
10 drops Citrus Bliss®
10 drops tulsi
10 drops Serenity®
20 drops Adaptiv™

GET-TO-IT BLEND*
Ingredients:
10 drops clary sage
15 drops bergamot
15 drops grapefruit
15 drops frankincense
10 drops lemon
25 drops tangerine

EXHAUSTION BLEND*
Ingredients:
10 drops eucalyptus
8 drops rosemary
7 drops bergamot
7 drops grapefruit

MOTIVATION BLEND*
Ingredients:
10 drops lime
10 drops wild orange
12 drops Douglas fir
7 drops spearmint

MENTAL CLARITY BLEND*
Ingredients:
12 drops lime
8 drops rosemary
4 drops cypress
2 drops peppermint

Diffuser Remedies

Directions:
Diffuse to replace discontented, agitated, nervous, or anxious feelings.

RELAX
Add 5 drops each petitgrain, tangerine, and bergamot mint to diffuser for 30-60 minutes and enjoy.

FROM STESSED TO CAREFREE
Ingredients:
7 drops green mandarin
2 drops clove
2 drops cardamom

STRESS

Bath Remedies

DE-STRESS BATH
Ingredients:
1 C Epsom salts
1/ C cup baking soda
10 drops lavender
or Serenity®

Directions:
Mix and add to warm bath water. Soak. Repeat 2-3x's per week.

This is a basic recipe. To individualize, select oils and add 10-15 drops to bath. Combining a few oils or using an existing blend is an excellent way to enjoy the benefits of multiple oils at once. Add ½-1 C milk or cream as a moisturizer.

Favorite bath recipes to choose from:

Bliss Bath– 7 drops each Serenity® and Roman chamomile

Calming Bath– 10 drops Roman chamomile

De-Stress & Focus Bath– 5 drops each Adaptiv™ and frankincense

Energizing & Calming Bath– 10 drops Citrus Bliss® and 2 drops melissa

Get-My-Heart-Back-in-the-Project– 2 drops ylang ylang and 6 drops wild orange

Grounding Bath– 5 drops each Balance® and Adaptiv™

Life-is-Good Blend– 2 drops green mandarin, 1 drop spearmint; then roll on neroli Touch® on before stepping into bath

Quiet-the-Mind Bath– 3 drops each sandalwood, lavender, and cedarwood

Reviving & Relaxing Bath– 10 drops Cheer® or Motivate®

Soothing Bath– 5 drops each Deep Blue® and AromaTouch®

Stop the Tantrums Bath– 3 drops each Serenity® and vetiver. Roll on Calmer™ before bath

Tension Tamer Bath– 4 drops each Serenity® and PastTense®

Warm, Relax, Revive the Weary Bath– 2 drops each ginger, wild orange, clove and lavender

For more ideas, download the app on Android or iOS.

THE URINARY TRACT consists of the kidneys, ureters, bladder, and urethra. The principal function of the urinary system is to maintain the volume and composition of body fluids within normal limits. This includes ridding the body of waste products that accumulate as a result of cellular metabolism. As a result, it is sometimes referred to as the excretory system. While it plays a major role in excretion, however, it relies on other organs to support this function.

The urinary system maintains appropriate fluid volumes, pH and chemical balances, and electrolyte levels through complex processes in the kidneys and by regulating the amount of water that is excreted in the urine. Urine is formed in the kidneys through a blood filtration process and carries waste products and excess fluid to the ureters, tubes made of smooth muscle fibers that propel urine toward the urinary bladder, where it is stored until it is expelled from the body.

The moving of urine from the bladder through the urethra and out of the body is called urination, or voiding.

The kidneys are also responsible for regulating sodium and potassium levels. No less important is the kidney's ability to remove drugs from the body, release hormones that regulate blood pressure, produce an active form of vitamin D, which promotes strong, healthy bones, and control the production of red blood cells.

Most individuals operate in a constant state of dehydration, which takes its toll on overall health, but particularly impacts kidney health. In addition to adequate water intake, there are some essential oils that are extremely effective in supporting kidney health and helping the body to quickly rid itself of UTI discomfort, infections, and even stones. While it is of utmost importance to utilize the services of medical professionals in the case of a prolonged or serious condition, essential oils can serve as a powerful first line of defense.

top solutions

Single Oils

Juniper berry— acts as diuretic, tonifies bladder, and supports urinary system (pg. 170)

Lemongrass, Siberian fir— decongest urinary tract and fight urinary infections (pgs. 180, 221)

Celery seed— acts as diuretic and calms urinary distress (pg. 122)

Lemon— helps dissolve stones and acts as diuretic (pg. 176)

Cypress— resolves incontinence and excessive water/fluid retention (pg. 139)

Thyme— supports healthy prostate and circulation, fights urinary infections (pg. 234)

Eucalyptus— relieves infection, stones (pg. 146)

Blends

DDR Prime®, Air-X™— antioxidant, cleanses and disinfects urinary tract (pgs. 140, 97)

Zendocrine®— supports proper liver and kidney function (pg. 251)

Slim & Sassy®— acts as diuretic and detoxifies (pg. 222)

On Guard®— promotes blood flow and elimination of waste (pg. 195)

Supplements

Alpha CRS®+, **DDR Prime® Softgels** (pg. 256), Microplex VMz®, **On Guard Softgels** and **Tablets** (pg. 262), Slim & Sassy® Softgels, Turmeric Duals Capsules, **Zendocrine® Complex** (pg. 272), **Zendocrine® Softgels** (pg. 273)

usage tips

For best success in supporting urinary conditions:

- **Internal:** Internal consumption is key. Use softgels or place oils in a capsule, under tongue, or in water and consume every few hours for acute situations.
- **Topical:** Place oils/blends over urinary areas of bladder/kidneys. Dilute with carrier oil as needed to prevent sensitivity. Other excellent application areas are the spine and bottoms of feet.
- **Aromatic:** Diffuse oils through night for nighttime concerns such as bed-wetting or prostate challenges.

Related Ailments

Bed-Wetting, Berger's Disease, Incontinence, Kidney Infection, Kidney Stones, Overactive Bladder, Poor Urine Flow, Ureter Infection, Urinary Tract Infection (UTI), Urination (Painful/Frequent)

By Related Properties

For more, see *Oil Properties* on pages 535-538

Anti-infectious— arborvitae, basil, bergamot, cardamom, cedarwood, cinnamon bark, citronella, clove, copaiba, cypress, eucalyptus, frankincense, geranium, litsea, marjoram, patchouli, Roman chamomile, rose, rosemary, tea tree, tulsi, turmeric

Anti-inflammatory— arborvitae, basil, bergamot, birch, black pepper, blue tansy, cardamom, cassia, cedarwood, cinnamon bark, copaiba, cypress, eucalyptus, fennel, frankincense, geranium, ginger, helichrysum, lavender, lemongrass, lime, litsea, manuka, melissa, myrrh, neroli, oregano, patchouli, peppermint, rosemary, sandalwood, Siberian fir, spearmint, spikenard, tangerine, tea tree, wild orange, wintergreen, yarrow|pom

Cleanser— arborvitae, cilantro, eucalyptus, grapefruit, juniper berry, lemon, thyme, wild orange

Detoxifier— arborvitae, cassia, cilantro, citronella, cypress, geranium, juniper berry, lemon, lime, litsea, patchouli, rosemary, tangerine, wild orange, yarrow|pom

Diuretic— arborvitae, basil, bergamot, birch, cardamom, cedarwood, celery seed, copaiba, cypress, eucalyptus, fennel, frankincense, geranium, grapefruit, helichrysum, juniper berry, lavender, lemon, lime, marjoram, patchouli, ravintsara, rosemary, sandalwood, Siberian fir, tangerine, thyme, wild orange, wintergreen

Purifier— arborvitae, cinnamon bark, eucalyptus, grapefruit, lemon, lemongrass, lime, manuka, marjoram, oregano, Siberian fir, tangerine, tea tree, wild orange, yarrow|pom

URINARY

conditions

Abdominal pain— coriander, grapefruit, ginger, lavender, oregano, rosemary, Purify; see *Digestive & Intestinal*

Bed-wetting*— black pepper, cinnamon bark, copaiba, cypress, frankincense, juniper berry, rosemary, spearmint, tulsi, Brave™, Peace®, Zendocrine®

Bladder Stones— celery seed

Disorders— basil, bergamot, birch, cypress, juniper berry, lavender, lemongrass, lime, rosemary, sandalwood, thyme, wintergreen, Air-X™, DDR Prime®, DigestZen®

Dribbling/minor leaks— cypress, marjoram, thyme, DDR Prime®

Edema— See "Water Retention" below

Excrete uric acid/toxins— cardamom, cypress, frankincense, juniper berry, lemon, petitgrain, rosemary, Balance®, Purify, Zendocrine®

Hesitancy, urine flow— basil, celery seed, cypress, ginger, thyme, Slim & Sassy®

Incontinence*— basil, copaiba, coriander, cypress, rosemary, spearmint, AromaTouch®, Forgive®

Incontinence, emotional (repression of emotions)— black pepper, cypress, ginger, juniper berry, lavender, thyme, vetiver, AromaTouch®, Zendocrine®; see *Mood & Behavior*

Infections, bladder— arborvitae, birch, bergamot, cedarwood, cinnamon bark, clove, copaiba, eucalyptus, fennel, juniper berry, lemon, lemongrass, rosemary, sandalwood, Siberian fir, spearmint, thyme, tulsi, wintergreen, Abōde™, Air-X™, Console®, On Guard®, Purify

Infections, kidney— bergamot, cardamom, cinnamon bark, coriander, fennel, juniper berry, lemon, lemongrass, neroli, rosemary, sandalwood, spearmint, thyme, Abōde™, Air-X™, DDR Prime®, On Guard®, Passion®, Purify

Infections, urinary— bergamot, blue tansy, cedarwood, cinnamon bark, citronella, copaiba, fennel, lemon, lemongrass, geranium, juniper berry, neroli, rosemary, sandalwood, Siberian fir, thyme, tulsi, yarrow|pom, Abōde™, Air-X™, DDR Prime®, On Guard®, Passion®, Purify

Ketones in urine— coriander, fennel, juniper berry, rosemary, thyme

Kidney stones*— birch, cinnamon bark, celery seed, clary sage, eucalyptus, fennel, geranium, juniper berry, lemon, sandalwood, spearmint, wild orange, wintergreen, Forgive®

Kidney, circulation— basil, coriander, juniper berry

Kidney, toxic— bergamot, cardamom, coriander, grapefruit, juniper berry, lemon, lemongrass, turmeric, Abōde™, Air-X™, Purify, Slim & Sassy®, Zendocrine®

Kidney, weak— geranium, helichrysum, juniper berry, lemongrass, rosemary

Low-force/volume urine stream— bergamot, cardamom, cinnamon bark, lemon, juniper berry, marjoram, thyme, AromaTouch®, Console®, Slim & Sassy®, Zendocrine®

Nausea/vomiting— bergamot, clove, fennel, ginger, lemon; see *Digestive & Intestinal*

Pelvic pressure— basil, cypress, clary sage, ginger, lavender, peppermint, Slim & Sassy®

Perspiration, lack of— cardamom, cilantro, ginger, juniper berry, lemongrass, oregano, Abōde™, Air-X™, Purify

Pus or blood in urine— basil, cardamom, frankincense, lemon, oregano, sandalwood, tea tree, Abōde™, Air-X™, Citrus Bliss®, DDR Prime®, On Guard®, Purify, Zendocrine®; see *Immune & Lymphatic*

Sharp/spastic pains in kidneys or bladder when urinating— basil, cardamom, cilantro, clary sage, cypress, grapefruit, juniper berry, lavender, lemon, marjoram, Roman chamomile, Siberian fir, thyme, PastTense®

Swollen ankles, toes, fingers— basil, cypress, frankincense, grapefruit, lemon, marjoram, patchouli, AromaTouch®

Urination, painful/burning/frequent*— basil, birch, cinnamon bark, juniper berry, lemongrass, sandalwood, AromaTouch®, On Guard®, Zendocrine®

Urgency of urination— cypress, frankincense, oregano, Balance®, DigestZen®

Water retention (edema)— blue tansy, cardamom, cedarwood, celery seed, cinnamon bark, cypress, Douglas fir, eucalyptus, fennel, frankincense, geranium, ginger, grapefruit, green mandarin, juniper berry, lemon, lemongrass, rosemary, Siberian fir, spikenard, tangerine, thyme, wild orange, wintergreen, AromaTouch®, Forgive®, Slim & Sassy®, Zendocrine®

 *See Protocols →

protocols

ROCKIN' RELIEF (for kidney stones)

Ingredients:

15 drops eucalyptus
15 drops wintergreen
15 drops lemongrass
15 drops lemon

Directions:

Combine in a 15mL bottle and fill remainder with carrier oil. Apply over lower back/kidney area every 20 minutes. **Note:** avoid alcohol, sugars, refined foods, and drink ample amounts of water.

FIRE EXTINGUISHER (supports resolving urinary burning/infection)

Ingredients:

6 drops DDR Prime®
4 drops lemon
4 drops juniper berry
4 drops lemongrass

Directions:

Combine in a 5mL roller bottle and fill remainder with carrier oil. Apply on lower abdomen/bladder area and/or on lower back/kidney area every 20 minutes during daytime hours until pain no longer occurs. Continue applying 3x's daily. Take 2 drops each of above oils in a capsule. **Note:** avoid alcohol, sugars, refined foods, and drink ample amounts of water.

IN CONTROL (bladder control— for incontinence/bed-wetting)

Ingredients:

1 drop juniper berry
1 drop cypress

Directions:

Combine in palm and apply across lower abdomen. Use for occasional inconvenient urges or 3-5 times a day for chronic control issues. Dilute as needed.

For more ideas, download the app on Android or iOS.

Weight

WEIGHT GAIN can result from an increase in muscle mass, fat deposits, or excess fluids such as water. The most common causes of weight gain are from excessive eating and poor nutrition. Food is made up of calories, or units of energy. Physical activity and normal body metabolism burn calories. When a person takes in more calories than the body uses, the extra calories are stored as fat subsequently enlarging or decreasing the "size" of fat cells depending on the balance of energy in the body. When fat cells build up or accumulate, it causes increased fat or obesity.

Other factors that may cause weight gain include medication, lack of lean muscle mass, inactivity, hypothyroidism, menopause, pregnancy, or slow metabolism. Sometimes toxicity levels within the body can encourage the body to hold onto fat. When there are too many toxins for the body to handle, the fats are diverted into fat cells—the only place in the body where natural insulation provides protection for vital body organs. Later, when individuals try to lose weight, despite effort it seems to prove to be next to impossible. These protective fat cells are programmed to guard the vital organs at all costs; therefore they cannot let go of their cargo.

Being overweight can bring about undesirable emotional effects such as depression, anxiety, and mood swings. Excess weight or obesity can cause exhaustion or fatigue and challenge individuals participating in various activities, a scenario especially difficult for overweight parents with active children. It causes undue stress on joints, bones, and muscles. Carrying excess fat can also dramatically increase the risk of developing deadly and debilitating diseases.

Essential oils and whole-food supplementation can be powerful allies in the process of maintaining a healthy weight and losing excess weight. Essential oils have the ability to coax toxic fat cells into releasing their contents, help break down the toxins, and, with proper hydration, flush them out of the body. Oils can also support the body's insulin response, reduce cravings, and provide a feeling of satiety. Supplements can give the cells the energy they need to carry out proper body function, including extra fuel for working out. Digestive enzymes help the body break down and utilize nutrients for maximum support.

top solutions

Single Oils

Grapefruit, Lime– curb cravings, reduce appetite, and induce fat burning (pgs. 154, 181)

Cinnamon bark– inhibits formation of new fat cells; balances blood sugar (pg. 126)

Peppermint– enhances sense of fullness; reduces cravings and appetite (pg. 202)

Ginger– encourages fat burning and metabolism; promotes satiation (pg. 153)

Pink and Black Pepper– enhance metabolism, help release toxins and fat (pgs. 206, 111)

Blends

Slim & Sassy®– balances metabolism, eliminates cravings, and lifts mood; acts as diuretic (pg. 222)

Zendocrine®– support body's ability to remove toxins and waste effectively (pg. 251)

DDR Prime®– improves function of the endocrine system and thyroid (pg. 140)

Supplements

Adaptiv™ Capsules (pg. 253), Alpha CRS®+, DigestZen® Softgels, **Fiber** (pg. 258), **Greens** (pg. 259), Microplex VMz®, PB Assist®+, Phytoestrogen Complex, **Protein** (pg. 266), Serenity® Softgels, **Sassy® Softgels** and **gum** (pg. 267), TerraGreens®, xEO Mega®, **Zendocrine® Complex** (pg. 272), Zendocrine ® Softgels (pg. 273)

WEIGHT

usage tips

For weight management, the focus is primarily on what and how much food is consumed (appetite) and how well it is utilized as fuel by the body (metabolism). Additionally, balancing other processes such as elimination, blood sugar, and hormones is necessary for long-lasting results. See suggested programs in "Protocols".

With that in mind, the following uses are recommended:

- **Internal:** Ingest oils for support with appetite, cravings and metabolism, including the ability to burn and release fat along with toxins, is very effective. Place drops of oils in a capsule for systemic support. Drink oils in water. Drop on tongue. Be generous with usage for this purpose.
- **Topical:** Use oils to assist the body to detox and target specific zones. Consider applying blends of oils to areas like the abdomen, thighs, buttocks, and arms as a treatment. Dilute with a carrier oil to prevent sensitivity especially with oils like cinnamon bark and Slim and Sassy®.
- **Aromatic:** Excellent for supporting appetite control. Inhale when needed. Diffuse throughout day.

Related Ailments

Excessive Appetite, Autointoxication, Cellulite, Loss of Appetite, Obesity, Overeating

By Related Properties

For more, see *Oil Properties* on pages 535-538

Analgesic– arborvitae, bergamot, black pepper, blue tansy, cassia, cinnamon bark, clary sage, clove, copaiba, coriander, cypress, eucalyptus, frankincense, helichrysum, jasmine, juniper berry, lavender, lemongrass, litsea, marjoram, oregano, peppermint, ravintsara, rosemary, Siberian fir, tulsi, wild orange, wintergreen, yarrow|pom

Antidepressant– basil, bergamot, clary sage, coriander, frankincense, geranium, grapefruit, jasmine, lavender, lemon, lemongrass, melissa, neroli, oregano, patchouli, ravintsara, rose, tangerine, wild orange

Calming– bergamot, birch, black pepper, blue tansy, cassia, clary sage, copaiba, coriander, fennel, frankincense, geranium, jasmine, juniper berry, lavender, litsea, magnolia, oregano, patchouli, Roman chamomile, sandalwood, tangerine, yarrow|pom

Detoxifier– arborvitae, cassia, cilantro, cypress, geranium, juniper berry, lemon, lime, litsea, patchouli, rosemary, tangerine, wild orange, yarrow|pom

Energizing– basil, clove, cypress, grapefruit, lemongrass, pink pepper, rosemary, Siberian fir, tangerine, wild orange, yarrow|pom

Steroidal– basil, birch, cedarwood, clove, fennel, patchouli, rosemary, thyme, tulsi

Stimulant– arborvitae, basil, bergamot, birch, black pepper, blue tansy, cardamom, cedarwood, cinnamon bark, clove, coriander, cypress, eucalyptus, fennel, ginger, grapefruit, juniper berry, lime, myrrh, patchouli, rosemary, Siberian fir, spearmint, tangerine, tea tree, thyme, tulsi, vetiver, wintergreen, ylang ylang

Stomachic– basil, blue tansy, cardamom, cinnamon bark, clary sage, coriander, fennel, ginger, juniper berry, marjoram, melissa, peppermint, pink pepper, rose, rosemary, tangerine, turmeric, wild orange, yarrow|pom

Uplifting– bergamot, cardamom, cedarwood, clary sage, cypress, grapefruit, lemon, lime, litsea, melissa, sandalwood, tangerine, wild orange, ylang ylang

conditions

Anorexia— See *Eating Disorders*

Appetite, excess*— bergamot, cassia, cinnamon bark, citronella, fennel, ginger, grapefruit, juniper berry, lemon, peppermint, Peace®, Slim & Sassy®; if due to nutritional deficiencies, see *Weight*— "Supplements"

Appetite, imbalanced— grapefruit, tangerine, wild orange, Slim & Sassy®

Appetite, loss of— bergamot, black pepper, cardamom, coriander, fennel, ginger, grapefruit, lemon, patchouli, spearmint, tangerine, thyme, Console®, DigestZen®, Passion®, PastTense®, Peace®, Purify, Slim & Sassy®

Blood sugar imbalance— cassia, cinnamon bark, coriander, fennel, green mandarin, pink pepper, rosemary, tulsi, Cheer®, On Guard®, Slim & Sassy®; see *Blood Sugar*

Cellulite*— birch, cypress, Douglas fir, eucalyptus, geranium, ginger, grapefruit, lemongrass, lemon, lime, pink pepper (obesity), rosemary, Siberian fir, spikenard, tangerine, Siberian fir, wild orange, wintergreen, Slim & Sassy®; see *Detoxification*

Cravings*— ginger, grapefruit, peppermint, Slim & Sassy®

Cravings, sugar— cassia, cinnamon bark, clove, grapefruit, Slim & Sassy®

Eating, over/binging/compulsive— bergamot, black pepper, cedarwood, cinnamon bark, ginger, grapefruit, juniper berry, lemon, oregano, patchouli, peppermint, Elevation, Slim & Sassy®

Edema/swelling/water retention— basil, cypress, ginger, green mandarin, juniper berry, lemon, lemongrass, patchouli, rosemary, tangerine, Slim & Sassy®; see *Urinary*

Emotional/stress-induced eating— bergamot, grapefruit, Slim & Sassy®; see *Eating Disorders, Mood & Behavior*

Energy, low/fatigue/exhaustion— basil, bergamot mint, green mandarin, lime, peppermint, pink pepper, rosemary, jasmine; see *Energy & Vitality*

Excessive weight/obese— birch, cinnamon bark, fennel, ginger, grapefruit, juniper berry, lemon, oregano, tangerine, wild orange, wintergreen, Slim & Sassy®

Fat, breakdown/dissolve— grapefruit, green mandarin, lemon, lime, neroli, spearmint, tangerine, Slim & Sassy®

Food addiction— basil, black pepper, cardamom, ginger, grapefruit, pink pepper, Slim & Sassy®; see *Addictions*

Hunger pains— fennel, myrrh, oregano, peppermint, InTune®; see *Digestion & Intestinal*

Inability to lose weight— cinnamon bark, coriander, spearmint, Slim & Sassy®, Zendocrine®; see *Candida, Detoxification*

Metabolism, slow*— cassia, clove, ginger, lemongrass, pink pepper, spearmint, tangerine, tulsi, Slim & Sassy®

Metabolism, too fast— ginger, Slim & Sassy®, myrrh, Breathe® drops

Overindulgence of food*— grapefruit, juniper berry, peppermint, Slim & Sassy®

Pancreas, inflamed— fennel, tulsi; see *Endocrine (Pancreas)*

Satiety/satiation, lack of— bergamot, fennel, ginger, grapefruit, peppermint

Sagging skin— helichrysum, grapefruit, AromaTouch®, Immortelle; see *Integumentary*

Sense of self, poor/self worth, lack of*— bergamot, grapefruit, jasmine, Elevation; see *Mood & Behavior*

Stretch marks— frankincense, geranium, lavender, sandalwood, tangerine, Immortelle; see *Integumentary*

Thyroid imbalances— coriander, clove, frankincense, ginger, rosemary, Immortelle, DDR Prime®; see *Endocrine (Thyroid, Adrenal)*

Toxicity*— lemon, grapefruit, rosemary, Air-X™, Slim & Sassy®, Zendocrine®; see *Detoxification*

*See Protocols on pg. 435

Weight Loss Program

	10-30 days (Pre-Cleanse)	10 days (Cleanse)	20 days (Restore)	30 days (Maintain)
UPON RISING	***Greens and/or Fiber with lemon and ginger essential oils in water***			
Morning Meal	Protein shake MicroPlex VMz® xEO Mega® Zendocrine® Complex TerraZyme®†	Protein shake MicroPlex VMz® xEO Mega® GX Assist® * Zendocrine® Softgels	Protein shake MicroPlex VMz® xEO Mega® TerraZyme® † PB Assist®+	Protein shake MicroPlex VMz® xEO Mega® [optional: TerraZyme®†]
BETWEEN MEALS	***Slim & Sassy® in or with water***			
Noon Meal	Protein shake TerraZyme®†	Protein shake GX Assist® *	Healthy Meal or Protein TerraZyme® †	Healthy Meal or Protein [optional: TerraZyme®†]
BETWEEN MEALS	***Slim & Sassy® in or with water***			
Evening Meal	Healthy Meal MicroPlex VMz® xEO Mega® Zendocrine® Complex TerraZyme®†	Healthy Meal MicroPlex VMz® xEO Mega® TerraZyme® † GX Assist® * Zendocrine® Softgels	Healthy Meal MicroPlex VMz® xEO Mega® TerraZyme® † PB Assist®	Healthy Meal MicroPlex VMx® xEO Mega® [optional: TerraZyme®†]
BETWEEN MEALS	***Slim & Sassy® in or with water***			
Exercise	Aerobic (20+ minutes 3x per week) Resistance (10+ minutes 3x per week) Flexibility (5-20 minutes daily)			

Take all supplements according to label recommnedations and based on personal needs and tolerance.
*GX Assist® - start with 1 softgel a day, increasing up to 3 per day as is comfortable.
†TerraZyme® - take 1-2 per meal

Note: Slim & Sassy® can be taken 5 drops 5x daily (mentioned 3x above) and/or combine with softgels
Make it your own program: Use common sense and seek the advice of a health care professional as needed for any health conditions.

WEIGHT

protocols

WEIGHT LOSS DETOX AND METABOLISM BOOST

- Take 5 drops Slim & Sassy® in capsule or water 2-5x's per day or 1-2 Slim & Sassy® Softgels 2-3x's/day
- Take 3 drops Zendocrine® in capsule 2x's a day.
- Take 1-2 capsules of TerraZyme® 20-30 minutes BEFORE every meal.
- Apply grapefruit to troubled areas. Dilute as needed or desired.
- Address thyroid— see *Endocrine (Thyroid)*. (pg. 340)
- Rub 1-2 drops Balance® and Motivate® on bottoms of feet AM and PM.
- As a morning meal, use Protein in a shake or smoothie. Add cinnamon bark, cassia, and/or citrus oil for flavor and added benefits.

BODY SLIMMING WRAP

Ingredients:

30 drops Slim & Sassy®
15 drops eucalyptus
15 drops peppermint
10 drops grapefruit
10 drops lavender
10 drops ClaryCalm®
5 drops wintergreen

Directions:

Mix oils in a 4 oz glass bottle with a sprayer top. Swirl. Fill remainder with fractionated coconut oil OR add oils to approximately 4 ozs of non-scented, natural lotion.

Instructions for use:

- Step 1: Take measurements of areas to be wrapped.
- Step 2: Spray or apply mixture to areas of concern.
- Step 3: Wrap with cotton fabric (e.g., muslin) or paper towel as a barrier between skin and plastic wrap so as not to absorb toxins from plastic (oils breakdown some plastics).
- Step 4: Wrap plastic around treated areas — 3-4 layers
- Step 5: Leave on for a few hours or overnight as desired.
- Step 6: Take measurements and record the difference.

NOTE: Drink plenty of water with lemon oil or before and after treatment as an excellent diuretic to help release toxins from fat.

WEIGHT LOSS TUMMY RUB

Ingredients:

20 drops fennel
20 drops grapefruit
20 drops pink pepper
20 drops Siberian fir

Directions:

Blend with carrier oil in a 15mL empty amber bottle and apply to abdomen. Enhance effects by consuming Slim & Sassy® in drinking water throughout the day.

CELLULITE/WEIGHT LOSS/DETOX BATH

Ingredients:

1 C Epsom salt
1 C baking soda
10 drops Slim & Sassy®

Directions:

Mix and add to warm bath. Soak 20 minutes or longer 2-3x's a week. Drink lots of water during. Add Slim & Sassy® to drinking water for enhanced results and as a habit throughout the day.

DRINKING WATER SUGGESTIONS

- **Cinnamon & lime**— boost metabolism
- **Lemon & spearmint**— uplift and cleanse liver
- **Peppermint**— curb appetite and cool
- **Green mandarin**— cleanse and refresh
- **Grapefruit**— boost immunity and diminish cellulite
- **Slim & Sassy®**— balance blood sugar and appetite

APPETITE CONTROL

Pick a blend below. Take in a capsule 2x's per day. Inhale aroma from cupped hands prior to eating and when cravings are triggered.

• Sexy Citrus

Ingredients:

2 drops grapefruit
1 drop lemon or lime
3 drops pink pepper
2 drops cinnamon

• Marvelous Mint

Ingredients:

2 drops peppermint
2 drops bergamot
3 drops green mandarin
1 drop fennel

• Herbal Mix

Ingredients:

2 drops basil
1 drop marjoram
1 drop cilantro
1 drop thyme
1 drop juniper berry

CRAVE AWAY

Place 1-3 drops grapefruit or tangerine in palms, rub together, cup over face/nose, and inhale deeply. Add a drop of patchouli if desired.

LOVE YOURSELF

Apply 1-2 drops each grapefruit and bergamot diluted to chest or diffuse to encourage a positive relationship with physical self.

WOMEN face health challenges specific to their gender including, but not limited to, the reproductive system, brain, heart, skeleton, and hormone issues. Many women suffer from high cortisol levels, which lead to fatigue, weight changes, depression, anxiety, and digestive problems. At all stages of life, most women do their best to maintain homeostasis while multitasking. Physical and emotional stress can be a cause and symptom of many women's issues.

The female reproductive system works closely with other systems, specifically the endocrine system. The female reproductive system includes the ovaries, fallopian tubes, uterus, cervix, external genitalia, and breasts. The ovaries are responsible for producing egg cells as well as secreting the hormones estrogen and progesterone. These hormones are vital to reproductive health and fertility, but they also play a role in the balance of a woman's emotional and physical health. They influence other body tissue and even bone mass. Hydration and nutrition can directly impact the production of these hormones. Women with lower body fat sometimes do not produce enough of the sex hormones and can encounter amenorrhea (an abnormal absence of menstruation) and decreased bone density.

For approximately forty years of their lives, women experience the menstruation cycle. This monthly cycle (26-35 days) involves egg development and release from the ovaries, the uterus preparing to receive a fertilized egg, and the shedding of the uterine lining if an egg is not fertilized. Many women experience difficulty during the second half of this cycle in the form of premenstrual syndrome and menstrual cramps. Irritability, anxiousness, bloating, headaches, and even migraines can be common at this time. The cycle is maintained through the secretion of the sex hormones. An imbalance of sex hormones can lead to a lack of period as well as irregular and/or extended bleeding. This can be linked to polycystic ovary syndrome or endometriosis.

As a woman ages, the sex hormones begin to diminish. Menopause refers to the time when menstruation no longer occurs due to diminished sex hormones, specifically after a lack of twelve periods. This change leads to periodic instability of functions in the body, and side effects such as hot flashes, mood swings, vaginal dryness, fluctuations in sexual desire, fatigue, forgetfulness, or urinary incontinence.

Nutrition and hydration are important keys to a woman's health. Daily supplements that include a whole food nutrient supplement, essential oil xEO Mega®, bone supplement complex, and phytoestrogen complex will help a woman's body be able to regulate hormones properly. The phytoestrogen complex is a natural form of estrogen-like therapy, assisting to balance not only a deficiency, but also any excess of the wrong kind and harmful estrogen metabolites. Whisper® can be applied to the wrists, ankles, and directly over the abdomen when symptoms of PMS and menopause are occurring. Grapefruit and thyme oils support healthy progesterone levels, the counterbalance hormone to estrogen. Also, mood-enhancing oils, including Elevation, Serenity®, Citrus Bliss®, and Balance®, can help with depression and other emotions that may be prevalent for women.

top solutions

Single Oils

Clary sage— enhances endocrine system function and balances hormones (pg. 133)

Rose— helps overcome frigidity and infertility; promotes healthy menstruation (pg. 215)

Geranium— supports hormone, emotional balance, and fertility (pg. 152)

Neroli and Ylang ylang— promotes healthy libido; relax (pgs. 193, 250)

Grapefruit, Pink pepper— support healthy progesterone levels and breast health (pgs. 154, 206)

Jasmine— promotes a healthy uterus, libido (pg. 169)

Ginger— promotes healthy menstruation and libido; relieves cramps (pg. 153)

Fennel— supports healthy estrogen levels, ovaries, and breast milk production (pg. 148)

Thyme, Oregano— supports healthy progesterone levels (pgs. 234, 196)

Blends

Whisper®— stabilizes mood and supports proper endocrine function (pg. 242)

ClaryCalm®— supports monthly cycle (pg. 132)

Adaptiv™— promotes adaptability, hormonal, and emotonal balance (pg. 96)

Motivate®— supports healthy reproductive function (pg. 190)

Supplements

Adaptiv™ Capsules (pg. 253), **Alpha CRS®+** (pg. 254), **Bone Nutrient Complex** (pg. 255), DDR Prime® Softgels, IQ Mega, **Microplex VMz®** (pg. 261), **Phytoestrogen Complex** (pg. 265), **xEO Mega®** (pg. 271), **Yarrow|Pom Capsules** (pg. 272)

usage tips

For best results for women's health:

- **Aromatic:** Women are very sensitive and emotionally responsive to aromas. Diffuse selected oils regularly to promote emotional stability. Additionally, use favorite oils to wear as perfume; applied to wrists and neck. Smell throughout the day. Reapply as needed.
- **Topical:** Apply selected oils to back of neck and shoulders or other areas of need (e.g., back for menstrual cramps) to reduce tension, soothe sore muscles, and reduce spasms. The bottoms of the feet and, more specifically, under the ankle bones, are significiant reflex points of application.

Related Ailments

Amenorrhea, Dysmenorrhea, Endometriosis, Estrogen Imbalance [Detoxification], Excessive Menstrual Bleeding, Female Hormonal Imbalance [Detoxification], Fibrocystic Breasts [Endocrine], Fibroids [Cellular Health], Hot Flashes, Infertility, Irregular Menstrual Cycle, Lack Of Ovulation, Libido (low) for Women, Menopause, Menorrhagia, Menstrual Pain, Ovarian Cyst, Pelvic Pain Syndrome, Perimenopause, PMS, Polycystic Ovary Syndrome (PCOS), Scanty Menstruation, Vaginal Yeast Infections [Candida], Vaginitis, Xenoestrogen

By Related Properties

For more, see *Oil Properties* on pages 535-538

Analgesic— arborvitae, basil, bergamot, birch, black pepper, blue tansy, cassia, cinnamon bark, clary sage, clove, copaiba, coriander, cypress, fennel, frankincense, ginger, helichrysum, jasmine, juniper berry, lavender, lemongrass, litsea, marjoram, oregano, peppermint, rosemary, Siberian fir, tulsi, tea tree, turmeric, wild orange, wintergreen, yarrow|pom

Antidepressant— basil, bergamot, cinnamon bark, clary sage, coriander, frankincense, geranium, grapefruit, jasmine, lemon, lemongrass, magnolia, melissa, neroli, oregano, patchouli, ravintsara, rose, sandalwood, tangerine, wild orange, ylang ylang

Antihemorrhagic— geranium, helichrysum, yarrow|pom

Aphrodisiac— black pepper, cardamom, cinnamon bark, clary sage, clove, coriander, ginger, jasmine, juniper berry, magnolia, neroli, patchouli, peppermint, pink pepper, ravintsara, rose, rosemary, sandalwood, spearmint, thyme, vanilla, vetiver, wild orange, ylang ylang

Detoxifier— arborvitae, cassia, celery seed, cilantro, cypress, geranium, juniper berry, lemon, lime, litsea, patchouli, rosemary, tangerine, turmeric, wild orange, yarrow|pom

Emmenagogue— arborvitae, basil, cassia, cedarwood, cinnamon bark, clary sage, fennel, ginger, jasmine, juniper berry, lavender, marjoram, myrrh, oregano, peppermint, Roman chamomile, rose, rosemary, spearmint, thyme, wintergreen, yarrow|pom

Galactagogue— basil, clary sage, fennel, jasmine, lemongrass, wintergreen

conditions

Breast, cellular health— clary sage, eucalyptus, frankincense, geranium, grapefruit, magnolia, pink pepper, DDR Prime®

Breast size, too small (want to enlarge)— black pepper, clary sage, fennel, geranium, myrrh, vetiver, yarrow|pom, ClaryCalm®, DDR Prime®, Peace®, Whisper® (oils will not cause already larger breasts to enlarge further)

Breasts, tender*— clary sage, fennel, geranium, helichrysum, lavender, lemon, myrrh, Roman chamomile, yarrow|pom, Citrus Bliss®, ClaryCalm®, DDR Prime®, Whisper®, Zendocrine®

Candida— See *Candida*

Cysts, ovarian— basil, clary sage, cypress, fennel, frankincense, geranium, grapefruit, lemon, rosemary, thyme, tulsi, ClaryCalm®, DDR Prime®, Purify, Slim & Sassy®, Whisper®, Zendocrine®; see *Blood Sugar*

Endometriosis— basil, bergamot, black pepper, clary sage, copaiba, cypress, eucalyptus, frankincense, geranium, ginger, lemongrass, neroli, oregano, rose, rosemary, sandalwood, thyme, ylang ylang, yarrow|pom, ClaryCalm®, DDR Prime®, Elevation, On Guard®, Peace®, Whisper®, Zendocrine®

Estrogen dominance— basil, clove, lemongrass, thyme, Forgive®, Purify, Zendocrine®

Estrogen, false/xenoestrogens— clary sage, ginger, grapefruit, lemon, oregano, thyme, ClaryCalm®, DDR Prime®, Zendocrine®; see *Candida, Detoxification*

Estrogen, imbalanced/low— basil, clary sage, coriander, cypress, lavender, neroli

Fibrocystic breasts— clary sage, eucalpytus, frankincense, grapefruit, magnolia, oregano, pink peper, thyme, DDR Prime®

Fibroids— basil, clary sage, eucalyptus, frankincense, helichrysum, lemon, lemongrass, tea tree, sandalwood, thyme, DDR Prime®, Peace®

Frigidity— jasmine, neroli, rose, ylang ylang, Adaptiv™, AromaTouch®, Passion®, Peace®, Whisper®; see "Aphrodisiacs" property, *Intimacy*

Genital warts— arborvitae, frankincense, geranium, lemongrass, melissa, thyme, Zendocrine®

Headache, migraine/cyclical— basil, clary sage, fennel, geranium, lavender, melissa, peppermint, rosemary, Roman chamomile, tulsi, ClaryCalm®, DDR Prime®, PastTense®, Whisper®

Hemorrhoids— cypress, helichrysum, myrrh, Roman chamomile, sandalwood, AromaTouch®, DigestZen®, Zendocrine®; see *Cardiovascular*

Hormones, imbalanced (general)— jasmine, geranium, magnolia, rose, ylang ylang, ClaryCalm®, Forgive®, Motivate®, Whisper®

Hot flashes— clary sage, eucalyptus, lemon, peppermint, spearmint, ClaryCalm®, Whisper®; see *Endocrine (Thyroid)*

Infertility*— basil, clary sage, copaiba, cypress, fennel, frankincense, geranium, jasmine, melissa, Roman chamomile, rose, rosemary, spikenard, thyme, ylang ylang, ClaryCalm®, DDR Prime®, Passion®, Purify, Whisper®, Zendocrine®; see *Candida, Blood Sugar*, "Progesterone, low" below

Low libido— black pepper, cardamom, cinnamon bark, clary sage, clove, ginger, jasmine, juniper berry, magnolia, neroli, patchouli, rose, rosemary, sandalwood, spearmint, thyme, vetiver, wild orange, ylang ylang, Passion®, Whisper®; see "Aphrodisiacs" property, *Intimacy*

Mammary gland support— clary sage, geranium, grapefruit, pink pepper, DDR Prime®, Whisper®; see "Breast Detox" recipe below

Menopause problems*— basil, clary sage, cypress, fennel, geranium, lavender, neroli, Roman chamomile, rosemary, thyme, wild orange, yarrow|pom, ClaryCalm®, Peace®, Whisper®, Zendocrine®

Menstruation (menses) cycle, irregular— cypress, fennel, jasmine, juniper berry, lavender, melissa, peppermint, rose, rosemary, thyme, yarrow|pom, Cheer®, ClaryCalm®, DDR Prime®, Deep Blue®, Forgive®, PastTense®, Whisper®

Menstruation (menses), heavy (menorrhagia)*— clary sage, cypress, fennel, frankincense, geranium, helichrysum, thyme, yarrow|pom, ClaryCalm®, DDR Prime®, Forgive®, Purify, Whisper®, Zendocrine®

Menstruation (menses), lack of/absence (amenorrhea)— basil, cedarwood, clary sage, geranium, juniper berry, Roman chamomile, rosemary, yarrow|pom, ClaryCalm®, DDR Prime®, Forgive®, Passion®, Whisper®, Zendocrine®

Menstruation (menses), overly light— basil, cinnamon bark, ginger, rosemary, ylang ylang, Citrus Bliss®, ClaryCalm®, DDR Prime®, Purify, Passion®, Whisper®, Zendocrine®

Menstruation (menses), painful (dysmenorrhea), uterine cramping— basil, black pepper, blue tansy, cardamom, celery seed, cinnamon bark, citronella, clary sage, copaiba, coriander, cypress, frankincense, ginger, lemongrass, jasmine, juniper berry, magnolia, neroli, peppermint, petitgrain, pink pepper, spikenard, Cheer®, ClaryCalm®, DDR Prime®, Purify, Whisper®, Zendocrine®

Menstruation (menses), prolonged— copaiba, frankincense, geranium, ClaryCalm®, DDR Prime®, Whisper®

Miscarriages (multiple)— blue tansy, clary sage, frankincense, grapefruit, lemon, oregano, thyme, Citrus Bliss®, ClaryCalm®, DDR Prime®, Purify, Whisper®, Zendocrine®

Night sweats— clary sage, eucalyptus, ginger, lime, peppermint, spearmint, AromaTouch®, ClaryCalm®, DDR Prime®, PastTense®, Whisper®, Zendocrine®; see *Endocrine (Thyroid), Immune & Lymphatic*

Ovarian cysts— See "*Cysts, ovarian*"

Ovaries— basil, clary sage, frankincense, geranium, rosemary, thyme, tulsi, ClaryCalm®, DDR Prime®, Zendocrine®

Ovulation, irregular— basil, clary sage, copaiba, jasmine, melissa, rose, ylang ylang, Zendocrine®

Pelvic pain— coriander, cypress, Douglas fir, geranium, ginger, marjoram, rosemary, thyme, ClaryCalm®, PastTense®

Perimenopause— cardamom, clary sage, cypress, fennel, lavender, Roman chamomile, rosemary, yarrow|pom, ClaryCalm®, DDR Prime®, Peace®, Whisper®, Zendocrine®

PMS*— bergamot, clary sage, copaiba, cypress, fennel, geranium, grapefruit, jasmine, lavender, magnolia, neroli, pink pepper, Roman chamomile, spikenard, Adaptiv™, Cheer®, ClaryCalm®, Peace®

Postpartum depression— See *Pregnancy, Labor & Nursing*

Progesterone, low— clove, geranium, grapefruit, oregano, thyme, ClaryCalm®, Whisper®, Zendocrine®

Uterus, cleansing and purifying— clary sage, geranium, jasmine, lemon, tea tree, rose, Citrus Bliss®, ClaryCalm®, Purify, Whisper®, Zendocrine®

Uterus, damaged/degenerated— frankincense, geranium, lemongrass, sandalwood, DDR Prime®, Whisper®

Uterus lining, unhealthy— celery seed, frankincense, geranium, grapefruit, jasmine, rose, DDR Prime®, Whisper®

Uterus, prolapsed/lack of tone— fennel, frankincense, juniper berry (stimulates uterine muscles), melissa, rose, wild orange, ClaryCalm®, Whisper®

Vaginal, candida/thrush— tea tree, myrrh, oregano, thyme, On Guard®, Purify, Slim & Sassy®, Zendocrine®; see *Candida*

Vaginal discharge— clary sage, frankincense, lavender (thick, yellow), DDR Prime®, On Guard®, Purify, Whisper®, Zendocrine®; see *Candida*

Vaginal dryness— clary sage, Balance®; see *Integumentary*

Vaginal infection/inflammation— clary sage, eucalyptus, frankincense, magnolia, rosemary, spearmint, DDR Prime®, On Guard®, Peace®, Whisper®, Zendocrine®

*See Protocols →

protocols

COOL YOUR HOT MESS (PMS)

Ingredients:

12 drops wild orange
6 drops clary sage
8 drops geranium
8 drops Roman chamomile
5 drops ylang ylang
5 drops black spruce

Directions:

Combine in a 5mL bottle/roller bottle and fill remainder with carrier oil. Apply to pulse points, back of neck, and palms. Then inhale deeply from cupped hands.

HE'LL NEVER KNOW (for symptoms of PMS/menopause)

Ingredients:

12 drops geranium
6 drops ylang ylang
4 drops clary sage

Directions:

Combine in a 5mL bottle/roller bottle and fill remainder with carrier oil. Apply over lower abdomen and lower back, wrists, and cup hands together over nose and mouth and inhale. Or apply ClaryCalm® in same manner.

MENORRHAGIA (heavy flow)

Ingredients:

4 drops geranium
3 drops helichrysum
2 drops cypress
3 drops yarrow|pom

Directions:

Add oils to a slightly used ClaryCalm® roll-on bottle. Shake to blend. Massage onto abdomen and pelvic area 2-3x daily, starting the week before menstruation.

BREAST DETOX

Consider repeating detox 2-4 times per year.

- Apply 4 drops frankincense to breasts twice daily for 30 days.
- Take DDR Prime® Softgels twice daily for 30 days.
- Apply diluted 2 drops each eucalyptus, grapefruit, Siberian fir, and/or pink pepper for additional targeted support.
- Take 2 drops each pink pepper and grapefruit in a capsule 2-3x's daily.

BREAST ENHANCER

Apply 1 drop vetiver, 4 drops clary sage, and then a layer of ClaryCalm® and Whisper across 2x's per day until desired results are achieved (generally a couple months).

NOTE: This suggestion is suited for women who have lost or never had breast mass due to intense exercise levels [e.g., runners or from breastfeeding]. Vetiver will not have a negative impact on women with larger breasts so it is unnecessary to avoid usage for other purposes.

FERTILITY BLEND

Ingredients:

7 drops clary sage
5 drops fennel
9 drops geranium
4 drops spikenard
4 drops patchouli

Directions:

Add oils to a slightly used rose roller bottle. Apply to lower abdomen twice daily, targeting ovary and uterus areas.

FERTILITY PROTOCOL

- **Diet:** See *Candida*
- **Supplementation:**
  - Alpha CRS®+, Microplex VMz®, xEO Mega®– take as directed
  - PB Assist®+– take 1 capsule 3x's a day; days 11-15 of monthly cycle; take 1 per day from day 16 thru end of month (onset of menstruation). Repeat until results are achieved. Then reduce to 1-2 capsules per day.
  - GX Assist®– take first 10 days of monthly cycle, 1 capsule 1-3x's a day. Stop taking upon conception.
  - Phytoestrogen Complex– take 1-2 capsules every day to help eliminate harmful estrogen metabolites and maintain healthy estrogen levels. Stop taking upon conception.
- **Essential oil use:**
  - Geranium– apply diluted 2x's a day over liver, adrenal, and kidney areas to support healthy progesterone levels.
  - Grapefruit & Thyme– take 2 drops each in a capsule twice daily to support healthy progesterone levels.
  - Spikenard– apply diluted under outside ankle bones.
  - Clary sage– apply 1 drop under each inside ankle bone. Stop using upon conception.

Follow program until becoming pregnant. Then discontinue GX Assist®, Phytoestrogen Complex, and Clary Sage. Continue everything else throughout pregnancy as desired or needed.

MOOD LIFTING PERFUME

In a 10mL roller bottle, combine 4 drops ylang ylang, 3 drops bergamot, 6 drops clary sage, 7 drops lavender, and 12 drops tangerine essential oils. Top with carrier oil. Apply to pulse points throughout the day. Consider layering with jasmine, magnolia, neroli, and/or rose.

CRAMP-LESS

Apply diluted magnolia topically, followed by 2-3 drops each copaiba and marjoram on lower abdomen. Layer geranium or ClaryCalm® as desired.

FIXUS (Pilaris Keratosis)

Ingredients:

15 drops lavender
15 drops geranium
15 drops tea tree
15 drops myrrh
15 drops oregano or thyme

Directions:

Combine in 2 oz glass spray bottle and fill remainder with carrier oil. Apply 3-5x's a day to affected area, shaking lightly before each use.

WOMEN'S HEALTH

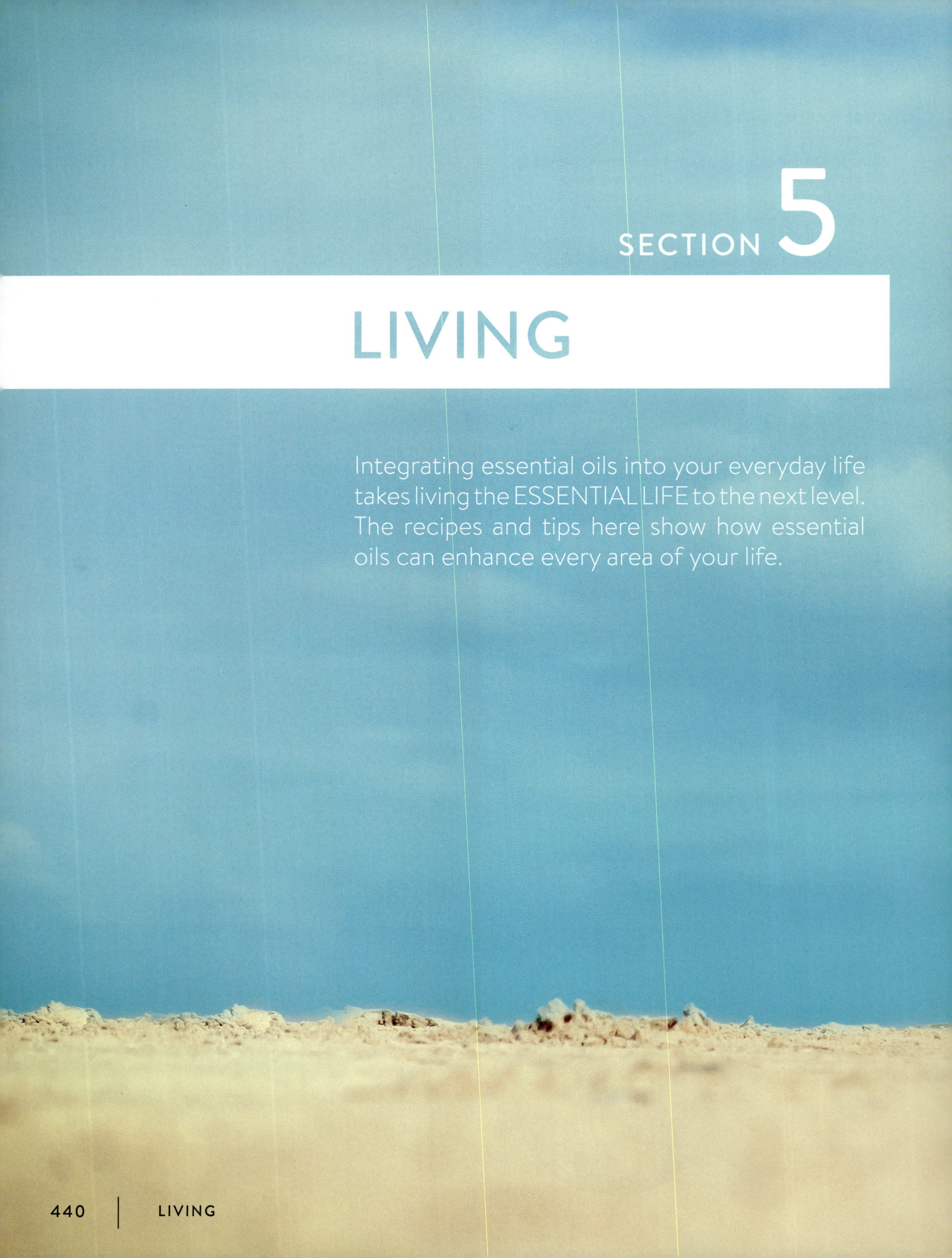

SECTION 5

LIVING

Integrating essential oils into your everyday life takes living the ESSENTIAL LIFE to the next level. The recipes and tips here show how essential oils can enhance every area of your life.

EVERYDAY *Oils*

Be Your Best Self with Essential Oils Daily:

1. Open your oils. Breathe them in. Put them on, in, and around you.
2. Make and keep them accessible.
3. Hook their use to a habit (e.g. during a bedtime routine, meal)

morning

Nourish

Wake Up— Arise or peppermint
Detox— Tangerine or grapefruit, DDR Prime®
Ground— Balance® or Anchor
Mediate— Align or frankincense & sandalwood
Workout— Deep Blue® or AromaTouch®
Uplift— Cheer®, Citrus Bliss®, Citrus Bloom™, or Elevation

Cleanse

Aftershave— Balance® or Amavi®
Deodorant— Amavi®, Balance®, Citrus Bloom™, Whisper®
House— Abōde™ collection

all day

Recover

Cravings— Slim & Sassy®, grapefruit, black pepper, or bergamot
Depression— Elevation or melissa
Frustration— Forgive® or Adaptiv™
Meltdowns— Serenity® or Balance®
Mental Fatigue— Rosemary and peppermint or spearmint, Motivate®
Tantrums— Calmer™, Roman chamomile, or Console®
Tension— PastTense® or AromaTouch®

Solve

Cuts— Tea tree and lavender
Bites— Lavender and Purify
Bruises— Helichrysum
Pain— Deep Blue® products or Rescuer™
Stress— Adaptiv™ or Peace®
Tummy Upset— DigestZen® or Tamer™

Optimize

Athletic Performance— Breathe® and Deep Blue®, AromaTouch®
Breath Freshener— Peppermint or beadlets
Focus & Homework— InTune®, vetiver and lavender, Motivate®, Thinker™, or cedarwood
Freshen Up— Cheer® or Motivate®
Presence— Anchor or Thinker™
Work/Life Performance— Motivate® or Brave™

evening

Relax

Bedtime— Serenity® & Serenity® Softgels, cedarwood
Still— Peace® or Balance®

Restore

Fine Lines, Wrinkles— Immortelle, frankincense or sandalwood, rose or black spruce
Protect— On Guard® or Stronger™
Sore Muscles & Feet— Deep Blue® or AromaTouch®

- To increase efficacy, add frankincense, heat, and/or massage.
- To increase absorption: use Touch® oils or apply carrier oil during topical application.
- For best results, use essential oils more frequently for acute situations, (e.g., every 20-60 minutes) and less often for more chronic conditions (e.g., 2-4 times per day).

Recipes

Cleaning

Dusting Spray

Ingredients:

1 C water, distilled or boiled and cooled
¼ cup vinegar
1 T olive oil
15 drops preferred essential oil (lemon, wild orange)

Directions:

Combine ingredients in a glass spray bottle. Shake before each use. Spray on a microfiber cloth and apply to surface to clean, polish, and keep dust away.

Upholstered Fabric Cleaner

Ingredients:

¼ C warm water
2 t castile soap
3 drops lime

Directions:

Mix ingredients in a glass container with a lid. Dip cloth in the mixture and dab onto the stain for quick spot treatments on any fabric. Store for future use in a cool, dry place.

Deodorizer

Ingredients:

2 T white vinegar
30 drops citronella
Purified water

Directions:

Using a 16 oz glass spray bottle, add all ingredients. Shake well before each use and store in cool, dry place. Spray on surfaces, carpets, pillows, curtains, and/or places smells linger.

Grill Cleaner

Ingredients:

Baking soda
3 t castile soap
20 drops lemon
White vinegar

Directions:

Combine soap and essential oil in a 16 oz glass bottle. Fill the remainder with vinegar. Sprinkle baking soda on grill and spray solution onto the baking soda. Let sit at least 30 minutes before scrubbing. Repeat steps as needed.

Refresh and Purify the Air

Ingredients:

12 drops Siberian fir
12 drops lemon eucalyptus
12 drops tea tree
12 drops peppermint

Directions:

Combine essential oils with 8 oz water in glass spray bottle. Spray on pillows, couch, or areas of heavy use, to refresh and cleanse the fabric. Allow to dry and vacuum to refresh the fabric.

Carpet Stain Remover

Ingredients:

4 C warm water, divided
½ t clear castile soap or dish soap
10 drops lemon

Directions:

Mix 2 cups water, soap, and essential oil. Soak a cloth in the mixture, wring out, and gently blot the stain. Use a clean cloth soaked in the remaining 2 cups water to remove the residue. Alternate the soap solution with the fresh water until the stain is gone. Remember to blot, not rub, to remove a carpet stain, as rubbing will ruin the carpet fibers.

Vinegar-Free Cleaner

Ingredients:

12 oz purified water
1 T unscented liquid castile soap
10 drops tea tree
5–10 drops citronella

Directions:

Fill a 16 oz glass spray bottle ¾ full with purified water. Add soap, essential oils, and top off with additional purified water. Shake well before each use.

Wood Polish

Ingredients:

1 C olive oil
½ C distilled water
30 drops lemon
10 drops wild orange

Directions:

Using a 16 oz glass spray bottle, add olive oil, water, and essential oils. Shake well (and at every use). Spray on wooden surface to polish wood and remove dust.

Toy Cleaner

Ingredients:

4 oz white vinegar
2 drops On Guard®

Directions:

Combine ingredients in an 4 oz glass spray bottle topped off with distilled water.

To Use: Spray on toys and all to dry completely.

Stainless Steel Cleaner

Ingredients:

2 oz liquid castile soap
5 drops lemon
5 drops On Guard®
5 drops Balance®
Distilled water

Directions:

Add ingredients to a 16 oz glass spray bottle. Top off with distilled water.

To Use: Spray on stainless steel appliances and wipe clean with a cloth.

Leather Cleaner

Ingredients:

¼ cup olive oil
½ cup white vinegar
3 drops eucalyptus

Directions:

Add ingredients to an 4 oz glass spray bottle and shake it well. Spray leather and wipe it clean with a cotton cloth. Please note, this recipe is safe for regular leather, not on suede.

Classic All-Purpose Cleaner

Ingredients:

1 C distilled water
1 C white vinegar
1 t natural dish soap
15 drops lemon
10 drops tea tree

Directions:

Using a 16 oz glass spray bottle, add water and vinegar. Add soap and essential oils. Shake well.

To Use: Spray on to clean surfaces, sinks, counters, floors, or most surfaces. Not necessary to rinse the surface.

CLEANING Bathroom

Disinfecting Cleaning Wipes

Ingredients:

12 thick and durable paper towels
1 C distilled water
½ C white vinegar
¼ C rubbing alcohol
5 drops lavender
5 drops lemon

Directions:

Cut paper towels in half and stack into a neat pile. Roll up and place in a quart size glass jar. Mix ingredients and pour over paper towels. Let absorb before using.

Window & Mirror Cleaner

Ingredients:

2 C water
2 T white vinegar
2 T rubbing alcohol
5 drops peppermint

Directions:

Add ingredients to a glass spray bottle and shake well.

To Use: Spray windows or mirrors and wipe dry. Store in cool place for up to two months.

Soap Scum Remover

Ingredients:

2 C hot water
¼–½ C borax
10 drops lemon

Directions:

Add ingredients to a glass spray bottle and shake well.

To Use: Spray surfaces and wipe dry. Store in cool, dry place for up to two months.

Mold & Mildew Preventer

Ingredients:

2 C water
30 drops tea tree
10 drops peppermint

Directions:

Add ingredients to a glass spray bottle and shake well.

To Use: Spray directly on mold or mildew. Do not rinse. Repeat as needed, daily or more frequently, as long as the surface dries in between applications.

Disinfecting Toilet Bowl Cleaner

Ingredients:

½ C baking soda
¼ C white vinegar
10 drops tea tree

Directions:

Mix ingredients to dissolve baking soda in a glass jar.

To Use: Add to toilet. Let sit up to 20 minutes. Scrub with a brush and flush.

LIVING
CLEANING
Kitchen

Oven Cleaner Paste

Ingredients:

1 C baking soda
½ C water
1 T dish or castile soap
10 drops lemon

Directions:

Combine ingredients in a bowl to form a paste.

To Use: Apply with a sponge and let sit up to 30 minutes. Wipe clean with clean cloth and water.

Oven Cleaner Spray

Ingredients:

1 C warm water
3 T baking soda
1 T castile soap
5 drops lemon
5 drops clove

Directions:

Add all ingredients to a glass spray bottle and shake to combine.

To Use: Spray liberally in the oven and let sit for 15 minutes. Wipe clean with cloth and water.

Drain Cleaner

Ingredients:

¼ C baking soda
¼ C distilled white vinegar
3 drops wild orange

Directions:

Pour essential oil directly down drain, followed by baking soda and then vinegar. Allow mix to sit for 15 minutes. Pour hot water down the drain, followed by cold water to unclog drains.

Smooth Scrub Cleanser

Ingredients:

¾ C rounded baking soda
¼ C unscented liquid castile soap
1 T water
1 T white vinegar
5-10 drops lemon

Directions:

In a glass jar with a lid, combine baking soda and soap, stir in water, vinegar and essential oil. The consistency should be a soft paste. Use to scrub soap scum, stains, brighten tub, tile and/or toilet, kitchen sink, or refrigerator.

To Use: Apply to area and let sit for 5-10 minutes and then scrub. Wipe clean with a damp cloth.

Sticker & Goo Remover

Ingredients:

1 T baking soda
1 T almond or vegetable oil
2 drops lemon

Directions:

Mix into a small glass bowl. Apply a small amount to the sticker or label and let sit for 1-2 minutes. Use a cloth, or rinse, to remove. Reapply, if needed.

Stove Cleaner

Ingredients:

¼ C baking soda
2 T natural dish detergent
5 drops lemon
White vinegar

Directions:

Combine first 3 ingredients. Add vinegar until mixture has an olive-oil consistency.

To Use: Rub mixture onto stove top. Let sit for 15-30 minutes. Use a damp scouring pad to scrub surface clean. Rinse with water.

Garbage Can Odor Tablets

Ingredients:

2 C baking soda
1 C Epsom salt
¼ C water
10 drops lemon
5 drops peppermint
Ice cube tray or small silicone mold

Directions:

Combine dry ingredients. Slowly add water, then oils, and stir. Carefully, transfer mixture to ice cube tray (silicone mold) without overfilling. Allow to dry overnight or until hardened.

To Use: Place one tablet in the bottom of the garbage can. Store remaining tablets in an airtight container. Replace tablets as needed.

Garbage Can Refresher

Ingredients:

2 C baking soda
1 C salt
5 drops Purify or Abōde™
5 drops lemon

Directions:

Combine baking soda and salt in a small glass jar. Sprinkle 2-4 T into the bottom of a fresh garbage bag. Add 4-5 drops essential oils to a cotton ball and add to the garbage bag. When bag is full, throw away as usual, adding the above to the new empty bag. *Baking soda and salt will help absorb odors and essential oils will refresh.

CLEANING

Laundry

Lemon Stain Remover

Ingredients:

½ C white vinegar
10 drops lemon
10 drops tea tree

Directions:

Combine ingredients in a 4 oz glass spray bottle. Fill remainder with water. Shake well. Spray onto stains before washing.

On Guard® Stain Remover

Ingredients:

2 T On Guard® Cleaner Concentrate
3 C water

Directions:

Add all ingredients to a large glass spray bottle (at least 24 oz). Spray stain and wash/dry as usual.

Baby Stain Remover Spray

Ingredients:

8 oz water
2 T borax
20 drops lemon

Directions:

Add to glass spray bottle and shake combine. Shake before each use. Spray on stain and wash as normal.

Washing Machine Cleaner

Ingredients:

¾ C white vinegar
10 drops tea tree
5 drops grapefruit

Directions:

In an 8 oz glass spray bottle, combine ingredients and shake well. Spray around the seal (rubber at the front of a front load washer), drum, and door of the washer. Using a cotton cloth, throughly wipe down. Remove soap dispenser tray; spray, wipe down, and put it back. Let air dry before doing laundry.

For top loading washers; use to wipe down the drum, inside and outside the lid, and bleach and soap dispenser. Use weekly or as needed.

Linen Spray

Ingredients:

1 C distilled water
1 T witch hazel
4 drops green mandarin

Directions:

Combine ingredients in a glass spray bottle. Spritz pillows and linens.

Reusable Dryer Sheet

Ingredients:

6"x 6"piece of cotton or wool cloth (recycled T-shirts, sweaters, or socks, etc.)
2–4 drops wild orange or other essential oil of choice

Directions:

Place cloth in a glass container with a lid. Add essential oil and allow to dry thoroughly. Place dryer sheet in dryer and dry clothes as usual. When cloth has lost its scent, repeat steps.

Hint: Store several cloths in a container. Add a fresh cloth to your dryer each laundry day.

Liquid Fabric Softener

Ingredients:

1 gallon white vinegar
2 C baking soda
20 drops clove
10 drops lemon

Directions:

Combine ingredients in a large glass jar.

To Use: Add ¼ to ½ cup per load.

Laundry Fragrance Booster

Ingredients:

Epsom salt
20-25 drops lavender, lemon, Citrus Bliss®, or scent of choice

Directions:

Add 3 pounds Epsom salt (or kosher salt) to a large glass jar. Add essential oils. Mix together making sure to equally spread the oils throughout the salt.

To Use: Add ½ cup to each wash cycle and wash as usual. It is safe for all types of washers.

Dryer Softener Balls

Ingredients:

100% wool yarn or 100% animal yarn
Pantyhose (reuse ones with runs in them)
4-6 drops essential oil of choice

Directions:

Take the end of the yarn and wrap it around the middle and index finger about 10 times. Remove it from fingers and wrap 2 or 3x's around the middle (It should look like a bow. Keep tightly wrapping the yarn, making a ball the size of a tennis ball. Cut and tuck the ends. Create four or more balls.

Cut one leg off pantyhose. Place one yarn ball into the bottom and tie a knot above the ball. Repeat until all have been added and secured. Once secured, felt (fusing together) the yarn by washing and drying on the highest heat setting. When the balls are dry, remove from the pantyhose, and add 4–6 drops essential oil. Toss in each dryer load with clothes.

Stain Stick

Ingredients:

2.5 oz bar castile soap
3 t water
4 drops tea tree

Directions:

Grate soap and place in microwave-safe bowl with water. Melt in microwave in 30-second intervals for about 1 ½ minutes. Once melted, let cool for 5 minutes and stir in essential oil. Pour into a container with a push-up bottom. Allow to cool to a solid state before using. Alternately, store in a small glass container/jar, and spot clean stains with a clean cotton cloth.

LIVING

LIVING

COOKING *with* Essential Oils

Adding essential oils to favorite recipes makes it easy to incorporate their healthful benefits throughout the day. There are many variables with dealing with essential oils for cooking. If you have ever used fresh herbs instead of dried, you know the flavor and the quantity used is different. The same rule applies to essential oils and cooking. The oils are super-concentrated in flavor and aroma. You may find that some essential oil brands are more potent than others— this has to do with sourcing and purity. Essential oils can add a very subtle or very strong taste to the final dishes, depending on how much is used. We like to enjoy and identify as many flavors in our foods as possible, so use caution and know that less is best. Start with a tiny amount, then add more, as needed. If you add too much, the flavor will dominate and can spoil the dish.

Oils have different viscosity as well, so some are thinner, and some are thicker. The type of opening in the bottle will affect the size of the drop. Using a dropper or syringe can help control what is dispersed. Another good option is to drip oil onto a utensil first, then pull from that amount what you want is needed to go into the dish or beverage.

You'll notice in the following recipes some interesting measurements that will help you add the right amount of essential oils to the recipes. The best way to control quantity is to use the toothpick method.

1 toothpick dip = Dip a toothpick into the essential oil and dip it once into the recipe.

1 toothpick swirl = Dip a toothpick into the essential oil and swirl it around in the recipe.

½ drop = Drop an essential oil into a spoon, then use the tip of a sharp knife to obtain the desired amount of oil and add it to the recipe.

Be sure to use a fresh toothpick with each use so as not to contaminate the essential oil bottles.

Hot, savory, or spicy herbs are particularly hard to judge (for example, basil oil may be much more subtle in flavor than oregano), so the general rule should be: if it isn't a citrus oil, use a toothpick until you test it or have a guaranteed recipe.

It's always best to mix essential oils with an olive or other oil/liquid when cooking to more evenly disperse the flavor in the dish.

Baking typically requires more oil flavoring than cooking does. For example, where you might use 2 or 3 toothpick swirls of oregano in spaghetti sauce, you might use 2 or 3 drops when making artisan bread.

Substituting Oils for Herbs

Substitute an oil for an herb to increase the health benefits and increase the flavor of any dish.

- **½ t dried herbs = 1½ t fresh herbs = 2-3 toothpick swirls**
- **1 t dried herbs = 1 T fresh herbs = 1 drop**

Substituting Oils for Citrus

- 1 t lemon extract = 1/8 t lemon = 16 drops
- 1 T lemon zest = 1/16 t lemon = 8-14 drops

COOKING *with* OILS CHART

	Meat	Chicken	Fish	Eggs	Cheese	Vegetables	Rice	Pasta	Desserts	Pastries	Bread	Cakes	Sorbets	Ice Cream	Fruit	Dressings
Basil	•	•	•			•	•	•								
Bergamot		•	•						•				•	•		
Black pepper	•	•	•	•		•	•	•			•				•	•
Cardamom	•	•	•	•		•	•		•	•	•	•	•	•	•	•
Cassia			•		•	•	•	•	•	•	•	•		•	•	•
Celery seed	•	•	•	•	•	•	•	•								•
Cilantro	•	•				•		•								
Cinnamon	•	•	•	•	•	•	•	•	•	•	•	•	•	•	•	•
Clove	•	•							•	•	•	•	•	•	•	•
Coriander	•	•				•		•								
Dill	•	•	•			•	•	•		•	•				•	•
Fennel			•			•	•	•	•	•	•	•			•	•
Ginger					•	•		•	•	•	•	•	•	•	•	•
Grapefruit				•		•	•	•	•	•			•	•		•
Green mandarin						•			•	•		•	•	•	•	•
Jasmine		•	•			•	•	•	•	•	•	•	•	•	•	
Lavender		•	•	•	•		•	•	•	•	•	•	•	•	•	
Lemongrass		•	•	•	•	•	•	•	•	•	•	•	•	•	•	•
Lime	•	•	•			•	•	•	•	•	•	•	•	•	•	•
Marjoram	•	•	•								•					•
Melissa		•	•	•	•	•	•						•	•	•	
Oregano	•	•	•	•	•	•	•	•			•					•
Peppermint						•			•	•		•	•	•	•	
Pink pepper	•	•	•	•		•	•	•			•				•	•
Rose		•		•	•		•		•	•	•	•	•	•	•	
Rosemary	•	•	•		•	•	•			•						•
Spearmint						•			•	•		•	•	•	•	
Tangerine	•	•	•				•	•	•	•	•	•	•	•	•	•
Thyme	•	•	•			•	•	•								•
Turmeric	•	•	•	•	•	•	•	•			•					•
Wild orange	•	•	•	•			•	•	•	•	•	•	•	•	•	•
Ylang ylang		•					•	•	•	•	•	•	•	•	•	

COOKING

Beverages

Sparkling Citrus Drink

Ingredients:

12 oz seltzer water
⅛–¼ t stevia, to taste
6 drops grapefruit
6 drops lemon

Directions:

Mix ingredients together and serve chilled or over ice. Garnish with a sprig of mint or a slice of lime, if desired.

Blueberry Lavender Lemonade

Ingredients:

1½ C lemon juice
8 C cold water
4 C blueberry lavender simple syrup (recipe below)
Blueberry Lavender Simple Syrup
- 1 C fresh blueberries
- 1 C granulated sugar
- 2 C water
- 6–8 drops lavender

Directions:

Combine the lemon juice, water, and simple syrup in a large jug. Serve over ice.

Blueberry Lavender Simple Syrup: Place blueberries, sugar, and water in a small saucepan and bring to a simmer, over medium heat. Reduce heat to low and simmer for 5 minutes. Remove from heat and allow to steep until completely cooled. Stir in essential oils. Store in glass jar in the refrigerator until ready to use.

Homemade Cola

Ingredients:

4 drops lime
4 drops orange
2 drops lemon
2 drops cardamom
⅛ t freshly grated nutmeg
2 drops cinnamon
4 t vanilla extract
4 t maple syrup, honey, or liquid stevia

Directions:

Mix ingredients. Add chilled cola to 8-10oz cold seltzer water.

Celery Seed Tea

Ingredients:

2–3 drops celery seed
1 C hot water

Directions:

Combine and drink up to 3 cups a day to stimulate digestion and enhance liver health.

Lime Rickey

Ingredients:

32 oz Concord grape juice
16 oz sparkling apple cider
4 drops lime
Lime slices, for garnish

Directions:

Add all ingredients into a large glass pitcher, stir, and serve over ice cubes.

Citrus Water

Ingredients:

16 oz water
1 drop lemon
1 drop orange
1 drop grapefruit
Sliced lemons, limes, berries or other fresh fruit, optional

Directions:

Add 16 oz water to glass or stainless steel drinking container. Add essential oils (1 drop at a time, to taste). Drink and enjoy throughout the day, repeating often.

Optional: add fresh fruit, veggies, and/or herbs.

tips

Try adding these essential oils to still or sparkling water for a delicious flavor (and zero calories!)

• Peppermint • Lemon • Cardamom • On Guard® • Grapefruit • Ginger • Lime • Grapefruit & Cassia • Cinnamon & Lime

Add essential oil to ice cube trays. To distinguish the flavor and add to the presentation, you can include a drop of food coloring, zest of fruit, or leaf (e.g. peppermint or basil; dried citrus looks appealing as well).

Green Berry Protein Shake

Ingredients:

8 oz almond milk (milk of choice)
2 scoops protein
1–2 C fresh or frozen berries
2 scoops Greens or 1 large handful fresh spinach
2 drops ginger
2 drops grapefruit
Optional: 1-2 scoops Fiber

Directions:

Add ingredients to blender. Blend until smooth and serve.

Frozen Blended Virgin Daiquiri

Ingredients:

1 C frozen strawberries
1 t vanilla extract
1–2 drops lime
1 C water
Stevia (sweetener of choice)

Directions:

Add ingredients to blender. Add sweetener and lime to taste. Add more water for a thinner consistency. For a creamy consistency, add plain yogurt.

Lemonade Bar

Prepared lemonade of choice (8 oz per person).
Fresh fruits, like raspberries, strawberries, lemons, and limes.
Toothpicks for adding essential oils.

Ingredients:

Choose one or more of these essential oils:
- Basil, 1 toothpick dip or to taste (great with raspberry lemonade)
- Lavender, 1 toothpick swirl or to taste
- Geranium, 1 toothpick swirl or to taste
- Ginger, 1 toothpick swirl or to taste
- Grapefruit, 3–4 toothpick swirls or to taste
- Lime, 2–3 toothpick swirls or to taste

Directions:

Pour prepared lemonade into glasses, allow guests to add fruit, and their choice of essential oils with the toothpicks.

Sparkling Lavender Lemonade

Ingredients:

Simple Syrup:
  1 C water
  1 C sugar
  2 drops lavender
1 C lemon juice (about 6 lemons)
3 C cold sparkling water
1 drop purple food coloring (optional)

Directions:

Make simple syrup by combining water and sugar in a small saucepan. Bring to a simmer until sugar is dissolved. Let cool to room temperature, add lavender.

Combine lemon juice, simple syrup, and water in 1-quart pitcher. Add food coloring if desired. Serve chilled with ice, lemon slices, and/or lavender sprigs.

COOKING Breads

Wheat Herb Bread

Ingredients:

2 drops thyme, sage, basil, rosemary, or oregano
1 ½ t honey (to taste)
1 ⅓ C warm water
1 package or 2 ¼ t active dry yeast
1 ½ t sea salt
2 to 2 ¼ C bread flour
1 ¾ C whole wheat flour

tips

Great bread recipe for dipping in favorite olive oil (see Sauces for ideas pg.484)

Directions:

Stir together essential oils and honey.

In a large bowl, combine water, yeast, and honey mixture. Let stand for 5 minutes.

In a separate bowl, combine salt and flours. Stir flour mixture gradually into water mixture, until flour has been absorbed, and the dough forms a ball.

Knead dough until it is moderately stiff, smooth, and elastic in mixer or by hand.

Lightly oil a bowl. Place dough in bowl, cover with a towel, and let rise until doubled in size.

Punch down dough and let rest for 10 minutes.

Grease an 8x4" loaf pan. Shape dough to form a loaf and place in pan. Let rise until doubled in size but not much higher than top of pan. Put into a cold oven.

Bake at 350°F oven for 25–30 minutes or until golden on top and sides pull away from pan.

Rosemary Artisan Sourdough Bread

Ingredients:

1 ½ C all-purpose flour
1 ½ C whole wheat flour
1 t salt
½ t active dry yeast
1 ½ C warm water
3–4 drops rosemary
¼ t Italian seasoning (optional)
¼ t garlic powder (optional)
¼ t black pepper (optional)
Fresh rosemary, roughly chopped, for garnish

Directions:

In a large bowl, stir the flours, salt, and yeast together. Add warm water and rosemary. Stir to combine. It's fine if it looks messy or on the dry side.

Cover the bowl, and set at room temperature for 8–24 hours (it is done sitting when it looks wet and bubbly and has doubled in size). Turn dough out onto a well-floured surface, and gently pull it into a squarish shape. Sprinkle on Italian seasoning, garlic powder, black pepper, and fresh rosemary. Fold the corners in like an envelope. Then flip the dough over and shape it into a ball. Let it rest for 30 minutes.

In the meantime, put a Dutch oven in the oven, and preheat to 450°F (230°C).

After the 30 minute rise, flip the bread over (seam side up) and cut an "x" in the dough, sprinkle with fresh rosemary, and carefully place it in the hot Dutch oven. Cover with the lid, and cook for 30 minutes. Remove the lid and bake for 10–20 minutes or until bread is golden brown.

tips

Essential oils can flavor butters and oils, salt and/or sugar for a savory, spicy, or sweet taste. For example, add cinnamon, stevia, and ground cinnamon to butter or oil for toast or biscuits. Add basil, thyme, and oregano to salt, and sprinkle on garlic bread or buttered pasta. Add tangerine, wild orange and/or grapefruit to sugar and sprinkle on muffins.

Pumpkin Bread

2 loaves Ingredients:

3 ½ C all purpose flour
1 t salt
2 t baking soda
2 ¾ C sugar
1 t baking powder
½ C coconut oil
½ C unsalted butter, softened
15 oz can pumpkin puree
4 large eggs
⅓ C water
1 C plain yogurt
2 drops cinnamon
1 drop clove
1 drop ginger
4 drops lemon
⅛ t nutmeg, freshly ground

Directions: *Preheat oven to 325°F*

Grease pans. In a small bowl, combine flour, baking soda, baking powder, salt, and sugar and set aside. In a mixing bowl, combine coconut oil, butter, pumpkin puree, water, yogurt, eggs, essential oils, and nutmeg.

With the mixer on low, slowly add the dry ingredients to the wet, scraping the sides often to make sure everything is well combined. Once combined, set on medium speed and mix for 2 minutes until light and fluffy.

Divide mixture into two pans and bake for 45–50 minutes or until a toothpick comes out clean, the center of the bread.

Lavender Lemon Banana Bread

Ingredients:

2 ripe bananas, mashed
1 egg
3 drops lavender
2 drops lemon
¼ C softened butter
1 ¾ C superfine cake flour
½ t salt
1 t vanilla
¾ t baking powder
¼ t baking soda
⅔ C sugar
1 T lemon zest
⅓ C sour cream

Directions: *Prevent oven to 350ºF.*

In mixing bowl, combine butter and sugar, mixing until creamy. Add in egg, sour cream, lemon zest, vanilla, essential oils, and bananas. Mix and set aside.

In separate bowl combine flour, baking soda, baking powder, and salt. Whisk together until blended.

In loaf pan, grease and dust with flour. Pour in batter until half full. Bake for 40–45 minutes. Remove and allow to cool briefly. Serve warm or cooled.

tips

Add corresponding essential oils instead of herbs to favorite bread recipes. Add orange-infused dried cranberries into sweet bread or muffin batters (see Snacks pg. 492).

Make bread dips by flavoring olive oil with rosemary, thyme, and basil to taste. Mix balsamic vinegar with the flavored olive oil and serve with fresh bread chunks or slices.

Ginger Spice Banana Bread

Ingredients:

4 medjool dates, washed and de-seeded
½ T maple syrup
½ C coconut flour (or almond flour)
½ t salt
¼ t baking soda
½ t nutmeg
6 eggs
½ T vanilla
¼ C coconut oil (warmed)
½ C very ripe bananas, mashed
½ C walnuts, chopped
½ C pecans, chopped
1 drops ginger
1 drop cinnamon

Directions: *Prevent oven to 350ºF.*

Place the dates and maple syrup in a food processor and chop and combine to make a paste-like mixture, then add to a large mixing bowl with the remaining ingredients and mix to combine.

Pour the batter into a greased loaf pan and bake for 30–40 minutes or until golden.

Specialty Frostings/Glazes

Directions:

Add 1–2 drops lemon or wild orange to glazes or frostings. If making a lemon or citrus cake or pastry, try a toothpick dip of lavender with 1 drop lemon in the glaze for a unique and delicious flavor combination.

Easy Bread or Muffin Add-Ins:

Add to favorite bran muffin or sweet bread recipe:

Ingredients:

1 C frozen berries (raspberries or blueberries work best)
2–3 drops wild orange, to taste

Add to veggie breads (such as pumpkin, carrot, or zucchini):

Ingredients:

1 drop cinnamon, to taste
1 toothpick swirl clove, to taste

LIVING

LIVING

COOKING Breakfast

Blueberry Cardamom Scones

Ingredients: Preheat oven to 375°F.

3 C all-purpose flour
⅓ C sugar
1 T baking powder
1 t salt
12 T butter, cut into pieces
1 pint blueberries
¾ C plus 2 T milk
2 drops cardamom
1 drops ginger
2 T turbinado sugar, for sprinkling

Directions:

Line a rimmed baking sheet with parchment paper.

In a bowl, combine flour, sugar, baking powder, and salt. Cut in the butter pieces until well combined. Toss in the fresh blueberries and milk, mix, and combine well.

Divide dough into 2 pieces and on a floured surface, form into a round disk, about 6" in diameter, using extra flour if needed. Slice each disk into 6 triangular scones. Place on lined baking sheet. Mix turbinado sugar, and essential oils in small bowl, and sprinkle tops of scones. Bake in a preheated oven for 25 to 30 minutes or until golden on top.

Grain-free Huevos Rancheros

Ingredients:

10–12 eggs
1 medium onion, finely chopped
1 red bell pepper, de-seeded and finely chopped
2 bunches green onions or one leek, finely chopped
2 tomatoes, finely chopped
½ to 1 drop oregano, to taste
¼ C fresh cilantro, finely chopped
1 t each of the following—cumin, coriander, oregano, and chili powder
½ T paprika
1 t Celtic sea salt or Himalayan pink salt
1 t pepper of choice—red pepper flakes or 1 drop black or pink pepper
4 cloves garlic, minced
¼ C coconut milk or yogurt, for added creaminess
½ C shredded cheese—Gruyere, Cheddar, or Colby Jack
2 drops lemon

Directions:

In a large cast iron or stainless steel skillet, saute onion until translucent and slightly browned. Add the green onions/leeks until they get a little soft. Add the tomatoes, garlic, and spices and toast for just a few minutes. Add the eggs and cook until desired consistency. Top with grated cheese. Serve right out of the skillet!

French Toast with Apple Cranberry Sauce

Ingredients:

Apple Cranberry Sauce:
- 1 C dried cranberries
- ½ C juice (grape, apple, or orange)
- 1 C berry preserves
- 1 Granny Smith apple, chopped
- 4 drops wild orange, divided
- 3 drops cinnamon, divided

3 eggs
¾ C milk
½ C butter, melted
½ t vanilla extract
⅛ t nutmeg
1 drop clove
1 drop ginger
2 drops cinnamon
2 drops wild orange
8 big slices of bread (Texas toast) or 12 regular slices

Directions:

Apple Cranberry Sauce: In a small stainless steel saucepan, combine cranberries, juice, preserves, and apples. Cook over low heat until the mixture comes to a low simmer. Remove from heat and stir in essential oils. Set aside.

Heat griddle to 375°F.

In a shallow dish, combine eggs, milk, butter, vanilla, nutmeg, and essential oils, stir well. Dip bread into the egg mixture, allowing extra to drip off before cooking. Cook on both sides until done. Spoon over the toast and serve immediately.

Dust with powdered sugar, if desired.

tips

Always use glass, ceramic, or metal bowls and spoons. Avoid plastic utensils and storage containers.

Make a yummy fruit dip as a side or topping by mixing 1 C vanilla yogurt with ½ C mashed berries and 1–2 drops lime.

Try adding essential oils to favorite breakfast drink or tea.

Salsa Scramble

Ingredients:

2 C cooked black beans
½ C salsa or more, to taste
½ t unrefined sea salt
½–1 drop lime, to taste
Bacon drippings
¼ t ground cumin to taste
Optional Toppings: Avocado, cheese, chives, diced tomatoes, cut up red peppers

Directions:

Place first 3 ingredients in a saucepan. Heat over medium heat until bubbling. Remove from heat and allow beans to cool for a few minutes then add essential oil.

Heat skillet over medium heat and add bacon drippings. Whip eggs with a bit of salt and pepper and cook to desired consistency. Combine black bean mixture and scrambled eggs in individual bowls, add optional toppings.

Orange Cinnamon Biscuits

Ingredients:

2 ½ C all-purpose flour
½ C cornstarch (plus more for rolling)
4 ½ t baking powder
½ t salt
½ C salted butter (cold)
1 C whole fat plain yogurt
2 t vanilla extract ½ t, divided
1 egg
6 drops tangerine
6 drops lemon
Filling:
- 2 T butter, softened
- ¼ C sugar
- 2 t ground cinnamon

Glaze:
- 2 T whole milk
- 10 drops wild orange
- 1 C powdered sugar

Directions:

Heat oven to 450°F. Line a baking sheet with parchment paper. In food processor, combine flour, cornstarch, baking powder, and salt until combined. Add ½ cup cold butter, pulse about 10 seconds until crumbly and the butter is pea sized and evenly distributed throughout the flour mixture. Add yogurt, vanilla, egg, and essential oils and pulse until dough ball forms.

Remove from food processor, onto counter that is lightly covered with cornstarch. Knead the dough a few times, turning it over onto itself, about 6–10 times. Don't overwork the dough. This will heat the dough and cause the butter to melt, resulting in gummy biscuits.

Roll out to 9x15 rectangle, about ¾ inch thick.

Filling: Spread softened butter over the dough, and sprinkle with sugar and cinnamon. Roll the long side of the dough up with the butter mixture on the inside. Slice into 15 sections (about 1 inch each).

Bake on middle rack at 450°F for 10 minutes until biscuits are lightly browned.

While the biscuits cool, mix together glaze ingredients in a small bowl. Stir until no lumps remain. Dip the biscuits into the glaze and allow to sit for 5 minutes before serving.

LIVING

COOKING

Desserts

Lemon or Lime Bars

Crust:

1 C butter, softened (not melted)
2 C flour
½ C powdered sugar
¼ t sea salt

Topping (after baking):

⅓ –½ C powdered sugar
1 drop lemon or lime

Filling:

4 eggs
2 C sugar
3 T lemon or lime juice
1 T water
¼ C cornstarch
6 drops lemon or lime (or more to taste)

Directions:

Crust: Combine ingredients with pastry blender. Press into the bottom of 9x13" pan (for nicer presentation, line pan with parchment paper, so bars lift neatly out of the pan).

Filling: Mix eggs and sugar till light and fluffy. Add the lemon or lime juice, essential oil, water and cornstarch. Pour mixture over semi-cooked crust and bake an additional 25–30 minutes.

Topping: Mix powdered sugar and citrus oil in baggie and shake it up. When bars are done, sprinkle with citrus-infused powdered sugar. Best served cold.

tips

Directions:

- *Mix 1-2 drops cassia in Greek yogurt, for a delicious fruit dip.*
- *Add 2-5 drops peppermint, wild orange, or spearmint to favorite chocolate brownie mix.*
- *Add lime to guacamole for a zesty treat.*

Strawberries Romanoff

Directions:

Wash and rinse 1 quart strawberries and allow to dry. Into sour cream or plain Greek yogurt, add 2 toothpick swirls lemon. Put brown sugar in a dish. Holding strawberry by the stem, dip into creamy essential oil mixture, then dab into brown sugar.

Ice Cream Log

Directions:

Prepare desired cake recipe as directed. Instead of using a 9" x 13" pan, prepare a jelly roll pan with nonstick spray. Place parchment paper 2" larger than pan on all sides, and spray nonstick spray on parchment paper.

Spread cake batter thinly onto parchment paper.

Move oven rack to top ⅓ of the oven and bake for 10–12 minutes at 350°F. Remove from oven. Lift cake out of pan by holding all corners of parchment paper. Let cool.

While cake is cooling, make ice cream mixture. Into 1 quart vanilla ice cream, softened to the consistency of a thick milkshake, add desired flavoring (e.g., peppermint, wild orange, lime, lemon, cinnamon, cardamom, chocolate chip pieces or sprinkles) to taste. Spread ice cream evenly on top of cooled cake mixture. Roll cake and ice cream using parchment paper, removing paper as you roll. Place roll onto a clean parchment-paper lined pan and freeze. Once frozen, wrap with plastic wrap to store in freezer. Slice and serve.

Pudding Variations

Use pudding variations for making trifles, parfaits, or cream pies.

Citrus: Add 1 drop lemon, lime, grapefruit, green mandarin, tangerine, or wild orange to warm pudding, after pudding has thickened slightly. If you want to add more, add in "toothpick dip" increments.

Flavored Chocolate: In a microwavable dish, melt 1 cup chocolate chips and stir into warm pudding, after pudding has thickened slightly. Add 3 toothpick swirls peppermint to taste; 1 drop wild orange; 2 toothpick swirls cinnamon, cassia, or cardamom, to taste.

Butterscotch: In a microwavable dish, melt 1 cup butterscotch chips and stir into warm pudding, after pudding has thickened slightly. Add 1 toothpick swirl of ginger to taste.

Banana: Chop a banana into small pieces; add to warm pudding. Add 1 toothpick swirl of tangerine or ginger.

Coconut: Add roasted coconut flakes to prepared pudding, a dollop of whipped cream, and sprinkle shredded coconut on top.

Coconut lime: Add roasted coconut flakes to prepared pudding together with 2–3 toothpick swirls lime, a dollop of whipped cream and sprinkle shredded coconut on top.

Lemon Cookies

Ingredients:

2 C all-purpose flour
2 t baking powder
½ t salt
10 T softened butter
1 C and 2 T organic sugar
1 large egg yolk
1 large egg
8–12 drops lemon
2 T whole milk

Directions: Preheat oven to 350°F.

In a medium bowl, combine first 7 ingredients. Add lemon to taste. Pour milk into bowl and mix well until dough is formed. Line a baking pan, and scoop cookie dough balls evenly in the pan. Bake at 350°F for 10 minutes. Let cookies cool.

Peppermint Brownies

Directions: Preheat oven to 350°F.

12 oz semi-sweet chocolate chips
¾ C salted butter
1 ¼ C organic sugar
1 T pure vanilla extract
4 large eggs
3 drops peppermint
1 t salt
1 C all purpose flour
1 C chocolate chips (for richer flavor)

Directions:

In a small microwaveable bowl, melt butter and chocolate together. Stir to ensure both melted and incorporated. Pour mixture into a medium size bowl. Add sugar, vanilla, eggs, and mix well. Add salt and stir again. Slowly fold in flour. For extra chocolate flavor, add additional chocolate chips and mix. Lightly dust 9 x 13 baking pan with flour and pour batter evenly into pan. Bake at 350°F for 30 minutes. Let cool for 10 minutes, before cutting.

COOKING

Dressings & Marinades

LIVING

tips

- Essential oils absorb well into meats and make great marinades.
- When making vinegar dressings, pair ingredients.
- Balsamic or red wine vinegar (dark vinegars) pairs with raspberry or strawberry salads, beef, and lamb.
- White wine vinegar, rice, or champagne vinegars (light vinegars) go well with chicken, fish, pears, chunks of grapefruit, mango, or orange.
- Candied nuts and feta cheese go well with both dressings.

Wild Orange Vinaigrette

Ingredients:

1 C extra virgin olive oil
1 t Dijon mustard
½–⅓ C balsamic vinegar
1–2 drops wild orange
2 T mayonnaise
½ C brown sugar
Sea salt
Black pepper to taste
(or 1-2 drops black or pink pepper)

Directions:

Combine ingredients in a food processor or blender until smooth. Store in a glass jar in the fridge for up to 1 month.

This dressing is good on all salads. Try Romaine lettuce, sliced apples, dried cranberries, and toasted sliced almonds.

Cinnamon Spice Dressing

Ingredients:

¼ C olive oil
2 T raw apple cider vinegar
2 drops cinnamon
1 drop clove
⅛ t fresh ground nutmeg
1 small garlic clove, finely minced
¼ t sea salt
⅛ t fresh ground pepper
(or 1 drop either black or pink pepper)

Directions:

Mix all ingredients and place in a jar. Shake well.

Great on a bed of baby spinach. Toss with thinly sliced apples. Top with toasted pine nuts and crumbled goat cheese.

Creamy Cucumber Dill Dressing

Ingredients:

1 seedless cucumber, chopped into chunks
4 T sour cream or plain Greek yogurt
(or a combination of the two)
1 T olive oil
1 T distilled white vinegar
1 drop dill
¼ t garlic powder
Black pepper to taste
(or 1-2 drops black or pink pepper)
Salt to taste

Directions:

Blend ingredients, in a blender, until smooth. Add spices to taste. Chill or serve immediately. Store in the refrigerator for up to a week.

NOTE: Add more sour cream/yogurt for a thicker dressing.

How to Make Wild Fermented Sauerkraut

Raw, unpasteurized sauerkraut delivers healthful probiotics to the digestive tract, increases body alkalinity, and increases nutrition absorption.

To make sauerkraut, you will need a knife, cutting board, large mixing bowl, non-porous crock or Mason jar, and weighted lid.

Chop or shred the cabbage into uniform sizes into a bowl. Two heads of cabbage fill a ½ gallon jar nicely. Add any desired spices (dill, caraway, juniper berry, and/or bay leaves). Add coarse sea salt and mix throughout, using your hands to massage the mixture. The cabbage will begin to produce liquid (brine).

Using a wooden tamper, create an anaerobic environment by removing the air bubbles as you pack the vegetable mixture tightly into a crock or jar. Push until the brine starts to rise to the top of the veggies. Place a saucer or plate on top of the vegetables, covering them as closely to the edges as possible. Alternatively, use outer cabbage leaves to make a seal. Place a weight on top of the packed vegetables. A jar of water works well. Cover completely with a cloth and secure with a rubber band to keep bugs out.

During the first week, tamp the mixture down daily to keep the veggies under the brine. Sometimes it takes a day or two to get the brine to stay above the veggies. This will help prevent mold from forming. Taste it after a week and see if you like it. You can let it ferment as long as you want, but most people prefer 2-4 weeks of fermentation in small batches. When it is too young, it will leave a carbonated feeling on the tongue, which disappears after about a week of fermentation.

The best temperature to ferment sauerkraut is 55–65°F. Put it in a pantry, root cellar, cupboard, or on the kitchen counter. A variation in this temperature is fine, but the best flavors develop within this range. When fermentation is complete, remove the "lid", scrape off the top layer, and enjoy the fresh, healthy, goodness below. Add essential oils after the sauerkraut is fermented.

Note: If mold forms, all is not lost. This is a test of your senses. Scrape off the mold and compost it. If the sauerkraut underneath smells okay, taste it. If it tastes "off," spit it out, and discard the batch!

Fermented Foods

Cortido (Sauerkraut Variation)*

Ingredients:

1 head/about 1000 g Napa cabbage, cored and outer leaves removed, shredded
2 T fine Celtic sea salt
1 C (140g) chopped carrots
1 green apple, peeled, thinly sliced
1 onion, peeled, thinly sliced
1 fresh jalapeño pepper, thinly sliced (deseed for less heat)
1 drop oregano
5 drops lime
Juice of half of a lime

Directions:

In a large non-metal bowl, mix cabbage with sea salt. Use clean hands to really work the salt into the cabbage. Allow to rest for 1–2 hours. The cabbage will wilt and brine (salty liquid) will develop.

Add the carrots, apple, onion, jalapeño, and lime juice to the cabbage. Mix well.

Basic Sauerkraut*

Ingredients:

1 to 1 ½ heads cabbage
1 T sea salt per pound of cabbage
1 onion
2 drops dill or coriander
2–3 T caraway seeds
2 drops lemon to a pint-size container of sauerkraut (after fermentation)

Red Cabbage & Apple Sauerkraut*

Ingredients:

1 to 1 ½ heads red cabbage, finely shredded
2 Granny Smith apples, cored and shredded
¼ C very thinly sliced red onion
1 T salt per pound of cabbage
5 whole peppercorns or 2 drops black pepper
2 drops clove
1 drop cardamom
¼ t coriander seeds
⅛ t cinnamon

Directions:

Combine cabbage, apple, and red onion. Sprinkle with salt and massage. In a small bowl, place the remaining ingredients. Crush with the back of a spoon or mortar and pestle. Add to cabbage mixture and follow basic recipe instructions.

Juniper Berry Sauerkraut*

Ingredients:

1 ½ to 2 heads red or green cabbage, shredded
1 to 1 ½ apples, peeled, cored, and coarsely chopped
1 T caraway seeds
1 drop juniper berry
1 T salt per pound of cabbage

*Follow How to Recipe.

Lemon and Ginger Kombucha

Ingredients:

750mL kombucha (homemade or store bought)
1 drop lemon
1 lemon wedge
1 drop ginger
750mL glass bottle (swing top ones work best)

Directions:

Pour homemade kombucha into a glass jar leaving a 2cm gap between the kombucha and the lid. Add essential oil and lemon wedge. Secure the lid and leave in a dark place to ferment for 2 days, then transfer to the fridge, and enjoy.

tips

Use essential oils to flavor fermented foods after the fermenting process is completed. Add a toothpick-dip of the oil of choice to taste.

Vanilla Orange Kombucha

Ingredients:

½ C sugar
750mL kombucha (homemade or store bought)
1-2 drops wild orange
Vanilla bean
750mL glass bottle (swing top ones work best)

Directions:

Pour the homemade kombucha into a glass jar leaving a 2cm gap between the kombucha and the lid. Add essential oil and a small piece of vanilla bean. Secure the lid and leave in a dark place to ferment for 2 days, then transfer to the fridge, and enjoy.

Try: Grapefruit and a cinnamon stick instead of wild orange and vanilla bean.

Kefir

Kefir is high in enzymes and probiotics and is alkalizing to the body. It stimulates mucosal immune response to protect from microbiological invasion of mucous membranes throughout the body. Kefir contains peptides that may restore normal immune function. Kefir is also good for lactose-intolerant people. The lactose found in milk is converted to lactic acid during the fermentation process.

Ingredients:

1 T milk kefir grains
8–16 oz goat or cow milk (raw, unpasteurized is best)

Directions:

Add kefir grains to raw milk in a jar with a lid. Let sit on the counter, at room temperature, for 24-72 hours, depending on how sour you like it, and how warm the house is. Shake gently a couple times a day, to redistribute the grains. When fermentation is complete, strain the milk and save the kefir grains to make a new batch. Put the strained kefir in a jar with a tight lid. Let sit at room temperature for a few hours to increase fizziness then store in refrigerator.

Blueberry Kefir Smoothie

Ingredients:

Blend together and drink immediately:

1 C blueberries
1 C kefir
2 large handfuls of greens
1 apple, seeded
1 drop lemon

Holiday COOKING

Pumpkin Pie

Ingredients:

- 2 C pureed pumpkin
- 1 large egg
- ¼ C egg whites
- ½ C milk (of choice)
- 3 t melted butter or coconut oil
- ⅓ C brown sugar or honey
- 2 T vanilla extract
- ¼ t ground nutmeg
- 2 drops clove
- 2 drops ginger
- 3 drops cassia or cinnamon
- 1 uncooked pie crust

Directions:

Preheat oven to 350°F. Add pie crust (homemade or store-bought) into a 9" pie pan.

In a food processor, blend ingredients until smooth. Add to pie pan. Bake for 30–45 minutes or until crust is lightly browned and center it set and not too wiggly. Let sit for at least 10 minutes, or until completely cooled. Store in the refrigerator.

Peppermint Bark

Ingredients:

- 1 pkg white almond bark
- 1 pkg chocolate almond bark
- 1 drop peppermint
- 4–8 crushed candy canes or 10–15 round peppermint candies

Directions:

Cover a cookie sheet with parchment paper. In a double boiler, heat chocolate bark until completely melted. Add essential oil and stir well. Carefully pour onto prepared cookie sheet and smooth it out. Place in the freezer. Clean the top of the double boiler. Add the white bark, heating until completely melted. While heating, add the candy to a zip-top bag and crush. Remove the chocolate layer from the freezer and carefully smooth the white bark on top of the chocolate. Top with crushed candy and return cookie sheet to the freezer until set (about 10 minutes).

Break apart and store in air tight containers.

Gingerbread Cookies

Ingredients:

1 ⅓ C buckwheat flour
⅔ C tapioca flour
⅔ C sorghum flour
1 T chia seed meal
1 T flax seed meal
⅓ C coconut palm sugar
½ t baking powder
½ t baking soda
¼ t salt
½ t nutmeg
2 drops cinnamon
2 drops ginger
2 drops clove
½ C coconut oil
¼ C unsweetened applesauce
3 T water
3 T molasses
1 t apple cider vinegar
45 drops liquid-Stevia

Directions: Preheat oven to 325°F

Preheat oven to 350°F. Combine dry ingredients in bowl and whisk. In a separate bowl, combine wet ingredients, including essential oils, until well combined. Add dry to wet ingredients on slow speed until combined. Dust work surface with a little flour and roll dough out to ¼-½" thick.

Cut out shapes with cookie cutters or free style them. Place onto cookie sheets and bake for 12–15 minutes or until done. Remove from oven and let cool. Top with icing if desired.

Cinnamon Hot Chocolate

Ingredients:

4 C chocolate milk
¼ C chocolate, chopped
2 t vanilla extract
1 drop cinnamon
2 t chocolate, shaved
Cinnamon sticks for garnish

Directions:

In a medium-sized saucepan, heat milk, chocolate and vanilla over low heat. Stir constantly until melted. Remove from heat, stir in essential oil, and garnish with a sprinkle of chocolate shavings and a cinnamon stick. Enjoy!

tips

- Create the scent of Christmas by diffusing Holiday Joy.
- Create Christmas pinecones by adding 1–2 drops cassia to a pinecone or spray a bowl of pinecones with Holiday Joy.
- Transform an artificial Christmas tree to a fresh smelling wonder by filling a small glass spray bottle with 20 drops Douglas fir, topped off with water and spray tree often.

Eggnog

Ingredients:

6 large egg yolks
½ C sugar
1 C heavy cream
2 C milk
½ t nutmeg
Pinch of salt
¼ t vanilla extract
1 drop cinnamon

Directions:

Whisk egg yolks and sugar together in a medium bowl until light and creamy. In a saucepan over medium-high heat, combine the cream, milk, nutmeg, and salt. Stir until mixture comes to a low simmer. Temper the milk into the egg mixture (add a big ladle of the hot milk mixture to the egg mixture, whisking vigorously. Repeat until all combined). Once combined, pour the mixture back into the saucepan, on the stove, whisking constantly, until mixture reaches 160°F. Remove from heat and stir in vanilla.

Pour eggnog into a pitcher, add cinnamon, and cover with plastic wrap. Refrigerate until chilled. Serve with whipped cream, if desired.

COOKING

Main Dishes

LIVING

Lemon & Thyme Roasted Chicken

Ingredients:

Whole chicken, giblets removed
4 T olive oil
4 drops lemon
4 drops thyme
Salt and pepper to taste
Sprinkle of dried oregano
1 lemon, sliced
1 onion, sliced

Directions: *Preheat oven to 350°F.*

Mix the oils, salt, and pepper together in a small bowl. Set aside. Place lemon and onion slices in the bottom of a roasting pan, and in the cavity of the chicken. Add a little water, just enough to barely cover the bottom of the pan. Add chicken to roasting pan, breast side up, and baste the chicken with the oil mixture. If there's some leftover, pour in the cavity of the chicken. Sprinkle top of the chicken with a dried oregano.

Cook in preheated oven until the internal temperature reaches 165°F (about 1 hour 45 minutes, depending on the size). Rest chicken at least 10 minutes before slicing.

enjoy

Sesame Orange Chicken

Ingredients:

1½ to 2 pounds chicken breast, cut into bite-size pieces
4 T coconut oil, divided
⅔ C soy sauce
2 inches fresh ginger, chopped
4 cloves garlic, minced
3 T tomato paste
¼ C honey (agave or a liquid sugar of choice)
½ t ground black pepper
Pinch of red pepper flakes
½ C water + 10–20 drops wild orange
1 T sesame seeds

Directions: *Preheat oven to 350°F.*

Heat 2 T coconut oil in a cast iron skillet. Add chicken and saute until beginning to brown on the outside and no longer pink on tne inside. Set aside.

In a medium saucepan, combine 2 T coconut oil and next 7 ingredients. Whisk together over low-medium heat and simmer 5 minutes. Remove from heat and blend until smooth. Transfer back to the pan. Add the water and wild orange mixture. Taste sauce and adjust as needed. Add chicken and stir to coat. Sprinkle with sesame seeds. Serve over spaghetti squash, cauli-rice, or starch of choice.

remember

Certain essential oils go best with certain dishes.

- **Chicken:** basil, bergamot, black pepper, cassia, cilantro, cinnamon, ginger, grapefruit, lemon, lemongrass, lime, rosemary, tangerine, sage, thyme, and wild orange.
- **Fish:** citrus oils, frankincense, lavender, spearmint, peppermint, pink pepper, and black pepper.
- **Red meats:** basil, black pepper, cassia, cilantro, cinnamon, clove, coriander, fennel, ginger, grapefruit, lemongrass, lime, marjoram, oregano, wild orange, rosemary, tangerine, and thyme.
- **Vegetables:** basil, black pepper, cardamom, cilantro, fennel, ginger, grapefruit, lemon, lemongrass, lime, and pink pepper.

Perfect Peppered Burger

Ingredients:

1 pound ground beef
Salt to taste
1 drop pink or black pepper (per patty)

Directions:

Preheat outdoor grill to high heat and lightly oil grate. Form ground burger into 4 patties, approximately ¾" t hick and salt to liking.

Place patties on the prepared grill. When meat juices appear on the top of the burgers, add essential oil on each patty. Cover and cook 6 to 8 minutes or to desired doneness.

Happy Spring Rolls

Ingredients:

Dressing:
4 oz rice wine vinegar
2 oz light sesame oil
2 T raw coconut aminos
1 T Mirin
3 drop ginger

Spring Rolls:
6 brown rice spring roll wrappers
1 red pepper, thinly sliced
1 carrot, julienned
1 cucumber, julienned
1 avocado, cut into slices
½ C cilantro, chopped (or toothpick swirl cilantro)

Directions:

Dip wrapper completely in water, and spread out flat on plate. Layer with vegetables, avocado, and cilantro, roll up tightly, folding ends in, while rolling up.

Combine dressing ingredients and serve with spring rolls.

Chicken Alfredo Stuffed Shells

Ingredients:

2 lbs chicken, cooked and shredded
12 oz jumbo shells, partially boiled and cooled
2 jars alfredo sauce
2 drops oregano
Salt to taste
1 drop pink or black pepper
Shredded parmesan

Directions: Preheat oven to 350°F.

Add shredded chicken, alfredo sauce, oregano and salt into a skillet. Add essential oil and mix to combine, adjust seasons to taste. Spread about ¼ of the mixture onto the bottom of a 9x13 baking dish. Fill each shell with remaining mixture and line in the baking dish. Sprinkle cheese over the shells.

Bake for 20 minutes and serve!

Veggie Pita Pizzas

Ingredients:

2 whole grain pita rounds
3–4 T Neufchatel cheese (or cream cheese)
1 drop basil
½ C fresh baby spinach
⅓ red pepper, thinly slices
1–2 mushrooms, thinly sliced
¼ C frozen sweet corn, thawed
½ C mozzarella cheese
⅛ t garlic power

Directions: Preheat oven or toaster oven to 450°F.

In a small bowl, stir basil into Neufchatel cheese. Spread mixture on both pitas. Layer on spinach, red pepper, mushrooms, and corn. Top with cheese and a sprinkle of garlic powder. Bake on cookie sheet or directly on oven rack until cheese is melted. Slice if desired and enjoy!

French Dip Pot Roast

Delish for dipping! Perfect for dinner!

Ingredients:

3 pounds roast
½ C soy sauce
1 drop thyme
1 drop rosemary
1 t garlic powder
1 bay leaf
2 C water
2 drops black or pink pepper
4–8 large romaine lettuce leaves, rinsed (or bread rolls)

Directions:

Place roast in a slow cooker. Add essential oils to soy sauce and pour over the roast. Add garlic powder, bay leaf, and water, and cook for 5–6 hours on high until meat is tender. Remove and rest roast. Reserve and pour juice into small dishes. Slice roast into thin slices. Pile meat onto lettuce leaf, and roll up burrito style, or place a roll. Serve with au jus for dipping.

Makes 6–8 servings

Acapulco Chicken

Marinade for boneless skinless chicken

Ingredients:

6 oz can pineapple juice
Zest and juice of 1 large orange
½ drop wild orange
1 good pinch of saffron, rubbed between fingers
4 large cloves garlic, finely minced
1" fresh ginger
1 drop cardamom
4-6 chicken pieces, pounded to even thickness

Directions:

Combine marinade in a glass bowl, add chicken, and marinate at least a ½ hour. Grill chicken until done. Add remaining marinade to pan on stove and bring to a boil, to serve with chicken, if desired. Note: This had raw chicken in it, so it **must** be boiled for a minute or two; Or boil it, and let it reduce until the chicken is done.

Serve with fresh cut pineapple pieces (grilled is amazing too!) and sliced green onions (if desired).

Serve with long grain rice cooked with 1–2 drops wild orange and the zest of an orange added.

Broccoli Beef

Ingredients:

½ C soy sauce
3 T water
2 T brown sugar
2 T cornstarch
1–2 drops ginger
1 ½ pounds thin sliced steak
2 C small broccoli florets

Directions:

Combine first 5 ingredients in a small bowl. Pour mixture over the sliced steak. Let marinate for at least 10 minutes. Preheat pan, and stir fry the broccoli to desired doneness then set aside. Allow pan to get hot again, and add the meat in batches, with olive oil. Cook about 5 minutes, stirring occasionally to brown all sides. Once all the meat is cooked, add the remaining marinade and broccoli to the pan, and stir. Cook until the mixture thickens. Serve over rice or starch of choice.

Pork Chops with Orange Sauce

Ingredients:

6 loin pork chops ¾ inch thick
1 T butter
1 medium onion diced
1 T flour
2 cubes bullion
1 C hot water
½ t minced parsley
1 T dry mustard
1 t salt
1 drop black or pink pepper
1 drop peppermint
1 drop lemon
3 drops wild orange (or more to taste, 1 drop at a time)
½ C water or orange juice

Directions:

Over medium heat, brown both sides of all the pork chops, and set aside. Add butter to pan, melt and saute onions for about 5 minutes or until soft. Dissolve bullion into hot water and set aside. Stir flour into onions, then slowly add water bullion mixture, stirring constantly. Cook for 5 minutes, then add parsley, salt, pepper, oils, and ½ cup of water or orange juice. Place chops in liquid, cover, and cook over low heat for 20–30 minutes, or until meat is 135°F internal temperature. Let rest 5–10 minutes before serving.

Heavenly Salad

Ingredients:

1 head romaine
½ head red-leaf lettuce
½ C red onion, chopped
2 medium artichokes, chopped
½ C sun-dried tomatoes, chopped
½ C olives (green, black or Kalamata)

Dressing:
1 lemon, zested and juiced
¼ C white wine vinegar
3–4 drops lemon
⅓ C extra virgin olive oil
Salt
Pepper (1-2 drops black or pink pepper)

Directions:

Add dressing ingredients to jar with a tight-fitting lid and shake vigorously to combine.

Top salad with some Parmesan Reggiano. Serve salad dressed and/or dressing on the side.

Celery Seed Salad Dressing

Ingredients:

½ C extra virgin olive oil
2 T balsamic vinegar
1 t apple cider vinegar
½ small onion, peeled and quartered
1 T raw honey
1 drop celery seed
A dash of garlic powder
Himalayan salt, to taste
Ground black pepper, to taste (black or pink pepper)

Directions:

Combine ingredients in blender until smooth. Add salt and pepper to taste. Refrigerate and shake before use.

Warm Roasted Butternut Squash & Quinoa Salad

Ingredients:

¾ C dried cranberries
¾ C baby spinach leaves
1 butternut squash, peeled and cubed
½ t coarse salt
½ large sweet onion, thinly sliced
4 C red quinoa, cooked and kept warm
1 ½ C wheat berries, cooked kept warm

Dressing:
1 T fresh lemon juice
1 T raw honey
1 T olive oil
Large pinch of salt
1 toothpick swirl black pepper

Directions:

Place the spinach and dried cranberries in a large bowl. Cover and set aside. Combine the dressing ingredients in a small bowl and whisk until combined. Set aside. Preheat the oven to 425°F. Line a cookie sheet with foil or parchment paper. Toss the squash with olive oil and salt. Spread evenly on a cookie sheet. Roast squash, in the top ⅓ of the oven for 15–20 minutes, until tender and golden brown. Remove from oven.

While the squash is roasting, add ½ T olive oil in a small saute pan and heat to medium/high. Add onion and saute for 2 minutes. Reduce heat to medium and saute for 5–6 minutes until lightly caramelized.

Combine the warm squash, onions, quinoa, and wheat berries to the bowl of spinach and cranberries. Toss together to slightly wilt the spinach. Add the dressing and toss until well-coated. Serve warm.

tips

- Use essential oils to infuse olive oil and make seasoned croutons.
- See Spiced Almond recipe in Snacks to add crunch to salads.
- Essential oils are a fantastic addition to pasta salads.
- Heat can break down certain components of essential oils. Whenever possible, add them after the heating process is complete.

Waldorf Salad

Ingredients:

5 apples, medium diced (soaked in On Guard® to prevent browning)
5 oz celery, small diced
5 oz grapes, halved
4 oz walnuts, course chopped
⅔ C mayo or plain Greek yogurt
7 drops lemon
Salt and pepper to taste

Directions:

Drain apples and pat dry. Combine may and essential oils together in the bottom of a medium to larger bowl. Add apples, celery, grapes, and walnuts to dressing and mix throughly.

Optional add-ins: mini marshmallows, raisins, dried cranberries, dried pineapple, red onion, cooked chicken or turkey, and/or broccoli.

Peach Jerk Sausage Salad with Citrus Dressing

Ingredients:

11 oz package peach jerk sausage (or flavored sausage of choice)
5 oz baby arugula
2 oranges or 4 clementines, peeled and sliced
1 C sugar snap peas, trimmed and thinly sliced
1 small jicama, peeled, cut into matchstick sized pieces
½ small red onion, thinly sliced

Dressing:
2 T freshly squeezed orange juice
2 T freshly squeezed lemon or lime juice
½ t kosher salt
¼ t ground cumin
1 drop black or pink pepper
¼ C extra-virgin olive oil
1 drop wild orange

Directions:

Dressing: Combine ingredients in a small bowl, whisking in olive oil until well combined. Set aside.

Cook the sausage according to the package instruction. Remove from heat, drain, and slice. Combine arugula, oranges, snap peas, jicama, and onion in a large bowl, top with sausage. Drizzle with salad dressing and toss to coat.

Marinara Sauce

Ingredients:

2 pounds Roma tomatoes, halved
1 onion, sliced
4 garlic cloves
Olive oil
Sea salt
Pepper
1 drop basil
1 toothpick oregano

Directions: Preheat oven to 350° F.

Place tomatoes, onions, and garlic on baking sheet. Add a generous amount of salt, pepper, and olive oil. Cook for 60–90 minutes or until tomatoes and onions begin to darken around the edges. Remove from oven and transfer to food processor or blender. Pulse until sauce reaches desired consistency. Add essential oils and stir.

Southwest Beef Marinade

Ingredients:

¼ C fresh cilantro, chopped
¼ C olive oil
¼ C lemon or lime juice
2 t salt
1 t cumin
1 t fresh garlic, minced
5 drops black pepper
7 drops lemon

Directions:

Combine all ingredients. Marinate beef for at least 1 hour in the refrigerator. Bring beef to room temperature before grilling. Delicious when served with a side of homemade guacamole.

Wild Orange Strawberry Jam

Ingredients:

⅔ C granulated sugar
2 T instant pectin
1 ⅔ C prepared strawberries
2–4 drops wild orange

Directions:

To prepare strawberries, wash in lemon, hull, and cut into small pieces. Mash with potato masher. Combine sugar and pectin in medium sized bowl, add prepared fruit, and stir to incorporate, add essential oils, and stir for 3 minutes. Pour into clean and sterilized jars, let rest for 30 minutes. Add lids. Store for up to 3 weeks in the refrigerator or 1 year in the freezer.

Other flavors to try: Peaches and ginger, peaches and cinnamon, or strawberries and lime.

Pizza Sauce

Ingredients:

6 oz can organic tomato paste
½ red onion, chopped
1 shallot, sliced
2 cloves garlic, minced
2 drops basil
½–1 drop oregano
1 t sea salt
2 T raw honey

Directions:

Combine ingredients in a blender until smooth. Add sauce to a pot, bring to a boil and simmer for 30–40 minutes. Use to top 1 large pizza crust.

tips

- Make a sweet glaze for chicken or fish by adding essential oils to honey and brushing on, before baking.
- Add lemon to homemade hollandaise sauce.
- Use essential oils to make a honey dip for cooked chicken wings.
- Make herbed butters for steaks by adding favorite savory oils to whipped butter.

Barbecue Sauce

Ingredients:

15 oz tomato sauce
¼ C apple cider vinegar
1 ½ T mustard
1 T lemon juice
1 T hickory liquid smoke
½ T sea salt
1 t garlic powder
1 t onion powder
1 t molasses
¼ C brown sugar
2–3 drops black or pink pepper
1 drop lemon

Directions:

Blend the ingredients in a blender on high for 1 minute. Transfer to a saucepan and heat. Replace in any dish calling for barbecue sauce.

enjoy!

LIVING

Warm Spiced Sugar

Ingredients:

2 T coarse cane sugar
1 drop cinnamon
1 drop cardamom
1 drop black or pink pepper
1 drop wild orange
1 drop clove
1 T salt

Directions:

Blend and reserve in a glass jar with a lid.

To Use: Sprinkle into tea, coffee, oatmeal, cookies, and/or toast.

Asian Seasoning Salt

Ingredients:

2 T sea salt
2 drops ginger
2 drops lemongrass
1 drop basil

Directions:

Blend and reserve in a glass jar with a lid.

To Use: Sprinkle and rub into chicken, pork, vegetables, and/or on salad.

Pesto

Ingredients:

3 C basil leaves, loosely packed
3 small or 2 large garlic cloves
¼ C pine nuts
⅔–¾ C olive oil
1 toothpick dip black or pink pepper
1 toothpick dip basil
1 toothpick dip lemon
½ C freshly grated Parmesan cheese

Directions:

Combine all ingredients in a food processor and chop till well-blended and has reached desired consistency. If using a blender, pulse-blend ½ at a time until desired consistency. Store in refrigerator in an air-tight container. Excellent on pasta, fish, or chicken.

enjoy!

Italian Seasoning Salt

Ingredients:

2 T sea salt
1 drop each: rosemary, basil, oregano, and thyme

Directions:

Blend and reserve in a glass jar with a lid.

To Use: Sprinkle on favorite pasta, soup, sauce, and/or meat as a rub.

Avocado Salsa

Ingredients:

6 medium roma tomatoes, seeded and diced
1 C red onion, chopped
1 large or 2 small jalapeños, seeded and chopped (¼ C)
3 medium avocados, peeled, cored, and diced
3 ½ T olive oil
3 T fresh lime juice
1 clove garlic, finely minced
½ t salt (more or less to taste)
½ C loosely packed cilantro leaves, chopped
Toothpick swirl cilantro
1-2 drops black or pink pepper
1-2 drops lime

Directions:

Place red onion in a strainer or sieve and rinse under cool water to remove harsh bite. Drain well. Add to a mixing bowl along with tomatoes, jalapeños, and avocados.

In a separate small mixing bowl, whisk together olive oil, lime juice, garlic, salt, and essential oils, until mixture is fully incorporated. Pour over avocado mixture, add cilantro leaves, then gently toss to evenly coat. Serve with tortilla chips or over Mexican entrees.

Tip: leave seeds and ribs in jalapeño to bring the heat!

Fresh Caprese Skewers

Ingredients:

½ C cherry tomato halves
¼ C mozzarella cheese ball halves
2 T balsamic vinegar
2–3 T olive oil
1–2 drop basil
Fresh basil leaves for garnish

Directions:

Combine olive oil and basil essential oil. Thread tomatoes and cheese onto mini skewers and drizzle with balsamic vinegar and oil mixture, top with fresh basil.

Clean-Eating Mac and Cheese

Ingredients:

½ C canned pumpkin puree
½ C plain Greek yogurt
8 oz package gluten-free pasta (pasta of choice)
2–4 drops black or pink pepper
⅛ t garlic powder
⅛ t paprika
¼ t salt
½ C shredded sharp cheddar cheese
2 t breadcrumb brand

Directions: Preheat at 350°F

Boil pasta according to package directions. In a separate bowl, combine ingredients, cooked pasta, and stir until incorporated. Spoon mixture into greased muffin tins. Top with breadcrumbs and bake for 10 minutes until crispy.

Guacamole

Ingredients:

2–3 ripe avocados
¼ C diced red onion
¼ C chopped cilantro
¼ C chopped tomato
Garlic powder to taste
Sea salt to taste
4–6 drops lime

Directions:

Mash avocados and mix ingredients together. Adjust seasonings and serve.

Italian Bread Dip

Ingredients:

¼ C olive oil
1–3 T balsamic vinegar to taste
½ t Italian seasoning
1 T Parmesan cheese
1–3 drops oregano
1 drop basil
1 drop rosemary
1 drop thyme

Directions:

Gently mix together all ingredients in a bowl large enough to dip into. Dip any Italian-style bread in and enjoy!

Zucchini Mushroom Pasta

Ingredients:

1-pound zucchini, julienned
1-pound mushrooms, sliced thin
3 T olive oil
1 C green onions, sliced thinly
2 cloves garlic, minced
1–2 toothpick dips basil, to taste
1 toothpick dip black or pink pepper
½ t sea salt
3 T butter, softened
¼ t sea salt and pepper (to taste)
2 t parsley
1 ½ C grated Parmesan cheese, divided
1 pound noodles

Directions:

Cook pasta in a large saucepan. In a large skillet over medium heat, saute onions until tender. Add garlic and cook another minute. Add zucchini and cook until fork tender. Season with salt and pepper, add mushrooms, and saute until tender. Remove from heat. When pasta is done, drain and put in serving bowl. Add essential oil to butter; toss with warm pasta, parsley, green onion, and ¾ cup grated Parmesan cheese. Top with remaining freshly grated Parmesan cheese.

tips

- Use a produce rinse for healthier and fresher tasting fruit, berries, and vegetables, including greens. Fill a clean glass or metal bowl with water. Add 1 T white vinegar and 2–3 drops lemon. Rinse produce and place on clean paper towels or cotton cloth to dry.
- For oven-roasted veggies, add your favorite essential oils to taste to olive oil. Add salt and pepper until you like the flavor. Pour oil mixture over veggies and toss to cover. Spread out on cookie sheet and roast just until tender. Serve.

Rosemary Garlic Mashed Potatoes

Ingredients:

5 pounds Yukon gold potatoes, peeled and diced
1 ½ t salt
1 t garlic powder
¾ heavy cream
6 T butter
3 T milk
1–2 drops rosemary, to taste
1 drop black or pink pepper

Directions:

Peel, dice, and boil the potatoes for 20–25 minutes or until soft. Drain potatoes and place in a bowl with butter. Allow butter to melt then add cream. Mash potatoes until desired consistency, adding milk as needed. Stir in essential oils, garlic, and salt to taste. Serve warm.

Sweet & Spicy Yogurt Topping

Ingredients:

⅔ C plain yogurt
1 t honey
½ to 1 drop cinnamon
¼ C granola or chopped nuts
Sea salt to taste

Directions:

Mix together and serve over yogurt.

Additional oil suggestions: lime, lemon, grapefruit, On Guard®, or get creative and try something new.

LIVING

Wild Orange Smoothie

Ingredients:

¾ C vanilla yogurt
¾ C skim milk (coconut milk or almond milk)
3–4 mandarin oranges or 1 large orange
1–2 drops wild orange
½ t vanilla extract
12–15 ice cubes

Directions:

Combine ingredients in a blender until smooth. Blend longer to break up extra pulp from the oranges.

Healthy Shamrock Shake

Ingredients:

1 banana, peeled
1 avocado, peeled and cubed
2 C light coconut milk
4 drops (or more) peppermint
4 drops organic liquid Stevia
1 C ice

Directions:

Place ingredients in a blender on high for 2 minutes until smooth. Top with coconut whipped cream, dark chocolate shavings, and strawberries. Serve and enjoy!

Berry Citrus Smoothie

Ingredients:

1 banana
2 C frozen mixed berries
1 C frozen mango
1 medium avocado, peeled and cubed
3 T raw hemp seeds
2 T chia seeds
1 scoop Greens
4 C water
2 drops wild orange
2 drops lime
Optional: 1 scoop Fiber

Directions:

Blend until smooth. Use organic fruits for optimal taste and health benefits. Serves 2–4, Enjoy!

Lavender Blueberry Raspberry Smoothie

Ingredients:

6 ice cubes
2 C almond milk
1 C frozen blueberries
1 C frozen raspberries
½–1 drop lavender
2 t chia seeds

Directions:

Blend all ingredients, in a blender, adding more milk if desired. 1–2 servings.

tips

- A single scoop of Protein or Vegan Protein offers 21 grams of protein; 42% of the daily value based on a 2,000 calorie diet, with only 1 gram of total sugar!
- Add extra nutrition to smoothies by adding any, all, or some of the following:
  - Ground flaxseed
  - Chia seeds
  - Coconut oil
  - Protein powder
  - Fiber powder
  - Green powder
- When blending, put liquid in first, followed by Greens, and chunks of fruit and ice.

Simple Veggie Smoothie

Ingredients:

Blend together:
2 C kale
1 C chopped tomato or grape tomatoes
¾ C chopped cucumber
1 toothpick swirl of pink or black pepper
1–2 C water, as desired for consistency
1 C ice
Dash salt

Paradise Smoothie

Ingredients:

Blend together:
½ C coconut milk
1 toothpick swirl lime
1 C kale
1 C spinach
1 C chopped pineapple
½ C frozen mango
4 frozen strawberries
1 banana
Water or ice, as needed for consistency

basic formula

2 C liquid base
2 C leafy greens
3 C fresh or frozen fruit
Essential oils to taste
Water and/or ice for consistency

LIVING

COOKING Snacks

Orange Creamsicle Cheesecake Fruit Dip

Ingredients:

16 oz cream OR neufchatel cheese, softened to room temperature
⅔ C vanilla Greek yogurt
6 T granulated sugar
2 t vanilla extract
4–6 drops wild orange
¼ t salt

Directions: Preheat oven to 350° F

In a large mixing bowl, beat the cream cheese on medium/high for about 2 minutes, until very smooth and fluffy. Scrape down the sides of the bowl as needed.

Add yogurt and continue to beat for another 1–2 minutes.

Add sugar, vanilla, essential oil, and salt; beat 1–2 minutes more until very smooth and creamy.

Makes about 3 cups. Serve with assorted fruits, cookies, or pretzels, as desired.

Lavender Lemon Cookies

Ingredients:

1 box lemon cake mix
½ C unsalted butter, melted
1 egg
8 drops lemon
½ C lavender colored candy melts (could also use white)
1–2 drops lavender

Directions: Preheat oven to 350° F

Grease a cookie sheet. In a large mixing bowl, combine cake mix, butter, egg and essential oil. Mix until combined. Using hands, roll out golf-ball-sized rounds. Place 1" apart on cookie sheet. While baking, place the candy melts in a microwave safe bowl and heat for 45 seconds. Stir until completely melted (microwave in 10-second increments, if needed). Add 1 drop lavender and taste, adding another drop if needed (while it may taste strong, remember the lemon cookie will balance this out). Set aside to cool slightly.

Remove the cookies from the oven and allow to sit on the cookie sheet for another 5–6 minutes. Using thumb or forefinger, gently press an indent or well into the center of each cookie. Using a small spoon, carefully place a teaspoon of the melted candy into the "well" of each cookie. Using the back of a spoon to smooth out the candy. Allow to cool completely until the candy has hardened.

White Chocolate Lemon Cashew Bites

Ingredients:

Lemon-Cashew Bites:
- 1 ¾ C cashew flour or almond flour
- 1 T lemon juice
- 1 T lemon zest (1 large lemon)
- 3 drops lemon
- 1 t vanilla extract
- 1 T coconut oil, melted
- 1 T coconut nectar (or liquid sweetener of choice)
- Pinch of salt

White Chocolate Coating:
- 4 T melted cacao butter
- 3 T raw coconut butter
- 1 T coconut nectar + 5 drops stevia (or an extra 1 T coconut nectar)
- 1 t vanilla extract

Directions:

Lemon-Cashew Bites: Add ingredients to food processor and pulse until combined. It should have a thick dough-like consistency, but not be too sticky or wet.

Roll the mixture into small balls. Place on parchment lined cookie sheet in the freezer.

White Chocolate Coating: Gently melt the cacao and coconut butter together, over a double boiler. Once melted, remove from heat, and add vanilla and sweetener.

Set aside to thicken slightly, at room temperature, stirring occasionally.

Dip each bite in coating mixture, until completely covered. Scoop out and tap to remove excess coating. Place on parchment lined cookie sheet and return to the freezer, until solid. Repeat coating dip, if desired.

Lemon Fruit Dip

Ingredients:

1 package cream cheese, softened
1 C sour cream
⅓ C sugar
2 t vanilla extract
1–2 drops lemon

Directions:

Mix ingredients with until smooth. Serve with fresh fruit. Store in a tightly sealed container in the refrigerator, up to 2 days.

COOKING

Soups

Nourishing Soup

Ingredients:

2-pounds bone-in chicken
1 ½-gallon filtered water
1-pound carrots, sliced
2 C winter squash, peeled and cubed
2-3 C vegetables; shredded cabbage, sliced mushrooms, peas, corn etc.
1 bunch chives, finely chopped
1 T + 1 t sea salt
2–3 drops lemongrass or basil, or a combination of both
½–1 drop ginger, to taste
1 clove garlic, minced

Directions:

Place chicken, water and sea salt into a large stockpot. Cook for 45 minutes on medium heat. Remove chicken from pot and cool slightly. When cool enough to handle, shred the chicken and discard the bones.

Add vegetables, and simmer until tender, stirring occasionally. Return chicken to the pot.

Add essential oils and garlic. Stir to combine. Taste and adjust as needed. Serve, garnished with green onions or chives.

Roasted Butternut Squash Soup

Ingredients:

¼ C medium onion, diced
¼ C celery, diced
¼ C carrot, diced
3 C butternut squash, peeled & cubed
2–3 C vegetable stock
½ C almond milk or milk of choice
1 t salt
½ t black pepper
2 drops cardamom
2 drops cinnamon

Directions:

Roast first 4 ingredients in 350 °F oven; when browned, add to saucepan. Add 2 cups stock, milk, salt and pepper. Bring to a simmer. Carefully puree until smooth. Add more stock, if needed, for desired consistency. Return to saucepan and add essential oils. Adjust seasoning as needed. Serve warm.

tips

- It has been found that smelling essential oils helps curb the appetite. Every few hours, just take a sniff of a savory essential oil and trick the brain into feeling satiated.
- Flavor Asian dishes with lemongrass, lemon, and ginger.
- Remember, less is more. Use the toothpick dip and swirl method. Adding more is much easier than wasting an entire dish.
- Flavor Italian dishes with basil, marjoram, oregano, rosemary, and thyme essential oils.

· Don't be intimidated; just realize that a drop goes a LONG way.

· Whenever possible, start with a toothpick swirl and taste the dish. Increase in small increments, until desired flavor is achieved.

Spiced Lentil Soup

Ingredients:

2 C onion, diced
2 large garlic cloves, minced
1–2 drops turmeric
1 drop cumin
1 toothpick swirl cinnamon
1 toothpick swirl cardamom
15 oz can diced tomatoes with juice
15 oz can coconut milk
¾ C uncooked red lentils, rinsed
3 ½ C low-sodium vegetable broth
½ t fine sea salt or to taste
1–2 drops black or pink pepper to taste
Red pepper flakes or cayenne pepper to taste
5 oz package baby spinach
2 t fresh lime juice or more to taste

Directions:

In a large pot, saute onion and garlic over medium heat for 4 to 5 minutes until softened.

Add tomatoes (with juice), coconut milk, lentils, broth, salt, and essential oils. Add red pepper flakes or cayenne, if using. Stir to combine. Increase heat to high and bring to a boil.

Once it boils, reduce and simmer, uncovered for 18-22 minutes until the lentils are tender.

Turn heat to low and stir in spinach until wilted. Add lime juice to taste. Stir in the essential oils until combined. Continue cooking for about 1 minute until fragrant.

Taste and adjust as needed. Ladle into bowls and serve with toasted bread and lime wedges.

enjoy!

Thai Soup

Ingredients:

1 C uncooked basmati rice
2 T unsalted butter
1 pound medium shrimp, peeled (or try chicken or tofu)
Kosher salt
2 cloves garlic, minced
1 onion, diced
1 red bell pepper, diced
1 T freshly grated ginger
1 drop ginger
2 T red curry paste
2 (12 oz) cans unsweetened coconut milk
4 C vegetable stock
2 drops black or pink pepper
2 drops lemon
Juice and zest of 1 lime
2 T fresh cilantro, chopped

Directions:

Cook basmati rice in a saucepan following package directions; set aside. Melt butter in a large Dutch oven over medium-high heat. Add shrimp and season with salt. Cook, stirring occasionally, until pink. Remove shrimp to a small bowl and set aside.

Add all vegetables to the Dutch oven. Cook, stirring occasionally, until tender about 3–4 minutes. Stir in ginger until fragrant. Mix in curry paste until well combined. Gradually whisk in coconut milk, vegetable stock, and essential oils; cook, stirring gently until fully incorporated. Bring to a boil; reduce heat and simmer until thickened. Stir in rice, shrimp, lime juice and zest, and cilantro. Season with salt and pepper to taste.

Garnish with lime wedges and cilantro. Serve and enjoy!

DIY Children

Bathtub Crayons

Ingredients:

Glycerin soap
Essential oils
Natural dye (soap making colors)
Silicone mold

Directions:

Cut glycerin soap into 1 oz pieces. Melt in a microwave-safe bowl for 15 seconds. Continue heating in 3-second increments until fully melted.

Add 1–2 drops essential oils per 2 oz of soap. Add dye color. Carefully pour into the mold until it's almost full. Avoid overfilling.

Repeat for additional crayon colors, and scents. Let dry in the mold for 24 hours.

Remove and store in airtight container. Allow to fully dry after bath time, before sealing container.

Oobleck Slime

Ingredients:

2 C cornstarch
1-1½ C water
3-6 drops essential oils (of choice)

Directions:

Combine essential oils with 1 cup water. Add cornstarch to a medium bowl and slowly add the water. Add additional water to have the correct consistency.

Diffuser Bracelets

Ingredients:

1 mm craft stretchy cord
Non polished lava stone beads
Craft beads for jewelry
Scissors
Essential oils

Directions:

Select craft and lava beads to make a bracelet. Select enough beads to encircle the wrist, plus a few extra beads. Lay out the beads in the order to be added on the cord.

Measure out cording. Double what the final size will need to be, just to make sure you have enough cording.

Note: This cord will stretch out over time, so do not make it too loose or it will not fit after time.

Tape one end of the cord to the table and carefully string lava and craft beads onto the other end. When the bracelet is finished, untape the other end and carefully tie the two ends together.

The more lava beads that are in the finished bracelet, the more area to place essential oils on.

Moon Sand

Ingredients:

8 C flour
1 C vegetable oil
8-10 drops essential oils

Directions:

In a large bowl, combine ingredients. Mix with hands until well-combined, adding more vegetable oil if needed, until a moldable consistency is achieved. Store in an airtight container.

Clay Diffuser

Ingredients:

Air drying clay
Rolling pin
Cookie cutters
Thin thread for hanging
Beads (for decoration)

Directions:

Separate a chunk of air drying clay and roll it out to 1–2cm thick. Use cookie cutters to cut shapes in the clay. Wiggle the cutter a little to ensure it is fully cut. Use a skewer to make a hole to hang the clay diffuser. Leave it to dry for the recommended time on the clay packet. When fully dry, add a string with beads or other decorations, if using. Add essential oils and enjoy a portable scent.

Bubbles

Ingredients:

1 C warm water
1 t sugar
2 T On Guard® foaming hand wash

Directions:

Mix sugar into warm water until dissolved. Add hand soap and stir to combine. Use recycled bubble wands, or make some from pipe cleaners.

Sensory Rice

Ingredients:

2 C rice
1-5 drops lavender (drops depend on intensity)
Purple food coloring
White vinegar
Ziptop bag
Pompoms
Spoons/scoops

Directions:

Add rice to zip-top bag. Drop lavender, food coloring, and few drops vinegar.

Mix the rice inside the bad. Until fully colored and scented. Pour into a small plastic tub with pompoms and spoons/scoops for quiet calming play for children.

See *Aromatherapy Playdough* for additional color/scented ideas.

Aromatherapy Play Dough

Ingredients:

2 C flour
2 C colored water
2 t cream of tarter
¾ C salt
1 T olive oil
10-15 drops essential oils

Directions:

Combine all ingredients, except essential oils in a large saucepan and stir until well combined. Place over medium heat, and stir until it forms a ball. Don't overcook, as it will lead the dough to dry out. Remove from heat and cool on parchment paper.

Once cooled, add essential oils, starting with 10 drops until desired aroma, kneading the oils into the dough.

Store in airtight containers.

Try these color/aroma choices:

Lemon– yellow	Balance®– blue
Lavender– purple	Lime– green
On Guard®– red	Wild orange– orange

Monster Repellent Spray

Ingredients:

20 drops lavender or Serenity®

Directions:

In a 2 oz glass spray bottle, add essential oils, and top off with water. Create a cute "monster" label and spray when needed. Shake before each use.

DIY

Gift Giving

Chapped Lip Balm

Ingredients:

1 T honey
2 T beeswax
1 T shea butter
2–5 drops spearmint
Optional: natural dye color
Lip balm tubes

Directions:

Heat first 3 ingredients and dye color, if using, on medium/low heat until melted. Remove from heat, add essential oil, and quickly pour into containers.

Additional flavor ideas: wild orange, peppermint, tangerine, lime, and/or lemon.

Glitter Body Spray

Ingredients:

3 t carrier oil
2 t gold mica
4 drops frankincense
(or essential oil of choice)
Distilled water

Directions:

Add to a 4 oz glass bottle, add carrier oil, mica, and essential oils. Top off with distilled water. Shake well (and before every use). Spray on body, face, and/or hair.

Bubble Bath

Ingredients:

½ C castile soap
¼ C vegetable glycerin
15 drops lemon
5 drops lavender

Directions:

Combine all ingredients in a 8 oz plastic squeeze bottle and top off with water. Shake well before use.

Scented Ornaments

Ingredients:

1 C baking soda
½ C cornstarch
½ C water
10-15 drops of cassia, Siberian fir, Holiday Joy, wild orange, or peppermint
Optional: Glitter and/or food coloring

Directions:

In a saucepan, heat first 3 ingredients over medium heat. Bring to a boil, stirring continuously. Once mixture has thickened into a dough-like consistency, remove from heat and mix in essential oil(s) and add glitter or food coloring, if using. Roll dough out and cut with cookie cutters. Use skewer or straw to make a hole in the top of each shape. Cool completely. String twine or ribbon to hang the ornament.

Siberian Citrus Candle

Ingredients:

13 oz soy wax
Candle dye (if desired)
Wick
Popsicle sticks
5 drops lavender
5 drops grapefruit
5 drops Citrus Bliss®
5 drops Siberian fir
Glass jar

Directions:

In a double boiler, melt wax slowly. Once melted, add colors, if using. Put wick in the center of the jar, and wrap the top of the wick around the popsicle stick to hold it up. Let the wax cool, about 30 minutes then add essential oils, and stir to combine.

Carefully pour wax into a jar and let sit at least 24 hours, before lighting.

tips

Mix favorite essential oils in a roller bottle to create signature scents and top off with a carrier oil. Great for gift giving.

Mood-Boosting Bath Salt

Ingredients:

1 C sea salt or Epsom salt
½ T jojoba oil (or carrier oil)
10 drops wild orange
10 drops grapefruit
10 drops tangerine

Directions:

Add essential oils to jojoba oil. Add Epsom salt to 16 oz glass jar and carefully combine oil mixture into salt until fully distributed.

To Use: Add a few tablespoons to tub while filling with warm water.

Additional oil ideas: Deep Blue® or AromaTouch® for a sore muscle soak. Serenity® for relaxing or preparing for bed.

Bath Bomb

Ingredients:

1 C baking soda
⅔ C Epsom salt
½ t mica (color on choice)
40 drops frankincense
10 drops myrrh
1 T coconut oil
½ C citric acid
Witch hazel
Bath Bomb Molds

Directions:

Combine baking soda, Epsom salt, and mica in a large bowl until well incorporated. Add essential oils and citric acid, combining until fully combined. Spray witch hazel over the mixture (it will get fizzy) until mixture can hold its shape. Once it can hold its shape, carefully pack into molds. Pack tightly. Keep in the mold for at least 24 hours, and completely dry. Gently remove from the mold and store in a cool dry place.

To Use: Add to bath water and soak!

Makeup Remover

Ingredients:

1 bag cotton balls/pads (for facial use)
2 T carrier oil
1 T witch hazel
4 drops lavender

Directions:

In a 4 oz glass bottle with dropper, ingredients, and shake well.

To Use: Add mixture to cotton pads. Wipe to remove makeup, leaving a clean and fresh sensation.

Garden

Plant Pest Control

Ingredients:

2 T castile soap
10 drops peppermint
10 drops lavender
5 drops cedarwood
5 drops lemongrass

Directions:

Combine all ingredients in a 16 oz glass spray bottle and top off with water. Spray early mornings or after the sun has set to prevent burning the leaves.

Fungus Suppressant

Ingredients:

20 drops tea tree

Directions:

In a small glass spray bottle, add essential oil and water to fill. Spray directly onto infected plants and surrounding soil, 1–2x's weekly.

did you know?

A staggering 85% of all plant disease is fungal-related. Avid gardeners love spending time outdoors, connecting with the earth and nurturing their plants, in the sun. Unfortunately, there are pests and fungal diseases that can impede growth or reduce the harvest of producing plants. Rather than turning to harmful chemicals to address these challenges, try all-natural solutions and keep the garden organic, and chemical-free.

Ant Spray

Ingredients:

¼ C witch hazel
10 drops peppermint

Directions:

Combine ingredients in a 4 oz glass spray bottle with water. Spray ant trails and areas ants have populated.

Pollinator Attractor

Ingredients:

5 drops wild orange

Directions:

Add essential oil to a glass spray bottle, topped off with water. Spray on flowers and buds to attract bees for pollination.

Pest Repellents

Repel pests with these essential oils:

- **Ants:** peppermint, spearmint
- **Aphids:** cedarwood, peppermint, spearmint
- **Beetles:** peppermint, thyme
- **Caterpillars:** spearmint, peppermint
- **Chiggers:** lavender, lemongrass, sage, thyme
- **Fleas:** peppermint, lemongrass, spearmint, lavender
- **Flies:** lavender, peppermint, rosemary, sage
- **Gnats:** patchouli, spearmint
- **Lice:** cedarwood, peppermint, spearmint
- **Mosquitoes:** lavender, lemongrass, arborvitae, TerraShield®
- **Moths:** cedarwood, lavender, peppermint, spearmint
- **Plant lice:** peppermint, spearmint
- **Rodents:** peppermint
- **Slugs:** cedarwood
- **Snails:** cedarwood, patchouli
- **Spiders:** peppermint, spearmint
- **Ticks:** lavender, lemongrass, sage, thyme
- **Weevils:** cedarwood, patchouli, sandalwood

Apply essential oils on soil, animals, plants, window seals, corners, and spray where pests reside.

Meditation & Yoga

To be used by individuals, in a one-on-one setting, or group session to create an environment that promotes healthy emotional processing and provides a process by which to overcome emotional paralysis.

LIVING

tips

Anytime during the day when unpleasant feelings emerge:

- Bring self back into alignment and apply Align.
- Seek to discover the purpose of the discontent and apply Anchor.
- Choose to move forward and apply Arise.

Step One: Align

Apply Align to the crown, base of spine, and bottoms of feet, as you begin the process of bringing self into a state of focus, alignment, and singlemindedness. Visualize the intention for your meditation. Invite yourself to feel and experience what it is you envision.

Step Two: Anchor

Once connection has been established with the intention for your meditation:

Apply Anchor. Get in touch with what is being felt, with and within the body, identifying what may be keeping you from moving forward, in life, in some way.

- Ask yourself: If I trust that all emotions have a higher or positive purpose and allow myself to accept and surrender to what I am feeling, then what is the higher intention for my troubled feelings?
- How are they alerting me to misalignment and inviting me to get out of my head and move into my heart? Continue asking until you identify the purpose of your feelings.
- Allow your awareness to anchor you, no longer fearful or avoiding how you feel but creating a space of safety that honors self.

Step Three: Arise

Once the higher intentions is identified:

Apply Arise to support your discoveries as you seek to understand the valuable partnership with the emotions you are feeling. Through acceptance, you are allowing your emotions to be part of your life, and in moving you forward. Be with your emotions and their higher intentions. Consciously find where within you, your power resides, so it can be accessed repeatedly.

Step Four: Repeat

Once you have connected with your higher intention:

Go back to Arise blend multiple times throughout the day to remind you of your intention. If you find yourself slipping back into old thinking, re-align yourself with Align or re-anchor with Anchor.

By choosing to accept how you feel, the very feelings most people avoid become a catalyst for moving you forward in life. With acknowledgment and focus of the higher meaning, the intention for your day is no longer cluttered, obscured, or shrouded by unnecessary confusion, overwhelm, or double mindedness, that typically arises when one is placed into a state of fight or flight when ruled by unacknowledged or unaddressed emotions.

Additional Technique

Ask yourself: What oil am I drawn to today? Smell your oils. Rub between your hands & inhale deeply. Set a daily intention. Reapply & smell whenever you need to be reminded of your intention. This practice is excellent just prior to a yoga practice.

LIVING
On the Go

Hand Sanitizer

Ingredients:

5 T aloe vera gel
4 T water
½ t vitamin E oil
10 drops On Guard®
5 drops wild orange

Directions:

Combine ingredients in a squeezable container. Shake well.

To Use: Apply a dime-size dollop to palms of hands and rub together until absorbed.

Car Air Freshener

Ingredients:

Wool felt
Twine
10 drops essential oils (any combo, or choice)

Directions:

Cut a 4" shape from the wool felt. Using a small hole punch, punch a hole in the top of the shape, thread twine through it, and knot. Apply essential oils and hang on the rear view mirror.

Reapply essential oils as needed.

Bedbugs-Be-Gone Spray

Ingredients:

10 drops Siberian fir or peppermint

Directions:

Combine essential oils in 2 oz glass spray bottle topped off with water. Spray on bedding and sheets to deter bedbugs. Spray in suitcases, so they can't stow away home with you.

Jet Lag Help

Ingredients:

8 drops lavender
8 drops rosemary
1 C Epsom salt

Directions:

Combine essential oils with Epsom salt. Add to warm bath water. Bathe and enjoy. Follow with a quick cold shower to help refresh and enliven.

Eyeglass Cleaner

Ingredients:

1 C white vinegar
¼ C water
5 drops lemon

Directions:

Mix ingredients in a small glass spray bottle, shake before use, and spray directly onto glass. Wipe with a scratch-free cloth.

LIVING

tips

- For a mosquito repellent, spray or apply TerraShield®.
- To relieve the discomfort of a poison ivy rash, apply lavender and Roman chamomile.
- For cooling or overheated; apply peppermint on the back of the neck, or add 10 drops lavender to a damp washcloth. Place on forehead or around the neck.

Bug Off

Ingredients:

16 drops patchouli
10 drops cedarwood
4 drops lemon eucalyptus
2 oz witch hazel

Directions:

Combine essential oils and witch hazel in a 4 oz glass spray bottle.

To Use: Shake well before each use. Spray on exposed skin and clothing every 2–4 hours.

Bug Repellent

Ingredients:

¼ C witch hazel
10 drops peppermint
6 drops eucalyptus
6 drops tea tree
5 drops cedarwood

Directions:

Add essential oils to a 4 oz glass spray bottle, top of witch hazel. Shake well before each use.

To Use: Apply to skin and clothing before heading outdoors. Reapply every 2-4 hours.

Cooling Spray

Ingredients:

1 oz water
1 oz witch hazel
4 drops peppermint
4 drops lavender

Directions:

In a 2 oz glass spray bottle, combine essential oils, water, and witch hazel. Shake well before each use.

To Use: Carefully spray directly on neck and face. Be careful around eyes.

Sunburn Spray

Ingredients:

1 C aloe vera juice
¼ C carrier oil
1 t vitamin E oil
8 drops lavender
8 drops tea tree
8 drops Roman chamomile

Directions:

Combine in a 16 oz glass spray bottle. Shake well and spray onto sunburned skin. Repeat as needed.

*Store in the refrigerator for extra cooling effects.

Did you know?

- Out of 2,000 sunscreens reviewed, more than 75% were found to contain toxic chemicals.
- Common side effects for commercial insect repellents include skin reactions, allergic rashes, and eye irritation.
- Many topical medicated creams for insect-bite itching and irritation have side effects, causing redness, irritation, and swelling.

Sunscreen

Ingredients:

2 T shea butter
⅓ C beeswax
2 T zinc oxide
½ C olive oil
½ C carrier oil
1 T raspberry seed oil
(avocado or pomegranate seed oil)
1 t vitamin E oil
10 drops helichrysum
5 drops myrrh
5 drops frankincense
5 drops arborvitae

Directions:

Heat shea butter and beeswax on medium/low until melted. Mix in zinc oxide. Remove from heat and add remaining ingredients. Let cool slightly then pour into 8 oz clear bottle.

Personal Care

did you know?

- Most deodorants and antiperspirants contain ingredients that research now links to breast cancer and Alzheimer's.
- Teeth whitening products can cause teeth sensitivity and lead to gum recession and irritation.
- Irritation of the oral mucous membranes, a burning feeling in the mouth, and the potential to increase the risk of pharyngeal and oral cancers are common side effects of mouthwash use.
- Incorporate all-natural essential oils into your personal care regimen to bypass negative side effects and harmful chemicals.
- For fine-lines, laugh lines, and wrinkles, moisturize with yarrow|pom as part of your nightly routine.
- For easy eye and makeup remover use fractionated coconut oil.
- For a quick breath freshener, pop a peppermint beadlet.
- To pull toxins from the body and improve overall health, try oil pulling. Oil pulling has been said to help with overall oral health while pulling unwanted toxins out of the body. Apply 1–2 t carrier oil into mouth. Add desired essential oils and swish around for 15-20 minutes, then spit out (in the trash, not down a drain). Rinse with warm water and brush teeth as usual. See pg. 330 for more.

Thickening Shampoo

Ingredients:

1 drop lemon eucalyptus
2 drops rosemary

Directions:

Add essential oils to approximately 1 teaspoon of shampoo.

To Use: Massage into scalp. Rinse well before conditioning.

Floral Hair Repair

Ingredients:

22 drops ylang ylang
13 drops rosemary
24 drops lavender
Carrier oil

Directions:

Combine essential oils in a 2 oz glass spray bottle. Top off with carrier oil. Shake well. Spray 2–3 x's (on wet or dry hair) before styling.

Texturizing Hair Spray

Ingredients:

½ C warm water
½ T sea salt
½–1 t carrier oil
4–5 drops lavender

Directions:

Add all ingredients to a 4 oz glass spray bottle and shake well before each use.

To Use: Spray over damp hair to help add more texture to dried and styled hair.

Dry Shampoo

Ingredients:

8 T arrowroot
½ T cocoa powder (adjust according to hair color)
5 drops tea tree

Directions:

Add powders to 3 ½ oz shaker bottle. Add essential oil and mix well. Sprinkle a light dusting on hair and comb it in through to the roots. Keep combing until the powder is completely worked into hair and scalp.

Black Mascara

Ingredients:

1 ½ t plant based glycerin or aloe vera gel
1 ½ t activated charcoal
3 t bentonite clay
1-2 drops lavender

Directions:

In a small bowl, combine ingredients. Add to a clean mascara tube with a pipette or oral syringe.

To Use: Apply 2-3 coats, allowing each to dry in between each layer.

Hint: Use cocoa powder (instead of activated charcoa) for brown mascara.

Night-time Facial Moisturizing

Ingredients:

2 T fractionated coconut oil
20–25 drops myrrh

Directions:

Combine fractionated coconut oil and myrrh in 1 oz roll-on bottle. Shake to combine.

To Use: Roll on face, neck, and chest after removing makeup for the night. Use fingers to massage into the skin.

Makeup-Setting Spray

Ingredients:

3 T water
1 T witch hazel
1 T aloe vera juice
3 drops lavender
3 drops ylang ylang

Directions:

In a small glass spray bottle, combine ingredients, and mix thoroughly. Shake before each use.

To Use: Apply to face after applying makeup for hours of extended wear.

Lengthen Lashes

Ingredients:

1 t sweet almond oil
1 t castor oil
3 drops lavender
1 drop rosemary

Directions:

Mix ingredients, in a clean empty mascara tube, or add to current mascara.

To Use: Apply a coat every night before going to bed.

tips

Strawberries have a slight bleaching effect (malic acid) and if used daily may help rid teeth of minor stains.

Puree or crush one strawberry with 1/2 t baking soda and mix well. Dip toothbrush in mixture and coat teeth, let sit for 5 minutes, then brush teeth as usual.

Sunkissed Skin Bronzer

Ingredients:

1 T cinnamon powder (red coloring)
1 t cocoa powder (brown coloring)
1 t freshly ground nutmeg powder (tan coloring)
2 t arrowroot powder (or cornstarch)
15 drops lavender or rosemary

Directions:

Adjust ingredients to specific shade and mix well in a small bowl. Break up any clumps until it's smooth. Place in a heavy walled jar.

To Use: Using a cotton pad, apply and enjoy a chemical-free bronzer.

Foot Soak

Ingredients:

10 drops lemon eucalyptus
10 drops tea tree
4 drops lavender
2 oz carrier oil
2 oz pink Himalayan salt

Directions:

Combine essential oils, carrier oil, and salt in a glass jar.

To Use: Add 1 T to foot bath or small tub of warm water. Mix until incorporated/dissolve salt. Soak feet for 10-15 minutes.

Cellulite Reducing Cream

Ingredients:

8 oz carrier oil
15mL copaiba (entire bottle)
30 drops clove

Directions:

Add carrier oil to a 12 oz glass bottle. Add essential oils. Make sure the mixture is mixed well and let rest overnight. Apply 2x's a day to help firm skin and reduce cellulite.

Personal Fragrance

Perfumes can be intoxicating, seductive, and evoke emotions and memories. However, there is a dark side to the perfume industry of which many are not aware. To protect trade secrets, commercial perfume manufacturers are permitted to withhold disclosing ingredients; many of which are potentially hazardous petrochemicals and other synthetic chemicals.

Did you know?

Sensitive to Fragrances?

It's no wonder, considering the average commercially produced fragrance contains 14 chemicals which often present themselves as allergies, sensitivity, headaches, skin reactions, or nausea when exposed.

Of these undisclosed ingredients, many can be classified as carcinogens, hormone disrupters, lead to sperm damage in men, and when worn by pregnant mothers, can lead to abnormal reproductive development in male fetuses.

Women's

Stand Alone

Reach for these standalone favorites:

Adaptiv™
Beautiful
Citrus Bloom™
Davana
Elevation
Hope®
Jasmine
Kintana
Magnolia
Neroli
Passion®
Whisper®

Love

Floral & Rosey

16 drops sandalwood
16 drops geranium
8 drops bergamot

Bliss

Floral Oriental

16 drops grapefruit
12 drops vetiver
8 drops ginger

Urban

Soft, Chic, Citrusy

16 drops sandalwood
16 drops bergamot
8 drops frankincense

Harmony

Fruity & Citrusy

24 drops frankincense
8 drops lemongrass
8 drops ylang ylang

Secret

Soft Powdery Floral

16 drops bergamot
12 drops ylang ylang
8 drops patchouli

Directions for all:

Combine oils in 10mL roller bottle then fill with carrier oil or 70% alcohol or vodka, Quadruple recipe and add to a 2 oz glass spray bottle. For best results, let sit for 2-3 days to allow blend to mature. Roll on pulse points and enjoy.

Unisex

Peace

Aquatic & Earthy

28 drops patchouli
12 drops grapefruit
4 drop ylang ylang

Pure

Green, fresh, citrus

12 drops bergamot
8 drops black pepper
8 drops frankincense
4 drop rosemary

Strong

Woodsy

12 drops bergamot
8 drops juniper
8 drops cedarwood
4 drop balsam or Siberian fir

Terra

Woodsy

12 drops bergamot
8 drops juniper
8 drops cedarwood
4 drop balsam or Siberian fir

Men's Cologne

Stand Alone

Reach for these standalone favorites:

Adaptiv™
Amavi®
Balance®
Douglas fir
Midnight Forest
Northern Escape

Earthy Spice

20 drops bergamot
15 drops Douglas fir
10 drops clove
8 drops lemon

Sweet Musk

30 drops lime
20 drops fennel
15 drops patchouli

Pick-Me-Up

30 drops cinnamon
12 drops cassia
10 drops peppermint
10 drops grapefruit

Woodsy Licorice

30 drops sandalwood
8 drops fennel
8 drops cypress
8 drops wild orange
8 drops lime
8 drops wintergreen

Orange Fir

15 drops bergamot
15 drops wild orange
10 drops basil
10 drops Siberian fir

Pets

Smell Good Pet Spray

Ingredients:

25 drops Abōde™ or favorite aroma

Directions:

Combine in a 4 oz glass spray bottle, top off with distilled water. Shake well and spray on pet for instant deodorizing and disinfecting relief.

Pet Shampoo

Ingredients:

1 C water
1 T castile soap
¼ t vitamin E
3 drops peppermint
2 drops Roman chamomile
2 drops Purify or Abōde™
1 drop cedarwood

Directions:

Place ingredients in a glass jar and mix well. Apply a quarter-size amount to pet and scrub vigorously. Rinse until no soap residue is left. Shampoo will be a bit watery but will leave pet clean and smelling great for days.

tips

SAFETY NOTICE

- Animals are smaller, so diluting essential oils is important.
- Avoid using tea tree for cats.

- Animals prefer certain aromas just as humans do. Experiment with various oils to see how the animals respond to the aroma. Always leave animals a way to remove themselves, if needed.
- For joint pain relief; rub frankincense and copaiba directly on pet joints.
- To help calm and relax a stressed pet; apply 2 to 3 drops lavender to ears and paws.

Flea Repellent Collar

Ingredients:

¼ t rubbing alcohol
4 garlic oil capsules
1 drop cedarwood
1 drop lavender
1 drop lemon
1 drop thyme

Directions:

Mix ingredients in a medium bowl. Soak a pet collar, in the mixture, for 25-30 minutes. Lay out to dry; place on animal's neck. Repeat 1-2x's a month, or as needed.

Dog Treats

Ingredients:

1 large banana
3 heaping T creamy peanut butter
1 large egg
2 C garbanzo bean flour
¼ C flax seed
3-5 drops peppermint, DigestZen®, frankincense, or cassia

Directions:

Preheat oven to 325°F. Combine banana, peanut butter, and egg. In a separate bowl, combine flour and flax seed. Mix wet and dry ingredients together. Add essential oil of choice. Roll dough on floured surface to ¼ inch thick. Using cookie cutters to cut "cookies." Bake for 25-30 minutes or until golden brown. Cool and store up to 2 weeks in an airtight container.

Doggie Paw Balm

Ingredients:

2 T shea butter
2 T coconut oil
1 t jojoba oil
2 T beeswax
1-2 drops lavender
1-2 drops frankincense
1-2 drops peppermint

Directions:

Over a double boiler, melt the shea butter, coconut oil, beeswax, and jojoba together. Remove from the heat and let it cool enough to touch. Add essential oils and pour into a jar. Let sit until firm.

To Use: Apply to sore paws, rubbing mixture into area very well.

Did you know?

- Common anti-flea solutions for dogs can cause adverse reactions, such as skin irritation, hair loss, vomiting, diarrhea, tremors, and seizures.
- Medication commonly used to treat painful arthritis in cats and dogs often causes serious damage to the stomach, liver, and kidneys.
- Most people don't realize that pure essential oils can provide all-natural solutions for animals as well as humans.

Calming Doggie Spray

Ingredients:

16 oz distilled water
5 drops lavender
5 drops roman chamomile

Directions:

Mix ingredients in a glass spray bottle. Shake well before each use.

To Use: Cover face and eyes of dog with a cloth, and lightly mist over the dog during times of stress.

Hint: Spray about 10 minutes before leaving pet alone, or before guests are to arrive.

No-Odor Kitty Litter

Ingredients:

25 drops Purify or Abōde™
4 C baking soda

Directions:

Combine in a large ziptop bag. Sprinkle 2 T into kitty litter when scooping box daily.

Cat Scratch Deterrent

Ingredients:

10 drops eucalyptus
10 drops lemon
1 C water

Directions:

Fill glass spray bottle with essential oils. Top off with water. Shake well before each use. Spray on areas cat is not allowed on or areas cat should not be scratching up.

Spring: CITRUS BLOOM™

Top Uses:

- Wear as a natural perfume to calm and uplift emotions and help ease feelings of tension or stress.
- Diffuse and apply to invite a feeling of being open to new possibilities, while overcoming challenges and moving into a sense of aligned happiness.

Blooming Mood

Roller Bottle Blend

Ingredients:

16 drops Citrus Bloom™
10 drops Balance®
6 drops lime

Directions:

Combine essential oils in 10mL roller bottle. Top off with fractionated coconut oil. Apply on pulse points, behind ears, and along neck to experience a unique mood-boosting aroma.

Summer: ISLAND MINT®

Top Uses:

- Diffuse to escape to a tropical oasis wherever you are, home, work, or traveling.
- Diffuse and apply to create feelings of positivity and happiness and abundant feelings of joy.

Tropical Escape

Room Spray

Ingredients:

10 drops Island Mint®
10 drops rosemary
10 drops eucalyptus

Directions:

Add essential oils with water to 16 oz glass spray bottle and shake to mix well. Spray to purify air, uplift moods, and remove offensive odors. Shake before each use.

Fall: HARVEST SPICE

Top Uses:

- Diffuse during family gatherings to celebrate and make wonderful memories with this heartwarming and comforting aroma.
- Wear as a signature scent to help encourage a sense of contentment and groundedness.

Warm & Cozy
Scented Lotion

Ingredients:

3 drops Harvest Spice
3 drops Siberian fir
2 drops Citrus Bliss®
2 drops ginger

Directions:

Add unscented lotion and essential oils to a 2 oz squeeze bottle. Stir and shake to mix thoroughly. Apply to moisturize while warming hands and feet after outdoor activity.

Winter: HYGGE™

Top Uses:

- Diffuse to bring a sense of harmony, togetherness, and closeness to gatherings.
- Wear to feel warm and collected and help overcome winter blahs.

Warm Winter Balm

Ingredients:

2 oz cocoa butter
2 oz beeswax
4 oz coconut oil
25 drops Hygge™

Directions:

Carefully melt cocoa butter and beeswax in a double boiler. Once melted, stir in coconut oil until incorporated. Cool. Add essential oils. Let sit until solid.

Rub generously on hands, elbows, heels, or anywhere needing extra care.

Holiday: HOLIDAY JOY & HOLIDAY PEACE

Top Uses:

- Diffuse to create a welcoming aroma for holiday gatherings, to purify the air, and uplift spirits.
- Diffuse to bring a tranquil, serene, and grounding feeling during the hectic holiday season.

Rest & Renew
Sugar Scrub

Ingredients:

16 drops Holiday Peace
16 drops Holiday Joy
½ C carrier oil
1 C brown or white granulated sugar

Directions:

Combine essential oils and carrier oil in a bowl and stir. Add sugar and mix well. Put in glass jar. Apply a small amount in circular motions on wet skin to exfoliate. Rinse.

SECTION 6

RESOURCES

Turn to these resources to explore research, deepen understanding of ailments, and to find oil properties.

OIL COMPOSITION *and* CHEMISTRY

Plants synthesize two types of oils: fixed oils and essential oils. Fixed oils consist of glycerol and fatty acids. Essential oils are a mix of volatile organic compounds that contribute to the fragrance and well-being of the plant. Essential oils are made up of many compound constituents that serve several purposes for the plant:

- Protection and responses to parasites such a bacteria, viruses, fungi, and other pests
- Restoration from wounds and physical damage
- Protection from sun and other elements
- Communication through fragrance to insects or other plants of the same genus

Essential oils are volatile oils that have an intrinsic nature or essence of the plant. Essential oils are more soluble in lipophilic solvents than in water. They are complex mixtures of chemical compounds, and every biological effect displayed by an essential oil is due to the actions of one or more of its constituents.

Essential oils are secondary metabolites in plants. The oils are isolated from plants through a process called hydrodistillation: passing boiling water through the plant material and vaporizing the essential oil from the plant. As the steam rises and condenses, the water and essential oil separate, and the oil product, the essential oil, is captured. The remaining water is aromatic and contains in much lower concentrations and in different ratios some of the constituents from the oil. This water is known as a hydrosol and is used and sold for its therapeutic benefits and its fragrance.

The chemical compounds in citrus essential oils come from the rind of the fruit. Most citrus essential oils are generally isolated by cold pressing rather than distillation. Citrus oils that are cold-pressed also include relatively large, nonvolatile molecules, including the phototoxic compounds. These compounds are not in distilled citrus oils.

Some fragrant oils, such as rose or jasmine are at times extracted with organic solvents, which produces concretes, absolutes, or resinoids.

Essential oils typically contain dozens of constituents with related, but distinct, chemical structures. Each constituent has its own characteristic and has different effects when used. Even though an essential oil contains many different types of compounds, usually one or two compounds dominate their action. For example, α-Pinene is the main compound that is responsible for the action of frankincense essential oil. Some constituents may comprise a small percentage of an oil but may play a significant role in its overall action. Because no two distillations are ever the same and because of many other variables such as elevation, harvest time, soil type, weather condition, etc., lists of compounds contained in an essential oil are usually stated as a range. For example, the compound α-Pinene may range from 41 percent to 80 percent of a frankincense essential oil (*Boswellia frereana*).

Because of their antimicrobial properties, essential oils are not generally subject to microbial contamination. Essential oils can be contaminated from unnatural constituents, distillation items, or adulterants. These include pesticides or herbicides, traces of solvent, and phthalates (plasticizing agents). Adulteration includes both intentional dilution and fabrication of an oil or parts of an essential oil. There are many ways and methods to test an essential oil for levels of purity. Testing by independent and properly equipped labs is critical to knowing an oil's purity and complete profile. Adulteration could increase toxicity of an oil. Only essential oils that are tested and verified pure therapeutic grade should be used for therapeutic benefits.

It's a complex task to evaluate and unravel the chemistry of an essential oil. Many compounds in an essential oil are present in minute amounts. They may be hard to detect except through testing by laboratories with a large enough database to identify all of the constituents. Some of the modern methods and analyses that are used to determine the chemical profile of an essential oil include:

- Gas Chromatography (GC)
- Mass Spectrometry (MS)
- High-Performance Liquid Chromatography (HPLC)
- Nuclear Magnetic Resonance Spectroscopy (NMR)
- Fourier Transform Infrared Spectroscopy (FTIS)
- Chiral GC Testing
- Isotope Carbon 14TPC/Microbial

The best testing involves a combination of several methods throughout the process from harvest to bottle.

Essential oils are made up of organic (carbon-based) compounds. The individual essential oil constituents contain atoms in addition to carbon(C), such as hydrogen(H) and oxygen(O). Learning the basics of essential oil chemical construction will help in understanding why different oils achieve different actions. For example, α-Pinene, a compound in frankincense essential oil, is written chemically as $C_{10}H_{16}$ This means the α-Pinene consists of ten carbon atoms and sixteen hydrogen atoms. The compound can also be shown as a diagram. The double line indicates a double bond in that part of the compound. Essential oil molecules are three-dimensional but are represented in the following diagram as two-dimensional.

[1] *Essential Oil Safety*, Robert Tisserand and Rodney Young, 2014, page 6.
[2] *Essential Oil Safety*, pg 7.
[3] *Essential Oil Safety*, pg 8.

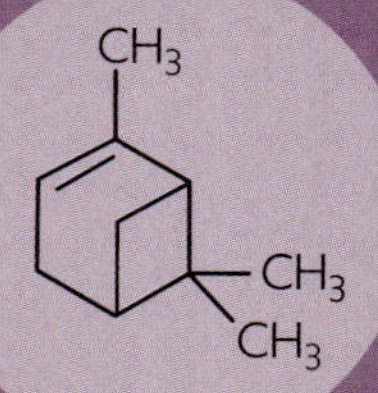

Essential oil constituents are built on a framework of isoprene units. Isoprene units consist of carbon and hydrogen atoms; their chemical makeup consists of five carbon atoms and eight hydrogen atoms. Their chemical signature is C_5H_8. Most of the compounds in essential oils consist of two to four isoprene units. These units are referred to as terpenes or terpenoids. Terpenoids are terpenes that have functional groups added to them. These functional groups are made up of mostly hydrogen and oxygen and include alcohols, phenols, aldehydes, esters, and ethers. Terpenes do not have a functional group added to them; they are often referred to as hydrocarbons. The simplest and most common class of terpenes found in essential oils is the monoterpene (a double isoprene unit with ten carbon atoms). The next group of terpenes is the sesquiterpenes, and the basic structure is composed of fifteen carbon atoms or three isoprene units. They have a larger molecular size than the monoterpenes and therefore are less volatile. See the following table for the classes of terpenes and the number of carbon atoms in each.

Monoterpene	10 carbon atoms	Most common
Sequiterpenes	15 carbon atoms	Larger size molecule and less volatile
Diterpenes	20 carbon atoms	Only in some essential oils
Triterpenes	30 carbon atoms	Can be present in absolutes
Tetraterpenes	40 carbon atoms	Not part of essential oils but found in cold-pressed citrus oils (β-carotene is an example)

All of the compounds or constituents in essential oils belong to a group. These groups are defined by the number of carbon atoms they have and the type of functional group assigned to them. For example α-Pinene is part of the monoterpene hydrocarbon group. It has ten carbon atoms and does not have a functional group as part of its molecular makeup, which makes it a hydrocarbon. It is unique from the other compounds in the group because of the number of hydrogen atoms and how the carbon and hydrogen atoms are bonded together. Another example is α-Santalol, a major compound in sandalwood essential oil. α-Santalol chemically is $C_{15}H_{24}O$ It has an oxygen functional group and fifteen carbon atoms, so it is part of the sesquiterpene alcohol group.

The compounds and the compound groups have been researched and found to exhibit certain common therapeutic benefits. Once a compound is identified as part of an essential oil and once the group to which it belongs is identified, the possible action of the essential oil can be determined. Essential oils are made up of many compounds. Some compounds make up a larger percentage of an oil, while others may only offer a trace of the total essential oil. Though compounds that comprise larger parts of an oil definitely help guide an oil's benefit, the smaller amounts play a part in the oil's actions.

The following table lists common groups of compounds in essential oils, examples of compounds in that group, the known therapeutic benefits of that group, and some of the essential oils that contain compounds in that group.

SUBSTITUTIONS

OIL	BY OUTCOME	BY CHEMISTRY
ABŌDE™ (Distilled Lime, Cassia, Litsea, Lemon Eucalyptus, Tea Tree, Arborvitae, Eucalyptus, Cilantro, Lavandin, Lemon, Myrtle)	Air-X™, Arborvitae, Cassia, Cilantro, Eucalyptus, Lemon Eucalyptus, Lemon Myrtle, Lime, Niaouli, Purify, Tea Tree	Purify
ADAPTIV™ (Wild Orange, Lavender, Copaiba, Spearmint, Magnolia, Rosemary, Neroli, Sweet Gum)	Cedarwood, Copaiba, Magnolia, Neroli, Rosemary, Wild Orange	Copaiba, Jasmine, Lavender, Neroli, Serenity®, Wild Orange
AIR-X™ (Litsea, Tangerine, Grapefruit, Frankincense, Cardamom)	Abōde™, Breathe®, DDR Prime®, HD Clear®, Lemongrass, Litsea, Melissa	Cardamom, Litsea
ALIGN (Bergamot, Coriander, Marjoram, Peppermint, Geranium, Basil, Jasmine Absolute, Rose)	Arborvitae, Black Spruce, Copaiba, Northern Escape	Basil, Coriander, Marjoram
AMAVI® (Buddha Wood, Balsam Fir, Black Pepper, Hinoki, Patchouli)	Balance®, Black Spruce, Hinoki	Black Pepper, Patchouli
ANCHOR (Lavender, Cedarwood, Frankincense, Cinnamon Bark, Sandalwood, Black Pepper, Patchouli)	Arborvitae, Balance®, Black Spruce, Cedarwood, Frankincense, Patchouli, Sandalwood	Cedarwood, Frankincense, Sandalwood, Patchouli
ARBORVITAE	Abōde™, Align, Anchor, Cedarwood, Clary Sage, Jasmine, Petitgrain, Roman Chamomile	Clary Sage, Jasmine, Petitgrain, Roman Chamomile
ARISE (Grapefruit, Lemon, Osmanthus, Melissa, Siberian Fir)	Beautiful, Citrus Bloom™, Elevation, Hinoki, Melissa	Beautiful, Melissa
AROMATOUCH® (Cypress, Peppermint, Marjoram, Basil, Grapefruit, Lavender)	Basil, Coriander, Cypress, Marjoram	Basil, Cypress, Grapefruit, Marjoram
BALANCE® (Spruce, Ho Wood, Frankincense, Blue Tansy, Blue Chamomile, Osmanthus)	Amavi®, Anchor, Black Spruce, Frankincense, Steady™	Black Spruce, Blue Tansy, Frankincense
BALSAM FIR	Balance®, Black Pepper, Black Spruce, Cypress, Douglas Fir, Frankincense, Pink Pepper, Steady™	Black Pepper, Cypress, Douglas Fir, Frankincense, Pink Pepper
BASIL	AromaTouch®, Coriander, Fennel, Marjoram, Rosemary, Tulsi	Coriander, Rosemary
BEAUTIFUL (Lime, Osmanthus, Bergamot, Frankincense)	Arise, Beautiful Body Mist, Citrus Bloom™, Elevation, Magnolia	Beautiful, Magnolia
BERGAMOT	Citrus Bliss®, Hope®, Magnolia, Neroli, Petitgrain, Pink Pepper, Whisper®	Magnolia, Neroli, Petitgrain
BERGAMOT MINT	Clary Sage, Island Mint®, Lavender, Petitgrain, Spearmint	Clary Sage, Lavender, Petitgrain
BIRCH	Deep Blue®, PastTense®, Wintergreen	Deep Blue®, Wintergreen
BLACK PEPPER	Balsam Fir, Copaiba, Hinoki, Juniper Berry, Yarrow|Pom, Ylang Ylang	Balsam Fir, Copaiba, Juniper Berry, Yarrow|Pom, Ylang Ylang
BLACK SPRUCE	Align, Amavi®, Anchor, Balance®, Forgive®, Hinoki, Jasmine, Lavender, Northern Escape, Petitgrain, Siberian Fir	Lavender, Petitgrain, Siberian Fir
BLUE TANSY	Deep Blue®, Juniper Berry, Roman Chamomile, Rosemary, Tulsi, Yarrow|Pom	Deep Blue®, Juniper Berry, Rosemary, Yarrow|Pom

RESOURCES

OIL	BY OUTCOME	BY CHEMISTRY
BRAVE™ (Wild Orange, Amyris, Osmanthus, Cinnamon)	Harvest Spice, Holiday Joy, Passion®, Wild Orange	Cinnamon, Holiday Joy, Passion, Wild Orange
BREATHE® (Laurel Leaf, Eucalyptus, Peppermint, Tea Tree, Lemon, Cardamom, Ravintsara, Ravensara)	Air-X™, Eucalyptus, Laurel Leaf, Peppermint, Ravintsara	Air-X™, Eucalyptus, Laurel, Peppermint, Ravintsara
CALMER™ (Lavender, Cananga, Buddha Wood, Roman Chamomile)	Console®, Lavender, Roman Chamomille, Serenity®, Ylang Ylang	Digestzen®, Serenity®, Tamer™
CARDAMOM	Celery Seed, Coriander, DigestZen®, Dill, Eucalyptus, Passion®	Breathe®, Celery Seed, Coriander, DigestZen®, Eucalyptus, Laurel leaf
CASSIA	Abōde™, Cinnamon	Cinnamon, Laurel Leaf, Lemon Mrytle, Summer Savory
CEDARWOOD	Adaptiv™, Anchor, Arborvitae, Copaiba, Frankincense, Holiday Peace, Hygge™, Sandalwood, Serenity®, Spikenard, Stronger™, TerraShield®	Copaiba, Ginger, Frankincense, Spikenard
CELERY SEED	Cardamom, Dill, Green Mandarin	Cardamom, Cumin, Dill, Green Mandarin
CHEER® (Wild Orange, Clove, Star Anise, Lemon Myrtle, Nutmeg, Vanilla Extract, Ginger, Cinnamon, Zdravetz)	Elevation, Harvest Spice, Holiday Joy, Motivate®, Vanilla, Wild Orange	Elevation, Harvest Spice, Holiday Joy, OnGuard®
CILANTRO	Abōde™, Citronella, Coriander, Lemon Eucalyptus, Marjoram, Melissa	Citronella, Coriander, Lemon Eucalyptus, Melissa
CINNAMON	Cassia, Clove, On Guard®, Passion®, Slim & Sassy®, Tulsi	Cassia, Clove, OnGuard®, Passion, Slim & Sassy®
CITRONELLA	Cilantro, Laurel Leaf, Lemon Eucalyptus, Rose, TerraShield®	Geranium, Laurel Leaf, Lemon Eucalyptus, Rose
CITRUS BLISS® (Wild Orange, Lemon, Grapefruit, Mandarin, Bergamot, Tangerine, Clementine, Vanilla Bean Absolute)	Citrus Bloom™, Grapefruit, Lemon, Red Mandarin, Tangerine, Vanilla, Wild Orange	Citrus Bloom™
CITRUS BLOOM™ (Wild Orange, Grapefruit, Lavender, Roman Chamomile, Magnolia)	Arise, Beautiful, Citrus Bliss®, Elevation, Magnolia	Citrus Bliss®
CLARYCALM®	Clary Sage, Geranium, Jasmine, Roman Chamomile, Serenity®, Ylang Ylang	Clary Sage, Digestzen, Geranium, Roman Chamomille, Serenity, Ylang Ylang
CLARY SAGE	Bergamot Mint, ClaryCalm®, Davana, Jasmine, Lavender, Magnolia, Petitgrain, Roman Chamomile	Arborvitae, Bergamot Mint, Clary Calm®, Jasmine, Lavender, Petitgrain, Roman Chamomile
CLEMENTINE	Grapefruit, Green Mandarin, Red Mandarin, Tangerine, Wild Orange	Grapefruit, Green Mandarin, Red Mandarin, Tangerine, Wild Orange
CLOVE	Cinnamon, DDR Prime®, On Guard®, Oregano, Thyme, Tulsi	Cinnamon, OnGuard®, Oregano, Thyme, Tulsi
CONSOLE® (Frankincense, Patchouli, Ylang Ylang, Labdanum, Amyris, Sandalwood, Rose, Osmanthus)	Calmer™, Deep Blue®, Frankincense, Geranium, Helichrysum, Myrrh, Patchouli, Rose, Ylang Ylang	Frankincense, InTune®, Patchouli, Rose, Sandalwood
COPAIBA	Adaptiv™, Align, Black Pepper, Cedarwood, Deep Blue®, Deep Blue® Stick, Rescuer™, Tulsi, Ylang Ylang	Black Pepper, Cedarwood, Deep Blue®, Rescuer™, Tulsi

SUBSTITUTIONS

OIL	BY OUTCOME	BY CHEMISTRY
CORIANDER	AromaTouch®, Basil, Cardamom, Cilantro, DigestZen®, Magnolia	Basil, Cardamom, Cilantro, Digestzen, Lavender, Magnolia
CUMIN	Celery Seed, DigestZen®, Dill, Summer Savory	Celery Seed, DigestZen®
CYPRESS	AromaTouch®, Douglas Fir, Hinoki, Juniper Berry, Neroli, Northern Escape, Siberian Fir	AromaTouch®, Balsam Fir, Douglas Fir, Hinoki, Neroli, Siberian Fir
DAVANA	Clary Sage, Frankincense, Geranium, Jasmine, Neroli, Rose	Extremely Unique
DDR PRIME® (Frankincense, Wild Orange, Litsea, Thyme, Clove, Summer Savory, Niaouli, Lemongrass)	Air-X™, Clove, Frankincense, Lemongrass, Pink Pepper, Thyme, Tulsi, Wild Orange	Frankincense, HD Clear®, Pink Pepper, Wild Orange
DEEP BLUE® (Wintergreen, Camphor, Peppermint, Ylang Ylang, Helichrysum, Blue Tansy, Blue Chamomile, Osmanthus)	Blue Tansy, Copaiba, Helichrysum, PastTense®, Peppermint, Rescuer™, Wintergreen	Blue Tansy, Copaiba, Rescuer™
DIGESTZEN® (Peppermint, Coriander, Ginger, Caraway, Cardamom, Fennel, Anise)	Cardamom, Coriander, Fennel, Ginger, Peppermint, Tamer™	Cardamom, Coriander, Cumin, Dill, Ginger, Peppermint, Tamer™
DILL	Cardamom, Celery Seed, DigestZen®, Fennel, Peppermint, Spearmint	Cardamom, Celery Seed, Cumin, DigestZen®, Peppermint, Spearmint
DOUGLAS FIR	Cypress, Frankincense, Northern Escape, Pink Pepper, Siberian Fir, Yarrow|Pom	Balsam Fir, Cypress, Frankincense, Hinoki, Yarrow|Pom
ELEVATION (Lavandin, Tangerine, Lavender, Amyris Bark, Clary Sage, Hawaiian Sandalwood, Ylang Ylang, Ho Wood, Osmanthus, Lemon Myrtle, Melissa)	Arise, Beautiful, Cheer®, Citrus Bloom™, Melissa	Cheer®
EUCALYPTUS	Abōde™, Breathe®, Cardamom, Laurel Leaf, Ravintsara, Rosemary	Breathe®, Cardamom, Laurel Leaf, Niaouli, Ravintsara, Rosemary
FENNEL	Basil, Cardamom, DigestZen®	DigestZen®
FORGIVE® (Spruce, Bergamot, Juniper Berry, Myrrh, Arborvitae, Nootka Tree, Thyme Leaf, Citronella)	Arborvitae, Black Spruce, Holiday Peace, Northern Escape, Thyme	Holiday Peace, Northern Escape, Zendocrine®
FRANKINCENSE	Anchor, Balance®, DDR Prime®, Douglas Fir, Ginger, Immortelle, InTune®, Myrrh, Pink Pepper, Siberian Fir, Spikenard, Stronger™, Turmeric	Balsam Fir, Balance, DDR Prime®, Douglas Fir, Hinoki, Immortelle, Pink Pepper
GERANIUM	ClaryCalm®, Console®, Davana, HD Clear®, Helichrysum, Lavender, Neroli, Rose, Zendrocrine®	Citronella, Lavender, Neroli, Palmarosa, Roman Chamomile, Rose, Zendocrine®
GINGER	Cedarwood, DigestZen®, Frankincense, Slim & Sassy®, Tamer™, Turmeric	Cedarwood, DigestZen®, Fennel, Slim & Sassy®
GRAPEFRUIT	Citrus Bliss®, Green Mandarin, Tangerine, Wild Orange	Clementine, Green Mandarin, Red Mandarin, Tangerine, Wild Orange
GREEN MANDARIN	Celery Seed, Grapefruit, Tangerine, Wild Orange	Celery Seed, Clementine, Grapefruit, Kumquat, Lemon, Red Mandarin, Tangerine, Wild Orange
HARVEST SPICE (Cassia, Clove, Eucalyptus, Cedarwood, Nutmeg, Cinnamon)	Brave™, Cheer®, Holiday Joy, On Guard®, Passion®, Tulsi	Cheer®

OIL	BY OUTCOME	BY CHEMISTRY
HD CLEAR® (Black Cumin Seed, Geranium, Ho Wood, Litsea, Eucalyptus, Tea Tree)	Abōde™, Air-X™, DDR Prime®, Forgive®, Geranium, Litsea, Tea Tree	DDR Prime®
HELICHRYSUM	Deep Blue®, Geranium, Immortelle, Ravintsara, Yarrow|Pom	Deep Blue®, Immortelle, Ravintsara, Yarrow|Pom
HINOKI	Amavi®, Black Pepper, Black Spruce, Cypress, Douglas Fir, Frankincense, Juniper Berry, Northern Escape, Siberian Fir	Amavi®, Black Pepper, Black Spruce, Cypress, Douglas Fir, Frankincense, Juniper Berry, Northern Escape, Siberian Fir
HOLIDAY JOY (Wild orange, Clove, Cassia, Siberian fir, Frankincense, Styrax, Ginger Co2, Balsam fir, Cistus)	Brave™, Cheer®, Harvest Spice, On Guard®, Passion®, Tulsi	Brave™, Cheer®, Harvest Spice, On Guard®, Passion®, Tulsi
HOLIDAY PEACE (Siberian Fir, Grapefruit, Douglas Fir, Himalayan Fir, Frankincense, Vetiver)	Cedarwood, Northern Escape, Siberian Fir	Cedarwood, Northern Escape, Siberian Fir
HOPE® (Bergamot, Ylang Ylang, Frankincense, Vanilla Bean Absolute)	Bergamot, Motivate®, Vanilla, Ylang Ylang	Bergamot, Motivate®, Vanilla, Ylang Ylang
HYGGE™ (Wild Orange, Cedarwood, Amyris, Frankincense, Myrrh, Cistus, Vetiver, Tonka Bean, Vanilla Absolute)	Anchor, Cedarwood, Frankincense, Harvest Spice, Holiday Joy, InTune®, Peace®, Steady™	Holiday Joy
HYSSOP	Manuka, Peppermint, Spearmint, Turmeric	Manuka, Peppermint, Spearmint, Turmeric
IMMORTELLE (Frankincense, Hawaiian Sandalwood, Lavender, Myrrh, Helichrysum, Rose)	Frankincense, Helichrysum, Lavender, Myrrh, Rose, Sandalwood, Yarrow|Pom	Frankincense, Rose, Sandalwood
INTUNE® (Amyris, Patchouli, Frankincense, Lime, Ylang Ylang, Hawaiian Sandalwood, Roman Chamomile)	Frankincense, Hawaiian Sandalwood, Patchouli, Peace®, Serenity®, Thinker™, Vetiver	Patchouli, Sandalwood, Steady
ISLAND MINT® (Lime, Lemon, Peppermint, Spruce)	Bergamot Mint, Peppermint, Spearmint, Tamer™	Unique
JASMINE	Arborvitae, Clary Sage, Davana, Magnolia, Neroli, Passion®, Petitgrain, Roman Chamomile, Rose, Whisper®, Ylang Ylang	Clary Sage, Petitgrain, Roman Chamomile
JUNIPER BERRY	Black Pepper, Blue Tansy, Celery Seed, Coriander, Cypress, Rosemary, Yarrow|Pom, Zendrocrine®	Black Pepper, Blue Tansy, Hinoki, Yarrow|Pom
KUMQUAT	Grapefruit, Green Mandarin, Tangerine, Wild Orange	Green Mandarin, Red Mandarin
LAUREL LEAF	Breathe®, Cardamom, Eucalyptus, Ravintsara, Rosemary	Cardamom, Eucalyptus, Niaouli, Ravintsara, Rosemary
LAVENDER	Adaptiv™, Anchor, Bergamot Mint, Black Pepper, Black Spruce, Calmer™, Clary Sage, Geranium, Immortelle, Petitgrain, Serenity®	Black Spruce, Clary Sage, Geranium, Petitgrain
LEMON	Citrus Bliss®, Green Mandarin, Lime, Purify	Lime, Green Mandarin, Red Mandarin
LEMON EUCALYPTUS	Abōde™, Cilantro, Citronella, TerraShield®	Cassia, Citronella, Lemon Myrtle

SUBSTITUTIONS

OIL	BY OUTCOME	BY CHEMISTRY
LEMON MYRTLE	Air-X™, Abōde™, Cassia, DDR Prime®, Lemon Eucalyptus, Litsea, Melissa	Cassia, Lemon Eucalyptus, Litsea
LEMONGRASS	Abōde™, Air-X™, DDR Prime®, Litsea, Melissa, TerraShield®	Air-X™, Lemon Myrtle, Litsea, Melissa
LIME	Abōde™, Black Pepper, Lemon, Purify	Lemon
LITSEA	Abōde™, Air-X™, Lemongrass, Lemon, Melissa, Stronger™	Lemongrass, Lemon Myrtle, Melissa
MAGNOLIA	Beautiful, Bergamot, Citrus Bloom™, Clary Sage, Coriander, Jasmine, Neroli, Petitgrain, Rose, Steady™, Ylang Ylang	Beautiful, Coriander, Rose
MANUKA	Patchouli, Spikenard, Ylang Ylang	Hyssop, Patchouli, Spikenard, Ylang Ylang
MARJORAM	AromaTouch®, Basil, Cilantro, PastTense®, Tea Tree	AromaTouch®, Basil, Cilantro, Peppermint, Tea Tree
MELISSA	Air-X™, Arise, Black Pepper, Cilantro, Elevation, Lemongrass, Litsea, On Guard™+ Softgels	Black Pepper, Cilantro, Citronella, Litsea, Lemongrass, Lemon Myrtle
MOTIVATE® (Peppermint, Clementine, Coriander, Basil, Yuzu, Melissa, Rosemary, Vanilla Bean Absolute)	AromaTouch®, Cheer®, Clementine, Hope®, Peppermint	Unique
MYRRH	Frankincense, Immortelle, InTune®, Patchouli, Sandalwood, Spikenard, Turmeric, Vetiver	Unique
NEROLI	Adaptiv™, Bergamot, Cypress, Geranium, Jasmine, Magnolia, Petitgrain	Cypress, Geranium, Petitgrain
NIAOULI	Breathe®, Eucalyptus, Laurel Leaf, Ravintsara	Eucalyptus, Laurel Leaf, Ravintsara
NOOTKA	Arborvitae, Cedarwood, Northern Escape	Cedarwood
NORTHERN ESCAPE	Align, Black Spruce, Cypress, Douglas Fir, Forgive®, Holiday Peace, Siberian Fir, Tulsi	Holiday Peace
ON GUARD® (Wild Orange, Clove, Cinnamon, Cinnamon, Eucalyptus, Rosemary)	Cheer®, Cinnamon, Clove, Harvest Spice, Holiday Joy, Passion®, Stronger™, Tulsi	Cinnamon, Clove, DDR Prime®, Passion, Stronger
OREGANO	Clove, On Guard™+ Softgels, Thyme	Clove, Thyme
OSMANTHUS	Beautiful, Magnolia	Magnolia
PALMAROSA	Citronella, Coriander, Geranium, Roman Chamomile	Citronella, Coriander, Geranium, Roman Chamomile
PASSION® (Cardamom, Cinnamon, Ginger, Clove, Sandalwood, Jasmine Absolute, Vanilla Bean Absolute, Damiana)	Cardamom, Cinnamon, Ginger, Harvest Spice, Holiday Joy, Jasmine, On Guard®	OnGuard®
PASTTENSE® (Wintergreen, Lavender, Peppermint, Frankincense, Cilantro, Marjoram, Roman Chamomile, Basil, Rosemary)	AromaTouch®, Basil, Deep Blue®, Marjoram, Motivate®, Peppermint, Wintergreen	AromaTouch®
PATCHOULI	Anchor, Console®, InTune®, Myrrh, Sandalwood, Spikenard, Vetiver, Whisper®	InTune®, Manuka, Sandalwood, Spikenard, Vetiver

OIL	BY OUTCOME	BY CHEMISTRY
PEACE® (Vetiver, Lavender, Ylang Ylang, Frankincense, Clary Sage, Marjoram, Labdanum Absolute, Spearmint)	Anchor, Hygge™, InTune®, Lavender, Serenity®, Thinker™, Vetiver, Ylang Ylang	Lavender, Serenity®, Vetiver
PEPPERMINT	Breathe®, Deep Blue®, DigestZen®, Island Mint®, Motivate®, PastTense®, Spearmint, Tamer™, Thinker™	Basil, Deep Blue®, DigestZen®, Dill, Hyssop, Spearmint
PETITGRAIN	Arborvitae, Bergamot Mint, Black Spruce, Clary Sage, Jasmine, Lavender, Magnolia, Neroli, Roman Chamomile	Arborvitae, Bergamot Mint, Black Spruce, Clary Sage, Jasmine, Lavender
PINK PEPPER	DDR Prime®, Douglas Fir, Frankincense	Balsam Fir, Douglas Fir, Frankincense
PURIFY (Lemon, Siberian Fir, Citronella, Lime, Tea Tree, Cilantro)	Abōde™, Cilantro, Citronella, Lemon, Lime, Siberian Fir, Tea Tree	Abōde™
RAVINTSARA	Breathe®, Eucalyptus, Helichrysum, Laurel Leaf	Eucalyptus, Helichrysum, Laurel Leaf, Niaouli
RED MANDARIN	Grapefruit, Green Mandarin, Lemon, Tangerine, Wild Orange	Lemon
RESCUER™ (Copaiba, Lavender, Spearmint, Zanthoxylum)	Copaiba, Deep Blue®, Deep Blue® Stick, Lavender, Spearmint	Copaiba, Deep Blue®
ROMAN CHAMOMILE	Arborvitae, Blue Tansy, Calmer™, ClaryCalm®, Clary Sage, Jasmine, Lavender, Palmarosa, Petitgrain, Serenity®	Arborvitae, Clary Sage, Jasmine, Palmarosa, Geranium
ROSE	Citronella, Console®, Davana, Geranium, Immortelle, Jasmine, Magnolia, Stronger™, Whisper®, Ylang Ylang	Citronella, Geranium, Immortelle, Magnolia
ROSEMARY	Basil, Blue Tansy, Eucalyptus, Juniper Berry, Laurel Leaf, Thinker™	Blue Tansy, Eucalyptus, Laurel Leaf
SANDALWOOD	Anchor, Cedarwood, Immortelle, InTune®, Myrrh, Patchouli, Spikenard, Vetiver	Patchouli, Vetiver
SERENITY® (Lavender, Cedarwood, Ho Wood, Ylang Ylang, Marjoram, Roman Chamomile, Vetiver, Vanilla Bean Absolute, Hawaiian Sandalwood)	Calmer™, Cedarwood, ClaryCalm®, Frankincense, Lavender, InTune®, Peace®, Ylang Ylang	Cedarwood, Lavender, Peace®
SIBERIAN FIR	Black Spruce, Cypress, Douglas Fir, Frankincense, Hinoki, Holiday Peace, Northern Escape, Purify	Black Spruce, Cypress
SLIM & SASSY® (Grapefruit, Lemon, Peppermint, Ginger, Cinnamon)	Cinnamon, Ginger, Grapefruit, Lemon, Peppermint	Cinnamon, Ginger, Grapefruit
SPEARMINT	Bergamot Mint, Island Mint®, Peppermint, Rescuer™, Tamer™, Turmeric	Dill, Hyssop, Peppermint, Turmeric
SPIKENARD	Cedarwood, Myrrh, Patchouli, Ylang Ylang	Cedarwood, Patchouli, Ylang Ylang
STEADY™ (Amyris, Balsam Fir, Coriander, Magnolia)	Balance®, Hygge™, InTune®, Magnolia	InTune®
STRONGER™ (Cedarwood, Litsea, Frankincense, Rose)	Cedarwood, Frankincense, Holiday Joy, Litsea, On Guard®, Rose	OnGuard®

SUBSTITUTIONS

OIL	BY OUTCOME	BY CHEMISTRY
SUMMER SAVORY	DDR Prime®, Melissa	Cumin, Melissa
TAMER™ (Spearmint, Japanese Peppermint, Ginger, Black Pepper, Parsley)	DigestZen®, Ginger, Island Mint®, Peppermint, Spearmint	Digestzen®
TANGERINE	Citrus Bliss®, Grapefruit, Green Mandarin, Wild Orange	Clementine, Grapefruit, Green Mandarin, Kumquat, Red Mandarin, Wild Orange
TEA TREE	Abōde™, HD Clear®, Marjoram	Marjoram, Neroli
TERRASHIELD® (Citronella, Lemongrass, Thyme, Cedarwood, Geranium, Peppermint, Sesame Seed Oil)	Abōde™, Arborvitae, Citronella, Lemon Eucalyptus, Lemongrass, Thyme	Arborvitae, Citronella, Lemongrass
THINKER™ (Vetiver, Peppermint, Clementine, Rosemary)	InTune®, Peace®, Peppermint, Rosemary, Vetiver	Vetiver
THYME	Clove, DDR Prime®, Forgive®, Oregano, TerraShield®, Tulsi	Clove, Oregano
TULSI	Basil, Blue Tansy, Clove, Copaiba, Coriander, Fennel	Blue Tansy, Clove, Copaiba, Ylang Ylang
TURMERIC	Ginger, Myrrh, Spearmint	Hyssop, Spearmint
VANILLA	Cheer®, Citrus Bliss®, Hope®, Whisper®	Unique
VETIVER	InTune®, Myrrh, Patchouli, Peace®, Sandalwood, Thinker™, Whisper®	Patchouli, Sandalwood
WHITE FIR	Arborvitae, Douglas Fir, Grapefruit, Neroli, Northern Escape, Pink Pepper, Siberian Fir	Siberian Fir, Black Pepper
WHISPER® (Patchouli, Bergamot, Sandalwood, Vanilla Bean Absolute, Rose, Jasmine, Cinnamon, Vetiver, Labdanum, Cocoa Seed, Ylang Ylang)	Bergamot, Jasmine, Neroli, Patchouli, Rose, Sandalwood, Vanilla, Vetiver, Ylang Ylang	Patchouli, Rose, Sandalwood
WILD ORANGE	Adaptiv™, Cheer®, Citrus Bliss®, DDR Prime®, Grapefruit, Green Mandarin, Tangerine	DDR Prime®, Clementine, Grapefruit, Green Mandarin, Red Mandarin, Tangerine
WINTERGREEN	AromaTouch®, Birch, Deep Blue®, PastTense®	Birch, Deep Blue
YARROW|POM	Black Pepper, Blue Tansy, Douglas Fir, Helichrysum, Immortelle, Juniper, Ylang Ylang	Black Pepper, Blue Tansy, Douglas Fir, Juniper Berry, Ylang Ylang
YLANG YLANG	Black Pepper, Calmer™, ClaryCalm®, Console®, Copaiba, Hope®, Jasmine, Magnolia, Peace®, Rose, Tulsi, Whisper®, Yarrow|Pom	Black Pepper, Yarrow|Pom
ZENDOCRINE® (Tangerine, Rosemary, Geranium, Juniper Berry, Cilantro)	Cilantro, Forgive®, Geranium, Juniper Berry, Rosemary, Tangerine	Forgive®, Geranium

RESOURCES

CHEMICAL COMPOUND GROUP AND EXAMPLES	THERAPEUTIC BENEFITS	OILS CONTAINING SOME OF THE GROUP	MOLECULAR STRUCTURE
Monoterpene Hydrocarbon *(a & β-pinene, limonene, sabinene, phellandrene)*	Inhibit the accumulation of toxins and help discharge existing toxins, anti-inflammatory, antibacterial, soothing to irritated tissues, insect repellent, cancer-preventative properties, cellular protective	basil, citrus oils, cypress, Douglas fir, frankincense, ginger, juniper berry, litsea, marjoram, tea tree, pink pepper, rosemary, Siberian fir, thyme, yarrow|pom	10 carbon terpenes
Sesquiterpene Hydrocarbon *(chamazulene, faresene, zingiberene)*	Anti-inflammatory, sedative, soothing, antibacterial, soothing to irritated skin and tissue, liver and glandular stimulant	black pepper, blue tansy, cedarwood, copaiba, ginger, helichrysum, myrrh, patchouli, spikenard, ylang ylang	15 carbon terpenes
Monoterpene Alcohols *(borneol, geraniol, linalool)*	Antimicrobial, supports immune system, restorative to skin, cleansing, antispasmodic, sedative, gentle, mild	basil, coriander, frankincense, geranium, lavender, magnolia, marjoram, tea tree, neroli, petitgrain, rose	10 carbon terpenoids bound to a hydroxyl group, high resistance to oxidation
Sesquiterpene Alcohols	Anti-allergenic, antibacterial, anti-inflammatory, liver and glandular stimulant	cedarwood, patchouli, sandalwood, vetiver, yarrow|pom	15 carbon terpenoids bound to a hydroxyl group bound to a carbon instead of a hydrogen
Esters *(geranyl acetate, linalyl acetate, methyl salicylate)*	Very calming, relaxing, and balancing, antifungal, antispasmodic, balancing to nervous system	arborvitae, bergamot, birch, cardamom, clary sage, helichrysum, jasmine, lavender, petitgrain, Roman chamomile, wintergreen, ylang ylang	Consists of a carboxyl group (carbon atom double-bonded to an oxygen atom)
Aldehydes *(citral, geranial, neral)*	Powerful aromas, calming to emotions, anti-infectious, anti-inflammatory, calming to autonomic nervous system, fever-reducing, hypotensive, tonic	cassia, cilantro, cinnamon, geranium, lemongrass, lime, litsea, marjoram, melissa	Consists of a carboxyl group (carbon atom double-bonded to an oxygen atom). Slightly fruity odor, can cause skin irritation
Ketones *(camphor, jasmone)*	Mucolytic, stimulate cell regeneration, promote the formation of tissue, analgesic, sedative	fennel, helichrysum, lavender, lemongrass, manuka, myrrh, peppermint, Roman chamomile, rosemary, spearmint, spikenard, turmeric, vetiver	Consists of a carboxyl group (carbon atom double-bonded Xto an oxygen atom)
Phenols *(carvacrol, eugenol, thymol)*	Powerful antibacterial, anti-infectious, antiseptic, very stimulating to the autonomic nervous system, analgesic, antifungal, cancer preventative	cinnamon, clove, oregano, thyme	Consists of a benzene ring—6 carbon atoms bound in a circle—and a hydroxyl group. May be irritating to skin, some concerns at high dosages for liver toxicity. Use for short periods of time.
Oxides *(1,8 cineole)*	Expectorant, mildly stimulating, respiratory support, pain relief, anti-inflammatory	basil, cardamom, clary sage, clove, cypress, eucalyptus, fennel, tea tree, peppermint, rosemary, thyme,	An oxygen atom has become bound between two carbon atoms.
Ethers *(estragole, anethole)*	Balancing to autonomic nervous system, soothing, sedative	basil, fennel, marjoram, ylang ylang,	Compounds in which an oxygen atom in the molecule is bonded to two carbon atoms.
Lactones *(coumarin)*	Expectorant properties	In very low amounts in some essential oils	Consists of an ester group integrated into a carbon ring system. Has a vanilla-like odor
Coumarins *(bergamottin)*		bergamot	phototoxic

BLENDING *and* LAYERING

When using essential oils, the desired outcome may best be accomplished by using more than one essential oil at a time. To do so, the oils may be layered topically, ingested separately, or placed together in a blend. Layering is defined as applying one essential oil to the skin, waiting for it to be absorbed, and then applying another oil over the first. This may be repeated several times until all the desired oils are applied. Massage expedites and improves this absorption process. Oils are absorbed rapidly into the skin, so the wait time can be short. A carrier oil, such as fractionated coconut oil, may be applied prior to or along with an oil application. In some cases, layering is a preferred method for topical use, as it requires less skill and knowledge than blending, and allows the oil selections to be varied at every application.

Layering is particularly useful when multiple concerns must be addressed simultaneously. For example, a sprained or twisted ankle may involve tendons or ligaments (connective tissue) as well as muscle or bone. Furthermore, bruising and swelling may be present. Increasing blood flow to the injury site would also be useful for healing. Each of these concerns may be addressed through the use of layering.

Here is an example of an injured tissue layering sequence:

- **1–2 drops of lemongrass**—for connective tissue: apply, massage lightly if possible, wait for absorption
- **1–2 drops of marjoram**—for muscle: apply, massage lightly if possible, wait for absorption
- **1–2 drops of cypress**—for circulation: apply, massage lightly if possible, wait for absorption
- **1–2 drops of helichrysum**—for pain: apply, massage lightly if possible, wait for absorption
- **1–2 drops of wintergreen**—for bone: apply, massage lightly if possible, wait for absorption

This layering sequence would be repeatedly applied to expedite healing. For example, application every 30–60 minutes for the first four applications may be followed by application every 4–6 hours the following few days. Finally, twice-a-day application may be used once the pain has mostly subsided and until complete healing has occurred.

In addition to layering the oils, there are times when creating an essential oil blend is a good or better way to achieve an intended result such as calming a mood, relaxing muscles, or supporting a distressed respiratory system. Blending is the process of combining multiple selected essential oils together in one bottle. The chemical profile of a blend is very different from each of the individual oils it contains. Combining essential oils together creates a synergistic effect, forming a new, unique molecular structure.

There is an art to blending, which is enhanced and improved by practice and through applying proven techniques and principles. Artistry and skill combine to creating a blend that is aromatically pleasing and that accomplishes the desired therapeutic outcome or goal. Since essential oils are potent and often expensive, care should be taken to blend appropriately so as not to waste essential oils or to create a blend that may cause an adverse reaction, such as a headache or skin sensitivity. There are many resources and educational classes on the art of blending essential oils.

One excellent resource is *Aromatherapy Workbook* by Marcel Lavabre. A study of the basic chemical makeup of essential oil aids in creating therapeutically effective blends. For a foundational understanding of the main chemical constituents in essential oils refer to the *Resources: Oil Composition & Chemistry* in this book.

BLENDING GUIDELINES

Some basic guidelines help in blending regardless of the method used:

1. The "Blends Well With" listings under each oil description in the "Natural Solutions: Oils" assist in selecting oils that blend well together.
2. Blends that have been professionally created are best used as they are.
3. Essential oils from the same botanical family usually blend well together.
4. Essential oils with similar constituents usually mix well together.
5. A blend should be aromatically pleasing.
6. It is best to use the smallest amount of oil possible when experimenting with a blend.
7. It is helpful to label your blend.
8. Be specific in defining your desired outcome.
9. Keeping a blending journal serves as a reference for making adjustments or remembering what worked.
10. As a beginner, it is best to start with blending four to six essential oils for a total of fifteen to twenty drops in the blend.

PLACE IN BLEND	NAME OF CLASSIFICATION	PERCENTAGE OF THE BLEND	CHARACTERISTICS	EXAMPLE OILS IN THIS CLASSIFICATION
First	Personifier	1-5%	Sharp, strong, and long-lasting aroma, dominant properties, strong therapeutic action	birch, black pepper, blue tansy, cassia, cardamom, cinnamon, clary sage, clove, copaiba, coriander, ginger, helichrysum, neroli, orange, peppermint, Roman chamomile, rose, spearmint, tangerine, vetiver, wintergreen, and ylang ylang
Second	Enhancer	50-80%	Enhances the properties of the other oils in the blend, not a sharp aroma; evaporates faster than the Personifier	arborvitae, basil, bergamot, birch, cassia, cedarwood, cinnamon, dill, eucalyptus, frankincense, geranium, grapefruit, jasmine, lavender, lemon, lemongrass, lime, litsea, manuka, marjoram, tea tree, melissa, orange, oregano, patchouli, rose, rosemary, thyme, wintergreen, and yarrow|pom
Third	Equalizer	10-15%	Creates balance and synergy among the oils in the blend	arborvitae, basil, bergamot, cederwood, cilantro, cypress, fennel, frankincense, geranium, ginger, jasmine, juniper berry, lavender, lemongrass, lime, litsea, marjoram, tea tree, melissa, myrrh, neroli, oregano, rose, sandalwood, Siberian fir, thyme
Fourth	Modifier	5-8%	Mild; evaporates quickly, adds harmony to the blend	bergamot, black pepper, cardamom, coriander, eucalyptus, fennel, grapefruit, jasmine, lavender, lemon, melissa, myrrh, neroli, rose, sandalwood, tangerine, and ylang ylang

There are differing opinions and experiences as to what order oils should be added to a blend. It is has been shown in a laboratory that in small amounts, such as blends for personal use, order doesn't matter. However, if blending in large amounts (e.g. companies that create their own blends en masse to sell) the order in which oils are added may be very important.

Blending Methods

There are three suggested techniques for creating essential oil blends:

1. Blending Classifications Method.
2. Odor Types/Notes Method.
3. Combination of Techniques (Chemical Compounds and Odor Types) Method.

An in-depth description of each of these methods or techniques is beyond the scope of this book, though a summary is included here for each method. Practice and study improves the ability to create effective and aromatically pleasing blends.

Blending Classification Method

This method uses the four blending classifications: personifier, enhancer, equalizer, and modifier. Below is a description of each classification.

The table on the bottom left provides an example of a blend for easing muscle strain using the Blending Classification Method. Using this recipe, mix the four oils in the order listed in a 10mL roller bottle and fill with a carrier oil such as fractionated coconut oil for dilution.

Odor Types/Notes

This second method focuses on the odor and odor intensity ascribed to each essential oil. The perfume industry has assigned perfume "notes" to essential oils. The three notes are base, middle, and top. These assignments can be used as a guide in creating a blend.

Top notes are light oils and often have fresh, sweet, citrusy, or fruity aromas. Middle notes are oils that have a floral, slight woody, or sweet aroma. Base notes are woody, heavy, earthy, rich, or deep. Some oils such as basil or fennel may be used in a blend as either a top or middle note. Clary sage and ylang ylang are examples of oils that may be used as either middle or base notes. When creating a blend, base notes are 5% to 20% of the blend, middle notes are 50% to 80%, and top notes are 5% to 20% of the blend. This blending method is more focused on aroma than therapeutic benefits.

Following is an example of a blend designed to ease muscle strain using the **Odor Types/Notes** method. Using this recipe, mix the four oils in the order listed in a 10mL roller bottle and fill with a carrier oil such as fractionated coconut oil for dilution.

CLASSIFICATION	AMOUNT*	ESSENTIAL OIL
Personifier	1 drop	cinnamon
Enhancer	8 drops	basil
Equalizer	2 drops	ginger
Modifier	4 drops	grapefruit

**based on a 15-drop blend*

ODOR TYPE/NOTE	AMOUNT*	OIL
Base Note	3 drops	sandalwood
Middle Note	3 drops	ginger
Middle Note	4 drops	cypress
Top Note	5 drops	wild orange

**based on a 15-drop blend*

Following is a table of single oils with their scent profile and assigned scent note. Knowing an oils scent note is critical in blending using the note type classification method.

OIL	SCENT PROFILE	SCENT NOTE
Arborvitae	Intense, medicinal, woody, earthy	Top to Middle
Basil	Herbaceous, spicy, anise-like, camphoraceous, lively	Top to Middle
Bergamot	Sweet, lively, citrusy, fruity	Top
Birch	Sweet, sharp, camphoraceous, fresh	Middle
Black pepper	Spicy, peppery, musky, warm, with herbaceous undertones.	Middle
Blue tansy	Sweet, slightly-floral, fruity	Middle
Cardamom	Sweet, spicy, balsamic, with floral undertones	Middle
Cassia	Spicy, warm, sweet	Middle
Cilantro	Herbaceous, citrusy, fresh	Top
Cinnamon	Spicy, earthy, sweet	Middle
Clary sage	Herbaceous, spicy, hay-like, sharp fixative	Middle to Base
Clove	Spicy, warming, slightly bitter, woody	Middle to Base
Copaiba	Sweet, woody	Base
Coriander	Woody, spicy, sweet	Middle
Cypress	Fresh, herbaceous, slightly woody with evergreen undertones	Middle
Dill	Fresh, sweet, herbaceous	Middle
Douglas fir	Clean, fresh, woody, sweet	Middle
Eucalyptus	Slightly camphorous, sweet, fruity	Middle
Fennel (sweet)	Sweet, somewhat spicy, licorice-like	Top to Middle
Frankincense	Rich, deep, warm, balsamic, sweet, with incense-like overtones	Base
Geranium	Sweet, green, citrus-rosy, fresh	Middle
Ginger	Sweet, spicy-woody, warm, tenacious, fresh, sharp	Middle
Grapefruit	Clean, fresh, bitter, citrusy	Top
Green mandarin	Sweet, bright, citrusy, tangy	Top
Helichrysum	Rich, sweet, fruity, with tea and honey undertones	Middle
Jasmine	Powerful, sweet, tenacious, floral with fruity-herbaceous undertones	Base
Juniper berry	Sweet, balsamic, tenacious	Middle
Kumquat	Refreshing, citrus, bright, rich	Top
Lavender	Floral, sweet, herbaceous, balsamic, woody undertones	Middle
Lemon	Sweet, sharp, clear, citrusy	Top
Lemongrass	Grassy, lemony, pungent, earthy, slightly bitter	Top

OIL	SCENT PROFILE	SCENT NOTE
Lime	Sweet, tart, intense, lively	Top
Litsea	Crisp, citrusy, fresh	Top
Magnolia	Sweet, fruity, exotic, rich, heady, radiant	Top
Manuka	Warm, rich, sweet	Middle
Marjoram	Herbaceous, green, spicy	Middle
Melissa	Delicate, lemony, spicy	Middle
Myrrh	Warm, earthy, woody, balsamic	Base
Neroli	Light, sweet-floral	Top or Base
Orange	Fresh, citrusy, fruity, sweet	Top
Oregano	Spicy, warm, herbaceous, sharp	Middle
Patchouli	Earthy, herbaceous, sweet, balsamic, rich, with woody undertones	Base
Peppermint	Minty, sharp, intense	Middle
Petitgrain	Fresh, floral, woody, slightly herbaceous	Top
Pink pepper	Intense, dry, warm, sweet-spicy with a faint floral note, slightly smoky undertone	Middle
Red mandarin	smooth, sweet-tart, citrusy, slightly floral undertone	Top
Roman chamomile	Fresh, sweet, fruity-herbaceous, apple-like, no tenacity	Middle
Rose	Floral, spicy, rich, deep, sensual, green, honey-like	Middle to Base
Rosemary	Herbaceous, strong, camphorous, with woody-balsamic and evergreen undertones	Middle
(Hawaiian) Sandalwood	Soft, woody, spicy, sweet, earthy, balsamic	Base
Siberian fir	Fresh, soft-pine	Middle to Top
Spearmint	Minty, slightly fruity, less bright than peppermint	Top
Spikenard	Earthy, woody, musty, spicy	Base
Tangerine	Fresh, sweet, citrusy	Top
Tea tree	Medicinal, fresh, woody, earthy, herbaceous	Middle
Thyme	Fresh, medicinal, herbaceous	Middle
Turmeric	Woody, spicy, fresh, warm	Base
Vetiver	Earthy, heavy, woody, smoky, balsamic	Base
Siberian fir	Fresh, woody, earthy, sweet	Middle
Wintergreen	Minty, camphorous, fresh	Top
Yarrow|pom	Fresh, green-herbaceous, woody	Middle
Ylang ylang	Sweet, heavy, euphoric, tropical floral, with spicy-balsamic undertones	Middle to Base

Combination of Techniques (Chemistry Compounds and Scent Types)

The first two blending methods are primarily focused on creating a pleasing aroma with secondary consideration to the end therapeutic goal. The Combination of Techniques method allows for both aroma and therapeutic effectiveness to be considered. When creating a blend, first set a specific end goal. Then select specific essential oils, based on desired therapeutic benefits from their chemical compounds. By also considering scent types, both an effective and aromatically pleasing blend is created. Refer to Oil Composition & Chemistry in previous section.

The steps to create a blend by considering essential oil chemical compounds and odor types are listed below. Fine-tuning these steps necessarily includes intuitive action and experience.

1. Select the desired outcome. The more specific the outcome, the more effective the blend will be.
2. Select the essential oil chemical compound groups that will best meet the goal.
3. Select approximately eight to fifteen essential oils from these groups to draw from.
4. Note the scent profile/note for each of the selected oils.
5. Select one oil as the base note, two to three oils as the middle notes, and one oil to be the top note (This is a guideline; use intuition and experience to alter.).
6. Decide how many drops will be used for each of the five oils selected. A fifteen-drop blend is a good ratio for a 5mL or 10mL bottle with a carrier oil.
7. Place the oils in the bottle and add the carrier oil. As the blend is used to meet the desired outcome, make notes in a blending journal.

The following is an example of using the steps to create a blend to ease muscle strain using Combination of Techniques Method.

Steps 1-2: the following table is used to identify the most helpful chemical compound groups to meet the blend goal. In this example, aldehydes, esters, sesquiterpene hydrocarbons, and ethers would be helpful.

Steps 3-4: the following is an example (see next page) of a list of oils chosen from the four selected chemical groups, which will help meet the desired outcome of easing muscle strain.

The letter next to each oil indicates the odor type assigned to that oil so as to assist with selection: (T) Top, (M) Middle, (B) Base.

CHEMICAL COMPOUND GROUP	THERAPEUTIC BENEFITS	OILS
Monoterpene Hydrocarbon	Cellular protective, anti-inflammatory, antibacterial	basil, citrus oils, cypress, Douglas fir, frankincense, ginger, juniper berry, litsea, neroli, pink pepper, rosemary, Siberian fir, tangerine, thyme, yarrow
Sesquiterpene Hydrocarbon	Anti-inflammatory, sedative, soothing, antibacterial	black pepper, blue tansy, cedarwood, copaiba, ginger, helichrysum, manuka, myrrh, patchouli, spikenard, Siberian fir, ylang ylang
Monoterpene Alcohols	Antimicrobial, somewhat stimulating, tonifying and restorative to the skin, cleansing, antispasmodic, sedative, gentle, mild	basil, cilantro, coriander, frankincense, geranium, lavender, magnolia, marjoram, tea tree, petitgrain, neroli, rose
Sesquiterpene Alcohols	Anti-allergenic, antibacterial, anti-inflammatory, liver and glandular stimulant	cedarwood, geranium, patchouli, sandalwood, vetiver, yarrow
Esters	Very calming, relaxing, balancing, antifungal, antispasmodic	arborvitae, bergamot, birch, cardamom, cassia, clary sage, clove, geranium, helichrysum, jasmine, lavender, peppermint, petitgrain, Roman chamomile, wintergreen, ylang ylang
Aldehydes	Strong aroma; calming to the emotions, anti-infectious, anti-inflammatory, calming overall, fever-reducing, hypotensive, and tonic; some are vasodilators	cassia, cinnamon, geranium, lemongrass, lime, litsea, marjoram, melissa, Roman chamomile
Ketones	Mucolytic, stimulate cell regeneration, promote the formation of tissue, analgesic, sedative	fennel, helichrysum, lavender, manuka, myrrh, peppermint, Roman chamomile, rosemary, spearmint, spikenard, turmeric, vetiver
Phenols	Powerful antibacterial, anti-infective, and antiseptic, very stimulating to the autonomic nervous system	cinnamon, clove, oregano, thyme
Oxides	Expectorant, mildly stimulating	basil, cardamom, clary sage, clove, cypress, fennel, tea tree, peppermint, rosemary, thyme
Ethers	Balancing to the autonomic nervous system, soothing, sedative	basil, fennel, eucalyptus, marjoram, myrrh, ylang ylang

Aldehyde:	lemongrass (T), Roman chamomile (M)
Esters:	Roman chamomile (M), geranium (M), ylang ylang (M to B)
Sesquiterpene Hydrocarbons:	cedarwood (B), Siberian fir (M), black pepper (M), ginger (M), ylang ylang (M to T)
Ethers:	basil (M to T), ylang ylang (M to T), marjoram (M)

Steps 5-7: Using the above list of selected oils, select five oils and the number of drops needed from each oil to create the blend that will equal a total of fifteen drops. The blend can be placed in a 5mL or 10mL roller bottle and topped off with a carrier oil to fill the bottle.

Base note:	cedarwood	(4 drops)
Middle note:	Roman chamomile	(2 drops)
Middle note:	ginger	(2 drops)
Middle note:	black pepper	(3 drops)
Top note:	ylang ylang	(4 drops)

When using essential oils for a therapeutic goal, it is often helpful to use more than one oil. Layering these oils following the suggested steps outlined here is beneficial to accomplish the desired outcome. When time permits, it may also be helpful to create a blend using oils selected based on their chemical compounds and their note type as outlined in this section. Intuition and experience improves blending skills.

Oil PROPERTIES GLOSSARY

Analgesic— relieves or allays pain

Anaphrodisiac— reduces sexual desire

Anti-allergenic— reduces allergic response

Antiarthritic— effective in treatment of arthritis

Antibacterial— kills or inhibits growth of bacteria

Anticarcinogenic— inhibits development of cancer

Anti-carcinoma— destroys or inhibits cancer cells

Anticatarrhal— removes excess mucus

Anticoagulant— prevents clotting of blood

Anticonvulsant— reduces convulsions

Antidepressant— effective in treatment against depression

Antiemetic— effective against nausea and vomiting

Antifungal— inhibits growth of fungi

Antihemorrhagic— promotes hemostasis; stops bleeding

Antihistamine— blocks histamine receptors; reduces allergic response

Anti-infectious— reduces/prevents infection

Anti-inflammatory— reduces inflammation

Antimicrobial— kills or inhibits microorganisms

Antimutagenic— reduces rate of genetic variants/mutation

Antioxidant— mitigates damage by free radicals

Anti-parasitic— destroys or inhibits growth/reproduction of parasites

Anti-rheumatic— mitigates pain and stiffness

Antiseptic— destroys microorganisms to prevent or treat infection on living tissue/skin

Antispasmodic— relieves spasms of involuntary muscles

Antitoxic— neutralizes or counteracts toxins

Anti-tumoral— inhibits growth of tumors

Antiviral— destroys viruses or suppresses replication

Aphrodisiac— heightens sexual desire

Astringent— contracts tissues, generally of the skin; reduces minor bleeding

Calming— pacifying

Cardiotonic— tones and vitalizes the heart

Carminative— reduces gas or bloating

Cleanser— cleanses body and/or household surfaces

Cytophylactic— stimulates cell growth

Decongestant— reduces respiratory congestion; opens airways

Deodorant— stops formation of odors

Detoxifier— removes toxins from the body tissues and organs

Digestive stimulant— stimulates digestion

Disinfectant— mitigates growth of microorganisms on inorganic surfaces

Diuretic— increases production and excretion of urine

Emmenagogue— regulates and induces menstruation

Energizing— generates and enhances energy

Expectorant— promotes discharge of phlegm and other fluids from the respiratory tract

Galactagogue— promotes lactation and increases milk supply

Grounding— assists one's sense of feeling centered and secure

Hypertensive— raises blood pressure

Hypotensive— lowers blood pressure

Immunostimulant— induces activation of the body's protective ability

Insect repellent— deters insects and bugs

Insecticidal— kills insects and bugs

Invigorating— revitalizes and rejuvenates

Laxative— stimulates bowel excretion

Mucolytic— loosens, thins, and breaks down mucus

Nervine— beneficial effect on nerves

Neuroprotective— protects nerves

Neurotonic— improves tone or force of nervous system

Purifier— eliminates impurities

Refreshing— renews; promotes feeling of freshness

Regenerative— promotes regeneration of body tissue

Relaxant— promotes relaxation; reduces tension

Restorative— encourages repair, recovery, restoration

Revitalizer— uplifts and energizes

Rubefacient— increases circulation; increases skin redness

Sedative— promotes calm and sleep; reduces agitation; tranquilizing

Steroidal— stimulates cortisone-like action

Stimulant— increases activity

Stomachic— assists digestion, promotes appetite

Tonic— promotes a feeling of vigor or well being

Uplifting— elevating; promotes sense of happiness and hope

Vasoconstrictor— restricts blood vessels; decreases blood flow; can increase blood pressure

Vasodilator— relaxes/dilates blood vessels; increases blood flow; can decrease blood pressure

Vermicide— kills parasitic worms

Vermifuge— stuns parasites

Warming— raises body and/or specific body tissue temperature—referred to as "localized warming"

Oil PROPERTIES CHART A-P

Oil Properties	analgesic	anaphrodisiac	anti-allergenic	antiarthritic	antibacterial	anticarcinogenic	anti-carcinoma	anticatarrhal	anticoagulant	anticonvulsant	antidepressant	antiemetic	antifungal	antihemorrhagic	antihistamine	anti-infectious	anti-inflammatory	antimicrobial	antimutagenic	antioxidant	anti-parasitic	antirheumatic	antiseptic	antispasmodic	antitoxic	anti-tumoral	antiviral	aphrodisiac	astringent	bactericidal	calming	cardiotonic	carminative	cleanser	cytophylactic	decongestant	deodorant	detoxifier
Arborvitae	•	•		•	•	•	•						•		•	•	•	•		•			•			•	•		•					•	•			•
Basil	•				•			•			•	•				•	•	•		•			•	•			•				•		•			•		
Bergamot	•				•						•		•			•	•				•		•	•	•						•		•				•	
Bergamot Mint	•										•		•				•			•	•			•							•							
Birch	•				•												•					•	•	•					•									
Black Pepper	•				•			•									•			•	•		•	•	•			•			•							
Black Spruce	•				•	•										•	•	•		•				•			•				•						•	
Blue Tansy	•		•	•	•								•		•		•	•			•	•		•			•				•		•					
Cardamom					•							•				•	•	•					•	•				•					•			•		
Cassia	•			•	•							•	•				•	•		•		•		•			•		•	•	•	•	•			•		•
Cedarwood					•								•			•	•						•						•									
Celery Seed	•				•												•			•											•							•
Cilantro					•								•					•		•										•			•	•				•
Cinnamon	•				•						•		•			•	•	•	•	•	•		•	•	•		•	•	•	•			•					
Citronella	•				•					•	•		•			•	•			•	•		•	•		•	•		•	•				•			•	•
Clary Sage	•				•				•	•	•		•				•	•					•	•				•	•		•		•				•	
Clove	•				•							•	•		•	•	•			•	•	•	•	•		•	•	•					•					
Copaiba	•			•	•		•					•	•			•	•	•	•	•		•	•			•	•				•	•	•			•	•	
Coriander	•				•						•	•	•				•	•		•		•		•	•			•			•		•				•	
Cypress	•				•								•			•	•	•				•	•	•					•			•	•			•	•	•
Dill					•						•		•				•	•						•			•						•					
Douglas fir	•				•															•			•						•									
Eucalyptus	•				•			•					•			•	•	•		•		•		•			•							•		•	•	
Fennel	•									•		•	•				•	•			•		•	•	•						•	•	•					
Frankincense	•					•	•	•			•					•	•	•		•	•		•			•			•		•				•			
Geranium			•		•					•	•		•	•		•	•						•	•	•				•	•	•				•		•	•
Ginger	•			•	•							•	•				•		•	•		•	•				•					•	•			•		
Grapefruit					•		•				•									•			•		•				•			•		•		•		
Green Mandarin					•	•						•					•	•		•			•	•					•		•		•	•				•
Helichrysum	•		•		•			•	•				•	•			•	•		•			•	•			•		•									
Hinoki	•				•							•					•						•						•								•	
Jasmine	•										•						•						•	•				•			•	•	•					
Juniper berry	•																			•	•	•	•	•	•			•	•		•	•	•	•				•
Kumquat					•		•						•				•	•		•			•				•		•				•	•	•			
Laurel Leaf	•				•			•									•	•		•					•													•
Lavender	•								•	•	•	•	•		•	•	•	•	•		•	•	•	•	•	•			•		•	•	•		•		•	
Lemon							•				•		•					•		•		•	•	•	•		•						•	•		•		•
Lemon Eucalyptus	•				•								•			•	•				•		•				•							•		•	•	
Lemongrass	•				•		•				•		•				•	•	•	•		•	•		•					•			•			•	•	
Lime					•												•			•		•	•	•			•											•
Litsea	•				•		•						•			•	•	•						•			•		•		•	•	•				•	•
Magnolia	•		•		•						•							•					•					•			•					•		•
Manuka			•	•	•								•		•		•	•				•	•				•					•			•		•	
Marjoram	•	•			•											•							•	•								•						
Melissa					•						•				•		•	•					•	•			•		•	•	•	•	•					
Myrrh					•	•	•	•					•			•	•	•					•			•	•		•			•	•					
Neroli				•	•			•		•	•						•	•	•	•			•	•				•					•		•		•	
Oregano	•				•						•		•				•	•		•	•	•	•				•				•	•	•					
Patchouli					•						•	•	•			•	•	•					•	•	•			•	•		•	•	•			•	•	•
Peppermint	•				•	•						•					•						•	•			•	•				•	•					
Petitgrain					•						•	•				•							•	•							•	•					•	•

RESOURCES

	digestive stimulant	disinfectant	diuretic	emmenagogue	energizing	expectorant	galactagogue	grounding	hypertensive	hypotensive	immunostimulant	insect repellent	insecticidal	invigorating	laxative	mucolytic	nervine	neuroprotective	neurotonic	purifier	refreshing	regenerative	relaxant	restorative	revitalizer	rubefacient	sedative	steroidal	stimulant	stomachic	tonic	uplifting	vasoconstrictor	vasodilator	vermicide	vermifuge	warming
Arborvitae		•	•	•		•					•	•							•	•									•	•	•					•	
Basil	•	•	•	•	•	•	•	•							•	•	•		•			•	•	•			•	•	•	•	•					•	
Bergamot	•		•		•										•				•							•	•	•	•		•	•				•	
Bergamot Mint														•																							
Birch		•	•									•														•		•	•		•						•
Black Pepper	•					•				•					•				•							•			•								•
Black Spruce						•		•								•	•			•				•		•		•	•	•		•					
Blue Tansy								•		•		•	•		•								•				•		•	•				•	•		
Cardamom	•		•			•																							•	•	•	•					
Cassia				•							•												•														•
Cedarwood			•	•		•		•				•	•			•						•	•				•	•	•		•	•				•	
Celery Seed	•		•						•			•								•			•				•			•							
Cilantro																																					
Cinnamon	•			•							•	•								•									•	•						•	•
Citronella			•									•	•																•	•	•	•					
Clary Sage	•			•			•	•		•						•	•		•				•				•			•	•	•			•		
Clove		•			•	•					•						•					•							•							•	•
Copaiba		•	•							•	•		•		•	•																		•			
Coriander	•												•									•			•		•		•	•	•						
Cypress			•		•			•								•			•		•		•						•		•	•	•				
Dill	•			•		•	•	•		•																			•								
Douglas fir			•		•	•									•												•		•	•							
Eucalyptus		•	•			•				•	•	•	•							•						•			•							•	•
Fennel	•		•	•		•	•	•			•				•	•							•					•	•	•	•					•	
Frankincense	•	•	•				•				•							•				•		•			•				•						
Geranium			•									•									•	•	•				•				•					•	
Ginger				•		•					•				•				•							•			•	•	•						•
Grapefruit	•	•	•		•									•						•	•								•		•	•					
Green Mandarin	•		•			•											•					•		•		•	•				•	•					
Helichrysum	•		•			•										•	•					•				•							•				
Hinoki								•			•																		•				•				
Jasmine				•		•	•	•	•													•	•				•										
Juniper berry	•		•	•													•								•	•	•		•	•	•						
Kumquat	•				•					•	•			•		•		•			•	•		•	•		•		•	•	•	•			•		
Laurel Leaf		•				•				•			•																								
Lavender			•	•						•			•				•	•				•	•			•	•				•				•	•	
Lemon		•	•		•					•	•		•	•		•					•				•	•					•	•				•	
Lemon Eucalyptus	•	•				•					•	•				•										•				•							
Lemongrass	•				•	•	•	•					•				•			•		•			•		•				•			•			•
Lime		•	•		•						•									•	•			•	•				•		•	•					
Litsea	•	•								•		•		•									•									•		•			
Magnolia								•								•		•		•			•			•	•			•							
Manuka										•										•		•	•		•									•			
Marjoram	•			•		•				•										•			•				•			•	•			•			•
Melissa									•		•						•										•			•	•	•					
Myrrh	•			•		•										•						•	•						•		•						
Neroli		•								•									•			•	•	•			•				•			•			•
Oregano	•	•		•		•					•									•															•		•
Patchouli	•		•						•		•	•	•				•					•		•			•	•	•		•						
Peppermint				•	•	•								•			•				•									•			•			•	•
Petitgrain											•												•				•				•	•					

Chart continues on next page→

Oil PROPERTIES CHART P-Y

Oil Properties	analgesic	anaphrodisiac	anti-allergenic	antiarthritic	antibacterial	anticarcinogenic	anti-carcinoma	anticatarrhal	anticoagulant	anticonvulsant	antidepressant	antiemetic	antifungal	antihemorrhagic	antihistamine	anti-infectious	anti-inflammatory	antimicrobial	antimutagenic	antioxidant	anti-parasitic	antirheumatic	antiseptic	antispasmodic	antitoxic	anti-tumoral	antiviral	aphrodisiac	astringent	bactericidal	calming	cardiotonic	carminative	cleanser	cytophylactic	decongestant	deodorant	detoxifier
Pink Pepper	•				•		•				•	•					•	•		•		•	•	•			•	•				•	•					
Ravintsara	•				•						•		•			•		•		•	•										•			•		•		
Red Mandarin					•	•						•	•				•	•		•			•	•		•	•		•		•		•	•	•			•
Roman chamomile																•	•				•			•							•	•	•					
Rose											•					•							•	•			•	•		•		•	•					
Rosemary	•				•		•	•					•			•	•	•		•	•	•	•	•				•	•		•	•	•		•			•
Sandalwood					•		•	•			•		•				•						•	•		•		•	•		•	•	•					
Siberian fir	•				•								•				•	•					•	•			•									•	•	
Spearmint					•			•					•				•						•	•				•				•	•					
Spikenard					•								•				•																				•	
Tangerine						•	•		•	•	•						•		•	•	•		•	•							•		•		•			•
Tea Tree	•				•								•			•	•			•	•		•				•									•		
Thyme					•								•					•		•	•	•	•	•	•		•	•				•	•	•				
Tulsi	•				•						•						•				•						•				•						•	
Turmeric	•		•		•	•	•			•			•				•	•	•	•	•		•			•	•						•			•		•
Vanilla																															•							
Vetiver																				•			•	•				•			•	•	•					
White fir	•			•				•														•	•				•		•		•					•	•	
Wild orange	•				•		•				•		•				•			•			•	•				•				•	•	•				•
Wintergreen	•																•					•	•	•					•		•	•	•					
Yarrow|Pom	•					•	•							•	•		•			•		•		•			•		•		•		•			•		•
Ylang ylang					•						•												•	•				•										

	digestive stimulant	disinfectant	diuretic	emmenagogue	energizing	expectorant	galactagogue	grounding	hypertensive	hypotensive	immunostimulant	insect repellent	insecticidal	invigorating	laxative	mucolytic	nervine	neuroprotective	neurotonic	purifier	refreshing	regenerative	relaxant	restorative	revitalizer	rubefacient	sedative	steroidal	stimulant	stomachic	tonic	uplifting	vasoconstrictor	vasodilator	vermicide	vermifuge	warming
Pink Pepper	•		•		•	•						•		•	•					•	•		•			•			•	•	•	•					•
Ravintsara		•			•	•					•			•		•							•														
Red Mandarin	•		•			•					•						•				•		•	•		•	•			•	•	•					
Roman chamomi e				•														•					•				•				•					•	
Rose				•											•		•										•			•	•						
Rosemary			•	•	•	•			•		•						•							•		•		•	•	•	•			•		•	
Sandalwood			•			•			•				•								•	•		•			•				•	•					
Siberian fir					•	•		•	•		•			•						•	•					•			•		•		•				
Spearmint	•			•	•						•		•	•										•					•								
Spikenard															•												•										
Tangerine	•		•		•										•	•				•				•			•		•	•	•	•					
Tea Tree	•					•		•			•		•						•	•	•	•							•							•	
Thyme			•	•		•			•		•	•	•				•	•								•		•	•					•		•	•
Tulsi																							•					•				•					
Turmeric	•					•						•						•					•				•			•							•
Vanilla																							•														
Vetiver								•			•	•	•					•								•	•		•		•					•	
White fir			•		•	•				•	•												•			•			•		•		•				
Wild orange	•		•		•						•			•						•	•	•								•	•	•				•	
Wintergreen		•	•	•			•	•						•							•							•	•						•	•	•
Yarrow|Pom	•			•	•	•				•	•				•	•				•		•					•	•		•	•						
Ylang Ylang								•		•	•	•											•				•		•		•	•	•				

Research Index BY OIL

ARBORVITAE

Effect of arborvitae seed oncognitive function and a-7nAChR protein expression of hippocampus in model rats with Alzheimer's disease, Cheng XL, Xiong XB, Xiang MQ, *Cell Biochem Biophys*, 2013

Conservative surgical management of stage IA endometrial carcinoma for fertility preservation, Mazzon I, Corrado G, Masciullo V, Morricone D, Ferrandina G, Scambia G., *Fertil Steril*, 2010

BASIL

RESEARCH: Cyclodextrin-Complexed Ocimum basilicum Leaves Essential Oil Increases Fos Protein Expression in the Central Nervous System and Produces an Antihyperalgesic Effect in Animal Models for Fibromyalgia, Nascimento SS, *International Journal of Molecular Sciences*, 2014

Central Properties and Chemical Composition of Ocimum basilicum Essential Oil, Ismail M, *Pharmaceutical Biology*, 2006

A comparative study of antiplaque and antigingivitis effects of herbal mouthrinse containing tea tree oil, clove, and basil with commercially available essential oil mouthrinse, Kothiwale SV, Patwardhan V, Gandhi M, Sohoni R, Kumar A, *Journal of Indian Society of Periodontology*, 2014

Protective effect of basil (Ocimum basilicum L.) against oxidative DNA damage and mutagenesis, Berić T, *Food and Chemical Toxicology*, 2008

Biological effects, antioxidant and anticancer activities of marigold and basil essential oils, Mahmoud GI, *Journal of Medicinal Plants Research*, 2013

Increased seizure latency and decreased severity of pentylenetetrazol-induced seizures in mice after essential oil administration, Koutroumanidou E, *Epilepsy Research and Treatment*, 2013

Antigiardial activity of Ocimum basilicum essential oil, de Almeida I, *Parasitology Research*, 2007

Antibacterial Effects of the Essential Oils of Commonly Consumed Medicinal Herbs Using an In Vitro Model, Soković M, *Molecules*, 2010

BERGAMOT

Anticancer activity of liposomal bergamot essential oil (BEO) on human neuroblastoma cells, Celia C, Trapasso E, Locatelli M, Navarra M, Ventura CA, Wolfram J, Carafa M, Morittu VM, Britti D, Di Marzio L, Paolino D, *Colloids and Surfaces*, 2013

The essential oil of bergamot enhances the levels of amino acid neurotransmitters in the hippocampus of rat: implication of monoterpene hydrocarbons, Morrone LA, Rombolà L, Pelle C, Corasaniti MT, Zappettini S, Paudice P, Bonanno G, Bagetta G, *Pharmacological Research*, 2007

The effects of inhalation of essential oils on the body weight, food efficiency rate and serum leptin of growing SD rats, Hur MH, Kim C, Kim CH, Ahn HC, Ahn HY, *Korean Society of Nursing Science*, 2006

BIRCH

Repelling properties of some plant materials on the tick Ixodes ricinus L., Thorsell W, Mikiver A, Tunón H, *Phytomedicine*, 2006

BLACK PEPPER

Black pepper and piperine reduce cholesterol uptake and enhance translocation of cholesterol transporter proteins, Duangjai A, *Journal of Natural Medicine*, 2013

Growth inhibition of pathogenic bacteria and some yeasts by selected essential oils and survival of L. monocytogenes and C. albicans in apple-carrot juice., Irkin R, *Foodborne Pathogens and Disease*, 2009

Antioxidative Properties and Inhibition of Key Enzymes Relevant to Type-2 Diabetes and Hypertension by Essential Oils from Black Pepper, Oboh G, *Advances in Pharmacological Sciences*, 2013

Black pepper essential oil to enhance intravenous catheter insertion in patients with poor vein visibility: a controlled study, Kristiniak S, Journal of Alternative and Complementary Medicine, 2012

Olfactory stimulation using black pepper oil facilitates oral feeding in pediatric patients receiving long-term enteral nutrition, Munakata M, *The Tohoku Journal of Experimental Medicine*, 2008

BLACK SPRUCE

Composition, antimicrobial and antioxidant activities of seven essential oils from the North American boreal forest.

Poaty B, Lahlah J, Porqueres F, Bouafif H.

World J Microbiol Biotechonol. 2015 Jun;31(6):907-19, doi: 10.1007s/11274-015-1845-y. Epub 2015 Mar 24

The antioxidant potential of the boreal samples was determined by the 1,1-diphenyl-2-picrylhydrazyl radical scavenging (concentration providing 50% inhibition ≥ 7 mg/ml) and reducing power methods. Finally, this investigation revealed some boreal EOs to be potential antimicrobial and antioxidant agents that would notably benefit products in the personal hygiene and care industry.

BLUE TANSY

Chemical composition, antibacterial activity and cytotoxicity of essential oils of Tanacetumparthenium in different developmental stages. Mohsenzadeh F, Chehregani A, Amiri H. Pharm Biol. 2011 Sep;49(9):920-6. doi: 10.3109/13880209.2011.556650. Epub 2011 May 19. PMID: 21592001

Select item 18568393 Parthenolide inhibits proliferation of fibroblast-like synoviocytes in vitro. Parada-Turska J. Mitura A, Brzana W, Jalonkski M, Majdan M, Rzeski W. Inflammation. 2008 Aug; 31(4):281-5. doi: 10.1007/s10753-008-9076-0. PMID: 18568393

CARDAMOM

Antimicrobial activity of the bioactive components of essential oils from Pakistani spices against Salmonella and other multi-drug resistant bacteria., Naveed R, Hussain I, *BMC Complementary and Alternative Medicine*, 2013

Gastroprotective effect of cardamom, Elettaria cardamomum Maton, fruits in rats, Jamal A, *Journal of Ethnopharmacology*, 2006

Aromatherapy as a Treatment for Postoperative Nausea: A randomized trial, Hunt R, *Anesthesia and Analgesia*, 2013

Treatment of irritable bowel syndrome with herbal preparations: results of a double-blind, randomized, placebo-controlled, multi-centre trial, Madisch A, *Alimentary Pharmacology and Therapeutics*, 2004

Identification of proapoptopic, anti-inflammatory, anti-proliferative, anti-invasive and anti-angiogenic targets of essential oils in cardamom by dual reverse virtual screening and binding pose analysis, Bhattacharjee B, *Asian Pacific Journal of Cancer Prevention*, 2013

Activity of Essential Oils Against Bacillus subtilis Spores, Lawrence HA, *Journal of Microbiology and Biotechnology*, 2009

CASSIA

Anti-inflammatory effects of essential oil from the leaves of Cinnamomum cassia and cinnamaldehyde on lipopolysaccharide-stimulated J774A.1 cells., Pannee C, *Journal of Advanced Pharmaceutical Technology & Research*, 2014

From type 2 diabetes to antioxidant activity: a systematic review of the safety and efficacy of common and cassia cinnamon bark., Dugoua JJ, Seely D, Perri D, Cooley K, Forelli T, Mills E, Koren G, *Canadian Journal of Physiology and Pharmacology*, 2007

A review on anti-inflammatory activity of monoterpenes, de Cássia da Silveira e Sá R, Andrade LN, de Sousa DP, *Molecules*, 2013

Cinnamomum cassia essential oil inhibits MSH-induced melanin production and oxidative stress in murine B16 melanoma cells, Chou ST, Chang WL, Chang CT, Hsu SL, Lin YC, Shih Y, *International Journal of Molecular Sciences*, 2013

Randomized clinical trial of a phytotherapic compound containing Pimpinella anisum, Foeniculum vulgare, Sambucus nigra, and Cassia augustifolia for chronic constipation, Picon PD, Picon RV, Costa AF, Sander GB, Amaral KM, Aboy AL, Henriques AT, *BMC Complementary and Alternative Medicine*, 2010

Antimicrobial activities of cinnamon oil and cinnamaldehyde from the Chinese medicinal herb Cinnamomum cassia Blume, Ooi LS, Li Y, Kam SL, Wang H, Wong EY, Ooi VE, *The American Journal of Chinese Medicine*, 2006

CEDARWOOD

Repellency of Essential Oils to Mosquitoes (Diptera: Culicidae), Barnard DR, *Journal of Medical Entomology*, 1999

Repellency of essential oils to mosquitoes (Diptera: Culicidae), Barnard DR, *Journal of Medical Entomology*, 1999

Fumigant toxicity of plant essential oils against Camptomyia corticalis (Diptera: Cecidomyiidae), Kim JR, Haribalan P, Son BK, Ahn YJ, *Journal of Economic Entomology*, 2012

Bactericidal activities of plant essential oils and some of their isolated constituents against Campylobacter jejuni, Escherichia coli, Listeria monocytogenes, and Salmonella enterica, Friedman M, Henika PR, Mandrell RE, *Journal of Food Protection*, 2002

Chemical composition and antibacterial activity of selected essential oils and some of their main compounds, Wanner J, Schmidt E, Bail S, Jirovetz L, Buchbauer G, Gochev V, Girova T, Atanasova T, Stoyanova A, *Natural Product Communications*, 2010

Randomized trial of aromatherapy: successful treatment for alopecia areata, Hay IC, Jamieson M, Ormerod AD, *Archives of Dermatology*, 1998

CILANTRO

Antimicrobial activity of individual and mixed fractions of dill, cilantro, coriander and eucalyptus essential oils. Delaquis PJ, Stanich K, Girard B, Mazza G, *International Journal of Food Microbiology*, 2002

CLARY SAGE

Changes in 5-hydroxytryptamine and Cortisol Plasma Levels in Menopausal Women After Inhalation of Clary Sage Oil, Lee KB, Cho E, Kang YS, *Phytotherapy Research*, 2014

Randomized controlled trial for Salvia sclarea or Lavandula angustifolia: differential effects on blood pressure in female patients with urinary incontinence undergoing urodynamic examination, Seol GH, Lee YH, Kang P, You JH, Park M, Min SS, *The Journal of Alternative and Complementary Medicine*, 2013

Antidepressant-like effect of Salvia sclarea is explained by modulation of dopamine activities in rats, Seol GH, Shim HS, Kim PJ, Moon HK, Lee KH, Shim I, Suh SH, Min SS, *Journal of Ethnopharmacology*, 2010

Aromatherapy massage on the abdomen for alleviating menstrual pain in high school girls: a

preliminary controlled clinical study, Hur MH, Lee MS, Seong KY, Lee MK, *Evidence-Based Complementary and Alternative Medicine*, 2012
Pain relief assessment by aromatic essential oil massage on outpatients with primary dysmenorrhea: a randomized, double-blind clinical trial, Ou MC, Hsu TF, Lai AC, Lin YT, Lin CC, *The Journal of Obstetrics and Gynecology Research*, 2012

CLOVE

Antimicrobial Activities of Clove and Thyme Extracts, Nzeako BC, Al-Kharousi ZS, Al-Mahrooqui Z, *Sultan Qaboos University Medical Journal*, 2006
Antimicrobial activity of clove oil and its potential in the treatment of vaginal candidiasis, Ahmad N, Alam MK, Shehbaz A, Khan A, Mannan A, Hakim SR, Bisht D, Owais M, *Journal of Drug Targeting*, 2005
Eugenol (an essential oil of clove) acts as an antibacterial agent against Salmonella typhi by disrupting the cellular membrane, Devi KP, Nisha SA, Sakthivel R, Pandian SK, *Journal of Ethnopharmacology*, 2010
The effect of clove and benzocaine versus placebo as topical anesthetics, Alqareer A, Alyahya A, Andersson L, *Journal of Dentistry*, 2006
Synergistic effect between clove oil and its major compounds and antibiotics against oral bacteria, Moon SE, Kim HY, Cha JD, *Archives of Oral Biology*, 2011
Antifungal activity of clove essential oil and its volatile vapour against dermatophytic fungi, Chee HY, Lee MH, *Mycobiology*, 2007
Microbicide activity of clove essential oil (Eugenia caryophyllata), Nuñez L, Aquino MD, *Brazilian Journal of Microbiology*, 2011
Anti-arthritic effect of eugenol on collagen-induced arthritis experimental model, Grespan R, Paludo M, Lemos Hde P, Barbosa CP, Bersani-Amado CA, Dalalio MM, Cuman RK, *Biological and Pharmaceutical Bulletin*, 2012
A novel aromatic oil compound inhibits microbial overgrowth on feet: a case study, Misner BD, *Journal of the International Society of Sports Nutrition*, 2007

COPAIBA

Bacteriostatic effect of copaiba oil (Copaifera officinalis) against Streptococcus mutans. Pieri FA et al. Braz Dent J. (2012)
Antimicrobial Activity of Copaiba (Copaifera officinalis) and Pracaxi (Pentaclethra macroloba) Oils against Staphylococcus Aureus: Importance in Compounding for Wound Care.Guimarães AL et al. Int J Pharm Compd. (2016)
Anti-Inflammatory and Antioxidant Actions of Copaiba Oil Are Related to Liver Cell Modifications in Arthritic Rats. Castro Ghizoni CV, Arssufi Ames AP, Lameira OA, Bersani Amado CA, Sá Nakanishi AB, Bracht L, Marçal Natali MR, Peralta RM, Bracht A, Comar JF. J Cell Biochem. 2017 Mar 21. doi: 10.1002/jcb.25998. [Epub ahead of print] PMID:28322470
Development and pharmacological evaluation of in vitro nanocarriers composed of lamellar silicates containing copaiba oil-resin for treatment of endometriosis. de Almeida Borges VR, da Silva JH, Barbosa SS, Nasciutti LE, Cabral LM, de Sousa VP. Mater Sci Eng C Mater Biol Appl. 2016 Jul 1;64:310-7. doi: 10.1016/j.msec.2016.03.094. Epub 2016 Mar 31.PMID: 27127058

CORIANDER

Coriandrum sativum L. protects human keratinocytes from oxidative stress by regulating oxidative defense systems., Park G, Kim HG, Kim YO, Park SH, Kim SY, Oh MS, *Skin Pharmacology and Physiology*, 2012
Antioxidant and Hepatoprotective Potential of Essential Oils of Coriander (Coriandrum sativum L.) and Caraway (Carum carvi L.) (Apiaceae), Samojlik I, Lakic N, Mimica-Dukic N, Dakovic-Svajcer K, Bozin B, *Journal of Agricultural and Food Chemistry*, 2010
Inhalation of coriander volatile oil increased anxiolytic-antidepressant-like behaviors and decreased oxidative status in beta-amyloid (1-42) rat model of Alzheimer's disease., Cioanca O, Hritcu L, Mihasan M, Trifan A, Hancianu M, *Physiology & Behavior*, 2014
Coriandrum sativum L. (Coriander) Essential Oil: Antifungal Activity and Mode of Action on Candida spp., and Molecular Targets Affected in Human Whole-Genome Expression, Freires Ide A, Murata RM, Furletti VF, Sartoratto A, Alencar SM, Figueira GM, de Oliveira Rodrigues JA, Duarte MC, Rosalen PL, *PLoS One*, 2014
Antimicrobial activity against bacteria with dermatological relevance and skin tolerance of the essential oil from Coriandrum sativum L. fruits, Casetti F, Bartelke S, Biehler K, Augustin M, Schempp CM, Frank U, *Phytotherapy Research*, 2012
Coriander (Coriandrum sativum L.) essential oil: its antibacterial activity and mode of action evaluated by flow cytometry, Silva F, Ferreira S, Queiroz JA, Domingues FC, *Journal of Medical Microbiology*, 2011

CYPRESS

Immunological and Psychological Benefits of Aromatherapy Massage, Kuriyama H, Watanabe S, Nakaya T, Shigemori I, Kita M, Yoshida N, Masaki D, Tadai T, Ozasa K, Fukui K, Imanishi J, *Evidence-Based Complementary and Alternative Medicine*, 2005
Chemical composition, bio-herbicidal and antifungal activities of essential oils isolated from Tunisian common cypress (Cupressus sempervirens L.), Ismail A, Lamia H, Mohsen H, Samia G, Bassem J, *Journal of Medicinal Plants Research*, 2013
Immunological and Psychological Benefits of Aromatherapy Massage, Kuriyama H, Watanabe S, Nakaya T, Shigemori I, Kita M, Yoshida N, Masaki D, Tadai T, Ozasa K, Fukui K, Imanishi J, *Evidence-Based Complementary and Alternative Medicine*, 2005
Effect of aromatherapy massage on abdominal fat and body image in post-menopausal women, Kim HJ, *Taehan Kanho Hakhoe Chi*, 2007
Evaluation of the Effects of Plant-derived Essential Oils on Central Nervous System Function Using Discrete Shuttle-type Conditioned Avoidance Response in Mice, Umezu T., *Phytotherapy Research*, 2012

DILL

Effects of Cd, Pb, and Cu on growth and essential oil contents in dill, peppermint, and basil, Zheljazkov VD, Craker LE, Xing B, *Environmental and Experimental Botany*, 2006
Dill (Anethum graveolens L.) seed essential oil induces Candida albicans apoptosis in a metacaspase-dependent manner, Chen Y, Zeng H, Tian J, Ban X, Ma B, Wang Y, Fungal Biology, 2014
Anethum graveolens: An Indian traditional medicinal herb and spice, Jana S, Shekhawat GS, *Pharmacognosy Review*, 2010
Hypolipidemic activity of Anethum graveolens in rats, Hajhashemi V, Abbasi N, *Phytotherapy Research*, 2008
Antifungal mechanism of essential oil from Anethum graveolens seeds against Candida albicans, Chen Y, Zeng H, Tian J, Ban X, Ma B, Wang Y, *Journal of Medical Microbiology*, 2013

DOUGLAS FIR

Antimicrobial activity of some Pacific Northwest woods against anaerobic bacteria and yeast. Johnston WH, Karchesy JJ, Constantine GH, Craig AM. Phytother Res. 2001 Nov;15(7):586-8.
Douglas-fir root-associated microorganisms with inhibitory activity towards fungal plant pathogens and human bacterial pathogens. Axelrood PE, Clarke AM, Radley R, Zemcov SJ. Can J Microbiol. 1996 Jul;42(7):690-700.
Food-related odor probes of brain reward circuits during hunger: a pilot FMRI study. Bragulat V, Dzemidzic M, Bruno C, Cox CA, Talavage T, Considine RV, Kareken DA.
Obesity (Silver Spring). 2010 Aug;18(8):1566-71. doi: 10.1038/oby.2010.57. Epub 2010 Mar 25.
Contemporary use of bark for medicine by two Salishan native elders of southeast Vancouver Island, Canada. Turner NJ, Hebda RJ. J Ethnopharmacol. 1990 Apr;29(1):59-72.

FENNEL

In vitro antifungal activity and mechanism of essential oil from fennel (Foeniculum vulgare L.) on dermatophyte species, Zeng H, Chen X, Liang J, *Journal of Medical Microbiology*, 2014
Antinociceptive activity of α-pinene and fenchone, Him A, Ozbek H, Turel I, Oner AC, *Pharmacology Online*, 2008
The palliation of nausea in hospice and palliative care patients with essential oils of Pimpinella anisum (aniseed), Foeniculum vulgare var. dulce (sweet fennel), Anthemis nobilis (Roman chamomile) and Mentha x piperita (peppermint), Gilligan NP, *International Journal of Aromatherapy*, 2005
Comparison of fennel and mefenamic acid for the treatment of primary dysmenorrhea, Namavar Jahromi B, Tartifizadeh A, Khabnadideh S, International Journal of Gynaecology and Obstetrics: *the Official Organ of the International Federation of Gynaecology and Obstetrics*, 2003
Carvacrol, a component of thyme oil, activates PPAR α and gamma and suppresses COX-2 expression, Hotta M, Nakata R, Katsukawa M, Hori K, Takahashi S, Inoue H., *Journal of Lipid Research*, 2010
Effects of herbal essential oil mixture as a dietary supplement on egg production in quail, Çabuk M, Eratak S, Alçicek A, Bozkurt M., *The Scientific World Journal*, 2014
Antimicrobial and antiplasmid activities of essential oils, Schelz Z, Molnar J, Hohmann J, *Fitoterapia*, 2006
Chemical composition, antimicrobial and antioxidant activities of anethole-rich oil from leaves of selected varieties of fennel [Foeniculum vulgare Mill. ssp. vulgare var. azoricum (Mill.) Thell], Senatore F, Oliviero F, Scandolera E, Taglialatela-Scafati O, Roscigno G, Zaccardelli M, De Falco E, *Fitoterapia*, 2013
Salinity impact on yield, water use, mineral and essential oil content of fennel (Foeniculum vulgare Mill.), Semiz GD, Unlukara A, Yurtseven E, Suarez DL, Telci I, *Journal of Agricultural Science*, 2012
Efficacy of plant essential oils on postharvest control of rots caused by fungi on different stone fruits in vivo, Lopez-Reyes JG, Spadaro D, Prelle A, Garibaldi A, Gullino ML, *Journal of Food Protection*, 2013

FRANKINCENSE

Frankincense oil derived from Boswellia carteri induces tumor cell specific cytotoxicity, Frank MB, Yang Q, Osban J, Azzarello JT, Saban MR, Saban R, Ashley RA, Welter JC, Fung KM, Lin HK, *BMC Complementary and Alternative Medicine*, 2009
Differential effects of selective frankincense (Ru Xiang) essential oil versus non-selective sandalwood (Tan Xiang) essential oil on cultured bladder cancer cells: a microarray and bioinformatics study, Dozmorov MG, Yang Q, Wu W, Wren J, Suhail MM, Woolley CL, Young DG, Fung KM, Lin HK, 2014
Composition and potential anticancer activities of essential oils obtained from myrrh and frankincense, Chen Y, Zhou C, Ge Z, Liu Y, Liu Y, Feng W, Li S, Chen G, Wei T, *Oncology Letters*, 2013
Volatile composition and antimicrobial activity of twenty commercial frankincense essential oil samples, Van Vuurena SF, Kamatoub GPP, Viljoenb, AM, South African Journal of Botany, 2010
Effects of Aroma Hand Massage on Pain, State Anxiety and Depression in Hospice Patients with Terminal Cancer, Chang SY, *Journal of Korean Academy of Nursing*, 2008
Evaluation of the Effects of Plant-derived Essential Oils on Central Nervous System Function Using Discrete Shuttle-type Conditioned Avoidance Response in Mice, Umezu T., *Phytotherapy Research*, 2012
Chemistry and immunomodulatory activity of frankincense oil, Mikhaeil BR, Maatooq GT, Badria FA, Amer MM, *Zeitschrift fur Naturforschung C*, 2003

GERANIUM

Bioactivity-guided investigation of geranium essential oils as natural tick repellents, Tabanca N, Wang M, Avonto C, Chittiboyina AG, Parcher JF, Carroll JF, Kramer M, Khan IA, *Journal of Agricultural and Food Chemistry*, 2013
The antibacterial activity of geranium oil against Gram-negative bacteria isolated from difficult-to- heal wounds, Sienkiewicz M, Poznacska-Kurowska K, Kaszuba A, Kowalczyk E, Burns, 2014
Suppression of neutrophil accumulation in mice by cutaneous application of geranium essential oil, Maruyama N, Sekimoto Y, Ishibashi H, Inouye S, Oshima H, Yamaguchi H, Abe S, *Journal of Inflammation* (London, England), 2005
Hypoglycemic and antioxidant effects of leaf essential oil of Pelargonium graveolens, L'Hér. in alloxan induced diabetic rats, Boukhris M, Bouaziz M, Feki I, Jemai H, El Feki A, Sayadi S, *Lipids in Health and Disease*, 2012
Antioxidant and Anticancer Activities of Citrus reticulate (Petitgrain Mandarin) and Pelargonium graveolens (Geranium) Essential Oils, Fayed SA, *Research Journal of Agriculture and Biological Sciences*, 2009
Aromatherapy Massage Affects Menopausal Symptoms in Korean Climacteric Women: A Pilot-Controlled Clinical Trial, Myung-HH, Yun Seok Y, Myeong SL, *Evidence-Based Complementary and Alternative Medicine*, 2008il, Mikhaeil BR, Maatooq GT, Badria FA, Amer MM, *Zeitschrift fur Naturforschung C*, 2003

GINGER

Gastroprotective activity of essential oils from turmeric and ginger, Liju VB, Jeena K, Kuttan R., *Journal of Basic and Clinical Physiology and Pharmacology*, 2014

Reversal of pyrogallol-induced delay in gastric emptying in rats by ginger (Zingiber officinale), Gupta YK, Sharma M, Methods and Findings in Experimental and Clinical Pharmacology, 2001

The essential oil of ginger, Zingiber officinale, and anaesthesia, Geiger JL, *International Journal of Aromatherapy*, 2005

Effectiveness of aromatherapy with light thai massage for cellular immunity improvement in colorectal cancer patients receiving chemotherapy, Khiewkhern S, Promthet S, Sukprasert A, Eunhpinitpong W, Bradshaw P, *Asian Pacific Journal of Cancer Prevention*, 2013

Antioxidant, anti-inflammatory and antinociceptive activities of essential oil from ginger, Jeena K, Liju VB, Kuttan R, *Indian Journal of Physiology and Pharmacology*, 2013

A brief review of current scientific evidence involving aromatherapy use for nausea and vomiting, Lua PL, Zakaria NS, *The Journal of Alternative and Complementary Medicine*, 2012

Anti-inflammatory effects of ginger and some of its components in human bronchial epithelial (BEAS-2B) cells, Podlogar JA, Verspohl EJ, *Phytotherapy Research*, 2012

Medicinal plants as antiemetics in the treatment of cancer: a review, Haniadka R, Popouri S, Palatty PL, Arora R, Baliga MS, *Integrative Cancer Therapies*, 2012

Inhibitory potential of ginger extracts against enzymes linked to type 2 diabetes, inflammation and induced oxidative stress, Rani MP, Padmakumari KP, Sankarikutty B, Cherian OL, Nisha VM, Raghu KG, *International Journal of Food Sciences and Nutrition*, 2011

Ginger: An herbal medicinal product with broad anti-inflammatory actions, Grzanna R, Lindmark L, Frondoza CG, *Journal of Medicinal Food*, 2005

GRAPERUIT

Olfactory stimulatory with grapefruit and lavender oils change autonomic nerve activity and physiological function, Nagai K, Niijima A, Horii Y, Shen J, Tanida M, *Autonomic Neuroscience: basic & clinical*, 2014

Minor Furanocoumarins and Coumarins in Grapefruit Peel Oil as Inhibitors of Human Cytochrome P450 3A4, César TB, Manthey JA, Myung K, *Journal of Natural Products*, 2009

Antimicrobial effects of essential oils in combination with chlorhexidine digluconate, Filoche SK, Soma K, Sissons CH, *Oral Microbiology and Immunology*, 2005

Inhibition of acetylcholinesterase activity by essential oil from Citrus paradisi, Miyazawa M, Tougo H, Ishihara M, *Natural Product Letters*, 2001

Olfactory stimulation with scent of essential oil of grapefruit affects autonomic neurotransmission and blood pressure, Tanida M, Niijima A, Shen J, Nakamura T, Nagai K, *Brain Research*, 2005

Mechanism of changes induced in plasma glycerol by scent stimulation with grapefruit and lavender essential oils, Shen J, Niijima A, Tanida M, Horii Y, Nakamura T, Nagai K, *Neuroscience Letters*, 2007

Olfactory stimulation with scent of grapefruit oil affects autonomic nerves, lipolysis and appetite in rats, Shen J, Niijima A, Tanida M, Horii Y, Maeda K, Nagai K, *Neuroscience Letters*, 2005

Effects of fragrance inhalation on sympathetic activity in normal adults, Haze S, Sakai K, Gozu Y, *The Japanese Journal of Pharmacology*, 2002

Effect of olfactory stimulation with flavor of grapefruit oil and lemon oil on the activity of sympathetic branch in the white adipose tissue of the epididymis, Niijima A, Nagai K, Experimental Biology and Medicine, 2003

Effect of aromatherapy massage on abdominal fat and body image in post-menopausal women, Kim HJ, *Taehan Kanho Hakhoe Chi*, 2007

HELICHRYSUM

Chemical composition and biological activity of the essential oil from Helichrysum microphyllum Cambess. ssp. tyrrhenicum Bacch., Brullo e Giusso growing in La Maddalena Archipelago, Sardinia., Ornano L, Venditti A, Sanna C, Ballero M, Maggi F, Lupidi G, Bramucci M, Quassinti L, Bianco A, *Journal of Oleo Science*, 2014

Arzanol, an anti-inflammatory and anti-HIV-1 phloroglucinol α-Pyrone from Helichrysum italicum ssp. microphyllum, Appendino G, Ottino M, Marquez N, Bianchi F, Giana A, Ballero M, Sterner O, Fiebich BL, Munoz E, *Journal of Natural Products*, 2007

Protective role of arzanol against lipid peroxidation in biological systems, Rosa A, Pollastro F, Atzeri A, Appendino G, Melis MP, Deiana M, Incani A, Loru D, Dessì MA, *Chemical and Physics of Lipids*, 2011

Arzanol, a prenylated heterodimeric phloroglucinyl pyrone, inhibits eicosanoid biosynthesis and exhibits anti-inflammatory efficacy in vivo, Bauer J, Koeberle A, Dehm F, Pollastro F, Appendino G, Northoff H, Rossi A, Sautebin L, Werz O, *Biochemical Pharmacology*, 2011

Anti-inflammatory and antioxidant properties of Helichrysum italicum, Sala A, Recio M, Giner RM, Máñez S, Tournier H, Schinella G, Ríos JL, *The Journal of Pharmacy and Pharmacology*, 2002

Effects of Helichrysum italicum extract on growth and enzymatic activity of Staphylococcus aureus, Nostro A, Bisignano G, Angela Cannatelli M, Crisafi G, Paola Germanò M, Alonzo V, *International Journal of Antimicrobial Agents*, 2001

Helichrysum italicum extract interferes with the production of enterotoxins by Staphylococcus aureus., Nostro A, Cannatelli MA, Musolino AD, Procopio F, Alonzo V, *Letters in Applied Microbiology*, 2002

Assessment of the anti-inflammatory activity and free radical scavenger activity of tiliroside., Sala A, Recio MC, Schinella GR, Máñez S, Giner RM, Cerdá-Nicolás M, Rosí JL, *European Journal of Pharmacology*, 2003

JASMINE

The influence of essential oils on human attention and alertness, Ilmberger J, Heuberger E, Mahrhofer C, Dessovic H, Kowarik D, Buchbauer G, *Chemical Senses*, 2001

The influence of essential oils on human vigilance, Heuberger E, Ilmberger J, *Natural Product Communications*, 2010

Effects of Aromatherapy Massage on Blood Pressure and Lipid Profile in Korean Climacteric Women, Myung-HH , Heeyoung OH, Myeong SL , Chan K, Ae-na C, Gil-ran S, *International Journal of Neuroscience*, 2007

Sedative effects of the jasmine tea odor and (R)-(-)-linalool, one of its major odor components, on autonomic nerve activity and mood states, Kuroda K, Inoue N, Ito Y, Kubota K, Sugimoto A, Kakuda T, Fushiki T, *European Journal of Applied Physiology*, 2005

Aromatherapy Massage Affects Menopausal Symptoms in Korean Climacteric Women: A Pilot-Controlled Clinical Trial, Myung-HH, Yun Seok Y, Myeong SL, *Evidence-Based Complementary and Alternative Medicine*, 2008

Stimulating effect of aromatherapy massage with jasmine oil, Hongratanaworakit T, *Natural Product Communications*, 2010

Activities of Ten Essential Oils towards Propionibacterium acnes and PC-3, A-549 and MCF-7 Cancer Cells, Zu Y, Yu H, Liang L, Fu Y, Efferth T, Liu X, Wu N, *Molecules*, 2010

JUNIPER BERRY

Fumigant toxicity of plant essential oils against Camptomyia corticalis (Diptera: Cecidomyiidae), Kim JR, Haribalan P, Son BK, Ahn YJ, *Journal of Economic Entomology*, 2012

Antimicrobial activity of juniper berry essential oil (Juniperus communis L., Cupressaceae), Pepeljnjak S, Kosalec I, Kalodera Z, Blazevic N, *Acta Pharmaceutica*, 2005

Antioxidant activities and volatile constituents of various essential oils, Wei A, Shibamoto T, *Journal of Agriculture and Food Chemistry*, 2007

KUMQUAT

AInhibitory effects of Fortunella japonica var. margarita and Citrus sunki essential oils on nitric oxide production and skinpathogens.

Acta Microabiologica et immunologica Hungarica Yang EJ; Kim SS; Moon JY; Oh TH; Baik JS; Lee NH; Hyun CG in this study, the essential oils of the citrus species C. sunki (CSE) and F. japonica var. margarita (FJE), both native to the island of Jeju, Korea, were examined for their anti-inflammatory and antimicrobial activities against skin pathogens. Four human skin pathogenic microorganisms, Staphylococcus epidermidis CCARM 3709, Propionibacterium acnes CCARM 0081, Malassezia furfur KCCM 12679, and Candida albicans KCCM 11282, were studied. CSE and FJE exhibited strong antimicrobial activity against most of the pathogenic bacteria and yeast strains that were tested. Interestingly, CSE and FJE even showed antimicrobial activity against antibiotic-resistant S. epidermidis CCARM 3710, S. epidermidis CCARM 3711, P. acnes CCARM9009, and P. acnes CCARM9010 strains. In addition, CSE and FJE reduced the lipopolysaccharide (LPS)-induced secretion of nitric oxide (NO) in RAW 264.7 cells, indicating that they have anti-inflammatory effects. Taken together, these findings indicate that CSE and FJE have great potential to be used in human skin health applications.

Analysis of biologically active oxyprenylated ferulic acid derivatives in citrus fruits. Plant Foods for Human Nutrition

Genovese S; Fiorito S; Locatelli M; Carlucci G; EpifanoF

4'-Geranyloxyferulic (GOFA) and boropinic acid have been discovered during the last decade as interesting phytochemicals having valuable pharmacological effects as cancer chemopreventive, anti-inflammatory, neuroprotective, and anti-Helicobacter pylori agents. A reverse-phase HPLC-UV/Vis method for the separation and quantification of the title oxyprenylated ferulic acid derivatives in extracts obtained from peels of nine edible Citrus and Fortunella fruits was successfully applied.

LAVENDER

An olfactory stimulus modifies nighttime sleep in young men and women, Goel N, Kim H, Lao RP, *Chronobiology International*, 2005

Effects of lavender aromatherapy on insomnia and depression in women college students, Lee IS, Lee GJ, *Taehan Kanho Hakhoe Chi*, 2006

Effects of lavender (lavandula angustifolia Mill.) and peppermint (Mentha cordifolia Opiz.) aromas on subjective vitality, speed, and agility, Cruz AB, Lee SE, Pagaduan JC, Kim TH, *The Asian International Journal of Life Sciences*, 2012

Topical lavender oil for the treatment of recurrent aphthous ulceration, Altaei DT, *American Journal of Dentistry*, 2012

Lavender essential oil inhalation suppresses allergic airway inflammation and mucous cell hyperplasia in a murine model of asthma, Ueno-lio T, Shibakura M, Yokota K, Aoe M, Hyoda T, Shinohata R, Kanehiro A, Tanimoto M, Kataoka M, *Life Sciences*, 2014

Lavender essential oil in the treatment of migraine headache: a placebo-controlled clinical trial, Sasannejad P, Saeedi M, Shoeibi A, Gorji A, Abbasi M, Foroughipour M, European Neurology, 2012

Effect of aromatherapy on symptoms of dysmenorrhea in college students: A randomized placebo-controlled clinical trial, Han SH, Hur MH, Buckle J, Choi J, Lee MS, *The Journal of Alternative and Complementary Medicine*, 2006

The effects of aromatherapy on pain, depression, and life satisfaction of arthritis patients, Kim MJ, Nam ES, Paik SI, *Taehan Kanho Hakhoe Chi*, 2005

Effect of lavender oil (Lavandula angustifolia) on cerebral edema and its possible mechanisms in an experimental model of stroke,Vakili A, Sharifat S, Akhavan MM, Bandegi AR, *Brain Research*, 2014

Two US practitioners' experience of using essential oils for wound care, Hartman D, Coetzee JC, *Journal of Wound Care*, 2002

Lavender and the nervous system, Koulivand PH, Khaleghi Ghadiri M, Gorji A, *Evidence-Based Complementary and Alternative Medicine*, 2013

LEMON

Screening of the antibacterial effects of a variety of essential oils on respiratory tract pathogens, using a modified dilution assay method, Inouye S, Yamaguchi H, Takizawa T, Journal of Infection and Chemotherapy: *Official Journal of the Japan Society of Chemotherapy*, 2001

Antioxidative effects of lemon oil and its components on copper induced oxidation of low density lipoprotein, Grassmann J, Schneider D, Weiser D, Elstner EF, Arzneimittel-Forschung, 2001

The effect of lemon inhalation aromatherapy on nausea and vomiting of pregnancy: a double-blinded, randomized, controlled clinical trial, Yavari Kia P, Safajou F, Shahnazi M, Nazemiyeh H, *Iranian Red Crescent Medical Journal*, 2014

Chemical composition of the essential oils of variegated pink-fleshed lemon (Citrus x limon L. Burm. f.) and their anti-inflammatory and antimicrobial activities, Hamdan D, Ashour ML, Mulyaningsih S, El-Shazly A, Wink M, *Zeitschrift Fur Naturforschung C-A Journal of Biosciences*, 2013

Essential oil from lemon peels inhibit key enzymes linked to neurodegenerative conditions and pro-oxidant induced lipid peroxidation, Oboh G, Olasehinde TA, Ademosun AO, *Journal of Oleo Science*, 2014

Effect of flavour components in lemon essential oil on physical or psychological stress, Fukumoto S, Morishita A, Furutachi K, Terashima T, Nakayama T, Yokogoshi H, *Stress and Health*, 2008

Cytological aspects on the effects of a nasal spray consisting of standardized extract of citrus

RESOURCES

lemon and essential oils in allergic rhinopathy, Ferrara L, Naviglio D, Armone Caruso A, *ISRN Pharmaceutics*, 2012
Aromatherapy as a safe and effective treatment for the management of agitation in severe dementia: the results of a double-blind, placebo-controlled trial with Melissa, Ballard CG, O'Brien JT, Reichelt K, Perry EK, *The Journal of Clinical Psychiatry*, 2002

LEMON EUCALYPTUS

Essential oil of Algerian Eucalyptus citriodora: Chemical composition, antifungal activity
Tolba H, Moghrani H, Benelmouffok A, Kellou D, Maachi R
J Mycol Med. 2015 Dec;25(4):e128-33. doi: 10.1016/j.mycmed.2015.10.009. Epub 2015 Dec 1
The chemical composition of the oil revealed the presence of 22 compounds accounting for 95.27% of the oil. The dominant compounds were citronellal (69.77%), citronellol (10.63%) and isopulegol (4.66%). The disc diffusion method, MIC and MFC determination, indicated that E. citriodora essential oil had a higher antifungal potential against the tested strains with inhibition zone diameter which varied from (12 to 90mm) and MIC and MFC values ranged from (0.6 to 5µL/mL and 1.25 to 5µL/mL) respectively.
The results of the present study indicated that E. citriodora essential oil may be used as a new antifungal agent recommended by the pharmaceutical industries.
Plant-based insect repellents: a review of their efficacy, development and testing
Marta Ferreira Maia, Sarah J Moore
Malar J. 2011; 10 (Suppl 1): S11.
Published online 2011 Mar 15. doi: 10.1186/1475-2875-10-S1-S11
PMD from lemon eucalyptus (Corymbia citriodora) extract
Corymbia citriodora (Myrtaceae), also known as lemon eucalyptus, is a potent natural repellent extracted from the leaves of lemon eucalyptus trees (Table (Table1).1). It was discovered in the 1960s during mass screenings of plants used in Chinese traditional medicine. Lemon eucalyptus essential oil, comprising 85% citronellal, is used by cosmetic industries due to its fresh smell. However, it was discovered that the waste distillate remaining after hydro-distillation of the essential oil was far more effective at repelling mosquitoes than the essential oil itself. Many plant extracts and oils repel mosquitoes, with their effect lasting from several minutes to several hours (Table (Table1).1). Their active ingredients tend to be highly volatile, so although they are effective repellents for a short period after application, they rapidly evaporate leaving the user unprotected. The exception to this is para-menthane 3, 8 diol, which has a lower vapour pressure than volatile monoterpines found in most plant oils and provides very high protection from a broad range of insect vectors over several hours, whereas the essential oil is repellent for around one hour. PMD is the only plant-based repellent that has been advocated for use in disease endemic areas by the CDC (Centres for Disease Control), due to its proven clinical efficacy to prevent malaria [26] and is considered to pose no risk to human health. It should be noted that the essential oil of lemon eucalyptus does not have EPA (Environmental Protection Agency) registration for use as an insect repellent.

LEMONGRASS

Protective effects of lemongrass (Cymbopogon citratus STAPF) essential oil on DNA damage and carcinogenesis in female Balb/C mice, Bidinotto LT, Costa CA, Salvadori DM, Costa M, Rodrigues MA, Barbisan LF, *Journal of Applied Toxicology*, 2011
The anti-biofilm activity of lemongrass (Cymbopogon flexuosus) and grapefruit (Citrus paradisi) essential oils against five strains of Staphylococcus aureus, Adukwu EC, Allen SC, Phillips CA, *Journal of Applied Microbiology*, 2012
Protective effect of lemongrass oil against dexamethasone induced hyperlipidemia in rats: possible role of decreased lecithin cholesterol acetyl transferase activity, Kumar VR, Inamdar MN, Nayeemunnisa, Viswanatha GL, *Asian Pacific Journal of Tropical Medicine*, 2011
The GABAergic system contributes to the anxiolytic-like effect of essential oil from Cymbopogon citratus (lemongrass), Costa CA, Kohn DO, de Lima VM, Gargano AC, Flório JC, Costa M, *Journal of Ethnopharmacology*, 2011
The effect of lemongrass EO highlights its potential against antibiotic resistant Staph. aureus in the healthcare environment, Adukwu EC, Allen SC, Phillips CA, *Journal of Applied Microbiology*, 2012
Anticancer activity of an essential oil from Cymbopogon flexuosus (lemongrass), Sharma PR, Mondhe DM, Muthiah S, Pal HC, Shahi AK, Saxena AK, Qazi GN, *Chemico-Biological Interactions*, 2009
Antimicrobial activity of juniper berry essential oil (Juniperus communis L., Cupressaceae), Pepeljnjak S, Kosalec I, Kalodera Z, Blazevic N, *Acta Pharmaceutica*, 2005
Antioxidant activities and volatile constituents of various essential oils, Wei A, Shibamoto T, *Journal of Agriculture and Food Chemistry*, 2007

LIME

Bactericidal activity of herbal volatile oil extracts against multidrug-resistant Acinetobacter baumannii, Intorasoot A, Chornchoem P, Sookkhee S, Intorasoot S, *Journal of Intercultural Ethnoparmacology*, 2017
Anticancer activity of Key Lime (Citrus aurantifolia), Narang N, Jiraungkoorskul W, *Pharmacognosy Review*, 2016
Anti-inflammatory properties and chemical characterization of the essential oils of four citrus species, Amorim JL, Simas DL, Pinheiro MM, Moreno DS, Alviano CS, da Silva AJ, Fernandes PD, *PLoS One*, 2016.
Essential oil from Citrus aurantifolia prevents ketotifen-induced weight-gain in mice, Asnaashari S, Delazar A, Habibi B, Vasfi R, NaharL, Hamedeyazdan S, Sarker SD, *Phytotherapy Research*, 2010.
Antioxidant effects of Citrus aurantifolia juice and peel extract on LDL oxidation, Boshtam M, Moshtaghian J, Naderi G, Asgary S, Nayeri H, *Journal of Research in Medical Sciences*, 2011.
Chemical composition and in-vitro antioxidant and antimicrobial activity of the essential oil of Citrus aurantifolia L leaves, Al-Aamri M, Al-Abousi N, Al-Jabri Sausan, Alam T, Khan S, *Journal of Taibah University Medical Sciences*, 2018

LITSEA

Anti-Inflammatory Effects of Boldine and Reticuline Isolated from Litsea cubeba through JAK2/STAT3 and NF-ÐB Signaling Pathways. Yang X, Gao X, Cao Y, Guo Q, Li S, Zhu Z, Zhao Y, Tu P, Chai X. Planta Med. 2017 Jun 26. doi: 10.1055/s-0043- 113447. [Epub ahead of print] PMID: 28651290
Essential Oil Compositions and Antimicrobial Activities of Various Parts of Litsea cubeba from Taiwan. Su YC, Ho CL. Nat Prod Commun. 2016 Apr;11(4):515-8. PMID: 27396208
Anti-inflammatory constituents from the root of Litsea cubeba in LPS-induced RAW 264.7 macrophages. Lin B, Sun LN, Xin HL, Nian H, Song HT, Jiang YP, Wei ZQ, Qin LP, Han T. Pharm Biol. 2016 Sep;54(9):1741-7. doi: 10.3109/13880209.2015.1126619. Epub 2016 Jan 5. PMID: 26731513
Antibacterial activity of Litsea cubeba (Lauraceae, May Chang) and its effects on the biological response of common carp Cyprinus carpio challenged with Aeromonas hydrophila. Nguyen HV, Caruso D, Lebrun M, Nguyen NT, Trinh TT, Meile JC, Chu-Ky S, Sarter S. J Appl Microbiol. 2016 Aug;121(2):341-51. doi: 10.1111/jam.13160. Epub 2016 Jun 30. PMID: 27124660

MAGNOLIA

Natural Product Research Farag, MA; Al-Mahdy, DA
The biological activities and the determined major volatile components in the Magnolia grandiflora and M. virginiana flowers extracts were compared. Volatile components were detected in the essential oil by dynamic headspace sampling (HS). 2-Phenylethanol (40% and 61%) was found as the main constituent in the essential oil and HS samples of M. virginiana, respectively. In the M. grandiflora oil sample, (E,E)-farnesol (18%) and 2-phenylethanol (10%) were found as main constituents, whereas germacrene D (17%) and β- bisabolene (17%) were the main components of the HS sample. The essential oil in M. virginiana displayed a moderate antioxidant activity relative to vitamin E, whereas both essential oils were active against human lung carcinoma and breast carcinoma cell lines, even at concentrations higher than 200 µg mL(-1).

MARJORAM

Comparative effects of Artemisia dracunculus, Satureja hortensis and Origanum majorana on inhibition of blood platelet adhesion, aggregation and secretion, Yazdanparast R, Shahriyary L, *Vascular Pharmacology*, 2008
The effects of aromatherapy on pain, depression, and life satisfaction of arthritis patients, Kim MJ, Nam ES, Paik SI, *Taehan Kanho Hakhoe Chi*, 2005
Immunological and Psychological Benefits of Aromatherapy Massage, Kuriyama H, Watanabe S, Nakaya T, Shigemori I, Kita M, Yoshida N, Masaki D, Tadai T, Ozasa K, Fukui K, Imanishi J, *Evidence-Based Complementary and Alternative Medicine*, 2005
Ovicidal and adulticidal activities of Origanum majorana essential oil constituents against insecticide-susceptible and pyrethroid/malathion-resistant Pediculus humanus capitis (Anoplura: Pediculidae), Yang YC, Lee SH, Clark JM, Ahn YJ, *Journal of Agricultural and Food Chemistry*, 2009
Essential oil inhalation on blood pressure and salivary cortisol levels in prehypertensive and hypertensive subjects, Kim IH, Kim C, Seong K, Hur MH, Lim HM, Lee MS, *Evidence-Based Complementary and Alternative Medicine*, 2012
Free radical scavenging and antiacetylcholinesterase activities of Origanum majorana L. essential oil, Mossa AT, Mawwar GA, *Human & Experimental Toxicology*, 2011
Pain relief assessment by aromatic essential oil massage on outpatients with primary dysmenorrhea: a randomized, double-blind clinical trial, Ou MC, Hsu TF, Lai AC, Lin YT, Lin CC, *The Journal of Obstetrics and Gynecology Research*, 2012

MELALEUCA

Essential oil of Melaleuca alternifolia for the treatment of oral candidiasis induced in an immunosuppressed mouse model, de Campos Rasteiro VM, da Costa AC, Araújo CF, de Barros PP, Rossoni
RD, Anbinder AL, Jorge AO, Junqueira JC, *BMC Complementary and Alternative Medicine*, 2014
Tea tree oil-induced transcriptional alterations in Staphylococcus aureus., Cuaron JA, Dulal S, Song Y, Singh AK, Montelongo CE, Yu W, Nagarajan V, Jayaswal RK, Wilkinson BJ, Gustafson JE, *Phytotherapy Research*, 2013
Susceptibility to Melaleuca alternifolia (tea tree) oil of yeasts isolated from the mouths of patients with advanced cancer, Bagg J, Jackson MS, Petrina Sweeney M, Ramage G, Davies AN, *Oral Oncology*, 2006
Cooling the burn wound: evaluation of different modalites., Jandera V, Hudson DA, de Wet PM, Innes PM, Rode H, Burns: *Journal of the International Society for Burn Injuries*, 2000
Anti-inflammatory effects of Melaleuca alternifolia essential oil on human polymorphonuclear neutrophils and monocytes, Caldefie-Chézet F, Guerry M, Chalchat JC, Fusillier C, Vasson MP, Guillot J, *Free Radical Research*, 2004
Tea tree oil reduces histamine-induced skin inflammation, Koh KJ, Pearce AL, Marshman G, Finlay-Jones JJ, Hart PH, British Journal of Dermatology, 2002
Terpinen-4-ol, the main component of Melaleuca alternifolia (tea tree) oil inhibits the in vitro growth of human melanoma cells, Calcabrini A, Stringaro A, Toccacieli L, Meschini S, Marra M, Colone M, Salvatore G, Mondello F, Arancia G, Molinari A, *Journal of Investigative Dermatology*, 2004
A comparative study of tea-tree oil versus benzoylperoxide in the treatment of acne, Bassett IB, Pannowitz DL, Barnetson RS, *Medical Journal of Australia*, 1990
Topically applied Melaleuca alternifolia (tea tree) oil causes direct anti-cancer cytotoxicity in subcutaneous tumour bearing mice, Ireland DJ, Greay SJ, Hooper CM, Kissick HT, Filion P, Riley TV, Beilharz MW, *Journal of Dermatological Science*, 2012
Tea tree oil as a novel anti-psoriasis weapon, Pazyar N, Yaghoobi R, *Skin Pharmacology and Physiology*, 2012

MELISSA

Low level of Lemon Balm (Melissa officinalis) essential oils showed hypoglycemic effects by altering the expression of glucose metabolism genes in db/db mice, Mi Ja Chung, Sung-Yun Cho and Sung-Joon Lee, *The Journal of the Federation of American Societies for Experimental Biology*, 2008
Apoptosis-Inducing Effects of Melissa officinalis L. Essential Oil in Glioblastoma Multiforme Cells, Queiroz RM, Takiya CM, Guimarães LP, Rocha Gda G, Alviano DS, Blank AF, Alviano CS, Gattass CR, *Cancer Investigation*, 2014
In Vivo Potential Anti-Inflammatory Activity of Melissa officinalis L. Essential Oil, Bounihi A, Hajjaj G, Alnamer R, Cherrah Y, Zellou A, *Advances in Pharmacological Sciences*, 2013
Antiviral activity of the volatile oils of Melissa officinalis L. against Herpes simplex virus type-2, Allahverdiyev A, Duran N, Ozguven M, Koltas S, *Phytomedicine*, 2004
Aromatherapy as a safe and effective treatment for the management of agitation in severe dementia: the results of a double-blind, placebo-controlled trial with Melissa, Ballard CG, O'Brien JT, Reichelt K, Perry EK, *The Journal of Clinical Psychiatry*, 2002
Chemical composition and in vitro antimicrobial activity of essential oil of Melissa officinalis L.

from Romania, Hăncianu M, Aprotosoaie AC, Gille E, Poiată A, Tuchiluş C, Spac A, Stănescu U, Revista Medico-Chirurgicala a Societatii de Medici si Naturalisti din Iasi, 2008

Chemical composition and larvicidal evaluation of Mentha, Salvia, and Melissa essential oils against the West Nile virus mosquito Culex pipiens, Koliopoulos G, Pitarokili D, Kioulos E, Michaelakis A, Tzakou O, *Parasitology Research*, 2010

MYRRH

Systematic Review of Complementary and Alternative Medicine Treatments in Inflammatory Bowel Diseases., Langhorst J, Wulfert H, Lauche R, Klose P, Cramer H, Dobos GJ,Korzenik,J, *Journal of Crohn's & Colitis*,2015

Clinical trial of aromatherapy on postpartum mother's perineal healing, Hur MH, Han SH, *Journal of Korean Academy of Nursing*, 2004

Composition and potential anticancer activities of essential oils obtained from myrrh and frankincense, Chen Y, Zhou C, Ge Z, Liu Y, Liu Y, Feng W, Li S, Chen G, Wei T, *Oncology Letters*, 2013

In vitro cytotoxic and anti-inflammatory effects of myrrh oil on human gingival fibroblasts and epithelial cells, Tipton DA, Lyle B, Babich H, Dabbous MKh, *Toxicology in Vitro*, 2003

Anti-inflammatory and analgesic activity of different extracts of Commiphora myrrha, Su S, Wang T, Duan JA, Zhou W, Hua YQ, Tang YP, Yu L, Qian DW, *Journal of Ethnopharmacology*, 2011

Myrrh: Medical Marvel or Myth of the Magi?, Nomicos EY, Holistic Nursing Practice, 2007

Chemical composition and antibacterial activity of selected essential oils and some of their main compounds, Wanner J, Schmidt E, Bail S, Jirovetz L, Buchbauer G, Gochev V, Girova T, Atanasova T, Stoyanova A, *Natural Product Communications*, 2010

The Effect of Commiphora molmol (Myrrh) in Treatment of Trichomoniasis vaginalis infection, El-Sherbiny GM, El Sherbiny ET, *Iranian Red Crescent Medical Journal*, 2011

Sesquiterpenoids from myrrh inhibit androgen receptor expression and function in human prostate cancer cells, Wang XL, Kong F, Shen T, Young CY, Lou HX, Yuan HQ, *Acta Pharmacologica Sinica*, 2011

NEROLI

Neroli oil (citrus aurantium) to have pharmacological effects on fatigue and insomnia, Essential oils used in aromatherapy, Babar Ali, Naser Ali Al-Wabel, Saiba Shams, Aftab Ahamand, Shah Alam Khan, Firoz Anwar, Asian Pacific Journal of Tropical Biomedicine, 2015.

Inhalation of neroli oil by postmenopausal women improved their quality of life related to menopausal symptoms, increased sexual desire, and reduced blood pressure. In addition, inhalation of neroli oil may reduce stress levels and stimulate the endocrine system. Choi, Seo Yeon et al. "Effects of Inhalation of Essential Oil of Citrus AurantiumL. Var. amara on Menopausal Symptoms, Stress, and Estrogen in Postmenopausal Women: A Randomized Controlled Trial."

Evidence-Based Complementary and Alternative Medicine, 2014

Aromatherapy with C. aurantium blossom oil is a simple, inexpensive, noninvasive, and effective intervention to reduce anxiety during labor. Namazi, Masoumeh et al. "Aromatherapy With Citrus Aurantium Oil and Anxiety During the First Stage of Labor." *Iranian Red Crescent Medical Journal* (2014)

Neroli EO (that is extracted from flowers of Citrus aurantium) demonstrated the capacity to reduce systolic pressure in patients undergoing colonoscopy. Stea, Susanna, Alina Beraudi, and Dalila De Pasquale. "Essential Oils for Complementary Treatment of Surgical Patients: State of the Art." *Evidence-Based Complementary and Alternative Medicine*, 2014.

The results suggest that neroli possesses biologically active constituent(s) that have anticonvulsant activity which supports the ethnomedicinal claims of the use of the plant in the management of seizure. Azanchi, T, H Shafaroodi, and J Asgarpanah. "Anticonvulsant activity of Citrus aurantium blossom essential oil (neroli): involvement of the GABAergic system." *Natural Products Communication*, 2014.

Results suggest that neroli possesses biologically active constituent(s) that have significant activity against acute and especially chronic inflammation, and have central and peripheral antinociceptive effects which support the ethnomedicinal claims of the use of the plant in the management of pain and inflammation. Asgarpanah, J, P Khadobakhsh, and H Shafaroodi. "Analgesic and anti-inflammatory activities of Citrus aurantium L. blossoms essential oil (neroli): involvement of the nitric oxide/

cyclic-guanosine monophostphate pathway." *Journal of Natural Medicines*, 2015.

OREGANO

Antiviral efficacy and mechanisms of action of oregano essential oil and its primary component carvacrol against murine norovirus, Gilling DH, Kitajima M, Torrey JR, Bright KR, *Journal of Applied Microbiology*, 2014

Origanum vulgare subsp. hirtum Essential Oil Prevented Biofilm Formation and Showed Antibacterial Activity against Planktonic and Sessile Bacterial Cells, Schillaci D, Napoli EM, Cusimano MG, Vitale M, Ruberto A, *Journal of Food Protection*, 2013

Oregano essential oil as an antimicrobial additive to detergent for hand washing and food contact surface cleaning, Rhoades J, Gialagkolidou K, Gogou M, Mavridou O, Blatsiotis N, Ritzoulis C, Likotrafiti E, *Journal of Applied Microbiology*, 2013

Evaluation of bacterial resistance to essential oils and antibiotics after exposure to oregano and cinnamon essential oils, Becerril R, Nerín C, Gómez-Lus R, *Foodborne Pathogens and Disease*, 2012

Supercritical fluid extraction of oregano (Origanum vulgare) essentials oils: anti-inflammatory properties based on cytokine response on THP-1 macrophages, Ocaña-Fuentes A, Arranz-Gutiérrez E, Señorans FJ, Reglero G, *Food and Chemical Toxicology*, 2010

Antioxidant and antimicrobial activities of essential oils obtained from oregano, Karakaya S, El SN, Karagözlü N, Sahin S, *Journal of Medicinal Food*, 2011

Anti-inflammatory and anti-ulcer activities of carvacrol, a monoterpene present in the essential oil of oregano, Silva FV, Guimarães AG, Silva ER, Sousa-Neto BP, Machado FD, Quintans-Júnior LJ, Arcanjo DD, Oliveira FA, Oliveira RC, *Journal of Medicinal Food*, 2012

PATCHOULI

Immunological and Psychological Benefits of Aromatherapy Massage, Kuriyama H, Watanabe S, Nakaya T, Shigemori I, Kita M, Yoshida N, Masaki D, Tadai T, Ozasa K, Fukui K, Imanishi J, *Evidence-Based Complementary and Alternative Medicine*, 2005

Chemical composition, bio-herbicidal and antifungal activities of essential oils isolated from Tunisian common cypress (Cupressus sempervirens L.), Ismail A, Lamia H, Mohsen H, Samia G, Bassem J, *Journal of Medicinal Plants Research*, 2013

Immunological and Psychological Benefits of Aromatherapy Massage, Kuriyama H, Watanabe S, Nakaya T, Shigemori I, Kita M, Yoshida N, Masaki D, Tadai T, Ozasa K, Fukui K, Imanishi J, *Evidence-Based Complementary and Alternative Medicine*, 2005

Effect of aromatherapy massage on abdominal fat and body image in post-menopausal women, Kim HJ, *Taehan Kanho Hakhoe Chi*, 2007

Evaluation of the Effects of Plant-derived Essential Oils on Central Nervous System Function Using Discrete Shuttle-type Conditioned Avoidance Response in Mice, Umezu T., *Phytotherapy Research*, 2012

PEPPERMINT

Screening of the antibacterial effects of a variety of essential oils on respiratory tract pathogens, using a modified dilution assay method, Inouye S, Yamaguchi H, Takizawa T, Journal of Infection and Chemotherapy: *Official Journal of the Japan Society of Chemotherapy*, 2001

The influence of essential oils on human attention and alertness, Ilmberger J, Heuberger E, Mahrhofer C, Dessovic H, Kowarik D, Buchbauer G, *Chemical Senses*, 2001

Enteric-coated, pH-dependent peppermint oil capsules for the treatment of irritable bowel syndrome in children, Kline RM, Kline JJ, Di Palma J, Barbero GJ, *The Journal of Pediatrics*, 2001

Cutaneous application of menthol 10% solution as an abortive treatment of migraine without aura: a randomised, double-blind, placebo-controlled, crossed-over study, Borhani Haghighi A, Motazedian S, Rezaii R, Mohammadi F, Salarian L, Pourmokhtari M, Khodaei S, Vossoughi M, Miri R, *The International Journal of Clinical Practice*, 2010

Peppermint oil for the treatment of irritable bowel syndrome: a systematic review and meta-analysis, Khanna R, MacDonald JK, Levesque BG, Journal of Clinical Gastroenterology, 2014

Effects of Peppermint and Cinnamon Odor Administration on Simulated Driving Alertness, Mood and Workload, Raudenbush B, Grayhem R, Sears T, Wilson I., *North American Journal of Psychology*, 2009

Preliminary investigation of the effect of peppermint oil on an objective measure of daytime sleepiness, Norrish MI, Dwyer KL, International journal of psychophysiology: official journal of the International Organization of Psychophysiology, 2005

Controlled breathing with or without peppermint aromatherapy for postoperative nausea and/or vomiting symptom relief: a randomized controlled trial, Sites DS, Johnson NT, Miller JA, Torbush PH, Hardin JS, Knowles SS, Nance J, Fox TH, Tart RC, *Journal of PeriAnesthesia Nursing*, 2014

Antioxidant components of naturally-occurring oils exhibit marked anti-inflammatory activity in epithelial cells of the human upper respiratory system, Gao M, Singh A, Macri K, Reynolds C, Singhal V, Biswal S, Spannhake EW, *Respiratory Research*, 2011

The effects of peppermint on exercise performance, Meamarbashi A, Rajabi A, *Journal of International Society of Sports Nutrition*, 2013

PETITGRAIN

Aromatherapy Improves Work Performance Through Balancing the Autonomic Nervous System, Huang L, *Capdevila L, J Altern Complement Med*, 2016

Characterization of radicals arising from oxidation of commercially-important essential oils, Mori HM, Iwahashi H., *Free Radic Res.* 2016

Determination of allergenic hydroperoxides in essential oils using gas chromatography with electron ionization mass spectrometry, Rudbäck J, Ramzy A, Karlberg AT, Nilsson U, J Sep Sci. 2014

Volatile constituents and antioxidant activity of peel, flowers and leaf oils of Citrus aurantium L. growing in Greece, Sarrou E, Chatzopoulou P, Dimassi-Theriou K, Therios I. *Molecules*, 2013

A sensitive method for determination of allergenic fragrance terpene hydroperoxides using liquid chromatography coupled with tandem mass spectrometry, Rudbäck J, Islam N, Nilsson U, Karlberg AT, J Sep Sci, 2013

Season's variation impact on Citrus aurantium leaves essential oil: chemical composition and biological activities, Ellouze I. Abderrabba M, Sabaou N, Mathieu F, Lebrihi A, Bouajila J, J Food Sci, 2012

Determination of petitgrain oils landmark parameters by using gas chromatography-combustion-isotope ratio mass spectrometry and enantioselective multidimensional gas chromatography, Schipilliti L, Bonaccorsi I, Sciarrone D, Dugo L, Mondello L, Dugo G., *Anal Bioanal Chem*, 2013

Chemotaxonomic investigations of peel and petitgrain essential oils from 17 citron cultivars, Venturini N, Curk F, Desjobert JM, Karp D, Costa J, Paolini J, Chem Biodivers. 2010

PINK PEPPER

Schinus molle L., native of South America, produces an active antibacterial essential oil extracted from the leaves and fruits. This work reports a complete study of its chemical composition and determines the antibacterial activity of Schinus molle L. essential oil and its main components. The results showed that the crude extract essential oil has a potent antibacterial effect on Staphylococcus aureus ATCC 25923, a strong / moderate effect on Escherichia coli ATCC 25922.

Schinus molle L. has been used in folk medicine as antibacterial, antiviral, topical antiseptic, antifungal, antioxidant, anti-inflammatory, anti-tumoural as well as antispasmodic and analgesic.

RED MANDARIN

Methyl-N-methylanthranilate, a pungent compound from Citrus reticulata Blanco leaves. Pharmacology Biology 2016 Correa E; Quinones W; Echeverri F

Terpenes are compounds found in essential oils. The compound responsible for the pungency of mandarin and other citrus leaves was isolated, and surprisingly it was identified as a methyl-N-methylanthranilate. This kind of molecule with this activity could be used to discover new analgesics in human therapy against pain.

In vitro comparative analysis of antiproliferative activity of essential oil from mandarin peel and its principal component limonene. *Natural Product Research* 2013

Manassero CA; Girotti JR; Mijailovsky S; Garcia de Bravo M; Polo M

The effects of the essential oil of mandarin peel (Corrientes, Argentina) and limonene (its major component) were studied on two human tumor cell lines growth (lung adenocarcinoma A549 and hepatocarcinoma HepG2). Both mandarin essential oil and limonene tested showed a strong dose-dependent effect on the growth inhibition of these cell lines. The essential oil was more effective in A549 than in HepG2 cells and more effective than limonene in both the cases. It is likely that minor components and limonene of the oil could exert additive or synergistic effects. Hence, mandarin essential oil could lead to the development

RESOURCES

of anti-tumor agent or complementary and alternative medicines for the treatment of diverse cancers.
Decoctions from Citrus reticulata Blanco seeds protect the uroepithelium against Escherichia coli invasion.
Journal of Ethnopharmacology
Vollmerhausen TL; Ramos NL; Dzung DT; Brauner A
Citrus reticulata treatment decreased 1 integrin expression and reduced bacterial invasion while adhesion of uroepithelial cells was not affected. Results show that Citrus reticulata has a protective effect on the uroepithelium as seen by reduced bacterial invasion of uroepithelial cells. These properties suggest that seeds from Citrus reticulata may have therapeutic potential in preventing UTI.

ROSEMARY
The effects of prolonged rose odor inhalation in two animal models of anxiety, Bradley BF, Starkey NJ, Brown SL, Lea RW, *Physiology & Behavior*, 2007
The metabolic responses to aerial diffusion of essential oils, Wu Y, Zhang Y, Xie G, Zhao A, Pan X, Chen T, Hu Y, Liu Y, Cheng Y. Chi Y, Yao L, Jia W, *PLoS One*, 2012
Essential oils and anxiolytic aromatherapy, Setzer WN, *Natural Product Communications*, 2009
The effects of clinical aromatherapy for anxiety and depression in the high risk postpartum woman – a pilot study, Conrad P, Adams C, Complementary Therapies in Clinical Practice, 2012
Anxiolytic-like effects of rose oil inhalation on the elevated plus-maze test in rats, de Almeida RN, Motta SC, de Brito Faturi C, Catallani B, Leite JR, *Pharmacology Biochemistry and Behavior*, 2004
Rose geranium essential oil as a source of new and safe anti-inflammatory drugs, Boukhatem MN, Kameli A, Ferhat MA, Saidi F, Mekarnia M, *The Libyan Journal of Medicine*, 2013
Effect of "rose essential oil" inhalation on stress-induced skin-barrier disruption in rats and humans, Fukada M, Kano E, Miyoshi M, Komaki R, Watanabe T, *Chemical Senses*, 2012
Effects of fragrance inhalation on sympathetic activity in normal adults, Haze S, Sakai K, Gozu Y, *The Japanese Journal of Pharmacology*, 2002
Relaxing effect of rose oil on humans, Hongratanaworakit T, *Natural Product Communications*, 2009

SANDALWOOD
Olfactory receptor neuron profiling using sandalwood odorants, Bieri S, Monastyrskaia K, Schilling B, *Chemical Senses*, 2004
Differential effects of selective frankincense (Ru Xiang) essential oil versus non-selective sandalwood (Tan Xiang) essential oil on cultured bladder cancer cells: a microarray and bioinformatics study, Dozmorov MG, Yang Q, Wu W, Wren J, Suhail MM, Woolley CL, Young DG, Fung KM, Lin HK, *Chinese Medicine*, 2014
Sandalwood oil prevent skin tumour development in CD1 mice, Dwivedi C, Zhang Y, *European Journal of Cancer Prevention*, 1999
Chemopreventive effects of α-santalol on skin tumor development in CD-1 and SENCAR mice, Dwivedi C, Guan X, Harmsen WL, Voss AL, Goetz-Parten DE, Koopman EM, Johnson KM, Valluri HB, Matthees DP, Cancer Epidemiology, *Biomarkers and Prevention*, 2003
α-santalol, a chemopreventive agent against skin cancer, causes G2/M cell cycle arrest in both p53-mutated human epidermoid carcinoma A431 cells and p53 wild-type human melanoma UACC-62 cells, Zhang X, Chen W, Guillermo R, Chandrasekher G, Kaushik RS, Young A, Fahmy H, Dwivedi C, *BMC Research Notes*, 2010
α-santalol, a derivative of sandalwood oil, induces apoptosis in human prostate cancer cells by causing caspase-3 activation, Bommareddy A, Rule B, VanWert AL, Santha S, Dwivedi C, *Phytomedicine*, 2012
Skin cancer chemopreventive agent, α-santalol, induces apoptotic death of human epidermoid carcinoma A431 cells via caspase activation together with dissipation of mitochondrial membrane potential and cytochrome c release,
Kaur M, Agarwal C, Singh RP, Guan X, Dwivedi C, Agarwal R, Carcinogenesis, 2005
Evaluation of in vivo anti-hyperglycemic and antioxidant potentials of α-santalol and sandalwood oil, Misra BB, Dey S, *Phytomedicine*, 2013

SIBERIAN FIR
General Toxicity and Antifungal Activity of a New Dental Gel with Essential Oil from Abies SibiricaL.Noreikaitė A, Ayupova R, Satbayeva E, Seitaliyeva A, Amirkulova M, Pichkhadze G, Datkhayev U, Stankevičius E. Med Sci Monit. 2017 Jan 29;23:521-527. PMID: 281320653
General Toxicity and Antifungal Activity of a New Dental Gel with Essential Oil from Abies SibiricaL.Noreikaitė A, Ayupova R, Satbayeva E, Seitaliyeva A, Amirkulova M, Pichkhadze G, Datkhayev U, Stankevičius E. Med Sci Monit. 2017 Jan 29;23:521-527. PMID: 28132065
Effects of Abies sibirica terpenes on cancer- and aging-associated pathways in human cells. Kudryavtseva A, Krasnov G Lipatova A, Alekseev B, Maganova F, Shaposhnikov M, Fedorova M, Snezhkina A, Moskalev A. Oncotarget. 2016 Dec 13;7(50):83744-83754. doi: 10.18632/oncotarget.13467. PMID: 27888805
In vitro effect of Knotolan, a new lignan from Abies sibirica, on the growth of hormone-dependent breast cancer cells. Zhukova OS, Fetisova LV, Trishin AV, Anisimova NY, Scherbakov AM, Yashunskii DV, Tsvetkov DE, Men'shov VM, Kiselevskii MV, Nifant'ev NE. Bull Exp Biol Med. 2010 Oct;149(4):511-4. English, Russian. Erratum in: Bull Exp Biol Med. 2011 Feb;150(4):556. Shcherbakov, A E [corrected to Scherbakov, A M]. PMID: 21234454

SPEARMINT
Aromatherapy as a Treatment for Postoperative Nausea: A randomized Trial, Hunt R, Dienemann J, Norton HJ, Hartley W, Hudgens A, Stern T, Divine G, *Anesthesia and Analgesia*, 2013
Inhibition by the essential oils of peppermint and spearmint of the growth of pathogenic bacteria, Imai H, Osawa K, Yasuda H, Hamashima H, Arai T, Sasatsu M, *Microbios*, 2001
Influence of the chirality of (R)-(-)- and (S)-(+)-carvone in the central nervous system: a comparative study, de Sousa DP, de Farias Nóbrega FF, de Almeida RN, *Chirality*, 2007
Comparison of essential oils from three plants for enhancement of antimicrobial activity of nitrofurantoin against enterobacteria, Rafii F, Shahverdi AR, Chemotherapy, 2007
Botanical perspectives on health peppermint: more than just an after-dinner mint, Spirling LI, Daniels IR, *Journal for the Royal Society for the Promotion of Health*, 2001
The effect of gender and ethnicity on children's attitudes and preferences for essential oils: a pilot study, Fitzgerald M, Culbert T, Finkelstein M, Green M, Johnson A, Chen S, Explore (New York, N.Y.), 2007

SPIKENARD
Aromatherapy as a Treatment for Postoperative Nausea: A randomized Trial, Hunt R, Dienemann J, Norton HJ, Hartley W, Hudgens A, Stern T, Divine G, *Anesthesia and Analgesia*, 2013
Inhibition by the essential oils of peppermint and spearmint of the growth of pathogenic bacteria, Imai H, Osawa K, Yasuda H, Hamashima H, Arai T, Sasatsu M, *Microbios*, 2001
Influence of the chirality of (R)-(-)- and (S)-(+)-carvone in the central nervous system: a comparative study, de Sousa DP, de Farias Nóbrega FF, de Almeida RN, *Chirality*, 2007
Comparison of essential oils from three plants for enhancement of antimicrobial activity of nitrofurantoin against enterobacteria, Rafii F, Shahverdi AR, Chemotherapy, 2007
Botanical perspectives on health peppermint: more than just an after-dinner mint, Spirling LI, Daniels IR, *Journal for the Royal Society for the Promotion of Health*, 2001
The effect of gender and ethnicity on children's attitudes and preferences for essential oils: a pilot study, Fitzgerald M, Culbert T, Finkelstein M, Green M, Johnson A, Chen S, Explore (New York, N.Y.), 2007

TANGERINE
Evaluation of the chemical constituents and the antimicrobial activity of the volatile oil of Citrus reticulata fruit (Tangerine fruit peel) from South West Nigeria, Ayoola GA, Johnson OO, Adelowotan T, Aibinu IE, Adenipekun E, Adepoju AA, Coker HAB, Odugbemi TO, *African Journal of Biotechnology*, 2008
In-vitro and in-vivo anti-Trichophyton activity of essential oils by vapour contact, Inouye S, Uchida K, Yamaguchi H, Mycoses, 2001
Antidepressant-like effect of carvacrol (5-Isopropyl-2-methylphenol) in mice: involvement of dopaminergic system, Melo FH, Moura BA, de Sousa DP, de Vasconcelos SM, Macedo DS, Fonteles MM, Viana GS, de Sousa FC, *Fundamental and Clinical Pharmacology*, 2011
Atomic force microscopy analysis shows surface structure changes in carvacrol-treated bacterial cells, La Storia A, Ercolini D, Marinello F, Di Pasqua R, Villani F, Mauriello G, *Research in Microbiology*, 2011
Screening of the antibacterial effects of a variety of essential oils on microorganisms responsible for respiratory infections, Fabio A, Cermelli C, Fabio G, Nicoletti P, Quaglio P, *Phytotherapy Research*, 2007
Stimulative and sedative effects of essential oils upon inhalation in mice, Lim WC, Seo JM, Lee CI, Pyo HB, Lee BC, *Archives of Pharmacal Research*, 2005

THYME
Antimicrobial Activities of Clove and Thyme Extracts, Nzeako BC, Al-Kharousi ZS, Al-Mahrooqui Z, *Sultan Qaboos University Medical Journal*, 2006
Effects of Thymol and Carvacrol, Constituents of Thymus vulgaris L. Essential Oil, on the Inflammatory Response, *Evidence-Based Complementary and Alternative Medicine*
Volume, 2012
Encapsulated thyme (Thymus vulgaris) essential oil used as a natural preservative in bakery product, Goncalves ND, Pena FL, Sartoratto A, Derlameline C, Duarte MCT, Antune AEC, Prata AS, *Food Res Int.*, 2017
Down-regulatory effect of Thymus vulgaris L. on growth and Tri4 gene expression in Fusarium oxysporum strains, Divband K, Shokri H, Khosravi AR, *Microbial Pathogenesis*, 2017
Antifungal Activity of Essential Oils Against Candida Species Isolated from Clinical Samples, Cordoba S, Vivot W, Szusz W, Albo G, *Mycopathologia*, 2019
Activity of Thymus capitatus essential oil components against in vitro cultured Echinococcus multilocularis metacestodes and germinal layer cells, Hizem A, Lundstrom-Stadelmann, M'rad S, Souial S, *Parasitology*, 2019
Combined effect of conventional antimicrobials with essential oils and their main components against resistant Streptococcus suis strains, de Aguiar FC, Solarte, AL, Tarradas C, Gomez-Gascon L, Astorga R, Maldonado A, Huerta B, *Letters in Applied Microbiology*, 2019

TURMERIC
Effects of Turmeric (Curcuma longa) on Skin Health Phytotherapy Research
Vaughn AR; Branum A; Sivamani RK
Turmeric (Curcuma longa) has anti-inflammatory, anti-inflammatory, antimicrobial, antioxidant, and antineuroplastic properties, and may be used to treat a variety of dermatologic diseases. Researchers studied effects of ingestion, topical use, and concurrent ingestion and topical use, and concurrent ingestion and topical use on a variety of skin conditions. Ten studies noted statistically signicant improvement in skin disease severity in the turmeric/curcumin treatment groups compared with control groups. Overall, there is early evidence that turmeric / curcumin products and supplements, both oral and topical, may provide therapeutic beneifts for skin health.
Is Curcumin a Possibility to Treat Inflammatory Bowel Diseases? Journal of Medicinal Food
Mazieiro R; Frizon RR; Barbalho SM' Goulart RA
Curcumin is a natural anti-inflammatory bowel diseases (such as Crohn's disease and Ulcerative colitis) IBD due to its remarkable anti-inflammatory properties.
Curcumin suppresses the progression of laryngeal squamous cell carcinoma through the upregulation of miR-145 and inhibition of the PI3K/Akt/mTOR pathway.
Onco Targets & Therapy/Zhy X; Zhu R
The administration of curcumin markedly suppressed cell proliferation, migration and invasion and induced cell cycle arrest and apoptosis in laryngeal squamous cell carcinoma cells (LSCC).
Curcuma longa L. alleviates skin inflammation
Inflammonpharmacology
Kumar A; Agarwal K; Singh M; Yadav P; Maurya AK; Yadav A; Tandon S; Chanda D; Bawankule DU
These findings of topical anti-inflammatory properties of EOCl provide a scientific basis for medicinal use of this plant material against inflammatory disorders.
Evaluation of the Antiproliferative Activity of Some Nanoparticulate Essential Oils Formulated in Microemulsion on Selected Human Carcinoma Cell Lines.
Current Clinical Pharmacology
Abd-Rabou AA; Edros AE
Some EOs and their microemulstions may potentially be used as natural adjuvants to classical anti-cancer drugs.

VETIVER
Effect of calcium on growth performance and essential oil of vetiver grass (Chrysopogon zizanioides) grown on lead contaminated soils, Danh LT, Truong P, Mammucari R, Foster N, International Journal of Phytoremediation, 2011
Effect of Vetiveria zizanioides Essential Oil on Melanogenesis in Melanoma Cells: Downregulation of Tyrosinase Expression and Suppression of Oxidative Stress, Peng HY, Lai CC, Lin CC, Chou ST, *The Scientific World Journal*, 2014
Constituents of south Indian vetiver oils, Mallavarapu GR, Syamasundar KV, Ramesh S, Rao BR, *Natural Product Communications*, 2012
In Vitro Antioxidant Activities of Essential Oils, Veerapan P, Khunkitti W, *Isan Journal of Pharmaceutical Sciences*, 2011
Antioxidant potential of the root of Vetiveria zizanioides (L.) Nash, Luqman S, Kumar R, Kaushik S, Srivastava S, Darokar MP, Khanuja SP, *Indian Journal of Biochemistry and Biophysics*, 2009
Volatiles emitted from the roots of Vetiveria zizanioides suppress the decline in attention during a visual display terminal taskvi, Matsubara E, Shimizu K, Fukagawa M, Ishizi Y, Kakoi C, Hatayama T, Nagano J, Okamoto T, Ohnuki K, Kondo R, *Biomedical Research*, 2012
Evaluation of the Effects of Plant-derived Essential Oils on Central Nervous System Function Using Discrete Shuttle-type Conditioned Avoidance Response in Mice, Umezu T, *Phytotherapy Research*, 2012

WHITE FIR
Repellency to Stomoxys calcitrans (Diptera: Muscidae) of Plant Essential Oils Alone or in Combination with Calophyllum inophyllum Nut Oil, Hieu TT, Kim SI, Lee SG, Ahn YJ, *Journal of Medical Etomology*, 2010
The battle against multi-resistant strains: Renaissance of antimicrobial essential oils as a promising force to fight hospital-acquired infections, Warnke PH, Becker ST, Podschun R, Sivananthan S, Springer IN, Russo PA, Wiltfang J, Fickenscher H, Sherry E, *Journal of Cranio-Maxillo-Facial Surgery*, 2009

WILD ORANGE
Antimicrobial Effect and Mode of Action of Terpeneless Cold Pressed Valencia Orange Essential Oil on Methicillin-Resistant Staphylococcus aureus, Muthaiyan A, Martin EM, Natesan S, Crandall PG, Wilkinson BJ, Ricke SC, *Journal of Applied Microbiology*, 2012
Insecticidal properties of volatile extracts of orange peels, Ezeonu FC, Chidume GI, Udedi SC, *Bioresource Technology*, 2001
An experimental study on the effectiveness of massage with aromatic ginger and orange essential oil for moderate-to-severe knee pain among the elderly in Hong Kong, Yip YB, Tam AC, *Complementary Therapies in Medicine*, 2008
Oil of bitter orange: new topical antifungal agent, Ramadan W, Mourad B, Ibrahim S, Sonbol F, *International Journal of Dermatology*, 1996
Ambient odor of orange in a dental office reduces anxiety and improves mood in female patients, Lehrner J, Eckersberger C, Walla P, Pötsch G, Deecke L, *Physiology and Behavior*, 2000
Effect of sweet orange aroma on experimental anxiety in humans., Goes TC, Antunes FD, Alves PB, Teixeira-Silva F, The Journal of Alternative and Complementary Medicine
Effect of aromatherapy on patients with Alzheimer's disease, Jimbo D, Kimura Y, Taniguchi M, Inoue M, Urakami K, *Psychogeriatrics*, 2009

WINTERGREEN
Comparison of oral aspirin versus topical applied methyl salicylate for platelet inhibition, Tanen DA, Danish DC, Reardon JM, Chisholm CB, Matteucci MJ, Riffenburgh RH, *Annals of Pharmacotherapy*, 2008
Fumigant toxicity of plant essential oils against Camptomyia corticalis (Diptera: Cecidomyiidae), Kim JR, Haribalan P, Son BK, Ahn YJ, *Journal of Economic Entomology*, 2012
Field evaluation of essential oils for reducing attraction by the Japanese beetle (Coleoptera: Scarabaeidae), Youssef NN, Oliver JB, Ranger CM, Reding ME, Moyseenko JJ, Klein MG, Pappas RS, *Journal of Economic Entomology*, 2009
Essential oils and their compositions as spatial repellents for pestiferous social wasps, Zhang QH, Schnidmiller RG, Hoover DR, *Pest Management Science*, 2013

YARROW
Chamazulene carboxylic acid and matricin: a natural profen and its natural prodrug, identified through similarity to synthetic drug substances, Ramadan M, Goeters S, Watzer B, Krause E, Lohmann K, Bauer R, Hempel B, Imming P, *Journal of Natural Products*, 2006
Comparative evaluation of 11 essential oils of different origin as functional antioxidants, antiradicals and antimicrobials in foods, Sacchetti G, Maietti S, Muzzoli M, Scaglianti M, Manfredini S, Radice M, Bruni R, *Food Chemistry*, 2005

YLANG YLANG
Relaxing Effect of Ylang ylang Oil on Humans after Transdermal Absorption, Hongratanaworakit T, Buchbauer G, *Phytotherapy Research*, 2006
Safety assessment of Ylang-Ylang (Cananga spp.) as a food ingredient., Burdock GA, Carabin IG, *Food and Chemical Toxicology*, 2008
Effects of Ylang-Ylang aroma on blood pressure and heart rate in healthy men, Jung DJ, Cha JY, Kim SE, Ko IG, Jee YS, *Journal of Exercise Rehabilitation*, 2013
Evaluation of the harmonizing effect of ylang-ylang oil on humans after inhalation, Hongratanaworakit T, Buchbauer G, *Planta Medica*, 2004
Essential oil inhalation on blood pressure and salivary cortisol levels in prehypertensive and hypertensive subjects, Kim IH, Kim C, Seong K, Hur MH, Lim HM, Lee MS, *Evidence-Based Complementary and Alternative Medicine*, 2012
The Effects of Herbal Essential Oils on the Oviposition-deterrent and Ovicidal Activities of Aedes aegypti (Linn.), Anopheles dirus (Peyton and Harrison) and Culex quinquefasciatus (Say), Siriporn P, Mayura S, *Tropical Biomedicine*, 2012
Evaluation of the Effects of Plant-derived Essential Oils on Central Nervous System Function Using Discrete Shuttle-type Conditioned Avoidance Response in Mice, Umezu T., *Phytotherapy Research*, 2012
Effects of aromatherapy on changes in the autonomic nervous system, aortic pulse wave velocity and aortic augmentation index in patients with essential hypertension, Cha JH, Lee SH, Yoo YS, *Journal of Korean Academy of Nursing*, 2010

Research Index BY TOPIC

ADDICTION

The effects of aromatherapy on nicotine craving on a U.S. campus: a small comparison study, Cordell B, Buckle J, *The Journal of Alternative and Complementary Medicine*, 2013

ALERTNESS

Effects of Peppermint and Cinnamon Odor Administration on Simulated Driving Alertness, Mood and Workload, Raudenbush B, Grayhem R, Sears T, Wilson I., *North American Journal of Psychology*, 2009

The influence of essential oils on human attention. I: alertness, Ilmberger J, Heuberger E, Mahrhofer C, Dessovic H, Kowarik D, Buchbauer G, *Chemical Senses*, 2001

The influence of essential oils on human vigilance, Heuberger E, Ilmberger J, *Natural Product Communications*, 2010

Volatiles emitted from the roots of Vetiveria zizanioides suppress the decline in attention during a visual display terminal task, Matsubara E, Shimizu K, Fukagawa M, Ishizi Y, Kakoi C, Hatayama T, Nagano J, Okamoto T, Ohnuki K, Kondo R, *Biomedical Research*, 2012

ALLERGIES

Cytological aspects on the effects of a nasal spray consisting of standardized extract of citrus lemon and essential oils in allergic rhinopathy, Ferrara L, Naviglio D, Armone Caruso A, *ISRN Pharm*, 2012

ALZHEIMER'S DISEASE

Effect of arborvitae seed on cognitive function and α7nAChR protein expression of hippocampus in model rats with Alzheimer's disease, Cheng XL, Xiong XB, Xiang MQ, *Cell Biochem Biophys*, 2013

Effect of aromatherapy on patients with Alzheimer's disease, Jimbo D, Kimura Y, Taniguchi M, Inoue M, Urakami K, *Psychogeriatrics*, 2009

Inhalation of coriander volatile oil increased anxiolytic-antidepressant-like behaviors and decreased oxidative status in beta-amyloid (1-42) rat model of Alzheimer's disease, Cioanca O, Hritcu L, Mihasan M, Trifan A, Hancianu M, *Physiology & Behavior*, 2014

ANTIBACTERIAL

Activity of Essential Oils Against Bacillus subtilis Spores, Lawrence HA, Palombo EA, *Journal of Microbiology and Biotechnology*, 2009

Antibacterial activity of essential oils and their major constituents against respiratory tract pathogens by gaseous contact, Inouye S, Takizawa T, Yamaguchi H, *The Journal of Antimicrobial Chemotherapy*, 2001

Antibacterial activity of Litsea cubeba (Lauraceae, May Chang) and its effects on the biological response of common carp Cyprinus carpio challenged with Aeromonas hydrophila. Nguyen HV, Caruso D, Lebrun M, Nguyen NT, Trinh TT, Meile JC, Chu-Ky S, Sarter S. J Appl Microbiol. 2016

Antibacterial activity of the essential oil from Rosmarinus officinalis and its major components against oral pathogens, Bernardes WA, Lucarini R, Tozatti MG, Flauzino LG, Soutza MG, Turatti IC, Andrade e Silva ML, Martins CH, da Silva Filho AA, Cunha WR, *Zeitschrift Fur Naturforschung C-A Journal of Biosciences*, 2010

Antibacterial and antioxidant properties of Mediterranean aromatic plants, Piccaglia R, Marotti M, Giovanelli E, Deans SG, Eaglesham E, *Industrial Crops and Products*, 1993

Antibacterial Effects of the Essential Oils of Commonly Consumed Medicinal Herbs Using an In Vitro Model, Soković M, Glamočlija J, Marin PD, Brkić D, van Griensven LJ, *Molecules*, 2010

Atomic force microscopy analysis shows surface structure changes in carvacrol-treated bacterial cells, La Storia A, Ercolini D, Marinello F, Di Pasqua R, Villani F, Mauriello G, *Research in Microbiology*, 2011

Bactericidal activities of plant essential oils and some of their isolated constituents against Campylobacter jejuni, Escherichia coli, Listeria monocytogenes, and Salmonella enterica, Friedman M, Henika PR, Mandrell RE, *Journal of Food Protection*, 2002

Bacteriostatic effect of copaiba oil (Copaifera officinalis) against Streptococcus mutans. Pieri FA et al. Braz Dent J. 2012

Chemical composition and antibacterial activity of selected essential oils and some of their main compounds, Wanner J, Schmidt E, Bail S, Jirovetz L, Buchbauer G, Gochev V, Girova T, Atanasova T, Stoyanova A, *Natural Product Communications*, 2010

Chemical composition, antibacterial activity and cytotoxicity of essential oils of Tanacetumparthenium in different developmental stages. Mohsenzadeh F, Chehregani A, Amiri H. Pharm Biol. 2011 Sep;49(9):920-6. doi: 10.3109/13880209.2011.556650. Epub, 2011

Coriander (Coriandrum sativum L.) essential oil: its antibacterial activity and mode of action evaluated by flow cytometry, Silva F, Ferreira S, Queiroz JA, Domingues FC, *Journal of Medical Microbiology*, 2011

Effects of Helichrysum italicum extract on growth and enzymatic activity of Staphylococcus aureus, Nostro A, Bisignano G, Angela Cannatelli M, Crisafi G, Paola Germanò M, Alonzo V, *International Journal of Antimicrobial Agents*, 2001

Eugenol (an essential oil of clove) acts as an antibacterial agent against Salmonella typhi by disrupting the cellular membrane, Devi KP, Nisha SA, Sakthivel R, Pandian SK, *Journal of Ethnopharmacology*, 2010

Evaluation of bacterial resistance to essential oils and antibiotics after exposure to oregano and cinnamon essential oils, Becerril R, Nerín C, Gómez-Lus R, *Foodborne Pathogens and Disease*, 2012

Growth inhibition of pathogenic bacteria and some yeasts by selected essential oils and survival of L. monocytogenes and C. albicans in apple-carrot juice., Irkin R, Korukluoglu M, *Foodborne Pathogens and Disease*, 2009

Helichrysum italicum extract interferes with the production of enterotoxins by Staphylococcus aureus., Nostro A, Cannatelli MA, Musolino AD, Procopio F, Alonzo V, *Letters in Applied Microbiology*, 2002

In vitro antibacterial activity of some plant essential oils, Prabuseenivasan S, Jayakumar M, Ignacimuthu S, *BMC Complementary and Alternative Medicine*, 2006

Inhibition by the essential oils of peppermint and spearmint of the growth of pathogenic bacteria, Imai H, Osawa K, Yasuda H, Hamashima H, Arai T, Sasatsu M, *Microbios*, 2001

Investigation of antibacterial activity of rosemary essential oil against Propionibacterium acnes with atomic force microscopy, Fu Y, Zu Y, Chen L, Efferth T, Liang H, Liu Z, Liu W, *Planta Medica*, 2007

Origanum vulgare subsp. hirtum Essential Oil Prevented Biofilm Formation and Showed Antibacterial Activity against Planktonic and Sessile Bacterial Cells, Schillaci D, Napoli EM, Cusimano MG, Vitale M, Ruberto A, *Journal of Food Protection*, 2013

Potential of rosemary oil to be used in drug-resistant infections, Luqman S, Dwivedi GR, Darokar MP, Kalra A, Khanuja SP, *Alternative Therapies in Health and Medicine*, 2007

Screening of the antibacterial effects of a variety of essential oils on microorganisms responsible for respiratory infections, Fabio A, Cermelli C, Fabio G, Nicoletti P, Quaglio P, *Phytotherapy Research*, 2007

Screening of the antibacterial effects of a variety of essential oils on respiratory tract pathogens, using a modified dilution assay method, Inouye S, Yamaguchi H, Takizawa T, *Journal of Infection and Chemotherapy: Official Journal of the Japan Society of Chemotherapy*, 2001

Some evidences on the mode of action of Cinnamomum verum bark essential oil, alone and in combination with piperacillin against a multi-drug resistant Escherichia coli strain, Yap PS, Krishnan T, Chan KG, Lim SH, *Journal of Microbiology and Biotechnology*, 2014

Sub-inhibitory stress with essential oil affects enterotoxins production and essential oil susceptibility in Staphylococcus aureus. Turchi B, Mancini S, Pistelli L, Najar B, Cerri D, Fratini F. Nat Prod Res. 2017.

Tea tree oil-induced transcriptional alterations in Staphylococcus aureus, Cuaron JA, Dulal S, Song Y, Singh AK, Montelongo CE, Yu W, Nagarajan V, Jayaswal RK, Wilkinson BJ, Gustafson JE, *Phytotherapy Research*, 2013

The anti-biofilm activity of lemongrass (Cymbopogon flexuosus) and grapefruit (Citrus paradisi) essential oils against five strains of Staphylococcus aureus, Adukwu EC, Allen SC, Phillips CA, *Journal of Applied Microbiology*, 2012

The antibacterial activity of geranium oil against Gram-negative bacteria isolated from difficult-to-heal wounds, Sienkiewicz M, Poznańska-Kurowska K, Kaszuba A, Kowalczyk E, *Burns*, 2014

The effect of lemongrass EO highlights its potential against antibiotic resistant Staph. aureus in the healthcare environment, Adukwu EC, Allen SC, Phillips CA, *Journal of Applied Microbiology*, 2012

The potential of use basil and rosemary essential oils as effective antibacterial agents, Sienkiewicz M, Łysakowska M, Pastuszka M, Bienias W, Kowalczyk E, *Molecules*, 2013

ANTIFUNGAL

Antibacterial, antifungal, and anticancer activities of volatile oils and extracts from stems, leaves, and flowers of Eucalyptus sideroxylon and Eucalyptus torquata, Ashour HM, *Cancer Biology and Therapy*, 2008

Antifungal activity of clove essential oil and its volatile vapour against dermatophytic fungi, Chee HY, Lee MH, *Mycobiology*, 2007

Antifungal mechanism of essential oil from Anethum graveolens seeds against Candida albicans, Chen Y, Zeng H, Tian J, Ban X, Ma B, Wang Y, *Journal of Medical Microbiology*, 2013

Antifungal, anti-biofilm and adhesion activity of the essential oil of Myrtus communis L. against Candida species, Cannas S, Molicotti P, Usai D, Maxia A, Zanetti S, *Natural Product Research*, 2014

Chemical composition, bio-herbicidal and antifungal activities of essential oils isolated from Tunisian common cypress (Cupressus sempervirens L.), Ismail A, Lamia H, Mohsen H, Samia G, Bassem J, *Journal of Medicinal Plants Research*, 2013

Coriandrum sativum L. (Coriander) Essential Oil: Antifungal Activity and Mode of Action on Candida spp., and Molecular Targets Affected in Human Whole-Genome Expression, Freires Ide A, Murata RM, Furletti VF, Sartoratto A, Alencar SM, Figueira GM, de Oliveira Rodrigues JA, Duarte MC, Rosalen PL, *PLoS One*, 2014

Dill (Anethum graveolens L.) seed essential oil induces Candida albicans apoptosis in a metacaspase-dependent manner, Chen Y, Zeng H, Tian J, Ban X, Ma B, Wang Y, *Fungal Biology*, 2014

In vitro antagonistic activity of monoterpenes and their mixtures against 'toe nail fungus' pathogens, Ramsewak RS, Nair MG, Stommel M, Selanders L, *Phytotherapy Research*, 2003

In-vitro and in-vivo anti-Trichophyton activity of essential oils by vapour contact, Inouye S, Uchida K, Yamaguchi H, *Mycoses*, 2001

Oil of bitter orange: new topical antifungal agent, Ramadan W, Mourad B, Ibrahim S, Sonbol F, *International Journal of Dermatology*, 1996

ANTIMICROBIAL
A novel aromatic oil compound inhibits microbial overgrowth on feet: a case study, Misner BD, *Journal of the International Society of Sports Nutrition*, 2007
Antimicrobial activities of cinnamon oil and cinnamaldehyde from the Chinese medicinal herb Cinnamomum cassia Blume, Ooi LS, Li Y, Kam SL, Wang H, Wong EY, Ooi VE, *The American Journal of Chinese Medicine*, 2006
Antimicrobial Activities of Clove and Thyme Extracts, Nzeako BC, Al-Kharousi ZS, Al-Mahrooqui Z, *Sultan Qaboos University Medical Journal*, 2006
Antimicrobial activity against bacteria with dermatological relevance and skin tolerance of the essential oil from Coriandrum sativum L. fruits, Casetti F, Bartelke S, Biehler K, Augustin M, Schempp CM, Frank U, *Phytotherapy Research*, 2012
Antimicrobial activity of clove oil and its potential in the treatment of vaginal candidiasis, Ahmad N, Alam MK, Shehbaz A, Khan A, Mannan A, Hakim SR, Bisht D, Owais M, *Journal of Drug Targeting*, 2005
Antimicrobial Activity of Copaiba (Copaifera officinalis) and Pracaxi (Pentaclethra macroloba) Oils against Staphylococcus Aureus: Importance in Compounding for Wound Care.Guimarães AL et al. Int J Pharm Compd. 2016
Antimicrobial activity of essential oils and five terpenoid compounds against Campylobacter jejuni in pure and mixed culture experiments, Kurekci C, Padmanabha J, Bishop-Hurley SL, Hassan E, Al Jassim RA, McSweeney CS, *International Journal of Food Microbiology*, 2013
Antimicrobial activity of individual and mixed fractions of dill, cilantro, coriander and eucalyptus essential oils, Delaquis PJ, Stanich K, Girard B, Mazza G, *International Journal of Food Microbiology*, 2002
Antimicrobial activity of juniper berry essential oil (Juniperus communis L., Cupressaceae), Pepeljnjak S, Kosalec I, Kalodera Z, Blazević N, *Acta Pharmaceutica*, 2005
Antimicrobial activity of the bioactive components of essential oils from Pakistani spices against Salmonella and other multi-drug resistant bacteria, Naveed R, Hussain I, Tawab A, Tariq M, Rahman M, Hameed S, Mahmood MS, Siddique AB, Iqbal M, *BMC Complementary and Alternative Medicine*, 2013
Antimicrobial Effect and Mode of Action of Terpeneless Cold Pressed Valencia Orange Essential Oil on Methicillin-Resistant Staphylococcus aureus, Muthaiyan A, Martin EM, Natesan S, Crandall PG, Wilkinson BJ, Ricke SC, *Journal of Applied Microbiology*, 2012
Antimicrobial effects of essential oils in combination with chlorhexidine digluconate, Filoche SK, Soma K, Sissons CH, *Oral Microbiology and Immunology*, 2005
Antimicrobial effects of Manuka honey on in vitro biofilm formation by Clostridium difficile. Piotrowski M, Karpiński P, Pituch H, van Belkum A, Obuch-Woszczatyński P. Eur J Clin Microbiol Infect Dis. 2017
Chemical composition and in vitro antimicrobial activity of essential oil of Melissa officinalis L. from Romania, Hăncianu M, Aprotosoaie AC, Gille E, Poiată A, Tuchiluş C, Spac A, Stănescu U, *Revista Medico-Chirurgicala a Societatii de Medici si Naturalisti din Iasi*, 2008
Comparative evaluation of 11 essential oils of different origin as functional antioxidants, antiradicals and antimicrobials in foods, Sacchetti G, Maietti S, Muzzoli M, Scaglianti M, Manfredini S, Radice M, Bruni R, *Food Chemistry*, 2005
Comparison of essential oils from three plants for enhancement of antimicrobial activity of nitrofurantoin against enterobacteria, Rafii F, Shahverdi AR, *Chemotherapy*, 2007
Essential Oil Compositions and Antimicrobial Activities of Various Parts of Litsea cubeba from Taiwan. Su YC, Ho CL. Nat Prod Commun. 2016
Essential Oil Compositions and Antimicrobial Activities of Various Parts of Litsea cubeba from Taiwan. Su YC, Ho CL. Nat Prod Commun. 2016
Evaluation of the antimicrobial properties of different parts of Citrus aurantifolia (lime fruit) as used locally, Aibinu I, Adenipekun T, Adelowotan T, Ogunsanya T, Odugbemi T, *African Journal of Traditional, Complementary, and Alternative Medicines*, 2006
Immune-Modifying and Antimicrobial Effects of Eucalyptus Oil and Simple Inhalation Devices, Sadlon AE, Lamson DW, *Alternative Medicine Review: A Journal of Clinical Therapeutic*, 2010
Microbicide activity of clove essential oil (Eugenia caryophyllata), Nuñez L, Aquino MD, *Brazilian Journal of Microbiology*, 2012
Oregano essential oil as an antimicrobial additive to detergent for hand washing and food contact surface cleaning, Rhoades J, Gialagkolidou K, Gogou M, Mavridou O, Blatsiotis N, Ritzoulis C, Likotrafiti E, *Journal of Applied Microbiology*, 2013
Study of the antimicrobial action of various essential oils extracted from Malagasy plants. II: Lauraceae, Raharivelomanana PJ, Terrom GP, Bianchini JP, Coulanges P, *Arch Inst Pasteur Madagascar*, 1989
The additive and synergistic antimicrobial effects of select frankincense and myrrh oils–a combination from the pharaonic pharmacopoeia, de Rapper S, Van Vuuren SF, Kamatou GP, Viljoen AM, Dagne E, *Letters in Applied Microbiology*, 2012
The battle against multi-resistant strains: Renaissance of antimicrobial essential oils as a promising force to fight hospital-acquired infections, Warnke PH, Becker ST, Podschun R, Sivananthan S, Springer IN, Russo PA, Wiltfang J, Fickenscher H, Sherry E, *Journal of Cranio-Maxillo-Facial Surgery*, 200
Volatile composition and antimicrobial activity of twenty commercial frankincense essential oil samples, Van Vuurena SF, Kamatoub GPP, Viljoenb, AM, *South African Journal of Botany*, 2010

ANTIOXIDANT
Anti-Inflammatory and Antioxidant Actions of Copaiba Oil Are Related to Liver Cell Modifications in Arthritic Rats. Castro Ghizoni CV, Arssufi Ames AP, Lameira OA, Bersani Amado CA, Sá Nakanishi AB, Bracht L, Marçal Natali MR, Peralta RM, Bracht A, Comar JF. J Cell Biochem. 2017
Antioxidant activities and volatile constituents of various essential oils, Wei A, Shibamoto T, *Journal of Agriculture and Food Chemistry*, 2007
Antioxidant activity of rosemary (Rosmarinus officinalis L.) essential oil and its hepatoprotective potential, Ra Kovi A, Milanovi I, Pavlovi NA, Ebovi T, Vukmirovi SA, Mikov M, *BMC Complementary and Alternative Medicine*, 2014
Antioxidant and antimicrobial activities of essential oils obtained from oregano, Karakaya S, El SN, Karagözlü N, Sahin S, *Journal of Medicinal Food*, 2011
Antioxidant and Hepatoprotective Potential of Essential Oils of Coriander (Coriandrum sativum L.) and Caraway (Carum carvi L.) (Apiaceae), Samojlik I, Lakić N, Mimica-Dukić N, Daković-Svajcer K, Bozin B, *Journal of Agricultural and Food Chemistry*, 2010
Antioxidant potential of the root of Vetiveria zizanioides (L.) Nash, Luqman S, Kumar R, Kaushik S, Srivastava S, Darokar MP, Khanuja SP, *Indian Journal of Biochemistry and Biophysics*, 2009
Antioxidative effects of lemon oil and its components on copper induced oxidation of low density lipoprotein, Grassmann J, Schneider D, Weiser D, Elstner EF, *Arzneimittel-Forschung*, 2001
Biological effects, antioxidant and anticancer activities of marigold and basil essential oils, Mahmoud GI, *Journal of Medicinal Plants Research*, 2013
Comparative evaluation of 11 essential oils of different origin as functional antioxidants, antiradicals and antimicrobials in foods, Sacchetti G, Maietti S, Muzzoli M, Scaglianti M, Manfredini S, Radice M, Bruni R, *Food Chemistry*, 2005
Evaluation of in vivo anti-hyperglycemic and antioxidant potentials of α-santalol and sandalwood oil, Misra BB, Dey S, *Phytomedicine*, 2013
In Vitro Antioxidant Activities of Essential Oils, Veerapan P, Khunkitti W, *Isan Journal of Pharmaceutical Sciences*, 2011
Minor Furanocoumarins and Coumarins in Grapefruit Peel Oil as Inhibitors of Human Cytochrome P450 3A4, César TB, Manthey JA, Myung K, *Journal of Natural Products*, 2009

ANTIVIRAL
Antiviral activities in plants endemic to madagascar, Hudson JB, Lee MK, Rasoanaivo P, *Pharm Biol*. 2000
Antiviral activity of the volatile oils of Melissa officinalis L. against Herpes simplex virus type-2, Allahverdiyev A, Duran N, Ozguven M, Koltas S, *Phytomedicine*, 2004
Antiviral efficacy and mechanisms of action of oregano essential oil and its primary component carvacrol against murine norovirus, Gilling DH, Kitajima M, Torrey JR, Bright KR, *Journal of Applied Microbiology*, 2014
Immunologic mechanism of Patchouli alcohol anti-H1N1 influenza virus may through regulation of the RLH signal pathway in vitro, Wu XL, Ju DH, Chen J, Yu B, Liu KL, He JX, Dai CQ, Wu S, Chang Z, Wang YP, Chen XY, *Current Microbiology*, 2013
Oral administration of patchouli alcohol isolated from Pogostemonis Herba augments protection against influenza viral infection in mice, Li YC, Peng SZ, Chen HM, Zhang FX, Xu PP, Xie JH, He JJ, Chen JN, Lai XP, Su ZR, International Immunopharmacology, 2012

ANXIETY
Ambient odor of orange in a dental office reduces anxiety and improves mood in female patients, Lehrner J, Eckersberger C, Walla P, Pötsch G, Deecke L, *Physiology and Behavior*, 2000
Anxiolytic-like effects of rose oil inhalation on the elevated plus-maze test in rats, de Almeida RN, Motta SC, de Brito Faturi C, Catallani B, Leite JR, *Pharmacology Biochemistry and Behavior*, 2004
Effect of sweet orange aroma on experimental anxiety in humans, Goes TC, Antunes FD, Alves PB, Teixeira-Silva F, *The Journal of Alternative and Complementary Medicine*
Essential oils and anxiolytic aromatherapy, Setzer WN, *Natural Product Communications*, 2009
The effects of prolonged rose odor inhalation in two animal models of anxiety, Bradley BF, Starkey NJ, Brown SL, Lea RW, *Physiology & Behavior*, 2007
The GABAergic system contributes to the anxiolytic-like effect of essential oil from Cymbopogon citratus (lemongrass), Costa CA, Kohn DO, de Lima VM, Gargano AC, Flório JC, Costa M, *Journal of Ethnopharmacology*, 2011

ARTHRITIS
Anti-arthritic effect of eugenol on collagen-induced arthritis experimental model, Grespan R, Paludo M, Lemos Hde P, Barbosa CP, Bersani-Amado CA, Dalalio MM, Cuman RK, *Biological and Pharmaceutical Bulletin*, 2012
The effects of aromatherapy on pain, depression, and life satisfaction of arthritis patients, Kim MJ, Nam ES, Paik SI, *Taehan Kanho Hakhoe Chi*, 2005

BEHAVIOR
Immunological and Psychological Benefits of Aromatherapy Massage, Kuriyama H, Watanabe S, Nakaya T, Shigemori I, Kita M, Yoshida N, Masaki D, Tadai T, Ozasa K, Fukui K, Imanishi J, *Evidence-Based Complementary and Alternative Medicine*, 2005
The effect of gender and ethnicity on children's attitudes and preferences for essential oils: a pilot study, Fitzgerald M, Culbert T, Finkelstein M, Green M, Johnson A, Chen S, *Explore (New York, N.Y.)*, 2007

BLOOD
Black pepper essential oil to enhance intravenous catheter insertion in patients with poor vein visibility: a controlled study, Kristiniak S, Harpel J, Breckenridge DM, Buckle J, *Journal of Alternative and Complementary Medicine*, 2012
Comparative screening of plant essential oils: Phenylpropanoid moiety as basic core for antiplatelet activity, Tognolini M, Barocelli E, Ballabeni V, Bruni R, Bianchi A, Chiavarini M, Impicciatore M, *Life Sciences*, 2006
Comparison of oral aspirin versus topical applied methyl salicylate for platelet inhibition, Tanen DA, Danish DC, Reardon JM, Chisholm CB, Matteucci MJ, Riffenburgh RH, *Annals of Pharmacotherapy*, 2008
Effects of a novel formulation of essential oils on glucose-insulin metabolism in diabetic and hypertensive rats: a pilot study, Talpur N, Echard B, Ingram C, Bagchi D, Preuss H, Diabetes, *Obesity and Metabolism*, 2005
Mechanism of changes induced in plasma glycerol by scent stimulation with grapefruit and lavender essential oils, Shen J, Niijima A, Tanida M, Horii Y, Nakamura T, Nagai K, *Neuroscience Letters*, 2007
Suppression of neutrophil accumulation in mice by cutaneous application of geranium essential oil, Maruyama N, Sekimoto Y, Ishibashi H, Inouye S, Oshima H, Yamaguchi H, Abe S, *Journal of Inflammation (London, England)*, 2005

BLOOD PRESSURE
Antioxidative Properties and Inhibition of Key Enzymes Relevant to Type-2 Diabetes and Hypertension by Essential Oils from Black Pepper, Oboh G, Ademosun AO, Odubanjo OV, Akinbola IA, *Advances in Pharmacological Sciences*, 2013
Effects of Aromatherapy Massage on Blood Pressure and Lipid Profile in Korean Climacteric Women, Myung-HH , Heeyoung OH, Myeong SL, Chan K, Ae-na C, Gil-ran S, *International Journal of Neuroscience*, 2007
Effects of Ylang-Ylang aroma on blood pressure and heart rate in healthy men, Jung DJ, Cha JY, Kim SE, Ko IG, Jee YS, *Journal of Exercise Rehabilitation*, 2013
Essential oil inhalation on blood pressure and salivary cortisol levels in prehypertensive and hypertensive subjects, Kim IH, Kim C, Seong K, Hur MH, Lim HM, Lee MS, *Evidence-Based Complementary and Alternative Medicine*, 2012

Inhibitory potential of omega-3 fatty and fenugreek essential oil on key enzymes of carbohydrate-digestion and hypertension in diabetes rats, Hamden K, Keskes H, Belhaj S, Mnafgui K, Feki A, Allouche N, *Lipids in Health and Disease*, 2011

Olfactory stimulation with scent of essential oil of grapefruit affects autonomic neurotransmission and blood pressure, Tanida M, Niijima A, Shen J, Nakamura T, Nagai K, *Brian Research*, 2005

Randomized controlled trial for Salvia sclarea or Lavandula angustifolia: differential effects on blood pressure in female patients with urinary incontinence undergoing urodynamic examination, Seol GH, Lee YH, Kang P, You JH, Park M, Min SS, *The Journal of Alternative and Complementary Medicine*, 2013

The effects of the inhalation method using essential oils on blood pressure and stress responses of clients with essential hypertension, Hwang JH, *Korean Society of Nursing Science*, 2006

Neroli EO (that is extracted from flowers of Citrus aurantium) demonstrated the capacity to reduce systolic pressure in patients undergoing colonoscopy. Stea, Susanna, Alina Beraudi, and Dalila De Pasquale. "Essential Oils for Complementary Treatment of Surgical Patients: State of
the Art." *Evidence-Based Complementary and Alternative Medicine*, 2014.

BRAIN

Effects of fragrance inhalation on sympathetic activity in normal adults, Haze S, Sakai K, Gozu Y, *The Japanese Journal of Pharmacology*, 2002

Essential oil from lemon peels inhibit key enzymes linked to neurodegenerative conditions and pro-oxidant induced lipid peroxidation, Oboh G, Olasehinde TA, Ademosun AO, *Journal of Oleo Science*, 2014

Inhibition of acetylcholinesterase activity by essential oil from Citrus paradisi, Miyazawa M, Tougo H, Ishihara M, *Natural Product Letters*, 2001

Neuropharmacology of the essential oil of bergamot, Bagetta G, Morrone LA, Rombolà L, Amantea D, Russo R, Berliocchi L, Sakurada S, Sakurada T, Rotiroti D, Corasaniti MT, *Fitoterapia*, 2010

Olfactory receptor neuron profiling using sandalwood odorants., Bieri S, Monastyrskaia K, Schilling B, *Chemical Senses*, 2004

Plasma 1,8-cineole correlates with cognitive performance following exposure to rosemary essential oil aroma, Moss M, Oliver L, *Therapeutic Advances in Psychopharmacology*, 2012

The essential oil of bergamot enhances the levels of amino acid neurotransmitters in the hippocampus of rat: implication of monoterpene hydrocarbons, Morrone LA, Rombolà L, Pelle C, Corasaniti MT, Zappettini S, Paudice P, Bonanno G, Bagetta G, *Pharmacological Research*, 2007

CANCER

α-santalol, a chemopreventive agent against skin cancer, causes G2/M cell cycle arrest in both p53-mutated human epidermoid carcinoma A431 cells and p53 wild-type human melanoma UACC-62 cells, Zhang X, Chen W, Guillermo R, Chandrasekher G, Kaushik RS, Young A, Fahmy H, Dwivedi C, *BMC Research Notes*, 2010

Anticancer activity of an essential oil from Cymbopogon flexuosus (lemongrass), Sharma PR, Mondhe DM, Muthiah S, Pal HC, Shahi AK, Saxena AK, Qazi GN, *Chemico-Biological Interactions*, 2009

Anticancer activity of liposomal bergamot essential oil (BEO) on human neuroblastoma cells, Celia C, Trapasso E, Locatelli M, Navarra M, Ventura CA, Wolfram J, Carafa M, Morittu VM, Britti D, Di Marzio L, Paolino D, *Colloids and Surfaces*, 2013

Antioxidant and Anticancer Activities of Citrus reticulate (Petitgrain Mandarin) and Pelargonium graveolens (Geranium) Essential Oils, Fayed SA, *Research Journal of Agriculture and Biological Sciences*, 2009

Apoptosis-mediated proliferation inhibition of human colon cancer cells by volatile principles of Citrus aurantifolia, Patil JR, Jayaprakasha GK, Chidambara Murthy KN, Tichy SE, Chetti MB, Patil BS, *Food Chemistry*, 2009

Biological effects, antioxidant and anticancer activities of marigold and basil essential oils, Mahmoud GI, *Journal of Medicinal Plants Research*, 2013

Composition and potential anticancer activities of essential oils obtained from myrrh and frankincense, Chen Y, Zhou C, Ge Z, Liu Y, Liu Y, Feng W, Li S, Chen G, Wei T, *Oncology Letters*, 2013

Conservative surgical management of stage IA endometrial carcinoma for fertility preservation, Mazzon I, Corrado G, Masciullo V, Morricone D, Ferrandina G, Scambia G, *Fertil Steril*, 2010

Differential effects of selective frankincense (Ru Xiang) essential oil versus non-selective sandalwood (Tan Xiang) essential oil on cultured bladder cancer cells: a microarray and bioinformatics study, Dozmorov MG, Yang Q, Wu W, Wren J, Suhail MM, Woolley CL, Young DG, Fung KM, Lin HK, *Chinese Medicine*, 2014

Effect of Vetiveria zizanioides Essential Oil on Melanogenesis in Melanoma Cells: Downregulation of Tyrosinase Expression and Suppression of Oxidative Stress, Peng HY, Lai CC, Lin CC, Chou ST, *The Scientific World Journal*, 2014

Effects of Abies sibirica terpenes on cancer- and aging-associated pathways in human cells. Kudryavtseva A, Krasnov G, Lipatova A, Alekseev B, Maganova F, Shaposhnikov M, Fedorova M, Snezhkina A, Moskalev A. Oncotarget. 2016 Medicinal plants as antiemetics in the treatment of cancer: a review, Haniadka R, Popouri S, Palatty PL, Arora R, Baliga MS, *Integrative Cancer Therapies*, 2012

In vitro effect of Knotolan, a new lignan from Abies sibirica, on the growth of hormone-dependent breast cancer cells. Zhukova OS, Fetisova LV, Trishin AV, Anisimova NY, Scherbakov AM, Yashunskii DV, Tsvetkov DE, Men'shov VM, Kiselevskii MV, Nifant'ev NE. Bull Exp Biol Med. 2010 Oct;149(4):511-4. English, Russian. Erratum in: Bull Exp Biol Med. 2011

Protective effects of lemon grass (Cymbopogon citratus STAPF) essential oil on DNA damage and carcinogenesis in female Balb/C mice, Bidinotto LT, Costa CA, Salvadori DM, Costa M, Rodrigues MA, Barbisan LF, *Journal of Applied Toxicology*, 2011

Sesquiterpenoids from myrrh inhibit androgen receptor expression and function in human prostate cancer cells, Wang XL, Kong F, Shen T, Young CY, Lou HX, Yuan HQ, *Acta Pharmacologica Sinica*, 2011

Skin cancer chemopreventive agent, {α}-santalol, induces apoptotic death of human epidermoid carcinoma A431 cells via caspase activation together with dissipation of mitochondrial membrane potential and cytochrome c release, Kaur M, Agarwal C, Singh RP, Guan X, Dwivedi C, Agarwal R, *Carcinogenesis*, 2005

Strawberry-Tree Honey Induces Growth Inhibition of Human Colon Cancer Cells and Increases ROS Generation: A Comparison with Manuka Honey. Afrin S, Forbes-Hernandez TY, Gasparrini M, Bompadre S, Quiles JL, Sanna G, Spano N, Giampieri F, Battino M. Int J Mol Sci. 2017

Terpinen-4-ol, the main component of Melaleuca alternifolia (tea tree) oil inhibits the in vitro growth of human melanoma cells, Calcabrini A, Stringaro A, Toccacieli L, Meschini S, Marra M, Colone M, Salvatore G, Mondello F, Arancia G, Molinari A, *Journal of Investigative Dermatology*, 2004

Topically applied Melaleuca alternifolia (tea tree) oil causes direct anti-cancer cytotoxicity in subcutaneous tumour bearing mice, Ireland DJ, Greay SJ, Hooper CM, Kissick HT, Filion P, Riley TV, Beilharz MW, *Journal of Dermatological Science*, 2012

α-Santalol, a derivative of sandalwood oil, induces apoptosis in human prostate cancer cells by causing caspase-3 activation, Bommareddy A, Rule B, VanWert AL, Santha S, Dwivedi C, *Phytomedicine*, 2012

CELLULAR REPAIR AND CELLULAR HEALTH

Carvacrol and rosemary essential oil manifest cytotoxic, DNA-protective and pro-apoptotic effect having no effect on DNA repair, Melusova M, Slamenova D, Kozics K, Jantova S, Horvathova E, *Neoplasma*, 2014

Effectiveness of aromatherapy with light thai massage for cellular immunity improvement in colorectal cancer patients receiving chemotherapy, Khiewkhern S, Promthet S, Sukprasert A, Eunhpinitpong W, Bradshaw P, *Asian Pacific Journal of Cancer Prevention*, 2013

Protective effect of basil (Ocimum basilicum L.) against oxidative DNA damage and mutagenesis, Berić T, Nikolić B, Stanojević J, Vuković-Gačić B, Knezević-Vukcević J, *Food and Chemical Toxicology*, 2008

CHEMICAL COMPOSITION AND PROPERTIES

Anethum graveolens: An Indian traditional medicinal herb and spice, Jana S, Shekhawat GS, *Pharmacognosy Review*, 2010

Antioxidant activities and volatile constituents of various essential oils, Wei A, Shibamoto T, *Journal of Agriculture and Food Chemistry*, 2007

Application of near-infrared spectroscopy in quality control and determination of adulteration of African essential oils, Juliani HR, Kapteyn J, Jones D, Koroch AR, Wang M, Charles D, Simon JE., Phytochem Anal. 2006 Mar-Apr

Botanical perspectives on health peppermint: more than just an after-dinner mint, Spirling LI, Daniels IR, *Journal for the Royal Society for the Promotion of Health*, 2001

Chamomile: A herbal medicine of the past with bright future, Srivastava JK, Shankar E, Gupta S, *Molecular Medicine Reports*, 2010

Chemical composition and antibacterial activity of selected essential oils and some of their main compounds, Wanner J, Schmidt E, Bail S, Jirovetz L, Buchbauer G, Gochev V, Girova T, Atanasova T, Stoyanova A, *Natural Product Communications*, 2010

Chemical composition and biological activity of the essential oil from Helichrysum microphyllum Cambess. ssp. tyrrhenicum Bacch., Brullo e Giusso growing in La Maddalena Archipelago, Sardinia., Ornano L, Venditti A, Sanna C, Ballero M, Maggi F, Lupidi G, Bramucci M, Quassinti L, Bianco A, *Journal of Oleo Science*, 2014

Chemical composition of the essential oils of variegated pink-fleshed lemon (Citrus x limon L. Burm. f.) and their anti-inflammatory and antimicrobial activities, Hamdan D, Ashour ML, Mulyaningsih S, El-Shazly A, Wink M, *Zeitschrift Fur Naturforschung C- A Journal of Biosciences*, 2013

Constituents of south Indian vetiver oils, Mallavarapu GR, Syamasundar KV, Ramesh S, Rao BR, *Natural Product Communications*, 2012

Determination of the absolute configuration of 6-alkylated α-pyrones from Ravensara crassifolia by LC-NMR., Queiroz EF, Wolfender JL, Raoelison G, Hostettmann K, *Phytochem Anal.* 2003

Evaluation of the chemical constituents and the antimicrobial activity of the volatile oil of Citrus reticulata fruit (Tangerine fruit peel) from South West Nigeria, Ayoola GA, Johnson OO, Adelowotan T, Aibinu IE, Adenipekun E, Adepoju AA, Coker HAB, Odugbemi TO, *African Journal of Biotechnology*, 2008

The Essential Oil of Bergamot Stimulates Reactive Oxygen Species Production in Human Polymorphonuclear Leukocytes, Cosentino M, Luini A, Bombelli R, Corasaniti MT, Bagetta G, Marino F, *Phytotherapy Research*, 2014

The essential oil of ginger, Zingiber officinale, and anaesthesia, Geiger JL, *International Journal of Aromatherapy*, 2005

Two 6-substituted 5,6-dihydro-α-pyrones from Ravensara anisata., Andrianaivoravelona JO, Sahpaz S, Terreaux C, Hostettmann K, Stoeckli-Evans H, Rasolondramanitra J, *Phytochemistry*. 1999

Volatile composition and biological activity of key lime Citrus aurantifolia essential oil, Spadaro F, Costa R, Circosta C, Occhiuto F, *Natural Product Communications*, 2012

Volatiles from steam-distilled leaves of some plant species from Madagascar and New Zealand and evaluation of their biological activity, Costa R, Pizzimenti F, Marotta F, Dugo P, Santi L, Mondello L, *Nat Prod Commun*, 2010

CHOLESTEROL

Hypolipidemic activity of Anethum graveolens in rats, Hajhashemi V, Abbasi N, *Phytotherapy Research*, 2008

Protective effect of lemongrass oil against dexamethasone induced hyperlipidemia in rats: possible role of decreased lecithin cholesterol acetyl transferase activity, Kumar VR, Inamdar MN, Nayeemunnisa, Viswanatha GL, *Asian Pacific Journal of Tropical Medicine*, 2011

Protective role of arzanol against lipid peroxidation in biological systems, Rosa A, Pollastro F, Atzeri A, Appendino G, Melis MP, Deiana M, Incani A, Loru D, Dessì MA, *Chemical and Physics of Lipids*, 2011

DECONGESTANT

Effect of inhaled menthol on citric acid induced cough in normal subjects, Morice AH, Marshall AE, Higgins KS, Grattan TJ, *Thorax*, 1994

Remedies for common family ailments: 10. Nasal decongestants, Sinclair A, *Professional Care of Mother and Child*, 1996

DEMENTIA

Aromatherapy as a safe and effective treatment for the management of agitation in severe dementia: the results of a double-blind, placebo-controlled trial with Melissa, Ballard CG, O'Brien JT, Reichelt K, Perry EK, *The Journal of Clinical Psychiatry*, 2002

DEPRESSION (INCLUDING POSTPARTUM)
Antidepressant-like effect of carvacrol (5-Isopropyl-2-methylphenol) in mice: involvement of dopaminergic system, Melo FH, Moura BA, de Sousa DP, de Vasconcelos SM, Macedo DS, Fonteles MM, Viana GS, de Sousa FC, *Fundamental and Clinical Pharmacology*, 2011
Antidepressant-like effect of Salvia sclarea is explained by modulation of dopamine activities in rats, Seol GH, Shim HS, Kim PJ, Moon HK, Lee KH, Shim I, Suh SH, Min SS, *Journal of Ethnopharmacology*, 2010
Effects of Aroma Hand Massage on Pain, State Anxiety and Depression in Hospice Patients with Terminal Cancer, Chang SY, *Journal of Korean Academy of Nursing*, 2008
Effects of lavender aromatherapy on insomnia and depression in women college students, Lee IS, Lee GJ, *Taehan Kanho Hakhoe Chi*, 2006
The effects of clinical aromatherapy for anxiety and depression in the high risk postpartum woman – a pilot study, Conrad P, Adams C, *Complimentary Therapy in Clinical Practice*, 2012

DIABETES
Ameliorative effect of the cinnamon oil from Cinnamomum zeylanicum upon early stage diabetic nephropathy, Mishra A, Bhatti R, Singh A, Singh Ishar MP, *Planta Medica*, 2010
Cinnamon bark extract improves glucose metabolism and lipid profile in the fructose-fed rat, Kannappan S, Jayaraman T, Rajasekar P, Ravichandran MK, Anuradha CV, *Singapore Medical Journal*, 2006
Comparative effects of Artemisia dracunculus, Satureja hortensis and Origanum majorana on inhibition of blood platelet adhesion, aggregation and secretion, Yazdanparast R, Shahriyary L, *Vascular Pharmacology*, 2008
Effects of a novel formulation of essential oils on glucose-insulin metabolism in diabetic and hypertensive rats: a pilot study, Talpur N, Echard B, Ingram C, Bagchi D, Preuss H, Diabetes, *Obesity and Metabolism*, 2005
From type 2 diabetes to antioxidant activity: a systematic review of the safety and efficacy of common and cassia cinnamon bark., Dugoua JJ, Seely D, Perri D, Cooley K, Forelli T, Mills E, Koren G, *Canadian Journal of Physiology and Pharmacology*, 2007
Hypoglycaemic effects of myrtle oil in normal and alloxan-diabetic rabbits, Sepici A, Gürbüz I, Cevik C, Yesilada E, *Journal of Ethnopharmacology*, 2004
Hypoglycemic and antioxidant effects of leaf essential oil of Pelargonium graveolens L'Hér. in alloxan induced diabetic rats, Boukhris M, Bouaziz M, Feki I, Jemai H, El Feki A, Sayadi S, *Lipids in Health and Disease*, 2012
Inhibitory potential of ginger extracts against enzymes linked to type 2 diabetes, inflammation and induced oxidative stress, Rani MP, Padmakumari KP, Sankarikutty B, Cherian OL, Nisha VM, Raghu KG, *International Journal of Food Sciences and Nutrition*, 2011

DIGESTION
Antigiardial activity of Ocimum basilicum essential oil, de Almeida I, Alviano DS, Vieira DP, Alves PB, Blank AF, Lopes AH, Alviano CS, Rosa Mdo S, *Parasitology Research*, 2007
Enteric-coated, pH-dependent peppermint oil capsules for the treatment of irritable bowel syndrome in children, Kline RM, Kline JJ, Di Palma J, Barbero GJ, *The Journal of Pediatrics*, 2001
Gastroprotective activity of essential oils from turmeric and ginger, Liju VB, Jeena K, Kuttan R, *Journal of Basic and Clinical Physiology and Pharmacology*, 2014
Gastroprotective effect of cardamom, Elettaria cardamomum Maton. fruits in rats., Jamal A, Javed K, Aslam M, Jafri MA, *Journal of Ethnopharmacology*, 2006
Olfactory stimulation using black pepper oil facilitates oral feeding in pediatric patients receiving long-term enteral nutrition, Munakata M, Kobayashi K, Niisato-Nezu J, Tanaka S, Kakisaka Y, Ebihara T, Ebihara S, Haginoya K, Tsuchiya S, Onuma A, *The Tohoku Journal of Experimental Medicine*, 2008
Peppermint oil for the treatment of irritable bowel syndrome: a systematic review and meta-analysis, Khanna R, MacDonald JK, Levesque BG, *Journal of Clinical Gastroenterology*, 2014
Randomized clinical trial of a phytotherapic compound containing Pimpinella anisum, Foeniculum vulgare, Sambucus nigra, and Cassia augustifolia for chronic constipation, Picon PD, Picon RV, Costa AF, Sander GB, Amaral KM, Aboy AL, Henriques AT, *BMC Complementary and Alternative Medicine*, 2010
Reversal of pyrogallol-induced delay in gastric emptying in rats by ginger (Zingiber officinale), Gupta YK, Sharma M, *Methods and Findings in Experimental and Clinical Pharmacology*, 2001
Systematic Review of Complementary and Alternative Medicine Treatments in Inflammatory Bowel Diseases, Langhorst J, Wulfert H, Lauche R, Klose P, Cramer H, Dobos GJ,Korzenik,J, *Journal of Crohn's & Colitis*,2015
The cinnamon-derived dietary factor cinnamic aldehyde activates the Nrf2-dependent antioxidant response in human epithelial colon cells, Wondrak GT, Villeneuve NF, Lamore SD, Bause AS, Jiang T, Zhang DD, *Molecules*, 2010
Treatment of irritable bowel syndrome with herbal preparations: results of a double-blind, randomized, placebo-controlled, multi-centre trial, Madisch A, Holtmann G, Plein K, Hotz J, *Alimentary pharmacology and & therapeutics*, 2004

FIBROMYALGIA
Cutaneous application of menthol 10% solution as an abortive treatment of migraine without aura: a randomised, double-blind, placebo-controlled, crossed-over study, Borhani Haghighi A, Motazedian S, Rezaii R, Mohammadi F, Salarian L, Pourmokhtari M, Khodaei S, Vossoughi M, Miri R, *The International Journal of Clinical Practice*, 2010
Lavender essential oil in the treatment of migraine headache: a placebo-controlled clinical trial, Sasannejad P, Saeedi M, Shoeibi A, Gorji A, Abbasi M, Foroughipour M, *European Neurology*, 2012

HERPES
Inhibitory effect of essential oils against herpes simplex virus type 2, Koch C, Reichling J, Schneele J, Schnitzler P, *Phytomedicine*, 2008
Susceptibility of drug-resistant clinical herpes simplex virus type 1 strains to essential oils of ginger, thyme, hyssop, and sandalwood, Schnitzler P, Koch C, Reichling J, *Antimicrobial Agents and Chemotherapy*, 2007

IMMUNE SYSTEM
Chemistry and immunomodulatory activity of frankincense oil, Mikhaeil BR, Maatooq GT, Badria FA, Amer MM, *Zeitschrift fur Naturforschung C*, 2003

INFLAMMATION AND PAIN
Anti-Inflammatory and Antioxidant Actions of Copaiba Oil Are Related to Liver Cell Modifications in Arthritic Rats. Castro Ghizoni CV, Arssufi Ames AP, Lameira OA, Bersani Amado CA, Sá Nakanishi AB, Bracht L, Marçal Natali MR, Peralta RM, Bracht A, Comar JF. J Cell Biochem. 2017
Anti-inflammatory constituents from the root of Litsea cubeba in LPS-induced RAW 264.7 macrophages. Lin B, Sun LN, Xin HL, Nian H, Song HT, Jiang YP, Wei ZQ, Qin LP, Han T. Pharm Biol. 2016
Anti-Inflammatory Effects of Boldine and Reticuline Isolated from Litsea cubeba through JAK2/STAT3 and NF-kB Signaling Pathways. Yang X, Gao X, Cao Y, Guo Q, Li S, Zhu Z, Zhao Y, Tu P, Chai X. Planta Med. 2017
A review on anti-inflammatory activity of monoterpenes, de Cássia da Silveira e Sá R, Andrade LN, de Sousa DP, *Molecules*, 2013
An experimental study on the effectiveness of massage with aromatic ginger and orange essential oil for moderate-to-severe knee pain among the elderly in Hong Kong, Yip YB, Tam AC, *Complementary Therapies in Medicine*, 2008
Anti-inflammatory activity of patchouli alcohol in RAW264.7 and HT-29 cells, Jeong JB, Shin YK, Lee SH, *Food and Chemical Toxicology*, 2013
Anti-inflammatory and analgesic activity of different extracts of Commiphora myrrha, Su S, Wang T, Duan JA, Zhou W, Hua YQ, Tang YP, Yu L, Qian DW, *Journal of Ethnopharmacology*, 2011
Anti-inflammatory and anti-ulcer activities of carvacrol, a monoterpene present in the essential oil of oregano, Silva FV, Guimarães AG, Silva ER, Sousa-Neto BP, Machado FD, Quintans-Júnior LJ, Arcanjo DD, Oliveira FA, Oliveira RC, *Journal of Medicinal Food*, 2012
Anti-inflammatory and antioxidant properties of Helichrysum italicum, Sala A, Recio M, Giner RM, Máñez S, Tournier H, Schinella G, Ríos JL, *The Journal of Pharmacy and Pharmacology*, 200
Anti-inflammatory effects of Melaleuca alternifolia essential oil on human polymorphonuclear neutrophils and monocytes, Caldefie-Chézet F, Guerry M, Chalchat JC, Fusillier C, Vasson MP, Guillot J, *Free Radical Research*, 2004
Antihypernociceptive activity of anethole in experimental inflammatory pain, Ritter AM, Domiciano TP, Verri WA Jr, Zarpelon AC, da Silva LG, Barbosa CP, Natali MR, Cuman RK, Bersani-Amado CA, *Inflammopharmacology*, 2013
Anti-inflammatory effects of essential oil from the leaves of Cinnamomum cassia and cinnamaldehyde on lipopolysaccharide-stimulated J774A.1 cells., Pannee C, Chandhanee I, Wacharee L, *Journal of Advanced Pharmaceutical Technology & Research*, 2014
Anti-inflammatory effects of ginger and some of its components in human bronchial epithelial (BEAS-2B) cells, Podlogar JA, Verspohl EJ, *Phytotherapy Research*, 2012
Antioxidant components of naturally-occurring oils exhibit marked anti-inflammatory activity in epithelial cells of the human upper respiratory system, Gao M, Singh A, Macri K, Reynolds C, Singhal V, Biswal S, Spannhake EW, *Respiratory Research*, 2011
Antioxidant, anti-inflammatory and antinociceptive activities of essential oil from ginger, Jeena K, Liju VB, Kuttan R, *Indian Journal of Physiology and Pharmacology*, 2013
Arzanol, a prenylated heterodimeric phloroglucinyl pyrone, inhibits eicosanoid biosynthesis and exhibits anti-inflammatory efficacy in vivo, Bauer J, Koeberle A, Dehm F, Pollastro F, Appendino G, Northoff H, Rossi A, Sautebin L, Werz O, *Biochemical Pharmacology*, 2011
Arzanol, an anti-inflammatory and anti-HIV-1 phloroglucinol α-Pyrone from Helichrysum italicum ssp. microphyllum, Appendino G, Ottino M, Marquez N, Bianchi F, Giana A, Ballero M, Sterner O, Fiebich BL, Munoz E, *Journal of Natural Products*, 2007
Assessment of the anti-inflammatory activity and free radical scavenger activity of tiliroside., Sala A, Recio MC, Schinella GR, Máñez S, Giner RM, Cerdá-Nicolás M, Rosí JL, *European Journal of Pharmacology*, 2003
Boswellia frereana (frankincense) suppresses cytokine-induced matrix metalloproteinase expression and production of pro-inflammatory molecules in articular cartilage., Blain EJ, Ali AY, Duance VC, *Phytotherapy Research*, 2012
Chamazulene carboxylic acid and matricin: a natural profen and its natural prodrug, identified through similarity to synthetic drug substances, Ramadan M, Goeters S, Watzer B, Krause E, Lohmann K, Bauer R, Hempel B, Imming P, *Journal of Natural Products*, 2006
Ginger: An herbal medicinal product with broad anti-inflammatory actions, Grzanna R, Lindmark L, Frondoza CG, *Journal of Medicinal Food*, 2005
Identification of proapoptopic, anti-inflammatory, anti-proliferative, anti-invasive and anti-angiogenic targets of
essential oils in cardamom by dual reverse virtual screening and binding pose analysis, Bhattacharjee B, Chatterjee J, *Asian Pacific Journal of Cancer Prevention*, 2013
In vitro cytotoxic and anti-inflammatory effects of myrrh oil on human gingival fibroblasts and epithelial cells, Tipton DA, Lyle B, Babich H, Dabbous MKh, *Toxicology in Vitro*, 2003
In Vivo Potential Anti-Inflammatory Activity of Melissa officinalis L. Essential Oil, Bounihi A, Hajjaj G, Alnamer R, Cherrah Y, Zellou A, *Advances in Pharmacological Sciences*, 2013
Inhibitory effect of anethole in nonimmune acute inflammation, Domiciano TP, Dalalio MM, Silva EL, Ritter AM, Estevão-Silva CF, Ramos FS, Caparroz-Assef SM, Cuman RK, Bersani-Amado CA, *Naunyn-Schmiedeberg's Archives of Pharmacology*, 2013
Lavender essential oil inhalation suppresses allergic airway inflammation and mucous cell hyperplasia in a murine model of asthma, Ueno-Iio T, Shibakura M, Yokota K, Aoe M, Hyoda T, Shinohata R, Kanehiro A, Tanimoto M, Kataoka M, *Life Sciences*, 2014
Parthenolide inhibits proliferation of fibroblast-like synoviocytes in vitro. Parada-Turska J. Mitura A, Brzana W, Jalonkski M, Majdan M, Rzeski W. Inflammation. 2008
Results suggest that neroli possesses biologically active constituent(s) that have significant activity against acute and especially chronic inflammation, and have central and peripheral antinociceptive effects which support the ethnomedicinal claims of the use of the plant in the management of pain and inflammation. Asgarpanah, J, P Khadobakhsh, and H Shafaroodi. "Analgesic and anti-inflammatory activities of Citrus aurantium L. blossoms essential oil (neroli): involvement of the nitric oxide/cyclic-guanosine monophostphate pathway." *Journal of Natural Medicines*, 2015
Rose geranium essential oil as a source of new and safe anti-inflammatory drugs, Boukhatem MN, Kameli A, Ferhat MA, Saidi F, Mekarnia M, *The Libyan Journal of Medicine*, 2013
Supercritical fluid extraction of oregano (Origanum vulgare) essentials oils: anti-inflammatory properties based on cytokine response on THP-1 macrophages, Ocaña-Fuentes A, Arranz-Gutiérrez E, Señorans FJ, Reglero G, *Food and Chemical Toxicology*, 2010

INSECT REPELLENT

Bioactivity-guided investigation of geranium essential oils as natural tick repellents, Tabanca N, Wang M, Avonto C, Chittiboyina AG, Parcher JF, Carroll JF, Kramer M, Khan IA, *Journal of Agricultural and Food Chemistry*, 2013

Essential oils and their compositions as spatial repellents for pestiferous social wasps., Zhang QH, Schnidmiller RG, *Hoover DR, Pest Management Science*, 2013

Field evaluation of essential oils for reducing attraction by the Japanese beetle (Coleoptera: Scarabaeidae), Youssef NN, Oliver JB, Ranger CM, Reding ME, Moyseenko JJ, Klein MG, Pappas RS, *Journal of Economic Entomology*, 2009

Fumigant toxicity of plant essential oils against Camptomyia corticalis (Diptera: Cecidomyiidae), Kim JR, Haribalan P, Son BK, Ahn YJ, *Journal of Economic Entomology*, 2012

Insecticidal properties of volatile extracts of orange peels, Ezeonu FC, Chidume GI, Udedi SC, *Bioresource Technology*, 2001

Repellency of Essential Oils to Mosquitoes (Diptera: Culicidae), Barnard DR, *Journal of Medical Entomology*, 1999

Repellency to Stomoxys calcitrans (Diptera: Muscidae) of Plant Essential Oils Alone or in Combination with Calophyllum inophyllum Nut Oil, Hieu TT, Kim SI, Lee SG, Ahn YJ, *Journal of Medical Etomology*, 2010

Repelling properties of some plant materials on the tick Ixodes ricinus L, Thorsell W, Mikiver A, Tunón H, *Phytomedicine*, 2006

MENOPAUSE

Aromatherapy Massage Affects Menopausal Symptoms in Korean Climacteric Women: A Pilot-Controlled Clinical Trial, Myung-HH, Yun Seok Y, Myeong SL, *Evidence-Based Complementary and Alternative Medicine*, 2008

Changes in 5-hydroxytryptamine and Cortisol Plasma Levels in Menopausal Women After Inhalation of Clary Sage Oil. Lee KB, Cho E, Kang YS, *Phytotherapy Research*, 2014

Effect of aromatherapy massage on abdominal fat and body image in post-menopausal women, Kim HJ, *Taehan Kanho Hakhoe Chi*, 2007

Inhalation of neroli oil by postmenopausal women improved their quality of life related to menopausal symptoms, increased sexual desire, and reduced blood pressure. In addition, inhalation of neroli oil may reduce stress levels and stimulate the endocrine system. Choi, Seo Yeon et al. "Effects of Inhalation of Essential Oil of Citrus AurantiumL Var. amara on Menopausal Symptoms, Stress, and Estrogen in Postmenopausal Women: A Randomized Controlled Trial." *Evidence-Based Complementary and Alternative Medicine*, 2014

MENSTRUAL

Effect of aromatherapy on symptoms of dysmenorrhea in college students: A randomized placebo-controlled clinical trial, Han SH, Hur MH, Buckle J, Choi J, Lee MS, *The Journal of Alternative and Complementary Medicine*, 2006

Pain relief assessment by aromatic essential oil massage on outpatients with primary dysmenorrhea: a randomized, double-blind clinical trial, Ou MC, Hsu TF, Lai AC, Lin YT, Lin CC, *The Journal of Obstetrics and Gynecology Research*, 2012

MIGRAINE

Cutaneous application of menthol 10% solution as an abortive treatment of migraine without aura: a randomised, double-blind, placebo-controlled, crossed-over study, Borhani Haghighi A, Motazedian S, Rezaii R, Mohammadi F, Salarian L, Pourmokhtari M, Khodaei S, Vossoughi M, Miri R, *The International Journal of Clinical Practice*, 2010

Lavender essential oil in the treatment of migraine headache: a placebo-controlled clinical trial, Sasannejad P, Saeedi M, Shoeibi A, Gorji A, Abbasi M, Foroughipour M, *European Neurology*, 2012

MOOD

Effects of fragrance inhalation on sympathetic activity in normal adults, Haze S, Sakai K, Gozu Y, *The Japanese Journal of Pharmacology*, 2002

Evaluation of the harmonizing effect of ylang-ylang oil on humans after inhalation, Hongratanaworakit T, Buchbauer G, *Planta Medica*, 2004

Relaxing effect of rose oil on humans, Hongratanaworakit T, *Natural Product Communications*, 2009

Relaxing Effect of Ylang ylang Oil on Humans after Transdermal Absorption, Hongratanaworakit T, Buchbauer G, *Phytotherapy Research*, 2006

NAUSEA

A brief review of current scientific evidence involving aromatherapy use for nausea and vomiting, Lua PL, Zakaria NS, *The Journal of Alternative and Complementary Medicine*, 2012

Aromatherapy as a Treatment for Postoperative Nausea: A randomized Trial, Hunt R, Dienemann J, Norton HJ, Hartley W, Hudgens A, Stern T, *Divine G, Anesthesia and Analgesia*, 2013

Controlled breathing with or without peppermint aromatherapy for postoperative nausea and/or vomiting symptom relief: a randomized controlled trial, Sites DS, Johnson NT, Miller JA, Torbush PH, Hardin JS, Knowles SS, Nance J, Fox TH, Tart RC, *Journal of PeriAnesthesia Nursing*, 2014

The effect of lemon inhalation aromatherapy on nausea and vomiting of pregnancy: a double-blinded, randomized, controlled clinical trial, Yavari Kia P, Safajou F, Shahnazi M, Nazemiyeh H, *Iranian Red Crescent Medical Journal*, 2014

The palliation of nausea in hospice and palliative care patients with essential oils of Pimpinella anisum (aniseed), Foeniculum vulgare var. dulce (sweet fennel), Anthemis nobilis (Roman chamomile) and Mentha × piperita (peppermint), Gilligan NP, *International Journal of Aromatherapy*, 2005

ORAL HEALTH

Efficacy of grapefruit, tangerine, lime, and lemon oils as solvents for softening gutta-percha in root canal retreatment procedures, Jantarat J, Malhotra W, Sutimuntanakul S, *Journal of Investigative and Clinical Dentistry*, 2013

Essential oil of Melaleuca alternifolia for the treatment of oral candidiasis induced in an immunosuppressed mouse model, de Campos Rasteiro VM, da Costa AC, Araújo CF, de Barros PP, Rossoni RD, Anbinder AL, Jorge AO, Junqueira JC, *BMC Complementary and Alternative Medicine*, 2014

General Toxicity and Antifungal Activity of a New Dental Gel with Essential Oil from Abies SibiricaL.Noreikaitė A, Ayupova R, Satbayeva E, Seitaliyeva A, Amirkulova M, Pichkhadze G, Datkhayev U, Stankevičius E. Med Sci Monit. 2017

Plants and other natural products used in the management of oral infections and improvement of oral health. Chinsembu KC. Acta Trop. 2016

Susceptibility to Melaleuca alternifolia (tea tree) oil of yeasts isolated from the mouths of patients with advanced cancer, Bagg J, Jackson MS, Petrina Sweeney M, Ramage G, Davies AN, *Oral Oncology*, 2006

Synergistic effect between clove oil and its major compounds and antibiotics against oral bacteria, Moon SE, Kim HY, Cha JD, *Archives of Oral Biology*, 2011

Topical lavender oil for the treatment of recurrent aphthous ulceration, Altaei DT, *American Journal of Dentistry*, 2012

PHYSICAL AGILITY

Effects of lavender (lavandula angustifolia Mill.) and peppermint (Mentha cordifolia Opiz.) aromas on subjective vitality, speed, and agility, Cruz AB, Lee SE, Pagaduan JC, Kim TH, *The Asian International Journal of Life Sciences*, 2012

The effects of peppermint on exercise performance, Meamarbashi A, Rajabi A, *Journal of International Society of Sports Nutrition*, 2013

PREGNANCY

Aromatherapy with C. aurantium blossom oil is a simple, inexpensive, noninvasive, and effective intervention to reduce anxiety during labor. Namazi, Masoumeh et al. "Aromatherapy With Citrus Aurantium Oil and Anxiety During the First Stage of Labor." Iranian Red Crescent Medical Journal , 2014

Clinical trial of aromatherapy on postpartum mother's perineal healing, Hur MH, Han SH, *Journal of Korean Academy of Nursing*, 2004

REPRODUCTIVE SYSTEM

Development and pharmacological evaluation of in vitro nanocarriers composed of lamellar silicates containing copaiba oil-resin for treatment of endometriosis. de Almeida Borges VR, da Silva JH, Barbosa SS, Nasciutti LE, Cabral LM, de Sousa VP. Mater Sci Eng C Mater Biol Appl. 2016

Effect of different terpene-containing essential oils on permeation of estradiol through hairless mouse skin, Monti D, Chetoni P, Burgalassi S, Najarro M, Saettone MF, Boldrini E, *International Journal of Pharmaceutics*, 2002

Effect of olfactory stimulation with flavor of grapefruit oil and lemon oil on the activity of sympathetic branch in the white adipose tissue of the epididymis, Niijima A, Nagai K, *Experimental Biology and Medicine*, 2003

The Effects of Herbal Essential Oils on the Oviposition-deterrent and Ovicidal Activities of Aedes aegypti (Linn.), Anopheles dirus (Peyton and Harrison) and Culex quinquefasciatus (Say), Siriporn P, Mayura S, *Tropical Biomedicine*, 2012

SEIZURES

Anticonvulsant and neuroprotective effects of Pimpinella anisum in rat brain, Fariba K, Mahmoud H, Diana M, Hassan A, Gholam RH, Mohamad B, Maryam J, Hadi K, Ali G, *BMC Complementary and Alternative Medicine*, 2012

Increased seizure latency and decreased severity of pentylenetetrazol-induced seizures in mice after essential oil administration, Koutroumanidou E, Kimbaris A, Kortsaris A, Bezirtzoglou E, Polissiou M, Charalabopoulos K, Pagonopoulou O, *Epilepsy Research and Treatment*, 2013

The results suggest that neroli possesses biologically active constituent(s) that have anticonvulsant activity which supports the ethnomedicinal claims of the use of the plant in the management of seizure. Azanchi, T, H Shafaroodi, and J Asgarpanah. "Anticonvulsant activity of Citrus aurantium blossom essential oil (neroli): involvement of the GABAergic system." Natural Products Communication, 2014.

SKIN

A comparative study of tea-tree oil versus benzoylperoxide in the treatment of acne, Bassett IB, Pannowitz DL, Barnetson RS, *Medical Journal of Australia*, 1990

Activities of Ten Essential Oils towards Propionibacterium acnes and PC-3, A-549 and MCF-7 Cancer Cells, Zu Y, Yu H, Liang L, Fu Y, Efferth T, Liu X, Wu N, *Molecules*, 2010

Cinnamomum cassia essential oil inhibits α-MSH-induced melanin production and oxidative stress in murine B16 melanoma cells, Chou ST, Chang WL, Chang CT, Hsu SL, Lin YC, Shih Y, *International Journal of Molecular Sciences*, 2013

Cooling the burn wound: evaluation of different modalites., Jandera V, Hudson DA, de Wet PM, Innes PM, Rode H, Burns: *Journal of the International Society for Burn Injuries*, 2000

Coriandrum sativum L. protects human keratinocytes from oxidative stress by regulating oxidative defense systems, Park G, Kim HG, Kim YO, Park SH, Kim SY, Oh MS, *Skin Pharmacology and Physiology*, 2012

Effects of Abies sibirica terpenes on cancer- and aging-associated pathways in human cells. Kudryavtseva A, Krasnov G, Lipatova A, Alekseev B, Maganova F, Shaposhnikov M, Fedorova M, Snezhkina A, Moskalev A. Oncotarget. 2016

Essential oil of Australian lemon myrtle (Backhousia citriodora) in the treatment of molluscum contagiosum in children, Burke BE, Baillie JE, Olson RD, *Biomedicine & Pharmacotherapy*, 2004

Randomized trial of aromatherapy: successful treatment for alopecia areata, Hay IC, Jamieson M, Ormerod AD,, *Archives of Dermatology*, 1998

Tea tree oil as a novel anti-psoriasis weapon, Pazyar N, Yaghoobi R, *Skin Pharmacology and Physiology*, 2012

Tea tree oil reduces histamine-induced skin inflammation, Koh KJ, Pearce AL, Marshman G, Finlay-Jones JJ, Hart PH, *British Journal of Dermatology*, 2002

The effect of clove and benzocaine versus placebo as topical anesthetics, Alqareer A, Alyahya A, Andersson L, *Journal of Dentistry*, 2006

Two US practitioners' experience of using essential oils for wound care, Hartman D, Coetzee JC, *Journal of Wound Care*, 2002

SLEEP

An olfactory stimulus modifies nighttime sleep in young men and women, Goel N, Kim H, Lao RP, *Chronobiology International*, 2005

Neroli oil (citrus aurantium) to have pharmacological effects on fatigue and insomnia, Essential oils used in aromatherapy, Babar Ali, Naser Ali Al-Wabel, Saiba Shams, Aftab Ahamand, Shah Alam Khan, Firoz Anwar, Asian Pacific Journal of Tropical Biomedicine, 2015.

Preliminary investigation of the effect of peppermint oil on an objective measure of daytime sleepiness, Norrish MI, Dwyer KL, *International Journal of Psychophysiology: Official Journal of*

the International Organization of Psychophysiology, 2005
Sedative effects of the jasmine tea odor and (R)-(-)-linalool, one of its major odor components, on autonomic nerve activity and mood states, Kuroda K, Inoue N, Ito Y, Kubota K, Sugimoto A, Kakuda T, Fushiki T, *European Journal of Applied Physiology*, 2005
Stimulating effect of aromatherapy massage with jasmine oil, Hongratanaworakit T, *Natural Product Communications*, 2010
Stimulative and sedative effects of essential oils upon inhalation in mice, Lim WC, Seo JM, Lee CI, Pyo HB, Lee BC, *Archives of Pharmacal Research*, 2005

STRESS
Effect of "rose essential oil" inhalation on stress-induced skin-barrier disruption in rats and humans, Fukada M, Kano E, Miyoshi M, Komaki R, Watanabe T, *Chemical Senses*, 2012
Effect of flavour components in lemon essential oil on physical or psychological stress, Fukumoto S, Morishita A, Furutachi K, Terashima T, Nakayama T, Yokogoshi H, *Stress and Health*, 2008
The physical effects of aromatherapy in alleviating work-related stress on elementary school teachers in taiwan, Liu SH, Lin TH, Chang KM, *Evidence-Based Complementary and Alternative Medicine*, 2013

STROKE
Effect of lavender oil (Lavandula angustifolia) on cerebral edema and its possible mechanisms in an experimental model of stroke,Vakili A, Sharifat S, Akhavan MM, Bandegi AR, *Brain Research*, 2014

TUMORS
Chemopreventive effects of α-santalol on skin tumor development in CD-1 and SENCAR mice, Dwivedi C, Guan X, Harmsen WL, Voss AL, Goetz-Parten DE, Koopman EM, Johnson KM, Valluri HB, Matthees DP, Cancer Epidemiology, *Biomarkers and Prevention*, 2003
Frankincense oil derived from Boswellia carteri induces tumor cell specific cytotoxicity, Frank MB, Yang Q, Osban J, Azzarello JT, Saban MR, Saban R, Ashley RA, Welter JC, Fung KM, Lin HK, *BMC Complementary and Alternative Medicine*, 2009
Sandalwood oil prevent skin tumour development in CD1 mice, Dwivedi C, Zhang Y, *European Journal of Cancer Prevention*, 1999

WEIGHT LOSS AND WEIGHT MANAGEMENT
Effect of aromatherapy massage on abdominal fat and body image in post-menopausal women, Kim HJ, *Taehan Kanho Hakhoe Chi*, 2007
Effects of herbal essential oil mixture as a dietary supplement on egg production in quail, Çabuk M, Eratak S, Alçicek A, Bozkurt M, *The Scientific World Journal*, 2014
Essential oil from Citrus aurantifolia prevents ketotifen-induced weight-gain in mice, Asnaashari S, Delazar A, Habibi B, Vasfi R, Nahar L, Hamedeyazdan S, Sarker SD, *Phytotherapy Research*, 2010
Low level of Lemon Balm (Melissa officinalis) essential oils showed hypoglycemic effects by altering the expression of glucose metabolism genes in db/db mice, Mi Ja Chung, Sung-Yun Cho and Sung-Joon Lee, *The Journal of the Federation of American Societies for Experimental Biology*, 2008
Olfactory stimulation with scent of grapefruit oil affects autonomic nerves, lipolysis and appetite in rats, Shen J, Niijima A, Tanida M, Horii Y, Maeda K, Nagai K, *Neuroscience Letters*, 2005
Safety assessment of Ylang-Ylang (Cananga spp.) as a food ingredient., Burdock GA, Carabin IG, *Food and Chemical Toxicology*, 2008
The effects of inhalation of essential oils on the body weight, food efficiency rate and serum leptin of growing SD rats, Hur MH, Kim C, Kim CH, Ahn HC, Ahn HY, *Korean Society of Nursing Science*, 2006
The metabolic responses to aerial diffusion of essential oils, Wu Y, Zhang Y, Xie G, Zhao A, Pan X, Chen T, Hu Y, Liu Y, Cheng Y, Chi Y, Yao L, Jia W, *PLoS One*, 2012

BIBLIOGRAPHY

About Brain Tumors. Barrow Neurological Institute. Thebarrow.org, 2014.

The American Heritage Medical Dictionary. Boston: Houghton Mifflin Co., 2007.

The Aromatic Practitioners Reference. Australia: Maria Mitchell, 2011.

The Aromatherapy Encyclopedia: A Concise Guide to Over 385 Plant Oils. Basic Health Publications, Inc.: Schiller, C. and Schiller, D., 2008.

Aromatherapy Workbook. London: Price, Shirley, Thorsons, 2000.

The Art of Aromatherapy. Essex: The C W Daniel Company Ltd, Tisserand, Robert, 2009.

The Aromatherapy Encyclopedia. Laguna Beach, CA: Basic Health Publications Inc, Schiller, Carol & Schiller, David, 2008.

Aromatherapy for Health Professionals, 3rd ed. London: Churchhill Livingstone Elsevier, Price, Shirley & Price, Len, 2007.

Aromatherapy A-Z. London, England: Random House, Davis Patricia, 2005.

BabyMed.com, 2014.

Churchill Livingstone Dictionary of Sport and Exercise Science and Medicine. Philadelphia: Churchill Livingstone, 2008.

Clinical Aromatherapy Essential Oils in Healthcare, 3rd ed. St Louis, MO: Elsevier, Buckle, Jane 2015.

Collins English Dictionary. London: Collins, 2000.

The Columbia Electronic Encyclopedia. New York, NY: Columbia University Press, 2012.

The Complete Aromatherapy & Essential Oils Handbook for Everyday Wellness. Toronto: Robert Rose Inc, Purchon, Nerys & Cantele, Lora, 2014.

The Complete Guide to Aromatherapy, 2nd ed. Brisbane, QLD: The International Centre of Holistic Aromatherapy, Battaglia, Salvatore, 2003.

The Directory of Essential Oils. London: Vermillion, Sellar, Wanda, 2005.

Dorland's Medical Dictionary for Health Consumers. 2014

Emotions & Essential Oils 3rd Edition. American Fork, Utah: Enlighten Alternative Healing, 2014.

The Encyclopedia of Essential Oils. London: Thorsons, Lawless, Julia, 2002.

Essential Oil Safety, 2nd ed. London: Churchill Livingstone Elsevier, Tisserand, Robert & Young, Rodney, 2013.

Essential Oils Desk Reference, 5th ed. USA: Life Science Publishing, 2011.

The Essential Oils Handbook. London: Duncan Baird Publishers Ltd, Harding, Jennie, 2008.

Essential Oils Integrative Medical Guide. USA: Essential Science Publishing, Young, D Gary, 2006.

Essentials of the Earth, 2nd ed. Idaho USA: Essential Oils Books LLC, James, R L, 2013.

Farlex Partner Medical Dictionary. Huntingdon Valley, PA: Farlex Inc. 2014.

The Fragrant Pharmacy. Moorebank, NSW: Transworld Publishers Ltd, Wormwood, Valerie A, 1993.

Gale Encyclopedia of Medicine. Farmington Hills, MI: Gale, 1999.

The Healing Intelligence of Essential Oils. Rockester, Vermont: Healing Arts Press, Schnacbelt Kurt, 2011.

The Huffington Post; HuffingtonPost.com, 2014.

The Human Body. New York, New York: Dorling Kindersley Publishing, Inc., 2001.

Illustrated Dictionary of Podiatry and Foot Science. New York: Churchill Livingstone, 2009.

MayoClinic.org, 2014 & 2015.

McGraw-Hill Concise Dictionary of Modern Medicine. New York: McGraw-Hill, 2006.

McGraw-Hill Dictionary of Scientific & Technical Terms 6th ed., New York: McGraw-Hill, 2003.

Mind Over Medicine. Hay House, Inc.: Rankin Lissa, 2014.

Molecules of Emotion. Simon & Schuster, Pert Candance B. Ph.D., 1999.

The Mood Cure. London, England: Penguin Books, Ross Julia MA, 2003.

Mosby's Dental Dictionary, 2nd ed. C.V. Mosby Co, 2008

Mosby's Dictionary of Complementary and Alternative Medicine. St. Louis, MO: Elsevier Mosby, 2005.

Mosby's Medical Dictionary 9th ed., Philadelphia: Elsevier, 2013.

Miller-Keane Encyclopedia and Dictionary of Medicine, Nursing, and Allied Health, 7th ed. Philadelphia: Saunders, 2003.

Patient.co.uk, 2014.

Random House Kernerman Webster's College Dictionary. New York: Random House, 1997.

Saunders Comprehensive Veterinary Dictionary. Edinburgh [Scotland]: Saunders Elsevier, 2012.

Segen's Medical Dictionary. New York: McGraw-Hill, 2006.

Stedman's Medical Dictionary for the Health Professions and Nursing. Philadelphia: Lippincott Williams & Wilkins, 2005.

WebMD.com, 2014.

INDEX

RESOURCES

RESOURCES

RESOURCES

GET AMAZING RESULTS
Anytime, Anywhere

ESSENTIAL LIFE BOOK 7.0

Comprehensive Reference Guide

The most trusted essential oil resource! With recommendations for 600+ ailments, expansive explorations of every body system and related symptoms and conditions, and answers to top health priorities, there is no better way to become your own essential oil expert.

THE ESSENTIAL BASICS

On-the-Go Guide

Access essential oil solutions when out and about! This travel size guide pairs A-Z ailment solutions with much of the core information provided in the comprehensive guide and fits easily into your purse or car.

THE ESSENTIAL QUICK REFERENCE

Share the Love

This A-Z reference is the perfect way to introduce essential oil safety, storage, and quality to the new user and beyond. Include a copy with every essential oil sample you share!